The Single Market Review

A G G R E G A T E   A N D   R E G I O N A L   I M P A C T

AGGREGATE RESULTS OF THE SINGLE MARKET PROGRAMME

The Single Market Review series

EUROPEAN COMMISSION

The Single Market Review

AGGREGATE AND REGIONAL IMPACT

AGGREGATE RESULTS OF THE SINGLE MARKET PROGRAMME

The Single Market Review

SUBSERIES VI: VOLUME 5

OFFICE FOR OFFICIAL PUBLICATIONS
OF THE EUROPEAN COMMUNITIES

KOGAN PAGE . EARTHSCAN

This report is part of a series of 39 studies commissioned from independent consultants in the context of a major review of the Single Market. The 1996 Single Market Review responds to a 1992 Council of Ministers Resolution calling on the European Commission to present an overall analysis of the effectiveness of measures taken in creating the Single Market. This review, which assesses the progress made in implementing the Single Market Programme, was coordinated by the Directorate-General 'Internal Market and Financial Services' (DG XV) and the Directorate-General 'Economic and Financial Affairs' (DG II) of the European Commission.

This document was prepared for the European Commission

by the

National Technical University of Athens

It does not, however, express the Commission's official views. Whilst every reasonable effort has been made to provide accurate information in regard to the subject matter covered, the Consultants are not responsible for any remaining errors. All recommendations are made by the Consultants for the purpose of discussion. Neither the Commission nor the Consultants accept liability for the consequences of actions taken on the basis of the information contained herein.

The European Commission would like to express thanks to the external experts and representatives of firms and industry bodies for their contribution to the 1996 Single Market Review, and to this report in particular.

Office for Official Publications of the European Communities
2 rue Mercier, L-2985 Luxembourg
ISBN 92-827-8810-5   Catalogue number: C1-72-96-005-EN-C

Kogan Page . Earthscan
120 Pentonville Road, London N1 9JN
ISBN 0 7494 2342 0

Table of contents

List of tables

List of figures

List of abbreviations

BLEU	Belgo-Luxembourg Economic Union
CES	Constant elasticity of substitution function
CET	Constant elasticity of transformation function
CGE	Computable general equilibrium
EC	European Community
ECU	European currency unit
EU	European Union
Eurostat	Statistical Office of the European Communities
GDP	Gross domestic product
GEM-E3	General equilibrium model for energy-economy-environment
GEM-E3-SM	Extended version of the GEM-E3 model, used in this study
IC	Imperfect competition
IM	Imperfect markets
I-O	Input-output tables
LES	Linear expenditure system
MES	Minimum efficiency scale
NTB	Non-tariff barriers
NTUA	National Technical University of Athens
PC	Perfect competition
RAS	Mathematical technique for balancing biproportional matrices
RW (or ROW)	Rest of the world (non-EU countries)
SAM	Social accounting matrix
SMP	Single Market Programme

Acknowledgements

This is the final report of a study on *Aggregate results of the single market programme*, undertaken by the National Technical University of Athens (NTUA) for the European Commission.

The core modelling team of the project involved the NTUA (P. Capros and T. Georgakopoulos), the Centre for Economic Studies of the Catholic University of Leuven (D. Van Regemorter and S. Proost) and the University of Middlesex (Dirk Willenbockel). Computer software support was successfully covered by Y. Antoniou and G. Atsabes, while data management was undertaken by A. Filipoupolitis (all from the NTUA).

Contributions were made by the University of Toulouse (N. Ladoux, M. Vielle, J.-J. Laffont) on benchmark data set preparation, Coherence, Belgium (D. Gusbin) on the collection of information from studies of the *Single Market Review 1996* and the University of Athens (Professor A. Sarris) on earlier methodological issues. Professor Erno Zalai (University of Budapest) also contributed in the modelling work, during his stay at NTUA (summer 1996). The authors would like to thank all members of the study steering committee for their helpful comments and suggestions, and for providing pre-publication copies of the other studies in the *Single Market Review* series.

1. Summary

1.1. Background

The present study deals with the overall appraisal of the macroeconomic implications of the European Union (EU) single market programme (SMP). The SMP, as introduced by the Single European Act, involved a large list of measures aimed at implementing the single market, by the end of 1992. The SMP involved a series of measures aiming at affecting the European economy in the following areas:

(a)   liberalization of trade of goods, through elimination of border and fiscal formalities and abolition of technical barriers to trade;
(b)   liberalization of cross-border public procurement;
(c)   general deregulation and more active enforcement of competition policy in all sectors;
(d)   liberalization of trade of factors, through, among others, abolition of capital mobility controls;
(e)   liberalization of cross-border service provision and abolition of restrictions to establishment.

1.2. Objective and scope

The objective of this study is to evaluate the SMP effects in an *ex post* manner by conducting simulations with an updated and adapted version of the GEM-E3 model,[1] an applied multi-country, multi-sectoral dynamic computable general equilibrium (CGE) model of the 12 EU Member States.

The *ex post* character of this evaluation is conceived in a twofold manner:

(a)   the study should use the actual performance of the EU economies, during the SMP implementation period; while
(b)   the primary effects of the SMP measures, as quantified by the sectoral studies[2] in an *ex post* manner, should provide the input to the CGE-based evaluation.

The study focuses solely on the CGE modelling methodology. A multitude of other CGE modelling analyses on the SMP effects, as reported in the literature, estimated the *ex ante* implications of SMP. The present study is the first one, attempting to carry out a global *ex post* evaluation, in the sense defined above.

1.3. *Monde* and *antimonde* related to the SMP

To evaluate a policy in an *ex post* manner, one must be able first to reproduce the reality (the observations), by using the model, and then to simulate a counterfactual scenario that excludes the measures under evaluation, in the present case the SMP measures. In the following we use the terms *monde* for the historical simulation and *antimonde* for the counterfactual one.

---

[1]   The GEM-E3 model was constructed by a collaborative project team, partially financed by the Joule Programme of the European Commission (DG XII/FI), and involved NTUA as a coordinator, KUL/CES, University of Toulouse, University of Mannheim, University of Strathclyde and CORE.

[2]   Such studies were commissioned by the European Commission within the 'Single Market Review' programme of the Directorates-General for the Internal Market and Financial Services (DG XV) and for Economic and Financial Affairs (DG II).

Apart from the difficulty of deriving quantitative assumptions, at the level of detail demanded in terms of the model, from the often qualitative or aggregate information provided by the sectoral studies, the study had to circumvent two major obstacles for the *ex post* analysis:

(a)   The first was a conceptual difficulty: the *monde* occurred as such not only because of the measures under evaluation but also because of a multitude of other changes. If the measures had not taken place, the *monde* would be different, still not observable, but also some of the other changes would perhaps be different as well. It is certain, therefore, that the *ex post* evaluation cannot avoid some degree of arbitrariness related to the separation of changes in part that will be attributed to the SMP and part that will be considered as non-attributable to the SMP. A transparent decision had then to be made regarding this distinction. For example, the following observed changes in the 1985–92 period were assumed as non-related to SMP completion: changes of tastes of consumers, as the shifts in favour of automobiles, services, communications and health care, shifts in the propensity of trade that cannot be explained by relative price changes and SMP measures, most of the observed technical progress, government policy, monetary indicators and price evolution in the rest of the world.

(b)   The second was a technical challenge: achieving a good replication of the observed economic statistics within a model run, termed 'dynamic calibration' of the model. In the literature, there is no formal method proposed for dynamic calibration of CGE models. In the context of this study such a procedure was designed and followed. Additional limitations arise, however, from the poor statistical information, at the level of detail required by the model, as available from EU statistical sources.[3]

1.4. The SMP measures in the model runs

The study attempts to quantitatively evaluate the implications of the *antimonde*, i.e. the impact of the non application of the SMP measures. The measures and primary effects assumed in this study to form the SMP, were considered as follows:

(a)   Non-tariff barriers (NTBs) associated to delays in custom control formalities involving losses in trade transactions. Formulated as iceberg-type losses in export volumes, they range from 1% to 2.5% of trade flow costs.

(b)   Extra trade costs necessary for compliance with foreign non-harmonized standards, labelling and packaging. Represented through *ad valorem* rates, of the order of 0.3% to 0.6% of trade costs, they also involve activity for market services associated to exports.

(c)   Costs of transport and banking activity associated to trade flows, also represented through *ad valorem* rates. They are likely to decrease because of efficiency gains in international transport and banking services supporting exports, entailing 0.1% up to 0.2% lower trade costs, differing by country.

(d)   The single market measures and the European Commission's initiatives in pursuing liberalization of sectors that were not included in the Single Market White Paper (European Commission, 1985) (e.g. insurance, telecommunications, air transport), incited economic agents to anticipate higher competition in all markets and achieve productivity gains. Based on sectoral studies, this has exerted particularly important effects on gains in the domain of X-inefficiencies in the banking and

---

3   This mainly concerned time series and input-output tables for the EU Member States, covering the post-1985 time period.

telecommunications sectors. For these sectors, an *ad hoc* higher productivity of labour and capital reaching 2.5% and 5%, respectively, in terms of fixed cost requirements, was introduced as primary SMP effect.

(e) Harmonization of standards and regulations, and generally the completion of the single market, make consumers perceive EU and domestic commodities as more homogeneous than before, minimizing distinctions in preferences over the geographic origin. This SMP effect is represented by a switch in the nesting of the consumers' preference structure reflecting market integration (in contrast to market segmentation, that prevailed before the SMP completion) and a subsequent increase in the price sensitivity of the consumers in their choice of EU products to reflect increasing homogeneity.

(f) The realization of the SMP increases the number of different commodity varieties that are available to EU consumers, for final demand, intermediate consumption, investment building or public procurement. It is assumed that efficiency gains are derived from the increased possibility of choice for the consumers. These gains, that permeate the whole economy are endogenously modelled only in one of the *monde* variants simulated with the model. Instead in other *monde* variants, because of analytical reasons that will be explained below, an exogenous improvement of total factor productivity (reaching 0.1% in all sectors) is assumed to be induced by the SMP. This improvement is considered implicitly to include some of the efficiency gains from increasing availability of varieties, but may also include additional effects of accelerated technology progress facilitated by the enlarged market. In any case, the variety effect acts through consumption, while the total factor productivity effect acts through production.

The study does not cover the analysis of other SMP issues, such as tax harmonization, structural funds, international capital mobility, labour mobility and public procurement. For the last two issues, sectoral studies indicated that they have induced little effect over the study period. Also, mainly because of lack of sectoral data, the present model version does not include a split of labour in different skills and a corresponding representation of household classes. Such a model extension would allow for improved insight of social distributional effects of the SMP.

1.5. Modelling methodology

The extended model, GEM-E3-SM, follows the standard methodology of computable general equilibrium frameworks, involving economic agents, producers and consumers, that compete through their demand and supply functions over a set of simultaneous markets of commodities and primary production factors, operating within a Walras economy (in which all economic transactions sum to zero, in equilibrium).

In addition, the extended model formulates a number of economic sectors (intermediate and equipment goods industries, banks and telecommunications) as being able to perform economies of scale and compete within an oligopolistic market regime. Firms operating in these sectors produce commodity varieties that are assumed not to be perfect substitutes in consumption. Bilateral EU trade flows, involving NTB and service-related trade costs, ensure a pan-European equilibrium. The model is dynamic, as simulating a time-dependent sequence of static equilibria depending on the updating of capital stock from endogenous investment.

The modelling framework simulates (and numerically calibrates) a mechanism through which market enlargement and the related increase of competition within the EU, can induce real growth effects.

Firms, perceiving more competition in the enlarged market, readjust their size, reduce price-cost margins and exploit economies of scale potential. This acts as a release of resources for the economy that become available for consumption and investment, entailing real growth effects.

Efficiency gains in exports and autonomous efficiency improvement in production act in a similar way: they allow for trade creation and a price fall. Additional efficiency gains for the consumer (final or intermediate), as he can choose from an increased variety of commodities within the enlarged market, add real growth effects.

Foreign trade, involving the EU and the rest of the world (RW) re-adjusts, through relative price changes. In a model variant,[4] this has been restrained by fixing the current account (as a % of EU GDP) and letting the real interest rate to adjust domestic activity, while in other model variants the current account of the EU could vary freely, allowing for possible terms of trade effects.

1.6. Design of model runs

The evaluation of the *ex post* effects of the SMP is based on dynamic model runs (and sensitivity tests) over the period 1985–91 (period observed) extended to 1994 (not observed). The baseline scenario is identical to the *monde* as this was dynamically calibrated. The *antimonde* simulation is defined as the removal of the SMP measures described above.

Table 1.1.   Summary of assumptions for the SMP simulations

Title of simulation	Explanation
Constraint case	The current account as a % of GDP is assumed fixed in each Member State. The real interest rate by country can adjust. A total factor productivity assumption, related to the SMP, is included.
Flexible case	Trade is freely adjusting in bilateral intra-EU trade and with respect to the rest of the world. The current account can vary freely, but real interest rates remain fixed. The EU can adjust its terms of trade *vis-à-vis* the rest of the world. A total factor productivity assumption, related to the SMP, is included.
Efficiency case	As in 'flexible case' regarding current account and the interest rate, but inclusive of endogenous efficiency gains coming from the increased variety of EU commodities in the enlarged market. No exogenous factor productivity gains are assumed.

Three main *antimonde* scenarios were constructed and simulated with the model, as shown in the table. The constraint case does not allow for possible terms of trade effects in the EU economies (in the sense of implying net inflow of resources from the RW to the EU), when

---

[4]   Such a modelling choice corresponds to the model's closure rule regarding the external sector.

comparing the *monde* to the *antimonde* simulations. The scenario assumes that in these two simulations, the level of current account by country as a % of GDP is kept unchanged, and to obtain this result, the economies can vary their real interest rates, so as to adjust their domestic activities in investment and consumption. That sort of 'external sector' closure rule, often used in CGE modelling, allows to evaluate the effects of a policy in the domestic economy only, as a result of the new allocation (of sectors, investment, consumption, etc.) induced by the policy. In this sense, the analytical benefit from constructing the constraint case simulation, is the evaluation of the pure internal effects of the SMP policy in each country, abstracting from any global gain or loss coming from the external sector. Of course, the intra-EU trade and the trade with the RW change, under the SMP in the constraint case, but this operates in such a way that the surplus or deficit (as a % of GDP) of each country with their trade partners remains unchanged.

The flexible and the efficiency simulation cases remove the assumption about the external sector constraint and let the current account change in level and in % of GDP in all EU countries, as an indirect consequence of the SMP. Hence, there is no need to vary the real interest rate, that is assumed to remain unchanged in the simulations. These two simulation cases accept by construction that terms of trade effects (for example net inflow from the RW), induced by the economy adjustment under the SMP, are possible in all the EU Member States. The allocation of activities and resources, induced by the SMP, has therefore more freedom to adjust, than in the constraint case, by redirecting transfers to more attractive countries both for the EU and the RW.

In a sense, the flexible and the efficiency cases provide results about the SMP that are more likely to have occurred as a consequence of the SMP, than in the constraint case. For example, empirical sectoral studies, within the 'Single Market Review' programme, confirmed that the SMP has implied net inflow of investment from the RW to the EU. Nevertheless, it can be also argued that these two simulation cases do not account for the possible re-adjustment of the RW attitude who may react as well, in view of the terms of trade changes with respect to the EU. Therefore, we consider that the range of results obtained from the constraint and the other two simulation cases is more valid than the individual results of any simulation case alone.

The flexible and the efficiency cases differ only in the representation of technical efficiency progress that has been partly induced by the SMP. The flexible case (and the constraint case) considers that the acceleration of technical progress, as a consequence of the SMP, occurs in the production side of the EU economies. It is assumed (and confirmed by many specialized studies) that, as producers face increased competition, they accelerate the incorporation of innovations in their production process and their products, while under the enlarged market, they can choose among a larger variety of commodities for their production and investment. In both cases, they improve in production efficiency. Given the complexity of this process and the lack of empirical evidence, it is assumed in the two simulation cases that the SMP induced in all sectors an exogenous gain in total factor productivity.

The efficiency case puts emphasis on the consumption side and only considers efficiency gains resulting from the increase in commodity varieties under the enlarged single market. Firms, in intermediate consumption and investment, private consumers and the government benefit from the availability of larger variety and can achieve efficiency gains, in the volume and costs of their consumption. In this simulation case, technical progress due to the enlargement of the market, is endogenously modelled, as an indirect consequence of the variety effect. The comparison of results from the efficiency case with those from the flexible case, gives analytical insight about the role of the variety effect mechanism, in the SMP evaluation. As it will be shown below, it widens the range of numerical results about the impact of the SMP, hence improving robustness of conclusions. Of course, the efficiency case does not include the total factor productivity assumption, since if added on top of the variety effect, double counting errors would have been introduced in the analysis.

The analysis is completed by a set of sensitivity simulation tests. For example, the study constructed a set of simulations assuming that in the *antimonde* there has been partial removal of SMP measures, for example regarding border controls only and not competition intensification. Such partial *antimondes* are built for analytical reasons, serving to evaluate isolated effects of individual measures. Additional sensitivity tests, for example regarding full capital mobility in the EU, or analysis of robustness of results regarding the assumptions in the numerical calibration of imperfect competition sectors, have also been undertaken.

Additional analysis effort was devoted, in the study, to the evaluation of long-run properties of the results about the impact of the SMP. The question was to estimate, through model runs, which of the overall SMP effects are transitory and which are likely to leave permanent traces on the EU economy. For this purpose, the efficiency case was simulated over a longer time period, in fact over 20 years, so as to approach a steady state solution of the model.

1.7. Results: evaluation of the SMP

The results and sensitivity tests generally suggest that the SMP has induced real activity gains and increased the volume of intra-EU trade. According to the model results, and considering the range estimated from the three main simulation cases, as mentioned above:

(a)   EU GDP in 1994 is estimated to have been 1.1% to 1.5% higher due to the single market, leading to a cumulative net gain ranging from ECU 174 billion to ECU 207 billion in the period 1988–94.

(b)   Real GDP increase is supported by a higher level of investment, increasing by 2.5% to 4.5% and consumption increasing by 0.8% to 1.6%.

(c)   Employment is also higher indicating the creation of 320,000 to 620,000 new jobs, in 1985–94, which represents, however, a small increase in total employment (0.25% to 0.49%).

(d)   The volume of trade has increased significantly: intra-EU trade, for example, is found 4% to 5% higher in 1994. Trade creation is also observed in the relations with the rest of the world.

(e)   In the manufacturing sectors the increase in intra-EU trade is even higher (7% to 8%) accompanied by higher industrial concentration and falling price/cost margins (0.8% to 0.9%) because of increasing competition. Equipment goods, construction and building materials are found to gain more from the SMP, than intermediate (metals, chemicals) and consumer goods. This is related to investment that boosts significantly more than private consumption.

(f)   Among the service sectors, noticeable is the performance of telecommunications and banking services that achieve 12% to 18% higher intra-EU trade and 4.0% to 6.0% lower fixed costs.

(g)   Relative to a non-EU foreign numeraire, the SMP induces a general decrease in domestic prices (reaching -0.6% down to -1.1% in 1994), as a result of the combined effects of efficiency gains in trade and production that over-compensate pressures on prices from the higher level of activity.

The main effects of the SMP are summarized in Table 1.2.

Table 1.2.   Overall impact of the SMP

Effects of the SMP on EUR-11	Constraint case	Flexible case	Efficiency case
GDP	+1.10%	+1.26%	+1.46%
Private consumption	+0.82%	+1.53%	+1.60%
Total investment	+2.67%	+4.52%	+4.53%
Total intra-EU trade	+3.99%	+4.63%	+4.74%
Employment	+0.25%	+0.48%	+0.49%
Labour productivity	+0.32%	+0.77%	+0.97%
Consumer price index	-1.19%	-0.74%	-0.65%
Real wage rate	+1.43%	+1.67%	+1.87%
Average mark-up	-0.79%	-0.92%	-0.92%
Current account as percent of GDP	0.00%	-0.68%	-0.62%

Note: Numbers indicate percent changes between *monde* and *antimonde* except current account which is absolute difference. The figures presented in this table refer to the last year of the simulation (i.e. 1994) of the three full *antimonde* scenarios.

If the the current account as a % of GDP is not constrained in the simulations, as in the flexible case (and the efficiency case), the EU economy is attractive for exporters from the rest of the world who bring resources into the EU contributing to increase activity, which boosts from the realization of the SMP. In this case, investment also increases, allowed to take its full amplitude. Gains from terms of trade effects, coming from the RW, are obtained in this case, and these are added to the gains from the SMP.

If the current account as a % of GDP is restrained from varying as a consequence of the SMP, as in the constraint case, the real interest rate increases to discourage investment and consumption so as to limit the needs for support of domestic activity from the rest of the world. Obviously, this reduces real growth effects but also contributes to lowering domestic prices. Terms of trade effects vanish, but real activity gains that are due to the better allocation of resources induced by the increased competition under the SMP remain.

As explained, the constraint case measures the effects of the SMP on the domestic EU economy alone, as a consequence of domestic readjustments. The results are suggesting clearly positive pure effects of the SMP for domestic activity and prices. Terms of trade gains from the RW largely explain the additional GDP effects, found in the flexible case, compared to the constraint case.

The efficiency case includes the pure gains from the SMP (as in the constraint case), the additional gains from terms of trade (as in the flexible case) but also an amplification of positive growth effects, as it induces efficiency gains through consumption, for which a bigger variety of commodities is available in the enlarged EU market. To avoid double counting, the efficiency case does not include the total factor productivity assumption, that has been introduced in the other two cases. Regarding the representation of the technical progress induced by the SMP, the efficiency case simulation is considered as an alternative to the simulations that accept an *ad hoc* total factor productivity assumption. The variety effect, endogenously present in the efficiency scenario only, acts in favour of moderating the upwards pressures on prices limiting the need for imports from the RW and releasing more domestic resources for consumption and investment.

The distributional impact of the SMP on the EU economic sectors are also worth mentioning. Given that investment is found to boost more than consumption, as a consequence of the SMP, sectors related to investment, such as equipment goods, construction and building materials, benefit more from the policy, in terms of activity and efficiency gains. EU production of consumption and agricultural goods is found stable, while chemicals and metal products slightly loose their share in the EU market. The activity of service sectors, albeit losses in activities related to the support of trade, progresses under the SMP and an internal EU trade market for services is found to be emerging.

The partial *antimonde* runs indicate that the removal of border controls and the efficiency in trade costs, if taken alone, mainly induce trade creation effects, leading to 2.6% more intra-EU trade, accompanied by a reduction of prices. GDP effects are positive but very small.

The enlargement of the market, higher competition and the increased substitutability among the EU commodities also contributes to trade creation (less than the border controls), but constitutes the main cause of real GDP, employment and investment growth effects.

Efficiency gains on the production side (X-efficiencies in sectors and total factor productivity gains) explain a small part of the achieved GDP growth: they account for 0.2% of extra GDP, in the flexible case. The efficiency case explaining technical progress from the variety effects on efficiency gains leads to a similar, even higher, performance.

The trade creation effects were found robust in all sensitivity tests. The results on real GDP growth, higher employment and higher investment effects from the SMP were also found robust in the tests. However, these results were found to vary in magnitude, though on the positive side, depending on the numerical calibration of imperfect competition sectors and the model's closure rule.

The long-run simulation that approaches the steady state of model dynamics, suggests that although the effects through EU foreign trade with the RW tend to re-equilibrate, indicating that the terms of trade effects are transitory, there are permanent effects from the SMP that remain in the EU economy in the long term, regarding GDP growth, investment, employment, production cost efficiency and the intra-EU trade. The long-run effects are found to be even more favourable for the evaluation of the SMP.

1.8. Limitations of the study

First, there is a fundamental limitation, arising from the fact that economics is not an experimental science. Since we cannot 'see' the *antimonde* experiment, our separation of changes into SMP-induced and non-SMP-induced effects involves a certain degree of arbitrariness.

A second limitation results from the poor statistical observation of the *monde* that decreases the reliability of the dynamic calibration. Perhaps structural changes not encountered in the statistically incomplete view of the EU could lead to a different quantitative *ex post* appraisal of the SMP, although unchanged in qualitative terms. The quantitative evaluation could also be more accurate, if updated engineering cost information on the imperfect competition sectors were available.

One issue that is incompletely covered in this study regards the effects of the SMP on price convergence. This is due to the particularities of standard CGE models, as they are calibrated on a single base year, for which they assume unit prices in all sectors and countries. Therefore, information about initial differentials in prices across countries and sectors is not basically incorporated into the model information, except those related to economies of scale potential in the imperfect competition sectors. These only contribute to price convergence, which has also been confirmed in the study results.

2. Introduction

2.1. Background to the study

Under a 1992 Council of Ministers Resolution the European Commission had to provide an overall analysis of the effectiveness of measures taken in view of the creation of the European single market. The measures are also termed the single market programme (SMP). In 1996, the European Commission launched an important set of studies aiming at *ex post* evaluation of the implications of the SMP on the European Union economy. The term 1996 Single Market Review is used for that set of studies. The majority of the studies cover specific economic sectors, while others focus on issues that have a horizontal character. Finally, two studies cover the modelling of the European economy at the aggregate level. The present report corresponds to one of these two studies, focusing in particular on the application of a Computable General Equilibrium (CGE) methodology.

The study had a total duration of five months and was supervised by a steering committee involving DG II, DG XV (both European Commission) and Professor F. Bourguignon acting as external referee.[5]

The project built on the existing CGE model GEM-E3 (**G**eneral **E**quilibrium **M**odel of **E**conomy, **E**nergy and **E**nvironment)[6] that was adapted and extended according to the needs of the study. The new version of the model is named GEM-E3-SM (SM standing for the Single Market).

The core modelling team of the project involved National Technical University of Athens (NTUA) (P. Capros and T. Georgakopoulos), KUL/CES (D. Van Regemorter and S. Proost) and University of Middlesex (Dirk Willenbockel).[7]

Contributions were made by the University of Toulouse (N. Ladoux, M. Vielle, J.-J. Laffont) on benchmark data set preparation, Coherence, Belgium (D. Gusbin) on the collection of information from studies of the 'Single Market Review' and University of Athens (Professor A. Sarris) on earlier methodological issues.

2.2. Objectives and scope of the study

The objective of the present study was to evaluate the SMP effects in an *ex post* manner by conducting simulations with an updated and adapted version of an existing multi-country, multi-sectoral dynamic computable general equilibrium (CGE) model of the 12 EU Member States.

---

[5] We would like to thank all members of the study steering committee for their helpful comments and suggestions. Of course, the project team bears sole responsibility for any errors or omissions.

[6] The GEM-E3 model was constructed by a collaborative project team, partially financed by the Joule Programme of the European Commission (DG XII/F1), and involved NTUA as a coordinator, KUL/CES, University of Toulouse, University of Mannheim, University of Strathclyde and CORE.

[7] Also, Professor Erno Zalai (University of Budapest) contributed in the modelling, during his stay at NTUA, in summer 1996.

The *ex post* character of this evaluation is conceived in a twofold manner:

(a)   the study should use the actual performance of the EU economies, during the SMP implementation period; while

(b)   the primary effects of the SMP measures, as quantified by the sectoral studies in an *ex post* manner, should provide the input to the CGE-based evaluation.

The study focuses solely on the CGE modelling methodology. A multitude of other CGE modelling analyses on the SMP effects, as reported in the literature, estimated the *ex ante* implications of SMP. The present study is the first one, attempting to carry out a global *ex post* evaluation, in the sense defined above.

To carry out an *ex post* evaluation, one must be able first to reproduce the reality (the observations), by using the model, and then to simulate a counterfactual scenario that excludes the measures under evaluation. In the following we use the term *monde* for the historical simulation and *antimonde* for the counterfactual one.

The difficulty of such an exercise arises from the assertions used for the *antimonde*. Of course, the *monde* occurred as such not only because of the measures under evaluation but also because of a multitude of other changes. If the measures had not taken place, the *monde* would be different, still not observable, but also some of the other changes would perhaps be different as well. It is certain, therefore, that the *ex post* evaluation cannot avoid some degree of arbitrariness related to the separation of changes in a part that will be attributed to the SMP and a part that will be considered as non-attributable to the SMP.

As it will be explained in detail in the remaining sections, a prerequisite of the above methodology is the accurate observation of the *monde*. Unfortunately, the Eurostat statistics are rather poor in this matter, at least at the level of detail required by the model. Furthermore, the sectoral statistics of Eurostat, as available at present, cover the years up to 1992, a period in which the SMP was not yet fully realized.

An additional difficulty arises from the very nature of the modelling approach, regarding the adjustment of the model-based baseline scenario to the *monde*, as actually observed. As it is known, a CGE model is strong in analysing distributional effects and counterfactual policies, but it is rather weak in economic forecasting. Other modelling approaches, nevertheless, that are strong in economic forecasting, for example the traditional macroeconometric models, are weak in policy analysis as their microeconomic foundations are substantially less elaborate than in the CGE models.

The challenge, therefore, for the present study was to achieve a good replication of the observed economic statistics within a model run. This is hereafter called dynamic calibration. In the literature, there is no formal method (even very few attempts) proposed for dynamic calibration of CGE models. In a following section we propose such a formal procedure for the GEM-E3-SM model.

As mentioned, the study starts from the existing CGE model GEM-E3. For the purpose of assessing in an *ex post* manner the impact of the SMP on the economies of EU Member States, the present study undertook a considerable revision and adaptation, regarding both the data and model specification.

2.3. Overview of the study

The study is presented in three parts. The first part is the main report, involving Sections 3 to 5, further discussed below. The second part is a technical report, presenting technical details about the model and the numerical assumptions (Appendix A). Finally, the third part contains a full set of numerical results (Appendix B).

To quantify the primary effects of the SMP measures in model-related terms, the study started from an exhaustive review of the Single Market Review results of sectoral studies, as commissioned by the European Commission. The objective, in this respect, was to produce a synthesis of sectoral evaluations so as to obtain well-founded quantitative assertions, as inputs for model runs. This is presented in Section 3.

Section 4 deals with the methodology followed for model extension and application. The model application is based on a general assertion stating that the EU economies in the pre-SMP period were characterized by important inefficiencies, that were generally due to the segmentation of markets. EU economies were characterized by:

(a)   inefficiencies in trade, as exports involved high costs for border control, compliance with foreign standards, packaging, labelling, bank services, etc.;
(b)   inefficiencies in production, since the average size of firms in a country was below the technically optimal efficiency level, resulting in high production costs;
(c)   inefficiencies in pricing (high price-cost margins), as firms were perceiving low competition within the segmented country markets;
(d)   inefficiencies in consumption, both final and intermediate consumers could only select from a limited variety of commodities.

The SMP measures attempt to remove those inefficiencies by integrating and harmonizing the EU country markets. Regarding model extensions, Section 4 describes the techniques that were necessary to incorporate inefficiencies in a general equilibrium model. Also, Section 4 describes the procedure for quantification of these inefficiencies, in other terms the static calibration to pre-SMP facts, and the dynamic calibration, so that the baseline model run replicates the *monde*.

Section 5 presents the application of the model to evaluate the global effects of the SMP. A number of model runs are designed for that purpose, each attempting to quantify the dynamic effects from the absence of one or more SMP measures. These model runs are termed simulated *antimonde*. Section 5 discusses the results for the SMP evaluation and considers a set of sensitivity tests.

3. The single market programme

3.1. Introduction

In 1985 Jacques Delors initiated a policy aimed at turning the European common market into a single market. By July 1987, the Member States adopted the Single European Act which involved a large list of measures aimed at implementing the single market, by the end of 1992. The SMP involves a series of measures intended to affect the European economy in the following areas (European Commission 1985, 1988; Pelkmans and Winters, 1988):

(a)   liberalization of trade of goods, through elimination of border and fiscal formalities and abolition of technical barriers to trade;
(b)   liberalization of cross-border public procurement;
(c)   general deregulation and more active enforcement of competition policy in all sectors;
(d)   liberalization of trade of factors, through among others abolition of capital mobility controls;
(e)   liberalization of cross-border service provisions and abolition of restrictions to establishment.

The single market measures and the Commission's initiatives in pursuing liberalization of sectors that were not included in the Single Market White Paper (e.g. insurance, telecommunications, air transports) brought economic agents to anticipate higher competition in all markets. Therefore, it is likely that changes induced by the SMP took place even before the 1992 completion deadline.

Reports suggested that there had been considerable progress towards SMP completion by 1993, especially in the relaxation of border checks and controls, the banking and transport sectors, the high technology sectors and the liberalization of capital movements (European Commission, 1994; Hoeller and Louppe, 1994). By April 1994, 86% of the total number of pieces of national legislation required as a result of Council measures had been adopted by the Member States. However, according to the Commission, despite the progress, delays have been significant in the areas of public procurement, insurance and company law, and intellectual and industrial property.

Although the SMP measures applied to all economic sectors, there is general consensus that some sectors are likely to be more affected than others, mainly through higher competition induced by market enlargement. These sectors mainly include intermediate and equipment goods, accounting for a rough 20% of total EU gross domestic production. Earlier studies on the SMP have put emphasis on such industrial sectors, and identified great potential of possible economies of scale and intra-sectoral restructuring that could result from the realization of the SMP.

3.2. Effects of the SMP: synthesis of sectoral studies

Several specific studies were commissioned by the EC,[8] in 1995 and 1996, to assess the impact of the single market measures on manufacturing and service sectors, on the dismantling of barriers, on trade and investment, on competition and scale effects.

An overview of the principal (and available) studies has been made, within the present study, to evaluate their possible contributions as input to the CGE model. More specifically, the following studies were examined:

Sub-panel 1

(a)   Chemicals
(b)   Motor vehicles

Sub-panel 2

(a)   Air transport
(b)   Road freight transport
(c)   Credit institutions and banking
(d)   Telecommunications: liberalized services

Sub-panel 3

(a)   Technical barriers to trade
(b)   Public procurement
(c)   Customs and fiscal formalities at frontiers

Sub-panel 4

(a)   Foreign direct investment
(b)   Trade patterns inside the single market
(c)   Trade creation and trade diversion

Sub-panel 5

(a)   Price competition and convergence
(b)   Competition issues
(c)   Economies of scale

Sub-panel 6

(a)   Trade, labour and capital flows: the less developed regions
(b)   Employment, trade and labour costs in manufacturing

Deriving precise quantitative assumptions in terms of the CGE model from these studies has been very difficult, as most of these provided only qualitative information or just aggregate indicators. Nevertheless, it was possible to derive the order of magnitude of the primary or sectoral effects of the SMP measures.

---

[8]   A description of the studies content is given in the EU document, Single Market Review 1996, Summary description of individual studies. See also list of published studies, page ii.

Several of the sectoral studies (e.g. some of those in Sub-panels 4 and 5) providing indication about overall indirect effects of the SMP, were overlapping with the present study's scope. Thus, they have been used for cross-checking only.

On the other hand, the above list did not include an update of the engineering information regarding the sectoral minimum efficient industrial scale (as was done by Pratten in 1988), so no *ex post* information was available about any direct efficiency gains in terms of production costs. For some sectors however, there was information in some studies regarding the detraction of prices likely due to increased competition and industrial concentration.

Examining the Eurostat Business Survey,[9] it is evident that the main effect as perceived by industrial executives, was trade liberalization and the removal of extra costs due to the absence of harmonization of legislation. The present study has put emphasis on quantifying these primary effects.

Some studies have concluded that the effects of the SMP where negligible during the pre-1992 period. For example, this was the case for public procurement and labour mobility across countries. For this reason these effects were not considered in the simulations.

3.2.1. The dismantling of border controls

Sectoral studies provide strong evidence indicating a considerable decrease of trade costs due to the dismantling of fiscal formalities at frontiers. The average cost per consignment in the EUR-12 has been found to have decreased by almost 60% between 1992 and 1995.

For model analysis purposes this cost decrease has to be further decomposed by cost item because economy in some items just represents efficiency gains, while in others it also implies a decrease in associated services. For this purpose, the effects from dismantling border controls are divided into the following three categories:

(a)   those involving costs from delays and physical controls within border formalities;
(b)   those that arise from compliance to foreign legislation; and
(c)   those associated with transport costs, banking and insurance services.

Effects from customs/duty formalities

In this study the direct cost saving effects from the removal of customs formalities are called non-tariff barriers[10] (NTBs). When effective, the NTBs involve delays in product delivery and other physical controls that lead to extra cost per consignment. *Ex ante* studies suggested that the extra cost from NTBs would amount to 2% of total intra-EU trade. *Ex post* evaluations based on detailed surveys indicate that the cost savings from the removal of NTBs represented a 1% to 1.5% reduction in trade costs.

---

[9]   *Single Market Review*, Results of the business survey, Luxembourg, Office for Official Publications of the EC, 1997.

[10]   The non-tariff barriers considered for the SMP do not include any quota restriction or any other form of quantity export restraints.

Effects from reduction of compliance costs

Cost savings in trade have also been achieved from the harmonization of norms and regulations across the EU countries. These accounted for 0.3% to 0.6% of total trade costs as suggested by *ex post* surveys. Significant discrepancies across countries are observed with Spain, Portugal, Greece and Italy benefiting more from harmonization. On the contrary, smaller cost reduction can be expected for the Benelux countries.

Harmonization also involves a decrease in the demand for those market services that were necessary for the transformation of the exported product regarding packaging, labelling and other norms.

Effects on trade costs from transport and banking services

Cost savings regarding the transport and banking costs components of exports are related to two types of effects of the SMP. First, the removal of frontier controls and harmonization implied shorter delays for freight transports and fewer administrative formalities for bank transactions. Second, the SMP allowed both the transport and banking sector to optimize their support of inter-country trade flows and transactions, further leading to efficiency gains in these activities.

For example, *ex post* surveys indicated that from the elimination of border delays alone, a 2% saving on hauliers' costs was effected. These cost reductions, in terms of hauliers' costs, again differ by country, ranging from 5% for Greece to 2.5% for central Europe. Of course, although the reduction of trade costs implies gains in efficiency, it will also result in a decrease in the demand of the transport and banking sectors.

3.2.2. Factor productivity effects

There is a general belief that market integration can accelerate technical progress, associated to production factors and thus induce growth. There has been no empirical evidence from the sectoral studies about the magnitude of such effects. Experts consulted about this matter, including those of the European Commission (DG II), believe that the single market has induced accelerated technical progress, acting in favour of total factor productivity gains of the order of 0.1% per annum in 1992, on average and for all sectors.

As mentioned above, some sectors were found to have more potential for competition-driven restructuring; for example in industries producing intermediate and equipment goods. These sectors also are more capital intensive, also needing more research and development capital, than other sectors.

Increased competition in such markets would push firms to accelerate intangible investment, so as to preserve competitiveness for their commodity varieties; this implies embedding innovation in their products, which as they are further used as intermediate or capital goods by other sectors, induce general technical progress.

The enlargement of the market also leads to higher degrees of product variety being available for consumption, intermediate inputs and investment. This further induces productivity and efficiency gains in all sectors.

Intra-sectoral restructuring in these intermediate and equipment goods industries, such as premature scrapping of old equipment, merging and reorganization of production (including specialization in the most efficient production lines), also leads to total factor productivity gains.

Empirical studies, including those that were commissioned within the 'Single Market Review', confirmed that there has been accelerated technical progress in the equipment and intermediate goods industry and in the use of their products in other sectors. However, since the period of the SMP coincided with a period of high technology evolution in these sectors world-wide, these studies were inconclusive about the impact of the SMP on the observed total factor productivity gains.

3.2.3. X-efficiency gains in service sectors

Although the SMP did not incorporate any direct measures for the service sectors, these have undergone significant restructuring involving efficiency gains in anticipation of the completion of the EU single market.

Several studies consider that these gains were of X-efficiency type, that is as if these sectors started optimizing their production only when perceiving potential competition from the opening of the market. These gains cannot be explained as scale effects (which are endogenously modelled in the study) so they were included as autonomous effects of the SMP.

Financial services

The SMP measures have resulted in an intensification of competition, but with only a limited impact on the prices of financial services during this period. Surveys indicated that this effect is more evident in countries like Spain, Portugal and Greece, which were among the most highly regulated. The level of market concentration has increased, there is an increase in cross-border acquisitions, joint ventures and strategic alliances. There are indications that part of the potential for economies of scale has been exploited and that the cost efficiency of the sector has increased, though all of it cannot be attributed to the SM. There is also an increase in trade in financial services, in off-balance-sheet activities, in investment management and in the corporate sector, but it is not clear whether it can be entirely attributed to the SMP.

Telecommunications services

The surveys indicate that there has been an evolution towards market integration and increasing competition, as the number of operators has increased and prices were dropping and converging. The decrease in prices has resulted from the decrease in equipment prices (20 to 30%) and through increased competition. It should be mentioned, however, that the liberalized services only represent 20% of total sales on the telecommunications markets.

Regarding the impact of the SM, the study on telecommunications services indicates that though the general evolution in this sector is mostly explained by autonomous technological change, the SM has allowed some European firms to participate in the technological breakthrough occurring in this sector and to become competitive at world level after restructuring of the supply side.

3.2.4. Indirect effects

Several of the sectoral studies provide indication about overall indirect effects of the SMP, on the issues of:

(a)   trade patterns by sector;
(b)   price convergence;
(c)   competition effects;
(d)   realization of economies of scale.

These effects are expected to be endogenously derived from the model simulations in the present study.

Trade patterns by sector

The question in the relevant sectoral study was to examine if the observed trade patterns confirms the expectation of increased competitiveness of EU industries in world markets and trade creation among EU partners.

Through an analysis of shares/coverage ratios, the study suggests that there have been some gains in competitiveness: there is a modest increase in the intra-EU coverage (measured by the exports on imports ratio for intra-EU trade) in all countries, as well as in the extra-EU coverage (with the exception of Italy, BLEU, Greece and Spain). There was a moderate erosion in domestic market shares, indicating some trade creation, but there was no indication of trade diversion. The same type of conclusions are drawn from the study on trade creation and trade diversion.

Price convergence by sector

The main results from the study on price competition and price convergence, which can be useful for the analysis in the context of this study are the following:

(a)   In general, the dispersion between prices decreased since 1988. The convergence in prices for consumer products and services tends to accelerate after the SMP.
(b)   The price dispersion is lowest in the sectors more open to trade or to non-EU producers' competition. Price convergence has been greater in Greece, Spain and Portugal (the catch-up effect of integration).
(c)   For products/services that are differentiated in terms of research and development or advertising, price diversity remained stable and rather high (household appliances, televisions, electronics, etc.). This, of course, cannot be attributed to the SMP, but rather is the result of autonomous technological evolution.

Evolution of competition in the single market

Sectoral studies indicated that within this period there has been a general increase of competition, a significant part of which can be attributed to market enlargement resulting from the SMP. Other factors have independently induced more competition, such as: external trade liberalization on a more global scale or sector specific reforms (e.g. air transport, motor vehicles) and technological developments (e.g. telecommunications).

Increased competition can explain the price/cost margin reduction which has been observed and has been found to be rather substantial: 5% to 10% for pharmaceuticals, 16% to 30% in office machinery (stable in Germany), 12% to 14% in France and Italy but 0% in Belgium and the UK for boiler-making are examples of results given in a preliminary report.

Realization of economies of scale/concentration

The study on the realization of economies of scale shows that although the average size of the firms, measured by real gross value added, increased over the period 1981–91, there is no structural break reflecting the anticipated influence of the imperfect market (IM) measures. There has been a significant increase in concentration of the industry at the EU level between 1987 and 1993, but the study does not give any clear conclusion on an eventual realization of economies of scale. The clearest impact on the average firm size has been observed in the R&D-intensive industries, though in absolute terms it remains small. International mergers and acquisitions have been one of the responses of firms towards EU integration and this might have been motivated by the exploitation of economies of scale in R&D and marketing rather than in production. Data availability has limited the possibility for quantitative estimates of these effects, so as to be comparable to the model results.

Regarding economies of scale, the study suggests that one of the most important contributions of the IM measures could be through pushing the firms towards their production frontiers; however, no data or study to confirm this is available.

Opening public procurement to competition

The study shows that, although in legal terms the opening of the public procurement market has been rather effective, it did not yet have very concrete results. No real price decrease or price convergence has been observed; some firms have indicated a slight increase in business because of the opening of foreign public sectors. The share of imports in public procurement has slightly increased (from 6.2% in 1987 to 10% in 1994 on average). The increase is higher in small countries and mainly concerns sectors with high technology content (medical equipment, railway rolling stock and office machinery).

4. Methodology

4.1. A review of literature on *ex ante* evaluation of the SMP with CGE models

The economics of 1992 (in other terms the effects of the SMP) have been researched very intensively in an *ex ante* sense (for the better known studies see Emerson *et al.*, 1988; European Commission, 1988; Winters and Venables, 1990; Winters, 1992a). The gains are presumed to arise from the following welfare enhancing mechanisms of freeing intra-EC trade:

(a)   an initial reduction in costs due to dismantling of trade barriers and customs formalities;
(b)   lower costs due to economies of scale;
(c)   reductions in price/cost margins due to stronger competition; and,
(d)   welfare gains due to non-price effects, such as enhanced innovation, a wider product range and organizational changes.

Empirical *ex ante* analyses, based on partial or sectoral equilibrium modelling, have estimated the EC-wide economic gains at between 2% and 7% of GDP, along with a 4% to 6% fall in prices, and the creation of between 2 and 4 million jobs (Emerson *et al.*, 1988; Catinat and Italianer, 1988; Gasiorek, Smith and Venables, 1992). However, these estimates seem to depend very much on particular assumptions, and some of them have been criticized in the scientific literature as being biased on the high side (e.g. Grossman, 1990; Winters, 1992b).

Empirical studies have pointed out that the SMP would necessitate considerable industrial restructuring, particularly of the intra-sectoral type. The prediction that all Member States would benefit, with the largest gains expected in the smaller southern countries, mainly because of a greater scope for exploiting scale economies. Dynamic effects could be even higher as induced by accelerated accumulation of more productive capital. Baldwin (1992), for instance, finds that such an effect can double the static welfare gains.

Baldwin and Venables (1995) have categorized several classes of effects that could lead to welfare gains from increased economic integration, such as envisaged by the SMP. They mentioned:

(a)   changes in wedges between private and social prices, arising from changes in tariffs, quantitative restrictions (if applicable), real trade costs, shifts in location of production, terms or trade effects, etc.;
(b)   changes in trade volumes, arising from effects such as reduction of cross-hauling of goods by monopolistic firms, changes in relative factor costs, changes in incomes and expenditures, etc.;
(c)   changes in firm level output and numbers of domestic firms arising from industrial rationalization;
(d)   changes in the number of available varieties of products available to consumers;
(e)   factor accumulation changes, arising by induced changes in factor prices, and X-efficiency effects.

Studies of the growth implications of EC integration, that were based on econometric estimations, are generally inconclusive in attempting to separate the effects of the SMP or just found small effects on growth. For example, Coe and Moghadam (1993) using regressions explaining output growth, including variables such as the share of intra-EC trade in total EC trade, suggest that in the period after 1987 the SMP is likely to have had a very small effect on growth, of the order of 0.25% on GDP per annum.

On the other hand, models with micro-foundations, such as the CGE models, illustrate higher potential gains from the SMP. For example, the studies by Gasiorek, Smith and Venables (1991 and 1992), and the earlier partial equilibrium study of Smith and Venables (1988), formulating imperfect competition and economies of scale, illustrated high gains induced from increased trade within market integration. As supported also by Branson and Winters (1990), the trade and welfare effects of trade liberalization are substantially higher when the CGE model formulates trade in the presence of imperfect competition and economies of scale, compared to results of pure perfect competition CGE approaches.

The CGE-based studies generally showed that the removal of border control measures, alone, would induce rather small effects on growth, but higher effects on trade creation. For example, Willenbockel (1994) finds an increase of 0.2%–0.3% of the UK's GDP and above 3% for the volume of trade.

The CGE approaches mainly explored the effects of market integration, compared to market segmentation that prevailed in the pre-SMP era. The numerical estimates of effects from market integration, as found in the scientific literature, are generally within a range of 0.5% to 1.5%, regarding static effects, which may reach 2.5% in a steady state. In the literature, the *ex ante* applications of CGE models differ in their estimates. Beside the numerical assumptions, the differences can be also attributed to the nature of the mechanism which the author is emphasizing.

In a series of approaches, authors formulate the fall of price cost margins as being induced directly from market integration. For example, Haaland and Wooton (1991) and Haaland and Norman (1992), assume that market integration removes price discrimination by market of destination, leading to the drop in mark-ups in the average. Others, for example Harrison, Rutherford and Tarr (1994) in a report to the World Bank, formulate changes as coming from a structural shift in the multiple stage budgeting hierarchy of consumers, asserting that integration leads to higher substitutability between domestic goods and goods imported from the EU. They found that the effects from market integration alone account for more than half of the total SMP effects on GDP.

Other approaches prefer to put emphasis on the direct link between higher competition and the firms' price setting behaviour. For example, Burniaux and Waelbroeck (1992) and Mercenier (1994), formulating oligopolistic behaviour of firms based on quantity conjectural variations, suggest that positive effects of the SMP are mainly derived from a rise in perceived elasticities of demand.

The issue regarding the formulation of conjectures, for the oligopolistic behaviour of firms competing in the imperfect competition markets, raised controversies in the literature. It is argued that changing conjectures involves arbitrariness that may lead to uncontrolled (or badly interpreted) results. If the conjectures are assumed to be zero, then a Nash–Cournot or a Nash–Bertrand oligopoly is represented.

4.2. The equilibrium framework of the GEM-E3 model

GEM-E3 is an applied general equilibrium model, for the EU Member States, involving multiple countries, linked through the endogenous trade of goods and services, multiple industrial sectors and economic agents, and multiple time period dynamics of capital accumulation and technology progress. In addition, the model covers the major aspects of public finance including all substantial taxes, social policy subsidies, public expenditures and deficit financing. The results of the model include projections of full input-output tables by country, national accounts, employment, capital, income distribution, balance of payments, public finance and household consumption.

The model follows the standard methodology of computable general equilibrium models, involving economic agents, producers and consumers, that compete through their demand and supply functions over a set of simultaneous markets of commodities and primary production factors. The model computes the set of prices that equilibrate demand and supply in all markets, ensuring that the net sum of payments and revenues are equalized within the whole of the economy.

Compared to other CGE models, GEM-E3 differs in that it is more detailed concerning: (a) production structure which is fully endogenous; (b) the consumption system, involving consumption by purpose, durable and non-durable commodities; (c) the bilateral trade flows between EU Member States; and (d) the representation of income distribution and fiscal instruments.

A stylized description of the model's equilibrium framework is given below. The equations involve a set of indices, defined as follows:

(a) i and j span the set of firms;

(b) it is assumed that each firm produces a single variety, indexed by v and u;

(c) varieties are grouped in commodity categories, which in the supply side are identical to economic sectors, denoted by indices ℓ and λ;

(d) thus i may produce a variety v and operate in a sector ℓ, corresponding to a commodity category ℓ in which variety v belongs;

(e) country indices are m and n, while h stands for the set of economic agents, namely households, firms, government and foreign countries.

The production possibility frontier of a firm i operating in sector ℓ, determines supply XD^S of a variety of commodity type ℓ produced by the firm, given that capital stock K is fixed in the period:

(1) $$XD^S_{i,m} = f\left(K_{i,m}, L_{i,m}, XI_{i,\lambda,m}\right)$$

Obviously (1) defines, in static terms, a positively sloped supply function for varieties. Given a total cost function, the firm determines derived demand for primary production factors (including labour L) and intermediate inputs XI defined at the level of commodity category λ:

(2) $\quad \dfrac{\partial XD_{i,m}}{\partial L_{i,m}} \cdot \dfrac{\partial C_{i,m}}{\partial XD_{i,m}} = p^{L}_{i,m}$ where p^{L} is gross wage rate, assumed to be depending on

labour market equilibrium, under an assumption of labour mobility across sectors.

(3) $\quad \dfrac{\partial XD_{i,m}}{\partial K_{i,m}} \cdot \dfrac{\partial C_{i,m}}{\partial XD_{i,m}} = p^{K}_{i,m}$

(4) $\quad \dfrac{\partial XD_{i,m}}{\partial XI_{i,\lambda,m}} \cdot \dfrac{\partial C_{i,m}}{\partial XD_{i,m}} = p^{Y}_{\lambda,m}$

where C is the total cost function. Since in static terms, stock of capital is fixed, equation (3) serves to derive the sectoral shadow price of capital p^{K}. The derived demand for intermediate inputs depends, in (4), on the aggregate price of commodity type λ in domestic absorption $p^{Y}_{\lambda,m}$.

A zero profit assumption, at the level of the sector ℓ, is asserted within the period. This implies that the number of firms $N_{\ell,m}$, involving all firms $i \in \ell$ that supply the same commodity type ℓ, is fully adjustable: entry and exit of firms is freely made within the period. The zero profit conditions, expressed in (5), involves a selling price for the commodity $p^{S}_{i,m}$ from firm i, which is related to total cost through an endogenous perceived price elasticity ψ, following a Lerner formula expressed in equation (6).

(5) $\quad \displaystyle\sum_{i=1, i\in\ell}^{N_{\ell,m}} p^{S}_{i,m} \cdot XD^{S}_{i,m} = \sum_{i=1, i\in\ell}^{N_{\ell,m}} C_{i,m}\left(p^{K}_{i,m}, p^{L}_{i,m}, p^{Y}_{\lambda,m}; K_{i,m}, L_{i,m}, XI_{i,\lambda,m}\right)$

(6) $\quad p^{S}_{i,m} = \left(1 - \dfrac{1}{\psi_{i,m}}\right)^{-1} \cdot \dfrac{\partial C_{i,m}}{\partial XD^{S}_{i,m}}$

Demand for commodities, decided by economic agents, is determined along a multiple stage budgeting process, involving commodity categories ℓ. Firms determine their demand for other commodities, as shown in (4), for intermediate consumption. They also demand capital goods, IP, to invest in capacity expansion. Thus, demand by all firms for commodity category ℓ is:

(7) $\quad Y^{F}_{\ell,m} = \displaystyle\sum_{i} XI_{i,\ell,m} + \sum_{i} IP_{i,\ell,m}$

where $IP_{i,\ell,m}$ depends on firms' investment in capacity expansion $I_{i,m}$.

Households maximize their inter-temporal utility under an inter-temporal budget constraint, to determine consumption and leisure. The formulation is such that it accommodates voluntary unemployment, corresponding to spare leisure. Real wage rate of equilibrium may incite people to enter the labour market, reduce leisure and obtain higher wage income for consumption and savings.

Optimality conditions for the first year (under a myopic expectations assumption), derived from the inter-temporal households' behaviour, is incorporated in the model. It simultaneously determines supply of labour by households and total budget attributed to consumption and savings, given disposable income. Total consumption is further allocated to consumption by purpose, which is further associated to demand for commodities.

Thus, demand for commodity categories ℓ is an indirect function of labour supply L_m^S (wage income), other revenues E and relative prices.

$$(8) \qquad Y_{\ell,m}^H = g\left(p_m^L \cdot L_m^S + E_m; p_{\ell,m}^Y, p_{\lambda,m}^Y\right)$$

$$(9) \qquad L_m^S = h\left(p_m^L \cdot L^T + E_m; p_{\ell,m}^Y\right)$$

where L^T stands for total time resources.

Governments' demands for commodities, $Y_{\ell,m}^G$ is left exogenous, associated to public consumption policy.

Foreign countries demand domestic commodity types, as derived from their own equilibrium:

$$(10) \qquad Y_{\ell,m,n}^W = M_{\ell,n,m}$$

Equations (7), (8) and (10) determine domestic and export absorption of commodity category ℓ, as follows:

$$(11) \qquad Y_{\ell,m} = Y_{\ell,m}^F + Y_{\ell,m}^G + Y_{\ell,m}^H + Y_{\ell,m}^W$$

Following an Armington assumption, domestic absorption of commodity category ℓ is satisfied by domestic production and imports that are considered as non-perfect substitutes. The aggregation function is defined by $Y_{\ell,m} = A\left(XD_{\ell,m}^D, M_{\ell,m,n}\right)$

where $XD_{\ell,m}^D$ stands for demand for domestically produced commodity category ℓ which aggregates domestic production of all varieties v by firms i that belong to sector ℓ, while $M_{\ell,m,n}$ is the similar aggregate supply of firms operating in the same sector of country origin n addressing their production to country m.

Under a budget constraint (12), which is as follows,

$$(12) \qquad p_{\ell,m}^Y \cdot Y_{\ell,m} = p_{\ell,m}^S \cdot XD_{\ell,m}^D + \sum_n p_{\ell,m,n}^M \cdot M_{\ell,m,n}$$

where $p_{\ell,m,n}^M = p_{\ell,n}^Y$ is the aggregate price of commodity category supplied by other countries, cost minimization determines derived demand for domestically produced commodities and imports by country of origin:

$$(13) \qquad \frac{\partial Y_{\ell,m}}{\partial XD_{\ell,m}^D} = \frac{p_{\ell,m}^S}{p_{\ell,m}^Y}$$

$$(14) \qquad \frac{\partial Y_{\ell,m}}{\partial M_{\ell,m,n}} = \frac{p_{\ell,m,n}^M}{p_{\ell,m}^Y}$$

where $p^{S}_{\ell,m}$ is the aggregate selling price of domestically produced commodity category ℓ.

Total savings in the economy, involving income distribution and fiscal policy relationships, is assumed to determine total investment:

$$(15) \quad \sum_{i} I_{i,m} = \sum_{h} S_{h,m}$$

which determines a global shadow price of capital $\overline{p}^{K}_{m}$, by assuming capital mobility across sectors, but not across countries. Sectoral investment $I_{i,m}$ is further determined by comparing sectoral shadow price of capital, as determined in equation (3), to a long-term exogenous rate of return of capital ($\rho + \delta$):

$$(16) \quad I_{i,m} = I\left(p^{K}_{i,m} \Big/ p^{K}_{i,m}, p^{Y}\left(\rho_{m} + \delta_{i,m}\right) \right)$$

Equilibrium conditions are, finally, defined for commodities and labour. Regarding commodity category ℓ, the firms $i \in \ell$ operating in the corresponding sector, supply a total volume, as in the left-hand side of (17).

Consumers, that is firms, households, government and foreign countries, having determined aggregate demand for domestically produced commodity categories, are assumed to consider that varieties, in the same commodity category, are not perfect substitutes. They consider then $\varphi(\ )$ as a transformation function aggregating varieties $XD^{D}_{v,m}$ that form a commodity category ℓ, so as to satisfy their aggregate demand for $XD^{D}_{\ell,m}$. Then equilibrium of commodity markets is defined at the sectoral level, as follows:

$$(17) \quad \sum_{i=1,i\in\ell}^{N_{\ell,m}} XD^{S}_{i,m} = \varphi_{\ell,m}\left(XD^{D}_{v,m}, \forall v = i \in \ell\right) = XD^{D}_{\ell,m}$$

The derived equilibrium aggregate price $p^{S}_{\ell,m}$ of commodity category ℓ serves to determine the selling price $p^{S}_{i,m}, \forall i = v \in \ell$ of firms i producing variety v, by maximizing the right-hand side of (17) transformation function (interpreted as consumer aggregation over imperfectly substitutable varieties) under a budget constraint, ensuring that total expenditure in varieties within a commodity category is equal to total receipts from selling those varieties.

Derivation leads to (18):

$$(18) \quad \frac{p^{S}_{i,m}}{p^{S}_{\ell,m}} = \frac{\partial \varphi_{\ell,m}\left(XD^{D}_{i,m}, \forall i = v \in \ell\right)}{\partial XD^{D}_{i,m}}$$

The price-cost margin (mark-up) used in (6), at the level of the firm, is interrelated with the transformation function $\varphi(\ )$ used in (17) and (18), to determine the shares of firms within each sector. The relationship depends on an *ad hoc* assumption about the competition regime that prevails in each economic sector. For example, in a following section, we will assume for some sectors that firms are symmetric and compete under a Nash–Cournot oligopolistic regime. For other sectors, we will assume that the number of firms is infinite, so that a perfect competition regime prevails.

As mentioned, labour mobility across firms, within each country, is assumed to prevail in the labour market. Thus (19) is the corresponding equilibrium condition, serving to determine the average wage rate of equilibrium p^L :

$$(19) \quad L_m^S = \sum_i L_{i,m}^D$$

Dynamics are introduced, implying that the model operates over a sequence of static equilibria, in which capital stock is updated with investment and scrapping, as follows:

$$(20) \quad K_{i,m}^{t+1} = \left(1 - \delta_{i,m}\right) \cdot K_{i,m}^t + I_{i,m}^t$$

where t denotes time.

4.3. Representation of inefficiencies related to the SMP

This section presents the specific implementation of inefficiencies, that are assumed to be removed (entirely or partially) by the realization of the SMP.

In the model's production side, the objective is to capture potential scale economy effects in those sectors that can achieve economies of scale within the enlarged EU market, after the completion of the SMP. The underlying economic assertion is that, prior to the SMP, firms in some sectors operated inefficiently due to the small scale of the countries, compared to the EU integrated scale. Empirical studies revealed that such potential in economies of scale are mainly concentrated in intermediate and equipment goods industries. This is presented in Section 4.3.1.

In the foreign trade part of the model, the objective is to represent extra trade costs that were due to border obstacles and non-harmonized regulation that prevailed prior to the SMP. It is expected that the removal of such obstacles and the harmonization will imply higher efficiency in trade flows and lower costs of trade, but also lower demand for associated services. This is presented in Section 4.3.2.

The enlargement of the market and the expected harmonization of commodity specifications, due to the completion of the SMP, will generally make the EU products more homogeneous, hence more substitutable for the consumers. In the Armington specification parts of the model, the objective is to represent structural changes of consumers' perception of substitutability. This is presented in Section 4.3.3.

The increase of product substitutability across the EU and the intra-sector restructuring in the supply side, are expected to change the perception of firms regarding competition. The SMP will thus imply, through higher competition in the enlarged market, changes in the oligopolistic, hence pricing, behaviour of firms, that is formulated in the corresponding part of the model. This is presented in Section 4.3.4.

The realization of the SMP is also expected to increase the number of different commodity varieties that will be available to EU consumers, for final demand, intermediate consumption, investment building or public procurement. The corresponding part of the model, seeks to capture efficiency gains that are derived from the increased possibility of choice for the consumers. This is presented in Section 4.3.5.

4.3.1. Changes in production: economies of scale

To represent potential economies of scale, in some sectors, a simple model of average cost functions is assumed, so as to also facilitate numerical calibration. Following Pratten (1988), it is assumed that, in these sectors, the total cost function (see Equation 5 in Section 4.2), is composed of a variable cost and a fixed cost part. The production technology is assumed to exhibit constant returns of scale, implying that the variable cost part of the cost function determines a variable average cost that coincides with the marginal cost function.

Firm-internal economies of scale in the sense of decreasing unit costs are introduced by incorporation of a recurrent annual fixed-cost element. Before the first unit of output can be produced using the production technology, fixed amounts of output-independent production factors must be hired in addition to variable, output-dependent input requirements just to maintain a firm's capacity to produce and sell its output variant. A firm's total cost function then takes the form:

$$C_{i,m}\left(XD_{i,m}\right)= h_{i,m}(\ )\cdot XD_{i,m} + F_{i,m} \quad \text{where} \quad F_{i,m} = F\left(p_{i,m}^{L}\cdot L_{i,m}^{f}, p_{i,m}^{K}\cdot K_{i,m}^{f}, \sum_{\ell} p_{i,\ell,m}^{Y}\cdot XI_{i,m}^{f}\right)$$

where $h(.)$ is a marginal cost function (identical to the unit average cost function) depending only on the prices of the production factors, F is total fixed cost and $L_{i,m}^{f}, K_{i,m}^{f}, XI_{i,m}^{f}$ are respectively fixed amounts of labour services, capital services and intermediate inputs, which are constant parameters numerically calibrated in accordance with the existing extraneous evidence on cost-scale relationships by industry.

Figure 4.1.   Minimum efficiency scale: a graphic description

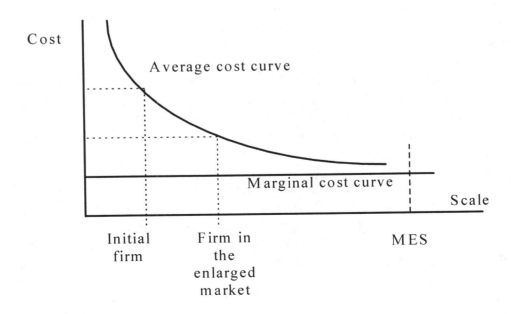

Figure 4.1 illustrates the assumed average and marginal cost curves. If production scale by firm increases, the share of fixed costs in total costs decreases resulting in efficiency gains. The curve in Figure 4.1 shows that costs are steeply declining when production is low, and almost flat when it is high. The lowest level of the curve, assumed never to be achievable, corresponds to the Minimum Efficiency Scale (MES). The concept is based on engineering considerations. The horizontal marginal cost curve is tangent to the average cost curve at the MES point. Firms mainly operate at a point that stands to the left of the MES. The degree to which they are, initially, within the deeply declining region of the average cost curve largely determines the degree of positive gains resulting from market enlargement.

4.3.2. Changes in trade: reduction of costs from border controls

Three types of border-related costs, regarding EU trade, are included in the model specification:

(a)   non-tariff barriers (NTBs);
(b)   costs required for compliance to foreign standards and other regulations;
(c)   transport and banking costs associated with international trade.

It is assumed that customs duties and quantitative restrictions on trade, for example quotas, had already been completely eliminated in the pre-SMP period within the EU and are not considered.

As mentioned, non-tariff trade barriers are here conceived as related to delays dictated by border formalities. In the model this is stylized by introducing pre-SMP intra-EC NTBs in a manner formally equivalent to the imposition of iceberg type transport costs. In this context, it is assumed that a fraction of any produced output unit designated for export melts away in the course of the subsequent additional transformation and administrative processes required to overcome trade barriers imposed by trade partners. Thus, part of home production destined to exports is lost and the importing country receives only a fraction of the produced quantity.

Removal of NTBs would then imply that to export the same quantity, the exporting country has to produce less. This allows for a release of some of the production capacity and results in relaxing supply constraints for the domestic country entailing lower equilibrium prices. On the importer country side, the effective price of imports would indirectly also be lower when removing NTBs.

NTBs are introduced in Equation (10) of Section 4.2:

$$(10a) \quad Y_{\ell,m,n}^{W} = \left(1 + NTB_{i,n,m}\right) M_{\ell,n,m}$$

indicating that $NTB_{i,n,m} \cdot M_{\ell,n,m}$ is the quantity that is never delivered.

Differences in standards and regulation, between the EU trading partners, were additional border barriers. The necessity to adapt products to differing technical standards, packaging, labelling and regulation entail costs in specialized market and non-market services that are added to the cost. The effects of standards differ from those of NTBs, since the harmonization of the former induces reduction of demand of exporters addressed to service sectors, while NTB removal has a supply effect, as explained.

To represent the effects of harmonizing standards and regulation[11] we formulate links between trade flows, in the sense that exporting goods also involves exporting some services. The latter are separated in the benchmark data in exports of services *per se* and exports that are linked to exports of other goods. Costs due to standards are generally formulated in an *ad valorem* fashion.

We similarly treat transport costs associated to trade flows. Exporting a good entails demand for transport services that are supplied by a variety of transport firms located in different countries. The allocation depends on geographical location of the exporter and the market shares of the countries in international transport activity. It is therefore complex to link trade flows exactly with transport activities. Similarly, bank services are dedicated to support export activity.

The model adopts a rather simplified approach that starts from computing country shares in international activity of transport of goods and considers that these shares remain fixed. Then a differential transport demand is associated to each trade flow. A reduction of transport costs, expected from SMP completion to reflect better combination of transport means and a more efficient restructuring of the international transport sector, would imply less demand for transport services and a lower cost for trade. The effects by country will differ, depending on distance (taken into account in country-specific coefficients) and on countries' share in the market of transports. Similar effects are formulated for bank services as the reduction of border formalities and harmonization is expected to reduce the need for banking services.

Total demand for these service sectors is then composed of their own demand $XD^D_{v,m}$ and the services demanded by other sectors, for the purpose of exporting:

$$\overline{XD^D_{\ell,m}} = XD^D_{\ell,m} + \sum_{\lambda} c_{\lambda,\ell,m,n} \cdot Y^W_{\lambda,m,n},$$

where $c_{\lambda,\ell,m,n}$ is the quantity of service ℓ needed per unit of export of commodity λ that is exported from country m to country n. The index ℓ concerns the market services needed for compliance, transport and banking.

It is assumed that the additional cost for these services is paid by the importer. The import price then becomes:

$$p^M_{\ell,m,n} = p^Y_{\ell,n} + \sum_{\lambda,\lambda \in \{services\}} c_{\lambda,\ell,n,m} \cdot p^Y_{\lambda,n}$$

After completion of the SMP, it is assumed that the parameters $c_{\lambda,\ell,m,n}$ are exogenously decreased at rates that depend on the country as explained above.

4.3.3. Changes in product substitutability in the EU

From the earlier stages of the Single Market Review, a conclusion was generally drawn that consumers having greater access to new regional markets will impose increased competition

---

[11]   Surveys show that in the opinion of entrepreneurs this harmonization will likely have one of the most noticeable impacts on trade.

on firms. Besides the enlargement of the market, due to border control removal, the effort towards harmonization of product standards and regulation will substantially increase the ability of buyers to substitute among the products of EU suppliers.

Standardization of products (uniformity standards, quality standards, interchangeability standards, licensing standards, anti-competitive standards), harmonization of technical regulation and indirect taxation, higher accessibility of foreign producers by domestic consumers[12] and other factors support the assertion that consumers will consider the domestic and the EU products as being more similar and hence more substitutable. This is considered as a change of preferences influencing substitutability of products by origin.

This change is formulated in the model at the level of multiple stage budgeting of the consumers reflected in a change of the nesting of the budgeting scheme.[13] While in the pre-SMP period consumers were assumed to choose first between domestic and imported goods and second between imported goods by origin (between EU and ROW and then among the EU Member States), the completion of the SMP will imply a change of this nesting: they will first decide how much to spend on commodities originating from the EU (whether domestic or imported from another EU country), and commodities originating from the ROW. Given the budget for EU commodities, they will further decide the allocation over those from the EU Member States, one of which is their own country.

This change of decision process reflects the fact that EU goods are closer substitutes than before, and no important difference exists anymore between domestic and other EU commodities. The representation of preferences as changing structure could be continuous by using flexible functional forms. This preference change does not imply a structural change of the welfare. Figure 4.2 shows the two nesting schemes, before and after the SMP as formulated in the model.

4.3.4. Changes in imperfect competition behaviour

It is assumed that the sectors which exhibit economies of scale potential coincide with those that operate under an imperfect competition (IC) market regime. It is formulated in the model that in these sectors (mainly intermediate and equipment goods industries) a finite number of symmetric firms operate, competing within an oligopolistic market regime. The model assumes that all other sectors are composed of infinite firms under perfect competition.

In the IC sectors, firms exerting oligopoly power set a mark-up over their marginal cost as defined by the Lerner formula (6) depending on their perception of the elasticity of demand $\psi_{i,m}$.

The exact specification of this elasticity depends on the type of oligopolistic market in which the firms are assumed to operate. Among the various oligopolistic market operation models,

---

[12]   Here consumers include households, producers acting as consumers for their intermediate consumption and government.

[13]   Alternative specifications of the integration process were also formulated but not kept in the final model version. These are presented in the technical report (Appendix B).

the Nash–Cournot[14] hypothesis involving zero and invariant conjectures was chosen for the current model version. In this context, the perception of the demand elasticity varies endogenously with market share variations, the number of firms operating within each market and changes in the competitive environment.

Figure 4.2.   Market segmentation versus market integration in GEM-E3-SM

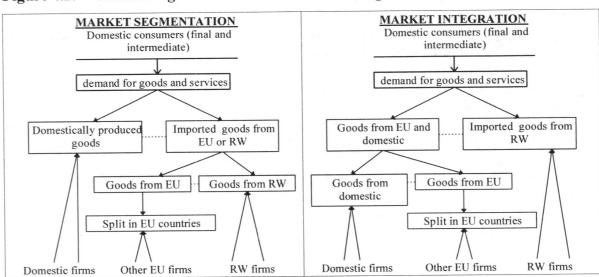

The formulas of perceived elasticities as introduced in the model, involving some simplification that was necessary because of the complexity of the model's demand structure, are as follows for the domestic market (dropping country and firm indices):

$$(21s)\quad -\frac{1}{\psi}=-\frac{1}{\sigma}+\frac{1}{N}\left[\frac{1}{\sigma}-\frac{1}{\sigma_{XD/M}}+V_{XD/Y}\left(\frac{1}{\sigma_{XD/M}}-\frac{1}{\Omega}\right)\right]$$

$$(21i)\quad -\frac{1}{\psi}=-\frac{1}{\sigma}+\frac{1}{N}\left[\frac{1}{\sigma}-\frac{1}{\sigma_{XD/EU}}+V_{XD/EU}\left(\frac{1}{\sigma_{XD/EU}}-\frac{1}{\sigma_{EU/RW}^{I}}\right)+V_{XD/Y}\left(\frac{1}{\sigma_{EU/RW}^{I}}-\frac{1}{\Omega}\right)\right]$$

Equation (21s) is activated under the market segmentation hypothesis, and (21i) under market integration. Parameter $\sigma_{XD/M}$ denotes the elasticity of substitution between domestically produced commodities and imports (in the case of market segmentation), while $\sigma_{XD/EU}$ and $\sigma_{EU/RW}^{I}$ are the elasticities of substitution between domestic goods and EU imports, and EU goods imported from the ROW respectively. The elasticity of substitution between varieties within a commodity category is denoted by σ. Finally, Ω is the aggregate price elasticity of

---

[14]   The Nash–Bertrand assumption was also formulated but not used in the final model version. Other models in the literature assume conjectural variation. We avoided such an assumption because of the implied arbitrariness of the applied analysis. Technical details on the computation of the mark-up are presented in the technical report (Appendix B).

demand for commodity categories. Endogenous value shares are introduced in (21), where $V_{a/b}$ denotes the value share of a in expenditure b.

The opening of the market as induced by the SMP, representing, as explained in the previous paragraph, a shift from (21s) to (21i), leads to a reduction of the perceived elasticity of demand ψ and consequently a drop of price/cost margins as in (20). This is obvious in (21) mainly because $\sigma^{I}_{XD/EU} > \sigma^{S}_{XD/M}$ (reflecting higher substitutability between EU commodities) but also because an additional term is added in (21i) representing the change of the nesting.

Similar formulas apply for the mark-ups on exports addressed by country m to other countries n that belong to the rest of the EU. In the case of market segmentation, the perceived elasticity for EU imports is:

$$(22s) \quad -\frac{1}{\psi^{S}_{m,n}} = -\frac{1}{\sigma_n} + \frac{1}{N_m}\left[\begin{array}{l}\dfrac{1}{\sigma_n} - \dfrac{1}{\sigma_{EU/EU}} + V_{M_{n,m}/M_{n}.EU}\left(\dfrac{1}{\sigma_{EU/EU}} - \dfrac{1}{\sigma^{S}_{EU/RW}}\right) \\[2ex] + V_{M_{n,m}/M_{n}}\left(\dfrac{1}{\sigma^{S}_{EU/RW}} - \dfrac{1}{\sigma_{XD/M}}\right) + V_{M_{n,m}/Y_{n}}\left(\dfrac{1}{\sigma_{XD/M}} - \dfrac{1}{\Omega}\right)\end{array}\right]$$

In the case of market integration, the perceived elasticity for EU imports is:

$$(22i) \quad -\frac{1}{\psi^{I}_{m,n}} = -\frac{1}{\sigma_n} + \frac{1}{N_m}\left[\begin{array}{l}\dfrac{1}{\sigma_n} - \dfrac{1}{\sigma_{EU/EU}} + V_{M_{n,m}/M_{n}.EU}\left(\dfrac{1}{\sigma_{EU/EU}} - \dfrac{1}{\sigma_{XD/EU}}\right) \\[2ex] + V_{M_{n,m}/EU}\left(\dfrac{1}{\sigma_{XD/EU}} - \dfrac{1}{\sigma^{I}_{EU/RW}}\right) + V_{M_{n,m}/Y_{n}}\left(\dfrac{1}{\sigma^{I}_{EU/RW}} - \dfrac{1}{\Omega}\right)\end{array}\right]$$

where $\sigma_{EU/EU}$ is the elasticity of substitution among EU products.

The perceived elasticity of demand for imports of country n from non-EU countries (ROW) is as in (23s) in case of market segmentation and as in (23i) under market integration.

$$(23s) \quad -\frac{1}{\psi_{RW}} = -\frac{1}{\sigma} + \frac{1}{N}\left[\frac{1}{\sigma} - \frac{1}{\sigma^{S}_{EU/RW}}\right]$$

$$(23i) \quad -\frac{1}{\psi_{RW}} = -\frac{1}{\sigma} + \frac{1}{N}\left[\frac{1}{\sigma} - \frac{1}{\sigma^{I}_{EU/RW}}\right]$$

where $\sigma_{EU/RW}$ is the elasticity of substitution between EU and ROW products.

Regarding mark-ups on exports to the EU, the fall of mark-ups when shifting from market segmentation to market integration is not certain. It depends on the difference between $\sigma^{S}_{SU/RW}$

and $\sigma_{\textit{xD/EU}}$ and the related value shares. With particular values one can obtain even an increase of mark-ups on exports to the EU. The values of elasticities of substitution in the model are such that they result almost in all cases in a drop of mark-ups for exports to the EU, as do the mark-ups for domestic sales. This reflects the assumption that the goods from the EU and the domestic goods were even in the early SMP period more substitutes than in the case of EU and ROW goods.

4.3.5. Efficiency from consumption of commodity varieties

Recall the market integration hierarchy of multiple stage budgeting of the consumers, as mentioned in the previous sub-section. There exists in that hierarchy a budgeting stage that compares domestically produced goods to the rest of EU goods. One can imagine that market integration has progressed even more, so as to let the consumer choose directly among varieties of commodities, in other words among firms of the EU, without paying any attention to the EU country of origin. Obviously, this would make the EU products even more substitutable. It is important to notice that this could also have an additional efficiency gain effect, induced by more advanced market integration. Figure 4.3 illustrates multiple stage budgeting under the integration and the more advanced market integration.

Figure 4.3. Advanced market integration

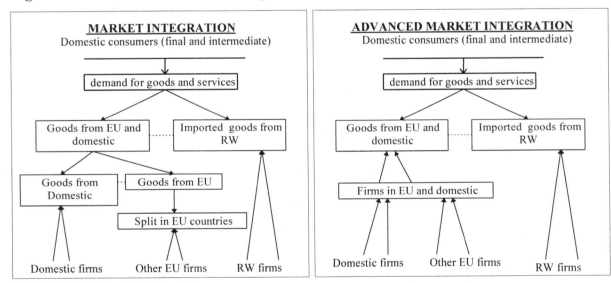

In the advanced market integration regime, not only is the drop of mark-ups more significant (since competition is more intense), but also there is scope for additional efficiency gains: since firms' origin is indistinguishable, this enables consumers to choose from a bigger pool of varieties, in all consumption uses (final, intermediate, investment, etc.). This constitutes an efficiency gain for consumption as illustrated in the following formulas.

In the case of symmetric firms operating in sector i , the transformation function $\varphi(\ )$ that aggregates for the consumer varieties within commodity category i can be of the following CES type:

$$\varphi_{\ell,m}(\ )= N_{\ell,m}^{\sigma/\sigma-1}$$

In the case of market integration as in the left-hand part of the equation above, a consumer in country m faces an aggregation $\varphi^{I}_{\ell,m}(\ ) = N^{\sigma/\sigma-1}_{\ell,m} + N^{\sigma/\sigma-1}_{\ell,n}$ where n denotes other EU firms exporting to country m. In the case of advanced market integration (right-hand part of the equation), the consumer faces an aggregation $\varphi^{AI}_{\ell,m}(\ ) = \left(N_{\ell,m} + N_{\ell,n}\right)^{\sigma/\sigma-1}$. Since the elasticity of the love of variety σ is always higher than 1, φ^{AI} is higher than φ^{I}. In other words, the consumer can obtain the same aggregate consumption quantity by using varieties in a more efficient way under advanced integration than under simple integration. Given the equilibrium condition (17), the advanced market integration regime exerts an overall efficiency gain effect in the economy.

The efficiency gain in aggregating variety quantities has a double effect on prices. On the one hand, it relaxes supply constraints in static terms leading to lower marginal costs and prices. On the other hand, the inverse transformation function $\varphi^{-1}_{\ell,m}(\ ) = N^{1/1-\sigma}_{\ell,m}$ which aggregates variety prices to form commodity category prices, also decreases when shifting to the advanced market integration regime. This will lead to further reduction in prices.

4.3.6. Illustration of growth effects

The establishment of the SMP measures can induce real growth effects if only through market enlargement (even without taking into account the effects of reducing trade costs) when the segmented economies can be characterized in the pre-SMP period as combining imperfect competition and economies of scale potential. It turned out that at least in terms of growth, the model results are mainly due to that mechanism. The following maquette model illustrates the mechanism of obtaining real growth effects.

Suppose that GDP, considered as a measure of growth, comprises only consumption produced by using capital and labour inputs. The economy's budget constraint as in (i) states that the value of GDP (identical to the value of consumption $P \cdot C$) exactly matches total production costs involving cost of labour $w \cdot \ell$, cost of capital $r \cdot K$ and a fixed cost term f (valued in terms of the wage rate w). Costs are conceived at the firm level, so total cost involves the number of firms N.

(i) $\qquad P \cdot C = w \cdot N \cdot \ell + r \cdot K + w \cdot f \cdot N$

The production possibility frontier of a firm (ii) is assumed to combine labour and capital through a Cobb–Douglas technology. Optimization of production of quantity xd leads to the derivation of demand for labour (iii) and a shadow price of capital stock (iv), as this remains fixed in static terms.

(ii) $\qquad xd = \ell^{a} \cdot \left(\dfrac{K}{N}\right)^{1-a}$

(iii) $\qquad \dfrac{w \cdot \ell}{P_{c} \cdot xd} = a$

(iv) $\dfrac{r \cdot K\!\!\!/_{\!\!n}}{P_c \cdot xd} = 1 - a$

where P_c is the marginal cost of production.

Under an imperfect competition assumption, firms set selling price P_s according to a Lerner formula (v) involving the perceived elasticity of demand ψ .

(v) $P_s = P_c \cdot \left(1 - \dfrac{1}{\psi}\right)^{-1}$

Assuming that firm-produced varieties are imperfect substitutes for the consumer and that all firms are symmetric, consumers satisfy their consumption needs C through an aggregation function as in (vi). Similarly, an aggregate consumption price is obtained by applying the inverse aggregation function (vii).

(vi) $C = N^{\sigma\!\!\!/_{\!\!\sigma-1}} \cdot xd$

(vii) $P = N^{1\!\!\!/_{\!\!1-\sigma}} \cdot P_s$

The formulation above ensures that firms will always operate at zero profits, i.e. that the mark-up will be such as to exactly compensate for the fixed cost. $P_s \cdot xd = P_d \cdot xd + w \cdot f$. As already explained, market enlargement within the SMP results in an increase of the perceived elasticity of demand ψ , hence a fall in mark-ups and a decrease in the number of symmetric firms under a zero-profit assertion. Solving the model (i)-(vii), the following formula is obtained for computing GDP:

$$GDP = C = N^{\sigma\!\!\!/_{\!\!\sigma-1}} \cdot a^a \cdot \left[f \cdot (\psi - 1)\right]^a \cdot \left(\dfrac{K}{N}\right)^{1-a}$$

Both changes induced by the SMP lead to an increase in GDP according to the above formula, since $0 < a < 1$, $\psi > 1$ and $\sigma \gg 1$. As the number of firms decreases, production by firm increases, better sharing fixed costs at the sectoral level, which is, under zero profit, equivalent to the drop of mark-ups.

Dynamically, GDP being bounded by fixed capital stock can further increase through the accumulation of investment induced by the increased shadow price of capital, since the GDP per capital unit ratio has increased in static terms.

4.4.   Model calibration

4.4.1.   Data sources and nomenclature

The choice of the sectoral nomenclature of the model was influenced by the following:

(a)   empirical studies that determined which sectors are likely to have a higher potential of economies of scale under the SMP;

(b)   the availability of data from Eurostat, in a unified structure for all Member States;

(c)   the computational complexity of the model.

Table 4.1 shows the industrial classification retained for the model. The abbreviation PC denotes a perfectly competitive sector, and IC an imperfectly competitive one.[15]

Table 4.1.   Industrial classification in GEM-E3-SM

No	Sector	Status	NACE-CLIO R25
1	Agriculture	PC	010
2	Fuel and power products	PC	060
3	Ferrous and non-ferrous ore and metals	IC	130
4	Chemical products	IC	170
5	Other energy-intensive industries	IC	150+190+470
6	Electrical goods	IC	250
7	Transport equipment	IC	280
8	Other equipment goods industries	IC	210+230
9	Consumer goods industries	PC	360+420+490+480
10	Building and construction	PC	530
11	Telecommunication services	IC	670
12	Transports	PC	610+630+650
13	Services of credit and insurance	IC	690
14	Other market services	PC	560+590+740
15	Non-market services	PC	860

Consumption of households by purpose involves the following categories (ND stands for non-durables and D for durables):

---

[15]   Sector 9 was also a candidate for inclusion in the IC sectors. Given, however, the heterogeneity of the industries included in this sector and the relatively low unexploited technical scale economy potential (Pratten, 1988) it was decided to treat it as PC.

Table 4.2.   Consumption in categories in GEM-E3-SM

No	Purpose	Status	Eurostat
1	Food, beverages and tobacco	ND	1
2	Clothing and footwear	ND	2
3	Housing and water	ND	31
4	Fuels and power	ND	32
5	Housing furniture and operation	ND	41+42+44+45+46
6	Heating and cooking appliances	D	43
7	Medical care and health expenses	ND	5
8	Transport equipment	D	61
9	Operation of transport equipment	ND	62
10	Purchased transport	ND	63
11	Telecommunication services	ND	64
12	Recreation, entertainment, culture, etc.	ND	7
13	Other services	ND	8

The data for the base year, namely 1985, were all based on Eurostat.

To build the Social Accounting Matrices, the model database used the following sources:[16] input-output tables (I-O), per Member State, compiled by Eurostat from national sources; consumption matrix, investment matrix and employment by sector, also compiled by Eurostat; national accounts by sector, also available from Eurostat.

Eurostat does not provide new observed I-O tables after 1985.[17] For a few countries post-1985 I-O tables, following the national methodology, are available, but it was not possible, with the resources within this project, to make them compatible with Eurostat 1985 tables. Full I-O tables have been made available only for France, for years other than 1985. These have been used to compute technical progress by sector and production factor.

[16]   Several of the tables were not homogeneous by country, because of different initial sources, and had to be aggregated and completed.

[17]   The I-O tables of 1991, as prepared by J. Beutel *et al.*, were evaluated, but were found inappropriate to serve as a database for the model for two main reasons: the structure of the intermediate consumption is created artificially (i.e. not through real data), using a type of advanced RAS method; the I-O tables are in current prices, which renders them inappropriate for the needs of the current study, as they are not directly comparable to 1985 data regarding changes in volumes and technical progress.

In the absence of complete Social Accounting Matrices for years other than 1985, the study had to rely only on sectoral time-series as provided by Eurostat.[18] The following time-series, have been used:

(a)   value added per sector (volume, value), factor prices and market prices;
(b)   exports and imports per sector (volume and value);
(c)   actual output (available for a few countries);
(d)   investment by ownership branch;
(e)   consumption of households by purpose (volume and value);
(f)   employment per sector;
(g)   national accounts per aggregate economic sector.

However, it was not possible to build a complete benchmark data set for 1993 or 1994, as several gaps existed in the Eurostat statistics.

Regarding foreign trade data, the Comext data source has been used. This served to compute a bilateral trade matrix for the model's sectors for 1985, but no evaluation of the evolution in the trade matrix has been possible as a break in the statistics occurred in 1988. The Comext data only concern trade of goods, while there is no other source for bilateral trade in services. A special Eurostat publication, used for this purpose, only contained aggregate data of service trade.

4.4.2.   Calibration of imperfect competition sectors and economies of scale

Numerical calibration of imperfect markets under economies of scale seeks to render consistent the numerical values of three sectoral parameters, namely the fixed part of production cost, the number of symmetric firms and the elasticity of substitution of varieties within a sector, with observed sectoral statistics comprising: volume of production in the sector and engineering information about economics of sectoral technology. As illustrated in the previous sub-section, the assumption of zero profit in the base year implies that the sectoral parameters are interrelated.

Engineering information about sectoral technology economics has been based on Pratten (1988). This study provides an estimation of the minimum efficient scale per sector and the cost increase gradient, i.e. the percentage increase of average cost of the firm when it produces at a level of one-third of the minimum efficiency scale.

The number of symmetric firms, by country and sector, has been approximated by computing Herfindahl indices for 1985 and 1992, from Eurostat data; these have been cross-checked with those by Bruce Lyons (East Anglia University) who provided such an index for the whole EU in 1988; statistical rank correlation analysis showed, for example, that the UK numbers were close to those of the whole EU.

The calibration procedure for IC sectors starts from the computation of the fixed cost per firm. This computation assumes that the firm operates at zero profit in the base year. The formula is as follows:

---

[18]   Cronos database.

$$Fixed\_Cost = \frac{\left(\frac{MES}{XD}\right) \cdot \left(Cost\_gradient\right) \cdot XD_{value}}{2 - \left(Cost\_gradient\right) \cdot \left[N \cdot \left(\frac{MES}{XD}\right) - 1\right]}$$

where N is the number of firms. Then, the sectoral value of mark-up can be determined, as it exactly covers the fixed cost, under a zero profit assumption for the base year. Also given the number of firms in the sector, the elasticity of substitution among varieties within each commodity category, is uniquely defined.[19]

4.4.3. Static calibration of the model

Static calibration of the CGE model follows a standard procedure, as in most CGE models. The starting data set includes the following:

(a)   values of production, consumption, investment, imports and exports per sector, which are available from the Social Accounting Matrix tables, which include I-O tables and National Accounts;

(b)   bilateral sectoral trade tables for the EU Member States and the ROW.

The calibration procedure is a model run, that assumes unit values for the export price and the price of absorption and a complete set of elasticity parameters. The calibration computes volumes, effective fiscal policy rates and a number of share parameters in production and consumption functions.

As the base year is assumed to be prior to the SMP, the calibration methodology implies that by definition all sectors have equal pre-tax prices in all countries. They only differ in the initial amount of fixed costs, that indicates their potential economy of scale. Because of the lack of statistical information, structural differences in sectoral prices across countries, other than the fixed costs, could not be incorporated in the model information, to support eventual price convergence analyses due to the completion of the SMP.

4.4.4. Dynamic calibration of the model

We define as dynamic calibration the exercise consisting in applying changes on the exogenous parameters of a model in order to reproduce an observed time-series data set after running the model dynamically. Once this is achieved, the model run over the past (often referred to as historical simulation) reproduces the observed *monde*.

As mentioned, a CGE type of model uses a single year benchmark data set for static calibration, which is a formal modelling procedure computing a set of structural model parameters, including, among others:

(a)   level parameters (δ in the case of CES functional forms) in trade, production and consumption functions;

(b)   utility and consumption allocation share parameters;

(c)   level parameters in investment functions;

---

[19]   Details are provided in the technical report (Appendix B).

(d)   technical coefficients in exogenous allocations, such as the investment and government consumption matrices;

(e)   effective rates for indirect taxation, direct taxation, duties, subsidies, social security and income transfers.

It is generally admitted that it is difficult to run historical simulations with a CGE model. This should not be attributed to the possible absence of econometric estimation of the model's elasticities, but rather to the fundamental assertion, in CGE models, regarding full utilization of the economy's resources (mainly capital stock and labour force).

Fluctuations in the rates of resource utilization are not usually represented in CGE models. Exceptionally, some model builders (including Bourguignon *et al.*, 1989, Capros *et al.* 1989) introduced short-run mechanisms and under-utilization in a CGE model. A technical difficulty is that this needs time-series and econometric estimation, while there still is no endogenous mechanism that would bring long-run general equilibrium from short-run disequilibrium or fluctuations.

Another source of bad performance in forecasting comes from the absence of macroeconomic reduced form functions in a CGE model. Other models (Keynesian, for example) that incorporate such reduced form macroeconomic functions (like Hendry's consumption function) use them to short-circuit some of the structural mechanisms of the model and indirectly constrain the solution. It is difficult in CGE models containing only formulations driven from microeconomic behaviour, to include the complexity needed to reproduce the properties of the reduced form functions.

To do the *ex post* evaluation of the SMP, the model has first to reproduce the *monde*. If the dynamic runs were based on simple extrapolation of exogenous variables, except those directly associated with the SMP completion, an *ex ante* evaluation would have been obtained, as in the literature.

The argument in favour of a good replication of the *monde* is that this would set the level that influences the accuracy of evaluation of the percentage change induced by the *antimonde* simulation. For example, structural changes, such as technical progress, change of household tastes, shifts in the propensity of trading, tax and income distribution policy, developments occurred in the ROW, etc., influence the properties of the model in terms of rates of change.

In formal terms, one can better understand the properties of a general equilibrium model, by applying the Johansen (1960) linearization operator on all the model's equations. The operator defined as:

$$\Delta \log(x) \cong \left(x_{\alpha\mu} - x_{\mu}\right)\Big/ x_{\mu}$$ where $x_{\alpha\mu}$ is the value in the *antimonde* and x_{μ} is the value in the

monde, linearizes[20] the model by involving two kinds of parameters, namely shares and rates

---

[20]   For example, when applying the operator on a part of equation involving $x + y$, the result is $sh_x \cdot \dot{x} + sh_y \cdot \dot{y}$ where sh_x, sh_y are shares and $\dot{x}, \dot{y}$ are rates of change.

of change. From the form of the linearized model, one can deduce the overall properties of the model (see also Deleau and Malgrange, 1981). When computing the overall rates of change from the *monde* and *antimonde* simulations, the numerical values of the rates depend on the shares of individual variables, unless the model uses constant elasticity of substitution functions. As a matter of fact, this is the case of many CGE models, a model property that leads to a model linear (or almost linear) in logarithms. The presence of the imperfect competition sectors and the economies of scale, implies that the GEM-E3-SM model is not linear in logarithms, or at least is significantly far from being almost linear in logarithms.

This discussion justifies why it was not possible to neglect the problem of obtaining a good replication of the *monde*. An additional problem comes from the poor statistical information about the *monde*, at the level of detail that is necessary for the CGE model.

As mentioned, it has been possible only to collect the following time series in volume and value: value added by sector (not decomposable in labour and capital); consumption of households (by purpose); exports and imports by product; investment by ownership branch; taxes, social security and income distribution; deflators; government consumption and investment; macroeconomic indicators. Changes in the I-O tables, cost structure and the use of production factors has been observed for France only.

In order to reduce arbitrariness in isolating the changes due to the SMP, the study had to make *a priori* choices about which of the observed changes should not be considered as resulting from completion of the SMP. The following changes have been considered exogenous (non-SMP):

(a)   changes of tastes of consumers; for example, the observed high consumption propensity towards automobiles, services, communications and health care;
(b)   shifts in the propensity of trade that cannot be explained by relative price changes and SMP measures;
(c)   technical progress (productivity gains) and other technology changes (measured as shifts in the use of the production factors not explained by relative price changes) except X-inefficiency gains and total factor productivity gains that were assumed to be associated with the SMP;
(d)   relocation of industries in the ROW, such as that resulting from the decline of basic metal processing in Europe (Sector 3);
(e)   government policy regarding consumption, investment, taxation and social security;
(f)   macroeconomic indicators, such as the exchange and the interest rates, as well as the ROW prices.

In addition, the dynamic calibration did not consider any change in the values of elasticities of substitution (in production, consumption, trade and in imperfect substitution among varieties), as assumed in the base year, except those that implicitly change because of competition regime switches due to the completion of the SMP. Of course, in the *monde* run, all effects attributed to the SMP have been included.

A formal (algorithmic) procedure has been designed to perform dynamic calibration. A first step has dealt with the correct projection of technical progress associated to the use of production factors and the structural technology changes in production.

In the absence of such information, except France, the study used the French detailed I-O tables of 1985, 1988 and 1991, and extrapolated results for all countries. Through a simple production model (specifically designed for that purpose), the implied technical progress rates (dynamically) embedded in the use of production factors has been computed. The estimated technical progress (and technology) changes computed for each country have been left unchanged in both the *monde* and *antimonde*.

The second step is the main task of dynamic calibration. For this purpose, a specific version of the CGE model has been designed, with the following features:

(a) all components of final demand and trade that have been observed in the monde, namely final consumption of households by purpose, volumes and deflators of imports and exports and investment by ownership branch, have been left exogenous to the dynamic calibration CGE model;

(b) the remaining CGE model corresponds to a closed economy in which all features of the CGE-E3-SM model have been included, such as production functions, costs and mark-ups in IM sectors, domestic markets for goods and labour, endogenous determination of the number of firms, income distribution and taxation; in this closed economy model the wage rate acts as numeraire, helping to set the general level of prices close to observed general inflation;

(c) as endogenous variables, apart from the usual ones, the model includes a set of structural and shift parameters that are compatible with the observed imports, exports and final consumption; these parameters are defined as shifts in the structural parameters (δ) of the Armington functions and in households' demand allocation; the simultaneity of these parameter computations with the rest of the model (including price adjustments, other influence factors and SMP measures) ensure that the model determines those shifts that are strictly necessary to fit the *monde*, acting on top of the effects of prices, public policy and SMP measures;

(d) the model incorporates representation of all SMP measures, such as NTBs, standards, transports, X-inefficiencies and changes of competition regime in Armington;

(e) the model computes rates of replacement of capital stock per sector (for all periods) to achieve a compatibility between the exogenous schedule of sectoral investment, the observed sectoral value added and the expected change of productivity of primary production factors;

(f) finally, the model computes shifts in the preference of households between consumption and leisure so as to make the observed outcome of the equilibrium in the labour market compatible.

Then, a dynamic simulation of this closed-economy calibration CGE model is performed as follows:

(a) all changes non-attributable to the SMP are kept exogenous, including tax and other government policy, technical progress, foreign prices, final demand components, exchange and interest rates, foreign prices and export prices;

(b) the dynamic run of the calibration model computes shifts in structural parameters;

(c) the computed figures of value added by sector are compared to the observed ones. By correcting a total factor productivity parameter by sector and after repeating the procedure, one can approximate observed figures of value added by sector and country.

Figure 4.4.   Dynamic calibration of a CGE model

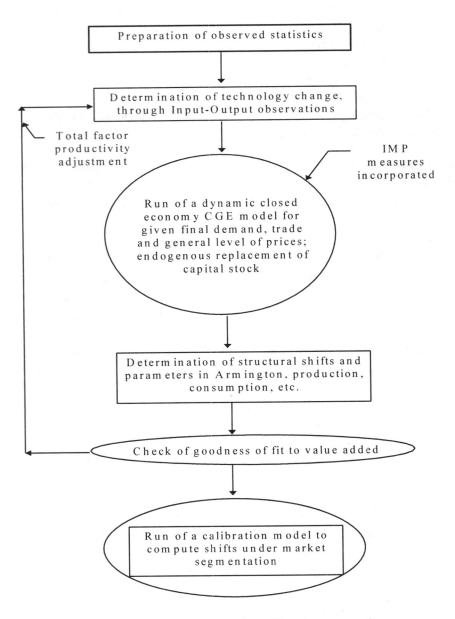

Figure 4.4 summarizes the dynamic calibration procedure.

It turned out that the endogenous determination of the rate of replacement of capital stock by sector (which has been kept constant in all further simulations) has been of critical importance for the success of dynamic calibration. Obviously, this approximates the changes in the rate of use of capital equipment endogenously, as it is allowed to take both positive and negative values in the dynamic calibration. Since the stock of capital acts as a supply constraint in the model, the level of sectoral prices and the simultaneous determination of the necessary shifts in trade propensity can be made compatible with each other.

When doing the *antimonde* simulation, in the main model runs, it is necessary to use shift parameters in the Armington specification that are compatible with the market segmentation regime (since in the *monde* calibration market integration regime is assumed to prevail). To do this, a conceptual problem arises. The shift parameters in the *monde* calibration have been computed in the presence of the SMP measures and regime changes, which facilitated the shift. If the SMP were not applied, the observation of history would have been different and the necessary shifts under market segmentation would also have been different.

Obviously, there is no way of computing these shifts under market segmentation directly from observations. It was therefore necessary to assume that the shifts under the hypothesis of market segmentation that lead to the observed (of course, within *monde* and not *antimonde* circumstances) imports, exports and other sectoral statistics, would be equal to those that would achieve the same trade figures in the *antimonde*. A specific variant of the dynamic calibration model under the market segmentation hypothesis was developed and used for the calibration of the Armington shifts in the *antimonde*.

After that step, all the information to run the *antimonde* simulation was available.

5. Model runs for evaluating the effects of the single market programme

5.1. Overview of the experiment

All the results presented below are derived from dynamic simulations performed with the GEM-E3-SM model (for all EUR-12 Member States, except Luxembourg) as presented in Chapter 4.

The study attempts to quantitatively evaluate the implications of the *antimonde*, i.e. the impact of the non-application of the SMP measures. The measures that were considered relate to the removal of border controls, the harmonization of standards, the enlargement of the market as perceived by consumers and firms, the cost reductions in transports and services associated to trade, X-efficiency gains in telecommunications and banking sectors and the factor productivity gains induced by the SMP.

The *monde* is defined as the situation in which the SMP measures take place, applied to an evolving economy, also in which factors not attributable to the SMP influence economic activity and technology change. The *antimonde*, on the other hand, is the situation in which the SMP measures do not take place, all other things being equal, in the sense that all factors not related to the SMP do take place and allow the economy to evolve. Of course, the independent factors combined with the absence of the SMP, i.e. the *antimonde*, dynamically bring the economy to a different evolution path.

The 'evaluation of the SMP' is then defined in a straightforward manner as the comparison of *antimonde* to *monde*, dynamically, year by year. In the study, the evaluation comes from comparing two model simulations, as is usually done in economic modelling. The baseline dynamic simulation represents the *monde*. The counterfactual dynamic model simulation represents the *antimonde*. This is constructed by changing the values of some exogenous model parameters, in particular by removing the SMP measures that have been incorporated in the baseline and by keeping all other exogenous variables to their numerical values as in the baseline scenario. The percentage change of the values of all endogenous variables of the counterfactual scenario, compared to their value in the baseline, gives an estimate of the effects of the SMP. Note that benefits from the SMP are found as losses of the *antimonde* scenario compared to the *monde* scenario, and vice-versa.

The procedure adopted can be characterized as an *ex post* evaluation of the SMP because the direct effects of the SMP take their numerical values based on *ex post* studies and surveys and because the *monde* is dynamically calibrated to fit the observed evolution of the economy of each EUR-11 Member State. Therefore, the baseline scenario is a historical simulation (in the sense of forecasting models) and if the dynamic calibration were perfect, it would exactly replicate the observed values of the endogenous variables.

5.2. Design of the experiment

5.2.1. Schedule of the SMP

As already explained, the numerical quantification of the SMP measures was drawn from the results of studies within the 1996 Single Market Review programme.

The completion of the SMP, which is part of the *monde*, is, of course, a continuous process that has lasted several years, even beyond 1992. It may also be the case that expectations of the SMP effects may have accelerated the effective completion even before 1992. For the purpose of the simulations, however, it was necessary to make an *a priori* assumption, within the *monde* about the schedule for SMP completion. For technical reasons related to the modelling application, that schedule had to be discrete, involving the implementation of concrete SMP measures. Given that most available statistics stopped in 1991, it was decided to use that year as representing the full implementation of the SMP. For reasons of computational convenience, it was also decided to use a three-year time path in the model and therefore only simulate the years 1985, 1988, 1991 (last observed) and 1994 (not observed).

In the context of the modelling application, these four periods do not really represent the respective years, but rather an abstraction trying to capture intermediate steps of the implementation of the SMP.

The following assumptions were made:

(a)   was prior to the SMP implementation, therefore the *monde* is not different from the *antimonde* in this year;

(b)   is the first year of partial SMP implementation involving the removal of NTBs, partial harmonization of standards, partial reduction of cost of transports and services associated to trade, partial X-efficiency gains in telecommunications and banks, partial increased total factor productivity and a switch in consumer preferences structure that changed the competition regime from market segmentation (in 1985) to market integration in 1988. Thus it is assumed that already in 1988, firms and consumers were behaving with the perception of the enlarged market. Delays regarding adjustment of border controls and harmonization deprived the EU from full SMP completion in 1988;

(c)   is assumed to be the year of full completion of the SMP, regarding border controls, efficiency gains and market integration. Thus, 1991 is the year in which changes that began in 1988, including harmonization standardization and product homogeneity across the EU, took place in their entirety;

(d)   involved no further progress regarding the SMP and is used to infer about longer-run effects.

5.2.2. Numerical assumptions for SMP measures

The modelling application concerns the following SMP measures and changes:

I.   Trade measures (in all sectors)

(a)   Removal of non-tariff barriers (NTBs).
(b)   Reduction in trade costs absorbed by market services for compliance to foreign product standards, labelling, packaging, etc.
(c)   Reduction and efficiency gains in costs of trade associated to international transports and banking services.

II.   Market integration (in all sectors except energy)

(a)   Shift in consumer preferences considering domestic and EU commodities as being closer substitutes.

(b)   Additional shift in consumer preferences considering domestic and EU varieties of commodities as being equally substitutable in forming commodity categories.

III.   Efficiency gains in production

(a)   X-efficiency gains in telecommunication and banking services.

(b)   Additional factor productivity gains (in all sectors).

Table 5.1 summarizes the assumed NTB rates by sector (assumed uniform across all EU Member States).

Table 5.1.   NTB rates by sector

Sector	Non-tariff barriers (%)
Agriculture	1.2
Energy	0.9
Metallic	1.6
Chemical	0.9
Non-metallic	1.54
Electrical goods	2.2
Transport equipment	2.73
Other equipment	1.7
Consumer goods	1.63
Building	1
Telecommunications	2.5
Transports	2.5
Banks	2.5
Services	1
Non-market	1

The above figures refer only to intra-EU trade. Trade with the rest of the world is assumed to have also benefited from the reduction of trade costs associated with border controls, but to a lesser extent. Thus, it is assumed that half of the reduction of the NTBs also applies to trade with the rest of the world.

Pre-SMP trade costs required for compliance to foreign standards and other regulation, labelling and packaging differ by country and sector. Because of a lack of detailed quantitative information in the sectoral studies, *ad hoc* values were chosen based as much as possible on these studies. On average, as a percentage of the value of a trade transaction, the standards costs are of the order of 0.3% to 0.5%. Within the SMP it is assumed that harmonization is complete, so trade costs for compliance to foreign standards are eliminated.

Table 5.2.   **Reduction of costs of compliance to standards attributed to the SMP (as % of corresponding export flow)**

	B	D	DK	F	GR	IRL	I	NL	P	E	UK
						Exporter					
Agriculture	-0.4	-0.5	-0.5	-0.5	-0.3	-0.5	-0.5	-0.4	-0.1	-0.5	-0.5
Energy	-0.4	-0.5	-0.5	-0.5	-0.3	-0.5	-0.5	-0.4	0.0	-0.5	-0.5
Metal industry	-0.4	-0.5	-0.5	-0.5	-0.3	-0.5	-0.5	-0.4	-0.1	-0.5	-0.5
Chemicals	-0.4	-0.5	-0.5	-0.5	-0.3	-0.5	-0.5	-0.4	0.0	-0.5	-0.5
Other energy intensive	-0.4	-0.5	-0.5	-0.5	-0.3	-0.4	-0.5	-0.4	0.0	-0.5	-0.4
Electrical	-0.4	-0.5	-0.5	-0.5	-0.3	-0.5	-0.5	-0.4	0.0	-0.5	-0.5
Transport equipment	-0.4	-0.5	-0.5	-0.5	-0.3	-0.5	-0.5	-0.4	0.0	-0.5	-0.5
Other equipment	-0.4	-0.5	-0.5	-0.5	-0.3	-0.5	-0.5	-0.4	0.0	-0.5	-0.5
Consumer goods	-0.4	-0.5	-0.5	-0.5	-0.3	-0.4	-0.5	-0.4	0.0	-0.5	-0.4

Trade costs associated to transports vary more widely, since they account for distance between trade partners. For example, total transport costs attain about 5% of trade flow for peripheral economies, while being of the order of 1.5% in Central Europe. The reduction of transport costs due to the SMP is difficult to estimate by country as some peripheral countries continued to bear high transport costs for their exports. Table 5.3 summarizes the numerical assumptions for the reduction attributed to the SMP.

Table 5.3.   **Reduction of international transport costs of exports attributed to the SMP (as % of corresponding export flow)**

	B	D	DK	F	GR	IRL	I	NL	P	E	UK
						Exporter					
Agriculture	-0.08	-0.04	-0.23	-0.05	-0.01	-0.07	-0.09	-0.15	-0.11	-0.13	-0.07
Energy	-0.14	-0.06	-0.33	-0.08	-0.01	-0.06	-0.06	-0.12	-0.17	-0.11	-0.06
Metal industry	-0.12	-0.08	-0.23	-0.07	0.00	-0.07	-0.09	-0.16	-0.17	-0.14	-0.07
Chemicals	-0.12	-0.07	-0.22	-0.08	0.00	-0.07	-0.09	-0.18	-0.10	-0.11	-0.07
Other energy intensive	-0.10	-0.07	-0.24	-0.09	-0.01	-0.07	-0.09	-0.16	-0.14	-0.15	-0.07
Electrical	-0.11	-0.09	-0.26	-0.09	-0.01	-0.07	-0.10	-0.22	-0.13	-0.13	-0.07
Transport equipment	-0.14	-0.10	-0.34	-0.08	0.00	-0.07	-0.10	-0.28	-0.10	-0.15	-0.07
Other equipment	-0.12	-0.08	-0.22	-0.09	-0.01	-0.07	-0.10	-0.22	-0.11	-0.14	-0.07
Consumer goods	-0.13	-0.08	-0.25	-0.08	-0.01	-0.06	-0.10	-0.19	-0.17	-0.15	-0.06

The total cost of bank services associated to trade was already in the pre-SMP period rather small, of the order of 0.5%. Banking costs are assumed to decrease, because of efficiency gains and harmonization, under the SMP. As different currencies are still applicable and harmonization of international banking transactions regulation has been rather limited in the 1985–92 period, the overall changes of trade costs related to bank services are very small as shown in Table 5.4.

Table 5.4. **Reduction of banking services costs attributed to the SMP (as % of corresponding export flow)**

	B	D	DK	F	GR	IRL	I	NL	P	E	UK
						Exporter					
Agriculture	0.00	0.00	-0.02	-0.02	0.00	-0.06	-0.02	-0.02	0.00	-0.01	-0.06
Energy	0.00	0.00	-0.02	-0.02	0.00	-0.07	-0.02	-0.01	-0.01	-0.01	-0.07
Metal industry	0.00	0.00	-0.02	-0.02	0.00	-0.07	-0.03	-0.02	-0.01	-0.01	-0.07
Chemicals	0.00	0.00	-0.02	-0.02	0.00	-0.07	-0.03	-0.02	-0.01	-0.01	-0.07
Other energy intensive	0.00	0.00	-0.02	-0.02	0.00	-0.07	-0.03	-0.01	-0.01	-0.01	-0.07
Electrical	0.00	0.00	-0.02	-0.02	0.00	-0.08	-0.03	-0.02	0.00	-0.01	-0.08
Transport equipment	0.00	0.00	-0.03	-0.02	0.00	-0.07	-0.03	-0.03	0.00	-0.01	-0.07
Other equipment	0.00	0.00	-0.02	-0.02	0.00	-0.08	-0.03	-0.02	-0.01	-0.01	-0.08
Consumer goods	0.00	0.00	-0.02	-0.02	0.00	-0.07	-0.03	-0.02	-0.01	-0.01	-0.07

Gains regarding X-inefficiencies in telecommunications and banking have been found to be substantial, in sectoral studies. However, these should also be partly attributed to the important global technology evolution in these sectors. Regarding the part attributed to the SMP, it is assumed that fixed costs in telecommunications decreased by 2% in 1988 and 5% in 1991 (representing about -1.2% in total sector cost), while in the banking sectors the corresponding reduction is assumed to be 1.5 and 2.5% for 1988 and 1991 respectively (about -0.5% in total sector cost).

Sectoral studies also suggested that the SMP induced an acceleration of technical progress in all sectors. Experts consulted about this matter, including those of the European Commission (DG II) believe that the single market has induced accelerated technical progress, acting in favour of total factor productivity gains, of the order of 0.1% per annum in 1991, on average and for all sectors.

Regarding the switch from market segmentation to market integration, the following values of elasticities were adopted:

Table 5.5. **Armington elasticities in GEM-E3-SM**

Sectors	Market segmentation		Market integration	
	Domestic and imported goods	EU imports and ROW imports	EU commodities (domestic and imported) and ROW imports	Domestic and EU imports[1]
Agriculture	2	3	2	5 - 7
Energy	0.8	1.1	0.8	0.7 - 0.7
Metal industry	1.5	3.6	1.5	5 - 7.6
Chemicals	1.8	4	1.8	5.6 - 8.4
Other energy intensive	2	4.4	2	6.2 - 9.2
Electrical goods	2	4.4	2	6.2 - 9.2
Transport equipment	1.5	3.6	1.5	5 - 7.6
Other equipment	1.5	3.6	1.5	5 - 7.6
Consumer goods	2	2.5	2	7 - 10.5
Building and construction	1.2	1.5	1.2	1.5 - 1.5
Telecommunications	1.2	3	1.2	4.2 - 6.3
Transports	1.5	2	1.5	2 - 2
Banking services	1.5	4	1.5	5.6 - 8.4
Market services	1.2	1.5	1.2	4.2 - 6.3
Non-market services	0.3	0.5	0.3	0.5 -0.5

[1] The first number in this column corresponds to the elasticity used in 1988 in the *monde*, while the second is the one used from 1991 onwards.

5.2.3. Design of the model runs

As mentioned, the *antimonde* experiment is a dynamic model simulation defined exactly as the baseline simulation, apart from the SMP measures which are removed as described in the previous sub-section.

For analytical reasons, and with a view to reducing uncertainty in concluding from model results, the study designed and simulated different cases that differ in the *a priori* assumptions regarding two issues:

(a)   the hypothesis whether or not terms of trade effects from the ROW to the EU (in the sense of net inflow of resources from the ROW to the EU, to consume and invest in the EU rather than in the ROW) are allowed in the simulation that evaluates the consequences of the SMP. Terms of trade effects can be avoided in the model simulations, by constraining the adjustment flexibility of the current account by country (as a % of GDP), for example by keeping it fixed in the counterfactual scenario at its level in the baseline scenario;

(b)   the hypothesis whether or not the simulation allows consumption (in all its forms) to experience efficiency gains from the availability of a larger variety of commodities in the enlarged market, under the SMP policy. Efficiency gains under the variety efficiency hypothesis exert indirect technical progress effects on production, leading to further efficiency gains, in production as well. There might also be other forms of technical progress (not induced by varieties) resulting from the SMP, such as accelerated incorporation of innovation in the products, as a consequence of increased competition (Barro and Sala-i-Martin, 1995). In analytical terms, one must therefore be careful to avoid double counting of effects of the SMP on technical progress.

In macroeconomic policy analysis, the *a priori* assumption about the way in which the external sector will adjust, in reacting to the policy, is important for understanding the effects of that policy. If the current account can adjust freely, allocation effects in the domestic economy are mixed with terms of trade effects, as it might be opportune for the foreign sectors to bring activity into the domestic economy. In public policy analysis (for example, taxation policy), to evaluate the 'pure' allocation effects of a policy in the domestic economy, it is often assumed that some mechanism acts to refrain foreign sectors from bringing or obtaining activity. For the same purpose, in CGE modelling it is quite common to fix the current account (as a % of GDP) in the counterfactual simulation at the level of the baseline simulation, so as to let domestic economy mechanisms act alone. Such an assumption is one of the possible closure assumptions in CGE modelling. If such a constraint is imposed on the current account equation of the CGE model, then an additional unknown variable must be computed endogenously. In the logic of the CGE models, such a variable must be a price. For example, in the case of the GEM-E3-SM model, it has been decided to endogenously compute the real interest rate in each EU Member State (which is normally exogenous), as a means of keeping fixed the country's current account as a percentage of GDP. The real interest rate influences mainly sectoral investment and secondly private consumption, through the consumption-savings choice. Under the current account constraint, the real interest rate adjusts consequently to refrain investment and consumption from bringing additional resources into the country from foreign ones, or vice versa to avoid leakage of domestic activity to foreign sectors.

In the design of scenario runs for the SMP, it was decided to contrast the evaluation of the SMP with respect to the assumption about the external sector closure rule of the model.

The constraint case scenario assumes then that the current account of each EU Member State as a percentage of GDP remains constant. Since no net inflow (or outflow) of resources is allowed for any country, this case mainly serves to evaluate the impact of the SMP through the domestic economy of each Member State. The main source of growth effects comes from efficiency gains in the domestic sectors, for example where economies of scale can be achieved. As the current account remains fixed, the real interest rate by country is allowed to vary, affecting investment and consumption in the domestic economies.

The flexible case scenario assumes, on the other hand, that the current account of any EU Member State can vary freely, while the real interest rate remains fixed. This case entails an additional potential source of growth, induced by terms of trade effects from the rest of the world and possibly a better allocation of resources within the EU as bilateral intra-EU trade is also allowed to adjust more freely, as not being constrained by the current account level of each country. Regarding the external sector closure assumption, the third simulation case, namely the efficiency case, is the same as the flexible case. These two differ in the representation of possible technical progress induced by the SMP.

The issue about potential efficiency gains in consumption (intermediate, final, investment, etc.) from increasing commodity variety has been discussed in Section 4.3.5. There, it was shown that if EU consumers perceive all domestic and EU varieties as equal though still imperfect substitutes, an efficiency gain is obtained compared to the case where different substitutability between the domestic bulk of varieties and the EU one is perceived. In terms of the SMP, such efficiency gains can be obtained under the assumption that within a commodity variety, there is no distinction by country of origin.

It is extremely difficult to quantify such an efficiency gain although there is strong evidence of an increase in varieties that are at the disposal of the consumer after the completion of the SMP. In modelling terms, the inclusion of this variety effect is conveyed through a further shift in market competition regime to advanced integration, as explained in Section 4.3.5.

To isolate the variety effect, the efficiency case scenario was designed. The scenario is exactly the same as the flexible case regarding current account flexibility, but it differs in the inclusion of efficiency gains from increasing commodity varieties and the exclusion of the *ad hoc* total factor productivity assumption (that has been included in both the constraint and the flexible cases). In fact, to avoid double counting, the *ad hoc* assumption about total factor productivity gains has been removed in the efficiency case. Therefore, the efficiency gains from bigger variety in the enlarged market are the only source of indirect technical progress effected in the simulation of the efficiency case as a result of the SMP.

Among the many sensitivity tests that were performed, two major cases are reported here. The first concerns capital mobility, for which it is assumed that it fully applies across the EU Member States in contrast to the main cases where capital is mobile only across sectors of the domestic economy. The second sensitivity attempts to evaluate the robustness of results when varying the numerical assumptions concerning the elasticity of substitution among firms' varieties in the IC sectors and the consequent change of the fixed part of costs in these sectors.

Finally, in order to find out which of the SMP effects are permanent and which are transitory, a longer-term dynamic model run was undertaken. The efficiency case was allowed to run over 20 years and end in 2006, instead of 1994. We have verified, in the numerical results, that in that year the model approaches a steady state.

Notice that all model runs use exactly the same value for the elasticity of substitution among firms' products (the so-called love of variety). By model construction, as the hypothesis about symmetric firms is retained, the consumer utility index is well defined in all scenarios. Preferences in scenarios are modified in such a way that indices of utility remain well defined, since the change of preferences, reflected in the change of the nesting of stepwise budgeting, does not alter the optimality of the initial allocation, in the sense that there is no disruption of the benchmark equilibrium. So, in terms of welfare, the *monde* and the *antimonde* are comparable across the simulation cases.

Table 5.6 summarizes the definition of the main simulation cases.

Table 5.6.   Definition of SMP simulations

Full *antimonde* simulations	
Title	*Explanation*
Constraint case	The current account is assumed fixed at the level of each Member State. The real interest rate can change. The *ad hoc* total factor productivity assumption is included.
Flexible case	Trade is freely adjusting in bilateral intra-EU trade and with respect to the rest of the world. The current account is free. Real interest rates are kept fixed. The *ad hoc* total factor productivity assumption is included.
Efficiency case	As in the flexible case, regarding current account and real interest rates. Inclusion of endogenous efficiency gains coming from the larger variety of EU commodities in the enlarged market. No exogenous total factor productivity gains are assumed.
Sensitivity *antimonde* simulations	
Mobile capital sensitivity	As in the flexible case, but capital is assumed perfectly mobile across countries in addition to mobility across sectors.
Variety sensitivity	As in the constraint case, but starting from different numerical values for the elasticity of substitution among varieties.
Long-run simulation	As in the efficiency case, but dynamic run up to 2006.

In addition to the full *antimonde* simulations, a set of partial *antimonde* simulations was constructed. This was done for analytical reasons, with a view to isolating and understanding the effects of individual SMP measures. Such a stepwise analysis also allows for examining whether or not the effects of individual measures are adding up to the full *antimonde* scenario. All the partial *antimonde* scenarios follow the flexible case closure rule regarding the current account.

Tables 5.7 and 5.8 summarize the assumptions of the main simulations and indicate the SMP measures not implemented in each of the partial *antimonde* cases.

Table 5.7. Definition of partial *antimonde* simulations

Title of partial *antimonde* run	Explanation
Border controls	Non-tariff barriers are restored in their 1985 status. Trade cost reductions for standards, transport and banking services are assumed not to have occurred.
Border controls and X-inefficiencies	As in border controls. Additionally, no X-efficiency gains are assumed to have been induced by the SMP.
Market segmentation	The switch of consumer preferences reflecting market integration is cancelled out; markets remain segmented.
Trade *antimonde*	The combination of the two scenarios above: restoration of border controls, no X-efficiency gains, segmented markets.
Full *antimonde*	As in trade *antimonde*; additionally, no total factor productivity gains.

Table 5.8. Description of sensitivity tests

SMP measures Name of scenario	Removal of NTBs	Harmonization of standards	Market regime (segmented/ integrated)	X-efficiency gains	Factor productivity gains
Full *monde*	Yes	Yes	Integrated	Yes	Yes
Border controls	No	No	Integrated	Yes	Yes
Border controls and X-inefficiency	No	No	Integrated	No	Yes
Market segmentation	Yes	Yes	Segmented	Yes	Yes
Trade *antimonde*	No	No	Segmented	No	Yes
Full *antimonde* (equivalent to the flexible case)	No	No	Segmented	No	No

5.2.4. Organization of model results

In Appendix B of this study, a full set of numerical results is provided. This set is organized as follows:

(a) results are presented first at the EUR-11 aggregate level and then by individual Member State;

(b) two sets of results are given: one presenting the three full *antimonde* simulations titled *The full antimonde scenario* and one isolating the impact of individual SMP measures titled *Decomposition of effects*.

Each set of results presents:

(a) aggregate indices of the economy (macroeconomic aggregates, deflators and cumulative effects);

(b) the effects on the sectors with economies of scale potential in terms of industrial concentration, efficiency (measured through the fixed cost) and mark-ups;

(c) the impact of the scenario at the sectoral level involving volumes (production, investment, consumption, trade, labour demand) and relative prices (marginal cost, cost of labour, trade prices).

All figures presenting numerical results correspond to percentages or absolute differences between the *antimonde* and the *monde* (except where otherwise indicated).

The signs of the percentage changes induced by the *antimonde* scenarios in comparison with the baseline *monde* scenario must be inverted to be interpreted as the effects of the SMP measures. A negative figure in the results indicates that the corresponding quantity is lower in the *antimonde* compared to the *monde* so the SMP has affected it positively. Conversely, a positive figure in the results indicates that corresponding quantity is higher in the *antimonde* compared to the *monde* so the SMP had a negative impact on it.

Notice that all numerical results are annual percentage changes (or percentage point changes) compared to the baseline simulation. They are not cumulative, except where specifically indicated.

5.3.   Main results and sensitivity analysis

In Section 5.3.1 the overall effects of the SMP inferred from the three main full *antimonde* scenarios are presented. To avoid confusion for the reader, results presented directly show the impact of the SMP and not the impact of the *antimonde* corresponding to the absence of the SMP.[21]

Sections 5.3.1 to 5.3.4 present the partial *antimonde* simulations.

5.3.1. The overall effects of the SMP

The results and sensitivity tests generally suggest that the SMP has induced real activity gains and increased the volume of intra-EU trade. According to the range of results obtained from the three main *antimonde* scenarios:

(a)   EU GDP in 1994 is estimated to have been 1.1% to 1.5% higher due to the single market leading to a cumulative net gain ranging from ECU 174 to 207 billion in the period 1988–94. Higher GDP is also obtained in all intermediate years, from 1988 to 1994. It is likely that the net gains continue to accumulate also after 1994, as the long-run simulation (approaching the steady state) indicates.

(b)   Real GDP increase is supported by a higher level of investment, increasing by 2.5% to 4.5% in 1994, and consumption increasing by 0.8% to 1.6%. Again, increases are found for all intermediate years and in the longer run.

(c)   Employment is also higher indicating the creation of 320,000 to 620,000 new jobs, still increasing towards the steady state.

(d)   The volume of trade is found to have increased significantly as a result of the SMP; intra-EU trade, for example, is found 4% to 5% higher in 1994. The intra-EU trade creation effect is persisting over the longer run. Trade creation is also observed in the relations with the rest of the world, especially in imports from the ROW.

(e)   In the manufacturing sectors, the increase in intra-EU trade is even higher (7% to 8%) accompanied by higher industrial concentration and falling price/cost margins (0.8% to 0.9%) because of increasing competition.

---

21   In other words, the signs of the results were inverted.

(f)   Among the service sectors, the performance of telecommunication and banking services is noticeable, achieving 12% to 18% higher intra-EU trade and 4.0% to 6.0% lower fixed costs.

(g)   Relative to a non-EU foreign numeraire, domestic prices generally drop (-0.6% down to -1.1% per annum), as a result of the combined effects of efficiency gains in trade and production (about -0.9% drop in price-cost margins, on average) that overcompensate pressures on prices from the higher level of activity.

The main effects of the SMP are summarized in Table 5.9.

Table 5.9.   Aggregate effects of the SMP

Effects of the SMP on EUR-11	Constraint case	Flexible case	Efficiency case
GDP	+1.10%	+1.26%	+1.46%
Private consumption	+0.82%	+1.53%	+1.60%
Total investment	+2.67%	+4.52%	+4.53%
Total intra-EU trade	+3.99%	+4.63%	+4.74%
Employment	+0.25%	+0.48%	+0.49%
Labour productivity	+0.32%	+0.77%	+0.97%
Consumer price index	-1.19%	-0.74%	-0.65%
Real wage rate	+1.43%	+1.67%	+1.87%
Average mark-up	-0.79%	-0.92%	-0.92%
Current account as percent of GDP	0.00%	-0.68%	-0.62%

Note: Numbers indicate percentage changes between *monde* and *antimonde*, except current account where difference is absolute. The figures presented in this table refer to the last year of the simulation (i.e. 1994) of the three full *antimonde* scenarios.

The basic mechanism in all three scenarios starts from the one illustrated in Section 4.3.6. In the first place, the increased competition related to the SMP implies a fall in mark-ups and a related exploitation of economies of scale, while industrial concentration adjusts for zero profits. Of course, this occurs in the imperfect competition sectors only, representing about 20% of the EU's GDP. This acts as a release of resources for the economy that become available for consumption and investment.

The resulting increase in domestic EU demand, in other terms an activity-boosting effect, tends to push prices upwards, because of constraints from fixed production capacity, which may overweigh, in a first approximation, cost contraction due to increased competition.

On the other hand, trade measures related to the SMP allow for a decrease of trade costs and further efficiency gains (direct through the NTBs and indirect through increasing the intra-EU volume of trade allowing for a better overall allocation). The direct effect of trade measures within the SMP is trade creation within the EU, allowing for a more efficient allocation between sectors and countries. Price effects of reduced trade costs, and efficiency gains from trade, tend to compensate the activity effects on prices. In the presence of positive activity effects, investments tend to increase so as to react to the increasing pressures on production capacity reflected on the shadow price of capital.

Through the mechanism presented in the stylized example in Section 4.3.5 and exemplified in the beginning of this section, the SMP had a positive impact on GDP. Although the order of magnitude of the gain appears to be sensitive in the modelling assumptions and differs across countries, a positive sign was obtained in all cases, with gains progressively increasing until the steady state. The three main *antimonde* simulations seem to place the GDP gains somewhere between 1.10% to 1.50%, with additional effects (going up to 2.4% in the efficiency case) expected towards the steady state. Sensitivity analysis further expands this band in both directions by an additional 0.2%.

If the current account is flexible, the EU economy is attractive for exporters from the rest of the world, who bring resources into the EU contributing to support increased activity. As the nominal exchange rate of the ECU with respect to the ROW currencies acts as numeraire in the EU economy (following the model), this situation is equivalent to a re-evaluation of the real exchange rate of the EU. In these terms the consumer price index and the production costs drop. The full adjustment of international trade in the flexible case and the corresponding ability to obtain terms of trade gains from the rest of the world (in other words, the rest of the world consents to a deterioration of the EU current account) allow for the full adjustment of demand and investment. This allows for GDP gains reaching 1.26% in 1994. In cumulative terms, this gain amounts to ECU 183 billion for the 1988–94 period. These results place the flexible case in the middle of the band of results.

If the current account is fixed, as in the constraint case, the real interest rate has to increase to discourage investment and consumption so as to limit the needs for support of domestic activity from the rest of the world. Obviously, this reduces real growth effects but also moderates the upward pressures on domestic prices. Terms of trade effects vanish, but real activity gains that are due to efficiency gains from higher competition and better allocation of resources from trade creation remain. Thus, the constraint case measures the effects of the SMP on the domestic EU economy taken alone. In the short term, GDP gains are similar to the flexible case, but the lower increase in investment results in subsequent periods in lower GDP gains reaching 1.10% in 1994, or a cumulative ECU 174 billion in the 1988–94 period. Regarding GDP effects, the constraint case is close to the low end of the band of results.

The efficiency case is similar to the flexible case, regarding current account adjustment, but includes the additional variety effect, without also including the total factor productivity assumption.[22] This simulation case amplifies activity gains as it induces an endogenous efficiency mechanism triggered by the SMP and acting through consumption of commodities, in private, intermediate, investment, etc. The variety effect implies that in consumption, less input is needed to derive the same effective volume of output. This can be seen, for example, in intermediate consumption, where having a bigger pool of varieties at a firm's disposal, the most suitable one will be selected, leading to increased efficiency. The variety effect acts in favour of moderating the upwards pressures on prices limiting the need for imports from the ROW and releasing more domestic resources for consumption and investment.

The type of additional effects that the efficiency case imposes in the model compared to the flexible case, are similar to technical progress effects, the difference being that total factor productivity applies on production while these efficiency gains apply on the demand side. It is therefore not surprising that the efficiency case leads to results similar to those of a total factor

---

[22]   Otherwise it would be double counting.

productivity increase,[23] which, however, in this case depends endogenously on the fluctuations of industrial concentration in each sector, as implied by the SMP. Although the assumption that increased variety induces efficiency gains seems rather straightforward, it is very difficult to substantiate and quantify in empirical terms. For this reason, it has not been incorporated in the other two cases.

In terms of GDP effects, it can be stated that the efficiency case presents the upper bound of the effects of the SMP. Compared to the flexible case, the efficiency case derives its additional gains neither from higher investment nor from financing from ROW, but rather from more efficient allocation of the domestic resources.

Allowing for endogenous efficiency gains being obtained from the increase in varieties perceived by the consumers within the SMP, GDP gains increase by an additional 20% reaching 1.46% in 1994 or a cumulative ECU 207 billion. At the steady state solution (obtained after year 2010 and not shown in the results), the total gain from the SMP increases even more.

Efficiency gains on the production side (X-efficiencies in service sectors and total factor productivity gains as imposed in the constraint and flexible cases) explain a small part of the achieved GDP growth: they account for only 0.2% of extra GDP, in the flexible case. The efficiency case, not including the total factor productivity assumption, but incorporating the variety effects, leads to an even higher performance (0.4% more GDP).

Table 5.10. Long-run impact of the SMP

Effects of the SMP on EUR-11 in the long-run solution	Efficiency Case
GDP	+2.4%
Private consumption	+2.2%
Total investment	+5.03%
Total intra-EU trade	+5.47%
Employment	+0.79%
Labour productivity	+1.6
Consumer price index	-0.93%
Real wage rate	+3.6
Average mark-up	-0.94

Note: Numbers indicate percentage changes except current account where difference is absolute. The figures refer to the last year of a long-run simulation (i.e. 2006) of the three full *antimonde* scenarios.

The dynamic effects are of interest for the SMP evaluation. After 20 years, growing investment allows for a re-establishment of normal values for the real shadow price of capital and a net drop in domestic prices relative to foreign ROW prices, gradually limiting requests for net imports from the ROW. Permanent effects on real domestic activity remain however: GDP, private consumption, employment, real wage rate and labour productivity are found

---

[23]   Several theoretical models link the expanding commodity varieties with technological progress (see Barro and Sala-i-Martin, 1995).

improved in the steady state, as shown in the table above. On the contrary, trade volume with the ROW and the current account tend to return to their baseline values, leaving no net effect.

Table 5.11 summarizes the trade relationships of the EU with the ROW as influenced by the SMP.

Table 5.11.   Impact of the SMP on the rest of the world

Effects of the SMP on trade with the ROW	Constraint case	Flexible case	Efficiency case	Long Run
Exports to the ROW (vol)	+0.14%	-1.03%	-0.85%	-0.23%
Imports from the ROW (vol)	+0.36%	+2.75%	+2.45%	+1.62%

Note: Numbers indicate percentage changes. The figures refer to the last year of the simulation i.e. 1994 for the three full *antimonde* scenarios and 2006 for the last column.

In the remainder of the section some key issues derived from the results are further discussed. These include:

(a)   increase in intra-EU trade, which is found to be significant in all scenarios and sensitivity tests;

(b)   increase in industrial concentration and drop in price/cost margins in the IC sectors, found to be significant in scenario runs that include perception of increased competition within the EU;

(c)   increase in investment, dynamic effects and the role of consumption and employment;

(d)   differential effects by industrial sector;

(e)   differential effects by country.

Increase in intra-EU trade: the most noticeable effect of the SMP concerns the intra-EU volume of trade. It is found significantly higher, increasing on average by 4.0% to 5.0% annually at the EUR-11 level. This increase is a combination of effects coming from the abolition of border controls and the perception of the enlargement of the market, domestic markets open in competition entailing higher substitutability among the EU commodities. The increase in intra-EU trade was found robust with respect both to the external sector closure assumption and to the consumption efficiency mechanism.

Trade creation is also observed with respect to the rest of the world, but to a lesser extent. Mainly imports from the ROW increase (by 2% to 3% per year in the flexible and efficiency cases – much less in the constraint case, because of the external sector closure assumption). The SMP did not deprive foreign suppliers from access to the EU market. Exports of the EU to the ROW, on the other hand, remain almost stabilized (increase of 0.1% in the constraint case) or are slightly reduced (in the other two cases). The abolition of border controls did induce lower EU prices and hence competitiveness gains with respect to the ROW, but this gain is diminished from the upwards pressures on EU marginal costs as EU domestic activity increases.

The combination of border control removal and economies of scale, which are only possible in IC sectors, is beneficial to trade creation. For example, intra-EU trade increased by 8.1% (for EUR-11 in 1994 in the flexible case) for transport equipment, and by 7.2% for metal industry products, while being of the order of about 5% to 6% for products of other IC sectors. Among the service sectors, banking and telecommunications have additionally benefited from autonomous efficiency gains leading to high performance in intra-EU trade creation: 12% and 18% respectively. Intra-EU trade in the perfect competition sectors generally increased, but at a significantly lower degree. For example, in the consumer goods and construction sectors trade increased by about 3%. The service sectors that bore negative activity effects from efficiency gains in trading goods within the EU showed a slightly negative net effect on their exports: this is the case of market services and transports.

In cumulative terms, the SMP resulted in additional trade volume amounting to ECU 123, 136 and 139 billion for the constraint, flexible and efficiency cases respectively, during the 1988-94 period.

Reduction of price/cost margins and increased industrial concentration in the sectors with economies of scale potential: integration, as modelled in the context of this study, increases the price sensitivity of intra-EU trade, thereby inducing mark-up decline. Through the change in consumer preferences, firms perceive an enlarged competition domain that forces them to lower profits.

The instantaneous adjustment of the number of firms leads to an increase in average firm size. This results in a better sharing of fixed costs, and savings in production. This effect is more pronounced in transport equipment and in the metal industries, where the number of symmetric firms in the sector (which is a measure of industrial concentration) is reduced by 11% to 13% in all cases. Fixed costs, as a percentage of total production costs within each sector, decrease significantly.

The reduction of price mark-ups (of the order of -0.8% down to -0.9% for EUR-12) occurred both for domestic sales and (to a lesser extent) EU-oriented exports. The most significant reduction in mark-ups is obtained in transport equipment (about -1.7% in the flexible case) and in the metal industry (-1.2%) while in the other IC sectors the reduction was found to be of lower magnitude (-0.4 to -0.6%). Mark-ups in sales addressed to the rest of the world remained almost unaffected.

Shift towards more investments: the freeing of resources that were not productive pre-SMP manifests itself as higher demand, pushing for increased production. The productive capacity is only constrained by the scarcity of capital stock in the economy as a whole, as capital is assumed to be mobile across sectors within the same country. In static terms, the need for more production leads to an increase in the real shadow price of capital (+1% in the flexible case in 1988) and hence to higher opportunity in investing. Thus, investment demand increases (+4.2% in 1988), considerably more than private consumption (+1.1% in 1988 in the same scenario). Apart from the important sectoral effects from this redirection of demand, higher investment also entails higher capital stock in the following years (through the capital accumulation mechanism) and hence lower prices (since the capital constraint will be relaxed) and higher production capacity. This is the main mechanism that leads to the persistence of the gains in growth in the long term. Investments at the EUR-11 level increase by 4.5% in 1994 in the flexible case and stabilize at a slightly higher level until the steady state.

In the constraint case, this effect is smaller, as the current account constraint is effective. In order to avoid the deterioration of the current account, real interest rates have to increase (compared to the *antimonde*) so as to discourage investment and limit the need for an inflow of foreign resources. Investment still increases but much less (+2.1% in 1988). Consumption is also affected negatively compared to the flexible case, increasing by only +0.6%. The fact that lower investment is involved in the constraint case explains the growth differential, compared to the other two cases: gains in GDP in the constraint case start from 0.58% in 1988 to reach 1.1% in 1994, while the flexible case although starting from a slightly lower base (+0.46% in 1988) evolves to a higher level (+1.26%). In the steady state, this difference is further amplified.

With respect to investment and growth, the efficiency case exhibits the same basic behaviour as the flexible case, though slightly more amplified.

Sectoral activity effects in the EU: as already explained, the SMP was found to lead to an increase in activity within the EU because of the combined effect of the exploitation of economies of scale potential and the efficiency gains in trade. This increase in turn provokes a considerable increase in investment and to a lesser extent in consumption.

This switch has important sectoral effects. Sectors linked to investment such as construction, building materials and equipment goods experience a higher increase in demand. Services, consumer goods and agriculture, on the other hand, increase just proportionately to the increase in private consumption.

In the constraint case, since penetration of imports from the ROW is moderated, the outcome is an increase in the demand for the products of all industrial sectors of the EU.

In the two other simulation cases, investments take their full amplitude, consumption increases, but at the same time imports from the ROW obtain a significant share of the additional activity. This last effect implies increased competition for domestic producers. Thus, two mechanisms moving in the opposite direction dictate the demand for domestically-produced goods in each sector (within the EU): higher demand and more competition from the ROW. The net outcome of these depends, of course, on the particular sector, especially its links to investment and its exposure to ROW competition. The model results show that:

(a)   sectors directly linked to investment such as construction, building materials (termed other intermediate goods in the model's classification) and equipment goods industry (electrical goods, transport equipment, etc.) benefit significantly from the SMP. For example, a 7.5% increase is observed in construction, 2.9% in transport equipment and 2.7% in the other equipment goods sector;

(b)   sectors with high income elasticity in consumption also benefit, especially if they do not face high competition from the ROW; such is the case of the service sectors. For example, domestic production in market services increases by 1.1%, and domestic production in telecommunications by 0.8%;

(c)   on the contrary, sectors open to foreign competition and not benefiting highly from investments can even experience decreasing domestic production: notable cases in this respect are the metal industries (-0.5%) and the chemical industries (-2.0%), both losing market share because of ROW import penetration (+2.7% and +2.9% respectively).

Increase in employment and labour productivity: the removal of border controls and the switch to a regime of market integration induce two opposing trends. Increased activity tends to increase employment, while production rationalization reduces fixed costs and hence the labour demand associated with them. The net effect is in favour of higher demand for labour, but only marginally so. Efficiency gains in trade also favour employment, because although efficiency decreases activity in some service sectors, the positive effects from trade creation overcompensate the better use of labour force, leading to additional job creation.

The aggregate increase in employment reaches 0.48% (corresponding to an increase of 610,000 employed persons) in 1994 at the EUR-11 aggregated level in the flexible case. The effect in the constraint case is about half as important (0.25%).

Increased labour demand also leads, through the labour supply elasticity (implied by the labour–leisure choice of the consumers), to a re-evaluation of the real wage rate of the order of 1.45%, up to 1.7% in the flexible case.

Labour demand increases less than production, leading to an increase in labour productivity. The fact that the use of labour as a production factor gets more limited within the SMP can also be attributed (apart from a general investment increase) to the fact that the main efficiency gains are obtained in the IC sectors, which are less labour intensive than other sectors and grow more than the other sectors.

Both the re-evaluation of the real wage rate and the gains in employment increase further towards the steady state.

Lower price levels: there are several complementary effects acting in favour of a reduction of the price level. These include:

(a)   the removal of NTBs coupled with trade cost reductions for standards, transport and banking services implied exporting efficiency resulting in lower trade costs, a relaxation of supply constraints, and hence a lower shadow price of capital and marginal costs;

(b)   the reduction of mark-ups induced by the higher level of competition also acts as cost saving;

(c)   in the long term, the high level of investment that results in capital accumulation and relaxation of pressures on production capacities moderates domestic pressures on marginal costs;

(d)   the gains in productivity of factors, induced by exogenously assumed improvement in the constraint and the flexible cases and by the variety effect in the efficiency case, are also contributing to lowering prices.

On the other hand, increased demand (as is the case especially in the flexible case) tends to increase the shadow price of capital and through that the marginal cost of production. The real wage rate also increases. In the constraint case, where the pressure from demand is moderated, the price fall is higher, reaching -1.2%. In the flexible case, this reduction is lower, reaching -0.6% in the steady state (relative to the ROW currency which is the numeraire).

Variable effects across countries: effects vary across different countries. A few points are worth mentioning:

(a)   Qualitatively the effects are of the same nature in all the EU countries. Private consumption, GDP, investment, volume of trade and employment all increase in all countries as a result of the SMP. Furthermore all countries experience similar dynamic patterns (permanent long-run effects everywhere) in terms of the effects of the SMP. The results differ in magnitude only.

(b)   Economies that were in 1985 already open and EU-oriented (like Belgium, for example, where trade amounted to 80% of GDP) seem to have profited the most from the SMP, experiencing GDP gains of up to 2.5% (in the constraint case, 1994), investments increase by 5% to 10%, higher private consumption by 1.5% to 2% and trade with the rest of the EU increasing by about 6% to 7%. Employment gains are also marginally higher than the EU average. Apart from Belgium, the Netherlands and Denmark exhibit the same behaviour. The gap between these countries and the EU average is more noticeable in the constraint case than in the flexible case.

(c)   Large countries with extensive domestic markets (Germany, France and the UK) do experience positive effects in terms of GDP, but these are slightly below the EU average. By construction, in the calibration, large countries have a lower potential of economies of scale per unit of potential increase in industrial concentration. The effect for Spain and Italy, on the other hand, depends on the effects of the closure assumption regarding the current account adjustment: in the constraint case, they are below the EU average, while in the flexible case their gains rise significantly.

(d)   Peripheral economies, especially of the south, also experience positive effects on activity, consumption and investment, but the magnitude of the benefits heavily depends upon the closure assumption. A flexible current account allows for a better allocation of resources within the EU, which seems to result in higher benefits for Portugal and Ireland, which in the flexible case benefit more than the EU average. In Greece, there appears to be an inter-temporal trade-off with very small initial gains (or even losses) becoming more significant in the last periods of the SMP. In the efficiency case, these countries gain substantially more than in other simulation cases, which probably reflects the low initial level of available commodity variety.

Figure 5.1.   The impact of the SMP by country

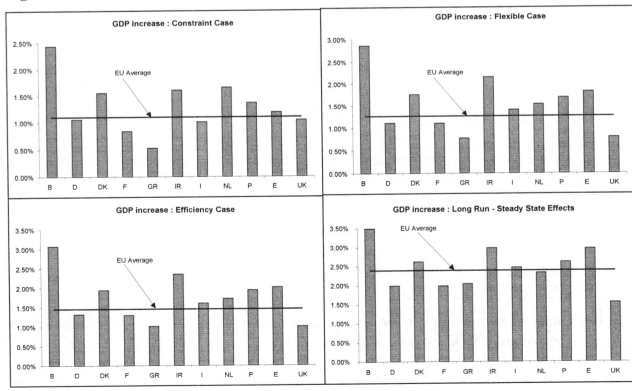

5.3.2. The effects of non-removal of non-tariff barriers (NTBs) and of non-harmonized standards

Harmonization of regulations, packaging, labelling and standards in intra-EU trade, exerts a multitude of effects. On the one hand, it implies lower costs of trade related to trade-specific services (for example, those entering the banking and the market services) while, on the other hand, it leads to a greater homogeneity of EU products, allowing the consumer to select them on an equal basis with home varieties. The first is a trade cost effect, the second is a competition effect.

The nature of trade cost effects is such that their reduction also entails less demand addressed to the non-market service sector and in particular to those service activities (e.g. those related to customs control) that covered this specific demand in the pre-SMP period.

In addition, harmonization, but generally also the single market, has led to efficiency gains in international transports and banking services associated to trade. For example, there is increased possibility for combined modal transportation and a cost-effective allocation of transport activity. Sectoral studies verified this statement.

To summarize, the border controls *antimonde* scenario combines the following SMP measures only:

(a)   non-removal of NTBs;
(b)   cost of trade due to non-harmonized standards, restored to their 1985 values;
(c)   cancellation of efficiency in intra-EU transports and banking services for trade.

The scenario is applied on the flexible case.

One of the primary effects of the SMP relates to the removal of NTBs. This is modelled as an increase in efficiency of exports in supplying a given demand for imports by another country (export volume effect), also implying a decrease of regulatory costs of transactions (import price effect).

With respect to the NTBs, the *antimonde* is assumed to restore the NTBs to their 1985 values, compared to the case of *monde* where the NTBs have been removed. In a first approximation, the removal of NTBs implies that exports require a lower volume of production, since no part of the exported goods melts away in border controls, as in the *antimonde*. It also implies indirectly, lower import costs for the importer. The latter effect leads to a shift towards EU imports.

In addition to these effects in the border controls scenario, the results show two distinct primary mechanisms:

(a)   The abolition of border controls and the increased efficiency of related services leads to lower demand for services, transports and the banking sector, that alone would act negatively on activity and employment. In the service and transport sectors, the *monde* illustrates a decrease in activity compared to the *antimonde*, of the order of 0.3% and 0.4%, in EUR-11 in 1994, respectively. Demand for bank services also decreases by 0.3%.

(b)   The reduced costs of intra-EU trade has a positive net effect on the volume of trade. This makes the economies of Member States benefit, from increased efficiency in trade and a more efficient overall allocation of resources within the EU, leading to a slight net increase of EUR-11 GDP (0.08% higher in the *monde* compared to the *antimonde* for EUR-11 in 1994).

(c)   Efficiency and relative price reduction within the EU entails competitiveness gains with respect to the ROW that lead to an improvement of the current account of the EU. Exports to the ROW increase by 0.6%.

On the domestic production side, exporting efficiency and the shift towards intra-EU trade (because of lower effective EU import prices) results in a relaxation of supply constraints, which leads to a decrease in marginal production costs. Similarly, lower EU import costs affect the price of the composite good resulting in a further decrease in prices (reflected in the decrease of the consumer price index by -0.3%). The net effect is an increase of the intra-EU volume of trade (2.6% in EUR-11) and a slight decrease of imports from the rest of the world (by -1.4%).

Private consumption decreases slightly for two reasons: exporting efficiency resulted in lower demand for the service sectors, while competitiveness gains (with respect to the ROW) make some of the domestic resources leak to the ROW.

In the IC sectors, firms face an overall slightly increased demand. Therefore, to adjust at zero profit, the number of equivalent firms increases slightly (by 1.3% in the chemical industry and by 1.7% in transport equipment), while the increase in trade also operates in the same direction, since it increases the price elasticity of demand as perceived by the firms. Under market segmentation, as assumed in this partial exercise, these two effects are rather small, leading in most cases to small decreases in the price/cost margins.

NTBs in the scenario assumptions concern all production sectors, whether IC or PC, which explains why PC sectors exhibit trends similar to the IC ones, especially regarding marginal costs decrease and relative stability of domestic production. Most gains are observed in agriculture (+1.1%), in the metal industry (+1.0%) and the equipment goods sectors (+0.8% to +0.9%).

The dominating effect in the border controls partial *antimonde* is the one implied by the restoration of the NTBs alone. The other measures related to border controls exert a trade-cost effect and a sectoral allocation one, but not a more fundamental efficiency gain effect, as the NTBs do.

The cumulative effect of border controls on the EUR-11 GDP is a gain of the order of ECU 15 billion, which is small compared to the full *antimonde* simulation, while the cumulative EU-trade volume increase amounts to ECU 81 billion, or about 60% of the total figure obtained in the full *antimonde* simulation. Thus, 60% of trade creation should be attributed to the removal of border controls, taken alone.

5.3.3.   The effects of market competition regime switch

Harmonization of standards (for example, uniformity, quality, interchangeability standards, etc.) and regulation, easy access for EU producers to other EU country markets and consumers' ability to select commodities independently of the country of origin. Combined with other factors related to the enlargement of the market, harmonization leads to higher substitutability between EU commodities.

Consumers, in their preferences, take advantage of higher price elasticities as EU products are more substitutable. Hence, producers anticipate higher competition within the enlarged market, tending to lower price cost margins within the EU markets.

This phenomenon, which is derived from the ability and willingness of EU buyers to substitute among the products of EU suppliers, is highly emphasized in the modelling approach and as will be shown in the following, constitutes a key feature to consider in interpreting the results.

In the GEM-E3-SM model representing the pre-SMP situation, a flexible demand structure is employed in which consumers have preferences for the product of firms depending on their region of origin. As a result of harmonization, this demand structure is assumed to change. This evolution is reflected by a change in the nesting of the consumers' preferences structure (the stepwise budgeting process in the Armington specification). A regime switching from market segmentation to market integration is assumed to have occurred in 1988 under the *monde* circumstances. Progress in the harmonization of products because of the advance of the SMP, in the following years (up to 1992 only), is modelled as an additional increase in the substitutability of EU commodities. However, the *antimonde* involves preservation of the consumer preference structure, i.e. one that reflects market segmentation and limited substitutability of domestic with rest of the EU commodities.

In the partial *antimonde* simulation that deals with the market integration process, the border control removal is not included.

The primary effect of the change of competition regime, reflects the definition of the perceived price elasticity of demand as explained in Section 4.3.4. The regime switching from segmentation to integration implies that domestic firms, instead of competing separately in their domestic market and in foreign markets, face a unified EU market which is considerably larger by nature. In this enlarged market, consumers are more price sensitive in their selection between home and EU-originating varieties than before (because of assumed change of preferences). Additionally, the market share of each firm is much smaller within the enlarged market. Within a Nash–Cournot competition model, the perceived elasticity of demand in this market becomes higher. Firms therefore reduce price/cost margins for products addressed to their domestic markets, but also to their EU export markets. Their mark-ups to the ROW remain, however, almost unchanged.

The reduction of the mark-ups would lead firms to losses, and so by adjusting the number of equivalent firms to obtain zero profits, industrial concentration in IC sectors increases. Production efficiency improves, in the sense of better sharing the sectoral fixed cost, allowing for economies of scale. These effects result in lower producer prices.

On the other hand, there is a variety effect from the production side, resulting from the decreasing number of firms within a sector. This happens despite the fact that there is no change in the love of variety from the consumer's perspective. The decrease of the number of firms exerts an efficiency loss effect in the economy, which acts in an opposite direction to the efficiency gains from economies of scale. However, the numerical calibration of the model is such that the loss from the variety effect is much smaller than the gains from production rationalization.[24]

Alternatively, an activity boosting effect acts on marginal production costs, hence on prices: if seen from the production side, a lower number of firms in a sector leads to more production per firm which in the short term exerts a pressure on capital stock use, further leading to higher marginal costs.

On the production side, therefore, two competing mechanisms are present, the net effect on sectoral prices being uncertain at first glance. However, the observed information used for calibrating the production side IC sectors is such that the mark-up effect far outweighs the variety effect coming from higher industrial concentration in the SMP.

The price sensitivity of the substitutions decided by the consumer also depends on the initial value shares of trade in consumption. An economy that was already open to foreign competition in 1985 (before market integration) will experience higher price sensitivity in consumers' decisions after the regime change. In addition, such economies also started from levels of mark-ups that were lower than in other more closed economies.

Thus, a regime switching to integration that would entail higher domestic activity for EU exports could lead to increasing marginal costs of production under fixed production capacity that could outweigh the price decrease due to the fall of mark-ups. On the contrary, in more closed economies, high initial mark-ups and lower price sensitivity after regime switching can imply the reverse: the effect of mark-ups may outweigh the activity boosting effects.

Independently of these price effects, the change of the preference structure induces, by construction, intra-EU trade creation regarding both exports and imports. Combined with the economy of scale effects, the regime switching to market integration leads to real GDP gains.

The numerical results obtained from the partial *antimonde* called market segmentation confirm the above mechanisms. The main effects of the switch to market integration are:

(a) GDP increases by 1.%;
(b) intra-EU trade increases by 3.5%. This increase occurs after 1991, when the level of advancement of market integration, reflected in the additional increase of the substitution elasticity of EU commodities, leads to a considerable reduction of export mark-ups;
(c) efficiency gains due to cost savings are obtained. Fixed costs as part of domestic production are reduced;
(d) investment increases significantly. Practically all investment increase found in the full *antimonde* scenarios ensues from the switch to market integration;
(e) private consumption increases (+1.4%);
(f) mark-ups are reduced in the domestic market and in EU exports;
(g) employment, labour productivity and the real wage rate increase;

---

[24]   One of the sensitivity tests aims to explore this effect by calibrating the IC sectors at a significantly lower level of love of variety. We retain the high numerical values in the main results, because large variety of commodities was already available for the EU consumers, even in the pre-SMP period, since the EU countries are among the most developed ones in the world. If the model was applied to less developed regions, then low degree of variety should have been retained for the numerical calibration of the IC sectors.

(h)   imports from the rest of the world increase considerably (more than +4%) to support domestic investment and consumption. Consequently, the current account as a percentage of GDP deteriorates (-1.1%).

On a cumulative basis the switch to market integration is responsible for most of the GDP gains observed in the flexible case, amounting to ECU 143 billion for the 1988–94 period, while the effect on intra-EU trade is comparable to that of the removal of border controls.

5.3.4.   The role of X-inefficiencies in services and of total factor productivity gains

The organizational effects, in telecommunications and banking are considered exogenous changes, not related to production cost minimization. Implicitly it is assumed that these sectors were experiencing diseconomies of scale in the pre-SMP period, being in reality oversized compared to minimum efficiency scale. Of course, this is not compatible with the formulation of a continuously decreasing average cost curve that means it would be impossible to approximate X-efficiency gains in an endogenous manner within the present model.

Exogenous total factor productivity gains associated with the SMP (of the order of 0.1% in 1994) are incorporated in the *monde* simulation (in the constraint and flexible cases only) and removed in the *antimonde* one.

The separate impact of the X-efficiency gains accounts for the difference between the border controls and the border controls and X-inefficiencies partial *antimonde* simulations, while total factor productivity separates the trade *antimonde* and the full *antimonde* scenarios.

Both exogenous assumptions exert productivity changes that act typically when changing technical progress parameters in perfect competition CGE models. Nevertheless, some additional effects are found in the IC sectors, implied by the assumption that the exogenous productivity gain assumptions act on the fixed cost part of the total cost function, rather than on the variable cost part. For example, X-efficiency deterioration involved in this *antimonde* scenario implies higher costs for these sectors but also higher demand for primary production factors according to their proportions within the sectoral fixed costs.

The indirect effects pervade the rest of the economy through the industrial links of the sectors. For example, X-efficiency gains in telecommunication and banking services transmit gains to other sectors through their intermediate consumption and to private consumption, depending on their relative importance in final demand. Given that within the dynamic evolution incorporated in the *monde* the growing importance of these two sectors in the EU economy has been observed, the negative effects of loss of X-efficiency in the *antimonde* would increase over time. Indeed, the results show both volume contraction and inflationary effects in all countries, when removing the SMP effects.

X-efficiency gains in the two service sectors, taken alone in the partial simulation, lead to very small aggregate effects at the EUR-11 level: GDP increases by 0.02% per annum (total cumulative gain ECU 2 billion), private consumption by less than 0.01% and employment by 13,000 more persons in employment. As these figures indicate, the indirect effects due to efficiency improvement outweigh the direct effect on employment due to lower fixed cost. Prices fall slightly.

X-efficiency gains have uniform implications across countries (since they were assumed to be similar in all countries). For this reason, no competitiveness effects occur within the EU.

The effects of total factor productivity gains are more significant. They account for about 0.2% of the GDP effect of the SMP under the flexible case. They also make a small contribution to the increase in intra-EU trade, private consumption and income.

Under the efficiency case, factor productivity gains are an indirect result of consumption efficiency in the enlarged market, as mentioned before.

5.4. Sensitivity analysis

Apart from the three main *antimonde* simulations, additional sensitivity tests were performed to evaluate the robustness of the results under different assumptions. The general finding of these tests is that the qualitative nature of the results presented in the previous sections is always the same, the quantitative one may vary. The variation is small in intra-EU trade (the lowest compared to the highest case in this respect do not differ by more than 25%) especially in the last years of the SMP. The fall in mark-ups is also relatively unaffected by the modelling assumptions. On the other hand, the order of magnitude of the gains in demand, employment and GDP are found to depend significantly on the modelling assumptions.

Two main sensitivity tests are presented in this section. The first aims to determine the impact of different calibration assumptions concerning the IC sectors, in order to find a lower bound for the impact of the SMP. The second assesses the impact of assuming capital to be perfectlty mobile across the EU as a result of the SMP.

5.5. Conservative assumptions in calibrating the IC sectors

The first sensitivity, termed conservative case, involves alternative assumptions concerning the numerical calibration of the IC sectors and the effects attributable to the SMP. This sensitivity test was meant to set a lower bound to the impact of the SMP, by using only the most conservative estimates. The main assumptions of the sensitivity tests are:

(a)   IC sectors are assumed to have a lower tendency for fluctuations in the mark-up, in the sense that their perceived elasticity is less affected by the change in the market regime and their market shares.

(b)   Integration occurs in 1988 in the *monde* as before, substitutability between EU commodities is, however, not assumed to increase further in 1991, as in the main *monde* scenario.

(c)   Implicitly, it is assumed that the economies of scale potential is more limited than in the baseline scenario.

(d)   No total factor productivity gains are assigned to the SMP.

(e)   The scenario is applied in the most conservative of the three main cases, namely the constraint case.

As expected, the benefits from the SMP for GDP and employment are found to be more limited, since the initial inefficiencies are by assumption calibrated to a lower level. The results point to the following:

(a)   The qualitative nature of the results seems to be stable. Although the exact numbers differ, higher GDP and consumption is still obtained, intra-EU trade increases, industrial concentration increases, investments accelerate, labour productivity increases and lower prices are obtained as a result of the SMP. Differences across countries are also maintained, with Belgium and the rest of the open economies (Netherlands, Denmark) benefiting more than the others.

(b)   In quantitative terms, it seems that the increase in the volume of intra-EU trade (4% in the constraint case compared to 3.6% in the conservative case) seems rather robust. The same can be said of the increase in the mark-ups, which dropped (for the EU as a whole), by roughly 0.8% – slightly lower than in the constraint case.

(c)   The increase in investments is roughly maintained. Investment increase is always much higher (as percentage change) than either consumption or total domestic absorption.

The exact value of the GDP and consumption gains are rather more sensitive. By limiting the potential for economies of scale, the price sensitivity of consumers and the responsiveness of firms while, on the other hand, emphasizing variety losses from the reduction of the number of firms, the conservative case allows for limited gains to be obtained from the SMP. Gains in terms of GDP amount only to 0.26% in the constraint case.

5.6. Capital mobility across the EU

In this sensitivity test, it is assumed that capital is fully mobile across countries and sectors of the EU. Capital mobility is considered as part of the SMP measures, on top of the measures included in the previous simulations, such as in the flexible case. In the *monde* simulation, full capital mobility operates, while in the *antimonde* capital mobility is allowed only within each country.

In static terms, the full capital mobility assumption means that the investment savings equality clears at the level of the EU, rather than at the level of each EU Member State as assumed in the other model runs. This clearing sets a unique rate of capital return at the EU level, which then influences sectoral and country-specific allocation of total available capital stock (which is fixed in static terms). In other words, capital is assumed to move freely from sector to sector (as in the other model runs) and simultaneously from country to country, without any constraint.

In dynamic terms, static capital mobility influences investment, which can more freely be redirected to the sectors (irrespective of country) that exhibit the higher relative shadow price of capital. The process is, however, constrained, in dynamic terms, by the turnover of total capital stock in the EU which evolves under the assumption of a fixed replacement rate. Obviously, such a model, incorporating perfect mobility of capital, is more flexible in allocation terms.

The results of the simulation show that the overall effects of the SMP on real GDP growth are lower in the beginning, being +0.15% in 1988 compared to +0.46% in the flexible case, but tend to amplify in the long run, and go beyond the results of the flexible case some time after 1994. A similar dynamic pattern is found for employment and private consumption. The trade creation effects, the boosting of investment and the fall of production costs and prices are quite similar to those in the flexible case. As will be shown, the distributional effects across countries are quite different.

In the shortrun, i.e. at the beginning of the SMP, capital goes to the sectors that have the highest shadow price of capital. It is not certain in the results whether the difference in the shadow prices of capital by country (for the same sector) reflects lack of capital or should be attributed to the SMP measures. For example, small countries (and especially the southern ones) are more attractive for capital, perhaps also because their size permits the preservation of higher price/cost margins differentials, even under the SMP. The most notable examples are Greece and Portugal which attract capital from northern countries, mainly from Germany, France and the UK.

The countries that benefit from the capital flows within the EU also benefit in terms of domestic activity (for example, GDP), but the differential gain is less than the one that would have been obtained if capital has stayed in the north. This is due to the Leontief multiplier in the southern countries (which is smaller than in the more vertically integrated economies of the north) and the domestic activity multiplier of exports which increases more in the south since it benefits from higher drops of the domestic marginal costs than the north (as capital goes to remedy pressures on marginal costs).

In the long run, however, higher returns are obtained, as the more efficient allocation of capital (allowed by its mobility) starts to manifest itself. As a conclusion, existence of a trade-off over time is inferred from the results: in the full capital mobility case, the EU has to tolerate lower short-run gains from the SMP at the EU level, requiring more tolerance in the larger countries (while smaller countries gain more), to obtain a higher overall performance in the long term.

6. Conclusions

The objective of this study was to evaluate the SMP effects in an *ex post* manner by conducting simulations based solely on a CGE modelling methodology. In practice, the study involves updating and adapting extensively an existing multi-country, multi-sectoral dynamic CGE model of the 12 EU Member States, namely the GEM-E3 model. We consider that the exercise has been, from a technical point of view, a success, since both the model was rendered computationally tractable and formal methodologies were devised to comply with the *ex post* nature of this study.

The *ex post* element was implemented in the following two ways:

(a)   first the study was designed to take into account the results from the sectoral and other studies commissioned under the Single Market Review programme;

(b)   the model was dynamically calibrated to simulate the observed reality – the *monde*.

Concerning the first *ex post* element, one limitation arose from the fact that the sectoral studies were mostly qualitative (and hence the extraction of quantitative hypotheses to be used in the simulations was not straightforward). Also, some information, such as the changes in total factor productivity induced by the SMP (which, incidentally, turned out to be significant for the exact magnitude of the results in two out of the three main simulation cases), was simply not validated in empirical terms.

On the second *ex post* element, the major difficulty arose from the bad quality of the Eurostat statistics for the post-1985 period, which rendered the dynamic calibration incomplete. Sensitivity tests, however, seem to indicate that the bad observation of the *monde* does not influence results very much.

Regarding the *ex post* calibration, we also found that the way of calibrating the IC sectors (regarding the initial magnitude of the mark-ups and the values of the love of variety) is important for the order of magnitude of the effects of the SMP. Since the work of Pratten (1988) which served as a basis for all CGE analyses of the SMP, there has been no updated (hence *ex post*) empirical estimation of the minimum efficiency scale, and a differentiation by country is still not available. Similarly, there have been no empirical attempts to estimate the love of variety elasticities, from a consumer's perspective. This omission is important for the accuracy of our *ex post* estimation.

Our results appear to be in conformity with most of the *ex ante* studies and well in the range set by these studies in numerical terms. However, the Cecchini report seems far too optimistic. This is due more to the initial assumptions about the SMP effects (which in the Cecchini report were much higher than the sectoral studies indicate) and the fact that the Cecchini study was based on the extrapolation of partial equilibrium results.

The results and sensitivity test confirm the following points:

(a)   The SMP induced a considerable increase in intra-EU trade; a 3% to 4% increase in intra-EU trade both seems reasonable and withstands alternative scenario assumptions. Trade creation was found also in the EU–ROW trade.

(b)   GDP and welfare gains were obtained in all Member States. The exact magnitude of these gains seems, however, to depend on the assumptions. The pure domestic allocation effects of the SMP are estimated to have induced a gain of 1.1% in GDP in the EU, in 1994, while under other modelling assumptions which relax external sector constraints or account for variety efficiency effect, the outcome is higher: it goes up to +1.5% in the best case. The tendency persists in the long run, leaving a permanent growth pattern in the EU economy.

(c)   GDP growth was found to be mainly driven by a substantial increase in investment, rather than in consumption, a result that has been validated in all sensitivity tests. The overall effect on employment was found to be positive, though small in magnitude. The increase in investments accounts for the persistence and slight increase of the effect in the long run.

(d)   Rationalization of production, exploitation of economies of scale through increased industrial concentration and reduction of price cost margins were observed in all cases. The average decrease of the mark-ups was found to have been of the order of 0.8% up to 0.9%, a result that is in accordance with sectoral studies. Again, this figure seems rather insensitive to alternative assumptions.

(e)   Effects differ significantly by country (where the economies which in 1985 were already open and EU-oriented seem to have profited the most) and by sector. Equipment goods and construction benefit more, followed by service sectors.

A number of issues were not covered in this study, such as tax harmonization, structural funds, international capital mobility, labour mobility and public procurement. For the last two issues, sectoral studies indicated that they induced little effects over the study period. All the above, if implemented, would, most probably, increase the effects of the SMP and alleviate the differences across countries. Also, mainly because of the lack of sectoral data, the present model version does not include a split of labour in different skills and a corresponding representation of household classes. Such a model extension would allow for improved insight of social distributional effects of the SMP.

As demonstrated in the long-run simulations, the effects of the SMP would also probably be higher if the sectoral studies and the existing Eurostat data went beyond 1992–93. It is likely, therefore, that some of the additional effects of the SMP in the long run may have been missed.

One final point is worth mentioning. It is certain that the SMP, through the opening of the EU markets to all EU products (whether domestic or imported), has increased the variety in the choice of the consumer (household, firm or government), thus inducing an autonomous efficiency increase in the economy. By endogenizing this mechanism in one of the model simulations, we have demonstrated that an *ad hoc* (not empirically validated) assumption about total factor productivity gains induced by the SMP is not necessary. For analytical reasons, it would be worth further elaborating on this issue, by explicitly linking the variety effects and the increased competition to the dynamics of technology progress and the resulting acceleration of incorporation of innovations in the EU products.

APPENDIX A

Technical report

A1. The GEM-E3-SM computable general equilibrium model

A general outline of the GEM-E3-SM model is presented in this Appendix.

Section A1.1 presents the general characteristics of the model, Section A1.2 presents a short description of the most significant features of the representation of the IC sectors and the incorporation of distortions in foreign trade that are supposed to be removed through the SMP.

A1.1. General characteristics of the model

The GEM-E3 model represents an Arrow–Debreu economy that exhibits price homogeneity and satisfies the Walras law. The economy involves consumption and production of a set of commodities. There is a one-to-one correspondence between commodities and production sectors. In some sectors (the ones in which perfect competition is assumed to prevail), it is assumed that a large number of firms operate, represented in the model by a representative firm. In the sectors where the regime is assumed to be imperfectly competitive, the number of firms is finite and endogenous. All commodities are considered as products and production factors. Primary production factors, i.e. capital and labour, are supplied by the economy's savings and households, respectively. The commodities are traded through transactions involving multiple countries. At each country level, the government is regulating income distribution by means of a set of taxes, subsidies, duties and social security contributions. Its behaviour is largely exogenous.

Capital is considered as an asset, financed by savings, and a physical production capacity. This capacity is fixed in static terms, constraining production possibilities. Investment, represented as an anticipation behaviour, ensures dynamic update of production capacity.

A1.1.1. Domestic supply of goods and services

As in the conventional definition of I-O tables, each production sector produced a single and homogeneous commodity, which is distinguishable from any other commodity. Production uses production factors that include labour, capital and intermediate consumption commodities. The latter are not distinguished from produced commodities.

The production possibility frontier is represented by a production function allowing for price-driven substitution between production factors. Changes in factor productivity are represented by exogenous technical progress trends embedded within each production factor.

The production function is specified so as to represent a nested decision about the optimal choice of production factors and exhibit constant returns to scale. In static terms, that is within a model run period, capital stock acts as a constraint inducing a decreasing return commodity supply. The optimal choice of production factors is derived through the Shephard lemma from profit maximization. Given the assumption about constant return of scale, this is equivalent to unit cost minimization.

Capital stock being fixed within the model run period (but updated only in dynamic runs), but mobile across sectors in the same country, the amount of capital stock utilized by each sector is then computed as a residual of a zero profit condition.

The sectoral investment equation formulates an anticipation behaviour that involves a comparison of the desired to the effective capital stock. The desired capital stock is derived from the production function as profit maximization, given a long-term rate of return of capital involving the cost of purchasing the capital stock, the interest rate and the capital replacement rates (Ando–Modigliani formula).

A1.1.2.   Behaviour of households

Household behaviour is based on an inter-temporal model of the household sector. In a first stage, the households decide each year on the allocation of their expected resources between present and future consumption of goods and leisure, by maximizing over their entire life horizon an inter-temporal utility function. This utility function has as arguments consumption of goods and leisure. Using a linear expenditure system (LES) formulation for the utility function, the household model can be written:

$$\max U(q(t)) = \int_{t=0}^{\infty} e^{-\delta t} \cdot u(q(t))dt \ , \ where \ u(q(t)) = \beta \cdot \log(q(t) - \gamma)$$

where $q(t)$ is a vector of two commodity flows (in our case consumption and leisure) and δ is the subjective discount rate of households. The γ s represent the subsistence quantities of consumption and leisure, while the β s are the share parameters of consumption and leisure in the LES function. The maximization is subject to an inter-temporal budget constraint, where w represents the total wealth the consumers expect for their lifetime including the value of their total time resources $y(t)$ (leisure and work time).

$$\dot{w}(t) = r \cdot w(t) + y(t) - p' \cdot q(t)$$

Solving this maximization problem under general assumptions regarding expectations, demand functions are derived that allocate the expected income of the households between expenditure on consumption goods, leisure and future consumption. These steady-state derived demand equations are only used in the model. They are of the following type:

$$p_i \cdot q_i = p_i \cdot \gamma_i + \mu \cdot \beta_i \cdot (z - p_i \cdot \gamma_i), \ i = \text{consumption, leisure}$$

where μ is the ratio of the consumer's subjective discount rate to the real interest rate and z denotes the expected resources (from wealth and time) for the current year.

The computed demand for leisure is used in the determination of the labour market equilibrium.

In a next step households allocate their total consumption expenditure between expenditure on non-durable consumption categories (food, culture, etc.) and services from durable goods (cars, heating systems, electric appliances).

Figure A1.1. Allocation of households' disposable income

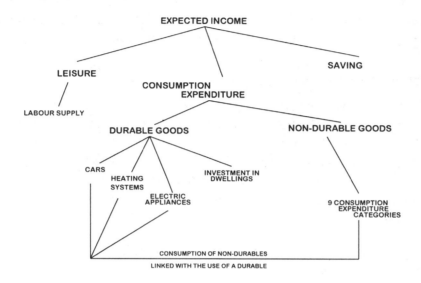

For this allocation an integrated model of consumer demand for non-durables and durables, developed by Conrad and Schröder (1991) is implemented with a LES variable expenditure function. The figure presents the general separability scheme of the consumption of households, as used in the model.

Special care is given to the evaluation of the user's cost of durable: it takes into account the price of the durable, the interest rate, the depreciation rate, any tax on the durable and the price of the non-durable goods, that the use of each durable entails (e.g. cars, which are a durable good, consume gasoline which is a non-durable good; therefore, the demand for new cars will also depend on the price of gasoline). The demand for durables is then obtained from the difference between the desired stock and the initial stock (which is the depreciated stock of the previous year).

The demand for consumption categories is then transformed into demand for products through a consumption transition matrix with fixed technical coefficients. The consumption transition matrix is also used to compute the consumption price by function, as the weighted average of the delivery prices of products to private consumption. Finally, a cost-of-living index, usually called the consumers price index, is derived as the ratio between value and volume of consumption.

Based on their available income, the households also decide how to allocate their savings between tangible and intangible assets. This is again accomplished through a LES so as to take into account the subsistence quantity of the stock of houses. The share of tangible and intangible assets is determined by the comparison of the average real rate of return of assets to the rental rate of houses (taking the depreciation into account).

Consumption is allocated between durable goods and non-durable consumption categories, defined by consumption purpose, as mentioned before.

Given time availability of households (depending also on population), labour supply is derived from the demand for leisure. Labour supply is an increasing function of the real wage rate.

Given that the model formulates a global market for labour, allowing for labour mobility across sectors (but not across countries), the cost of labour by sector depends on the wage rate of equilibrium plus the social security contributions of employers.

A1.1.3.   Absorption, domestic demand and imports

The demand of products by consumers, producers and the public sector constitutes total domestic demand. Total demand is further allocated between domestic and imported products, following an Armington specification that defines a composite commodity which combines domestically produced and imported goods. These are considered as non-perfect substitutes. The buyer (domestic) seeks to minimize his total cost and decides the mix of imported and domestic products so that the marginal rate of substitution equals the ratio of domestic to imported product prices. The buyer's total cost is called absorption.

Domestic demand for domestically produced goods is derived from applying the Shephard lemma to unit cost minimization:

The model does not cover the whole planet and thus the behaviour of the rest of the world (ROW) is left exogenous: imports demanded by the ROW depends on the export prices that the EU countries set and exports from the ROW to the EU occur at a fix price.

Figure A1.2. Bilateral trade flows in GEM-E3-SM

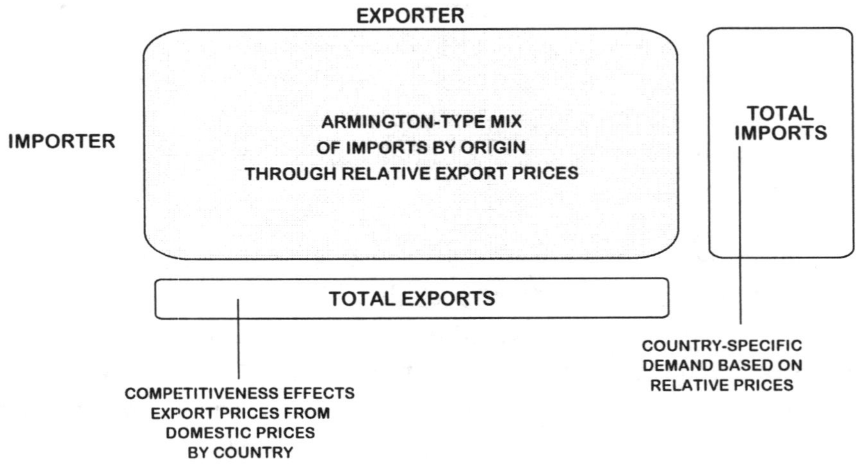

The imports demanded by the ROW are flexibly satisfied by exports originating from the EU countries. The latter consider the profitability of exporting to the ROW, exporting to the EU or addressing the goods to their domestic markets. Via these profitability considerations, the EU countries set their export prices. An export supply function represents these mechanisms: it determines a supply price for the domestic market and a supply price for the export markets, guaranteeing at the same time for the firm the equilibrium between its resources and its costs. Within the EU, exports are considered homogeneous. This means that the producer sets a single export price for EU countries and another export price for the ROW.

Imports demanded by the EU countries from the ROW are supplied flexibly by the latter. However, the EU countries consider the optimal allocation of their total imports over the countries of origin, according to the relative import prices. The EU countries buy imports at the prices set by the supplying countries following their export supply behaviour. Of course, the supplying countries may gain or loose market shares according to their price setting. When importing, the EU countries compute an index of mean import price according to their optimal allocation by country of origin. This mean import price is then compared to the domestic prices in order to allocate demand between imports and domestic production (cf. Armington assumption).

Given total import demand, derived from the allocation of the country demand for the composite good, each country addresses specific demand for imports to partner countries.

It is possible to verify analytically that, under the above formulation, the balance of the trade matrix in value and the global Walras law are verified in all cases.

A1.1.4. Consumption prices and indirect taxation

In this perfect competition version of the model, cost-price wedges can only be attributed to taxation.

All consumption prices depend on the prices of the composite commodities, which as mentioned further depend on the prices of domestic goods addressed to the domestic market and the prices of imports. *Ad valorem* and excise taxation is represented.

A1.1.5. Surplus or deficit of agents

The real sector of the model is grouped within the framework of a Social Accounting Matrix (SAM) (see Figure A1.3), which ensures consistency and equilibrium of flows from production to the agents and back to consumption. The construction of the SAM is the starting point of the model building work. The definition of the set of prices ensures the consistency of the SAM, also in current currency, a fact which is finally reflected in the above condition, which states that the algebraic sum of net savings over the set of agents is, by construction, equal to zero.

Figure A1.3. The social accounting matrix (SAM)

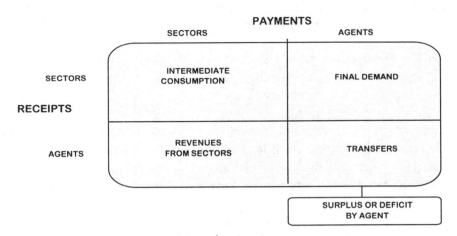

The economic agents are households, firms, government and ROW. The sources of income for consumers and producers are labour and capital rewarding. Respectively the sources of income for government are transfers and taxes. The agents use income for consumption or investment. Finally, the surplus of deficit by agent equals net savings minus investment.

In the following figures we only present a reduced form of the SAM in which we directly determine the surplus or deficit of the economic agents:

A1.1.6.   Equilibrium of the real side of the model

Figure A1.4. Demand–supply equilibrium in GEM-E3-SM

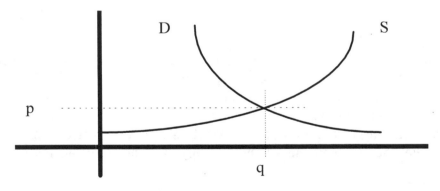

The demand–supply interaction in the markets of commodities is defined. It serves to determine the selling price P_i , which, in fact, is also the unit cost and the marginal cost of domestic production.

The model assumes a competitive regime in the labour market. Given that the allocation of the time constraint of workers in leisure and work is flexible, the supply of labour is not fixed, allowing for varying level of employment. Additional employment, if demand for labour allows, is attributable to increasing active population and not to reducing unemployment. In other words, this regime corresponds to voluntary unemployment. Depending on the values used in model calibration, the implicit elasticity of labour supply with respect to the real wage rate can be different from zero. This situation can also be interpreted as a reduced form of a wage bargaining model.

Alternative labour market closure rules are possible to reflect the existence of non-voluntary unemployment. A model version, for example, incorporates a Philips curve formulation to determine the wage rate and allows for unemployment.

A1.1.7. Model closure

It can be verified that the algebraic sum of the surplus or deficits of all the economic agents equals to zero by model construction. Also, the sum of the trade deficits over all countries (inclusive of the ROW) are always zero by model construction, so the Walras law is always verified (and thus not included in the model text).

If the real interest rate is exogenous, then the surplus or deficit of the ROW, in other words the current account, is free to vary. If we fix the current account to a pre-specified level (or fix the ratio of the current account as a percentage of GDP), then the model computes the real interest rate.

In both cases, the exchange rate is exogenous and acts as a numeraire.

A1.2. Extensions for the incorporation of imperfect competition

This section presents the extensions and changes of the model specification that are necessary for the evaluation of the effects of the SMP.

(a)   In the model's production side, the objective is to capture potential scale economy effects, price-cost margin effects and supply variety effects associated with changes in the market structure of imperfectly competitive industries triggered by the single market completion programme.

(b)   The underlying economic assertion is that, prior to the SMP, firms operated inefficiently due to the small scale of the countries, compared to the EU integrated scale. The potential from increasing returns to scale is expected to allow for positive gains from the enlarged market.

(c)   In the demand side, the aim is to represent structural changes in consumers' behaviour regarding the consideration of substitutability between domestic, EU and ROW commodities.

(d)   The underlying economic assumption is that, through the single market, domestic and EU goods become more close substitutes, implying stronger competition between firms within the enlarged market, hence changes of perceived elasticity of demand leading to lower cost mark-ups.

(e)   In the foreign trade part of the model, the motivation of model changes is to represent extra costs due to border obstacles and non-harmonized regulation that prevailed prior to the SMP.

(f)   It is expected that the removal of such obstacles and harmonization will imply higher efficiency in trade flows and lower costs of trade, but also lower demand for associated services.

(g)   Regarding model dynamics, the model changes concern the mechanism of adjustment of the capital stock. Fixing the capital stock by sector brings out a short-run character of model functioning, as is also the case of assuming that the number of firms remains fixed in the imperfect competitive sectors. The aim of the retained specification is to make endogenous both the capital allocation across the sectors (total capital stock remaining fixed in the period) and the adjustment of the number of firms under a zero profit condition in the presence of positive mark-ups.

(h)   Therefore, to ensure comparability between the *monde* and *antimonde* scenarios we retain a specification that includes long-run properties within the model run period. The dynamics mainly regard, then, the update of total capital stock.

(i)   Concerning model closure, we keep the competitive equilibrium regime in the labour market.[25] However, the calibration is such that the reaction of labour supply to changes of the real wage rate is rather flexible, as we account for the availability of work time resources (because of the existence of unemployment).

(j)   Model specification has been substantially changed regarding costs associated to trade flows. Three types of border-related costs, regarding EU trade are represented:
   (i)   non-tariff barriers (NTBs);
   (ii) costs due to standards and other regulation;
   (iii) transport costs.

A1.3. Alternative formulations tested

Apart from the main model text, a number of alternative formulations were implemented and tested successfully. However, they were not implemented in the final model version, that was used to produce the results presented.

The main alternative specifications that were utilized but were not kept in the final model version appear below:

(a)   **Nash–Bertrand assumptions for the IC sectors.** The main convenience of the Nash–Bertrand conjectures on imperfect competition is the simplicity of the derivation of the formulas for the perceived price elasticity of demand. The drawback was that using the realistic number of symmetric firms (as calibrated through the Herfindahl index) the price elasticity was very insensitive to changes in the behaviour of the consumers. Thus, mark-ups changed very little and the overall behaviour of the model was very similar to the version with perfect competition. It seemed that the Nash–Bertrand assumptions would probably underestimate the impact of the SMP.

(b)   **Number of firms not adjusting to zero profits within each period.** Another alternative specification was also tested, namely that firm numbers in a sector adapt according to a dynamic adaptation mechanism

(c) $n(t+1) - n(t) = -g \cdot [n(t) - n^*(t)], \qquad 0 < g \le 1$, where n^* is the hypothetical number of firms consistent with zero profits in the industry, and the parameter g controls the speed of adjustment. The convenience of this approach is that the number of firms within each period is fixed, so the computational burden is much lower. On the other hand, among several other shortcomings (such as the arbitrariness in the selection of g, potential cyclical or erratic behaviour in the model dynamics) there was also another reason that dictated the use of the instantaneous adjustment: since the base year is, by calibration, a year where the number of firms is the one consistent with zero profits and that the last period of the simulation should also be in equilibrium (otherwise the two could not be directly comparable) there was no clear way that these two could be achieved without assuming that the intermediate years should also have the number of firms consistent with zero profits.

(d) **Producer-driven approach for market integration.** In this approach, no matter whether firms are assumed to play Cournot or Bertrand, their supply behaviour also depends on the extent to which they can engage in third-degree price discrimination by setting different supply prices for different regional markets, which in turn depends on whether regional markets are segmented or integrated in the sense of Markusen and Venables (1988). Here regional markets are called 'integrated' if cross-border arbitrage ensures the equalization of supply prices for any homogeneous product across countries of destination within the integrated area, so that price discrimination for sales to the integrated area is impossible and consumer prices across regions within the area can only differ due to the presence of trade costs. Regional markets are called 'segmented', on the other hand, if the absence of international arbitrage between countries allows firms to set different prices to consumers located in different market segments for the same homogeneous product. Following the lead of Smith and Venables' (1988) partial equilibrium study, a number of *ex ante* CGE analyses have simulated the single market creation by combining border costs removal with a competitive regime switch from national market segmentation within the EC to EC-wide market integration. This approach was abandoned for two reasons: first, it is difficult to justify on empirical grounds the disappearance of price discrimination that this method implies and, second, this approach has the indirect effect that mark-ups for exports increase as a result of the SMP, something again not supported by the sectoral studies.

(e) **A CET export supply function.** In this formulation a sort of market segmentation between domestic and export supply is incorporated, allowing for price differentiation. Since this supply behaviour is now explicitly incorporated through the determination of the mark-ups, there was not much room to keep such a formulation allowing for an additional mark-up on top of that computed through the perceived elasticity of demand.

A1.4. Derivation of the formula for the perceived elasticity of demand

In the following the derivation of the formula for the perceived elasticity of demand ψ in the domestic market (the computation for the export market follows the same rules) under market segmentation and market integration assumptions are presented. The derivation follows the Nash–Cournot assumptions. The names of all the variables follow their respective names in the GEM-E3-SM model.

Consider the optimization problem facing a firm selling into its domestic market. The firm wishes to maximize its profit Π given as a difference between its revenues from selling a quantity $xxdf$ at a price $pxdf$, and the cost that the production of this quantity entailed, namely $pd \cdot xxdf$, where pd is the marginal cost of supply which is considered as exogenous in this derivation.

(1) $\Pi_{xxdf} = pxdf \cdot xxdf - pd \cdot xxdf$

First order conditions for profit maximization then give:

(2) $\quad \dfrac{\partial \Pi}{\partial xxdf} = \dfrac{\partial pxdf}{\partial xxdf} \cdot xxdf + pxdf - pd = 0 \Rightarrow pd = pxdf\left(1 + \dfrac{1}{\dfrac{\partial xxdf / xxdf}{\partial pxdf / pxdf}}\right)$

or by substituting $\dfrac{1}{\psi} = -\dfrac{\partial pxdf}{\partial xxdf} \cdot \dfrac{xxdf}{pxdf}$

(3) $\quad pd = pxdf\left(1 - \dfrac{1}{\psi}\right)$

where ψ is the perceived elasticity of demand.

Within the IC sectors, the products of the various firms located within the same industrial sector are treated as horizontally differentiated, imperfect substitutes. The specification of the consumer demand specification is rooted on Dixit and Stiglitz's love of variety conception.

Assuming symmetric firms, total demand for a commodity category XXD is derived as a CES-aggregator of the demand for each individual firm (assuming that N symmetrical firms operate within the sector).

(4) $\quad XXD = \left[\displaystyle\sum_{i=1}^{N}(xxd_i)^{\sigma-\frac{1}{\sigma}}\right]^{\frac{\sigma}{\sigma-1}} = N^{\frac{\sigma}{\sigma-1}} \cdot xxd$

The aggregate dual associated price index PXD is then

(5) $\quad PXD = \left[\displaystyle\sum_{i=1}^{N}(pxd_i)^{1-\sigma}\right]^{\frac{1}{1-\sigma}} = N^{\frac{1}{1-\sigma}} \cdot pxd$

where s_i is the elasticity of substitution between firm-specific product varieties (the love of variety elasticity of substitution).

The derived demand function for individual firm-specific products is derived from applying Shephard's lemma to the unit cost function (5):

(6) $\quad xxd = XXD \cdot \left(\dfrac{PXD}{pxd}\right)^{\sigma}$ or $\dfrac{xxdf}{XXD} = \left(\dfrac{PXD}{pxdf}\right)^{\sigma}$

Through (6) an inverse demand function can be specified as:

(7) $\quad pxdf = PXD \cdot \left(\dfrac{XXD}{xxdf}\right)^{\frac{1}{\sigma}} = PXD \cdot XXD^{\frac{1}{\sigma}} \cdot xxdf^{-\frac{1}{\sigma}}$

The above equation can then be used to evaluate the perceived price elasticity. At first the derivative $\dfrac{\partial pxdf}{\partial xxdf}$ will be computed:

$$\frac{\partial pxdf}{\partial xxdf} = PXD \cdot XXD^{\frac{1}{\sigma}} \cdot \left(-\frac{1}{\sigma}\right) \cdot xxdf^{1\frac{1}{\sigma}-1} + XXD^{\frac{1}{\sigma}} \cdot xxdf^{-\frac{1}{\sigma}} \cdot \frac{\partial PXD}{\partial xxdf} +$$

$$+ PXD \cdot xxdf^{-\frac{1}{\sigma}} \cdot \frac{1}{\sigma} \cdot XXD^{\frac{1}{\sigma}-1} \cdot \frac{\partial XXD}{\partial xxdf}$$

(8) $\quad \dfrac{\partial pxdf}{\partial xxdf} = -\dfrac{1}{\sigma} \cdot \dfrac{pxdf}{xxdf} + \dfrac{1}{\sigma} \cdot \dfrac{pxdf}{XXD} \cdot \dfrac{\partial XXD}{\partial xxdf} + \dfrac{pxdf}{PXD} \cdot \dfrac{\partial PXD}{\partial xxdf}$

The left-hand side of (8) is known if $\dfrac{\partial XXD}{\partial xxdf}$, $\dfrac{\partial PXD}{\partial xxdf}$ are known.

(i)   Computation of $\dfrac{\partial XXD}{\partial xxdf}$:

(9)
$$\frac{\partial XXD}{\partial xxdf_i} = \left[\sum xxdf_i^{\frac{\sigma-1}{\sigma}}\right]^{\frac{\sigma}{\sigma-1}-1} \cdot xxdf^{\frac{\sigma-1}{\sigma}-1} \Rightarrow \frac{\partial XXD}{\partial xxdf_i} = \left[XXD^{\frac{\sigma-1}{\sigma}}\right]^{\frac{1}{\sigma-1}} \cdot xxdf^{-\frac{1}{\sigma}}$$

$$\Rightarrow \frac{\partial XXD}{\partial xxdf} = \left(\frac{XXD}{xxdf}\right)^{\frac{1}{\sigma}}$$

(ii)   Computation of $\dfrac{\partial PXD}{\partial xxdf}$:

(10) $\quad \dfrac{\partial PXD}{\partial xxdf} = \dfrac{\partial PXD}{\partial XXD} \cdot \dfrac{\partial XXD}{\partial xxdf}$, with $\dfrac{\partial XXD}{\partial xxdf}$ being computed as before.

Substituting (9) and (10) into (8) the perceived price elasticity of demand can be computed.

(11)
$$\frac{\partial pxdf / pxdf}{\partial xxdf / xxdf} = -\frac{1}{\sigma} + \frac{1}{\sigma} \cdot \frac{pxdf}{XXD} \cdot \left(\frac{XXD}{xxdf}\right)^{\frac{1}{\sigma}} \cdot \frac{xxdf}{pxdf} + \frac{\partial PXD}{\partial XXD} \cdot \left(\frac{XXD}{xxdf}\right)^{\frac{1}{\sigma}} \cdot \frac{pxdf}{PXD} \cdot \frac{xxdf}{pxdf}$$

$$\Rightarrow -\frac{1}{\psi} = -\frac{1}{\sigma} + \frac{1}{\sigma} \cdot \frac{pxdf \cdot xxdf}{PXD \cdot XXD} + \frac{\partial PXD}{\partial XXD} \cdot \frac{pxdf \cdot xxdf}{PXD \cdot XXD} \cdot \frac{XXD}{PXD}$$

or writing the above in terms of value shares

(12) $\quad \dfrac{\partial pxdf / pxdf}{\partial xxd / xxdf} = -\dfrac{1}{\sigma} + \dfrac{1}{\sigma} VSH_{(xxdf/XXD)} + \dfrac{\partial PXD/PXD}{\partial XXD/XXD} \cdot VSH_{(xxdf/XXD)}$

The term $\dfrac{\partial PXD/PXD}{\partial XXD/XXD}$ that appears on (12) corresponds to the demand elasticity of the upper level of the Armington nesting structure. Equation (12) applies both to the market segmentation and to the market integration nesting structure.

A1.4.1.   Market segmentation

Recalling the nesting of the Armington within market segmentation,

(13) $Y = \left(\delta_1 \cdot XXD^{s-1/s} + \delta_2 \cdot IMP^{s-1/s} \right)^{s/s-1}$

Following the same procedure as above (equations (8) to (12)) a formula for $\dfrac{\partial PXD/PXD}{\partial XXD/XXD}$ can be derived:

(14)
$$\frac{\partial PXD/PXD}{\partial XXD/XXD} = -\frac{1}{s} + \frac{1}{s} \cdot \frac{PXD \cdot XXD}{PY \cdot Y} + \frac{\partial PY}{\partial Y} \cdot \frac{PXD \cdot XXD}{PY \cdot Y} \cdot \frac{Y}{PY} =$$
$$= -\frac{1}{s} + \frac{1}{s} VSH_{(XXD/Y)} + VSH_{(XXD/Y)} \cdot \frac{\partial PY/PY}{\partial Y/Y}$$

In the model, as well as in reality, the demand for the composite good is the sum of demand behaviour of different economic agents using the commodities for different purposes. The composite good includes demand by households, demand for intermediate production inputs, demand by government, etc. The complexity of formulations (for example, households' behaviour is formulated as a LES system involving consumption by purpose that is further transformed into consumption by product) makes impossible the exact computation of the price elasticity of demand.

It is reasonably assumed, instead, that individual firms do not have full information about the complex determination of the composite good, or that the cost of gathering and processing information together with the computational complexity involved in finding their true demand functions precludes firms from making use of all available information. Instead firms are characterized by bounded rationality at this stage and make simplifying working assumptions about the demand elasticity. Specifically, firms are taken to assume that top-level composite demand by any region is governed by a constant elasticity demand function:

$Y = a(PY)^{-\Omega}$

Setting $\Omega = 0$ would be equivalent to the assumption that firms ignore the effects of changes in their supply price on top level demands, while setting $\Omega = 1$ is equivalent to assuming that firms perceive total expenditure values to be unaffected by their actions.

Because now $Y = PY^{-\Omega}$, $\dfrac{\partial Y/Y}{\partial PY/PY} = -\Omega$, so substituting back to (14) gives:

$$(15) \quad \frac{\partial PXD/PXD}{\partial XXD/XXD} = -\frac{1}{s} + \frac{1}{s}VSH_{(XXD/Y)} - \frac{1}{\Omega}VSHARE_{(XXD/Y)}$$

Replacing (15) into (12) gives (noticing that $VSH_{(xxdf/XXD)} = \frac{1}{N}$, because of the assumption of symmetrical firms):

$$(16) \quad -\frac{1}{\psi} = \frac{\partial pxdf/pxdf}{\partial xxdf/xxdf} = -\frac{1}{\sigma} + \frac{1}{N \cdot \sigma} + \frac{1}{N} \cdot \left[-\frac{1}{s} + \frac{1}{s} \cdot VSH_{(XXD/Y)} - \frac{1}{\Omega} \cdot VSH_{(XXD/Y)} \right]$$

A1.4.2. Market integration

In the case of market integration, the nesting of the Armington is as follows: first consumers allocate their demand between EU products YEU (domestic and imported) and ROW imports (equation (17)) and then between domestic products and EU imports (equation (18)).

$$(17) \quad Y = \left(\delta_1 \cdot YEU^{s3-1/s3} + \delta_2 \cdot IMPRW^{s3-1/s3} \right)^{s3/s3-1}$$

$$(18) \quad YEU = \left(\delta_1 \cdot XXD^{s2-1/s2} + \delta_2 \cdot IMPEU^{s2-1/s2} \right)^{s2/s2-1}$$

Starting again from (12) and applying the same procedure as before we obtain:

$$(19) \quad \frac{\partial PXD/PXD}{\partial XXD/XXD} = -\frac{1}{s_2} + \frac{1}{s_2} \cdot \frac{PXD \cdot XXD}{PYEU \cdot YEU} + \frac{\partial PYEU/PYEU}{\partial YEU/YEU} \cdot \frac{PXD \cdot XXD}{PYEU \cdot YEU} \quad \text{from the}$$

second level of the Armington and

$$(20) \quad \frac{\partial PYDO/PYDO}{\partial YDO/YDO} = -\frac{1}{s3} + \frac{1}{s3} \cdot \frac{PYEU \cdot YEU}{PY \cdot Y} + \frac{\partial PY/PY}{\partial Y/Y} \cdot \frac{PYEU \cdot YEU}{PY \cdot Y}$$

from the upper level.

Applying the same assumption of firms' perception on the elasticity of demand as in the case of market integration, and replacing (19) and (20) in (12) the function for the perceived elasticity of demand in the case of market integration is derived:

$$\frac{\partial pxdf/pxdf}{\partial xxdf/xxdf} = -\frac{1}{\sigma} + \frac{1}{N \cdot \sigma} + \frac{1}{N} \cdot \left[-\frac{1}{s_2} + \frac{1}{s_2}VSH_{(XXD/YEU)} + \frac{\partial PYEU/PYEU}{\partial YEU/YEU} \cdot VSH_{(XXD/YEU)} \right]$$

and finally

$$-\frac{1}{\psi} = -\frac{1}{\sigma} + \frac{1}{N \cdot \sigma} + \frac{1}{N} \cdot \left[-\frac{1}{s_2} + \frac{1}{s_2}VSH_{(XXD/YEU)} + VSH_{(XXD/YEU)} \left(-\frac{1}{s_3} + \frac{1}{s_3}VSH_{(YEU/Y)} - \frac{1}{\Omega}VSH_{(YEU/Y)} \right) \right]$$

or alternatively, rearranging the above:

(21)

$$-\frac{1}{\psi} = -\frac{1}{\sigma} + \frac{1}{N} \cdot \left(\frac{1}{\sigma} - \frac{1}{s_2}\right) + \frac{VSH_{(XXD/YEU)}}{N} \cdot \left(\frac{1}{s_2} - \frac{1}{s_3}\right) + \frac{VSH_{(XXD/YEU)} \cdot VSH_{(YEU/Y)}}{N} \cdot \left(\frac{1}{s_3} - \frac{1}{\Omega}\right)$$

A2. Model database

A2.1. Nomenclature

Table A2.1 shows the new sectoral nomenclature of the model. The abbreviation PC denotes a perfectly competitive sector, while IC an imperfectly competitive one.

Table A2.1. PC and IC sectors in GEM-E3-SM

No	Sector name	Status	NACE-CLIO R25
1	Agriculture	PC	010
2	Fuel and power products	PC	060
3	Ferrous and non-ferrous ore and metals	IC	130
4	Chemical products	IC	170
5	Other energy-intensive industries	IC	150+190+470
6	Electrical goods	IC	250
7	Transport equipment	IC	280
8	Other equipment goods industries	IC	210+230
9	Consumer goods industries	PC	360+420+490+480
10	Building and construction	PC	530
11	Telecommunication services	IC	670
12	Transports	PC	610+630+650
13	Services of credit and insurance	IC	690
14	Other market services	PC	560+590+740
15	Non-market services	PC	860

The choice of imperfectly competitive sectors is based on the results by Pratten (1988) who identified the sectors with significant unexploited potential of economies of scale and the *ex ante* evaluations of the SMP, as surveyed in the literature.

Sector 9 was also a candidate for inclusion in the IC sectors; given, however, the heterogeneity of the industries included in this sector and the relatively low unexploited technical scale economy potential (Pratten, 1988), it was decided to treat it as PC.

Consumption of households by purpose has also changed. The new classification is shown in Table A2.2 (ND stands for non-durables and D for durables):

Table A2.2.   Durable and non-durable consumption categories

No	Purpose name	Status	Eurostat
1	Food, beverages and tobacco	ND	1
2	Clothing and footwear	ND	2
3	Housing and water	ND	31
4	Fuels and power	ND	32
5	Housing furniture and operation	ND	41+42+44+45+46
6	Heating and cooking appliances	D	43
7	Medical care and health expenses	ND	5
8	Transport equipment	D	61
9	Operation of transport equipment	ND	62
10	Purchased transport	ND	63
11	Telecommunication services	ND	64
12	Recreation, entertainment, culture, etc.	ND	7
13	Other services	ND	8

A2.2.   Benchmark year data set

The data for the base year, namely 1985, were all based on Eurostat.

A2.2.1.   Social accounting matrix (SAM) for the benchmark year

To build the SAMs, the following data were used:

(a)   I-O tables, per Member State, compiled by Eurostat from national sources; the tables were not homogeneous by country, because of different initial sources; they had to be aggregated and completed for some Member States.

(b)   Consumption matrix, investment matrix and employment by sector, also compiled by Eurostat. We did aggregation and completion.

(c)   National accounts by sector from the Cronos database of Eurostat, that (after aggregation) have been used to complete the income distribution part of the SAM by country.

Two types of data have been gathered from the new Cronos database:

(a)   the national accounts, detailed tables by branch;

(b)   the national accounts, detailed tables by sector, non-financial transactions.

For 1985, the first category of data has been used to compute the consumption and the investment matrix for the countries for which they were not available. The employment by branch was also derived from these data. The second category was used to complete, after aggregation, the income distribution part of the SAM by country.

A software in spreadsheet is available (by NTUA) to prepare the data needed for GEM-E3 starting from the original SAM.

A2.2.2.   Foreign trade data

The Comext data have been used to compute a bilateral trade matrix for the GEM-E3 branches for 1985, but no evaluation of the evolution in the trade matrix has been possible.

Different problems have been encountered:

(a)   Quality of the data: though trade matrix computed from the imports and from the exports data (which are separate), it seems impossible to make a clear link between both types of data and the differences can be sometimes very large (up to 25%) without any clear explanation. It has therefore been impossible to derive CIF/FOB relations from these data. Also, from 1993 the discrepancies increase, partly explained by the new procedure implemented (due to the SM) for collecting the data.

(b)   Nimexe–NACE classification: the data for 1985 were in Nimexe classification and had to be aggregated in the new NACE classification of GEM-E3. After 1988 the classification changed implying a break of continuity of the time series. This is the reason for the impossibility to build a time-series of trade matrices.

(c)   The Comext data only concern trade of goods and there are no other sources for the disaggregation by country of the external trade in services of one country. A special Eurostat publication, used for this matter, published only aggregate data of service trade. We had to assume the allocation of services trade by country.

(d)   The Comext data are very different from the I-O exports and imports data by branch and we have not yet been able to receive a clear explanation. The national account data for exports and imports by branch (in new Cronos) are too bad to be used (Eurostat is currently modifying them).

The 1985 trade matrix has been used to calibrate costs of services and transports associated to trade of other goods.

A2.3.   Time series for dynamic calibration

A2.3.1.   Time series for dynamic calibration

In the absence of SAMs for years other than 1985, we were obliged to only use sectoral time series as provided by the Cronos database of Eurostat. We have collected the following time series, that have been aggregated to the model's classification:

(a)   value added per sector (volume, value), factor prices (gaps exist) and market prices;
(b)   exports and imports per sector (volume and value);
(c)   actual output (available for a few countries);
(d)   investment by ownership branch (gaps exist);
(e)   consumption of households by purpose (volume and value);
(f)   employment per sector (gaps exist);
(g)   national accounts per sector.

However, it was not possible to build a complete benchmark data set for 1993 or 1994, as a complete set of data for each country and with the sectoral disaggregation needed only exist up to 1991.

The available data have therefore been used to ensure an evolution in the dynamic simulations with GEM-E3 which is compatible with this statistical information. They have served as targets for the dynamic calibration. Practically, the time series concern some of the margins of the I-O tables and the income distribution structure.

A2.3.2.   Social accounting matrix for the post-1985 years

Eurostat does not provide new observed I-O tables after 1985. For a few countries post-1985 I-O tables, following the national methodology, are available, but it was not possible, with the resources within this project, to make them compatible with Eurostat 1985 tables. We had access only to a time series of French I-O table, that were used to compute technical progress.

The I-O tables of 1991, as prepared by J. Beutel *et al.*, were evaluated, but were found inappropriate to serve as a database for the model for two main reasons:

(a)   the structure of the intermediate consumption is created artificially (i.e. not through real data), using a type of advanced RAS method;
(b)   the I-O tables are in current prices, which renders them inappropriate for the needs of the current project.

A3. Model calibration for representing the *monde*

A3.1. Static calibration

A3.1.1. Industrial concentration: computation of the Herfindahl index

Information on the firm size distribution in all three-digit industries:

(a)   number of firms in each firm size class;
(b)   total output value in each size class.

The computation of model firm numbers proceeds as follows:

1.   compute Herfindahl index H_i for each three-digit industry (as explained below);
2.   compute the implied number of symmetric firms n_i in each three-digit industry simply by taking the reciprocal value of H_i :

$$n_i = \frac{1}{H_i}$$

3.   compute the firms number used in the model as output-weighted average of the three-digit level n_i figures:

$$n = \sum_i W_i \cdot n_i$$

i : index over three-digit industries in a model sector

W_i: output (gross production value) of sub-industry i divided by the output of model industry

n : firm numbers used in the model.

The Herfindahl index H_i in step 1 is computed as follows.

In general, the Herfindahl index is defined as:

$$H = \sum_j MS_j^2$$

i.e. sum of the squared market shares of each firm, where j is the index over all firms in an industry and MS_j is the market share (output share) of firm j.

In practice, Census of Production data provide numbers of firms by size class and one has to assume for the computation that all firms within a discrete size class are equal sized.

A practical example for the UK 1985 may be helpful.

Let us take Chemicals (model sector 4). According to the UK SIC classification, the sector consists of seven three-digit industries (251, 255, 256, 257, 258, 259, 260). Let us take sector 251 (basic industrial chemicals) as an example. The UK 1985 Census of Production gives the information presented in Table A3.1.

Table A3.1.   Illustration of the computation of the Herfindahl index

Size class k	Enterprise size by number of employees (1)	No of enterprises n_k (2)	Gross output per size class (£ million) X_k (3)
1	1–99	935	1,065
2	100–199	34	600
3	200–499	35	1,523
4	500–999	12	1,184
5	1,000–1,499	7	1,299
6	1,500 and over	8	6,767
			12,439
			$= \sum_{k=1}^{6} X_k$

The output share of a typical firm in size class k is then

$$\frac{(X_k / n_k)}{\sum X_k} := MS_k$$

(e.g. $MS_1 = (1065/935)/12439$)

and $H_i = \sum_{k=1}^{6} n_k \cdot (MS_k)^2 = 0.039822$

$$\Rightarrow n_i = \frac{1}{H_i} = 25.1$$

The same procedure is then repeated for the other six sub-industries and the n for model sector 4 is computed as an output-weighted average over the seven sub-industries.

A3.2.2.   Calibration for IC sectors

The above statistics have been complemented with specific information to calibrate the imperfect market formulations based on:

(a)   the Pratten (1988) study regarding the engineering estimation of the minimum efficient scales per sector and the cost increase gradient (related to the number of firms);

(b)   Herfindahl indices computed for 1985 and 1992: these have been compared to similar information available by Bruce Lyons (University of East Anglia) who provided such an index for the whole EU and 1988; statistical rank correlation analysis showed, for example, that the UK numbers were close to those of the whole EU.

The starting data set includes the following:

(a)   values of production, absorption, imports and exports per sector, which are available from the SAM tables;

(b) the minimum efficiency scale per unit of domestic production, computed from the engineering data of Pratten;

(c) the cost gradient, i.e. the percent increase of average cost of the firm when it produces 1/3 of the minimum efficiency scale (available from Pratten);

(d) the number of firms per sector, computed as the inverse of a sectoral Herfindahl index.

The calibration procedure starts from the computation of the fixed cost per firm. This computation assumes that the firm operates at zero profit in the base year. The formula is derived as follows. The cost gradient is defined as the increase in average cost AC when production of a firm is reduced from the MES to 1/3 of the MES.

$$Cost\_gradient = \frac{AC(\tfrac{1}{3} \cdot MES) - AC(MES)}{AC(MES)} = \frac{MC + \dfrac{3 Fixed\_Cost}{MES} - MC - \dfrac{Fixed\_Cost}{MES}}{MC + \dfrac{Fixed\_Cost}{MES}}$$

or

$$Cost\_gadient = \frac{\dfrac{2 Fixed\_Cost}{MES}}{MC + \dfrac{Fixed\_Cost}{MES}}$$

(1) where MC is the marginal cost.

Assuming now zero-profits $AC = MC + \dfrac{Fixed\_Cost}{XD_{Firm}}$ (2)

Combining the two above equations, and letting N be the number of firms:

$$Cost\_gradient = \frac{\dfrac{2 \cdot Fixed\_Cost}{MES}}{AC - \dfrac{Fixed\_Cost}{XD_{Firm}} + \dfrac{Fixed\_Cost}{MES}} = \frac{\dfrac{2 \cdot Fixed\_Cost}{MES}}{AC - \dfrac{N \cdot Fixed\_Cost}{XD_{Value}} + \dfrac{Fixed\_Cost}{MES}}$$

$$Cost\_gradient = \frac{\dfrac{2 \cdot Fixed\_Cost}{MES / XD_{Branch}}}{XD_{Branch} + \dfrac{Fixed\_Cost}{MES / XD_{Branch}} - N \cdot Fixed\_Cost}$$

from which the fixed cost can be derived

$$Fixed\_Cost = \frac{\left(MES / XD_{branch} \right) \cdot \left(Cost\_gradient \right) \cdot XD_{branch}}{2 - \left(Cost\_gradient \right) \cdot \left[N \cdot \left(MES / XD_{branch} \right) - 1 \right]}$$

The calibration procedure runs, then, a simultaneous system of equations per sector involving:

(a) unit price assumption for the export price and the price of absorption;

(b)   the relationship between marginal costs and selling prices to domestic markets, exports to the EU and exports to the ROW, involving the mark-ups under a segmentation hypothesis;

(c)   the analytical formulas of the mark-ups, including the elasticities of substitution in the love of variety of domestic, EU and ROW consumption, the number of firms and the value shares (known from the SAM);

(d)   a zero profit condition per sector;

(e)   a domestic production equilibrium condition for volumes.

This system is iteratively solved for the elasticities of substitution in the love of variety of domestic consumption, the mark-ups, the selling prices and the volumes of production and exports. Once this completed, a set of recursive equations compute the rest of the calibration as in any CGE model (there we use the code from the original GEM-E3 model).

Table A3.2 illustrates the calibration of IC sectors.

Table A3.2. Calibration of the IC sectors (1985)

Sectors	MES as % of production	Cost gradient at 1/3 of MES	Herfindahl index	Fixed cost as % of domestic production	Mark-ups in %		Variety
					Dom-estic	EU exports	
Belgium							
Metallic	53.2%	8%	0.167	11.1%	18.7%	9.8%	36.0
Chemical	31.6%	7%	0.143	7.4%	13.4%	6.4%	49.0
Non-metallic	6.1%	7%	0.056	4.0%	5.7%	2.9%	72.0
Electrical goods	132.6%	7%	0.333	12.6%	28.3%	11.3%	45.0
Transport equipment	83.2%	9%	0.250	13.7%	27.0%	12.3%	32.0
Other equipment	21.4%	7%	0.111	6.3%	11.3%	5.7%	45.0
Telecomms	165.5%	9%	0.250	23.8%	33.3%	10.6%	240.0
Banks	68.2%	10%	0.167	17.7%	21.8%	6.1%	60.0
Germany							
Metallic	9.7%	8%	0.056	6.4%	7.7%	4.7%	45.0
Chemical	3.9%	10%	0.045	4.4%	5.7%	3.4%	66.0
Non-metallic	0.6%	7%	0.011	2.0%	2.1%	1.5%	92.0
Electrical goods	2.0%	7%	0.025	2.8%	3.4%	2.3%	80.0
Transport equipment	29.9%	9%	0.125	10.2%	15.8%	9.2%	40.0
Other equipment	0.7%	7%	0.013	1.8%	2.2%	1.7%	96.0
Telecomms	93.0%	10%	0.200	19.7%	25.2%	11.4%	300.0
Banks	33.6%	7%	0.100	10.9%	12.2%	3.6%	100.0
Denmark							
Metallic	161.5%	8%	0.333	15.9%	34.5%	13.1%	30.0
Chemical	112.5%	10%	0.333	15.1%	32.4%	11.3%	39.0
Non-metallic	8.5%	7%	0.056	5.6%	6.8%	3.1%	54.0
Electrical goods	95.7%	7%	0.250	12.2%	22.5%	8.3%	40.0
Transport equipment	130.5%	9%	0.333	15.7%	34.7%	13.2%	30.0
Other equipment	4.8%	7%	0.042	3.9%	5.5%	3.3%	48.0
Telecomms	298.2%	10%	0.333	32.0%	50.1%	13.7%	180.0
Banks	93.6%	7%	0.167	16.9%	21.3%	6.0%	60.0
France							
Metallic	13.7%	8%	0.071	6.9%	9.3%	5.3%	39.2
Chemical	6.7%	7%	0.050	4.7%	6.1%	3.3%	60.0
Non-metallic	0.8%	7%	0.013	2.4%	2.5%	1.7%	77.0
Electrical goods	13.1%	7%	0.071	6.2%	8.3%	3.9%	56.0
Transport equipment	17.9%	9%	0.100	7.9%	11.8%	6.1%	50.0
Other equipment	2.7%	7%	0.026	3.6%	4.4%	3.1%	46.8
Telecomms	106.7%	9%	0.200	20.1%	25.4%	8.4%	300.0
Banks	22.6%	10%	0.100	10.6%	12.1%	4.3%	100.0
Greece							
Metallic	71.9%	8%	0.200	12.3%	22.4%	8.6%	35.0
Chemical	35.9%	10%	0.167	10.2%	16.2%	7.0%	36.0
Non-metallic	7.8%	7%	0.056	5.2%	6.3%	2.6%	72.0
Electrical goods	85.9%	7%	0.200	13.5%	19.1%	7.4%	35.0
Transport equipment	132.3%	9%	0.250	20.1%	26.8%	10.6%	28.0
Other equipment	30.9%	7%	0.100	9.8%	11.4%	6.1%	30.0
Telecomms	321.8%	10%	0.333	33.7%	50.8%	13.0%	180.0
Banks	101.0%	7%	0.167	18.0%	22.0%	5.9%	60.0
Italy							
Metallic	39.1%	8%	0.111	12.0%	15.3%	7.3%	27.0
Chemical	4.9%	10%	0.048	5.1%	6.0%	2.9%	63.0
Non-metallic	1.0%	7%	0.014	2.7%	2.9%	1.9%	69.0
Electrical goods	19.3%	7%	0.083	7.7%	10.0%	4.4%	48.0
Transport equipment	13.9%	9%	0.083	7.4%	9.8%	4.4%	60.0
Other equipment	1.4%	7%	0.018	2.7%	3.2%	2.2%	66.0
Telecomms	157.3%	10%	0.250	24.9%	33.8%	10.5%	240.0
Banks	32.0%	7%	0.100	10.4%	12.0%	4.3%	100.0

Table A3.2.   Calibration of the IC sectors (1985) (continued)

Sectors	MES as % of production	Cost gradient at 1/3 of MES	Herfindahl index	Fixed cost as % of domestic production	Mark-ups in % Dom-estic	EU exports	Variety
Netherlands							
Metallic	98.0%	8%	0.250	13.2%	26.7%	11.3%	32.0
Chemical	3.4%	10%	0.050	3.5%	5.2%	3.1%	70.0
Non-metallic	15.8%	7%	0.083	6.8%	9.1%	3.9%	60.0
Electrical goods	73.6%	7%	0.250	9.6%	19.9%	8.6%	48.0
Transport equipment	36.9%	9%	0.167	9.5%	16.5%	7.1%	48.0
Other equipment	21.0%	7%	0.111	6.2%	11.0%	5.7%	45.0
Telecomms	149.6%	10%	0.250	24.0%	32.8%	11.1%	240.0
Banks	95.7%	7%	0.167	17.2%	21.8%	6.8%	60.0
Portugal							
Metallic	149.9%	8%	0.250	18.9%	30.2%	10.7%	28.0
Chemical	23.6%	10%	0.111	10.1%	13.1%	5.6%	36.0
Non-metallic	17.2%	7%	0.083	7.4%	10.3%	4.0%	48.0
Electrical goods	185.3%	7%	0.333	16.8%	33.1%	11.5%	27.0
Transport equipment	173.7%	9%	0.333	19.9%	39.0%	13.5%	27.0
Other equipment	34.2%%	7%	0.111	9.7%	13.3%	6.8%	27.0
Telecomms	317.1%	10%	0.333	33.4%	50.7%	13.0%	180.0
Banks	100.0%	7%	0.167	17.9%	22.0%	5.9%	60.0
Spain							
Metallic	111.2%	8%	0.200	17.8%	26.4%	9.1%	35.0
Chemical	14.3%	10%	0.083	8.3%	10.4%	4.5%	42.0
Non-metallic	4.0%	7%	0.033	4.4%	5.0%	2.5%	60.0
Electrical goods	29.5%	7%	0.100	9.7%	12.0%	4.8%	40.0
Transport equipment	24.2%	9%	0.111	9.4%	13.3%	5.4%	54.0
Other equipment	7.1%	7%	0.050	4.7%	6.0%	3.2%	60.0
Telecomms	152.3%	10%	0.250	24.3%	33.7%	10.5%	240.0
Banks	41.8%	7%	0.111	12.0%	13.7%	4.0%	90.0
UK							
Metallic	7.5%	8%	0.050	5.5%	7.1%	4.2%	40.0
Chemical	2.4%	10%	0.037	3.3%	4.4%	2.4%	81.0
Non-metallic	0.7%	7%	0.012	2.2%	2.4%	1.5%	83.0
Electrical goods	5.8%	7%	0.043	4.6%	5.8%	3.4%	46.0
Transport equipment	8.0%	9%	0.067	5.4%	7.4%	3.5%	75.0
Other equipment	0.5%	7%	0.011	1.6%	1.9%	1.3%	108.0
Telecomms	91.0%	10%	0.200	19.3%	25.0%	11.6%	300.0
Banks	21.3%	7%	0.083	8.5%	9.9%	5.0%	120.0
Ireland							
Metallic	95.3%	8%	0.250	12.9%	26.1%	10.7%	28.0
Chemical	27.7%	10%	0.167	8.1%	15.8%	7.1%	36.0
Non-metallic	92.0%	7%	0.200	15.1%	23.7%	8.5%	25.0
Electrical goods	19.6%	7%	0.125	5.4%	9.8%	4.7%	56.0
Transport equipment	72.7%	9%	0.250	12.2%	25.0%	10.7%	28.0
Other equipment	9.3%	7%	0.067	4.6%	7.6%	4.3%	45.0
Telecomms	309.2%	10%	0.333	32.8%	50.6%	13.3%	180.0
Banks	96.4%	7%	0.167	17.3%	21.5%	6.0%	60.0

A3.2. Dynamic calibration for representing the *monde*

Table A3.3. Goodness of fit of the dynamic calibration model: France

(numbers indicate % changes)

Sectors	01	02	03	04	05	06	07	08	09	10	11	12	13	14	15
Change in value added (in volume)															
(1985-88)															
Observed data	3.0%	-5.0%	18.0%	10.0%	9.0%	5.0%	10.0%	4.0%	9.0%	12.0%	24.0%	14.0%	11.0%	12.0%	5.0%
Computed value	0.9%	-3.7%	11.7%	8.1%	9.0%	2.4%	9.5%	4.0%	6.3%	10.9%	19.8%	7.7%	7.1%	7.5%	6.7%
(1988-91)															
Observed data	1.0%	5.0%	0.0%	9.0%	7.0%	9.0%	-4.0%	6.0%	9.0%	7.0%	33.0%	4.0%	-12.0%	10.0%	5.0%
Computed value	3.2%	10.4%	3.0%	13.2%	22.0%	21.2%	-1.4%	10.3%	12.3%	10.0%	28.3%	6.8%	-11.5%	16.9%	7.0%
Change in imports (in volume)															
(1985-88)															
Observed data	12.1%	3.0%	15.3%	27.7%	29.4%	39.9%	43.6%	42.7%	29.0%	-	4.4%	11.7%	48.8%	-17.4%	-
Computed value	12.1%	3.0%	15.3%	27.7%	29.4%	39.9%	43.6%	42.7%	29.0%	-	4.4%	11.7%	48.8%	-17.4%	-
(1988-91)															
Observed data	16.9%	10.6%	13.4%	21.4%	15.5%	32.9%	16.6%	16.5%	18.2%	-	8.5%	37.6%	60.8%	-7.2%	-
Computed value	16.9%	10.6%	13.4%	21.4%	15.5%	32.9%	16.6%	16.5%	18.2%	-	8.5%	37.6%	60.8%	-7.2%	-
Change in exports (in volume)															
(1985-88)															
Observed data	16.4%	17.1%	2.9%	14.8%	8.8%	5.5%	10.5%	7.5%	17.9%	-	-16.5%	2.3%	31.9%	-22.8%	-
Computed value	16.4%	17.1%	2.9%	14.8%	8.8%	5.5%	10.5%	7.5%	17.9%	-	-16.5%	2.3%	31.9%	-22.8%	-
(1988-91)															
Observed data	1.6%	22.8%	8.9%	17.2%	24.5%	40.8%	19.2%	22.8%	20.1%	-	21.8%	18.5%	52.1%	-4.5%	-
Computed value	1.6%	22.8%	8.9%	17.2%	24.5%	40.8%	19.2%	22.8%	20.1%	-	21.8%	18.5%	52.1%	-4.5%	-
Change in investments by ownership branch (in volume)															
(1985-88)															
Observed data	9.5%	-19.0%	-6.6%	34.8%	54.3%	-0.9%	50.8%	11.0%	23.3%	16.1%	-17.6%	33.4%	37.3%	24.4%	24.2%
Computed value	9.5%	-19.0%	-6.5%	34.8%	54.3%	-0.9%	50.8%	11.0%	23.3%	16.1%	-17.6%	33.4%	37.3%	24.4%	24.2%
(1988-91)															
Observed data	0.0%	-7.5%	-7.7%	14.1%	9.6%	8.7%	22.8%	8.5%	6.2%	8.3%	39.0%	16.4%	19.5%	9.6%	15.0%
Computed value	0.1%	-7.5%	-7.7%	14.1%	9.6%	8.7%	22.8%	8.4%	6.2%	8.3%	38.9%	16.4%	19.5%	9.6%	15.0%
Deflator of value added															
(1985-88)															
Observed data	1.9%	1.2%	4.3%	22.9%	18.3%	13.3%	21.5%	8.5%	11.8%	13.7%	-12.0%	3.7%	17.5%	17.4%	9.0%
Computed value	2.5%	-1.8%	4.5%	14.8%	13.2%	14.5%	16.8%	12.3%	14.0%	10.9%	-10.3%	10.1%	11.0%	14.5%	11.7%

	1985-88		1988-91	
	Real	Computed	Real	Computed
Consumer's price index	10.7%	9.7%	7.1%	6.9%
Gross domestic product	9.0%	8.6%	7.0%	7.6%

The goodness of fit for the other countries was perfect for the volume of exports and imports, consumption and investment, but there were some small discrepancies in the figures obtained for the value added in volume and deflator.

APPENDIX B

Numerical results

The numbers in all the tables presenting numerical results were solely derived using the GEM-E3-SM method.

Where '#VALUE!' and '#DIV/0!' appear, percent differences are not defined because value is zero in the *monde*.

Table B1.1.
The full *antimonde* scenario: macroeconomic aggregates for EUR-11

Macroeconomic Aggregates (vol.) (% change from *monde*)	Constraint Case			Flexible Case			Efficiency Case		
	1988	1991	1994	1988	1991	1994	1988	1991	1994
GDP fact. pr.	-0.58%	-0.85%	-1.10%	-0.46%	-0.90%	-1.26%	-0.49%	-1.01%	-1.46%
Priv. Consumption	-0.58%	-0.65%	-0.82%	-1.11%	-1.30%	-1.53%	-1.12%	-1.34%	-1.60%
Absorption	-0.48%	-0.57%	-0.72%	-1.31%	-1.58%	-1.82%	-1.32%	-1.62%	-1.88%
Total Investment	-2.07%	-2.20%	-2.67%	-4.24%	-4.39%	-4.52%	-4.24%	-4.39%	-4.53%
Total Exports to RW	0.25%	-0.06%	-0.14%	1.56%	1.24%	1.03%	1.53%	1.14%	0.85%
Total Imports from RW	-0.70%	-0.33%	-0.36%	-3.47%	-3.04%	-2.75%	-3.43%	-2.87%	-2.45%
Total Intra-EU Trade	-2.67%	-3.71%	-3.99%	-1.29%	-4.42%	-4.63%	-1.31%	-4.49%	-4.74%
Employment (diff. from *monde*, 10³ persons)	-136	-207	-317	-270	-431	-610	-272	-437	-621
Disposable Income (deflated)	-0.59%	-0.65%	-0.83%	-1.17%	-1.36%	-1.59%	-1.18%	-1.39%	-1.66%

Macroeconomic Ratios (abs. diff. from *monde*)	Constraint Case			Flexible Case			Efficiency Case		
	1988	1991	1994	1988	1991	1994	1988	1991	1994
Current Account as % of GDP	0.00%	0.00%	0.00%	0.81%	0.73%	0.68%	0.80%	0.70%	0.62%
Public Deficit as % of GDP	-0.35%	-0.45%	-0.61%	-0.31%	-0.42%	-0.54%	-0.32%	-0.45%	-0.59%
Labour Productivity	-0.47%	-0.68%	-0.84%	-0.25%	-0.55%	-0.77%	-0.28%	-0.67%	-0.97%
Investment/GDP	-0.31%	-0.28%	-0.32%	-1.78%	-1.76%	-1.74%	-1.78%	-1.74%	-1.70%
Priv.Cons./GDP	0.00%	0.12%	0.17%	-0.39%	-0.24%	-0.16%	-0.38%	-0.20%	-0.08%

Deflators (% change from *monde*)	Constraint Case			Flexible Case			Efficiency Case		
	1988	1991	1994	1988	1991	1994	1988	1991	1994
Consumer Price Index	0.45%	1.04%	1.19%	0.90%	0.77%	0.74%	0.88%	0.72%	0.65%
Real Wage Rate	-0.69%	-1.03%	-1.38%	-0.63%	-1.18%	-1.67%	-0.66%	-1.29%	-1.87%
Marginal Costs	0.35%	0.98%	1.13%	0.56%	0.45%	0.41%	0.55%	0.42%	0.36%
Producer Prices	0.45%	1.09%	1.23%	0.63%	0.56%	0.52%	0.62%	0.53%	0.46%
Average change in mark-ups (abs. diff.)	0.64%	0.76%	0.79%	0.58%	0.87%	0.92%	0.58%	0.87%	0.92%
Shadow Price of Capital	-0.07%	0.80%	1.08%	-0.10%	0.53%	0.99%	-0.12%	0.44%	0.83%
Terms-of-Trade RW	-0.51%	0.06%	0.24%	-5.12%	-4.05%	-3.36%	-5.03%	-3.71%	-2.77%

Implicit change in real exchange rate of EU	0.25%	0.99%	1.14%	-4.20%	-2.94%	-2.16%	-4.11%	-2.57%	-1.51%

Trade Regime	Segmentation			Segmentation			Segmentation		
Cumul. GDP in bill. ECU	-17	-84	-174	-14	-81	-183	-15	-90	-207
Cumul. Intra-EU trade in bill. ECU	-13	-64	-123	-7	-61	-136	-7	-62	-139

Table B1.2.
The full *antimonde* scenario: effects on IC sectors for EUR-11

% change from *monde*

Metal Industries	Constraint Case			Flexible Case			Efficiency Case		
	1988	1991	1994	1988	1991	1994	1988	1991	1994
Production per firm	-7.71%	-9.04%	-9.20%	-6.61%	-11.07%	-11.27%	-6.63%	-11.15%	-11.41%
Real Marginal Costs	0.98%	1.50%	1.68%	1.90%	1.81%	1.64%	1.89%	1.77%	1.57%
Real Producer Prices	1.54%	2.18%	2.37%	2.31%	2.50%	2.35%	2.31%	2.47%	2.29%
Mark-ups domestic (abs. diff.)	0.76%	0.83%	0.84%	0.72%	0.88%	0.90%	0.72%	0.89%	0.91%
Fixed Costs per firm	0.84%	1.32%	1.43%	-2.21%	-1.11%	-0.54%	-2.14%	-0.83%	-0.04%
Number of Firms	6.31%	7.05%	6.93%	8.09%	11.45%	11.13%	8.07%	11.36%	10.98%
Sigma of Love of Variety	0.00%	0.00%	0.00%	0.00%	0.00%	0.00%	0.00%	0.00%	0.00%

Chemical	Constraint Case			Flexible Case			Efficiency Case		
	1988	1991	1994	1988	1991	1994	1988	1991	1994
Production per firm	-6.47%	-8.01%	-8.16%	-5.09%	-8.66%	-8.91%	-5.12%	-8.75%	-9.06%
Real Marginal Costs	0.60%	1.13%	1.30%	1.31%	1.14%	1.04%	1.30%	1.10%	0.98%
Real Producer Prices	0.86%	1.46%	1.62%	1.49%	1.46%	1.37%	1.49%	1.43%	1.31%
Mark-ups domestic (abs. diff.)	0.45%	0.48%	0.48%	0.36%	0.50%	0.51%	0.36%	0.50%	0.51%
Fixed Costs per firm	0.45%	0.88%	0.95%	-2.53%	-1.58%	-1.03%	-2.46%	-1.30%	-0.54%
Number of Firms	5.06%	5.64%	5.55%	8.07%	11.09%	10.78%	8.05%	11.01%	10.63%
Sigma of Love of Variety	0.00%	0.00%	0.00%	0.00%	0.00%	0.00%	0.00%	0.00%	0.00%

Other Intensive Industries	Constraint Case			Flexible Case			Efficiency Case		
	1988	1991	1994	1988	1991	1994	1988	1991	1994
Production per firm	-2.95%	-3.37%	-3.54%	-3.64%	-5.94%	-6.12%	-3.66%	-6.00%	-6.23%
Real Marginal Costs	0.48%	1.07%	1.19%	0.68%	0.52%	0.41%	0.68%	0.50%	0.37%
Real Producer Prices	0.54%	1.14%	1.26%	0.76%	0.64%	0.53%	0.75%	0.61%	0.49%
Mark-ups domestic (abs. diff.)	0.06%	0.07%	0.07%	0.09%	0.12%	0.13%	0.09%	0.12%	0.13%
Fixed Costs per firm	0.00%	0.29%	0.30%	-3.30%	-2.51%	-1.99%	-3.23%	-2.22%	-1.48%
Number of Firms	2.08%	2.34%	2.23%	1.38%	2.60%	2.47%	1.37%	2.58%	2.44%
Sigma of Love of Variety	0.00%	0.00%	0.00%	0.00%	0.00%	0.00%	0.00%	0.00%	0.00%

Electrical goods	Constraint Case			Flexible Case			Efficiency Case		
	1988	1991	1994	1988	1991	1994	1988	1991	1994
Production per firm	-7.38%	-8.44%	-8.63%	-7.11%	-11.05%	-11.28%	-7.14%	-11.16%	-11.46%
Real Marginal Costs	0.55%	1.08%	1.17%	0.76%	0.61%	0.47%	0.75%	0.58%	0.42%
Real Producer Prices	0.81%	1.41%	1.50%	0.99%	0.98%	0.84%	0.99%	0.95%	0.80%
Mark-ups domestic (abs. diff.)	0.46%	0.49%	0.50%	0.51%	0.57%	0.58%	0.51%	0.57%	0.58%
Fixed Costs per firm	0.32%	0.69%	0.71%	-3.10%	-2.22%	-1.70%	-3.03%	-1.93%	-1.19%
Number of Firms	4.37%	5.16%	4.93%	4.27%	6.62%	6.40%	4.25%	6.52%	6.24%
Sigma of Love of Variety	0.00%	0.00%	0.00%	0.00%	0.00%	0.00%	0.00%	0.00%	0.00%

Transport equipment	Constraint Case			Flexible Case			Efficiency Case		
	1988	1991	1994	1988	1991	1994	1988	1991	1994
Production per firm	-9.14%	-11.34%	-11.55%	-9.76%	-14.59%	-14.68%	-9.79%	-14.67%	-14.82%
Real Marginal Costs	0.95%	1.47%	1.57%	1.21%	1.39%	1.22%	1.21%	1.37%	1.19%
Real Producer Prices	1.60%	2.35%	2.47%	1.86%	2.35%	2.19%	1.86%	2.34%	2.17%
Mark-ups domestic (abs. diff.)	1.08%	1.23%	1.29%	1.41%	1.67%	1.67%	1.41%	1.67%	1.68%
Fixed Costs per firm	0.95%	1.35%	1.38%	-2.71%	-1.60%	-1.08%	-2.64%	-1.31%	-0.56%
Number of Firms	11.17%	11.96%	11.43%	8.86%	13.66%	13.73%	8.84%	13.62%	13.67%
Sigma of Love of Variety	0.00%	0.00%	0.00%	0.00%	0.00%	0.00%	0.00%	0.00%	0.00%

Other Equipment	Constraint Case			Flexible Case			Efficiency Case		
	1988	1991	1994	1988	1991	1994	1988	1991	1994
Production per firm	-8.32%	-9.43%	-9.56%	-8.32%	-12.07%	-12.26%	-8.34%	-12.14%	-12.39%
Real Marginal Costs	0.59%	1.13%	1.22%	0.80%	0.62%	0.47%	0.79%	0.59%	0.42%
Real Producer Prices	0.75%	1.33%	1.42%	0.94%	0.83%	0.68%	0.94%	0.80%	0.63%
Mark-ups domestic (abs. diff.)	0.29%	0.32%	0.32%	0.33%	0.42%	0.42%	0.33%	0.42%	0.42%
Fixed Costs per firm	0.36%	0.67%	0.70%	-2.91%	-2.04%	-1.52%	-2.84%	-1.75%	-1.02%
Number of Firms	6.28%	7.42%	7.25%	4.80%	6.64%	6.37%	4.77%	6.56%	6.22%
Sigma of Love of Variety	0.00%	0.00%	0.00%	0.00%	0.00%	0.00%	0.00%	0.00%	0.00%

Telecommunications	Constraint Case			Flexible Case			Efficiency Case		
	1988	1991	1994	1988	1991	1994	1988	1991	1994
Production per firm	0.37%	0.67%	0.53%	-1.97%	-4.09%	-4.44%	-1.99%	-4.15%	-4.53%
Real Marginal Costs	0.51%	1.38%	1.56%	-0.01%	-0.01%	0.07%	-0.01%	-0.02%	0.06%
Real Producer Prices	1.27%	2.30%	2.45%	0.06%	0.12%	0.18%	0.06%	0.11%	0.16%
Mark-ups domestic (abs. diff.)	0.83%	0.98%	0.94%	-0.05%	-0.27%	-0.30%	-0.05%	-0.28%	-0.32%
Fixed Costs per firm	3.96%	5.95%	5.86%	-5.80%	-6.35%	-5.95%	-5.73%	-6.08%	-5.48%
Number of Firms	-0.31%	-0.65%	-0.54%	2.02%	4.28%	4.36%	2.03%	4.30%	4.40%
Sigma of Love of Variety	0.00%	0.00%	0.00%	0.00%	0.00%	0.00%	0.00%	0.00%	0.00%

Banks	Constraint Case			Flexible Case			Efficiency Case		
	1988	1991	1994	1988	1991	1994	1988	1991	1994
Production per firm	1.36%	1.53%	1.41%	-1.17%	-2.11%	-2.42%	-1.19%	-2.16%	-2.52%
Real Marginal Costs	0.41%	1.23%	1.38%	0.02%	0.01%	0.10%	0.02%	0.00%	0.07%
Real Producer Prices	0.68%	1.51%	1.66%	0.04%	0.03%	0.11%	0.04%	0.01%	0.08%
Mark-ups domestic (abs. diff.)	0.28%	0.28%	0.27%	-0.02%	-0.08%	-0.08%	-0.02%	-0.08%	-0.08%
Fixed Costs per firm	3.15%	4.22%	4.18%	-5.28%	-5.31%	-4.80%	-5.21%	-5.02%	-4.30%
Number of Firms	-0.58%	-0.46%	-0.37%	1.52%	3.33%	3.47%	1.52%	3.35%	3.49%
Sigma of Love of Variety	0.00%	0.00%	0.00%	0.00%	0.00%	0.00%	0.00%	0.00%	0.00%

Table B1.3.

The full *antimonde* scenario: sectoral results for EUR-11 (volumes)

% change from *monde*

Agriculture	Constraint Case			Flexible Case			Efficiency Case		
	1988	1991	1994	1988	1991	1994	1988	1991	1994
Domestic Production - vol.	0.0%	-0.2%	-0.5%	2.5%	1.5%	0.9%	2.4%	1.3%	0.5%
Imports - vol.	-0.4%	0.6%	0.9%	-3.3%	-2.5%	-1.9%	-3.2%	-2.2%	-1.5%
Exports - vol.	0.4%	0.0%	-0.2%	1.5%	1.1%	0.8%	1.5%	1.0%	0.6%
Absorption - vol.	-0.1%	0.0%	0.0%	0.9%	0.4%	0.0%	0.8%	0.3%	-0.2%
Investment - vol.	3.2%	2.9%	2.0%	-3.1%	-3.6%	-3.9%	-3.1%	-3.6%	-4.0%
Labour Demand - vol.	-0.1%	-0.3%	-0.4%	2.7%	1.7%	1.4%	2.7%	1.6%	1.2%
Private Consumption - vol.	-1.2%	-0.8%	-0.8%	-0.8%	-1.2%	-1.4%	-0.8%	-1.2%	-1.5%
Supply to domestic - vol.	0.4%	0.3%	0.1%	2.6%	2.1%	1.5%	2.6%	1.9%	1.1%
Intra-EU Trade - vol	-3.5%	-4.2%	-4.5%	-0.1%	-2.2%	-2.6%	-0.1%	-2.3%	-2.8%

Energy	Constraint Case			Flexible Case			Efficiency Case		
	1988	1991	1994	1988	1991	1994	1988	1991	1994
Domestic Production - vol.	-0.6%	-0.9%	-1.1%	1.3%	0.8%	0.3%	1.3%	0.7%	0.1%
Imports - vol.	-0.3%	0.0%	0.0%	-1.1%	-1.0%	-0.9%	-1.1%	-0.9%	-0.8%
Exports - vol.	0.0%	-0.1%	-0.2%	0.6%	0.5%	0.4%	0.6%	0.4%	0.3%
Absorption - vol.	-0.3%	-0.3%	-0.4%	0.3%	-0.1%	-0.4%	0.3%	-0.1%	-0.5%
Investment - vol.	-5.3%	-5.5%	-5.9%	-3.5%	-3.7%	-3.9%	-3.5%	-3.8%	-4.0%
Labour Demand - vol.	-0.9%	-1.2%	-1.4%	1.7%	1.0%	0.5%	1.7%	0.9%	0.4%
Private Consumption - vol.	-0.2%	0.2%	0.2%	-0.8%	-1.1%	-1.3%	-0.8%	-1.1%	-1.3%
Supply to domestic - vol.	-0.2%	-0.4%	-0.5%	1.1%	0.6%	0.2%	1.1%	0.5%	0.0%
Intra-EU Trade - vol	-1.9%	-2.5%	-2.9%	1.0%	0.5%	0.2%	1.0%	0.4%	0.0%

Metal Industries	Constraint Case			Flexible Case			Efficiency Case		
	1988	1991	1994	1988	1991	1994	1988	1991	1994
Domestic Production - vol.	-1.3%	-2.0%	-2.3%	1.7%	1.0%	0.5%	1.7%	0.8%	0.2%
Imports - vol.	-0.5%	-0.4%	-0.4%	-3.0%	-3.0%	-2.7%	-3.0%	-2.8%	-2.4%
Exports - vol.	0.0%	-0.3%	-0.4%	1.2%	0.9%	0.7%	1.2%	0.8%	0.5%
Absorption - vol.	-0.4%	-0.8%	-1.0%	0.0%	-0.4%	-0.7%	0.0%	-0.5%	-0.9%
Investment - vol.	-4.1%	-4.9%	-5.5%	-3.1%	-3.6%	-3.9%	-3.2%	-3.7%	-4.0%
Labour Demand - vol.	-0.1%	-0.6%	-0.8%	4.0%	5.9%	5.2%	4.0%	5.7%	5.0%
Private Consumption - vol.	-1.2%	-0.9%	-0.9%	-0.9%	-1.2%	-1.5%	-0.9%	-1.3%	-1.6%
Supply to domestic - vol.	-0.4%	-1.0%	-1.3%	3.3%	6.6%	5.9%	3.2%	6.4%	5.5%
Intra-EU Trade - vol	-2.4%	-3.2%	-3.4%	-1.8%	-7.1%	-7.2%	-1.8%	-7.1%	-7.2%

Chemical	Constraint Case			Flexible Case			Efficiency Case		
	1988	1991	1994	1988	1991	1994	1988	1991	1994
Domestic Production - vol.	-1.0%	-1.8%	-2.0%	3.4%	2.6%	2.0%	3.4%	2.4%	1.7%
Imports - vol.	-0.2%	0.2%	0.3%	-3.7%	-3.2%	-2.9%	-3.7%	-3.0%	-2.5%
Exports - vol.	0.0%	-0.3%	-0.4%	1.7%	1.4%	1.2%	1.7%	1.3%	1.0%
Absorption - vol.	-0.5%	-0.6%	-0.7%	1.1%	0.6%	0.2%	1.1%	0.5%	0.1%
Investment - vol.	-3.6%	-4.3%	-4.9%	-2.5%	-2.9%	-3.1%	-2.5%	-2.9%	-3.2%
Labour Demand - vol.	-0.6%	-1.2%	-1.3%	4.3%	4.2%	3.7%	4.3%	4.1%	3.5%
Private Consumption - vol.	-1.2%	-0.8%	-0.8%	-0.8%	-1.1%	-1.4%	-0.8%	-1.2%	-1.5%
Supply to domestic - vol.	-0.8%	-1.6%	-1.8%	4.6%	6.6%	6.1%	4.6%	6.4%	5.7%
Intra-EU Trade - vol	-1.0%	-1.0%	-1.2%	-0.3%	-4.0%	-4.2%	-0.3%	-4.1%	-4.3%

Other Intensive Industries	Constraint Case			Flexible Case			Efficiency Case		
	1988	1991	1994	1988	1991	1994	1988	1991	1994
Domestic Production - vol.	0.1%	-0.2%	-0.4%	-1.1%	-1.4%	-1.7%	-1.1%	-1.5%	-1.9%
Imports - vol.	-1.7%	-1.1%	-1.1%	-5.7%	-4.9%	-4.4%	-5.7%	-4.6%	-3.9%
Exports - vol.	0.2%	-0.1%	-0.2%	1.7%	1.3%	1.1%	1.6%	1.2%	0.9%
Absorption - vol.	-0.2%	-0.4%	-0.7%	-2.2%	-2.4%	-2.6%	-2.2%	-2.4%	-2.7%
Investment - vol.	-2.2%	-2.5%	-3.1%	-4.7%	-4.8%	-5.0%	-4.7%	-4.8%	-5.0%
Labour Demand - vol.	0.2%	-0.1%	-0.2%	-0.5%	-0.6%	-0.8%	-0.6%	-0.6%	-0.9%
Private Consumption - vol.	-0.1%	-0.4%	-0.8%	-1.4%	-1.3%	-1.5%	-1.4%	-1.4%	-1.6%
Supply to domestic - vol.	0.5%	0.3%	0.0%	-1.0%	-0.3%	-0.7%	-1.0%	-0.4%	-0.8%
Intra-EU Trade - vol	-3.8%	-4.8%	-5.0%	-2.8%	-6.3%	-6.4%	-2.8%	-6.3%	-6.5%

Electrical goods	Constraint Case			Flexible Case			Efficiency Case		
	1988	1991	1994	1988	1991	1994	1988	1991	1994
Domestic Production - vol.	-0.2%	-0.7%	-1.1%	0.0%	-0.6%	-1.1%	-0.1%	-0.8%	-1.4%
Imports - vol.	-1.6%	-1.4%	-1.7%	-5.9%	-5.2%	-4.9%	-5.9%	-5.0%	-4.5%
Exports - vol.	0.5%	0.2%	0.1%	2.0%	1.6%	1.4%	2.0%	1.5%	1.2%
Absorption - vol.	-0.6%	-1.1%	-1.6%	-3.8%	-3.8%	-4.0%	-3.8%	-3.9%	-4.1%
Investment - vol.	0.8%	0.1%	-0.9%	-4.4%	-4.9%	-5.2%	-4.4%	-5.0%	-5.3%
Labour Demand - vol.	0.7%	0.4%	0.1%	1.3%	1.8%	1.5%	1.2%	1.7%	1.3%
Private Consumption - vol.	2.8%	0.9%	-0.9%	-3.9%	-2.4%	-2.3%	-4.0%	-2.4%	-2.4%
Supply to domestic - vol.	0.7%	0.5%	-0.1%	-0.3%	2.3%	1.8%	-0.3%	2.1%	1.4%
Intra-EU Trade - vol	-3.4%	-5.0%	-5.4%	-2.1%	-6.1%	-6.3%	-2.1%	-6.2%	-6.5%

Transport equipment	Constraint Case			Flexible Case			Efficiency Case		
	1988	1991	1994	1988	1991	1994	1988	1991	1994
Domestic Production - vol.	0.5%	-1.2%	-1.8%	-1.5%	-2.7%	-2.9%	-1.5%	-2.8%	-3.1%
Imports - vol.	0.5%	-1.1%	-2.0%	-5.9%	-6.0%	-5.7%	-5.9%	-5.8%	-5.3%
Exports - vol.	0.6%	0.2%	0.2%	1.9%	1.5%	1.3%	1.9%	1.4%	1.1%
Absorption - vol.	2.1%	-0.6%	-1.7%	-4.6%	-5.6%	-5.5%	-4.6%	-5.6%	-5.6%
Investment - vol.	2.5%	0.6%	-0.7%	-4.5%	-4.8%	-4.9%	-4.6%	-4.8%	-5.0%
Labour Demand - vol.	2.7%	1.5%	1.0%	1.8%	5.7%	5.6%	1.8%	5.6%	5.5%
Private Consumption - vol.	12.7%	3.0%	-0.7%	-4.3%	-2.3%	-1.8%	-4.3%	-2.3%	-1.9%
Supply to domestic - vol.	3.6%	1.5%	0.4%	-1.2%	3.0%	2.9%	-1.2%	2.9%	2.7%
Intra-EU Trade - vol	-2.7%	-5.6%	-6.2%	-3.5%	-8.1%	-8.1%	-3.5%	-8.1%	-8.2%

Other Equipment

	Constraint Case			Flexible Case			Efficiency Case		
	1988	1991	1994	1988	1991	1994	1988	1991	1994
Domestic Production - vol.	-0.4%	-0.8%	-1.1%	-1.3%	-2.2%	-2.7%	-1.3%	-2.3%	-3.0%
Imports - vol.	-1.3%	-1.2%	-1.5%	-5.0%	-4.7%	-4.5%	-5.0%	-4.6%	-4.2%
Exports - vol.	0.2%	-0.1%	-0.2%	1.8%	1.4%	1.2%	1.8%	1.3%	1.0%
Absorption - vol.	-0.5%	-0.7%	-1.1%	-4.8%	-5.3%	-5.6%	-4.8%	-5.4%	-5.7%
Investment - vol.	5.3%	4.6%	3.5%	-4.8%	-5.2%	-5.5%	-4.8%	-5.3%	-5.6%
Labour Demand - vol.	0.0%	-0.2%	-0.4%	-0.3%	-0.6%	-0.9%	-0.4%	-0.7%	-1.1%
Private Consumption - vol.	-1.0%	-0.9%	-1.1%	-1.5%	-1.7%	-2.0%	-1.5%	-1.8%	-2.1%
Supply to domestic - vol.	0.8%	0.6%	0.1%	-2.1%	-0.8%	-1.4%	-2.1%	-1.0%	-1.7%
Intra-EU Trade - vol	-2.8%	-3.6%	-3.9%	-2.8%	-5.2%	-5.4%	-2.8%	-5.3%	-5.5%

Consumer goods

	Constraint Case			Flexible Case			Efficiency Case		
	1988	1991	1994	1988	1991	1994	1988	1991	1994
Domestic Production - vol.	0.1%	0.1%	-0.1%	1.5%	0.8%	0.4%	1.4%	0.7%	0.1%
Imports - vol.	-1.1%	-0.2%	-0.1%	-4.2%	-3.5%	-3.0%	-4.2%	-3.2%	-2.6%
Exports - vol.	0.3%	-0.1%	-0.3%	2.2%	1.7%	1.4%	2.1%	1.6%	1.2%
Absorption - vol.	-0.6%	-0.5%	-0.6%	-0.4%	-0.7%	-1.0%	-0.4%	-0.8%	-1.1%
Investment - vol.	5.2%	5.0%	4.1%	-3.5%	-3.9%	-4.1%	-3.5%	-3.9%	-4.2%
Labour Demand - vol.	0.0%	0.1%	0.0%	1.7%	0.9%	0.7%	1.7%	0.8%	0.6%
Private Consumption - vol.	-1.1%	-0.8%	-0.8%	-0.8%	-1.1%	-1.3%	-0.8%	-1.1%	-1.4%
Supply to domestic - vol.	0.5%	0.7%	0.6%	1.4%	1.5%	1.0%	1.4%	1.3%	0.8%
Intra-EU Trade - vol	-4.6%	-5.7%	-6.0%	-0.8%	-3.0%	-3.3%	-0.8%	-3.1%	-3.4%

Construction

	Constraint Case			Flexible Case			Efficiency Case		
	1988	1991	1994	1988	1991	1994	1988	1991	1994
Domestic Production - vol.	-2.1%	-2.1%	-2.5%	-7.1%	-7.3%	-7.5%	-7.1%	-7.3%	-7.5%
Imports - vol.	-7.0%	-7.4%	-7.9%	-3.5%	-3.6%	-3.7%	-3.5%	-3.6%	-3.7%
Exports - vol.	0.1%	0.0%	0.0%	0.5%	0.4%	0.3%	0.5%	0.3%	0.2%
Absorption - vol.	-2.2%	-2.2%	-2.5%	-7.1%	-7.3%	-7.5%	-7.1%	-7.3%	-7.5%
Investment - vol.	-1.2%	-1.2%	-2.1%	-7.6%	-7.7%	-7.8%	-7.6%	-7.7%	-7.8%
Labour Demand - vol.	-1.8%	-1.8%	-2.1%	-6.8%	-6.9%	-7.0%	-6.8%	-6.9%	-6.9%
Private Consumption - vol.	-1.2%	-0.9%	-0.9%	-0.8%	-1.1%	-1.4%	-0.8%	-1.1%	-1.4%
Supply to domestic - vol.	-2.1%	-2.1%	-2.5%	-7.1%	-7.3%	-7.5%	-7.1%	-7.3%	-7.5%
Intra-EU Trade - vol	-1.4%	-1.8%	-2.1%	-3.2%	-3.3%	-3.4%	-3.2%	-3.3%	-3.4%

Telecommunications

	Constraint Case			Flexible Case			Efficiency Case		
	1988	1991	1994	1988	1991	1994	1988	1991	1994
Domestic Production - vol.	-0.8%	-0.7%	-0.8%	-0.1%	-0.5%	-0.8%	-0.1%	-0.5%	-0.8%
Imports - vol.	-1.7%	-0.7%	-0.6%	-5.7%	-5.5%	-5.1%	-5.6%	-5.3%	-4.8%
Exports - vol.	0.6%	0.3%	0.3%	1.0%	0.9%	0.7%	1.0%	0.8%	0.6%
Absorption - vol.	-0.8%	-0.7%	-0.8%	-0.4%	-0.6%	-0.9%	-0.4%	-0.6%	-0.9%
Investment - vol.	-4.6%	-4.1%	-4.2%	-4.2%	-4.4%	-4.5%	-4.2%	-4.4%	-4.5%
Labour Demand - vol.	2.7%	3.3%	3.4%	0.0%	-0.6%	-0.7%	0.0%	-0.6%	-0.6%
Private Consumption - vol.	-1.7%	-1.4%	-1.4%	-0.8%	-1.2%	-1.5%	-0.8%	-1.2%	-1.6%
Supply to domestic - vol.	-0.6%	-0.5%	-0.5%	0.3%	1.1%	0.8%	0.3%	1.1%	0.8%
Intra-EU Trade - vol	-6.7%	-8.9%	-8.9%	-7.0%	-18.0%	-18.1%	-7.0%	-18.1%	-18.2%

Transports

	Constraint Case			Flexible Case			Efficiency Case		
	1988	1991	1994	1988	1991	1994	1988	1991	1994
Domestic Production - vol.	-0.4%	-0.4%	-0.4%	0.2%	0.0%	-0.2%	0.2%	0.0%	-0.3%
Imports - vol.	-0.6%	-0.5%	-0.5%	0.1%	0.0%	-0.1%	0.1%	0.0%	-0.2%
Exports - vol.	0.2%	0.1%	0.1%	0.7%	0.5%	0.5%	0.6%	0.5%	0.4%
Absorption - vol.	-0.6%	-0.5%	-0.5%	-0.5%	-0.7%	-1.0%	-0.5%	-0.7%	-1.0%
Investment - vol.	-5.3%	-5.3%	-5.5%	-4.1%	-4.2%	-4.3%	-4.1%	-4.2%	-4.3%
Labour Demand - vol.	-0.4%	-0.4%	-0.4%	0.3%	0.3%	0.1%	0.3%	0.3%	0.1%
Private Consumption - vol.	-1.6%	-1.1%	-1.1%	-0.9%	-1.4%	-1.7%	-1.0%	-1.4%	-1.8%
Supply to domestic - vol.	-0.4%	-0.4%	-0.4%	0.2%	0.0%	-0.2%	0.2%	0.0%	-0.3%
Intra-EU Trade - vol	-0.1%	-0.3%	-0.3%	1.1%	1.2%	1.1%	1.1%	1.2%	1.0%

Banks

	Constraint Case			Flexible Case			Efficiency Case		
	1988	1991	1994	1988	1991	1994	1988	1991	1994
Domestic Production - vol.	-0.2%	0.0%	0.0%	0.1%	0.1%	-0.2%	0.0%	0.0%	-0.3%
Imports - vol.	-2.9%	-1.5%	-1.4%	-5.7%	-4.9%	-4.4%	-5.6%	-4.7%	-4.0%
Exports - vol.	0.2%	-0.1%	-0.1%	1.0%	0.8%	0.7%	1.0%	0.7%	0.6%
Absorption - vol.	-0.4%	-0.2%	-0.3%	-0.1%	0.0%	-0.3%	-0.1%	-0.1%	-0.4%
Investment - vol.	-3.1%	-2.9%	-3.3%	-4.2%	-4.2%	-4.3%	-4.2%	-4.2%	-4.3%
Labour Demand - vol.	3.2%	3.5%	3.6%	0.1%	-0.4%	-0.5%	0.1%	-0.4%	-0.5%
Private Consumption - vol.	-1.8%	-1.3%	-1.3%	-1.0%	-1.5%	-1.9%	-1.0%	-1.6%	-2.0%
Supply to domestic - vol.	-0.2%	0.1%	0.0%	0.2%	0.7%	0.4%	0.2%	0.6%	0.3%
Intra-EU Trade - vol	-6.6%	-8.5%	-8.3%	-4.7%	-11.7%	-12.0%	-4.7%	-11.7%	-12.0%

Services

	Constraint Case			Flexible Case			Efficiency Case		
	1988	1991	1994	1988	1991	1994	1988	1991	1994
Domestic Production - vol.	-0.3%	-0.4%	-0.5%	-0.7%	-0.8%	-1.1%	-0.7%	-0.9%	-1.2%
Imports - vol.	-1.4%	-0.6%	-0.6%	-3.4%	-2.8%	-2.4%	-3.3%	-2.6%	-2.1%
Exports - vol.	0.2%	-0.1%	-0.2%	1.0%	0.8%	0.6%	1.0%	0.7%	0.5%
Absorption - vol.	-0.6%	-0.6%	-0.7%	-1.0%	-1.3%	-1.5%	-1.0%	-1.3%	-1.6%
Investment - vol.	-0.9%	-0.9%	-1.4%	-4.5%	-4.6%	-4.7%	-4.5%	-4.6%	-4.7%
Labour Demand - vol.	-0.3%	-0.3%	-0.4%	-0.5%	-0.6%	-0.6%	-0.5%	-0.6%	-0.6%
Private Consumption - vol.	-0.9%	-0.8%	-0.9%	-1.0%	-1.4%	-1.6%	-1.1%	-1.4%	-1.7%
Supply to domestic - vol.	-0.5%	-0.5%	-0.6%	-1.0%	-1.3%	-1.6%	-1.0%	-1.3%	-1.6%
Intra-EU Trade - vol	0.0%	-0.7%	-0.8%	1.9%	2.8%	2.7%	1.9%	2.8%	2.7%

Non market

	Constraint Case			Flexible Case			Efficiency Case		
	1988	1991	1994	1988	1991	1994	1988	1991	1994
Domestic Production - vol.	-0.1%	-0.1%	-0.1%	-0.1%	-0.2%	-0.2%	-0.1%	-0.2%	-0.2%
Imports - vol.	-0.3%	-0.3%	-0.3%	-0.1%	-0.2%	-0.2%	-0.2%	-0.2%	-0.2%
Exports - vol.	0.0%	0.0%	0.0%	0.2%	0.2%	0.2%	0.2%	0.2%	0.1%
Absorption - vol.	-0.1%	-0.1%	-0.1%	-0.1%	-0.2%	-0.2%	-0.1%	-0.2%	-0.2%
Investment - vol.	-6.9%	-6.9%	-7.0%	-4.1%	-4.1%	-4.1%	-4.1%	-4.1%	-4.1%
Labour Demand - vol.	-0.2%	-0.1%	-0.1%	-0.1%	-0.1%	-0.1%	-0.1%	0.0%	0.0%
Private Consumption - vol.	-0.9%	-0.8%	-0.9%	-1.0%	-1.2%	-1.4%	-1.0%	-1.2%	-1.4%
Supply to domestic - vol.	-0.1%	-0.1%	-0.1%	-0.1%	-0.2%	-0.2%	-0.1%	-0.2%	-0.2%
Intra-EU Trade - vol	0.4%	0.3%	0.4%	0.1%	0.1%	0.1%	0.1%	0.1%	0.1%

Table B1.4.
The full *antimonde* scenario: sectoral results for EUR-11 (prices)

% change from *monde*

Agriculture	Constraint Case			Flexible Case			Efficiency Case		
	1988	1991	1994	1988	1991	1994	1988	1991	1994
Real Marginal Costs	0.33%	1.06%	1.32%	0.72%	0.72%	0.85%	0.71%	0.69%	0.80%
Real Cost of Labour	-0.17%	0.50%	0.37%	-0.74%	-0.94%	-1.50%	-0.76%	-1.04%	-1.68%
Real Deflator of Absorption	0.47%	1.03%	1.23%	1.53%	1.38%	1.36%	1.51%	1.30%	1.21%
Real Price of Exports-RW	-0.28%	0.42%	0.81%	0.61%	0.60%	0.73%	0.60%	0.57%	0.68%

Energy	Constraint Case			Flexible Case			Efficiency Case		
	1988	1991	1994	1988	1991	1994	1988	1991	1994
Marginal Costs	0.38%	0.93%	1.15%	1.36%	1.13%	1.10%	1.34%	1.03%	0.93%
Cost of Labour	-0.05%	0.48%	0.30%	-0.81%	-1.15%	-1.48%	-0.83%	-1.23%	-1.63%
Deflator of Absorption	0.48%	0.84%	0.98%	2.50%	2.04%	1.83%	2.46%	1.88%	1.54%
Price of Exports-RW	0.23%	0.80%	1.04%	1.45%	1.16%	1.12%	1.42%	1.05%	0.94%

Metal Industries	Constraint Case			Flexible Case			Efficiency Case		
	1988	1991	1994	1988	1991	1994	1988	1991	1994
Marginal Costs	0.98%	1.50%	1.68%	1.90%	1.81%	1.64%	1.89%	1.77%	1.57%
Cost of Labour	-1.12%	-0.83%	-1.03%	-2.06%	-4.87%	-5.14%	-2.08%	-4.96%	-5.31%
Deflator of Absorption	1.41%	1.80%	1.92%	3.02%	2.87%	2.62%	3.00%	2.78%	2.45%
Price of Exports-RW	0.70%	1.24%	1.45%	1.78%	1.65%	1.52%	1.77%	1.61%	1.46%

Chemical	Constraint Case			Flexible Case			Efficiency Case		
	1988	1991	1994	1988	1991	1994	1988	1991	1994
Marginal Costs	0.60%	1.13%	1.30%	1.31%	1.14%	1.04%	1.30%	1.10%	0.98%
Cost of Labour	-0.51%	-0.20%	-0.40%	-0.95%	-1.85%	-2.24%	-0.98%	-1.97%	-2.46%
Deflator of Absorption	0.90%	1.29%	1.39%	2.47%	2.27%	2.08%	2.44%	2.19%	1.93%
Price of Exports-RW	0.25%	0.77%	0.96%	1.17%	0.92%	0.84%	1.16%	0.89%	0.79%

Other Intensive Industries	Constraint Case			Flexible Case			Efficiency Case		
	1988	1991	1994	1988	1991	1994	1988	1991	1994
Marginal Costs	0.48%	1.07%	1.19%	0.68%	0.52%	0.41%	0.68%	0.50%	0.37%
Cost of Labour	-0.24%	0.17%	-0.04%	-0.85%	-1.44%	-1.93%	-0.88%	-1.55%	-2.13%
Deflator of Absorption	0.66%	1.17%	1.27%	1.15%	0.96%	0.81%	1.14%	0.91%	0.73%
Price of Exports-RW	0.22%	0.90%	1.09%	0.72%	0.57%	0.47%	0.72%	0.54%	0.42%

Electrical goods	Constraint Case			Flexible Case			Efficiency Case		
	1988	1991	1994	1988	1991	1994	1988	1991	1994
Marginal Costs	0.55%	1.08%	1.17%	0.76%	0.61%	0.47%	0.75%	0.58%	0.42%
Cost of Labour	-0.71%	-0.41%	-0.61%	-1.07%	-2.19%	-2.69%	-1.09%	-2.31%	-2.90%
Deflator of Absorption	1.22%	1.59%	1.65%	2.29%	2.04%	1.77%	2.26%	1.94%	1.61%
Price of Exports-RW	0.15%	0.66%	0.79%	0.67%	0.51%	0.38%	0.66%	0.48%	0.34%

Transport equipment	Constraint Case			Flexible Case			Efficiency Case		
	1988	1991	1994	1988	1991	1994	1988	1991	1994
Marginal Costs	0.95%	1.47%	1.57%	1.21%	1.39%	1.22%	1.21%	1.37%	1.19%
Cost of Labour	-1.13%	-0.97%	-1.18%	-2.06%	-5.60%	-6.07%	-2.10%	-5.74%	-6.32%
Deflator of Absorption	1.98%	2.39%	2.48%	2.84%	3.09%	2.85%	2.82%	3.04%	2.74%
Price of Exports-RW	0.53%	1.03%	1.20%	1.12%	1.17%	1.00%	1.12%	1.16%	0.97%

Other Equipment	Constraint Case			Flexible Case			Efficiency Case		
	1988	1991	1994	1988	1991	1994	1988	1991	1994
Marginal Costs	0.59%	1.13%	1.22%	0.80%	0.62%	0.47%	0.79%	0.59%	0.42%
Cost of Labour	-0.25%	0.07%	-0.16%	-0.81%	-1.58%	-2.09%	-0.84%	-1.70%	-2.30%
Deflator of Absorption	1.05%	1.38%	1.43%	2.06%	1.81%	1.55%	2.06%	1.72%	1.39%
Price of Exports-RW	0.28%	0.79%	0.92%	0.78%	0.56%	0.43%	0.77%	0.53%	0.39%

Consumer goods	Constraint Case			Flexible Case			Efficiency Case		
	1988	1991	1994	1988	1991	1994	1988	1991	1994
Marginal Costs	0.50%	1.13%	1.31%	0.91%	0.77%	0.71%	0.91%	0.75%	0.67%
Cost of Labour	-0.15%	0.28%	0.07%	-0.58%	-0.81%	-1.37%	-0.61%	-0.92%	-1.56%
Deflator of Absorption	0.72%	1.21%	1.35%	1.67%	1.43%	1.27%	1.65%	1.36%	1.16%
Price of Exports-RW	-0.03%	0.62%	0.89%	0.87%	0.64%	0.60%	0.87%	0.62%	0.56%

Construction	Constraint Case			Flexible Case			Efficiency Case		
	1988	1991	1994	1988	1991	1994	1988	1991	1994
Marginal Costs	0.36%	0.99%	1.12%	0.48%	0.35%	0.28%	0.48%	0.33%	0.25%
Cost of Labour	-0.63%	-0.22%	-0.43%	-0.75%	-1.23%	-1.72%	-0.77%	-1.34%	-1.92%
Deflator of Absorption	0.36%	0.99%	1.12%	0.48%	0.35%	0.29%	0.48%	0.33%	0.25%
Price of Exports-RW	-0.23%	0.17%	0.32%	0.52%	0.05%	-0.02%	0.51%	0.03%	-0.05%

Telecommunications	Constraint Case			Flexible Case			Efficiency Case		
	1988	1991	1994	1988	1991	1994	1988	1991	1994
Marginal Costs	0.51%	1.38%	1.56%	-0.01%	-0.01%	0.07%	-0.01%	-0.02%	0.06%
Cost of Labour	-1.73%	-1.29%	-1.46%	-0.61%	-0.77%	-1.25%	-0.64%	-0.88%	-1.45%
Deflator of Absorption	1.22%	2.16%	2.30%	0.15%	-0.03%	0.01%	0.14%	-0.06%	-0.03%
Price of Exports-RW	0.91%	1.81%	1.97%	-0.15%	-0.29%	-0.21%	-0.16%	-0.30%	-0.23%

Transports	Constraint Case			Flexible Case			Efficiency Case		
	1988	1991	1994	1988	1991	1994	1988	1991	1994
Marginal Costs	0.16%	0.78%	0.92%	0.30%	0.13%	0.07%	0.29%	0.09%	0.00%
Cost of Labour	-0.35%	0.08%	-0.09%	-0.68%	-1.23%	-1.69%	-0.70%	-1.33%	-1.87%
Deflator of Absorption	0.51%	1.06%	1.18%	0.47%	0.27%	0.20%	0.46%	0.23%	0.12%
Price of Exports-RW	-0.01%	0.58%	0.74%	0.31%	0.10%	0.05%	0.31%	0.06%	-0.02%

Banks	Constraint Case			Flexible Case			Efficiency Case		
	1988	1991	1994	1988	1991	1994	1988	1991	1994
Marginal Costs	0.41%	1.23%	1.38%	0.02%	0.01%	0.10%	0.02%	0.00%	0.07%
Cost of Labour	-2.38%	-1.87%	-2.06%	-0.51%	-0.23%	-0.64%	-0.54%	-0.33%	-0.82%
Deflator of Absorption	0.71%	1.51%	1.65%	0.04%	-0.05%	0.02%	0.03%	-0.07%	-0.01%
Price of Exports-RW	0.47%	1.31%	1.47%	0.10%	0.04%	0.12%	0.10%	0.03%	0.09%

Services	Constraint Case			Flexible Case			Efficiency Case		
	1988	1991	1994	1988	1991	1994	1988	1991	1994
Marginal Costs	0.17%	0.88%	1.06%	0.12%	0.14%	0.25%	0.12%	0.12%	0.21%
Cost of Labour	-0.47%	0.00%	-0.17%	-0.68%	-1.09%	-1.59%	-0.71%	-1.20%	-1.78%
Deflator of Absorption	0.21%	0.90%	1.08%	0.14%	0.16%	0.26%	0.14%	0.13%	0.22%
Price of Exports-RW	-0.18%	0.55%	0.78%	0.04%	-0.05%	0.05%	0.03%	-0.08%	0.01%

Non market	Constraint Case			Flexible Case			Efficiency Case		
	1988	1991	1994	1988	1991	1994	1988	1991	1994
Marginal Costs	0.05%	0.57%	0.56%	0.04%	-0.27%	-0.51%	0.03%	-0.30%	-0.57%
Cost of Labour	-0.30%	0.13%	-0.04%	-0.57%	-1.07%	-1.53%	-0.60%	-1.18%	-1.72%
Deflator of Absorption	0.05%	0.57%	0.57%	0.05%	-0.26%	-0.50%	0.05%	-0.29%	-0.56%
Price of Exports-RW	0.23%	0.73%	0.74%	0.37%	0.13%	0.00%	0.36%	0.10%	-0.06%

Table B1.5.
Decomposition of effects: macroeconomic aggregates for EUR-11

Macroeconomic Aggregates (vol.) (% change from *monde*)	Border Controls			Border controls and x-ineff.			Market segmentation			Trade *antimonde*			Full *antimonde*		
	1988	1991	1994	1988	1991	1994	1988	1991	1994	1988	1991	1994	1988	1991	1994
GDP fact. pr.	-0.04%	-0.08%	-0.08%	-0.05%	-0.09%	-0.10%	-0.33%	-0.70%	-1.01%	-0.37%	-0.75%	-1.07%	-0.46%	-0.90%	-1.26%
Priv. Consumption	0.15%	0.14%	0.14%	0.15%	0.14%	0.14%	-1.09%	-1.23%	-1.43%	-1.07%	-1.23%	-1.44%	-1.11%	-1.30%	-1.53%
Absorption	0.02%	-0.01%	-0.01%	0.02%	0.00%	-0.01%	-1.23%	-1.45%	-1.67%	-1.28%	-1.53%	-1.75%	-1.31%	-1.58%	-1.82%
Total Investment	0.03%	0.03%	0.03%	0.03%	0.03%	0.04%	-4.24%	-4.39%	-4.52%	-4.23%	-4.38%	-4.51%	-4.24%	-4.39%	-4.52%
Total Exports to RW	-0.53%	-0.61%	-0.61%	-0.54%	-0.62%	-0.63%	1.92%	1.63%	1.45%	1.62%	1.33%	1.15%	1.56%	1.24%	1.03%
Total Imports from RW	1.22%	1.39%	1.40%	1.23%	1.41%	1.43%	-4.72%	-4.45%	-4.24%	-3.61%	-3.25%	-3.03%	-3.47%	-3.04%	-2.75%
Total Intra-EU Trade	-1.01%	-2.59%	-2.59%	-1.02%	-2.61%	-2.61%	-0.54%	-3.46%	-3.62%	-1.17%	-4.26%	-4.42%	-1.29%	-4.42%	-4.63%
Employment (diff. from *monde*, 10³ persons)	-3	-7	-6	-10	-20	-19	-243	-385	-563	-257	-406	-585	-270	-431	-610
Disposable Income (deflated)	0.16%	0.16%	0.16%	0.16%	0.16%	0.15%	-1.16%	-1.29%	-1.50%	-1.12%	-1.29%	-1.50%	-1.17%	-1.36%	-1.59%

Macroeconomic Ratios (abs. diff. from *monde*)	Border Controls			Border controls and x-ineff.			Market segmentation			Trade *antimonde*			Full *antimonde*		
	1988	1991	1994	1988	1991	1994	1988	1991	1994	1988	1991	1994	1988	1991	1994
Current Account as % of GDP	-0.24%	-0.27%	-0.27%	-0.24%	-0.28%	-0.28%	1.15%	1.12%	1.09%	0.85%	0.79%	0.76%	0.81%	0.73%	0.68%
Public Deficit as % of GDP	0.06%	0.06%	0.06%	0.06%	0.05%	0.05%	-0.31%	-0.39%	-0.49%	-0.28%	-0.38%	-0.48%	-0.31%	-0.42%	-0.54%
Labour Productivity	-0.04%	-0.07%	-0.08%	-0.04%	-0.08%	-0.09%	-0.14%	-0.39%	-0.56%	-0.16%	-0.43%	-0.60%	-0.25%	-0.55%	-0.77%
Investment/GDP	0.02%	0.03%	0.03%	0.03%	0.04%	0.04%	-1.81%	-1.80%	-1.79%	-1.80%	-1.78%	-1.78%	-1.78%	-1.76%	-1.74%
Priv.Cons./GDP	0.12%	0.14%	0.14%	0.12%	0.14%	0.14%	-0.46%	-0.32%	-0.26%	-0.42%	-0.29%	-0.23%	-0.39%	-0.24%	-0.16%

Deflators (% change from *monde*)	Border Controls			Border controls and x-ineff.			Market segmentation			Trade *antimonde*			Full *antimonde*		
	1988	1991	1994	1988	1991	1994	1988	1991	1994	1988	1991	1994	1988	1991	1994
Consumer Price Index	-0.23%	-0.25%	-0.26%	-0.23%	-0.26%	-0.27%	0.96%	0.83%	0.81%	0.92%	0.81%	0.79%	0.90%	0.77%	0.74%
Real Wage Rate	-0.05%	-0.08%	-0.08%	-0.07%	-0.11%	-0.12%	-0.46%	-0.90%	-1.33%	-0.53%	-1.02%	-1.46%	-0.63%	-1.18%	-1.67%
Marginal Costs	-0.15%	-0.17%	-0.18%	-0.15%	-0.17%	-0.18%	0.60%	0.48%	0.45%	0.57%	0.47%	0.44%	0.56%	0.45%	0.41%
Producer Prices	-0.15%	-0.16%	-0.16%	-0.15%	-0.17%	-0.17%	0.67%	0.59%	0.56%	0.65%	0.58%	0.55%	0.63%	0.56%	0.52%
Shadow Price of Capital	0.04%	-0.02%	-0.04%	0.05%	0.00%	-0.02%	-0.09%	0.53%	1.02%	-0.04%	0.60%	1.10%	-0.10%	0.53%	0.99%
Terms-of-Trade RW	2.04%	2.31%	2.33%	2.06%	2.34%	2.37%	-6.42%	-5.48%	-4.90%	-5.31%	-4.33%	-3.74%	-5.12%	-4.05%	-3.36%

Real Exchange Rate	Border Controls			Border controls and x-ineff.			Market segmentation			Trade *antimonde*			Full *antimonde*		
	1988	1991	1994	1988	1991	1994	1988	1991	1994	1988	1991	1994	1988	1991	1994
Real Exchange Rate	3.99%	4.30%	4.32%	4.01%	4.34%	4.37%	-7.15%	-6.01%	-5.36%	-4.40%	-3.24%	-2.56%	-4.20%	-2.94%	-2.16%

Trade Regime	Integration			Integration			Segmentation			Segmentation			Segmentation		
Cumul. GDP in bill. ECU	-1	-7	-15	-1	-9	-17	-10	-61	-143	-11	-67	-153	-14	-81	-183
Cumul. Intra-EU trade in bill. ECU	-5	-39	-81	-5	-39	-82	-3	-43	-102	-6	-58	-130	-7	-61	-136

Table B1.6.
Decomposition of effects: effects on IC sectors for EUR-11

% change from *monde*

Metal Industries

	Border Controls			Border controls and x-ineff.			Market segmentation			Trade *antimonde*			Full *antimonde*		
	1988	1991	1994	1988	1991	1994	1988	1991	1994	1988	1991	1994	1988	1991	1994
Production per firm	-0.85%	-1.80%	-1.80%	-0.85%	-1.80%	-1.81%	-5.75%	-10.05%	-10.20%	-6.50%	-10.92%	-11.07%	-6.61%	-11.07%	-11.27%
Marginal Costs	3.56%	3.84%	3.86%	3.58%	3.88%	3.91%	-5.18%	-4.18%	-3.69%	-2.50%	-1.43%	-0.91%	-2.30%	-1.14%	-0.52%
Producer Prices	3.62%	3.98%	3.99%	3.65%	4.01%	4.04%	-4.83%	-3.59%	-3.08%	-2.09%	-0.74%	-0.22%	-1.88%	-0.44%	0.19%
Mark-ups domestic (abs. diff.)	0.05%	0.08%	0.08%	0.05%	0.08%	0.08%	0.66%	0.81%	0.83%	0.71%	0.87%	0.88%	0.72%	0.88%	0.90%
Fixed Costs per firm	3.55%	3.83%	3.84%	3.57%	3.85%	3.88%	-5.06%	-4.12%	-3.65%	-2.37%	-1.35%	-0.85%	-2.21%	-1.11%	-0.54%
Number of Firms	-0.01%	0.56%	0.56%	-0.01%	0.57%	0.56%	8.69%	12.17%	11.88%	8.17%	11.55%	11.26%	8.09%	11.45%	11.13%
Sigma of Love of Variety	0.00%	0.00%	0.00%	0.00%	0.00%	0.00%	0.00%	0.00%	0.00%	0.00%	0.00%	0.00%	0.00%	0.00%	0.00%

Chemical

	Border Controls			Border controls and x-ineff.			Market segmentation			Trade *antimonde*			Full *antimonde*		
	1988	1991	1994	1988	1991	1994	1988	1991	1994	1988	1991	1994	1988	1991	1994
Production per firm	-0.65%	-1.68%	-1.69%	-0.66%	-1.70%	-1.71%	-4.81%	-8.23%	-8.43%	-5.00%	-8.53%	-8.73%	-5.09%	-8.66%	-8.91%
Marginal Costs	3.79%	4.08%	4.10%	3.82%	4.12%	4.15%	-5.86%	-4.94%	-4.37%	-3.08%	-2.09%	-1.50%	-2.89%	-1.81%	-1.12%
Producer Prices	3.82%	4.15%	4.17%	3.84%	4.18%	4.22%	-5.69%	-4.63%	-4.06%	-2.89%	-1.77%	-1.17%	-2.70%	-1.48%	-0.79%
Mark-ups domestic (abs. diff.)	0.00%	0.03%	0.03%	0.00%	0.03%	0.03%	0.37%	0.50%	0.51%	0.36%	0.49%	0.50%	0.36%	0.50%	0.51%
Fixed Costs per firm	3.74%	4.03%	4.04%	3.76%	4.05%	4.08%	-5.46%	-4.65%	-4.19%	-2.67%	-1.79%	-1.31%	-2.53%	-1.58%	-1.03%
Number of Firms	0.62%	1.34%	1.34%	0.62%	1.34%	1.33%	7.84%	10.97%	10.69%	8.13%	11.19%	10.91%	8.07%	11.09%	10.78%
Sigma of Love of Variety	0.00%	0.00%	0.00%	0.00%	0.00%	0.00%	0.00%	0.00%	0.00%	0.00%	0.00%	0.00%	0.00%	0.00%	0.00%

Other Intensive Industries

	Border Controls			Border controls and x-ineff.			Market segmentation			Trade *antimonde*			Full *antimonde*		
	1988	1991	1994	1988	1991	1994	1988	1991	1994	1988	1991	1994	1988	1991	1994
Production per firm	-0.53%	-1.29%	-1.30%	-0.53%	-1.30%	-1.30%	-3.27%	-5.47%	-5.63%	-3.58%	-5.85%	-6.01%	-3.64%	-5.94%	-6.12%
Marginal Costs	3.80%	4.10%	4.11%	3.83%	4.13%	4.16%	-6.42%	-5.47%	-4.92%	-3.71%	-2.71%	-2.13%	-3.51%	-2.42%	-1.75%
Producer Prices	3.81%	4.12%	4.14%	3.84%	4.15%	4.18%	-6.36%	-5.36%	-4.81%	-3.63%	-2.59%	-2.02%	-3.44%	-2.31%	-1.64%
Mark-ups domestic (abs. diff.)	0.00%	0.01%	0.01%	0.00%	0.01%	0.01%	0.08%	0.12%	0.12%	0.09%	0.12%	0.13%	0.09%	0.12%	0.13%
Fixed Costs per firm	3.78%	3.98%	4.00%	3.79%	4.00%	4.02%	-6.22%	-5.52%	-5.09%	-3.43%	-2.71%	-2.26%	-3.30%	-2.51%	-1.99%
Number of Firms	0.25%	0.68%	0.68%	0.25%	0.69%	0.69%	1.40%	2.63%	2.51%	1.39%	2.61%	2.49%	1.38%	2.60%	2.47%
Sigma of Love of Variety	0.00%	0.00%	0.00%	0.00%	0.00%	0.00%	0.00%	0.00%	0.00%	0.00%	0.00%	0.00%	0.00%	0.00%	0.00%

Electrical goods

	Border Controls			Border controls and x-ineff.			Market segmentation			Trade *antimonde*			Full *antimonde*		
	1988	1991	1994	1988	1991	1994	1988	1991	1994	1988	1991	1994	1988	1991	1994
Production per firm	-0.98%	-2.21%	-2.22%	-0.99%	-2.23%	-2.24%	-6.33%	-10.07%	-10.24%	-7.00%	-10.89%	-11.06%	-7.11%	-11.05%	-11.28%
Marginal Costs	3.82%	4.12%	4.14%	3.85%	4.15%	4.18%	-6.36%	-5.40%	-4.88%	-3.63%	-2.61%	-2.07%	-3.44%	-2.33%	-1.70%
Producer Prices	3.87%	4.22%	4.23%	3.89%	4.25%	4.28%	-6.16%	-5.08%	-4.55%	-3.39%	-2.25%	-1.71%	-3.20%	-1.97%	-1.32%
Mark-ups domestic (abs. diff.)	0.03%	0.06%	0.06%	0.03%	0.06%	0.06%	0.50%	0.55%	0.56%	0.51%	0.57%	0.57%	0.51%	0.57%	0.58%
Fixed Costs per firm	3.84%	4.10%	4.11%	3.86%	4.12%	4.14%	-6.06%	-5.29%	-4.86%	-3.24%	-2.43%	-1.98%	-3.10%	-2.22%	-1.70%
Number of Firms	0.28%	1.01%	1.00%	0.28%	1.02%	1.00%	4.47%	6.90%	6.72%	4.34%	6.72%	6.53%	4.27%	6.62%	6.40%
Sigma of Love of Variety	0.00%	0.00%	0.00%	0.00%	0.00%	0.00%	0.00%	0.00%	0.00%	0.00%	0.00%	0.00%	0.00%	0.00%	0.00%

Transport equipment

	Border Controls			Border controls and x-ineff.			Market segmentation			Trade *antimonde*			Full *antimonde*		
	1988	1991	1994	1988	1991	1994	1988	1991	1994	1988	1991	1994	1988	1991	1994
Production per firm	-0.67%	-1.65%	-1.65%	-0.68%	-1.66%	-1.67%	-9.33%	-14.01%	-14.07%	-9.67%	-14.47%	-14.53%	-9.76%	-14.59%	-14.68%
Marginal Costs	3.84%	4.17%	4.19%	3.86%	4.21%	4.24%	-5.96%	-4.71%	-4.22%	-3.18%	-1.85%	-1.34%	-2.98%	-1.55%	-0.95%
Producer Prices	3.88%	4.28%	4.30%	3.91%	4.32%	4.35%	-5.36%	-3.81%	-3.32%	-2.54%	-0.90%	-0.38%	-2.34%	-0.59%	0.02%
Mark-ups domestic (abs. diff.)	0.00%	0.06%	0.06%	0.00%	0.06%	0.06%	1.42%	1.67%	1.68%	1.40%	1.66%	1.67%	1.41%	1.67%	1.67%
Fixed Costs per firm	3.82%	4.12%	4.13%	3.83%	4.14%	4.17%	-5.68%	-4.72%	-4.29%	-2.86%	-1.82%	-1.38%	-2.71%	-1.60%	-1.08%
Number of Firms	0.76%	1.72%	1.70%	0.76%	1.73%	1.71%	8.78%	13.64%	13.70%	8.90%	13.72%	13.79%	8.86%	13.66%	13.73%
Sigma of Love of Variety	0.00%	0.00%	0.00%	0.00%	0.00%	0.00%	0.00%	0.00%	0.00%	0.00%	0.00%	0.00%	0.00%	0.00%	0.00%

Other Equipment

	Border Controls			Border controls and x-ineff.			Market segmentation			Trade *antimonde*			Full *antimonde*		
	1988	1991	1994	1988	1991	1994	1988	1991	1994	1988	1991	1994	1988	1991	1994
Production per firm	-0.86%	-1.69%	-1.70%	-0.87%	-1.71%	-1.71%	-7.48%	-11.06%	-11.20%	-8.23%	-11.94%	-12.09%	-8.32%	-12.07%	-12.26%
Marginal Costs	3.79%	4.09%	4.11%	3.81%	4.12%	4.15%	-6.30%	-5.37%	-4.86%	-3.59%	-2.60%	-2.07%	-3.40%	-2.32%	-1.69%
Producer Prices	3.81%	4.12%	4.14%	3.83%	4.15%	4.18%	-6.18%	-5.19%	-4.67%	-3.45%	-2.40%	-1.86%	-3.25%	-2.12%	-1.48%
Mark-ups domestic (abs. diff.)	0.01%	0.03%	0.03%	0.01%	0.03%	0.03%	0.32%	0.41%	0.41%	0.33%	0.41%	0.42%	0.33%	0.42%	0.42%
Fixed Costs per firm	3.78%	4.03%	4.05%	3.80%	4.05%	4.08%	-5.86%	-5.11%	-4.69%	-3.05%	-2.24%	-1.80%	-2.91%	-2.04%	-1.52%
Number of Firms	0.09%	0.76%	0.76%	0.09%	0.77%	0.76%	5.20%	7.12%	6.88%	4.86%	6.74%	6.49%	4.80%	6.64%	6.37%
Sigma of Love of Variety	0.00%	0.00%	0.00%	0.00%	0.00%	0.00%	0.00%	0.00%	0.00%	0.00%	0.00%	0.00%	0.00%	0.00%	0.00%

Telecommunications

	Border Controls			Border controls and x-ineff.			Market segmentation			Trade *antimonde*			Full *antimonde*		
	1988	1991	1994	1988	1991	1994	1988	1991	1994	1988	1991	1994	1988	1991	1994
Production per firm	0.05%	0.07%	0.07%	-0.58%	-1.25%	-1.25%	-1.36%	-2.87%	-3.19%	-1.32%	-2.84%	-3.15%	-1.97%	-4.09%	-4.44%
Marginal Costs	4.00%	4.31%	4.34%	4.03%	4.35%	4.39%	-7.15%	-6.02%	-5.28%	-4.40%	-3.24%	-2.48%	-4.20%	-2.95%	-2.09%
Producer Prices	3.97%	4.27%	4.30%	3.81%	3.95%	3.99%	-6.90%	-5.53%	-4.81%	-4.16%	-2.76%	-2.01%	-4.14%	-2.82%	-1.98%
Mark-ups domestic (abs. diff.)	-0.03%	-0.04%	-0.04%	-0.27%	-0.52%	-0.53%	0.22%	0.25%	0.22%	0.20%	0.23%	0.20%	-0.05%	-0.27%	-0.30%
Fixed Costs per firm	3.90%	4.17%	4.19%	2.42%	1.22%	1.24%	-7.25%	-6.49%	-6.15%	-4.56%	-3.80%	-3.44%	-5.80%	-6.35%	-5.95%
Number of Firms	0.10%	0.17%	0.17%	0.78%	1.58%	1.59%	1.28%	2.84%	2.90%	1.34%	2.91%	2.97%	2.02%	4.28%	4.36%
Sigma of Love of Variety	0.00%	0.00%	0.00%	0.00%	0.00%	0.00%	0.00%	0.00%	0.00%	0.00%	0.00%	0.00%	0.00%	0.00%	0.00%

Banks

	Border Controls			Border controls and x-ineff.			Market segmentation			Trade *antimonde*			Full *antimonde*		
	1988	1991	1994	1988	1991	1994	1988	1991	1994	1988	1991	1994	1988	1991	1994
Production per firm	0.09%	0.17%	0.17%	-0.34%	-0.69%	-0.70%	-0.78%	-1.30%	-1.59%	-0.70%	-1.20%	-1.50%	-1.17%	-2.11%	-2.42%
Marginal Costs	4.00%	4.30%	4.31%	4.02%	4.33%	4.36%	-7.12%	-5.99%	-5.25%	-4.37%	-3.22%	-2.44%	-4.18%	-2.93%	-2.07%
Producer Prices	3.98%	4.27%	4.29%	3.95%	4.21%	4.24%	-7.05%	-5.88%	-5.13%	-4.30%	-3.11%	-2.34%	-4.16%	-2.92%	-2.05%
Mark-ups domestic (abs. diff.)	-0.01%	-0.02%	-0.02%	-0.07%	-0.14%	-0.14%	0.05%	0.05%	0.05%	0.04%	0.04%	0.04%	-0.02%	-0.08%	-0.08%
Fixed Costs per firm	3.94%	4.19%	4.21%	3.04%	2.39%	2.41%	-7.31%	-6.55%	-6.13%	-4.58%	-3.83%	-3.38%	-5.28%	-5.31%	-4.80%
Number of Firms	0.20%	0.37%	0.37%	0.64%	1.30%	1.31%	0.97%	2.30%	2.44%	1.08%	2.45%	2.58%	1.52%	3.33%	3.47%
Sigma of Love of Variety	0.00%	0.00%	0.00%	0.00%	0.00%	0.00%	0.00%	0.00%	0.00%	0.00%	0.00%	0.00%	0.00%	0.00%	0.00%

Table B1.7.
Decomposition of effects: sectoral results for EUR-11 (volumes)

% change from *monde*

Agriculture

	Border Controls			Border controls and x-ineff.			Market segmentation			Trade *antimonde*			Full *antimonde*		
	1988	1991	1994	1988	1991	1994	1988	1991	1994	1988	1991	1994	1988	1991	1994
Domestic Production - vol.	-0.9%	-1.1%	-1.1%	-0.9%	-1.1%	-1.1%	3.2%	2.5%	1.8%	2.6%	1.7%	1.1%	2.5%	1.5%	0.9%
Imports - vol.	1.9%	2.1%	2.1%	1.9%	2.1%	2.1%	-4.9%	-4.2%	-3.8%	-3.4%	-2.7%	-2.2%	-3.3%	-2.5%	-1.9%
Exports - vol.	-0.7%	-0.8%	-0.8%	-0.7%	-0.8%	-0.8%	2.0%	1.7%	1.4%	1.6%	1.2%	0.9%	1.5%	1.1%	0.8%
Absorption - vol.	-0.2%	-0.4%	-0.3%	-0.2%	-0.4%	-0.4%	1.1%	0.7%	0.3%	0.9%	0.5%	0.1%	0.9%	0.4%	0.0%
Investment - vol.	-0.4%	-0.5%	-0.5%	-0.4%	-0.5%	-0.5%	-2.8%	-3.2%	-3.4%	-3.1%	-3.5%	-3.8%	-3.1%	-3.6%	-3.9%
Labour Demand - vol.	-0.8%	-0.9%	-0.9%	-0.8%	-0.9%	-0.9%	3.4%	2.4%	2.2%	2.8%	1.8%	1.5%	2.7%	1.7%	1.4%
Private Consumption - vol.	0.1%	0.1%	0.1%	0.1%	0.1%	0.1%	-0.8%	-1.1%	-1.4%	-0.8%	-1.1%	-1.4%	-0.8%	-1.2%	-1.4%
Supply to domestic - vol.	-0.6%	-0.3%	-0.3%	-0.6%	-0.4%	-0.4%	3.2%	2.8%	2.2%	2.8%	2.3%	1.7%	2.6%	2.1%	1.5%
Intra-EU Trade - vol	-1.9%	-3.9%	-3.9%	-1.9%	-4.0%	-4.0%	1.5%	-0.3%	-0.7%	0.0%	-2.0%	-2.4%	-0.1%	-2.2%	-2.6%

Energy

	Border Controls			Border controls and x-ineff.			Market segmentation			Trade *antimonde*			Full *antimonde*		
	1988	1991	1994	1988	1991	1994	1988	1991	1994	1988	1991	1994	1988	1991	1994
Domestic Production - vol.	-0.3%	-0.4%	-0.4%	-0.3%	-0.4%	-0.4%	1.6%	1.1%	0.7%	1.4%	0.9%	0.5%	1.3%	0.8%	0.3%
Imports - vol.	0.7%	0.8%	0.8%	0.7%	0.8%	0.8%	-1.5%	-1.4%	-1.3%	-1.1%	-1.0%	-0.9%	-1.1%	-1.0%	-0.9%
Exports - vol.	-0.3%	-0.3%	-0.3%	-0.3%	-0.4%	-0.4%	0.9%	0.7%	0.6%	0.7%	0.5%	0.4%	0.6%	0.5%	0.4%
Absorption - vol.	0.0%	0.0%	0.0%	0.0%	0.0%	0.0%	0.4%	0.1%	-0.2%	0.3%	0.0%	-0.2%	0.3%	-0.1%	-0.4%
Investment - vol.	-0.2%	-0.2%	-0.2%	-0.2%	-0.2%	-0.2%	-3.3%	-3.6%	-3.8%	-3.4%	-3.7%	-3.9%	-3.5%	-3.7%	-3.9%
Labour Demand - vol.	-0.5%	-0.8%	-0.8%	-0.5%	-0.8%	-0.8%	2.0%	1.5%	1.0%	1.7%	1.1%	0.6%	1.7%	1.0%	0.5%
Private Consumption - vol.	0.1%	0.1%	0.2%	0.1%	0.1%	0.2%	-0.8%	-1.0%	-1.2%	-0.7%	-1.0%	-1.2%	-0.8%	-1.1%	-1.3%
Supply to domestic - vol.	-0.3%	-0.4%	-0.4%	-0.3%	-0.4%	-0.4%	1.4%	1.0%	0.6%	1.2%	0.8%	0.4%	1.1%	0.6%	0.2%
Intra-EU Trade - vol	-0.4%	-0.5%	-0.5%	-0.4%	-0.5%	-0.6%	1.3%	1.0%	0.7%	1.0%	0.6%	0.3%	1.0%	0.5%	0.2%

Metal Industries

	Border Controls			Border controls and x-ineff.			Market segmentation			Trade *antimonde*			Full *antimonde*		
	1988	1991	1994	1988	1991	1994	1988	1991	1994	1988	1991	1994	1988	1991	1994
Domestic Production - vol.	-0.7%	-1.0%	-1.0%	-0.7%	-1.0%	-1.0%	3.1%	2.6%	2.2%	1.9%	1.2%	0.8%	1.7%	1.0%	0.5%
Imports - vol.	1.1%	1.2%	1.2%	1.1%	1.2%	1.3%	-4.7%	-4.8%	-4.7%	-3.2%	-3.2%	-3.0%	-3.0%	-3.0%	-2.7%
Exports - vol.	-0.6%	-0.7%	-0.7%	-0.6%	-0.7%	-0.7%	1.7%	1.4%	1.3%	1.3%	1.0%	0.8%	1.2%	0.9%	0.7%
Absorption - vol.	-0.3%	-0.5%	-0.5%	-0.3%	-0.5%	-0.5%	0.8%	0.5%	0.2%	0.1%	-0.3%	-0.6%	0.0%	-0.4%	-0.7%
Investment - vol.	-0.4%	-0.6%	-0.6%	-0.4%	-0.6%	-0.6%	-2.5%	-2.9%	-3.1%	-3.1%	-3.5%	-3.8%	-3.1%	-3.6%	-3.9%
Labour Demand - vol.	-0.8%	-0.9%	-0.9%	-0.8%	-0.9%	-0.9%	5.2%	7.3%	6.7%	4.1%	6.0%	5.4%	4.0%	5.9%	5.2%
Private Consumption - vol.	0.1%	0.1%	0.1%	0.1%	0.1%	0.1%	-0.8%	-1.2%	-1.4%	-0.8%	-1.2%	-1.4%	-0.9%	-1.2%	-1.5%
Supply to domestic - vol.	-0.1%	0.9%	0.9%	-0.1%	0.9%	0.8%	4.2%	7.7%	7.1%	3.4%	6.8%	6.2%	3.3%	6.6%	5.9%
Intra-EU Trade - vol	-1.5%	-3.1%	-3.1%	-1.5%	-3.1%	-3.1%	0.1%	-5.0%	-5.0%	-1.7%	-6.9%	-6.9%	-1.8%	-7.1%	-7.2%

Chemical

	Border Controls			Border controls and x-ineff.			Market segmentation			Trade *antimonde*			Full *antimonde*		
	1988	1991	1994	1988	1991	1994	1988	1991	1994	1988	1991	1994	1988	1991	1994
Domestic Production - vol.	0.0%	-0.2%	-0.2%	0.0%	-0.2%	-0.2%	3.4%	2.8%	2.4%	3.6%	2.8%	2.3%	3.4%	2.6%	2.0%
Imports - vol.	1.0%	1.1%	1.2%	1.0%	1.2%	1.2%	-4.9%	-4.7%	-4.5%	-3.9%	-3.5%	-3.3%	-3.7%	-3.2%	-2.9%
Exports - vol.	-0.3%	-0.4%	-0.4%	-0.3%	-0.4%	-0.4%	1.9%	1.6%	1.4%	1.8%	1.5%	1.3%	1.7%	1.4%	1.2%
Absorption - vol.	-0.1%	-0.2%	-0.2%	-0.1%	-0.2%	-0.2%	1.2%	0.8%	0.5%	1.2%	0.7%	0.4%	1.1%	0.6%	0.2%
Investment - vol.	0.0%	-0.1%	-0.1%	0.0%	-0.1%	-0.1%	-2.5%	-2.8%	-3.0%	-2.5%	-2.8%	-3.0%	-2.5%	-2.9%	-3.1%
Labour Demand - vol.	0.1%	0.0%	0.0%	0.1%	0.0%	0.0%	4.2%	4.2%	3.8%	4.4%	4.3%	3.8%	4.3%	4.2%	3.7%
Private Consumption - vol.	0.1%	0.1%	0.1%	0.1%	0.1%	0.1%	-0.7%	-1.1%	-1.3%	-0.7%	-1.1%	-1.3%	-0.8%	-1.1%	-1.4%
Supply to domestic - vol.	0.8%	2.1%	2.1%	0.8%	2.1%	2.1%	4.5%	6.6%	6.1%	4.7%	6.8%	6.3%	4.6%	6.6%	6.1%
Intra-EU Trade - vol	-1.2%	-3.0%	-3.0%	-1.2%	-3.0%	-3.0%	0.4%	-2.9%	-3.1%	-0.2%	-3.8%	-4.0%	-0.3%	-4.0%	-4.2%

Other Intensive Industries

	Border Controls			Border controls and x-ineff.			Market segmentation			Trade *antimonde*			Full *antimonde*		
	1988	1991	1994	1988	1991	1994	1988	1991	1994	1988	1991	1994	1988	1991	1994
Domestic Production - vol.	-0.1%	-0.2%	-0.2%	-0.1%	-0.2%	-0.2%	-0.8%	-1.0%	-1.3%	-1.0%	-1.3%	-1.6%	-1.1%	-1.4%	-1.7%
Imports - vol.	1.8%	2.1%	2.1%	1.8%	2.1%	2.1%	-7.9%	-7.4%	-7.1%	-6.0%	-5.3%	-5.0%	-5.7%	-4.9%	-4.4%
Exports - vol.	-0.5%	-0.6%	-0.6%	-0.5%	-0.6%	-0.6%	2.0%	1.7%	1.5%	1.7%	1.4%	1.2%	1.7%	1.3%	1.1%
Absorption - vol.	0.0%	-0.1%	-0.1%	0.0%	0.0%	0.0%	-2.1%	-2.2%	-2.4%	-2.2%	-2.3%	-2.6%	-2.2%	-2.4%	-2.6%
Investment - vol.	-0.1%	-0.1%	-0.1%	-0.1%	-0.1%	-0.1%	-4.5%	-4.7%	-4.8%	-4.6%	-4.8%	-5.0%	-4.7%	-4.8%	-5.0%
Labour Demand - vol.	-0.1%	-0.1%	-0.1%	-0.1%	-0.1%	-0.1%	-0.4%	-0.4%	-0.6%	-0.5%	-0.6%	-0.8%	-0.5%	-0.6%	-0.8%
Private Consumption - vol.	0.2%	0.1%	0.1%	0.2%	0.1%	0.1%	-1.4%	-1.2%	-1.4%	-1.4%	-1.2%	-1.4%	-1.4%	-1.3%	-1.5%
Supply to domestic - vol.	0.2%	0.8%	0.8%	0.2%	0.8%	0.8%	-0.9%	-0.2%	-0.5%	-0.9%	-0.3%	-0.6%	-1.0%	-0.3%	-0.7%
Intra-EU Trade - vol	-1.6%	-3.9%	-3.9%	-1.6%	-3.9%	-3.9%	-1.6%	-4.9%	-5.0%	-2.7%	-6.1%	-6.3%	-2.8%	-6.3%	-6.4%

Electrical goods

	Border Controls			Border controls and x-ineff.			Market segmentation			Trade antimonde			Full antimonde		
	1988	1991	1994	1988	1991	1994	1988	1991	1994	1988	1991	1994	1988	1991	1994
Domestic Production - vol.	-0.5%	-0.8%	-0.8%	-0.5%	-0.8%	-0.8%	0.7%	0.4%	0.0%	0.1%	-0.4%	-0.8%	0.0%	-0.6%	-1.1%
Imports - vol.	1.5%	1.7%	1.7%	1.5%	1.7%	1.8%	-7.6%	-7.1%	-6.9%	-6.1%	-5.5%	-5.3%	-5.9%	-5.2%	-4.9%
Exports - vol.	-0.6%	-0.7%	-0.7%	-0.6%	-0.7%	-0.7%	2.4%	2.1%	1.9%	2.1%	1.7%	1.5%	2.0%	1.6%	1.4%
Absorption - vol.	0.0%	-0.1%	-0.1%	0.0%	-0.1%	-0.1%	-3.6%	-3.5%	-3.7%	-3.7%	-3.8%	-3.9%	-3.8%	-3.8%	-4.0%
Investment - vol.	-0.3%	-0.4%	-0.4%	-0.3%	-0.4%	-0.4%	-4.0%	-4.5%	-4.7%	-4.3%	-4.8%	-5.1%	-4.4%	-4.9%	-5.2%
Labour Demand - vol.	-0.5%	-0.7%	-0.7%	-0.5%	-0.7%	-0.7%	1.9%	2.7%	2.4%	1.4%	2.0%	1.7%	1.3%	1.8%	1.5%
Private Consumption - vol.	0.6%	0.3%	0.2%	0.6%	0.3%	0.2%	-4.0%	-2.2%	-2.1%	-3.8%	-2.2%	-2.1%	-3.9%	-2.4%	-2.3%
Supply to domestic - vol.	0.3%	1.5%	1.5%	0.3%	1.5%	1.5%	0.0%	2.7%	2.2%	-0.1%	2.5%	2.0%	-0.3%	2.3%	1.8%
Intra-EU Trade - vol	-1.6%	-3.6%	-3.6%	-1.6%	-3.6%	-3.6%	-0.5%	-4.2%	-4.3%	-1.9%	-5.9%	-6.0%	-2.1%	-6.1%	-6.3%

Transport equipment

	Border Controls			Border controls and x-ineff.			Market segmentation			Trade antimonde			Full antimonde		
	1988	1991	1994	1988	1991	1994	1988	1991	1994	1988	1991	1994	1988	1991	1994
Domestic Production - vol.	0.0%	-0.3%	-0.3%	0.0%	-0.3%	-0.3%	-1.1%	-2.2%	-2.3%	-1.3%	-2.5%	-2.6%	-1.5%	-2.7%	-2.9%
Imports - vol.	1.4%	1.6%	1.6%	1.4%	1.6%	1.6%	-7.9%	-8.3%	-8.1%	-6.1%	-6.3%	-6.1%	-5.9%	-6.0%	-5.7%
Exports - vol.	-0.6%	-0.7%	-0.7%	-0.6%	-0.7%	-0.7%	2.3%	2.0%	1.8%	2.0%	1.7%	1.5%	1.9%	1.5%	1.3%
Absorption - vol.	0.2%	0.0%	0.0%	0.2%	0.0%	0.0%	-4.6%	-5.4%	-5.4%	-4.6%	-5.5%	-5.5%	-4.6%	-5.6%	-5.5%
Investment - vol.	0.0%	-0.1%	-0.1%	0.0%	-0.1%	-0.1%	-4.4%	-4.6%	-4.7%	-4.5%	-4.7%	-4.9%	-4.5%	-4.8%	-4.9%
Labour Demand - vol.	0.2%	0.5%	0.5%	0.2%	0.5%	0.5%	1.9%	5.8%	5.7%	1.9%	5.7%	5.7%	1.8%	5.7%	5.6%
Private Consumption - vol.	0.5%	0.2%	0.1%	0.5%	0.2%	0.1%	-4.2%	-2.0%	-1.7%	-4.1%	-2.1%	-1.7%	-4.3%	-2.3%	-1.8%
Supply to domestic - vol.	1.1%	2.4%	2.4%	1.1%	2.4%	2.4%	-1.3%	2.9%	2.8%	-1.1%	3.1%	3.0%	-1.2%	3.0%	2.9%
Intra-EU Trade - vol	-0.9%	-2.3%	-2.3%	-0.9%	-2.3%	-2.3%	-2.7%	-7.1%	-7.1%	-3.4%	-8.0%	-7.9%	-3.5%	-8.1%	-8.1%

Other Equipment

	Border Controls			Border controls and x-ineff.			Market segmentation			Trade antimonde			Full antimonde		
	1988	1991	1994	1988	1991	1994	1988	1991	1994	1988	1991	1994	1988	1991	1994
Domestic Production - vol.	-0.7%	-0.9%	-0.9%	-0.7%	-0.9%	-0.9%	-0.2%	-0.9%	-1.3%	-1.1%	-1.9%	-2.4%	-1.3%	-2.2%	-2.7%
Imports - vol.	1.4%	1.6%	1.6%	1.4%	1.6%	1.6%	-7.1%	-7.0%	-6.9%	-5.2%	-5.0%	-4.9%	-5.0%	-4.7%	-4.5%
Exports - vol.	-0.8%	-0.9%	-0.9%	-0.8%	-0.9%	-0.9%	2.3%	2.0%	1.8%	1.9%	1.5%	1.3%	1.8%	1.4%	1.2%
Absorption - vol.	-0.2%	-0.3%	-0.3%	-0.2%	-0.3%	-0.3%	-4.4%	-4.9%	-5.2%	-4.7%	-5.3%	-5.6%	-4.8%	-5.3%	-5.6%
Investment - vol.	-0.4%	-0.4%	-0.4%	-0.4%	-0.4%	-0.4%	-4.3%	-4.7%	-5.0%	-4.7%	-5.2%	-5.4%	-4.8%	-5.2%	-5.5%
Labour Demand - vol.	-0.8%	-1.0%	-1.0%	-0.8%	-1.0%	-1.0%	0.6%	0.5%	0.2%	-0.3%	-0.5%	-0.7%	-0.3%	-0.6%	-0.9%
Private Consumption - vol.	0.2%	0.2%	0.2%	0.2%	0.2%	0.2%	-1.4%	-1.6%	-1.8%	-1.4%	-1.6%	-1.9%	-1.5%	-1.7%	-2.0%
Supply to domestic - vol.	0.2%	1.5%	1.5%	0.2%	1.5%	1.5%	-1.6%	-0.4%	-0.9%	-2.0%	-0.7%	-1.2%	-2.1%	-0.8%	-1.4%
Intra-EU Trade - vol	-1.3%	-2.7%	-2.8%	-1.3%	-2.8%	-2.8%	-1.3%	-3.5%	-3.6%	-2.7%	-5.0%	-5.2%	-2.8%	-5.2%	-5.4%

Consumer goods

	Border Controls			Border controls and x-ineff.			Market segmentation			Trade antimonde			Full antimonde		
	1988	1991	1994	1988	1991	1994	1988	1991	1994	1988	1991	1994	1988	1991	1994
Domestic Production - vol.	-0.3%	-0.4%	-0.4%	-0.3%	-0.4%	-0.4%	1.7%	1.2%	0.8%	1.6%	1.0%	0.6%	1.5%	0.8%	0.4%
Imports - vol.	1.5%	1.8%	1.8%	1.5%	1.8%	1.8%	-5.4%	-4.9%	-4.5%	-4.4%	-3.7%	-3.4%	-4.2%	-3.5%	-3.0%
Exports - vol.	-0.7%	-0.8%	-0.8%	-0.7%	-0.8%	-0.8%	2.6%	2.2%	1.9%	2.2%	1.8%	1.6%	2.2%	1.7%	1.4%
Absorption - vol.	0.0%	0.0%	0.0%	0.0%	0.0%	0.0%	-0.4%	-0.6%	-0.9%	-0.4%	-0.7%	-0.9%	-0.4%	-0.7%	-1.0%
Investment - vol.	-0.2%	-0.3%	-0.3%	-0.2%	-0.3%	-0.3%	-3.4%	-3.7%	-3.9%	-3.5%	-3.8%	-4.1%	-3.5%	-3.9%	-4.1%
Labour Demand - vol.	-0.3%	-0.2%	-0.2%	-0.2%	-0.2%	-0.2%	1.9%	1.2%	1.0%	1.8%	1.0%	0.8%	1.7%	0.9%	0.7%
Private Consumption - vol.	0.1%	0.1%	0.1%	0.1%	0.1%	0.1%	-0.8%	-1.0%	-1.2%	-0.7%	-1.0%	-1.2%	-0.8%	-1.1%	-1.3%
Supply to domestic - vol.	0.2%	1.0%	1.0%	0.2%	0.9%	0.9%	1.5%	1.6%	1.2%	1.5%	1.6%	1.2%	1.4%	1.5%	1.0%
Intra-EU Trade - vol	-1.8%	-4.1%	-4.1%	-1.8%	-4.2%	-4.2%	0.0%	-2.0%	-2.2%	-0.7%	-2.9%	-3.1%	-0.8%	-3.0%	-3.3%

Construction

	Border Controls			Border controls and x-ineff.			Market segmentation			Trade antimonde			Full antimonde		
	1988	1991	1994	1988	1991	1994	1988	1991	1994	1988	1991	1994	1988	1991	1994
Domestic Production - vol.	0.1%	0.2%	0.2%	0.1%	0.2%	0.2%	-7.2%	-7.4%	-7.6%	-7.1%	-7.3%	-7.5%	-7.1%	-7.3%	-7.5%
Imports - vol.	0.1%	0.1%	0.1%	0.1%	0.1%	0.1%	-3.6%	-3.7%	-3.8%	-3.5%	-3.6%	-3.7%	-3.5%	-3.6%	-3.7%
Exports - vol.	-0.3%	-0.3%	-0.3%	-0.3%	-0.3%	-0.3%	0.7%	0.6%	0.5%	0.5%	0.4%	0.3%	0.5%	0.4%	0.3%
Absorption - vol.	0.1%	0.2%	0.2%	0.1%	0.2%	0.2%	-7.2%	-7.4%	-7.6%	-7.1%	-7.3%	-7.5%	-7.1%	-7.3%	-7.5%
Investment - vol.	0.1%	0.1%	0.1%	0.1%	0.2%	0.1%	-7.6%	-7.8%	-7.9%	-7.6%	-7.7%	-7.9%	-7.6%	-7.7%	-7.8%
Labour Demand - vol.	0.1%	0.2%	0.2%	0.2%	0.1%	0.2%	-7.0%	-7.1%	-7.2%	-6.9%	-7.0%	-7.1%	-6.8%	-6.9%	-7.0%
Private Consumption - vol.	0.1%	0.1%	0.1%	0.1%	0.1%	0.1%	-0.8%	-1.0%	-1.3%	-0.8%	-1.0%	-1.3%	-0.8%	-1.1%	-1.4%
Supply to domestic - vol.	0.1%	0.2%	0.2%	0.1%	0.2%	0.2%	-7.2%	-7.4%	-7.6%	-7.1%	-7.3%	-7.5%	-7.1%	-7.3%	-7.5%
Intra-EU Trade - vol	0.3%	0.4%	0.4%	0.4%	0.4%	0.4%	-3.5%	-3.6%	-3.7%	-3.2%	-3.3%	-3.4%	-3.2%	-3.3%	-3.4%

Telecommunications

	Border Controls			Border controls and x-ineff.			Market segmentation			Trade *antimonde*			Full *antimonde*		
	1988	1991	1994	1988	1991	1994	1988	1991	1994	1988	1991	1994	1988	1991	1994
Domestic Production - vol.	0.1%	0.2%	0.2%	0.2%	0.2%	0.2%	-0.2%	-0.6%	-0.9%	-0.1%	-0.6%	-0.8%	-0.1%	-0.5%	-0.8%
Imports - vol.	0.9%	1.1%	1.1%	0.8%	0.9%	1.0%	-6.2%	-6.0%	-5.7%	-5.8%	-5.6%	-5.3%	-5.7%	-5.5%	-5.1%
Exports - vol.	-0.2%	-0.3%	-0.3%	-0.2%	-0.2%	-0.3%	1.1%	1.0%	0.8%	1.1%	0.9%	0.8%	1.0%	0.9%	0.7%
Absorption - vol.	0.1%	0.1%	0.1%	0.1%	0.2%	0.2%	-0.5%	-0.7%	-0.9%	-0.4%	-0.7%	-0.9%	-0.4%	-0.6%	-0.9%
Investment - vol.	0.1%	0.1%	0.2%	0.1%	0.2%	0.2%	-4.3%	-4.5%	-4.6%	-4.3%	-4.5%	-4.6%	-4.2%	-4.4%	-4.5%
Labour Demand - vol.	0.1%	0.1%	0.1%	-0.3%	-0.6%	-0.6%	0.2%	0.0%	0.0%	0.3%	0.1%	0.0%	0.0%	-0.6%	-0.7%
Private Consumption - vol.	0.1%	0.1%	0.1%	0.1%	0.2%	0.2%	-0.8%	-1.2%	-1.5%	-0.8%	-1.2%	-1.5%	-0.8%	-1.2%	-1.5%
Supply to domestic - vol.	0.1%	0.1%	0.1%	0.1%	0.3%	0.3%	0.2%	1.0%	0.8%	0.3%	1.0%	0.8%	0.3%	1.1%	0.8%
Intra-EU Trade - vol	0.5%	0.4%	0.4%	0.2%	-0.7%	-0.7%	-7.2%	-18.1%	-18.2%	-6.9%	-17.9%	-18.0%	-7.0%	-18.0%	-18.1%

Transports

	Border Controls			Border controls and x-ineff.			Market segmentation			Trade *antimonde*			Full *antimonde*		
	1988	1991	1994	1988	1991	1994	1988	1991	1994	1988	1991	1994	1988	1991	1994
Domestic Production - vol.	0.4%	0.4%	0.4%	0.4%	0.5%	0.5%	-0.2%	-0.3%	-0.6%	0.2%	0.1%	-0.2%	0.2%	0.0%	-0.2%
Imports - vol.	0.1%	0.1%	0.1%	0.1%	0.1%	0.1%	0.0%	-0.1%	-0.2%	0.1%	0.0%	-0.1%	0.1%	0.0%	-0.1%
Exports - vol.	-0.1%	-0.2%	-0.2%	-0.1%	-0.2%	-0.2%	0.7%	0.6%	0.5%	0.7%	0.6%	0.5%	0.7%	0.5%	0.5%
Absorption - vol.	0.1%	0.1%	0.1%	0.1%	0.1%	0.1%	-0.5%	-0.7%	-0.9%	-0.5%	-0.7%	-0.9%	-0.5%	-0.7%	-1.0%
Investment - vol.	0.2%	0.2%	0.2%	0.2%	0.2%	0.2%	-4.3%	-4.4%	-4.5%	-4.1%	-4.2%	-4.3%	-4.1%	-4.2%	-4.3%
Labour Demand - vol.	0.2%	0.3%	0.3%	0.2%	0.3%	0.3%	0.1%	0.0%	-0.2%	0.3%	0.2%	0.0%	0.3%	0.3%	0.1%
Private Consumption - vol.	0.1%	0.2%	0.2%	0.1%	0.2%	0.2%	-0.9%	-1.3%	-1.6%	-0.9%	-1.3%	-1.6%	-0.9%	-1.4%	-1.7%
Supply to domestic - vol.	0.4%	0.4%	0.4%	0.4%	0.5%	0.5%	-0.2%	-0.3%	-0.6%	0.2%	0.1%	-0.2%	0.2%	0.0%	-0.2%
Intra-EU Trade - vol	1.1%	1.3%	1.3%	1.1%	1.3%	1.3%	0.0%	0.0%	-0.2%	1.1%	1.2%	1.1%	1.1%	1.2%	1.1%

Banks

	Border Controls			Border controls and x-ineff.			Market segmentation			Trade *antimonde*			Full *antimonde*		
	1988	1991	1994	1988	1991	1994	1988	1991	1994	1988	1991	1994	1988	1991	1994
Domestic Production - vol.	0.2%	0.3%	0.3%	0.2%	0.3%	0.3%	0.0%	0.0%	-0.3%	0.1%	0.1%	-0.1%	0.1%	0.1%	-0.2%
Imports - vol.	1.1%	1.4%	1.4%	1.1%	1.3%	1.4%	-6.6%	-6.0%	-5.6%	-5.9%	-5.3%	-4.9%	-5.7%	-4.9%	-4.4%
Exports - vol.	-0.2%	-0.3%	-0.3%	-0.2%	-0.3%	-0.3%	1.1%	0.9%	0.8%	1.0%	0.8%	0.7%	1.0%	0.8%	0.7%
Absorption - vol.	0.2%	0.3%	0.3%	0.2%	0.3%	0.3%	-0.1%	-0.1%	-0.3%	0.0%	0.0%	-0.2%	-0.1%	0.0%	-0.3%
Investment - vol.	0.1%	0.2%	0.2%	0.1%	0.2%	0.2%	-4.3%	-4.3%	-4.4%	-4.2%	-4.2%	-4.3%	-4.2%	-4.2%	-4.3%
Labour Demand - vol.	0.1%	0.2%	0.2%	0.0%	-0.1%	-0.1%	0.1%	-0.2%	-0.4%	0.2%	-0.1%	-0.2%	0.1%	-0.4%	-0.5%
Private Consumption - vol.	0.1%	0.2%	0.2%	0.1%	0.2%	0.2%	-1.0%	-1.4%	-1.8%	-0.9%	-1.4%	-1.8%	-1.0%	-1.5%	-1.9%
Supply to domestic - vol.	0.2%	0.3%	0.3%	0.2%	0.3%	0.3%	0.2%	0.6%	0.4%	0.2%	0.7%	0.5%	0.2%	0.7%	0.4%
Intra-EU Trade - vol	0.7%	0.6%	0.6%	0.6%	0.2%	0.2%	-5.3%	-12.3%	-12.6%	-4.7%	-11.6%	-11.8%	-4.7%	-11.7%	-12.0%

Services

	Border Controls			Border controls and x-ineff.			Market segmentation			Trade *antimonde*			Full *antimonde*		
	1988	1991	1994	1988	1991	1994	1988	1991	1994	1988	1991	1994	1988	1991	1994
Domestic Production - vol.	0.3%	0.3%	0.3%	0.3%	0.3%	0.3%	-0.8%	-1.0%	-1.3%	-0.6%	-0.8%	-1.1%	-0.7%	-0.8%	-1.1%
Imports - vol.	1.8%	2.0%	2.0%	1.8%	2.0%	2.0%	-4.9%	-4.4%	-4.1%	-3.5%	-3.0%	-2.7%	-3.4%	-2.8%	-2.4%
Exports - vol.	-0.6%	-0.6%	-0.6%	-0.6%	-0.6%	-0.6%	1.5%	1.2%	1.1%	1.1%	0.9%	0.7%	1.0%	0.8%	0.6%
Absorption - vol.	0.1%	0.1%	0.1%	0.2%	0.1%	0.1%	-1.0%	-1.2%	-1.5%	-1.0%	-1.2%	-1.5%	-1.0%	-1.3%	-1.5%
Investment - vol.	0.1%	0.2%	0.2%	0.1%	0.2%	0.2%	-4.6%	-4.7%	-4.8%	-4.5%	-4.6%	-4.7%	-4.5%	-4.6%	-4.7%
Labour Demand - vol.	0.3%	0.3%	0.3%	0.3%	0.4%	0.4%	-0.7%	-0.9%	-0.9%	-0.5%	-0.6%	-0.7%	-0.5%	-0.6%	-0.6%
Private Consumption - vol.	0.1%	0.1%	0.1%	0.1%	0.1%	0.1%	-1.0%	-1.3%	-1.5%	-1.0%	-1.3%	-1.5%	-1.0%	-1.4%	-1.6%
Supply to domestic - vol.	0.1%	0.1%	0.1%	0.1%	0.2%	0.1%	-1.0%	-1.2%	-1.5%	-1.0%	-1.2%	-1.5%	-1.0%	-1.3%	-1.6%
Intra-EU Trade - vol	2.3%	3.1%	3.1%	2.3%	3.1%	3.1%	-0.3%	0.1%	0.0%	1.9%	2.8%	2.8%	1.9%	2.8%	2.7%

Non market

	Border Controls			Border controls and x-ineff.			Market segmentation			Trade *antimonde*			Full *antimonde*		
	1988	1991	1994	1988	1991	1994	1988	1991	1994	1988	1991	1994	1988	1991	1994
Domestic Production - vol.	0.0%	0.0%	0.0%	0.0%	0.0%	0.0%	-0.1%	-0.2%	-0.2%	-0.1%	-0.2%	-0.2%	-0.1%	-0.2%	-0.2%
Imports - vol.	0.0%	0.0%	0.0%	0.0%	0.0%	0.0%	-0.1%	-0.2%	-0.2%	-0.1%	-0.2%	-0.2%	-0.1%	-0.2%	-0.2%
Exports - vol.	-0.1%	-0.2%	-0.2%	-0.1%	-0.2%	-0.2%	0.3%	0.3%	0.3%	0.3%	0.2%	0.2%	0.2%	0.2%	0.2%
Absorption - vol.	0.0%	0.0%	0.0%	0.0%	0.0%	0.0%	-0.1%	-0.2%	-0.2%	-0.1%	-0.2%	-0.2%	-0.1%	-0.2%	-0.2%
Investment - vol.	0.0%	0.0%	0.0%	0.0%	0.0%	0.0%	-4.1%	-4.2%	-4.2%	-4.1%	-4.2%	-4.2%	-4.1%	-4.1%	-4.1%
Labour Demand - vol.	0.0%	0.0%	0.0%	0.0%	0.0%	0.1%	-0.1%	-0.2%	-0.2%	-0.1%	-0.2%	-0.2%	-0.1%	-0.1%	-0.1%
Private Consumption - vol.	0.1%	0.2%	0.2%	0.1%	0.2%	0.2%	-0.9%	-1.1%	-1.3%	-0.9%	-1.1%	-1.3%	-1.0%	-1.2%	-1.4%
Supply to domestic - vol.	0.0%	0.0%	0.0%	0.0%	0.0%	0.0%	-0.1%	-0.2%	-0.2%	-0.1%	-0.2%	-0.2%	-0.1%	-0.2%	-0.2%
Intra-EU Trade - vol	0.3%	0.3%	0.3%	0.3%	0.3%	0.3%	-0.1%	0.1%	-0.2%	0.1%	0.1%	0.1%	0.1%	0.1%	0.1%

Table B1.8.
Decomposition of effects: sectoral results for EUR-11 (prices)

% change from monde

Agriculture

	Border Controls			Border controls and x-ineff.			Market segmentation			Trade antimonde			Full antimonde		
	1988	1991	1994	1988	1991	1994	1988	1991	1994	1988	1991	1994	1988	1991	1994
Marginal Costs	-0.18%	-0.20%	-0.20%	-0.17%	-0.19%	-0.19%	0.73%	0.71%	0.83%	0.72%	0.72%	0.85%	0.72%	0.72%	0.85%
Cost of Labour	0.02%	-0.14%	-0.15%	0.01%	-0.17%	-0.18%	-0.65%	-0.79%	-1.29%	-0.66%	-0.81%	-1.33%	-0.74%	-0.94%	-1.50%
Deflator of Absorption	-0.50%	-0.54%	-0.55%	-0.50%	-0.54%	-0.54%	1.70%	1.52%	1.52%	1.56%	1.42%	1.42%	1.53%	1.38%	1.36%
Price of Exports-RW	-0.13%	-0.15%	-0.16%	-0.12%	-0.14%	-0.14%	0.59%	0.54%	0.67%	0.61%	0.59%	0.73%	0.61%	0.60%	0.73%

Energy

	Border Controls			Border controls and x-ineff.			Market segmentation			Trade antimonde			Full antimonde		
	1988	1991	1994	1988	1991	1994	1988	1991	1994	1988	1991	1994	1988	1991	1994
Marginal Costs	-0.46%	-0.53%	-0.53%	-0.46%	-0.53%	-0.54%	1.59%	1.36%	1.36%	1.42%	1.20%	1.20%	1.36%	1.13%	1.10%
Cost of Labour	0.16%	0.33%	0.33%	0.15%	0.30%	0.30%	-0.74%	-1.08%	-1.36%	-0.72%	-1.02%	-1.31%	-0.81%	-1.15%	-1.48%
Deflator of Absorption	-0.92%	-1.02%	-1.03%	-0.92%	-1.03%	-1.05%	2.97%	2.52%	2.36%	2.59%	2.17%	2.00%	2.50%	2.04%	1.83%
Price of Exports-RW	-0.50%	-0.57%	-0.58%	-0.50%	-0.57%	-0.59%	1.70%	1.42%	1.42%	1.50%	1.23%	1.23%	1.45%	1.16%	1.12%

Metal Industries

	Border Controls			Border controls and x-ineff.			Market segmentation			Trade antimonde			Full antimonde		
	1988	1991	1994	1988	1991	1994	1988	1991	1994	1988	1991	1994	1988	1991	1994
Marginal Costs	-0.43%	-0.46%	-0.46%	-0.44%	-0.46%	-0.46%	1.97%	1.83%	1.67%	1.90%	1.81%	1.65%	1.90%	1.81%	1.64%
Cost of Labour	0.03%	-0.21%	-0.20%	0.02%	-0.23%	-0.22%	-1.76%	-4.36%	-4.57%	-1.95%	-4.70%	-4.91%	-2.06%	-4.87%	-5.14%
Deflator of Absorption	-0.65%	-0.67%	-0.68%	-0.66%	-0.68%	-0.69%	3.14%	2.91%	2.68%	3.05%	2.91%	2.68%	3.02%	2.87%	2.62%
Price of Exports-RW	-0.42%	-0.47%	-0.47%	-0.42%	-0.47%	-0.48%	1.80%	1.60%	1.48%	1.77%	1.64%	1.52%	1.78%	1.65%	1.52%

Chemical

	Border Controls			Border controls and x-ineff.			Market segmentation			Trade antimonde			Full antimonde		
	1988	1991	1994	1988	1991	1994	1988	1991	1994	1988	1991	1994	1988	1991	1994
Marginal Costs	-0.20%	-0.22%	-0.22%	-0.20%	-0.22%	-0.22%	1.28%	1.08%	0.99%	1.32%	1.15%	1.06%	1.31%	1.14%	1.04%
Cost of Labour	-0.04%	-0.10%	-0.09%	-0.06%	-0.13%	-0.13%	-0.77%	-1.56%	-1.88%	-0.85%	-1.69%	-2.03%	-0.95%	-1.85%	-2.24%
Deflator of Absorption	-0.19%	-0.19%	-0.19%	-0.20%	-0.20%	-0.20%	2.30%	2.04%	1.87%	2.50%	2.32%	2.15%	2.47%	2.27%	2.08%
Price of Exports-RW	-0.15%	-0.19%	-0.19%	-0.15%	-0.19%	-0.19%	1.09%	0.80%	0.73%	1.18%	0.93%	0.86%	1.17%	0.92%	0.84%

Other Intensive Industries

	Border Controls			Border controls and x-ineff.			Market segmentation			Trade antimonde			Full antimonde		
	1988	1991	1994	1988	1991	1994	1988	1991	1994	1988	1991	1994	1988	1991	1994
Marginal Costs	-0.19%	-0.21%	-0.21%	-0.19%	-0.21%	-0.21%	0.73%	0.55%	0.44%	0.69%	0.53%	0.43%	0.68%	0.52%	0.41%
Cost of Labour	-0.05%	-0.12%	-0.12%	-0.07%	-0.15%	-0.15%	-0.65%	-1.13%	-1.56%	-0.75%	-1.28%	-1.72%	-0.85%	-1.44%	-1.93%
Deflator of Absorption	-0.22%	-0.23%	-0.23%	-0.23%	-0.24%	-0.24%	1.16%	0.94%	0.81%	1.17%	0.99%	0.85%	1.15%	0.96%	0.81%
Price of Exports-RW	-0.17%	-0.19%	-0.19%	-0.17%	-0.19%	-0.19%	0.73%	0.55%	0.45%	0.73%	0.58%	0.48%	0.72%	0.57%	0.47%

Electrical goods

	Border Controls			Border controls and x-ineff.			Market segmentation			Trade *antimonde*			Full *antimonde*		
	1988	1991	1994	1988	1991	1994	1988	1991	1994	1988	1991	1994	1988	1991	1994
Marginal Costs	-0.17%	-0.18%	-0.18%	-0.17%	-0.18%	-0.18%	0.78%	0.62%	0.48%	0.77%	0.63%	0.49%	0.76%	0.61%	0.47%
Cost of Labour	-0.04%	-0.13%	-0.12%	-0.05%	-0.16%	-0.16%	-0.88%	-1.90%	-2.32%	-0.97%	-2.03%	-2.47%	-1.07%	-2.19%	-2.69%
Deflator of Absorption	-0.39%	-0.40%	-0.41%	-0.40%	-0.41%	-0.42%	2.31%	2.02%	1.79%	2.33%	2.10%	1.86%	2.29%	2.04%	1.77%
Price of Exports-RW	-0.13%	-0.19%	-0.19%	-0.14%	-0.19%	-0.19%	0.63%	0.44%	0.32%	0.68%	0.52%	0.39%	0.67%	0.51%	0.38%

Transport equipment

	Border Controls			Border controls and x-ineff.			Market segmentation			Trade *antimonde*			Full *antimonde*		
	1988	1991	1994	1988	1991	1994	1988	1991	1994	1988	1991	1994	1988	1991	1994
Marginal Costs	-0.15%	-0.13%	-0.13%	-0.15%	-0.13%	-0.13%	1.19%	1.30%	1.14%	1.21%	1.39%	1.22%	1.21%	1.39%	1.22%
Cost of Labour	-0.18%	-0.66%	-0.66%	-0.20%	-0.70%	-0.69%	-1.80%	-5.09%	-5.49%	-1.95%	-5.41%	-5.83%	-2.06%	-5.60%	-6.07%
Deflator of Absorption	-0.17%	-0.10%	-0.10%	-0.18%	-0.11%	-0.11%	2.67%	2.81%	2.59%	2.86%	3.12%	2.89%	2.84%	3.09%	2.85%
Price of Exports-RW	-0.16%	-0.19%	-0.19%	-0.16%	-0.20%	-0.20%	1.03%	1.01%	0.84%	1.11%	1.16%	0.99%	1.12%	1.17%	1.00%

Other Equipment

	Border Controls			Border controls and x-ineff.			Market segmentation			Trade *antimonde*			Full *antimonde*		
	1988	1991	1994	1988	1991	1994	1988	1991	1994	1988	1991	1994	1988	1991	1994
Marginal Costs	-0.20%	-0.21%	-0.21%	-0.20%	-0.22%	-0.22%	0.85%	0.64%	0.50%	0.81%	0.63%	0.49%	0.80%	0.62%	0.47%
Cost of Labour	0.00%	0.04%	0.05%	-0.02%	0.01%	0.01%	-0.63%	-1.31%	-1.75%	-0.71%	-1.42%	-1.87%	-0.81%	-1.58%	-2.09%
Deflator of Absorption	-0.43%	-0.43%	-0.43%	-0.43%	-0.44%	-0.44%	2.15%	1.82%	1.59%	2.13%	1.88%	1.64%	2.08%	1.81%	1.55%
Price of Exports-RW	-0.17%	-0.21%	-0.21%	-0.17%	-0.21%	-0.21%	0.77%	0.52%	0.40%	0.78%	0.56%	0.44%	0.78%	0.56%	0.43%

Consumer goods

	Border Controls			Border controls and x-ineff.			Market segmentation			Trade *antimonde*			Full *antimonde*		
	1988	1991	1994	1988	1991	1994	1988	1991	1994	1988	1991	1994	1988	1991	1994
Marginal Costs	-0.25%	-0.28%	-0.28%	-0.25%	-0.27%	-0.27%	0.95%	0.79%	0.73%	0.91%	0.77%	0.71%	0.91%	0.77%	0.71%
Cost of Labour	-0.09%	-0.21%	-0.22%	-0.11%	-0.25%	-0.26%	-0.42%	-0.56%	-1.06%	-0.48%	-0.66%	-1.18%	-0.58%	-0.81%	-1.37%
Deflator of Absorption	-0.37%	-0.40%	-0.40%	-0.37%	-0.40%	-0.40%	1.71%	1.43%	1.30%	1.69%	1.46%	1.32%	1.67%	1.43%	1.27%
Price of Exports-RW	-0.17%	-0.20%	-0.20%	-0.17%	-0.20%	-0.20%	0.84%	0.57%	0.52%	0.87%	0.64%	0.60%	0.87%	0.64%	0.60%

Construction

	Border Controls			Border controls and x-ineff.			Market segmentation			Trade *antimonde*			Full *antimonde*		
	1988	1991	1994	1988	1991	1994	1988	1991	1994	1988	1991	1994	1988	1991	1994
Marginal Costs	-0.13%	-0.15%	-0.15%	-0.13%	-0.15%	-0.15%	0.50%	0.35%	0.30%	0.48%	0.35%	0.29%	0.48%	0.35%	0.28%
Cost of Labour	-0.04%	-0.06%	-0.06%	-0.06%	-0.08%	-0.09%	-0.58%	-0.98%	-1.40%	-0.65%	-1.07%	-1.51%	-0.75%	-1.23%	-1.72%
Deflator of Absorption	-0.13%	-0.15%	-0.15%	-0.13%	-0.15%	-0.15%	0.50%	0.36%	0.30%	0.49%	0.35%	0.29%	0.48%	0.35%	0.29%
Price of Exports-RW	-0.06%	-0.14%	-0.14%	-0.06%	-0.14%	-0.14%	0.48%	0.03%	-0.03%	0.53%	0.07%	0.01%	0.52%	0.05%	-0.02%

Telecommunications

	Border Controls			Border controls and x-ineff.			Market segmentation			Trade antimonde			Full antimonde		
	1988	1991	1994	1988	1991	1994	1988	1991	1994	1988	1991	1994	1988	1991	1994
Marginal Costs	0.01%	0.01%	0.02%	0.01%	0.01%	0.02%	0.00%	-0.01%	0.08%	0.00%	0.00%	0.08%	-0.01%	-0.01%	0.07%
Cost of Labour	-0.02%	-0.01%	-0.01%	-0.06%	-0.07%	-0.08%	-0.43%	-0.49%	-0.91%	-0.49%	-0.56%	-1.00%	-0.61%	-0.77%	-1.25%
Deflator of Absorption	-0.04%	-0.06%	-0.05%	-0.23%	-0.44%	-0.43%	0.34%	0.35%	0.40%	0.33%	0.34%	0.39%	0.15%	-0.03%	0.01%
Price of Exports-RW	0.02%	0.03%	0.04%	-0.04%	-0.09%	-0.08%	-0.08%	-0.16%	-0.08%	-0.10%	-0.18%	-0.10%	-0.15%	-0.29%	-0.21%

Transports

	Border Controls			Border controls and x-ineff.			Market segmentation			Trade antimonde			Full antimonde		
	1988	1991	1994	1988	1991	1994	1988	1991	1994	1988	1991	1994	1988	1991	1994
Marginal Costs	-0.16%	-0.19%	-0.19%	-0.16%	-0.19%	-0.20%	0.39%	0.23%	0.19%	0.33%	0.16%	0.12%	0.30%	0.13%	0.07%
Cost of Labour	0.14%	0.13%	0.13%	0.12%	0.11%	0.10%	-0.67%	-1.16%	-1.56%	-0.59%	-1.08%	-1.50%	-0.68%	-1.23%	-1.69%
Deflator of Absorption	-0.19%	-0.23%	-0.23%	-0.19%	-0.23%	-0.23%	0.56%	0.37%	0.32%	0.49%	0.31%	0.26%	0.47%	0.27%	0.20%
Price of Exports-RW	-0.14%	-0.18%	-0.18%	-0.14%	-0.18%	-0.19%	0.39%	0.19%	0.15%	0.34%	0.13%	0.10%	0.31%	0.10%	0.05%

Banks

	Border Controls			Border controls and x-ineff.			Market segmentation			Trade antimonde			Full antimonde		
	1988	1991	1994	1988	1991	1994	1988	1991	1994	1988	1991	1994	1988	1991	1994
Marginal Costs	0.01%	0.00%	-0.01%	0.01%	0.00%	-0.01%	0.02%	0.02%	0.11%	0.03%	0.02%	0.12%	0.02%	0.01%	0.10%
Cost of Labour	0.07%	0.14%	0.14%	0.04%	0.12%	0.12%	-0.38%	-0.03%	-0.38%	-0.39%	-0.04%	-0.41%	-0.51%	-0.23%	-0.64%
Deflator of Absorption	-0.02%	-0.04%	-0.04%	-0.07%	-0.15%	-0.16%	0.10%	0.07%	0.15%	0.10%	0.06%	0.15%	0.04%	-0.05%	0.02%
Price of Exports-RW	0.01%	0.01%	0.01%	0.00%	-0.01%	-0.02%	0.11%	0.07%	0.16%	0.12%	0.07%	0.16%	0.10%	0.04%	0.12%

Services

	Border Controls			Border controls and x-ineff.			Market segmentation			Trade antimonde			Full antimonde		
	1988	1991	1994	1988	1991	1994	1988	1991	1994	1988	1991	1994	1988	1991	1994
Marginal Costs	-0.05%	-0.07%	-0.07%	-0.05%	-0.06%	-0.07%	0.14%	0.16%	0.27%	0.14%	0.16%	0.28%	0.12%	0.14%	0.25%
Cost of Labour	-0.01%	-0.02%	-0.02%	-0.03%	-0.05%	-0.05%	-0.54%	-0.86%	-1.30%	-0.59%	-0.94%	-1.39%	-0.68%	-1.09%	-1.59%
Deflator of Absorption	-0.06%	-0.09%	-0.09%	-0.06%	-0.08%	-0.08%	0.17%	0.18%	0.29%	0.16%	0.18%	0.29%	0.14%	0.16%	0.26%
Price of Exports-RW	-0.02%	-0.04%	-0.05%	-0.02%	-0.04%	-0.04%	0.04%	-0.05%	0.07%	0.05%	-0.04%	0.08%	0.04%	-0.05%	0.05%

Non market

	Border Controls			Border controls and x-ineff.			Market segmentation			Trade antimonde			Full antimonde		
	1988	1991	1994	1988	1991	1994	1988	1991	1994	1988	1991	1994	1988	1991	1994
Marginal Costs	-0.09%	-0.11%	-0.10%	-0.09%	-0.11%	-0.12%	0.11%	-0.18%	-0.40%	0.07%	-0.22%	-0.45%	0.04%	-0.27%	-0.51%
Cost of Labour	-0.05%	-0.08%	-0.08%	-0.07%	-0.11%	-0.11%	-0.41%	-0.83%	-1.23%	-0.48%	-0.93%	-1.34%	-0.57%	-1.07%	-1.53%
Deflator of Absorption	-0.09%	-0.11%	-0.11%	-0.10%	-0.12%	-0.12%	0.13%	-0.16%	-0.38%	0.08%	-0.21%	-0.44%	0.05%	-0.26%	-0.50%
Price of Exports-RW	-0.01%	0.03%	0.04%	-0.02%	0.03%	0.03%	0.41%	0.19%	0.08%	0.40%	0.18%	0.06%	0.37%	0.13%	0.00%

Table B2.1.
The full *antimonde* scenario: macroeconomic aggregates for Belgium

Macroeconomic Aggregates (vol.) (% change from *monde*)	Constraint Case			Flexible Case			Efficiency Case		
	1988	1991	1994	1988	1991	1994	1988	1991	1994
GDP fact. pr.	-1.61%	-1.99%	-2.44%	-1.39%	-2.52%	-2.86%	-1.42%	-2.64%	-3.07%
Priv. Consumption	-1.81%	-1.95%	-2.15%	-1.85%	-2.34%	-2.47%	-1.85%	-2.34%	-2.48%
Absorption	-2.42%	-2.61%	-2.87%	-2.85%	-5.64%	-5.72%	-2.86%	-5.66%	-5.75%
Total Investment	-9.38%	-9.87%	-10.61%	-4.46%	-4.76%	-4.89%	-4.46%	-4.76%	-4.90%
Total Exports to RW	-1.06%	-1.37%	-1.74%	1.40%	1.19%	0.99%	1.38%	1.09%	0.81%
Total Imports from RW	-2.20%	-2.28%	-2.43%	-3.85%	-5.07%	-4.70%	-3.80%	-4.90%	-4.40%
Total Intra-EU Trade	-2.31%	-2.36%	-2.50%	-1.76%	-5.59%	-5.70%	-1.77%	-5.65%	-5.80%
Employment (diff. from *monde*, 10³ persons)	-15	-20	-26	-15	-12	-17	-15	-12	-17
Disposable Income (deflated)	-1.87%	-2.02%	-2.22%	-1.92%	-2.42%	-2.56%	-1.92%	-2.42%	-2.57%

Macroeconomic Ratios (abs. diff. from *monde*)	Constraint Case			Flexible Case			Efficiency Case		
	1988	1991	1994	1988	1991	1994	1988	1991	1994
Current Account as % of GDP	0.00%	0.00%	0.00%	0.00%	0.53%	0.55%	0.01%	0.55%	0.59%
Public Deficit as % of GDP	-0.39%	-0.43%	-0.49%	-1.00%	-1.56%	-1.65%	-1.01%	-1.57%	-1.68%
Labour Productivity	-1.19%	-1.42%	-1.70%	-0.98%	-2.18%	-2.38%	-1.01%	-2.30%	-2.60%
Investment/GDP	-1.31%	-1.34%	-1.39%	-1.37%	-1.28%	-1.27%	-1.36%	-1.26%	-1.23%
Priv.Cons./GDP	-0.13%	0.03%	0.20%	-0.31%	0.13%	0.27%	-0.29%	0.21%	0.41%

Deflators (% change from *monde*)	Constraint Case			Flexible Case			Efficiency Case		
	1988	1991	1994	1988	1991	1994	1988	1991	1994
Consumer Price Index	-0.94%	-0.66%	-0.40%	1.33%	1.02%	0.91%	1.31%	0.92%	0.73%
Real Wage Rate	-1.49%	-1.95%	-2.49%	-1.28%	-2.11%	-2.54%	-1.31%	-2.22%	-2.74%
Marginal Costs	-1.02%	-0.73%	-0.46%	1.33%	1.70%	1.56%	1.31%	1.64%	1.44%
Producer Prices	-0.69%	-0.40%	-0.12%	1.57%	1.89%	1.76%	1.55%	1.83%	1.64%
Average change in mark-ups (abs. diff.)	2.26%	2.39%	2.49%	1.93%	1.59%	1.73%	1.94%	1.60%	1.74%
Shadow Price of Capital	-3.27%	-2.24%	-1.26%	-1.09%	-1.84%	-1.18%	-1.11%	-1.96%	-1.38%
Terms-of-Trade RW	-1.42%	-1.15%	-0.88%	-4.69%	-4.11%	-3.40%	-4.61%	-3.78%	-2.83%

Implicit change in real exchange rate	-2.07%	-1.66%	-1.27%	-4.63%	-3.94%	-3.07%	-4.53%	-3.53%	-2.35%

Trade Regime	Segmentation	Segmentation	Segmentation

Table B2.2.
The full *antimonde* scenario: effects on IC sectors for Belgium

% change from *monde*

Metal Industries

	Constraint Case			Flexible Case			Efficiency Case		
	1988	1991	1994	1988	1991	1994	1988	1991	1994
Production per firm	-12.37%	-12.44%	-12.59%	-12.67%	-20.23%	-20.17%	-12.68%	-20.25%	-20.21%
Real Marginal Costs	1.00%	1.12%	1.27%	0.43%	2.18%	3.12%	0.53%	2.59%	3.84%
Real Producer Prices	2.39%	2.51%	2.68%	1.71%	4.21%	5.15%	1.81%	4.63%	5.89%
Mark-ups domestic (abs. diff.)	3.19%	3.20%	3.22%	3.68%	5.08%	5.07%	3.68%	5.08%	5.06%
Fixed Costs per firm	0.86%	0.93%	1.00%	-0.88%	0.02%	0.49%	-0.82%	0.27%	0.92%
Number of Firms	7.39%	7.30%	7.15%	6.05%	2.31%	2.91%	6.05%	2.43%	3.11%
Sigma of Love of Variety	0.00%	0.00%	0.00%	0.00%	0.00%	0.00%	0.00%	0.00%	0.00%

Chemical

	Constraint Case			Flexible Case			Efficiency Case		
	1988	1991	1994	1988	1991	1994	1988	1991	1994
Production per firm	-11.80%	-11.94%	-12.13%	-10.84%	-16.09%	-16.31%	-10.87%	-16.19%	-16.48%
Real Marginal Costs	0.19%	0.37%	0.57%	-0.80%	0.76%	1.89%	-0.69%	1.22%	2.69%
Real Producer Prices	1.08%	1.26%	1.48%	-0.07%	1.82%	2.96%	0.04%	2.28%	3.78%
Mark-ups domestic (abs. diff.)	3.35%	3.36%	3.38%	3.52%	4.47%	4.49%	3.52%	4.47%	4.49%
Fixed Costs per firm	0.28%	0.36%	0.42%	-1.85%	-1.07%	-0.49%	-1.77%	-0.78%	0.02%
Number of Firms	9.14%	9.01%	8.83%	10.82%	12.66%	12.27%	10.79%	12.49%	11.97%
Sigma of Love of Variety	0.00%	0.00%	0.00%	0.00%	0.00%	0.00%	0.00%	0.00%	0.00%

Other Intensive Industries

	Constraint Case			Flexible Case			Efficiency Case		
	1988	1991	1994	1988	1991	1994	1988	1991	1994
Production per firm	-7.94%	-8.11%	-8.33%	-10.05%	-14.59%	-14.78%	-10.07%	-14.65%	-14.88%
Real Marginal Costs	-1.26%	-1.06%	-0.89%	-2.42%	-1.23%	-0.11%	-2.31%	-0.77%	0.69%
Real Producer Prices	-0.94%	-0.74%	-0.56%	-2.05%	-0.69%	0.43%	-1.94%	-0.23%	1.25%
Mark-ups domestic (abs. diff.)	0.61%	0.61%	0.62%	0.75%	1.00%	1.01%	0.75%	1.00%	1.01%
Fixed Costs per firm	-1.21%	-1.12%	-1.08%	-3.57%	-3.20%	-2.64%	-3.50%	-2.90%	-2.12%
Number of Firms	10.12%	10.02%	9.82%	12.39%	26.51%	26.33%	12.38%	26.44%	26.22%
Sigma of Love of Variety	0.00%	0.00%	0.00%	0.00%	0.00%	0.00%	0.00%	0.00%	0.00%

Electrical goods

	Constraint Case			Flexible Case			Efficiency Case		
	1988	1991	1994	1988	1991	1994	1988	1991	1994
Production per firm	-16.36%	-16.34%	-16.49%	-13.05%	-17.97%	-18.20%	-13.09%	-18.08%	-18.40%
Real Marginal Costs	0.11%	0.25%	0.39%	-1.42%	-0.02%	1.05%	-1.31%	0.44%	1.86%
Real Producer Prices	2.22%	2.35%	2.50%	-0.12%	1.63%	2.72%	-0.01%	2.10%	3.56%
Mark-ups domestic (abs. diff.)	10.94%	10.94%	11.00%	11.46%	13.10%	13.12%	11.46%	13.11%	13.14%
Fixed Costs per firm	0.21%	0.26%	0.27%	-2.55%	-1.97%	-1.44%	-2.48%	-1.67%	-0.92%
Number of Firms	7.09%	7.26%	7.12%	5.17%	1.09%	1.12%	5.13%	0.90%	0.79%
Sigma of Love of Variety	0.00%	0.00%	0.00%	0.00%	0.00%	0.00%	0.00%	0.00%	0.00%

Transport equipment

	Constraint Case			Flexible Case			Efficiency Case		
	1988	1991	1994	1988	1991	1994	1988	1991	1994
Production per firm	-21.25%	-21.23%	-21.36%	-21.61%	-29.03%	-29.00%	-21.63%	-29.08%	-29.08%
Real Marginal Costs	2.75%	2.85%	2.98%	0.86%	3.22%	4.22%	0.98%	3.69%	5.06%
Real Producer Prices	5.85%	5.93%	6.08%	3.38%	6.45%	7.47%	3.49%	6.94%	8.32%
Mark-ups domestic (abs. diff.)	10.56%	10.55%	10.60%	11.57%	13.96%	13.93%	11.57%	13.96%	13.94%
Fixed Costs per firm	2.79%	2.82%	2.84%	-0.30%	1.24%	1.74%	-0.23%	1.55%	2.27%
Number of Firms	7.82%	7.93%	7.81%	0.79%	-18.99%	-18.40%	0.78%	-19.02%	-18.44%
Sigma of Love of Variety	0.00%	0.00%	0.00%	0.00%	0.00%	0.00%	0.00%	0.00%	0.00%

Other Equipment

	Constraint Case			Flexible Case			Efficiency Case		
	1988	1991	1994	1988	1991	1994	1988	1991	1994
Production per firm	-14.30%	-14.39%	-14.53%	-13.21%	-17.46%	-17.64%	-13.24%	-17.55%	-17.79%
Real Marginal Costs	0.00%	0.15%	0.29%	-1.38%	0.07%	1.12%	-1.27%	0.53%	1.93%
Real Producer Prices	0.91%	1.06%	1.20%	-0.68%	0.97%	2.03%	-0.57%	1.43%	2.85%
Mark-ups domestic (abs. diff.)	3.93%	3.93%	3.95%	4.58%	5.59%	5.60%	4.59%	5.59%	5.61%
Fixed Costs per firm	0.02%	0.08%	0.11%	-2.57%	-1.94%	-1.41%	-2.50%	-1.65%	-0.90%
Number of Firms	11.77%	11.65%	11.44%	9.18%	11.85%	11.63%	9.15%	11.73%	11.42%
Sigma of Love of Variety	0.00%	0.00%	0.00%	0.00%	0.00%	0.00%	0.00%	0.00%	0.00%

Telecommunications

	Constraint Case			Flexible Case			Efficiency Case		
	1988	1991	1994	1988	1991	1994	1988	1991	1994
Production per firm	-1.36%	-1.17%	-1.54%	-2.53%	-4.37%	-4.79%	-2.54%	-4.43%	-4.90%
Real Marginal Costs	-2.81%	-2.19%	-1.79%	-4.31%	-3.53%	-2.18%	-4.19%	-3.04%	-1.32%
Real Producer Prices	-2.19%	-1.36%	-0.99%	-4.15%	-3.35%	-2.01%	-4.03%	-2.87%	-1.15%
Mark-ups domestic (abs. diff.)	0.63%	0.92%	0.87%	0.14%	-0.34%	-0.36%	0.14%	-0.35%	-0.38%
Fixed Costs per firm	-1.52%	0.20%	0.08%	-7.32%	-9.05%	-8.60%	-7.24%	-8.76%	-8.10%
Number of Firms	1.75%	1.06%	1.19%	4.34%	10.94%	10.98%	4.35%	10.96%	11.01%
Sigma of Love of Variety	0.00%	0.00%	0.00%	0.00%	0.00%	0.00%	0.00%	0.00%	0.00%

Banks

	Constraint Case			Flexible Case			Efficiency Case		
	1988	1991	1994	1988	1991	1994	1988	1991	1994
Production per firm	-0.02%	-0.03%	-0.27%	-0.77%	0.00%	-0.27%	-0.78%	-0.05%	-0.36%
Real Marginal Costs	-2.91%	-2.53%	-2.30%	-4.24%	-3.43%	-2.21%	-4.12%	-2.95%	-1.37%
Real Producer Prices	-2.76%	-2.30%	-2.08%	-4.30%	-3.81%	-2.59%	-4.18%	-3.33%	-1.75%
Mark-ups domestic (abs. diff.)	0.18%	0.27%	0.27%	-0.06%	-0.47%	-0.47%	-0.06%	-0.48%	-0.47%
Fixed Costs per firm	-2.06%	-1.27%	-1.28%	-6.58%	-7.65%	-7.11%	-6.51%	-7.35%	-6.58%
Number of Firms	0.39%	0.00%	0.00%	1.98%	5.72%	5.71%	1.98%	5.73%	5.72%
Sigma of Love of Variety	0.00%	0.00%	0.00%	0.00%	0.00%	0.00%	0.00%	0.00%	0.00%

Table B2.3.
The full *antimonde* scenario: sectoral results for Belgium (volumes)

% change from *monde*

Agriculture	Constraint Case			Flexible Case			Efficiency Case		
	1988	1991	1994	1988	1991	1994	1988	1991	1994
Domestic Production - vol.	4.5%	3.8%	2.9%	5.7%	16.5%	14.5%	5.7%	16.3%	14.1%
Imports - vol.	-1.9%	-1.8%	-1.7%	-2.2%	0.1%	0.5%	-2.2%	0.3%	0.9%
Exports - vol.	1.1%	0.7%	0.4%	1.5%	1.4%	1.1%	1.5%	1.3%	0.9%
Absorption - vol	1.8%	1.4%	1.0%	1.8%	5.5%	4.8%	1.8%	5.4%	4.7%
Investment - vol	-4.8%	-5.9%	-7.4%	-1.7%	3.2%	2.3%	-1.7%	3.1%	2.2%
Labour Demand - vol.	4.5%	4.0%	3.5%	5.7%	16.6%	14.8%	5.7%	16.4%	14.6%
Private Consumption - vol.	-1.5%	-1.9%	-2.0%	-1.4%	-2.2%	-2.5%	-1.4%	-2.2%	-2.5%
Supply to domestic - vol.	6.3%	5.3%	4.2%	7.3%	19.7%	17.7%	7.2%	19.4%	17.3%
Intra-EU Trade - vol	0.0%	0.0%	0.0%	0.5%	-0.6%	-1.1%	0.5%	-0.7%	-1.3%

Energy	Constraint Case			Flexible Case			Efficiency Case		
	1988	1991	1994	1988	1991	1994	1988	1991	1994
Domestic Production - vol.	-0.3%	-0.7%	-1.3%	1.4%	2.4%	2.3%	1.4%	2.4%	2.2%
Imports - vol.	-1.1%	-1.4%	-1.6%	-1.5%	-1.5%	-1.2%	-1.5%	-1.4%	-1.1%
Exports - vol.	-0.4%	-0.9%	-1.6%	0.6%	0.6%	0.5%	0.6%	0.5%	0.4%
Absorption - vol.	-0.8%	-1.1%	-1.4%	-0.2%	-0.6%	-0.8%	-0.2%	-0.7%	-0.8%
Investment - vol.	-8.8%	-9.3%	-10.1%	-3.3%	-2.9%	-2.9%	-3.4%	-2.9%	-2.9%
Labour Demand - vol.	0.0%	-0.4%	-0.9%	1.7%	2.8%	2.8%	1.7%	2.8%	2.8%
Private Consumption - vol.	-1.2%	-1.6%	-1.9%	-1.0%	-1.6%	-1.9%	-1.0%	-1.6%	-1.9%
Supply to domestic - vol.	-0.1%	-0.6%	-1.0%	0.9%	0.6%	0.3%	0.9%	0.5%	0.2%
Intra-EU Trade - vol	0.0%	0.0%	0.0%	0.7%	1.1%	1.0%	0.7%	1.0%	0.9%

Metal Industries	Constraint Case			Flexible Case			Efficiency Case		
	1988	1991	1994	1988	1991	1994	1988	1991	1994
Domestic Production - vol.	-5.9%	-6.1%	-6.3%	-7.4%	-18.4%	-17.8%	-7.4%	-18.3%	-17.7%
Imports - vol.	-1.2%	-1.2%	-1.3%	-4.4%	-8.1%	-7.7%	-4.4%	-8.0%	-7.4%
Exports - vol.	-4.0%	-4.1%	-4.4%	0.8%	0.5%	0.3%	0.8%	0.4%	0.2%
Absorption - vol.	-4.6%	-4.7%	-4.9%	-6.1%	-15.1%	-14.6%	-6.1%	-15.0%	-14.5%
Investment - vol.	-13.5%	-13.9%	-14.6%	-7.1%	-12.2%	-12.0%	-7.1%	-12.1%	-11.9%
Labour Demand - vol.	-4.2%	-4.3%	-4.6%	-5.7%	-16.2%	-15.6%	-5.7%	-16.1%	-15.4%
Private Consumption - vol.	-0.7%	-0.9%	-1.0%	-0.7%	-1.1%	-1.3%	-0.7%	-1.1%	-1.3%
Supply to domestic - vol.	-9.0%	-9.2%	-9.6%	-7.8%	-18.0%	-17.3%	-7.8%	-18.0%	-17.2%
Intra-EU Trade - vol	0.0%	0.0%	0.0%	-3.5%	-9.8%	-9.7%	-3.5%	-9.8%	-9.7%

Chemical	Constraint Case			Flexible Case			Efficiency Case		
	1988	1991	1994	1988	1991	1994	1988	1991	1994
Domestic Production - vol.	-3.7%	-4.0%	-4.4%	-1.2%	-5.5%	-6.0%	-1.3%	-5.7%	-6.5%
Imports - vol.	2.8%	2.6%	2.5%	-3.3%	-3.5%	-3.2%	-3.3%	-3.3%	-2.9%
Exports - vol.	-1.1%	-1.4%	-1.7%	1.6%	1.4%	1.1%	1.5%	1.3%	1.0%
Absorption - vol.	-1.8%	-2.0%	-2.3%	-0.5%	-2.7%	-3.2%	-0.5%	-2.9%	-3.4%
Investment - vol.	-11.8%	-12.3%	-13.1%	-4.5%	-6.4%	-6.7%	-4.5%	-6.5%	-6.9%
Labour Demand - vol.	-2.5%	-2.8%	-3.1%	-0.1%	-4.0%	-4.5%	-0.1%	-4.2%	-4.8%
Private Consumption - vol.	-1.2%	-1.6%	-1.8%	-1.1%	-1.8%	-2.1%	-1.1%	-1.8%	-2.1%
Supply to domestic - vol.	-9.8%	-10.2%	-10.7%	-3.3%	-6.0%	-6.8%	-3.3%	-6.3%	-7.3%
Intra-EU Trade - vol	0.0%	0.0%	0.0%	0.1%	-2.5%	-2.8%	0.1%	-2.6%	-3.0%

Other Intensive Industries	Constraint Case			Flexible Case			Efficiency Case		
	1988	1991	1994	1988	1991	1994	1988	1991	1994
Domestic Production - vol.	1.4%	1.1%	0.7%	1.1%	8.1%	7.7%	1.1%	7.9%	7.4%
Imports - vol.	-7.1%	-7.1%	-7.3%	-5.8%	-5.8%	-5.3%	-5.7%	-5.5%	-4.8%
Exports - vol.	0.9%	0.6%	0.2%	1.8%	1.7%	1.5%	1.8%	1.6%	1.3%
Absorption - vol.	-2.9%	-3.0%	-3.3%	-3.4%	-4.9%	-5.0%	-3.4%	-4.9%	-5.0%
Investment - vol.	-7.6%	-8.1%	-9.0%	-3.7%	-0.5%	-0.7%	-3.7%	-0.6%	-0.8%
Labour Demand - vol.	1.9%	1.7%	1.3%	1.8%	9.0%	8.7%	1.7%	9.0%	8.6%
Private Consumption - vol.	-1.8%	-1.5%	-1.6%	-2.1%	-2.1%	-1.8%	-2.1%	-2.0%	-1.8%
Supply to domestic - vol.	2.0%	1.8%	1.3%	3.1%	15.9%	15.5%	3.1%	15.7%	15.3%
Intra-EU Trade - vol	0.0%	0.0%	0.0%	-2.4%	-5.3%	-5.5%	-2.4%	-5.4%	-5.6%

Electrical goods	Constraint Case			Flexible Case			Efficiency Case		
	1988	1991	1994	1988	1991	1994	1988	1991	1994
Domestic Production - vol.	-10.4%	-10.3%	-10.6%	-8.6%	-17.1%	-17.3%	-8.6%	-17.3%	-17.8%
Imports - vol.	3.1%	3.7%	3.5%	-6.3%	-7.3%	-6.7%	-6.2%	-7.1%	-6.3%
Exports - vol.	-3.1%	-3.3%	-3.6%	1.9%	1.5%	1.3%	1.8%	1.4%	1.1%
Absorption - vol.	-7.9%	-7.2%	-7.4%	-7.9%	-11.9%	-11.6%	-7.9%	-12.0%	-11.7%
Investment - vol.	-17.7%	-18.0%	-19.0%	-7.9%	-11.8%	-12.0%	-8.0%	-11.9%	-12.2%
Labour Demand - vol.	-7.7%	-7.5%	-7.7%	-6.6%	-14.8%	-14.9%	-6.6%	-15.0%	-15.3%
Private Consumption - vol.	-7.5%	-4.2%	-4.0%	-8.4%	-6.0%	-3.9%	-8.4%	-5.9%	-3.8%
Supply to domestic - vol.	-32.0%	-31.4%	-31.7%	-25.7%	-38.0%	-37.8%	-25.8%	-38.2%	-38.2%
Intra-EU Trade - vol	0.0%	0.0%	0.0%	-1.0%	-3.5%	-3.6%	-1.1%	-3.6%	-3.8%

Transport equipment	Constraint Case			Flexible Case			Efficiency Case		
	1988	1991	1994	1988	1991	1994	1988	1991	1994
Domestic Production - vol.	-15.1%	-15.0%	-15.2%	-21.0%	-42.5%	-42.1%	-21.0%	-42.6%	-42.2%
Imports - vol.	0.6%	1.0%	0.8%	-8.6%	-15.8%	-15.3%	-8.6%	-15.7%	-15.1%
Exports - vol.	-7.8%	-7.9%	-8.2%	0.8%	-0.2%	-0.4%	0.8%	-0.3%	-0.6%
Absorption - vol.	-10.3%	-10.0%	-10.2%	-14.5%	-31.3%	-30.8%	-14.5%	-31.3%	-30.8%
Investment - vol.	-20.6%	-20.9%	-21.9%	-13.1%	-23.0%	-22.8%	-13.1%	-23.0%	-22.8%
Labour Demand - vol.	-11.3%	-11.1%	-11.3%	-17.9%	-39.6%	-39.1%	-17.9%	-39.6%	-39.1%
Private Consumption - vol.	-8.3%	-4.3%	-4.3%	-7.2%	-5.0%	-2.8%	-7.2%	-5.0%	-2.8%
Supply to domestic - vol.	-31.3%	-31.0%	-31.2%	-32.3%	-58.4%	-57.8%	-32.3%	-58.4%	-57.9%
Intra-EU Trade - vol	0.0%	0.0%	0.0%	-5.9%	-13.3%	-13.1%	-5.9%	-13.3%	-13.2%

Other Equipment

	Constraint Case			Flexible Case			Efficiency Case		
	1988	1991	1994	1988	1991	1994	1988	1991	1994
Domestic Production - vol.	-4.2%	-4.4%	-4.7%	-5.2%	-7.7%	-8.1%	-5.3%	-7.9%	-8.4%
Imports - vol.	-4.2%	-4.5%	-5.0%	-5.3%	-6.2%	-5.9%	-5.3%	-6.0%	-5.7%
Exports - vol.	-1.6%	-1.8%	-2.0%	1.6%	1.4%	1.2%	1.6%	1.3%	1.0%
Absorption - vol.	-6.3%	-6.6%	-7.1%	-6.9%	-10.0%	-10.2%	-6.9%	-10.0%	-10.3%
Investment - vol.	-11.9%	-12.8%	-14.1%	-6.4%	-7.5%	-7.7%	-6.4%	-7.5%	-7.9%
Labour Demand - vol.	-2.5%	-2.7%	-2.9%	-3.8%	-5.9%	-6.2%	-3.8%	-6.0%	-6.4%
Private Consumption - vol.	-2.4%	-2.5%	-2.7%	-2.6%	-3.0%	-3.1%	-2.6%	-3.0%	-3.1%
Supply to domestic - vol.	-13.2%	-13.6%	-14.3%	-12.2%	-16.5%	-16.8%	-12.3%	-16.7%	-17.2%
Intra-EU Trade - vol	0.0%	0.0%	0.0%	-2.4%	-3.9%	-4.0%	-2.5%	-3.9%	-4.2%

Consumer goods

	Constraint Case			Flexible Case			Efficiency Case		
	1988	1991	1994	1988	1991	1994	1988	1991	1994
Domestic Production - vol.	2.7%	2.3%	1.7%	2.9%	7.5%	6.7%	2.9%	7.3%	6.5%
Imports - vol.	-3.9%	-4.2%	-4.3%	-3.3%	-2.4%	-2.1%	-3.2%	-2.1%	-1.7%
Exports - vol.	0.6%	0.2%	-0.3%	2.1%	1.9%	1.6%	2.0%	1.8%	1.3%
Absorption - vol.	-0.4%	-0.7%	-1.0%	-0.5%	0.1%	-0.2%	-0.5%	0.1%	-0.3%
Investment - vol.	-6.1%	-7.1%	-8.7%	-2.8%	-0.7%	-1.1%	-2.8%	-0.8%	-1.2%
Labour Demand - vol.	3.2%	2.9%	2.4%	3.4%	8.2%	7.5%	3.4%	8.1%	7.4%
Private Consumption - vol.	-1.3%	-1.7%	-1.8%	-1.3%	-2.0%	-2.3%	-1.3%	-2.0%	-2.3%
Supply to domestic - vol.	7.6%	7.1%	6.4%	6.9%	20.0%	18.8%	6.9%	19.8%	18.5%
Intra-EU Trade - vol	0.0%	0.0%	0.0%	-0.5%	-2.0%	-2.4%	-0.6%	-2.1%	-2.5%

Construction

	Constraint Case			Flexible Case			Efficiency Case		
	1988	1991	1994	1988	1991	1994	1988	1991	1994
Domestic Production - vol.	-7.0%	-7.4%	-7.9%	-6.8%	-6.7%	-6.9%	-6.8%	-6.7%	-6.9%
Imports - vol.	-7.0%	-7.4%	-7.9%	#VALUE!	#VALUE!	#VALUE!	#VALUE!	#VALUE!	#VALUE!
Exports - vol.	1.0%	0.9%	0.7%	0.5%	0.5%	0.4%	0.5%	0.4%	0.3%
Absorption - vol.	-7.4%	-7.8%	-8.4%	-7.1%	-7.0%	-7.2%	-7.1%	-7.0%	-7.2%
Investment - vol.	-15.8%	-16.5%	-17.7%	-7.6%	-7.6%	-7.8%	-7.6%	-7.6%	-7.7%
Labour Demand - vol.	-6.8%	-7.1%	-7.5%	-6.6%	-6.4%	-6.5%	-6.6%	-6.4%	-6.4%
Private Consumption - vol.	-1.3%	-1.8%	-2.0%	-1.1%	-1.9%	-2.4%	-1.1%	-1.9%	-2.4%
Supply to domestic - vol.	-7.0%	-7.4%	-7.9%	-6.8%	-6.7%	-6.9%	-6.8%	-6.7%	-6.9%
Intra-EU Trade - vol	0.0%	0.0%	0.0%	-3.3%	-3.3%	-3.4%	-3.3%	-3.3%	-3.4%

Telecommunications

	Constraint Case			Flexible Case			Efficiency Case		
	1988	1991	1994	1988	1991	1994	1988	1991	1994
Domestic Production - vol.	0.4%	-0.1%	-0.4%	1.7%	6.1%	5.7%	1.7%	6.0%	5.6%
Imports - vol.	-11.7%	-11.3%	-11.1%	-7.0%	-7.1%	-6.8%	-6.9%	-6.9%	-6.4%
Exports - vol.	-0.1%	-1.0%	-1.5%	1.3%	1.4%	1.3%	1.3%	1.4%	1.2%
Absorption - vol.	-0.6%	-0.9%	-1.1%	-0.3%	0.3%	0.0%	-0.3%	0.3%	0.0%
Investment - vol.	-8.0%	-8.1%	-8.5%	-3.5%	-1.5%	-1.7%	-3.5%	-1.5%	-1.7%
Labour Demand - vol.	1.6%	1.8%	1.7%	2.0%	6.4%	6.2%	2.0%	6.4%	6.2%
Private Consumption - vol.	-1.5%	-2.1%	-2.4%	-1.2%	-2.0%	-2.4%	-1.2%	-2.0%	-2.5%
Supply to domestic - vol.	0.4%	0.0%	-0.3%	2.0%	8.2%	7.8%	2.0%	8.2%	7.8%
Intra-EU Trade - vol	0.0%	0.0%	0.0%	-6.7%	-19.1%	-19.2%	-6.7%	-19.1%	-19.2%

Transports

	Constraint Case			Flexible Case			Efficiency Case		
	1988	1991	1994	1988	1991	1994	1988	1991	1994
Domestic Production - vol.	0.2%	0.0%	-0.1%	1.0%	0.6%	0.3%	1.0%	0.5%	0.2%
Imports - vol.	0.2%	0.0%	-0.1%	0.5%	0.3%	0.2%	0.5%	0.3%	0.1%
Exports - vol.	1.4%	1.4%	1.3%	0.8%	0.8%	0.7%	0.8%	0.7%	0.6%
Absorption - vol.	-1.2%	-1.6%	-1.9%	-1.3%	-2.8%	-3.1%	-1.3%	-2.8%	-3.2%
Investment - vol.	-9.0%	-9.3%	-9.7%	-3.9%	-4.1%	-4.2%	-3.9%	-4.1%	-4.2%
Labour Demand - vol.	0.3%	0.2%	0.1%	1.2%	0.7%	0.6%	1.2%	0.8%	0.6%
Private Consumption - vol.	-1.7%	-2.3%	-2.6%	-1.5%	-2.5%	-3.0%	-1.5%	-2.5%	-3.0%
Supply to domestic - vol.	0.2%	0.0%	-0.1%	1.0%	0.6%	0.3%	1.0%	0.5%	0.2%
Intra-EU Trade - vol	0.0%	0.0%	0.0%	1.9%	2.3%	2.1%	1.9%	2.2%	2.1%

Banks

	Constraint Case			Flexible Case			Efficiency Case		
	1988	1991	1994	1988	1991	1994	1988	1991	1994
Domestic Production - vol.	0.4%	0.0%	-0.3%	1.2%	5.7%	5.4%	1.2%	5.7%	5.3%
Imports - vol.	-18.9%	-18.8%	-18.8%	-6.6%	-5.9%	-5.5%	-6.6%	-5.6%	-5.0%
Exports - vol.	1.1%	1.4%	1.8%	1.3%	1.3%	1.2%	1.2%	1.2%	1.1%
Absorption - vol.	-0.2%	-0.6%	-0.8%	0.3%	2.9%	2.5%	0.3%	2.8%	2.5%
Investment - vol.	-8.1%	-8.4%	-9.1%	-3.8%	-1.7%	-1.9%	-3.8%	-1.7%	-1.9%
Labour Demand - vol.	0.8%	0.7%	0.6%	1.1%	5.2%	5.0%	1.1%	5.2%	5.1%
Private Consumption - vol.	-1.5%	-2.1%	-2.3%	-1.4%	-2.3%	-2.8%	-1.4%	-2.3%	-2.8%
Supply to domestic - vol.	0.4%	-0.1%	-0.3%	1.1%	5.7%	5.4%	1.1%	5.6%	5.3%
Intra-EU Trade - vol	0.0%	0.0%	0.0%	-7.5%	-19.7%	-20.0%	-7.5%	-19.7%	-19.9%

Services

	Constraint Case			Flexible Case			Efficiency Case		
	1988	1991	1994	1988	1991	1994	1988	1991	1994
Domestic Production - vol.	0.0%	-0.3%	-0.7%	0.4%	2.3%	1.9%	0.4%	2.3%	1.9%
Imports - vol.	-10.5%	-10.4%	-10.1%	-4.2%	-4.3%	-3.9%	-4.1%	-4.1%	-3.5%
Exports - vol.	5.2%	4.3%	3.8%	1.2%	1.2%	1.0%	1.2%	1.2%	0.9%
Absorption - vol.	-1.6%	-1.8%	-2.1%	-1.6%	-2.2%	-2.4%	-1.6%	-2.2%	-2.4%
Investment - vol.	-8.8%	-9.4%	-10.3%	-4.1%	-3.3%	-3.4%	-4.1%	-3.2%	-3.4%
Labour Demand - vol.	0.1%	-0.1%	-0.2%	0.5%	2.5%	2.3%	0.5%	2.5%	2.3%
Private Consumption - vol.	-1.8%	-2.0%	-2.2%	-1.8%	-2.4%	-2.6%	-1.8%	-2.4%	-2.6%
Supply to domestic - vol.	-0.8%	-1.0%	-1.3%	-1.0%	0.0%	-0.4%	-1.0%	-0.1%	-0.4%
Intra-EU Trade - vol	0.0%	0.0%	0.0%	1.7%	0.5%	0.5%	1.7%	0.5%	0.4%

Non market

	Constraint Case			Flexible Case			Efficiency Case		
	1988	1991	1994	1988	1991	1994	1988	1991	1994
Domestic Production - vol.	-0.1%	-0.1%	-0.1%	-0.1%	-0.1%	-0.1%	-0.1%	-0.1%	-0.1%
Imports - vol.	-	-	-	#VALUE!	#VALUE!	#VALUE!	#VALUE!	#VALUE!	#VALUE!
Exports - vol.	-	-	-	#VALUE!	#VALUE!	#VALUE!	#VALUE!	#VALUE!	#VALUE!
Absorption - vol.	-0.1%	-0.1%	-0.1%	-0.1%	-0.1%	-0.1%	-0.1%	-0.1%	-0.1%
Investment - vol.	-8.9%	-9.0%	-9.1%	-4.2%	-4.2%	-4.2%	-4.2%	-4.2%	-4.1%
Labour Demand - vol.	0.0%	0.0%	0.0%	0.0%	0.0%	0.0%	0.0%	0.1%	0.1%
Private Consumption - vol.	-1.4%	-1.7%	-1.9%	-1.3%	-1.9%	-2.2%	-1.3%	-1.9%	-2.2%
Supply to domestic - vol.	-0.1%	-0.1%	-0.1%	-0.1%	-0.1%	-0.1%	-0.1%	-0.1%	-0.1%
Intra-EU Trade - vol	0.0%	0.0%	0.0%	#DIV/0!	#DIV/0!	#DIV/0!	#DIV/0!	#DIV/0!	#DIV/0!

Table B2.4.
The full *antimonde* scenario: sectoral results for Belgium (prices)

% change from *monde*

Agriculture	Constraint Case			Flexible Case			Efficiency Case		
	1988	1991	1994	1988	1991	1994	1988	1991	1994
Real Marginal Costs	-1.14%	-0.60%	-0.03%	1.12%	0.76%	0.91%	1.11%	0.69%	0.78%
Real Cost of Labour	-3.56%	-3.61%	-3.76%	-1.28%	-2.11%	-2.54%	-1.31%	-2.22%	-2.74%
Real Deflator of Absorption	-0.01%	0.24%	0.49%	2.74%	2.66%	2.49%	2.70%	2.49%	2.20%
Real Price of Exports-RW	-1.14%	-0.60%	-0.03%	1.12%	0.76%	0.91%	1.11%	0.69%	0.78%

Energy	Constraint Case			Flexible Case			Efficiency Case		
	1988	1991	1994	1988	1991	1994	1988	1991	1994
Marginal Costs	-0.65%	-0.40%	-0.13%	1.85%	1.52%	1.37%	1.81%	1.37%	1.10%
Cost of Labour	-3.56%	-3.61%	-3.76%	-1.28%	-2.11%	-2.54%	-1.31%	-2.22%	-2.74%
Deflator of Absorption	0.21%	0.30%	0.40%	3.14%	3.00%	2.70%	3.09%	2.79%	2.33%
Price of Exports-RW	-0.65%	-0.40%	-0.13%	1.85%	1.52%	1.37%	1.81%	1.37%	1.10%

Metal Industries	Constraint Case			Flexible Case			Efficiency Case		
	1988	1991	1994	1988	1991	1994	1988	1991	1994
Marginal Costs	1.00%	1.12%	1.27%	3.78%	4.01%	3.64%	3.75%	3.91%	3.45%
Cost of Labour	-3.56%	-3.61%	-3.76%	-1.28%	-2.11%	-2.54%	-1.31%	-2.22%	-2.74%
Deflator of Absorption	2.20%	2.25%	2.32%	5.48%	6.09%	5.60%	5.43%	5.90%	5.27%
Price of Exports-RW	2.21%	2.33%	2.49%	3.49%	3.90%	3.50%	3.46%	3.79%	3.30%

Chemical	Constraint Case			Flexible Case			Efficiency Case		
	1988	1991	1994	1988	1991	1994	1988	1991	1994
Marginal Costs	0.19%	0.37%	0.57%	2.55%	2.60%	2.42%	2.53%	2.53%	2.30%
Cost of Labour	-3.56%	-3.61%	-3.76%	-1.28%	-2.11%	-2.54%	-1.31%	-2.22%	-2.74%
Deflator of Absorption	1.58%	1.65%	1.72%	4.22%	4.71%	4.44%	4.19%	4.60%	4.25%
Price of Exports-RW	0.73%	0.92%	1.13%	2.15%	2.12%	1.95%	2.13%	2.06%	1.84%

Other Intensive Industries	Constraint Case			Flexible Case			Efficiency Case		
	1988	1991	1994	1988	1991	1994	1988	1991	1994
Marginal Costs	-1.26%	-1.06%	-0.89%	0.93%	0.61%	0.41%	0.91%	0.54%	0.30%
Cost of Labour	-3.56%	-3.61%	-3.76%	-1.28%	-2.11%	-2.54%	-1.31%	-2.22%	-2.74%
Deflator of Absorption	0.34%	0.44%	0.53%	2.30%	2.45%	2.18%	2.28%	2.35%	2.01%
Price of Exports-RW	-1.14%	-0.95%	-0.77%	0.77%	0.26%	0.07%	0.75%	0.20%	-0.04%

Electrical goods	Constraint Case			Flexible Case			Efficiency Case		
	1988	1991	1994	1988	1991	1994	1988	1991	1994
Marginal Costs	0.11%	0.25%	0.39%	1.92%	1.81%	1.57%	1.91%	1.75%	1.47%
Cost of Labour	-3.56%	-3.61%	-3.76%	-1.28%	-2.11%	-2.54%	-1.31%	-2.22%	-2.74%
Deflator of Absorption	3.87%	3.89%	3.93%	4.94%	5.52%	5.18%	4.91%	5.40%	4.97%
Price of Exports-RW	1.40%	1.54%	1.69%	1.49%	1.72%	1.48%	1.48%	1.68%	1.40%

Transport equipment	Constraint Case			Flexible Case			Efficiency Case		
	1988	1991	1994	1988	1991	1994	1988	1991	1994
Marginal Costs	2.75%	2.85%	2.98%	4.21%	5.05%	4.75%	4.20%	5.00%	4.66%
Cost of Labour	-3.56%	-3.61%	-3.76%	-1.28%	-2.11%	-2.54%	-1.31%	-2.22%	-2.74%
Deflator of Absorption	5.13%	5.15%	5.19%	6.34%	7.97%	7.58%	6.32%	7.87%	7.40%
Price of Exports-RW	4.60%	4.69%	4.83%	4.15%	6.52%	6.18%	4.14%	6.48%	6.11%

Other Equipment	Constraint Case			Flexible Case			Efficiency Case		
	1988	1991	1994	1988	1991	1994	1988	1991	1994
Marginal Costs	0.00%	0.15%	0.29%	1.96%	1.90%	1.65%	1.95%	1.84%	1.54%
Cost of Labour	-3.56%	-3.61%	-3.76%	-1.28%	-2.11%	-2.54%	-1.31%	-2.22%	-2.74%
Deflator of Absorption	1.89%	1.92%	1.96%	3.79%	4.13%	3.76%	3.76%	4.00%	3.52%
Price of Exports-RW	0.65%	0.80%	0.95%	1.66%	1.50%	1.25%	1.64%	1.44%	1.14%

Consumer goods	Constraint Case			Flexible Case			Efficiency Case		
	1988	1991	1994	1988	1991	1994	1988	1991	1994
Marginal Costs	-0.76%	-0.51%	-0.25%	1.61%	1.34%	1.19%	1.59%	1.27%	1.05%
Cost of Labour	-3.56%	-3.61%	-3.76%	-1.28%	-2.11%	-2.54%	-1.31%	-2.22%	-2.74%
Deflator of Absorption	0.64%	0.72%	0.80%	3.45%	3.40%	3.02%	3.41%	3.22%	2.71%
Price of Exports-RW	-0.76%	-0.51%	-0.25%	1.61%	1.34%	1.19%	1.59%	1.27%	1.05%

Construction	Constraint Case			Flexible Case			Efficiency Case		
	1988	1991	1994	1988	1991	1994	1988	1991	1994
Marginal Costs	-1.43%	-1.12%	-0.84%	0.76%	0.40%	0.31%	0.75%	0.34%	0.20%
Cost of Labour	-3.56%	-3.61%	-3.76%	-1.28%	-2.11%	-2.54%	-1.31%	-2.22%	-2.74%
Deflator of Absorption	-1.36%	-1.07%	-0.79%	0.77%	0.43%	0.33%	0.76%	0.37%	0.22%
Price of Exports-RW	-1.43%	-1.12%	-0.84%	0.76%	0.40%	0.31%	0.75%	0.34%	0.20%

Telecommunications	Constraint Case			Flexible Case			Efficiency Case		
	1988	1991	1994	1988	1991	1994	1988	1991	1994
Marginal Costs	-2.81%	-2.19%	-1.79%	-0.96%	-1.69%	-1.65%	-0.97%	-1.73%	-1.71%
Cost of Labour	-3.56%	-3.61%	-3.76%	-1.28%	-2.11%	-2.54%	-1.31%	-2.22%	-2.74%
Deflator of Absorption	-2.02%	-1.24%	-0.91%	-0.46%	-1.18%	-1.19%	-0.47%	-1.24%	-1.27%
Price of Exports-RW	0.27%	0.98%	1.37%	-1.34%	-2.63%	-2.60%	-1.35%	-2.67%	-2.67%

Transports	Constraint Case			Flexible Case			Efficiency Case		
	1988	1991	1994	1988	1991	1994	1988	1991	1994
Marginal Costs	-2.44%	-1.96%	-1.51%	-0.30%	-0.91%	-0.81%	-0.32%	-0.97%	-0.92%
Cost of Labour	-3.56%	-3.61%	-3.76%	-1.28%	-2.11%	-2.54%	-1.31%	-2.22%	-2.74%
Deflator of Absorption	-1.81%	-1.39%	-1.01%	-0.09%	-0.60%	-0.54%	-0.11%	-0.67%	-0.66%
Price of Exports-RW	-2.44%	-1.96%	-1.51%	-0.30%	-0.91%	-0.81%	-0.32%	-0.97%	-0.92%

Banks	Constraint Case			Flexible Case			Efficiency Case		
	1988	1991	1994	1988	1991	1994	1988	1991	1994
Marginal Costs	-2.91%	-2.53%	-2.30%	-0.89%	-1.60%	-1.69%	-0.90%	-1.64%	-1.76%
Cost of Labour	-3.56%	-3.61%	-3.76%	-1.28%	-2.11%	-2.54%	-1.31%	-2.22%	-2.74%
Deflator of Absorption	-2.64%	-2.19%	-1.97%	-0.87%	-1.85%	-1.93%	-0.88%	-1.89%	-2.01%
Price of Exports-RW	-1.67%	-1.27%	-1.04%	-0.97%	-1.82%	-1.91%	-0.98%	-1.86%	-1.99%

Services	Constraint Case			Flexible Case			Efficiency Case		
	1988	1991	1994	1988	1991	1994	1988	1991	1994
Marginal Costs	-2.55%	-2.06%	-1.60%	-0.40%	-1.03%	-0.91%	-0.42%	-1.08%	-1.01%
Cost of Labour	-3.56%	-3.61%	-3.76%	-1.28%	-2.11%	-2.54%	-1.31%	-2.22%	-2.74%
Deflator of Absorption	-2.28%	-1.82%	-1.39%	-0.29%	-0.82%	-0.72%	-0.31%	-0.88%	-0.83%
Price of Exports-RW	-2.55%	-2.06%	-1.60%	-0.40%	-1.03%	-0.91%	-0.42%	-1.08%	-1.01%

Non market	Constraint Case			Flexible Case			Efficiency Case		
	1988	1991	1994	1988	1991	1994	1988	1991	1994
Marginal Costs	-2.99%	-2.96%	-3.01%	-0.75%	-1.44%	-1.78%	-0.76%	-1.49%	-1.88%
Cost of Labour	-3.56%	-3.61%	-3.76%	-1.28%	-2.11%	-2.54%	-1.31%	-2.22%	-2.74%
Deflator of Absorption	-2.99%	-2.96%	-3.01%	-0.75%	-1.44%	-1.78%	-0.76%	-1.49%	-1.88%
Price of Exports-RW	-2.99%	-2.96%	-3.01%	-0.75%	-1.44%	-1.78%	-0.76%	-1.49%	-1.88%

Table B2.5.
Decomposition of effects: macroeconomic aggregates for Belgium

Macroeconomic Aggregates (vol.) (% change from monde)	Border Controls			Border controls and x-ineff.			Market segmentation			Trade antimonde			Full antimonde		
	1988	1991	1994	1988	1991	1994	1988	1991	1994	1988	1991	1994	1988	1991	1994
GDP fact. pr.	-0.09%	-0.23%	-0.24%	-0.09%	-0.25%	-0.26%	-1.20%	-2.23%	-2.52%	-1.29%	-2.37%	-2.66%	-1.39%	-2.52%	-2.86%
Priv. Consumption	0.23%	0.13%	0.13%	0.23%	0.13%	0.13%	-1.86%	-2.24%	-2.36%	-1.82%	-2.29%	-2.41%	-1.85%	-2.34%	-2.47%
Absorption	-0.21%	-0.57%	-0.57%	-0.21%	-0.56%	-0.56%	-2.45%	-5.03%	-5.09%	-2.80%	-5.57%	-5.63%	-2.85%	-5.64%	-5.72%
Total Investment	0.03%	0.01%	0.01%	0.04%	0.01%	0.01%	-4.45%	-4.73%	-4.85%	-4.45%	-4.75%	-4.88%	-4.46%	-4.76%	-4.89%
Total Exports to RW	-0.54%	-0.59%	-0.60%	-0.55%	-0.60%	-0.61%	1.80%	1.63%	1.44%	1.46%	1.28%	1.09%	1.40%	1.19%	0.99%
Total Imports from RW	1.22%	1.19%	1.20%	1.23%	1.21%	1.23%	-5.19%	-6.50%	-6.21%	-3.98%	-5.28%	-4.98%	-3.85%	-5.07%	-4.70%
Total Intra-EU Trade	-0.93%	-2.19%	-2.19%	-0.94%	-2.20%	-2.21%	-0.87%	-4.44%	-4.50%	-1.66%	-5.46%	-5.52%	-1.76%	-5.59%	-5.70%
Employment (diff. from monde , 10³ persons)	1	1	1	1	1	1	-14	-11	-16	-15	-12	-17	-15	-12	-17
Disposable Income (deflated)	0.23%	0.14%	0.14%	0.24%	0.14%	0.14%	-1.93%	-2.32%	-2.45%	-1.89%	-2.37%	-2.50%	-1.92%	-2.42%	-2.56%

Macroeconomic Ratios (abs. diff. from monde)	Border Controls			Border controls and x-ineff.			Market segmentation			Trade antimonde			Full antimonde		
	1988	1991	1994	1988	1991	1994	1988	1991	1994	1988	1991	1994	1988	1991	1994
Current Account as % of GDP	-0.06%	0.03%	0.04%	-0.06%	0.04%	0.04%	-0.07%	0.37%	0.38%	-0.03%	0.48%	0.49%	0.00%	0.53%	0.55%
Public Deficit as % of GDP	0.06%	-0.03%	-0.03%	0.06%	-0.03%	-0.03%	-0.96%	-1.43%	-1.51%	-0.97%	-1.51%	-1.59%	-1.00%	-1.56%	-1.65%
Labour Productivity	-0.11%	-0.26%	-0.26%	-0.12%	-0.27%	-0.28%	-0.80%	-1.93%	-2.07%	-0.88%	-2.04%	-2.19%	-0.98%	-2.18%	-2.38%
Investment/GDP	0.03%	0.04%	0.04%	0.03%	0.05%	0.05%	-1.40%	-1.32%	-1.31%	-1.38%	-1.30%	-1.30%	-1.37%	-1.28%	-1.27%
Priv.Cons./GDP	0.21%	0.24%	0.24%	0.22%	0.26%	0.26%	-0.45%	-0.01%	0.11%	-0.36%	0.05%	0.17%	-0.31%	0.13%	0.27%

Deflators (% change from monde)	Border Controls			Border controls and x-ineff.			Market segmentation			Trade antimonde			Full antimonde		
	1988	1991	1994	1988	1991	1994	1988	1991	1994	1988	1991	1994	1988	1991	1994
Consumer Price Index	-0.41%	-0.41%	-0.41%	-0.42%	-0.43%	-0.44%	1.46%	1.12%	1.03%	1.38%	1.10%	1.01%	1.33%	1.02%	0.91%
Real Wage Rate	-0.10%	-0.21%	-0.21%	-0.11%	-0.24%	-0.25%	-1.06%	-1.77%	-2.14%	-1.19%	-1.96%	-2.34%	-1.28%	-2.11%	-2.54%
Marginal Costs	-0.28%	-0.23%	-0.23%	-0.28%	-0.23%	-0.23%	1.36%	1.64%	1.52%	1.35%	1.73%	1.60%	1.33%	1.70%	1.56%
Producer Prices	-0.27%	-0.20%	-0.20%	-0.27%	-0.21%	-0.22%	1.60%	1.84%	1.72%	1.59%	1.93%	1.81%	1.57%	1.89%	1.76%
Shadow Price of Capital	-0.02%	-0.21%	-0.22%	0.00%	-0.17%	-0.18%	-0.95%	-1.60%	-0.91%	-1.02%	-1.75%	-1.05%	-1.09%	-1.84%	-1.18%
Terms-of-Trade RW	2.09%	2.25%	2.27%	2.12%	2.29%	2.32%	-6.09%	-5.62%	-5.01%	-4.86%	-4.37%	-3.74%	-4.69%	-4.11%	-3.40%
Real Exchange Rate	4.32%	4.46%	4.48%	4.35%	4.50%	4.54%	-7.78%	-7.11%	-6.38%	-4.81%	-4.23%	-3.46%	-4.63%	-3.94%	-3.07%
Trade Regime	Integration			Integration			Segmentation			Segmentation			Segmentation		

Table B2.6.
Decomposition of effects: effects on IC sectors for Belgium

% change from *monde*

Metal Industries

	Border Controls			Border controls and x-ineff.			Market segmentation			Trade *antimonde*			Full *antimonde*		
	1988	1991	1994	1988	1991	1994	1988	1991	1994	1988	1991	1994	1988	1991	1994
Production per firm	-1.16%	-2.44%	-2.45%	-1.16%	-2.44%	-2.45%	-11.45%	-18.84%	-18.73%	-12.57%	-20.10%	-19.99%	-12.67%	-20.23%	-20.17%
Marginal Costs	3.46%	3.69%	3.70%	3.48%	3.72%	3.75%	-3.82%	-3.08%	-2.69%	-1.03%	-0.19%	0.22%	-0.85%	0.07%	0.57%
Producer Prices	3.57%	3.90%	3.91%	3.58%	3.92%	3.95%	-2.71%	-1.27%	-0.89%	0.24%	1.83%	2.23%	0.43%	2.11%	2.61%
Mark-ups domestic (abs. diff.)	0.12%	0.31%	0.31%	0.12%	0.31%	0.31%	3.46%	4.79%	4.77%	3.66%	5.06%	5.03%	3.68%	5.08%	5.07%
Fixed Costs per firm	3.45%	3.68%	3.69%	3.46%	3.70%	3.72%	-3.79%	-3.06%	-2.68%	-1.01%	-0.17%	0.22%	-0.88%	0.02%	0.49%
Number of Firms	0.10%	0.21%	0.23%	0.11%	0.23%	0.25%	7.24%	3.83%	4.48%	6.15%	2.45%	3.08%	6.05%	2.31%	2.91%
Sigma of Love of Variety	0.00%	0.00%	0.00%	0.00%	0.00%	0.00%	0.00%	0.00%	0.00%	0.00%	0.00%	0.00%	0.00%	0.00%	0.00%

Chemical

	Border Controls			Border controls and x-ineff.			Market segmentation			Trade *antimonde*			Full *antimonde*		
	1988	1991	1994	1988	1991	1994	1988	1991	1994	1988	1991	1994	1988	1991	1994
Production per firm	-1.32%	-2.94%	-2.95%	-1.33%	-2.96%	-2.97%	-10.10%	-14.97%	-15.13%	-10.73%	-15.92%	-16.08%	-10.84%	-16.09%	-16.31%
Marginal Costs	4.08%	4.33%	4.34%	4.10%	4.37%	4.40%	-5.39%	-4.84%	-4.27%	-2.27%	-1.63%	-1.03%	-2.08%	-1.34%	-0.65%
Producer Prices	4.16%	4.50%	4.52%	4.18%	4.54%	4.57%	-4.73%	-3.90%	-3.32%	-1.55%	-0.59%	0.02%	-1.35%	-0.29%	0.42%
Mark-ups domestic (abs. diff.)	0.07%	0.22%	0.22%	0.07%	0.22%	0.22%	3.50%	4.40%	4.41%	3.51%	4.45%	4.46%	3.52%	4.47%	4.49%
Fixed Costs per firm	4.06%	4.33%	4.34%	4.07%	4.35%	4.38%	-5.12%	-4.53%	-4.04%	-1.99%	-1.29%	-0.78%	-1.85%	-1.07%	-0.49%
Number of Firms	0.16%	0.12%	0.12%	0.16%	0.10%	0.09%	10.92%	13.16%	12.82%	10.91%	12.81%	12.47%	10.82%	12.66%	12.27%
Sigma of Love of Variety	0.00%	0.00%	0.00%	0.00%	0.00%	0.00%	0.00%	0.00%	0.00%	0.00%	0.00%	0.00%	0.00%	0.00%	0.00%

Other Intensive Industries

	Border Controls			Border controls and x-ineff.			Market segmentation			Trade *antimonde*			Full *antimonde*		
	1988	1991	1994	1988	1991	1994	1988	1991	1994	1988	1991	1994	1988	1991	1994
Production per firm	-1.39%	-3.25%	-3.25%	-1.39%	-3.25%	-3.26%	-9.31%	-13.85%	-14.02%	-10.00%	-14.52%	-14.69%	-10.05%	-14.59%	-14.78%
Marginal Costs	4.02%	4.16%	4.18%	4.04%	4.19%	4.22%	-6.78%	-6.48%	-5.92%	-3.87%	-3.59%	-3.00%	-3.70%	-3.33%	-2.66%
Producer Prices	4.07%	4.27%	4.29%	4.09%	4.31%	4.34%	-6.44%	-5.98%	-5.42%	-3.50%	-3.05%	-2.46%	-3.33%	-2.79%	-2.11%
Mark-ups domestic (abs. diff.)	0.02%	0.06%	0.06%	0.02%	0.06%	0.06%	0.75%	0.99%	1.00%	0.75%	1.00%	1.00%	0.75%	1.00%	1.01%
Fixed Costs per firm	3.99%	4.15%	4.16%	4.00%	4.16%	4.19%	-6.60%	-6.28%	-5.81%	-3.70%	-3.38%	-2.89%	-3.57%	-3.20%	-2.64%
Number of Firms	0.65%	2.69%	2.70%	0.66%	2.70%	2.71%	12.47%	26.60%	26.43%	12.41%	26.54%	26.36%	12.39%	26.51%	26.33%
Sigma of Love of Variety	0.00%	0.00%	0.00%	0.00%	0.00%	0.00%	0.00%	0.00%	0.00%	0.00%	0.00%	0.00%	0.00%	0.00%	0.00%

Electrical goods

	Border Controls			Border controls and x-ineff.			Market segmentation			Trade *antimonde*			Full *antimonde*		
	1988	1991	1994	1988	1991	1994	1988	1991	1994	1988	1991	1994	1988	1991	1994
Production per firm	-1.97%	-3.82%	-3.83%	-1.98%	-3.84%	-3.85%	-11.37%	-16.02%	-16.17%	-12.90%	-17.74%	-17.90%	-13.05%	-17.97%	-18.20%
Marginal Costs	4.05%	4.24%	4.26%	4.07%	4.27%	4.30%	-5.90%	-5.44%	-4.93%	-2.88%	-2.40%	-1.86%	-2.71%	-2.13%	-1.50%
Producer Prices	4.23%	4.55%	4.57%	4.25%	4.59%	4.62%	-4.82%	-4.05%	-3.52%	-1.60%	-0.78%	-0.22%	-1.40%	-0.48%	0.17%
Mark-ups domestic (abs. diff.)	0.20%	0.50%	0.51%	0.20%	0.50%	0.51%	11.21%	12.74%	12.75%	11.42%	13.04%	13.04%	11.46%	13.10%	13.12%
Fixed Costs per firm	4.03%	4.23%	4.24%	4.04%	4.25%	4.28%	-5.70%	-5.23%	-4.78%	-2.69%	-2.17%	-1.70%	-2.55%	-1.97%	-1.44%
Number of Firms	0.06%	0.02%	0.01%	0.06%	0.00%	-0.01%	5.84%	2.02%	2.08%	5.29%	1.26%	1.33%	5.17%	1.09%	1.12%
Sigma of Love of Variety	0.00%	0.00%	0.00%	0.00%	0.00%	0.00%	0.00%	0.00%	0.00%	0.00%	0.00%	0.00%	0.00%	0.00%	0.00%

Transport equipment

	Border Controls			Border controls and x-ineff.			Market segmentation			Trade antimonde			Full antimonde		
	1988	1991	1994	1988	1991	1994	1988	1991	1994	1988	1991	1994	1988	1991	1994
Production per firm	-1.33%	-2.71%	-2.72%	-1.33%	-2.72%	-2.73%	-20.59%	-27.58%	-27.51%	-21.51%	-28.89%	-28.82%	-21.61%	-29.03%	-29.00%
Marginal Costs	4.02%	4.26%	4.28%	4.04%	4.29%	4.33%	-3.80%	-2.55%	-2.11%	-0.62%	0.80%	1.27%	-0.42%	1.11%	1.68%
Producer Prices	4.14%	4.48%	4.50%	4.16%	4.52%	4.55%	-1.51%	0.36%	0.81%	1.88%	4.01%	4.48%	2.09%	4.34%	4.92%
Mark-ups domestic (abs. diff.)	0.09%	0.30%	0.30%	0.09%	0.30%	0.31%	11.43%	13.57%	13.55%	11.54%	13.92%	13.88%	11.57%	13.96%	13.93%
Fixed Costs per firm	4.00%	4.25%	4.27%	4.02%	4.27%	4.30%	-3.64%	-2.35%	-1.95%	-0.46%	1.01%	1.43%	-0.30%	1.24%	1.74%
Number of Firms	0.41%	0.16%	0.15%	0.41%	0.15%	0.13%	1.22%	-18.06%	-17.46%	0.88%	-18.89%	-18.27%	0.79%	-18.99%	-18.40%
Sigma of Love of Variety	0.00%	0.00%	0.00%	0.00%	0.00%	0.00%	0.00%	0.00%	0.00%	0.00%	0.00%	0.00%	0.00%	0.00%	0.00%

Other Equipment

	Border Controls			Border controls and x-ineff.			Market segmentation			Trade antimonde			Full antimonde		
	1988	1991	1994	1988	1991	1994	1988	1991	1994	1988	1991	1994	1988	1991	1994
Production per firm	-1.31%	-2.43%	-2.43%	-1.31%	-2.44%	-2.45%	-11.94%	-15.94%	-16.06%	-13.11%	-17.31%	-17.43%	-13.21%	-17.46%	-17.64%
Marginal Costs	3.97%	4.17%	4.19%	3.99%	4.21%	4.24%	-5.82%	-5.34%	-4.84%	-2.85%	-2.31%	-1.79%	-2.67%	-2.04%	-1.42%
Producer Prices	4.03%	4.29%	4.30%	4.05%	4.32%	4.35%	-5.21%	-4.55%	-4.05%	-2.15%	-1.42%	-0.89%	-1.96%	-1.14%	-0.51%
Mark-ups domestic (abs. diff.)	0.07%	0.17%	0.17%	0.07%	0.17%	0.17%	4.50%	5.48%	5.48%	4.58%	5.57%	5.58%	4.58%	5.59%	5.60%
Fixed Costs per firm	3.95%	4.16%	4.18%	3.96%	4.18%	4.21%	-5.68%	-5.18%	-4.74%	-2.71%	-2.14%	-1.68%	-2.57%	-1.94%	-1.41%
Number of Firms	-0.20%	0.23%	0.24%	-0.20%	0.23%	0.22%	10.00%	12.93%	12.75%	9.25%	11.97%	11.78%	9.18%	11.85%	11.63%
Sigma of Love of Variety	0.00%	0.00%	0.00%	0.00%	0.00%	0.00%	0.00%	0.00%	0.00%	0.00%	0.00%	0.00%	0.00%	0.00%	0.00%

Telecommunications

	Border Controls			Border controls and x-ineff.			Market segmentation			Trade antimonde			Full antimonde		
	1988	1991	1994	1988	1991	1994	1988	1991	1994	1988	1991	1994	1988	1991	1994
Production per firm	0.14%	0.33%	0.33%	-0.65%	-1.35%	-1.36%	-1.91%	-3.07%	-3.46%	-1.75%	-2.85%	-3.25%	-2.53%	-4.37%	-4.79%
Marginal Costs	4.27%	4.28%	4.31%	4.29%	4.33%	4.37%	-8.63%	-8.63%	-7.84%	-5.76%	-5.90%	-5.07%	-5.59%	-5.63%	-4.72%
Producer Prices	4.22%	4.19%	4.21%	4.00%	3.78%	3.82%	-8.20%	-7.94%	-7.15%	-5.37%	-5.25%	-4.42%	-5.43%	-5.46%	-4.55%
Mark-ups domestic (abs. diff.)	-0.05%	-0.08%	-0.09%	-0.41%	-0.81%	-0.81%	0.55%	0.45%	0.42%	0.51%	0.40%	0.38%	0.14%	-0.34%	-0.36%
Fixed Costs per firm	4.20%	4.24%	4.25%	2.36%	0.58%	0.60%	-8.58%	-8.60%	-8.21%	-5.75%	-5.89%	-5.47%	-7.32%	-9.05%	-8.60%
Number of Firms	0.11%	0.30%	0.30%	0.97%	2.28%	2.29%	3.38%	9.02%	9.05%	3.48%	9.14%	9.16%	4.34%	10.94%	10.98%
Sigma of Love of Variety	0.00%	0.00%	0.00%	0.00%	0.00%	0.00%	0.00%	0.00%	0.00%	0.00%	0.00%	0.00%	0.00%	0.00%	0.00%

Banks

	Border Controls			Border controls and x-ineff.			Market segmentation			Trade antimonde			Full antimonde		
	1988	1991	1994	1988	1991	1994	1988	1991	1994	1988	1991	1994	1988	1991	1994
Production per firm	0.07%	0.22%	0.22%	-0.45%	-0.77%	-0.78%	-0.28%	1.01%	0.77%	-0.21%	1.12%	0.86%	-0.77%	0.00%	-0.27%
Marginal Costs	4.23%	4.26%	4.27%	4.25%	4.29%	4.32%	-8.54%	-8.52%	-7.85%	-5.68%	-5.78%	-5.08%	-5.52%	-5.54%	-4.76%
Producer Prices	4.21%	4.21%	4.22%	4.12%	4.01%	4.04%	-8.49%	-8.68%	-8.00%	-5.64%	-5.97%	-5.26%	-5.58%	-5.92%	-5.13%
Mark-ups domestic (abs. diff.)	-0.02%	-0.04%	-0.04%	-0.15%	-0.32%	-0.32%	0.08%	-0.20%	-0.19%	0.07%	-0.22%	-0.21%	-0.06%	-0.47%	-0.47%
Fixed Costs per firm	4.20%	4.23%	4.25%	3.07%	1.97%	2.00%	-8.50%	-8.49%	-8.01%	-5.66%	-5.76%	-5.26%	-6.58%	-7.65%	-7.11%
Number of Firms	0.07%	0.24%	0.24%	0.61%	1.45%	1.45%	1.38%	4.54%	4.54%	1.43%	4.61%	4.60%	1.98%	5.72%	5.71%
Sigma of Love of Variety	0.00%	0.00%	0.00%	0.00%	0.00%	0.00%	0.00%	0.00%	0.00%	0.00%	0.00%	0.00%	0.00%	0.00%	0.00%

Table B2.7.
Decomposition of effects: sectoral results for Belgium (volumes)

% change from *monde*

Agriculture

	Border Controls			Border controls and x-ineff.			Market segmentation			Trade *antimonde*			Full *antimonde*		
	1988	1991	1994	1988	1991	1994	1988	1991	1994	1988	1991	1994	1988	1991	1994
Domestic Production - vol.	-1.5%	-0.5%	-0.5%	-1.6%	-0.6%	-0.6%	7.3%	18.0%	16.0%	5.9%	16.7%	14.8%	5.7%	16.5%	14.5%
Imports - vol.	1.6%	1.8%	1.8%	1.6%	1.8%	1.8%	-4.0%	-1.9%	-1.5%	-2.4%	-0.1%	0.2%	-2.2%	0.1%	0.5%
Exports - vol.	-0.7%	-0.8%	-0.8%	-0.7%	-0.8%	-0.8%	2.1%	2.0%	1.7%	1.6%	1.5%	1.2%	1.5%	1.4%	1.1%
Absorption - vol.	-0.7%	-0.7%	-0.7%	-0.7%	-0.7%	-0.7%	2.4%	6.1%	5.5%	1.9%	5.5%	4.9%	1.8%	5.5%	4.8%
Investment - vol.	-0.8%	-0.3%	-0.3%	-0.8%	-0.3%	-0.3%	-1.0%	3.9%	3.0%	-1.6%	3.3%	2.4%	-1.7%	3.2%	2.3%
Labour Demand - vol.	-1.5%	-0.5%	-0.5%	-1.5%	-0.5%	-0.5%	7.2%	17.9%	16.2%	5.8%	16.7%	15.0%	5.7%	16.6%	14.8%
Private Consumption - vol.	0.2%	0.2%	0.2%	0.2%	0.2%	0.2%	-1.5%	-2.2%	-2.4%	-1.4%	-2.2%	-2.5%	-1.4%	-2.2%	-2.5%
Supply to domestic - vol.	-1.0%	1.5%	1.5%	-1.0%	1.4%	1.4%	8.5%	21.0%	19.1%	7.4%	19.9%	18.0%	7.3%	19.7%	17.7%
Intra-EU Trade - vol	-1.9%	-3.4%	-3.4%	-1.9%	-3.4%	-3.4%	2.1%	1.2%	0.6%	0.6%	-0.4%	-0.9%	0.5%	-0.6%	-1.1%

Energy

	Border Controls			Border controls and x-ineff.			Market segmentation			Trade *antimonde*			Full *antimonde*		
	1988	1991	1994	1988	1991	1994	1988	1991	1994	1988	1991	1994	1988	1991	1994
Domestic Production - vol.	-0.2%	0.1%	0.1%	-0.2%	0.0%	0.1%	1.6%	2.7%	2.6%	1.4%	2.4%	2.3%	1.4%	2.4%	2.3%
Imports - vol.	1.0%	1.0%	1.1%	1.0%	1.1%	1.1%	-2.2%	-2.1%	-1.9%	-1.6%	-1.5%	-1.3%	-1.5%	-1.5%	-1.2%
Exports - vol.	-0.3%	-0.3%	-0.3%	-0.3%	-0.3%	-0.4%	0.9%	0.8%	0.7%	0.7%	0.6%	0.5%	0.6%	0.6%	0.5%
Absorption - vol.	-0.1%	-0.1%	-0.1%	-0.1%	-0.1%	-0.1%	0.1%	-0.3%	-0.4%	-0.1%	-0.6%	-0.7%	-0.2%	-0.6%	-0.8%
Investment - vol.	-0.1%	0.0%	0.0%	-0.1%	0.0%	0.0%	-3.3%	-2.8%	-2.8%	-3.4%	-2.9%	-3.0%	-3.3%	-2.9%	-2.9%
Labour Demand - vol.	-0.2%	0.0%	0.0%	-0.2%	0.0%	0.0%	1.9%	3.0%	3.0%	1.7%	2.8%	2.7%	1.7%	2.8%	2.8%
Private Consumption - vol.	0.1%	0.1%	0.1%	0.1%	0.1%	0.1%	-1.0%	-1.6%	-1.8%	-1.0%	-1.6%	-1.8%	-1.0%	-1.6%	-1.9%
Supply to domestic - vol.	-0.3%	-0.3%	-0.3%	-0.3%	-0.3%	-0.3%	1.2%	1.0%	0.8%	1.0%	0.6%	0.4%	0.9%	0.6%	0.3%
Intra-EU Trade - vol	-0.3%	-0.3%	-0.3%	-0.3%	-0.3%	-0.3%	1.1%	1.5%	1.4%	0.7%	1.1%	1.0%	0.7%	1.1%	1.0%

Metal Industries

	Border Controls			Border controls and x-ineff.			Market segmentation			Trade *antimonde*			Full *antimonde*		
	1988	1991	1994	1988	1991	1994	1988	1991	1994	1988	1991	1994	1988	1991	1994
Domestic Production - vol.	-1.1%	-2.2%	-2.2%	-1.0%	-2.2%	-2.2%	-5.0%	-15.7%	-15.1%	-7.2%	-18.1%	-17.5%	-7.4%	-18.4%	-17.8%
Imports - vol.	0.8%	0.5%	0.5%	0.8%	0.6%	0.6%	-5.6%	-9.3%	-8.9%	-4.6%	-8.3%	-7.9%	-4.4%	-8.1%	-7.7%
Exports - vol.	-0.6%	-0.6%	-0.6%	-0.6%	-0.6%	-0.6%	1.3%	1.0%	0.9%	0.9%	0.6%	0.4%	0.8%	0.5%	0.3%
Absorption - vol.	-0.8%	-1.8%	-1.7%	-0.8%	-1.7%	-1.7%	-4.4%	-13.0%	-12.5%	-6.0%	-14.9%	-14.4%	-6.1%	-15.1%	-14.6%
Investment - vol.	-0.6%	-1.2%	-1.2%	-0.6%	-1.2%	-1.2%	-6.0%	-10.9%	-10.7%	-7.1%	-12.1%	-11.9%	-7.1%	-12.2%	-12.0%
Labour Demand - vol.	-1.0%	-2.1%	-2.1%	-1.0%	-2.1%	-2.0%	-3.5%	-13.7%	-13.0%	-5.5%	-16.0%	-15.4%	-5.7%	-16.2%	-15.6%
Private Consumption - vol.	0.1%	0.1%	0.1%	0.1%	0.1%	0.1%	-0.7%	-1.1%	-1.2%	-0.7%	-1.1%	-1.2%	-0.7%	-1.1%	-1.3%
Supply to domestic - vol.	-0.1%	0.3%	0.3%	-0.1%	0.3%	0.3%	-5.6%	-15.6%	-14.7%	-7.6%	-17.8%	-17.0%	-7.8%	-18.0%	-17.3%
Intra-EU Trade - vol	-1.3%	-2.7%	-2.7%	-1.3%	-2.7%	-2.7%	-1.5%	-7.6%	-7.4%	-3.3%	-9.6%	-9.4%	-3.5%	-9.8%	-9.7%

Chemical

	Border Controls			Border controls and x-ineff.			Market segmentation			Trade *antimonde*			Full *antimonde*		
	1988	1991	1994	1988	1991	1994	1988	1991	1994	1988	1991	1994	1988	1991	1994
Domestic Production - vol.	-1.2%	-2.8%	-2.8%	-1.2%	-2.9%	-2.9%	-0.3%	-3.8%	-4.2%	-1.0%	-5.2%	-5.6%	-1.2%	-5.5%	-6.0%
Imports - vol.	0.9%	0.7%	0.7%	0.9%	0.7%	0.7%	-4.9%	-5.3%	-5.2%	-3.6%	-3.8%	-3.7%	-3.3%	-3.5%	-3.2%
Exports - vol.	-0.4%	-0.5%	-0.5%	-0.4%	-0.5%	-0.5%	1.8%	1.7%	1.5%	1.6%	1.5%	1.3%	1.6%	1.4%	1.1%
Absorption - vol.	-0.9%	-1.9%	-1.9%	-0.9%	-2.0%	-2.0%	0.3%	-1.5%	-1.9%	-0.3%	-2.5%	-3.0%	-0.5%	-2.7%	-3.2%
Investment - vol.	-0.6%	-1.4%	-1.4%	-0.6%	-1.4%	-1.4%	-4.1%	-5.7%	-6.0%	-4.4%	-6.3%	-6.6%	-4.5%	-6.4%	-6.7%
Labour Demand - vol.	-1.1%	-2.6%	-2.6%	-1.1%	-2.7%	-2.7%	0.7%	-2.4%	-2.9%	0.1%	-3.7%	-4.1%	-0.1%	-4.0%	-4.5%
Private Consumption - vol.	0.1%	0.1%	0.1%	0.1%	0.1%	0.1%	-1.0%	-1.7%	-2.0%	-1.0%	-1.7%	-2.1%	-1.1%	-1.8%	-2.1%
Supply to domestic - vol.	0.4%	1.1%	1.1%	0.4%	1.1%	1.1%	-2.9%	-5.1%	-5.8%	-3.1%	-5.7%	-6.4%	-3.3%	-6.0%	-6.8%
Intra-EU Trade - vol	-1.2%	-2.8%	-2.8%	-1.2%	-2.8%	-2.8%	1.0%	-1.1%	-1.3%	0.2%	-2.3%	-2.5%	0.1%	-2.5%	-2.8%

Other Intensive Industries

	Border Controls			Border controls and x-ineff.			Market segmentation			Trade *antimonde*			Full *antimonde*		
	1988	1991	1994	1988	1991	1994	1988	1991	1994	1988	1991	1994	1988	1991	1994
Domestic Production - vol.	-0.7%	-0.6%	-0.6%	-0.7%	-0.6%	-0.6%	2.0%	9.1%	8.7%	1.2%	8.2%	7.8%	1.1%	8.1%	7.7%
Imports - vol.	1.9%	2.1%	2.1%	1.9%	2.1%	2.1%	-8.5%	-8.7%	-8.4%	-6.1%	-6.2%	-5.8%	-5.8%	-5.8%	-5.3%
Exports - vol.	-0.6%	-0.6%	-0.6%	-0.6%	-0.6%	-0.6%	2.2%	2.2%	2.0%	1.8%	1.8%	1.6%	1.8%	1.7%	1.5%
Absorption - vol.	-0.3%	-0.7%	-0.7%	-0.3%	-0.7%	-0.7%	-2.9%	-4.2%	-4.3%	-3.3%	-4.8%	-4.9%	-3.4%	-4.9%	-5.0%
Investment - vol.	-0.4%	-0.5%	-0.3%	-0.4%	-0.3%	-0.3%	-3.3%	-0.1%	-0.3%	-3.7%	-0.5%	-0.7%	-3.7%	-0.5%	-0.7%
Labour Demand - vol.	-0.7%	-0.5%	-0.5%	-0.7%	-0.5%	-0.5%	2.6%	9.9%	9.6%	1.8%	9.1%	8.8%	1.8%	9.0%	8.7%
Private Consumption - vol.	0.2%	0.1%	0.1%	0.2%	0.1%	0.1%	-2.1%	-1.9%	-1.8%	-2.1%	-2.0%	-1.8%	-2.1%	-2.1%	-1.8%
Supply to domestic - vol.	1.0%	4.5%	4.5%	1.0%	4.5%	4.5%	3.4%	16.2%	15.9%	3.2%	16.0%	15.7%	3.1%	15.9%	15.5%
Intra-EU Trade - vol	-1.4%	-2.9%	-2.9%	-1.4%	-2.9%	-2.9%	-1.3%	-4.2%	-4.3%	-2.3%	-5.2%	-5.4%	-2.4%	-5.3%	-5.5%

Electrical goods

	Border Controls			Border controls and x-ineff.			Market segmentation			Trade antimonde			Full antimonde		
	1988	1991	1994	1988	1991	1994	1988	1991	1994	1988	1991	1994	1988	1991	1994
Domestic Production - vol.	-1.9%	-3.8%	-3.8%	-1.9%	-3.8%	-3.9%	-6.2%	-14.3%	-14.4%	-8.3%	-16.7%	-16.8%	-8.6%	-17.1%	-17.3%
Imports - vol.	1.7%	1.5%	1.5%	1.7%	1.5%	1.5%	-8.6%	-9.8%	-9.4%	-6.5%	-7.7%	-7.2%	-6.3%	-7.3%	-6.7%
Exports - vol.	-0.7%	-0.7%	-0.7%	-0.7%	-0.8%	-0.8%	2.4%	2.1%	1.9%	1.9%	1.6%	1.4%	1.9%	1.5%	1.3%
Absorption - vol.	-0.5%	-1.7%	-1.7%	-0.5%	-1.7%	-1.7%	-6.9%	-10.5%	-10.1%	-7.7%	-11.7%	-11.4%	-7.9%	-11.9%	-11.6%
Investment - vol.	-1.0%	-1.9%	-1.9%	-1.0%	-1.9%	-1.9%	-6.9%	-10.6%	-10.7%	-7.8%	-11.7%	-11.8%	-7.9%	-11.8%	-12.0%
Labour Demand - vol.	-1.8%	-3.5%	-3.5%	-1.8%	-3.5%	-3.5%	-4.4%	-12.3%	-12.3%	-6.4%	-14.5%	-14.6%	-6.6%	-14.8%	-14.9%
Private Consumption - vol.	1.0%	0.0%	0.1%	1.0%	0.0%	0.1%	-8.5%	-5.5%	-3.6%	-8.3%	-5.9%	-3.8%	-8.4%	-6.0%	-3.9%
Supply to domestic - vol.	0.6%	0.8%	0.8%	0.6%	0.7%	0.7%	-24.8%	-37.0%	-36.8%	-25.5%	-37.8%	-37.5%	-25.7%	-38.0%	-37.8%
Intra-EU Trade - vol	-1.4%	-2.7%	-2.7%	-1.4%	-2.7%	-2.7%	0.6%	-1.5%	-1.6%	-0.9%	-3.3%	-3.3%	-1.0%	-3.5%	-3.6%

Transport equipment

	Border Controls			Border controls and x-ineff.			Market segmentation			Trade antimonde			Full antimonde		
	1988	1991	1994	1988	1991	1994	1988	1991	1994	1988	1991	1994	1988	1991	1994
Domestic Production - vol.	-0.9%	-2.5%	-2.6%	-0.9%	-2.6%	-2.6%	-19.6%	-40.7%	-40.2%	-20.8%	-42.3%	-41.8%	-21.0%	-42.5%	-42.1%
Imports - vol.	1.3%	0.9%	0.9%	1.4%	0.9%	0.9%	-10.6%	-17.4%	-17.1%	-8.8%	-16.0%	-15.6%	-8.6%	-15.8%	-15.3%
Exports - vol.	-0.7%	-0.8%	-0.8%	-0.7%	-0.8%	-0.8%	1.4%	0.4%	0.3%	0.9%	-0.1%	-0.3%	0.8%	-0.2%	-0.4%
Absorption - vol.	-0.3%	-1.7%	-1.7%	-0.3%	-1.7%	-1.7%	-13.7%	-30.0%	-29.5%	-14.4%	-31.2%	-30.6%	-14.5%	-31.3%	-30.8%
Investment - vol.	-0.5%	-1.3%	-1.3%	-0.5%	-1.3%	-1.3%	-12.5%	-22.2%	-22.0%	-13.0%	-22.9%	-22.7%	-13.1%	-23.0%	-22.8%
Labour Demand - vol.	-0.8%	-2.3%	-2.3%	-0.8%	-2.3%	-2.4%	-16.7%	-37.9%	-37.4%	-17.8%	-39.5%	-38.9%	-17.9%	-39.6%	-39.1%
Private Consumption - vol.	0.8%	0.0%	0.0%	0.7%	0.0%	0.0%	-7.2%	-4.6%	-2.6%	-7.1%	-4.9%	-2.7%	-7.2%	-5.0%	-2.8%
Supply to domestic - vol.	0.9%	0.5%	0.5%	0.9%	0.5%	0.4%	-31.6%	-57.5%	-56.9%	-32.2%	-58.2%	-57.7%	-32.3%	-58.4%	-57.8%
Intra-EU Trade - vol	-0.9%	-2.3%	-2.3%	-0.9%	-2.3%	-2.3%	-4.9%	-11.8%	-11.7%	-5.8%	-13.1%	-13.0%	-5.9%	-13.3%	-13.1%

Other Equipment

	Border Controls			Border controls and x-ineff.			Market segmentation			Trade antimonde			Full antimonde		
	1988	1991	1994	1988	1991	1994	1988	1991	1994	1988	1991	1994	1988	1991	1994
Domestic Production - vol.	-1.5%	-2.2%	-2.2%	-1.5%	-2.2%	-2.2%	-3.1%	-5.1%	-5.4%	-5.1%	-7.4%	-7.7%	-5.2%	-7.7%	-8.1%
Imports - vol.	1.3%	1.3%	1.3%	1.3%	1.3%	1.3%	-7.6%	-8.6%	-8.5%	-5.5%	-6.4%	-6.3%	-5.3%	-6.2%	-5.9%
Exports - vol.	-0.8%	-0.9%	-0.9%	-0.8%	-0.9%	-0.9%	2.3%	2.1%	1.9%	1.7%	1.5%	1.3%	1.6%	1.4%	1.2%
Absorption - vol.	-0.7%	-1.2%	-1.2%	-0.7%	-1.2%	-1.2%	-5.9%	-8.7%	-8.9%	-6.8%	-9.9%	-10.1%	-6.9%	-10.0%	-10.2%
Investment - vol.	-0.8%	-1.1%	-1.1%	-0.8%	-1.1%	-1.1%	-5.4%	-6.3%	-6.5%	-6.3%	-7.4%	-7.6%	-6.4%	-7.5%	-7.7%
Labour Demand - vol.	-1.5%	-2.1%	-2.1%	-1.5%	-2.1%	-2.1%	-1.8%	-3.4%	-3.7%	-3.7%	-5.7%	-5.9%	-3.8%	-5.9%	-6.2%
Private Consumption - vol.	0.3%	0.1%	0.1%	0.3%	0.1%	0.1%	-2.6%	-2.9%	-3.0%	-2.6%	-3.0%	-3.0%	-2.6%	-3.0%	-3.1%
Supply to domestic - vol.	0.5%	3.0%	3.0%	0.5%	3.0%	3.0%	-11.2%	-15.3%	-15.6%	-12.1%	-16.3%	-16.6%	-12.2%	-16.5%	-16.8%
Intra-EU Trade - vol	-1.2%	-2.2%	-2.2%	-1.2%	-2.2%	-2.2%	-0.8%	-1.9%	-2.0%	-2.3%	-3.7%	-3.8%	-2.4%	-3.9%	-4.0%

Consumer goods

	Border Controls			Border controls and x-ineff.			Market segmentation			Trade antimonde			Full antimonde		
	1988	1991	1994	1988	1991	1994	1988	1991	1994	1988	1991	1994	1988	1991	1994
Domestic Production - vol.	-1.1%	-1.2%	-1.2%	-1.1%	-1.2%	-1.2%	3.7%	8.4%	7.7%	3.0%	7.6%	6.9%	2.9%	7.5%	6.7%
Imports - vol.	1.4%	1.6%	1.6%	1.4%	1.6%	1.7%	-4.4%	-3.6%	-3.4%	-3.4%	-2.6%	-2.3%	-3.3%	-2.4%	-2.1%
Exports - vol.	-0.7%	-0.8%	-0.8%	-0.7%	-0.8%	-0.8%	2.6%	2.4%	2.2%	2.2%	2.0%	1.7%	2.1%	1.9%	1.6%
Absorption - vol.	-0.2%	-0.2%	-0.2%	-0.2%	-0.2%	-0.2%	-0.2%	0.5%	0.1%	-0.4%	0.2%	-0.2%	-0.5%	0.1%	-0.2%
Investment - vol.	-0.6%	-0.7%	-0.7%	-0.6%	-0.7%	-0.7%	-2.4%	-0.3%	-0.7%	-2.8%	-0.7%	-1.1%	-2.8%	-0.7%	-1.1%
Labour Demand - vol.	-1.1%	-1.2%	-1.2%	-1.1%	-1.3%	-1.3%	4.2%	9.0%	8.4%	3.5%	8.2%	7.6%	3.4%	8.2%	7.5%
Private Consumption - vol.	0.2%	0.2%	0.1%	0.2%	0.2%	0.1%	-1.3%	-1.9%	-2.2%	-1.3%	-2.0%	-2.2%	-1.3%	-2.0%	-2.3%
Supply to domestic - vol.	1.2%	5.9%	5.9%	1.1%	5.8%	5.8%	7.4%	20.4%	19.4%	7.1%	20.2%	19.2%	6.9%	20.0%	18.8%
Intra-EU Trade - vol	-1.5%	-3.2%	-3.2%	-1.5%	-3.3%	-3.3%	0.2%	-1.1%	-1.4%	-0.5%	-2.0%	-2.3%	-0.5%	-2.0%	-2.4%

Construction

	Border Controls			Border controls and x-ineff.			Market segmentation			Trade antimonde			Full antimonde		
	1988	1991	1994	1988	1991	1994	1988	1991	1994	1988	1991	1994	1988	1991	1994
Domestic Production - vol.	0.3%	0.3%	0.3%	0.3%	0.4%	0.4%	-7.0%	-6.9%	-7.1%	-6.8%	-6.7%	-6.9%	-6.8%	-6.7%	-6.9%
Imports - vol.	#VALUE!	#VALUE!	#VALUE!	#VALUE!	#VALUE!	#VALUE!	#VALUE!	#VALUE!	#VALUE!	#VALUE!	#VALUE!	#VALUE!	#VALUE!	#VALUE!	#VALUE!
Exports - vol.	-0.3%	-0.3%	-0.3%	-0.3%	-0.3%	-0.3%	0.7%	0.7%	0.6%	0.5%	0.5%	0.4%	0.5%	0.5%	0.4%
Absorption - vol.	0.3%	0.4%	0.4%	0.3%	0.4%	0.4%	-7.7%	-7.2%	-7.4%	-7.1%	-7.0%	-7.2%	-7.1%	-7.0%	-7.2%
Investment - vol.	0.1%	0.2%	0.2%	0.1%	0.2%	0.2%	-7.7%	-7.7%	-7.8%	-7.6%	-7.7%	-7.8%	-7.6%	-7.6%	-7.8%
Labour Demand - vol.	0.3%	0.3%	0.3%	0.3%	0.4%	0.4%	-6.8%	-6.7%	-6.8%	-6.6%	-6.5%	-6.6%	-6.6%	-6.4%	-6.5%
Private Consumption - vol.	0.1%	0.1%	0.1%	0.1%	0.1%	0.1%	-1.1%	-1.9%	-2.3%	-1.1%	-1.9%	-2.3%	-1.1%	-1.9%	-2.4%
Supply to domestic - vol.	0.3%	0.3%	0.3%	0.3%	0.4%	0.4%	-7.0%	-6.9%	-7.1%	-6.8%	-6.7%	-6.9%	-6.8%	-6.7%	-6.9%
Intra-EU Trade - vol	0.3%	0.3%	0.3%	0.3%	0.3%	0.3%	-3.5%	-3.5%	-3.6%	-3.3%	-3.3%	-3.4%	-3.3%	-3.3%	-3.4%

Telecommunications

	Border Controls			Border controls and x-ineff.			Market segmentation			Trade antimonde			Full antimonde		
	1988	1991	1994	1988	1991	1994	1988	1991	1994	1988	1991	1994	1988	1991	1994
Domestic Production - vol.	0.2%	0.6%	0.6%	0.3%	0.9%	0.9%	1.4%	5.7%	5.3%	1.7%	6.0%	5.6%	1.7%	6.1%	5.7%
Imports - vol.	1.1%	1.1%	1.1%	1.0%	0.9%	0.9%	-7.6%	-7.7%	-7.5%	-7.0%	-7.2%	-6.9%	-7.0%	-7.1%	-6.8%
Exports - vol.	-0.2%	-0.2%	-0.2%	-0.2%	-0.2%	-0.2%	1.4%	1.5%	1.4%	1.3%	1.4%	1.3%	1.3%	1.4%	1.3%
Absorption - vol.	0.2%	0.3%	0.3%	0.3%	0.5%	0.5%	-0.5%	0.0%	-0.3%	-0.3%	0.2%	-0.1%	-0.3%	0.3%	0.0%
Investment - vol.	0.2%	0.4%	0.4%	0.2%	0.5%	0.5%	-3.7%	-1.8%	-2.0%	-3.6%	-1.6%	-1.8%	-3.5%	-1.5%	-1.7%
Labour Demand - vol.	0.2%	0.5%	0.5%	-0.1%	0.1%	0.1%	2.1%	6.8%	6.6%	2.3%	7.1%	6.9%	2.0%	6.4%	6.2%
Private Consumption - vol.	0.1%	0.1%	0.1%	0.2%	0.3%	0.3%	-1.3%	-2.1%	-2.5%	-1.2%	-2.1%	-2.5%	-1.2%	-2.0%	-2.4%
Supply to domestic - vol.	0.2%	0.5%	0.5%	0.3%	1.0%	1.0%	1.8%	7.9%	7.5%	1.9%	8.1%	7.7%	2.0%	8.2%	7.8%
Intra-EU Trade - vol	0.4%	0.2%	0.2%	0.1%	-1.2%	-1.2%	-6.9%	-19.3%	-19.3%	-6.6%	-19.0%	-19.1%	-6.7%	-19.1%	-19.2%

Transports

	Border Controls			Border controls and x-ineff.			Market segmentation			Trade antimonde			Full antimonde		
	1988	1991	1994	1988	1991	1994	1988	1991	1994	1988	1991	1994	1988	1991	1994
Domestic Production - vol.	1.1%	1.3%	1.3%	1.1%	1.3%	1.3%	0.0%	-0.6%	-0.8%	1.1%	0.6%	0.4%	1.0%	0.6%	0.3%
Imports - vol.	0.5%	0.6%	0.6%	0.5%	0.6%	0.6%	0.0%	-0.3%	-0.4%	0.5%	0.3%	0.2%	0.5%	0.3%	0.2%
Exports - vol.	-0.2%	-0.2%	-0.2%	-0.2%	-0.2%	-0.2%	0.8%	0.8%	0.7%	0.8%	0.8%	0.7%	0.8%	0.8%	0.7%
Absorption - vol.	-0.2%	-0.4%	-0.4%	-0.2%	-0.4%	-0.4%	-0.9%	-2.3%	-2.6%	-1.3%	-2.8%	-3.1%	-1.3%	-2.8%	-3.1%
Investment - vol.	0.5%	0.6%	0.6%	0.5%	0.6%	0.6%	-4.3%	-4.7%	-4.8%	-3.9%	-4.1%	-4.2%	-3.9%	-4.1%	-4.2%
Labour Demand - vol.	1.1%	1.3%	1.3%	1.1%	1.3%	1.3%	0.1%	-0.5%	-0.7%	1.1%	0.7%	0.5%	1.2%	0.7%	0.6%
Private Consumption - vol.	0.2%	0.2%	0.2%	0.2%	0.2%	0.2%	-1.5%	-2.5%	-2.9%	-1.5%	-2.5%	-3.0%	-1.5%	-2.5%	-3.0%
Supply to domestic - vol.	1.1%	1.3%	1.3%	1.1%	1.3%	1.3%	0.0%	-0.6%	-0.8%	1.1%	0.6%	0.4%	1.0%	0.6%	0.3%
Intra-EU Trade - vol	1.9%	2.4%	2.4%	1.9%	2.4%	2.4%	0.1%	0.1%	-0.1%	1.9%	2.3%	2.2%	1.9%	2.3%	2.1%

Banks

	Border Controls			Border controls and x-ineff.			Market segmentation			Trade antimonde			Full antimonde		
	1988	1991	1994	1988	1991	1994	1988	1991	1994	1988	1991	1994	1988	1991	1994
Domestic Production - vol.	0.1%	0.5%	0.5%	0.2%	0.7%	0.7%	1.1%	5.6%	5.3%	1.2%	5.8%	5.5%	1.2%	5.7%	5.4%
Imports - vol.	1.3%	1.4%	1.4%	1.2%	1.3%	1.3%	-7.7%	-7.0%	-6.7%	-6.8%	-6.1%	-5.9%	-6.6%	-5.9%	-5.5%
Exports - vol.	-0.2%	-0.2%	-0.2%	-0.2%	-0.2%	-0.2%	1.4%	1.4%	1.3%	1.3%	1.3%	1.2%	1.3%	1.3%	1.2%
Absorption - vol.	0.1%	0.3%	0.3%	0.2%	0.5%	0.5%	0.3%	2.8%	2.5%	0.4%	2.9%	2.6%	0.3%	2.9%	2.5%
Investment - vol.	0.1%	0.3%	0.3%	0.1%	0.4%	0.4%	-3.8%	-1.8%	-2.0%	-3.8%	-1.8%	-1.9%	-3.8%	-1.7%	-1.9%
Labour Demand - vol.	0.1%	0.4%	0.4%	0.0%	0.2%	0.2%	1.2%	5.4%	5.3%	1.3%	5.6%	5.4%	1.1%	5.2%	5.0%
Private Consumption - vol.	0.2%	0.2%	0.1%	0.2%	0.2%	0.2%	-1.4%	-2.2%	-2.6%	-1.3%	-2.2%	-2.7%	-1.4%	-2.3%	-2.8%
Supply to domestic - vol.	0.1%	0.4%	0.4%	0.2%	0.6%	0.6%	1.0%	5.6%	5.3%	1.1%	5.7%	5.4%	1.1%	5.7%	5.4%
Intra-EU Trade - vol	0.5%	-0.1%	-0.1%	0.3%	-0.9%	-0.9%	-7.7%	-20.0%	-20.2%	-7.4%	-19.6%	-19.9%	-7.5%	-19.7%	-20.0%

Services

	Border Controls			Border controls and x-ineff.			Market segmentation			Trade antimonde			Full antimonde		
	1988	1991	1994	1988	1991	1994	1988	1991	1994	1988	1991	1994	1988	1991	1994
Domestic Production - vol.	0.7%	1.0%	1.0%	0.7%	1.0%	1.0%	-0.2%	1.6%	1.2%	0.4%	2.4%	2.0%	0.4%	2.3%	1.9%
Imports - vol.	1.9%	1.9%	1.9%	1.9%	1.9%	1.9%	-5.6%	-5.7%	-5.3%	-4.3%	-4.5%	-4.1%	-4.2%	-4.3%	-3.9%
Exports - vol.	-0.6%	-0.6%	-0.6%	-0.6%	-0.6%	-0.6%	1.7%	1.7%	1.5%	1.3%	1.3%	1.1%	1.2%	1.2%	1.0%
Absorption - vol.	0.1%	0.5%	0.5%	0.1%	0.5%	0.5%	-1.5%	-2.0%	-2.2%	-1.6%	-2.1%	-2.3%	-1.6%	-2.2%	-2.4%
Investment - vol.	0.3%	0.5%	0.5%	0.3%	0.5%	0.5%	-4.4%	-3.6%	-3.8%	-4.1%	-3.3%	-3.5%	-4.1%	-3.3%	-3.4%
Labour Demand - vol.	0.7%	1.1%	1.0%	0.7%	1.1%	1.1%	-0.2%	1.7%	1.4%	0.4%	2.4%	2.2%	0.5%	2.5%	2.3%
Private Consumption - vol.	0.2%	0.1%	0.1%	0.2%	0.1%	0.1%	-1.8%	-2.3%	-2.5%	-1.7%	-2.3%	-2.5%	-1.8%	-2.4%	-2.6%
Supply to domestic - vol.	0.0%	0.0%	0.0%	0.0%	0.0%	0.0%	-0.9%	0.2%	-0.1%	-1.0%	0.0%	-0.3%	-1.0%	0.0%	-0.4%
Intra-EU Trade - vol	2.6%	3.5%	3.5%	2.6%	3.6%	3.5%	-0.6%	-2.5%	-2.5%	1.6%	0.5%	0.4%	1.7%	0.5%	0.5%

Non market

	Border Controls			Border controls and x-ineff.			Market segmentation			Trade antimonde			Full antimonde		
	1988	1991	1994	1988	1991	1994	1988	1991	1994	1988	1991	1994	1988	1991	1994
Domestic Production - vol.	0.0%	0.0%	0.0%	0.0%	0.0%	0.0%	-0.1%	-0.1%	-0.1%	-0.1%	-0.1%	-0.1%	-0.1%	-0.1%	-0.1%
Imports - vol.	#VALUE!	#VALUE!	#VALUE!	#VALUE!	#VALUE!	#VALUE!	#VALUE!	#VALUE!	#VALUE!	#VALUE!	#VALUE!	#VALUE!	#VALUE!	#VALUE!	#VALUE!
Exports - vol.	#VALUE!	#VALUE!	#VALUE!	#VALUE!	#VALUE!	#VALUE!	#VALUE!	#VALUE!	#VALUE!	#VALUE!	#VALUE!	#VALUE!	#VALUE!	#VALUE!	#VALUE!
Absorption - vol.	0.0%	0.0%	0.0%	0.0%	0.0%	0.0%	-0.1%	-0.1%	-0.1%	-0.1%	-0.1%	-0.1%	-0.1%	-0.1%	-0.1%
Investment - vol.	0.0%	0.0%	0.0%	0.0%	0.0%	0.0%	-4.2%	-4.2%	-4.2%	-4.2%	-4.2%	-4.2%	-4.2%	-4.2%	-4.2%
Labour Demand - vol.	0.0%	0.0%	0.0%	0.0%	0.0%	0.0%	0.0%	0.0%	-0.1%	0.0%	0.0%	-0.1%	0.0%	0.0%	0.0%
Private Consumption - vol.	0.2%	0.1%	0.1%	0.2%	0.1%	0.1%	-1.3%	-1.9%	-2.1%	-1.3%	-1.9%	-2.2%	-1.3%	-1.9%	-2.2%
Supply to domestic - vol.	0.0%	0.0%	0.0%	0.0%	0.0%	0.0%	-0.1%	-0.1%	-0.1%	-0.1%	-0.1%	-0.1%	-0.1%	-0.1%	-0.1%
Intra-EU Trade - vol	#DIV/0!	#DIV/0!	#DIV/0!	#DIV/0!	#DIV/0!	#DIV/0!	#DIV/0!	#DIV/0!	#DIV/0!	#DIV/0!	#DIV/0!	#DIV/0!	#DIV/0!	#DIV/0!	#DIV/0!

Table B2.8.
Decomposition of effects: sectoral results for Belgium (prices)

% change from *monde*

Agriculture

	Border Controls			Border controls and x-ineff.			Market segmentation			Trade *antimonde*			Full *antimonde*		
	1988	1991	1994	1988	1991	1994	1988	1991	1994	1988	1991	1994	1988	1991	1994
Marginal Costs	-0.40%	-0.42%	-0.42%	-0.39%	-0.41%	-0.41%	1.22%	0.82%	0.98%	1.14%	0.78%	0.94%	1.12%	0.76%	0.91%
Cost of Labour	-0.10%	-0.21%	-0.21%	-0.11%	-0.24%	-0.25%	-1.06%	-1.77%	-2.14%	-1.19%	-1.96%	-2.34%	-1.28%	-2.11%	-2.54%
Deflator of Absorption	-0.94%	-0.87%	-0.87%	-0.94%	-0.87%	-0.88%	3.08%	2.89%	2.76%	2.79%	2.74%	2.61%	2.74%	2.66%	2.49%
Price of Exports-RW	-0.40%	-0.42%	-0.42%	-0.39%	-0.41%	-0.41%	1.22%	0.82%	0.98%	1.14%	0.78%	0.94%	1.12%	0.76%	0.91%

Energy

	Border Controls			Border controls and x-ineff.			Market segmentation			Trade *antimonde*			Full *antimonde*		
	1988	1991	1994	1988	1991	1994	1988	1991	1994	1988	1991	1994	1988	1991	1994
Marginal Costs	-0.70%	-0.69%	-0.70%	-0.70%	-0.70%	-0.71%	2.15%	1.77%	1.66%	1.91%	1.62%	1.51%	1.85%	1.52%	1.37%
Cost of Labour	-0.10%	-0.21%	-0.21%	-0.11%	-0.24%	-0.25%	-1.06%	-1.77%	-2.14%	-1.19%	-1.96%	-2.34%	-1.28%	-2.11%	-2.54%
Deflator of Absorption	-1.00%	-0.93%	-0.94%	-1.01%	-0.95%	-0.96%	3.55%	3.29%	3.06%	3.23%	3.13%	2.89%	3.14%	3.00%	2.70%
Price of Exports-RW	-0.70%	-0.69%	-0.70%	-0.70%	-0.70%	-0.71%	2.15%	1.77%	1.66%	1.91%	1.62%	1.51%	1.85%	1.52%	1.37%

Metal Industries

	Border Controls			Border controls and x-ineff.			Market segmentation			Trade *antimonde*			Full *antimonde*		
	1988	1991	1994	1988	1991	1994	1988	1991	1994	1988	1991	1994	1988	1991	1994
Marginal Costs	-0.86%	-0.77%	-0.77%	-0.87%	-0.79%	-0.79%	3.96%	4.03%	3.68%	3.79%	4.04%	3.68%	3.78%	4.01%	3.64%
Cost of Labour	-0.10%	-0.21%	-0.21%	-0.11%	-0.24%	-0.25%	-1.06%	-1.77%	-2.14%	-1.19%	-1.96%	-2.34%	-1.28%	-2.11%	-2.54%
Deflator of Absorption	-1.15%	-1.01%	-1.01%	-1.17%	-1.03%	-1.04%	5.73%	6.13%	5.68%	5.53%	6.17%	5.71%	5.48%	6.09%	5.60%
Price of Exports-RW	-0.87%	-0.79%	-0.78%	-0.88%	-0.80%	-0.80%	3.62%	3.85%	3.47%	3.49%	3.92%	3.53%	3.49%	3.90%	3.50%

Chemical

	Border Controls			Border controls and x-ineff.			Market segmentation			Trade *antimonde*			Full *antimonde*		
	1988	1991	1994	1988	1991	1994	1988	1991	1994	1988	1991	1994	1988	1991	1994
Marginal Costs	-0.24%	-0.13%	-0.13%	-0.24%	-0.14%	-0.14%	2.39%	2.28%	2.11%	2.55%	2.60%	2.43%	2.55%	2.60%	2.42%
Cost of Labour	-0.10%	-0.21%	-0.21%	-0.11%	-0.24%	-0.25%	-1.06%	-1.77%	-2.14%	-1.19%	-1.96%	-2.34%	-1.28%	-2.11%	-2.54%
Deflator of Absorption	-0.12%	0.12%	0.12%	-0.13%	0.11%	0.10%	3.82%	4.03%	3.79%	4.24%	4.74%	4.50%	4.22%	4.71%	4.44%
Price of Exports-RW	-0.25%	-0.14%	-0.14%	-0.25%	-0.14%	-0.14%	2.00%	1.80%	1.64%	2.14%	2.12%	1.95%	2.15%	2.12%	1.95%

Other Intensive Industries

	Border Controls			Border controls and x-ineff.			Market segmentation			Trade *antimonde*			Full *antimonde*		
	1988	1991	1994	1988	1991	1994	1988	1991	1994	1988	1991	1994	1988	1991	1994
Marginal Costs	-0.30%	-0.30%	-0.30%	-0.31%	-0.31%	-0.31%	1.00%	0.63%	0.46%	0.94%	0.64%	0.46%	0.93%	0.61%	0.41%
Cost of Labour	-0.10%	-0.21%	-0.21%	-0.11%	-0.24%	-0.25%	-1.06%	-1.77%	-2.14%	-1.19%	-1.96%	-2.34%	-1.28%	-2.11%	-2.54%
Deflator of Absorption	-0.27%	-0.08%	-0.08%	-0.27%	-0.10%	-0.10%	2.19%	2.18%	1.94%	2.32%	2.49%	2.25%	2.30%	2.45%	2.18%
Price of Exports-RW	-0.31%	-0.35%	-0.35%	-0.32%	-0.36%	-0.36%	0.85%	0.30%	0.13%	0.79%	0.30%	0.11%	0.77%	0.26%	0.07%

Electrical goods

	Border Controls			Border controls and x-ineff.			Market segmentation			Trade *antimonde*			Full *antimonde*		
	1988	1991	1994	1988	1991	1994	1988	1991	1994	1988	1991	1994	1988	1991	1994
Marginal Costs	-0.27%	-0.22%	-0.22%	-0.27%	-0.23%	-0.23%	1.88%	1.67%	1.45%	1.93%	1.83%	1.60%	1.92%	1.81%	1.57%
Cost of Labour	-0.10%	-0.21%	-0.21%	-0.11%	-0.24%	-0.25%	-1.06%	-1.77%	-2.14%	-1.19%	-1.96%	-2.34%	-1.28%	-2.11%	-2.54%
Deflator of Absorption	-0.27%	-0.05%	-0.04%	-0.28%	-0.06%	-0.07%	4.63%	4.95%	4.64%	4.96%	5.56%	5.24%	4.94%	5.52%	5.18%
Price of Exports-RW	-0.28%	-0.23%	-0.22%	-0.28%	-0.23%	-0.23%	1.41%	1.51%	1.28%	1.49%	1.72%	1.49%	1.49%	1.72%	1.48%

Transport equipment

	Border Controls			Border controls and x-ineff.			Market segmentation			Trade *antimonde*			Full *antimonde*		
	1988	1991	1994	1988	1991	1994	1988	1991	1994	1988	1991	1994	1988	1991	1994
Marginal Costs	-0.31%	-0.20%	-0.20%	-0.31%	-0.21%	-0.21%	3.98%	4.57%	4.27%	4.19%	5.04%	4.73%	4.21%	5.05%	4.75%
Cost of Labour	-0.10%	-0.21%	-0.21%	-0.11%	-0.24%	-0.25%	-1.06%	-1.77%	-2.14%	-1.19%	-1.96%	-2.34%	-1.28%	-2.11%	-2.54%
Deflator of Absorption	-0.34%	-0.16%	-0.16%	-0.34%	-0.18%	-0.18%	5.98%	7.23%	6.87%	6.36%	7.99%	7.62%	6.34%	7.97%	7.58%
Price of Exports-RW	-0.34%	-0.21%	-0.21%	-0.34%	-0.22%	-0.22%	3.89%	5.90%	5.56%	4.13%	6.49%	6.14%	4.15%	6.52%	6.18%

Other Equipment

	Border Controls			Border controls and x-ineff.			Market segmentation			Trade *antimonde*			Full *antimonde*		
	1988	1991	1994	1988	1991	1994	1988	1991	1994	1988	1991	1994	1988	1991	1994
Marginal Costs	-0.35%	-0.29%	-0.28%	-0.36%	-0.30%	-0.30%	1.96%	1.78%	1.53%	1.97%	1.92%	1.67%	1.96%	1.90%	1.65%
Cost of Labour	-0.10%	-0.21%	-0.21%	-0.11%	-0.24%	-0.25%	-1.06%	-1.77%	-2.14%	-1.19%	-1.96%	-2.34%	-1.28%	-2.11%	-2.54%
Deflator of Absorption	-0.52%	-0.32%	-0.31%	-0.53%	-0.34%	-0.34%	3.73%	3.84%	3.50%	3.83%	4.20%	3.85%	3.79%	4.13%	3.76%
Price of Exports-RW	-0.35%	-0.30%	-0.29%	-0.35%	-0.31%	-0.31%	1.64%	1.35%	1.11%	1.66%	1.51%	1.26%	1.66%	1.50%	1.25%

Consumer goods

	Border Controls			Border controls and x-ineff.			Market segmentation			Trade *antimonde*			Full *antimonde*		
	1988	1991	1994	1988	1991	1994	1988	1991	1994	1988	1991	1994	1988	1991	1994
Marginal Costs	-0.50%	-0.47%	-0.47%	-0.50%	-0.48%	-0.48%	1.73%	1.38%	1.24%	1.62%	1.37%	1.22%	1.61%	1.34%	1.19%
Cost of Labour	-0.10%	-0.21%	-0.21%	-0.11%	-0.24%	-0.25%	-1.06%	-1.77%	-2.14%	-1.19%	-1.96%	-2.34%	-1.28%	-2.11%	-2.54%
Deflator of Absorption	-0.81%	-0.69%	-0.69%	-0.82%	-0.71%	-0.71%	3.60%	3.41%	3.07%	3.50%	3.49%	3.15%	3.45%	3.40%	3.02%
Price of Exports-RW	-0.50%	-0.47%	-0.47%	-0.50%	-0.48%	-0.48%	1.73%	1.38%	1.24%	1.62%	1.37%	1.22%	1.61%	1.34%	1.19%

Construction

	Border Controls			Border controls and x-ineff.			Market segmentation			Trade *antimonde*			Full *antimonde*		
	1988	1991	1994	1988	1991	1994	1988	1991	1994	1988	1991	1994	1988	1991	1994
Marginal Costs	-0.30%	-0.32%	-0.32%	-0.30%	-0.32%	-0.32%	0.85%	0.45%	0.37%	0.78%	0.43%	0.34%	0.76%	0.40%	0.31%
Cost of Labour	-0.10%	-0.21%	-0.21%	-0.11%	-0.24%	-0.25%	-1.06%	-1.77%	-2.14%	-1.19%	-1.96%	-2.34%	-1.28%	-2.11%	-2.54%
Deflator of Absorption	-0.30%	-0.32%	-0.32%	-0.30%	-0.32%	-0.32%	0.86%	0.48%	0.40%	0.79%	0.45%	0.37%	0.77%	0.43%	0.33%
Price of Exports-RW	-0.30%	-0.32%	-0.32%	-0.30%	-0.32%	-0.32%	0.85%	0.45%	0.37%	0.78%	0.43%	0.34%	0.76%	0.40%	0.31%

Telecommunications

	Border Controls			Border controls and x-ineff.			Market segmentation			Trade antimonde			Full antimonde		
	1988	1991	1994	1988	1991	1994	1988	1991	1994	1988	1991	1994	1988	1991	1994
Marginal Costs	-0.06%	-0.18%	-0.17%	-0.05%	-0.17%	-0.16%	-0.85%	-1.52%	-1.46%	-0.95%	-1.67%	-1.61%	-0.96%	-1.69%	-1.65%
Cost of Labour	-0.10%	-0.21%	-0.21%	-0.11%	-0.24%	-0.25%	-1.06%	-1.77%	-2.14%	-1.19%	-1.96%	-2.34%	-1.28%	-2.11%	-2.54%
Deflator of Absorption	-0.14%	-0.26%	-0.25%	-0.40%	-0.76%	-0.76%	-0.08%	-0.51%	-0.48%	-0.19%	-0.66%	-0.64%	-0.46%	-1.18%	-1.19%
Price of Exports-RW	-0.07%	-0.21%	-0.20%	-0.15%	-0.41%	-0.40%	-1.14%	-2.28%	-2.23%	-1.25%	-2.46%	-2.42%	-1.34%	-2.63%	-2.60%

Transports

	Border Controls			Border controls and x-ineff.			Market segmentation			Trade antimonde			Full antimonde		
	1988	1991	1994	1988	1991	1994	1988	1991	1994	1988	1991	1994	1988	1991	1994
Marginal Costs	-0.18%	-0.28%	-0.28%	-0.17%	-0.28%	-0.28%	-0.17%	-0.73%	-0.62%	-0.27%	-0.86%	-0.74%	-0.30%	-0.91%	-0.81%
Cost of Labour	-0.10%	-0.21%	-0.21%	-0.11%	-0.24%	-0.25%	-1.06%	-1.77%	-2.14%	-1.19%	-1.96%	-2.34%	-1.28%	-2.11%	-2.54%
Deflator of Absorption	-0.23%	-0.32%	-0.32%	-0.23%	-0.32%	-0.32%	0.06%	-0.42%	-0.34%	-0.06%	-0.55%	-0.47%	-0.09%	-0.60%	-0.54%
Price of Exports-RW	-0.18%	-0.28%	-0.28%	-0.17%	-0.28%	-0.28%	-0.17%	-0.73%	-0.62%	-0.27%	-0.86%	-0.74%	-0.30%	-0.91%	-0.81%

Banks

	Border Controls			Border controls and x-ineff.			Market segmentation			Trade antimonde			Full antimonde		
	1988	1991	1994	1988	1991	1994	1988	1991	1994	1988	1991	1994	1988	1991	1994
Marginal Costs	-0.09%	-0.21%	-0.21%	-0.10%	-0.22%	-0.22%	-0.76%	-1.40%	-1.47%	-0.87%	-1.55%	-1.62%	-0.89%	-1.60%	-1.69%
Cost of Labour	-0.10%	-0.21%	-0.21%	-0.11%	-0.24%	-0.25%	-1.06%	-1.77%	-2.14%	-1.19%	-1.96%	-2.34%	-1.28%	-2.11%	-2.54%
Deflator of Absorption	-0.12%	-0.24%	-0.24%	-0.24%	-0.50%	-0.50%	-0.63%	-1.43%	-1.49%	-0.74%	-1.59%	-1.65%	-0.87%	-1.85%	-1.93%
Price of Exports-RW	-0.10%	-0.22%	-0.22%	-0.12%	-0.28%	-0.28%	-0.81%	-1.58%	-1.64%	-0.92%	-1.73%	-1.81%	-0.97%	-1.82%	-1.91%

Services

	Border Controls			Border controls and x-ineff.			Market segmentation			Trade antimonde			Full antimonde		
	1988	1991	1994	1988	1991	1994	1988	1991	1994	1988	1991	1994	1988	1991	1994
Marginal Costs	-0.15%	-0.26%	-0.26%	-0.15%	-0.26%	-0.26%	-0.28%	-0.86%	-0.73%	-0.37%	-0.98%	-0.85%	-0.40%	-1.03%	-0.91%
Cost of Labour	-0.10%	-0.21%	-0.21%	-0.11%	-0.24%	-0.25%	-1.06%	-1.77%	-2.14%	-1.19%	-1.96%	-2.34%	-1.28%	-2.11%	-2.54%
Deflator of Absorption	-0.18%	-0.27%	-0.27%	-0.18%	-0.27%	-0.27%	-0.16%	-0.65%	-0.54%	-0.26%	-0.77%	-0.66%	-0.29%	-0.82%	-0.72%
Price of Exports-RW	-0.15%	-0.26%	-0.26%	-0.15%	-0.26%	-0.26%	-0.28%	-0.86%	-0.73%	-0.37%	-0.98%	-0.85%	-0.40%	-1.03%	-0.91%

Non market

	Border Controls			Border controls and x-ineff.			Market segmentation			Trade antimonde			Full antimonde		
	1988	1991	1994	1988	1991	1994	1988	1991	1994	1988	1991	1994	1988	1991	1994
Marginal Costs	-0.13%	-0.22%	-0.22%	-0.14%	-0.24%	-0.25%	-0.60%	-1.24%	-1.54%	-0.71%	-1.37%	-1.69%	-0.75%	-1.44%	-1.78%
Cost of Labour	-0.10%	-0.21%	-0.21%	-0.11%	-0.24%	-0.25%	-1.06%	-1.77%	-2.14%	-1.19%	-1.96%	-2.34%	-1.28%	-2.11%	-2.54%
Deflator of Absorption	-0.13%	-0.22%	-0.22%	-0.14%	-0.24%	-0.25%	-0.60%	-1.24%	-1.54%	-0.71%	-1.37%	-1.69%	-0.75%	-1.44%	-1.78%
Price of Exports-RW	-0.13%	-0.22%	-0.22%	-0.14%	-0.24%	-0.25%	-0.60%	-1.24%	-1.54%	-0.71%	-1.37%	-1.69%	-0.75%	-1.44%	-1.78%

Table B3.1.

The full *antimonde* scenario: macroeconomic aggregates for Denmark

Macroeconomic Aggregates (vol.) (% change from *monde*)	Constraint Case			Flexible Case			Efficiency Case		
	1988	1991	1994	1988	1991	1994	1988	1991	1994
GDP fact. pr.	-0.82%	-1.27%	-1.56%	-0.71%	-1.38%	-1.76%	-0.73%	-1.48%	-1.94%
Priv. Consumption	-0.97%	-1.24%	-1.53%	-1.24%	-1.58%	-1.91%	-1.25%	-1.63%	-1.99%
Absorption	-0.82%	-1.06%	-1.23%	-1.56%	-1.82%	-2.02%	-1.56%	-1.85%	-2.06%
Total Investment	-4.15%	-4.80%	-5.13%	-4.36%	-4.52%	-4.63%	-4.36%	-4.52%	-4.64%
Total Exports to RW	-0.32%	-1.34%	-1.67%	1.48%	1.19%	0.99%	1.46%	1.09%	0.81%
Total Imports from RW	-1.80%	-2.15%	-2.28%	-3.25%	-3.02%	-2.74%	-3.21%	-2.86%	-2.46%
Total Intra-EU Trade	-0.84%	-0.98%	-1.01%	-0.67%	-3.35%	-3.62%	-0.69%	-3.42%	-3.75%
Employment (diff. from *monde*, 10^3 persons)	-2	-2	-3	-6	-5	-6	-6	-4	-5
Disposable Income (deflated)	-1.15%	-1.39%	-1.70%	-1.74%	-2.03%	-2.33%	-1.75%	-2.05%	-2.36%

Macroeconomic Ratios (abs. diff. from *monde*)	Constraint Case			Flexible Case			Efficiency Case		
	1988	1991	1994	1988	1991	1994	1988	1991	1994
Current Account as % of GDP	0.00%	0.00%	0.00%	-0.48%	-0.28%	-0.28%	-0.48%	-0.27%	-0.26%
Public Deficit as % of GDP	-0.04%	-0.11%	-0.14%	-0.53%	-0.68%	-0.77%	-0.53%	-0.71%	-0.82%
Labour Productivity	-0.74%	-1.21%	-1.43%	-0.45%	-1.20%	-1.54%	-0.48%	-1.32%	-1.74%
Investment/GDP	-0.69%	-0.73%	-0.74%	-1.80%	-1.72%	-1.69%	-1.79%	-1.70%	-1.65%
Priv.Cons./GDP	-0.08%	0.02%	0.02%	-0.30%	-0.11%	-0.08%	-0.29%	-0.08%	-0.03%

Deflators (% change from *monde*)	Constraint Case			Flexible Case			Efficiency Case		
	1988	1991	1994	1988	1991	1994	1988	1991	1994
Consumer Price Index	-0.24%	0.26%	0.49%	1.19%	1.02%	0.97%	1.18%	0.95%	0.86%
Real Wage Rate	-0.83%	-1.28%	-1.73%	-0.67%	-1.16%	-1.68%	-0.69%	-1.27%	-1.87%
Marginal Costs	-0.51%	0.05%	0.25%	0.49%	0.42%	0.38%	0.49%	0.39%	0.33%
Producer Prices	-0.37%	0.22%	0.42%	0.62%	0.57%	0.55%	0.61%	0.55%	0.50%
Average change in mark-ups (abs. diff.)	0.96%	1.21%	1.26%	0.97%	1.32%	1.42%	0.98%	1.33%	1.43%
Shadow Price of Capital	-1.36%	-0.60%	0.01%	-0.77%	-0.42%	0.30%	-0.79%	-0.49%	0.19%
Terms-of-Trade RW	-1.12%	-0.57%	-0.34%	-4.84%	-3.93%	-3.25%	-4.76%	-3.61%	-2.68%

Implicit change in real exchange rate	-0.73%	-0.09%	0.12%	-3.91%	-2.93%	-2.20%	-3.82%	-2.57%	-1.57%

Trade Regime	*Segmentation*			*Segmentation*			*Segmentation*		

Table B3.2.
The full *antimonde* scenario: effects on IC sectors for Denmark

% change from *monde*

Metal Industries

	Constraint Case			Flexible Case			Efficiency Case		
	1988	1991	1994	1988	1991	1994	1988	1991	1994
Production per firm	-25.69%	-35.97%	-36.08%	-18.64%	-24.38%	-24.59%	-18.66%	-24.44%	-24.71%
Real Marginal Costs	0.46%	1.08%	1.30%	-1.55%	-0.11%	1.06%	-1.44%	0.32%	1.81%
Real Producer Prices	4.73%	7.20%	7.44%	1.01%	3.02%	4.23%	1.11%	3.46%	5.00%
Mark-ups domestic (abs. diff.)	*17.78%*	*20.81%*	*20.87%*	*17.90%*	*20.25%*	*20.28%*	*17.91%*	*20.27%*	*20.30%*
Fixed Costs per firm	0.43%	0.95%	1.04%	-2.06%	-1.19%	-0.65%	-2.00%	-0.92%	-0.18%
Number of Firms	11.26%	8.62%	8.53%	10.67%	-0.37%	-0.77%	10.65%	-0.48%	-0.95%
Sigma of Love of Variety	0.00%	0.00%	0.00%	0.00%	0.00%	0.00%	0.00%	0.00%	0.00%

Chemical

	Constraint Case			Flexible Case			Efficiency Case		
	1988	1991	1994	1988	1991	1994	1988	1991	1994
Production per firm	-15.24%	-20.95%	-21.14%	-10.46%	-13.97%	-14.22%	-10.48%	-14.04%	-14.34%
Real Marginal Costs	0.43%	1.10%	1.33%	-1.53%	-0.08%	1.13%	-1.42%	0.35%	1.89%
Real Producer Prices	2.82%	4.41%	4.66%	-0.03%	1.80%	3.03%	0.07%	2.24%	3.80%
Mark-ups domestic (abs. diff.)	*10.18%*	*12.41%*	*12.45%*	*8.93%*	*10.26%*	*10.30%*	*8.94%*	*10.27%*	*10.32%*
Fixed Costs per firm	0.64%	1.19%	1.23%	-1.69%	-0.86%	-0.39%	-1.63%	-0.60%	0.07%
Number of Firms	6.73%	4.75%	4.67%	7.15%	2.24%	1.91%	7.13%	2.16%	1.77%
Sigma of Love of Variety	0.00%	0.00%	0.00%	0.00%	0.00%	0.00%	0.00%	0.00%	0.00%

Other Intensive Industries

	Constraint Case			Flexible Case			Efficiency Case		
	1988	1991	1994	1988	1991	1994	1988	1991	1994
Production per firm	-3.24%	-4.15%	-4.31%	-4.03%	-6.17%	-6.33%	-4.04%	-6.23%	-6.43%
Real Marginal Costs	-0.18%	0.31%	0.47%	-2.28%	-0.95%	0.17%	-2.17%	-0.51%	0.94%
Real Producer Prices	0.01%	0.54%	0.69%	-2.05%	-0.61%	0.51%	-1.94%	-0.17%	1.28%
Mark-ups domestic (abs. diff.)	*0.21%*	*0.22%*	*0.22%*	*0.29%*	*0.38%*	*0.38%*	*0.29%*	*0.38%*	*0.38%*
Fixed Costs per firm	-0.18%	0.19%	0.20%	-2.77%	-2.04%	-1.59%	-2.71%	-1.77%	-1.12%
Number of Firms	3.99%	5.20%	5.18%	3.54%	6.13%	6.16%	3.54%	6.12%	6.15%
Sigma of Love of Variety	0.00%	0.00%	0.00%	0.00%	0.00%	0.00%	0.00%	0.00%	0.00%

Electrical goods

	Constraint Case			Flexible Case			Efficiency Case		
	1988	1991	1994	1988	1991	1994	1988	1991	1994
Production per firm	-12.80%	-17.12%	-17.25%	-11.36%	-16.12%	-16.19%	-11.38%	-16.19%	-16.30%
Real Marginal Costs	0.14%	0.61%	0.71%	-1.99%	-0.65%	0.40%	-1.88%	-0.22%	1.15%
Real Producer Prices	1.73%	2.75%	2.85%	-0.70%	1.13%	2.19%	-0.60%	1.56%	2.95%
Mark-ups domestic (abs. diff.)	*4.75%*	*5.67%*	*5.68%*	*4.84%*	*5.91%*	*5.94%*	*4.84%*	*5.93%*	*5.96%*
Fixed Costs per firm	0.16%	0.52%	0.49%	-2.50%	-1.75%	-1.35%	-2.44%	-1.49%	-0.90%
Number of Firms	9.78%	10.91%	10.90%	7.72%	6.89%	7.06%	7.70%	6.84%	6.97%
Sigma of Love of Variety	0.00%	0.00%	0.00%	0.00%	0.00%	0.00%	0.00%	0.00%	0.00%

Transport equipment

	Constraint Case			Flexible Case			Efficiency Case		
	1988	1991	1994	1988	1991	1994	1988	1991	1994
Production per firm	-18.73%	-25.66%	-25.62%	-15.88%	-19.64%	-19.48%	-15.89%	-19.65%	-19.50%
Real Marginal Costs	0.46%	0.90%	0.97%	-1.47%	-0.18%	0.78%	-1.36%	0.23%	1.51%
Real Producer Prices	3.50%	5.15%	5.20%	0.74%	2.40%	3.35%	0.84%	2.82%	4.08%
Mark-ups domestic (abs. diff.)	*15.90%*	*19.16%*	*19.38%*	*15.39%*	*17.33%*	*17.39%*	*15.40%*	*17.35%*	*17.43%*
Fixed Costs per firm	0.37%	0.73%	0.71%	-2.12%	-1.38%	-1.00%	-2.06%	-1.14%	-0.57%
Number of Firms	11.85%	11.66%	11.47%	8.17%	4.80%	5.26%	8.16%	4.79%	5.24%
Sigma of Love of Variety	0.00%	0.00%	0.00%	0.00%	0.00%	0.00%	0.00%	0.00%	0.00%

Other Equipment

	Constraint Case			Flexible Case			Efficiency Case		
	1988	1991	1994	1988	1991	1994	1988	1991	1994
Production per firm	-8.64%	-11.35%	-11.48%	-8.87%	-12.36%	-12.51%	-8.89%	-12.42%	-12.62%
Real Marginal Costs	-0.11%	0.34%	0.45%	-2.26%	-0.94%	0.13%	-2.16%	-0.51%	0.89%
Real Producer Prices	0.23%	0.78%	0.89%	-1.94%	-0.50%	0.58%	-1.84%	-0.07%	1.34%
Mark-ups domestic (abs. diff.)	*0.96%*	*1.08%*	*1.09%*	*1.09%*	*1.37%*	*1.38%*	*1.09%*	*1.38%*	*1.38%*
Fixed Costs per firm	-0.10%	0.24%	0.21%	-2.78%	-2.05%	-1.65%	-2.72%	-1.79%	-1.19%
Number of Firms	9.39%	12.31%	12.22%	7.88%	11.70%	11.77%	7.87%	11.66%	11.71%
Sigma of Love of Variety	0.00%	0.00%	0.00%	0.00%	0.00%	0.00%	0.00%	0.00%	0.00%

Telecommunications

	Constraint Case			Flexible Case			Efficiency Case		
	1988	1991	1994	1988	1991	1994	1988	1991	1994
Production per firm	-1.78%	-1.86%	-2.09%	-2.41%	-4.92%	-5.26%	-2.42%	-4.98%	-5.36%
Real Marginal Costs	-0.65%	0.13%	0.46%	-3.55%	-2.09%	-0.70%	-3.43%	-1.61%	0.14%
Real Producer Prices	0.16%	1.19%	1.47%	-3.10%	-1.32%	0.04%	-2.99%	-0.85%	-0.87%
Mark-ups domestic (abs. diff.)	*1.01%*	*1.11%*	*1.03%*	*0.51%*	*0.14%*	*0.06%*	*0.51%*	*0.12%*	*0.02%*
Fixed Costs per firm	0.10%	1.58%	1.51%	-5.14%	-5.65%	-5.27%	-5.08%	-5.38%	-4.80%
Number of Firms	1.42%	1.67%	1.78%	3.06%	6.67%	6.81%	3.06%	6.70%	6.86%
Sigma of Love of Variety	0.00%	0.00%	0.00%	0.00%	0.00%	0.00%	0.00%	0.00%	0.00%

Banks

	Constraint Case			Flexible Case			Efficiency Case		
	1988	1991	1994	1988	1991	1994	1988	1991	1994
Production per firm	0.07%	1.94%	1.96%	-1.40%	1.30%	2.17%	-1.41%	1.30%	2.16%
Real Marginal Costs	-1.10%	-0.72%	-0.74%	-3.53%	-2.35%	-1.36%	-3.43%	-1.91%	-0.59%
Real Producer Prices	-0.96%	-0.79%	-0.82%	-3.48%	-2.92%	-2.09%	-3.37%	-2.49%	-1.34%
Mark-ups domestic (abs. diff.)	*0.11%*	*-0.25%*	*-0.27%*	*0.03%*	*-0.98%*	*-1.20%*	*0.03%*	*-1.00%*	*-1.22%*
Fixed Costs per firm	-0.19%	0.80%	0.70%	-5.22%	-5.60%	-5.24%	-5.16%	-5.34%	-4.77%
Number of Firms	4.31%	6.54%	6.62%	6.06%	16.54%	18.49%	6.07%	16.66%	18.67%
Sigma of Love of Variety	0.00%	0.00%	0.00%	0.00%	0.00%	0.00%	0.00%	0.00%	0.00%

Table B3.3.
The full *antimonde* scenario: sectoral results for Denmark (volumes)

% change from *monde*

Agriculture	Constraint Case			Flexible Case			Efficiency Case		
	1988	1991	1994	1988	1991	1994	1988	1991	1994
Domestic Production - vol.	0.9%	1.0%	0.5%	2.1%	1.4%	0.4%	2.1%	1.2%	0.0%
Imports - vol.	-2.0%	-1.7%	-1.3%	-3.2%	-2.4%	-1.9%	-3.1%	-2.2%	-1.5%
Exports - vol.	-1.3%	-2.7%	-3.7%	1.4%	1.1%	0.8%	1.4%	1.0%	0.6%
Absorption - vol.	0.8%	1.3%	1.1%	1.2%	0.9%	0.3%	1.2%	0.8%	0.1%
Investment - vol.	0.9%	0.3%	-0.5%	-3.3%	-3.6%	-4.0%	-3.3%	-3.7%	-4.1%
Labour Demand - vol.	0.9%	1.2%	0.8%	2.1%	1.6%	0.9%	2.0%	1.4%	0.6%
Private Consumption - vol.	-1.6%	-1.4%	-1.5%	-0.8%	-1.4%	-1.8%	-0.8%	-1.4%	-1.9%
Supply to domestic - vol.	1.4%	2.0%	1.5%	2.8%	2.6%	1.7%	2.7%	2.4%	1.3%
Intra-EU Trade - vol	0.0%	0.0%	0.0%	-1.2%	-4.0%	-4.6%	-1.2%	-4.1%	-4.8%

Energy	Constraint Case			Flexible Case			Efficiency Case		
	1988	1991	1994	1988	1991	1994	1988	1991	1994
Domestic Production - vol.	-0.3%	-0.8%	-1.1%	0.8%	-0.2%	-0.6%	0.7%	-0.3%	-0.8%
Imports - vol.	-0.7%	-0.7%	-0.7%	-1.1%	-1.2%	-1.1%	-1.1%	-1.2%	-1.1%
Exports - vol.	-1.0%	-1.7%	-2.2%	0.6%	0.4%	0.3%	0.6%	0.4%	0.3%
Absorption - vol.	-0.4%	-0.6%	-0.7%	-0.2%	-0.9%	-1.2%	-0.3%	-1.0%	-1.3%
Investment - vol.	-6.1%	-6.7%	-7.1%	-3.7%	-4.1%	-4.3%	-3.7%	-4.2%	-4.4%
Labour Demand - vol.	-0.2%	-0.7%	-0.9%	1.0%	0.1%	-0.2%	1.0%	0.0%	-0.3%
Private Consumption - vol.	-0.5%	-0.3%	-0.5%	-0.6%	-1.1%	-1.4%	-0.7%	-1.1%	-1.5%
Supply to domestic - vol.	-0.1%	-0.5%	-0.8%	1.0%	0.1%	-0.4%	0.9%	0.0%	-0.6%
Intra-EU Trade - vol	0.0%	0.0%	0.0%	0.4%	-0.6%	-0.9%	0.4%	-0.7%	-1.0%

Metal Industries	Constraint Case			Flexible Case			Efficiency Case		
	1988	1991	1994	1988	1991	1994	1988	1991	1994
Domestic Production - vol.	-17.3%	-30.4%	-30.6%	-10.0%	-24.7%	-25.2%	-10.0%	-24.8%	-25.4%
Imports - vol.	5.4%	11.3%	11.2%	-2.4%	-3.4%	-3.2%	-2.4%	-3.3%	-3.0%
Exports - vol.	-3.1%	-6.4%	-6.7%	1.5%	0.8%	0.6%	1.4%	0.7%	0.4%
Absorption - vol.	-2.4%	-5.2%	-5.2%	-3.1%	-6.5%	-6.5%	-3.1%	-6.5%	-6.5%
Investment - vol.	-20.6%	-33.5%	-33.7%	-8.5%	-15.3%	-15.6%	-8.6%	-15.4%	-15.6%
Labour Demand - vol.	-13.4%	-25.8%	-25.9%	-7.2%	-21.9%	-22.3%	-7.3%	-22.0%	-22.5%
Private Consumption - vol.	-0.9%	-0.7%	-0.8%	-0.4%	-0.7%	-1.0%	-0.4%	-0.8%	-1.0%
Supply to domestic - vol.	-40.4%	-58.9%	-59.0%	-32.3%	-52.0%	-52.4%	-32.4%	-52.2%	-52.7%
Intra-EU Trade - vol	0.0%	0.0%	0.0%	3.2%	2.8%	2.6%	3.2%	2.7%	2.4%

Chemical	Constraint Case			Flexible Case			Efficiency Case		
	1988	1991	1994	1988	1991	1994	1988	1991	1994
Domestic Production - vol.	-9.5%	-17.2%	-17.5%	-4.1%	-12.0%	-12.6%	-4.1%	-12.2%	-12.8%
Imports - vol.	9.3%	19.5%	19.4%	-2.2%	-2.5%	-2.3%	-2.2%	-2.3%	-2.0%
Exports - vol.	-1.7%	-3.8%	-4.1%	1.7%	1.2%	1.0%	1.6%	1.1%	0.8%
Absorption - vol.	-2.2%	-4.1%	-4.3%	-1.5%	-4.0%	-4.4%	-1.6%	-4.1%	-4.5%
Investment - vol.	-13.2%	-20.8%	-21.2%	-5.9%	-9.6%	-9.8%	-5.9%	-9.6%	-9.9%
Labour Demand - vol.	-6.9%	-13.8%	-14.0%	-2.2%	-9.9%	-10.3%	-2.3%	-10.0%	-10.4%
Private Consumption - vol.	-1.6%	-1.3%	-1.5%	-0.6%	-1.3%	-1.7%	-0.7%	-1.3%	-1.8%
Supply to domestic - vol.	-23.1%	-36.8%	-37.0%	-14.4%	-26.3%	-27.0%	-14.4%	-26.5%	-27.3%
Intra-EU Trade - vol	0.0%	0.0%	0.0%	3.3%	2.2%	1.9%	3.2%	2.1%	1.8%

Other Intensive Industries	Constraint Case			Flexible Case			Efficiency Case		
	1988	1991	1994	1988	1991	1994	1988	1991	1994
Domestic Production - vol.	0.6%	0.8%	0.6%	-0.6%	-0.4%	-0.6%	-0.7%	-0.5%	-0.7%
Imports - vol.	-5.5%	-7.6%	-7.6%	-4.9%	-4.5%	-4.1%	-4.9%	-4.2%	-3.6%
Exports - vol.	-0.6%	-1.5%	-1.7%	1.5%	1.3%	1.1%	1.5%	1.1%	0.9%
Absorption - vol.	-1.1%	-1.5%	-1.6%	-2.5%	-3.1%	-3.3%	-2.5%	-3.1%	-3.3%
Investment - vol.	-3.2%	-3.4%	-3.8%	-4.3%	-4.2%	-4.3%	-4.3%	-4.2%	-4.3%
Labour Demand - vol.	0.9%	1.2%	1.1%	-0.2%	0.2%	0.2%	-0.2%	0.2%	0.1%
Private Consumption - vol.	-1.7%	-1.5%	-1.6%	-0.9%	-1.5%	-1.9%	-0.9%	-1.6%	-2.0%
Supply to domestic - vol.	1.1%	1.7%	1.5%	0.0%	1.8%	1.6%	0.0%	1.7%	1.5%
Intra-EU Trade - vol	0.0%	0.0%	0.0%	-3.2%	-7.8%	-8.0%	-3.2%	-7.9%	-8.2%

Electrical goods	Constraint Case			Flexible Case			Efficiency Case		
	1988	1991	1994	1988	1991	1994	1988	1991	1994
Domestic Production - vol.	-4.3%	-8.1%	-8.2%	-4.5%	-10.3%	-10.3%	-4.6%	-10.5%	-10.5%
Imports - vol.	0.2%	2.4%	2.2%	-4.4%	-4.4%	-4.0%	-4.4%	-4.2%	-3.7%
Exports - vol.	-1.2%	-3.0%	-3.2%	1.8%	1.5%	1.3%	1.8%	1.4%	1.1%
Absorption - vol.	-2.7%	-3.8%	-4.0%	-4.4%	-6.0%	-6.1%	-4.4%	-6.0%	-6.1%
Investment - vol.	-5.1%	-9.6%	-10.0%	-6.0%	-8.7%	-8.8%	-6.0%	-8.8%	-8.8%
Labour Demand - vol.	-2.3%	-5.5%	-5.6%	-2.7%	-8.1%	-7.9%	-2.8%	-8.1%	-8.0%
Private Consumption - vol.	-1.9%	-1.7%	-2.2%	-2.0%	-2.5%	-2.8%	-2.0%	-2.6%	-3.0%
Supply to domestic - vol.	-8.4%	-14.8%	-14.9%	-9.2%	-14.8%	-14.8%	-9.2%	-15.0%	-15.0%
Intra-EU Trade - vol	0.0%	0.0%	0.0%	0.1%	-2.1%	-2.3%	0.1%	-2.2%	-2.4%

Transport equipment	Constraint Case			Flexible Case			Efficiency Case		
	1988	1991	1994	1988	1991	1994	1988	1991	1994
Domestic Production - vol.	-9.1%	-17.0%	-17.1%	-9.0%	-15.8%	-15.2%	-9.0%	-15.8%	-15.3%
Imports - vol.	8.2%	10.2%	9.0%	-3.8%	-3.0%	-2.7%	-3.8%	-2.9%	-2.5%
Exports - vol.	-1.8%	-4.5%	-4.7%	1.7%	1.3%	1.2%	1.7%	1.2%	1.0%
Absorption - vol.	1.8%	-3.0%	-3.9%	-6.3%	-5.5%	-5.1%	-6.3%	-5.5%	-5.1%
Investment - vol.	-9.7%	-18.1%	-18.5%	-7.9%	-11.1%	-10.9%	-8.0%	-11.1%	-10.9%
Labour Demand - vol.	-5.9%	-13.0%	-13.0%	-6.4%	-12.9%	-12.3%	-6.4%	-12.9%	-12.3%
Private Consumption - vol.	11.0%	0.6%	-1.8%	-6.6%	-3.5%	-2.5%	-6.6%	-3.5%	-2.5%
Supply to domestic - vol.	-26.7%	-43.8%	-44.3%	-27.6%	-38.2%	-37.7%	-27.7%	-38.3%	-37.9%
Intra-EU Trade - vol	0.0%	0.0%	0.0%	1.9%	2.4%	2.4%	1.9%	2.3%	2.3%

Other Equipment

	Constraint Case			Flexible Case			Efficiency Case		
	1988	1991	1994	1988	1991	1994	1988	1991	1994
Domestic Production - vol.	-0.1%	-0.4%	-0.7%	-1.7%	-2.1%	-2.2%	-1.7%	-2.2%	-2.4%
Imports - vol.	-3.7%	-5.4%	-5.7%	-5.0%	-4.8%	-4.6%	-4.9%	-4.7%	-4.3%
Exports - vol.	-0.5%	-1.1%	-1.3%	1.6%	1.3%	1.1%	1.6%	1.2%	0.9%
Absorption - vol.	-2.2%	-3.2%	-3.6%	-5.7%	-6.6%	-6.7%	-5.7%	-6.7%	-6.8%
Investment - vol.	1.5%	0.1%	-0.6%	-5.0%	-5.2%	-5.3%	-5.0%	-5.2%	-5.4%
Labour Demand - vol.	0.6%	0.4%	0.3%	-1.0%	-1.1%	-1.1%	-1.0%	-1.2%	-1.1%
Private Consumption - vol.	0.6%	-0.1%	-2.1%	-4.9%	-4.1%	-3.5%	-5.0%	-4.2%	-3.7%
Supply to domestic - vol.	0.9%	1.2%	0.9%	-3.0%	0.6%	0.6%	-3.1%	0.5%	0.5%
Intra-EU Trade - vol	0.0%	0.0%	0.0%	-2.9%	-5.4%	-5.5%	-2.9%	-5.4%	-5.6%

Consumer goods

	Constraint Case			Flexible Case			Efficiency Case		
	1988	1991	1994	1988	1991	1994	1988	1991	1994
Domestic Production - vol.	1.2%	1.8%	1.4%	1.8%	1.5%	0.8%	1.7%	1.3%	0.5%
Imports - vol.	-6.1%	-8.3%	-8.3%	-3.8%	-3.3%	-3.0%	-3.7%	-3.1%	-2.6%
Exports - vol.	-0.2%	-1.0%	-1.4%	2.0%	1.6%	1.3%	1.9%	1.5%	1.1%
Absorption - vol.	-0.8%	-0.7%	-0.9%	-0.7%	-1.2%	-1.6%	-0.7%	-1.3%	-1.7%
Investment - vol.	2.9%	2.4%	1.6%	-3.3%	-3.5%	-3.8%	-3.3%	-3.5%	-3.9%
Labour Demand - vol.	1.5%	2.1%	1.8%	2.1%	1.9%	1.4%	2.0%	1.8%	1.2%
Private Consumption - vol.	-1.4%	-1.2%	-1.3%	-0.7%	-1.2%	-1.6%	-0.7%	-1.3%	-1.6%
Supply to domestic - vol.	2.7%	4.5%	4.1%	2.7%	4.5%	3.7%	2.6%	4.3%	3.4%
Intra-EU Trade - vol	0.0%	0.0%	0.0%	-1.8%	-5.3%	-5.6%	-1.8%	-5.4%	-5.7%

Construction

	Constraint Case			Flexible Case			Efficiency Case		
	1988	1991	1994	1988	1991	1994	1988	1991	1994
Domestic Production - vol.	-2.9%	-3.2%	-3.4%	-6.1%	-6.1%	-6.3%	-6.1%	-6.1%	-6.3%
Imports - vol.	-	-	-	#VALUE!	#VALUE!	#VALUE!	#VALUE!	#VALUE!	#VALUE!
Exports - vol.	-	-	-	#VALUE!	#VALUE!	#VALUE!	#VALUE!	#VALUE!	#VALUE!
Absorption - vol.	-2.9%	-3.2%	-3.4%	-6.1%	-6.1%	-6.3%	-6.1%	-6.1%	-6.3%
Investment - vol.	-4.4%	-5.3%	-5.9%	-7.1%	-7.1%	-7.2%	-7.1%	-7.1%	-7.2%
Labour Demand - vol.	-2.8%	-3.0%	-3.1%	-5.9%	-5.9%	-5.9%	-5.9%	-5.8%	-5.8%
Private Consumption - vol.	#DIV/0!	#DIV/0!	#DIV/0!	#DIV/0!	#DIV/0!	#DIV/0!	#DIV/0!	#DIV/0!	#DIV/0!
Supply to domestic - vol.	-2.9%	-3.2%	-3.4%	-6.1%	-6.1%	-6.3%	-6.1%	-6.1%	-6.3%
Intra-EU Trade - vol	0.0%	0.0%	0.0%	#DIV/0!	#DIV/0!	#DIV/0!	#DIV/0!	#DIV/0!	#DIV/0!

Telecommunications

	Constraint Case			Flexible Case			Efficiency Case		
	1988	1991	1994	1988	1991	1994	1988	1991	1994
Domestic Production - vol.	-0.4%	-0.2%	-0.3%	0.6%	1.4%	1.2%	0.6%	1.4%	1.1%
Imports - vol.	-8.9%	-12.7%	-12.6%	-6.3%	-6.2%	-5.9%	-6.2%	-6.0%	-5.6%
Exports - vol.	-2.5%	-5.6%	-5.9%	1.1%	1.0%	0.9%	1.1%	1.0%	0.8%
Absorption - vol.	-0.8%	-0.6%	-0.7%	-0.3%	-0.3%	-0.5%	-0.3%	-0.3%	-0.5%
Investment - vol.	-5.4%	-5.0%	-5.1%	-3.9%	-3.5%	-3.5%	-3.9%	-3.4%	-3.5%
Labour Demand - vol.	1.4%	2.5%	2.6%	0.8%	2.0%	2.0%	0.8%	2.0%	2.1%
Private Consumption - vol.	-2.1%	-1.9%	-2.1%	-0.6%	-1.4%	-2.0%	-0.7%	-1.5%	-2.1%
Supply to domestic - vol.	-0.2%	0.3%	0.2%	1.1%	4.0%	3.8%	1.1%	4.0%	3.7%
Intra-EU Trade - vol	0.0%	0.0%	0.0%	-6.9%	-18.0%	-18.1%	-6.9%	-18.0%	-18.2%

Transports

	Constraint Case			Flexible Case			Efficiency Case		
	1988	1991	1994	1988	1991	1994	1988	1991	1994
Domestic Production - vol.	-0.3%	-0.5%	-0.6%	0.4%	0.2%	0.0%	0.4%	0.2%	-0.1%
Imports - vol.	-0.3%	-0.5%	-0.6%	0.2%	0.1%	0.0%	0.2%	0.1%	-0.1%
Exports - vol.	0.5%	0.0%	-0.1%	0.6%	0.5%	0.5%	0.6%	0.5%	0.4%
Absorption - vol.	-0.7%	-0.8%	-0.9%	-0.6%	-1.0%	-1.3%	-0.6%	-1.0%	-1.3%
Investment - vol.	-6.3%	-6.7%	-6.8%	-4.1%	-4.2%	-4.3%	-4.1%	-4.1%	-4.2%
Labour Demand - vol.	-0.2%	-0.4%	-0.4%	0.5%	0.4%	0.3%	0.5%	0.4%	0.3%
Private Consumption - vol.	-1.8%	-1.6%	-1.8%	-0.8%	-1.5%	-2.0%	-0.8%	-1.6%	-2.1%
Supply to domestic - vol.	-0.3%	-0.5%	-0.6%	0.4%	0.2%	0.0%	0.4%	0.2%	-0.1%
Intra-EU Trade - vol	0.0%	0.0%	0.0%	2.0%	2.4%	2.3%	2.0%	2.4%	2.2%

Banks

	Constraint Case			Flexible Case			Efficiency Case		
	1988	1991	1994	1988	1991	1994	1988	1991	1994
Domestic Production - vol.	4.4%	8.6%	8.7%	4.6%	18.1%	21.1%	4.6%	18.2%	21.2%
Imports - vol.	-13.3%	-20.5%	-20.8%	-4.1%	-0.3%	0.8%	-4.1%	0.0%	1.3%
Exports - vol.	0.0%	-0.9%	-0.5%	1.1%	1.0%	1.0%	1.1%	1.0%	0.9%
Absorption - vol.	2.8%	5.7%	5.7%	3.1%	12.0%	13.8%	3.1%	12.1%	13.9%
Investment - vol.	0.3%	4.2%	4.1%	-2.1%	4.0%	5.3%	-2.1%	4.1%	5.5%
Labour Demand - vol.	4.7%	8.8%	9.0%	4.6%	17.3%	20.2%	4.7%	17.5%	20.5%
Private Consumption - vol.	-2.0%	-1.8%	-2.0%	-0.9%	-1.7%	-2.3%	-0.9%	-1.7%	-2.4%
Supply to domestic - vol.	4.7%	9.3%	9.4%	4.9%	19.9%	23.0%	5.0%	20.0%	23.2%
Intra-EU Trade - vol	0.0%	0.0%	0.0%	-4.9%	-13.7%	-14.6%	-4.9%	-13.8%	-14.7%

Services

	Constraint Case			Flexible Case			Efficiency Case		
	1988	1991	1994	1988	1991	1994	1988	1991	1994
Domestic Production - vol.	-0.4%	-0.3%	-0.5%	-0.7%	-0.6%	-1.0%	-0.7%	-0.7%	-1.0%
Imports - vol.	-8.3%	-12.2%	-12.2%	-3.5%	-3.1%	-2.7%	-3.4%	-2.9%	-2.4%
Exports - vol.	2.4%	1.8%	1.5%	1.0%	0.8%	0.6%	1.0%	0.8%	0.5%
Absorption - vol.	-1.1%	-1.2%	-1.3%	-1.2%	-1.6%	-1.9%	-1.2%	-1.6%	-2.0%
Investment - vol.	-3.4%	-3.7%	-4.1%	-4.5%	-4.5%	-4.6%	-4.5%	-4.5%	-4.6%
Labour Demand - vol.	-0.4%	-0.1%	-0.1%	-0.6%	-0.4%	-0.6%	-0.6%	-0.4%	-0.5%
Private Consumption - vol.	-1.5%	-1.4%	-1.7%	-1.0%	-1.5%	-2.0%	-1.0%	-1.6%	-2.1%
Supply to domestic - vol.	-0.7%	-0.4%	-0.6%	-1.1%	-1.2%	-1.5%	-1.1%	-1.2%	-1.6%
Intra-EU Trade - vol	0.0%	0.0%	0.0%	0.6%	-0.4%	-0.5%	0.6%	-0.4%	-0.5%

Non market

	Constraint Case			Flexible Case			Efficiency Case		
	1988	1991	1994	1988	1991	1994	1988	1991	1994
Domestic Production - vol.	-0.1%	-0.1%	-0.1%	-0.1%	-0.1%	-0.2%	-0.1%	-0.1%	-0.2%
Imports - vol.	-	-	-	#VALUE!	#VALUE!	#VALUE!	#VALUE!	#VALUE!	#VALUE!
Exports - vol.	1.4%	1.2%	1.3%	0.3%	0.2%	0.2%	0.3%	0.2%	0.2%
Absorption - vol.	-0.1%	-0.1%	-0.1%	-0.1%	-0.1%	-0.2%	-0.1%	-0.1%	-0.2%
Investment - vol.	-7.5%	-7.6%	-7.6%	-4.2%	-4.2%	-4.2%	-4.1%	-4.1%	-4.1%
Labour Demand - vol.	-0.1%	-0.1%	0.0%	0.0%	0.0%	0.0%	0.1%	0.1%	0.1%
Private Consumption - vol.	-1.8%	-1.6%	-1.8%	-1.0%	-1.7%	-2.2%	-1.0%	-1.7%	-2.3%
Supply to domestic - vol.	-0.1%	-0.1%	-0.1%	-0.1%	-0.1%	-0.2%	-0.1%	-0.1%	-0.2%
Intra-EU Trade - vol	0.0%	0.0%	0.0%	0.4%	0.3%	0.3%	0.3%	0.3%	0.3%

Table B3.4.

The full *antimonde* scenario: sectoral results for Denmark (prices)

% change from *monde*

Agriculture	Constraint Case			Flexible Case			Efficiency Case		
	1988	1991	1994	1988	1991	1994	1988	1991	1994
Real Marginal Costs	-0.27%	0.41%	0.83%	0.72%	0.79%	1.03%	0.71%	0.77%	1.00%
Real Cost of Labour	-1.56%	-1.37%	-1.62%	-0.67%	-1.16%	-1.68%	-0.69%	-1.27%	-1.87%
Real Deflator of Absorption	-0.09%	0.47%	0.82%	1.38%	1.33%	1.43%	1.36%	1.26%	1.31%
Real Price of Exports-RW	-0.27%	0.41%	0.83%	0.72%	0.79%	1.03%	0.71%	0.77%	1.00%

Energy	Constraint Case			Flexible Case			Efficiency Case		
	1988	1991	1994	1988	1991	1994	1988	1991	1994
Marginal Costs	-0.14%	0.34%	0.66%	1.61%	1.42%	1.40%	1.59%	1.30%	1.21%
Cost of Labour	-1.56%	-1.37%	-1.62%	-0.67%	-1.16%	-1.68%	-0.69%	-1.27%	-1.87%
Deflator of Absorption	0.24%	0.46%	0.61%	3.09%	2.66%	2.40%	3.04%	2.46%	2.04%
Price of Exports-RW	-0.14%	0.34%	0.66%	1.61%	1.42%	1.40%	1.59%	1.30%	1.21%

Metal Industries	Constraint Case			Flexible Case			Efficiency Case		
	1988	1991	1994	1988	1991	1994	1988	1991	1994
Marginal Costs	0.46%	1.08%	1.30%	1.70%	1.66%	1.57%	1.69%	1.62%	1.51%
Cost of Labour	-1.56%	-1.37%	-1.62%	-0.67%	-1.16%	-1.68%	-0.69%	-1.27%	-1.87%
Deflator of Absorption	2.98%	3.84%	3.86%	5.34%	5.49%	5.12%	5.30%	5.32%	4.82%
Price of Exports-RW	2.69%	6.29%	6.53%	0.65%	1.69%	1.65%	0.64%	1.67%	1.60%

Chemical	Constraint Case			Flexible Case			Efficiency Case		
	1988	1991	1994	1988	1991	1994	1988	1991	1994
Marginal Costs	0.43%	1.10%	1.33%	1.72%	1.69%	1.65%	1.71%	1.65%	1.58%
Cost of Labour	-1.56%	-1.37%	-1.62%	-0.67%	-1.16%	-1.68%	-0.69%	-1.27%	-1.87%
Deflator of Absorption	3.12%	4.20%	4.27%	5.30%	5.52%	5.30%	5.28%	5.40%	5.08%
Price of Exports-RW	2.64%	5.78%	6.03%	1.11%	1.49%	1.49%	1.10%	1.46%	1.43%

Other Intensive Industries	Constraint Case			Flexible Case			Efficiency Case		
	1988	1991	1994	1988	1991	1994	1988	1991	1994
Marginal Costs	-0.18%	0.31%	0.47%	0.97%	0.82%	0.69%	0.96%	0.79%	0.64%
Cost of Labour	-1.56%	-1.37%	-1.62%	-0.67%	-1.16%	-1.68%	-0.69%	-1.27%	-1.87%
Deflator of Absorption	0.34%	0.67%	0.78%	1.99%	1.81%	1.59%	1.98%	1.72%	1.45%
Price of Exports-RW	0.14%	0.95%	1.10%	0.93%	0.75%	0.62%	0.92%	0.72%	0.56%

Electrical goods	Constraint Case			Flexible Case			Efficiency Case		
	1988	1991	1994	1988	1991	1994	1988	1991	1994
Marginal Costs	0.14%	0.61%	0.71%	1.26%	1.12%	0.92%	1.25%	1.08%	0.85%
Cost of Labour	-1.56%	-1.37%	-1.62%	-0.67%	-1.16%	-1.68%	-0.69%	-1.27%	-1.87%
Deflator of Absorption	2.41%	2.83%	2.87%	4.03%	4.05%	3.73%	4.00%	3.92%	3.50%
Price of Exports-RW	1.49%	3.55%	3.66%	0.83%	0.73%	0.52%	0.82%	0.69%	0.45%

Transport equipment	Constraint Case			Flexible Case			Efficiency Case		
	1988	1991	1994	1988	1991	1994	1988	1991	1994
Marginal Costs	0.46%	0.90%	0.97%	1.78%	1.58%	1.30%	1.77%	1.53%	1.21%
Cost of Labour	-1.56%	-1.37%	-1.62%	-0.67%	-1.16%	-1.68%	-0.69%	-1.27%	-1.87%
Deflator of Absorption	3.22%	3.77%	3.79%	5.80%	5.61%	5.11%	5.75%	5.39%	4.72%
Price of Exports-RW	2.73%	6.30%	6.41%	0.99%	1.11%	0.78%	0.97%	1.05%	0.68%

Other Equipment	Constraint Case			Flexible Case			Efficiency Case		
	1988	1991	1994	1988	1991	1994	1988	1991	1994
Marginal Costs	-0.11%	0.34%	0.45%	0.98%	0.82%	0.65%	0.97%	0.79%	0.59%
Cost of Labour	-1.56%	-1.37%	-1.62%	-0.67%	-1.16%	-1.68%	-0.69%	-1.27%	-1.87%
Deflator of Absorption	1.13%	1.31%	1.35%	2.58%	2.46%	2.19%	2.55%	2.36%	2.00%
Price of Exports-RW	0.16%	0.91%	1.02%	0.89%	0.69%	0.51%	0.88%	0.65%	0.45%

Consumer goods	Constraint Case			Flexible Case			Efficiency Case		
	1988	1991	1994	1988	1991	1994	1988	1991	1994
Marginal Costs	-0.12%	0.43%	0.70%	1.11%	1.00%	0.99%	1.11%	0.98%	0.95%
Cost of Labour	-1.56%	-1.37%	-1.62%	-0.67%	-1.16%	-1.68%	-0.69%	-1.27%	-1.87%
Deflator of Absorption	0.40%	0.75%	0.92%	2.28%	2.05%	1.87%	2.26%	1.95%	1.70%
Price of Exports-RW	-0.12%	0.43%	0.70%	1.11%	1.00%	0.99%	1.11%	0.98%	0.95%

Construction	Constraint Case			Flexible Case			Efficiency Case		
	1988	1991	1994	1988	1991	1994	1988	1991	1994
Marginal Costs	-0.35%	0.13%	0.28%	0.70%	0.54%	0.42%	0.69%	0.52%	0.38%
Cost of Labour	-1.56%	-1.37%	-1.62%	-0.67%	-1.16%	-1.68%	-0.69%	-1.27%	-1.87%
Deflator of Absorption	-0.35%	0.13%	0.28%	0.70%	0.54%	0.42%	0.69%	0.52%	0.38%
Price of Exports-RW	-0.35%	0.13%	0.28%	0.70%	0.54%	0.42%	0.69%	0.52%	0.38%

Telecommunications	Constraint Case			Flexible Case			Efficiency Case		
	1988	1991	1994	1988	1991	1994	1988	1991	1994
Marginal Costs	-0.65%	0.13%	0.46%	-0.30%	-0.32%	-0.18%	-0.30%	-0.31%	-0.16%
Cost of Labour	-1.56%	-1.37%	-1.62%	-0.67%	-1.16%	-1.68%	-0.69%	-1.27%	-1.87%
Deflator of Absorption	0.16%	0.96%	1.22%	0.23%	0.09%	0.18%	0.23%	0.08%	0.16%
Price of Exports-RW	3.23%	7.09%	7.42%	-0.67%	-1.12%	-1.00%	-0.66%	-1.12%	-1.00%

Transports	Constraint Case			Flexible Case			Efficiency Case		
	1988	1991	1994	1988	1991	1994	1988	1991	1994
Marginal Costs	-0.69%	-0.16%	0.10%	0.25%	0.14%	0.17%	0.24%	0.11%	0.13%
Cost of Labour	-1.56%	-1.37%	-1.62%	-0.67%	-1.16%	-1.68%	-0.69%	-1.27%	-1.87%
Deflator of Absorption	-0.65%	-0.12%	0.14%	0.25%	0.14%	0.17%	0.25%	0.12%	0.13%
Price of Exports-RW	-0.69%	-0.16%	0.10%	0.25%	0.14%	0.17%	0.24%	0.11%	0.13%

Banks	Constraint Case			Flexible Case			Efficiency Case		
	1988	1991	1994	1988	1991	1994	1988	1991	1994
Marginal Costs	-1.10%	-0.72%	-0.74%	-0.29%	-0.59%	-0.84%	-0.30%	-0.61%	-0.89%
Cost of Labour	-1.56%	-1.37%	-1.62%	-0.67%	-1.16%	-1.68%	-0.69%	-1.27%	-1.87%
Deflator of Absorption	-0.73%	-0.65%	-0.68%	-0.14%	-1.11%	-1.48%	-0.15%	-1.15%	-1.54%
Price of Exports-RW	0.04%	1.49%	1.47%	-0.53%	-1.25%	-1.58%	-0.54%	-1.28%	-1.64%

Services	Constraint Case			Flexible Case			Efficiency Case		
	1988	1991	1994	1988	1991	1994	1988	1991	1994
Marginal Costs	-0.91%	-0.32%	-0.01%	-0.15%	-0.16%	0.00%	-0.15%	-0.18%	-0.02%
Cost of Labour	-1.56%	-1.37%	-1.62%	-0.67%	-1.16%	-1.68%	-0.69%	-1.27%	-1.87%
Deflator of Absorption	-0.80%	-0.24%	0.05%	-0.13%	-0.14%	0.02%	-0.14%	-0.15%	-0.01%
Price of Exports-RW	-0.91%	-0.32%	-0.01%	-0.15%	-0.16%	0.00%	-0.15%	-0.18%	-0.02%

Non market	Constraint Case			Flexible Case			Efficiency Case		
	1988	1991	1994	1988	1991	1994	1988	1991	1994
Marginal Costs	-1.06%	-0.73%	-0.79%	-0.09%	-0.43%	-0.75%	-0.10%	-0.47%	-0.82%
Cost of Labour	-1.56%	-1.37%	-1.62%	-0.67%	-1.16%	-1.68%	-0.69%	-1.27%	-1.87%
Deflator of Absorption	-1.06%	-0.73%	-0.79%	-0.09%	-0.43%	-0.75%	-0.10%	-0.47%	-0.82%
Price of Exports-RW	-1.06%	-0.73%	-0.79%	-0.09%	-0.43%	-0.75%	-0.10%	-0.47%	-0.82%

Table B3.5.
Decomposition of effects: macroeconomic aggregates for Denmark

Macroeconomic Aggregates (vol.) (% change from monde)	Border Controls			Border controls and x-ineff.			Market segmentation			Trade antimonde			Full antimonde		
	1988	1991	1994	1988	1991	1994	1988	1991	1994	1988	1991	1994	1988	1991	1994
GDP fact. pr.	0.02%	-0.06%	-0.06%	0.01%	-0.09%	-0.09%	-0.65%	-1.27%	-1.61%	-0.62%	-1.25%	-1.59%	-0.71%	-1.38%	-1.76%
Priv. Consumption	-0.19%	-0.17%	-0.17%	-0.20%	-0.18%	-0.18%	-0.85%	-1.13%	-1.44%	-1.18%	-1.49%	-1.80%	-1.24%	-1.58%	-1.91%
Absorption	0.03%	0.03%	0.03%	0.04%	0.05%	0.05%	-1.48%	-1.71%	-1.89%	-1.53%	-1.79%	-1.97%	-1.56%	-1.82%	-2.02%
Total Investment	0.06%	0.07%	0.07%	0.06%	0.07%	0.07%	-4.38%	-4.53%	-4.64%	-4.36%	-4.52%	-4.63%	-4.36%	-4.52%	-4.63%
Total Exports to RW	-0.43%	-0.52%	-0.52%	-0.43%	-0.53%	-0.54%	1.72%	1.46%	1.28%	1.54%	1.28%	1.09%	1.48%	1.19%	0.99%
Total Imports from RW	1.09%	1.27%	1.28%	1.10%	1.29%	1.31%	-4.37%	-4.31%	-4.11%	-3.38%	-3.22%	-3.01%	-3.25%	-3.02%	-2.74%
Total Intra-EU Trade	-1.26%	-3.16%	-3.17%	-1.27%	-3.20%	-3.21%	0.07%	-2.43%	-2.67%	-0.56%	-3.20%	-3.43%	-0.67%	-3.35%	-3.62%
Employment (diff. from monde, 10³ persons)	4	4	4	4	4	4	-9	-7	-8	-6	-4	-6	-6	-5	-6
Disposable Income (deflated)	0.16%	0.22%	0.23%	0.15%	0.21%	0.22%	-1.62%	-1.85%	-2.13%	-1.70%	-1.96%	-2.23%	-1.74%	-2.03%	-2.33%

Macroeconomic Ratios (abs. diff. from monde)	Border Controls			Border controls and x-ineff.			Market segmentation			Trade antimonde			Full antimonde		
	1988	1991	1994	1988	1991	1994	1988	1991	1994	1988	1991	1994	1988	1991	1994
Current Account as % of GDP	-0.27%	-0.27%	-0.26%	-0.27%	-0.26%	-0.25%	-0.32%	-0.14%	-0.15%	-0.50%	-0.31%	-0.31%	-0.48%	-0.28%	-0.28%
Public Deficit as % of GDP	0.04%	0.04%	0.04%	0.04%	0.03%	0.03%	-0.54%	-0.69%	-0.77%	-0.51%	-0.65%	-0.73%	-0.53%	-0.68%	-0.77%
Labour Productivity	-0.13%	-0.23%	-0.23%	-0.14%	-0.26%	-0.27%	-0.30%	-1.01%	-1.30%	-0.37%	-1.08%	-1.37%	-0.45%	-1.20%	-1.54%
Investment/GDP	0.02%	0.04%	0.04%	0.03%	0.05%	0.05%	-1.81%	-1.75%	-1.73%	-1.81%	-1.75%	-1.73%	-1.80%	-1.72%	-1.69%
Priv.Cons./GDP	-0.12%	-0.06%	-0.06%	-0.12%	-0.05%	-0.05%	-0.11%	0.08%	0.10%	-0.32%	-0.13%	-0.11%	-0.30%	-0.11%	-0.08%

Deflators (% change from monde)	Border Controls			Border controls and x-ineff.			Market segmentation			Trade antimonde			Full antimonde		
	1988	1991	1994	1988	1991	1994	1988	1991	1994	1988	1991	1994	1988	1991	1994
Consumer Price Index	-0.17%	-0.26%	-0.27%	-0.17%	-0.28%	-0.29%	1.11%	0.93%	0.90%	1.22%	1.06%	1.03%	1.19%	1.02%	0.97%
Real Wage Rate	-0.20%	-0.22%	-0.22%	-0.22%	-0.26%	-0.26%	-0.36%	-0.77%	-1.23%	-0.57%	-1.00%	-1.47%	-0.67%	-1.16%	-1.68%
Marginal Costs	-0.10%	-0.15%	-0.16%	-0.09%	-0.16%	-0.16%	0.46%	0.37%	0.34%	0.50%	0.43%	0.40%	0.49%	0.42%	0.38%
Producer Prices	-0.08%	-0.12%	-0.13%	-0.09%	-0.14%	-0.14%	0.58%	0.53%	0.51%	0.63%	0.60%	0.57%	0.62%	0.57%	0.55%
Real Shadow Price of Capital	0.35%	0.32%	0.31%	0.38%	0.36%	0.34%	-0.98%	-0.63%	0.11%	-0.74%	-0.40%	0.35%	-0.77%	-0.42%	0.30%
Terms-of-Trade RW	1.59%	1.90%	1.91%	1.61%	1.94%	1.97%	-5.68%	-4.87%	-4.28%	-5.01%	-4.19%	-3.59%	-4.84%	-3.93%	-3.25%

	Border Controls			Border controls and x-ineff.			Market segmentation			Trade antimonde			Full antimonde		
Real Exchange Rate	3.59%	3.99%	4.01%	3.61%	4.04%	4.07%	-6.41%	-5.51%	-4.89%	-4.08%	-3.19%	-2.56%	-3.91%	-2.93%	-2.20%

	Border Controls			Border controls and x-ineff.			Market segmentation			Trade antimonde			Full antimonde		
Trade Regime	Integration			Integration			Segmentation			Segmentation			Segmentation		

Table B3.6.
Decomposition of effects: effects on IC sectors for Denmark

% change from *monde*

Metal Industries

	Border Controls			Border controls and x-ineff.			Market segmentation			Trade *antimonde*			Full *antimonde*		
	1988	1991	1994	1988	1991	1994	1988	1991	1994	1988	1991	1994	1988	1991	1994
Production per firm	-1.39%	-3.61%	-3.62%	-1.39%	-3.63%	-3.65%	-17.48%	-22.90%	-23.08%	-18.53%	-24.22%	-24.38%	-18.64%	-24.38%	-24.59%
Marginal Costs	3.37%	3.69%	3.70%	3.40%	3.73%	3.76%	-4.83%	-4.02%	-3.49%	-2.39%	-1.53%	-0.98%	-2.21%	-1.27%	-0.63%
Producer Prices	3.53%	4.06%	4.08%	3.55%	4.10%	4.13%	-2.52%	-1.21%	-0.64%	0.15%	1.57%	2.15%	0.34%	1.86%	2.54%
Mark-ups domestic (abs. diff.)	0.14%	0.34%	0.33%	0.14%	0.34%	0.34%	17.76%	20.08%	20.10%	17.87%	20.21%	20.23%	17.90%	20.25%	20.28%
Fixed Costs per firm	3.32%	3.63%	3.64%	3.33%	3.65%	3.68%	-4.61%	-3.85%	-3.40%	-2.19%	-1.38%	-0.90%	-2.06%	-1.19%	-0.65%
Number of Firms	0.58%	1.75%	1.76%	0.58%	1.70%	1.71%	11.01%	0.00%	-0.38%	10.74%	-0.28%	-0.65%	10.67%	-0.37%	-0.77%
Sigma of Love of Variety	0.00%	0.00%	0.00%	0.00%	0.00%	0.00%	0.00%	0.00%	0.00%	0.00%	0.00%	0.00%	0.00%	0.00%	0.00%

Chemical

	Border Controls			Border controls and x-ineff.			Market segmentation			Trade *antimonde*			Full *antimonde*		
	1988	1991	1994	1988	1991	1994	1988	1991	1994	1988	1991	1994	1988	1991	1994
Production per firm	-0.78%	-2.57%	-2.58%	-0.79%	-2.60%	-2.60%	-10.45%	-13.85%	-14.07%	-10.38%	-13.85%	-14.06%	-10.46%	-13.97%	-14.22%
Marginal Costs	3.54%	3.87%	3.89%	3.56%	3.91%	3.94%	-4.91%	-4.09%	-3.51%	-2.36%	-1.50%	-0.90%	-2.19%	-1.24%	-0.55%
Producer Prices	3.63%	4.17%	4.19%	3.65%	4.21%	4.24%	-3.45%	-2.28%	-1.68%	-0.88%	0.37%	0.99%	-0.70%	0.64%	1.35%
Mark-ups domestic (abs. diff.)	0.12%	0.38%	0.37%	0.12%	0.38%	0.37%	9.07%	10.38%	10.41%	8.92%	10.24%	10.27%	8.93%	10.26%	10.30%
Fixed Costs per firm	3.44%	3.76%	3.77%	3.45%	3.78%	3.81%	-4.35%	-3.64%	-3.24%	-1.81%	-1.04%	-0.62%	-1.69%	-0.86%	-0.39%
Number of Firms	1.21%	2.09%	2.10%	1.21%	2.07%	2.07%	6.71%	1.85%	1.54%	7.20%	2.30%	2.00%	7.15%	2.24%	1.91%
Sigma of Love of Variety	0.00%	0.00%	0.00%	0.00%	0.00%	0.00%	0.00%	0.00%	0.00%	0.00%	0.00%	0.00%	0.00%	0.00%	0.00%

Other Intensive Industries

	Border Controls			Border controls and x-ineff.			Market segmentation			Trade *antimonde*			Full *antimonde*		
	1988	1991	1994	1988	1991	1994	1988	1991	1994	1988	1991	1994	1988	1991	1994
Production per firm	-0.40%	-1.26%	-1.25%	-0.41%	-1.27%	-1.27%	-3.87%	-5.94%	-6.07%	-3.97%	-6.09%	-6.22%	-4.03%	-6.17%	-6.33%
Marginal Costs	3.44%	3.78%	3.80%	3.46%	3.82%	3.85%	-5.51%	-4.79%	-4.30%	-3.11%	-2.36%	-1.85%	-2.94%	-2.11%	-1.51%
Producer Prices	3.46%	3.85%	3.86%	3.48%	3.88%	3.91%	-5.29%	-4.47%	-3.97%	-2.89%	-2.03%	-1.51%	-2.72%	-1.77%	-1.17%
Mark-ups domestic (abs. diff.)	0.00%	0.01%	0.01%	0.00%	0.01%	0.01%	0.30%	0.38%	0.39%	0.29%	0.38%	0.38%	0.29%	0.38%	0.38%
Fixed Costs per firm	3.37%	3.70%	3.72%	3.38%	3.72%	3.75%	-5.26%	-4.61%	-4.24%	-2.89%	-2.21%	-1.83%	-2.77%	-2.04%	-1.59%
Number of Firms	0.85%	2.22%	2.24%	0.86%	2.21%	2.23%	3.42%	6.00%	6.04%	3.56%	6.15%	6.19%	3.54%	6.13%	6.16%
Sigma of Love of Variety	0.00%	0.00%	0.00%	0.00%	0.00%	0.00%	0.00%	0.00%	0.00%	0.00%	0.00%	0.00%	0.00%	0.00%	0.00%

Electrical goods

	Border Controls			Border controls and x-ineff.			Market segmentation			Trade *antimonde*			Full *antimonde*		
	1988	1991	1994	1988	1991	1994	1988	1991	1994	1988	1991	1994	1988	1991	1994
Production per firm	-1.09%	-3.16%	-3.16%	-1.09%	-3.17%	-3.18%	-10.89%	-15.45%	-15.49%	-11.27%	-16.01%	-16.04%	-11.36%	-16.12%	-16.19%
Marginal Costs	3.45%	3.79%	3.81%	3.47%	3.82%	3.86%	-5.24%	-4.52%	-4.09%	-2.81%	-2.05%	-1.60%	-2.65%	-1.81%	-1.28%
Producer Prices	3.56%	4.10%	4.12%	3.57%	4.13%	4.17%	-4.04%	-2.87%	-2.43%	-1.54%	-0.29%	0.17%	-1.37%	-0.03%	0.50%
Mark-ups domestic (abs. diff.)	0.10%	0.29%	0.29%	0.10%	0.29%	0.29%	4.85%	5.93%	5.95%	4.83%	5.90%	5.93%	4.84%	5.91%	5.94%
Fixed Costs per firm	3.39%	3.73%	3.74%	3.40%	3.74%	3.77%	-5.02%	-4.36%	-4.04%	-2.61%	-1.91%	-1.57%	-2.50%	-1.75%	-1.35%
Number of Firms	1.42%	3.05%	3.06%	1.43%	3.04%	3.05%	7.59%	6.76%	6.94%	7.77%	6.96%	7.15%	7.72%	6.89%	7.06%
Sigma of Love of Variety	0.00%	0.00%	0.00%	0.00%	0.00%	0.00%	0.00%	0.00%	0.00%	0.00%	0.00%	0.00%	0.00%	0.00%	0.00%

Transport equipment

	Border Controls			Border controls and x-ineff.			Market segmentation			Trade antimonde			Full antimonde		
	1988	1991	1994	1988	1991	1994	1988	1991	1994	1988	1991	1994	1988	1991	1994
Production per firm	-0.47%	-1.88%	-1.88%	-0.47%	-1.89%	-1.89%	-15.77%	-19.50%	-19.34%	-15.83%	-19.62%	-19.45%	-15.88%	-19.64%	-19.48%
Marginal Costs	3.33%	3.65%	3.67%	3.35%	3.68%	3.71%	-4.71%	-4.05%	-3.70%	-2.29%	-1.58%	-1.22%	-2.13%	-1.34%	-0.90%
Producer Prices	3.39%	3.86%	3.88%	3.40%	3.89%	3.92%	-2.57%	-1.54%	-1.21%	-0.09%	1.00%	1.35%	0.07%	1.24%	1.67%
Mark-ups domestic (abs. diff.)	0.18%	0.46%	0.46%	0.18%	0.46%	0.47%	15.34%	17.31%	17.39%	15.37%	17.30%	17.36%	15.39%	17.33%	17.39%
Fixed Costs per firm	3.31%	3.63%	3.64%	3.32%	3.64%	3.67%	-4.64%	-4.00%	-3.69%	-2.23%	-1.55%	-1.22%	-2.12%	-1.38%	-1.00%
Number of Firms	0.92%	1.96%	1.94%	0.92%	1.97%	1.94%	8.30%	4.86%	5.27%	8.24%	4.87%	5.33%	8.17%	4.80%	5.26%
Sigma of Love of Variety	0.00%	0.00%	0.00%	0.00%	0.00%	0.00%	0.00%	0.00%	0.00%	0.00%	0.00%	0.00%	0.00%	0.00%	0.00%

Other Equipment

	Border Controls			Border controls and x-ineff.			Market segmentation			Trade antimonde			Full antimonde		
	1988	1991	1994	1988	1991	1994	1988	1991	1994	1988	1991	1994	1988	1991	1994
Production per firm	-0.76%	-1.80%	-1.80%	-0.76%	-1.82%	-1.82%	-8.39%	-11.83%	-11.95%	-8.80%	-12.26%	-12.38%	-8.87%	-12.36%	-12.51%
Marginal Costs	3.45%	3.80%	3.82%	3.47%	3.83%	3.86%	-5.50%	-4.79%	-4.34%	-3.09%	-2.35%	-1.88%	-2.93%	-2.10%	-1.55%
Producer Prices	3.48%	3.86%	3.88%	3.49%	3.89%	3.92%	-5.20%	-4.37%	-3.92%	-2.77%	-1.91%	-1.43%	-2.61%	-1.66%	-1.10%
Mark-ups domestic (abs. diff.)	0.02%	0.07%	0.07%	0.02%	0.07%	0.07%	1.08%	1.37%	1.37%	1.08%	1.37%	1.38%	1.09%	1.37%	1.38%
Fixed Costs per firm	3.39%	3.73%	3.74%	3.39%	3.74%	3.77%	-5.27%	-4.63%	-4.30%	-2.89%	-2.22%	-1.87%	-2.78%	-2.05%	-1.65%
Number of Firms	0.75%	1.88%	1.87%	0.76%	1.87%	1.86%	7.98%	11.79%	11.87%	7.92%	11.75%	11.83%	7.88%	11.70%	11.77%
Sigma of Love of Variety	0.00%	0.00%	0.00%	0.00%	0.00%	0.00%	0.00%	0.00%	0.00%	0.00%	0.00%	0.00%	0.00%	0.00%	0.00%

Telecommunications

	Border Controls			Border controls and x-ineff.			Market segmentation			Trade antimonde			Full antimonde		
	1988	1991	1994	1988	1991	1994	1988	1991	1994	1988	1991	1994	1988	1991	1994
Production per firm	0.17%	0.30%	0.30%	-0.32%	-0.78%	-0.79%	-2.06%	-4.17%	-4.48%	-1.91%	-3.96%	-4.27%	-2.41%	-4.92%	-5.26%
Marginal Costs	3.67%	4.05%	4.07%	3.69%	4.10%	4.14%	-6.77%	-5.90%	-5.15%	-4.40%	-3.54%	-2.76%	-4.21%	-3.25%	-2.38%
Producer Prices	3.54%	3.87%	3.89%	3.33%	3.50%	3.53%	-6.02%	-4.58%	-3.86%	-3.73%	-2.31%	-1.56%	-3.77%	-2.48%	-1.64%
Mark-ups domestic (abs. diff.)	-0.12%	-0.15%	-0.15%	-0.49%	-0.92%	-0.92%	0.97%	0.98%	0.90%	0.90%	0.92%	0.85%	0.51%	0.14%	0.06%
Fixed Costs per firm	3.42%	3.78%	3.80%	2.21%	1.36%	1.38%	-6.35%	-5.76%	-5.44%	-4.13%	-3.56%	-3.22%	-5.14%	-5.65%	-5.27%
Number of Firms	0.23%	0.42%	0.42%	0.78%	1.68%	1.69%	2.42%	5.48%	5.61%	2.52%	5.57%	5.69%	3.06%	6.67%	6.81%
Sigma of Love of Variety	0.00%	0.00%	0.00%	0.00%	0.00%	0.00%	0.00%	0.00%	0.00%	0.00%	0.00%	0.00%	0.00%	0.00%	0.00%

Banks

	Border Controls			Border controls and x-ineff.			Market segmentation			Trade antimonde			Full antimonde		
	1988	1991	1994	1988	1991	1994	1988	1991	1994	1988	1991	1994	1988	1991	1994
Production per firm	0.83%	1.63%	1.64%	0.38%	0.89%	0.92%	-1.41%	1.60%	2.49%	-0.90%	2.32%	3.21%	-1.40%	1.30%	2.17%
Marginal Costs	3.47%	3.84%	3.86%	3.48%	3.86%	3.90%	-6.57%	-5.94%	-5.56%	-4.35%	-3.73%	-3.34%	-4.20%	-3.51%	-3.05%
Producer Prices	3.32%	3.55%	3.56%	3.22%	3.33%	3.35%	-6.34%	-6.19%	-5.97%	-4.20%	-4.11%	-3.88%	-4.15%	-4.08%	-3.78%
Mark-ups domestic (abs. diff.)	-0.16%	-0.35%	-0.36%	-0.29%	-0.66%	-0.68%	0.24%	-0.63%	-0.84%	0.15%	-0.74%	-0.95%	0.03%	-0.98%	-1.20%
Fixed Costs per firm	3.43%	3.80%	3.82%	2.36%	1.67%	1.69%	-6.53%	-5.94%	-5.63%	-4.33%	-3.76%	-3.44%	-5.22%	-5.60%	-5.24%
Number of Firms	0.99%	2.45%	2.53%	1.61%	4.11%	4.23%	5.10%	14.78%	16.69%	5.50%	15.33%	17.25%	6.06%	16.54%	18.49%
Sigma of Love of Variety	0.00%	0.00%	0.00%	0.00%	0.00%	0.00%	0.00%	0.00%	0.00%	0.00%	0.00%	0.00%	0.00%	0.00%	0.00%

Table B3.7.
Decomposition of effects: sectoral results for Denmark (volumes)

% change from *monde*

Agriculture

	Border Controls			Border controls and x-ineff.			Market segmentation			Trade *antimonde*			Full *antimonde*		
	1988	1991	1994	1988	1991	1994	1988	1991	1994	1988	1991	1994	1988	1991	1994
Domestic Production - vol.	-1.1%	-2.1%	-2.1%	-1.1%	-2.2%	-2.2%	2.8%	2.3%	1.4%	2.3%	1.6%	0.7%	2.1%	1.4%	0.4%
Imports - vol.	1.7%	1.8%	1.9%	1.8%	1.9%	1.9%	-4.5%	-3.9%	-3.4%	-3.3%	-2.7%	-2.2%	-3.2%	-2.4%	-1.9%
Exports - vol.	-0.6%	-0.7%	-0.7%	-0.6%	-0.8%	-0.8%	1.9%	1.5%	1.3%	1.5%	1.2%	0.9%	1.4%	1.1%	0.8%
Absorption - vol.	-0.3%	-0.7%	-0.7%	-0.3%	-0.8%	-0.8%	1.3%	1.2%	0.6%	1.3%	1.0%	0.4%	1.2%	0.9%	0.3%
Investment - vol.	-0.5%	-1.0%	-1.0%	-0.6%	-1.1%	-1.1%	-3.0%	-3.2%	-3.6%	-3.2%	-3.5%	-3.9%	-3.3%	-3.6%	-4.0%
Labour Demand - vol.	-1.0%	-1.9%	-2.0%	-1.0%	-2.0%	-2.0%	2.5%	2.3%	1.6%	2.1%	1.7%	1.0%	2.1%	1.6%	0.9%
Private Consumption - vol.	-0.2%	-0.2%	-0.2%	-0.2%	-0.2%	-0.2%	-0.5%	-1.0%	-1.4%	-0.7%	-1.3%	-1.7%	-0.8%	-1.4%	-1.8%
Supply to domestic - vol.	-0.7%	-1.0%	-1.0%	-0.8%	-1.0%	-1.0%	3.2%	3.2%	2.4%	2.9%	2.8%	1.9%	2.8%	2.6%	1.7%
Intra-EU Trade - vol	-1.9%	-4.8%	-4.8%	-1.9%	-4.9%	-4.9%	0.0%	-2.3%	-2.9%	-1.1%	-3.8%	-4.4%	-1.2%	-4.0%	-4.6%

Energy

	Border Controls			Border controls and x-ineff.			Market segmentation			Trade *antimonde*			Full *antimonde*		
	1988	1991	1994	1988	1991	1994	1988	1991	1994	1988	1991	1994	1988	1991	1994
Domestic Production - vol.	-0.3%	-0.5%	-0.5%	-0.3%	-0.5%	-0.5%	0.9%	0.1%	-0.3%	0.8%	-0.1%	-0.5%	0.8%	-0.2%	-0.6%
Imports - vol.	0.6%	0.7%	0.7%	0.6%	0.7%	0.7%	-1.5%	-1.6%	-1.6%	-1.2%	-1.2%	-1.2%	-1.1%	-1.2%	-1.1%
Exports - vol.	-0.2%	-0.3%	-0.3%	-0.3%	-0.3%	-0.3%	0.7%	0.6%	0.5%	0.6%	0.5%	0.4%	0.6%	0.4%	0.3%
Absorption - vol.	0.0%	0.0%	0.0%	0.0%	-0.1%	-0.1%	-0.2%	-0.8%	-1.1%	-0.2%	-0.9%	-1.1%	-0.2%	-0.9%	-1.2%
Investment - vol.	-0.2%	-0.3%	-0.3%	-0.2%	-0.3%	-0.3%	-3.6%	-4.0%	-4.2%	-3.6%	-4.1%	-4.3%	-3.7%	-4.1%	-4.3%
Labour Demand - vol.	-0.3%	-0.5%	-0.5%	-0.3%	-0.5%	-0.5%	1.1%	0.3%	0.0%	1.0%	0.1%	-0.2%	1.0%	0.1%	-0.2%
Private Consumption - vol.	-0.1%	-0.1%	-0.1%	-0.1%	-0.1%	-0.1%	-0.5%	-0.8%	-1.1%	-0.6%	-1.1%	-1.4%	-0.6%	-1.1%	-1.4%
Supply to domestic - vol.	-0.3%	-0.5%	-0.5%	-0.3%	-0.5%	-0.5%	1.2%	0.4%	-0.1%	1.0%	0.2%	-0.3%	1.0%	0.1%	-0.4%
Intra-EU Trade - vol	-0.7%	-1.0%	-1.0%	-0.7%	-1.0%	-1.0%	1.0%	0.2%	-0.1%	0.5%	-0.5%	-0.8%	0.4%	-0.6%	-0.9%

Metal Industries

	Border Controls			Border controls and x-ineff.			Market segmentation			Trade *antimonde*			Full *antimonde*		
	1988	1991	1994	1988	1991	1994	1988	1991	1994	1988	1991	1994	1988	1991	1994
Domestic Production - vol.	-0.8%	-1.9%	-1.9%	-0.8%	-2.0%	-2.0%	-8.4%	-22.9%	-23.4%	-9.8%	-24.4%	-24.9%	-10.0%	-24.7%	-25.2%
Imports - vol.	1.2%	1.4%	1.4%	1.2%	1.4%	1.4%	-4.3%	-5.5%	-5.4%	-2.6%	-3.7%	-3.5%	-2.4%	-3.4%	-3.2%
Exports - vol.	-0.5%	-0.6%	-0.6%	-0.5%	-0.6%	-0.6%	1.8%	1.2%	1.1%	1.5%	0.9%	0.7%	1.5%	0.8%	0.6%
Absorption - vol.	0.3%	0.3%	0.3%	0.3%	0.3%	0.3%	-2.8%	-6.0%	-6.1%	-3.0%	-6.4%	-6.4%	-3.1%	-6.5%	-6.5%
Investment - vol.	-0.4%	-1.0%	-1.0%	-0.4%	-1.0%	-1.0%	-7.8%	-14.5%	-14.7%	-8.5%	-15.2%	-15.5%	-8.5%	-15.3%	-15.6%
Labour Demand - vol.	-0.6%	-1.5%	-1.5%	-0.6%	-1.6%	-1.6%	-5.9%	-20.3%	-20.8%	-7.1%	-21.7%	-22.1%	-7.2%	-21.9%	-22.3%
Private Consumption - vol.	-0.1%	-0.1%	-0.1%	-0.1%	-0.1%	-0.1%	-0.3%	-0.5%	-0.7%	-0.4%	-0.7%	-0.9%	-0.4%	-0.7%	-1.0%
Supply to domestic - vol.	2.0%	4.0%	4.0%	2.0%	3.9%	3.9%	-32.0%	-51.8%	-52.2%	-32.2%	-51.9%	-52.3%	-32.3%	-52.0%	-52.4%
Intra-EU Trade - vol	-1.4%	-2.8%	-2.8%	-1.4%	-2.8%	-2.8%	5.5%	5.5%	5.3%	3.4%	3.1%	3.0%	3.2%	2.8%	2.6%

Chemical

	Border Controls			Border controls and x-ineff.			Market segmentation			Trade *antimonde*			Full *antimonde*		
	1988	1991	1994	1988	1991	1994	1988	1991	1994	1988	1991	1994	1988	1991	1994
Domestic Production - vol.	0.4%	-0.5%	-0.5%	0.4%	-0.6%	-0.6%	-4.4%	-12.3%	-12.7%	-3.9%	-11.9%	-12.3%	-4.1%	-12.0%	-12.6%
Imports - vol.	0.9%	1.0%	1.0%	0.9%	1.0%	1.0%	-3.5%	-4.1%	-3.9%	-2.4%	-2.8%	-2.7%	-2.2%	-2.5%	-2.3%
Exports - vol.	-0.2%	-0.3%	-0.3%	-0.2%	-0.3%	-0.3%	1.7%	1.3%	1.1%	1.7%	1.3%	1.1%	1.7%	1.2%	1.0%
Absorption - vol.	0.0%	-0.3%	-0.3%	0.0%	-0.3%	-0.3%	-1.5%	-3.9%	-4.2%	-1.5%	-4.0%	-4.3%	-1.5%	-4.0%	-4.4%
Investment - vol.	0.2%	-0.3%	-0.3%	0.2%	-0.3%	-0.3%	-6.1%	-9.7%	-9.9%	-5.8%	-9.5%	-9.7%	-5.9%	-9.6%	-9.8%
Labour Demand - vol.	0.6%	-0.1%	-0.1%	0.6%	-0.2%	-0.2%	-2.7%	-10.2%	-10.6%	-2.2%	-9.8%	-10.2%	-2.2%	-9.9%	-10.3%
Private Consumption - vol.	-0.2%	-0.2%	-0.2%	-0.2%	-0.2%	-0.2%	-0.4%	-0.9%	-1.2%	-0.6%	-1.2%	-1.6%	-0.6%	-1.3%	-1.7%
Supply to domestic - vol.	2.3%	3.5%	3.5%	2.3%	3.4%	3.4%	-15.1%	-27.0%	-27.6%	-14.2%	-26.2%	-26.8%	-14.4%	-26.3%	-27.0%
Intra-EU Trade - vol	-1.2%	-2.8%	-2.8%	-1.2%	-2.9%	-2.9%	4.1%	3.3%	3.1%	3.4%	2.4%	2.2%	3.3%	2.2%	1.9%

Other Intensive Industries

	Border Controls			Border controls and x-ineff.			Market segmentation			Trade *antimonde*			Full *antimonde*		
	1988	1991	1994	1988	1991	1994	1988	1991	1994	1988	1991	1994	1988	1991	1994
Domestic Production - vol.	0.4%	0.9%	1.0%	0.4%	0.9%	0.9%	-0.6%	-0.3%	-0.4%	-0.6%	-0.3%	-0.4%	-0.6%	-0.4%	-0.6%
Imports - vol.	1.5%	1.9%	1.9%	1.5%	1.9%	1.9%	-6.7%	-6.5%	-6.2%	-5.2%	-4.8%	-4.5%	-4.9%	-4.5%	-4.1%
Exports - vol.	-0.4%	-0.5%	-0.5%	-0.4%	-0.5%	-0.5%	1.7%	1.5%	1.4%	1.6%	1.3%	1.2%	1.5%	1.3%	1.1%
Absorption - vol.	0.2%	0.3%	0.3%	0.2%	0.3%	0.3%	-2.5%	-3.0%	-3.2%	-2.5%	-3.1%	-3.2%	-2.5%	-3.1%	-3.3%
Investment - vol.	0.2%	0.4%	0.5%	0.2%	0.4%	0.4%	-4.2%	-4.1%	-4.2%	-4.2%	-4.2%	-4.2%	-4.3%	-4.2%	-4.3%
Labour Demand - vol.	0.5%	1.0%	1.1%	0.5%	1.0%	1.0%	-0.3%	0.2%	0.2%	-0.2%	0.2%	0.2%	-0.2%	0.2%	0.2%
Private Consumption - vol.	-0.2%	-0.2%	-0.2%	-0.2%	-0.2%	-0.2%	-0.5%	-1.1%	-1.4%	-0.8%	-1.4%	-1.8%	-0.9%	-1.5%	-1.9%
Supply to domestic - vol.	1.0%	2.7%	2.8%	1.0%	2.7%	2.7%	-0.1%	1.7%	1.5%	0.1%	1.9%	1.8%	0.0%	1.8%	1.6%
Intra-EU Trade - vol	-2.3%	-5.1%	-5.1%	-2.3%	-5.1%	-5.1%	-1.6%	-6.0%	-6.2%	-3.1%	-7.7%	-7.8%	-3.2%	-7.8%	-8.0%

Electrical goods

Electrical goods	Border Controls			Border controls and x-ineff.			Market segmentation			Trade *antimonde*			Full *antimonde*		
	1988	1991	1994	1988	1991	1994	1988	1991	1994	1988	1991	1994	1988	1991	1994
Domestic Production - vol.	0.3%	-0.2%	-0.2%	0.3%	-0.2%	-0.2%	-4.1%	-9.7%	-9.6%	-4.4%	-10.2%	-10.0%	-4.5%	-10.3%	-10.3%
Imports - vol.	1.4%	1.7%	1.7%	1.4%	1.7%	1.7%	-6.2%	-6.5%	-6.3%	-4.6%	-4.7%	-4.4%	-4.4%	-4.4%	-4.0%
Exports - vol.	-0.4%	-0.5%	-0.5%	-0.5%	-0.5%	-0.6%	2.1%	1.8%	1.6%	1.9%	1.6%	1.4%	1.8%	1.5%	1.3%
Absorption - vol.	0.1%	0.1%	0.1%	0.1%	0.1%	0.1%	-4.2%	-5.8%	-5.8%	-4.4%	-6.0%	-6.0%	-4.4%	-6.0%	-6.1%
Investment - vol.	0.1%	-0.1%	-0.1%	0.1%	-0.1%	-0.1%	-5.8%	-8.4%	-8.5%	-6.0%	-8.7%	-8.7%	-6.0%	-8.7%	-8.8%
Labour Demand - vol.	0.5%	0.2%	0.2%	0.5%	0.1%	0.1%	-2.5%	-7.7%	-7.5%	-2.6%	-8.0%	-7.8%	-2.7%	-8.1%	-7.9%
Private Consumption - vol.	-0.4%	-0.2%	-0.2%	-0.4%	-0.3%	-0.3%	-1.3%	-1.8%	-2.2%	-1.9%	-2.4%	-2.7%	-2.0%	-2.5%	-2.8%
Supply to domestic - vol.	2.4%	4.9%	4.9%	2.4%	4.9%	4.9%	-9.4%	-15.1%	-15.0%	-9.1%	-14.6%	-14.6%	-9.2%	-14.8%	-14.8%
Intra-EU Trade - vol	-1.7%	-3.6%	-3.6%	-1.7%	-3.6%	-3.6%	1.8%	-0.1%	-0.2%	0.3%	-1.9%	-2.0%	0.1%	-2.1%	-2.3%

Transport equipment

Transport equipment	Border Controls			Border controls and x-ineff.			Market segmentation			Trade *antimonde*			Full *antimonde*		
	1988	1991	1994	1988	1991	1994	1988	1991	1994	1988	1991	1994	1988	1991	1994
Domestic Production - vol.	0.4%	0.0%	0.0%	0.4%	0.0%	0.0%	-8.8%	-15.6%	-15.1%	-8.9%	-15.7%	-15.2%	-9.0%	-15.8%	-15.2%
Imports - vol.	0.7%	0.8%	0.8%	0.7%	0.9%	0.9%	-4.7%	-4.2%	-4.0%	-3.9%	-3.2%	-2.9%	-3.8%	-3.0%	-2.7%
Exports - vol.	-0.4%	-0.5%	-0.5%	-0.4%	-0.5%	-0.5%	2.0%	1.6%	1.5%	1.8%	1.4%	1.3%	1.7%	1.3%	1.2%
Absorption - vol.	0.0%	0.1%	0.1%	0.0%	0.1%	0.1%	-5.8%	-5.3%	-5.0%	-6.3%	-5.4%	-5.1%	-6.3%	-5.5%	-5.1%
Investment - vol.	0.2%	0.0%	0.0%	0.2%	0.0%	-0.1%	-7.8%	-11.0%	-10.9%	-7.9%	-11.1%	-10.9%	-7.9%	-11.1%	-10.9%
Labour Demand - vol.	0.5%	0.2%	0.2%	0.5%	0.2%	0.2%	-6.3%	-12.9%	-12.3%	-6.3%	-12.9%	-12.3%	-6.4%	-12.9%	-12.3%
Private Consumption - vol.	-0.3%	0.0%	0.0%	-0.3%	0.0%	0.0%	-5.4%	-2.8%	-2.1%	-6.5%	-3.4%	-2.3%	-6.6%	-3.5%	-2.5%
Supply to domestic - vol.	1.9%	3.9%	3.9%	1.9%	3.9%	3.9%	-27.1%	-38.0%	-37.6%	-27.5%	-38.1%	-37.5%	-27.6%	-38.2%	-37.7%
Intra-EU Trade - vol	-1.2%	-2.3%	-2.3%	-1.2%	-2.3%	-2.3%	3.8%	4.5%	4.5%	2.1%	2.6%	2.7%	1.9%	2.4%	2.4%

Other Equipment

Other Equipment	Border Controls			Border controls and x-ineff.			Market segmentation			Trade *antimonde*			Full *antimonde*		
	1988	1991	1994	1988	1991	1994	1988	1991	1994	1988	1991	1994	1988	1991	1994
Domestic Production - vol.	0.0%	0.0%	0.0%	0.0%	0.0%	0.0%	-1.1%	-1.4%	-1.5%	-1.6%	-2.0%	-2.0%	-1.7%	-2.1%	-2.2%
Imports - vol.	1.4%	1.6%	1.6%	1.4%	1.6%	1.7%	-7.1%	-7.3%	-7.2%	-5.1%	-5.1%	-5.0%	-5.0%	-4.8%	-4.6%
Exports - vol.	-0.7%	-0.8%	-0.8%	-0.7%	-0.8%	-0.8%	2.1%	1.8%	1.6%	1.7%	1.4%	1.3%	1.6%	1.3%	1.1%
Absorption - vol.	0.0%	-0.1%	-0.1%	0.0%	-0.1%	-0.1%	-5.4%	-6.3%	-6.5%	-5.7%	-6.6%	-6.7%	-5.7%	-6.6%	-6.7%
Investment - vol.	0.0%	0.0%	0.0%	0.0%	0.0%	0.0%	-4.6%	-4.8%	-5.0%	-4.9%	-5.1%	-5.3%	-5.0%	-5.2%	-5.3%
Labour Demand - vol.	0.1%	0.1%	0.1%	0.1%	0.1%	0.1%	-0.5%	-0.7%	-0.6%	-0.9%	-1.1%	-1.0%	-1.0%	-1.1%	-1.1%
Private Consumption - vol.	-0.6%	-0.2%	-0.1%	-0.7%	-0.2%	-0.1%	-3.5%	-3.2%	-2.9%	-4.7%	-3.9%	-3.3%	-4.9%	-4.1%	-3.5%
Supply to domestic - vol.	2.2%	5.6%	5.6%	2.2%	5.6%	5.6%	-3.1%	0.5%	0.5%	-2.9%	0.7%	0.8%	-2.9%	0.6%	0.6%
Intra-EU Trade - vol	-1.3%	-2.8%	-2.8%	-1.3%	-2.8%	-2.8%	-1.5%	-3.9%	-4.0%	-2.8%	-5.2%	-5.3%	-2.9%	-5.4%	-5.5%

Consumer goods

Consumer goods	Border Controls			Border controls and x-ineff.			Market segmentation			Trade *antimonde*			Full *antimonde*		
	1988	1991	1994	1988	1991	1994	1988	1991	1994	1988	1991	1994	1988	1991	1994
Domestic Production - vol.	-0.3%	-0.7%	-0.7%	-0.3%	-0.7%	-0.8%	1.9%	1.8%	1.2%	1.9%	1.7%	1.1%	1.8%	1.5%	0.8%
Imports - vol.	1.2%	1.4%	1.4%	1.2%	1.4%	1.4%	-4.6%	-4.2%	-4.0%	-3.9%	-3.5%	-3.3%	-3.8%	-3.3%	-3.0%
Exports - vol.	-0.5%	-0.7%	-0.7%	-0.5%	-0.7%	-0.7%	2.3%	1.9%	1.7%	2.1%	1.7%	1.5%	2.0%	1.6%	1.3%
Absorption - vol.	-0.1%	-0.3%	-0.3%	-0.1%	-0.3%	-0.3%	-0.5%	-1.0%	-1.3%	-0.6%	-1.2%	-1.5%	-0.7%	-1.2%	-1.6%
Investment - vol.	-0.2%	-0.4%	-0.4%	-0.2%	-0.4%	-0.4%	-3.2%	-3.3%	-3.6%	-3.3%	-3.4%	-3.7%	-3.3%	-3.5%	-3.8%
Labour Demand - vol.	-0.3%	-0.6%	-0.6%	-0.3%	-0.7%	-0.7%	2.0%	2.0%	1.6%	2.1%	2.0%	1.5%	2.1%	1.9%	1.4%
Private Consumption - vol.	-0.1%	-0.1%	-0.1%	-0.1%	-0.2%	-0.1%	-0.4%	-0.9%	-1.2%	-0.6%	-1.2%	-1.5%	-0.7%	-1.2%	-1.6%
Supply to domestic - vol.	0.8%	2.6%	2.6%	0.8%	2.5%	2.5%	2.7%	4.7%	4.0%	2.8%	4.7%	4.0%	2.7%	4.5%	3.7%
Intra-EU Trade - vol	-2.1%	-5.2%	-5.2%	-2.1%	-5.2%	-5.2%	-1.3%	-4.6%	-4.8%	-1.7%	-5.2%	-5.5%	-1.8%	-5.3%	-5.6%

Construction

Construction	Border Controls			Border controls and x-ineff.			Market segmentation			Trade *antimonde*			Full *antimonde*		
	1988	1991	1994	1988	1991	1994	1988	1991	1994	1988	1991	1994	1988	1991	1994
Domestic Production - vol.	#VALUE!	#VALUE!	#VALUE!	0.2%	0.3%	0.3%	-6.2%	-6.2%	-6.4%	-6.1%	-6.2%	-6.4%	-6.1%	-6.1%	-6.3%
Imports - vol.	0.3%	0.3%	0.3%	#VALUE!	#VALUE!	#VALUE!	#VALUE!	#VALUE!	#VALUE!	#VALUE!	#VALUE!	#VALUE!	#VALUE!	#VALUE!	#VALUE!
Exports - vol.	#VALUE!	#VALUE!	#VALUE!	#VALUE!	#VALUE!	#VALUE!	#VALUE!	#VALUE!	#VALUE!	#VALUE!	#VALUE!	#VALUE!	#VALUE!	#VALUE!	#VALUE!
Absorption - vol.	0.2%	0.3%	0.3%	0.2%	0.3%	0.3%	-6.2%	-6.2%	-6.4%	-6.1%	-6.2%	-6.4%	-6.1%	-6.1%	-6.3%
Investment - vol.	0.1%	0.1%	0.1%	0.1%	0.1%	0.1%	-7.1%	-7.1%	-7.3%	-7.1%	-7.1%	-7.3%	-7.1%	-7.1%	-7.2%
Labour Demand - vol.	0.2%	0.3%	0.3%	0.2%	0.3%	0.3%	-6.1%	-6.1%	-6.2%	-6.0%	-6.0%	-6.1%	-5.9%	-5.9%	-5.9%
Private Consumption - vol.	#DIV/0!	#DIV/0!	#DIV/0!	#DIV/0!	#DIV/0!	#DIV/0!	#DIV/0!	#DIV/0!	#DIV/0!	#DIV/0!	#DIV/0!	#DIV/0!	#DIV/0!	#DIV/0!	#DIV/0!
Supply to domestic - vol.	0.2%	0.3%	0.3%	0.2%	0.3%	0.3%	-6.2%	-6.2%	-6.4%	-6.1%	-6.2%	-6.4%	-6.1%	-6.1%	-6.3%
Intra-EU Trade - vol	#DIV/0!	#DIV/0!	#DIV/0!	#DIV/0!	#DIV/0!	#DIV/0!	#DIV/0!	#DIV/0!	#DIV/0!	#DIV/0!	#DIV/0!	#DIV/0!	#DIV/0!	#DIV/0!	#DIV/0!

Telecommunications

	Border Controls			Border controls and x-ineff.			Market segmentation			Trade *antimonde*			Full *antimonde*		
	1988	1991	1994	1988	1991	1994	1988	1991	1994	1988	1991	1994	1988	1991	1994
Domestic Production - vol.	0.4%	0.7%	0.7%	0.5%	0.9%	0.9%	0.3%	1.1%	0.9%	0.6%	1.4%	1.2%	0.6%	1.4%	1.2%
Imports - vol.	0.7%	0.9%	0.9%	0.5%	0.7%	0.7%	-6.7%	-6.5%	-6.3%	-6.4%	-6.3%	-6.0%	-6.3%	-6.2%	-5.9%
Exports - vol.	-0.2%	-0.2%	-0.2%	-0.1%	-0.2%	-0.2%	1.1%	1.0%	0.9%	1.1%	1.0%	0.9%	1.1%	1.0%	0.9%
Absorption - vol.	0.1%	0.2%	0.2%	0.1%	0.3%	0.3%	-0.4%	-0.3%	-0.5%	-0.4%	-0.4%	-0.5%	-0.3%	-0.3%	-0.5%
Investment - vol.	0.2%	0.4%	0.4%	0.3%	0.5%	0.5%	-4.0%	-3.7%	-3.8%	-3.9%	-3.5%	-3.6%	-3.9%	-3.5%	-3.5%
Labour Demand - vol.	0.4%	0.6%	0.6%	-0.2%	-0.5%	-0.4%	1.2%	3.0%	3.0%	1.4%	3.3%	3.3%	0.8%	2.0%	2.0%
Private Consumption - vol.	-0.2%	-0.3%	-0.3%	-0.2%	-0.1%	-0.1%	-0.4%	-1.1%	-1.6%	-0.6%	-1.5%	-2.0%	-0.6%	-1.4%	-2.0%
Supply to domestic - vol.	0.2%	0.4%	0.4%	0.3%	0.8%	0.8%	1.0%	3.9%	3.7%	1.0%	3.9%	3.7%	1.1%	4.0%	3.8%
Intra-EU Trade - vol	0.3%	0.0%	0.0%	-0.1%	-1.3%	-1.3%	-7.3%	-18.4%	-18.5%	-6.8%	-17.8%	-17.9%	-6.9%	-18.0%	-18.1%

Transports

	Border Controls			Border controls and x-ineff.			Market segmentation			Trade *antimonde*			Full *antimonde*		
	1988	1991	1994	1988	1991	1994	1988	1991	1994	1988	1991	1994	1988	1991	1994
Domestic Production - vol.	0.5%	0.6%	0.6%	0.5%	0.6%	0.6%	-0.1%	-0.4%	-0.6%	0.4%	0.2%	0.0%	0.4%	0.2%	0.0%
Imports - vol.	0.3%	0.3%	0.3%	0.3%	0.3%	0.3%	0.0%	-0.2%	-0.3%	0.2%	0.1%	0.0%	0.2%	0.1%	0.0%
Exports - vol.	-0.1%	-0.1%	-0.1%	-0.1%	-0.1%	-0.1%	0.6%	0.6%	0.5%	0.6%	0.6%	0.5%	0.6%	0.5%	0.5%
Absorption - vol.	0.2%	0.2%	0.2%	0.2%	0.2%	0.2%	-0.7%	-1.1%	-1.3%	-0.6%	-1.0%	-1.3%	-0.6%	-1.0%	-1.3%
Investment - vol.	0.3%	0.3%	0.3%	0.3%	0.3%	0.3%	-4.3%	-4.4%	-4.5%	-4.1%	-4.2%	-4.3%	-4.1%	-4.2%	-4.3%
Labour Demand - vol.	0.5%	0.6%	0.6%	0.5%	0.7%	0.7%	-0.1%	-0.3%	-0.4%	0.5%	0.3%	0.2%	0.5%	0.4%	0.3%
Private Consumption - vol.	-0.2%	-0.2%	-0.2%	-0.2%	-0.2%	-0.2%	-0.4%	-1.0%	-1.5%	-0.7%	-1.4%	-1.9%	-0.8%	-1.5%	-2.0%
Supply to domestic - vol.	0.5%	0.6%	0.6%	0.5%	0.6%	0.6%	-0.1%	-0.4%	-0.6%	0.4%	0.2%	0.0%	0.4%	0.2%	0.0%
Intra-EU Trade - vol	2.0%	2.5%	2.5%	2.0%	2.5%	2.5%	0.1%	0.1%	0.0%	2.0%	2.4%	2.3%	2.0%	2.4%	2.3%

Banks

	Border Controls			Border controls and x-ineff.			Market segmentation			Trade *antimonde*			Full *antimonde*		
	1988	1991	1994	1988	1991	1994	1988	1991	1994	1988	1991	1994	1988	1991	1994
Domestic Production - vol.	1.8%	4.1%	4.2%	2.0%	5.0%	5.2%	3.6%	16.6%	19.6%	4.6%	18.0%	21.0%	4.6%	18.1%	21.1%
Imports - vol.	1.3%	2.2%	2.2%	1.2%	2.4%	2.4%	-5.1%	-1.5%	-0.6%	-4.3%	-0.6%	0.3%	-4.1%	-0.3%	0.8%
Exports - vol.	-0.1%	-0.2%	-0.2%	-0.1%	-0.2%	-0.2%	1.1%	1.0%	1.0%	1.1%	1.1%	1.0%	1.1%	1.0%	1.0%
Absorption - vol.	1.3%	2.8%	2.9%	1.4%	3.5%	3.5%	2.4%	11.1%	12.9%	3.1%	12.0%	13.8%	3.1%	12.0%	13.8%
Investment - vol.	0.9%	2.1%	2.1%	1.0%	2.5%	2.6%	-2.5%	3.4%	4.7%	-2.2%	3.9%	5.3%	-2.1%	4.0%	5.3%
Labour Demand - vol.	1.7%	3.8%	3.9%	1.7%	4.3%	4.5%	3.9%	16.3%	19.2%	4.8%	17.6%	20.5%	4.6%	17.3%	20.2%
Private Consumption - vol.	-0.3%	-0.3%	-0.3%	-0.3%	-0.3%	-0.3%	-0.5%	-1.1%	-1.6%	-0.8%	-1.6%	-2.1%	-0.9%	-1.7%	-2.3%
Supply to domestic - vol.	1.7%	4.1%	4.2%	1.9%	5.1%	5.3%	4.2%	18.7%	21.8%	4.9%	19.8%	23.0%	4.9%	19.9%	23.0%
Intra-EU Trade - vol	-0.2%	-1.1%	-1.1%	-0.4%	-1.8%	-1.8%	-5.4%	-14.3%	-15.2%	-4.9%	-13.6%	-14.6%	-4.9%	-13.7%	-14.6%

Services

	Border Controls			Border controls and x-ineff.			Market segmentation			Trade *antimonde*			Full *antimonde*		
	1988	1991	1994	1988	1991	1994	1988	1991	1994	1988	1991	1994	1988	1991	1994
Domestic Production - vol.	0.3%	0.4%	0.4%	0.3%	0.4%	0.4%	-0.8%	-0.8%	-1.1%	-0.6%	-0.6%	-0.9%	-0.7%	-0.6%	-1.0%
Imports - vol.	1.6%	1.8%	1.8%	1.6%	1.8%	1.8%	-4.6%	-4.3%	-4.0%	-3.6%	-3.2%	-2.9%	-3.5%	-3.1%	-2.7%
Exports - vol.	-0.5%	-0.6%	-0.6%	-0.5%	-0.6%	-0.6%	1.4%	1.2%	1.0%	1.1%	0.9%	0.7%	1.0%	0.8%	0.6%
Absorption - vol.	0.0%	0.0%	0.0%	0.0%	0.0%	0.0%	-1.0%	-1.4%	-1.7%	-1.2%	-1.5%	-1.8%	-1.2%	-1.6%	-1.9%
Investment - vol.	0.1%	0.2%	0.2%	0.1%	0.2%	0.2%	-4.6%	-4.6%	-4.7%	-4.5%	-4.5%	-4.7%	-4.5%	-4.5%	-4.6%
Labour Demand - vol.	0.3%	0.5%	0.5%	0.4%	0.5%	0.5%	-0.9%	-0.8%	-0.9%	-0.7%	-0.5%	-0.6%	-0.6%	-0.4%	-0.6%
Private Consumption - vol.	-0.2%	-0.2%	-0.2%	-0.2%	-0.2%	-0.2%	-0.6%	-1.1%	-1.5%	-0.9%	-1.4%	-1.8%	-1.0%	-1.5%	-2.0%
Supply to domestic - vol.	0.0%	0.1%	0.1%	0.0%	0.1%	0.1%	-1.0%	-1.0%	-1.3%	-1.1%	-1.1%	-1.5%	-1.1%	-1.2%	-1.5%
Intra-EU Trade - vol	1.4%	1.8%	1.8%	1.4%	1.8%	1.8%	-0.9%	-2.5%	-2.5%	0.7%	-0.4%	-0.5%	0.6%	-0.4%	-0.5%

Non market

	Border Controls			Border controls and x-ineff.			Market segmentation			Trade *antimonde*			Full *antimonde*		
	1988	1991	1994	1988	1991	1994	1988	1991	1994	1988	1991	1994	1988	1991	1994
Domestic Production - vol.	0.0%	0.0%	0.0%	0.0%	0.0%	0.0%	0.0%	-0.1%	-0.1%	-0.1%	-0.1%	-0.1%	-0.1%	-0.1%	-0.2%
Imports - vol.	#VALUE!	#VALUE!	#VALUE!	#VALUE!	#VALUE!	#VALUE!	#VALUE!	#VALUE!	#VALUE!	#VALUE!	#VALUE!	#VALUE!	#VALUE!	#VALUE!	#VALUE!
Exports - vol.	-0.1%	-0.1%	-0.1%	0.0%	0.0%	0.0%	0.3%	0.3%	0.3%	0.3%	0.2%	0.2%	0.3%	0.2%	0.2%
Absorption - vol.	0.0%	0.0%	0.0%	0.0%	0.0%	0.0%	0.0%	-0.1%	-0.1%	-0.1%	-0.1%	-0.1%	-0.1%	-0.1%	-0.2%
Investment - vol.	0.0%	0.0%	0.0%	0.0%	0.0%	0.0%	-4.2%	-4.2%	-4.2%	-4.2%	-4.2%	-4.2%	-4.2%	-4.2%	-4.2%
Labour Demand - vol.	0.0%	0.0%	0.0%	0.4%	0.5%	0.5%	0.0%	0.0%	0.0%	0.0%	0.0%	0.0%	0.0%	0.0%	0.0%
Private Consumption - vol.	-0.2%	-0.2%	-0.2%	-0.2%	-0.2%	-0.2%	-0.6%	-1.2%	-1.6%	-1.0%	-1.6%	-2.0%	-1.0%	-1.7%	-2.2%
Supply to domestic - vol.	0.0%	0.0%	0.0%	0.0%	0.0%	0.0%	0.0%	-0.1%	-0.1%	-0.1%	-0.1%	-0.1%	-0.1%	-0.1%	-0.2%
Intra-EU Trade - vol	0.5%	0.5%	0.5%	0.5%	0.5%	0.5%	-0.2%	-0.2%	-0.2%	0.4%	0.3%	0.3%	0.4%	0.3%	0.3%

Table B3.8.
Decomposition of effects: sectoral results for Denmark (prices)

% change from *monde*

Agriculture

	Border Controls			Border controls and x-ineff.			Market segmentation			Trade *antimonde*			Full *antimonde*		
	1988	1991	1994	1988	1991	1994	1988	1991	1994	1988	1991	1994	1988	1991	1994
Marginal Costs	0.03%	-0.04%	-0.04%	0.04%	-0.02%	-0.03%	0.52%	0.56%	0.79%	0.70%	0.77%	1.01%	0.72%	0.79%	1.03%
Cost of Labour	-0.20%	-0.22%	-0.22%	-0.22%	-0.26%	-0.26%	-0.36%	-0.77%	-1.23%	-0.57%	-1.00%	-1.47%	-0.67%	-1.16%	-1.68%
Deflator of Absorption	-0.25%	-0.36%	-0.36%	-0.25%	-0.35%	-0.36%	1.31%	1.23%	1.34%	1.39%	1.34%	1.46%	1.38%	1.33%	1.43%
Price of Exports-RW	0.03%	-0.04%	-0.04%	0.04%	-0.02%	-0.03%	0.52%	0.56%	0.79%	0.70%	0.77%	1.01%	0.72%	0.79%	1.03%

Energy

	Border Controls			Border controls and x-ineff.			Market segmentation			Trade *antimonde*			Full *antimonde*		
	1988	1991	1994	1988	1991	1994	1988	1991	1994	1988	1991	1994	1988	1991	1994
Marginal Costs	-0.47%	-0.60%	-0.61%	-0.46%	-0.60%	-0.62%	1.72%	1.51%	1.53%	1.66%	1.48%	1.49%	1.61%	1.42%	1.40%
Cost of Labour	-0.20%	-0.22%	-0.22%	-0.22%	-0.26%	-0.26%	-0.36%	-0.77%	-1.23%	-0.57%	-1.00%	-1.47%	-0.67%	-1.16%	-1.68%
Deflator of Absorption	-0.94%	-1.15%	-1.16%	-0.95%	-1.17%	-1.19%	3.39%	2.95%	2.75%	3.18%	2.80%	2.58%	3.09%	2.66%	2.40%
Price of Exports-RW	-0.47%	-0.60%	-0.61%	-0.46%	-0.60%	-0.62%	1.72%	1.51%	1.53%	1.66%	1.48%	1.49%	1.61%	1.42%	1.40%

Metal Industries

	Border Controls			Border controls and x-ineff.			Market segmentation			Trade *antimonde*			Full *antimonde*		
	1988	1991	1994	1988	1991	1994	1988	1991	1994	1988	1991	1994	1988	1991	1994
Marginal Costs	-0.21%	-0.31%	-0.31%	-0.21%	-0.31%	-0.32%	1.58%	1.48%	1.40%	1.70%	1.66%	1.58%	1.70%	1.66%	1.57%
Cost of Labour	-0.20%	-0.22%	-0.22%	-0.22%	-0.28%	-0.28%	-0.36%	-0.77%	-1.23%	-0.57%	-1.00%	-1.47%	-0.67%	-1.16%	-1.68%
Deflator of Absorption	-0.62%	-0.82%	-0.83%	-0.63%	-0.85%	-0.86%	5.10%	5.12%	4.80%	5.40%	5.59%	5.26%	5.34%	5.49%	5.12%
Price of Exports-RW	-0.28%	-0.49%	-0.49%	-0.28%	-0.49%	-0.49%	0.53%	1.48%	1.44%	0.65%	1.68%	1.64%	0.65%	1.69%	1.65%

Chemical

	Border Controls			Border controls and x-ineff.			Market segmentation			Trade *antimonde*			Full *antimonde*		
	1988	1991	1994	1988	1991	1994	1988	1991	1994	1988	1991	1994	1988	1991	1994
Marginal Costs	-0.05%	-0.12%	-0.13%	-0.05%	-0.13%	-0.13%	1.49%	1.41%	1.38%	1.72%	1.69%	1.66%	1.72%	1.69%	1.65%
Cost of Labour	-0.20%	-0.22%	-0.22%	-0.22%	-0.26%	-0.26%	-0.36%	-0.77%	-1.23%	-0.57%	-1.00%	-1.47%	-0.67%	-1.16%	-1.68%
Deflator of Absorption	0.10%	0.00%	-0.01%	0.10%	-0.02%	-0.03%	4.60%	4.68%	4.48%	5.35%	5.59%	5.39%	5.30%	5.52%	5.30%
Price of Exports-RW	-0.16%	-0.31%	-0.32%	-0.16%	-0.32%	-0.32%	0.93%	1.26%	1.25%	1.11%	1.50%	1.49%	1.11%	1.49%	1.49%

Other Intensive Industries

	Border Controls			Border controls and x-ineff.			Market segmentation			Trade *antimonde*			Full *antimonde*		
	1988	1991	1994	1988	1991	1994	1988	1991	1994	1988	1991	1994	1988	1991	1994
Marginal Costs	-0.14%	-0.21%	-0.21%	-0.15%	-0.22%	-0.22%	0.90%	0.72%	0.60%	0.97%	0.83%	0.71%	0.97%	0.82%	0.69%
Cost of Labour	-0.20%	-0.22%	-0.22%	-0.22%	-0.26%	-0.26%	-0.36%	-0.77%	-1.23%	-0.57%	-1.00%	-1.47%	-0.67%	-1.16%	-1.68%
Deflator of Absorption	-0.24%	-0.34%	-0.34%	-0.24%	-0.35%	-0.36%	1.84%	1.60%	1.41%	2.02%	1.85%	1.66%	1.99%	1.81%	1.59%
Price of Exports-RW	-0.15%	-0.24%	-0.24%	-0.16%	-0.25%	-0.25%	0.86%	0.65%	0.53%	0.93%	0.76%	0.63%	0.93%	0.75%	0.62%

Electrical goods

	Border Controls			Border controls and x-ineff.			Market segmentation			Trade antimonde			Full antimonde		
	1988	1991	1994	1988	1991	1994	1988	1991	1994	1988	1991	1994	1988	1991	1994
Marginal Costs	-0.14%	-0.20%	-0.20%	-0.14%	-0.22%	-0.22%	1.16%	0.98%	0.80%	1.27%	1.14%	0.95%	1.26%	1.12%	0.92%
Cost of Labour	-0.20%	-0.22%	-0.22%	-0.22%	-0.26%	-0.26%	-0.36%	-0.77%	-1.23%	-0.57%	-1.00%	-1.47%	-0.67%	-1.16%	-1.68%
Deflator of Absorption	-0.20%	-0.30%	-0.30%	-0.21%	-0.33%	-0.33%	3.64%	3.56%	3.28%	4.08%	4.13%	3.84%	4.03%	4.05%	3.73%
Price of Exports-RW	-0.23%	-0.39%	-0.39%	-0.23%	-0.40%	-0.41%	0.75%	0.61%	0.42%	0.84%	0.75%	0.55%	0.83%	0.73%	0.52%

Transport equipment

	Border Controls			Border controls and x-ineff.			Market segmentation			Trade antimonde			Full antimonde		
	1988	1991	1994	1988	1991	1994	1988	1991	1994	1988	1991	1994	1988	1991	1994
Marginal Costs	-0.25%	-0.34%	-0.34%	-0.26%	-0.36%	-0.36%	1.70%	1.46%	1.19%	1.79%	1.61%	1.34%	1.78%	1.58%	1.30%
Cost of Labour	-0.20%	-0.22%	-0.22%	-0.22%	-0.26%	-0.26%	-0.36%	-0.77%	-1.23%	-0.57%	-1.00%	-1.47%	-0.67%	-1.16%	-1.68%
Deflator of Absorption	-0.77%	-1.01%	-1.02%	-0.78%	-1.05%	-1.06%	5.68%	5.43%	4.99%	5.90%	5.76%	5.31%	5.80%	5.61%	5.11%
Price of Exports-RW	-0.36%	-0.55%	-0.55%	-0.36%	-0.57%	-0.57%	0.92%	0.99%	0.69%	1.00%	1.13%	0.81%	0.99%	1.11%	0.78%

Other Equipment

	Border Controls			Border controls and x-ineff.			Market segmentation			Trade antimonde			Full antimonde		
	1988	1991	1994	1988	1991	1994	1988	1991	1994	1988	1991	1994	1988	1991	1994
Marginal Costs	-0.14%	-0.20%	-0.20%	-0.14%	-0.21%	-0.21%	0.91%	0.72%	0.56%	0.99%	0.84%	0.68%	0.98%	0.82%	0.65%
Cost of Labour	-0.20%	-0.22%	-0.22%	-0.22%	-0.26%	-0.26%	-0.36%	-0.77%	-1.23%	-0.57%	-1.00%	-1.47%	-0.67%	-1.16%	-1.68%
Deflator of Absorption	-0.16%	-0.22%	-0.22%	-0.17%	-0.24%	-0.25%	2.26%	2.03%	1.78%	2.62%	2.53%	2.27%	2.58%	2.46%	2.19%
Price of Exports-RW	-0.14%	-0.22%	-0.22%	-0.15%	-0.23%	-0.23%	0.82%	0.59%	0.42%	0.90%	0.71%	0.54%	0.89%	0.69%	0.51%

Consumer goods

	Border Controls			Border controls and x-ineff.			Market segmentation			Trade antimonde			Full antimonde		
	1988	1991	1994	1988	1991	1994	1988	1991	1994	1988	1991	1994	1988	1991	1994
Marginal Costs	-0.17%	-0.25%	-0.25%	-0.16%	-0.25%	-0.25%	1.01%	0.86%	0.84%	1.10%	0.99%	0.97%	1.11%	1.00%	0.99%
Cost of Labour	-0.20%	-0.22%	-0.22%	-0.22%	-0.26%	-0.26%	-0.36%	-0.77%	-1.23%	-0.57%	-1.00%	-1.47%	-0.67%	-1.16%	-1.68%
Deflator of Absorption	-0.30%	-0.42%	-0.42%	-0.31%	-0.43%	-0.44%	2.11%	1.82%	1.67%	2.31%	2.09%	1.93%	2.28%	2.05%	1.87%
Price of Exports-RW	-0.17%	-0.25%	-0.25%	-0.16%	-0.25%	-0.25%	1.01%	0.86%	0.84%	1.10%	0.99%	0.97%	1.11%	1.00%	0.99%

Construction

	Border Controls			Border controls and x-ineff.			Market segmentation			Trade antimonde			Full antimonde		
	1988	1991	1994	1988	1991	1994	1988	1991	1994	1988	1991	1994	1988	1991	1994
Marginal Costs	-0.10%	-0.16%	-0.16%	-0.11%	-0.17%	-0.17%	0.63%	0.45%	0.34%	0.70%	0.54%	0.43%	0.70%	0.54%	0.42%
Cost of Labour	-0.20%	-0.22%	-0.22%	-0.22%	-0.26%	-0.26%	-0.36%	-0.77%	-1.23%	-0.57%	-1.00%	-1.47%	-0.67%	-1.16%	-1.68%
Deflator of Absorption	-0.10%	-0.16%	-0.16%	-0.11%	-0.17%	-0.17%	0.63%	0.45%	0.34%	0.70%	0.54%	0.43%	0.70%	0.54%	0.42%
Price of Exports-RW	-0.10%	-0.16%	-0.16%	-0.11%	-0.17%	-0.17%	0.63%	0.45%	0.34%	0.70%	0.54%	0.43%	0.70%	0.54%	0.42%

Telecommunications

	Border Controls			Border controls and x-ineff.			Market segmentation			Trade *antimonde*			Full *antimonde*		
	1988	1991	1994	1988	1991	1994	1988	1991	1994	1988	1991	1994	1988	1991	1994
Marginal Costs	0.08%	0.05%	0.06%	0.09%	0.06%	0.07%	-0.36%	-0.39%	-0.25%	-0.32%	-0.35%	-0.21%	-0.30%	-0.32%	-0.18%
Cost of Labour	-0.20%	-0.22%	-0.22%	-0.22%	-0.26%	-0.26%	-0.36%	-0.77%	-1.23%	-0.57%	-1.00%	-1.47%	-0.67%	-1.16%	-1.68%
Deflator of Absorption	0.01%	-0.04%	-0.03%	-0.23%	-0.53%	-0.52%	0.41%	0.50%	0.58%	0.46%	0.55%	0.64%	0.23%	0.09%	0.18%
Price of Exports-RW	0.05%	0.00%	0.00%	-0.02%	-0.17%	-0.16%	-0.65%	-1.04%	-0.92%	-0.62%	-1.02%	-0.90%	-0.67%	-1.12%	-1.00%

Transports

	Border Controls			Border controls and x-ineff.			Market segmentation			Trade *antimonde*			Full *antimonde*		
	1988	1991	1994	1988	1991	1994	1988	1991	1994	1988	1991	1994	1988	1991	1994
Marginal Costs	-0.10%	-0.16%	-0.17%	-0.10%	-0.16%	-0.17%	0.24%	0.13%	0.16%	0.25%	0.14%	0.17%	0.25%	0.14%	0.17%
Cost of Labour	-0.20%	-0.22%	-0.22%	-0.22%	-0.26%	-0.26%	-0.36%	-0.77%	-1.23%	-0.57%	-1.00%	-1.47%	-0.67%	-1.16%	-1.68%
Deflator of Absorption	-0.10%	-0.16%	-0.16%	-0.09%	-0.16%	-0.17%	0.24%	0.12%	0.16%	0.26%	0.15%	0.18%	0.25%	0.14%	0.17%
Price of Exports-RW	-0.10%	-0.16%	-0.17%	-0.10%	-0.16%	-0.17%	0.24%	0.13%	0.16%	0.25%	0.14%	0.17%	0.25%	0.14%	0.17%

Banks

	Border Controls			Border controls and x-ineff.			Market segmentation			Trade *antimonde*			Full *antimonde*		
	1988	1991	1994	1988	1991	1994	1988	1991	1994	1988	1991	1994	1988	1991	1994
Marginal Costs	-0.12%	-0.15%	-0.15%	-0.13%	-0.18%	-0.18%	-0.17%	-0.43%	-0.67%	-0.26%	-0.54%	-0.78%	-0.29%	-0.59%	-0.84%
Cost of Labour	-0.20%	-0.22%	-0.22%	-0.22%	-0.26%	-0.26%	-0.36%	-0.77%	-1.23%	-0.57%	-1.00%	-1.47%	-0.67%	-1.16%	-1.68%
Deflator of Absorption	-0.20%	-0.37%	-0.37%	-0.32%	0.65%	-0.66%	0.08%	-0.74%	-1.08%	-0.02%	-0.87%	-1.22%	-0.14%	-1.11%	-1.48%
Price of Exports-RW	-0.16%	-0.27%	-0.28%	-0.20%	-0.38%	-0.38%	-0.37%	-1.02%	-1.33%	-0.48%	-1.15%	-1.47%	-0.53%	-1.25%	-1.58%

Services

	Border Controls			Border controls and x-ineff.			Market segmentation			Trade *antimonde*			Full *antimonde*		
	1988	1991	1994	1988	1991	1994	1988	1991	1994	1988	1991	1994	1988	1991	1994
Marginal Costs	0.05%	0.01%	0.01%	0.06%	0.02%	0.01%	-0.22%	-0.24%	-0.07%	-0.15%	-0.16%	0.01%	-0.15%	-0.16%	0.00%
Cost of Labour	-0.20%	-0.22%	-0.22%	-0.22%	-0.26%	-0.26%	-0.36%	-0.77%	-1.23%	-0.57%	-1.00%	-1.47%	-0.67%	-1.16%	-1.68%
Deflator of Absorption	0.06%	0.01%	0.01%	0.07%	0.02%	0.01%	-0.22%	-0.23%	-0.07%	-0.13%	-0.14%	0.02%	-0.13%	-0.14%	0.02%
Price of Exports-RW	0.05%	0.01%	0.01%	0.06%	0.02%	0.01%	-0.22%	-0.24%	-0.07%	-0.15%	-0.16%	0.01%	-0.15%	-0.16%	0.00%

Non market

	Border Controls			Border controls and x-ineff.			Market segmentation			Trade *antimonde*			Full *antimonde*		
	1988	1991	1994	1988	1991	1994	1988	1991	1994	1988	1991	1994	1988	1991	1994
Marginal Costs	-0.17%	-0.21%	-0.20%	-0.18%	-0.23%	-0.23%	0.05%	-0.26%	-0.57%	-0.06%	-0.37%	-0.68%	-0.09%	-0.43%	-0.75%
Cost of Labour	-0.20%	-0.22%	-0.22%	-0.22%	-0.26%	-0.26%	-0.36%	-0.77%	-1.23%	-0.57%	-1.00%	-1.47%	-0.67%	-1.16%	-1.68%
Deflator of Absorption	-0.17%	-0.21%	-0.20%	-0.18%	-0.23%	-0.23%	0.05%	-0.26%	-0.57%	-0.06%	-0.37%	-0.68%	-0.09%	-0.43%	-0.75%
Price of Exports-RW	-0.17%	-0.21%	-0.20%	-0.18%	-0.23%	-0.23%	0.05%	-0.26%	-0.57%	-0.06%	-0.37%	-0.68%	-0.09%	-0.43%	-0.75%

Table B4.1.
The full *antimonde* scenario: macroeconomic aggregates for France

Macroeconomic Aggregates (vol.) (% change from *monde*)	Constraint Case 1988	Constraint Case 1991	Constraint Case 1994	Flexible Case 1988	Flexible Case 1991	Flexible Case 1994	Efficiency Case 1988	Efficiency Case 1991	Efficiency Case 1994
GDP fact. pr.	-0.45%	-0.64%	-0.84%	-0.35%	-0.76%	-1.11%	-0.38%	-0.87%	-1.30%
Priv. Consumption	-0.42%	-0.43%	-0.55%	-0.85%	-1.04%	-1.26%	-0.86%	-1.09%	-1.33%
Absorption	-0.30%	-0.35%	-0.49%	-1.19%	-1.40%	-1.65%	-1.20%	-1.45%	-1.72%
Total Investment	-1.71%	-1.70%	-2.14%	-4.21%	-4.35%	-4.48%	-4.21%	-4.36%	-4.49%
Total Exports to RW	-1.28%	-2.34%	-2.56%	1.71%	1.35%	1.13%	1.68%	1.24%	0.94%
Total Imports from RW	-1.98%	-2.31%	-2.39%	-3.33%	-2.76%	-2.49%	-3.29%	-2.60%	-2.20%
Total Intra-EU Trade	-0.73%	-0.24%	-0.23%	-1.15%	-4.06%	-4.28%	-1.17%	-4.13%	-4.39%
Employment (diff. from *monde*, 10³ persons)	-24	-33	-49	-43	-78	-113	-43	-80	-115
Disposable Income (deflated)	-0.44%	-0.44%	-0.57%	-0.88%	-1.08%	-1.30%	-0.89%	-1.12%	-1.38%

Macroeconomic Ratios (abs. diff. from *monde*)	Constraint Case 1988	Constraint Case 1991	Constraint Case 1994	Flexible Case 1988	Flexible Case 1991	Flexible Case 1994	Efficiency Case 1988	Efficiency Case 1991	Efficiency Case 1994
Current Account as % of GDP	0.00%	0.00%	0.00%	-1.23%	-1.14%	-1.05%	-1.21%	-1.09%	-0.97%
Public Deficit as % of GDP	-0.01%	-0.01%	-0.05%	-0.25%	-0.39%	-0.54%	-0.26%	-0.43%	-0.60%
Labour Productivity	-0.34%	-0.49%	-0.61%	-0.15%	-0.39%	-0.58%	-0.18%	-0.50%	-0.77%
Investment/GDP	-0.25%	-0.21%	-0.26%	-1.74%	-1.72%	-1.71%	-1.74%	-1.70%	-1.67%
Priv.Cons./GDP	0.02%	0.13%	0.18%	-0.31%	-0.17%	-0.09%	-0.29%	-0.13%	-0.02%

Deflators (% change from *monde*)	Constraint Case 1988	Constraint Case 1991	Constraint Case 1994	Flexible Case 1988	Flexible Case 1991	Flexible Case 1994	Efficiency Case 1988	Efficiency Case 1991	Efficiency Case 1994
Consumer Price Index	0.44%	1.08%	1.22%	0.75%	0.68%	0.68%	0.74%	0.65%	0.62%
Real Wage Rate	-0.49%	-0.70%	-0.94%	-0.47%	-0.96%	-1.40%	-0.49%	-1.06%	-1.58%
Marginal Costs	0.35%	1.04%	1.18%	0.41%	0.34%	0.32%	0.41%	0.32%	0.29%
Producer Prices	0.42%	1.13%	1.27%	0.47%	0.43%	0.41%	0.46%	0.41%	0.38%
Average change in mark-ups (abs. diff.)	0.48%	0.63%	0.64%	0.44%	0.73%	0.77%	0.44%	0.74%	0.78%
Shadow Price of Capital	0.01%	0.89%	1.13%	-0.06%	0.44%	1.00%	-0.08%	0.36%	0.86%
Terms-of-Trade RW	-0.24%	0.38%	0.52%	-5.35%	-4.23%	-3.52%	-5.26%	-3.89%	-2.92%

	Constraint Case	Flexible Case	Efficiency Case
Implicit change in real exchange rate	0.28%	-4.36%	-4.27%
	1.08%	-3.09%	-2.72%
	1.21%	-2.32%	-1.68%

	Constraint Case	Flexible Case	Efficiency Case
Trade Regime	*Segmentation*	*Segmentation*	*Segmentation*

Table B4.2.
The full *antimonde* scenario: effects on IC sectors for France

% change from *monde*

Metal Industries	Constraint Case			Flexible Case			Efficiency Case		
	1988	1991	1994	1988	1991	1994	1988	1991	1994
Production per firm	-7.41%	-9.70%	-9.83%	-5.27%	-9.97%	-10.13%	-5.30%	-10.05%	-10.27%
Real Marginal Costs	0.81%	1.33%	1.46%	-2.32%	-0.68%	0.38%	-2.21%	-0.25%	1.14%
Real Producer Prices	1.32%	2.01%	2.14%	-1.97%	-0.02%	1.05%	-1.86%	0.42%	1.81%
Mark-ups domestic (abs. diff.)	0.74%	0.82%	0.83%	0.59%	0.92%	0.93%	0.59%	0.92%	0.94%
Fixed Costs per firm	0.70%	1.16%	1.21%	-2.70%	-1.64%	-1.12%	-2.63%	-1.36%	-0.63%
Number of Firms	7.12%	8.76%	8.63%	8.85%	14.28%	13.94%	8.82%	14.16%	13.75%
Sigma of Love of Variety	0.00%	0.00%	0.00%	0.00%	0.00%	0.00%	0.00%	0.00%	0.00%

Chemical	Constraint Case			Flexible Case			Efficiency Case		
	1988	1991	1994	1988	1991	1994	1988	1991	1994
Production per firm	-4.97%	-6.81%	-6.92%	-2.78%	-6.12%	-6.35%	-2.81%	-6.22%	-6.51%
Real Marginal Costs	0.55%	1.13%	1.28%	-2.78%	-1.17%	-0.06%	-2.67%	-0.73%	0.72%
Real Producer Prices	0.78%	1.45%	1.60%	-2.66%	-0.91%	0.22%	-2.54%	-0.46%	1.00%
Mark-ups domestic (abs. diff.)	0.35%	0.39%	0.39%	0.20%	0.36%	0.37%	0.20%	0.36%	0.37%
Fixed Costs per firm	0.43%	0.94%	1.01%	-3.18%	-2.17%	-1.59%	-3.11%	-1.88%	-1.08%
Number of Firms	4.34%	5.50%	5.45%	7.39%	10.37%	10.06%	7.37%	10.25%	9.86%
Sigma of Love of Variety	0.00%	0.00%	0.00%	0.00%	0.00%	0.00%	0.00%	0.00%	0.00%

Other Intensive Industries	Constraint Case			Flexible Case			Efficiency Case		
	1988	1991	1994	1988	1991	1994	1988	1991	1994
Production per firm	-1.33%	-1.89%	-2.03%	-1.72%	-2.81%	-2.97%	-1.73%	-2.88%	-3.09%
Real Marginal Costs	0.45%	1.07%	1.19%	-3.28%	-1.66%	-0.57%	-3.17%	-1.21%	0.24%
Real Producer Prices	0.48%	1.12%	1.23%	-3.24%	-1.60%	-0.50%	-3.13%	-1.15%	0.30%
Mark-ups domestic (abs. diff.)	0.03%	0.04%	0.04%	0.04%	0.06%	0.06%	0.04%	0.06%	0.06%
Fixed Costs per firm	0.35%	0.91%	0.94%	-3.73%	-2.72%	-2.17%	-3.66%	-2.42%	-1.65%
Number of Firms	1.75%	1.98%	1.85%	0.60%	1.27%	1.14%	0.59%	1.24%	1.10%
Sigma of Love of Variety	0.00%	0.00%	0.00%	0.00%	0.00%	0.00%	0.00%	0.00%	0.00%

Electrical goods	Constraint Case			Flexible Case			Efficiency Case		
	1988	1991	1994	1988	1991	1994	1988	1991	1994
Production per firm	-3.68%	-5.32%	-5.54%	-3.65%	-6.90%	-7.16%	-3.68%	-7.02%	-7.35%
Real Marginal Costs	0.41%	1.04%	1.14%	-3.39%	-1.77%	-0.67%	-3.28%	-1.32%	0.13%
Real Producer Prices	0.63%	1.37%	1.48%	-3.17%	-1.37%	-0.26%	-3.06%	-0.91%	0.55%
Mark-ups domestic (abs. diff.)	0.31%	0.35%	0.38%	0.37%	0.52%	0.53%	0.37%	0.52%	0.53%
Fixed Costs per firm	0.32%	0.88%	0.91%	-3.85%	-2.84%	-2.31%	-3.77%	-2.55%	-1.79%
Number of Firms	5.15%	6.15%	5.81%	4.04%	7.75%	7.50%	4.02%	7.65%	7.33%
Sigma of Love of Variety	0.00%	0.00%	0.00%	0.00%	0.00%	0.00%	0.00%	0.00%	0.00%

Transport equipment	Constraint Case			Flexible Case			Efficiency Case		
	1988	1991	1994	1988	1991	1994	1988	1991	1994
Production per firm	-7.80%	-10.82%	-11.04%	-7.17%	-11.83%	-11.95%	-7.20%	-11.94%	-12.12%
Real Marginal Costs	0.76%	1.35%	1.46%	-2.97%	-1.31%	-0.26%	-2.85%	-0.84%	0.57%
Real Producer Prices	1.37%	2.22%	2.34%	-2.45%	-0.43%	0.63%	-2.33%	0.04%	1.46%
Mark-ups domestic (abs. diff.)	1.02%	1.21%	1.26%	1.11%	1.60%	1.60%	1.11%	1.60%	1.61%
Fixed Costs per firm	0.63%	1.18%	1.23%	-3.47%	-2.35%	-1.79%	-3.39%	-2.04%	-1.25%
Number of Firms	10.37%	12.01%	11.48%	7.93%	14.55%	14.51%	7.92%	14.47%	14.38%
Sigma of Love of Variety	0.00%	0.00%	0.00%	0.00%	0.00%	0.00%	0.00%	0.00%	0.00%

Other Equipment	Constraint Case			Flexible Case			Efficiency Case		
	1988	1991	1994	1988	1991	1994	1988	1991	1994
Production per firm	-6.34%	-8.10%	-8.22%	-5.42%	-8.36%	-8.62%	-5.45%	-8.45%	-8.78%
Real Marginal Costs	0.45%	1.08%	1.19%	-3.33%	-1.70%	-0.58%	-3.22%	-1.24%	0.22%
Real Producer Prices	0.67%	1.37%	1.48%	-3.15%	-1.42%	-0.29%	-3.04%	-0.96%	0.51%
Mark-ups domestic (abs. diff.)	0.37%	0.43%	0.43%	0.36%	0.49%	0.50%	0.36%	0.50%	0.50%
Fixed Costs per firm	0.35%	0.91%	0.94%	-3.78%	-2.76%	-2.21%	-3.70%	-2.46%	-1.69%
Number of Firms	7.07%	8.58%	8.36%	5.13%	8.10%	7.63%	5.10%	7.97%	7.41%
Sigma of Love of Variety	0.00%	0.00%	0.00%	0.00%	0.00%	0.00%	0.00%	0.00%	0.00%

Telecommunications	Constraint Case			Flexible Case			Efficiency Case		
	1988	1991	1994	1988	1991	1994	1988	1991	1994
Production per firm	-0.27%	0.20%	0.09%	-1.15%	-2.51%	-2.89%	-1.17%	-2.57%	-2.99%
Real Marginal Costs	0.64%	1.72%	1.94%	-3.94%	-2.06%	0.69%	-3.82%	-1.59%	0.14%
Real Producer Prices	0.86%	2.07%	2.25%	-4.04%	-2.29%	-0.95%	-3.92%	-1.83%	-0.14%
Mark-ups domestic (abs. diff.)	0.25%	0.38%	0.34%	-0.15%	-0.40%	-0.44%	-0.16%	-0.41%	-0.45%
Fixed Costs per firm	1.50%	3.66%	3.61%	-6.01%	-6.58%	-6.17%	-5.94%	-6.32%	-5.70%
Number of Firms	-0.41%	-0.74%	-0.62%	0.89%	1.95%	2.06%	0.90%	1.97%	2.10%
Sigma of Love of Variety	0.00%	0.00%	0.00%	0.00%	0.00%	0.00%	0.00%	0.00%	0.00%

Banks	Constraint Case			Flexible Case			Efficiency Case		
	1988	1991	1994	1988	1991	1994	1988	1991	1994
Production per firm	-0.43%	-0.23%	-0.29%	-1.16%	-2.30%	-2.65%	-1.17%	-2.35%	-2.74%
Real Marginal Costs	0.47%	1.44%	1.60%	-3.96%	-2.12%	-0.81%	-3.84%	-1.66%	0.00%
Real Producer Prices	0.56%	1.54%	1.69%	-3.94%	-2.12%	-0.80%	-3.83%	-1.66%	0.01%
Mark-ups domestic (abs. diff.)	0.09%	0.08%	0.07%	0.00%	-0.04%	-0.04%	0.00%	-0.04%	-0.04%
Fixed Costs per firm	0.90%	2.15%	2.14%	-5.39%	-5.27%	-4.76%	-5.32%	-4.98%	-4.25%
Number of Firms	0.40%	0.58%	0.67%	1.07%	1.99%	2.00%	1.07%	2.00%	2.01%
Sigma of Love of Variety	0.00%	0.00%	0.00%	0.00%	0.00%	0.00%	0.00%	0.00%	0.00%

Table B4.3.
The full *antimonde* scenario: sectoral results for France (volumes)

% change from *monde*

Agriculture	Constraint Case			Flexible Case			Efficiency Case		
	1988	1991	1994	1988	1991	1994	1988	1991	1994
Domestic Production - vol.	-0.4%	-0.7%	-0.9%	2.6%	0.9%	0.0%	2.6%	0.7%	-0.4%
Imports - vol.	-1.6%	-0.5%	-0.1%	-3.7%	-2.7%	-2.1%	-3.6%	-2.5%	-1.7%
Exports - vol.	-2.9%	-4.4%	-4.9%	1.6%	1.1%	0.8%	1.5%	1.0%	0.6%
Absorption - vol.	-0.2%	0.0%	-0.1%	1.4%	0.6%	0.1%	1.4%	0.5%	-0.1%
Investment - vol.	3.2%	3.1%	2.3%	-3.0%	-3.8%	-4.2%	-3.0%	-3.9%	-4.3%
Labour Demand - vol.	-0.4%	-0.6%	-0.6%	2.7%	1.2%	0.6%	2.7%	1.1%	0.4%
Private Consumption - vol.	-1.2%	-0.7%	-0.6%	-0.6%	-0.9%	-1.2%	-0.6%	-1.0%	-1.2%
Supply to domestic - vol.	0.0%	0.1%	-0.1%	2.6%	1.6%	0.8%	2.5%	1.4%	0.5%
Intra-EU Trade - vol	0.0%	0.0%	0.0%	0.5%	-2.2%	-2.8%	0.5%	-2.3%	-3.0%

Energy	Constraint Case			Flexible Case			Efficiency Case		
	1988	1991	1994	1988	1991	1994	1988	1991	1994
Domestic Production - vol.	-0.4%	-0.5%	-0.6%	1.0%	0.4%	0.1%	0.9%	0.3%	-0.1%
Imports - vol.	-0.2%	0.1%	0.1%	-0.8%	-0.8%	-0.7%	-0.8%	-0.7%	-0.7%
Exports - vol.	-2.7%	-3.7%	-4.1%	0.7%	0.5%	0.4%	0.7%	0.5%	0.3%
Absorption - vol.	-0.2%	-0.1%	-0.1%	0.2%	-0.2%	-0.4%	0.2%	-0.2%	-0.5%
Investment - vol.	-4.9%	-5.0%	-5.2%	-3.6%	-3.8%	-4.0%	-3.6%	-3.9%	-4.0%
Labour Demand - vol.	-0.4%	-0.5%	-0.5%	1.2%	0.7%	0.5%	1.2%	0.7%	0.4%
Private Consumption - vol.	-0.2%	0.4%	0.4%	-0.7%	-1.0%	-1.2%	-0.7%	-1.0%	-1.2%
Supply to domestic - vol.	-0.1%	-0.1%	-0.2%	0.8%	0.3%	0.0%	0.8%	0.2%	-0.2%
Intra-EU Trade - vol	0.0%	0.0%	0.0%	0.8%	0.2%	0.1%	0.7%	0.2%	-0.1%

Metal Industries	Constraint Case			Flexible Case			Efficiency Case		
	1988	1991	1994	1988	1991	1994	1988	1991	1994
Domestic Production - vol.	-0.8%	-1.8%	-2.0%	3.1%	2.9%	2.4%	3.1%	2.7%	2.1%
Imports - vol.	-0.2%	-0.3%	-0.5%	-3.2%	-2.6%	-2.4%	-3.2%	-2.4%	-2.1%
Exports - vol.	-2.4%	-3.4%	-3.6%	1.4%	1.0%	0.9%	1.3%	0.9%	0.7%
Absorption - vol.	0.2%	-0.3%	-0.5%	0.6%	0.6%	0.3%	0.6%	0.5%	0.1%
Investment - vol.	-3.1%	-4.0%	-4.5%	-2.5%	-2.7%	-2.9%	-2.6%	-2.7%	-3.0%
Labour Demand - vol.	-0.2%	-1.0%	-1.2%	3.7%	3.9%	3.5%	3.7%	3.8%	3.3%
Private Consumption - vol.	-0.6%	-0.3%	-0.3%	-0.3%	-0.4%	-0.5%	-0.3%	-0.5%	-0.6%
Supply to domestic - vol.	0.6%	-0.3%	-0.6%	5.0%	10.3%	9.6%	5.0%	10.0%	9.2%
Intra-EU Trade - vol	0.0%	0.0%	0.0%	-1.2%	-6.0%	-6.1%	-1.2%	-6.0%	-6.2%

Chemical	Constraint Case			Flexible Case			Efficiency Case		
	1988	1991	1994	1988	1991	1994	1988	1991	1994
Domestic Production - vol.	-0.9%	-1.7%	-1.9%	4.4%	3.6%	3.1%	4.4%	3.4%	2.7%
Imports - vol.	-0.3%	0.6%	0.7%	-3.9%	-3.3%	-3.0%	-3.8%	-3.1%	-2.6%
Exports - vol.	-1.3%	-2.3%	-2.5%	1.8%	1.5%	1.3%	1.8%	1.4%	1.1%
Absorption - vol.	-0.4%	-0.5%	-0.6%	1.4%	0.9%	0.5%	1.4%	0.8%	0.3%
Investment - vol.	-3.1%	-3.8%	-4.3%	-2.0%	-2.4%	-2.7%	-2.0%	-2.5%	-2.8%
Labour Demand - vol.	-0.5%	-1.3%	-1.4%	4.7%	4.2%	3.7%	4.7%	4.0%	3.5%
Private Consumption - vol.	-1.2%	-0.7%	-0.6%	-0.5%	-0.9%	-1.1%	-0.5%	-0.9%	-1.2%
Supply to domestic - vol.	-0.5%	-1.2%	-1.3%	5.2%	7.2%	6.5%	5.2%	6.9%	6.1%
Intra-EU Trade - vol	0.0%	0.0%	0.0%	0.2%	-3.5%	-3.7%	0.2%	-3.6%	-3.9%

Other Intensive Industries	Constraint Case			Flexible Case			Efficiency Case		
	1988	1991	1994	1988	1991	1994	1988	1991	1994
Domestic Production - vol.	0.4%	0.1%	-0.2%	-1.1%	-1.6%	-1.9%	-1.2%	-1.7%	-2.0%
Imports - vol.	-3.8%	-4.2%	-4.2%	-6.1%	-5.2%	-4.7%	-6.1%	-4.9%	-4.2%
Exports - vol.	-1.7%	-2.6%	-2.8%	1.8%	1.4%	1.2%	1.7%	1.3%	1.0%
Absorption - vol.	0.1%	-0.1%	-0.4%	-2.2%	-2.4%	-2.6%	-2.2%	-2.4%	-2.7%
Investment - vol.	-1.7%	-2.0%	-2.5%	-4.7%	-4.9%	-5.0%	-4.7%	-4.9%	-5.1%
Labour Demand - vol.	0.5%	0.2%	-0.1%	-0.9%	-1.3%	-1.5%	-0.9%	-1.3%	-1.5%
Private Consumption - vol.	0.6%	0.1%	-0.3%	-1.0%	-0.8%	-0.9%	-1.0%	-0.9%	-1.0%
Supply to domestic - vol.	0.8%	0.6%	0.3%	-1.1%	-0.7%	-1.0%	-1.2%	-0.7%	-1.1%
Intra-EU Trade - vol	0.0%	0.0%	0.0%	-2.7%	-5.9%	-6.0%	-2.7%	-5.9%	-6.1%

Electrical goods	Constraint Case			Flexible Case			Efficiency Case		
	1988	1991	1994	1988	1991	1994	1988	1991	1994
Domestic Production - vol.	1.3%	0.5%	-0.1%	0.2%	0.3%	-0.2%	0.2%	0.1%	-0.6%
Imports - vol.	-3.8%	-5.6%	-6.1%	-6.9%	-5.9%	-5.5%	-6.8%	-5.7%	-5.0%
Exports - vol.	-1.1%	-2.3%	-2.5%	2.2%	1.7%	1.5%	2.1%	1.6%	1.3%
Absorption - vol.	0.6%	-0.4%	-1.1%	-3.8%	-3.5%	-3.7%	-3.8%	-3.5%	-3.8%
Investment - vol.	3.0%	2.3%	1.2%	-4.1%	-4.1%	-4.3%	-4.1%	-4.1%	-4.5%
Labour Demand - vol.	1.7%	1.0%	0.6%	0.8%	1.2%	0.8%	0.7%	1.0%	0.6%
Private Consumption - vol.	7.6%	2.8%	-0.3%	-3.8%	-2.2%	-2.1%	-3.8%	-2.3%	-2.2%
Supply to domestic - vol.	2.7%	2.3%	1.5%	-0.3%	2.8%	2.3%	-0.3%	2.6%	2.0%
Intra-EU Trade - vol	0.0%	0.0%	0.0%	-2.5%	-6.8%	-6.9%	-2.5%	-6.8%	-7.1%

Transport equipment	Constraint Case			Flexible Case			Efficiency Case		
	1988	1991	1994	1988	1991	1994	1988	1991	1994
Domestic Production - vol.	1.8%	-0.1%	-0.8%	0.2%	1.0%	0.8%	0.1%	0.8%	0.5%
Imports - vol.	-0.3%	-4.8%	-6.0%	-6.3%	-5.3%	-4.9%	-6.2%	-5.1%	-4.5%
Exports - vol.	-1.7%	-3.1%	-3.2%	2.0%	1.6%	1.4%	2.0%	1.5%	1.2%
Absorption - vol.	3.9%	0.6%	-0.7%	-3.2%	-2.6%	-2.7%	-3.3%	-2.7%	-2.7%
Investment - vol.	4.0%	2.1%	0.8%	-3.8%	-3.5%	-3.6%	-3.9%	-3.6%	-3.7%
Labour Demand - vol.	2.6%	1.0%	0.4%	1.1%	2.4%	2.4%	1.1%	2.3%	2.2%
Private Consumption - vol.	12.5%	3.3%	-0.2%	-3.1%	-1.9%	-1.6%	-3.1%	-2.0%	-1.7%
Supply to domestic - vol.	6.4%	4.0%	2.6%	0.4%	6.9%	6.8%	0.3%	6.7%	6.6%
Intra-EU Trade - vol	0.0%	0.0%	0.0%	-2.9%	-6.5%	-6.5%	-2.9%	-6.5%	-6.6%

Other Equipment	Constraint Case			Flexible Case			Efficiency Case		
	1988	1991	1994	1988	1991	1994	1988	1991	1994
Domestic Production - vol.	0.3%	-0.2%	-0.6%	-0.6%	-0.9%	-1.7%	-0.6%	-1.2%	-2.0%
Imports - vol.	-1.7%	-1.9%	-2.2%	-5.4%	-4.9%	-4.7%	-5.4%	-4.7%	-4.4%
Exports - vol.	-1.2%	-2.1%	-2.2%	1.9%	1.5%	1.3%	1.9%	1.4%	1.0%
Absorption - vol.	0.1%	-0.1%	-0.5%	-5.0%	-5.4%	-5.7%	-5.0%	-5.4%	-5.8%
Investment - vol.	6.3%	5.8%	4.7%	-4.4%	-4.7%	-5.0%	-4.5%	-4.7%	-5.2%
Labour Demand - vol.	0.7%	0.3%	0.0%	-0.1%	-0.2%	-0.8%	-0.1%	-0.3%	-1.0%
Private Consumption - vol.	-0.5%	-0.5%	-0.8%	-1.2%	-1.3%	-1.6%	-1.2%	-1.4%	-1.7%
Supply to domestic - vol.	1.8%	1.6%	1.1%	-1.7%	0.2%	-0.5%	-1.7%	0.0%	-0.9%
Intra-EU Trade - vol	0.0%	0.0%	0.0%	-2.6%	-4.9%	-5.1%	-2.7%	-4.9%	-5.2%

Consumer goods	Constraint Case			Flexible Case			Efficiency Case		
	1988	1991	1994	1988	1991	1994	1988	1991	1994
Domestic Production - vol.	0.1%	0.2%	0.1%	2.1%	1.4%	0.7%	2.0%	1.2%	0.4%
Imports - vol.	-4.8%	-5.0%	-4.7%	-4.4%	-3.4%	-2.8%	-4.3%	-3.1%	-2.3%
Exports - vol.	-1.6%	-2.6%	-2.9%	2.3%	1.8%	1.5%	2.3%	1.7%	1.2%
Absorption - vol.	-0.6%	-0.4%	-0.4%	-0.1%	-0.4%	-0.7%	-0.1%	-0.5%	-0.8%
Investment - vol.	6.0%	6.2%	5.4%	-3.2%	-3.6%	-3.9%	-3.2%	-3.6%	-4.0%
Labour Demand - vol.	0.2%	0.3%	0.3%	2.3%	1.8%	1.3%	2.3%	1.6%	1.1%
Private Consumption - vol.	-1.1%	-0.7%	-0.6%	-0.6%	-0.8%	-1.1%	-0.6%	-0.9%	-1.1%
Supply to domestic - vol.	0.5%	0.9%	0.8%	1.7%	1.7%	1.2%	1.7%	1.6%	0.9%
Intra-EU Trade - vol	0.0%	0.0%	0.0%	-0.8%	-3.0%	-3.3%	-0.8%	-3.1%	-3.4%

Construction	Constraint Case			Flexible Case			Efficiency Case		
	1988	1991	1994	1988	1991	1994	1988	1991	1994
Domestic Production - vol.	-2.0%	-1.9%	-2.3%	-7.3%	-7.5%	-7.8%	-7.3%	-7.6%	-7.8%
Imports - vol.	-	-	-	#VALUE!	#VALUE!	#VALUE!	#VALUE!	#VALUE!	#VALUE!
Exports - vol.	-	-	-	#VALUE!	#VALUE!	#VALUE!	#VALUE!	#VALUE!	#VALUE!
Absorption - vol.	-2.0%	-1.9%	-2.3%	-7.3%	-7.5%	-7.8%	-7.3%	-7.6%	-7.8%
Investment - vol.	-0.5%	-0.4%	-1.2%	-7.6%	-7.8%	-7.9%	-7.6%	-7.7%	-7.8%
Labour Demand - vol.	-1.9%	-1.8%	-2.1%	-7.2%	-7.3%	-7.4%	-7.2%	-7.2%	-7.3%
Private Consumption - vol.	-1.4%	-0.8%	-0.7%	-0.6%	-1.0%	-1.3%	-0.6%	-1.0%	-1.3%
Supply to domestic - vol.	-2.0%	-1.9%	-2.3%	-7.3%	-7.5%	-7.8%	-7.3%	-7.6%	-7.8%
Intra-EU Trade - vol	0.0%	0.0%	0.0%	#DIV/0!	#DIV/0!	#DIV/0!	#DIV/0!	#DIV/0!	#DIV/0!

Telecommunications	Constraint Case			Flexible Case			Efficiency Case		
	1988	1991	1994	1988	1991	1994	1988	1991	1994
Domestic Production - vol.	-0.7%	-0.5%	-0.5%	-0.3%	-0.6%	-0.9%	-0.3%	-0.6%	-0.9%
Imports - vol.	-5.5%	-5.9%	-5.7%	-6.3%	-6.1%	-5.8%	-6.2%	-6.0%	-5.5%
Exports - vol.	-3.2%	-6.1%	-6.3%	1.1%	0.9%	0.7%	1.1%	0.8%	0.6%
Absorption - vol.	-0.7%	-0.5%	-0.5%	-0.3%	-0.6%	-0.8%	-0.3%	-0.6%	-0.9%
Investment - vol.	-4.4%	-3.7%	-3.8%	-4.3%	-4.4%	-4.5%	-4.3%	-4.4%	-4.4%
Labour Demand - vol.	0.2%	0.9%	1.0%	-0.5%	-0.9%	-1.0%	-0.5%	-0.9%	-0.9%
Private Consumption - vol.	-1.7%	-1.2%	-1.1%	-0.5%	-0.9%	-1.3%	-0.6%	-1.0%	-1.4%
Supply to domestic - vol.	-0.6%	-0.5%	-0.5%	-0.2%	-0.2%	-0.5%	-0.2%	-0.3%	-0.6%
Intra-EU Trade - vol	0.0%	0.0%	0.0%	-4.7%	-14.3%	-14.5%	-4.7%	-14.4%	-14.5%

Transports	Constraint Case			Flexible Case			Efficiency Case		
	1988	1991	1994	1988	1991	1994	1988	1991	1994
Domestic Production - vol.	-0.4%	-0.4%	-0.4%	0.0%	-0.2%	-0.4%	0.0%	-0.2%	-0.5%
Imports - vol.	-0.4%	-0.4%	-0.4%	0.0%	-0.1%	-0.2%	0.0%	-0.1%	-0.2%
Exports - vol.	0.1%	-0.4%	-0.3%	0.7%	0.6%	0.5%	0.7%	0.5%	0.4%
Absorption - vol.	-0.5%	-0.4%	-0.4%	-0.5%	-0.7%	-1.0%	-0.5%	-0.7%	-1.0%
Investment - vol.	-5.0%	-5.0%	-5.1%	-4.1%	-4.2%	-4.4%	-4.1%	-4.2%	-4.3%
Labour Demand - vol.	-0.3%	-0.3%	-0.3%	0.1%	0.0%	-0.1%	0.1%	0.0%	-0.1%
Private Consumption - vol.	-1.6%	-1.0%	-0.8%	-0.7%	-1.1%	-1.4%	-0.7%	-1.2%	-1.5%
Supply to domestic - vol.	-0.4%	-0.4%	-0.4%	0.0%	-0.2%	-0.4%	0.0%	-0.2%	-0.5%
Intra-EU Trade - vol	0.0%	0.0%	0.0%	0.9%	1.0%	0.9%	0.9%	1.0%	0.9%

Banks	Constraint Case			Flexible Case			Efficiency Case		
	1988	1991	1994	1988	1991	1994	1988	1991	1994
Domestic Production - vol.	0.0%	0.4%	0.4%	-0.1%	-0.3%	-0.7%	-0.1%	-0.4%	-0.8%
Imports - vol.	-9.8%	-11.8%	-11.7%	-5.8%	-5.2%	-4.7%	-5.7%	-5.0%	-4.3%
Exports - vol.	-1.2%	-2.2%	-1.8%	1.1%	0.9%	0.7%	1.1%	0.8%	0.6%
Absorption - vol.	-0.3%	0.1%	0.1%	-0.3%	-0.6%	-0.9%	-0.3%	-0.6%	-1.0%
Investment - vol.	-2.0%	-1.2%	-1.5%	-4.3%	-4.4%	-4.5%	-4.2%	-4.3%	-4.5%
Labour Demand - vol.	0.4%	1.0%	1.1%	-0.1%	-0.2%	-0.4%	0.0%	-0.2%	-0.4%
Private Consumption - vol.	-1.6%	-0.9%	-0.8%	-0.8%	-1.2%	-1.5%	-0.8%	-1.2%	-1.6%
Supply to domestic - vol.	0.0%	0.4%	0.4%	-0.1%	0.0%	-0.3%	-0.1%	-0.1%	-0.4%
Intra-EU Trade - vol	0.0%	0.0%	0.0%	-3.6%	-9.3%	-9.5%	-3.6%	-9.3%	-9.5%

Services	Constraint Case			Flexible Case			Efficiency Case		
	1988	1991	1994	1988	1991	1994	1988	1991	1994
Domestic Production - vol.	-0.3%	-0.3%	-0.4%	-0.6%	-0.8%	-1.1%	-0.6%	-0.9%	-1.1%
Imports - vol.	-2.7%	-2.0%	-1.9%	-3.0%	-2.2%	-1.8%	-3.0%	-2.1%	-1.5%
Exports - vol.	1.6%	0.6%	0.5%	1.1%	0.8%	0.6%	1.1%	0.7%	0.5%
Absorption - vol.	-0.5%	-0.4%	-0.5%	-0.9%	-1.1%	-1.4%	-0.9%	-1.2%	-1.5%
Investment - vol.	-0.7%	-0.7%	-1.1%	-4.4%	-4.5%	-4.6%	-4.4%	-4.5%	-4.6%
Labour Demand - vol.	-0.3%	-0.2%	-0.3%	-0.5%	-0.5%	-0.6%	-0.4%	-0.5%	-0.5%
Private Consumption - vol.	-0.8%	-0.6%	-0.7%	-0.8%	-1.1%	-1.3%	-0.8%	-1.1%	-1.4%
Supply to domestic - vol.	-0.5%	-0.4%	-0.5%	-0.9%	-1.2%	-1.4%	-0.9%	-1.2%	-1.5%
Intra-EU Trade - vol	0.0%	0.0%	0.0%	2.0%	3.0%	2.9%	2.0%	3.0%	2.8%

Non market	Constraint Case			Flexible Case			Efficiency Case		
	1988	1991	1994	1988	1991	1994	1988	1991	1994
Domestic Production - vol.	-0.1%	-0.1%	-0.1%	-0.1%	-0.1%	-0.1%	-0.1%	-0.1%	-0.1%
Imports - vol.	-	-	-	#VALUE!	#VALUE!	#VALUE!	#VALUE!	#VALUE!	#VALUE!
Exports - vol.	-	-	-	#VALUE!	#VALUE!	#VALUE!	#VALUE!	#VALUE!	#VALUE!
Absorption - vol.	-0.1%	-0.1%	-0.1%	-0.1%	-0.1%	-0.1%	-0.1%	-0.1%	-0.1%
Investment - vol.	-6.9%	-6.8%	-6.9%	-4.1%	-4.1%	-4.1%	-4.1%	-4.1%	-4.1%
Labour Demand - vol.	-0.1%	0.0%	0.0%	0.0%	0.1%	0.1%	0.1%	0.1%	0.2%
Private Consumption - vol.	-1.0%	-0.6%	-0.6%	-0.6%	-0.9%	-1.1%	-0.6%	-0.9%	-1.2%
Supply to domestic - vol.	-0.1%	-0.1%	-0.1%	-0.1%	-0.1%	-0.1%	-0.1%	-0.1%	-0.1%
Intra-EU Trade - vol	0.0%	0.0%	0.0%	#DIV/0!	#DIV/0!	#DIV/0!	#DIV/0!	#DIV/0!	#DIV/0!

Table B4.4.
The full *antimonde* scenario: sectoral results for France (prices)

% change from *monde*

Agriculture	Constraint Case			Flexible Case			Efficiency Case		
	1988	1991	1994	1988	1991	1994	1988	1991	1994
Real Marginal Costs	0.48%	1.21%	1.45%	0.71%	0.84%	1.06%	0.70%	0.83%	1.04%
Real Cost of Labour	-0.21%	0.38%	0.28%	-0.47%	-0.96%	-1.40%	-0.49%	-1.06%	-1.58%
Real Deflator of Absorption	0.53%	1.16%	1.37%	1.20%	1.21%	1.34%	1.19%	1.17%	1.26%
Real Price of Exports-RW	0.48%	1.21%	1.45%	0.71%	0.84%	1.06%	0.70%	0.83%	1.04%

Energy	Constraint Case			Flexible Case			Efficiency Case		
	1988	1991	1994	1988	1991	1994	1988	1991	1994
Marginal Costs	0.48%	1.06%	1.24%	1.33%	1.15%	1.09%	1.31%	1.06%	0.95%
Cost of Labour	-0.21%	0.38%	0.28%	-0.47%	-0.96%	-1.40%	-0.49%	-1.06%	-1.58%
Deflator of Absorption	0.52%	0.89%	1.01%	2.50%	2.08%	1.87%	2.47%	1.93%	1.61%
Price of Exports-RW	0.48%	1.06%	1.24%	1.33%	1.15%	1.09%	1.31%	1.06%	0.95%

Metal Industries	Constraint Case			Flexible Case			Efficiency Case		
	1988	1991	1994	1988	1991	1994	1988	1991	1994
Marginal Costs	0.81%	1.33%	1.46%	1.57%	1.44%	1.29%	1.56%	1.41%	1.23%
Cost of Labour	-0.21%	0.38%	0.28%	-0.47%	-0.96%	-1.40%	-0.49%	-1.06%	-1.58%
Deflator of Absorption	1.30%	1.63%	1.71%	2.95%	2.88%	2.63%	2.93%	2.79%	2.48%
Price of Exports-RW	1.32%	2.34%	2.48%	1.41%	1.17%	1.02%	1.40%	1.13%	0.96%

Chemical	Constraint Case			Flexible Case			Efficiency Case		
	1988	1991	1994	1988	1991	1994	1988	1991	1994
Marginal Costs	0.55%	1.13%	1.28%	1.11%	0.95%	0.86%	1.11%	0.92%	0.82%
Cost of Labour	-0.21%	0.38%	0.28%	-0.47%	-0.96%	-1.40%	-0.49%	-1.06%	-1.58%
Deflator of Absorption	0.78%	1.16%	1.26%	2.34%	2.13%	1.95%	2.32%	2.06%	1.83%
Price of Exports-RW	0.73%	1.61%	1.76%	1.02%	0.82%	0.74%	1.02%	0.80%	0.69%

Other Intensive Industries	Constraint Case			Flexible Case			Efficiency Case		
	1988	1991	1994	1988	1991	1994	1988	1991	1994
Marginal Costs	0.45%	1.07%	1.19%	0.61%	0.46%	0.35%	0.61%	0.45%	0.33%
Cost of Labour	-0.21%	0.38%	0.28%	-0.47%	-0.96%	-1.40%	-0.49%	-1.06%	-1.58%
Deflator of Absorption	0.59%	1.12%	1.23%	0.98%	0.80%	0.68%	0.98%	0.78%	0.63%
Price of Exports-RW	0.47%	1.17%	1.28%	0.61%	0.46%	0.35%	0.61%	0.44%	0.33%

Electrical goods	Constraint Case			Flexible Case			Efficiency Case		
	1988	1991	1994	1988	1991	1994	1988	1991	1994
Marginal Costs	0.41%	1.04%	1.14%	0.50%	0.35%	0.25%	0.50%	0.34%	0.22%
Cost of Labour	-0.21%	0.38%	0.28%	-0.47%	-0.96%	-1.40%	-0.49%	-1.06%	-1.58%
Deflator of Absorption	0.99%	1.44%	1.53%	1.76%	1.57%	1.38%	1.74%	1.51%	1.27%
Price of Exports-RW	0.54%	1.58%	1.69%	0.44%	0.23%	0.13%	0.44%	0.22%	0.11%

Transport equipment	Constraint Case			Flexible Case			Efficiency Case		
	1988	1991	1994	1988	1991	1994	1988	1991	1994
Marginal Costs	0.76%	1.35%	1.46%	0.92%	0.82%	0.66%	0.92%	0.82%	0.66%
Cost of Labour	-0.21%	0.38%	0.28%	-0.47%	-0.96%	-1.40%	-0.49%	-1.06%	-1.58%
Deflator of Absorption	1.89%	2.36%	2.47%	2.31%	2.59%	2.41%	2.30%	2.57%	2.39%
Price of Exports-RW	1.34%	2.67%	2.80%	0.71%	0.41%	0.25%	0.71%	0.41%	0.26%

Other Equipment	Constraint Case			Flexible Case			Efficiency Case		
	1988	1991	1994	1988	1991	1994	1988	1991	1994
Marginal Costs	0.45%	1.08%	1.19%	0.56%	0.43%	0.34%	0.56%	0.42%	0.32%
Cost of Labour	-0.21%	0.38%	0.28%	-0.47%	-0.96%	-1.40%	-0.49%	-1.06%	-1.58%
Deflator of Absorption	1.03%	1.36%	1.43%	2.01%	1.77%	1.55%	1.99%	1.70%	1.43%
Price of Exports-RW	0.62%	1.43%	1.54%	0.52%	0.37%	0.29%	0.52%	0.36%	0.27%

Consumer goods	Constraint Case			Flexible Case			Efficiency Case		
	1988	1991	1994	1988	1991	1994	1988	1991	1994
Marginal Costs	0.49%	1.14%	1.32%	0.75%	0.67%	0.67%	0.75%	0.67%	0.67%
Cost of Labour	-0.21%	0.38%	0.28%	-0.47%	-0.96%	-1.40%	-0.49%	-1.06%	-1.58%
Deflator of Absorption	0.68%	1.19%	1.33%	1.38%	1.20%	1.13%	1.37%	1.17%	1.08%
Price of Exports-RW	0.49%	1.14%	1.32%	0.75%	0.67%	0.67%	0.75%	0.67%	0.67%

Construction	Constraint Case			Flexible Case			Efficiency Case		
	1988	1991	1994	1988	1991	1994	1988	1991	1994
Marginal Costs	0.37%	1.03%	1.15%	0.38%	0.26%	0.20%	0.38%	0.26%	0.19%
Cost of Labour	-0.21%	0.38%	0.28%	-0.47%	-0.96%	-1.40%	-0.49%	-1.06%	-1.58%
Deflator of Absorption	0.37%	1.03%	1.15%	0.38%	0.26%	0.20%	0.38%	0.26%	0.19%
Price of Exports-RW	0.37%	1.03%	1.15%	0.38%	0.26%	0.20%	0.38%	0.26%	0.19%

Telecommunications	Constraint Case			Flexible Case			Efficiency Case		
	1988	1991	1994	1988	1991	1994	1988	1991	1994
Marginal Costs	0.64%	1.72%	1.94%	-0.04%	0.07%	0.23%	-0.04%	0.07%	0.24%
Cost of Labour	-0.21%	0.38%	0.28%	-0.47%	-0.96%	-1.40%	-0.49%	-1.06%	-1.58%
Deflator of Absorption	0.86%	2.03%	2.22%	-0.12%	-0.20%	-0.07%	-0.12%	-0.21%	-0.08%
Price of Exports-RW	3.30%	6.19%	6.41%	-0.10%	-0.07%	0.09%	-0.10%	-0.07%	0.09%

Transports	Constraint Case			Flexible Case			Efficiency Case		
	1988	1991	1994	1988	1991	1994	1988	1991	1994
Marginal Costs	0.24%	0.92%	1.03%	0.28%	0.16%	0.12%	0.27%	0.13%	0.06%
Cost of Labour	-0.21%	0.38%	0.28%	-0.47%	-0.96%	-1.40%	-0.49%	-1.06%	-1.58%
Deflator of Absorption	0.45%	1.06%	1.16%	0.37%	0.22%	0.17%	0.36%	0.18%	0.10%
Price of Exports-RW	0.24%	0.92%	1.03%	0.28%	0.16%	0.12%	0.27%	0.13%	0.06%

Banks	Constraint Case			Flexible Case			Efficiency Case		
	1988	1991	1994	1988	1991	1994	1988	1991	1994
Marginal Costs	0.47%	1.44%	1.60%	-0.06%	0.00%	0.11%	-0.07%	0.00%	0.10%
Cost of Labour	-0.21%	0.38%	0.28%	-0.47%	-0.96%	-1.40%	-0.49%	-1.06%	-1.58%
Deflator of Absorption	0.59%	1.53%	1.68%	-0.01%	0.01%	0.12%	-0.02%	0.00%	0.10%
Price of Exports-RW	1.35%	2.96%	3.12%	-0.09%	-0.05%	0.06%	-0.09%	-0.05%	0.05%

Services	Constraint Case			Flexible Case			Efficiency Case		
	1988	1991	1994	1988	1991	1994	1988	1991	1994
Marginal Costs	0.20%	0.96%	1.12%	0.05%	0.10%	0.21%	0.05%	0.08%	0.18%
Cost of Labour	-0.21%	0.38%	0.28%	-0.47%	-0.96%	-1.40%	-0.49%	-1.06%	-1.58%
Deflator of Absorption	0.22%	0.96%	1.11%	0.07%	0.11%	0.22%	0.06%	0.09%	0.18%
Price of Exports-RW	0.20%	0.96%	1.12%	0.05%	0.10%	0.21%	0.05%	0.08%	0.18%

Non market	Constraint Case			Flexible Case			Efficiency Case		
	1988	1991	1994	1988	1991	1994	1988	1991	1994
Marginal Costs	0.08%	0.70%	0.71%	-0.02%	-0.31%	-0.56%	-0.02%	-0.34%	-0.62%
Cost of Labour	-0.21%	0.38%	0.28%	-0.47%	-0.96%	-1.40%	-0.49%	-1.06%	-1.58%
Deflator of Absorption	0.08%	0.70%	0.71%	-0.02%	-0.31%	-0.56%	-0.02%	-0.34%	-0.62%
Price of Exports-RW	0.08%	0.70%	0.71%	-0.02%	-0.31%	-0.56%	-0.02%	-0.34%	-0.62%

Table B4.5.
Decomposition of effects: macroeconomic aggregates for France

Macroeconomic Aggregates (vol.) (% change from monde)

	Border Controls			Border controls and x-ineff.			Market segmentation			Trade antimonde			Full antimonde		
	1988	1991	1994	1988	1991	1994	1988	1991	1994	1988	1991	1994	1988	1991	1994
GDP fact. pr.	-0.04%	-0.06%	-0.07%	-0.04%	-0.07%	-0.08%	-0.23%	-0.58%	-0.88%	-0.26%	-0.62%	-0.93%	-0.35%	-0.76%	-1.11%
Priv. Consumption	0.08%	0.06%	0.06%	0.07%	0.06%	0.06%	-0.82%	-0.96%	-1.15%	-0.81%	-0.98%	-1.18%	-0.85%	-1.04%	-1.26%
Absorption	-0.01%	-0.03%	-0.03%	-0.01%	-0.03%	-0.03%	-1.12%	-1.29%	-1.51%	-1.15%	-1.35%	-1.58%	-1.19%	-1.40%	-1.65%
Total Investment	0.02%	0.02%	0.02%	0.02%	0.02%	0.02%	-4.21%	-4.34%	-4.46%	-4.20%	-4.34%	-4.46%	-4.21%	-4.35%	-4.48%
Total Exports to RW	-0.55%	-0.62%	-0.62%	-0.56%	-0.63%	-0.64%	2.10%	1.77%	1.58%	1.78%	1.45%	1.25%	1.71%	1.35%	1.13%
Total Imports from RW	1.17%	1.31%	1.32%	1.18%	1.34%	1.35%	-4.83%	-4.46%	-4.28%	-3.50%	-3.01%	-2.81%	-3.33%	-2.76%	-2.49%
Total Intra-EU Trade	-0.98%	-2.53%	-2.54%	-0.99%	-2.54%	-2.55%	-0.31%	-3.01%	-3.17%	-1.01%	-3.88%	-4.03%	-1.15%	-4.06%	-4.28%
Employment (diff. from monde, 10³ persons)	-4	-6	-6	-5	-10	-10	-35	-66	-100	-40	-73	-107	-43	-78	-113
Disposable Income (deflated)	0.08%	0.06%	0.06%	0.08%	0.06%	0.06%	-0.85%	-0.99%	-1.19%	-0.84%	-1.01%	-1.22%	-0.88%	-1.08%	-1.30%

Macroeconomic Ratios (abs. diff. from monde)

	Border Controls			Border controls and x-ineff.			Market segmentation			Trade antimonde			Full antimonde		
	1988	1991	1994	1988	1991	1994	1988	1991	1994	1988	1991	1994	1988	1991	1994
Current Account as % of GDP	0.01%	0.03%	0.03%	0.02%	0.04%	0.04%	-1.31%	-1.26%	-1.19%	-1.27%	-1.20%	-1.13%	-1.23%	-1.14%	-1.05%
Public Deficit as % of GDP	-0.01%	-0.02%	-0.03%	-0.02%	-0.03%	-0.03%	-0.19%	-0.30%	-0.43%	-0.22%	-0.34%	-0.47%	-0.25%	-0.39%	-0.54%
Labour Productivity	-0.02%	-0.03%	-0.04%	-0.02%	-0.03%	-0.03%	-0.07%	-0.27%	-0.41%	-0.08%	-0.28%	-0.43%	-0.15%	-0.39%	-0.58%
Investment/GDP	0.02%	0.02%	0.02%	0.02%	0.02%	0.03%	-1.77%	-1.75%	-1.75%	-1.76%	-1.74%	-1.74%	-1.74%	-1.72%	-1.71%
Priv.Cons./GDP	0.07%	0.08%	0.08%	0.07%	0.08%	0.08%	-0.36%	-0.23%	-0.17%	-0.34%	-0.22%	-0.15%	-0.31%	-0.17%	-0.09%

Deflators (% change from monde)

	Border Controls			Border controls and x-ineff.			Market segmentation			Trade antimonde			Full antimonde		
	1988	1991	1994	1988	1991	1994	1988	1991	1994	1988	1991	1994	1988	1991	1994
Consumer Price Index	-0.13%	-0.13%	-0.13%	-0.13%	-0.13%	-0.14%	0.78%	0.70%	0.71%	0.77%	0.71%	0.73%	0.75%	0.68%	0.68%
Real Wage Rate	-0.05%	-0.08%	-0.09%	-0.06%	-0.10%	-0.11%	-0.33%	-0.74%	-1.12%	-0.38%	-0.83%	-1.22%	-0.47%	-0.96%	-1.40%
Marginal Costs	-0.08%	-0.09%	-0.09%	-0.08%	-0.08%	-0.08%	0.43%	0.34%	0.33%	0.42%	0.35%	0.34%	0.41%	0.34%	0.32%
Producer Prices	-0.08%	-0.08%	-0.08%	-0.08%	-0.08%	-0.08%	0.49%	0.43%	0.42%	0.48%	0.44%	0.43%	0.47%	0.43%	0.41%
Real Shadow Price of Capital	0.07%	0.07%	0.07%	0.09%	0.11%	0.10%	-0.05%	0.45%	1.03%	-0.01%	0.52%	1.11%	-0.06%	0.44%	1.00%
Terms-of-Trade RW	2.00%	2.24%	2.26%	2.02%	2.27%	2.30%	-6.66%	-5.66%	-5.06%	-5.54%	-4.52%	-3.91%	-5.35%	-4.23%	-3.52%
Real Exchange Rate	3.89%	4.14%	4.16%	3.91%	4.17%	4.21%	-7.31%	-6.15%	-5.51%	-4.56%	-3.38%	-2.71%	-4.36%	-3.09%	-2.32%
Trade Regime	Integration			Integration			Segmentation			Segmentation			Segmentation		

Table B4.6.
Decomposition of effects: effects on IC sectors for France

% change from *monde*

Metal Industries

	Border Controls			Border controls and x-ineff.			Market segmentation			Trade *antimonde*			Full *antimonde*		
	1988	1991	1994	1988	1991	1994	1988	1991	1994	1988	1991	1994	1988	1991	1994
Production per firm	-0.91%	-1.91%	-1.91%	-0.92%	-1.91%	-1.92%	-4.37%	-8.94%	-9.05%	-5.16%	-9.82%	-9.93%	-5.27%	-9.97%	-10.13%
Marginal Costs	3.62%	3.88%	3.90%	3.64%	3.92%	3.94%	-5.71%	-4.73%	-4.23%	-2.98%	-1.93%	-1.41%	-2.79%	-1.64%	-1.02%
Producer Prices	3.68%	4.01%	4.02%	3.70%	4.04%	4.06%	-5.43%	-4.16%	-3.66%	-2.64%	-1.27%	-0.75%	-2.44%	-0.98%	-0.35%
Mark-ups domestic (abs. diff.)	0.04%	0.08%	0.08%	0.04%	0.08%	0.08%	0.55%	0.87%	0.88%	0.58%	0.91%	0.92%	0.59%	0.92%	0.93%
Fixed Costs per firm	3.58%	3.85%	3.86%	3.60%	3.87%	3.89%	-5.57%	-4.65%	-4.23%	-2.85%	-1.86%	-1.41%	-2.70%	-1.64%	-1.12%
Number of Firms	-0.20%	0.06%	0.06%	-0.20%	0.07%	0.07%	9.47%	15.03%	14.74%	8.93%	14.41%	14.11%	8.85%	14.28%	13.94%
Sigma of Love of Variety	0.00%	0.00%	0.00%	0.00%	0.00%	0.00%	0.00%	0.00%	0.00%	0.00%	0.00%	0.00%	0.00%	0.00%	0.00%

Chemical

	Border Controls			Border controls and x-ineff.			Market segmentation			Trade *antimonde*			Full *antimonde*		
	1988	1991	1994	1988	1991	1994	1988	1991	1994	1988	1991	1994	1988	1991	1994
Production per firm	-0.46%	-1.32%	-1.32%	-0.47%	-1.33%	-1.33%	-2.59%	-5.83%	-6.01%	-2.68%	-5.97%	-6.15%	-2.78%	-6.12%	-6.35%
Marginal Costs	3.73%	3.98%	4.00%	3.75%	4.01%	4.04%	-6.20%	-5.24%	-4.68%	-3.44%	-2.42%	-1.84%	-3.25%	-2.14%	-1.46%
Producer Prices	3.75%	4.04%	4.05%	3.77%	4.07%	4.10%	-6.09%	-4.98%	-4.42%	-3.32%	-2.16%	-1.57%	-3.13%	-1.87%	-1.18%
Mark-ups domestic (abs. diff.)	0.00%	0.02%	0.02%	0.00%	0.02%	0.02%	0.21%	0.36%	0.37%	0.19%	0.35%	0.36%	0.20%	0.36%	0.37%
Fixed Costs per firm	3.70%	3.95%	3.96%	3.72%	3.97%	4.00%	-6.09%	-5.19%	-4.71%	-3.34%	-2.39%	-1.89%	-3.18%	-2.17%	-1.59%
Number of Firms	0.47%	1.14%	1.15%	0.47%	1.15%	1.15%	7.15%	10.16%	9.90%	7.47%	10.48%	10.21%	7.39%	10.37%	10.06%
Sigma of Love of Variety	0.00%	0.00%	0.00%	0.00%	0.00%	0.00%	0.00%	0.00%	0.00%	0.00%	0.00%	0.00%	0.00%	0.00%	0.00%

Other Intensive Industries

	Border Controls			Border controls and x-ineff.			Market segmentation			Trade *antimonde*			Full *antimonde*		
	1988	1991	1994	1988	1991	1994	1988	1991	1994	1988	1991	1994	1988	1991	1994
Production per firm	-0.27%	-0.62%	-0.62%	-0.27%	-0.62%	-0.63%	-1.47%	-2.49%	-2.62%	-1.65%	-2.72%	-2.85%	-1.72%	-2.81%	-2.97%
Marginal Costs	3.79%	4.04%	4.05%	3.81%	4.07%	4.10%	-6.70%	-5.71%	-5.17%	-3.95%	-2.92%	-2.36%	-3.75%	-2.63%	-1.97%
Producer Prices	3.79%	4.05%	4.07%	3.81%	4.08%	4.11%	-6.67%	-5.65%	-5.12%	-3.91%	-2.86%	-2.30%	-3.71%	-2.56%	-1.90%
Mark-ups domestic (abs. diff.)	0.00%	0.00%	0.00%	0.00%	0.00%	0.00%	0.04%	0.05%	0.06%	0.04%	0.06%	0.06%	0.04%	0.06%	0.06%
Fixed Costs per firm	3.76%	4.01%	4.02%	3.77%	4.03%	4.05%	-6.63%	-5.72%	-5.27%	-3.89%	-2.94%	-2.47%	-3.73%	-2.72%	-2.17%
Number of Firms	0.17%	0.47%	0.47%	0.18%	0.49%	0.49%	0.62%	1.31%	1.19%	0.62%	1.29%	1.18%	0.60%	1.27%	1.14%
Sigma of Love of Variety	0.00%	0.00%	0.00%	0.00%	0.00%	0.00%	0.00%	0.00%	0.00%	0.00%	0.00%	0.00%	0.00%	0.00%	0.00%

Electrical goods

	Border Controls			Border controls and x-ineff.			Market segmentation			Trade *antimonde*			Full *antimonde*		
	1988	1991	1994	1988	1991	1994	1988	1991	1994	1988	1991	1994	1988	1991	1994
Production per firm	-0.65%	-1.54%	-1.54%	-0.66%	-1.54%	-1.56%	-3.10%	-6.22%	-6.43%	-3.54%	-6.74%	-6.95%	-3.65%	-6.90%	-7.16%
Marginal Costs	3.81%	4.06%	4.08%	3.83%	4.09%	4.12%	-6.82%	-5.82%	-5.28%	-4.06%	-3.02%	-2.46%	-3.86%	-2.73%	-2.07%
Producer Prices	3.85%	4.15%	4.17%	3.87%	4.18%	4.21%	-6.64%	-5.46%	-4.92%	-3.85%	-2.62%	-2.06%	-3.64%	-2.33%	-1.66%
Mark-ups domestic (abs. diff.)	0.01%	0.03%	0.03%	0.01%	0.03%	0.03%	0.36%	0.51%	0.52%	0.36%	0.52%	0.52%	0.37%	0.52%	0.53%
Fixed Costs per firm	3.78%	4.03%	4.04%	3.80%	4.05%	4.08%	-6.75%	-5.84%	-5.41%	-4.00%	-3.06%	-2.60%	-3.85%	-2.84%	-2.31%
Number of Firms	0.24%	1.03%	1.03%	0.25%	1.04%	1.04%	4.14%	7.88%	7.64%	4.10%	7.83%	7.60%	4.04%	7.75%	7.50%
Sigma of Love of Variety	0.00%	0.00%	0.00%	0.00%	0.00%	0.00%	0.00%	0.00%	0.00%	0.00%	0.00%	0.00%	0.00%	0.00%	0.00%

Transport equipment

	Border Controls			Border controls and x-ineff.			Market segmentation			Trade *antimonde*			Full *antimonde*		
	1988	1991	1994	1988	1991	1994	1988	1991	1994	1988	1991	1994	1988	1991	1994
Production per firm	-0.61%	-1.53%	-1.54%	-0.62%	-1.54%	-1.55%	-6.75%	-11.32%	-11.40%	-7.07%	-11.69%	-11.75%	-7.17%	-11.83%	-11.95%
Marginal Costs	3.84%	4.11%	4.13%	3.86%	4.14%	4.18%	-6.46%	-5.45%	-4.97%	-3.65%	-2.58%	-2.07%	-3.44%	-2.27%	-1.66%
Producer Prices	3.88%	4.22%	4.24%	3.90%	4.25%	4.29%	-5.98%	-4.64%	-4.15%	-3.13%	-1.71%	-1.20%	-2.91%	-1.39%	-0.77%
Mark-ups domestic (abs. diff.)	0.00%	0.06%	0.06%	0.00%	0.06%	0.06%	1.12%	1.61%	1.61%	1.11%	1.59%	1.59%	1.11%	1.60%	1.60%
Fixed Costs per firm	3.83%	4.10%	4.12%	3.84%	4.12%	4.15%	-6.44%	-5.45%	-5.00%	-3.63%	-2.59%	-2.11%	-3.47%	-2.35%	-1.79%
Number of Firms	0.50%	1.08%	1.09%	0.50%	1.09%	1.10%	7.82%	14.44%	14.40%	7.99%	14.62%	14.59%	7.93%	14.55%	14.51%
Sigma of Love of Variety	0.00%	0.00%	0.00%	0.00%	0.00%	0.00%	0.00%	0.00%	0.00%	0.00%	0.00%	0.00%	0.00%	0.00%	0.00%

Other Equipment

	Border Controls			Border controls and x-ineff.			Market segmentation			Trade *antimonde*			Full *antimonde*		
	1988	1991	1994	1988	1991	1994	1988	1991	1994	1988	1991	1994	1988	1991	1994
Production per firm	-0.66%	-1.26%	-1.26%	-0.66%	-1.27%	-1.28%	-4.80%	-7.65%	-7.86%	-5.33%	-8.23%	-8.44%	-5.42%	-8.36%	-8.62%
Marginal Costs	3.81%	4.06%	4.08%	3.83%	4.09%	4.12%	-6.76%	-5.75%	-5.20%	-4.00%	-2.95%	-2.37%	-3.80%	-2.66%	-1.98%
Producer Prices	3.83%	4.10%	4.12%	3.85%	4.13%	4.17%	-6.61%	-5.51%	-4.95%	-3.82%	-2.67%	-2.09%	-3.62%	-2.38%	-1.69%
Mark-ups domestic (abs. diff.)	0.01%	0.02%	0.02%	0.01%	0.02%	0.02%	0.35%	0.48%	0.49%	0.36%	0.49%	0.50%	0.36%	0.49%	0.50%
Fixed Costs per firm	3.78%	4.03%	4.04%	3.79%	4.05%	4.07%	-6.68%	-5.77%	-5.32%	-3.93%	-2.98%	-2.51%	-3.78%	-2.76%	-2.21%
Number of Firms	-0.01%	0.67%	0.67%	-0.01%	0.67%	0.66%	5.53%	8.55%	8.12%	5.21%	8.22%	7.78%	5.13%	8.10%	7.63%
Sigma of Love of Variety	0.00%	0.00%	0.00%	0.00%	0.00%	0.00%	0.00%	0.00%	0.00%	0.00%	0.00%	0.00%	0.00%	0.00%	0.00%

Telecommunications

	Border Controls			Border controls and x-ineff.			Market segmentation			Trade *antimonde*			Full *antimonde*		
	1988	1991	1994	1988	1991	1994	1988	1991	1994	1988	1991	1994	1988	1991	1994
Production per firm	0.01%	0.03%	0.02%	-0.66%	-1.33%	-1.34%	-0.46%	-1.14%	-1.49%	-0.44%	-1.13%	-1.49%	-1.15%	-2.51%	-2.89%
Marginal Costs	3.93%	4.19%	4.22%	3.96%	4.23%	4.28%	-7.37%	-6.11%	-5.31%	-4.61%	-3.32%	-2.50%	-4.41%	-3.02%	-2.09%
Producer Prices	3.91%	4.16%	4.19%	3.75%	3.84%	3.88%	-7.29%	-5.98%	-5.21%	-4.54%	-3.21%	-2.41%	-4.51%	-3.25%	-2.35%
Mark-ups domestic (abs. diff.)	-0.02%	-0.03%	-0.04%	-0.25%	-0.48%	-0.48%	0.09%	0.07%	0.04%	0.07%	0.05%	0.02%	-0.15%	-0.40%	-0.44%
Fixed Costs per firm	3.82%	4.05%	4.07%	2.26%	0.92%	0.95%	-7.40%	-6.58%	-6.23%	-4.69%	-3.87%	-3.51%	-6.01%	-6.58%	-6.17%
Number of Firms	0.08%	0.11%	0.12%	0.79%	1.55%	1.56%	0.13%	0.45%	0.55%	0.17%	0.49%	0.59%	0.89%	1.95%	2.06%
Sigma of Love of Variety	0.00%	0.00%	0.00%	0.00%	0.00%	0.00%	0.00%	0.00%	0.00%	0.00%	0.00%	0.00%	0.00%	0.00%	0.00%

Banks

	Border Controls			Border controls and x-ineff.			Market segmentation			Trade *antimonde*			Full *antimonde*		
	1988	1991	1994	1988	1991	1994	1988	1991	1994	1988	1991	1994	1988	1991	1994
Production per firm	0.13%	0.24%	0.24%	-0.33%	-0.69%	-0.69%	-0.76%	-1.46%	-1.78%	-0.66%	-1.34%	-1.67%	-1.16%	-2.30%	-2.65%
Marginal Costs	3.91%	4.16%	4.18%	3.94%	4.20%	4.23%	-7.38%	-6.16%	-5.40%	-4.63%	-3.38%	-2.59%	-4.43%	-3.09%	-2.21%
Producer Prices	3.89%	4.13%	4.14%	3.87%	4.07%	4.09%	-7.31%	-6.05%	-5.29%	-4.57%	-3.28%	-2.50%	-4.41%	-3.08%	-2.20%
Mark-ups domestic (abs. diff.)	-0.02%	-0.03%	-0.03%	-0.07%	-0.14%	-0.14%	0.07%	0.08%	0.08%	0.06%	0.07%	0.07%	0.00%	-0.04%	-0.04%
Fixed Costs per firm	3.84%	4.07%	4.09%	2.94%	2.25%	2.27%	-7.41%	-6.50%	-6.06%	-4.69%	-3.78%	-3.32%	-5.39%	-5.27%	-4.76%
Number of Firms	0.16%	0.29%	0.29%	0.61%	1.19%	1.19%	0.52%	0.97%	0.99%	0.62%	1.10%	1.11%	1.07%	1.99%	2.00%
Sigma of Love of Variety	0.00%	0.00%	0.00%	0.00%	0.00%	0.00%	0.00%	0.00%	0.00%	0.00%	0.00%	0.00%	0.00%	0.00%	0.00%

Table B4.7.
Decomposition of effects: sectoral results for France (volumes)

% change from monde

Agriculture

	Border Controls			Border controls and x-ineff.			Market segmentation			Trade antimonde			Full antimonde		
	1988	1991	1994	1988	1991	1994	1988	1991	1994	1988	1991	1994	1988	1991	1994
Domestic Production - vol.	-0.8%	-1.2%	-1.2%	-0.9%	-1.2%	-1.3%	3.4%	1.8%	1.0%	2.8%	1.1%	0.3%	2.6%	0.9%	0.0%
Imports - vol.	2.0%	2.2%	2.3%	2.1%	2.3%	2.3%	-5.4%	-4.7%	-4.2%	-3.8%	-3.0%	-2.5%	-3.7%	-2.7%	-2.1%
Exports - vol.	-0.7%	-0.8%	-0.8%	-0.7%	-0.8%	-0.8%	2.1%	1.7%	1.4%	1.6%	1.2%	0.9%	1.6%	1.1%	0.8%
Absorption - vol.	-0.3%	-0.4%	-0.4%	-0.3%	-0.4%	-0.4%	1.6%	1.0%	0.5%	1.4%	0.7%	0.2%	1.4%	0.6%	0.1%
Investment - vol.	-0.4%	-0.6%	-0.6%	-0.4%	-0.6%	-0.6%	-2.7%	-3.4%	-3.7%	-3.0%	-3.7%	-4.1%	-3.0%	-3.8%	-4.2%
Labour Demand - vol.	-0.8%	-1.2%	-1.2%	-0.8%	-1.2%	-1.2%	3.4%	2.1%	1.5%	2.8%	1.4%	0.8%	2.7%	1.2%	0.6%
Private Consumption - vol.	0.1%	0.1%	0.1%	0.1%	0.1%	0.1%	-0.6%	-0.9%	-1.1%	-0.6%	-0.9%	-1.1%	-0.6%	-0.9%	-1.2%
Supply to domestic - vol.	-0.5%	-0.3%	-0.4%	-0.5%	-0.4%	-0.4%	3.0%	2.1%	1.4%	2.7%	1.7%	1.0%	2.6%	1.6%	0.8%
Intra-EU Trade - vol.	-1.8%	-3.8%	-3.8%	-1.8%	-3.9%	-3.9%	2.0%	-0.3%	-0.8%	0.7%	-1.9%	-2.4%	0.5%	-2.2%	-2.8%

Energy

	Border Controls			Border controls and x-ineff.			Market segmentation			Trade antimonde			Full antimonde		
	1988	1991	1994	1988	1991	1994	1988	1991	1994	1988	1991	1994	1988	1991	1994
Domestic Production - vol.	-0.2%	-0.2%	-0.2%	-0.2%	-0.2%	-0.2%	1.2%	0.7%	0.4%	1.1%	0.5%	0.3%	1.0%	0.4%	0.1%
Imports - vol.	0.5%	0.6%	0.6%	0.5%	0.6%	0.6%	-1.2%	-1.1%	-1.0%	-0.8%	-0.8%	-0.7%	-0.8%	-0.8%	-0.7%
Exports - vol.	-0.3%	-0.3%	-0.3%	-0.3%	-0.3%	-0.3%	0.9%	0.7%	0.6%	0.7%	0.5%	0.4%	0.7%	0.5%	0.4%
Absorption - vol.	0.0%	0.0%	0.0%	0.0%	0.0%	0.0%	0.3%	0.0%	-0.2%	0.2%	-0.1%	-0.3%	0.2%	-0.2%	-0.4%
Investment - vol.	-0.1%	-0.1%	-0.1%	-0.1%	-0.1%	-0.1%	-3.5%	-3.7%	-3.8%	-3.5%	-3.8%	-3.9%	-3.6%	-3.8%	-4.0%
Labour Demand - vol.	-0.2%	-0.2%	-0.2%	-0.2%	-0.2%	-0.2%	1.3%	0.9%	0.7%	1.2%	0.7%	0.5%	1.2%	0.7%	0.5%
Private Consumption - vol.	0.1%	0.1%	0.1%	0.1%	0.1%	0.1%	-0.7%	-0.9%	-1.1%	-0.7%	-0.9%	-1.1%	-0.7%	-1.0%	-1.2%
Supply to domestic - vol.	-0.2%	-0.2%	-0.2%	-0.2%	-0.2%	-0.2%	1.0%	0.6%	0.3%	0.9%	0.4%	0.1%	0.8%	0.3%	0.0%
Intra-EU Trade - vol.	-0.3%	-0.4%	-0.4%	-0.4%	-0.4%	-0.4%	1.1%	0.7%	0.6%	0.8%	0.3%	0.2%	0.8%	0.2%	0.1%

Metal Industries

	Border Controls			Border controls and x-ineff.			Market segmentation			Trade antimonde			Full antimonde		
	1988	1991	1994	1988	1991	1994	1988	1991	1994	1988	1991	1994	1988	1991	1994
Domestic Production - vol.	-1.1%	-1.9%	-1.8%	-1.1%	-1.8%	-1.8%	4.7%	4.7%	4.4%	3.3%	3.2%	2.8%	3.1%	2.9%	2.4%
Imports - vol.	1.2%	1.3%	1.3%	1.2%	1.3%	1.3%	-5.3%	-5.0%	-4.9%	-3.4%	-2.9%	-2.8%	-3.2%	-2.6%	-2.4%
Exports - vol.	-0.6%	-0.7%	-0.7%	-0.6%	-0.7%	-0.7%	1.9%	1.6%	1.4%	1.4%	1.1%	1.0%	1.4%	1.0%	0.9%
Absorption - vol.	-0.5%	-0.8%	-0.8%	-0.5%	-0.8%	-0.8%	1.4%	1.5%	1.2%	0.7%	0.8%	0.5%	0.6%	0.6%	0.3%
Investment - vol.	-0.6%	-1.0%	-0.9%	-0.6%	-0.9%	-0.9%	-1.8%	-1.8%	-2.0%	-2.5%	-2.6%	-2.8%	-2.5%	-2.7%	-2.9%
Labour Demand - vol.	-1.1%	-1.7%	-1.7%	-1.1%	-1.7%	-1.7%	5.2%	5.6%	5.3%	3.9%	4.1%	3.8%	3.7%	3.9%	3.5%
Private Consumption - vol.	0.0%	0.0%	0.0%	0.0%	0.0%	0.0%	-0.3%	-0.4%	-0.5%	-0.3%	-0.4%	-0.5%	-0.3%	-0.4%	-0.5%
Supply to domestic - vol.	-0.3%	0.5%	0.5%	-0.3%	0.5%	0.5%	5.9%	11.3%	10.7%	5.2%	10.5%	9.9%	5.0%	10.3%	9.6%
Intra-EU Trade - vol.	-1.5%	-2.9%	-2.9%	-1.5%	-2.9%	-2.9%	0.7%	-3.9%	-4.0%	-1.1%	-5.8%	-5.8%	-1.2%	-6.0%	-6.1%

Chemical

	Border Controls			Border controls and x-ineff.			Market segmentation			Trade antimonde			Full antimonde		
	1988	1991	1994	1988	1991	1994	1988	1991	1994	1988	1991	1994	1988	1991	1994
Domestic Production - vol.	0.0%	-0.2%	-0.2%	0.0%	-0.2%	-0.2%	4.4%	3.7%	3.3%	4.6%	3.9%	3.4%	4.4%	3.6%	3.1%
Imports - vol.	0.9%	1.1%	1.1%	0.9%	1.1%	1.2%	-5.2%	-4.9%	-4.7%	-4.1%	-3.6%	-3.4%	-3.9%	-3.3%	-3.0%
Exports - vol.	-0.3%	-0.4%	-0.4%	-0.3%	-0.4%	-0.4%	2.0%	1.7%	1.5%	1.9%	1.6%	1.4%	1.8%	1.5%	1.3%
Absorption - vol.	-0.1%	-0.2%	-0.2%	-0.1%	-0.2%	-0.2%	1.6%	1.1%	0.8%	1.5%	1.0%	0.6%	1.4%	0.9%	0.5%
Investment - vol.	0.0%	-0.1%	-0.1%	0.0%	-0.1%	-0.1%	-2.1%	-2.4%	-2.6%	-2.0%	-2.3%	-2.6%	-2.0%	-2.4%	-2.7%
Labour Demand - vol.	0.0%	0.0%	0.0%	0.0%	0.0%	0.0%	4.6%	4.2%	3.8%	4.9%	4.4%	4.0%	4.7%	4.2%	3.7%
Private Consumption - vol.	0.0%	0.0%	0.0%	0.0%	0.0%	0.0%	-0.5%	-0.8%	-1.0%	-0.5%	-0.8%	-1.0%	-0.5%	-0.9%	-1.1%
Supply to domestic - vol.	0.5%	1.7%	1.7%	0.5%	1.7%	1.7%	5.1%	7.1%	6.5%	5.3%	7.4%	6.8%	5.2%	7.2%	6.5%
Intra-EU Trade - vol.	-1.0%	-2.7%	-2.7%	-1.0%	-2.7%	-2.8%	0.9%	-2.5%	-2.7%	0.3%	-3.3%	-3.4%	0.2%	-3.5%	-3.7%

Other Intensive Industries

	Border Controls			Border controls and x-ineff.			Market segmentation			Trade antimonde			Full antimonde		
	1988	1991	1994	1988	1991	1994	1988	1991	1994	1988	1991	1994	1988	1991	1994
Domestic Production - vol.	-0.1%	-0.2%	-0.1%	-0.1%	-0.1%	-0.1%	-0.9%	-1.2%	-1.5%	-1.0%	-1.5%	-1.7%	-1.1%	-1.6%	-1.9%
Imports - vol.	1.8%	2.1%	2.1%	1.8%	2.1%	2.1%	-8.6%	-8.0%	-7.8%	-6.4%	-5.6%	-5.3%	-6.1%	-5.2%	-4.7%
Exports - vol.	-0.5%	-0.6%	-0.6%	-0.5%	-0.6%	-0.6%	2.1%	1.8%	1.6%	1.8%	1.5%	1.3%	1.8%	1.4%	1.2%
Absorption - vol.	0.0%	-0.1%	-0.1%	0.0%	-0.1%	-0.1%	-2.1%	-2.2%	-2.4%	-2.2%	-2.3%	-2.5%	-2.2%	-2.4%	-2.6%
Investment - vol.	-0.1%	-0.1%	-0.1%	-0.1%	-0.1%	-0.1%	-4.5%	-4.7%	-4.9%	-4.6%	-4.9%	-5.0%	-4.7%	-4.9%	-5.0%
Labour Demand - vol.	0.1%	-0.1%	-0.1%	0.0%	0.0%	0.0%	-0.7%	-1.0%	-1.2%	-0.9%	-1.3%	-1.4%	-0.9%	-1.3%	-1.5%
Private Consumption - vol.	0.1%	0.0%	0.0%	0.1%	0.0%	0.0%	-1.0%	-0.7%	-0.8%	-0.9%	-0.8%	-0.9%	-1.0%	-0.9%	-0.9%
Supply to domestic - vol.	0.2%	0.8%	0.8%	0.2%	0.8%	0.8%	-1.1%	-0.6%	-0.9%	-1.1%	-0.6%	-0.9%	-1.1%	-0.7%	-1.0%
Intra-EU Trade - vol.	-1.6%	-3.7%	-3.7%	-1.6%	-3.7%	-3.7%	-1.5%	-4.4%	-4.5%	-2.6%	-5.7%	-5.8%	-2.7%	-5.9%	-6.0%

Electrical goods

	Border Controls 1988	1991	1994	Border controls and x-ineff. 1988	1991	1994	Market segmentation 1988	1991	1994	Trade antimonde 1988	1991	1994	Full antimonde 1988	1991	1994
Domestic Production - vol.	-0.4%	-0.5%	-0.5%	-0.4%	-0.5%	-0.5%	0.9%	1.2%	0.7%	0.4%	0.6%	0.1%	0.2%	0.3%	-0.2%
Imports - vol.	1.7%	1.9%	1.9%	1.7%	2.0%	2.0%	-8.9%	-8.3%	-8.0%	-7.1%	-6.3%	-6.0%	-6.9%	-5.9%	-5.5%
Exports - vol.	-0.6%	-0.7%	-0.7%	-0.6%	-0.7%	-0.7%	2.6%	2.2%	2.0%	2.2%	1.9%	1.6%	2.2%	1.7%	1.5%
Absorption - vol.	0.0%	-0.1%	-0.1%	0.0%	-0.1%	-0.1%	-3.6%	-3.3%	-3.5%	-3.7%	-3.4%	-3.6%	-3.8%	-3.5%	-3.7%
Investment - vol.	-0.2%	-0.3%	-0.3%	-0.2%	-0.3%	-0.3%	-3.8%	-3.7%	-3.9%	-4.0%	-4.0%	-4.2%	-4.1%	-4.1%	-4.3%
Labour Demand - vol.	-0.4%	-0.4%	-0.4%	-0.4%	-0.4%	-0.4%	1.3%	1.9%	1.5%	0.9%	1.3%	1.0%	0.8%	1.2%	0.8%
Private Consumption - vol.	0.5%	0.1%	0.1%	0.4%	0.0%	0.0%	-3.7%	-1.9%	-1.9%	-3.6%	-2.0%	-1.9%	-3.8%	-2.2%	-2.1%
Supply to domestic - vol.	0.4%	1.5%	1.5%	0.4%	1.5%	1.5%	-0.2%	-0.2%	2.5%	-0.2%	2.9%	2.5%	-0.3%	2.8%	2.3%
Intra-EU Trade - vol	-1.5%	-3.4%	-3.4%	-1.5%	-3.4%	-3.4%	-0.9%	-5.0%	-5.1%	-2.3%	-6.5%	-6.6%	-2.5%	-6.8%	-6.9%

Transport equipment

	Border Controls 1988	1991	1994	Border controls and x-ineff. 1988	1991	1994	Market segmentation 1988	1991	1994	Trade antimonde 1988	1991	1994	Full antimonde 1988	1991	1994
Domestic Production - vol.	-0.1%	-0.5%	-0.5%	-0.1%	-0.5%	-0.5%	0.5%	1.5%	1.4%	0.4%	1.2%	1.1%	0.2%	1.0%	0.8%
Imports - vol.	1.6%	1.8%	1.8%	1.6%	1.8%	1.9%	-8.8%	-8.3%	-8.0%	-6.5%	-5.7%	-5.5%	-6.3%	-5.3%	-4.9%
Exports - vol.	-0.6%	-0.7%	-0.7%	-0.6%	-0.7%	-0.7%	2.5%	2.2%	2.0%	2.1%	1.8%	1.6%	2.0%	1.6%	1.4%
Absorption - vol.	0.1%	0.0%	0.0%	0.1%	0.0%	0.0%	-3.1%	-2.5%	-2.5%	-3.2%	-2.6%	-2.6%	-3.2%	-2.6%	-2.7%
Investment - vol.	-0.1%	-0.2%	-0.2%	-0.1%	-0.2%	-0.2%	-3.7%	-3.3%	-3.4%	-3.8%	-3.4%	-3.5%	-3.8%	-3.5%	-3.6%
Labour Demand - vol.	-0.1%	-0.3%	-0.3%	-0.1%	-0.3%	-0.3%	1.4%	2.7%	2.7%	1.2%	2.6%	2.5%	1.1%	2.4%	2.4%
Private Consumption - vol.	0.2%	0.0%	0.1%	0.2%	0.0%	0.0%	-2.9%	-1.7%	-1.5%	-3.0%	-1.8%	-1.5%	-3.1%	-1.9%	-1.6%
Supply to domestic - vol.	1.0%	2.3%	2.4%	1.0%	2.4%	2.4%	0.1%	6.6%	6.5%	0.5%	7.0%	7.0%	0.4%	6.9%	6.8%
Intra-EU Trade - vol	-0.8%	-2.1%	-2.1%	-0.8%	-2.1%	-2.1%	-2.3%	-5.7%	-5.7%	-2.8%	-6.3%	-6.3%	-2.9%	-6.5%	-6.5%

Other Equipment

	Border Controls 1988	1991	1994	Border controls and x-ineff. 1988	1991	1994	Market segmentation 1988	1991	1994	Trade antimonde 1988	1991	1994	Full antimonde 1988	1991	1994
Domestic Production - vol.	-0.7%	-0.6%	-0.6%	-0.7%	-0.6%	-0.6%	0.5%	0.3%	-0.4%	-0.4%	-0.7%	-1.3%	-0.6%	-0.9%	-1.7%
Imports - vol.	1.5%	1.7%	1.7%	1.5%	1.7%	1.8%	-7.8%	-7.6%	-7.5%	-5.6%	-5.2%	-5.1%	-5.4%	-4.9%	-4.7%
Exports - vol.	-0.8%	-0.9%	-0.9%	-0.8%	-0.9%	-0.9%	2.5%	2.1%	1.9%	2.0%	1.6%	1.4%	1.9%	1.5%	1.3%
Absorption - vol.	-0.2%	-0.2%	-0.2%	-0.2%	-0.2%	-0.2%	-4.8%	-5.0%	-5.4%	-5.0%	-5.3%	-5.6%	-5.0%	-5.4%	-5.7%
Investment - vol.	-0.3%	-0.3%	-0.3%	-0.3%	-0.3%	-0.3%	-4.0%	-4.1%	-4.5%	-4.4%	-4.6%	-4.9%	-4.4%	-4.7%	-5.0%
Labour Demand - vol.	-0.6%	-0.5%	-0.5%	-0.6%	-0.5%	-0.5%	0.8%	0.9%	0.4%	0.0%	0.0%	-0.5%	-0.1%	-0.2%	-0.8%
Private Consumption - vol.	0.1%	0.1%	0.1%	0.1%	0.1%	0.1%	-1.2%	-1.2%	-1.5%	-1.2%	-1.3%	-1.5%	-1.2%	-1.3%	-1.6%
Supply to domestic - vol.	0.3%	1.9%	1.9%	0.3%	1.9%	1.9%	-1.4%	0.5%	-0.2%	-1.6%	0.4%	-0.3%	-1.7%	0.2%	-0.5%
Intra-EU Trade - vol	-1.3%	-2.6%	-2.6%	-1.3%	-2.6%	-2.6%	-1.2%	-3.1%	-3.3%	-2.5%	-4.7%	-4.8%	-2.6%	-4.9%	-5.1%

Consumer goods

	Border Controls 1988	1991	1994	Border controls and x-ineff. 1988	1991	1994	Market segmentation 1988	1991	1994	Trade antimonde 1988	1991	1994	Full antimonde 1988	1991	1994
Domestic Production - vol.	-0.3%	-0.3%	-0.3%	-0.3%	-0.3%	-0.3%	2.3%	1.7%	1.1%	2.2%	1.5%	1.0%	2.1%	1.4%	0.7%
Imports - vol.	1.6%	1.9%	1.9%	1.7%	1.9%	1.9%	-6.8%	-6.3%	-5.9%	-4.7%	-3.9%	-3.5%	-4.4%	-3.4%	-2.8%
Exports - vol.	-0.7%	-0.8%	-0.8%	-0.7%	-0.8%	-0.8%	2.8%	2.3%	2.0%	2.4%	2.0%	1.7%	2.3%	1.8%	1.5%
Absorption - vol.	-0.1%	-0.1%	-0.1%	-0.1%	-0.1%	-0.1%	0.0%	-0.3%	-0.6%	-0.1%	-0.4%	-0.6%	-0.1%	-0.4%	-0.7%
Investment - vol.	-0.2%	-0.2%	-0.2%	-0.2%	-0.2%	-0.2%	-3.1%	-3.4%	-3.7%	-3.2%	-3.5%	-3.8%	-3.2%	-3.6%	-3.9%
Labour Demand - vol.	-0.3%	-0.3%	-0.3%	-0.3%	-0.3%	-0.3%	2.5%	2.0%	1.6%	2.4%	1.9%	1.4%	2.3%	1.8%	1.3%
Private Consumption - vol.	0.0%	0.1%	0.1%	0.0%	0.1%	0.0%	-0.5%	-0.8%	-1.0%	-0.5%	-0.8%	-1.0%	-0.6%	-0.8%	-1.1%
Supply to domestic - vol.	0.2%	1.0%	0.9%	0.2%	0.9%	0.9%	1.8%	1.8%	1.3%	1.8%	1.9%	1.4%	1.7%	1.7%	1.2%
Intra-EU Trade - vol	-1.7%	-4.0%	-4.0%	-1.7%	-4.0%	-4.0%	0.4%	-1.5%	-1.7%	-0.6%	-2.8%	-3.0%	-0.8%	-3.0%	-3.3%

Construction

	Border Controls 1988	1991	1994	Border controls and x-ineff. 1988	1991	1994	Market segmentation 1988	1991	1994	Trade antimonde 1988	1991	1994	Full antimonde 1988	1991	1994
Domestic Production - vol.	0.1%	-0.1%	0.1%	-0.3%	-0.3%	-0.3%	-7.4%	-7.6%	-7.8%	-7.3%	-7.5%	-7.7%	-7.3%	-7.5%	-7.8%
Imports - vol.	#VALUE!	#VALUE!	#VALUE!	#VALUE!	#VALUE!	#VALUE!	#VALUE!	#VALUE!	#VALUE!	#VALUE!	#VALUE!	#VALUE!	#VALUE!	#VALUE!	#VALUE!
Exports - vol.	0.1%	0.1%	0.1%	0.1%	0.1%	0.1%	-7.4%	-7.6%	-7.8%	-7.3%	-7.5%	-7.7%	-7.3%	-7.5%	-7.8%
Absorption - vol.	0.0%	0.0%	0.0%	0.0%	0.0%	0.0%	-7.6%	-7.8%	-7.9%	-7.6%	-7.8%	-7.9%	-7.6%	-7.8%	-7.9%
Investment - vol.	0.1%	0.1%	0.1%	0.1%	0.2%	0.2%	-7.3%	-7.4%	-7.6%	-7.2%	-7.4%	-7.5%	-7.2%	-7.3%	-7.4%
Labour Demand - vol.	0.0%	0.1%	0.1%	0.0%	0.1%	0.1%	-0.5%	-0.9%	-1.1%	-0.5%	-0.9%	-1.2%	-0.6%	-1.0%	-1.3%
Private Consumption - vol.	0.1%	0.1%	0.1%	0.1%	0.1%	0.1%	-7.4%	-7.6%	-7.8%	-7.3%	-7.5%	-7.7%	-7.3%	-7.5%	-7.8%
Supply to domestic - vol.	0.1%	0.1%	0.1%	0.1%	0.1%	0.1%	-7.4%	-7.6%	-7.8%	-7.3%	-7.5%	-7.7%	-7.3%	-7.5%	-7.8%
Intra-EU Trade - vol	#DIV/0!	#DIV/0!	#DIV/0!	#DIV/0!	#DIV/0!	#DIV/0!	#DIV/0!	#DIV/0!	#DIV/0!	#DIV/0!	#DIV/0!	#DIV/0!	#DIV/0!	#DIV/0!	#DIV/0!

Telecommunications

	Border Controls			Border controls and x-ineff.			Market segmentation			Trade *antimonde*			Full *antimonde*		
	1988	1991	1994	1988	1991	1994	1988	1991	1994	1988	1991	1994	1988	1991	1994
Domestic Production - vol.	0.1%	0.1%	0.1%	0.1%	0.2%	0.2%	-0.3%	-0.7%	-0.9%	-0.3%	-0.6%	-0.9%	-0.3%	-0.6%	-0.9%
Imports - vol.	0.8%	1.0%	1.0%	0.8%	0.8%	0.9%	-6.9%	-6.7%	-6.4%	-6.4%	-6.3%	-6.0%	-6.3%	-6.1%	-5.8%
Exports - vol.	-0.2%	-0.2%	-0.2%	-0.2%	-0.2%	-0.2%	1.2%	1.0%	0.8%	1.1%	0.9%	0.8%	1.1%	0.9%	0.7%
Absorption - vol.	0.1%	0.1%	0.1%	0.1%	0.2%	0.2%	-0.4%	-0.6%	-0.9%	-0.4%	-0.6%	-0.8%	-0.3%	-0.6%	-0.8%
Investment - vol.	0.1%	0.1%	0.1%	0.1%	0.2%	0.2%	-4.3%	-4.5%	-4.6%	-4.3%	-4.5%	-4.6%	-4.3%	-4.4%	-4.5%
Labour Demand - vol.	0.1%	0.2%	0.2%	-0.3%	-0.7%	-0.7%	-0.2%	-0.2%	-0.3%	-0.1%	-0.1%	-0.2%	-0.5%	-0.9%	-1.0%
Private Consumption - vol.	0.0%	0.0%	0.0%	0.1%	0.1%	0.1%	-0.5%	-0.9%	-1.2%	-0.5%	-1.0%	-1.3%	-0.5%	-0.9%	-1.3%
Supply to domestic - vol.	0.1%	0.1%	0.1%	0.1%	0.2%	0.2%	-0.2%	-0.3%	-0.6%	-0.2%	-0.3%	-0.5%	-0.2%	-0.2%	-0.5%
Intra-EU Trade - vol.	0.6%	0.5%	0.5%	0.3%	-0.4%	-0.5%	-5.0%	-14.5%	-14.6%	-4.6%	-14.1%	-14.2%	-4.7%	-14.3%	-14.5%

Transports

	Border Controls			Border controls and x-ineff.			Market segmentation			Trade *antimonde*			Full *antimonde*		
	1988	1991	1994	1988	1991	1994	1988	1991	1994	1988	1991	1994	1988	1991	1994
Domestic Production - vol.	0.3%	0.3%	0.3%	0.3%	0.3%	0.5%	-0.2%	-0.4%	-0.7%	0.0%	-0.2%	-0.4%	0.0%	-0.2%	-0.4%
Imports - vol.	0.1%	0.2%	0.2%	0.1%	0.2%	0.2%	-0.1%	-0.2%	-0.3%	0.0%	-0.1%	-0.2%	0.0%	-0.1%	-0.2%
Exports - vol.	-0.1%	-0.1%	-0.1%	-0.1%	-0.1%	-0.1%	0.7%	0.6%	0.5%	0.7%	0.6%	0.5%	0.7%	0.6%	0.5%
Absorption - vol.	0.1%	0.1%	0.1%	0.1%	0.1%	0.1%	-0.5%	-0.7%	-0.9%	-0.4%	-0.7%	-0.9%	-0.5%	-0.7%	-1.0%
Investment - vol.	0.1%	0.1%	0.1%	0.1%	0.1%	0.1%	-4.3%	-4.4%	-4.5%	-4.2%	-4.3%	-4.4%	-4.1%	-4.2%	-4.4%
Labour Demand - vol.	0.3%	0.3%	0.3%	0.3%	0.3%	0.3%	-0.2%	-0.3%	-0.5%	0.1%	0.0%	-0.2%	0.1%	0.0%	-0.1%
Private Consumption - vol.	0.1%	0.1%	0.1%	0.1%	0.1%	0.1%	-0.7%	-1.0%	-1.3%	-0.7%	-1.0%	-1.3%	-0.7%	-1.1%	-1.4%
Supply to domestic - vol.	0.3%	0.3%	0.3%	0.3%	0.3%	0.3%	-0.2%	-0.4%	-0.7%	0.0%	-0.2%	-0.4%	0.0%	-0.2%	-0.4%
Intra-EU Trade - vol.	1.0%	1.2%	1.2%	1.0%	1.2%	1.2%	-0.1%	-0.1%	-0.2%	1.0%	1.1%	0.9%	0.9%	1.0%	0.9%

Banks

	Border Controls			Border controls and x-ineff.			Market segmentation			Trade *antimonde*			Full *antimonde*		
	1988	1991	1994	1988	1991	1994	1988	1991	1994	1988	1991	1994	1988	1991	1994
Domestic Production - vol.	0.3%	0.5%	0.5%	0.3%	0.5%	0.5%	-0.2%	-0.5%	-0.8%	0.0%	-0.2%	-0.6%	-0.1%	-0.3%	-0.7%
Imports - vol.	1.1%	1.4%	1.4%	1.1%	1.3%	1.3%	-6.9%	-6.4%	-6.1%	-6.0%	-5.6%	-5.3%	-5.8%	-5.2%	-4.7%
Exports - vol.	-0.2%	-0.2%	-0.2%	-0.2%	-0.2%	-0.2%	1.2%	1.0%	0.8%	1.1%	0.9%	0.8%	1.1%	0.9%	0.7%
Absorption - vol.	0.2%	0.4%	0.4%	0.2%	0.4%	0.4%	-0.4%	-0.7%	-1.0%	-0.3%	-0.5%	-0.8%	-0.3%	-0.6%	-0.9%
Investment - vol.	0.2%	0.3%	0.3%	0.2%	0.3%	0.3%	-4.3%	-4.5%	-4.6%	-4.3%	-4.3%	-4.5%	-4.3%	-4.4%	-4.5%
Labour Demand - vol.	0.3%	0.5%	0.5%	0.1%	0.1%	0.2%	-0.1%	-0.1%	-0.3%	0.1%	0.1%	0.0%	-0.1%	-0.2%	-0.4%
Private Consumption - vol.	0.1%	0.1%	0.1%	0.1%	0.1%	0.1%	-0.7%	-1.1%	-1.4%	-0.7%	-1.1%	-1.4%	-0.8%	-1.2%	-1.5%
Supply to domestic - vol.	0.2%	0.4%	0.4%	0.2%	0.4%	0.4%	-0.1%	-0.1%	-0.4%	0.0%	0.1%	-0.2%	-0.1%	0.0%	-0.3%
Intra-EU Trade - vol.	0.6%	0.6%	0.6%	0.5%	0.3%	0.3%	-4.1%	-9.8%	-10.0%	-3.5%	-9.1%	-9.3%	-3.6%	-9.3%	-9.5%

Services

	Border Controls			Border controls and x-ineff.			Market segmentation			Trade *antimonde*			Full *antimonde*		
	1988	1991	1994	1988	1991	1994	1988	1991	1994	1988	1991	1994	1988	1991	1994
Domestic Production - vol.	0.2%	0.3%	0.3%	0.2%	0.3%	0.3%	-0.7%	-0.9%	-1.2%	-0.5%	-0.8%	-1.0%	-0.6%	-0.8%	-1.1%
Imports - vol.	1.7%	1.9%	1.9%	1.7%	1.9%	1.9%	-5.8%	-5.1%	-4.8%	-3.3%	-2.6%	-2.3%	-3.0%	-2.2%	-1.8%
Exports - vol.	-0.6%	-0.6%	-0.6%	-0.6%	-0.6%	-0.6%	1.5%	1.3%	1.1%	1.1%	0.9%	0.7%	1.1%	0.8%	0.6%
Absorption - vol.	0.0%	0.0%	0.0%	0.0%	0.0%	0.0%	-0.9%	-1.1%	-1.3%	-0.9%	-1.1%	-1.3%	-0.9%	-1.1%	-1.4%
Investment - vol.	0.1%	0.1%	0.1%	0.1%	0.1%	0.2%	-4.5%	-4.6%	-4.7%	-4.4%	-4.5%	-4.6%	-4.4%	-4.5%	-4.6%
Labour Demand - vol.	0.2%	0.3%	0.3%	0.3%	0.3%	0.3%	-0.7%	-0.7%	-0.8%	-0.5%	-0.5%	-0.6%	-0.5%	-0.5%	-0.6%
Private Consumption - vol.	0.1%	0.1%	0.1%	0.1%	0.1%	0.1%	-0.8%	-1.0%	-1.2%	-0.8%	-1.0%	-1.2%	-0.8%	-1.1%	-1.3%
Supply to domestic - vol.	0.0%	0.0%	0.0%	0.0%	0.1%	0.1%	-0.8%	-1.1%	-1.3%	-0.9%	-1.1%	-1.4%	-0.9%	-1.2%	-1.4%
Intra-EU Trade - vol.	2.3%	3.0%	3.0%	2.3%	3.0%	3.0%	-0.1%	0.4%	0.3%	2.0%	3.0%	2.9%	2.0%	3.0%	2.9%

Non market

	Border Controls			Border controls and x-ineff.			Market segmentation			Trade *antimonde*			Full *antimonde*		
	1988	1991	1994	1988	1991	1994	1988	1991	1994	1988	1991	1994	1988	1991	1994
Domestic Production - vol.	0.0%	0.0%	0.0%	0.0%	0.0%	0.0%	-0.1%	-0.1%	-0.1%	-0.1%	-0.1%	-0.1%	-0.1%	-0.1%	-0.1%
Imports - vol.	#VALUE!	#VALUE!	#VALUE!	#VALUE!	#VALUE!	#VALUE!	#VALUE!	#VALUE!	#VALUE!	#VALUE!	#VALUE!	#VALUE!	#VALUE!	#VALUE!	#VALUE!
Exports - vol.	#VALUE!	#VALUE!	#VALUE!	#VALUE!	#VALUE!	#VALUE!	#VALUE!	#VALUE!	#VALUE!	#VALUE!	#VALUE!	#VALUE!	#VALUE!	#VALUE!	#VALUE!
Absorption - vol.	0.0%	0.0%	0.0%	0.0%	0.0%	0.0%	-0.1%	-0.1%	-0.1%	-0.1%	-0.1%	-0.1%	-0.1%	-0.1%	-0.1%
Investment - vol.	0.0%	0.0%	0.0%	0.0%	0.0%	0.0%	-4.1%	-4.1%	-4.1%	-4.1%	-4.1%	-4.1%	-4.1%	-4.1%	-4.1%
Labour Demand - vol.	0.0%	0.0%	0.0%	0.0%	0.1%	0.0%	0.0%	0.0%	0.0%	0.0%	0.0%	0.0%	0.0%	0.1%	0.0%
Private Consumption - vol.	0.0%	0.0%	0.0%	0.0%	0.0%	0.0%	-0.6%	-0.8%	-1.0%	-0.6%	-0.8%	-1.1%	-0.6%	-0.9%	-1.1%
Supply to domestic - vol.	0.0%	0.0%	0.0%	0.0%	0.0%	0.0%	-0.1%	-0.1%	-0.1%	-0.1%	-0.1%	-0.1%	-0.1%	-0.1%	-0.1%
Intra-EU Trade - vol.	#DIV/0!	#DIV/0!	#DIV/0!	#DIV/0!	#DIV/0!	#DIV/0!	#DIV/0!	#DIV/0!	#DIV/0!	#DIV/0!	#DIV/0!	#DIV/0!	#DIV/0!	#DIV/0!	#DIV/0!

Table B4.8.
Decomposition of effects: sectoral results for France (prices)

% change from *monde*

Agriculture

	Border Controls			Border controls and x-ineff.			Market segmentation			Trade *antimonde*			Full *antimonde*		
	1988	1991	1994	1988	1991	1994	1988	1991	1994	1988	1991	1994	1988	1991	1994
Marginal Costs	-0.08%	-0.08%	-0.08%	-0.07%	-0.06%	-0.06%	0.68%	0.78%	0.99%	0.70%	0.83%	1.04%	0.71%	0.84%	1.06%
Cost of Labour	-0.05%	-0.08%	-0.09%	-0.06%	-0.10%	-0.11%	-0.33%	-0.74%	-1.12%	-0.38%	-0.83%	-1.22%	-0.47%	-0.96%	-1.40%
Deflator of Absorption	-0.26%	-0.27%	-0.27%	-0.26%	-0.26%	-0.26%	1.27%	1.24%	1.37%	1.21%	1.22%	1.35%	1.20%	1.21%	1.34%
Price of Exports-RW	-0.08%	-0.08%	-0.08%	-0.07%	-0.06%	-0.06%	0.68%	0.78%	0.99%	0.70%	0.83%	1.04%	0.71%	0.84%	1.06%

Energy

	Border Controls			Border controls and x-ineff.			Market segmentation			Trade *antimonde*			Full *antimonde*		
	1988	1991	1994	1988	1991	1994	1988	1991	1994	1988	1991	1994	1988	1991	1994
Marginal Costs	-0.41%	-0.44%	-0.45%	-0.41%	-0.44%	-0.45%	1.55%	1.36%	1.33%	1.38%	1.21%	1.18%	1.33%	1.15%	1.09%
Cost of Labour	-0.05%	-0.08%	-0.09%	-0.06%	-0.10%	-0.11%	-0.33%	-0.74%	-1.12%	-0.38%	-0.83%	-1.22%	-0.47%	-0.96%	-1.40%
Deflator of Absorption	-0.79%	-0.85%	-0.86%	-0.80%	-0.86%	-0.87%	2.93%	2.50%	2.35%	2.59%	2.19%	2.03%	2.50%	2.08%	1.87%
Price of Exports-RW	-0.41%	-0.44%	-0.45%	-0.41%	-0.44%	-0.45%	1.55%	1.36%	1.33%	1.38%	1.21%	1.18%	1.33%	1.15%	1.09%

Metal Industries

	Border Controls			Border controls and x-ineff.			Market segmentation			Trade *antimonde*			Full *antimonde*		
	1988	1991	1994	1988	1991	1994	1988	1991	1994	1988	1991	1994	1988	1991	1994
Marginal Costs	-0.27%	-0.26%	-0.26%	-0.27%	-0.26%	-0.26%	1.60%	1.42%	1.28%	1.58%	1.45%	1.31%	1.57%	1.44%	1.29%
Cost of Labour	-0.05%	-0.08%	-0.09%	-0.06%	-0.10%	-0.11%	-0.33%	-0.74%	-1.12%	-0.38%	-0.83%	-1.22%	-0.47%	-0.96%	-1.40%
Deflator of Absorption	-0.41%	-0.35%	-0.35%	-0.41%	-0.35%	-0.36%	2.94%	2.77%	2.54%	2.98%	2.92%	2.69%	2.95%	2.88%	2.63%
Price of Exports-RW	-0.27%	-0.26%	-0.26%	-0.27%	-0.26%	-0.26%	1.43%	1.14%	1.00%	1.41%	1.17%	1.03%	1.41%	1.17%	1.02%

Chemical

	Border Controls			Border controls and x-ineff.			Market segmentation			Trade *antimonde*			Full *antimonde*		
	1988	1991	1994	1988	1991	1994	1988	1991	1994	1988	1991	1994	1988	1991	1994
Marginal Costs	-0.16%	-0.16%	-0.16%	-0.16%	-0.16%	-0.16%	1.11%	0.91%	0.83%	1.12%	0.95%	0.87%	1.11%	0.95%	0.86%
Cost of Labour	-0.05%	-0.08%	-0.09%	-0.06%	-0.10%	-0.11%	-0.33%	-0.74%	-1.12%	-0.38%	-0.83%	-1.22%	-0.47%	-0.96%	-1.40%
Deflator of Absorption	-0.11%	-0.08%	-0.08%	-0.11%	-0.08%	-0.08%	2.18%	1.90%	1.74%	2.38%	2.17%	2.02%	2.34%	2.13%	1.95%
Price of Exports-RW	-0.17%	-0.18%	-0.18%	-0.17%	-0.18%	-0.18%	1.02%	0.79%	0.71%	1.03%	0.83%	0.75%	1.02%	0.82%	0.74%

Other Intensive Industries

	Border Controls			Border controls and x-ineff.			Market segmentation			Trade *antimonde*			Full *antimonde*		
	1988	1991	1994	1988	1991	1994	1988	1991	1994	1988	1991	1994	1988	1991	1994
Marginal Costs	-0.10%	-0.11%	-0.11%	-0.10%	-0.11%	-0.11%	0.61%	0.44%	0.34%	0.61%	0.46%	0.35%	0.61%	0.46%	0.35%
Cost of Labour	-0.05%	-0.08%	-0.09%	-0.06%	-0.10%	-0.11%	-0.33%	-0.74%	-1.12%	-0.38%	-0.83%	-1.22%	-0.47%	-0.96%	-1.40%
Deflator of Absorption	-0.09%	-0.07%	-0.07%	-0.09%	-0.07%	-0.07%	0.94%	0.72%	0.60%	0.99%	0.81%	0.69%	0.98%	0.80%	0.68%
Price of Exports-RW	-0.10%	-0.11%	-0.11%	-0.10%	-0.11%	-0.11%	0.61%	0.44%	0.33%	0.61%	0.46%	0.35%	0.61%	0.46%	0.35%

Electrical goods

	Border Controls			Border controls and x-ineff.			Market segmentation			Trade *antimonde*			Full *antimonde*		
	1988	1991	1994	1988	1991	1994	1988	1991	1994	1988	1991	1994	1988	1991	1994
Marginal Costs	-0.08%	-0.08%	-0.08%	-0.08%	-0.08%	-0.08%	0.50%	0.33%	0.23%	0.50%	0.35%	0.25%	0.50%	0.35%	0.25%
Cost of Labour	-0.05%	-0.08%	-0.09%	-0.06%	-0.10%	-0.11%	-0.33%	-0.74%	-1.12%	-0.38%	-0.83%	-1.22%	-0.47%	-0.96%	-1.40%
Deflator of Absorption	-0.15%	-0.12%	-0.12%	-0.16%	-0.12%	-0.13%	1.69%	1.45%	1.28%	1.78%	1.61%	1.43%	1.76%	1.57%	1.38%
Price of Exports-RW	-0.08%	-0.10%	-0.10%	-0.08%	-0.10%	-0.10%	0.44%	0.21%	0.11%	0.44%	0.23%	0.13%	0.44%	0.23%	0.13%

Transport equipment

	Border Controls			Border controls and x-ineff.			Market segmentation			Trade *antimonde*			Full *antimonde*		
	1988	1991	1994	1988	1991	1994	1988	1991	1994	1988	1991	1994	1988	1991	1994
Marginal Costs	-0.05%	-0.03%	-0.03%	-0.05%	-0.03%	-0.03%	0.85%	0.70%	0.54%	0.91%	0.80%	0.64%	0.92%	0.82%	0.66%
Cost of Labour	-0.05%	-0.08%	-0.09%	-0.06%	-0.10%	-0.11%	-0.33%	-0.74%	-1.12%	-0.38%	-0.83%	-1.22%	-0.47%	-0.96%	-1.40%
Deflator of Absorption	0.13%	0.27%	0.27%	0.13%	0.26%	0.26%	2.01%	2.15%	1.98%	2.30%	2.58%	2.41%	2.31%	2.59%	2.41%
Price of Exports-RW	-0.07%	-0.07%	-0.07%	-0.07%	-0.07%	-0.07%	0.64%	0.31%	0.15%	0.70%	0.39%	0.23%	0.71%	0.41%	0.25%

Other Equipment

	Border Controls			Border controls and x-ineff.			Market segmentation			Trade *antimonde*			Full *antimonde*		
	1988	1991	1994	1988	1991	1994	1988	1991	1994	1988	1991	1994	1988	1991	1994
Marginal Costs	-0.08%	-0.08%	-0.08%	-0.08%	-0.08%	-0.08%	0.55%	0.39%	0.31%	0.56%	0.43%	0.34%	0.56%	0.43%	0.34%
Cost of Labour	-0.05%	-0.08%	-0.09%	-0.06%	-0.10%	-0.11%	-0.33%	-0.74%	-1.12%	-0.38%	-0.83%	-1.22%	-0.47%	-0.96%	-1.40%
Deflator of Absorption	-0.20%	-0.15%	-0.15%	-0.21%	-0.16%	-0.16%	1.96%	1.63%	1.45%	2.04%	1.81%	1.62%	2.01%	1.77%	1.55%
Price of Exports-RW	-0.08%	-0.09%	-0.09%	-0.08%	-0.09%	-0.09%	0.51%	0.34%	0.26%	0.52%	0.37%	0.29%	0.52%	0.37%	0.29%

Consumer goods

	Border Controls			Border controls and x-ineff.			Market segmentation			Trade *antimonde*			Full *antimonde*		
	1988	1991	1994	1988	1991	1994	1988	1991	1994	1988	1991	1994	1988	1991	1994
Marginal Costs	-0.13%	-0.13%	-0.13%	-0.12%	-0.12%	-0.12%	0.74%	0.63%	0.63%	0.74%	0.65%	0.65%	0.75%	0.67%	0.67%
Cost of Labour	-0.05%	-0.08%	-0.09%	-0.06%	-0.10%	-0.11%	-0.33%	-0.74%	-1.12%	-0.38%	-0.83%	-1.22%	-0.47%	-0.96%	-1.40%
Deflator of Absorption	-0.17%	-0.16%	-0.16%	-0.17%	-0.15%	-0.15%	1.34%	1.12%	1.05%	1.38%	1.21%	1.15%	1.38%	1.20%	1.13%
Price of Exports-RW	-0.13%	-0.13%	-0.13%	-0.12%	-0.12%	-0.12%	0.74%	0.63%	0.63%	0.74%	0.65%	0.65%	0.75%	0.67%	0.67%

Construction

	Border Controls			Border controls and x-ineff.			Market segmentation			Trade *antimonde*			Full *antimonde*		
	1988	1991	1994	1988	1991	1994	1988	1991	1994	1988	1991	1994	1988	1991	1994
Marginal Costs	-0.06%	-0.07%	-0.07%	-0.06%	-0.07%	-0.07%	0.38%	0.24%	0.18%	0.38%	0.26%	0.20%	0.38%	0.26%	0.20%
Cost of Labour	-0.05%	-0.08%	-0.09%	-0.06%	-0.10%	-0.11%	-0.33%	-0.74%	-1.12%	-0.38%	-0.83%	-1.22%	-0.47%	-0.96%	-1.40%
Deflator of Absorption	-0.06%	-0.07%	-0.07%	-0.06%	-0.07%	-0.07%	0.38%	0.24%	0.18%	0.38%	0.26%	0.20%	0.38%	0.26%	0.20%
Price of Exports-RW	-0.06%	-0.07%	-0.07%	-0.06%	-0.07%	-0.07%	0.38%	0.24%	0.18%	0.38%	0.26%	0.20%	0.38%	0.26%	0.20%

Telecommunications

	Border Controls			Border controls and x-ineff.			Market segmentation			Trade antimonde			Full antimonde		
	1988	1991	1994	1988	1991	1994	1988	1991	1994	1988	1991	1994	1988	1991	1994
Marginal Costs	0.04%	0.05%	0.06%	0.05%	0.06%	0.07%	-0.06%	0.04%	0.20%	-0.05%	0.05%	0.22%	-0.04%	0.07%	0.23%
Cost of Labour	-0.05%	-0.08%	-0.09%	-0.06%	-0.10%	-0.11%	-0.33%	-0.74%	-1.12%	-0.38%	-0.83%	-1.22%	-0.47%	-0.96%	-1.40%
Deflator of Absorption	0.02%	0.02%	0.03%	-0.16%	-0.35%	-0.34%	0.05%	0.14%	0.27%	0.05%	0.14%	0.28%	-0.12%	-0.20%	-0.07%
Price of Exports-RW	0.04%	0.04%	0.05%	-0.01%	-0.06%	-0.04%	-0.07%	0.01%	0.16%	-0.06%	0.02%	0.18%	-0.10%	-0.07%	0.09%

Transports

	Border Controls			Border controls and x-ineff.			Market segmentation			Trade antimonde			Full antimonde		
	1988	1991	1994	1988	1991	1994	1988	1991	1994	1988	1991	1994	1988	1991	1994
Marginal Costs	-0.11%	-0.12%	-0.13%	-0.11%	-0.12%	-0.13%	0.34%	0.23%	0.20%	0.30%	0.19%	0.16%	0.28%	0.16%	0.12%
Cost of Labour	-0.05%	-0.08%	-0.09%	-0.06%	-0.10%	-0.11%	-0.33%	-0.74%	-1.12%	-0.38%	-0.83%	-1.22%	-0.47%	-0.96%	-1.40%
Deflator of Absorption	-0.11%	-0.13%	-0.13%	-0.11%	-0.13%	-0.13%	0.43%	0.29%	0.26%	0.39%	0.25%	0.21%	0.37%	0.22%	0.17%
Price of Exports-RW	-0.11%	-0.12%	-0.13%	-0.11%	-0.12%	-0.13%	0.34%	0.23%	0.20%	0.30%	0.19%	0.16%	0.28%	0.16%	0.12%

Banks

	Border Controls			Border controls and x-ineff.			Market segmentation			Trade antimonde			Full antimonde		
	1988	1991	1994	1988	1991	1994	1988	1991	1994	1988	1991	1994	1988	1991	1994
Marginal Costs	0.02%	0.02%	0.02%	0.03%	0.03%	0.02%	-0.07%	-0.01%	0.11%	-0.07%	0.00%	0.12%	-0.06%	0.00%	0.11%
Cost of Labour	-0.05%	-0.08%	-0.09%	-0.06%	-0.10%	-0.11%	-0.33%	-0.74%	-1.12%	-0.38%	-0.83%	-1.22%	-0.47%	-0.96%	-1.40%
Deflator of Absorption	0.01%	-0.01%	-0.01%	-0.05%	-0.11%	-0.11%	0.04%	0.11%	0.23%	0.04%	0.11%	0.23%	-0.01%	0.01%	0.12%
Price of Exports-RW	0.02%	0.01%	0.01%	0.01%	0.00%	-0.01%	-0.08%	-0.03%	0.09%	-0.08%	-0.03%	0.09%	-0.09%	-0.05%	0.06%

Services

	Border Controls			Border controls and x-ineff.			Market segmentation			Trade antimonde			Full antimonde		
	1988	1991	1994	1988	1991	1994	1988	1991	1994	1988	1991	1994	1988	1991	1994
Marginal Costs	-0.01%	-0.02%	-0.02%	-0.01%	-0.01%	-0.02%	0.06%	0.11%	0.22%	0.06%	0.11%	0.23%	0.05%	0.10%	0.21%
Cost of Labour	-0.05%	-0.08%	-0.09%	-0.06%	-0.10%	-0.11%	-0.33%	-0.74%	-1.12%	-0.38%	-0.83%	-1.22%	-0.47%	-0.96%	-1.40%
Deflator of Absorption	-0.02%	-0.03%	-0.03%	-0.01%	-0.02%	-0.02%	0.08%	0.12%	0.23%	0.08%	0.12%	0.24%	0.07%	0.11%	0.22%
Price of Exports-RW	-0.01%	-0.02%	-0.02%	-0.01%	-0.01%	-0.02%	0.06%	0.11%	0.22%	0.06%	0.11%	0.23%	0.05%	0.10%	0.21%

Non market

	Border Controls			Border controls and x-ineff.			Market segmentation			Trade antimonde			Full antimonde		
	1988	1991	1994	1988	1991	1994	1988	1991	1994	1988	1991	1994	1988	1991	1994
Marginal Costs	-0.06%	-0.07%	-0.08%	-0.06%	-0.08%	-0.08%	0.03%	-0.24%	-0.47%	0.01%	-0.28%	-0.51%	-0.02%	-0.31%	-0.56%
Cost of Labour	-0.05%	-0.08%	-0.09%	-0.06%	-0.10%	-0.11%	-0.33%	-0.74%	-1.12%	-0.38%	-0.83%	-1.22%	-0.47%	-0.96%	-1.40%
Deflator of Absorption	-0.06%	-0.07%	-0.08%	-0.06%	-0.08%	-0.08%	0.03%	-0.24%	-0.47%	0.01%	-0.28%	-0.51%	-0.02%	-0.31%	-0.56%
Price of Exports-RW	-0.06%	-0.07%	-0.08%	-0.06%	-0.08%	-0.08%	0.03%	-0.24%	-0.47%	0.01%	-0.28%	-0.51%	-0.02%	-0.31%	-0.56%

Table B5.1.

The full *antimonde* scenario: macroeconomic aggregates for Germany

Macroeconomic Aggregates (vol.) (% change from *monde*)	Constraint Case			Flexible Case			Efficiency Case		
	1988	1991	1994	1988	1991	1994	1988	1991	1994
GDP fact. pr.	-0.49%	-0.81%	-1.06%	-0.38%	-0.76%	-1.11%	-0.41%	-0.89%	-1.33%
Priv. Consumption	-0.49%	-0.63%	-0.84%	-1.14%	-1.33%	-1.58%	-1.15%	-1.37%	-1.66%
Absorption	-0.29%	-0.41%	-0.56%	-1.10%	-1.20%	-1.43%	-1.11%	-1.24%	-1.50%
Total Investment	-1.41%	-1.67%	-2.16%	-4.21%	-4.35%	-4.48%	-4.22%	-4.36%	-4.49%
Total Exports to RW	-1.24%	-2.03%	-2.17%	1.65%	1.32%	1.11%	1.62%	1.21%	0.92%
Total Imports from RW	-1.80%	-2.11%	-2.15%	-3.72%	-3.05%	-2.73%	-3.67%	-2.87%	-2.40%
Total Intra-EU Trade	-0.44%	-0.09%	-0.11%	-1.56%	-5.06%	-5.24%	-1.58%	-5.12%	-5.35%
Employment (diff. from *monde*, 10³ persons)	-28	-43	-64	-49	-86	-121	-49	-88	-124
Disposable Income (deflated)	-0.51%	-0.65%	-0.87%	-1.17%	-1.37%	-1.63%	-1.18%	-1.41%	-1.71%

Macroeconomic Ratios (abs. diff. from *monde*)	Constraint Case			Flexible Case			Efficiency Case		
	1988	1991	1994	1988	1991	1994	1988	1991	1994
Current Account as % of GDP	0.00%	0.00%	0.00%	-1.31%	-1.27%	-1.22%	-1.30%	-1.23%	-1.14%
Public Deficit as % of GDP	0.00%	-0.03%	-0.07%	-0.24%	-0.33%	-0.46%	-0.25%	-0.36%	-0.51%
Labour Productivity	-0.38%	-0.64%	-0.81%	-0.19%	-0.43%	-0.64%	-0.22%	-0.54%	-0.84%
Investment/GDP	-0.19%	-0.18%	-0.23%	-1.81%	-1.79%	-1.78%	-1.81%	-1.77%	-1.73%
Priv.Cons./GDP	0.00%	0.10%	0.12%	-0.43%	-0.32%	-0.27%	-0.41%	-0.27%	-0.19%

Deflators (% change from *monde*)	Constraint Case			Flexible Case			Efficiency Case		
	1988	1991	1994	1988	1991	1994	1988	1991	1994
Consumer Price Index	0.66%	1.18%	1.30%	0.95%	0.84%	0.83%	0.93%	0.79%	0.74%
Real Wage Rate	-0.62%	-0.99%	-1.33%	-0.64%	-1.16%	-1.65%	-0.67%	-1.29%	-1.87%
Marginal Costs	0.58%	1.11%	1.22%	0.52%	0.39%	0.36%	0.51%	0.36%	0.31%
Producer Prices	0.64%	1.19%	1.30%	0.58%	0.50%	0.46%	0.57%	0.47%	0.41%
Average change in mark-ups (abs. diff.)	0.39%	0.52%	0.53%	0.50%	0.86%	0.90%	0.50%	0.86%	0.90%
Shadow Price of Capital	0.33%	1.03%	1.24%	0.09%	0.56%	1.12%	0.07%	0.47%	0.97%
Terms-of-Trade RW	-0.12%	0.36%	0.47%	-5.04%	-4.03%	-3.37%	-4.96%	-3.69%	-2.78%

| Implicit change in real exchange rate | 0.53% | 1.17% | 1.27% | -4.06% | -2.82% | -2.05% | -3.96% | -2.45% | -1.40% |

Trade Regime	Segmentation			Segmentation			Segmentation		

Table B5.2.
The full *antimonde* scenario: effects on IC sector for Germany

% change from *monde*

Metal Industries	Constraint Case			Flexible Case			Efficiency Case		
	1988	1991	1994	1988	1991	1994	1988	1991	1994
Production per firm	-3.39%	-4.42%	-4.55%	-2.32%	-3.90%	-4.05%	-2.35%	-4.01%	-4.23%
Real Marginal Costs	1.04%	1.50%	1.68%	-1.57%	-0.09%	0.98%	-1.45%	0.37%	1.79%
Real Producer Prices	1.25%	1.77%	1.96%	-1.42%	0.15%	1.23%	-1.31%	0.62%	2.05%
Mark-ups domestic (abs. diff.)	0.21%	0.23%	0.23%	0.16%	0.20%	0.21%	0.16%	0.20%	0.22%
Fixed Costs per firm	0.88%	1.24%	1.33%	-2.19%	-1.30%	-0.78%	-2.12%	-1.01%	-0.28%
Number of Firms	3.05%	3.75%	3.67%	5.57%	9.79%	9.60%	5.54%	9.65%	9.36%
Sigma of Love of Variety	0.00%	0.00%	0.00%	0.00%	0.00%	0.00%	0.00%	0.00%	0.00%

Chemical	Constraint Case			Flexible Case			Efficiency Case		
	1988	1991	1994	1988	1991	1994	1988	1991	1994
Production per firm	-3.53%	-4.96%	-5.08%	-2.70%	-5.14%	-5.34%	-2.73%	-5.24%	-5.50%
Real Marginal Costs	0.70%	1.18%	1.30%	-2.34%	-0.78%	0.37%	-2.23%	-0.32%	1.18%
Real Producer Prices	0.85%	1.39%	1.51%	-2.23%	-0.56%	0.59%	-2.12%	-0.10%	1.41%
Mark-ups domestic (abs. diff.)	0.25%	0.27%	0.28%	0.16%	0.25%	0.26%	0.16%	0.26%	0.27%
Fixed Costs per firm	0.56%	0.93%	0.95%	-2.94%	-1.99%	-1.43%	-2.87%	-1.71%	-0.94%
Number of Firms	2.95%	3.78%	3.74%	7.13%	9.65%	9.50%	7.11%	9.55%	9.32%
Sigma of Love of Variety	0.00%	0.00%	0.00%	0.00%	0.00%	0.00%	0.00%	0.00%	0.00%

Other Intensive Industries	Constraint Case			Flexible Case			Efficiency Case		
	1988	1991	1994	1988	1991	1994	1988	1991	1994
Production per firm	-0.99%	-1.52%	-1.65%	-1.68%	-2.69%	-2.88%	-1.69%	-2.75%	-2.98%
Real Marginal Costs	0.61%	1.11%	1.20%	-2.81%	-1.22%	-0.06%	-2.69%	-0.75%	0.77%
Real Producer Prices	0.62%	1.13%	1.23%	-2.77%	-1.17%	-0.01%	-2.66%	-0.70%	0.82%
Mark-ups domestic (abs. diff.)	0.02%	0.02%	0.02%	0.03%	0.04%	0.04%	0.03%	0.04%	0.04%
Fixed Costs per firm	0.48%	0.86%	0.86%	-3.43%	-2.50%	-1.96%	-3.36%	-2.21%	-1.45%
Number of Firms	0.94%	1.18%	1.10%	0.62%	0.83%	0.69%	0.61%	0.81%	0.66%
Sigma of Love of Variety	0.00%	0.00%	0.00%	0.00%	0.00%	0.00%	0.00%	0.00%	0.00%

Electrical goods	Constraint Case			Flexible Case			Efficiency Case		
	1988	1991	1994	1988	1991	1994	1988	1991	1994
Production per firm	-1.66%	-2.72%	-2.84%	-2.56%	-4.57%	-4.78%	-2.59%	-4.67%	-4.94%
Real Marginal Costs	0.51%	0.97%	1.02%	-2.95%	-1.40%	-0.29%	-2.84%	-0.94%	0.52%
Real Producer Prices	0.56%	1.04%	1.09%	-2.88%	-1.28%	-0.17%	-2.77%	-0.82%	0.64%
Mark-ups domestic (abs. diff.)	0.10%	0.10%	0.10%	0.10%	0.14%	0.15%	0.10%	0.14%	0.15%
Fixed Costs per firm	0.40%	0.75%	0.70%	-3.60%	-2.71%	-2.24%	-3.53%	-2.43%	-1.75%
Number of Firms	1.64%	2.49%	2.40%	4.35%	7.87%	7.66%	4.33%	7.78%	7.52%
Sigma of Love of Variety	0.00%	0.00%	0.00%	0.00%	0.00%	0.00%	0.00%	0.00%	0.00%

Transport equipment	Constraint Case			Flexible Case			Efficiency Case		
	1988	1991	1994	1988	1991	1994	1988	1991	1994
Production per firm	-4.63%	-6.91%	-7.10%	-5.41%	-9.21%	-9.40%	-5.44%	-9.31%	-9.55%
Real Marginal Costs	0.72%	1.21%	1.31%	-2.63%	-1.00%	0.14%	-2.52%	-0.53%	0.97%
Real Producer Prices	1.19%	1.91%	2.03%	-2.11%	-0.11%	1.04%	-1.99%	0.37%	1.89%
Mark-ups domestic (abs. diff.)	0.52%	0.59%	0.64%	0.88%	1.23%	1.23%	0.88%	1.23%	1.24%
Fixed Costs per firm	0.60%	0.98%	0.98%	-3.26%	-2.25%	-1.72%	-3.18%	-1.95%	-1.20%
Number of Firms	5.60%	6.55%	6.25%	5.60%	11.12%	10.87%	5.59%	11.07%	10.79%
Sigma of Love of Variety	0.00%	0.00%	0.00%	0.00%	0.00%	0.00%	0.00%	0.00%	0.00%

Other Equipment	Constraint Case			Flexible Case			Efficiency Case		
	1988	1991	1994	1988	1991	1994	1988	1991	1994
Production per firm	-3.09%	-4.20%	-4.30%	-2.87%	-4.30%	-4.48%	-2.89%	-4.39%	-4.64%
Real Marginal Costs	0.57%	1.03%	1.08%	-2.85%	-1.32%	-0.23%	-2.73%	-0.85%	-0.59%
Real Producer Prices	0.63%	1.10%	1.16%	-2.80%	-1.25%	-0.15%	-2.68%	-0.78%	-0.67%
Mark-ups domestic (abs. diff.)	0.07%	0.08%	0.08%	0.09%	0.12%	0.12%	0.09%	0.12%	0.12%
Fixed Costs per firm	0.45%	0.81%	0.77%	-3.51%	-2.60%	-2.10%	-3.43%	-2.31%	-1.60%
Number of Firms	3.01%	3.82%	3.70%	2.43%	3.66%	3.48%	2.41%	3.57%	3.33%
Sigma of Love of Variety	0.00%	0.00%	0.00%	0.00%	0.00%	0.00%	0.00%	0.00%	0.00%

Telecommunications	Constraint Case			Flexible Case			Efficiency Case		
	1988	1991	1994	1988	1991	1994	1988	1991	1994
Production per firm	-1.25%	-1.05%	-1.22%	-2.40%	-4.95%	-5.35%	-2.42%	-5.01%	-5.47%
Real Marginal Costs	0.87%	1.73%	1.88%	-3.45%	-1.63%	-0.23%	-3.33%	-1.14%	0.62%
Real Producer Prices	1.28%	2.30%	2.42%	-3.35%	-1.42%	-0.04%	-3.23%	-0.94%	-0.80%
Mark-ups domestic (abs. diff.)	0.36%	0.50%	0.46%	-0.03%	-0.24%	-0.27%	-0.03%	-0.25%	-0.28%
Fixed Costs per firm	1.69%	3.60%	3.42%	-5.88%	-6.57%	-6.22%	-5.82%	-6.32%	-5.77%
Number of Firms	0.53%	0.33%	0.44%	2.32%	4.36%	4.46%	2.33%	4.38%	4.51%
Sigma of Love of Variety	0.00%	0.00%	0.00%	0.00%	0.00%	0.00%	0.00%	0.00%	0.00%

Banks	Constraint Case			Flexible Case			Efficiency Case		
	1988	1991	1994	1988	1991	1994	1988	1991	1994
Production per firm	-0.46%	-0.24%	-0.37%	-0.99%	-1.81%	-2.18%	-1.01%	-1.87%	-2.28%
Real Marginal Costs	0.76%	1.54%	1.66%	-3.40%	-1.57%	-0.19%	-3.28%	-1.09%	0.66%
Real Producer Prices	0.84%	1.62%	1.73%	-3.41%	-1.62%	-0.23%	3.29%	-1.14%	0.61%
Mark-ups domestic (abs. diff.)	0.09%	0.08%	0.08%	0.00%	-0.06%	-0.06%	0.00%	-0.06%	-0.06%
Fixed Costs per firm	1.06%	2.02%	1.95%	-5.02%	-4.90%	-4.39%	-4.95%	-4.62%	-3.89%
Number of Firms	-0.47%	-0.39%	-0.32%	0.34%	0.88%	0.89%	0.35%	0.90%	0.91%
Sigma of Love of Variety	0.00%	0.00%	0.00%	0.00%	0.00%	0.00%	0.00%	0.00%	0.00%

Table B5.3.
The full *antimonde* scenario: sectoral results for Germany (volumes)

% change from *monde*

Agriculture	Constraint Case			Flexible Case			Efficiency Case		
	1988	1991	1994	1988	1991	1994	1988	1991	1994
Domestic Production - vol.	0.0%	-0.2%	-0.4%	2.5%	0.8%	0.2%	2.5%	0.6%	-0.2%
Imports - vol.	-1.1%	-0.5%	-0.4%	-3.1%	-2.4%	-1.9%	-3.0%	-2.2%	-1.5%
Exports - vol.	-3.7%	-4.8%	-5.3%	1.4%	1.0%	0.8%	1.4%	0.9%	0.6%
Absorption - vol.	-0.1%	0.0%	-0.1%	0.6%	-0.2%	-0.5%	0.6%	-0.3%	-0.7%
Investment - vol.	4.3%	3.8%	2.9%	-3.0%	-3.7%	-4.0%	-3.0%	-3.8%	-4.1%
Labour Demand - vol.	0.1%	0.0%	-0.1%	2.8%	1.3%	0.9%	2.7%	1.1%	0.7%
Private Consumption - vol.	-1.2%	-0.9%	-0.9%	-0.9%	-1.3%	-1.6%	-0.9%	-1.4%	-1.7%
Supply to domestic - vol.	0.3%	0.2%	0.0%	2.9%	1.5%	0.9%	2.8%	1.3%	0.5%
Intra-EU Trade - vol	0.0%	0.0%	0.0%	0.0%	-1.5%	-1.9%	0.0%	-1.6%	-2.1%

Energy	Constraint Case			Flexible Case			Efficiency Case		
	1988	1991	1994	1988	1991	1994	1988	1991	1994
Domestic Production - vol.	-0.1%	-0.3%	-0.4%	1.2%	0.8%	0.5%	1.2%	0.7%	0.3%
Imports - vol.	0.0%	0.3%	0.3%	-1.3%	-1.0%	-0.9%	-1.3%	-0.9%	-0.8%
Exports - vol.	-2.4%	-3.1%	-3.4%	0.6%	0.5%	0.4%	0.6%	0.4%	0.3%
Absorption - vol.	0.0%	0.0%	0.0%	0.4%	0.2%	-0.1%	0.4%	0.1%	-0.2%
Investment - vol.	-4.5%	-4.7%	-5.0%	-3.5%	-3.7%	-3.8%	-3.5%	-3.7%	-3.9%
Labour Demand - vol.	-0.1%	-0.2%	-0.2%	1.4%	1.1%	0.9%	1.4%	1.0%	0.7%
Private Consumption - vol.	0.1%	0.4%	0.3%	-0.7%	-1.0%	-1.2%	-0.7%	-1.0%	-1.3%
Supply to domestic - vol.	0.0%	-0.1%	-0.2%	1.2%	0.8%	0.5%	1.1%	0.7%	0.2%
Intra-EU Trade - vol	0.0%	0.0%	0.0%	0.7%	0.3%	0.1%	0.7%	0.2%	-0.1%

Metal Industries	Constraint Case			Flexible Case			Efficiency Case		
	1988	1991	1994	1988	1991	1994	1988	1991	1994
Domestic Production - vol.	-0.4%	-0.8%	-1.0%	3.1%	5.5%	5.2%	3.1%	5.2%	4.7%
Imports - vol.	-0.9%	-1.2%	-1.2%	-2.5%	-1.3%	-1.1%	-2.5%	-1.2%	-0.8%
Exports - vol.	-2.3%	-3.1%	-3.3%	1.2%	0.9%	0.7%	1.1%	0.8%	0.5%
Absorption - vol.	0.0%	-0.3%	-0.4%	1.5%	3.0%	2.7%	1.5%	2.8%	2.5%
Investment - vol.	-2.5%	-3.0%	-3.5%	-2.5%	-1.4%	-1.6%	-2.5%	-1.5%	-1.8%
Labour Demand - vol.	-0.1%	-0.4%	-0.6%	3.6%	6.1%	5.9%	3.5%	5.9%	5.5%
Private Consumption - vol.	-1.6%	-1.2%	-1.3%	-1.3%	-1.8%	-2.2%	-1.3%	-1.9%	-2.3%
Supply to domestic - vol.	0.3%	0.1%	-0.1%	4.3%	9.4%	9.0%	4.2%	9.1%	8.5%
Intra-EU Trade - vol	0.0%	0.0%	0.0%	-2.1%	-7.8%	-7.9%	-2.1%	-7.9%	-8.0%

Chemical	Constraint Case			Flexible Case			Efficiency Case		
	1988	1991	1994	1988	1991	1994	1988	1991	1994
Domestic Production - vol.	-0.7%	-1.4%	-1.5%	4.2%	4.0%	3.7%	4.2%	3.8%	3.3%
Imports - vol.	-0.1%	0.6%	0.7%	-3.7%	-3.0%	-2.6%	-3.6%	-2.8%	-2.2%
Exports - vol.	-1.2%	-1.9%	-2.1%	1.8%	1.4%	1.2%	1.7%	1.3%	1.0%
Absorption - vol.	-0.2%	-0.5%	-0.5%	1.6%	1.5%	1.2%	1.6%	1.4%	1.1%
Investment - vol.	-2.7%	-3.5%	-4.0%	-2.1%	-2.3%	-2.4%	-2.2%	-2.3%	-2.5%
Labour Demand - vol.	-0.4%	-1.0%	-1.2%	4.6%	4.5%	4.3%	4.5%	4.4%	4.0%
Private Consumption - vol.	-0.7%	-0.7%	-0.9%	-1.1%	-1.3%	-1.5%	-1.1%	-1.3%	-1.6%
Supply to domestic - vol.	-0.3%	-0.9%	-1.1%	5.3%	7.7%	7.3%	5.2%	7.4%	6.9%
Intra-EU Trade - vol	0.0%	0.0%	0.0%	-0.5%	-4.5%	-4.6%	-0.5%	-4.5%	-4.8%

Other Intensive Industries	Constraint Case			Flexible Case			Efficiency Case		
	1988	1991	1994	1988	1991	1994	1988	1991	1994
Domestic Production - vol.	-0.1%	-0.4%	-0.6%	-1.1%	-1.9%	-2.2%	-1.1%	-2.0%	-2.3%
Imports - vol.	-3.1%	-3.4%	-3.4%	-5.8%	-4.9%	-4.5%	-5.7%	-4.6%	-4.0%
Exports - vol.	-1.8%	-2.5%	-2.7%	1.7%	1.3%	1.1%	1.6%	1.2%	0.9%
Absorption - vol.	-0.2%	-0.4%	-0.6%	-2.1%	-2.2%	-2.5%	-2.1%	-2.3%	-2.5%
Investment - vol.	-1.9%	-2.3%	-2.9%	-4.6%	-5.0%	-5.2%	-4.6%	-5.0%	-5.2%
Labour Demand - vol.	0.0%	-0.2%	-0.4%	-0.9%	-1.6%	-1.8%	-0.9%	-1.6%	-1.8%
Private Consumption - vol.	-0.7%	-0.8%	-1.1%	-1.4%	-1.6%	-1.8%	-1.5%	-1.6%	-1.9%
Supply to domestic - vol.	0.3%	0.1%	-0.1%	-0.9%	-0.6%	-1.0%	-0.9%	-0.7%	-1.1%
Intra-EU Trade - vol	0.0%	0.0%	0.0%	-2.9%	-6.6%	-6.7%	-2.9%	-6.6%	-6.8%

Electrical goods	Constraint Case			Flexible Case			Efficiency Case		
	1988	1991	1994	1988	1991	1994	1988	1991	1994
Domestic Production - vol.	0.0%	-0.3%	-0.5%	1.7%	2.9%	2.5%	1.6%	2.8%	2.2%
Imports - vol.	-4.2%	-5.0%	-5.2%	-6.3%	-5.6%	-5.2%	-6.3%	-5.3%	-4.8%
Exports - vol.	-1.1%	-1.8%	-1.9%	2.0%	1.7%	1.4%	2.0%	1.5%	1.2%
Absorption - vol.	-0.8%	-1.0%	-1.3%	-3.0%	-2.9%	-3.1%	-3.0%	-2.9%	-3.2%
Investment - vol.	2.0%	1.5%	0.7%	-3.4%	-2.9%	-3.1%	-3.5%	-3.0%	-3.2%
Labour Demand - vol.	0.2%	0.0%	-0.1%	2.1%	3.5%	3.3%	2.0%	3.4%	3.1%
Private Consumption - vol.	-0.4%	-0.7%	-1.0%	-1.5%	-1.5%	-1.8%	-1.5%	-1.6%	-1.9%
Supply to domestic - vol.	0.7%	0.8%	0.5%	1.7%	5.9%	5.4%	1.7%	5.7%	5.1%
Intra-EU Trade - vol	0.0%	0.0%	0.0%	-2.3%	-7.2%	-7.3%	-2.3%	-7.2%	-7.5%

Transport equipment	Constraint Case			Flexible Case			Efficiency Case		
	1988	1991	1994	1988	1991	1994	1988	1991	1994
Domestic Production - vol.	0.7%	-0.8%	-1.3%	-0.1%	0.9%	0.5%	-0.2%	0.7%	0.2%
Imports - vol.	-2.7%	-7.4%	-8.1%	-5.7%	-4.7%	-4.3%	-5.7%	-4.5%	-4.0%
Exports - vol.	-1.9%	-3.1%	-3.3%	1.9%	1.6%	1.4%	1.9%	1.5%	1.1%
Absorption - vol.	2.4%	-0.2%	-1.0%	-3.3%	-2.4%	-2.5%	-3.3%	-2.5%	-2.6%
Investment - vol.	3.0%	1.1%	0.0%	-4.1%	-3.7%	-3.9%	-4.1%	-3.7%	-4.0%
Labour Demand - vol.	1.4%	0.2%	-0.2%	0.8%	2.4%	2.1%	0.8%	2.3%	2.0%
Private Consumption - vol.	9.9%	1.4%	-1.2%	-4.0%	-2.2%	-1.9%	-4.1%	-2.4%	-2.1%
Supply to domestic - vol.	4.2%	2.5%	1.5%	0.5%	7.7%	7.3%	0.5%	7.6%	7.1%
Intra-EU Trade - vol	0.0%	0.0%	0.0%	-3.6%	-8.6%	-8.6%	-3.7%	-8.6%	-8.7%

Other Equipment	Constraint Case			Flexible Case			Efficiency Case		
	1988	1991	1994	1988	1991	1994	1988	1991	1994
Domestic Production - vol.	-0.2%	-0.5%	-0.8%	-0.5%	-0.8%	-1.2%	-0.5%	-1.0%	-1.5%
Imports - vol.	-2.0%	-2.5%	-2.8%	-5.1%	-4.6%	-4.4%	-5.1%	-4.4%	-4.1%
Exports - vol.	-1.2%	-1.7%	-1.8%	1.8%	1.4%	1.2%	1.8%	1.3%	1.0%
Absorption - vol.	0.0%	-0.3%	-0.6%	-4.1%	-4.3%	-4.6%	-4.1%	-4.3%	-4.7%
Investment - vol.	6.3%	5.4%	4.3%	-4.4%	-4.6%	-4.9%	-4.5%	-4.7%	-5.0%
Labour Demand - vol.	0.0%	-0.2%	-0.4%	-0.1%	-0.3%	-0.5%	-0.1%	-0.4%	-0.7%
Private Consumption - vol.	-1.4%	-1.0%	-1.1%	-1.1%	-1.5%	-1.9%	-1.1%	-1.6%	-2.0%
Supply to domestic - vol.	0.9%	0.7%	0.4%	-1.5%	-0.1%	-0.5%	-1.6%	-0.2%	-0.7%
Intra-EU Trade - vol	0.0%	0.0%	0.0%	-2.6%	-5.2%	-5.4%	-2.6%	-5.3%	-5.5%

Consumer goods	Constraint Case			Flexible Case			Efficiency Case		
	1988	1991	1994	1988	1991	1994	1988	1991	1994
Domestic Production - vol.	0.1%	0.0%	-0.2%	1.2%	0.3%	-0.1%	1.2%	0.1%	-0.4%
Imports - vol.	-3.4%	-3.7%	-3.6%	-4.4%	-3.7%	-3.2%	-4.4%	-3.4%	-2.7%
Exports - vol.	-1.7%	-2.5%	-2.7%	2.1%	1.7%	1.4%	2.1%	1.5%	1.1%
Absorption - vol.	-0.4%	-0.4%	-0.5%	-0.6%	-0.9%	-1.1%	-0.6%	-0.9%	-1.2%
Investment - vol.	6.5%	6.0%	4.9%	-3.6%	-4.1%	-4.3%	-3.6%	-4.1%	-4.4%
Labour Demand - vol.	0.2%	0.2%	0.1%	1.6%	0.7%	0.5%	1.5%	0.6%	0.3%
Private Consumption - vol.	-0.7%	-0.6%	-0.7%	-1.0%	-1.1%	-1.3%	-1.0%	-1.1%	-1.4%
Supply to domestic - vol.	0.5%	0.6%	0.4%	1.2%	0.9%	0.5%	1.2%	0.8%	0.3%
Intra-EU Trade - vol	0.0%	0.0%	0.0%	-0.9%	-3.0%	-3.3%	-0.9%	-3.1%	-3.4%

Construction	Constraint Case			Flexible Case			Efficiency Case		
	1988	1991	1994	1988	1991	1994	1988	1991	1994
Domestic Production - vol.	-1.6%	-1.7%	-2.1%	-7.0%	-7.3%	-7.5%	-7.0%	-7.3%	-7.5%
Imports - vol.	-1.6%	-1.7%	-2.1%	-3.5%	-3.6%	-3.7%	-3.5%	-3.6%	-3.7%
Exports - vol.	0.0%	-0.2%	-0.2%	0.5%	0.4%	0.3%	0.5%	0.3%	0.2%
Absorption - vol.	-1.6%	-1.8%	-2.1%	-7.1%	-7.4%	-7.6%	-7.1%	-7.4%	-7.6%
Investment - vol.	0.2%	-0.3%	-1.2%	-7.6%	-7.7%	-7.8%	-7.5%	-7.7%	-7.8%
Labour Demand - vol.	-1.5%	-1.6%	-1.9%	-6.9%	-7.0%	-7.1%	-6.8%	-6.9%	-7.0%
Private Consumption - vol.	1.6%	0.2%	-0.5%	-1.9%	-1.1%	-1.1%	-1.9%	-1.2%	-1.2%
Supply to domestic - vol.	-1.6%	-1.7%	-2.1%	-7.0%	-7.3%	-7.5%	-7.0%	-7.3%	-7.5%
Intra-EU Trade - vol	0.0%	0.0%	0.0%	-3.3%	-3.4%	-3.5%	-3.3%	-3.4%	-3.5%

Telecommunications	Constraint Case			Flexible Case			Efficiency Case		
	1988	1991	1994	1988	1991	1994	1988	1991	1994
Domestic Production - vol.	-0.7%	-0.7%	-0.8%	-0.1%	-0.8%	-1.1%	-0.1%	-0.8%	-1.2%
Imports - vol.	-4.5%	-4.9%	-4.8%	-6.2%	-6.0%	-5.6%	-6.1%	-5.8%	-5.3%
Exports - vol.	-4.5%	-6.8%	-6.9%	1.0%	0.9%	0.7%	1.0%	0.8%	0.6%
Absorption - vol.	-0.7%	-0.7%	-0.7%	-0.4%	-0.7%	-1.0%	-0.4%	-0.7%	-1.0%
Investment - vol.	-4.3%	-3.9%	-4.0%	-4.2%	-4.5%	-4.6%	-4.2%	-4.5%	-4.6%
Labour Demand - vol.	0.5%	1.1%	1.2%	0.1%	-0.3%	-0.3%	0.1%	-0.2%	-0.3%
Private Consumption - vol.	-1.5%	-1.3%	-1.3%	-0.8%	-1.3%	-1.7%	-0.8%	-1.3%	-1.8%
Supply to domestic - vol.	-0.5%	-0.4%	-0.5%	0.4%	1.2%	0.9%	0.4%	1.2%	0.8%
Intra-EU Trade - vol	0.0%	0.0%	0.0%	-7.7%	-18.8%	-18.9%	-7.7%	-18.8%	-18.9%

Transports	Constraint Case			Flexible Case			Efficiency Case		
	1988	1991	1994	1988	1991	1994	1988	1991	1994
Domestic Production - vol.	-0.3%	-0.3%	-0.4%	0.4%	0.2%	0.0%	0.4%	0.2%	-0.1%
Imports - vol.	-0.3%	-0.3%	-0.4%	0.2%	0.1%	0.0%	0.2%	0.1%	0.0%
Exports - vol.	-0.1%	-0.3%	-0.2%	0.6%	0.5%	0.4%	0.6%	0.5%	0.4%
Absorption - vol.	-0.4%	-0.3%	-0.4%	-0.1%	-0.3%	-0.6%	-0.1%	-0.4%	-0.7%
Investment - vol.	-4.7%	-4.8%	-5.0%	-4.0%	-4.1%	-4.2%	-4.0%	-4.1%	-4.2%
Labour Demand - vol.	-0.2%	-0.2%	-0.2%	0.6%	0.5%	0.3%	0.6%	0.5%	0.3%
Private Consumption - vol.	-1.3%	-1.0%	-1.1%	-1.0%	-1.4%	-1.7%	-1.0%	-1.4%	-1.8%
Supply to domestic - vol.	-0.3%	-0.3%	-0.4%	0.4%	0.2%	0.0%	0.4%	0.2%	-0.1%
Intra-EU Trade - vol	0.0%	0.0%	0.0%	1.1%	1.2%	1.1%	1.1%	1.2%	1.0%

Banks	Constraint Case			Flexible Case			Efficiency Case		
	1988	1991	1994	1988	1991	1994	1988	1991	1994
Domestic Production - vol.	-0.9%	-0.6%	-0.7%	-0.7%	-0.9%	-1.3%	-0.7%	-1.0%	-1.4%
Imports - vol.	-10.0%	-12.1%	-12.0%	-6.0%	-5.4%	-5.0%	-5.9%	-5.2%	-4.6%
Exports - vol.	-1.4%	-2.1%	-1.7%	1.0%	0.8%	0.7%	1.0%	0.7%	0.6%
Absorption - vol.	-1.0%	-0.7%	-0.8%	-0.7%	-1.1%	-1.4%	-0.7%	-1.1%	-1.5%
Investment - vol.	-2.7%	-2.2%	-2.5%	-4.5%	-4.6%	-4.8%	-4.5%	-4.6%	-4.8%
Labour Demand - vol.	-0.4%	0.1%	0.1%	-0.6%	-0.9%	-1.0%	-0.6%	-0.8%	-1.0%
Private Consumption - vol.	-1.7%	-1.2%	-1.3%	-1.1%	-1.6%	-2.1%	-1.1%	-1.7%	-2.2%
Supply to domestic - vol.	-0.9%	-0.6%	-0.7%	-0.6%	-0.9%	-1.3%	-0.7%	-0.9%	-1.4%
Intra-EU Trade - vol	0.0%	0.0%	0.0%	-4.8%	-10.8%	-10.9%	-4.8%	-10.8%	-10.9%

Services	Constraint Case			Flexible Case			Efficiency Case		
	1988	1991	1994	1988	1991	1994	1988	1991	1994
Domestic Production - vol.	-0.3%	-0.4%	-0.5%	-0.7%	-1.1%	-1.4%	-0.7%	-1.2%	-1.5%
Imports - vol.	-2.2%	-1.7%	-1.6%	-3.2%	-2.5%	-2.1%	-3.2%	-2.3%	-1.8%
Exports - vol.	3.7%	2.7%	2.6%	1.0%	0.7%	0.5%	1.0%	0.6%	0.4%
Absorption - vol.	-0.5%	-0.5%	-0.6%	-0.9%	-1.1%	-1.4%	-0.9%	-1.2%	-1.5%
Investment - vol.	-0.4%	-0.6%	-1.2%	-4.5%	-4.7%	-4.8%	-4.5%	-4.7%	-4.8%
Labour Demand - vol.	-0.2%	-0.2%	-0.2%	-0.6%	-0.7%	-0.8%	-0.6%	-0.7%	-0.8%
Private Consumption - vol.	-1.0%	-0.9%	-1.0%	-1.0%	-1.4%	-1.7%	-1.0%	-1.4%	-1.8%
Supply to domestic - vol.	-0.5%	-0.5%	-0.6%	-1.0%	-1.3%	-1.6%	-1.0%	-1.4%	-1.7%
Intra-EU Trade - vol	0.0%	0.0%	0.0%	2.9%	4.3%	4.2%	2.9%	4.3%	4.2%

Non market	Constraint Case			Flexible Case			Efficiency Case		
	1988	1991	1994	1988	1991	1994	1988	1991	1994
Domestic Production - vol.	0.0%	0.0%	0.0%	-0.1%	-0.1%	-0.1%	-0.1%	-0.1%	-0.1%
Imports - vol.	0.0%	0.0%	0.0%	0.0%	0.0%	-0.1%	0.0%	0.0%	-0.1%
Exports - vol.	0.6%	0.5%	0.5%	0.3%	0.2%	0.2%	0.2%	0.2%	0.1%
Absorption - vol.	0.0%	0.0%	0.0%	-0.1%	-0.1%	-0.1%	-0.1%	-0.1%	-0.1%
Investment - vol.	-6.7%	-6.8%	-6.9%	-4.1%	-4.1%	-4.1%	-4.1%	-4.1%	-4.1%
Labour Demand - vol.	0.0%	0.0%	0.1%	0.1%	0.1%	0.1%	0.1%	0.2%	0.2%
Private Consumption - vol.	-0.6%	-0.7%	-0.9%	-1.2%	-1.3%	-1.6%	-1.2%	-1.4%	-1.7%
Supply to domestic - vol.	0.0%	0.0%	0.0%	-0.1%	-0.1%	-0.1%	-0.1%	-0.1%	-0.1%
Intra-EU Trade - vol	0.0%	0.0%	0.0%	0.1%	0.1%	0.1%	0.1%	0.1%	0.1%

Table B5.4.
The full *antimonde* scenario : sectoral results for Germany (prices)

% change from *monde*

Agriculture	Constraint Case			Flexible Case			Efficiency Case		
	1988	1991	1994	1988	1991	1994	1988	1991	1994
Real Marginal Costs	0.68%	1.26%	1.45%	0.85%	0.85%	0.96%	0.84%	0.81%	0.90%
Real Cost of Labour	-0.09%	0.18%	-0.06%	-0.64%	-1.16%	-1.65%	-0.67%	-1.29%	-1.87%
Real Deflator of Absorption	0.73%	1.11%	1.24%	1.91%	1.67%	1.60%	1.89%	1.56%	1.41%
Real Price of Exports-RW	0.68%	1.26%	1.45%	0.85%	0.85%	0.96%	0.84%	0.81%	0.90%

Energy	Constraint Case			Flexible Case			Efficiency Case		
	1988	1991	1994	1988	1991	1994	1988	1991	1994
Marginal Costs	0.66%	1.15%	1.30%	1.24%	1.01%	0.92%	1.22%	0.91%	0.76%
Cost of Labour	-0.09%	0.18%	-0.06%	-0.64%	-1.16%	-1.65%	-0.67%	-1.29%	-1.87%
Deflator of Absorption	0.64%	0.97%	1.07%	2.21%	1.78%	1.57%	2.17%	1.63%	1.31%
Price of Exports-RW	0.66%	1.15%	1.30%	1.24%	1.01%	0.92%	1.22%	0.91%	0.76%

Metal Industries	Constraint Case			Flexible Case			Efficiency Case		
	1988	1991	1994	1988	1991	1994	1988	1991	1994
Marginal Costs	1.04%	1.50%	1.68%	1.85%	1.57%	1.38%	1.84%	1.53%	1.32%
Cost of Labour	-0.09%	0.18%	-0.06%	-0.64%	-1.16%	-1.65%	-0.67%	-1.29%	-1.87%
Deflator of Absorption	1.16%	1.50%	1.64%	2.58%	2.22%	1.96%	2.56%	2.14%	1.81%
Price of Exports-RW	1.49%	2.31%	2.50%	1.77%	1.42%	1.24%	1.76%	1.39%	1.18%

Chemical	Constraint Case			Flexible Case			Efficiency Case		
	1988	1991	1994	1988	1991	1994	1988	1991	1994
Marginal Costs	0.70%	1.18%	1.30%	1.07%	0.88%	0.77%	1.07%	0.85%	0.71%
Cost of Labour	-0.09%	0.18%	-0.06%	-0.64%	-1.16%	-1.65%	-0.67%	-1.29%	-1.87%
Deflator of Absorption	0.83%	1.18%	1.26%	2.10%	1.85%	1.66%	2.08%	1.77%	1.52%
Price of Exports-RW	0.77%	1.50%	1.63%	1.00%	0.78%	0.67%	0.99%	0.74%	0.61%

Other Intensive Industries	Constraint Case			Flexible Case			Efficiency Case		
	1988	1991	1994	1988	1991	1994	1988	1991	1994
Marginal Costs	0.61%	1.11%	1.20%	0.61%	0.43%	0.34%	0.60%	0.41%	0.29%
Cost of Labour	-0.09%	0.18%	-0.06%	-0.64%	-1.16%	-1.65%	-0.67%	-1.29%	-1.87%
Deflator of Absorption	0.70%	1.13%	1.22%	1.01%	0.79%	0.66%	1.00%	0.75%	0.58%
Price of Exports-RW	0.59%	1.15%	1.24%	0.61%	0.43%	0.34%	0.60%	0.41%	0.29%

Electrical goods	Constraint Case			Flexible Case			Efficiency Case		
	1988	1991	1994	1988	1991	1994	1988	1991	1994
Marginal Costs	0.51%	0.97%	1.02%	0.47%	0.25%	0.11%	0.46%	0.22%	0.05%
Cost of Labour	-0.09%	0.18%	-0.06%	-0.64%	-1.16%	-1.65%	-0.67%	-1.29%	-1.87%
Deflator of Absorption	0.89%	1.20%	1.23%	1.76%	1.43%	1.17%	1.73%	1.34%	1.01%
Price of Exports-RW	0.43%	1.01%	1.05%	0.44%	0.21%	0.06%	0.44%	0.18%	0.00%

Transport equipment	Constraint Case			Flexible Case			Efficiency Case		
	1988	1991	1994	1988	1991	1994	1988	1991	1994
Marginal Costs	0.72%	1.21%	1.31%	0.78%	0.66%	0.54%	0.78%	0.64%	0.50%
Cost of Labour	-0.09%	0.18%	-0.06%	-0.64%	-1.16%	-1.65%	-0.67%	-1.29%	-1.87%
Deflator of Absorption	1.33%	1.74%	1.85%	2.11%	2.26%	2.07%	2.09%	2.21%	1.98%
Price of Exports-RW	1.56%	2.87%	2.99%	0.60%	0.28%	0.17%	0.59%	0.26%	0.13%

Other Equipment	Constraint Case			Flexible Case			Efficiency Case		
	1988	1991	1994	1988	1991	1994	1988	1991	1994
Marginal Costs	0.57%	1.03%	1.08%	0.57%	0.34%	0.17%	0.56%	0.31%	0.12%
Cost of Labour	-0.09%	0.18%	-0.06%	-0.64%	-1.16%	-1.65%	-0.67%	-1.29%	-1.87%
Deflator of Absorption	0.82%	1.13%	1.17%	1.58%	1.26%	1.01%	1.56%	1.18%	0.87%
Price of Exports-RW	0.66%	1.19%	1.25%	0.56%	0.33%	0.16%	0.55%	0.30%	0.11%

Consumer goods	Constraint Case			Flexible Case			Efficiency Case		
	1988	1991	1994	1988	1991	1994	1988	1991	1994
Marginal Costs	0.69%	1.19%	1.32%	0.94%	0.77%	0.70%	0.93%	0.74%	0.65%
Cost of Labour	-0.09%	0.18%	-0.06%	-0.64%	-1.16%	-1.65%	-0.67%	-1.29%	-1.87%
Deflator of Absorption	0.81%	1.19%	1.29%	1.72%	1.42%	1.26%	1.70%	1.34%	1.13%
Price of Exports-RW	0.69%	1.19%	1.32%	0.94%	0.77%	0.70%	0.93%	0.74%	0.65%

Construction	Constraint Case			Flexible Case			Efficiency Case		
	1988	1991	1994	1988	1991	1994	1988	1991	1994
Marginal Costs	0.51%	1.00%	1.07%	0.37%	0.20%	0.11%	0.36%	0.18%	0.06%
Cost of Labour	-0.09%	0.18%	-0.06%	-0.64%	-1.16%	-1.65%	-0.67%	-1.29%	-1.87%
Deflator of Absorption	0.51%	1.00%	1.07%	0.37%	0.20%	0.11%	0.37%	0.18%	0.06%
Price of Exports-RW	0.51%	1.00%	1.07%	0.37%	0.20%	0.11%	0.36%	0.18%	0.06%

Telecommunications	Constraint Case			Flexible Case			Efficiency Case		
	1988	1991	1994	1988	1991	1994	1988	1991	1994
Marginal Costs	0.87%	1.73%	1.88%	-0.04%	0.03%	0.17%	-0.04%	0.02%	0.15%
Cost of Labour	-0.09%	0.18%	-0.06%	-0.64%	-1.16%	-1.65%	-0.67%	-1.29%	-1.87%
Deflator of Absorption	1.21%	2.13%	2.24%	0.12%	0.03%	0.13%	0.11%	0.01%	0.09%
Price of Exports-RW	5.38%	8.11%	8.25%	-0.19%	-0.27%	-0.15%	-0.20%	-0.29%	-0.17%

Transports	Constraint Case			Flexible Case			Efficiency Case		
	1988	1991	1994	1988	1991	1994	1988	1991	1994
Marginal Costs	0.51%	1.05%	1.14%	0.26%	0.16%	0.15%	0.25%	0.13%	0.09%
Cost of Labour	-0.09%	0.18%	-0.06%	-0.64%	-1.16%	-1.65%	-0.67%	-1.29%	-1.87%
Deflator of Absorption	0.72%	1.20%	1.29%	0.32%	0.18%	0.16%	0.31%	0.14%	0.09%
Price of Exports-RW	0.51%	1.05%	1.14%	0.26%	0.16%	0.15%	0.25%	0.13%	0.09%

Banks	Constraint Case			Flexible Case			Efficiency Case		
	1988	1991	1994	1988	1991	1994	1988	1991	1994
Marginal Costs	0.76%	1.54%	1.66%	0.02%	0.08%	0.21%	0.01%	0.07%	0.19%
Cost of Labour	-0.09%	0.18%	-0.06%	-0.64%	-1.16%	-1.65%	-0.67%	-1.29%	-1.87%
Deflator of Absorption	0.85%	1.62%	1.74%	0.02%	0.04%	0.17%	0.01%	0.02%	0.14%
Price of Exports-RW	1.53%	2.93%	3.06%	0.01%	0.06%	0.19%	0.00%	0.05%	0.16%

Services	Constraint Case			Flexible Case			Efficiency Case		
	1988	1991	1994	1988	1991	1994	1988	1991	1994
Marginal Costs	0.50%	1.12%	1.28%	0.22%	0.31%	0.48%	0.21%	0.28%	0.43%
Cost of Labour	-0.09%	0.18%	-0.06%	-0.64%	-1.16%	-1.65%	-0.67%	-1.29%	-1.87%
Deflator of Absorption	0.51%	1.12%	1.28%	0.22%	0.30%	0.47%	0.21%	0.27%	0.42%
Price of Exports-RW	0.50%	1.12%	1.28%	0.22%	0.31%	0.48%	0.21%	0.28%	0.43%

Non market	Constraint Case			Flexible Case			Efficiency Case		
	1988	1991	1994	1988	1991	1994	1988	1991	1994
Marginal Costs	0.36%	0.79%	0.77%	0.07%	-0.20%	-0.43%	0.06%	-0.23%	-0.48%
Cost of Labour	-0.09%	0.18%	-0.06%	-0.64%	-1.16%	-1.65%	-0.67%	-1.29%	-1.87%
Deflator of Absorption	0.36%	0.79%	0.77%	0.07%	-0.20%	-0.43%	0.07%	-0.23%	-0.48%
Price of Exports-RW	0.36%	0.79%	0.77%	0.07%	-0.20%	-0.43%	0.06%	-0.23%	-0.48%

Table B5.5.
Decomposition of effects: macroeconomic aggregates for Germany

Macroeconomic Aggregates (vol.) (% change from monde)	Border Controls			Border controls and x-ineff.			Market segmentation			Trade antimonde			Full antimonde		
	1988	1991	1994	1988	1991	1994	1988	1991	1994	1988	1991	1994	1988	1991	1994
GDP fact. pr.	-0.05%	-0.09%	-0.09%	-0.06%	-0.10%	-0.11%	-0.23%	-0.56%	-0.85%	-0.27%	-0.61%	-0.91%	-0.38%	-0.76%	-1.11%
Priv. Consumption	0.15%	0.15%	0.15%	0.15%	0.14%	0.14%	-1.10%	-1.23%	-1.47%	-1.08%	-1.25%	-1.48%	-1.14%	-1.33%	-1.58%
Absorption	0.01%	0.01%	0.01%	0.02%	0.01%	0.01%	-1.01%	-1.08%	-1.28%	-1.06%	-1.15%	-1.36%	-1.10%	-1.20%	-1.43%
Total Investment	0.04%	0.04%	0.04%	0.04%	0.05%	0.05%	-4.23%	-4.36%	-4.48%	-4.21%	-4.34%	-4.47%	-4.21%	-4.35%	-4.48%
Total Exports to RW	-0.55%	-0.64%	-0.65%	-0.56%	-0.65%	-0.66%	2.02%	1.72%	1.54%	1.71%	1.41%	1.23%	1.65%	1.32%	1.11%
Total Imports from RW	1.31%	1.53%	1.54%	1.32%	1.55%	1.57%	-4.99%	-4.50%	-4.27%	-3.86%	-3.27%	-3.02%	-3.72%	-3.05%	-2.73%
Total Intra-EU Trade	-1.10%	-2.89%	-2.90%	-1.10%	-2.91%	-2.91%	-0.84%	-4.17%	-4.30%	-1.44%	-4.90%	-5.03%	-1.56%	-5.06%	-5.24%
Employment (diff. from monde, 10³ persons)	-5	-4	-4	-7	-7	-7	-38	-71	-106	-46	-81	-116	-49	-86	-121
Disposable Income (deflated)	0.16%	0.15%	0.15%	0.15%	0.15%	0.14%	-1.13%	-1.27%	-1.51%	-1.11%	-1.28%	-1.53%	-1.17%	-1.37%	-1.63%

Macroeconomic Ratios (abs. diff. from monde)	Border Controls			Border controls and x-ineff.			Market segmentation			Trade antimonde			Full antimonde		
	1988	1991	1994	1988	1991	1994	1988	1991	1994	1988	1991	1994	1988	1991	1994
Current Account as % of GDP	-0.05%	-0.04%	-0.04%	-0.05%	-0.04%	-0.03%	-1.35%	-1.35%	-1.32%	-1.35%	-1.33%	-1.30%	-1.31%	-1.27%	-1.22%
Public Deficit as % of GDP	0.06%	0.06%	0.06%	0.06%	0.05%	0.05%	-0.23%	-0.29%	-0.40%	-0.20%	-0.28%	-0.39%	-0.24%	-0.33%	-0.46%
Labour Productivity	-0.03%	-0.07%	-0.07%	-0.03%	-0.07%	-0.08%	-0.08%	-0.28%	-0.44%	-0.09%	-0.29%	-0.46%	-0.19%	-0.43%	-0.64%
Investment/GDP	0.03%	0.04%	0.04%	0.03%	0.04%	0.04%	-1.85%	-1.84%	-1.83%	-1.83%	-1.82%	-1.82%	-1.81%	-1.79%	-1.78%
Priv.Cons./GDP	0.11%	0.13%	0.13%	0.12%	0.13%	0.14%	-0.48%	-0.38%	-0.34%	-0.45%	-0.36%	-0.32%	-0.43%	-0.32%	-0.27%

Deflators (% change from monde)	Border Controls			Border controls and x-ineff.			Market segmentation			Trade antimonde			Full antimonde		
	1988	1991	1994	1988	1991	1994	1988	1991	1994	1988	1991	1994	1988	1991	1994
Consumer Price Index	-0.23%	-0.26%	-0.26%	-0.23%	-0.26%	-0.27%	1.00%	0.89%	0.90%	0.97%	0.88%	0.89%	0.95%	0.84%	0.83%
Real Wage Rate	-0.06%	-0.09%	-0.09%	-0.08%	-0.12%	-0.12%	-0.45%	-0.88%	-1.30%	-0.53%	-0.99%	-1.43%	-0.64%	-1.16%	-1.65%
Marginal Costs	-0.15%	-0.17%	-0.17%	-0.15%	-0.17%	-0.17%	0.55%	0.42%	0.40%	0.53%	0.41%	0.39%	0.52%	0.39%	0.36%
Producer Prices	-0.14%	-0.16%	-0.16%	-0.15%	-0.16%	-0.17%	0.62%	0.53%	0.51%	0.60%	0.52%	0.50%	0.58%	0.50%	0.46%
Real Shadow Price of Capital	0.10%	0.10%	0.09%	0.12%	0.13%	0.12%	0.06%	0.52%	1.11%	0.14%	0.62%	1.23%	0.09%	0.56%	1.12%
Terms-of-Trade RW	1.96%	2.25%	2.27%	1.98%	2.28%	2.31%	-6.23%	-5.36%	-4.81%	-5.22%	-4.30%	-3.74%	-5.04%	-4.03%	-3.37%

	Border Controls			Border controls and x-ineff.			Market segmentation			Trade antimonde			Full antimonde		
Real Exchange Rate	3.98%	4.31%	4.33%	4.01%	4.34%	4.38%	-6.98%	-5.88%	-5.25%	-4.25%	-3.11%	-2.45%	-4.06%	-2.82%	-2.05%

Trade Regime	Integration			Integration			Segmentation			Segmentation			Segmentation		

Table B5.6.
Decomposition of effects: effects on IC sectors for Germany

% change from *monde*

Metal Industries

	Border Controls			Border controls and x-ineff.			Market segmentation			Trade *antimonde*			Full *antimonde*		
	1988	1991	1994	1988	1991	1994	1988	1991	1994	1988	1991	1994	1988	1991	1994
Production per firm	-0.51%	-0.93%	-0.94%	-0.51%	-0.94%	-0.95%	-1.73%	-3.20%	-3.30%	-2.22%	-3.76%	-3.85%	-2.32%	-3.90%	-4.05%
Marginal Costs	3.47%	3.75%	3.77%	3.49%	3.78%	3.82%	-5.03%	-4.26%	-3.80%	-2.41%	-1.55%	-1.08%	-2.21%	-1.25%	-0.67%
Producer Prices	3.50%	3.81%	3.83%	3.52%	3.84%	3.87%	-4.92%	-4.06%	-3.60%	-2.27%	-1.32%	-0.84%	-2.06%	-1.01%	-0.42%
Mark-ups domestic (abs. diff.)	0.02%	0.03%	0.03%	0.02%	0.03%	0.03%	0.13%	0.17%	0.17%	0.16%	0.19%	0.20%	0.16%	0.20%	0.21%
Fixed Costs per firm	3.44%	3.72%	3.73%	3.45%	3.74%	3.77%	-4.96%	-4.22%	-3.80%	-2.35%	-1.53%	-1.09%	-2.19%	-1.30%	-0.78%
Number of Firms	-0.01%	0.66%	0.66%	-0.01%	0.66%	0.65%	6.12%	10.46%	10.31%	5.64%	9.91%	9.75%	5.57%	9.79%	9.60%
Sigma of Love of Variety	0.00%	0.00%	0.00%	0.00%	0.00%	0.00%	0.00%	0.00%	0.00%	0.00%	0.00%	0.00%	0.00%	0.00%	0.00%

Chemical

	Border Controls			Border controls and x-ineff.			Market segmentation			Trade *antimonde*			Full *antimonde*		
	1988	1991	1994	1988	1991	1994	1988	1991	1994	1988	1991	1994	1988	1991	1994
Production per firm	-0.46%	-1.21%	-1.21%	-0.47%	-1.22%	-1.22%	-2.55%	-4.90%	-5.05%	-2.62%	-5.02%	-5.17%	-2.70%	-5.14%	-5.34%
Marginal Costs	3.79%	4.09%	4.11%	3.81%	4.12%	4.15%	-5.92%	-5.03%	-4.49%	-3.17%	-2.21%	-1.65%	-2.98%	-1.94%	-1.28%
Producer Prices	3.81%	4.14%	4.16%	3.83%	4.17%	4.20%	-5.81%	-4.83%	-4.29%	-3.05%	-2.00%	-1.44%	-2.87%	-1.72%	-1.06%
Mark-ups domestic (abs. diff.)	0.00%	0.02%	0.02%	0.00%	0.02%	0.02%	0.17%	0.26%	0.27%	0.16%	0.25%	0.26%	0.16%	0.25%	0.26%
Fixed Costs per firm	3.75%	4.05%	4.06%	3.77%	4.07%	4.10%	-5.82%	-5.00%	-4.54%	-3.08%	-2.20%	-1.72%	-2.94%	-1.99%	-1.43%
Number of Firms	0.60%	1.30%	1.30%	0.60%	1.31%	1.30%	6.84%	9.41%	9.29%	7.19%	9.74%	9.62%	7.13%	9.65%	9.50%
Sigma of Love of Variety	0.00%	0.00%	0.00%	0.00%	0.00%	0.00%	0.00%	0.00%	0.00%	0.00%	0.00%	0.00%	0.00%	0.00%	0.00%

Other Intensive Industries

	Border Controls			Border controls and x-ineff.			Market segmentation			Trade *antimonde*			Full *antimonde*		
	1988	1991	1994	1988	1991	1994	1988	1991	1994	1988	1991	1994	1988	1991	1994
Production per firm	-0.32%	-0.70%	-0.70%	-0.33%	-0.71%	-0.72%	-1.43%	-2.37%	-2.53%	-1.62%	-2.61%	-2.76%	-1.68%	-2.69%	-2.88%
Marginal Costs	3.80%	4.10%	4.12%	3.82%	4.13%	4.17%	-6.33%	-5.42%	-4.87%	-3.63%	-2.66%	-2.09%	-3.45%	-2.38%	-1.72%
Producer Prices	3.81%	4.11%	4.13%	3.83%	4.15%	4.18%	-6.30%	-5.37%	-4.83%	-3.60%	-2.62%	-2.04%	-3.41%	-2.34%	-1.67%
Mark-ups domestic (abs. diff.)	0.00%	0.00%	0.00%	0.00%	0.00%	0.00%	0.03%	0.04%	0.04%	0.03%	0.04%	0.04%	0.03%	0.04%	0.04%
Fixed Costs per firm	3.75%	4.05%	4.06%	3.77%	4.07%	4.10%	-6.25%	-5.43%	-4.99%	-3.57%	-2.71%	-2.25%	-3.43%	-2.50%	-1.96%
Number of Firms	0.14%	0.28%	0.28%	0.14%	0.29%	0.28%	0.64%	0.90%	0.77%	0.64%	0.86%	0.73%	0.62%	0.83%	0.69%
Sigma of Love of Variety	0.00%	0.00%	0.00%	0.00%	0.00%	0.00%	0.00%	0.00%	0.00%	0.00%	0.00%	0.00%	0.00%	0.00%	0.00%

Electrical goods

	Border Controls			Border controls and x-ineff.			Market segmentation			Trade *antimonde*			Full *antimonde*		
	1988	1991	1994	1988	1991	1994	1988	1991	1994	1988	1991	1994	1988	1991	1994
Production per firm	-0.68%	-1.36%	-1.37%	-0.68%	-1.37%	-1.38%	-2.07%	-4.00%	-4.17%	-2.48%	-4.46%	-4.62%	-2.56%	-4.57%	-4.78%
Marginal Costs	3.82%	4.13%	4.15%	3.85%	4.16%	4.19%	-6.47%	-5.58%	-5.08%	-3.77%	-2.83%	-2.31%	-3.59%	-2.57%	-1.95%
Producer Prices	3.84%	4.16%	4.18%	3.86%	4.19%	4.23%	-6.41%	-5.48%	-4.97%	-3.70%	-2.71%	-2.19%	-3.52%	-2.45%	-1.83%
Mark-ups domestic (abs. diff.)	0.01%	0.02%	0.02%	0.01%	0.02%	0.02%	0.09%	0.14%	0.14%	0.10%	0.14%	0.14%	0.10%	0.14%	0.15%
Fixed Costs per firm	3.78%	4.08%	4.09%	3.79%	4.09%	4.12%	-6.41%	-5.62%	-5.23%	-3.73%	-2.90%	-2.50%	-3.60%	-2.71%	-2.24%
Number of Firms	0.03%	0.46%	0.46%	0.03%	0.47%	0.47%	4.53%	8.12%	7.95%	4.42%	7.96%	7.79%	4.35%	7.87%	7.66%
Sigma of Love of Variety	0.00%	0.00%	0.00%	0.00%	0.00%	0.00%	0.00%	0.00%	0.00%	0.00%	0.00%	0.00%	0.00%	0.00%	0.00%

Transport equipment

	Border Controls			Border controls and x-ineff.			Market segmentation			Trade antimonde			Full antimonde		
	1988	1991	1994	1988	1991	1994	1988	1991	1994	1988	1991	1994	1988	1991	1994
Production per firm	-0.61%	-1.41%	-1.41%	-0.62%	-1.42%	-1.43%	-5.05%	-8.77%	-8.93%	-5.32%	-9.10%	-9.25%	-5.41%	-9.21%	-9.40%
Marginal Costs	3.81%	4.13%	4.15%	3.84%	4.17%	4.20%	-6.18%	-5.23%	-4.71%	-3.46%	-2.45%	-1.90%	-3.27%	-2.16%	-1.52%
Producer Prices	3.87%	4.26%	4.28%	3.89%	4.30%	4.33%	-5.71%	-4.41%	-3.88%	-2.95%	-1.57%	-1.01%	-2.75%	-1.28%	-0.62%
Mark-ups domestic (abs. diff.)	0.01%	0.12%	0.12%	0.01%	0.12%	0.12%	0.89%	1.24%	1.24%	0.87%	1.22%	1.23%	0.88%	1.23%	1.23%
Fixed Costs per firm	3.78%	4.09%	4.11%	3.79%	4.11%	4.14%	-6.10%	-5.23%	-4.79%	-3.40%	-2.47%	-2.01%	-3.26%	-2.25%	-1.72%
Number of Firms	0.43%	0.75%	0.73%	0.42%	0.74%	0.72%	5.49%	11.04%	10.79%	5.65%	11.18%	10.93%	5.60%	11.12%	10.87%
Sigma of Love of Variety	0.00%	0.00%	0.00%	0.00%	0.00%	0.00%	0.00%	0.00%	0.00%	0.00%	0.00%	0.00%	0.00%	0.00%	0.00%

Other Equipment

	Border Controls			Border controls and x-ineff.			Market segmentation			Trade antimonde			Full antimonde		
	1988	1991	1994	1988	1991	1994	1988	1991	1994	1988	1991	1994	1988	1991	1994
Production per firm	-0.64%	-1.08%	-1.08%	-0.65%	-1.09%	-1.09%	-2.33%	-3.70%	-3.83%	-2.79%	-4.19%	-4.33%	-2.87%	-4.30%	-4.48%
Marginal Costs	3.79%	4.10%	4.12%	3.81%	4.13%	4.16%	-6.36%	-5.49%	-5.01%	-3.67%	-2.75%	-2.25%	-3.49%	-2.48%	-1.88%
Producer Prices	3.80%	4.11%	4.13%	3.83%	4.14%	4.18%	-6.32%	-5.43%	-4.95%	-3.62%	-2.68%	-2.17%	-3.44%	-2.41%	-1.81%
Mark-ups domestic (abs. diff.)	0.01%	0.01%	0.01%	0.01%	0.01%	0.01%	0.09%	0.12%	0.12%	0.09%	0.12%	0.12%	0.09%	0.12%	0.12%
Fixed Costs per firm	3.76%	4.06%	4.08%	3.77%	4.08%	4.10%	-6.31%	-5.52%	-5.11%	-3.64%	-2.80%	-2.37%	-3.51%	-2.60%	-2.10%
Number of Firms	-0.16%	0.05%	0.05%	-0.16%	0.06%	0.06%	2.82%	4.10%	3.95%	2.49%	3.74%	3.59%	2.43%	3.66%	3.48%
Sigma of Love of Variety	0.00%	0.00%	0.00%	0.00%	0.00%	0.00%	0.00%	0.00%	0.00%	0.00%	0.00%	0.00%	0.00%	0.00%	0.00%

Telecommunications

	Border Controls			Border controls and x-ineff.			Market segmentation			Trade antimonde			Full antimonde		
	1988	1991	1994	1988	1991	1994	1988	1991	1994	1988	1991	1994	1988	1991	1994
Production per firm	0.01%	0.00%	0.00%	-0.68%	-1.44%	-1.45%	-1.68%	-3.55%	-3.93%	-1.68%	-3.57%	-3.95%	-2.40%	-4.95%	-5.35%
Marginal Costs	4.03%	4.36%	4.39%	4.05%	4.39%	4.44%	-7.03%	-5.87%	-5.09%	-4.28%	-3.07%	-2.27%	-4.09%	-2.79%	-1.89%
Producer Prices	4.00%	4.33%	4.36%	3.84%	4.01%	4.06%	-6.74%	-5.30%	-4.55%	-4.01%	-2.51%	-1.72%	-3.99%	-2.58%	-1.70%
Mark-ups domestic (abs. diff.)	-0.03%	-0.03%	-0.03%	-0.25%	-0.49%	-0.49%	0.22%	0.25%	0.22%	0.20%	0.23%	0.20%	-0.03%	-0.24%	-0.27%
Fixed Costs per firm	3.90%	4.19%	4.21%	2.28%	0.97%	1.00%	-7.15%	-6.42%	-6.12%	-4.50%	-3.75%	-3.43%	-5.88%	-6.57%	-6.22%
Number of Firms	0.09%	0.10%	0.11%	0.84%	1.67%	1.68%	1.50%	2.76%	2.85%	1.56%	2.82%	2.90%	2.32%	4.36%	4.46%
Sigma of Love of Variety	0.00%	0.00%	0.00%	0.00%	0.00%	0.00%	0.00%	0.00%	0.00%	0.00%	0.00%	0.00%	0.00%	0.00%	0.00%

Banks

	Border Controls			Border controls and x-ineff.			Market segmentation			Trade antimonde			Full antimonde		
	1988	1991	1994	1988	1991	1994	1988	1991	1994	1988	1991	1994	1988	1991	1994
Production per firm	0.03%	0.04%	0.04%	-0.40%	-0.81%	-0.81%	-0.52%	-0.89%	-1.24%	-0.52%	-0.90%	-1.25%	-0.99%	-1.81%	-2.18%
Marginal Costs	4.01%	4.33%	4.34%	4.03%	4.37%	4.40%	-6.98%	-5.82%	-5.04%	-4.23%	-3.02%	-2.21%	-4.04%	-2.74%	-1.84%
Producer Prices	3.99%	4.31%	4.32%	3.97%	4.25%	4.28%	-6.93%	-5.77%	-4.99%	-4.19%	-2.98%	-2.17%	-4.04%	-2.78%	-1.89%
Mark-ups domestic (abs. diff.)	-0.01%	-0.02%	-0.02%	-0.07%	-0.12%	-0.12%	0.06%	0.06%	0.06%	0.05%	0.05%	0.05%	0.00%	-0.06%	-0.06%
Fixed Costs per firm	3.91%	4.21%	4.23%	3.05%	2.48%	2.51%	-7.03%	-6.18%	-5.75%	-4.35%	-3.47%	-3.02%	-5.02%	-4.90%	-4.39%
Number of Firms	0.12%	0.15%	0.15%	0.54%	1.00%	1.00%	-0.14%	-0.02%	-0.01%	-0.08%	0.04%	0.05%	0.34%	0.88%	0.89%
Sigma of Love of Variety	0.00%	0.00%	0.00%	0.00%	0.00%	0.00%	0.00%	0.00%	0.00%	0.00%	0.00%	0.00%	0.00%	0.00%	0.00%

Table B5.7.
Decomposition of effects: sectoral results for Germany (volumes)

% change from *monde*

Agriculture

	Border Controls			Border controls and x-ineff.			Market segmentation			Trade *antimonde*			Full *antimonde*		
	1988	1991	1994	1988	1991	1994	1988	1991	1994	1988	1991	1994	1988	1991	1994
Domestic Production - vol.	-0.6%	-0.2%	-0.2%	-0.6%	-0.2%	-0.2%	3.2%	1.6%	1.1%	2.7%	1.1%	0.5%	2.5%	0.8%	0.2%
Imports - vol.	1.9%	2.2%	2.2%	1.9%	2.3%	2.3%	-4.7%	-4.3%	-3.9%	-3.2%	-2.7%	-2.2%	-3.1%	-2.4%	-1.9%
Exports - vol.	-0.7%	-0.8%	-0.8%	-0.7%	-0.8%	-0.8%	1.9%	1.6%	1.3%	1.5%	1.1%	0.9%	1.4%	1.0%	0.8%
Absorption - vol.	-0.1%	0.1%	0.1%	-0.1%	0.1%	0.1%	0.7%	0.0%	-0.3%	0.6%	-0.1%	-0.4%	0.6%	-0.2%	-0.5%
Investment - vol.	-0.3%	-0.1%	-0.1%	-0.3%	-0.1%	-0.1%	-2.7%	-3.4%	-3.7%	-2.9%	-3.7%	-3.9%	-3.0%	-3.7%	-4.0%
Labour Demand - vol.	-0.6%	-0.1%	-0.1%	-0.6%	-0.1%	-0.1%	3.3%	1.9%	1.6%	2.8%	1.4%	1.1%	2.8%	1.3%	0.9%
Private Consumption - vol.	0.1%	0.2%	0.2%	0.1%	0.2%	0.2%	-0.9%	-1.2%	-1.5%	-0.9%	-1.2%	-1.5%	-0.9%	-1.3%	-1.6%
Supply to domestic - vol.	-0.5%	0.3%	0.3%	-0.5%	0.3%	0.3%	3.5%	2.2%	1.6%	3.0%	1.7%	1.1%	2.9%	1.5%	0.9%
Intra-EU Trade - vol	-2.0%	-4.0%	-4.0%	-2.1%	-4.1%	-4.1%	1.7%	0.5%	0.1%	0.1%	-1.3%	-1.7%	0.0%	-1.5%	-1.9%

Energy

	Border Controls			Border controls and x-ineff.			Market segmentation			Trade *antimonde*			Full *antimonde*		
	1988	1991	1994	1988	1991	1994	1988	1991	1994	1988	1991	1994	1988	1991	1994
Domestic Production - vol.	-0.3%	-0.3%	-0.3%	-0.3%	-0.3%	-0.3%	1.5%	1.1%	0.8%	1.3%	0.9%	0.7%	1.2%	0.8%	0.5%
Imports - vol.	0.8%	1.0%	1.0%	0.9%	1.0%	1.0%	-1.8%	-1.6%	-1.5%	-1.3%	-1.0%	-0.9%	-1.3%	-1.0%	-0.9%
Exports - vol.	-0.3%	-0.3%	-0.3%	-0.3%	-0.4%	-0.4%	0.9%	0.7%	0.6%	0.7%	0.5%	0.4%	0.6%	0.5%	0.4%
Absorption - vol.	0.0%	0.0%	0.0%	0.0%	0.0%	0.0%	0.5%	0.3%	0.1%	0.4%	0.3%	0.1%	0.4%	0.2%	-0.1%
Investment - vol.	-0.2%	-0.2%	-0.2%	-0.2%	-0.2%	-0.2%	-3.4%	-3.5%	-3.7%	-3.5%	-3.6%	-3.8%	-3.5%	-3.7%	-3.8%
Labour Demand - vol.	-0.3%	-0.3%	-0.3%	-0.3%	-0.3%	-0.3%	1.6%	1.3%	1.1%	1.5%	1.2%	0.9%	1.4%	1.1%	0.9%
Private Consumption - vol.	0.1%	0.1%	0.1%	0.1%	0.1%	0.1%	-0.7%	-1.0%	-1.2%	-0.7%	-1.0%	-1.2%	-0.7%	-1.0%	-1.2%
Supply to domestic - vol.	-0.3%	-0.3%	-0.3%	-0.3%	-0.3%	-0.3%	1.5%	1.1%	0.8%	1.3%	0.9%	0.6%	1.2%	0.8%	0.5%
Intra-EU Trade - vol	-0.6%	-0.7%	-0.7%	-0.6%	-0.7%	-0.7%	1.3%	1.0%	0.8%	0.8%	0.4%	0.2%	0.7%	0.3%	0.1%

Metal Industries

	Border Controls			Border controls and x-ineff.			Market segmentation			Trade *antimonde*			Full *antimonde*		
	1988	1991	1994	1988	1991	1994	1988	1991	1994	1988	1991	1994	1988	1991	1994
Domestic Production - vol.	-0.5%	-0.3%	-0.3%	-0.5%	-0.3%	-0.3%	4.3%	6.9%	6.7%	3.3%	5.8%	5.5%	3.1%	5.5%	5.2%
Imports - vol.	1.1%	1.4%	1.4%	1.1%	1.4%	1.4%	-4.1%	-3.2%	-3.0%	-2.7%	-1.6%	-1.4%	-2.5%	-1.3%	-1.1%
Exports - vol.	-0.6%	-0.6%	-0.6%	-0.6%	-0.7%	-0.7%	1.6%	1.4%	1.2%	1.2%	1.0%	0.8%	1.2%	0.9%	0.7%
Absorption - vol.	-0.3%	-0.3%	-0.3%	-0.3%	-0.3%	-0.3%	2.2%	3.9%	3.6%	1.6%	3.1%	2.9%	1.5%	3.0%	2.7%
Investment - vol.	-0.3%	-0.2%	-0.2%	-0.3%	-0.2%	-0.2%	-2.0%	-0.8%	-1.0%	-2.5%	-1.4%	-1.5%	-2.5%	-1.4%	-1.6%
Labour Demand - vol.	-0.5%	-0.2%	-0.2%	-0.5%	-0.2%	-0.3%	4.6%	7.4%	7.2%	3.7%	6.3%	6.1%	3.6%	6.1%	5.9%
Private Consumption - vol.	0.2%	0.2%	0.2%	0.2%	0.2%	0.2%	-1.2%	-1.7%	-2.1%	-1.2%	-1.7%	-2.1%	-1.3%	-1.8%	-2.2%
Supply to domestic - vol.	-0.2%	0.8%	0.8%	-0.2%	0.8%	0.8%	5.3%	10.6%	10.2%	4.4%	9.6%	9.3%	4.3%	9.4%	9.0%
Intra-EU Trade - vol	-1.6%	-3.4%	-3.4%	-1.6%	-3.4%	-3.4%	-0.1%	-5.8%	-5.8%	-1.9%	-7.6%	-7.6%	-2.1%	-7.8%	-7.9%

Chemical

	Border Controls			Border controls and x-ineff.			Market segmentation			Trade *antimonde*			Full *antimonde*		
	1988	1991	1994	1988	1991	1994	1988	1991	1994	1988	1991	1994	1988	1991	1994
Domestic Production - vol.	0.1%	0.1%	0.1%	0.1%	0.1%	0.1%	4.1%	4.0%	3.8%	4.4%	4.2%	3.9%	4.2%	4.0%	3.7%
Imports - vol.	1.0%	1.3%	1.3%	1.0%	1.3%	1.3%	-4.9%	-4.5%	-4.3%	-3.9%	-3.3%	-3.1%	-3.7%	-3.0%	-2.6%
Exports - vol.	-0.3%	-0.4%	-0.4%	-0.3%	-0.4%	-0.4%	1.9%	1.6%	1.4%	1.8%	1.5%	1.3%	1.8%	1.4%	1.2%
Absorption - vol.	0.0%	0.0%	0.0%	0.0%	0.0%	0.0%	1.7%	1.6%	1.3%	1.7%	1.5%	1.3%	1.6%	1.5%	1.2%
Investment - vol.	0.1%	0.0%	0.0%	0.1%	0.0%	0.0%	-2.2%	-2.3%	-2.4%	-2.1%	-2.2%	-2.3%	-2.1%	-2.3%	-2.4%
Labour Demand - vol.	0.2%	0.1%	0.1%	0.2%	0.1%	0.1%	4.4%	4.5%	4.3%	4.7%	4.7%	4.5%	4.6%	4.5%	4.3%
Private Consumption - vol.	0.1%	0.1%	0.1%	0.1%	0.1%	0.1%	-1.1%	-1.2%	-1.4%	-1.1%	-1.2%	-1.4%	-1.1%	-1.3%	-1.5%
Supply to domestic - vol.	0.7%	2.0%	2.0%	0.7%	2.0%	2.0%	5.1%	7.5%	7.2%	5.4%	7.8%	7.5%	5.3%	7.7%	7.3%
Intra-EU Trade - vol	-1.2%	-3.2%	-3.2%	-1.2%	-3.2%	-3.2%	0.1%	-3.6%	-3.7%	-0.3%	-4.3%	-4.4%	-0.5%	-4.5%	-4.6%

Other Intensive Industries

	Border Controls			Border controls and x-ineff.			Market segmentation			Trade *antimonde*			Full *antimonde*		
	1988	1991	1994	1988	1991	1994	1988	1991	1994	1988	1991	1994	1988	1991	1994
Domestic Production - vol.	-0.2%	-0.4%	-0.4%	-0.2%	-0.4%	-0.4%	-0.8%	-1.5%	-1.8%	-1.0%	-1.8%	-2.1%	-1.1%	-1.9%	-2.2%
Imports - vol.	1.8%	2.0%	2.0%	1.8%	2.1%	2.1%	-7.9%	-7.3%	-7.0%	-6.1%	-5.3%	-5.0%	-5.8%	-4.9%	-4.5%
Exports - vol.	-0.5%	-0.6%	-0.6%	-0.5%	-0.6%	-0.6%	2.0%	1.7%	1.5%	1.7%	1.4%	1.2%	1.7%	1.3%	1.1%
Absorption - vol.	-0.1%	-0.1%	-0.1%	-0.1%	-0.1%	-0.1%	-1.9%	-2.0%	-2.3%	-2.0%	-2.2%	-2.4%	-2.1%	-2.2%	-2.5%
Investment - vol.	-0.2%	-0.2%	-0.2%	-0.1%	-0.2%	-0.2%	-4.5%	-4.9%	-5.0%	-4.6%	-5.0%	-5.2%	-4.6%	-5.0%	-5.2%
Labour Demand - vol.	-0.2%	-0.4%	-0.4%	-0.2%	-0.4%	-0.4%	-0.7%	-1.3%	-1.5%	-0.8%	-1.6%	-1.8%	-0.9%	-1.6%	-1.8%
Private Consumption - vol.	0.2%	0.2%	0.2%	0.2%	0.2%	0.2%	-1.4%	-1.4%	-1.7%	-1.4%	-1.5%	-1.7%	-1.4%	-1.6%	-1.8%
Supply to domestic - vol.	0.1%	0.5%	0.5%	0.2%	0.5%	0.5%	-0.8%	-0.5%	-0.8%	-0.9%	-0.6%	-0.9%	-0.9%	-0.6%	-1.0%
Intra-EU Trade - vol	-1.7%	-4.1%	-4.1%	-1.7%	-4.1%	-4.1%	-1.8%	-5.2%	-5.3%	-2.8%	-6.4%	-6.5%	-2.9%	-6.6%	-6.7%

Electrical goods

	Border Controls			Border controls and x-ineff.			Market segmentation			Trade *antimonde*			Full *antimonde*		
	1988	1991	1994	1988	1991	1994	1988	1991	1994	1988	1991	1994	1988	1991	1994
Domestic Production - vol.	-0.6%	-0.9%	-0.9%	-0.6%	-0.9%	-0.9%	2.4%	3.8%	3.5%	1.8%	3.2%	2.8%	1.7%	2.9%	2.5%
Imports - vol.	1.5%	1.7%	1.7%	1.5%	1.7%	1.8%	-7.8%	-7.3%	-7.1%	-6.5%	-5.9%	-5.6%	-6.3%	-5.6%	-5.2%
Exports - vol.	-0.6%	-0.7%	-0.7%	-0.6%	-0.7%	-0.7%	2.4%	2.1%	1.9%	2.1%	1.8%	1.6%	2.0%	1.7%	1.4%
Absorption - vol.	-0.1%	-0.2%	-0.2%	-0.1%	-0.2%	-0.2%	-2.8%	-2.6%	-2.8%	-3.0%	-2.8%	-3.0%	-3.0%	-2.9%	-3.1%
Investment - vol.	-0.3%	-0.4%	-0.4%	-0.3%	-0.4%	-0.5%	-3.1%	-2.5%	-2.7%	-3.4%	-2.8%	-3.0%	-3.4%	-2.9%	-3.1%
Labour Demand - vol.	-0.6%	-0.9%	-0.9%	-0.6%	-0.9%	-0.9%	2.7%	4.3%	4.0%	2.2%	3.7%	3.4%	2.1%	3.5%	3.3%
Private Consumption - vol.	0.2%	0.2%	0.2%	0.2%	0.2%	0.2%	-1.5%	-1.4%	-1.6%	-1.5%	-1.4%	-1.7%	-1.5%	-1.5%	-1.8%
Supply to domestic - vol.	0.0%	1.1%	1.1%	0.0%	1.1%	1.1%	2.1%	6.3%	5.9%	1.8%	6.1%	5.6%	1.7%	5.9%	5.4%
Intra-EU Trade - vol	-1.6%	-3.8%	-3.8%	-1.6%	-3.8%	-3.8%	-0.9%	-5.6%	-5.7%	-2.2%	-7.0%	-7.1%	-2.3%	-7.2%	-7.3%

Transport equipment

	Border Controls			Border controls and x-ineff.			Market segmentation			Trade *antimonde*			Full *antimonde*		
	1988	1991	1994	1988	1991	1994	1988	1991	1994	1988	1991	1994	1988	1991	1994
Domestic Production - vol.	-0.2%	-0.7%	-0.7%	-0.2%	-0.7%	-0.7%	0.2%	1.3%	0.9%	0.0%	1.1%	0.7%	-0.1%	0.9%	0.5%
Imports - vol.	1.5%	1.7%	1.7%	1.5%	1.7%	1.7%	-7.7%	-7.0%	-6.8%	-5.9%	-5.0%	-4.8%	-5.7%	-4.7%	-4.3%
Exports - vol.	-0.6%	-0.7%	-0.7%	-0.6%	-0.7%	-0.8%	2.4%	2.1%	1.9%	2.0%	1.7%	1.5%	1.9%	1.6%	1.4%
Absorption - vol.	0.2%	0.0%	0.0%	0.2%	0.0%	0.0%	-3.2%	-2.3%	-2.4%	-3.2%	-2.4%	-2.4%	-3.3%	-2.4%	-2.5%
Investment - vol.	-0.1%	-0.3%	-0.3%	-0.1%	-0.3%	-0.4%	-4.0%	-3.5%	-3.8%	-4.1%	-3.6%	-3.9%	-4.1%	-3.7%	-3.9%
Labour Demand - vol.	-0.1%	-0.5%	-0.6%	-0.1%	-0.5%	-0.6%	1.0%	2.6%	2.4%	0.9%	2.5%	2.2%	0.8%	2.4%	2.1%
Private Consumption - vol.	0.5%	0.2%	0.1%	0.5%	0.2%	0.1%	-4.0%	-2.0%	-1.8%	-3.9%	-2.1%	-1.8%	-4.0%	-2.2%	-1.9%
Supply to domestic - vol.	0.7%	1.6%	1.6%	0.7%	1.6%	1.6%	0.5%	7.7%	7.3%	0.6%	7.8%	7.4%	0.5%	7.7%	7.3%
Intra-EU Trade - vol	-0.8%	-2.3%	-2.3%	-0.8%	-2.3%	-2.3%	-3.1%	-7.9%	-7.9%	-3.5%	-8.4%	-8.5%	-3.6%	-8.6%	-8.6%

Other Equipment

	Border Controls			Border controls and x-ineff.			Market segmentation			Trade *antimonde*			Full *antimonde*		
	1988	1991	1994	1988	1991	1994	1988	1991	1994	1988	1991	1994	1988	1991	1994
Domestic Production - vol.	-0.8%	-1.0%	-1.0%	-0.8%	-1.0%	-1.0%	0.4%	0.2%	0.0%	-0.4%	-0.6%	-0.9%	-0.5%	-0.8%	-1.2%
Imports - vol.	1.4%	1.6%	1.6%	1.4%	1.6%	1.6%	-7.0%	-6.7%	-6.6%	-5.3%	-4.9%	-4.7%	-5.1%	-4.6%	-4.4%
Exports - vol.	-0.8%	-0.9%	-0.9%	-0.8%	-0.9%	-0.9%	2.4%	2.0%	1.8%	1.9%	1.5%	1.3%	1.8%	1.4%	1.2%
Absorption - vol.	-0.2%	-0.3%	-0.3%	-0.2%	-0.3%	-0.3%	-3.8%	-3.9%	-4.2%	-4.0%	-4.2%	-4.5%	-4.1%	-4.3%	-4.6%
Investment - vol.	-0.4%	-0.5%	-0.5%	-0.4%	-0.5%	-0.5%	-4.0%	-4.2%	-4.4%	-4.4%	-4.6%	-4.8%	-4.4%	-4.6%	-4.9%
Labour Demand - vol.	-0.8%	-1.0%	-1.0%	-0.8%	-1.0%	-1.0%	0.7%	0.7%	0.5%	0.0%	-0.2%	-0.3%	-0.1%	-0.3%	-0.5%
Private Consumption - vol.	0.1%	0.2%	0.2%	0.1%	0.2%	0.2%	-1.0%	-1.4%	-1.7%	-1.0%	-1.4%	-1.8%	-1.1%	-1.5%	-1.9%
Supply to domestic - vol.	0.0%	0.9%	0.9%	0.0%	0.9%	0.9%	-1.1%	0.4%	0.1%	-1.5%	0.1%	-0.3%	-1.5%	-0.1%	-0.5%
Intra-EU Trade - vol	-1.3%	-2.9%	-2.9%	-1.3%	-2.9%	-2.9%	-1.3%	-3.7%	-3.8%	-2.5%	-5.0%	-5.2%	-2.6%	-5.2%	-5.4%

Consumer goods

	Border Controls			Border controls and x-ineff.			Market segmentation			Trade *antimonde*			Full *antimonde*		
	1988	1991	1994	1988	1991	1994	1988	1991	1994	1988	1991	1994	1988	1991	1994
Domestic Production - vol.	-0.2%	-0.1%	-0.1%	-0.2%	-0.1%	-0.1%	1.5%	0.6%	0.3%	1.3%	0.4%	0.1%	1.2%	0.3%	-0.1%
Imports - vol.	1.5%	1.8%	1.8%	1.6%	1.9%	1.9%	-5.4%	-4.8%	-4.5%	-4.6%	-3.9%	-3.5%	-4.4%	-3.7%	-3.2%
Exports - vol.	-0.7%	-0.8%	-0.8%	-0.7%	-0.8%	-0.8%	2.5%	2.1%	1.9%	2.2%	1.8%	1.5%	2.1%	1.7%	1.4%
Absorption - vol.	0.1%	0.1%	0.1%	0.1%	0.1%	0.1%	-0.6%	-0.8%	-1.0%	-0.6%	-0.8%	-1.0%	-0.6%	-0.9%	-1.1%
Investment - vol.	-0.1%	-0.1%	-0.1%	-0.1%	-0.1%	-0.1%	-3.5%	-3.9%	-4.1%	-3.5%	-4.0%	-4.2%	-3.6%	-4.1%	-4.3%
Labour Demand - vol.	-0.2%	-0.1%	-0.1%	-0.2%	-0.1%	-0.1%	1.7%	0.9%	0.7%	1.6%	0.8%	0.6%	1.6%	0.7%	0.5%
Private Consumption - vol.	0.1%	0.1%	0.1%	0.1%	0.1%	0.1%	-0.9%	-1.0%	-1.2%	-0.9%	-1.0%	-1.2%	-1.0%	-1.1%	-1.3%
Supply to domestic - vol.	0.3%	1.1%	1.1%	0.3%	1.1%	1.1%	1.4%	1.1%	0.8%	1.3%	1.1%	0.7%	1.2%	0.9%	0.5%
Intra-EU Trade - vol	-2.0%	-4.6%	-4.6%	-2.0%	-4.6%	-4.6%	-0.1%	-2.1%	-2.3%	-0.8%	-2.9%	-3.1%	-0.9%	-3.0%	-3.3%

Construction

	Border Controls			Border controls and x-ineff.			Market segmentation			Trade *antimonde*			Full *antimonde*		
	1988	1991	1994	1988	1991	1994	1988	1991	1994	1988	1991	1994	1988	1991	1994
Domestic Production - vol.	0.1%	0.2%	0.2%	0.2%	0.2%	0.2%	-7.1%	-7.4%	-7.6%	-7.0%	-7.3%	-7.5%	-7.0%	-7.3%	-7.5%
Imports - vol.	0.1%	0.2%	0.1%	0.1%	0.1%	0.1%	-3.6%	-3.7%	-3.8%	-3.5%	-3.6%	-3.7%	-3.5%	-3.6%	-3.7%
Exports - vol.	-0.3%	-0.3%	-0.3%	-0.3%	-0.3%	-0.3%	0.7%	0.6%	0.5%	0.5%	0.4%	0.3%	0.5%	0.4%	0.3%
Absorption - vol.	0.2%	0.2%	0.2%	0.2%	0.2%	0.2%	-7.2%	-7.5%	-7.7%	-7.1%	-7.4%	-7.6%	-7.1%	-7.4%	-7.6%
Investment - vol.	0.1%	0.1%	0.1%	0.1%	0.1%	0.1%	-7.6%	-7.8%	-7.9%	-7.6%	-7.7%	-7.9%	-7.6%	-7.7%	-7.8%
Labour Demand - vol.	0.2%	0.1%	0.1%	0.2%	0.2%	0.2%	-7.0%	-7.2%	-7.3%	-6.9%	-7.1%	-7.2%	-6.9%	-7.0%	-7.1%
Private Consumption - vol.	0.3%	0.1%	0.1%	0.3%	0.1%	0.1%	-1.9%	-1.0%	-1.0%	-1.8%	-1.1%	-1.1%	-1.9%	-1.1%	-1.1%
Supply to domestic - vol.	0.1%	0.2%	0.2%	0.2%	0.2%	0.2%	-7.1%	-7.4%	-7.6%	-7.0%	-7.3%	-7.5%	-7.0%	-7.3%	-7.5%
Intra-EU Trade - vol	0.3%	0.3%	0.3%	0.3%	0.3%	0.3%	-3.5%	-3.6%	-3.7%	-3.3%	-3.4%	-3.5%	-3.3%	-3.4%	-3.5%

Telecommunications

	Border Controls			Border controls and x-ineff.			Market segmentation			Trade *antimonde*			Full *antimonde*		
	1988	1991	1994	1988	1991	1994	1988	1991	1994	1988	1991	1994	1988	1991	1994
Domestic Production - vol.	0.1%	0.1%	0.1%	0.2%	0.2%	0.2%	-0.2%	-0.9%	-1.2%	-0.1%	-0.9%	-1.2%	-0.1%	-0.8%	-1.1%
Imports - vol.	0.9%	1.0%	1.1%	0.8%	0.9%	0.9%	-6.7%	-6.5%	-6.2%	-6.2%	-6.1%	-5.8%	-6.2%	-6.0%	-5.6%
Exports - vol.	-0.2%	-0.3%	-0.3%	-0.2%	-0.2%	-0.3%	1.1%	0.9%	0.8%	1.1%	0.9%	0.8%	1.0%	0.9%	0.7%
Absorption - vol.	0.1%	0.1%	0.1%	0.1%	0.2%	0.2%	-0.5%	-0.7%	-1.0%	-0.5%	-0.8%	-1.0%	-0.4%	-0.7%	-1.0%
Investment - vol.	0.1%	0.1%	0.1%	0.1%	0.2%	0.2%	-4.1%	-4.6%	-4.7%	-4.3%	-4.6%	-4.7%	-4.2%	-4.5%	-4.6%
Labour Demand - vol.	0.1%	0.1%	0.1%	-0.3%	-0.6%	-0.6%	0.4%	0.4%	0.3%	0.5%	0.5%	0.4%	0.1%	-0.3%	-0.3%
Private Consumption - vol.	0.1%	0.1%	0.1%	0.1%	0.2%	0.2%	-0.8%	-1.3%	-1.6%	-0.8%	-1.3%	-1.6%	-0.8%	-1.3%	-1.7%
Supply to domestic - vol.	0.0%	0.0%	0.0%	0.1%	0.3%	0.3%	0.4%	1.2%	0.9%	0.4%	1.1%	0.8%	0.4%	1.2%	0.9%
Intra-EU Trade - vol	0.4%	0.3%	0.3%	1.1%	1.3%	1.3%	-7.9%	-18.8%	-18.9%	-7.6%	-18.7%	-18.7%	-7.7%	-18.8%	-18.9%

Transports

	Border Controls			Border controls and x-ineff.			Market segmentation			Trade *antimonde*			Full *antimonde*		
	1988	1991	1994	1988	1991	1994	1988	1991	1994	1988	1991	1994	1988	1991	1994
Domestic Production - vol.	0.3%	0.3%	0.3%	0.3%	0.3%	0.3%	0.2%	0.0%	-0.3%	0.3%	0.3%	0.0%	0.4%	0.2%	0.0%
Imports - vol.	0.1%	0.2%	0.2%	0.1%	0.2%	0.2%	0.1%	0.0%	-0.1%	0.2%	0.1%	0.0%	0.2%	0.1%	0.0%
Exports - vol.	-0.1%	-0.2%	-0.2%	-0.1%	-0.2%	-0.2%	0.7%	0.6%	0.5%	0.7%	0.6%	0.5%	0.6%	0.5%	0.4%
Absorption - vol.	0.0%	0.0%	0.0%	0.1%	0.1%	0.1%	-0.1%	-0.3%	-0.5%	-0.1%	-0.3%	-0.6%	-0.1%	-0.3%	-0.6%
Investment - vol.	0.1%	0.2%	0.2%	0.1%	0.1%	0.2%	-4.1%	-4.2%	-4.3%	-4.0%	-4.1%	-4.2%	-4.0%	-4.1%	-4.2%
Labour Demand - vol.	0.3%	0.3%	0.4%	0.3%	0.4%	0.4%	0.2%	0.1%	-0.1%	0.5%	0.4%	0.3%	0.6%	0.5%	0.3%
Private Consumption - vol.	0.1%	0.2%	0.2%	0.1%	0.2%	0.2%	-0.9%	-1.3%	-1.6%	-0.9%	-1.3%	-1.6%	-1.0%	-1.4%	-1.7%
Supply to domestic - vol.	0.3%	0.3%	0.3%	0.3%	0.3%	0.3%	0.2%	0.0%	-0.3%	0.4%	0.3%	0.0%	0.4%	0.2%	0.0%
Intra-EU Trade - vol	1.1%	1.3%	1.3%	1.1%	1.3%	1.3%	0.0%	0.0%	-0.1%	1.1%	1.2%	1.1%	1.1%	1.2%	1.1%

Banks

	Border Controls			Border controls and x-ineff.			Market segmentation			Trade *antimonde*			Full *antimonde*		
	1988	1991	1994	1988	1991	1994	1988	1991	1994	1988	1991	1994	1988	1991	1994
Domestic Production - vol.	0.1%	0.2%	0.2%	0.1%	0.2%	0.2%	-0.7%	-0.9%	-1.3%	-0.6%	-0.9%	-1.2%	-0.7%	-0.9%	-1.3%
Imports - vol.	1.1%	1.4%	1.4%	1.1%	1.3%	1.3%	-7.0%	-6.6%	-6.3%	-6.2%	-5.8%	-5.5%	-6.0%	-5.4%	-5.0%
Exports - vol.	-0.2%	-0.3%	-0.3%	-0.2%	-0.3%	-0.3%	1.1%	0.9%	0.8%	1.0%	0.8%	0.7%	1.0%	0.8%	0.7%
Absorption - vol.	0.1%	0.2%	0.2%	0.1%	0.2%	0.2%	-0.7%	-1.0%	-1.4%	-0.7%	-1.0%	-1.3%	-0.7%	-1.1%	-1.4%
Investment - vol.	0.1%	0.1%	0.1%	0.1%	0.1%	0.1%	-4.6%	-4.7%	-4.8%	-4.5%	-4.6%	-4.8%	-4.5%	-4.6%	-4.8%
Labour Demand - vol.	0.2%	0.2%	0.2%	0.0%	-0.2%	-0.2%	-0.5%	-0.6%	-0.7%	-0.4%	-0.5%	-0.7%	-0.6%	-0.9%	-1.0%
Private Consumption - vol.	0.1%	0.2%	0.2%	0.1%	0.2%	0.2%	-1.0%	-1.5%	-1.9%	-1.0%	-1.5%	-2.0%	-1.1%	-1.6%	-2.1%
Supply to domestic - vol.	0.1%	0.2%	0.2%	0.1%	0.2%	0.2%	-0.7%	-0.9%	-1.2%	-0.6%	-0.8%	-1.2%	-0.6%	-0.9%	-1.3%
Intra-EU Trade - vol	0.3%	0.2%	0.2%	0.2%	-0.2%	-0.2%	-5.1%	-11.1%	-11.1%	-4.8%	-10.7%	-10.8%	-4.8%	-10.8%	-10.9%

Services

	Border Controls			Border controls and x-ineff.			Market segmentation			Trade *antimonde*			Full *antimonde*		
	1988	1991	1994	1988	1991	1994	1988	1991	1994	1988	1991	1994	1988	1991	1994
Domestic Production - vol.	0.3%	0.3%	0.3%	0.3%	0.3%	0.3%	-0.9%	-1.3%	-1.6%	-0.7%	-1.1%	-1.3%	-0.7%	-1.1%	-1.4%
Imports - vol.	1.8%	2.0%	2.0%	1.8%	2.0%	2.0%	-4.6%	-4.0%	-3.7%	-3.3%	-2.7%	-2.3%	-3.2%	-2.5%	-2.1%
Exports - vol.	-0.6%	-0.6%	-0.6%	-0.6%	-0.6%	-0.6%	1.4%	1.2%	1.0%	1.0%	0.8%	0.6%	1.0%	0.7%	0.5%
Absorption - vol.	0.1%	0.1%	0.1%	0.1%	0.1%	0.1%	-0.9%	-1.1%	-1.3%	-0.9%	-1.1%	-1.4%	-0.9%	-1.1%	-1.4%
Investment - vol.	0.1%	0.2%	0.2%	0.1%	0.2%	0.2%	-4.6%	-4.8%	-4.9%	-4.5%	-4.7%	-4.8%	-4.5%	-4.7%	-4.8%
Labour Demand - vol.	0.3%	0.4%	0.4%	0.3%	0.4%	0.4%	-0.8%	-1.1%	-1.2%	-0.6%	-0.8%	-0.9%	-0.6%	-0.7%	-0.8%
Private Consumption - vol.	0.1%	0.1%	0.1%	0.1%	0.1%	0.1%	-1.0%	-1.3%	-1.6%	-1.0%	-1.3%	-1.6%	-1.0%	-1.4%	-1.7%
Supply to domestic - vol.	0.1%	0.1%	0.1%	0.1%	0.1%	0.1%	-0.9%	-1.3%	-1.5%	-0.9%	-1.3%	-1.6%	-1.0%	-1.3%	-1.6%
Intra-EU Trade - vol	3.2%	4.2%	4.3%	3.2%	4.3%	4.3%	-0.1%	0.5%	0.4%	3.0%	4.4%	4.3%	2.9%	4.3%	4.2%

Non market

	Border Controls			Border controls and x-ineff.			Market segmentation			Trade *antimonde*			Full *antimonde*		
	1988	1991	1994	1988	1991	1994	1988	1991	1994	1988	1991	1994	1988	1991	1994
Domestic Production - vol.	0.0%	0.0%	0.0%	0.0%	0.0%	0.0%	-0.1%	-0.1%	-0.1%	-0.1%	-0.1%	-0.1%	-0.1%	-0.1%	-0.1%
Imports - vol.	0.0%	0.0%	0.0%	0.0%	0.0%	0.0%	0.0%	0.0%	-0.1%	0.0%	0.0%	-0.1%	0.0%	0.0%	-0.1%
Exports - vol.	-0.1%	-0.2%	-0.2%	-0.1%	-0.2%	-0.2%	0.4%	0.3%	0.3%	0.3%	0.2%	0.2%	0.3%	0.2%	0.2%
Absorption - vol.	0.0%	0.0%	0.0%	0.0%	0.0%	0.0%	-0.1%	-0.1%	-0.1%	-0.1%	-0.1%	-0.1%	-0.1%	-0.1%	-0.1%
Investment - vol.	0.0%	0.0%	0.0%	0.0%	0.0%	0.0%	-4.1%	-4.1%	-4.1%	-4.1%	-4.1%	-4.1%	-4.1%	-4.1%	-4.1%
Labour Demand - vol.	0.0%	0.0%	0.0%	0.0%	0.0%	0.0%	0.0%	0.0%	0.0%	0.0%	0.0%	0.0%	0.1%	0.1%	0.1%
Private Consumption - vol.	0.2%	0.2%	0.1%	0.2%	0.1%	0.1%	-1.1%	-1.2%	-1.5%	-1.1%	-1.3%	-1.5%	-1.2%	-1.3%	-1.6%
Supply to domestic - vol.	0.0%	0.0%	0.0%	0.0%	0.0%	0.0%	-0.1%	-0.1%	-0.1%	-0.1%	-0.1%	-0.1%	-0.1%	-0.1%	-0.1%
Intra-EU Trade - vol	0.2%	0.2%	0.2%	0.2%	0.2%	0.2%	-0.1%	-0.1%	-0.1%	0.1%	0.1%	0.1%	0.1%	0.1%	0.1%

Table B5.8.
Decomposition of effects: sectoral results for Germany (prices)

% change from *monde*

Agriculture

	Border Controls			Border controls and x-ineff.			Market segmentation			Trade *antimonde*			Full *antimonde*		
	1988	1991	1994	1988	1991	1994	1988	1991	1994	1988	1991	1994	1988	1991	1994
Marginal Costs	-0.19%	-0.22%	-0.22%	-0.18%	-0.20%	-0.21%	0.86%	0.84%	0.96%	0.85%	0.85%	0.97%	0.85%	0.85%	0.96%
Cost of Labour	-0.06%	-0.09%	-0.09%	-0.08%	-0.12%	-0.12%	-0.45%	-0.88%	-1.30%	-0.53%	-0.99%	-1.43%	-0.64%	-1.16%	-1.65%
Deflator of Absorption	-0.61%	-0.68%	-0.68%	-0.61%	-0.68%	-0.68%	2.12%	1.86%	1.82%	1.96%	1.73%	1.69%	1.91%	1.67%	1.60%
Price of Exports-RW	-0.19%	-0.22%	-0.22%	-0.18%	-0.20%	-0.21%	0.86%	0.84%	0.96%	0.85%	0.85%	0.97%	0.85%	0.85%	0.96%

Energy

	Border Controls			Border controls and x-ineff.			Market segmentation			Trade *antimonde*			Full *antimonde*		
	1988	1991	1994	1988	1991	1994	1988	1991	1994	1988	1991	1994	1988	1991	1994
Marginal Costs	-0.45%	-0.51%	-0.51%	-0.45%	-0.51%	-0.52%	1.45%	1.22%	1.17%	1.29%	1.08%	1.02%	1.24%	1.01%	0.92%
Cost of Labour	-0.06%	-0.09%	-0.09%	-0.08%	-0.12%	-0.12%	-0.45%	-0.88%	-1.30%	-0.53%	-0.99%	-1.43%	-0.64%	-1.16%	-1.65%
Deflator of Absorption	-0.80%	-0.90%	-0.90%	-0.80%	-0.90%	-0.92%	2.58%	2.17%	2.02%	2.29%	1.90%	1.73%	2.21%	1.78%	1.57%
Price of Exports-RW	-0.45%	-0.51%	-0.51%	-0.45%	-0.51%	-0.52%	1.45%	1.22%	1.17%	1.29%	1.08%	1.02%	1.24%	1.01%	0.92%

Metal Industries

	Border Controls			Border controls and x-ineff.			Market segmentation			Trade *antimonde*			Full *antimonde*		
	1988	1991	1994	1988	1991	1994	1988	1991	1994	1988	1991	1994	1988	1991	1994
Marginal Costs	-0.52%	-0.56%	-0.56%	-0.52%	-0.56%	-0.56%	1.95%	1.63%	1.45%	1.84%	1.56%	1.37%	1.85%	1.57%	1.38%
Cost of Labour	-0.06%	-0.09%	-0.09%	-0.08%	-0.12%	-0.12%	-0.45%	-0.88%	-1.30%	-0.53%	-0.99%	-1.43%	-0.64%	-1.16%	-1.65%
Deflator of Absorption	-0.70%	-0.75%	-0.75%	-0.71%	-0.76%	-0.76%	2.73%	2.33%	2.09%	2.60%	2.25%	2.00%	2.58%	2.22%	1.96%
Price of Exports-RW	-0.52%	-0.57%	-0.57%	-0.52%	-0.57%	-0.57%	1.86%	1.48%	1.30%	1.76%	1.41%	1.23%	1.77%	1.42%	1.24%

Chemical

	Border Controls			Border controls and x-ineff.			Market segmentation			Trade *antimonde*			Full *antimonde*		
	1988	1991	1994	1988	1991	1994	1988	1991	1994	1988	1991	1994	1988	1991	1994
Marginal Costs	-0.20%	-0.22%	-0.22%	-0.20%	-0.22%	-0.22%	1.06%	0.85%	0.76%	1.08%	0.89%	0.79%	1.07%	0.88%	0.77%
Cost of Labour	-0.06%	-0.09%	-0.09%	-0.08%	-0.12%	-0.12%	-0.45%	-0.88%	-1.30%	-0.53%	-0.99%	-1.43%	-0.64%	-1.16%	-1.65%
Deflator of Absorption	-0.20%	-0.22%	-0.22%	-0.21%	-0.22%	-0.23%	1.97%	1.67%	1.51%	2.13%	1.89%	1.73%	2.10%	1.85%	1.66%
Price of Exports-RW	-0.20%	-0.24%	-0.24%	-0.20%	-0.24%	-0.24%	0.99%	0.75%	0.66%	1.01%	0.79%	0.69%	1.00%	0.78%	0.67%

Other Intensive Industries

	Border Controls			Border controls and x-ineff.			Market segmentation			Trade *antimonde*			Full *antimonde*		
	1988	1991	1994	1988	1991	1994	1988	1991	1994	1988	1991	1994	1988	1991	1994
Marginal Costs	-0.18%	-0.21%	-0.21%	-0.18%	-0.21%	-0.21%	0.65%	0.47%	0.38%	0.62%	0.44%	0.35%	0.61%	0.43%	0.34%
Cost of Labour	-0.06%	-0.09%	-0.09%	-0.08%	-0.12%	-0.12%	-0.45%	-0.88%	-1.30%	-0.53%	-0.99%	-1.43%	-0.64%	-1.16%	-1.65%
Deflator of Absorption	-0.23%	-0.26%	-0.26%	-0.24%	-0.26%	-0.27%	1.04%	0.80%	0.68%	1.03%	0.82%	0.70%	1.01%	0.79%	0.66%
Price of Exports-RW	-0.18%	-0.21%	-0.21%	-0.18%	-0.21%	-0.21%	0.65%	0.46%	0.38%	0.62%	0.44%	0.35%	0.61%	0.43%	0.34%

Electrical goods

	Border Controls			Border controls and x-ineff.			Market segmentation			Trade *antimonde*			Full *antimonde*		
	1988	1991	1994	1988	1991	1994	1988	1991	1994	1988	1991	1994	1988	1991	1994
Marginal Costs	-0.16%	-0.18%	-0.18%	-0.16%	-0.18%	-0.19%	0.51%	0.30%	0.17%	0.48%	0.28%	0.14%	0.47%	0.25%	0.11%
Cost of Labour	-0.06%	-0.09%	-0.09%	-0.08%	-0.12%	-0.12%	-0.45%	-0.88%	-1.30%	-0.53%	-0.99%	-1.43%	-0.64%	-1.16%	-1.65%
Deflator of Absorption	-0.41%	-0.44%	-0.44%	-0.41%	-0.45%	-0.45%	1.83%	1.50%	1.28%	1.80%	1.50%	1.27%	1.76%	1.43%	1.17%
Price of Exports-RW	-0.16%	-0.19%	-0.19%	-0.16%	-0.19%	-0.19%	0.49%	0.26%	0.13%	0.46%	0.23%	0.10%	0.44%	0.21%	0.06%

Transport equipment

	Border Controls			Border controls and x-ineff.			Market segmentation			Trade *antimonde*			Full *antimonde*		
	1988	1991	1994	1988	1991	1994	1988	1991	1994	1988	1991	1994	1988	1991	1994
Marginal Costs	-0.17%	-0.18%	-0.18%	-0.17%	-0.18%	-0.18%	0.80%	0.65%	0.54%	0.79%	0.66%	0.54%	0.78%	0.66%	0.54%
Cost of Labour	-0.06%	-0.09%	-0.09%	-0.08%	-0.12%	-0.12%	-0.45%	-0.88%	-1.30%	-0.53%	-0.99%	-1.43%	-0.64%	-1.16%	-1.65%
Deflator of Absorption	-0.23%	-0.14%	-0.14%	-0.23%	-0.14%	-0.14%	2.05%	2.14%	1.97%	2.12%	2.28%	2.10%	2.11%	2.26%	2.07%
Price of Exports-RW	-0.19%	-0.21%	-0.21%	-0.19%	-0.21%	-0.21%	0.62%	0.29%	0.18%	0.60%	0.28%	0.17%	0.60%	0.28%	0.17%

Other Equipment

	Border Controls			Border controls and x-ineff.			Market segmentation			Trade *antimonde*			Full *antimonde*		
	1988	1991	1994	1988	1991	1994	1988	1991	1994	1988	1991	1994	1988	1991	1994
Marginal Costs	-0.19%	-0.21%	-0.21%	-0.19%	-0.22%	-0.22%	0.62%	0.39%	0.24%	0.58%	0.36%	0.20%	0.57%	0.34%	0.17%
Cost of Labour	-0.06%	-0.09%	-0.09%	-0.08%	-0.12%	-0.12%	-0.45%	-0.88%	-1.30%	-0.53%	-0.99%	-1.43%	-0.64%	-1.16%	-1.65%
Deflator of Absorption	-0.43%	-0.46%	-0.46%	-0.44%	-0.46%	-0.47%	1.69%	1.35%	1.13%	1.62%	1.32%	1.09%	1.58%	1.26%	1.01%
Price of Exports-RW	-0.19%	-0.21%	-0.21%	-0.19%	-0.22%	-0.22%	0.61%	0.37%	0.22%	0.57%	0.34%	0.19%	0.56%	0.33%	0.16%

Consumer goods

	Border Controls			Border controls and x-ineff.			Market segmentation			Trade *antimonde*			Full *antimonde*		
	1988	1991	1994	1988	1991	1994	1988	1991	1994	1988	1991	1994	1988	1991	1994
Marginal Costs	-0.25%	-0.29%	-0.29%	-0.25%	-0.28%	-0.28%	0.98%	0.79%	0.73%	0.94%	0.77%	0.71%	0.94%	0.77%	0.70%
Cost of Labour	-0.06%	-0.09%	-0.09%	-0.08%	-0.12%	-0.12%	-0.45%	-0.88%	-1.30%	-0.53%	-0.99%	-1.43%	-0.64%	-1.16%	-1.65%
Deflator of Absorption	-0.41%	-0.46%	-0.46%	-0.41%	-0.46%	-0.46%	1.77%	1.46%	1.32%	1.74%	1.46%	1.32%	1.72%	1.42%	1.26%
Price of Exports-RW	-0.25%	-0.29%	-0.29%	-0.25%	-0.28%	-0.28%	0.98%	0.79%	0.73%	0.94%	0.77%	0.71%	0.94%	0.77%	0.70%

Construction

	Border Controls			Border controls and x-ineff.			Market segmentation			Trade *antimonde*			Full *antimonde*		
	1988	1991	1994	1988	1991	1994	1988	1991	1994	1988	1991	1994	1988	1991	1994
Marginal Costs	-0.13%	-0.15%	-0.15%	-0.13%	-0.15%	-0.15%	0.40%	0.24%	0.15%	0.38%	0.22%	0.13%	0.37%	0.20%	0.11%
Cost of Labour	-0.06%	-0.09%	-0.09%	-0.08%	-0.12%	-0.12%	-0.45%	-0.88%	-1.30%	-0.53%	-0.99%	-1.43%	-0.64%	-1.16%	-1.65%
Deflator of Absorption	-0.13%	-0.15%	-0.15%	-0.13%	-0.15%	-0.15%	0.40%	0.24%	0.15%	0.38%	0.22%	0.13%	0.37%	0.20%	0.11%
Price of Exports-RW	-0.13%	-0.15%	-0.15%	-0.13%	-0.15%	-0.15%	0.40%	0.24%	0.15%	0.38%	0.22%	0.13%	0.37%	0.20%	0.11%

Telecommunications

	Border Controls			Border controls and x-ineff.			Market segmentation			Trade *antimonde*			Full *antimonde*		
	1988	1991	1994	1988	1991	1994	1988	1991	1994	1988	1991	1994	1988	1991	1994
Marginal Costs	0.05%	0.05%	0.06%	0.04%	0.05%	0.06%	-0.05%	0.02%	0.16%	-0.03%	0.04%	0.18%	-0.04%	0.03%	0.17%
Cost of Labour	-0.06%	-0.09%	-0.09%	-0.08%	-0.12%	-0.12%	-0.45%	-0.88%	-1.30%	-0.53%	-0.99%	-1.43%	-0.64%	-1.16%	-1.65%
Deflator of Absorption	0.00%	-0.01%	0.00%	-0.19%	-0.37%	-0.37%	0.29%	0.39%	0.49%	0.30%	0.40%	0.50%	0.12%	0.03%	0.13%
Price of Exports-RW	0.04%	0.04%	0.05%	-0.02%	-0.08%	-0.07%	-0.15%	-0.17%	-0.04%	-0.14%	-0.16%	-0.03%	-0.19%	-0.27%	-0.15%

Transports

	Border Controls			Border controls and x-ineff.			Market segmentation			Trade *antimonde*			Full *antimonde*		
	1988	1991	1994	1988	1991	1994	1988	1991	1994	1988	1991	1994	1988	1991	1994
Marginal Costs	-0.11%	-0.13%	-0.14%	-0.11%	-0.13%	-0.14%	0.31%	0.22%	0.22%	0.28%	0.19%	0.19%	0.26%	0.16%	0.15%
Cost of Labour	-0.06%	-0.09%	-0.09%	-0.08%	-0.12%	-0.12%	-0.45%	-0.88%	-1.30%	-0.53%	-0.99%	-1.43%	-0.64%	-1.16%	-1.65%
Deflator of Absorption	-0.12%	-0.16%	-0.16%	-0.13%	-0.16%	-0.17%	0.37%	0.24%	0.24%	0.34%	0.21%	0.20%	0.32%	0.18%	0.16%
Price of Exports-RW	-0.11%	-0.13%	-0.14%	-0.11%	-0.13%	-0.14%	0.31%	0.22%	0.22%	0.28%	0.19%	0.19%	0.26%	0.16%	0.15%

Banks

	Border Controls			Border controls and x-ineff.			Market segmentation			Trade *antimonde*			Full *antimonde*		
	1988	1991	1994	1988	1991	1994	1988	1991	1994	1988	1991	1994	1988	1991	1994
Marginal Costs	0.02%	0.02%	0.01%	0.03%	0.03%	0.02%	0.00%	0.07%	0.21%	0.02%	0.09%	0.23%	0.02%	0.08%	0.21%
Cost of Labour	-0.06%	-0.09%	-0.09%	-0.08%	-0.12%	-0.12%	-0.45%	-0.88%	-1.30%	-0.53%	-0.99%	-1.43%	-0.64%	-1.16%	-1.65%
Deflator of Absorption	0.01%	0.00%	-0.01%	-0.04%	-0.10%	-0.11%	0.06%	0.12%	0.27%	0.07%	0.14%	0.28%	0.02%	0.04%	0.17%
Price of Exports-RW	0.02%	0.01%	0.01%	0.01%	0.00%	-0.01%	0.01%	0.07%	0.21%	0.02%	0.09%	0.23%	0.01%	0.06%	0.19%

Services

	Border Controls			Border controls and x-ineff.			Market segmentation			Trade *antimonde*			Full *antimonde*		
	1988	1991	1994	1988	1991	1994	1988	1991	1994	1988	1991	1994	1988	1991	1994
Marginal Costs	-0.03%	-0.04%	-0.04%	-0.02%	-0.03%	-0.03%	0.21%	0.29%	0.47%	0.23%	0.32%	0.50%	0.22%	0.31%	0.48%
Cost of Labour	-0.06%	-0.09%	-0.09%	-0.08%	-0.12%	-0.12%	-0.45%	-0.88%	-1.30%	-0.53%	-0.99%	-1.43%	-0.64%	-1.16%	-1.65%
Deflator of Absorption	-0.03%	-0.05%	-0.05%	-0.02%	-0.03%	-0.04%	0.21%	0.29%	0.46%	0.23%	0.31%	0.49%	0.22%	0.30%	0.47%
Price of Exports-RW	-0.03%	-0.04%	-0.04%	-0.02%	-0.03%	-0.03%	0.21%	0.29%	0.47%	0.23%	0.32%	0.50%	0.22%	0.31%	0.48%

Non market

	Border Controls			Border controls and x-ineff.			Market segmentation			Trade *antimonde*			Full *antimonde*		
	1988	1991	1994	1988	1991	1994	1988	1991	1994	1988	1991	1994	1988	1991	1994
Marginal Costs	-0.10%	-0.12%	-0.12%	-0.10%	-0.13%	-0.13%	0.13%	-0.12%	-0.33%	0.09%	-0.17%	-0.39%	0.07%	-0.20%	-0.43%
Cost of Labour	-0.06%	-0.09%	-0.09%	-0.08%	-0.12%	-0.12%	-0.45%	-0.88%	-1.30%	-0.53%	-0.99%	-1.43%	-0.64%	-1.16%	-1.65%
Deflator of Absorption	-0.10%	-0.12%	-0.12%	-0.11%	-0.13%	-0.13%	0.14%	-0.12%	-0.33%	0.10%	-0.17%	-0.38%	0.07%	-0.20%	-0.43%
Price of Exports-RW	-0.10%	-0.12%	-0.12%	-0.10%	-0.13%	-0.13%	0.13%	-0.12%	-0.33%	0.09%	-0.17%	-0.39%	0.07%	-0.20%	-0.43%

Table B6.1.

The full *antimonde* scenario: macroeconomic aggregates for Greece

Macroeconomic Aggregates (vol.) (% change from *monde*)	Constraint Case			Flexible Case			Efficiency Case		
	1988	1991	1994	1988	1991	1994	1988	1991	1994
GDP fact. pr.	-0.31%	-0.40%	-0.53%	-0.16%	-0.32%	-0.78%	-0.19%	-0.46%	-1.01%
Priv. Consumption	-0.39%	-0.02%	0.03%	-0.88%	-0.82%	-1.14%	-0.89%	-0.86%	-1.21%
Absorption	-0.41%	-0.14%	-0.11%	-1.44%	-1.76%	-2.03%	-1.45%	-1.80%	-2.09%
Total Investment	-2.30%	0.12%	0.62%	-4.45%	-4.67%	-4.79%	-4.45%	-4.67%	-4.79%
Total Exports to RW	-0.61%	-2.75%	-3.52%	1.50%	1.18%	0.96%	1.48%	1.07%	0.78%
Total Imports from RW	-1.66%	-1.48%	-1.42%	-3.27%	-2.99%	-2.74%	-3.23%	-2.84%	-2.49%
Total Intra-EU Trade	0.15%	0.85%	0.80%	0.15%	-1.52%	-1.79%	0.13%	-1.60%	-1.93%
Employment (diff. from *monde*, 10³ persons)	8	5	2	18	15	7	17	14	5
Disposable Income (deflated)	-0.42%	-0.02%	0.03%	-0.95%	-0.88%	-1.22%	-0.96%	-0.92%	-1.30%

Macroeconomic Ratios (abs. diff. from *monde*)	Constraint Case			Flexible Case			Efficiency Case		
	1988	1991	1994	1988	1991	1994	1988	1991	1994
Current Account as % of GDP	0.00%	0.00%	0.00%	-1.18%	-1.56%	-1.51%	-1.18%	-1.53%	-1.44%
Public Deficit as % of GDP	-0.07%	-0.05%	-0.05%	-0.27%	-0.38%	-0.50%	-0.28%	-0.42%	-0.57%
Labour Productivity	-0.51%	-0.53%	-0.58%	-0.62%	-0.72%	-0.96%	-0.64%	-0.82%	-1.13%
Investment/GDP	-0.36%	0.10%	0.21%	-1.74%	-1.80%	-1.77%	-1.73%	-1.78%	-1.72%
Priv.Cons./GDP	-0.05%	0.27%	0.39%	-0.50%	-0.34%	-0.24%	-0.48%	-0.28%	-0.14%

Deflators (% change from *monde*)	Constraint Case			Flexible Case			Efficiency Case		
	1988	1991	1994	1988	1991	1994	1988	1991	1994
Consumer Price Index	0.12%	1.44%	1.98%	0.92%	0.73%	0.71%	0.90%	0.67%	0.62%
Real Wage Rate	-0.04%	-0.17%	-0.37%	0.32%	0.14%	-0.50%	0.29%	0.00%	-0.76%
Marginal Costs	-0.03%	1.47%	2.05%	0.61%	0.52%	0.47%	0.60%	0.47%	0.39%
Producer Prices	0.09%	1.60%	2.18%	0.71%	0.62%	0.57%	0.69%	0.57%	0.50%
Average change in mark-ups (abs. diff.)	0.86%	0.99%	1.00%	0.78%	0.83%	0.89%	0.78%	0.84%	0.90%
Shadow Price of Capital	-1.26%	0.34%	1.02%	-1.38%	-1.44%	-0.71%	-1.40%	-1.50%	-0.81%
Terms-of-Trade RW	-0.71%	0.60%	1.12%	-4.82%	-3.79%	-3.08%	-4.74%	-3.46%	-2.50%

| Implicit change in real exchange rate | -0.12% | 1.73% | 2.44% | -4.15% | -2.93% | -2.13% | -4.05% | -2.54% | -1.44% |

| Trade Regime | *Segmentation* | | | *Segmentation* | | | *Segmentation* | | |

Table B6.2.
The full *antimonde* scenario: effects on IC sectors for Greece

% change from *monde*

Metal Industries	Constraint Case			Flexible Case			Efficiency Case		
	1988	1991	1994	1988	1991	1994	1988	1991	1994
Production per firm	-12.89%	-17.26%	-17.47%	-11.09%	-16.16%	-16.18%	-11.10%	-16.19%	-16.23%
Real Marginal Costs	1.13%	2.20%	2.59%	-1.83%	-0.55%	0.62%	-1.72%	-0.11%	1.39%
Real Producer Prices	2.77%	4.42%	4.84%	-0.54%	1.29%	2.45%	-0.43%	1.73%	3.24%
Mark-ups domestic (abs. diff.)	4.59%	5.39%	5.44%	4.78%	5.99%	6.00%	4.78%	6.00%	6.01%
Fixed Costs per firm	1.16%	2.13%	2.43%	-1.28%	-0.22%	0.21%	-1.22%	0.03%	0.63%
Number of Firms	9.29%	10.26%	10.02%	8.48%	6.94%	7.25%	8.48%	7.01%	7.36%
Sigma of Love of Variety	0.00%	0.00%	0.00%	0.00%	0.00%	0.00%	0.00%	0.00%	0.00%

Chemical	Constraint Case			Flexible Case			Efficiency Case		
	1988	1991	1994	1988	1991	1994	1988	1991	1994
Production per firm	-15.08%	-19.97%	-20.21%	-11.83%	-15.83%	-16.06%	-11.86%	-15.92%	-16.22%
Real Marginal Costs	0.44%	1.72%	2.20%	-3.07%	-1.78%	-0.49%	-2.95%	-1.30%	0.35%
Real Producer Prices	2.03%	3.86%	4.36%	-1.91%	-0.26%	1.05%	-1.79%	0.23%	1.90%
Mark-ups domestic (abs. diff.)	3.88%	4.77%	4.82%	3.68%	4.57%	4.59%	3.68%	4.58%	4.60%
Fixed Costs per firm	0.60%	1.75%	2.11%	-2.32%	-1.26%	-0.80%	-2.25%	-0.99%	-0.33%
Number of Firms	12.30%	12.45%	12.13%	15.03%	16.80%	16.76%	15.01%	16.70%	16.59%
Sigma of Love of Variety	0.00%	0.00%	0.00%	0.00%	0.00%	0.00%	0.00%	0.00%	0.00%

Other Intensive Industries	Constraint Case			Flexible Case			Efficiency Case		
	1988	1991	1994	1988	1991	1994	1988	1991	1994
Production per firm	-3.99%	-4.83%	-4.99%	-4.66%	-6.36%	-6.54%	-4.68%	-6.41%	-6.64%
Real Marginal Costs	0.47%	1.72%	2.19%	-2.94%	-1.70%	-0.47%	-2.82%	-1.24%	0.34%
Real Producer Prices	0.68%	1.97%	2.45%	-2.69%	-1.37%	-0.13%	-2.57%	-0.90%	0.68%
Mark-ups domestic (abs. diff.)	0.28%	0.30%	0.30%	0.38%	0.47%	0.47%	0.38%	0.47%	0.47%
Fixed Costs per firm	0.59%	1.71%	2.09%	-2.24%	-1.24%	-0.82%	-2.18%	-0.98%	-0.37%
Number of Firms	5.01%	6.44%	6.39%	3.14%	4.51%	4.68%	3.15%	4.58%	4.81%
Sigma of Love of Variety	0.00%	0.00%	0.00%	0.00%	0.00%	0.00%	0.00%	0.00%	0.00%

Electrical goods	Constraint Case			Flexible Case			Efficiency Case		
	1988	1991	1994	1988	1991	1994	1988	1991	1994
Production per firm	-14.76%	-19.08%	-19.51%	-16.25%	-21.55%	-21.70%	-16.27%	-21.62%	-21.83%
Real Marginal Costs	1.02%	2.26%	2.71%	-2.47%	-1.09%	0.14%	-2.36%	-0.61%	0.98%
Real Producer Prices	3.12%	5.03%	5.56%	-0.36%	1.70%	2.95%	-0.23%	2.19%	3.81%
Mark-ups domestic (abs. diff.)	3.31%	4.02%	4.15%	3.91%	4.79%	4.80%	3.91%	4.79%	4.81%
Fixed Costs per firm	1.11%	2.25%	2.60%	-1.88%	-0.71%	-0.25%	-1.81%	-0.43%	0.22%
Number of Firms	13.97%	16.15%	15.49%	4.23%	-1.89%	-1.75%	4.22%	-1.91%	-1.76%
Sigma of Love of Variety	0.00%	0.00%	0.00%	0.00%	0.00%	0.00%	0.00%	0.00%	0.00%

Transport equipment	Constraint Case			Flexible Case			Efficiency Case		
	1988	1991	1994	1988	1991	1994	1988	1991	1994
Production per firm	-20.67%	-26.30%	-27.16%	-22.65%	-26.99%	-27.26%	-22.68%	-27.10%	-27.45%
Real Marginal Costs	0.37%	1.84%	2.37%	-3.40%	-2.13%	-0.97%	-3.28%	-1.67%	-0.16%
Real Producer Prices	4.94%	7.92%	8.75%	1.30%	3.57%	4.78%	1.42%	4.06%	5.65%
Mark-ups domestic (abs. diff.)	6.42%	8.36%	8.78%	6.69%	7.95%	7.98%	6.69%	7.96%	8.01%
Fixed Costs per firm	0.49%	1.87%	2.30%	-2.75%	-1.72%	-1.40%	-2.69%	-1.47%	-0.96%
Number of Firms	26.03%	27.57%	26.18%	20.46%	27.29%	27.44%	20.43%	27.22%	27.33%
Sigma of Love of Variety	0.00%	0.00%	0.00%	0.00%	0.00%	0.00%	0.00%	0.00%	0.00%

Other Equipment	Constraint Case			Flexible Case			Efficiency Case		
	1988	1991	1994	1988	1991	1994	1988	1991	1994
Production per firm	-25.24%	-31.35%	-31.56%	-26.72%	-33.91%	-34.02%	-26.74%	-33.96%	-34.10%
Real Marginal Costs	0.70%	1.99%	2.45%	-2.91%	-1.57%	-0.34%	-2.79%	-1.10%	0.49%
Real Producer Prices	3.28%	5.24%	5.74%	-0.30%	1.77%	3.02%	-0.18%	2.26%	3.88%
Mark-ups domestic (abs. diff.)	3.18%	3.91%	3.94%	3.39%	4.25%	4.24%	3.39%	4.25%	4.25%
Fixed Costs per firm	0.87%	2.03%	2.39%	-2.20%	-1.08%	-0.67%	-2.13%	-0.81%	-0.21%
Number of Firms	27.99%	29.88%	29.52%	19.20%	13.04%	13.53%	19.19%	13.16%	13.73%
Sigma of Love of Variety	0.00%	0.00%	0.00%	0.00%	0.00%	0.00%	0.00%	0.00%	0.00%

Telecommunications	Constraint Case			Flexible Case			Efficiency Case		
	1988	1991	1994	1988	1991	1994	1988	1991	1994
Production per firm	0.39%	1.21%	1.30%	-0.88%	-1.73%	-2.03%	-0.89%	-1.77%	-2.10%
Real Marginal Costs	-0.29%	1.41%	2.03%	-4.47%	-3.18%	-1.91%	-4.35%	-2.69%	-1.04%
Real Producer Prices	0.24%	2.26%	2.81%	-4.60%	-3.64%	-2.41%	-4.49%	-3.16%	-1.58%
Mark-ups domestic (abs. diff.)	0.81%	1.25%	1.15%	-0.21%	-0.72%	-0.78%	-0.22%	-0.75%	-0.83%
Fixed Costs per firm	1.70%	5.20%	5.72%	-5.38%	-6.04%	-5.84%	-5.32%	-5.80%	-5.42%
Number of Firms	-1.05%	-1.62%	-1.49%	0.31%	1.00%	1.08%	0.31%	1.03%	1.15%
Sigma of Love of Variety	0.00%	0.00%	0.00%	0.00%	0.00%	0.00%	0.00%	0.00%	0.00%

Banks	Constraint Case			Flexible Case			Efficiency Case		
	1988	1991	1994	1988	1991	1994	1988	1991	1994
Production per firm	0.45%	0.62%	0.54%	-0.15%	-0.69%	-1.07%	-0.16%	-0.75%	-1.17%
Real Marginal Costs	-0.36%	1.25%	1.88%	-4.54%	-3.27%	-1.72%	-4.42%	-2.76%	-0.82%
Real Producer Prices	-0.24%	1.40%	2.01%	-4.49%	-3.26%	-1.72%	-4.36%	-2.75%	-0.83%
Mark-ups domestic (abs. diff.)	0.14%	0.17%	0.16%	0.07%	0.01%	-0.01%	0.07%	0.01%	-0.02%
Fixed Costs per firm	0.71%	2.68%	3.17%	-4.07%	-3.74%	-3.31%	-4.00%	-3.46%	-2.82%
Number of Firms	-0.27%	-0.37%	-0.32%	0.06%	0.46%	0.55%	0.06%	0.49%	0.60%
Sigma of Love of Variety	0.00%	0.00%	0.00%	0.00%	0.00%	0.00%	0.00%	0.00%	0.00%

Table B6.3.
The full *antimonde* scenario: sectoral results for Greece (volumes)

% change from *monde*

Agriculture

	Constraint Case			Flexible Case			Efficiency Case		
	1988	1991	1994	1988	1991	1994	1988	1991	1994
Domestic Production - vol.	1.0%	1.1%	0.8%	3.2%	4.6%	3.8%	3.1%	4.4%	3.5%
Imports - vol.	-6.2%	-7.0%	-6.0%	-4.3%	-2.9%	-2.3%	-4.2%	-2.6%	-1.8%
Exports - vol.	-0.5%	-4.0%	-5.5%	1.8%	1.4%	1.1%	1.7%	1.3%	0.9%
Absorption - vol.	0.5%	0.8%	0.7%	1.6%	2.3%	1.7%	1.6%	2.2%	1.5%
Investment - vol.	4.1%	9.0%	9.7%	-3.2%	-2.6%	-2.9%	-3.3%	-2.7%	-3.0%
Labour Demand - vol.	0.8%	0.9%	0.8%	2.7%	4.2%	3.8%	2.7%	4.1%	3.6%
Private Consumption - vol.	-0.7%	-0.4%	-0.1%	-0.4%	-0.6%	-0.9%	-0.4%	-0.7%	-1.0%
Supply to domestic - vol.	1.2%	1.5%	1.4%	2.6%	3.9%	3.2%	2.5%	3.7%	2.9%
Intra-EU Trade - vol	0.0%	0.0%	0.0%	1.5%	-0.4%	-0.8%	1.5%	-0.5%	-1.0%

Energy

	Constraint Case			Flexible Case			Efficiency Case		
	1988	1991	1994	1988	1991	1994	1988	1991	1994
Domestic Production - vol.	-0.4%	-1.2%	-1.5%	0.6%	0.2%	0.3%	0.5%	0.2%	0.2%
Imports - vol.	-0.4%	-0.1%	0.0%	-1.1%	-1.1%	-0.9%	-1.1%	-1.0%	-0.9%
Exports - vol.	-1.2%	-2.6%	-3.3%	0.5%	0.4%	0.3%	0.5%	0.4%	0.3%
Absorption - vol.	-0.2%	-0.4%	-0.4%	-0.5%	-0.9%	-0.9%	-0.5%	-0.9%	-1.0%
Investment - vol.	-4.9%	-4.1%	-4.1%	-3.7%	-3.9%	-3.9%	-3.7%	-3.9%	-3.9%
Labour Demand - vol.	-0.3%	-1.0%	-1.3%	0.7%	0.4%	0.5%	0.7%	0.4%	0.6%
Private Consumption - vol.	0.8%	1.6%	2.0%	-0.5%	-0.6%	-0.7%	-0.5%	-0.6%	-0.7%
Supply to domestic - vol.	-0.1%	-0.6%	-0.8%	0.7%	0.1%	-0.1%	0.7%	0.0%	-0.3%
Intra-EU Trade - vol	0.0%	0.0%	0.0%	-0.1%	0.0%	0.5%	-0.1%	0.1%	0.7%

Metal Industries

	Constraint Case			Flexible Case			Efficiency Case		
	1988	1991	1994	1988	1991	1994	1988	1991	1994
Domestic Production - vol.	-4.8%	-8.8%	-9.2%	-3.5%	-10.3%	-10.1%	-3.6%	-10.3%	-10.1%
Imports - vol.	2.6%	5.2%	5.2%	-3.9%	-5.5%	-5.1%	-3.9%	-5.3%	-4.8%
Exports - vol.	-2.4%	-4.6%	-5.0%	1.1%	0.7%	0.5%	1.0%	0.6%	0.4%
Absorption - vol.	-2.0%	-3.6%	-3.8%	-4.6%	-9.2%	-9.1%	-4.6%	-9.1%	-9.0%
Investment - vol.	-6.9%	-8.6%	-8.7%	-5.5%	-8.7%	-8.6%	-5.5%	-8.6%	-8.5%
Labour Demand - vol.	-3.0%	-6.5%	-6.9%	-2.0%	-8.4%	-8.1%	-2.0%	-8.3%	-7.9%
Private Consumption - vol.	-0.4%	-0.3%	-0.1%	-0.2%	-0.4%	-0.4%	-0.2%	-0.4%	-0.5%
Supply to domestic - vol.	-8.1%	-14.4%	-14.9%	-7.4%	-14.5%	-14.2%	-7.4%	-14.5%	-14.1%
Intra-EU Trade - vol	0.0%	0.0%	0.0%	-0.5%	-4.0%	-4.0%	-0.5%	-4.0%	-4.1%

Chemical

	Constraint Case			Flexible Case			Efficiency Case		
	1988	1991	1994	1988	1991	1994	1988	1991	1994
Domestic Production - vol.	-4.6%	-10.0%	-10.5%	1.4%	-1.7%	-2.0%	1.4%	-1.9%	-2.3%
Imports - vol.	3.1%	6.7%	6.9%	-3.2%	-2.5%	-2.2%	-3.2%	-2.3%	-1.8%
Exports - vol.	-0.9%	-2.9%	-3.4%	1.8%	1.5%	1.3%	1.8%	1.4%	1.1%
Absorption - vol.	-0.7%	-1.7%	-1.8%	0.6%	0.1%	-0.2%	0.6%	0.0%	-0.4%
Investment - vol.	-6.7%	-9.7%	-9.8%	-3.4%	-4.8%	-5.0%	-3.4%	-4.9%	-5.1%
Labour Demand - vol.	-2.8%	-7.7%	-8.2%	2.8%	0.1%	-0.1%	2.8%	0.0%	-0.3%
Private Consumption - vol.	-0.6%	-0.4%	-0.2%	-0.3%	-0.5%	-0.7%	-0.3%	-0.5%	-0.7%
Supply to domestic - vol.	-8.1%	-16.4%	-17.0%	-1.5%	-5.1%	-5.4%	-1.6%	-5.3%	-5.8%
Intra-EU Trade - vol	0.0%	0.0%	0.0%	2.4%	2.1%	1.8%	2.4%	2.0%	1.7%

Other Intensive Industries

	Constraint Case			Flexible Case			Efficiency Case		
	1988	1991	1994	1988	1991	1994	1988	1991	1994
Domestic Production - vol.	0.8%	1.3%	1.1%	-1.7%	-2.1%	-2.2%	-1.7%	-2.1%	-2.1%
Imports - vol.	-4.9%	-4.8%	-4.1%	-5.2%	-4.6%	-4.1%	-5.1%	-4.3%	-3.6%
Exports - vol.	-0.4%	-1.6%	-2.0%	1.4%	1.1%	0.9%	1.4%	1.0%	0.7%
Absorption - vol.	-0.8%	-0.1%	0.1%	-3.3%	-4.0%	-4.1%	-3.3%	-4.0%	-4.0%
Investment - vol.	-1.2%	1.8%	2.1%	-4.8%	-5.1%	-5.1%	-4.8%	-5.0%	-5.1%
Labour Demand - vol.	1.2%	1.7%	1.6%	-1.3%	-1.7%	-1.6%	-1.3%	-1.6%	-1.5%
Private Consumption - vol.	-0.5%	-0.1%	-0.1%	-0.8%	-0.8%	-1.0%	-0.8%	-0.8%	-1.1%
Supply to domestic - vol.	1.3%	2.3%	2.1%	-2.2%	-2.1%	-2.1%	-2.2%	-2.1%	-2.0%
Intra-EU Trade - vol	0.0%	0.0%	0.0%	-1.5%	-4.0%	-4.4%	-1.5%	-4.1%	-4.6%

Electrical goods

	Constraint Case			Flexible Case			Efficiency Case		
	1988	1991	1994	1988	1991	1994	1988	1991	1994
Domestic Production - vol.	-2.8%	-6.0%	-7.0%	-12.7%	-23.0%	-23.1%	-12.7%	-23.1%	-23.2%
Imports - vol.	0.2%	2.9%	2.3%	-7.0%	-7.3%	-6.9%	-7.0%	-7.0%	-6.5%
Exports - vol.	-2.8%	-5.9%	-6.5%	1.6%	1.0%	0.8%	1.5%	0.9%	0.6%
Absorption - vol.	-0.8%	-0.4%	-1.2%	-8.5%	-11.3%	-11.5%	-8.5%	-11.3%	-11.5%
Investment - vol.	-0.5%	-0.1%	-0.5%	-9.7%	-14.5%	-14.5%	-9.7%	-14.5%	-14.6%
Labour Demand - vol.	-0.4%	-3.0%	-4.0%	-10.4%	-20.4%	-20.3%	-10.4%	-20.4%	-20.3%
Private Consumption - vol.	4.0%	6.4%	3.2%	-6.0%	-2.2%	-2.5%	-6.1%	-2.2%	-2.6%
Supply to domestic - vol.	-2.5%	-5.7%	-6.9%	-15.4%	-25.3%	-25.3%	-15.4%	-25.4%	-25.4%
Intra-EU Trade - vol	0.0%	0.0%	0.0%	-0.7%	-1.0%	-1.3%	-0.8%	-1.1%	-1.4%

Transport equipment

	Constraint Case			Flexible Case			Efficiency Case		
	1988	1991	1994	1988	1991	1994	1988	1991	1994
Domestic Production - vol.	0.0%	-6.0%	-8.1%	-6.8%	-7.1%	-7.3%	-6.9%	-7.3%	-7.6%
Imports - vol.	3.9%	4.9%	3.0%	-4.0%	-2.8%	-2.7%	-4.0%	-2.7%	-2.5%
Exports - vol.	1.6%	0.1%	-0.3%	2.3%	2.1%	1.9%	2.3%	1.9%	1.7%
Absorption - vol.	3.2%	2.5%	0.6%	-4.8%	-3.1%	-3.4%	-4.8%	-3.2%	-3.4%
Investment - vol.	2.3%	-0.1%	-1.7%	-7.1%	-7.2%	-7.4%	-7.1%	-7.3%	-7.5%
Labour Demand - vol.	5.2%	0.5%	-1.4%	-1.7%	-0.9%	-0.9%	-1.7%	-1.0%	-1.1%
Private Consumption - vol.	7.5%	7.0%	3.1%	-4.6%	-1.4%	-1.6%	-4.6%	-1.4%	-1.6%
Supply to domestic - vol.	0.6%	-5.9%	-8.2%	-7.2%	-7.3%	-7.5%	-7.3%	-7.5%	-7.8%
Intra-EU Trade - vol	0.0%	0.0%	0.0%	1.6%	2.2%	1.7%	1.6%	2.0%	1.4%

Other Equipment	Constraint Case			Flexible Case			Efficiency Case		
	1988	1991	1994	1988	1991	1994	1988	1991	1994
Domestic Production - vol.	-4.3%	-10.8%	-11.4%	-12.7%	-25.3%	-25.1%	-12.7%	-25.3%	-25.1%
Imports - vol.	-1.2%	-1.6%	-1.6%	-5.8%	-7.8%	-7.5%	-5.7%	-7.6%	-7.2%
Exports - vol.	-0.8%	-2.6%	-3.1%	1.7%	1.2%	1.0%	1.6%	1.0%	0.8%
Absorption - vol.	-1.6%	-3.4%	-3.5%	-7.5%	-13.3%	-13.4%	-7.6%	-13.4%	-13.4%
Investment - vol.	2.1%	0.0%	0.3%	-9.7%	-15.5%	-15.5%	-9.7%	-15.5%	-15.5%
Labour Demand - vol.	-1.4%	-7.5%	-7.9%	-9.9%	-22.3%	-21.9%	-9.9%	-22.2%	-21.8%
Private Consumption - vol.	-0.7%	0.0%	0.0%	-1.5%	-1.2%	-1.7%	-1.5%	-1.3%	-1.8%
Supply to domestic - vol.	-3.9%	-11.0%	-11.6%	-13.6%	-27.3%	-27.0%	-13.7%	-27.2%	-27.0%
Intra-EU Trade - vol	0.0%	0.0%	0.0%	-1.9%	-3.5%	-3.8%	-1.9%	-3.6%	-3.9%

Consumer goods	Constraint Case			Flexible Case			Efficiency Case		
	1988	1991	1994	1988	1991	1994	1988	1991	1994
Domestic Production - vol.	1.1%	1.2%	0.9%	2.7%	3.7%	2.8%	2.6%	3.4%	2.4%
Imports - vol.	-9.6%	-11.9%	-11.0%	-5.0%	-3.9%	-3.3%	-4.9%	-3.5%	-2.8%
Exports - vol.	-0.4%	-3.0%	-4.1%	2.4%	1.9%	1.6%	2.3%	1.7%	1.3%
Absorption - vol.	-0.2%	0.2%	0.3%	0.2%	0.3%	-0.1%	0.2%	0.3%	-0.2%
Investment - vol.	6.8%	12.6%	13.3%	-3.2%	-2.8%	-3.2%	-3.3%	-2.9%	-3.3%
Labour Demand - vol.	1.1%	1.3%	1.1%	2.6%	3.7%	3.0%	2.6%	3.5%	2.8%
Private Consumption - vol.	-0.8%	-0.4%	-0.2%	-0.4%	-0.6%	-0.9%	-0.4%	-0.6%	-0.9%
Supply to domestic - vol.	1.5%	2.5%	2.4%	1.9%	3.5%	2.8%	1.9%	3.3%	2.5%
Intra-EU Trade - vol	0.0%	0.0%	0.0%	-0.1%	-2.7%	-3.1%	-0.1%	-2.8%	-3.2%

Construction	Constraint Case			Flexible Case			Efficiency Case		
	1988	1991	1994	1988	1991	1994	1988	1991	1994
Domestic Production - vol.	-2.2%	0.0%	0.4%	-7.9%	-8.2%	-8.4%	-7.9%	-8.2%	-8.4%
Imports - vol.	-	-	-	#VALUE!	#VALUE!	#VALUE!	#VALUE!	#VALUE!	#VALUE!
Exports - vol.	-	-	-	#VALUE!	#VALUE!	#VALUE!	#VALUE!	#VALUE!	#VALUE!
Absorption - vol.	-2.2%	0.0%	0.4%	-7.9%	-8.2%	-8.4%	-7.9%	-8.2%	-8.4%
Investment - vol.	-0.7%	5.4%	6.7%	-7.9%	-8.0%	-8.2%	-7.9%	-8.0%	-8.1%
Labour Demand - vol.	-2.2%	0.0%	0.6%	-8.0%	-8.1%	-8.2%	-7.9%	-8.1%	-8.1%
Private Consumption - vol.	-1.0%	-0.6%	-0.3%	-0.4%	-0.7%	-1.1%	-0.4%	-0.7%	-1.2%
Supply to domestic - vol.	-2.2%	0.0%	0.4%	-7.9%	-8.2%	-8.4%	-7.9%	-8.2%	-8.4%
Intra-EU Trade - vol	0.0%	0.0%	0.0%	#DIV/0!	#DIV/0!	#DIV/0!	#DIV/0!	#DIV/0!	#DIV/0!

Telecommunications	Constraint Case			Flexible Case			Efficiency Case		
	1988	1991	1994	1988	1991	1994	1988	1991	1994
Domestic Production - vol.	-0.7%	-0.4%	-0.2%	-0.6%	-0.7%	-1.0%	-0.6%	-0.8%	-1.0%
Imports - vol.	-6.5%	-6.7%	-5.9%	-5.7%	-5.6%	-5.3%	-5.6%	-5.4%	-5.0%
Exports - vol.	-2.9%	-7.2%	-7.7%	1.0%	0.9%	0.8%	1.0%	0.8%	0.7%
Absorption - vol.	-0.7%	-0.4%	-0.2%	-0.6%	-0.8%	-1.0%	-0.6%	-0.8%	-1.0%
Investment - vol.	-5.2%	-3.4%	-2.8%	-4.4%	-4.5%	-4.6%	-4.4%	-4.4%	-4.5%
Labour Demand - vol.	0.0%	0.8%	1.0%	-1.0%	-1.7%	-1.7%	-1.0%	-1.6%	-1.6%
Private Consumption - vol.	-1.2%	-0.9%	-0.6%	-0.3%	-0.6%	-0.9%	-0.3%	-0.6%	-1.0%
Supply to domestic - vol.	-0.7%	-0.4%	-0.2%	-0.6%	-0.7%	-0.9%	-0.6%	-0.7%	-1.0%
Intra-EU Trade - vol	0.0%	0.0%	0.0%	-6.7%	-17.9%	-18.3%	-6.7%	-18.0%	-18.4%

Transports	Constraint Case			Flexible Case			Efficiency Case		
	1988	1991	1994	1988	1991	1994	1988	1991	1994
Domestic Production - vol.	-1.0%	-0.4%	-0.1%	-1.5%	-1.7%	-1.9%	-1.5%	-1.7%	-2.0%
Imports - vol.	-1.0%	-0.4%	-0.1%	-0.7%	-0.8%	-1.0%	-0.7%	-0.8%	-1.0%
Exports - vol.	0.4%	-0.7%	-0.9%	0.6%	0.5%	0.4%	0.6%	0.5%	0.4%
Absorption - vol.	-1.0%	-0.4%	-0.1%	-1.5%	-1.7%	-2.0%	-1.5%	-1.7%	-2.0%
Investment - vol.	-5.6%	-3.5%	-2.8%	-4.8%	-4.9%	-5.1%	-4.8%	-4.9%	-5.0%
Labour Demand - vol.	-0.9%	-0.3%	0.1%	-1.4%	-1.6%	-1.8%	-1.4%	-1.6%	-1.7%
Private Consumption - vol.	-1.3%	-0.8%	-0.4%	-0.7%	-1.0%	-1.4%	-0.7%	-1.1%	-1.5%
Supply to domestic - vol.	-1.0%	-0.4%	-0.1%	-1.5%	-1.7%	-1.9%	-1.5%	-1.7%	-2.0%
Intra-EU Trade - vol	0.0%	0.0%	0.0%	-0.6%	-0.7%	-0.8%	-0.6%	-0.7%	-0.8%

Banks	Constraint Case			Flexible Case			Efficiency Case		
	1988	1991	1994	1988	1991	1994	1988	1991	1994
Domestic Production - vol.	0.2%	0.2%	0.2%	-0.1%	-0.2%	-0.5%	-0.1%	-0.3%	-0.6%
Imports - vol.	-15.3%	-20.9%	-20.2%	-4.6%	-4.6%	-4.1%	-4.5%	-4.3%	-3.6%
Exports - vol.	-0.4%	-2.7%	-2.9%	1.0%	0.9%	0.7%	1.0%	0.8%	0.6%
Absorption - vol.	0.1%	0.0%	0.0%	-0.2%	-0.4%	-0.7%	-0.2%	-0.5%	-0.8%
Investment - vol.	-2.3%	0.1%	0.6%	-4.2%	-4.3%	-4.4%	-4.2%	-4.3%	-4.4%
Labour Demand - vol.	0.5%	0.8%	0.8%	-0.6%	-0.9%	-1.0%	-0.5%	-0.9%	-0.9%
Private Consumption - vol.	-1.4%	-0.9%	-0.4%	-0.7%	-1.1%	-1.6%	-0.7%	-1.2%	-1.7%
Supply to domestic - vol.	0.2%	0.2%	0.2%	-0.1%	-0.2%	-0.5%	-0.1%	-0.3%	-0.6%
Intra-EU Trade - vol	0.0%	0.0%	0.0%	-4.4%	-12.5%	-12.5%	-4.4%	-12.5%	-12.4%

Services	Constraint Case			Flexible Case			Efficiency Case		
	1988	1991	1994	1988	1991	1994	1988	1991	1994
Domestic Production - vol.	-0.4%	-0.1%	0.0%	-0.4%	-0.5%	-0.9%	-0.4%	-0.6%	-1.0%
Imports - vol.	-6.9%	-8.5%	-7.7%	-3.3%	-2.7%	-2.3%	-3.2%	-2.5%	-2.0%
Exports - vol.	0.8%	-0.6%	-1.1%	1.0%	0.8%	0.6%	1.0%	0.7%	0.5%
Absorption - vol.	-0.7%	-0.4%	-0.1%	-0.7%	-0.9%	-1.3%	-0.7%	-1.0%	-1.4%
Investment - vol.	-0.7%	2.7%	3.4%	-4.4%	-4.4%	-4.6%	-4.4%	-4.4%	-4.6%
Labour Demand - vol.	-0.5%	-0.1%	0.1%	-0.6%	-0.6%	-0.8%	-0.6%	-0.6%	-0.7%
Private Consumption - vol.	-1.0%	-0.6%	-0.3%	-0.6%	-0.8%	-1.2%	-0.6%	-0.9%	-1.3%
Supply to domestic - vol.	-0.5%	-0.1%	0.1%	-0.7%	-0.9%	-1.2%	-0.7%	-0.9%	-1.3%
Intra-EU Trade - vol	0.0%	0.0%	0.0%	1.0%	1.6%	1.5%	1.0%	1.6%	1.4%

Non market	Constraint Case			Flexible Case			Efficiency Case		
	1988	1991	1994	1988	1991	1994	1988	1991	1994
Domestic Production - vol.	0.0%	0.0%	0.0%	0.0%	0.0%	0.0%	0.0%	0.0%	0.0%
Imports - vol.	0.0%	0.0%	0.0%	0.0%	0.0%	0.0%	0.0%	0.0%	0.0%
Exports - vol.	-	-	-	#VALUE!	#VALUE!	#VALUE!	#VALUE!	#VALUE!	#VALUE!
Absorption - vol.	0.0%	0.0%	0.0%	0.0%	0.0%	0.0%	0.0%	0.0%	0.0%
Investment - vol.	-6.8%	-6.0%	-5.9%	-4.1%	-4.1%	-4.1%	-4.1%	-4.1%	-4.1%
Labour Demand - vol.	0.1%	0.2%	0.2%	0.1%	0.1%	0.1%	0.1%	0.1%	0.2%
Private Consumption - vol.	-0.5%	-0.3%	-0.1%	-0.3%	-0.4%	-0.5%	-0.3%	-0.4%	-0.6%
Supply to domestic - vol.	0.0%	0.0%	0.0%	0.0%	0.0%	0.0%	0.0%	0.0%	0.0%
Intra-EU Trade - vol	0.0%	0.0%	0.0%	0.0%	0.0%	0.0%	0.0%	0.0%	0.0%

Table B6.4.
The full *antimonde* scenario: sectoral results for Greece (prices)

% change from *monde*

Agriculture	Constraint Case			Flexible Case			Efficiency Case		
	1988	1991	1994	1988	1991	1994	1988	1991	1994
Real Marginal Costs	-0.45%	1.13%	1.76%	-0.15%	-0.25%	-0.06%	-0.16%	-0.28%	-0.12%
Real Cost of Labour	-0.16%	1.56%	2.07%	0.32%	0.14%	-0.50%	0.29%	0.00%	-0.76%
Real Deflator of Absorption	-0.32%	1.12%	1.70%	0.13%	0.02%	0.17%	0.12%	-0.02%	0.09%
Real Price of Exports-RW	-0.45%	1.13%	1.76%	-0.15%	-0.25%	-0.06%	-0.16%	-0.28%	-0.12%

Energy	Constraint Case			Flexible Case			Efficiency Case		
	1988	1991	1994	1988	1991	1994	1988	1991	1994
Marginal Costs	0.12%	1.10%	1.52%	2.11%	1.61%	1.38%	2.07%	1.45%	1.09%
Cost of Labour	-0.16%	1.56%	2.07%	0.32%	0.14%	-0.50%	0.29%	0.00%	-0.76%
Deflator of Absorption	0.31%	0.81%	1.02%	3.61%	2.83%	2.36%	3.54%	2.57%	1.91%
Price of Exports-RW	0.12%	1.10%	1.52%	2.11%	1.61%	1.38%	2.07%	1.45%	1.09%

Metal Industries	Constraint Case			Flexible Case			Efficiency Case		
	1988	1991	1994	1988	1991	1994	1988	1991	1994
Marginal Costs	1.13%	2.20%	2.59%	2.64%	2.51%	2.24%	2.62%	2.42%	2.08%
Cost of Labour	-0.16%	1.56%	2.07%	0.32%	0.14%	-0.50%	0.29%	0.00%	-0.76%
Deflator of Absorption	2.68%	3.42%	3.60%	4.92%	5.05%	4.68%	4.88%	4.90%	4.42%
Price of Exports-RW	2.50%	5.20%	5.61%	2.17%	2.12%	1.83%	2.15%	2.03%	1.66%

Chemical	Constraint Case			Flexible Case			Efficiency Case		
	1988	1991	1994	1988	1991	1994	1988	1991	1994
Marginal Costs	0.44%	1.72%	2.20%	1.40%	1.28%	1.13%	1.39%	1.23%	1.04%
Cost of Labour	-0.16%	1.56%	2.07%	0.32%	0.14%	-0.50%	0.29%	0.00%	-0.76%
Deflator of Absorption	1.68%	2.38%	2.54%	3.52%	3.55%	3.32%	3.49%	3.45%	3.14%
Price of Exports-RW	1.38%	3.90%	4.40%	0.80%	0.60%	0.45%	0.78%	0.55%	0.35%

Other Intensive Industries	Constraint Case			Flexible Case			Efficiency Case		
	1988	1991	1994	1988	1991	1994	1988	1991	1994
Marginal Costs	0.47%	1.72%	2.19%	1.53%	1.36%	1.15%	1.51%	1.29%	1.03%
Cost of Labour	-0.16%	1.56%	2.07%	0.32%	0.14%	-0.50%	0.29%	0.00%	-0.76%
Deflator of Absorption	0.87%	1.70%	2.01%	2.34%	2.14%	1.87%	2.31%	2.03%	1.68%
Price of Exports-RW	0.80%	2.38%	2.85%	1.49%	1.31%	1.10%	1.48%	1.24%	0.97%

Electrical goods	Constraint Case			Flexible Case			Efficiency Case		
	1988	1991	1994	1988	1991	1994	1988	1991	1994
Marginal Costs	1.02%	2.26%	2.71%	1.99%	1.97%	1.76%	1.98%	1.92%	1.67%
Cost of Labour	-0.16%	1.56%	2.07%	0.32%	0.14%	-0.50%	0.29%	0.00%	-0.76%
Deflator of Absorption	2.49%	3.17%	3.39%	3.75%	3.95%	3.66%	3.72%	3.85%	3.48%
Price of Exports-RW	2.06%	4.69%	5.19%	1.81%	2.06%	1.83%	1.80%	2.00%	1.74%

Transport equipment	Constraint Case			Flexible Case			Efficiency Case		
	1988	1991	1994	1988	1991	1994	1988	1991	1994
Marginal Costs	0.37%	1.84%	2.37%	1.07%	0.93%	0.65%	1.06%	0.87%	0.53%
Cost of Labour	-0.16%	1.56%	2.07%	0.32%	0.14%	-0.50%	0.29%	0.00%	-0.76%
Deflator of Absorption	2.49%	3.14%	3.33%	4.87%	4.52%	4.02%	4.82%	4.31%	3.65%
Price of Exports-RW	1.40%	5.46%	6.11%	-0.26%	-0.88%	-1.18%	-0.28%	-0.95%	-1.30%

Other Equipment	Constraint Case			Flexible Case			Efficiency Case		
	1988	1991	1994	1988	1991	1994	1988	1991	1994
Marginal Costs	0.70%	1.99%	2.45%	1.56%	1.49%	1.28%	1.54%	1.43%	1.18%
Cost of Labour	-0.16%	1.56%	2.07%	0.32%	0.14%	-0.50%	0.29%	0.00%	-0.76%
Deflator of Absorption	1.71%	2.06%	2.15%	2.91%	2.88%	2.58%	2.88%	2.76%	2.36%
Price of Exports-RW	1.04%	3.24%	3.72%	1.07%	1.16%	0.93%	1.05%	1.09%	0.82%

Consumer goods	Constraint Case			Flexible Case			Efficiency Case		
	1988	1991	1994	1988	1991	1994	1988	1991	1994
Marginal Costs	-0.07%	1.42%	2.03%	0.41%	0.30%	0.34%	0.41%	0.30%	0.33%
Cost of Labour	-0.16%	1.56%	2.07%	0.32%	0.14%	-0.50%	0.29%	0.00%	-0.76%
Deflator of Absorption	0.15%	1.44%	1.95%	0.85%	0.71%	0.69%	0.84%	0.68%	0.64%
Price of Exports-RW	-0.07%	1.42%	2.03%	0.41%	0.30%	0.34%	0.41%	0.30%	0.33%

Construction	Constraint Case			Flexible Case			Efficiency Case		
	1988	1991	1994	1988	1991	1994	1988	1991	1994
Marginal Costs	0.32%	1.66%	2.19%	1.05%	0.94%	0.85%	1.04%	0.90%	0.78%
Cost of Labour	-0.16%	1.56%	2.07%	0.32%	0.14%	-0.50%	0.29%	0.00%	-0.76%
Deflator of Absorption	0.32%	1.66%	2.19%	1.05%	0.94%	0.85%	1.04%	0.90%	0.78%
Price of Exports-RW	0.32%	1.66%	2.19%	1.05%	0.94%	0.85%	1.04%	0.90%	0.78%

Telecommunications	Constraint Case			Flexible Case			Efficiency Case		
	1988	1991	1994	1988	1991	1994	1988	1991	1994
Marginal Costs	-0.29%	1.41%	2.03%	0.00%	-0.12%	-0.29%	-0.01%	-0.15%	-0.36%
Cost of Labour	-0.16%	1.56%	2.07%	0.32%	0.14%	-0.50%	0.29%	0.00%	-0.76%
Deflator of Absorption	0.25%	2.27%	2.81%	-0.13%	-0.58%	-0.79%	-0.15%	-0.64%	-0.90%
Price of Exports-RW	3.39%	8.24%	8.88%	-0.04%	-0.23%	-0.42%	-0.05%	-0.28%	-0.50%

Transports	Constraint Case			Flexible Case			Efficiency Case		
	1988	1991	1994	1988	1991	1994	1988	1991	1994
Marginal Costs	0.09%	1.55%	2.11%	0.83%	0.63%	0.47%	0.81%	0.56%	0.35%
Cost of Labour	-0.16%	1.56%	2.07%	0.32%	0.14%	-0.50%	0.29%	0.00%	-0.76%
Deflator of Absorption	0.21%	1.59%	2.12%	0.88%	0.66%	0.50%	0.86%	0.59%	0.37%
Price of Exports-RW	0.09%	1.55%	2.11%	0.83%	0.63%	0.47%	0.81%	0.56%	0.35%

Banks	Constraint Case			Flexible Case			Efficiency Case		
	1988	1991	1994	1988	1991	1994	1988	1991	1994
Marginal Costs	-0.36%	1.25%	1.88%	-0.08%	-0.21%	-0.09%	-0.08%	-0.23%	-0.13%
Cost of Labour	-0.16%	1.56%	2.07%	0.32%	0.14%	-0.50%	0.29%	0.00%	-0.76%
Deflator of Absorption	-0.22%	1.41%	2.02%	-0.01%	-0.19%	-0.09%	-0.01%	-0.21%	-0.14%
Price of Exports-RW	0.91%	3.61%	4.25%	-0.08%	-0.23%	-0.12%	-0.08%	-0.24%	-0.16%

Services	Constraint Case			Flexible Case			Efficiency Case		
	1988	1991	1994	1988	1991	1994	1988	1991	1994
Marginal Costs	-0.29%	1.25%	1.88%	0.07%	-0.05%	0.08%	0.06%	-0.07%	0.04%
Cost of Labour	-0.16%	1.56%	2.07%	0.32%	0.14%	-0.50%	0.29%	0.00%	-0.76%
Deflator of Absorption	-0.26%	1.25%	1.86%	0.09%	-0.03%	0.09%	0.08%	-0.05%	0.05%
Price of Exports-RW	-0.29%	1.25%	1.88%	0.07%	-0.05%	0.08%	0.06%	-0.07%	0.04%

Non market	Constraint Case			Flexible Case			Efficiency Case		
	1988	1991	1994	1988	1991	1994	1988	1991	1994
Marginal Costs	0.04%	1.69%	2.25%	0.57%	0.42%	-0.03%	0.56%	0.35%	-0.15%
Cost of Labour	-0.16%	1.56%	2.07%	0.32%	0.14%	-0.50%	0.29%	0.00%	-0.76%
Deflator of Absorption	0.04%	1.69%	2.25%	0.57%	0.42%	-0.03%	0.55%	0.35%	-0.15%
Price of Exports-RW	0.04%	1.69%	2.25%	0.57%	0.42%	-0.03%	0.56%	0.35%	-0.15%

Table B6.5.
Decomposition of effects: macroeconomic aggregates for Greece

Macroeconomic Aggregates (vol.) (% change from *monde*)	Border Controls			Border controls and x-ineff.			Market segmentation			Trade *antimonde*			Full *antimonde*		
	1988	1991	1994	1988	1991	1994	1988	1991	1994	1988	1991	1994	1988	1991	1994
GDP fact. pr.	-0.14%	-0.30%	-0.30%	-0.15%	-0.32%	-0.33%	-0.01%	-0.09%	-0.50%	-0.06%	-0.17%	-0.58%	-0.16%	-0.32%	-0.78%
Priv. Consumption	0.15%	0.06%	0.07%	0.15%	0.06%	0.06%	-0.92%	-0.82%	-1.11%	-0.84%	-0.75%	-1.05%	-0.88%	-0.82%	-1.14%
Absorption	0.10%	0.12%	0.12%	0.10%	0.12%	0.13%	-1.45%	-1.75%	-2.00%	-1.41%	-1.72%	-1.97%	-1.44%	-1.76%	-2.03%
Total Investment	0.07%	0.10%	0.11%	0.07%	0.11%	0.11%	-4.48%	-4.69%	-4.81%	-4.45%	-4.66%	-4.79%	-4.45%	-4.67%	-4.79%
Total Exports to RW	-0.58%	-0.70%	-0.70%	-0.59%	-0.71%	-0.71%	1.93%	1.67%	1.48%	1.57%	1.27%	1.07%	1.50%	1.18%	0.96%
Total Imports from RW	1.31%	1.66%	1.66%	1.32%	1.68%	1.68%	-4.60%	-4.54%	-4.36%	-3.39%	-3.17%	-2.99%	-3.27%	-2.99%	-2.74%
Total Intra-EU Trade	-0.97%	-2.33%	-2.35%	-0.98%	-2.34%	-2.35%	0.92%	-0.56%	-0.75%	0.29%	-1.31%	-1.52%	0.15%	-1.52%	-1.79%
Employment (diff. from *monde*, 10³ persons)	-2	-3	-3	-2	-3	-3	20	18	9	19	17	8	18	15	7
Disposable Income (deflated)	0.16%	0.07%	0.07%	0.16%	0.06%	0.06%	-0.99%	-0.87%	-1.19%	-0.90%	-0.81%	-1.12%	-0.95%	-0.88%	-1.22%

Macroeconomic Ratios (abs. diff. from *monde*)	Border Controls			Border controls and x-ineff.			Market segmentation			Trade *antimonde*			Full *antimonde*		
	1988	1991	1994	1988	1991	1994	1988	1991	1994	1988	1991	1994	1988	1991	1994
Current Account as % of GDP	0.07%	0.25%	0.26%	0.07%	0.26%	0.27%	-1.24%	-1.64%	-1.60%	-1.21%	-1.61%	-1.56%	-1.18%	-1.56%	-1.51%
Public Deficit as % of GDP	-0.07%	-0.08%	-0.08%	-0.07%	-0.09%	-0.09%	-0.18%	-0.27%	-0.37%	-0.24%	-0.33%	-0.44%	-0.27%	-0.38%	-0.50%
Labour Productivity	-0.08%	-0.23%	-0.23%	-0.09%	-0.25%	-0.26%	-0.51%	-0.55%	-0.74%	-0.54%	-0.60%	-0.80%	-0.62%	-0.72%	-0.96%
Investment/GDP	0.05%	0.10%	0.10%	0.06%	0.11%	0.11%	-1.78%	-1.86%	-1.83%	-1.76%	-1.83%	-1.80%	-1.74%	-1.80%	-1.77%
Priv.Cons./GDP	0.20%	0.25%	0.25%	0.20%	0.26%	0.27%	-0.63%	-0.50%	-0.42%	-0.54%	-0.40%	-0.32%	-0.50%	-0.34%	-0.24%

Deflators (% change from *monde*)	Border Controls			Border controls and x-ineff.			Market segmentation			Trade *antimonde*			Full *antimonde*		
	1988	1991	1994	1988	1991	1994	1988	1991	1994	1988	1991	1994	1988	1991	1994
Consumer Price Index	-0.30%	-0.34%	-0.35%	-0.31%	-0.35%	-0.36%	1.04%	0.87%	0.88%	0.95%	0.78%	0.78%	0.92%	0.73%	0.71%
Real Wage Rate	-0.17%	-0.34%	-0.34%	-0.18%	-0.36%	-0.36%	0.47%	0.37%	-0.20%	0.43%	0.30%	-0.28%	0.32%	0.14%	-0.50%
Marginal Costs	-0.24%	-0.30%	-0.31%	-0.24%	-0.30%	-0.31%	0.71%	0.63%	0.60%	0.63%	0.55%	0.51%	0.61%	0.52%	0.47%
Producer Prices	-0.23%	-0.28%	-0.28%	-0.24%	-0.29%	-0.29%	0.81%	0.74%	0.71%	0.73%	0.66%	0.62%	0.71%	0.62%	0.57%
Real Shadow Price of Capital	0.27%	0.49%	0.47%	0.28%	0.52%	0.50%	-1.40%	-1.46%	-0.72%	-1.34%	-1.38%	-0.62%	-1.38%	-1.44%	-0.71%
Terms-of-Trade RW	2.10%	2.50%	2.51%	2.13%	2.54%	2.56%	-6.24%	-5.42%	-4.82%	-5.01%	-4.07%	-3.45%	-4.82%	-3.79%	-3.08%
Real Exchange Rate	4.26%	4.75%	4.77%	4.28%	4.79%	4.83%	-7.37%	-6.40%	-5.74%	-4.37%	-3.25%	-2.56%	-4.15%	-2.93%	-2.13%
Trade Regime	Integration			Integration			Segmentation			Segmentation			Segmentation		

Table B6.6.
Decomposition of effects: effects on IC sectors for Greece

% change from *monde*

Metal Industries

	Border Controls			Border controls and x-ineff.			Market segmentation			Trade *antimonde*			Full *antimonde*		
	1988	1991	1994	1988	1991	1994	1988	1991	1994	1988	1991	1994	1988	1991	1994
Production per firm	-0.72%	-1.78%	-1.78%	-0.72%	-1.78%	-1.78%	-10.46%	-15.63%	-15.61%	-10.98%	-16.04%	-16.02%	-11.09%	-16.16%	-16.18%
Marginal Costs	3.56%	3.89%	3.91%	3.58%	3.92%	3.95%	-4.46%	-3.60%	-3.19%	-1.68%	-0.67%	-0.24%	-1.50%	-0.41%	0.11%
Producer Prices	3.63%	4.06%	4.08%	3.65%	4.09%	4.12%	-3.28%	-1.88%	-1.47%	-0.41%	1.15%	1.58%	-0.22%	1.42%	1.95%
Mark-ups domestic (abs. diff.)	0.04%	0.09%	0.09%	0.04%	0.09%	0.09%	4.71%	5.93%	5.93%	4.77%	5.98%	5.98%	4.78%	5.99%	6.00%
Fixed Costs per firm	3.49%	3.79%	3.81%	3.50%	3.81%	3.83%	-4.16%	-3.31%	-2.97%	-1.41%	-0.41%	-0.06%	-1.28%	-0.22%	0.21%
Number of Firms	0.79%	2.27%	2.29%	0.79%	2.29%	2.32%	8.80%	7.23%	7.56%	8.54%	7.02%	7.34%	8.48%	6.94%	7.25%
Sigma of Love of Variety	0.00%	0.00%	0.00%	0.00%	0.00%	0.00%	0.00%	0.00%	0.00%	0.00%	0.00%	0.00%	0.00%	0.00%	0.00%

Chemical

	Border Controls			Border controls and x-ineff.			Market segmentation			Trade *antimonde*			Full *antimonde*		
	1988	1991	1994	1988	1991	1994	1988	1991	1994	1988	1991	1994	1988	1991	1994
Production per firm	-0.48%	-1.53%	-1.53%	-0.48%	-1.54%	-1.55%	-11.76%	-15.68%	-15.87%	-11.73%	-15.68%	-15.87%	-11.83%	-15.83%	-16.06%
Marginal Costs	4.00%	4.42%	4.43%	4.03%	4.45%	4.48%	-5.93%	-5.07%	-4.55%	-2.94%	-1.92%	-1.37%	-2.75%	-1.64%	-0.99%
Producer Prices	4.04%	4.54%	4.55%	4.06%	4.57%	4.60%	-4.81%	-3.61%	-3.07%	-1.79%	-0.42%	0.15%	-1.59%	-0.12%	0.55%
Mark-ups domestic (abs. diff.)	0.02%	0.10%	0.10%	0.02%	0.10%	0.10%	3.71%	4.60%	4.61%	3.67%	4.56%	4.58%	3.68%	4.57%	4.59%
Fixed Costs per firm	3.91%	4.27%	4.28%	3.92%	4.29%	4.31%	-5.43%	-4.59%	-4.22%	-2.46%	-1.46%	-1.08%	-2.32%	-1.26%	-0.80%
Number of Firms	1.02%	2.03%	2.05%	1.01%	2.03%	2.05%	14.74%	16.54%	16.52%	15.09%	16.88%	16.86%	15.03%	16.80%	16.76%
Sigma of Love of Variety	0.00%	0.00%	0.00%	0.00%	0.00%	0.00%	0.00%	0.00%	0.00%	0.00%	0.00%	0.00%	0.00%	0.00%	0.00%

Other Intensive Industries

	Border Controls			Border controls and x-ineff.			Market segmentation			Trade *antimonde*			Full *antimonde*		
	1988	1991	1994	1988	1991	1994	1988	1991	1994	1988	1991	1994	1988	1991	1994
Production per firm	-0.27%	-0.63%	-0.63%	-0.28%	-0.63%	-0.64%	-4.49%	-6.15%	-6.31%	-4.60%	-6.28%	-6.43%	-4.66%	-6.36%	-6.54%
Marginal Costs	3.80%	4.18%	4.19%	3.82%	4.21%	4.24%	-5.65%	-4.83%	-4.35%	-2.80%	-1.83%	-1.33%	-2.62%	-1.56%	-0.97%
Producer Prices	3.81%	4.20%	4.22%	3.83%	4.23%	4.26%	-5.41%	-4.50%	-4.03%	-2.55%	-1.50%	-0.99%	-2.36%	-1.23%	-0.63%
Mark-ups domestic (abs. diff.)	0.00%	0.00%	0.00%	0.00%	0.00%	0.00%	0.38%	0.47%	0.47%	0.38%	0.47%	0.47%	0.38%	0.47%	0.47%
Fixed Costs per firm	3.69%	4.01%	4.03%	3.70%	4.03%	4.06%	-5.19%	-4.38%	-4.05%	-2.38%	-1.43%	-1.08%	-2.24%	-1.24%	-0.82%
Number of Firms	0.77%	2.09%	2.13%	0.78%	2.11%	2.15%	3.13%	4.47%	4.65%	3.15%	4.51%	4.69%	3.14%	4.51%	4.68%
Sigma of Love of Variety	0.00%	0.00%	0.00%	0.00%	0.00%	0.00%	0.00%	0.00%	0.00%	0.00%	0.00%	0.00%	0.00%	0.00%	0.00%

Electrical goods

	Border Controls			Border controls and x-ineff.			Market segmentation			Trade *antimonde*			Full *antimonde*		
	1988	1991	1994	1988	1991	1994	1988	1991	1994	1988	1991	1994	1988	1991	1994
Production per firm	-0.29%	-1.54%	-1.54%	-0.29%	-1.54%	-1.55%	-15.92%	-21.08%	-21.16%	-16.12%	-21.38%	-21.48%	-16.25%	-21.55%	-21.70%
Marginal Costs	3.87%	4.25%	4.26%	3.89%	4.28%	4.31%	-5.30%	-4.35%	-3.89%	-2.35%	-1.24%	-0.75%	-2.15%	-0.95%	-0.37%
Producer Prices	3.90%	4.40%	4.42%	3.92%	4.43%	4.46%	-3.29%	-1.72%	-1.25%	-0.25%	1.52%	2.02%	-0.03%	1.84%	2.44%
Mark-ups domestic (abs. diff.)	-0.08%	-0.04%	-0.04%	-0.08%	-0.04%	-0.04%	3.94%	4.80%	4.81%	3.90%	4.77%	4.79%	3.91%	4.79%	4.80%
Fixed Costs per firm	3.80%	4.14%	4.16%	3.81%	4.16%	4.18%	-4.96%	-4.01%	-3.65%	-2.03%	-0.92%	-0.54%	-1.88%	-0.71%	-0.25%
Number of Firms	2.23%	4.70%	4.72%	2.23%	4.73%	4.76%	4.03%	-1.97%	-1.80%	4.31%	-1.80%	-1.65%	4.23%	-1.89%	-1.75%
Sigma of Love of Variety	0.00%	0.00%	0.00%	0.00%	0.00%	0.00%	0.00%	0.00%	0.00%	0.00%	0.00%	0.00%	0.00%	0.00%	0.00%

Transport equipment

	Border Controls			Border controls and x-ineff.			Market segmentation			Trade antimonde			Full antimonde		
	1988	1991	1994	1988	1991	1994	1988	1991	1994	1988	1991	1994	1988	1991	1994
Production per firm	-0.12%	-0.37%	-0.40%	-0.13%	-0.39%	-0.42%	-22.42%	-26.65%	-26.87%	-22.55%	-26.86%	-27.10%	-22.65%	-26.99%	-27.26%
Marginal Costs	3.97%	4.35%	4.37%	3.99%	4.38%	4.41%	-6.18%	-5.33%	-4.92%	-3.25%	-2.26%	-1.82%	-3.07%	-1.99%	-1.48%
Producer Prices	3.97%	4.39%	4.41%	3.99%	4.42%	4.45%	-1.68%	0.11%	0.56%	1.42%	3.41%	3.89%	1.62%	3.70%	4.28%
Mark-ups domestic (abs. diff.)	0.00%	0.04%	0.05%	0.00%	0.04%	0.05%	6.64%	7.86%	7.88%	6.67%	7.92%	7.96%	6.69%	7.95%	7.98%
Fixed Costs per firm	3.87%	4.20%	4.22%	3.88%	4.22%	4.24%	-5.78%	-4.94%	-4.70%	-2.88%	-1.90%	-1.64%	-2.75%	-1.72%	-1.40%
Number of Firms	1.00%	2.90%	2.87%	1.00%	2.90%	2.88%	20.70%	27.73%	27.93%	20.55%	27.41%	27.58%	20.46%	27.29%	27.44%
Sigma of Love of Variety	0.00%	0.00%	0.00%	0.00%	0.00%	0.00%	0.00%	0.00%	0.00%	0.00%	0.00%	0.00%	0.00%	0.00%	0.00%

Other Equipment

	Border Controls			Border controls and x-ineff.			Market segmentation			Trade antimonde			Full antimonde		
	1988	1991	1994	1988	1991	1994	1988	1991	1994	1988	1991	1994	1988	1991	1994
Production per firm	0.44%	1.28%	1.28%	0.43%	1.27%	1.27%	-26.53%	-33.71%	-33.79%	-26.65%	-33.81%	-33.90%	-26.72%	-33.91%	-34.02%
Marginal Costs	3.91%	4.29%	4.31%	3.93%	4.32%	4.35%	-5.72%	-4.81%	-4.34%	-2.78%	-1.71%	-1.22%	-2.59%	-1.43%	-0.85%
Producer Prices	3.87%	4.20%	4.21%	3.89%	4.23%	4.26%	-3.20%	-1.59%	-1.11%	-0.18%	1.61%	2.12%	0.02%	1.91%	2.52%
Mark-ups domestic (abs. diff.)	-0.05%	-0.12%	-0.12%	-0.05%	-0.12%	-0.12%	3.38%	4.24%	4.24%	3.39%	4.24%	4.24%	3.39%	4.25%	4.24%
Fixed Costs per firm	3.80%	4.14%	4.15%	3.82%	4.15%	4.18%	-5.24%	-4.34%	-4.02%	-2.34%	-1.28%	-0.94%	-2.20%	-1.08%	-0.67%
Number of Firms	2.47%	9.06%	9.10%	2.47%	9.07%	9.12%	19.31%	13.13%	13.64%	19.27%	13.13%	13.64%	19.20%	13.04%	13.53%
Sigma of Love of Variety	0.00%	0.00%	0.00%	0.00%	0.00%	0.00%	0.00%	0.00%	0.00%	0.00%	0.00%	0.00%	0.00%	0.00%	0.00%

Telecommunications

	Border Controls			Border controls and x-ineff.			Market segmentation			Trade antimonde			Full antimonde		
	1988	1991	1994	1988	1991	1994	1988	1991	1994	1988	1991	1994	1988	1991	1994
Production per firm	0.00%	-0.04%	-0.04%	-0.67%	-1.36%	-1.36%	-0.19%	-0.37%	-0.66%	-0.18%	-0.37%	-0.65%	-0.88%	-1.73%	-2.03%
Marginal Costs	4.21%	4.67%	4.69%	4.24%	4.70%	4.74%	-7.33%	-6.45%	-5.94%	-4.34%	-3.32%	-2.78%	-4.15%	-3.04%	-2.41%
Producer Prices	4.16%	4.59%	4.61%	3.80%	3.84%	3.87%	-7.08%	-6.14%	-5.67%	-4.11%	-3.03%	-2.53%	-4.28%	-3.50%	-2.91%
Mark-ups domestic (abs. diff.)	-0.09%	-0.11%	-0.12%	-0.64%	-1.24%	-1.25%	0.41%	0.49%	0.44%	0.37%	0.44%	0.39%	-0.21%	-0.72%	-0.78%
Fixed Costs per firm	4.05%	4.39%	4.41%	2.24%	0.77%	0.80%	-6.76%	-5.90%	-5.76%	-3.82%	-2.82%	-2.67%	-5.38%	-6.04%	-5.84%
Number of Firms	0.10%	0.15%	0.15%	0.85%	1.67%	1.68%	-0.51%	-0.59%	-0.52%	-0.46%	-0.53%	-0.46%	0.31%	1.00%	1.08%
Sigma of Love of Variety	0.00%	0.00%	0.00%	0.00%	0.00%	0.00%	0.00%	0.00%	0.00%	0.00%	0.00%	0.00%	0.00%	0.00%	0.00%

Banks

	Border Controls			Border controls and x-ineff.			Market segmentation			Trade antimonde			Full antimonde		
	1988	1991	1994	1988	1991	1994	1988	1991	1994	1988	1991	1994	1988	1991	1994
Production per firm	-0.05%	-0.11%	-0.10%	-0.38%	-0.75%	-0.75%	0.24%	0.05%	-0.31%	0.22%	0.03%	-0.34%	-0.15%	-0.69%	-1.07%
Marginal Costs	4.21%	4.73%	4.74%	4.21%	4.71%	4.74%	-7.37%	-6.51%	-5.73%	-4.41%	-3.40%	-2.58%	-4.22%	-3.13%	-2.22%
Producer Prices	4.17%	4.68%	4.69%	4.10%	4.52%	4.55%	-7.25%	-6.36%	-5.59%	-4.29%	-3.25%	-2.45%	-4.17%	-3.12%	-2.23%
Mark-ups domestic (abs. diff.)	-0.04%	-0.06%	-0.06%	-0.12%	-0.22%	-0.22%	0.17%	0.20%	0.18%	0.15%	0.18%	0.16%	0.07%	0.01%	-0.01%
Fixed Costs per firm	3.95%	4.33%	4.34%	3.24%	2.88%	2.90%	-6.43%	-5.60%	-5.26%	-3.54%	-2.58%	-2.21%	-4.07%	-3.74%	-3.31%
Number of Firms	0.17%	0.23%	0.23%	0.50%	0.91%	0.92%	-0.36%	-0.30%	-0.22%	-0.28%	-0.22%	-0.13%	0.06%	0.46%	0.55%
Sigma of Love of Variety	0.00%	0.00%	0.00%	0.00%	0.00%	0.00%	0.00%	0.00%	0.00%	0.00%	0.00%	0.00%	0.00%	0.00%	0.00%

Table B6.7.
Decomposition of effects: sectoral results for Greece (volumes)

% change from *monde*

Agriculture

	Border Controls			Border controls and x-ineff.			Market segmentation			Trade *antimonde*			Full *antimonde*		
	1988	1991	1994	1988	1991	1994	1988	1991	1994	1988	1991	1994	1988	1991	1994
Domestic Production - vol.	-0.7%	-1.5%	-1.5%	-0.7%	-1.5%	-1.5%	3.5%	5.1%	4.4%	3.3%	4.7%	4.0%	3.2%	4.6%	3.8%
Imports - vol.	2.5%	2.8%	2.8%	2.6%	2.8%	2.8%	-6.7%	-5.6%	-5.1%	-4.5%	-3.2%	-2.7%	-4.3%	-2.9%	-2.3%
Exports - vol.	-0.8%	-1.0%	-1.0%	-0.8%	-1.0%	-1.0%	2.4%	2.1%	1.8%	1.8%	1.5%	1.2%	1.8%	1.4%	1.1%
Absorption - vol.	-0.4%	-0.9%	-0.9%	-0.4%	-0.9%	-1.0%	1.8%	2.6%	2.0%	1.7%	2.4%	1.9%	1.6%	2.3%	1.7%
Investment - vol.	-0.3%	-0.7%	-0.7%	-0.3%	-0.7%	-0.7%	-3.1%	-2.4%	-2.7%	-3.2%	-2.5%	-2.9%	-3.2%	-2.6%	-2.9%
Labour Demand - vol.	-0.6%	-1.3%	-1.3%	-0.6%	-1.3%	-1.3%	2.9%	4.5%	4.1%	2.7%	4.2%	3.9%	2.7%	4.2%	3.8%
Private Consumption - vol.	0.0%	0.0%	0.0%	0.0%	0.0%	0.0%	-0.4%	-0.6%	-0.9%	-0.4%	-0.6%	-0.8%	-0.4%	-0.6%	-0.9%
Supply to domestic - vol.	-0.5%	-1.0%	-1.0%	-0.5%	-1.0%	-1.0%	2.8%	4.2%	3.5%	2.7%	4.0%	3.3%	2.6%	3.9%	3.2%
Intra-EU Trade - vol	-1.6%	-3.5%	-3.5%	-1.6%	-3.5%	-3.5%	2.7%	1.1%	0.7%	1.6%	-0.2%	-0.6%	1.5%	-0.4%	-0.8%

Energy

	Border Controls			Border controls and x-ineff.			Market segmentation			Trade *antimonde*			Full *antimonde*		
	1988	1991	1994	1988	1991	1994	1988	1991	1994	1988	1991	1994	1988	1991	1994
Domestic Production - vol.	0.5%	1.0%	1.0%	0.5%	1.0%	1.0%	0.2%	-0.5%	-0.4%	0.6%	0.3%	0.3%	0.6%	0.2%	0.3%
Imports - vol.	0.7%	0.9%	0.9%	0.7%	0.9%	0.9%	-1.5%	-1.6%	-1.5%	-1.1%	-1.1%	-1.0%	-1.1%	-1.1%	-0.9%
Exports - vol.	-0.3%	-0.3%	-0.3%	-0.3%	-0.3%	-0.3%	0.7%	0.6%	0.5%	0.5%	0.4%	0.4%	0.5%	0.4%	0.3%
Absorption - vol.	0.4%	0.7%	0.7%	0.4%	0.7%	0.7%	-0.7%	-1.2%	-1.3%	-0.4%	-0.8%	-0.9%	-0.5%	-0.9%	-0.9%
Investment - vol.	0.2%	0.4%	0.4%	0.2%	0.4%	0.4%	-3.8%	-4.2%	-4.2%	-3.7%	-3.9%	-3.9%	-3.7%	-3.9%	-3.9%
Labour Demand - vol.	0.5%	0.9%	0.9%	0.5%	0.9%	0.9%	0.4%	-0.3%	-0.2%	0.8%	0.4%	0.5%	0.7%	0.4%	0.5%
Private Consumption - vol.	0.1%	0.2%	0.2%	0.1%	0.2%	0.2%	-0.6%	-0.7%	-0.8%	-0.5%	-0.6%	-0.7%	-0.5%	-0.6%	-0.7%
Supply to domestic - vol.	-0.1%	0.0%	0.0%	-0.1%	0.0%	0.0%	0.9%	0.2%	0.0%	0.8%	0.2%	0.0%	0.7%	0.1%	-0.1%
Intra-EU Trade - vol	1.4%	2.2%	2.2%	1.4%	2.3%	2.3%	-1.1%	-1.6%	-1.1%	-0.1%	0.0%	0.5%	-0.1%	0.0%	0.5%

Metal Industries

	Border Controls			Border controls and x-ineff.			Market segmentation			Trade *antimonde*			Full *antimonde*		
	1988	1991	1994	1988	1991	1994	1988	1991	1994	1988	1991	1994	1988	1991	1994
Domestic Production - vol.	0.1%	0.4%	0.5%	0.1%	0.5%	0.5%	-2.6%	-9.5%	-9.2%	-3.4%	-10.1%	-9.9%	-3.5%	-10.3%	-10.1%
Imports - vol.	1.6%	2.3%	2.3%	1.6%	2.3%	2.4%	-6.1%	-7.8%	-7.6%	-4.1%	-5.7%	-5.5%	-3.9%	-5.5%	-5.1%
Exports - vol.	-0.6%	-0.6%	-0.7%	-0.6%	-0.7%	-0.7%	1.5%	1.2%	1.1%	1.1%	0.8%	0.7%	1.1%	0.7%	0.5%
Absorption - vol.	0.5%	1.5%	1.5%	0.6%	1.5%	1.5%	-4.2%	-8.8%	-8.7%	-4.5%	-9.1%	-9.0%	-4.6%	-9.2%	-9.1%
Investment - vol.	0.0%	0.1%	0.1%	0.0%	0.1%	0.2%	-5.1%	-8.3%	-8.2%	-5.5%	-8.6%	-8.5%	-5.5%	-8.7%	-8.6%
Labour Demand - vol.	0.1%	0.6%	0.6%	0.1%	0.6%	0.7%	-1.2%	-7.7%	-7.3%	-1.9%	-8.3%	-7.9%	-2.0%	-8.4%	-8.1%
Private Consumption - vol.	0.0%	0.0%	0.0%	0.0%	0.0%	0.0%	-0.2%	-0.4%	-0.5%	-0.2%	-0.3%	-0.5%	-0.2%	-0.4%	-0.5%
Supply to domestic - vol.	1.5%	4.3%	4.4%	1.5%	4.3%	4.4%	-6.8%	-14.0%	-13.7%	-7.2%	-14.4%	-14.0%	-7.4%	-14.5%	-14.2%
Intra-EU Trade - vol	-0.9%	-1.8%	-1.8%	-0.9%	-1.8%	-1.8%	1.0%	-2.6%	-2.6%	-0.3%	-3.8%	-3.8%	-0.5%	-4.0%	-4.0%

Chemical

	Border Controls			Border controls and x-ineff.			Market segmentation			Trade *antimonde*			Full *antimonde*		
	1988	1991	1994	1988	1991	1994	1988	1991	1994	1988	1991	1994	1988	1991	1994
Domestic Production - vol.	0.5%	0.5%	0.5%	0.5%	0.5%	0.5%	1.2%	-1.7%	-2.0%	1.6%	-1.4%	-1.7%	1.4%	-1.7%	-2.0%
Imports - vol.	1.2%	1.5%	1.5%	1.3%	1.5%	1.5%	-4.9%	-4.7%	-4.5%	-3.5%	-2.9%	-2.7%	-3.2%	-2.5%	-2.2%
Exports - vol.	-0.4%	-0.5%	-0.5%	-0.4%	-0.5%	-0.5%	2.1%	1.8%	1.6%	1.9%	1.6%	1.4%	1.8%	1.5%	1.3%
Absorption - vol.	0.0%	-0.2%	-0.2%	0.0%	-0.2%	-0.2%	0.7%	0.2%	-0.1%	0.7%	0.2%	-0.1%	0.6%	0.1%	-0.2%
Investment - vol.	0.3%	0.2%	0.2%	0.3%	0.2%	0.2%	-3.5%	-4.9%	-5.0%	-3.3%	-4.7%	-4.9%	-3.4%	-4.8%	-5.0%
Labour Demand - vol.	0.6%	0.7%	0.7%	0.6%	0.6%	0.7%	2.6%	0.0%	-0.2%	2.9%	0.3%	0.1%	2.8%	0.1%	-0.1%
Private Consumption - vol.	0.0%	0.0%	0.0%	0.0%	0.0%	0.0%	-0.3%	-0.5%	-0.7%	-0.3%	-0.4%	-0.6%	-0.3%	-0.5%	-0.7%
Supply to domestic - vol.	1.7%	3.3%	3.3%	1.7%	3.3%	3.3%	-1.9%	-5.5%	-5.7%	-1.4%	-5.0%	-5.2%	-1.5%	-5.1%	-5.4%
Intra-EU Trade - vol	-0.8%	-1.8%	-1.8%	-0.8%	-1.8%	-1.8%	3.0%	3.0%	2.7%	2.6%	2.3%	2.1%	2.4%	2.1%	1.8%

Other Intensive Industries

	Border Controls			Border controls and x-ineff.			Market segmentation			Trade *antimonde*			Full *antimonde*		
	1988	1991	1994	1988	1991	1994	1988	1991	1994	1988	1991	1994	1988	1991	1994
Domestic Production - vol.	0.5%	1.4%	1.5%	0.5%	1.5%	1.5%	-1.5%	-2.0%	-1.9%	-1.6%	-2.0%	-2.0%	-1.7%	-2.1%	-2.2%
Imports - vol.	1.9%	2.4%	2.4%	1.9%	2.4%	2.4%	-7.5%	-7.3%	-7.0%	-5.5%	-5.0%	-4.7%	-5.2%	-4.6%	-4.1%
Exports - vol.	-0.5%	-0.6%	-0.6%	-0.5%	-0.6%	-0.7%	1.8%	1.5%	1.4%	1.5%	1.2%	1.0%	1.4%	1.1%	0.9%
Absorption - vol.	0.3%	0.5%	0.6%	0.3%	0.6%	0.6%	-3.3%	-4.0%	-4.1%	-3.3%	-4.0%	-4.1%	-3.3%	-4.0%	-4.1%
Investment - vol.	0.2%	0.7%	0.7%	0.2%	0.7%	0.7%	-4.8%	-5.0%	-5.0%	-4.8%	-5.0%	-5.1%	-4.8%	-5.1%	-5.1%
Labour Demand - vol.	0.5%	1.5%	1.5%	0.5%	1.5%	1.6%	-1.2%	-1.6%	-1.5%	-1.3%	-1.7%	-1.6%	-1.3%	-1.7%	-1.6%
Private Consumption - vol.	0.1%	0.1%	0.1%	0.1%	0.0%	0.1%	-0.9%	-0.8%	-1.0%	-0.8%	-0.7%	-1.0%	-0.8%	-0.8%	-1.0%
Supply to domestic - vol.	0.9%	2.6%	2.6%	0.9%	2.6%	2.6%	-2.2%	-2.1%	-2.1%	-2.2%	-2.1%	-2.0%	-2.2%	-2.1%	-2.1%
Intra-EU Trade - vol	-1.8%	-3.8%	-3.8%	-1.8%	-3.8%	-3.8%	-0.1%	-2.4%	-2.8%	-1.4%	-3.8%	-4.1%	-1.5%	-4.0%	-4.4%

Electrical goods

	Border Controls			Border controls and x-ineff.			Market segmentation			Trade antimonde			Full antimonde		
	1988	1991	1994	1988	1991	1994	1988	1991	1994	1988	1991	1994	1988	1991	1994
Domestic Production - vol.	1.9%	3.1%	3.1%	1.9%	3.1%	3.1%	-12.5%	-22.6%	-22.6%	-12.5%	-22.8%	-22.8%	-12.7%	-23.0%	-23.1%
Imports - vol.	2.3%	2.7%	2.7%	2.3%	2.7%	2.8%	-9.6%	-10.1%	-9.9%	-7.3%	-7.6%	-7.4%	-7.0%	-7.3%	-6.9%
Exports - vol.	-0.6%	-0.7%	-0.7%	-0.6%	-0.7%	-0.7%	2.0%	1.6%	1.4%	1.6%	1.1%	1.0%	1.6%	1.0%	0.8%
Absorption - vol.	1.1%	1.3%	1.3%	1.1%	1.3%	1.3%	-8.7%	-11.2%	-11.3%	-8.4%	-11.2%	-11.4%	-8.5%	-11.3%	-11.5%
Investment - vol.	0.9%	1.5%	1.5%	0.9%	1.5%	1.5%	-9.6%	-14.3%	-14.3%	-9.6%	-14.4%	-14.4%	-9.7%	-14.5%	-14.5%
Labour Demand - vol.	1.9%	3.3%	3.3%	1.9%	3.3%	3.3%	-10.3%	-20.1%	-19.9%	-10.2%	-20.2%	-20.1%	-10.4%	-20.4%	-20.3%
Private Consumption - vol.	1.4%	0.3%	0.2%	1.4%	0.3%	0.2%	-6.7%	-2.2%	-2.5%	-5.9%	-2.0%	-2.4%	-6.0%	-2.2%	-2.5%
Supply to domestic - vol.	3.2%	6.1%	6.1%	3.2%	6.1%	6.2%	-15.7%	-25.4%	-25.4%	-15.2%	-25.1%	-25.1%	-15.4%	-25.3%	-25.3%
Intra-EU Trade - vol	-1.2%	-2.8%	-2.8%	-1.2%	-2.8%	-2.8%	0.4%	0.5%	0.3%	-0.6%	-0.8%	-1.0%	-0.7%	-1.0%	-1.3%

Transport equipment

	Border Controls			Border controls and x-ineff.			Market segmentation			Trade antimonde			Full antimonde		
	1988	1991	1994	1988	1991	1994	1988	1991	1994	1988	1991	1994	1988	1991	1994
Domestic Production - vol.	0.9%	2.5%	2.5%	0.9%	2.5%	2.4%	-6.4%	-6.3%	-6.4%	-6.6%	-6.8%	-7.0%	-6.8%	-7.1%	-7.3%
Imports - vol.	1.3%	1.3%	1.3%	1.3%	1.3%	1.3%	-5.5%	-4.5%	-4.5%	-4.2%	-3.0%	-3.0%	-4.0%	-2.8%	-2.7%
Exports - vol.	-0.7%	-0.7%	-0.7%	-0.7%	-0.7%	-0.7%	2.8%	2.6%	2.5%	2.4%	2.2%	2.0%	2.3%	2.1%	1.9%
Absorption - vol.	0.7%	0.6%	0.5%	0.7%	0.6%	0.5%	-5.0%	-3.1%	-3.3%	-4.7%	-3.1%	-3.3%	-4.8%	-3.1%	-3.4%
Investment - vol.	0.4%	1.2%	1.2%	0.4%	1.2%	1.2%	-6.9%	-6.8%	-7.0%	-7.0%	-7.1%	-7.3%	-7.1%	-7.2%	-7.4%
Labour Demand - vol.	0.9%	2.6%	2.5%	0.9%	2.6%	2.6%	-1.3%	-0.2%	-0.2%	-1.6%	-0.7%	-0.7%	-1.7%	-0.9%	-0.9%
Private Consumption - vol.	1.0%	0.3%	0.2%	1.0%	0.2%	0.1%	-5.0%	-1.4%	-1.6%	-4.5%	-1.3%	-1.5%	-4.6%	-1.4%	-1.6%
Supply to domestic - vol.	1.1%	3.0%	3.0%	1.1%	3.0%	2.9%	-6.8%	-6.5%	-6.6%	-7.1%	-7.0%	-7.2%	-7.2%	-7.3%	-7.5%
Intra-EU Trade - vol	-1.3%	-2.4%	-2.5%	-1.3%	-2.5%	-2.5%	3.8%	5.0%	4.6%	1.8%	2.6%	2.2%	1.6%	2.2%	1.7%

Other Equipment

	Border Controls			Border controls and x-ineff.			Market segmentation			Trade antimonde			Full antimonde		
	1988	1991	1994	1988	1991	1994	1988	1991	1994	1988	1991	1994	1988	1991	1994
Domestic Production - vol.	2.9%	10.5%	10.5%	2.9%	10.5%	10.5%	-12.3%	-25.0%	-24.8%	-12.5%	-25.1%	-24.9%	-12.7%	-25.3%	-25.1%
Imports - vol.	2.2%	4.1%	4.1%	2.2%	4.1%	4.1%	-8.4%	-10.6%	-10.5%	-6.0%	-8.1%	-7.9%	-5.8%	-7.8%	-7.5%
Exports - vol.	-0.8%	-0.8%	-0.9%	-0.8%	-0.9%	-0.9%	2.3%	1.9%	1.7%	1.7%	1.3%	1.1%	1.7%	1.2%	1.0%
Absorption - vol.	1.1%	4.2%	4.3%	1.1%	4.3%	4.3%	-7.4%	-13.2%	-13.2%	-7.5%	-13.3%	-13.3%	-7.5%	-13.3%	-13.4%
Investment - vol.	1.4%	5.1%	5.2%	1.4%	5.1%	5.2%	-9.6%	-15.4%	-15.4%	-9.7%	-15.5%	-15.4%	-9.7%	-15.5%	-15.5%
Labour Demand - vol.	2.9%	10.4%	10.4%	2.9%	10.4%	10.5%	-9.6%	-22.1%	-21.7%	-9.8%	-22.2%	-21.8%	-9.9%	-22.3%	-21.9%
Private Consumption - vol.	0.3%	0.1%	0.1%	0.3%	0.1%	0.1%	-1.6%	-1.2%	-1.6%	-1.4%	-1.1%	-1.6%	-1.5%	-1.2%	-1.7%
Supply to domestic - vol.	3.5%	12.1%	12.2%	3.5%	12.1%	12.2%	-13.4%	-27.1%	-26.8%	-13.5%	-27.1%	-26.8%	-13.6%	-27.3%	-27.0%
Intra-EU Trade - vol	-0.5%	-0.2%	-0.2%	-0.5%	-0.2%	-0.2%	-0.6%	-2.1%	-2.3%	-1.8%	-3.3%	-3.5%	-1.9%	-3.5%	-3.8%

Consumer goods

	Border Controls			Border controls and x-ineff.			Market segmentation			Trade antimonde			Full antimonde		
	1988	1991	1994	1988	1991	1994	1988	1991	1994	1988	1991	1994	1988	1991	1994
Domestic Production - vol.	-0.6%	-1.5%	-1.5%	-0.6%	-1.5%	-1.5%	2.9%	4.1%	3.3%	2.8%	3.9%	3.1%	2.7%	3.7%	2.8%
Imports - vol.	1.9%	2.3%	2.3%	2.0%	2.3%	2.3%	-6.4%	-5.5%	-5.1%	-5.2%	-4.2%	-3.7%	-5.0%	-3.9%	-3.3%
Exports - vol.	-0.8%	-1.0%	-1.0%	-0.8%	-1.0%	-1.0%	3.0%	2.6%	2.3%	2.5%	2.1%	1.7%	2.4%	1.9%	1.6%
Absorption - vol.	-0.1%	-0.4%	-0.4%	-0.1%	-0.4%	-0.4%	0.2%	0.4%	0.0%	0.2%	0.4%	0.0%	0.2%	0.3%	-0.1%
Investment - vol.	-0.3%	-0.7%	-0.7%	-0.3%	-0.7%	-0.7%	-3.2%	-2.6%	-3.0%	-3.2%	-2.7%	-3.1%	-3.2%	-2.8%	-3.2%
Labour Demand - vol.	-0.6%	-1.4%	-1.4%	-0.6%	-1.4%	-1.4%	2.8%	4.0%	3.3%	2.7%	3.8%	3.2%	2.6%	3.7%	3.0%
Private Consumption - vol.	0.0%	0.0%	0.0%	0.0%	0.0%	0.0%	-0.4%	-0.6%	-0.8%	-0.3%	-0.5%	-0.8%	-0.4%	-0.6%	-0.9%
Supply to domestic - vol.	0.0%	0.0%	0.0%	0.0%	0.0%	0.0%	2.0%	3.6%	2.9%	2.0%	3.6%	2.9%	1.9%	3.5%	2.8%
Intra-EU Trade - vol	-1.6%	-4.1%	-4.1%	-1.6%	-4.1%	-4.1%	0.3%	-2.0%	-2.3%	0.1%	-2.5%	-2.8%	-0.1%	-2.7%	-3.1%

Construction

	Border Controls			Border controls and x-ineff.			Market segmentation			Trade antimonde			Full antimonde		
	1988	1991	1994	1988	1991	1994	1988	1991	1994	1988	1991	1994	1988	1991	1994
Domestic Production - vol.	0.1%	0.1%	0.1%	0.1%	0.1%	0.1%	-8.0%	-8.2%	-8.5%	-7.9%	-8.1%	-8.4%	-7.9%	-8.2%	-8.4%
Imports - vol.	#VALUE!	#VALUE!	#VALUE!	#VALUE!	#VALUE!	#VALUE!	#VALUE!	#VALUE!	#VALUE!	#VALUE!	#VALUE!	#VALUE!	#VALUE!	#VALUE!	#VALUE!
Exports - vol.	0.1%	0.1%	0.1%	0.1%	0.1%	0.1%	-8.0%	-8.1%	-8.2%	-7.9%	-8.1%	-8.4%	-7.9%	-8.2%	-8.4%
Absorption - vol.	0.1%	0.1%	0.1%	0.1%	0.1%	0.1%	-8.0%	-8.3%	-8.4%	-8.0%	-8.2%	-8.3%	-7.9%	-8.0%	-8.2%
Investment - vol.	0.1%	0.2%	0.2%	0.2%	0.2%	0.2%	-8.1%	-8.3%	-8.4%	-8.0%	-8.2%	-8.3%	-8.0%	-8.1%	-8.2%
Labour Demand - vol.	0.0%	0.0%	0.0%	0.0%	0.0%	0.0%	-0.4%	-0.7%	-1.0%	-0.3%	-0.6%	-1.0%	-0.4%	-0.7%	-1.1%
Private Consumption - vol.	0.1%	0.1%	0.1%	0.1%	0.1%	0.1%	-8.0%	-8.2%	-8.4%	-7.9%	-8.1%	-8.2%	-7.9%	-8.1%	-8.2%
Supply to domestic - vol.	0.0%	0.0%	0.0%	0.0%	0.0%	0.0%	-8.0%	-8.3%	-8.4%	-7.9%	-8.1%	-8.4%	-7.9%	-8.2%	-8.4%
Intra-EU Trade - vol	#DIV/0!	#DIV/0!	#DIV/0!	#DIV/0!	#DIV/0!	#DIV/0!	#DIV/0!	#DIV/0!	#DIV/0!	#DIV/0!	#DIV/0!	#DIV/0!	#DIV/0!	#DIV/0!	#DIV/0!

Telecommunications

	Border Controls			Border controls and x-ineff.			Market segmentation			Trade *antimonde*			Full *antimonde*		
	1988	1991	1994	1988	1991	1994	1988	1991	1994	1988	1991	1994	1988	1991	1994
Domestic Production - vol.	0.1%	0.1%	0.1%	0.2%	0.3%	0.3%	-0.7%	-1.0%	-1.2%	-0.6%	-0.9%	-1.1%	-0.6%	-0.7%	-1.0%
Imports - vol.	1.0%	1.2%	1.3%	0.8%	0.9%	0.9%	-6.2%	-6.0%	-5.9%	-5.6%	-5.5%	-5.3%	-5.7%	-5.6%	-5.3%
Exports - vol.	-0.2%	-0.3%	-0.3%	-0.2%	-0.3%	-0.3%	1.1%	1.0%	0.9%	1.0%	0.9%	0.8%	1.0%	0.9%	0.8%
Absorption - vol.	0.1%	0.1%	0.1%	0.2%	0.3%	0.3%	-0.7%	-1.0%	-1.2%	-0.7%	-0.9%	-1.1%	-0.6%	-0.8%	-1.0%
Investment - vol.	0.1%	0.1%	0.1%	0.1%	0.2%	0.2%	-4.5%	-4.6%	-4.8%	-4.5%	-4.6%	-4.7%	-4.4%	-4.5%	-4.6%
Labour Demand - vol.	0.1%	0.2%	0.2%	-0.3%	-0.8%	-0.7%	-0.7%	-0.9%	-0.9%	-0.4%	-0.8%	-0.8%	-1.0%	-1.7%	-1.7%
Private Consumption - vol.	0.0%	0.0%	0.0%	0.1%	0.2%	0.3%	-0.4%	-0.8%	-1.1%	-0.4%	-0.7%	-1.0%	-0.3%	-0.6%	-0.9%
Supply to domestic - vol.	0.1%	0.1%	0.1%	0.2%	0.3%	0.3%	-0.7%	-1.0%	-1.2%	-0.6%	-0.9%	-1.1%	-0.6%	-0.7%	-0.9%
Intra-EU Trade - vol.	0.3%	0.5%	0.4%	-0.2%	-1.6%	-1.6%	-6.6%	-17.6%	-17.9%	-6.5%	-17.7%	-18.0%	-6.7%	-17.9%	-18.3%

Transports

	Border Controls			Border controls and x-ineff.			Market segmentation			Trade *antimonde*			Full *antimonde*		
	1988	1991	1994	1988	1991	1994	1988	1991	1994	1988	1991	1994	1988	1991	1994
Domestic Production - vol.	0.1%	0.1%	0.1%	0.1%	0.1%	0.1%	-1.6%	-1.8%	-2.0%	-1.5%	-1.7%	-1.9%	-1.5%	-1.7%	-1.9%
Imports - vol.	0.1%	0.1%	0.1%	0.1%	0.1%	0.1%	-0.8%	-0.9%	-1.0%	-0.7%	-0.8%	-1.0%	-0.7%	-0.8%	-1.0%
Exports - vol.	-0.1%	-0.2%	-0.2%	-0.1%	-0.2%	-0.2%	0.7%	0.6%	0.5%	0.6%	0.5%	0.5%	0.6%	0.5%	0.4%
Absorption - vol.	0.1%	0.1%	0.1%	0.1%	0.1%	0.1%	-1.6%	-1.8%	-2.1%	-1.5%	-1.7%	-2.0%	-1.5%	-1.7%	-2.0%
Investment - vol.	0.1%	0.1%	0.1%	0.1%	0.1%	0.1%	-4.9%	-5.0%	-5.1%	-4.8%	-4.9%	-5.1%	-4.8%	-4.9%	-5.1%
Labour Demand - vol.	0.1%	0.2%	0.2%	0.1%	0.2%	0.2%	-1.6%	-1.8%	-2.0%	-1.5%	-1.7%	-1.8%	-1.4%	-1.6%	-1.8%
Private Consumption - vol.	0.1%	0.1%	0.1%	0.1%	0.2%	0.1%	-0.7%	-1.1%	-1.4%	-0.6%	-1.0%	-1.3%	-0.7%	-1.0%	-1.4%
Supply to domestic - vol.	0.1%	0.1%	0.1%	0.1%	0.1%	0.1%	-1.6%	-1.8%	-2.0%	-1.5%	-1.7%	-1.9%	-1.5%	-1.7%	-1.9%
Intra-EU Trade - vol.	0.2%	0.2%	0.2%	0.2%	0.2%	0.2%	-0.7%	-0.8%	-1.0%	-0.6%	-0.7%	-0.8%	-0.6%	-0.7%	-0.8%

Banks

	Border Controls			Border controls and x-ineff.			Market segmentation			Trade *antimonde*			Full *antimonde*		
	1988	1991	1994	1988	1991	1994	1988	1991	1994	1988	1991	1994	1988	1991	1994
Domestic Production - vol.	0.1%	0.1%	0.1%	0.1%	0.2%	0.2%	-0.1%	-0.3%	-0.5%	-0.1%	-0.2%	-0.5%	-0.1%	-0.2%	-0.5%
Imports - vol.	1.2%	1.6%	1.6%	1.2%	1.5%	1.5%	-5.7%	-5.9%	-5.6%	-4.8%	-4.9%	-4.6%	-4.6%	-4.6%	-4.1%
Exports - vol.	-0.2%	-0.3%	-0.3%	-0.2%	-0.3%	-0.3%	1.2%	1.0%	0.9%	1.1%	0.9%	0.8%	1.0%	0.9%	0.7%
Absorption - vol.	0.1%	0.2%	0.2%	0.1%	0.2%	0.2%	-0.2%	-0.5%	-0.7%	-0.1%	-0.4%	-0.7%	-0.2%	-0.4%	-0.7%
Investment - vol.	0.1%	0.1%	0.1%	0.1%	0.1%	0.1%	-4.3%	-4.3%	-4.5%	-4.2%	-4.3%	-4.4%	-4.2%	-4.3%	-4.4%
Labour Demand - vol.	0.2%	0.2%	0.2%	-0.1%	-0.4%	-0.4%	-0.3%	-0.4%	-0.5%	-0.3%	-0.3%	-0.4%	-0.6%	-0.9%	-1.0%
Private Consumption - vol.	0.1%	0.1%	0.1%	0.1%	0.1%	0.1%	-0.7%	-1.1%	-1.6%	-0.7%	-1.0%	-1.5%	-0.7%	-1.1%	-1.6%
Supply to domestic - vol.	0.1%	0.1%	0.1%	0.1%	0.2%	0.2%	-0.1%	-0.3%	-0.5%	-0.1%	-0.2%	-0.5%	-0.1%	-0.2%	-0.5%
Intra-EU Trade - vol.	0.4%	1.5%	1.5%	0.2%	0.7%	0.7%	-4.4%	-12.5%	-12.4%	-4.3%	-12.4%	-12.3%	-4.4%	-12.5%	-12.5%

Services

	Border Controls			Border controls and x-ineff.			Market segmentation			Trade *antimonde*			Full *antimonde*		
	1988	1991	1994	1988	1991	1994	1988	1991	1994	1988	1991	1994	1988	1991	1994
Domestic Production - vol.	0.1%	0.0%	0.0%	0.1%	0.0%	0.0%	-0.4%	-0.5%	-0.9%	-0.3%	-0.4%	-0.8%	-0.4%	-0.5%	-0.9%
Imports - vol.	1.9%	2.2%	2.2%	1.9%	2.2%	2.2%	-4.8%	-4.4%	-4.1%	-3.4%	-2.9%	-2.6%	-3.3%	-2.7%	-2.3%
Exports - vol.	-0.6%	-0.7%	-0.7%	-0.6%	-0.7%	-0.7%	1.5%	1.3%	1.2%	1.1%	0.9%	0.7%	1.0%	0.8%	0.6%
Absorption - vol.	0.1%	0.0%	0.0%	0.1%	0.0%	0.0%	-0.7%	-0.9%	-1.3%	-0.7%	-0.9%	-1.2%	-0.7%	-0.9%	-1.3%
Investment - vol.	0.0%	0.0%	0.0%	0.0%	0.0%	0.0%	-4.4%	-4.4%	-4.6%	-4.4%	-4.4%	-4.6%	-4.4%	-4.4%	-4.6%
Labour Demand - vol.	0.1%	0.1%	0.1%	0.2%	0.1%	0.1%	-0.7%	-0.8%	-0.9%	-0.6%	-0.6%	-0.8%	-0.6%	-0.6%	-0.8%
Private Consumption - vol.	0.1%	0.0%	0.1%	0.1%	0.0%	0.0%	-0.6%	-0.8%	-1.2%	-0.5%	-0.8%	-1.1%	-0.6%	-0.8%	-1.2%
Supply to domestic - vol.	0.0%	-0.1%	-0.1%	0.0%	-0.1%	-0.1%	-0.6%	-0.8%	-1.2%	-0.6%	-0.8%	-1.1%	-0.7%	-0.9%	-1.2%
Intra-EU Trade - vol.	1.2%	1.5%	1.5%	1.2%	1.5%	1.6%	0.0%	0.8%	0.7%	1.1%	1.7%	1.6%	1.0%	1.6%	1.5%

Non market

	Border Controls			Border controls and x-ineff.			Market segmentation			Trade *antimonde*			Full *antimonde*		
	1988	1991	1994	1988	1991	1994	1988	1991	1994	1988	1991	1994	1988	1991	1994
Domestic Production - vol.	0.0%	0.0%	0.0%	0.0%	0.0%	0.0%	0.0%	0.0%	0.0%	0.0%	0.0%	0.0%	0.0%	0.0%	0.0%
Imports - vol.	0.0%	0.0%	0.0%	0.0%	0.0%	0.0%	0.0%	0.0%	0.0%	0.0%	0.0%	0.0%	0.0%	0.0%	0.0%
Exports - vol.	#VALUE!	#VALUE!	#VALUE!	#VALUE!	#VALUE!	#VALUE!	#VALUE!	#VALUE!	#VALUE!	#VALUE!	#VALUE!	#VALUE!	#VALUE!	#VALUE!	#VALUE!
Absorption - vol.	0.0%	0.0%	0.0%	0.0%	0.0%	0.0%	-4.1%	-4.1%	-4.1%	-4.1%	-4.1%	-4.1%	-4.1%	-4.1%	-4.1%
Investment - vol.	0.0%	0.0%	0.0%	0.0%	0.0%	0.0%	0.0%	0.0%	0.0%	0.0%	0.0%	0.0%	0.1%	0.1%	0.1%
Labour Demand - vol.	0.0%	0.0%	0.0%	0.0%	0.0%	0.1%	0.0%	0.0%	0.0%	0.0%	0.0%	0.0%	-0.3%	-0.4%	-0.5%
Private Consumption - vol.	0.0%	0.0%	0.0%	0.0%	0.0%	0.0%	-0.2%	-0.4%	-0.5%	-0.2%	-0.4%	-0.5%	0.0%	0.0%	0.0%
Supply to domestic - vol.	0.0%	-0.1%	0.0%	0.0%	0.0%	0.0%	0.0%	0.0%	0.0%	0.0%	0.0%	0.0%	0.0%	0.0%	0.0%
Intra-EU Trade - vol.	1.2%	1.5%	0.0%	0.0%	0.0%	0.0%	0.0%	0.0%	0.0%	0.0%	0.0%	0.0%	0.0%	0.0%	0.0%

Table B6.8
Decomposition of effects: sectoral results for Greece (prices)

% change from *monde*

Agriculture

	Border Controls			Border controls and x-ineff.			Market segmentation			Trade *antimonde*			Full *antimonde*		
	1988	1991	1994	1988	1991	1994	1988	1991	1994	1988	1991	1994	1988	1991	1994
Marginal Costs	-0.02%	0.02%	0.01%	-0.01%	0.03%	0.03%	-0.12%	-0.22%	-0.03%	-0.13%	-0.23%	-0.03%	-0.15%	-0.25%	-0.06%
Cost of Labour	-0.17%	-0.34%	-0.34%	-0.18%	-0.36%	-0.36%	0.47%	0.37%	-0.20%	0.43%	0.30%	-0.28%	0.32%	0.14%	-0.50%
Deflator of Absorption	-0.10%	-0.09%	-0.09%	-0.10%	-0.07%	-0.08%	0.19%	0.08%	0.24%	0.16%	0.05%	0.21%	0.13%	0.02%	0.17%
Price of Exports-RW	-0.02%	0.02%	0.01%	-0.01%	0.03%	0.03%	-0.12%	-0.22%	-0.03%	-0.13%	-0.23%	-0.03%	-0.15%	-0.25%	-0.06%

Energy

	Border Controls			Border controls and x-ineff.			Market segmentation			Trade *antimonde*			Full *antimonde*		
	1988	1991	1994	1988	1991	1994	1988	1991	1994	1988	1991	1994	1988	1991	1994
Marginal Costs	-1.09%	-1.28%	-1.29%	-1.10%	-1.29%	-1.31%	2.78%	2.38%	2.21%	2.20%	1.74%	1.56%	2.11%	1.61%	1.38%
Cost of Labour	-0.17%	-0.34%	-0.34%	-0.18%	-0.36%	-0.36%	0.47%	0.37%	-0.20%	0.43%	0.30%	-0.28%	0.32%	0.14%	-0.50%
Deflator of Absorption	-1.80%	-2.12%	-2.13%	-1.82%	-2.14%	-2.17%	4.72%	4.09%	3.72%	3.76%	3.05%	2.65%	3.61%	2.83%	2.36%
Price of Exports-RW	-1.09%	-1.28%	-1.29%	-1.10%	-1.29%	-1.31%	2.78%	2.38%	2.21%	2.20%	1.74%	1.56%	2.11%	1.61%	1.38%

Metal Industries

	Border Controls			Border controls and x-ineff.			Market segmentation			Trade *antimonde*			Full *antimonde*		
	1988	1991	1994	1988	1991	1994	1988	1991	1994	1988	1991	1994	1988	1991	1994
Marginal Costs	-0.70%	-0.86%	-0.86%	-0.70%	-0.87%	-0.88%	2.91%	2.80%	2.55%	2.68%	2.57%	2.32%	2.64%	2.51%	2.24%
Cost of Labour	-0.17%	-0.34%	-0.34%	-0.18%	-0.36%	-0.36%	0.47%	0.37%	-0.20%	0.43%	0.30%	-0.28%	0.32%	0.14%	-0.50%
Deflator of Absorption	-0.95%	-1.17%	-1.17%	-0.96%	-1.19%	-1.19%	5.19%	5.32%	5.00%	5.00%	5.16%	4.83%	4.92%	5.05%	4.68%
Price of Exports-RW	-0.75%	-1.00%	-1.00%	-0.75%	-1.01%	-1.02%	2.43%	2.40%	2.14%	2.21%	2.18%	1.90%	2.17%	2.12%	1.83%

Chemical

	Border Controls			Border controls and x-ineff.			Market segmentation			Trade *antimonde*			Full *antimonde*		
	1988	1991	1994	1988	1991	1994	1988	1991	1994	1988	1991	1994	1988	1991	1994
Marginal Costs	-0.25%	-0.33%	-0.34%	-0.26%	-0.34%	-0.34%	1.44%	1.32%	1.19%	1.43%	1.32%	1.19%	1.40%	1.28%	1.13%
Cost of Labour	-0.17%	-0.34%	-0.34%	-0.18%	-0.36%	-0.36%	0.47%	0.37%	-0.20%	0.43%	0.30%	-0.28%	0.32%	0.14%	-0.50%
Deflator of Absorption	-0.17%	-0.28%	-0.28%	-0.18%	-0.29%	-0.30%	3.29%	3.28%	3.09%	3.58%	3.63%	3.43%	3.52%	3.55%	3.32%
Price of Exports-RW	-0.30%	-0.44%	-0.44%	-0.30%	-0.44%	-0.45%	0.87%	0.67%	0.54%	0.83%	0.64%	0.50%	0.80%	0.60%	0.45%

Other Intensive Industries

	Border Controls			Border controls and x-ineff.			Market segmentation			Trade *antimonde*			Full *antimonde*		
	1988	1991	1994	1988	1991	1994	1988	1991	1994	1988	1991	1994	1988	1991	1994
Marginal Costs	-0.46%	-0.58%	-0.58%	-0.46%	-0.58%	-0.59%	1.72%	1.57%	1.39%	1.57%	1.42%	1.23%	1.53%	1.36%	1.15%
Cost of Labour	-0.17%	-0.34%	-0.34%	-0.18%	-0.36%	-0.36%	0.47%	0.37%	-0.20%	0.43%	0.30%	-0.28%	0.32%	0.14%	-0.50%
Deflator of Absorption	-0.56%	-0.71%	-0.71%	-0.57%	-0.73%	-0.73%	2.52%	2.33%	2.11%	2.40%	2.22%	1.98%	2.34%	2.14%	1.87%
Price of Exports-RW	-0.47%	-0.60%	-0.61%	-0.47%	-0.61%	-0.62%	1.68%	1.52%	1.34%	1.53%	1.36%	1.17%	1.49%	1.31%	1.10%

Electrical goods

	Border Controls			Border controls and x-ineff.			Market segmentation			Trade *antimonde*			Full *antimonde*		
	1988	1991	1994	1988	1991	1994	1988	1991	1994	1988	1991	1994	1988	1991	1994
Marginal Costs	-0.39%	-0.51%	-0.51%	-0.39%	-0.52%	-0.52%	2.07%	2.04%	1.85%	2.02%	2.01%	1.80%	1.99%	1.97%	1.76%
Cost of Labour	-0.17%	-0.34%	-0.34%	-0.18%	-0.36%	-0.36%	0.47%	0.37%	-0.20%	0.43%	0.30%	-0.28%	0.32%	0.14%	-0.50%
Deflator of Absorption	-0.46%	-0.66%	-0.66%	-0.47%	-0.68%	-0.68%	3.70%	3.87%	3.62%	3.80%	4.03%	3.77%	3.75%	3.95%	3.66%
Price of Exports-RW	-0.49%	-0.71%	-0.71%	-0.49%	-0.72%	-0.72%	1.90%	2.13%	1.92%	1.83%	2.09%	1.88%	1.81%	2.06%	1.83%

Transport equipment

	Border Controls			Border controls and x-ineff.			Market segmentation			Trade *antimonde*			Full *antimonde*		
	1988	1991	1994	1988	1991	1994	1988	1991	1994	1988	1991	1994	1988	1991	1994
Marginal Costs	-0.29%	-0.41%	-0.41%	-0.30%	-0.42%	-0.42%	1.18%	1.07%	0.82%	1.11%	0.99%	0.73%	1.07%	0.93%	0.65%
Cost of Labour	-0.17%	-0.34%	-0.34%	-0.18%	-0.36%	-0.36%	0.47%	0.37%	-0.20%	0.43%	0.30%	-0.28%	0.32%	0.14%	-0.50%
Deflator of Absorption	-1.12%	-1.40%	-1.40%	-1.13%	-1.43%	-1.44%	5.26%	4.97%	4.55%	4.99%	4.69%	4.25%	4.87%	4.52%	4.02%
Price of Exports-RW	-0.38%	-0.66%	-0.66%	-0.38%	-0.67%	-0.67%	-0.12%	-0.71%	-0.98%	-0.23%	-0.82%	-1.10%	-0.26%	-0.88%	-1.18%

Other Equipment

	Border Controls			Border controls and x-ineff.			Market segmentation			Trade *antimonde*			Full *antimonde*		
	1988	1991	1994	1988	1991	1994	1988	1991	1994	1988	1991	1994	1988	1991	1994
Marginal Costs	-0.35%	-0.46%	-0.46%	-0.35%	-0.47%	-0.47%	1.65%	1.59%	1.40%	1.59%	1.53%	1.34%	1.56%	1.49%	1.28%
Cost of Labour	-0.17%	-0.34%	-0.34%	-0.18%	-0.36%	-0.36%	0.47%	0.37%	-0.20%	0.43%	0.30%	-0.28%	0.32%	0.14%	-0.50%
Deflator of Absorption	-0.51%	-0.73%	-0.72%	-0.52%	-0.74%	-0.74%	2.97%	2.91%	2.65%	2.98%	2.98%	2.71%	2.91%	2.88%	2.58%
Price of Exports-RW	-0.43%	-0.72%	-0.72%	-0.43%	-0.73%	-0.73%	1.18%	1.26%	1.06%	1.10%	1.20%	0.99%	1.07%	1.16%	0.93%

Consumer goods

	Border Controls			Border controls and x-ineff.			Market segmentation			Trade *antimonde*			Full *antimonde*		
	1988	1991	1994	1988	1991	1994	1988	1991	1994	1988	1991	1994	1988	1991	1994
Marginal Costs	-0.14%	-0.15%	-0.16%	-0.13%	-0.15%	-0.15%	0.43%	0.32%	0.35%	0.40%	0.29%	0.32%	0.41%	0.30%	0.34%
Cost of Labour	-0.17%	-0.34%	-0.34%	-0.18%	-0.36%	-0.36%	0.47%	0.37%	-0.20%	0.43%	0.30%	-0.28%	0.32%	0.14%	-0.50%
Deflator of Absorption	-0.21%	-0.25%	-0.25%	-0.21%	-0.24%	-0.24%	0.88%	0.74%	0.72%	0.86%	0.72%	0.70%	0.85%	0.71%	0.69%
Price of Exports-RW	-0.14%	-0.15%	-0.16%	-0.13%	-0.15%	-0.15%	0.43%	0.32%	0.35%	0.40%	0.29%	0.32%	0.41%	0.30%	0.34%

Construction

	Border Controls			Border controls and x-ineff.			Market segmentation			Trade *antimonde*			Full *antimonde*		
	1988	1991	1994	1988	1991	1994	1988	1991	1994	1988	1991	1994	1988	1991	1994
Marginal Costs	-0.28%	-0.35%	-0.35%	-0.28%	-0.35%	-0.35%	1.14%	1.02%	0.95%	1.07%	0.96%	0.88%	1.05%	0.94%	0.85%
Cost of Labour	-0.17%	-0.34%	-0.34%	-0.18%	-0.36%	-0.36%	0.47%	0.37%	-0.20%	0.43%	0.30%	-0.28%	0.32%	0.14%	-0.50%
Deflator of Absorption	-0.28%	-0.35%	-0.35%	-0.28%	-0.35%	-0.35%	1.14%	1.02%	0.95%	1.07%	0.96%	0.88%	1.05%	0.94%	0.85%
Price of Exports-RW	-0.28%	-0.35%	-0.35%	-0.28%	-0.35%	-0.35%	1.14%	1.02%	0.95%	1.07%	0.96%	0.88%	1.05%	0.94%	0.85%

Telecommunications

	Border Controls			Border controls and x-ineff.			Market segmentation			Trade antimonde			Full antimonde		
	1988	1991	1994	1988	1991	1994	1988	1991	1994	1988	1991	1994	1988	1991	1994
Marginal Costs	-0.04%	-0.09%	-0.08%	-0.05%	-0.09%	-0.09%	0.04%	-0.05%	-0.20%	0.03%	-0.07%	-0.23%	0.00%	-0.12%	-0.29%
Cost of Labour	-0.17%	-0.34%	-0.34%	-0.18%	-0.36%	-0.36%	0.47%	0.37%	-0.20%	0.43%	0.30%	-0.28%	0.32%	0.14%	-0.50%
Deflator of Absorption	-0.10%	-0.17%	-0.16%	-0.49%	-0.96%	-0.96%	0.30%	0.26%	0.08%	0.27%	0.22%	0.03%	-0.13%	-0.58%	-0.79%
Price of Exports-RW	-0.06%	-0.10%	-0.10%	-0.16%	-0.30%	-0.30%	0.10%	0.02%	-0.14%	0.08%	-0.01%	-0.17%	-0.04%	-0.23%	-0.42%

Transports

	Border Controls			Border controls and x-ineff.			Market segmentation			Trade antimonde			Full antimonde		
	1988	1991	1994	1988	1991	1994	1988	1991	1994	1988	1991	1994	1988	1991	1994
Marginal Costs	-0.34%	-0.42%	-0.43%	-0.34%	-0.43%	-0.44%	1.01%	0.84%	0.71%	0.87%	0.69%	0.56%	0.83%	0.63%	0.47%
Cost of Labour	-0.17%	-0.34%	-0.34%	-0.18%	-0.36%	-0.36%	0.47%	0.37%	-0.20%	0.43%	0.30%	-0.28%	0.32%	0.14%	-0.50%
Deflator of Absorption	-0.36%	-0.45%	-0.46%	-0.36%	-0.46%	-0.47%	1.07%	0.90%	0.77%	0.92%	0.73%	0.59%	0.88%	0.66%	0.50%
Price of Exports-RW	-0.34%	-0.42%	-0.43%	-0.34%	-0.43%	-0.44%	1.01%	0.84%	0.71%	0.87%	0.69%	0.56%	0.83%	0.63%	0.47%

Banks

	Border Controls			Border controls and x-ineff.			Market segmentation			Trade antimonde			Full antimonde		
	1988	1991	1994	1988	1991	1994	1988	1991	1994	1988	1991	1994	1988	1991	1994
Marginal Costs	-0.05%	-0.03%	-0.03%	-0.08%	-0.08%	-0.09%	-0.01%	-0.11%	0.01%	-0.04%	-0.15%	-0.02%	-0.08%	-0.21%	-0.09%
Cost of Labour	-0.17%	-0.34%	-0.34%	-0.18%	-0.36%	-0.36%	0.47%	0.37%	-0.20%	0.43%	0.30%	-0.28%	0.32%	0.14%	-0.50%
Deflator of Absorption	-0.09%	-0.09%	-0.09%	-0.19%	-0.29%	-0.30%	0.14%	0.06%	0.17%	0.10%	0.02%	0.13%	-0.01%	-0.19%	-0.09%
Price of Exports-RW	-0.06%	-0.04%	-0.04%	-0.10%	-0.12%	-0.13%	0.01%	-0.10%	0.02%	-0.03%	-0.14%	-0.01%	-0.08%	-0.23%	-0.12%

Services

	Border Controls			Border controls and x-ineff.			Market segmentation			Trade antimonde			Full antimonde		
	1988	1991	1994	1988	1991	1994	1988	1991	1994	1988	1991	1994	1988	1991	1994
Marginal Costs	-0.09%	-0.08%	-0.08%	-0.09%	-0.08%	-0.08%	0.12%	0.00%	0.13%	0.08%	-0.04%	0.10%	0.07%	-0.05%	0.08%
Cost of Labour	-0.17%	-0.34%	-0.34%	-0.18%	-0.36%	-0.36%	0.47%	0.37%	-0.20%	0.43%	0.30%	-0.28%	0.32%	0.14%	-0.50%
Deflator of Absorption	-0.11%	-0.11%	-0.11%	-0.11%	-0.11%	-0.11%	0.15%	0.04%	0.17%	0.10%	-0.01%	0.11%	0.09%	-0.03%	0.09%
Price of Exports-RW	-0.09%	-0.08%	-0.08%	-0.09%	-0.08%	-0.08%	0.12%	0.00%	0.13%	0.08%	-0.04%	0.10%	0.07%	-0.05%	0.08%

Non market

	Border Controls			Border controls and x-ineff.			Market segmentation			Trade antimonde			Full antimonde		
	1988	1991	1994	1988	1991	1994	1988	1991	1994	1988	1991	1994	1988	1991	1994
Marginal Costs	-0.21%	-0.34%	-0.34%	-0.22%	-0.35%	-0.36%	0.67%	0.55%	0.15%	0.62%	0.49%	0.07%	0.57%	0.42%	-0.03%
Cost of Labour	-0.17%	-0.34%	-0.34%	-0.18%	-0.36%	-0.36%	0.47%	0.37%	-0.20%	0.43%	0.30%	-0.28%	0.32%	0.14%	-0.50%
Deflator of Absorption	-0.21%	-0.34%	-0.34%	-0.22%	-0.36%	-0.36%	0.67%	0.55%	0.15%	0.62%	0.48%	0.07%	0.57%	0.42%	-0.03%
Price of Exports-RW	-0.21%	-0.34%	-0.34%	-0.22%	-0.35%	-0.36%	0.67%	0.55%	0.15%	0.62%	0.49%	0.07%	0.57%	0.42%	-0.03%

Table B7.1.
The full *antimonde* scenario: macroeconomic aggregates for Ireland

Macroeconomic Aggregates (vol.) (% change from *monde*)	Constraint Case			Flexible Case			Efficiency Case		
	1988	1991	1994	1988	1991	1994	1988	1991	1994
GDP fact. pr.	-0.90%	-1.26%	-1.61%	-0.71%	-1.78%	-2.15%	-0.74%	-1.90%	-2.36%
Priv. Consumption	-1.51%	-1.75%	-2.02%	-1.81%	-2.67%	-2.92%	-1.82%	-2.71%	-2.99%
Absorption	-0.89%	-1.08%	-1.29%	-1.82%	-2.54%	-2.77%	-1.83%	-2.57%	-2.82%
Total Investment	-4.30%	-4.85%	-5.43%	-4.30%	-4.48%	-4.60%	-4.30%	-4.48%	-4.61%
Total Exports to RW	-0.19%	-0.43%	-0.67%	1.66%	1.43%	1.20%	1.63%	1.32%	1.01%
Total Imports from RW	-1.55%	-1.64%	-1.77%	-4.76%	-4.96%	-4.63%	-4.71%	-4.76%	-4.27%
Total Intra-EU Trade	-1.32%	-1.37%	-1.51%	-1.33%	-3.40%	-3.57%	-1.34%	-3.43%	-3.64%
Employment (diff. from *monde*, 10³ persons)	-2	-3	-5	-3	-3	-4	-3	-3	-4
Disposable Income (deflated)	-1.60%	-1.85%	-2.13%	-1.91%	-2.81%	-3.08%	-1.93%	-2.85%	-3.15%

Macroeconomic Ratios (abs. diff. from *monde*)	Constraint Case			Flexible Case			Efficiency Case		
	1988	1991	1994	1988	1991	1994	1988	1991	1994
Current Account as % of GDP	0.00%	0.00%	0.00%	-0.93%	-0.44%	-0.38%	-0.91%	-0.40%	-0.30%
Public Deficit as % of GDP	-0.14%	-0.17%	-0.20%	-0.37%	-0.71%	-0.80%	-0.38%	-0.74%	-0.86%
Labour Productivity	-0.70%	-0.94%	-1.18%	-0.43%	-1.54%	-1.78%	-0.47%	-1.65%	-1.99%
Investment/GDP	-0.72%	-0.76%	-0.82%	-1.80%	-1.64%	-1.62%	-1.80%	-1.62%	-1.58%
Priv.Cons./GDP	-0.38%	-0.31%	-0.25%	-0.69%	-0.56%	-0.49%	-0.68%	-0.51%	-0.40%

Deflators (% change from *monde*)	Constraint Case			Flexible Case			Efficiency Case		
	1988	1991	1994	1988	1991	1994	1988	1991	1994
Consumer Price Index	0.20%	0.33%	0.41%	1.30%	1.29%	1.25%	1.28%	1.23%	1.15%
Real Wage Rate	-1.17%	-1.62%	-2.07%	-1.10%	-2.12%	-2.59%	-1.13%	-2.24%	-2.80%
Marginal Costs	-0.28%	-0.12%	-0.03%	0.65%	0.62%	0.61%	0.64%	0.59%	0.55%
Producer Prices	-0.16%	0.00%	0.09%	0.68%	0.76%	0.75%	0.68%	0.73%	0.69%
Average change in mark-ups (abs. diff.)	0.84%	0.91%	0.96%	0.31%	1.16%	1.24%	0.31%	1.16%	1.26%
Shadow Price of Capital	-1.11%	-0.76%	-0.45%	-0.03%	0.20%	0.72%	-0.06%	0.10%	0.55%
Terms-of-Trade RW	-0.77%	-0.58%	-0.44%	-4.76%	-4.15%	-3.51%	-4.68%	-3.82%	-2.94%

Implicit change in real exchange rate	-0.67%	-0.49%	-0.39%	-4.10%	-3.41%	-2.78%	-4.01%	-3.05%	-2.14%

Trade Regime	*Segmentation*			*Segmentation*			*Segmentation*		

Table B7.2.
The full *antimonde* scenario: effects on IC sectors for Ireland

% change from *monde*

Metal Industries	Constraint Case			Flexible Case			Efficiency Case		
	1988	1991	1994	1988	1991	1994	1988	1991	1994
Production per firm	-13.76%	-13.83%	-13.95%	-3.82%	-17.58%	-17.75%	-3.85%	-17.68%	-17.92%
Real Marginal Costs	0.47%	0.60%	0.68%	-1.91%	-0.02%	1.07%	-1.80%	0.43%	1.85%
Real Producer Prices	2.31%	2.43%	2.52%	-1.52%	1.65%	2.75%	-1.41%	2.11%	3.55%
Mark-ups domestic (abs. diff.)	10.10%	10.11%	10.12%	2.84%	10.50%	10.51%	2.84%	10.51%	10.53%
Fixed Costs per firm	0.55%	0.55%	0.50%	-2.89%	-2.05%	-1.57%	-2.82%	-1.78%	-1.08%
Number of Firms	8.03%	8.05%	8.02%	5.17%	15.43%	15.39%	5.16%	15.35%	15.26%
Sigma of Love of Variety	0.00%	0.00%	0.00%	0.00%	0.00%	0.00%	0.00%	0.00%	0.00%

Chemical	Constraint Case			Flexible Case			Efficiency Case		
	1988	1991	1994	1988	1991	1994	1988	1991	1994
Production per firm	-5.24%	-5.45%	-5.69%	-0.55%	-8.97%	-9.73%	-0.57%	-9.04%	-9.85%
Real Marginal Costs	0.04%	0.29%	0.50%	-2.03%	-0.04%	1.25%	-1.92%	0.40%	2.03%
Real Producer Prices	0.50%	0.75%	0.96%	-1.96%	0.56%	1.89%	-1.85%	1.01%	2.67%
Mark-ups domestic (abs. diff.)	3.77%	3.77%	3.79%	0.38%	3.81%	3.86%	0.38%	3.82%	3.87%
Fixed Costs per firm	0.52%	0.55%	0.54%	-2.53%	-1.57%	-1.04%	-2.47%	-1.30%	-0.55%
Number of Firms	4.48%	4.44%	4.35%	3.98%	9.53%	8.94%	3.96%	9.43%	8.77%
Sigma of Love of Variety	0.00%	0.00%	0.00%	0.00%	0.00%	0.00%	0.00%	0.00%	0.00%

Other Intensive Industries	Constraint Case			Flexible Case			Efficiency Case		
	1988	1991	1994	1988	1991	1994	1988	1991	1994
Production per firm	-5.46%	-5.54%	-5.64%	-2.41%	-8.50%	-8.38%	-2.42%	-8.54%	-8.44%
Real Marginal Costs	-0.13%	-0.06%	-0.06%	-2.48%	-0.88%	0.13%	-2.37%	-0.43%	0.91%
Real Producer Prices	0.70%	0.76%	0.77%	-2.15%	0.24%	1.22%	-2.04%	0.69%	2.01%
Mark-ups domestic (abs. diff.)	1.88%	1.89%	1.90%	0.41%	1.79%	1.77%	0.41%	1.79%	1.77%
Fixed Costs per firm	-0.16%	-0.20%	-0.31%	-3.57%	-3.07%	-2.64%	-3.50%	-2.79%	-2.16%
Number of Firms	4.96%	4.94%	4.91%	0.78%	6.22%	6.36%	0.77%	6.21%	6.35%
Sigma of Love of Variety	0.00%	0.00%	0.00%	0.00%	0.00%	0.00%	0.00%	0.00%	0.00%

Electrical goods	Constraint Case			Flexible Case			Efficiency Case		
	1988	1991	1994	1988	1991	1994	1988	1991	1994
Production per firm	-5.42%	-5.50%	-5.63%	-4.86%	-14.89%	-14.95%	-4.87%	-14.90%	-14.96%
Real Marginal Costs	0.28%	0.41%	0.49%	-1.76%	-0.07%	0.97%	-1.65%	0.36%	1.72%
Real Producer Prices	0.58%	0.70%	0.79%	-1.53%	0.59%	1.63%	-1.43%	1.02%	2.38%
Mark-ups domestic (abs. diff.)	2.50%	2.51%	2.51%	0.59%	2.93%	2.93%	0.59%	2.93%	2.93%
Fixed Costs per firm	0.42%	0.39%	0.32%	-2.63%	-2.06%	-1.68%	-2.57%	-1.81%	-1.24%
Number of Firms	4.83%	4.83%	4.79%	0.21%	5.25%	5.30%	0.20%	5.23%	5.27%
Sigma of Love of Variety	0.00%	0.00%	0.00%	0.00%	0.00%	0.00%	0.00%	0.00%	0.00%

Transport equipment	Constraint Case			Flexible Case			Efficiency Case		
	1988	1991	1994	1988	1991	1994	1988	1991	1994
Production per firm	-12.74%	-12.58%	-12.54%	-6.48%	-17.51%	-16.80%	-6.47%	-17.42%	-16.64%
Real Marginal Costs	0.58%	0.56%	0.49%	-1.64%	-0.12%	0.69%	-1.54%	0.30%	1.42%
Real Producer Prices	2.16%	2.11%	2.02%	-1.04%	1.40%	2.15%	-0.94%	1.81%	2.86%
Mark-ups domestic (abs. diff.)	81.17%	81.89%	81.97%	3.79%	12.28%	12.21%	3.79%	12.28%	12.20%
Fixed Costs per firm	0.48%	0.39%	0.25%	-2.80%	-2.33%	-2.03%	-2.74%	-2.09%	-1.61%
Number of Firms	7.97%	7.65%	7.63%	3.32%	14.55%	15.35%	3.32%	14.60%	15.44%
Sigma of Love of Variety	0.00%	0.00%	0.00%	0.00%	0.00%	0.00%	0.00%	0.00%	0.00%

Other Equipment	Constraint Case			Flexible Case			Efficiency Case		
	1988	1991	1994	1988	1991	1994	1988	1991	1994
Production per firm	-5.05%	-5.17%	-5.33%	-6.61%	-13.84%	-13.84%	-6.61%	-13.79%	-13.74%
Real Marginal Costs	0.83%	0.99%	1.13%	-0.78%	1.04%	2.03%	-0.68%	1.44%	2.75%
Real Producer Prices	1.07%	1.23%	1.37%	-0.51%	1.57%	2.56%	-0.41%	1.97%	3.27%
Mark-ups domestic (abs. diff.)	1.58%	1.58%	1.59%	0.71%	1.96%	1.95%	0.71%	1.95%	1.95%
Fixed Costs per firm	0.97%	0.99%	0.98%	-1.53%	-0.80%	-0.42%	-1.48%	-0.57%	-0.03%
Number of Firms	3.45%	3.43%	3.35%	-1.92%	-0.06%	0.07%	-1.91%	0.06%	0.27%
Sigma of Love of Variety	0.00%	0.00%	0.00%	0.00%	0.00%	0.00%	0.00%	0.00%	0.00%

Telecommunications	Constraint Case			Flexible Case			Efficiency Case		
	1988	1991	1994	1988	1991	1994	1988	1991	1994
Production per firm	-0.67%	-0.60%	-0.80%	-1.38%	-3.23%	-3.45%	-1.39%	-3.27%	-3.51%
Real Marginal Costs	-0.54%	-0.17%	-0.04%	-3.16%	-1.69%	-0.50%	-3.04%	-1.21%	0.35%
Real Producer Prices	-0.19%	0.31%	0.42%	-3.09%	-1.43%	-0.27%	-2.97%	-0.96%	0.56%
Mark-ups domestic (abs. diff.)	0.57%	0.77%	0.72%	-0.01%	-0.22%	-0.26%	-0.01%	-0.24%	-0.30%
Fixed Costs per firm	-0.13%	0.71%	0.56%	-5.35%	-6.13%	-5.75%	-5.28%	-5.85%	-5.25%
Number of Firms	-0.05%	-0.32%	-0.25%	0.26%	1.13%	1.19%	0.27%	1.16%	1.24%
Sigma of Love of Variety	0.00%	0.00%	0.00%	0.00%	0.00%	0.00%	0.00%	0.00%	0.00%

Banks	Constraint Case			Flexible Case			Efficiency Case		
	1988	1991	1994	1988	1991	1994	1988	1991	1994
Production per firm	-0.92%	-0.91%	-1.09%	-0.75%	-1.37%	-1.48%	-0.76%	-1.41%	-1.54%
Real Marginal Costs	-0.81%	-0.58%	-0.54%	-3.31%	-1.96%	-0.86%	-3.19%	-1.49%	-0.05%
Real Producer Prices	-0.58%	-0.31%	-0.28%	-3.36%	-2.09%	-1.01%	-3.24%	-1.63%	-0.21%
Mark-ups domestic (abs. diff.)	0.29%	0.34%	0.33%	-0.03%	-0.11%	-0.13%	-0.04%	-0.12%	-0.14%
Fixed Costs per firm	-0.39%	0.07%	-0.10%	-5.40%	-6.13%	-5.76%	-5.33%	-5.85%	-5.27%
Number of Firms	1.62%	1.43%	1.44%	1.41%	4.03%	4.16%	1.42%	4.06%	4.20%
Sigma of Love of Variety	0.00%	0.00%	0.00%	0.00%	0.00%	0.00%	0.00%	0.00%	0.00%

Table B7.3.
The full *antimonde* scenario: sectoral results for Ireland (volumes)

% change from *monde*

Agriculture	Constraint Case			Flexible Case			Efficiency Case		
	1988	1991	1994	1988	1991	1994	1988	1991	1994
Domestic Production - vol.	1.1%	0.8%	0.4%	2.2%	3.2%	2.4%	2.2%	3.0%	2.0%
Imports - vol.	-1.6%	-1.3%	-1.1%	-3.5%	-2.4%	-1.8%	-3.5%	-2.1%	-1.4%
Exports - vol.	0.2%	-0.4%	-1.1%	1.5%	1.2%	0.9%	1.4%	1.1%	0.7%
Absorption - vol.	0.8%	0.6%	0.3%	1.4%	2.0%	1.3%	1.3%	1.8%	1.0%
Investment - vol.	-0.2%	-1.1%	-2.1%	-3.3%	-2.8%	-3.1%	-3.3%	-2.9%	-3.3%
Labour Demand - vol.	1.2%	1.0%	0.8%	2.4%	3.7%	3.2%	2.4%	3.6%	2.9%
Private Consumption - vol.	-1.6%	-1.7%	-1.9%	-1.4%	-2.4%	-2.8%	-1.4%	-2.4%	-2.9%
Supply to domestic - vol.	1.2%	0.9%	0.5%	2.3%	3.5%	2.7%	2.2%	3.3%	2.3%
Intra-EU Trade - vol	0.0%	0.0%	0.0%	-0.3%	-2.3%	-2.7%	-0.3%	-2.5%	-2.9%

Energy	Constraint Case			Flexible Case			Efficiency Case		
	1988	1991	1994	1988	1991	1994	1988	1991	1994
Domestic Production - vol.	0.2%	0.0%	-0.3%	0.9%	0.5%	0.0%	0.8%	0.4%	-0.2%
Imports - vol.	-1.1%	-1.1%	-1.2%	-2.0%	-1.7%	-1.5%	-2.0%	-1.6%	-1.4%
Exports - vol.	-0.2%	-0.7%	-1.3%	0.7%	0.6%	0.5%	0.7%	0.6%	0.4%
Absorption - vol.	-0.4%	-0.5%	-0.7%	-0.3%	-0.8%	-1.2%	-0.3%	-0.9%	-1.4%
Investment - vol.	-6.0%	-6.4%	-6.8%	-3.7%	-3.9%	-4.1%	-3.7%	-3.9%	-4.1%
Labour Demand - vol.	0.3%	0.1%	-0.1%	1.1%	0.9%	0.5%	1.1%	0.8%	0.3%
Private Consumption - vol.	-1.0%	-1.1%	-1.3%	-1.2%	-2.0%	-2.4%	-1.2%	-2.1%	-2.5%
Supply to domestic - vol.	0.2%	0.0%	-0.3%	0.6%	0.2%	-0.3%	0.5%	0.0%	-0.5%
Intra-EU Trade - vol	0.0%	0.0%	0.0%	0.2%	-0.3%	-0.6%	0.2%	-0.4%	-0.8%

Metal Industries	Constraint Case			Flexible Case			Efficiency Case		
	1988	1991	1994	1988	1991	1994	1988	1991	1994
Domestic Production - vol.	-6.8%	-6.9%	-7.1%	1.2%	-4.9%	-5.1%	1.1%	-5.0%	-5.4%
Imports - vol.	2.4%	2.3%	2.2%	-4.0%	-4.1%	-3.8%	-3.9%	-3.9%	-3.5%
Exports - vol.	-0.4%	-0.4%	-0.5%	1.5%	1.5%	1.3%	1.5%	1.4%	1.1%
Absorption - vol.	-2.1%	-2.2%	-2.3%	-2.6%	-5.1%	-5.2%	-2.6%	-5.1%	-5.2%
Investment - vol.	-11.4%	-11.7%	-12.1%	-3.7%	-6.4%	-6.5%	-3.7%	-6.5%	-6.6%
Labour Demand - vol.	-4.7%	-4.8%	-4.8%	1.8%	-2.6%	-2.8%	1.8%	-2.8%	-3.0%
Private Consumption - vol.	-0.8%	-0.9%	-1.0%	-0.7%	-1.2%	-1.4%	-0.7%	-1.2%	-1.4%
Supply to domestic - vol.	-20.6%	-20.7%	-20.9%	-1.2%	-10.2%	-10.4%	-1.2%	-10.4%	-10.6%
Intra-EU Trade - vol	0.0%	0.0%	0.0%	0.1%	-1.5%	-1.7%	0.1%	-1.6%	-1.8%

Chemical	Constraint Case			Flexible Case			Efficiency Case		
	1988	1991	1994	1988	1991	1994	1988	1991	1994
Domestic Production - vol.	-1.0%	-1.2%	-1.6%	3.4%	-0.3%	-1.7%	3.4%	-0.5%	-1.9%
Imports - vol.	2.7%	2.7%	2.6%	-3.2%	-2.4%	-2.2%	-3.2%	-2.2%	-1.9%
Exports - vol.	0.7%	0.5%	0.2%	1.8%	1.6%	1.3%	1.8%	1.5%	1.2%
Absorption - vol.	-0.3%	-0.4%	-0.6%	1.3%	0.2%	-0.5%	1.3%	0.1%	-0.7%
Investment - vol.	-6.0%	-6.4%	-7.0%	-2.7%	-4.3%	-4.9%	-2.7%	-4.4%	-5.0%
Labour Demand - vol.	-0.3%	-0.4%	-0.7%	3.6%	0.9%	-0.3%	3.6%	0.8%	-0.4%
Private Consumption - vol.	-1.7%	-1.8%	-2.0%	-1.3%	-2.4%	-2.9%	-1.4%	-2.4%	-2.9%
Supply to domestic - vol.	-7.2%	-7.6%	-8.1%	5.1%	3.3%	1.8%	5.1%	3.0%	1.3%
Intra-EU Trade - vol	0.0%	0.0%	0.0%	1.4%	-0.8%	-1.5%	1.4%	-0.8%	-1.6%

Other Intensive Industries	Constraint Case			Flexible Case			Efficiency Case		
	1988	1991	1994	1988	1991	1994	1988	1991	1994
Domestic Production - vol.	-0.8%	-0.9%	-1.0%	-1.7%	-2.8%	-2.6%	-1.7%	-2.9%	-2.6%
Imports - vol.	-0.9%	-1.1%	-1.3%	-5.6%	-4.7%	-4.2%	-5.5%	-4.4%	-3.7%
Exports - vol.	0.6%	0.6%	0.6%	1.7%	1.6%	1.4%	1.7%	1.5%	1.2%
Absorption - vol.	-1.2%	-1.4%	-1.6%	-2.6%	-3.1%	-3.1%	-2.6%	-3.1%	-3.2%
Investment - vol.	-5.5%	-5.9%	-6.4%	-5.0%	-5.6%	-5.5%	-5.0%	-5.6%	-5.4%
Labour Demand - vol.	0.3%	0.2%	0.1%	-1.1%	-1.3%	-1.0%	-1.1%	-1.3%	-0.9%
Private Consumption - vol.	-1.2%	-1.4%	-1.7%	-2.3%	-2.7%	-2.5%	-2.4%	-2.7%	-2.6%
Supply to domestic - vol.	-1.5%	-1.6%	-1.8%	-1.1%	-0.4%	-0.3%	-1.2%	-0.4%	-0.4%
Intra-EU Trade - vol	0.0%	0.0%	0.0%	-1.9%	-3.6%	-3.6%	-1.9%	-3.6%	-3.6%

Electrical goods	Constraint Case			Flexible Case			Efficiency Case		
	1988	1991	1994	1988	1991	1994	1988	1991	1994
Domestic Production - vol.	-0.8%	-0.9%	-1.1%	-4.7%	-10.4%	-10.4%	-4.7%	-10.4%	-10.5%
Imports - vol.	-1.4%	-1.5%	-1.7%	-6.1%	-6.8%	-6.4%	-6.0%	-6.6%	-6.0%
Exports - vol.	0.1%	0.0%	-0.1%	1.8%	1.6%	1.4%	1.7%	1.5%	1.2%
Absorption - vol.	-2.0%	-2.1%	-2.3%	-6.5%	-9.7%	-9.5%	-6.5%	-9.6%	-9.3%
Investment - vol.	-3.2%	-3.8%	-4.5%	-6.3%	-9.0%	-9.0%	-6.3%	-9.0%	-9.0%
Labour Demand - vol.	-0.1%	0.0%	-0.1%	-3.9%	-8.9%	-8.8%	-3.9%	-8.9%	-8.7%
Private Consumption - vol.	-2.4%	-2.6%	-3.3%	-6.3%	-6.0%	-4.7%	-6.3%	-6.1%	-4.8%
Supply to domestic - vol.	-4.5%	-4.7%	-5.1%	-2.6%	-6.1%	-6.2%	-2.7%	-6.2%	-6.4%
Intra-EU Trade - vol	0.0%	0.0%	0.0%	-2.9%	-6.3%	-6.3%	-2.9%	-6.3%	-6.4%

Transport equipment	Constraint Case			Flexible Case			Efficiency Case		
	1988	1991	1994	1988	1991	1994	1988	1991	1994
Domestic Production - vol.	-5.8%	-5.9%	-5.9%	-3.4%	-5.5%	-4.0%	-3.4%	-5.4%	-3.8%
Imports - vol.	-0.4%	-1.8%	-2.3%	-5.5%	-5.0%	-4.5%	-5.5%	-4.9%	-4.2%
Exports - vol.	-0.1%	0.0%	0.1%	1.8%	1.9%	1.8%	1.7%	1.8%	1.6%
Absorption - vol.	-2.2%	-3.5%	-4.0%	-5.9%	-6.0%	-5.3%	-5.9%	-6.0%	-5.3%
Investment - vol.	-7.3%	-8.0%	-8.5%	-5.4%	-6.5%	-5.9%	-5.4%	-6.4%	-5.7%
Labour Demand - vol.	-3.8%	-3.8%	-3.8%	-2.2%	-3.2%	-1.7%	-2.1%	-3.0%	-1.3%
Private Consumption - vol.	2.9%	-2.1%	-3.3%	-6.7%	-5.5%	-3.3%	-6.8%	-5.6%	-3.4%
Supply to domestic - vol.	-22.5%	-23.6%	-23.9%	-5.2%	-13.7%	-12.5%	-5.3%	-13.7%	-12.5%
Intra-EU Trade - vol	0.0%	0.0%	0.0%	-1.2%	-1.3%	-0.9%	-1.2%	-1.3%	-1.0%

Other Equipment	Constraint Case			Flexible Case			Efficiency Case		
	1988	1991	1994	1988	1991	1994	1988	1991	1994
Domestic Production - vol.	-1.8%	-1.9%	-2.2%	-8.4%	-13.9%	-13.8%	-8.4%	-13.7%	-13.5%
Imports - vol.	-1.3%	-1.4%	-1.6%	-5.4%	-6.7%	-6.4%	-5.3%	-6.5%	-6.0%
Exports - vol.	-1.3%	-1.4%	-1.6%	1.2%	0.9%	0.7%	1.2%	0.8%	0.6%
Absorption - vol.	-1.8%	-2.0%	-2.3%	-7.8%	-11.6%	-11.6%	-7.8%	-11.5%	-11.3%
Investment - vol.	-1.4%	-2.2%	-3.2%	-7.8%	-10.4%	-10.4%	-7.8%	-10.3%	-10.2%
Labour Demand - vol.	-1.0%	-1.0%	-1.1%	-7.5%	-12.5%	-12.2%	-7.5%	-12.3%	-11.9%
Private Consumption - vol.	-2.4%	-2.5%	-2.8%	-2.6%	-3.8%	-4.1%	-2.6%	-3.8%	-4.2%
Supply to domestic - vol.	-3.5%	-3.8%	-4.2%	-6.8%	-11.6%	-11.6%	-6.8%	-11.5%	-11.5%
Intra-EU Trade - vol	0.0%	0.0%	0.0%	-5.2%	-8.4%	-8.3%	-5.2%	-8.3%	-8.2%

Consumer goods	Constraint Case			Flexible Case			Efficiency Case		
	1988	1991	1994	1988	1991	1994	1988	1991	1994
Domestic Production - vol.	1.0%	0.7%	0.3%	1.9%	2.6%	1.9%	1.9%	2.3%	1.4%
Imports - vol.	-3.9%	-3.8%	-3.9%	-4.3%	-3.8%	-3.5%	-4.2%	-3.6%	-3.0%
Exports - vol.	0.3%	0.0%	-0.4%	2.1%	1.9%	1.6%	2.1%	1.7%	1.3%
Absorption - vol.	-0.8%	-1.0%	-1.2%	-0.7%	-1.3%	-1.7%	-0.7%	-1.4%	-1.9%
Investment - vol.	1.1%	0.1%	-0.9%	-3.4%	-3.1%	-3.4%	-3.4%	-3.2%	-3.6%
Labour Demand - vol.	1.3%	1.1%	0.9%	2.4%	3.3%	2.7%	2.3%	3.1%	2.4%
Private Consumption - vol.	-1.6%	-1.7%	-1.9%	-1.4%	-2.3%	-2.7%	-1.4%	-2.4%	-2.8%
Supply to domestic - vol.	1.7%	1.4%	1.0%	1.8%	3.3%	2.6%	1.8%	3.1%	2.2%
Intra-EU Trade - vol	0.0%	0.0%	0.0%	-0.1%	-1.3%	-1.6%	-0.1%	-1.4%	-1.8%

Construction	Constraint Case			Flexible Case			Efficiency Case		
	1988	1991	1994	1988	1991	1994	1988	1991	1994
Domestic Production - vol.	-3.4%	-3.8%	-4.2%	-6.0%	-6.0%	-6.2%	-6.0%	-6.0%	-6.2%
Imports - vol.	-	-	-	#VALUE!	#VALUE!	#VALUE!	#VALUE!	#VALUE!	#VALUE!
Exports - vol.	-	-	-	#VALUE!	#VALUE!	#VALUE!	#VALUE!	#VALUE!	#VALUE!
Absorption - vol.	-3.4%	-3.8%	-4.2%	-6.0%	-6.0%	-6.2%	-6.0%	-6.0%	-6.2%
Investment - vol.	-6.1%	-6.9%	-7.8%	-7.1%	-7.2%	-7.3%	-7.1%	-7.2%	-7.3%
Labour Demand - vol.	-3.2%	-3.5%	-3.9%	-5.7%	-5.6%	-5.7%	-5.7%	-5.6%	-5.6%
Private Consumption - vol.	#DIV/0!	#DIV/0!	#DIV/0!	#DIV/0!	#DIV/0!	#DIV/0!	#DIV/0!	#DIV/0!	#DIV/0!
Supply to domestic - vol.	-3.4%	-3.8%	-4.2%	-6.0%	-6.0%	-6.2%	-6.0%	-6.0%	-6.2%
Intra-EU Trade - vol	0.0%	0.0%	0.0%	#DIV/0!	#DIV/0!	#DIV/0!	#DIV/0!	#DIV/0!	#DIV/0!

Telecommunications	Constraint Case			Flexible Case			Efficiency Case		
	1988	1991	1994	1988	1991	1994	1988	1991	1994
Domestic Production - vol.	-0.7%	-0.9%	-1.0%	-1.1%	-2.1%	-2.3%	-1.1%	-2.1%	-2.3%
Imports - vol.	-6.6%	-6.2%	-6.2%	-7.1%	-7.4%	-7.1%	-7.0%	-7.2%	-6.8%
Exports - vol.	0.6%	0.0%	-0.1%	1.0%	1.0%	0.9%	1.0%	0.9%	0.8%
Absorption - vol.	-0.9%	-1.1%	-1.2%	-1.0%	-1.2%	-1.4%	-1.0%	-1.2%	-1.4%
Investment - vol.	-6.2%	-6.1%	-6.3%	-4.7%	-5.2%	-5.2%	-4.7%	-5.1%	-5.1%
Labour Demand - vol.	0.5%	1.3%	1.2%	-1.3%	-2.3%	-2.3%	-1.3%	-2.2%	-2.2%
Private Consumption - vol.	-1.9%	-2.2%	-2.5%	-1.4%	-2.5%	-3.0%	-1.5%	-2.6%	-3.1%
Supply to domestic - vol.	-0.8%	-1.0%	-1.1%	-0.9%	-0.8%	-1.0%	-0.9%	-0.8%	-1.0%
Intra-EU Trade - vol	0.0%	0.0%	0.0%	-3.1%	-10.6%	-10.5%	-3.1%	-10.6%	-10.6%

Transports	Constraint Case			Flexible Case			Efficiency Case		
	1988	1991	1994	1988	1991	1994	1988	1991	1994
Domestic Production - vol.	-0.4%	-0.5%	-0.7%	0.3%	-0.1%	-0.4%	0.3%	-0.1%	-0.5%
Imports - vol.	-0.4%	-0.5%	-0.7%	0.2%	0.0%	-0.2%	0.2%	-0.1%	-0.2%
Exports - vol.	0.8%	0.6%	0.5%	0.7%	0.6%	0.6%	0.7%	0.6%	0.5%
Absorption - vol.	-1.0%	-1.1%	-1.3%	-1.0%	-1.7%	-2.0%	-1.0%	-1.7%	-2.1%
Investment - vol.	-6.7%	-7.0%	-7.3%	-4.0%	-4.3%	-4.4%	-4.0%	-4.3%	-4.4%
Labour Demand - vol.	-0.3%	-0.4%	-0.5%	0.5%	0.2%	0.0%	0.5%	0.2%	0.0%
Private Consumption - vol.	-2.2%	-2.3%	-2.5%	-1.5%	-2.7%	-3.3%	-1.5%	-2.8%	-3.4%
Supply to domestic - vol.	-0.4%	-0.5%	-0.7%	0.3%	-0.1%	-0.4%	0.3%	-0.1%	-0.5%
Intra-EU Trade - vol	0.0%	0.0%	0.0%	1.1%	1.1%	1.0%	1.1%	1.1%	1.0%

Banks	Constraint Case			Flexible Case			Efficiency Case		
	1988	1991	1994	1988	1991	1994	1988	1991	1994
Domestic Production - vol.	0.7%	0.5%	0.3%	0.7%	2.6%	2.6%	0.6%	2.6%	2.6%
Imports - vol.	-8.7%	-8.6%	-8.7%	-5.5%	-5.0%	-4.6%	-5.4%	-4.7%	-4.2%
Exports - vol.	0.7%	0.4%	0.2%	1.1%	1.0%	0.9%	1.1%	1.0%	0.8%
Absorption - vol.	0.1%	-0.1%	-0.3%	0.1%	1.0%	0.8%	0.1%	0.9%	0.8%
Investment - vol.	-3.9%	-4.0%	-4.5%	-3.9%	-3.1%	-3.1%	-3.9%	-3.0%	-3.0%
Labour Demand - vol.	1.4%	1.5%	1.5%	0.6%	2.5%	2.7%	0.6%	2.6%	2.7%
Private Consumption - vol.	-2.1%	-2.2%	-2.5%	-1.6%	-2.9%	-3.5%	-1.7%	-3.0%	-3.6%
Supply to domestic - vol.	0.7%	0.5%	0.4%	0.5%	2.4%	2.3%	0.5%	2.3%	2.3%
Intra-EU Trade - vol	0.0%	0.0%	0.0%	-1.2%	-4.5%	-4.7%	-1.2%	-4.6%	-4.7%

Services	Constraint Case			Flexible Case			Efficiency Case		
	1988	1991	1994	1988	1991	1994	1988	1991	1994
Domestic Production - vol.	-1.0%	-1.3%	-1.5%	-0.3%	-0.1%	-0.4%	-0.3%	-0.2%	-0.4%
Imports - vol.	-4.2%	-4.3%	-4.5%	-3.7%	-3.6%	-3.3%	-3.6%	-3.4%	-3.0%
Exports - vol.	-3.0%	-4.8%	-4.9%	1.1%	1.0%	0.8%	1.1%	0.9%	0.7%
Absorption - vol.	-1.0%	-1.2%	-1.4%	-1.4%	-1.8%	-2.0%	-1.4%	-1.8%	-2.1%
Investment - vol.	-4.7%	-5.3%	-5.9%	-4.4%	-4.3%	-4.4%	-4.4%	-4.3%	-4.4%
Labour Demand - vol.	-0.8%	-1.0%	-1.1%	-0.1%	0.3%	0.3%	-0.1%	0.3%	0.3%
Private Consumption - vol.	-1.6%	-1.9%	-2.2%	-1.9%	-2.9%	-3.2%	-2.0%	-2.9%	-3.2%
Supply to domestic - vol.	-0.8%	-1.1%	-1.3%	-1.3%	-1.6%	-1.8%	-1.3%	-1.6%	-1.9%
Intra-EU Trade - vol	0.0%	0.0%	0.0%	6.9%	10.3%	10.3%	6.9%	10.3%	10.3%

Non market	Constraint Case			Flexible Case			Efficiency Case		
	1988	1991	1994	1988	1991	1994	1988	1991	1994
Domestic Production - vol.	-0.2%	-0.3%	-0.3%	-0.5%	-0.8%	-0.8%	-0.5%	-0.8%	-0.8%
Imports - vol.	-0.2%	-0.3%	-0.3%	-0.2%	-0.4%	-0.4%	-0.2%	-0.4%	-0.4%
Exports - vol.	1.6%	1.7%	1.8%	0.3%	0.3%	0.3%	0.3%	0.3%	0.2%
Absorption - vol.	-0.3%	-0.3%	-0.3%	-0.5%	-0.8%	-0.8%	-0.5%	-0.8%	-0.8%
Investment - vol.	-7.8%	-7.9%	-7.9%	-4.3%	-4.3%	-4.3%	-4.3%	-4.3%	-4.3%
Labour Demand - vol.	-0.2%	-0.2%	-0.2%	-0.4%	-0.6%	-0.6%	-0.4%	-0.5%	-0.5%
Private Consumption - vol.	-1.7%	-1.9%	-2.1%	-1.6%	-2.6%	-3.0%	-1.7%	-2.7%	-3.1%
Supply to domestic - vol.	-0.2%	-0.3%	-0.3%	-0.5%	-0.8%	-0.8%	-0.5%	-0.8%	-0.8%
Intra-EU Trade - vol	0.0%	0.0%	0.0%	0.2%	0.1%	0.1%	0.2%	0.1%	0.1%

Table B7.4.

The full *antimonde* scenario: sectoral results for Ireland (prices)

% change from *monde*

Agriculture	Constraint Case			Flexible Case			Efficiency Case		
	1988	1991	1994	1988	1991	1994	1988	1991	1994
Real Marginal Costs	-0.20%	0.14%	0.43%	0.77%	0.98%	1.25%	0.76%	0.96%	1.22%
Real Cost of Labour	-1.84%	-2.11%	-2.47%	-1.10%	-2.12%	-2.59%	-1.13%	-2.24%	-2.80%
Real Deflator of Absorption	-0.05%	0.24%	0.50%	1.11%	1.31%	1.54%	1.10%	1.27%	1.47%
Real Price of Exports-RW	-0.20%	0.14%	0.43%	0.77%	0.98%	1.25%	0.76%	0.96%	1.22%

Energy	Constraint Case			Flexible Case			Efficiency Case		
	1988	1991	1994	1988	1991	1994	1988	1991	1994
Marginal Costs	-0.24%	-0.01%	0.18%	0.79%	0.87%	1.03%	0.78%	0.80%	0.92%
Cost of Labour	-1.84%	-2.11%	-2.47%	-1.10%	-2.12%	-2.59%	-1.13%	-2.24%	-2.80%
Deflator of Absorption	0.30%	0.41%	0.50%	1.85%	2.07%	2.18%	1.82%	1.97%	2.00%
Price of Exports-RW	-0.24%	-0.01%	0.18%	0.79%	0.87%	1.03%	0.78%	0.80%	0.92%

Metal Industries	Constraint Case			Flexible Case			Efficiency Case		
	1988	1991	1994	1988	1991	1994	1988	1991	1994
Marginal Costs	0.47%	0.60%	0.68%	1.08%	1.27%	1.25%	1.08%	1.24%	1.19%
Cost of Labour	-1.84%	-2.11%	-2.47%	-1.10%	-2.12%	-2.59%	-1.13%	-2.24%	-2.80%
Deflator of Absorption	2.70%	2.72%	2.73%	3.12%	4.23%	4.13%	3.09%	4.13%	3.95%
Price of Exports-RW	-0.07%	0.06%	0.14%	0.69%	0.05%	0.03%	0.68%	0.01%	-0.03%

Chemical	Constraint Case			Flexible Case			Efficiency Case		
	1988	1991	1994	1988	1991	1994	1988	1991	1994
Marginal Costs	0.04%	0.29%	0.50%	0.97%	1.25%	1.44%	0.96%	1.21%	1.37%
Cost of Labour	-1.84%	-2.11%	-2.47%	-1.10%	-2.12%	-2.59%	-1.13%	-2.24%	-2.80%
Deflator of Absorption	1.50%	1.57%	1.64%	2.82%	3.82%	3.80%	2.80%	3.72%	3.63%
Price of Exports-RW	-0.20%	0.06%	0.27%	0.79%	0.81%	1.02%	0.78%	0.78%	0.96%

Other Intensive Industries	Constraint Case			Flexible Case			Efficiency Case		
	1988	1991	1994	1988	1991	1994	1988	1991	1994
Marginal Costs	-0.13%	-0.06%	-0.06%	0.52%	0.41%	0.31%	0.51%	0.38%	0.25%
Cost of Labour	-1.84%	-2.11%	-2.47%	-1.10%	-2.12%	-2.59%	-1.13%	-2.24%	-2.80%
Deflator of Absorption	1.29%	1.33%	1.34%	1.45%	2.02%	1.91%	1.44%	1.97%	1.82%
Price of Exports-RW	-0.41%	-0.34%	-0.33%	0.49%	0.16%	0.05%	0.48%	0.12%	-0.01%

Electrical goods	Constraint Case			Flexible Case			Efficiency Case		
	1988	1991	1994	1988	1991	1994	1988	1991	1994
Marginal Costs	0.28%	0.41%	0.49%	1.24%	1.22%	1.15%	1.22%	1.17%	1.06%
Cost of Labour	-1.84%	-2.11%	-2.47%	-1.10%	-2.12%	-2.59%	-1.13%	-2.24%	-2.80%
Deflator of Absorption	1.84%	1.86%	1.88%	3.52%	3.82%	3.55%	3.47%	3.66%	3.26%
Price of Exports-RW	0.08%	0.21%	0.29%	1.23%	1.04%	0.97%	1.22%	0.99%	0.89%

Transport equipment	Constraint Case			Flexible Case			Efficiency Case		
	1988	1991	1994	1988	1991	1994	1988	1991	1994
Marginal Costs	0.58%	0.56%	0.49%	1.36%	1.17%	0.88%	1.34%	1.11%	0.76%
Cost of Labour	-1.84%	-2.11%	-2.47%	-1.10%	-2.12%	-2.59%	-1.13%	-2.24%	-2.80%
Deflator of Absorption	2.81%	2.82%	2.81%	3.82%	4.33%	4.01%	3.78%	4.17%	3.73%
Price of Exports-RW	0.03%	0.03%	-0.04%	1.10%	0.00%	-0.37%	1.09%	-0.07%	-0.50%

Other Equipment	Constraint Case			Flexible Case			Efficiency Case		
	1988	1991	1994	1988	1991	1994	1988	1991	1994
Marginal Costs	0.83%	0.99%	1.13%	2.22%	2.33%	2.22%	2.20%	2.25%	2.09%
Cost of Labour	-1.84%	-2.11%	-2.47%	-1.10%	-2.12%	-2.59%	-1.13%	-2.24%	-2.80%
Deflator of Absorption	1.51%	1.56%	1.59%	3.52%	3.75%	3.47%	3.48%	3.58%	3.17%
Price of Exports-RW	0.77%	0.94%	1.08%	2.26%	2.33%	2.22%	2.24%	2.25%	2.08%

Consumer goods	Constraint Case			Flexible Case			Efficiency Case		
	1988	1991	1994	1988	1991	1994	1988	1991	1994
Marginal Costs	-0.02%	0.21%	0.38%	0.92%	0.91%	0.97%	0.92%	0.91%	0.96%
Cost of Labour	-1.84%	-2.11%	-2.47%	-1.10%	-2.12%	-2.59%	-1.13%	-2.24%	-2.80%
Deflator of Absorption	0.62%	0.74%	0.84%	2.01%	2.06%	2.01%	1.99%	2.00%	1.90%
Price of Exports-RW	-0.02%	0.21%	0.38%	0.92%	0.91%	0.97%	0.92%	0.91%	0.96%

Construction	Constraint Case			Flexible Case			Efficiency Case		
	1988	1991	1994	1988	1991	1994	1988	1991	1994
Marginal Costs	-0.28%	-0.23%	-0.25%	0.35%	0.14%	0.00%	0.34%	0.11%	-0.04%
Cost of Labour	-1.84%	-2.11%	-2.47%	-1.10%	-2.12%	-2.59%	-1.13%	-2.24%	-2.80%
Deflator of Absorption	-0.28%	-0.23%	-0.25%	0.35%	0.14%	0.00%	0.34%	0.11%	-0.04%
Price of Exports-RW	-0.28%	-0.23%	-0.25%	0.35%	0.14%	0.00%	0.34%	0.11%	-0.04%

Telecommunications	Constraint Case			Flexible Case			Efficiency Case		
	1988	1991	1994	1988	1991	1994	1988	1991	1994
Marginal Costs	-0.54%	-0.17%	-0.04%	-0.17%	-0.40%	-0.31%	-0.17%	-0.40%	-0.31%
Cost of Labour	-1.84%	-2.11%	-2.47%	-1.10%	-2.12%	-2.59%	-1.13%	-2.24%	-2.80%
Deflator of Absorption	-0.12%	0.37%	0.48%	-0.11%	-0.46%	-0.40%	-0.12%	-0.47%	-0.43%
Price of Exports-RW	-0.37%	0.03%	0.17%	-0.20%	-0.53%	-0.45%	-0.20%	-0.54%	-0.46%

Transports	Constraint Case			Flexible Case			Efficiency Case		
	1988	1991	1994	1988	1991	1994	1988	1991	1994
Marginal Costs	-0.52%	-0.40%	-0.36%	0.14%	-0.15%	-0.20%	0.14%	-0.18%	-0.24%
Cost of Labour	-1.84%	-2.11%	-2.47%	-1.10%	-2.12%	-2.59%	-1.13%	-2.24%	-2.80%
Deflator of Absorption	0.41%	0.49%	0.52%	0.38%	0.23%	0.20%	0.37%	0.20%	0.14%
Price of Exports-RW	-0.52%	-0.40%	-0.36%	0.14%	-0.15%	-0.20%	0.14%	-0.18%	-0.24%

Banks	Constraint Case			Flexible Case			Efficiency Case		
	1988	1991	1994	1988	1991	1994	1988	1991	1994
Marginal Costs	-0.81%	-0.58%	-0.54%	-0.31%	-0.67%	-0.67%	-0.32%	-0.68%	-0.71%
Cost of Labour	-1.84%	-2.11%	-2.47%	-1.10%	-2.12%	-2.59%	-1.13%	-2.24%	-2.80%
Deflator of Absorption	-0.39%	-0.13%	-0.10%	-0.19%	-0.55%	-0.55%	-0.20%	-0.57%	-0.59%
Price of Exports-RW	-0.86%	-0.62%	-0.59%	-0.37%	-0.83%	-0.84%	-0.37%	-0.84%	-0.87%

Services	Constraint Case			Flexible Case			Efficiency Case		
	1988	1991	1994	1988	1991	1994	1988	1991	1994
Marginal Costs	-0.87%	-0.70%	-0.61%	-0.10%	-0.35%	-0.30%	-0.11%	-0.38%	-0.35%
Cost of Labour	-1.84%	-2.11%	-2.47%	-1.10%	-2.12%	-2.59%	-1.13%	-2.24%	-2.80%
Deflator of Absorption	-0.80%	-0.64%	-0.56%	-0.08%	-0.31%	-0.25%	-0.09%	-0.34%	-0.30%
Price of Exports-RW	-0.87%	-0.70%	-0.61%	-0.10%	-0.35%	-0.30%	-0.11%	-0.38%	-0.35%

Non market	Constraint Case			Flexible Case			Efficiency Case		
	1988	1991	1994	1988	1991	1994	1988	1991	1994
Marginal Costs	-1.30%	-1.41%	-1.61%	-0.55%	-1.26%	-1.55%	-0.56%	-1.30%	-1.63%
Cost of Labour	-1.84%	-2.11%	-2.47%	-1.10%	-2.12%	-2.59%	-1.13%	-2.24%	-2.80%
Deflator of Absorption	-1.29%	-1.40%	-1.60%	-0.55%	-1.25%	-1.54%	-0.56%	-1.29%	-1.62%
Price of Exports-RW	-1.30%	-1.41%	-1.61%	-0.55%	-1.26%	-1.55%	-0.56%	-1.30%	-1.63%

Table B7.5.
Decomposition of effects: macroeconomic aggregates for Ireland

Macroeconomic Aggregates (vol.) (% change from monde)	Border Controls			Border controls and x-ineff.			Market segmentation			Trade antimonde			Full antimonde		
	1988	1991	1994	1988	1991	1994	1988	1991	1994	1988	1991	1994	1988	1991	1994
GDP fact. pr.	-0.21%	-0.39%	-0.39%	-0.22%	-0.41%	-0.42%	-0.37%	-1.30%	-1.62%	-0.59%	-1.61%	-1.93%	-0.71%	-1.78%	-2.15%
Priv. Consumption	-0.17%	-0.45%	-0.45%	-0.18%	-0.46%	-0.46%	-1.53%	-2.20%	-2.43%	-1.75%	-2.57%	-2.80%	-1.81%	-2.67%	-2.92%
Absorption	-0.26%	-0.47%	-0.47%	-0.25%	-0.46%	-0.45%	-1.50%	-2.08%	-2.30%	-1.78%	-2.48%	-2.70%	-1.82%	-2.54%	-2.77%
Total Investment	0.05%	0.04%	0.04%	0.05%	0.04%	0.04%	-4.32%	-4.50%	-4.62%	-4.29%	-4.47%	-4.60%	-4.30%	-4.48%	-4.60%
Total Exports to RW	-0.53%	-0.56%	-0.57%	-0.54%	-0.57%	-0.58%	2.06%	1.87%	1.67%	1.72%	1.52%	1.33%	1.66%	1.43%	1.20%
Total Imports from RW	1.16%	1.11%	1.14%	1.18%	1.14%	1.17%	-6.19%	-6.52%	-6.29%	-4.92%	-5.21%	-4.96%	-4.76%	-4.96%	-4.63%
Total Intra-EU Trade	-0.69%	-1.69%	-1.69%	-0.70%	-1.70%	-1.69%	-0.36%	-2.15%	-2.30%	-1.23%	-3.27%	-3.41%	-1.33%	-3.40%	-3.57%
Employment (diff. from monde, 10³ persons)	-1	0	0	-1	-1	-1	-3	-2	-3	-3	-2	-4	-3	-3	-4
Disposable Income (deflated)	-0.18%	-0.48%	-0.47%	-0.19%	-0.49%	-0.49%	-1.62%	-2.32%	-2.56%	-1.84%	-2.71%	-2.95%	-1.91%	-2.81%	-3.08%

Macroeconomic Ratios (abs. diff. from monde)	Border Controls			Border controls and x-ineff.			Market segmentation			Trade antimonde			Full antimonde		
	1988	1991	1994	1988	1991	1994	1988	1991	1994	1988	1991	1994	1988	1991	1994
Current Account as % of GDP	0.24%	0.37%	0.37%	0.24%	0.37%	0.37%	-1.20%	-0.80%	-0.76%	-0.97%	-0.50%	-0.46%	-0.93%	-0.44%	-0.38%
Public Deficit as % of GDP	-0.19%	-0.26%	-0.25%	-0.19%	-0.26%	-0.26%	-0.18%	-0.47%	-0.54%	-0.34%	-0.66%	-0.74%	-0.37%	-0.71%	-0.80%
Labour Productivity	-0.16%	-0.36%	-0.36%	-0.16%	-0.36%	-0.37%	-0.14%	-1.12%	-1.31%	-0.33%	-1.39%	-1.58%	-0.43%	-1.54%	-1.78%
Investment/GDP	0.07%	0.11%	0.11%	0.07%	0.11%	0.11%	-1.89%	-1.75%	-1.74%	-1.83%	-1.68%	-1.67%	-1.80%	-1.64%	-1.62%
Priv.Cons./GDP	0.02%	-0.04%	-0.03%	0.02%	-0.03%	-0.03%	-0.72%	-0.56%	-0.51%	-0.72%	-0.61%	-0.55%	-0.69%	-0.56%	-0.49%

Deflators (% change from monde)	Border Controls			Border controls and x-ineff.			Market segmentation			Trade antimonde			Full antimonde		
	1988	1991	1994	1988	1991	1994	1988	1991	1994	1988	1991	1994	1988	1991	1994
Consumer Price Index	0.02%	0.17%	0.17%	0.02%	0.17%	0.16%	1.23%	1.14%	1.12%	1.32%	1.33%	1.31%	1.30%	1.29%	1.25%
Real Wage Rate	-0.24%	-0.43%	-0.43%	-0.26%	-0.47%	-0.47%	-0.73%	-1.57%	-1.97%	-0.99%	-1.95%	-2.36%	-1.10%	-2.12%	-2.59%
Marginal Costs	-0.02%	0.04%	0.04%	-0.02%	0.05%	0.04%	0.63%	0.56%	0.56%	0.66%	0.64%	0.64%	0.65%	0.62%	0.61%
Producer Prices	-0.01%	0.07%	0.06%	-0.01%	0.06%	0.05%	0.66%	0.70%	0.70%	0.70%	0.79%	0.79%	0.68%	0.76%	0.75%
Real Shadow Price of Capital	0.22%	0.26%	0.25%	0.25%	0.31%	0.29%	-0.13%	0.09%	0.64%	0.02%	0.27%	0.82%	-0.03%	0.20%	0.72%
Terms-of-Trade RW	1.76%	1.84%	1.85%	1.78%	1.87%	1.89%	-5.99%	-5.47%	-4.93%	-4.92%	-4.40%	-3.85%	-4.76%	-4.15%	-3.51%
Real Exchange Rate	3.66%	3.64%	3.65%	3.68%	3.66%	3.69%	-7.04%	-6.37%	-5.85%	-4.27%	-3.68%	-3.13%	-4.10%	-3.41%	-2.78%
Trade Regime	Integration			Integration			Segmentation			Segmentation			Segmentation		

GEM-E3-SM results

Table B7.6.
Decomposition of effects: effects on IC sectors for Ireland

% change from *monde*

Metal Industries

	Border Controls			Border controls and x-ineff.			Market segmentation			Trade *antimonde*			Full *antimonde*		
	1988	1991	1994	1988	1991	1994	1988	1991	1994	1988	1991	1994	1988	1991	1994
Production per firm	-2.36%	-4.17%	-4.17%	-2.36%	-4.15%	-4.16%	-0.93%	-14.29%	-14.41%	-3.67%	-17.41%	-17.53%	-3.82%	-17.58%	-17.75%
Marginal Costs	3.70%	3.80%	3.82%	3.72%	3.83%	3.86%	-6.04%	-5.29%	-4.78%	-3.18%	-2.39%	-1.86%	-3.02%	-2.14%	-1.52%
Producer Prices	3.95%	4.16%	4.18%	3.97%	4.18%	4.21%	-5.94%	-4.01%	-3.50%	-2.80%	-0.74%	-0.20%	-2.62%	-0.47%	0.16%
Mark-ups domestic (abs. diff.)	0.23%	0.31%	0.31%	0.23%	0.31%	0.31%	2.48%	10.04%	10.04%	2.82%	10.47%	10.49%	2.84%	10.50%	10.51%
Fixed Costs per firm	3.67%	3.78%	3.79%	3.68%	3.79%	3.81%	-5.86%	-5.13%	-4.72%	-3.01%	-2.24%	-1.82%	-2.89%	-2.05%	-1.57%
Number of Firms	-0.74%	-1.03%	-1.02%	-0.73%	-0.99%	-0.98%	6.29%	16.98%	16.96%	5.23%	15.52%	15.49%	5.17%	15.43%	15.39%
Sigma of Love of Variety	0.00%	0.00%	0.00%	0.00%	0.00%	0.00%	0.00%	0.00%	0.00%	0.00%	0.00%	0.00%	0.00%	0.00%	0.00%

Chemical

	Border Controls			Border controls and x-ineff.			Market segmentation			Trade *antimonde*			Full *antimonde*		
	1988	1991	1994	1988	1991	1994	1988	1991	1994	1988	1991	1994	1988	1991	1994
Production per firm	-1.16%	-2.55%	-2.55%	-1.18%	-2.61%	-2.60%	0.42%	-7.61%	-8.35%	-0.45%	-8.82%	-9.54%	-0.55%	-8.97%	-9.73%
Marginal Costs	3.83%	3.93%	3.95%	3.86%	3.98%	4.00%	-6.25%	-5.40%	-4.69%	-3.30%	-2.42%	-1.69%	-3.13%	-2.16%	-1.34%
Producer Prices	3.91%	4.09%	4.10%	3.94%	4.14%	4.16%	-6.24%	-4.91%	-4.16%	-3.23%	-1.83%	-1.06%	-3.06%	-1.56%	-0.70%
Mark-ups domestic (abs. diff.)	0.03%	0.14%	0.14%	0.03%	0.14%	0.14%	0.38%	3.76%	3.81%	0.37%	3.79%	3.84%	0.38%	3.81%	3.86%
Fixed Costs per firm	3.78%	3.95%	3.96%	3.80%	3.96%	3.99%	-5.63%	-4.80%	-4.35%	-2.66%	-1.77%	-1.30%	-2.53%	-1.57%	-1.04%
Number of Firms	-0.10%	-0.28%	-0.28%	-0.10%	-0.30%	-0.30%	3.92%	9.76%	9.19%	4.04%	9.65%	9.07%	3.98%	9.53%	8.94%
Sigma of Love of Variety	0.00%	0.00%	0.00%	0.00%	0.00%	0.00%	0.00%	0.00%	0.00%	0.00%	0.00%	0.00%	0.00%	0.00%	0.00%

Other Intensive Industries

	Border Controls			Border controls and x-ineff.			Market segmentation			Trade *antimonde*			Full *antimonde*		
	1988	1991	1994	1988	1991	1994	1988	1991	1994	1988	1991	1994	1988	1991	1994
Production per firm	-0.68%	-1.58%	-1.56%	-0.67%	-1.55%	-1.54%	-1.67%	-7.69%	-7.56%	-2.36%	-8.45%	-8.32%	-2.41%	-8.50%	-8.38%
Marginal Costs	3.66%	3.69%	3.70%	3.68%	3.71%	3.73%	-6.52%	-6.00%	-5.56%	-3.74%	-3.24%	-2.79%	-3.58%	-3.00%	-2.47%
Producer Prices	3.76%	3.89%	3.90%	3.77%	3.90%	3.93%	-6.29%	-5.02%	-4.61%	-3.41%	-2.13%	-1.70%	-3.25%	-1.89%	-1.38%
Mark-ups domestic (abs. diff.)	0.00%	0.01%	0.01%	0.00%	0.01%	0.00%	0.40%	1.78%	1.78%	0.41%	1.79%	1.78%	0.41%	1.79%	1.77%
Fixed Costs per firm	3.63%	3.65%	3.67%	3.64%	3.66%	3.68%	-6.45%	-5.97%	-5.63%	-3.68%	-3.24%	-2.87%	-3.57%	-3.07%	-2.64%
Number of Firms	0.10%	0.94%	0.97%	0.11%	0.98%	1.01%	0.75%	6.12%	6.24%	0.77%	6.19%	6.33%	0.78%	6.22%	6.36%
Sigma of Love of Variety	0.00%	0.00%	0.00%	0.00%	0.00%	0.00%	0.00%	0.00%	0.00%	0.00%	0.00%	0.00%	0.00%	0.00%	0.00%

Electrical goods

	Border Controls			Border controls and x-ineff.			Market segmentation			Trade *antimonde*			Full *antimonde*		
	1988	1991	1994	1988	1991	1994	1988	1991	1994	1988	1991	1994	1988	1991	1994
Production per firm	-1.17%	-2.44%	-2.43%	-1.17%	-2.43%	-2.42%	-3.31%	-13.13%	-13.15%	-4.76%	-14.80%	-14.81%	-4.86%	-14.89%	-14.95%
Marginal Costs	3.59%	3.67%	3.68%	3.61%	3.69%	3.72%	-5.83%	-5.25%	-4.78%	-3.02%	-2.44%	-1.95%	-2.86%	-2.19%	-1.63%
Producer Prices	3.64%	3.76%	3.78%	3.66%	3.78%	3.81%	-5.67%	-4.69%	-4.22%	-2.80%	-1.77%	-1.29%	-2.64%	-1.53%	-0.96%
Mark-ups domestic (abs. diff.)	0.03%	0.09%	0.09%	0.03%	0.09%	0.09%	0.52%	2.84%	2.84%	0.58%	2.92%	2.92%	0.59%	2.93%	2.93%
Fixed Costs per firm	3.52%	3.60%	3.61%	3.52%	3.60%	3.63%	-5.51%	-5.01%	-4.70%	-2.74%	-2.23%	-1.90%	-2.63%	-2.06%	-1.68%
Number of Firms	-0.29%	-0.26%	-0.23%	-0.28%	-0.24%	-0.21%	0.88%	6.19%	6.24%	0.29%	5.37%	5.42%	0.21%	5.25%	5.30%
Sigma of Love of Variety	0.00%	0.00%	0.00%	0.00%	0.00%	0.00%	0.00%	0.00%	0.00%	0.00%	0.00%	0.00%	0.00%	0.00%	0.00%

Transport equipment

	Border Controls			Border controls and x-ineff.			Market segmentation			Trade *antimonde*			Full *antimonde*		
	1988	1991	1994	1988	1991	1994	1988	1991	1994	1988	1991	1994	1988	1991	1994
Production per firm	-0.28%	-0.62%	-0.62%	-0.25%	-0.55%	-0.55%	-5.88%	-17.07%	-16.37%	-6.49%	-17.62%	-16.93%	-6.48%	-17.51%	-16.80%
Marginal Costs	3.49%	3.53%	3.55%	3.50%	3.54%	3.57%	-5.63%	-5.20%	-4.95%	-2.88%	-2.45%	-2.19%	-2.74%	-2.24%	-1.90%
Producer Prices	3.51%	3.58%	3.59%	3.52%	3.58%	3.61%	-5.10%	-3.76%	-3.58%	-2.28%	-0.92%	-0.71%	-2.14%	-0.72%	-0.45%
Mark-ups domestic (abs. diff.)	-0.08%	-0.06%	-0.07%	-0.09%	-0.06%	-0.07%	3.83%	12.35%	12.30%	3.79%	12.29%	12.23%	3.79%	12.28%	12.21%
Fixed Costs per firm	3.48%	3.52%	3.53%	3.48%	3.52%	3.54%	-5.63%	-5.21%	-4.98%	-2.89%	-2.48%	-2.23%	-2.80%	-2.33%	-2.03%
Number of Firms	0.34%	1.00%	1.06%	0.36%	1.05%	1.12%	3.20%	14.32%	15.03%	3.33%	14.52%	15.27%	3.32%	14.55%	15.35%
Sigma of Love of Variety	0.00%	0.00%	0.00%	0.00%	0.00%	0.00%	0.00%	0.00%	0.00%	0.00%	0.00%	0.00%	0.00%	0.00%	0.00%

Other Equipment

	Border Controls			Border controls and x-ineff.			Market segmentation			Trade *antimonde*			Full *antimonde*		
	1988	1991	1994	1988	1991	1994	1988	1991	1994	1988	1991	1994	1988	1991	1994
Production per firm	-0.57%	-1.29%	-1.28%	-0.57%	-1.29%	-1.28%	-5.48%	-12.54%	-12.51%	-6.54%	-13.78%	-13.74%	-6.61%	-13.84%	-13.84%
Marginal Costs	3.35%	3.49%	3.51%	3.37%	3.52%	3.55%	-4.74%	-4.08%	-3.65%	-2.04%	-1.33%	-0.88%	-1.88%	-1.08%	-0.56%
Producer Prices	3.37%	3.53%	3.55%	3.39%	3.56%	3.59%	-4.52%	-3.62%	-3.19%	-1.78%	-0.80%	-0.36%	-1.62%	-0.56%	-0.03%
Mark-ups domestic (abs. diff.)	0.00%	0.04%	0.04%	0.00%	0.04%	0.04%	0.66%	1.89%	1.88%	0.71%	1.95%	1.95%	0.71%	1.96%	1.95%
Fixed Costs per firm	3.25%	3.41%	3.42%	3.26%	3.42%	3.44%	-4.29%	-3.68%	-3.38%	-1.64%	-0.96%	-0.64%	-1.53%	-0.80%	-0.42%
Number of Firms	0.08%	0.03%	0.04%	0.08%	0.05%	0.06%	-1.23%	0.96%	1.09%	-1.87%	0.00%	0.12%	-1.92%	-0.06%	0.07%
Sigma of Love of Variety	0.00%	0.00%	0.00%	0.00%	0.00%	0.00%	0.00%	0.00%	0.00%	0.00%	0.00%	0.00%	0.00%	0.00%	0.00%

Telecommunications

	Border Controls			Border controls and x-ineff.			Market segmentation			Trade *antimonde*			Full *antimonde*		
	1988	1991	1994	1988	1991	1994	1988	1991	1994	1988	1991	1994	1988	1991	1994
Production per firm	0.22%	0.48%	0.47%	-0.16%	-0.36%	-0.37%	-1.12%	-2.64%	-2.83%	-0.99%	-2.47%	-2.67%	-1.38%	-3.23%	-3.45%
Marginal Costs	3.71%	3.66%	3.68%	3.73%	3.68%	3.72%	-7.19%	-6.74%	-6.14%	-4.44%	-4.07%	-3.44%	-4.27%	-3.81%	-3.09%
Producer Prices	3.58%	3.43%	3.45%	3.41%	3.10%	3.14%	-6.86%	-6.03%	-5.45%	-4.17%	-3.44%	-2.84%	-4.19%	-3.55%	-2.86%
Mark-ups domestic (abs. diff.)	-0.12%	-0.17%	-0.16%	-0.42%	-0.77%	-0.77%	0.39%	0.51%	0.47%	0.31%	0.40%	0.37%	-0.01%	-0.22%	-0.26%
Fixed Costs per firm	3.55%	3.44%	3.46%	2.60%	1.52%	1.54%	-7.22%	-7.06%	-6.74%	-4.58%	-4.54%	-4.20%	-5.35%	-6.13%	-5.75%
Number of Firms	0.16%	0.24%	0.23%	0.57%	1.05%	1.05%	-0.27%	0.17%	0.22%	-0.15%	0.31%	0.35%	0.26%	1.13%	1.19%
Sigma of Love of Variety	0.00%	0.00%	0.00%	0.00%	0.00%	0.00%	0.00%	0.00%	0.00%	0.00%	0.00%	0.00%	0.00%	0.00%	0.00%

Banks

	Border Controls			Border controls and x-ineff.			Market segmentation			Trade *antimonde*			Full *antimonde*		
	1988	1991	1994	1988	1991	1994	1988	1991	1994	1988	1991	1994	1988	1991	1994
Production per firm	0.53%	1.21%	1.20%	0.14%	0.43%	0.41%	-0.71%	-1.26%	-1.35%	-0.33%	-0.54%	-0.64%	-0.75%	-1.37%	-1.48%
Marginal Costs	3.65%	3.58%	3.59%	3.67%	3.59%	3.62%	-7.28%	-6.92%	-6.39%	-4.57%	-4.32%	-3.76%	-4.41%	-4.08%	-3.45%
Producer Prices	3.54%	3.33%	3.35%	3.47%	3.19%	3.22%	-7.18%	-6.77%	-6.26%	-4.54%	-4.30%	-3.77%	-4.46%	-4.21%	-3.60%
Mark-ups domestic (abs. diff.)	-0.09%	-0.18%	-0.18%	-0.18%	-0.37%	-0.37%	0.13%	0.18%	0.16%	0.06%	0.08%	0.06%	-0.03%	-0.11%	-0.13%
Fixed Costs per firm	3.54%	3.41%	3.42%	2.69%	1.71%	1.73%	-7.34%	-7.21%	-6.91%	-4.72%	-4.73%	-4.40%	-5.40%	-6.13%	-5.76%
Number of Firms	0.39%	0.89%	0.88%	0.80%	1.75%	1.74%	0.73%	2.75%	2.88%	1.00%	3.19%	3.31%	1.41%	4.03%	4.16%
Sigma of Love of Variety	0.00%	0.00%	0.00%	0.00%	0.00%	0.00%	0.00%	0.00%	0.00%	0.00%	0.00%	0.00%	0.00%	0.00%	0.00%

Table B7.7.
Decomposition of effects: sectoral results for Ireland (volumes)

% change from *monde*

Agriculture

	Border Controls 1988	1991	1994	Border controls and x-ineff. 1988	1991	1994	Market segmentation 1988	1991	1994	Trade antimonde 1988	1991	1994	Full antimonde 1988	1991	1994
Domestic Production - vol.	-1.4%	-1.6%	-1.6%	-1.4%	-1.6%	-1.6%	3.3%	4.6%	3.8%	2.3%	3.4%	2.7%	2.2%	3.2%	2.4%
Imports - vol.	1.7%	1.7%	1.7%	1.8%	1.7%	1.7%	-5.5%	-4.5%	-4.1%	-3.7%	-2.6%	-2.2%	-3.5%	-2.4%	-1.8%
Exports - vol.	-0.7%	-0.7%	-0.7%	-0.7%	-0.7%	-0.7%	2.0%	1.8%	1.5%	1.5%	1.3%	1.0%	1.5%	1.2%	0.9%
Absorption - vol.	-1.1%	-1.4%	-1.5%	-1.1%	-1.5%	-1.5%	2.1%	2.8%	2.3%	1.5%	2.1%	1.5%	1.4%	2.0%	1.3%
Investment - vol.	-0.6%	-0.7%	-0.7%	-0.6%	-0.7%	-0.7%	-2.9%	-2.3%	-2.6%	-3.3%	-2.8%	-3.1%	-3.3%	-2.8%	-3.1%
Labour Demand - vol.	-1.3%	-1.4%	-1.4%	-1.3%	-1.4%	-1.4%	3.3%	4.9%	4.4%	2.4%	3.8%	3.3%	2.4%	3.7%	3.2%
Private Consumption - vol.	-0.1%	-0.4%	-0.4%	-0.1%	-0.4%	-0.5%	-1.2%	-2.0%	-2.4%	-1.4%	-2.3%	-2.7%	-1.4%	-2.4%	-2.8%
Supply to domestic - vol.	-1.1%	-1.2%	-1.2%	-1.2%	-1.2%	-1.2%	3.0%	4.5%	3.7%	2.4%	3.7%	2.9%	2.3%	3.5%	2.7%
Intra-EU Trade - vol	-1.7%	-3.4%	-3.4%	-1.8%	-3.4%	-3.4%	1.5%	0.0%	-0.3%	-0.2%	-2.2%	-2.5%	-0.3%	-2.3%	-2.7%

Energy

	Border Controls 1988	1991	1994	Border controls and x-ineff. 1988	1991	1994	Market segmentation 1988	1991	1994	Trade antimonde 1988	1991	1994	Full antimonde 1988	1991	1994
Domestic Production - vol.	-0.4%	-0.6%	-0.6%	-0.4%	-0.6%	-0.6%	1.3%	1.2%	0.7%	1.0%	0.6%	0.2%	0.9%	0.5%	0.0%
Imports - vol.	1.1%	1.2%	1.2%	1.1%	1.2%	1.2%	-2.8%	-2.5%	-2.4%	-2.0%	-1.8%	-1.6%	-2.0%	-1.7%	-1.5%
Exports - vol.	-0.3%	-0.4%	-0.4%	-0.3%	-0.4%	-0.4%	1.0%	0.9%	0.8%	0.7%	0.6%	0.5%	0.7%	0.6%	0.5%
Absorption - vol.	-0.3%	-0.6%	-0.6%	-0.3%	-0.6%	-0.6%	0.0%	-0.3%	-0.7%	-0.2%	-0.7%	-1.1%	-0.3%	-0.8%	-1.2%
Investment - vol.	-0.2%	-0.3%	-0.3%	-0.2%	-0.3%	-0.3%	-3.5%	-3.6%	-3.8%	-3.7%	-3.8%	-4.0%	-3.7%	-3.9%	-4.1%
Labour Demand - vol.	-0.4%	-0.5%	-0.5%	-0.4%	-0.5%	-0.5%	1.4%	1.4%	1.0%	1.1%	0.9%	0.5%	1.1%	0.9%	0.5%
Private Consumption - vol.	-0.1%	-0.3%	-0.4%	-0.1%	-0.3%	-0.4%	-1.0%	-1.7%	-2.0%	-1.1%	-2.0%	-2.3%	-1.2%	-2.0%	-2.4%
Supply to domestic - vol.	-0.3%	-0.4%	-0.5%	-0.3%	-0.4%	-0.5%	0.9%	0.6%	0.2%	0.6%	0.3%	-0.2%	0.6%	0.2%	-0.3%
Intra-EU Trade - vol	-0.6%	-0.9%	-0.9%	-0.6%	-0.9%	-0.9%	0.7%	0.5%	0.2%	0.2%	-0.2%	-0.5%	0.2%	-0.3%	-0.6%

Metal Industries

	Border Controls 1988	1991	1994	Border controls and x-ineff. 1988	1991	1994	Market segmentation 1988	1991	1994	Trade antimonde 1988	1991	1994	Full antimonde 1988	1991	1994
Domestic Production - vol.	-3.1%	-5.2%	-5.2%	-3.1%	-5.1%	-5.1%	5.3%	0.3%	0.1%	1.4%	-4.6%	-4.8%	1.2%	-4.9%	-5.1%
Imports - vol.	1.2%	1.0%	1.0%	1.2%	1.1%	1.1%	-6.3%	-6.6%	-6.4%	-4.2%	-4.4%	-4.2%	-4.0%	-4.1%	-3.8%
Exports - vol.	-0.7%	-0.7%	-0.7%	-0.7%	-0.7%	-0.7%	2.1%	2.1%	1.9%	1.6%	1.6%	1.4%	1.5%	1.5%	1.3%
Absorption - vol.	-0.9%	-1.7%	-1.7%	-0.9%	-1.7%	-1.7%	-1.3%	-3.4%	-3.5%	-2.5%	-5.1%	-5.2%	-2.6%	-5.1%	-5.2%
Investment - vol.	-1.5%	-2.6%	-2.6%	-1.5%	-2.5%	-2.5%	-1.8%	-4.1%	-4.2%	-3.6%	-6.3%	-6.4%	-3.7%	-6.4%	-6.5%
Labour Demand - vol.	-2.8%	-4.7%	-4.7%	-2.8%	-4.7%	-4.6%	5.6%	2.0%	1.9%	2.0%	-2.5%	-2.6%	1.8%	-2.6%	-2.8%
Private Consumption - vol.	-0.1%	-0.2%	-0.2%	-0.1%	-0.2%	-0.2%	-0.6%	-1.0%	-1.1%	-0.6%	-1.1%	-1.3%	-0.7%	-1.2%	-1.4%
Supply to domestic - vol.	-1.0%	-0.4%	-0.4%	-1.0%	-0.4%	-0.3%	0.4%	-8.5%	-8.6%	-1.1%	-10.1%	-10.2%	-1.2%	-10.2%	-10.4%
Intra-EU Trade - vol	-1.4%	-2.5%	-2.5%	-1.4%	-2.5%	-2.5%	2.3%	1.2%	1.0%	0.2%	-1.4%	-1.5%	0.1%	-1.5%	-1.7%

Chemical

	Border Controls 1988	1991	1994	Border controls and x-ineff. 1988	1991	1994	Market segmentation 1988	1991	1994	Trade antimonde 1988	1991	1994	Full antimonde 1988	1991	1994
Domestic Production - vol.	-1.3%	-2.8%	-2.8%	-1.3%	-2.9%	-2.9%	4.4%	1.4%	0.1%	3.6%	0.0%	-1.3%	3.4%	-0.3%	-1.7%
Imports - vol.	0.7%	0.7%	0.7%	0.8%	0.7%	0.7%	-4.6%	-4.1%	-4.0%	-3.5%	-2.7%	-2.7%	-3.2%	-2.4%	-2.2%
Exports - vol.	-0.3%	-0.4%	-0.4%	-0.3%	-0.4%	-0.4%	2.0%	1.8%	1.6%	1.9%	1.7%	1.5%	1.8%	1.6%	1.3%
Absorption - vol.	-0.9%	-1.6%	-1.6%	-0.9%	-1.6%	-1.7%	2.0%	1.3%	0.6%	1.4%	0.4%	-0.4%	1.3%	0.2%	-0.5%
Investment - vol.	-0.6%	-1.4%	-1.4%	-0.6%	-1.4%	-1.4%	-2.3%	-3.6%	-4.2%	-2.6%	-4.3%	-4.8%	-2.7%	-4.3%	-4.9%
Labour Demand - vol.	-1.1%	-2.5%	-2.5%	-1.1%	-2.6%	-2.6%	4.3%	2.3%	1.2%	3.7%	1.1%	-0.1%	3.6%	0.9%	-0.3%
Private Consumption - vol.	-0.2%	-0.4%	-0.4%	-0.2%	-0.4%	-0.5%	-1.1%	-2.0%	-2.4%	-1.3%	-2.3%	-2.8%	-1.3%	-2.4%	-2.9%
Supply to domestic - vol.	-0.5%	0.2%	0.2%	-0.5%	0.1%	0.1%	5.4%	3.8%	2.4%	5.3%	3.5%	2.1%	5.1%	3.3%	1.8%
Intra-EU Trade - vol	-1.0%	-2.2%	-2.2%	-1.0%	-2.2%	-2.2%	2.3%	0.7%	0.0%	1.5%	-0.6%	-1.2%	1.4%	-0.8%	-1.5%

Other Intensive Industries

	Border Controls 1988	1991	1994	Border controls and x-ineff. 1988	1991	1994	Market segmentation 1988	1991	1994	Trade antimonde 1988	1991	1994	Full antimonde 1988	1991	1994
Domestic Production - vol.	-0.6%	-0.7%	-0.6%	-0.6%	-0.6%	-0.5%	-0.9%	-2.0%	-1.8%	-1.6%	-2.8%	-2.5%	-1.7%	-2.8%	-2.6%
Imports - vol.	1.7%	1.8%	1.9%	1.8%	1.9%	1.9%	-8.2%	-7.7%	-7.4%	-5.9%	-5.1%	-4.8%	-5.6%	-4.7%	-4.2%
Exports - vol.	-0.5%	-0.5%	-0.5%	-0.5%	-0.5%	-0.5%	2.1%	2.0%	1.8%	1.8%	1.7%	1.5%	1.7%	1.6%	1.4%
Absorption - vol.	-0.3%	-0.4%	-0.4%	-0.2%	-0.4%	-0.4%	-2.3%	-2.7%	-2.8%	-2.6%	-3.1%	-3.1%	-2.6%	-3.1%	-3.1%
Investment - vol.	-0.3%	-0.3%	-0.3%	-0.3%	-0.3%	-0.3%	-4.7%	-5.2%	-5.1%	-5.0%	-5.6%	-5.5%	-5.0%	-5.6%	-5.5%
Labour Demand - vol.	-0.4%	-0.4%	-0.4%	-0.4%	-0.3%	-0.3%	-0.6%	-0.7%	-0.4%	-1.1%	-1.3%	-1.0%	-1.1%	-1.3%	-1.0%
Private Consumption - vol.	-0.2%	-0.5%	-0.4%	-0.2%	-0.5%	-0.4%	-2.0%	-2.2%	-2.1%	-2.3%	-2.6%	-2.4%	-2.3%	-2.7%	-2.5%
Supply to domestic - vol.	0.2%	1.3%	1.4%	0.2%	1.4%	1.4%	-1.1%	-0.5%	-0.5%	-1.1%	-0.4%	-0.3%	-1.1%	-0.4%	-0.3%
Intra-EU Trade - vol	-0.9%	-2.1%	-2.0%	-0.9%	-2.0%	-2.0%	-0.7%	-2.3%	-2.3%	-1.8%	-3.6%	-3.5%	-1.9%	-3.6%	-3.6%

Electrical goods

	Border Controls			Border controls and x-ineff.			Market segmentation			Trade *antimonde*			Full *antimonde*		
	1988	1991	1994	1988	1991	1994	1988	1991	1994	1988	1991	1994	1988	1991	1994
Domestic Production - vol.	-1.5%	-2.7%	-2.7%	-1.4%	-2.7%	-2.6%	-2.5%	-7.7%	-7.7%	-4.5%	-10.2%	-10.2%	-4.7%	-10.4%	-10.4%
Imports - vol.	1.1%	0.9%	1.0%	1.1%	1.0%	1.0%	-7.4%	-8.3%	-8.1%	-6.2%	-7.1%	-6.7%	-6.1%	-6.8%	-6.4%
Exports - vol.	-0.5%	-0.6%	-0.6%	-0.5%	-0.6%	-0.6%	2.2%	2.0%	1.8%	1.8%	1.7%	1.5%	1.8%	1.6%	1.4%
Absorption - vol.	-0.6%	-1.3%	-1.2%	-0.6%	-1.2%	-1.1%	-5.3%	-8.2%	-8.0%	-6.4%	-9.6%	-9.4%	-6.5%	-9.7%	-9.5%
Investment - vol.	-0.7%	-1.3%	-1.3%	-0.7%	-1.3%	-1.3%	-5.3%	-7.8%	-7.8%	-6.3%	-8.9%	-8.9%	-6.3%	-9.0%	-9.0%
Labour Demand - vol.	-1.3%	-2.5%	-2.4%	-1.3%	-2.4%	-2.4%	-1.9%	-6.5%	-6.4%	-3.8%	-8.8%	-8.7%	-3.9%	-8.9%	-8.8%
Private Consumption - vol.	-0.5%	-1.2%	-0.7%	-0.6%	-1.3%	-0.7%	-5.4%	-4.9%	-4.0%	-6.1%	-5.8%	-4.5%	-6.3%	-6.0%	-4.7%
Supply to domestic - vol.	-0.8%	0.5%	0.7%	-0.9%	0.6%	0.7%	-1.1%	-4.4%	-4.5%	-2.4%	-5.8%	-5.8%	-2.6%	-6.1%	-6.2%
Intra-EU Trade - vol	-1.2%	-2.3%	-2.3%	-1.2%	-2.3%	-2.3%	-0.9%	-3.9%	-3.9%	-2.7%	-6.1%	-6.1%	-2.9%	-6.3%	-6.3%

Transport equipment

	Border Controls			Border controls and x-ineff.			Market segmentation			Trade *antimonde*			Full *antimonde*		
	1988	1991	1994	1988	1991	1994	1988	1991	1994	1988	1991	1994	1988	1991	1994
Domestic Production - vol.	0.1%	0.4%	0.6%	0.1%	0.5%	0.6%	-2.9%	-5.2%	-3.8%	-3.4%	-5.7%	-4.2%	-3.4%	-5.5%	-4.0%
Imports - vol.	1.1%	1.2%	1.3%	1.1%	1.2%	1.3%	-7.3%	-7.1%	-6.7%	-5.7%	-5.3%	-4.8%	-5.5%	-5.0%	-4.5%
Exports - vol.	-0.5%	-0.5%	-0.5%	-0.5%	-0.5%	-0.5%	2.2%	2.3%	2.3%	1.8%	2.0%	1.9%	1.8%	1.9%	1.8%
Absorption - vol.	0.0%	-0.2%	0.0%	0.0%	-0.2%	0.0%	-5.7%	-5.8%	-5.2%	-5.8%	-6.0%	-5.3%	-5.9%	-6.0%	-5.3%
Investment - vol.	0.0%	0.1%	0.2%	0.0%	0.2%	0.2%	-5.2%	-6.3%	-5.8%	-5.4%	-6.6%	-6.0%	-5.4%	-6.5%	-5.9%
Labour Demand - vol.	0.1%	0.5%	0.6%	0.2%	0.6%	0.7%	-1.8%	-3.1%	-1.7%	-2.2%	-3.4%	-2.0%	-2.2%	-3.2%	-1.7%
Private Consumption - vol.	-0.5%	-1.2%	-0.5%	-0.5%	-1.2%	-0.5%	-5.8%	-4.5%	-2.8%	-6.5%	-5.3%	-3.1%	-6.7%	-5.5%	-3.3%
Supply to domestic - vol.	0.3%	2.8%	3.1%	0.4%	2.9%	3.1%	-5.2%	-13.8%	-12.8%	-5.1%	-13.6%	-12.4%	-5.2%	-13.7%	-12.5%
Intra-EU Trade - vol	-0.6%	-1.0%	-0.9%	-0.6%	-0.9%	-0.9%	0.1%	0.2%	0.5%	-1.1%	-1.2%	-0.8%	-1.2%	-1.3%	-0.9%

Other Equipment

	Border Controls			Border controls and x-ineff.			Market segmentation			Trade *antimonde*			Full *antimonde*		
	1988	1991	1994	1988	1991	1994	1988	1991	1994	1988	1991	1994	1988	1991	1994
Domestic Production - vol.	-0.5%	-1.3%	-1.2%	-0.5%	-1.2%	-1.2%	-6.6%	-11.7%	-11.6%	-8.3%	-13.8%	-13.6%	-8.4%	-13.9%	-13.8%
Imports - vol.	1.0%	0.8%	0.8%	1.0%	0.9%	0.9%	-6.7%	-8.0%	-7.8%	-5.5%	-6.8%	-6.7%	-5.4%	-6.7%	-6.4%
Exports - vol.	-0.6%	-0.7%	-0.7%	-0.6%	-0.7%	-0.7%	1.7%	1.5%	1.3%	1.3%	1.0%	0.8%	1.2%	0.9%	0.7%
Absorption - vol.	-0.4%	-1.0%	-1.0%	-0.4%	-1.0%	-0.9%	-6.6%	-10.1%	-10.0%	-7.7%	-11.6%	-11.5%	-7.8%	-11.6%	-11.6%
Investment - vol.	-0.3%	-0.7%	-0.7%	-0.3%	-0.7%	-0.7%	-7.0%	-9.4%	-9.4%	-7.8%	-10.4%	-10.3%	-7.8%	-10.4%	-10.4%
Labour Demand - vol.	-0.4%	-1.1%	-1.1%	-0.4%	-1.1%	-1.0%	-5.9%	-10.5%	-10.2%	-7.4%	-12.4%	-12.2%	-7.5%	-12.5%	-12.2%
Private Consumption - vol.	-0.2%	-0.6%	-0.6%	-0.3%	-0.7%	-0.6%	-2.2%	-3.1%	-3.4%	-2.5%	-3.6%	-3.9%	-2.6%	-3.8%	-4.1%
Supply to domestic - vol.	-0.5%	0.4%	0.4%	-0.5%	0.4%	0.4%	-5.2%	-9.7%	-9.7%	-6.7%	-11.4%	-11.4%	-6.8%	-11.6%	-11.6%
Intra-EU Trade - vol	-0.5%	-1.3%	-1.3%	-0.5%	-1.3%	-1.3%	-3.6%	-6.5%	-6.4%	-5.1%	-8.3%	-8.2%	-5.2%	-8.4%	-8.3%

Consumer goods

	Border Controls			Border controls and x-ineff.			Market segmentation			Trade *antimonde*			Full *antimonde*		
	1988	1991	1994	1988	1991	1994	1988	1991	1994	1988	1991	1994	1988	1991	1994
Domestic Production - vol.	-1.1%	-1.5%	-1.5%	-1.1%	-1.5%	-1.6%	2.6%	3.4%	2.8%	2.0%	2.8%	2.2%	1.9%	2.6%	1.9%
Imports - vol.	1.4%	1.5%	1.5%	1.4%	1.5%	1.5%	-5.4%	-5.1%	-4.8%	-4.4%	-4.0%	-3.8%	-4.3%	-3.8%	-3.5%
Exports - vol.	-0.6%	-0.7%	-0.7%	-0.6%	-0.7%	-0.7%	2.6%	2.4%	2.1%	2.2%	2.0%	1.7%	2.1%	1.9%	1.6%
Absorption - vol.	-0.4%	-0.7%	-0.8%	-0.4%	-0.7%	-0.8%	-0.3%	-0.7%	-1.1%	-0.7%	-1.2%	-1.6%	-0.7%	-1.3%	-1.7%
Investment - vol.	-0.5%	-0.7%	-0.7%	-0.5%	-0.7%	-0.7%	-3.1%	-2.8%	-3.1%	-3.3%	-3.1%	-3.4%	-3.4%	-3.1%	-3.4%
Labour Demand - vol.	-1.0%	-1.4%	-1.4%	-1.1%	-1.4%	-1.4%	2.9%	3.9%	3.5%	2.4%	3.4%	2.9%	2.4%	3.3%	2.7%
Private Consumption - vol.	-0.1%	-0.4%	-0.4%	-0.1%	-0.4%	-0.4%	-1.2%	-1.9%	-2.3%	-1.3%	-2.2%	-2.6%	-1.4%	-2.3%	-2.7%
Supply to domestic - vol.	-0.3%	0.7%	0.7%	-0.3%	0.7%	0.6%	2.2%	3.7%	3.1%	1.9%	3.5%	2.9%	1.8%	3.3%	2.6%
Intra-EU Trade - vol	-1.2%	-2.6%	-2.6%	-1.2%	-2.6%	-2.6%	0.6%	-0.3%	-0.6%	0.0%	-1.2%	-1.5%	-0.1%	-1.3%	-1.6%

Construction

	Border Controls			Border controls and x-ineff.			Market segmentation			Trade *antimonde*			Full *antimonde*		
	1988	1991	1994	1988	1991	1994	1988	1991	1994	1988	1991	1994	1988	1991	1994
Domestic Production - vol.	0.3%	0.5%	0.5%	0.4%	0.5%	0.5%	-6.3%	-6.4%	-6.6%	-6.0%	-6.1%	-6.3%	-6.0%	-6.0%	-6.2%
Imports - vol.	#VALUE!	#VALUE!	#VALUE!	#VALUE!	#VALUE!	#VALUE!	#VALUE!	#VALUE!	#VALUE!	#VALUE!	#VALUE!	#VALUE!	#VALUE!	#VALUE!	#VALUE!
Exports - vol.	#VALUE!	#VALUE!	#VALUE!	#VALUE!	#VALUE!	#VALUE!	#VALUE!	#VALUE!	#VALUE!	#VALUE!	#VALUE!	#VALUE!	#VALUE!	#VALUE!	#VALUE!
Absorption - vol.	0.3%	0.5%	0.5%	0.4%	0.5%	0.5%	-6.3%	-6.4%	-6.6%	-6.0%	-6.1%	-6.3%	-6.0%	-6.0%	-6.2%
Investment - vol.	0.2%	0.2%	0.2%	0.2%	0.2%	0.2%	-7.3%	-7.4%	-7.5%	-7.2%	-7.3%	-7.4%	-7.1%	-7.2%	-7.3%
Labour Demand - vol.	0.4%	0.5%	0.5%	0.4%	0.6%	0.6%	-6.1%	-6.1%	-6.3%	-5.8%	-5.7%	-5.9%	-5.7%	-5.6%	-5.7%
Private Consumption - vol.	#DIV/0!	#DIV/0!	#DIV/0!	#DIV/0!	#DIV/0!	#DIV/0!	#DIV/0!	#DIV/0!	#DIV/0!	#DIV/0!	#DIV/0!	#DIV/0!	#DIV/0!	#DIV/0!	#DIV/0!
Supply to domestic - vol.	0.3%	0.5%	0.5%	0.4%	0.5%	0.5%	-6.3%	-6.4%	-6.6%	-6.0%	-6.1%	-6.3%	-6.0%	-6.0%	-6.2%
Intra-EU Trade - vol	#DIV/0!	#DIV/0!	#DIV/0!	#DIV/0!	#DIV/0!	#DIV/0!	#DIV/0!	#DIV/0!	#DIV/0!	#DIV/0!	#DIV/0!	#DIV/0!	#DIV/0!	#DIV/0!	#DIV/0!

Telecommunications

	Border Controls			Border controls and x-ineff.			Market segmentation			Trade *antimonde*			Full *antimonde*		
	1988	1991	1994	1988	1991	1994	1988	1991	1994	1988	1991	1994	1988	1991	1994
Domestic Production - vol.	0.4%	0.7%	0.7%	0.4%	0.7%	0.7%	-1.4%	-2.5%	-2.6%	-1.1%	-2.2%	-2.3%	-1.1%	-2.1%	-2.3%
Imports - vol.	0.7%	0.7%	0.7%	0.6%	0.5%	0.6%	-7.7%	-8.0%	-7.9%	-7.2%	-7.5%	-7.3%	-7.1%	-7.4%	-7.1%
Exports - vol.	-0.2%	-0.2%	-0.2%	-0.2%	-0.1%	-0.1%	1.1%	1.1%	1.0%	1.1%	1.0%	0.9%	1.0%	1.0%	0.9%
Absorption - vol.	0.2%	0.3%	0.3%	0.3%	0.4%	0.4%	-1.2%	-1.4%	-1.6%	-1.0%	-1.3%	-1.5%	-1.0%	-1.2%	-1.4%
Investment - vol.	0.2%	0.4%	0.4%	0.2%	0.4%	0.4%	-4.9%	-5.4%	-5.4%	-4.8%	-5.3%	-5.3%	-4.7%	-5.2%	-5.2%
Labour Demand - vol.	0.3%	0.5%	0.5%	0.3%	0.5%	0.5%	-0.9%	-1.2%	-1.2%	-0.6%	-1.0%	-1.0%	-1.3%	-2.3%	-2.3%
Private Consumption - vol.	-0.2%	-0.4%	-0.5%	-0.2%	-0.3%	-0.4%	-1.2%	-2.2%	-2.6%	-1.4%	-2.5%	-3.0%	-1.5%	-2.7%	-3.0%
Supply to domestic - vol.	0.2%	0.3%	0.3%	0.3%	0.4%	0.4%	-1.1%	-1.1%	-1.3%	-0.9%	-0.9%	-1.1%	-0.9%	-0.8%	-1.0%
Intra-EU Trade - vol	1.2%	2.2%	2.2%	1.0%	1.3%	1.3%	-3.6%	-11.1%	-11.0%	-3.0%	-10.4%	-10.3%	-3.1%	-10.6%	-10.5%

Transports

	Border Controls			Border controls and x-ineff.			Market segmentation			Trade *antimonde*			Full *antimonde*		
	1988	1991	1994	1988	1991	1994	1988	1991	1994	1988	1991	1994	1988	1991	1994
Domestic Production - vol.	0.6%	0.6%	0.6%	0.6%	0.7%	0.6%	-0.3%	-0.7%	-1.0%	0.3%	0.0%	-0.3%	0.3%	-0.1%	-0.4%
Imports - vol.	0.3%	0.3%	0.3%	0.3%	0.3%	0.3%	-0.2%	-0.4%	-0.5%	0.2%	0.0%	-0.2%	0.2%	0.0%	-0.2%
Exports - vol.	-0.1%	-0.1%	-0.1%	-0.1%	-0.1%	-0.1%	0.7%	0.7%	0.6%	0.7%	0.6%	0.6%	0.7%	0.6%	0.6%
Absorption - vol.	-0.1%	-0.3%	-0.4%	-0.1%	-0.3%	-0.3%	-0.8%	-1.4%	-1.7%	-0.9%	-1.7%	-2.0%	-1.0%	-1.7%	-2.0%
Investment - vol.	0.3%	0.3%	0.3%	0.3%	0.3%	0.3%	-4.3%	-4.6%	-4.7%	-4.0%	-4.3%	-4.4%	-4.0%	-4.3%	-4.4%
Labour Demand - vol.	0.7%	0.7%	0.7%	0.7%	0.7%	0.7%	-0.2%	-0.6%	-0.8%	0.5%	0.2%	-0.1%	0.5%	0.2%	0.0%
Private Consumption - vol.	-0.2%	-0.5%	-0.5%	-0.2%	-0.5%	-0.6%	-1.3%	-2.3%	-2.7%	-1.4%	-2.6%	-3.1%	-1.5%	-2.7%	-3.3%
Supply to domestic - vol.	0.6%	0.6%	0.6%	0.6%	0.7%	0.7%	-0.3%	-0.7%	-1.0%	0.3%	0.0%	-0.3%	0.3%	-0.1%	-0.4%
Intra-EU Trade - vol	1.1%	1.3%	1.3%	1.1%	1.3%	1.3%	0.0%	-0.2%	-0.3%	1.1%	1.2%	1.0%	1.1%	1.1%	1.0%

Banks

	Border Controls			Border controls and x-ineff.			Market segmentation			Trade *antimonde*			Full *antimonde*		
	1988	1991	1994	1988	1991	1994	1988	1991	1994	1988	1991	1994	1988	1991	1994
Domestic Production - vol.	0.9%	2.1%	2.1%	0.9%	2.2%	2.2%	0.0%	1.5%	1.5%	0.7%	2.6%	2.7%	0.7%	2.6%	2.6%
Imports - vol.	1.1%	1.3%	1.3%	1.0%	1.2%	1.2%	-6.7%	-6.3%	-6.1%	-5.7%	-5.3%	-5.1%	-5.5%	-5.0%	-4.6%
Exports - vol.	-0.2%	-0.1%	-0.1%	-0.2%	-0.1%	-0.1%	1.2%	1.1%	1.0%	1.1%	1.1%	1.1%	1.1%	1.0%	0.9%
Absorption - vol.	0.6%	1.2%	1.2%	0.6%	1.3%	1.3%	-0.3%	0.3%	0.2%	0.1%	1.0%	0.9%	0.1%	1.0%	0.8%
Investment - vol.	0.5%	1.1%	1.0%	0.5%	1.1%	1.1%	-4.3%	-3.6%	-3.6%	-4.0%	-3.1%	-3.1%	-3.9%	-3.1%	-3.1%
Labour Demand - vol.	0.8%	1.9%	1.9%	0.6%	1.5%	1.5%	0.2%	1.9%	2.1%	0.8%	3.0%	3.1%	0.6%	2.5%	2.7%
Private Consumption - vol.	-0.2%	-0.5%	-0.6%	-0.2%	-0.5%	-0.6%	-1.4%	-2.4%	-2.9%	-1.6%	-2.8%	-3.4%	-1.6%	-2.9%	-3.5%
Supply to domestic - vol.	0.6%	1.5%	1.5%	0.7%	1.6%	1.6%	0.1%	1.6%	1.6%	0.5%	2.4%	2.3%	0.5%	2.4%	2.3%
Intra-EU Trade - vol	1.3%	2.0%	2.0%	1.2%	1.8%	1.7%	-2.3%	-6.4%	-6.6%	-1.2%	-4.4%	-4.6%	-1.2%	-4.5%	-4.7%

Services

	Border Controls			Border controls and x-ineff.			Market segmentation			Trade *antimonde*			Full *antimonde*		
	1988	1991	1994	1988	1991	1994	1988	1991	1994	1988	1991	1994	1988	1991	1994
Domestic Production - vol.	0.8%	1.1%	1.2%	0.9%	1.2%	1.2%	-1.1%	-1.0%	-1.2%	-0.3%	-0.1%	-0.3%	-0.3%	-0.1%	-0.4%
Imports - vol.	1.6%	1.5%	1.5%	1.6%	1.5%	1.5%	-5.0%	-4.9%	-4.7%	-3.8%	-3.7%	-3.5%	-3.7%	-3.6%	-3.3%
Exports - vol.	-0.5%	-0.5%	-0.5%	-0.5%	-0.5%	-0.5%	1.5%	1.4%	1.3%	1.1%	1.0%	0.9%	1.1%	1.0%	0.8%
Absorption - vol.	0.0%	-0.1%	-0.1%	0.0%	-0.1%	-0.1%	-1.3%	-1.6%	-1.9%	-1.3%	-1.7%	-2.0%	-1.4%	-1.8%	-2.0%
Investment - vol.	0.4%	0.6%	0.6%	0.4%	0.6%	0.6%	-4.7%	-4.7%	-4.8%	-4.4%	-4.3%	-4.4%	-4.4%	-4.3%	-4.4%
Labour Demand - vol.	0.9%	1.3%	1.3%	0.9%	1.3%	1.3%	-1.0%	-0.8%	-0.8%	-0.1%	0.2%	0.2%	-0.1%	0.3%	0.3%
Private Consumption - vol.	-0.2%	-0.5%	-0.5%	-0.2%	-0.5%	-0.5%	-1.6%	-2.4%	-2.6%	-1.9%	-2.8%	-3.0%	-1.9%	-2.9%	-3.2%
Supply to domestic - vol.	0.0%	-0.1%	-0.1%	0.0%	0.0%	0.0%	-1.3%	-1.5%	-1.7%	-1.3%	-1.6%	-1.8%	-1.3%	-1.6%	-1.8%
Intra-EU Trade - vol	7.5%	10.9%	10.9%	7.5%	10.9%	10.9%	-0.2%	0.5%	0.5%	6.9%	10.3%	10.3%	6.9%	10.3%	10.3%

Non market

	Border Controls			Border controls and x-ineff.			Market segmentation			Trade *antimonde*			Full *antimonde*		
	1988	1991	1994	1988	1991	1994	1988	1991	1994	1988	1991	1994	1988	1991	1994
Domestic Production - vol.	0.0%	0.0%	0.0%	0.0%	0.0%	0.0%	-0.5%	-0.7%	-0.7%	-0.5%	-0.8%	-0.8%	-0.5%	-0.8%	-0.8%
Imports - vol.	0.0%	0.0%	0.0%	0.0%	0.0%	0.0%	-0.2%	-0.4%	-0.4%	-0.2%	-0.4%	-0.4%	-0.2%	-0.4%	-0.4%
Exports - vol.	-0.1%	-0.1%	-0.1%	-0.1%	-0.1%	-0.1%	0.4%	0.4%	0.4%	0.3%	0.3%	0.3%	0.3%	0.3%	0.3%
Absorption - vol.	0.0%	0.0%	0.0%	0.0%	0.0%	0.0%	-0.5%	-0.7%	-0.8%	-0.5%	-0.8%	-0.8%	-0.5%	-0.8%	-0.8%
Investment - vol.	0.0%	0.0%	0.0%	0.0%	0.0%	0.0%	-4.3%	-4.3%	-4.3%	-4.3%	-4.3%	-4.4%	-4.3%	-4.3%	-4.3%
Labour Demand - vol.	0.0%	0.0%	0.0%	0.0%	0.0%	0.0%	-0.4%	-0.6%	-0.7%	-0.4%	-0.7%	-0.7%	-0.4%	-0.6%	-0.6%
Private Consumption - vol.	-0.2%	-0.4%	-0.5%	-0.2%	-0.4%	-0.5%	-1.4%	-2.2%	-2.5%	-1.6%	-2.5%	-2.9%	-1.6%	-2.6%	-3.0%
Supply to domestic - vol.	0.0%	0.0%	0.0%	0.0%	0.0%	0.0%	-0.5%	-0.7%	-0.7%	-0.5%	-0.8%	-0.8%	-0.5%	-0.8%	-0.8%
Intra-EU Trade - vol	0.4%	0.4%	0.4%	0.4%	0.4%	0.4%	-0.2%	0.5%	-0.3%	0.2%	0.1%	0.1%	0.2%	0.1%	0.1%

Table B7.8.
Decomposition of effects: sectoral results for Ireland (prices)

% change from *monde*

Agriculture

	Border Controls			Border controls and x-ineff.			Market segmentation			Trade *antimonde*			Full *antimonde*		
	1988	1991	1994	1988	1991	1994	1988	1991	1994	1988	1991	1994	1988	1991	1994
Marginal Costs	0.14%	0.25%	0.25%	0.16%	0.29%	0.28%	0.61%	0.73%	1.00%	0.76%	0.95%	1.23%	0.77%	0.98%	1.25%
Cost of Labour	-0.24%	-0.43%	-0.43%	-0.26%	-0.47%	-0.47%	-0.73%	-1.57%	-1.97%	-0.99%	-1.95%	-2.36%	-1.10%	-2.12%	-2.59%
Deflator of Absorption	0.07%	0.22%	0.22%	0.09%	0.25%	0.25%	0.98%	1.08%	1.31%	1.10%	1.30%	1.53%	1.11%	1.31%	1.54%
Price of Exports-RW	0.14%	0.25%	0.25%	0.16%	0.29%	0.28%	0.61%	0.73%	1.00%	0.76%	0.95%	1.23%	0.77%	0.98%	1.25%

Energy

	Border Controls			Border controls and x-ineff.			Market segmentation			Trade *antimonde*			Full *antimonde*		
	1988	1991	1994	1988	1991	1994	1988	1991	1994	1988	1991	1994	1988	1991	1994
Marginal Costs	0.11%	0.23%	0.23%	0.12%	0.25%	0.24%	0.72%	0.71%	0.90%	0.82%	0.90%	1.09%	0.79%	0.87%	1.03%
Cost of Labour	-0.24%	-0.43%	-0.43%	-0.26%	-0.47%	-0.47%	-0.73%	-1.57%	-1.97%	-0.99%	-1.95%	-2.36%	-1.10%	-2.12%	-2.59%
Deflator of Absorption	0.12%	0.41%	0.41%	0.13%	0.43%	0.42%	1.71%	1.77%	1.90%	1.89%	2.12%	2.26%	1.85%	2.07%	2.18%
Price of Exports-RW	0.11%	0.23%	0.23%	0.12%	0.25%	0.24%	0.72%	0.71%	0.90%	0.82%	0.90%	1.09%	0.79%	0.87%	1.03%

Metal Industries

	Border Controls			Border controls and x-ineff.			Market segmentation			Trade *antimonde*			Full *antimonde*		
	1988	1991	1994	1988	1991	1994	1988	1991	1994	1988	1991	1994	1988	1991	1994
Marginal Costs	0.04%	0.17%	0.17%	0.04%	0.17%	0.17%	1.00%	1.08%	1.07%	1.09%	1.28%	1.27%	1.08%	1.27%	1.25%
Cost of Labour	-0.24%	-0.43%	-0.43%	-0.26%	-0.47%	-0.47%	-0.73%	-1.57%	-1.97%	-0.99%	-1.95%	-2.36%	-1.10%	-2.12%	-2.59%
Deflator of Absorption	0.10%	0.48%	0.48%	0.10%	0.48%	0.47%	2.82%	3.64%	3.56%	3.14%	4.28%	4.19%	3.12%	4.23%	4.13%
Price of Exports-RW	0.10%	0.27%	0.27%	0.11%	0.27%	0.27%	0.53%	-0.20%	-0.22%	0.69%	0.06%	0.04%	0.69%	0.05%	0.03%

Chemical

	Border Controls			Border controls and x-ineff.			Market segmentation			Trade *antimonde*			Full *antimonde*		
	1988	1991	1994	1988	1991	1994	1988	1991	1994	1988	1991	1994	1988	1991	1994
Marginal Costs	0.17%	0.30%	0.29%	0.18%	0.32%	0.32%	0.79%	0.97%	1.16%	0.97%	1.25%	1.44%	0.97%	1.27%	1.44%
Cost of Labour	-0.24%	-0.43%	-0.43%	-0.26%	-0.47%	-0.47%	-0.73%	-1.57%	-1.97%	-0.99%	-1.95%	-2.36%	-1.10%	-2.12%	-2.59%
Deflator of Absorption	0.36%	0.72%	0.72%	0.36%	0.73%	0.72%	2.37%	3.10%	3.10%	2.85%	3.86%	3.86%	2.82%	3.82%	3.80%
Price of Exports-RW	0.17%	0.31%	0.31%	0.18%	0.34%	0.33%	0.62%	0.54%	0.75%	0.79%	0.81%	1.02%	0.79%	0.81%	1.02%

Other Intensive Industries

	Border Controls			Border controls and x-ineff.			Market segmentation			Trade *antimonde*			Full *antimonde*		
	1988	1991	1994	1988	1991	1994	1988	1991	1994	1988	1991	1994	1988	1991	1994
Marginal Costs	0.00%	0.05%	0.05%	0.00%	0.05%	0.05%	0.52%	0.37%	0.28%	0.54%	0.44%	0.35%	0.52%	0.41%	0.31%
Cost of Labour	-0.24%	-0.43%	-0.43%	-0.26%	-0.47%	-0.47%	-0.73%	-1.57%	-1.97%	-0.99%	-1.95%	-2.36%	-1.10%	-2.12%	-2.59%
Deflator of Absorption	0.17%	0.39%	0.39%	0.17%	0.38%	0.38%	1.27%	1.70%	1.61%	1.47%	2.05%	1.96%	1.45%	2.02%	1.91%
Price of Exports-RW	0.00%	0.01%	0.01%	-0.01%	0.00%	0.00%	0.49%	0.13%	0.04%	0.51%	0.18%	0.09%	0.49%	0.16%	0.05%

Electrical goods

	Border Controls			Border controls and x-ineff.			Market segmentation			Trade *antimonde*			Full *antimonde*		
	1988	1991	1994	1988	1991	1994	1988	1991	1994	1988	1991	1994	1988	1991	1994
Marginal Costs	-0.07%	0.03%	0.03%	-0.07%	0.03%	0.03%	1.21%	1.12%	1.07%	1.25%	1.24%	1.18%	1.24%	1.22%	1.15%
Cost of Labour	-0.24%	-0.43%	-0.43%	-0.26%	-0.47%	-0.47%	-0.73%	-1.57%	-1.97%	-0.99%	-1.95%	-2.36%	-1.10%	-2.12%	-2.59%
Deflator of Absorption	-0.26%	0.02%	0.02%	-0.27%	0.02%	0.01%	3.47%	3.61%	3.38%	3.58%	3.93%	3.69%	3.52%	3.82%	3.55%
Price of Exports-RW	-0.06%	0.04%	0.04%	-0.06%	0.04%	0.04%	1.18%	0.93%	0.87%	1.24%	1.06%	1.00%	1.23%	1.04%	0.97%

Transport equipment

	Border Controls			Border controls and x-ineff.			Market segmentation			Trade *antimonde*			Full *antimonde*		
	1988	1991	1994	1988	1991	1994	1988	1991	1994	1988	1991	1994	1988	1991	1994
Marginal Costs	-0.18%	-0.11%	-0.11%	-0.18%	-0.12%	-0.12%	1.41%	1.17%	0.90%	1.39%	1.22%	0.94%	1.36%	1.17%	0.88%
Cost of Labour	-0.24%	-0.43%	-0.43%	-0.26%	-0.47%	-0.47%	-0.73%	-1.57%	-1.97%	-0.99%	-1.95%	-2.36%	-1.10%	-2.12%	-2.59%
Deflator of Absorption	-0.23%	0.06%	0.06%	-0.23%	0.05%	0.04%	3.72%	4.02%	3.74%	3.87%	4.43%	4.14%	3.82%	4.33%	4.01%
Price of Exports-RW	-0.20%	-0.21%	-0.21%	-0.21%	-0.22%	-0.23%	1.17%	0.05%	-0.29%	1.13%	0.05%	-0.29%	1.10%	0.00%	-0.37%

Other Equipment

	Border Controls			Border controls and x-ineff.			Market segmentation			Trade *antimonde*			Full *antimonde*		
	1988	1991	1994	1988	1991	1994	1988	1991	1994	1988	1991	1994	1988	1991	1994
Marginal Costs	-0.31%	-0.14%	-0.14%	-0.31%	-0.14%	-0.14%	2.30%	2.29%	2.20%	2.23%	2.35%	2.25%	2.22%	2.33%	2.22%
Cost of Labour	-0.24%	-0.43%	-0.43%	-0.26%	-0.47%	-0.47%	-0.73%	-1.57%	-1.97%	-0.99%	-1.95%	-2.36%	-1.10%	-2.12%	-2.59%
Deflator of Absorption	-0.59%	-0.33%	-0.33%	-0.60%	-0.33%	-0.34%	3.77%	3.83%	3.59%	3.59%	3.85%	3.61%	3.52%	3.75%	3.47%
Price of Exports-RW	-0.31%	-0.14%	-0.14%	-0.31%	-0.14%	-0.14%	2.33%	2.27%	2.17%	2.27%	2.35%	2.25%	2.26%	2.33%	2.22%

Consumer goods

	Border Controls			Border controls and x-ineff.			Market segmentation			Trade *antimonde*			Full *antimonde*		
	1988	1991	1994	1988	1991	1994	1988	1991	1994	1988	1991	1994	1988	1991	1994
Marginal Costs	0.03%	0.13%	0.14%	0.03%	0.15%	0.15%	0.84%	0.74%	0.79%	0.91%	0.89%	0.94%	0.92%	0.91%	0.97%
Cost of Labour	-0.24%	-0.43%	-0.43%	-0.26%	-0.47%	-0.47%	-0.73%	-1.57%	-1.97%	-0.99%	-1.95%	-2.36%	-1.10%	-2.12%	-2.59%
Deflator of Absorption	0.02%	0.26%	0.27%	0.02%	0.27%	0.27%	1.87%	1.78%	1.73%	2.01%	2.08%	2.03%	2.01%	2.06%	2.01%
Price of Exports-RW	0.03%	0.13%	0.14%	0.03%	0.15%	0.15%	0.84%	0.74%	0.79%	0.91%	0.89%	0.94%	0.92%	0.91%	0.97%

Construction

	Border Controls			Border controls and x-ineff.			Market segmentation			Trade *antimonde*			Full *antimonde*		
	1988	1991	1994	1988	1991	1994	1988	1991	1994	1988	1991	1994	1988	1991	1994
Marginal Costs	-0.03%	-0.01%	0.00%	-0.03%	-0.02%	-0.02%	0.38%	0.16%	0.03%	0.37%	0.17%	0.04%	0.35%	0.14%	0.00%
Cost of Labour	-0.24%	-0.43%	-0.43%	-0.26%	-0.47%	-0.47%	-0.73%	-1.57%	-1.97%	-0.99%	-1.95%	-2.36%	-1.10%	-2.12%	-2.59%
Deflator of Absorption	-0.03%	-0.01%	0.00%	-0.03%	-0.02%	-0.02%	0.38%	0.16%	0.03%	0.37%	0.17%	0.04%	0.35%	0.14%	0.00%
Price of Exports-RW	-0.03%	-0.01%	0.00%	-0.03%	-0.02%	-0.02%	0.38%	0.16%	0.03%	0.37%	0.17%	0.04%	0.35%	0.14%	0.00%

Telecommunications

	Border Controls			Border controls and x-ineff.			Market segmentation			Trade *antimonde*			Full *antimonde*		
	1988	1991	1994	1988	1991	1994	1988	1991	1994	1988	1991	1994	1988	1991	1994
Marginal Costs	0.04%	0.02%	0.03%	0.05%	0.03%	0.03%	-0.15%	-0.37%	-0.29%	-0.17%	-0.40%	-0.31%	-0.17%	-0.40%	-0.31%
Cost of Labour	-0.24%	-0.43%	-0.43%	-0.26%	-0.47%	-0.47%	-0.73%	-1.57%	-1.97%	-0.99%	-1.95%	-2.36%	-1.10%	-2.12%	-2.59%
Deflator of Absorption	-0.04%	-0.08%	-0.07%	-0.24%	-0.49%	-0.48%	0.14%	0.02%	0.08%	0.09%	-0.06%	0.00%	-0.11%	-0.46%	-0.40%
Price of Exports-RW	0.02%	-0.01%	0.00%	-0.03%	-0.11%	-0.10%	-0.12%	-0.39%	-0.31%	-0.15%	-0.44%	-0.36%	-0.20%	-0.53%	-0.45%

Transports

	Border Controls			Border controls and x-ineff.			Market segmentation			Trade *antimonde*			Full *antimonde*		
	1988	1991	1994	1988	1991	1994	1988	1991	1994	1988	1991	1994	1988	1991	1994
Marginal Costs	-0.04%	-0.05%	-0.05%	-0.05%	-0.06%	-0.07%	0.20%	-0.08%	-0.12%	0.16%	-0.12%	-0.16%	0.14%	-0.15%	-0.20%
Cost of Labour	-0.24%	-0.43%	-0.43%	-0.26%	-0.47%	-0.47%	-0.73%	-1.57%	-1.97%	-0.99%	-1.95%	-2.36%	-1.10%	-2.12%	-2.59%
Deflator of Absorption	0.01%	0.09%	0.09%	0.00%	0.09%	0.09%	0.44%	0.29%	0.27%	0.39%	0.26%	0.24%	0.38%	0.23%	0.20%
Price of Exports-RW	-0.04%	-0.05%	-0.05%	-0.05%	-0.06%	-0.07%	0.20%	-0.08%	-0.12%	0.16%	-0.12%	-0.16%	0.14%	-0.15%	-0.20%

Banks

	Border Controls			Border controls and x-ineff.			Market segmentation			Trade *antimonde*			Full *antimonde*		
	1988	1991	1994	1988	1991	1994	1988	1991	1994	1988	1991	1994	1988	1991	1994
Marginal Costs	-0.01%	-0.06%	-0.06%	-0.01%	-0.07%	-0.07%	-0.24%	-0.55%	-0.54%	-0.29%	-0.64%	-0.63%	-0.31%	-0.67%	-0.67%
Cost of Labour	-0.24%	-0.43%	-0.43%	-0.26%	-0.47%	-0.47%	-0.73%	-1.57%	-1.97%	-0.99%	-1.95%	-2.36%	-1.10%	-2.12%	-2.59%
Deflator of Absorption	-0.06%	-0.15%	-0.15%	-0.14%	-0.33%	-0.33%	-0.01%	-0.23%	-0.21%	-0.10%	-0.37%	-0.35%	-0.19%	-0.55%	-0.55%
Price of Exports-RW	-0.03%	-0.10%	-0.10%	-0.05%	-0.14%	-0.15%	-0.27%	-0.66%	-0.66%	-0.33%	-0.77%	-0.76%	-0.37%	-0.83%	-0.84%

Services

	Border Controls			Border controls and x-ineff.			Market segmentation			Trade *antimonde*			Full *antimonde*		
	1988	1991	1994	1988	1991	1994	1988	1991	1994	1988	1991	1994	1988	1991	1994
Marginal Costs	0.00%	-0.02%	-0.02%	0.00%	-0.02%	-0.03%	-0.06%	-0.29%	-0.22%	-0.08%	-0.32%	-0.26%	-0.10%	-0.35%	-0.30%
Cost of Labour	-0.24%	-0.43%	-0.43%	-0.26%	-0.47%	-0.47%	-0.73%	-1.57%	-1.97%	-0.99%	-1.95%	-2.36%	-1.10%	-2.12%	-2.59%
Deflator of Absorption	0.01%	0.00%	0.00%	0.01%	0.00%	-0.01%	-0.03%	-0.25%	-0.18%	-0.06%	-0.28%	-0.21%	-0.08%	-0.31%	-0.25%
Price of Exports-RW	0.00%	-0.02%	-0.02%	0.00%	-0.02%	-0.03%	-0.06%	-0.29%	-0.22%	-0.08%	-0.32%	-0.26%	-0.10%	-0.35%	-0.30%

Non market

	Border Controls			Border controls and x-ineff.			Market segmentation			Trade *antimonde*			Full *antimonde*		
	1988	1991	1994	1988	1991	1994	1988	1991	1994	1988	1991	1994	1988	1991	1994
Marginal Costs	-0.16%	-0.27%	-0.27%	-0.17%	-0.30%	-0.30%	-0.34%	-0.95%	-1.21%	-0.50%	-1.18%	-1.45%	-0.55%	-1.26%	-1.55%
Cost of Labour	-0.24%	-0.43%	-0.43%	-0.26%	-0.47%	-0.47%	-0.73%	-1.57%	-1.97%	-0.99%	-1.95%	-2.36%	-1.10%	-2.12%	-2.59%
Deflator of Absorption	-0.15%	-0.27%	-0.26%	-0.17%	-0.29%	-0.29%	-0.33%	-0.94%	-1.20%	-0.50%	-1.17%	-1.44%	-0.55%	-1.25%	-1.54%
Price of Exports-RW	-0.16%	-0.27%	-0.27%	-0.17%	-0.30%	-0.30%	-0.34%	-0.95%	-1.21%	-0.50%	-1.18%	-1.45%	-0.55%	-1.26%	-1.55%

Table B8.1.
The full *antimonde* scenario: macroeconomic aggregates for Italy

Macroeconomic Aggregates (vol.) (% change from *monde*)	Constraint Case			Flexible Case			Efficiency Case		
	1988	1991	1994	1988	1991	1994	1988	1991	1994
GDP fact. pr.	-0.47%	-0.76%	-1.01%	-0.53%	-0.99%	-1.41%	-0.56%	-1.11%	-1.60%
Priv. Consumption	-0.36%	-0.41%	-0.57%	-1.05%	-1.24%	-1.48%	-1.06%	-1.27%	-1.55%
Absorption	-0.21%	-0.32%	-0.48%	-1.31%	-1.46%	-1.75%	-1.33%	-1.50%	-1.82%
Total Investment	-1.19%	-1.31%	-1.83%	-4.26%	-4.41%	-4.56%	-4.26%	-4.41%	-4.57%
Total Exports to RW	-1.47%	-2.67%	-2.91%	1.66%	1.26%	1.03%	1.63%	1.15%	0.84%
Total Imports from RW	-1.62%	-1.82%	-1.88%	-3.31%	-2.67%	-2.41%	-3.27%	-2.51%	-2.13%
Total Intra-EU Trade	-0.08%	0.61%	0.64%	-1.87%	-5.46%	-5.66%	-1.89%	-5.52%	-5.76%
Employment (diff. from *monde*, 10^3 persons)	-33	-50	-72	-45	-91	-132	-46	-92	-135
Disposable Income (deflated)	-0.39%	-0.43%	-0.61%	-1.12%	-1.31%	-1.58%	-1.13%	-1.35%	-1.65%

Macroeconomic Ratios (abs. diff. from *monde*)	Constraint Case			Flexible Case			Efficiency Case		
	1988	1991	1994	1988	1991	1994	1988	1991	1994
Current Account as % of GDP	0.00%	0.00%	0.00%	-1.26%	-1.22%	-1.13%	-1.25%	-1.18%	-1.07%
Public Deficit as % of GDP	0.01%	0.00%	-0.03%	-0.36%	-0.43%	-0.55%	-0.36%	-0.45%	-0.60%
Labour Productivity	-0.33%	-0.54%	-0.70%	-0.33%	-0.60%	-0.84%	-0.36%	-0.71%	-1.02%
Investment/GDP	-0.16%	-0.12%	-0.18%	-1.91%	-1.87%	-1.85%	-1.90%	-1.85%	-1.81%
Priv.Cons./GDP	0.07%	0.22%	0.28%	-0.33%	-0.15%	-0.05%	-0.32%	-0.11%	0.03%

Deflators (% change from *monde*)	Constraint Case			Flexible Case			Efficiency Case		
	1988	1991	1994	1988	1991	1994	1988	1991	1994
Consumer Price Index	0.78%	1.61%	1.78%	0.84%	0.69%	0.67%	0.83%	0.64%	0.59%
Real Wage Rate	-0.57%	-0.91%	-1.23%	-0.63%	-1.24%	-1.77%	-0.66%	-1.35%	-1.96%
Marginal Costs	0.73%	1.62%	1.78%	0.52%	0.35%	0.30%	0.51%	0.32%	0.25%
Producer Prices	0.79%	1.69%	1.85%	0.58%	0.45%	0.40%	0.57%	0.42%	0.35%
Average change in mark-ups (abs. diff.)	0.44%	0.55%	0.57%	0.50%	0.82%	0.86%	0.50%	0.82%	0.86%
Shadow Price of Capital	0.48%	1.48%	1.64%	-0.03%	0.33%	0.71%	-0.05%	0.24%	0.55%
Terms-of-Trade RW	0.13%	0.98%	1.16%	-5.24%	-3.96%	-3.24%	-5.15%	-3.62%	-2.64%

| Implicit change in real exchange rate | 0.74% | 1.76% | 1.93% | -4.34% | -2.82% | -2.02% | -4.24% | -2.45% | -1.37% |

Trade Regime	Segmentation			Segmentation			Segmentation		

Table B8.2.
The full *antimonde* scenario: effects on IC sectors for Italy

% change from *monde*

Metal Industries	Constraint Case			Flexible Case			Efficiency Case		
	1988	1991	1994	1988	1991	1994	1988	1991	1994
Production per firm	-4.63%	-6.00%	-6.19%	-3.77%	-5.97%	-6.30%	-3.80%	-6.08%	-6.48%
Real Marginal Costs	1.01%	1.83%	2.03%	-2.37%	-0.53%	0.68%	-2.26%	-0.08%	1.47%
Real Producer Prices	1.56%	2.55%	2.77%	-1.93%	0.17%	1.41%	-1.81%	0.63%	2.22%
Mark-ups domestic (abs. diff.)	0.64%	0.75%	0.77%	0.66%	0.82%	0.86%	0.66%	0.83%	0.88%
Fixed Costs per firm	0.87%	1.57%	1.68%	-2.93%	-1.79%	-1.18%	-2.86%	-1.50%	-0.68%
Number of Firms	4.87%	5.52%	5.37%	6.94%	11.58%	10.92%	6.92%	11.45%	10.70%
Sigma of Love of Variety	0.00%	0.00%	0.00%	0.00%	0.00%	0.00%	0.00%	0.00%	0.00%

Chemical	Constraint Case			Flexible Case			Efficiency Case		
	1988	1991	1994	1988	1991	1994	1988	1991	1994
Production per firm	-3.76%	-4.92%	-5.04%	-2.16%	-3.92%	-4.17%	-2.18%	-4.02%	-4.34%
Real Marginal Costs	0.87%	1.68%	1.87%	-2.53%	-0.67%	0.55%	-2.41%	-0.22%	1.34%
Real Producer Prices	1.06%	1.92%	2.12%	-2.41%	-0.47%	0.75%	-2.30%	-0.02%	1.55%
Mark-ups domestic (abs. diff.)	0.22%	0.25%	0.26%	0.15%	0.22%	0.23%	0.15%	0.22%	0.23%
Fixed Costs per firm	0.73%	1.41%	1.50%	-3.04%	-1.92%	-1.33%	-2.97%	-1.62%	-0.82%
Number of Firms	3.32%	3.81%	3.77%	6.60%	9.39%	9.09%	6.58%	9.29%	8.92%
Sigma of Love of Variety	0.00%	0.00%	0.00%	0.00%	0.00%	0.00%	0.00%	0.00%	0.00%

Other Intensive Industries	Constraint Case			Flexible Case			Efficiency Case		
	1988	1991	1994	1988	1991	1994	1988	1991	1994
Production per firm	-0.82%	-1.28%	-1.43%	-1.28%	-2.13%	-2.37%	-1.29%	-2.19%	-2.47%
Real Marginal Costs	0.81%	1.67%	1.83%	-3.01%	-1.10%	0.13%	-2.90%	-0.64%	0.94%
Real Producer Prices	0.83%	1.69%	1.86%	-2.98%	-1.05%	0.19%	-2.86%	-0.59%	0.99%
Mark-ups domestic (abs. diff.)	0.02%	0.02%	0.02%	0.04%	0.05%	0.05%	0.04%	0.05%	0.05%
Fixed Costs per firm	0.69%	1.42%	1.49%	-3.56%	-2.41%	-1.85%	-3.48%	-2.12%	-1.33%
Number of Firms	0.73%	0.84%	0.71%	-0.50%	-0.36%	-0.57%	-0.50%	-0.37%	-0.59%
Sigma of Love of Variety	0.00%	0.00%	0.00%	0.00%	0.00%	0.00%	0.00%	0.00%	0.00%

Electrical goods	Constraint Case			Flexible Case			Efficiency Case		
	1988	1991	1994	1988	1991	1994	1988	1991	1994
Production per firm	-3.33%	-4.75%	-5.04%	-4.23%	-7.02%	-7.32%	-4.26%	-7.13%	-7.51%
Real Marginal Costs	0.89%	1.73%	1.89%	-2.96%	-1.05%	0.17%	-2.84%	-0.59%	0.99%
Real Producer Prices	1.14%	2.09%	2.27%	-2.64%	-0.53%	0.70%	-2.52%	-0.06%	1.53%
Mark-ups domestic (abs. diff.)	0.28%	0.32%	0.35%	0.50%	0.60%	0.62%	0.50%	0.61%	0.62%
Fixed Costs per firm	0.78%	1.50%	1.57%	-3.52%	-2.36%	-1.80%	-3.44%	-2.06%	-1.27%
Number of Firms	4.11%	4.95%	4.58%	3.01%	5.63%	5.23%	2.99%	5.52%	5.05%
Sigma of Love of Variety	0.00%	0.00%	0.00%	0.00%	0.00%	0.00%	0.00%	0.00%	0.00%

Transport equipment	Constraint Case			Flexible Case			Efficiency Case		
	1988	1991	1994	1988	1991	1994	1988	1991	1994
Production per firm	-5.94%	-8.88%	-9.31%	-7.53%	-10.74%	-10.93%	-7.55%	-10.82%	-11.07%
Real Marginal Costs	0.90%	1.74%	1.89%	-2.94%	-1.04%	0.15%	-2.83%	-0.57%	0.97%
Real Producer Prices	1.34%	2.42%	2.60%	-2.41%	-0.28%	0.92%	-2.29%	0.19%	1.75%
Mark-ups domestic (abs. diff.)	0.46%	0.65%	0.73%	0.94%	1.12%	1.12%	0.94%	1.12%	1.12%
Fixed Costs per firm	0.79%	1.52%	1.58%	-3.52%	-2.35%	-1.80%	-3.45%	-2.05%	-1.27%
Number of Firms	11.77%	12.41%	11.58%	8.74%	18.02%	17.83%	8.73%	17.98%	17.77%
Sigma of Love of Variety	0.00%	0.00%	0.00%	0.00%	0.00%	0.00%	0.00%	0.00%	0.00%

Other Equipment	Constraint Case			Flexible Case			Efficiency Case		
	1988	1991	1994	1988	1991	1994	1988	1991	1994
Production per firm	-3.70%	-5.04%	-5.20%	-3.63%	-5.61%	-5.90%	-3.66%	-5.71%	-6.07%
Real Marginal Costs	0.85%	1.70%	1.86%	-3.04%	-1.12%	0.10%	-2.92%	-0.66%	0.92%
Real Producer Prices	0.94%	1.83%	1.99%	-2.94%	-0.98%	0.25%	-2.83%	-0.51%	1.07%
Mark-ups domestic (abs. diff.)	0.12%	0.14%	0.14%	0.17%	0.21%	0.22%	0.17%	0.22%	0.22%
Fixed Costs per firm	0.73%	1.46%	1.53%	-3.60%	-2.44%	-1.88%	-3.53%	-2.14%	-1.34%
Number of Firms	3.81%	4.62%	4.37%	2.31%	3.35%	2.86%	2.28%	3.24%	2.66%
Sigma of Love of Variety	0.00%	0.00%	0.00%	0.00%	0.00%	0.00%	0.00%	0.00%	0.00%

Telecommunications	Constraint Case			Flexible Case			Efficiency Case		
	1988	1991	1994	1988	1991	1994	1988	1991	1994
Production per firm	-0.23%	0.14%	0.05%	-1.08%	-2.46%	-2.74%	-1.09%	-2.52%	-2.83%
Real Marginal Costs	0.88%	1.97%	2.09%	-3.78%	-1.78%	-0.53%	-3.66%	-1.32%	0.30%
Real Producer Prices	1.15%	2.41%	2.51%	-3.89%	-1.98%	-0.73%	-3.78%	-1.52%	0.08%
Mark-ups domestic (abs. diff.)	0.30%	0.47%	0.43%	-0.20%	-0.49%	-0.50%	-0.20%	-0.50%	-0.52%
Fixed Costs per firm	1.74%	3.89%	3.83%	-5.88%	-6.17%	-5.77%	-5.81%	-5.90%	-5.30%
Number of Firms	-0.27%	-0.60%	-0.53%	0.98%	1.98%	2.00%	0.98%	2.00%	2.04%
Sigma of Love of Variety	0.00%	0.00%	0.00%	0.00%	0.00%	0.00%	0.00%	0.00%	0.00%

Banks	Constraint Case			Flexible Case			Efficiency Case		
	1988	1991	1994	1988	1991	1994	1988	1991	1994
Production per firm	-0.39%	-0.29%	-0.36%	-0.94%	-1.90%	-2.08%	-0.96%	-1.95%	-2.18%
Real Marginal Costs	0.82%	1.90%	2.00%	-3.83%	-1.79%	-0.50%	-3.71%	-1.32%	0.31%
Real Producer Prices	0.91%	2.02%	2.11%	-3.84%	-1.84%	-0.56%	-3.73%	-1.38%	0.25%
Mark-ups domestic (abs. diff.)	0.08%	0.09%	0.08%	-0.05%	-0.13%	-0.14%	-0.05%	-0.13%	-0.14%
Fixed Costs per firm	1.33%	2.75%	2.72%	-5.53%	-5.34%	-4.87%	-5.46%	-5.06%	-4.38%
Number of Firms	1.11%	1.25%	1.31%	2.66%	4.42%	4.57%	2.66%	4.44%	4.59%
Sigma of Love of Variety	0.00%	0.00%	0.00%	0.00%	0.00%	0.00%	0.00%	0.00%	0.00%

Table B8.3.
The full *antimonde* scenario: sectoral results for Italy (volumes)

% change from *monde*

Agriculture	Constraint Case			Flexible Case			Efficiency Case		
	1988	1991	1994	1988	1991	1994	1988	1991	1994
Domestic Production - vol.	-0.5%	-0.8%	-0.9%	2.9%	1.7%	1.2%	2.9%	1.6%	0.9%
Imports - vol.	-1.7%	-0.6%	-0.4%	-3.8%	-3.0%	-2.4%	-3.8%	-2.7%	-2.0%
Exports - vol.	-3.6%	-5.5%	-6.0%	1.6%	1.2%	0.9%	1.6%	1.0%	0.7%
Absorption - vol.	-0.5%	-0.4%	-0.5%	0.9%	0.1%	-0.3%	0.9%	0.0%	-0.4%
Investment - vol.	3.4%	3.0%	2.2%	-2.9%	-3.4%	-3.7%	-2.9%	-3.5%	-3.8%
Labour Demand - vol.	-0.4%	-0.6%	-0.6%	3.1%	2.1%	1.9%	3.0%	2.0%	1.7%
Private Consumption - vol.	-1.0%	-0.6%	-0.6%	-0.7%	-1.1%	-1.3%	-0.7%	-1.1%	-1.4%
Supply to domestic - vol.	-0.2%	-0.4%	-0.5%	2.8%	1.9%	1.3%	2.8%	1.7%	1.0%
Intra-EU Trade - vol	0.0%	0.0%	0.0%	-0.2%	-2.7%	-3.1%	-0.3%	-2.8%	-3.3%

Energy	Constraint Case			Flexible Case			Efficiency Case		
	1988	1991	1994	1988	1991	1994	1988	1991	1994
Domestic Production - vol.	-0.2%	-0.5%	-0.6%	1.1%	0.6%	0.2%	1.1%	0.5%	0.0%
Imports - vol.	0.1%	0.5%	0.5%	-0.9%	-0.8%	-0.7%	-0.9%	-0.7%	-0.7%
Exports - vol.	-1.9%	-2.7%	-3.0%	0.6%	0.4%	0.3%	0.6%	0.4%	0.3%
Absorption - vol.	0.0%	0.0%	0.0%	0.1%	-0.1%	-0.4%	0.1%	-0.1%	-0.5%
Investment - vol.	-4.8%	-5.0%	-5.3%	-3.5%	-3.8%	-3.9%	-3.5%	-3.8%	-4.0%
Labour Demand - vol.	-0.2%	-0.4%	-0.5%	1.4%	0.9%	0.6%	1.4%	0.9%	0.5%
Private Consumption - vol.	0.1%	0.5%	0.5%	-0.8%	-1.1%	-1.3%	-0.8%	-1.1%	-1.3%
Supply to domestic - vol.	-0.1%	-0.3%	-0.4%	1.2%	0.7%	0.3%	1.2%	0.6%	0.1%
Intra-EU Trade - vol	0.0%	0.0%	0.0%	0.6%	-0.2%	-0.2%	0.5%	-0.2%	-0.3%

Metal Industries	Constraint Case			Flexible Case			Efficiency Case		
	1988	1991	1994	1988	1991	1994	1988	1991	1994
Domestic Production - vol.	0.0%	-0.8%	-1.2%	2.9%	4.9%	3.9%	2.9%	4.7%	3.5%
Imports - vol.	-0.5%	-0.4%	-0.5%	-3.5%	-2.6%	-2.4%	-3.4%	-2.4%	-2.1%
Exports - vol.	-2.5%	-4.0%	-4.2%	1.5%	1.1%	0.9%	1.4%	1.0%	0.7%
Absorption - vol.	0.4%	0.0%	-0.3%	-0.4%	0.2%	-0.4%	-0.4%	0.1%	-0.5%
Investment - vol.	-2.3%	-3.2%	-3.8%	-2.7%	-1.8%	-2.3%	-2.7%	-1.9%	-2.4%
Labour Demand - vol.	0.7%	0.1%	-0.2%	3.6%	6.0%	5.1%	3.6%	5.8%	4.8%
Private Consumption - vol.	#DIV/0!	#DIV/0!	#DIV/0!	#DIV/0!	#DIV/0!	#DIV/0!	#DIV/0!	#DIV/0!	#DIV/0!
Supply to domestic - vol.	0.8%	0.2%	-0.2%	3.3%	7.5%	6.4%	3.2%	7.2%	6.0%
Intra-EU Trade - vol	0.0%	0.0%	0.0%	-2.6%	-8.1%	-8.1%	-2.6%	-8.1%	-8.2%

Chemical	Constraint Case			Flexible Case			Efficiency Case		
	1988	1991	1994	1988	1991	1994	1988	1991	1994
Domestic Production - vol.	-0.6%	-1.3%	-1.5%	4.3%	5.1%	4.5%	4.3%	4.9%	4.2%
Imports - vol.	-0.5%	0.6%	0.7%	-4.0%	-3.2%	-2.8%	-4.0%	-2.9%	-2.4%
Exports - vol.	-1.5%	-2.6%	-2.9%	1.8%	1.4%	1.2%	1.8%	1.3%	1.0%
Absorption - vol.	-0.3%	-0.5%	-0.6%	1.4%	1.4%	1.0%	1.4%	1.3%	0.9%
Investment - vol.	-2.8%	-3.5%	-4.0%	-2.1%	-1.8%	-2.0%	-2.1%	-1.8%	-2.1%
Labour Demand - vol.	-0.3%	-0.9%	-1.1%	4.6%	5.6%	5.2%	4.6%	5.5%	4.9%
Private Consumption - vol.	-1.0%	-0.6%	-0.6%	-0.6%	-1.0%	-1.2%	-0.6%	-1.0%	-1.3%
Supply to domestic - vol.	-0.3%	-0.9%	-1.1%	4.6%	6.8%	6.2%	4.6%	6.6%	5.8%
Intra-EU Trade - vol	0.0%	0.0%	0.0%	-1.3%	-5.5%	-5.7%	-1.3%	-5.6%	-5.8%

Other Intensive Industries	Constraint Case			Flexible Case			Efficiency Case		
	1988	1991	1994	1988	1991	1994	1988	1991	1994
Domestic Production - vol.	-0.1%	-0.5%	-0.7%	-1.8%	-2.5%	-2.9%	-1.8%	-2.6%	-3.0%
Imports - vol.	-3.5%	-3.4%	-3.4%	-6.3%	-5.2%	-4.8%	-6.2%	-4.9%	-4.2%
Exports - vol.	-1.9%	-3.1%	-3.3%	1.7%	1.3%	1.1%	1.7%	1.2%	0.9%
Absorption - vol.	-0.1%	-0.3%	-0.5%	-2.7%	-2.9%	-3.2%	-2.7%	-2.9%	-3.3%
Investment - vol.	-2.2%	-2.5%	-3.1%	-5.0%	-5.3%	-5.5%	-5.0%	-5.3%	-5.5%
Labour Demand - vol.	0.0%	-0.3%	-0.6%	-1.6%	-2.2%	-2.5%	-1.6%	-2.2%	-2.5%
Private Consumption - vol.	-1.0%	-0.7%	-0.7%	-1.1%	-1.4%	-1.7%	-1.1%	-1.4%	-1.8%
Supply to domestic - vol.	0.2%	0.0%	-0.3%	-2.0%	-1.9%	-2.3%	-2.0%	-1.9%	-2.4%
Intra-EU Trade - vol	0.0%	0.0%	0.0%	-3.1%	-7.0%	-7.2%	-3.1%	-7.1%	-7.3%

Electrical goods	Constraint Case			Flexible Case			Efficiency Case		
	1988	1991	1994	1988	1991	1994	1988	1991	1994
Domestic Production - vol.	0.7%	0.0%	-0.7%	-1.3%	-1.8%	-2.5%	-1.4%	-2.0%	-2.8%
Imports - vol.	-4.3%	-6.1%	-6.6%	-6.9%	-5.8%	-5.4%	-6.9%	-5.5%	-4.9%
Exports - vol.	-2.0%	-3.6%	-3.9%	2.0%	1.6%	1.3%	2.0%	1.4%	1.1%
Absorption - vol.	0.1%	-0.6%	-1.3%	-4.6%	-4.2%	-4.5%	-4.6%	-4.2%	-4.6%
Investment - vol.	2.4%	1.7%	0.4%	-4.8%	-5.0%	-5.4%	-4.8%	-5.1%	-5.5%
Labour Demand - vol.	1.1%	0.6%	0.0%	-0.6%	-0.7%	-1.2%	-0.7%	-0.9%	-1.5%
Private Consumption - vol.	4.6%	1.7%	-0.7%	-5.1%	-2.6%	-2.5%	-5.1%	-2.7%	-2.7%
Supply to domestic - vol.	1.8%	1.6%	0.8%	-1.8%	0.5%	-0.1%	-1.9%	0.3%	-0.5%
Intra-EU Trade - vol	0.0%	0.0%	0.0%	-3.5%	-8.1%	-8.2%	-3.5%	-8.1%	-8.3%

Transport equipment	Constraint Case			Flexible Case			Efficiency Case		
	1988	1991	1994	1988	1991	1994	1988	1991	1994
Domestic Production - vol.	5.1%	2.4%	1.2%	0.6%	5.3%	5.0%	0.5%	5.2%	4.7%
Imports - vol.	-0.2%	-6.8%	-8.3%	-6.8%	-5.5%	-5.1%	-6.7%	-5.3%	-4.7%
Exports - vol.	-1.8%	-3.4%	-3.7%	2.1%	1.7%	1.4%	2.0%	1.5%	1.2%
Absorption - vol.	6.1%	1.5%	-0.2%	-4.8%	-3.4%	-3.4%	-4.8%	-3.4%	-3.5%
Investment - vol.	7.1%	4.2%	2.4%	-3.8%	-1.7%	-1.9%	-3.9%	-1.7%	-2.0%
Labour Demand - vol.	5.8%	3.4%	2.3%	1.5%	6.8%	6.6%	1.5%	6.7%	6.5%
Private Consumption - vol.	23.1%	5.9%	-0.3%	-5.1%	-2.2%	-1.7%	-5.2%	-2.3%	-1.8%
Supply to domestic - vol.	9.6%	6.4%	4.6%	0.1%	9.4%	9.1%	0.1%	9.3%	8.9%
Intra-EU Trade - vol	0.0%	0.0%	0.0%	-4.3%	-9.1%	-9.1%	-4.4%	-9.1%	-9.1%

Other Equipment	Constraint Case			Flexible Case			Efficiency Case		
	1988	1991	1994	1988	1991	1994	1988	1991	1994
Domestic Production - vol.	0.0%	-0.7%	-1.1%	-1.4%	-2.5%	-3.2%	-1.5%	-2.7%	-3.6%
Imports - vol.	-2.2%	-2.6%	-3.0%	-5.7%	-5.1%	-4.9%	-5.7%	-4.9%	-4.6%
Exports - vol.	-1.7%	-2.7%	-3.0%	1.9%	1.4%	1.1%	1.8%	1.3%	0.9%
Absorption - vol.	0.3%	0.0%	-0.5%	-5.2%	-5.5%	-5.9%	-5.2%	-5.6%	-6.1%
Investment - vol.	5.9%	5.1%	3.9%	-4.9%	-5.4%	-5.8%	-4.9%	-5.5%	-5.9%
Labour Demand - vol.	0.2%	-0.3%	-0.6%	-1.0%	-1.8%	-2.4%	-1.0%	-1.9%	-2.6%
Private Consumption - vol.	-1.2%	-0.8%	-0.9%	-1.3%	-1.6%	-2.0%	-1.3%	-1.7%	-2.1%
Supply to domestic - vol.	1.3%	1.1%	0.5%	-2.8%	-1.8%	-2.5%	-2.8%	-2.0%	-2.8%
Intra-EU Trade - vol	0.0%	0.0%	0.0%	-3.1%	-6.2%	-6.5%	-3.1%	-6.3%	-6.6%

Consumer goods	Constraint Case			Flexible Case			Efficiency Case		
	1988	1991	1994	1988	1991	1994	1988	1991	1994
Domestic Production - vol.	-0.5%	-0.7%	-0.8%	1.6%	0.3%	-0.2%	1.5%	0.1%	-0.5%
Imports - vol.	-3.6%	-3.2%	-3.0%	-4.9%	-3.9%	-3.4%	-4.8%	-3.7%	-2.9%
Exports - vol.	-2.1%	-3.4%	-3.7%	2.3%	1.7%	1.4%	2.3%	1.6%	1.2%
Absorption - vol.	-0.6%	-0.5%	-0.5%	-0.2%	-0.7%	-1.0%	-0.2%	-0.7%	-1.1%
Investment - vol.	5.3%	5.0%	4.1%	-3.5%	-4.1%	-4.4%	-3.5%	-4.2%	-4.5%
Labour Demand - vol.	-0.4%	-0.5%	-0.6%	1.8%	0.7%	0.4%	1.8%	0.6%	0.2%
Private Consumption - vol.	-0.9%	-0.5%	-0.5%	-0.6%	-1.0%	-1.2%	-0.7%	-1.0%	-1.3%
Supply to domestic - vol.	-0.1%	0.0%	-0.1%	1.2%	0.8%	0.3%	1.2%	0.6%	0.1%
Intra-EU Trade - vol	0.0%	0.0%	0.0%	-0.7%	-3.7%	-4.0%	-0.7%	-3.8%	-4.1%

Construction	Constraint Case			Flexible Case			Efficiency Case		
	1988	1991	1994	1988	1991	1994	1988	1991	1994
Domestic Production - vol.	-1.4%	-1.5%	-1.8%	-7.5%	-7.7%	-7.9%	-7.5%	-7.7%	-7.9%
Imports - vol.	-1.4%	-1.5%	-1.8%	#VALUE!	#VALUE!	#VALUE!	#VALUE!	#VALUE!	#VALUE!
Exports - vol.	-0.1%	-0.7%	-0.8%	0.5%	0.4%	0.3%	0.5%	0.3%	0.2%
Absorption - vol.	-1.4%	-1.5%	-1.8%	-7.5%	-7.7%	-7.9%	-7.5%	-7.7%	-7.9%
Investment - vol.	0.1%	0.0%	-0.9%	-7.7%	-7.9%	-8.0%	-7.7%	-7.8%	-7.9%
Labour Demand - vol.	-1.4%	-1.3%	-1.6%	-7.3%	-7.4%	-7.5%	-7.3%	-7.3%	-7.4%
Private Consumption - vol.	-1.2%	-0.7%	-0.7%	-0.7%	-1.2%	-1.5%	-0.7%	-1.2%	-1.6%
Supply to domestic - vol.	-1.4%	-1.5%	-1.8%	-7.5%	-7.7%	-7.9%	-7.5%	-7.7%	-7.9%
Intra-EU Trade - vol	0.0%	0.0%	0.0%	-3.7%	-3.8%	-3.9%	-3.7%	-3.8%	-3.9%

Telecommunications	Constraint Case			Flexible Case			Efficiency Case		
	1988	1991	1994	1988	1991	1994	1988	1991	1994
Domestic Production - vol.	-0.5%	-0.5%	-0.5%	-0.1%	-0.5%	-0.8%	-0.1%	-0.6%	-0.9%
Imports - vol.	-3.3%	-3.0%	-3.0%	-5.5%	-5.2%	-4.9%	-5.5%	-5.0%	-4.6%
Exports - vol.	-3.2%	-5.8%	-5.9%	1.1%	0.9%	0.8%	1.1%	0.8%	0.7%
Absorption - vol.	-0.5%	-0.4%	-0.4%	-0.3%	-0.4%	-0.7%	-0.3%	-0.5%	-0.8%
Investment - vol.	-4.2%	-3.7%	-3.8%	-4.2%	-4.4%	-4.5%	-4.2%	-4.3%	-4.4%
Labour Demand - vol.	0.3%	1.0%	1.0%	-0.3%	-0.9%	-1.0%	-0.3%	-0.9%	-0.9%
Private Consumption - vol.	-1.4%	-1.1%	-1.0%	-0.7%	-1.1%	-1.4%	-0.7%	-1.1%	-1.5%
Supply to domestic - vol.	-0.4%	-0.3%	-0.3%	0.0%	0.1%	-0.1%	0.0%	0.1%	-0.2%
Intra-EU Trade - vol	0.0%	0.0%	0.0%	-5.4%	-15.9%	-15.9%	-5.4%	-15.9%	-16.0%

Transports	Constraint Case			Flexible Case			Efficiency Case		
	1988	1991	1994	1988	1991	1994	1988	1991	1994
Domestic Production - vol.	-0.2%	-0.4%	-0.4%	-0.2%	-0.3%	-0.7%	-0.2%	-0.4%	-0.7%
Imports - vol.	-0.2%	-0.4%	-0.4%	-0.1%	-0.2%	-0.3%	-0.1%	-0.2%	-0.4%
Exports - vol.	-0.1%	-0.6%	-0.6%	0.7%	0.5%	0.4%	0.6%	0.5%	0.4%
Absorption - vol.	-0.3%	-0.3%	-0.4%	-0.8%	-0.9%	-1.2%	-0.8%	-0.9%	-1.3%
Investment - vol.	-4.8%	-4.9%	-5.2%	-4.2%	-4.3%	-4.4%	-4.2%	-4.3%	-4.4%
Labour Demand - vol.	-0.2%	-0.3%	-0.3%	-0.1%	-0.1%	-0.3%	-0.1%	-0.1%	-0.3%
Private Consumption - vol.	-1.0%	-0.6%	-0.7%	-1.0%	-1.3%	-1.6%	-1.0%	-1.4%	-1.7%
Supply to domestic - vol.	-0.2%	-0.4%	-0.4%	-0.2%	-0.3%	-0.7%	-0.2%	-0.4%	-0.7%
Intra-EU Trade - vol	0.0%	0.0%	0.0%	1.3%	1.5%	1.3%	1.3%	1.4%	1.3%

Banks	Constraint Case			Flexible Case			Efficiency Case		
	1988	1991	1994	1988	1991	1994	1988	1991	1994
Domestic Production - vol.	0.7%	1.0%	0.9%	1.7%	2.4%	2.4%	1.7%	2.4%	2.3%
Imports - vol.	-7.9%	-9.8%	-9.7%	-5.4%	-4.4%	-4.0%	-5.4%	-4.2%	-3.6%
Exports - vol.	-1.0%	-1.9%	-1.6%	1.1%	0.9%	0.7%	1.1%	0.8%	0.7%
Absorption - vol.	0.4%	0.6%	0.6%	1.1%	1.5%	1.4%	1.1%	1.5%	1.3%
Investment - vol.	-1.3%	-0.7%	-1.1%	-3.5%	-3.1%	-3.1%	-3.5%	-3.1%	-3.1%
Labour Demand - vol.	1.1%	1.6%	1.6%	1.7%	2.5%	2.6%	1.7%	2.5%	2.7%
Private Consumption - vol.	-1.6%	-0.9%	-0.9%	-1.1%	-1.7%	-2.1%	-1.1%	-1.7%	-2.2%
Supply to domestic - vol.	0.8%	1.1%	1.1%	1.8%	3.0%	2.9%	1.8%	3.0%	2.9%
Intra-EU Trade - vol	0.0%	0.0%	0.0%	-4.6%	-10.9%	-11.2%	-4.6%	-10.9%	-11.2%

Services	Constraint Case			Flexible Case			Efficiency Case		
	1988	1991	1994	1988	1991	1994	1988	1991	1994
Domestic Production - vol.	-0.4%	-0.3%	-0.4%	-0.7%	-1.0%	-1.3%	-0.7%	-1.1%	-1.4%
Imports - vol.	-2.4%	-1.6%	-1.5%	-3.4%	-2.5%	-2.1%	-3.3%	-2.3%	-1.8%
Exports - vol.	2.0%	1.1%	0.9%	1.1%	0.7%	0.5%	1.0%	0.7%	0.4%
Absorption - vol.	-0.5%	-0.4%	-0.5%	-0.9%	-1.1%	-1.4%	-0.9%	-1.1%	-1.5%
Investment - vol.	-0.7%	-0.7%	-1.2%	-4.5%	-4.6%	-4.8%	-4.5%	-4.6%	-4.8%
Labour Demand - vol.	-0.3%	-0.2%	-0.2%	-0.5%	-0.7%	-0.8%	-0.5%	-0.6%	-0.8%
Private Consumption - vol.	-0.8%	-0.6%	-0.7%	-1.0%	-1.3%	-1.6%	-1.0%	-1.3%	-1.7%
Supply to domestic - vol.	-0.4%	-0.4%	-0.5%	-0.9%	-1.3%	-1.6%	-0.9%	-1.3%	-1.7%
Intra-EU Trade - vol	0.0%	0.0%	0.0%	2.2%	4.8%	4.8%	2.2%	4.8%	4.8%

Non market	Constraint Case			Flexible Case			Efficiency Case		
	1988	1991	1994	1988	1991	1994	1988	1991	1994
Domestic Production - vol.	0.0%	0.0%	0.0%	0.0%	0.0%	0.0%	0.0%	0.0%	-0.1%
Imports - vol.	-	-	-	#VALUE!	#VALUE!	#VALUE!	#VALUE!	#VALUE!	#VALUE!
Exports - vol.	0.6%	0.3%	0.3%	0.3%	0.2%	0.2%	0.3%	0.2%	0.2%
Absorption - vol.	0.0%	0.0%	0.0%	0.0%	0.0%	0.0%	0.0%	0.0%	-0.1%
Investment - vol.	-6.8%	-6.8%	-6.8%	-4.1%	-4.1%	-4.1%	-4.1%	-4.1%	-4.1%
Labour Demand - vol.	0.0%	0.0%	0.0%	0.1%	0.1%	0.1%	0.1%	0.2%	0.2%
Private Consumption - vol.	-0.4%	-0.3%	-0.4%	-0.6%	-0.7%	-0.9%	-0.6%	-0.7%	-0.9%
Supply to domestic - vol.	0.0%	0.0%	0.0%	0.0%	0.0%	0.0%	0.0%	0.0%	-0.1%
Intra-EU Trade - vol	0.0%	0.0%	0.0%	0.4%	0.3%	0.3%	0.4%	0.3%	0.3%

Table B8.4.
The full *antimonde* scenario: sectoral results for Italy (prices)

% change from *monde*

Agriculture	Constraint Case			Flexible Case			Efficiency Case		
	1988	1991	1994	1988	1991	1994	1988	1991	1994
Real Marginal Costs	0.72%	1.65%	1.84%	0.47%	0.44%	0.52%	0.46%	0.42%	0.47%
Real Cost of Labour	0.16%	0.85%	0.70%	-0.63%	-1.24%	-1.77%	-0.66%	-1.35%	-1.96%
Real Deflator of Absorption	0.74%	1.48%	1.63%	1.23%	1.01%	0.98%	1.21%	0.94%	0.86%
Real Price of Exports-RW	0.72%	1.65%	1.84%	0.47%	0.44%	0.52%	0.46%	0.42%	0.47%

Energy	Constraint Case			Flexible Case			Efficiency Case		
	1988	1991	1994	1988	1991	1994	1988	1991	1994
Marginal Costs	0.75%	1.42%	1.60%	2.05%	1.54%	1.31%	2.01%	1.39%	1.05%
Cost of Labour	0.16%	0.85%	0.70%	-0.63%	-1.24%	-1.77%	-0.66%	-1.35%	-1.96%
Deflator of Absorption	0.65%	1.04%	1.14%	3.40%	2.54%	2.12%	3.35%	2.32%	1.72%
Price of Exports-RW	0.75%	1.42%	1.60%	2.05%	1.54%	1.31%	2.01%	1.39%	1.05%

Metal Industries	Constraint Case			Flexible Case			Efficiency Case		
	1988	1991	1994	1988	1991	1994	1988	1991	1994
Marginal Costs	1.01%	1.83%	2.03%	1.33%	1.05%	0.94%	1.32%	1.02%	0.88%
Cost of Labour	0.16%	0.85%	0.70%	-0.63%	-1.24%	-1.77%	-0.66%	-1.35%	-1.96%
Deflator of Absorption	1.33%	1.94%	2.10%	2.52%	2.09%	1.89%	2.50%	2.01%	1.75%
Price of Exports-RW	1.87%	3.52%	3.74%	1.14%	0.72%	0.62%	1.13%	0.69%	0.57%

Chemical	Constraint Case			Flexible Case			Efficiency Case		
	1988	1991	1994	1988	1991	1994	1988	1991	1994
Marginal Costs	0.87%	1.68%	1.87%	1.18%	0.91%	0.80%	1.17%	0.88%	0.75%
Cost of Labour	0.16%	0.85%	0.70%	-0.63%	-1.24%	-1.77%	-0.66%	-1.35%	-1.96%
Deflator of Absorption	0.94%	1.54%	1.68%	2.07%	1.69%	1.51%	2.05%	1.62%	1.40%
Price of Exports-RW	1.15%	2.25%	2.44%	1.10%	0.80%	0.69%	1.10%	0.78%	0.65%

Other Intensive Industries	Constraint Case			Flexible Case			Efficiency Case		
	1988	1991	1994	1988	1991	1994	1988	1991	1994
Marginal Costs	0.81%	1.67%	1.83%	0.69%	0.47%	0.38%	0.69%	0.45%	0.34%
Cost of Labour	0.16%	0.85%	0.70%	-0.63%	-1.24%	-1.77%	-0.66%	-1.35%	-1.96%
Deflator of Absorption	0.85%	1.64%	1.79%	0.97%	0.71%	0.60%	0.96%	0.68%	0.54%
Price of Exports-RW	0.86%	1.80%	1.97%	0.69%	0.48%	0.39%	0.69%	0.45%	0.35%

Electrical goods	Constraint Case			Flexible Case			Efficiency Case		
	1988	1991	1994	1988	1991	1994	1988	1991	1994
Marginal Costs	0.89%	1.73%	1.89%	0.75%	0.52%	0.42%	0.74%	0.51%	0.39%
Cost of Labour	0.16%	0.85%	0.70%	-0.63%	-1.24%	-1.77%	-0.66%	-1.35%	-1.96%
Deflator of Absorption	1.25%	1.88%	2.03%	1.85%	1.51%	1.33%	1.84%	1.46%	1.24%
Price of Exports-RW	1.17%	2.50%	2.67%	0.69%	0.42%	0.32%	0.69%	0.41%	0.30%

Transport equipment	Constraint Case			Flexible Case			Efficiency Case		
	1988	1991	1994	1988	1991	1994	1988	1991	1994
Marginal Costs	0.90%	1.74%	1.89%	0.76%	0.54%	0.41%	0.76%	0.52%	0.38%
Cost of Labour	0.16%	0.85%	0.70%	-0.63%	-1.24%	-1.77%	-0.66%	-1.35%	-1.96%
Deflator of Absorption	1.60%	2.29%	2.44%	2.17%	2.06%	1.87%	2.16%	2.03%	1.81%
Price of Exports-RW	1.39%	2.94%	3.12%	0.57%	0.12%	0.00%	0.56%	0.11%	-0.03%

Other Equipment	Constraint Case			Flexible Case			Efficiency Case		
	1988	1991	1994	1988	1991	1994	1988	1991	1994
Marginal Costs	0.85%	1.70%	1.86%	0.67%	0.45%	0.36%	0.66%	0.44%	0.33%
Cost of Labour	0.16%	0.85%	0.70%	-0.63%	-1.24%	-1.77%	-0.66%	-1.35%	-1.96%
Deflator of Absorption	1.05%	1.65%	1.77%	1.57%	1.22%	1.04%	1.55%	1.17%	0.94%
Price of Exports-RW	0.98%	1.96%	2.12%	0.65%	0.44%	0.34%	0.65%	0.42%	0.32%

Consumer goods	Constraint Case			Flexible Case			Efficiency Case		
	1988	1991	1994	1988	1991	1994	1988	1991	1994
Marginal Costs	0.83%	1.70%	1.90%	0.80%	0.61%	0.56%	0.80%	0.60%	0.53%
Cost of Labour	0.16%	0.85%	0.70%	-0.63%	-1.24%	-1.77%	-0.66%	-1.35%	-1.96%
Deflator of Absorption	0.88%	1.63%	1.80%	1.33%	1.02%	0.91%	1.32%	0.98%	0.83%
Price of Exports-RW	0.83%	1.70%	1.90%	0.80%	0.61%	0.56%	0.80%	0.60%	0.53%

Construction	Constraint Case			Flexible Case			Efficiency Case		
	1988	1991	1994	1988	1991	1994	1988	1991	1994
Marginal Costs	0.77%	1.67%	1.85%	0.45%	0.33%	0.31%	0.45%	0.32%	0.28%
Cost of Labour	0.16%	0.85%	0.70%	-0.63%	-1.24%	-1.77%	-0.66%	-1.35%	-1.96%
Deflator of Absorption	0.77%	1.67%	1.85%	0.45%	0.33%	0.31%	0.45%	0.32%	0.28%
Price of Exports-RW	0.77%	1.67%	1.85%	0.45%	0.33%	0.31%	0.45%	0.32%	0.28%

Telecommunications	Constraint Case			Flexible Case			Efficiency Case		
	1988	1991	1994	1988	1991	1994	1988	1991	1994
Marginal Costs	0.88%	1.97%	2.09%	-0.08%	-0.21%	-0.27%	-0.08%	-0.22%	-0.30%
Cost of Labour	0.16%	0.85%	0.70%	-0.63%	-1.24%	-1.77%	-0.66%	-1.35%	-1.96%
Deflator of Absorption	1.12%	2.31%	2.41%	-0.13%	-0.48%	-0.56%	-0.13%	-0.50%	-0.60%
Price of Exports-RW	4.19%	7.58%	7.70%	-0.16%	-0.38%	-0.45%	-0.16%	-0.40%	-0.48%

Transports	Constraint Case			Flexible Case			Efficiency Case		
	1988	1991	1994	1988	1991	1994	1988	1991	1994
Marginal Costs	0.64%	1.51%	1.64%	0.43%	0.23%	0.15%	0.41%	0.19%	0.07%
Cost of Labour	0.16%	0.85%	0.70%	-0.63%	-1.24%	-1.77%	-0.66%	-1.35%	-1.96%
Deflator of Absorption	0.71%	1.54%	1.67%	0.49%	0.27%	0.18%	0.48%	0.22%	0.10%
Price of Exports-RW	0.64%	1.51%	1.64%	0.43%	0.23%	0.15%	0.41%	0.19%	0.07%

Banks	Constraint Case			Flexible Case			Efficiency Case		
	1988	1991	1994	1988	1991	1994	1988	1991	1994
Marginal Costs	0.82%	1.90%	2.00%	-0.12%	-0.21%	-0.25%	-0.13%	-0.23%	-0.28%
Cost of Labour	0.16%	0.85%	0.70%	-0.63%	-1.24%	-1.77%	-0.66%	-1.35%	-1.96%
Deflator of Absorption	0.95%	1.98%	2.08%	-0.05%	-0.23%	-0.28%	-0.06%	-0.25%	-0.32%
Price of Exports-RW	1.70%	3.42%	3.53%	-0.19%	-0.32%	-0.36%	-0.19%	-0.34%	-0.40%

Services	Constraint Case			Flexible Case			Efficiency Case		
	1988	1991	1994	1988	1991	1994	1988	1991	1994
Marginal Costs	0.68%	1.67%	1.86%	0.19%	0.25%	0.38%	0.19%	0.23%	0.33%
Cost of Labour	0.16%	0.85%	0.70%	-0.63%	-1.24%	-1.77%	-0.66%	-1.35%	-1.96%
Deflator of Absorption	0.69%	1.64%	1.83%	0.22%	0.26%	0.38%	0.21%	0.23%	0.33%
Price of Exports-RW	0.68%	1.67%	1.86%	0.19%	0.25%	0.38%	0.19%	0.23%	0.33%

Non market	Constraint Case			Flexible Case			Efficiency Case		
	1988	1991	1994	1988	1991	1994	1988	1991	1994
Marginal Costs	0.40%	1.15%	1.11%	-0.14%	-0.60%	-0.98%	-0.15%	-0.64%	-1.05%
Cost of Labour	0.16%	0.85%	0.70%	-0.63%	-1.24%	-1.77%	-0.66%	-1.35%	-1.96%
Deflator of Absorption	0.40%	1.15%	1.11%	-0.14%	-0.60%	-0.98%	-0.15%	-0.64%	-1.05%
Price of Exports-RW	0.40%	1.15%	1.11%	-0.14%	-0.60%	-0.98%	-0.15%	-0.64%	-1.05%

Table B8.5.
Decomposition of effects: macroeconomic aggregates for Italy

Macroeconomic Aggregates (vol.) (% change from monde)	Border Controls			Border controls and x-ineff.			Market segmentation			Trade antimonde			Full antimonde		
	1988	1991	1994	1988	1991	1994	1988	1991	1994	1988	1991	1994	1988	1991	1994
GDP fact. pr.	-0.02%	-0.05%	-0.06%	-0.03%	-0.07%	-0.08%	-0.41%	-0.81%	-1.18%	-0.43%	-0.85%	-1.22%	-0.53%	-0.99%	-1.41%
Priv. Consumption	0.16%	0.17%	0.17%	0.16%	0.16%	0.16%	-1.06%	-1.20%	-1.43%	-1.01%	-1.17%	-1.40%	-1.05%	-1.24%	-1.48%
Absorption	0.06%	0.06%	0.06%	0.06%	0.06%	0.06%	-1.27%	-1.38%	-1.64%	-1.28%	-1.41%	-1.68%	-1.31%	-1.46%	-1.75%
Total Investment	0.02%	0.03%	0.03%	0.03%	0.03%	0.03%	-4.26%	-4.40%	-4.54%	-4.25%	-4.39%	-4.54%	-4.26%	-4.41%	-4.56%
Total Exports to RW	-0.53%	-0.62%	-0.63%	-0.54%	-0.63%	-0.64%	2.01%	1.64%	1.45%	1.73%	1.35%	1.16%	1.66%	1.26%	1.03%
Total Imports from RW	1.15%	1.35%	1.35%	1.17%	1.37%	1.38%	-4.38%	-3.88%	-3.70%	-3.44%	-2.85%	-2.66%	-3.31%	-2.67%	-2.41%
Total Intra-EU Trade	-1.33%	-3.36%	-3.36%	-1.33%	-3.37%	-3.38%	-1.08%	-4.45%	-4.59%	-1.73%	-5.27%	-5.41%	-1.87%	-5.46%	-5.66%
Employment (diff. from monde, 10³ persons)	-2	-7	-7	-3	-9	-9	-40	-80	-121	-43	-86	-127	-45	-91	-132
Disposable Income (deflated)	0.17%	0.18%	0.18%	0.17%	0.17%	0.17%	-1.13%	-1.27%	-1.52%	-1.08%	-1.25%	-1.49%	-1.12%	-1.31%	-1.58%

Macroeconomic Ratios (abs. diff. from monde)	Border Controls			Border controls and x-ineff.			Market segmentation			Trade antimonde			Full antimonde		
	1988	1991	1994	1988	1991	1994	1988	1991	1994	1988	1991	1994	1988	1991	1994
Current Account as % of GDP	-0.05%	-0.05%	-0.05%	-0.05%	-0.04%	-0.04%	-1.31%	-1.30%	-1.23%	-1.30%	-1.28%	-1.21%	-1.26%	-1.22%	-1.13%
Public Deficit as % of GDP	0.10%	0.11%	0.11%	0.10%	0.10%	0.10%	-0.38%	-0.42%	-0.54%	-0.33%	-0.38%	-0.50%	-0.36%	-0.43%	-0.55%
Labour Productivity	-0.02%	-0.02%	-0.03%	-0.02%	-0.03%	-0.04%	-0.23%	-0.46%	-0.65%	-0.25%	-0.48%	-0.67%	-0.33%	-0.60%	-0.84%
Investment/GDP	0.02%	0.03%	0.03%	0.02%	0.03%	0.03%	-1.93%	-1.91%	-1.89%	-1.92%	-1.90%	-1.88%	-1.91%	-1.87%	-1.85%
Priv.Cons./GDP	0.12%	0.14%	0.14%	0.12%	0.15%	0.15%	-0.42%	-0.25%	-0.16%	-0.37%	-0.21%	-0.12%	-0.33%	-0.15%	-0.05%

Deflators (% change from monde)	Border Controls			Border controls and x-ineff.			Market segmentation			Trade antimonde			Full antimonde		
	1988	1991	1994	1988	1991	1994	1988	1991	1994	1988	1991	1994	1988	1991	1994
Consumer Price Index	-0.23%	-0.27%	-0.27%	-0.23%	-0.27%	-0.28%	0.92%	0.77%	0.77%	0.87%	0.73%	0.73%	0.84%	0.69%	0.67%
Real Wage Rate	-0.03%	-0.08%	-0.08%	-0.04%	-0.10%	-0.11%	-0.50%	-1.01%	-1.48%	-0.54%	-1.10%	-1.58%	-0.63%	-1.24%	-1.77%
Marginal Costs	-0.17%	-0.20%	-0.20%	-0.17%	-0.20%	-0.21%	0.57%	0.41%	0.37%	0.53%	0.37%	0.34%	0.52%	0.35%	0.30%
Producer Prices	-0.16%	-0.19%	-0.19%	-0.17%	-0.19%	-0.20%	0.64%	0.51%	0.47%	0.60%	0.48%	0.44%	0.58%	0.45%	0.40%
Real Shadow Price of Capital	0.05%	0.07%	0.06%	0.05%	0.08%	0.07%	0.01%	0.38%	0.79%	0.04%	0.42%	0.84%	-0.03%	0.33%	0.71%
Terms-of-Trade RW	1.99%	2.29%	2.31%	2.02%	2.33%	2.36%	-6.47%	-5.30%	-4.70%	-5.44%	-4.25%	-3.62%	-5.24%	-3.96%	-3.24%

	Border Controls			Border controls and x-ineff.			Market segmentation			Trade antimonde			Full antimonde		
Real Exchange Rate	3.95%	4.30%	4.32%	3.98%	4.34%	4.37%	-7.23%	-5.84%	-5.18%	-4.55%	-3.13%	-2.44%	-4.34%	-2.82%	-2.02%

Trade Regime	Integration			Integration			Segmentation			Segmentation			Segmentation		

Table B8.6.
Decomposition of effects: effects on IC sectors for Italy

% change from *monde*

Metal Industries

	Border Controls			Border controls and x-ineff.			Market segmentation			Trade *antimonde*			Full *antimonde*		
	1988	1991	1994	1988	1991	1994	1988	1991	1994	1988	1991	1994	1988	1991	1994
Production per firm	-0.49%	-1.00%	-1.01%	-0.50%	-1.02%	-1.03%	-3.30%	-5.41%	-5.69%	-3.67%	-5.83%	-6.12%	-3.77%	-5.97%	-6.30%
Marginal Costs	3.58%	3.87%	3.88%	3.60%	3.90%	3.93%	-5.80%	-4.71%	-4.16%	-3.21%	-2.07%	-1.49%	-3.01%	-1.77%	-1.09%
Producer Prices	3.63%	3.98%	4.00%	3.66%	4.02%	4.05%	-5.42%	-4.09%	-3.51%	-2.77%	-1.38%	-0.77%	-2.56%	-1.07%	-0.35%
Mark-ups domestic (abs. diff.)	0.02%	0.03%	0.04%	0.02%	0.04%	0.04%	0.62%	0.79%	0.83%	0.65%	0.81%	0.85%	0.66%	0.82%	0.86%
Fixed Costs per firm	3.53%	3.81%	3.83%	3.55%	3.84%	3.87%	-5.66%	-4.65%	-4.14%	-3.09%	-2.02%	-1.50%	-2.93%	-1.79%	-1.18%
Number of Firms	0.24%	1.23%	1.21%	0.24%	1.22%	1.19%	7.22%	11.91%	11.28%	7.00%	11.67%	11.03%	6.94%	11.58%	10.92%
Sigma of Love of Variety	0.00%	0.00%	0.00%	0.00%	0.00%	0.00%	0.00%	0.00%	0.00%	0.00%	0.00%	0.00%	0.00%	0.00%	0.00%

Chemical

	Border Controls			Border controls and x-ineff.			Market segmentation			Trade *antimonde*			Full *antimonde*		
	1988	1991	1994	1988	1991	1994	1988	1991	1994	1988	1991	1994	1988	1991	1994
Production per firm	-0.15%	-0.54%	-0.54%	-0.16%	-0.56%	-0.56%	-2.13%	-3.84%	-4.05%	-2.07%	-3.79%	-4.00%	-2.16%	-3.92%	-4.17%
Marginal Costs	3.70%	4.00%	4.02%	3.73%	4.04%	4.07%	-6.03%	-4.93%	-4.37%	-3.36%	-2.21%	-1.62%	-3.16%	-1.91%	-1.22%
Producer Prices	3.71%	4.03%	4.05%	3.73%	4.07%	4.10%	-5.92%	-4.74%	-4.18%	-3.25%	-2.02%	-1.42%	-3.05%	-1.71%	-1.02%
Mark-ups domestic (abs. diff.)	-0.01%	0.00%	0.00%	-0.01%	0.00%	0.00%	0.16%	0.22%	0.23%	0.15%	0.21%	0.22%	0.15%	0.22%	0.23%
Fixed Costs per firm	3.66%	3.94%	3.96%	3.67%	3.97%	4.00%	-5.86%	-4.86%	-4.38%	-3.20%	-2.15%	-1.65%	-3.04%	-1.92%	-1.33%
Number of Firms	0.76%	1.97%	1.97%	0.75%	1.96%	1.96%	6.41%	9.20%	8.93%	6.65%	9.46%	9.19%	6.60%	9.39%	9.09%
Sigma of Love of Variety	0.00%	0.00%	0.00%	0.00%	0.00%	0.00%	0.00%	0.00%	0.00%	0.00%	0.00%	0.00%	0.00%	0.00%	0.00%

Other Intensive Industries

	Border Controls			Border controls and x-ineff.			Market segmentation			Trade *antimonde*			Full *antimonde*		
	1988	1991	1994	1988	1991	1994	1988	1991	1994	1988	1991	1994	1988	1991	1994
Production per firm	-0.25%	-0.57%	-0.58%	-0.25%	-0.58%	-0.59%	-1.07%	-1.86%	-2.07%	-1.22%	-2.04%	-2.25%	-1.28%	-2.13%	-2.37%
Marginal Costs	3.75%	4.06%	4.07%	3.77%	4.09%	4.13%	-6.49%	-5.32%	-4.74%	-3.85%	-2.64%	-2.04%	-3.65%	-2.34%	-1.64%
Producer Prices	3.75%	4.07%	4.09%	3.78%	4.11%	4.14%	-6.46%	-5.28%	-4.69%	-3.82%	-2.59%	-1.98%	-3.61%	-2.29%	-1.58%
Mark-ups domestic (abs. diff.)	0.00%	0.00%	0.00%	0.00%	0.00%	0.00%	0.04%	0.05%	0.05%	0.04%	0.05%	0.05%	0.04%	0.05%	0.05%
Fixed Costs per firm	3.69%	3.98%	4.00%	3.70%	4.01%	4.03%	-6.33%	-5.30%	-4.84%	-3.72%	-2.65%	-2.16%	-3.56%	-2.41%	-1.85%
Number of Firms	0.16%	0.32%	0.32%	0.16%	0.32%	0.32%	-0.49%	-0.31%	-0.52%	-0.49%	-0.34%	-0.54%	-0.50%	-0.36%	-0.57%
Sigma of Love of Variety	0.00%	0.00%	0.00%	0.00%	0.00%	0.00%	0.00%	0.00%	0.00%	0.00%	0.00%	0.00%	0.00%	0.00%	0.00%

Electrical goods

	Border Controls			Border controls and x-ineff.			Market segmentation			Trade *antimonde*			Full *antimonde*		
	1988	1991	1994	1988	1991	1994	1988	1991	1994	1988	1991	1994	1988	1991	1994
Production per firm	-0.54%	-1.49%	-1.51%	-0.55%	-1.51%	-1.53%	-3.80%	-6.42%	-6.67%	-4.11%	-6.85%	-7.10%	-4.23%	-7.02%	-7.32%
Marginal Costs	3.79%	4.11%	4.12%	3.81%	4.14%	4.18%	-6.48%	-5.33%	-4.77%	-3.80%	-2.60%	-2.01%	-3.59%	-2.29%	-1.60%
Producer Prices	3.83%	4.21%	4.23%	3.85%	4.25%	4.28%	-6.20%	-4.87%	-4.29%	-3.49%	-2.09%	-1.49%	-3.28%	-1.77%	-1.07%
Mark-ups domestic (abs. diff.)	0.00%	0.02%	0.02%	0.00%	0.02%	0.02%	0.50%	0.60%	0.61%	0.50%	0.60%	0.61%	0.50%	0.60%	0.62%
Fixed Costs per firm	3.74%	4.05%	4.07%	3.76%	4.08%	4.10%	-6.35%	-5.32%	-4.85%	-3.68%	-2.60%	-2.12%	-3.52%	-2.36%	-1.80%
Number of Firms	0.63%	1.59%	1.55%	0.63%	1.57%	1.53%	3.02%	5.69%	5.32%	3.07%	5.71%	5.33%	3.01%	5.63%	5.23%
Sigma of Love of Variety	0.00%	0.00%	0.00%	0.00%	0.00%	0.00%	0.00%	0.00%	0.00%	0.00%	0.00%	0.00%	0.00%	0.00%	0.00%

Transport equipment

	Border Controls			Border controls and x-ineff.			Market segmentation			Trade *antimonde*			Full *antimonde*		
	1988	1991	1994	1988	1991	1994	1988	1991	1994	1988	1991	1994	1988	1991	1994
Production per firm	-0.35%	-1.21%	-1.23%	-0.36%	-1.23%	-1.25%	-7.37%	-10.53%	-10.69%	-7.43%	-10.62%	-10.77%	-7.53%	-10.74%	-10.93%
Marginal Costs	3.80%	4.12%	4.14%	3.83%	4.16%	4.19%	-6.47%	-5.33%	-4.79%	-3.79%	-2.59%	-2.03%	-3.58%	-2.28%	-1.62%
Producer Prices	3.82%	4.20%	4.22%	3.85%	4.24%	4.27%	-5.97%	-4.60%	-4.05%	-3.26%	-1.83%	-1.26%	-3.05%	-1.52%	-0.84%
Mark-ups domestic (abs. diff.)	-0.02%	0.01%	0.01%	-0.02%	0.01%	0.01%	0.96%	1.13%	1.14%	0.94%	1.12%	1.12%	0.94%	1.12%	1.12%
Fixed Costs per firm	3.77%	4.08%	4.09%	3.78%	4.10%	4.13%	-6.36%	-5.31%	-4.86%	-3.69%	-2.59%	-2.12%	-3.52%	-2.35%	-1.80%
Number of Firms	1.06%	2.51%	2.47%	1.05%	2.50%	2.46%	8.53%	17.80%	17.59%	8.78%	18.07%	17.87%	8.74%	18.02%	17.83%
Sigma of Love of Variety	0.00%	0.00%	0.00%	0.00%	0.00%	0.00%	0.00%	0.00%	0.00%	0.00%	0.00%	0.00%	0.00%	0.00%	0.00%

Other Equipment

	Border Controls			Border controls and x-ineff.			Market segmentation			Trade *antimonde*			Full *antimonde*		
	1988	1991	1994	1988	1991	1994	1988	1991	1994	1988	1991	1994	1988	1991	1994
Production per firm	-0.65%	-1.26%	-1.27%	-0.66%	-1.28%	-1.29%	-3.07%	-4.96%	-5.20%	-3.53%	-5.47%	-5.71%	-3.63%	-5.61%	-5.90%
Marginal Costs	3.79%	4.10%	4.12%	3.81%	4.14%	4.17%	-6.55%	-5.39%	-4.82%	-3.88%	-2.67%	-2.08%	-3.67%	-2.36%	-1.67%
Producer Prices	3.80%	4.14%	4.15%	3.83%	4.17%	4.21%	-6.47%	-5.27%	-4.69%	-3.79%	-2.53%	-1.93%	-3.58%	-2.22%	-1.52%
Mark-ups domestic (abs. diff.)	0.01%	0.02%	0.02%	0.01%	0.02%	0.02%	0.16%	0.21%	0.21%	0.17%	0.21%	0.22%	0.17%	0.21%	0.22%
Fixed Costs per firm	3.74%	4.04%	4.06%	3.76%	4.07%	4.10%	-6.42%	-5.38%	-4.92%	-3.77%	-2.68%	-2.20%	-3.60%	-2.44%	-1.88%
Number of Firms	0.08%	0.53%	0.52%	0.08%	0.52%	0.50%	2.62%	3.74%	3.28%	2.39%	3.47%	3.01%	2.31%	3.35%	2.86%
Sigma of Love of Variety	0.00%	0.00%	0.00%	0.00%	0.00%	0.00%	0.00%	0.00%	0.00%	0.00%	0.00%	0.00%	0.00%	0.00%	0.00%

Telecommunications

	Border Controls			Border controls and x-ineff.			Market segmentation			Trade *antimonde*			Full *antimonde*		
	1988	1991	1994	1988	1991	1994	1988	1991	1994	1988	1991	1994	1988	1991	1994
Production per firm	0.05%	0.07%	0.07%	-0.54%	-1.14%	-1.15%	-0.49%	-1.28%	-1.54%	-0.45%	-1.25%	-1.51%	-1.08%	-2.46%	-2.74%
Marginal Costs	3.94%	4.28%	4.30%	3.96%	4.32%	4.36%	-7.29%	-6.02%	-5.42%	-4.62%	-3.33%	-2.70%	-4.42%	-3.03%	-2.30%
Producer Prices	3.91%	4.23%	4.26%	3.72%	3.86%	3.90%	-7.19%	-5.81%	-5.21%	-4.53%	-3.12%	-2.50%	-4.53%	-3.22%	-2.50%
Mark-ups domestic (abs. diff.)	-0.03%	-0.05%	-0.05%	-0.37%	-0.61%	-0.61%	0.09%	0.09%	0.08%	0.08%	0.07%	0.07%	-0.20%	-0.49%	-0.50%
Fixed Costs per firm	3.86%	4.16%	4.18%	2.44%	1.32%	1.34%	-7.34%	-6.37%	-6.04%	-4.71%	-3.73%	-3.39%	-5.88%	-6.17%	-5.77%
Number of Firms	0.08%	0.11%	0.12%	0.70%	1.39%	1.40%	0.31%	0.67%	0.69%	0.34%	0.71%	0.72%	0.98%	1.98%	2.00%
Sigma of Love of Variety	0.00%	0.00%	0.00%	0.00%	0.00%	0.00%	0.00%	0.00%	0.00%	0.00%	0.00%	0.00%	0.00%	0.00%	0.00%

Banks

	Border Controls			Border controls and x-ineff.			Market segmentation			Trade *antimonde*			Full *antimonde*		
	1988	1991	1994	1988	1991	1994	1988	1991	1994	1988	1991	1994	1988	1991	1994
Production per firm	0.13%	0.17%	0.17%	-0.35%	-0.80%	-0.80%	-0.56%	-1.05%	-1.21%	-0.41%	-0.87%	-1.03%	-0.94%	-1.90%	-2.08%
Marginal Costs	3.95%	4.29%	4.30%	3.97%	4.32%	4.35%	-7.34%	-6.03%	-5.39%	-4.66%	-3.32%	-2.66%	-4.46%	-3.03%	-2.27%
Producer Prices	3.93%	4.26%	4.27%	3.90%	4.19%	4.22%	-7.29%	-5.96%	-5.33%	-4.63%	-3.28%	-2.62%	-4.48%	-3.08%	-2.33%
Mark-ups domestic (abs. diff.)	-0.02%	-0.02%	-0.02%	-0.08%	-0.14%	-0.15%	0.03%	0.01%	0.00%	0.01%	-0.01%	-0.02%	-0.05%	-0.13%	-0.14%
Fixed Costs per firm	3.89%	4.20%	4.22%	2.92%	2.23%	2.25%	-7.41%	-6.37%	-5.98%	-4.77%	-3.71%	-3.31%	-5.53%	-5.34%	-4.87%
Number of Firms	0.17%	0.23%	0.23%	0.66%	1.25%	1.26%	2.03%	3.25%	3.40%	2.17%	3.43%	3.57%	2.66%	4.42%	4.57%
Sigma of Love of Variety	0.00%	0.00%	0.00%	0.00%	0.00%	0.00%	0.00%	0.00%	0.00%	0.00%	0.00%	0.00%	0.00%	0.00%	0.00%

Table B8.7.
Decomposition of effects: sectoral effects for Italy (volumes)

% change from monde

Agriculture

	Border Controls			Border controls and x-ineff.			Market segmentation			Trade antimonde			Full antimonde		
	1988	1991	1994	1988	1991	1994	1988	1991	1994	1988	1991	1994	1988	1991	1994
Domestic Production - vol.	-0.7%	-0.9%	-0.9%	-0.2%	-0.9%	-0.9%	3.5%	2.4%	1.9%	3.1%	1.9%	1.4%	2.9%	1.7%	1.2%
Imports - vol.	2.0%	2.2%	2.2%	2.0%	2.2%	2.2%	-5.5%	-4.8%	-4.4%	-4.0%	-3.2%	-2.8%	-3.8%	-3.0%	-2.4%
Exports - vol.	-0.7%	-0.8%	-0.8%	-0.7%	-0.8%	-0.8%	2.1%	1.7%	1.4%	1.7%	1.2%	1.0%	1.6%	1.2%	0.9%
Absorption - vol.	-0.2%	-0.5%	-0.5%	-0.3%	-0.5%	-0.5%	1.1%	0.3%	0.0%	1.0%	0.2%	-0.2%	0.9%	0.1%	-0.3%
Investment - vol.	-0.4%	-0.5%	-0.5%	-0.4%	-0.5%	-0.5%	-2.6%	-3.1%	-3.3%	-2.9%	-3.4%	-3.6%	-2.9%	-3.4%	-3.7%
Labour Demand - vol.	-0.7%	-0.9%	-0.8%	-0.7%	-0.9%	-0.8%	3.6%	2.7%	2.5%	3.1%	2.2%	2.0%	3.1%	2.1%	1.9%
Private Consumption - vol.	0.1%	0.1%	0.2%	0.1%	0.1%	0.2%	-0.7%	-1.0%	-1.3%	-0.7%	-1.0%	-1.3%	-0.7%	-1.1%	-1.3%
Supply to domestic - vol.	-0.5%	-0.5%	-0.4%	-0.6%	-0.5%	-0.5%	3.3%	2.4%	1.9%	2.9%	2.0%	1.5%	2.8%	1.9%	1.3%
Intra-EU Trade - vol	-2.1%	-4.4%	-4.4%	-2.1%	-4.4%	-4.4%	1.4%	-0.8%	-1.1%	-0.1%	-2.6%	-2.9%	-0.2%	-2.7%	-3.1%

Energy

	Border Controls			Border controls and x-ineff.			Market segmentation			Trade antimonde			Full antimonde		
	1988	1991	1994	1988	1991	1994	1988	1991	1994	1988	1991	1994	1988	1991	1994
Domestic Production - vol.	-0.2%	-0.1%	0.2%	-0.2%	-0.1%	-0.1%	1.3%	0.8%	0.4%	1.2%	0.7%	0.4%	1.1%	0.6%	0.2%
Imports - vol.	0.5%	0.7%	0.7%	0.5%	0.7%	0.7%	-1.3%	-1.1%	-1.1%	-1.0%	-0.8%	-0.8%	-0.9%	-0.8%	-0.7%
Exports - vol.	-0.2%	-0.3%	-0.3%	-0.2%	-0.3%	-0.3%	0.7%	0.6%	0.5%	0.6%	0.4%	0.4%	0.6%	0.4%	0.3%
Absorption - vol.	0.1%	0.2%	0.2%	0.1%	0.2%	0.2%	0.1%	-0.1%	-0.3%	0.2%	0.0%	-0.3%	0.1%	-0.1%	-0.4%
Investment - vol.	-0.2%	-0.1%	-0.1%	-0.2%	-0.1%	-0.1%	-3.4%	-3.7%	-3.8%	-3.4%	-3.7%	-3.9%	-3.5%	-3.8%	-3.9%
Labour Demand - vol.	-0.3%	-0.2%	-0.2%	-0.3%	-0.2%	-0.2%	1.6%	1.1%	0.8%	1.4%	1.0%	0.7%	1.4%	0.9%	0.6%
Private Consumption - vol.	0.2%	0.2%	0.2%	0.2%	0.2%	0.2%	-0.9%	-1.1%	-1.3%	-0.8%	-1.0%	-1.2%	-0.8%	-1.1%	-1.3%
Supply to domestic - vol.	-0.3%	-0.3%	-0.3%	-0.3%	-0.3%	-0.3%	1.5%	1.0%	0.6%	1.3%	0.9%	0.4%	1.2%	0.7%	0.3%
Intra-EU Trade - vol	-0.2%	0.0%	-0.1%	-0.2%	0.0%	-0.1%	0.8%	0.0%	0.0%	0.6%	-0.2%	-0.2%	0.6%	-0.2%	-0.2%

Metal Industries

	Border Controls			Border controls and x-ineff.			Market segmentation			Trade antimonde			Full antimonde		
	1988	1991	1994	1988	1991	1994	1988	1991	1994	1988	1991	1994	1988	1991	1994
Domestic Production - vol.	-0.2%	0.2%	0.2%	-0.3%	0.2%	0.2%	3.7%	5.9%	4.9%	3.1%	5.2%	4.2%	2.9%	4.9%	3.9%
Imports - vol.	1.3%	1.6%	1.6%	1.4%	1.6%	1.6%	-5.3%	-4.7%	-4.7%	-3.6%	-2.8%	-2.8%	-3.5%	-2.6%	-2.4%
Exports - vol.	-0.6%	-0.7%	-0.7%	-0.6%	-0.7%	-0.7%	1.9%	1.6%	1.4%	1.5%	1.2%	1.0%	1.5%	1.1%	0.9%
Absorption - vol.	-0.1%	0.1%	0.0%	-0.1%	0.0%	0.0%	0.0%	0.6%	0.1%	-0.3%	0.3%	-0.2%	-0.4%	0.2%	-0.4%
Investment - vol.	-0.2%	0.1%	0.1%	-0.2%	0.1%	0.0%	-2.3%	-1.4%	-1.8%	-2.6%	-1.7%	-2.2%	-2.7%	-1.8%	-2.3%
Labour Demand - vol.	-0.2%	0.3%	0.3%	-0.2%	0.3%	0.3%	4.3%	6.8%	6.0%	3.7%	6.2%	5.3%	3.6%	6.0%	5.1%
Private Consumption - vol.	#DIV/0!	#DIV/0!	#DIV/0!	#DIV/0!	#DIV/0!	#DIV/0!	#DIV/0!	#DIV/0!	#DIV/0!	#DIV/0!	#DIV/0!	#DIV/0!	#DIV/0!	#DIV/0!	#DIV/0!
Supply to domestic - vol.	0.2%	1.4%	1.4%	0.2%	1.4%	1.3%	3.8%	8.1%	7.0%	3.4%	7.7%	6.6%	3.3%	7.5%	6.4%
Intra-EU Trade - vol	-1.8%	-3.6%	-3.6%	-1.8%	-3.6%	-3.6%	-0.6%	-6.0%	-6.0%	-2.4%	-7.8%	-7.8%	-2.6%	-8.1%	-8.1%

Chemical

	Border Controls			Border controls and x-ineff.			Market segmentation			Trade antimonde			Full antimonde		
	1988	1991	1994	1988	1991	1994	1988	1991	1994	1988	1991	1994	1988	1991	1994
Domestic Production - vol.	0.6%	1.4%	1.4%	0.6%	1.4%	1.4%	4.1%	5.0%	4.5%	4.4%	5.3%	4.8%	4.3%	5.1%	4.5%
Imports - vol.	1.0%	1.4%	1.4%	1.0%	1.4%	1.4%	-5.2%	-4.7%	-4.4%	-4.3%	-3.5%	-3.3%	-4.0%	-3.2%	-2.8%
Exports - vol.	-0.3%	-0.4%	-0.4%	-0.3%	-0.4%	-0.4%	1.9%	1.6%	1.4%	1.9%	1.5%	1.3%	1.8%	1.4%	1.2%
Absorption - vol.	0.1%	0.3%	0.3%	0.1%	0.3%	0.3%	1.5%	1.5%	1.2%	1.5%	1.5%	1.1%	1.4%	1.4%	1.0%
Investment - vol.	0.3%	0.7%	0.7%	0.3%	0.7%	0.7%	-2.2%	-1.8%	-2.1%	-2.1%	-1.7%	-1.9%	-2.1%	-1.8%	-2.0%
Labour Demand - vol.	0.6%	1.4%	1.4%	0.6%	1.4%	1.4%	4.4%	5.4%	5.0%	4.7%	5.8%	5.3%	4.6%	5.6%	5.2%
Private Consumption - vol.	0.1%	0.1%	0.1%	0.1%	0.1%	0.1%	-0.6%	-1.0%	-1.2%	-0.6%	-0.9%	-1.2%	-0.6%	-1.0%	-1.2%
Supply to domestic - vol.	0.9%	2.4%	2.4%	0.9%	2.4%	2.4%	4.4%	6.6%	6.1%	4.7%	6.9%	6.4%	4.6%	6.8%	6.2%
Intra-EU Trade - vol	-1.7%	-3.8%	-3.8%	-1.7%	-3.8%	-3.8%	-0.4%	-4.4%	-4.5%	-1.1%	-5.3%	-5.5%	-1.3%	-5.5%	-5.7%

Other Intensive Industries

	Border Controls			Border controls and x-ineff.			Market segmentation			Trade antimonde			Full antimonde		
	1988	1991	1994	1988	1991	1994	1988	1991	1994	1988	1991	1994	1988	1991	1994
Domestic Production - vol.	-0.1%	-0.3%	-0.3%	-0.1%	-0.3%	-0.3%	-1.6%	-2.2%	-2.6%	-1.7%	-2.4%	-2.8%	-1.8%	-2.5%	-2.9%
Imports - vol.	1.8%	2.1%	2.1%	1.8%	2.1%	2.2%	-8.4%	-7.6%	-7.3%	-6.6%	-5.6%	-5.3%	-6.3%	-5.2%	-4.8%
Exports - vol.	-0.5%	-0.6%	-0.6%	-0.5%	-0.6%	-0.6%	2.1%	1.7%	1.5%	1.8%	1.4%	1.2%	1.7%	1.3%	1.1%
Absorption - vol.	0.0%	0.0%	0.0%	0.0%	0.0%	0.0%	-2.6%	-2.7%	-3.0%	-2.7%	-2.8%	-3.1%	-2.7%	-2.9%	-3.2%
Investment - vol.	-0.1%	-0.1%	-0.1%	-0.1%	-0.1%	-0.1%	-4.9%	-5.2%	-5.4%	-5.0%	-5.3%	-5.5%	-5.0%	-5.3%	-5.5%
Labour Demand - vol.	-0.1%	-0.2%	-0.2%	-0.1%	-0.2%	-0.2%	-1.4%	-2.0%	-2.3%	-1.6%	-2.1%	-2.5%	-1.6%	-2.2%	-2.5%
Private Consumption - vol.	0.2%	0.2%	0.2%	0.2%	0.2%	0.2%	-1.1%	-1.4%	-1.6%	-1.1%	-1.3%	-1.6%	-1.1%	-1.4%	-1.7%
Supply to domestic - vol.	0.2%	0.5%	0.5%	0.2%	0.5%	0.5%	-1.9%	-1.7%	-2.1%	-1.9%	-1.8%	-2.2%	-2.0%	-1.9%	-2.3%
Intra-EU Trade - vol	-1.8%	-4.5%	-4.5%	-1.8%	-4.5%	-4.5%	-1.9%	-5.6%	-5.7%	-2.9%	-6.8%	-7.0%	-3.1%	-7.0%	-7.2%

	Border Controls			Border controls and x-ineff.			Market segmentation			Trade *antimonde*			Full *antimonde*		
	1988	1991	1994	1988	1991	1994	1988	1991	1994	1988	1991	1994	1988	1991	1994
Electrical goods															
Domestic Production - vol.	0.1%	0.1%	0.0%	0.1%	0.0%	0.0%	-0.9%	-1.1%	-1.7%	-1.2%	-1.5%	-2.1%	-1.3%	-1.8%	-2.5%
Imports - vol.	1.8%	2.1%	2.1%	1.8%	2.1%	2.1%	-8.9%	-8.1%	-7.9%	-7.2%	-6.2%	-5.9%	-6.9%	-5.8%	-5.4%
Exports - vol.	-0.6%	-0.7%	-0.7%	-0.6%	-0.7%	-0.7%	2.4%	2.0%	1.8%	2.1%	1.7%	1.5%	2.0%	1.6%	1.3%
Absorption - vol.	0.3%	0.2%	0.2%	0.3%	0.2%	0.2%	-4.6%	-4.0%	-4.3%	-4.6%	-4.1%	-4.4%	-4.6%	-4.2%	-4.5%
Investment - vol.	0.0%	0.0%	0.0%	0.0%	0.0%	0.0%	-4.6%	-4.7%	-5.0%	-4.7%	-4.9%	-5.2%	-4.8%	-5.0%	-5.4%
Labour Demand - vol.	0.1%	0.2%	0.1%	0.1%	0.2%	0.1%	-0.3%	-0.2%	-0.7%	-0.5%	-0.5%	-1.0%	-0.6%	-0.7%	-1.2%
Private Consumption - vol.	1.0%	0.4%	0.2%	1.0%	0.4%	0.2%	-5.3%	-2.4%	-2.4%	-4.9%	-2.4%	-2.4%	-5.1%	-2.6%	-2.5%
Supply to domestic - vol.	0.9%	2.1%	2.0%	0.8%	2.0%	2.0%	-1.8%	0.6%	0.0%	-1.7%	0.7%	0.1%	-1.8%	0.5%	-0.1%
Intra-EU Trade - vol	-1.9%	-4.2%	-4.2%	-1.9%	-4.2%	-4.2%	-2.0%	-6.3%	-6.4%	-3.3%	-7.8%	-7.9%	-3.5%	-8.1%	-8.2%
Transport equipment															
Domestic Production - vol.	0.7%	1.3%	1.2%	0.7%	1.2%	1.2%	0.5%	5.4%	5.0%	0.7%	5.5%	5.2%	0.6%	5.3%	5.0%
Imports - vol.	1.6%	1.9%	1.9%	1.7%	1.9%	1.9%	-9.1%	-8.2%	-8.0%	-7.0%	-5.9%	-5.6%	-6.8%	-5.5%	-5.1%
Exports - vol.	-0.6%	-0.7%	-0.7%	-0.6%	-0.7%	-0.7%	2.5%	2.1%	1.9%	2.1%	1.8%	1.6%	2.1%	1.7%	1.4%
Absorption - vol.	0.4%	0.3%	0.2%	0.4%	0.3%	0.2%	-4.8%	-3.3%	-3.4%	-4.8%	-3.3%	-3.3%	-4.8%	-3.4%	-3.4%
Investment - vol.	0.3%	0.6%	0.6%	0.3%	0.6%	0.6%	-3.9%	-1.7%	-1.9%	-3.8%	-1.6%	-1.8%	-3.8%	-1.7%	-1.9%
Labour Demand - vol.	0.7%	1.4%	1.3%	0.7%	1.3%	1.3%	1.4%	6.7%	6.5%	1.6%	6.9%	6.7%	1.5%	6.8%	6.6%
Private Consumption - vol.	0.7%	0.3%	0.1%	0.7%	0.3%	0.1%	-5.2%	-2.0%	-1.5%	-5.0%	-2.1%	-1.6%	-5.1%	-2.2%	-1.7%
Supply to domestic - vol.	1.6%	3.5%	3.4%	1.6%	3.5%	3.4%	-0.2%	9.1%	8.7%	0.2%	9.5%	9.2%	0.1%	9.4%	9.1%
Intra-EU Trade - vol	-1.2%	-2.8%	-2.8%	-1.2%	-2.8%	-2.8%	-3.6%	-8.2%	-8.2%	-4.2%	-8.9%	-8.9%	-4.3%	-9.1%	-9.1%
Other Equipment															
Domestic Production - vol.	-0.6%	-0.7%	-0.7%	-0.6%	-0.8%	-0.8%	-0.5%	-1.4%	-2.1%	-1.2%	-2.2%	-2.9%	-1.4%	-2.5%	-3.2%
Imports - vol.	1.5%	1.8%	1.8%	1.5%	1.8%	1.8%	-7.9%	-7.6%	-7.5%	-5.9%	-5.4%	-5.3%	-5.7%	-5.1%	-4.9%
Exports - vol.	-0.8%	-0.9%	-0.9%	-0.8%	-0.9%	-0.9%	2.4%	2.0%	1.8%	2.0%	1.5%	1.3%	1.9%	1.4%	1.1%
Absorption - vol.	-0.1%	-0.2%	-0.2%	-0.2%	-0.2%	-0.2%	-4.9%	-5.2%	-5.6%	-5.1%	-5.4%	-5.8%	-5.2%	-5.5%	-5.9%
Investment - vol.	-0.3%	-0.4%	-0.4%	-0.3%	-0.4%	-0.4%	-4.5%	-5.0%	-5.3%	-4.8%	-5.3%	-5.7%	-4.9%	-5.4%	-5.8%
Labour Demand - vol.	-0.6%	-0.7%	-0.7%	-0.6%	-0.7%	-0.7%	-0.2%	-0.9%	-1.4%	-0.9%	-1.6%	-2.2%	-1.0%	-1.8%	-2.4%
Private Consumption - vol.	0.2%	0.2%	0.2%	0.2%	0.2%	0.2%	-1.3%	-1.6%	-1.9%	-1.2%	-1.5%	-1.9%	-1.3%	-1.6%	-2.0%
Supply to domestic - vol.	0.3%	1.4%	1.4%	0.3%	1.4%	1.3%	-2.5%	-1.5%	-2.2%	-2.7%	-1.6%	-2.3%	-2.8%	-1.8%	-2.5%
Intra-EU Trade - vol	-1.4%	-3.2%	-3.2%	-1.4%	-3.2%	-3.2%	-1.7%	-4.6%	-4.8%	-2.9%	-6.0%	-6.2%	-3.1%	-6.2%	-6.5%
Consumer goods															
Domestic Production - vol.	-0.4%	-0.9%	-0.9%	-0.5%	-0.9%	-0.9%	1.9%	0.7%	0.3%	1.7%	0.5%	0.0%	1.6%	0.3%	-0.2%
Imports - vol.	1.5%	1.8%	1.8%	1.6%	1.8%	1.9%	-5.8%	-5.1%	-4.7%	-5.0%	-4.2%	-3.8%	-4.9%	-3.9%	-3.4%
Exports - vol.	-0.7%	-0.8%	-0.8%	-0.7%	-0.8%	-0.8%	2.7%	2.2%	1.9%	2.4%	1.9%	1.6%	2.3%	1.7%	1.4%
Absorption - vol.	-0.1%	-0.2%	-0.2%	-0.1%	-0.2%	-0.2%	-0.1%	-0.5%	-0.8%	-0.1%	-0.6%	-0.9%	-0.2%	-0.7%	-1.0%
Investment - vol.	-0.3%	-0.5%	-0.5%	-0.3%	-0.5%	-0.5%	-3.4%	-3.9%	-4.2%	-3.5%	-4.1%	-4.3%	-3.5%	-4.1%	-4.4%
Labour Demand - vol.	-0.4%	-0.9%	-0.9%	-0.5%	-0.9%	-0.9%	2.1%	1.1%	0.8%	1.9%	0.8%	0.5%	1.8%	0.7%	0.4%
Private Consumption - vol.	0.1%	0.1%	0.1%	0.1%	0.1%	0.1%	-0.6%	-0.9%	-1.2%	-0.6%	-0.9%	-1.1%	-0.6%	-1.0%	-1.2%
Supply to domestic - vol.	0.0%	0.3%	0.3%	0.0%	0.3%	0.3%	1.4%	1.0%	0.5%	1.3%	0.9%	0.5%	1.2%	0.8%	0.3%
Intra-EU Trade - vol	-2.0%	-5.0%	-5.0%	-2.0%	-5.0%	-5.0%	0.1%	-2.6%	-2.8%	-0.5%	-3.5%	-3.7%	-0.7%	-3.7%	-4.0%
Construction															
Domestic Production - vol.	#VALUE!	0.2%	0.2%	0.1%	0.2%	0.2%	#VALUE!	-7.8%	-8.0%	#VALUE!	-7.7%	-7.9%	#VALUE!	-7.7%	-7.9%
Imports - vol.	-0.3%	-0.3%	-0.3%	-0.3%	-0.3%	-0.3%	0.7%	0.6%	0.5%	0.5%	0.4%	0.3%	0.5%	0.4%	0.3%
Exports - vol.	0.1%	0.2%	0.2%	0.1%	0.1%	0.1%	-7.6%	-7.8%	-8.0%	-7.5%	-7.7%	-7.9%	-7.5%	-7.7%	-7.9%
Absorption - vol.	0.1%	0.2%	0.2%	0.2%	0.2%	0.2%	-7.5%	-7.6%	-7.7%	-7.4%	-7.5%	-7.6%	-7.3%	-7.4%	-7.5%
Investment - vol.	0.2%	0.1%	0.2%	0.1%	0.1%	0.1%	-7.5%	-7.6%	-7.7%	-7.4%	-7.5%	-7.6%	-7.3%	-7.4%	-7.5%
Labour Demand - vol.	0.1%	0.2%	0.2%	0.1%	0.1%	0.2%	-0.7%	-1.2%	-1.5%	-0.7%	-1.1%	-1.5%	-0.7%	-1.2%	-1.5%
Private Consumption - vol.	0.1%	0.1%	0.1%	0.1%	0.2%	0.2%	-7.6%	-7.8%	-8.0%	-7.5%	-7.7%	-7.9%	-7.5%	-7.7%	-7.9%
Supply to domestic - vol.	0.1%	0.2%	0.2%	0.1%	0.1%	0.1%	1.4%	1.0%	0.5%	1.3%	0.9%	0.5%	1.2%	0.8%	0.3%
Intra-EU Trade - vol	0.1%	0.1%	0.1%	0.1%	0.1%	0.1%	-3.8%	-3.9%	-4.0%	-3.7%	-3.8%	-3.9%	-3.7%	-3.8%	-3.9%

	Border Controls			Border controls and x-ineff.			Market segmentation			Trade antimonde			Full antimonde		
	1988	1991	1994	1988	1991	1994	1988	1991	1994	1988	1991	1994	1988	1991	1994
Telecommunications															
Domestic Production - vol.	0.2%	0.2%	0.2%	0.2%	0.2%	0.2%	-0.2%	-0.6%	-0.9%	-0.1%	-0.6%	-0.8%	-0.1%	-0.5%	-0.8%
Imports - vol.	0.8%	1.0%	1.1%	0.7%	0.9%	0.9%	-5.9%	-5.5%	-5.3%	-5.6%	-5.2%	-5.0%	-5.5%	-5.2%	-4.9%
Exports - vol.	-0.2%	-0.2%	-0.3%	-0.2%	-0.2%	-0.2%	1.2%	0.9%	0.9%	1.1%	0.9%	0.8%	1.1%	0.9%	0.8%
Absorption - vol.	0.1%	0.1%	0.1%	0.1%	0.2%	0.2%	-0.3%	-0.5%	-0.8%	-0.3%	-0.5%	-0.7%	-0.3%	-0.4%	-0.7%
Investment - vol.	0.1%	0.1%	0.2%	0.1%	0.2%	0.2%	-4.3%	-4.5%	-4.6%	-4.2%	-4.4%	-4.6%	-4.2%	-4.4%	-4.5%
Labour Demand - vol.	0.1%	0.2%	0.2%	-0.3%	-0.7%	-0.7%	0.0%	-0.1%	-0.2%	0.1%	0.0%	-0.1%	-0.3%	-0.9%	-1.0%
Private Consumption - vol.	0.1%	0.1%	0.2%	0.2%	0.3%	0.3%	-0.7%	-1.2%	-1.4%	-0.7%	-1.1%	-1.4%	-0.7%	-1.1%	-1.4%
Supply to domestic - vol.	0.1%	0.1%	0.1%	0.1%	0.3%	0.3%	0.0%	0.1%	-0.2%	0.0%	0.1%	-0.2%	0.0%	0.1%	-0.1%
Intra-EU Trade - vol	0.7%	0.6%	0.6%	0.3%	-0.6%	-0.6%	-5.8%	-16.1%	-16.2%	-5.3%	-15.6%	-15.7%	-5.4%	-15.9%	-15.9%
Transports															
Domestic Production - vol.	0.2%	0.3%	0.3%	0.2%	0.3%	0.3%	-0.4%	-0.5%	-0.8%	-0.2%	-0.3%	-0.6%	-0.2%	-0.3%	-0.7%
Imports - vol.	0.1%	0.1%	0.1%	0.1%	0.1%	0.1%	-0.2%	-0.3%	-0.4%	-0.1%	-0.1%	-0.3%	-0.1%	-0.2%	-0.3%
Exports - vol.	-0.1%	-0.1%	-0.1%	-0.1%	-0.1%	-0.2%	0.7%	0.6%	0.5%	0.7%	0.5%	0.5%	0.7%	0.5%	0.4%
Absorption - vol.	0.1%	0.1%	0.1%	0.1%	0.1%	0.1%	-0.7%	-0.8%	-1.2%	-0.7%	-0.9%	-1.2%	-0.8%	-0.9%	-1.2%
Investment - vol.	0.1%	0.1%	0.1%	0.1%	0.1%	0.1%	-4.3%	-4.4%	-4.5%	-4.2%	-4.3%	-4.5%	-4.2%	-4.3%	-4.4%
Labour Demand - vol.	0.2%	0.3%	0.3%	0.2%	0.3%	0.3%	-0.3%	-0.4%	-0.6%	-0.1%	-0.1%	-0.4%	-0.1%	-0.1%	-0.3%
Private Consumption - vol.	0.2%	0.2%	0.2%	0.2%	0.2%	0.2%	-1.0%	-1.3%	-1.6%	-0.9%	-1.3%	-1.5%	-1.0%	-1.3%	-1.6%
Supply to domestic - vol.	0.2%	0.3%	0.3%	0.2%	0.3%	0.3%	-0.4%	-0.5%	-0.8%	-0.2%	-0.3%	-0.6%	-0.2%	-0.3%	-0.7%
Intra-EU Trade - vol	1.4%	1.7%	1.7%	1.4%	1.7%	1.7%	-0.1%	-0.1%	-0.2%	1.3%	1.5%	1.4%	1.3%	1.5%	1.3%
Banks															
Domestic Production - vol.	0.3%	0.4%	0.4%	0.3%	0.4%	0.5%	1.5%	2.2%	2.1%	1.7%	2.5%	2.5%	1.7%	2.4%	2.4%
Imports - vol.	1.1%	1.4%	1.4%	1.1%	1.4%	1.4%	-6.4%	-5.5%	-5.2%	-5.7%	-4.8%	-4.4%	-5.4%	-4.4%	-4.0%
Exports - vol.	-0.2%	-0.2%	-0.3%	-0.2%	-0.2%	-0.3%	1.2%	1.0%	0.9%	1.1%	0.9%	0.8%	1.1%	0.9%	0.7%
Absorption - vol.	0.2%	0.3%	0.3%	0.2%	0.3%	0.3%	0.9%	1.3%	1.2%	1.1%	1.6%	1.5%	1.1%	1.5%	1.4%
Investment - vol.	0.2%	0.2%	0.2%	0.2%	0.3%	0.3%	-3.6%	-3.3%	-3.3%	-3.5%	-3.1%	-3.1%	-3.5%	-3.1%	-3.1%
Labour Demand - vol.	0.3%	0.4%	0.4%	0.2%	0.1%	0.2%	1.6%	2.5%	2.6%	1.9%	2.8%	3.0%	1.7%	2.5%	2.6%
Private Consumption - vol.	0.2%	0.3%	0.3%	0.2%	0.3%	0.3%	-1.2%	-1.7%	-2.0%	-1.1%	-1.6%	-2.0%	-1.1%	-1.7%	-2.1%
Supply to domestic - vol.	0.2%	0.3%	0.3%	0.3%	0.4%	0.4%	1.6%	2.8%	2.8%	1.8%	3.1%	3.0%	1.8%	3.0%	2.9%
Intra-EU Trade - vol	0.4%	0.5%	0.5%	0.3%	0.1%	0.0%	-5.0%	-11.4%	-11.6%	-4.5%	-10.8%	-11.0%	-4.6%	-10.9%	-11.2%
Services															
Domestic Production - vol.	0.2%	0.3%	0.3%	0.2%	0.3%	0.3%	-0.8%	-1.1%	-1.4%	-0.6%	-1.0%	-1.3%	-0.7%	-1.0%	-1.3%
Imports - vol.	1.8%	2.0%	2.0%	1.8%	2.0%	2.0%	-4.7%	-4.0%	-3.7%	-3.5%	-2.7%	-2.4%	-3.4%	-2.5%	-2.1%
Exports - vol.	-0.6%	-0.6%	-0.6%	-0.6%	-0.6%	-0.6%	1.5%	1.2%	1.0%	1.1%	0.8%	0.6%	1.1%	0.7%	0.5%
Absorption - vol.	0.1%	0.1%	0.1%	0.1%	0.1%	0.1%	-0.9%	-1.1%	-1.4%	-0.8%	-1.1%	-1.4%	-0.9%	-1.1%	-1.4%
Investment - vol.	0.1%	0.1%	0.1%	0.1%	0.1%	0.1%	-4.5%	-4.7%	-4.8%	-4.5%	-4.6%	-4.8%	-4.5%	-4.6%	-4.8%
Labour Demand - vol.	0.2%	0.3%	0.3%	0.3%	0.3%	0.3%	-0.7%	-0.9%	-1.0%	-0.5%	-0.7%	-0.8%	-0.5%	-0.7%	-0.8%
Private Consumption - vol.	0.1%	0.2%	0.2%	0.1%	0.2%	0.2%	-1.0%	-1.3%	-1.5%	-0.9%	-1.2%	-1.5%	-1.0%	-1.3%	-1.6%
Supply to domestic - vol.	0.1%	0.1%	0.1%	0.1%	0.1%	0.1%	-0.9%	-1.2%	-1.5%	-0.8%	-1.2%	-1.5%	-0.9%	-1.3%	-1.6%
Intra-EU Trade - vol	2.0%	2.9%	2.9%	2.0%	2.9%	3.0%	0.2%	2.2%	2.2%	2.2%	4.9%	4.9%	2.2%	4.8%	4.8%
Non market															
Domestic Production - vol.	0.0%	0.0%	0.0%	0.0%	0.0%	0.0%	0.0%	0.0%	0.0%	0.0%	0.0%	0.0%	0.0%	0.0%	0.0%
Imports - vol.	#VALUE!	#VALUE!	#VALUE!	#VALUE!	#VALUE!	#VALUE!	0.4%	0.3%	0.3%	0.3%	0.2%	0.2%	#VALUE!	#VALUE!	#VALUE!
Exports - vol.	-0.1%	-0.2%	-0.2%	-0.1%	-0.2%	-0.2%	0.0%	0.0%	0.0%	0.0%	0.0%	0.0%	0.2%	0.2%	0.2%
Absorption - vol.	0.0%	0.0%	0.0%	0.0%	0.0%	0.0%	-4.1%	-4.1%	-4.1%	-4.1%	-4.1%	-4.1%	0.0%	0.0%	0.0%
Investment - vol.	0.0%	0.0%	0.0%	0.0%	0.0%	0.0%	0.0%	0.0%	0.0%	0.0%	0.0%	0.0%	-4.1%	-4.1%	-4.1%
Labour Demand - vol.	0.1%	0.1%	0.1%	0.1%	0.1%	0.1%	-0.6%	-0.7%	-0.8%	-0.5%	-0.7%	-0.8%	0.1%	0.1%	0.1%
Private Consumption - vol.	0.0%	0.0%	0.1%	0.0%	0.0%	0.0%	0.0%	0.0%	0.0%	0.0%	0.0%	0.0%	-0.6%	-0.7%	-0.9%
Supply to domestic - vol.	0.0%	0.0%	0.0%	0.0%	0.0%	0.0%	0.0%	0.0%	0.0%	0.0%	0.0%	0.0%	0.0%	0.0%	0.0%
Intra-EU Trade - vol	0.5%	0.5%	0.5%	0.5%	0.5%	0.5%	-0.1%	-0.2%	-0.2%	0.4%	0.3%	0.3%	0.4%	0.3%	0.3%

Table B8.8.
Decomposition of effects: sectoral results for Italy (prices)

% change from *monde*

Agriculture

	Border Controls			Border controls and x-ineff.			Market segmentation			Trade *antimonde*			Full *antimonde*		
	1988	1991	1994	1988	1991	1994	1988	1991	1994	1988	1991	1994	1988	1991	1994
Marginal Costs	-0.13%	-0.15%	-0.15%	-0.13%	-0.15%	-0.15%	0.51%	0.47%	0.55%	0.48%	0.46%	0.54%	0.47%	0.44%	0.52%
Cost of Labour	-0.03%	-0.08%	-0.08%	-0.04%	-0.10%	-0.11%	-0.50%	-1.01%	-1.48%	-0.54%	-1.10%	-1.58%	-0.63%	-1.24%	-1.77%
Deflator of Absorption	-0.39%	-0.44%	-0.44%	-0.39%	-0.44%	-0.44%	1.37%	1.15%	1.14%	1.27%	1.07%	1.05%	1.23%	1.01%	0.98%
Price of Exports-RW	-0.13%	-0.15%	-0.15%	-0.13%	-0.15%	-0.15%	0.51%	0.47%	0.55%	0.48%	0.46%	0.54%	0.47%	0.44%	0.52%

Energy

	Border Controls			Border controls and x-ineff.			Market segmentation			Trade *antimonde*			Full *antimonde*		
	1988	1991	1994	1988	1991	1994	1988	1991	1994	1988	1991	1994	1988	1991	1994
Marginal Costs	-0.85%	-0.98%	-0.99%	-0.86%	-0.99%	-1.01%	2.52%	2.05%	1.89%	2.14%	1.67%	1.48%	2.05%	1.54%	1.31%
Cost of Labour	-0.03%	-0.08%	-0.08%	-0.04%	-0.10%	-0.11%	-0.50%	-1.01%	-1.48%	-0.54%	-1.10%	-1.58%	-0.63%	-1.24%	-1.77%
Deflator of Absorption	-1.41%	-1.61%	-1.62%	-1.42%	-1.63%	-1.65%	4.18%	3.38%	3.05%	3.53%	2.73%	2.38%	3.40%	2.54%	2.12%
Price of Exports-RW	-0.85%	-0.98%	-0.99%	-0.86%	-0.99%	-1.01%	2.52%	2.05%	1.89%	2.14%	1.67%	1.48%	2.05%	1.54%	1.31%

Metal Industries

	Border Controls			Border controls and x-ineff.			Market segmentation			Trade *antimonde*			Full *antimonde*		
	1988	1991	1994	1988	1991	1994	1988	1991	1994	1988	1991	1994	1988	1991	1994
Marginal Costs	-0.37%	-0.43%	-0.43%	-0.37%	-0.43%	-0.44%	1.43%	1.13%	1.03%	1.34%	1.06%	0.95%	1.33%	1.05%	0.94%
Cost of Labour	-0.03%	-0.08%	-0.08%	-0.04%	-0.10%	-0.11%	-0.50%	-1.01%	-1.48%	-0.54%	-1.10%	-1.58%	-0.63%	-1.24%	-1.77%
Deflator of Absorption	-0.57%	-0.65%	-0.65%	-0.58%	-0.66%	-0.67%	2.64%	2.17%	1.99%	2.56%	2.14%	1.96%	2.52%	2.09%	1.89%
Price of Exports-RW	-0.38%	-0.47%	-0.47%	-0.38%	-0.47%	-0.48%	1.24%	0.80%	0.72%	1.14%	0.73%	0.64%	1.14%	0.72%	0.62%

Chemical

	Border Controls			Border controls and x-ineff.			Market segmentation			Trade *antimonde*			Full *antimonde*		
	1988	1991	1994	1988	1991	1994	1988	1991	1994	1988	1991	1994	1988	1991	1994
Marginal Costs	-0.25%	-0.29%	-0.30%	-0.25%	-0.30%	-0.30%	1.20%	0.91%	0.81%	1.19%	0.92%	0.81%	1.18%	0.91%	0.80%
Cost of Labour	-0.03%	-0.08%	-0.08%	-0.04%	-0.10%	-0.11%	-0.50%	-1.01%	-1.48%	-0.54%	-1.10%	-1.58%	-0.63%	-1.24%	-1.77%
Deflator of Absorption	-0.22%	-0.27%	-0.28%	-0.23%	-0.28%	-0.29%	1.96%	1.54%	1.38%	2.10%	1.73%	1.57%	2.07%	1.69%	1.51%
Price of Exports-RW	-0.26%	-0.32%	-0.32%	-0.26%	-0.32%	-0.33%	1.13%	0.81%	0.71%	1.11%	0.81%	0.71%	1.10%	0.80%	0.69%

Other Intensive Industries

	Border Controls			Border controls and x-ineff.			Market segmentation			Trade *antimonde*			Full *antimonde*		
	1988	1991	1994	1988	1991	1994	1988	1991	1994	1988	1991	1994	1988	1991	1994
Marginal Costs	-0.20%	-0.24%	-0.24%	-0.20%	-0.24%	-0.25%	0.74%	0.52%	0.44%	0.70%	0.49%	0.40%	0.69%	0.47%	0.38%
Cost of Labour	-0.03%	-0.08%	-0.08%	-0.04%	-0.10%	-0.11%	-0.50%	-1.01%	-1.48%	-0.54%	-1.10%	-1.58%	-0.63%	-1.24%	-1.77%
Deflator of Absorption	-0.23%	-0.26%	-0.27%	-0.23%	-0.27%	-0.27%	1.00%	0.74%	0.64%	0.98%	0.73%	0.63%	0.97%	0.71%	0.60%
Price of Exports-RW	-0.20%	-0.24%	-0.24%	-0.20%	-0.25%	-0.25%	0.75%	0.52%	0.44%	0.70%	0.49%	0.40%	0.69%	0.48%	0.39%

Electrical goods

	Border Controls			Border controls and x-ineff.			Market segmentation			Trade *antimonde*			Full *antimonde*		
	1988	1991	1994	1988	1991	1994	1988	1991	1994	1988	1991	1994	1988	1991	1994
Marginal Costs	-0.16%	-0.19%	-0.19%	-0.16%	-0.20%	-0.20%	0.75%	0.51%	0.41%	0.75%	0.53%	0.42%	0.75%	0.52%	0.42%
Cost of Labour	-0.03%	-0.08%	-0.08%	-0.04%	-0.10%	-0.11%	-0.50%	-1.01%	-1.48%	-0.54%	-1.10%	-1.58%	-0.63%	-1.24%	-1.77%
Deflator of Absorption	-0.24%	-0.27%	-0.27%	-0.25%	-0.28%	-0.28%	1.80%	1.42%	1.26%	1.87%	1.55%	1.38%	1.85%	1.51%	1.33%
Price of Exports-RW	-0.17%	-0.22%	-0.22%	-0.17%	-0.23%	-0.23%	0.70%	0.42%	0.32%	0.70%	0.42%	0.33%	0.69%	0.42%	0.32%

Transport equipment

	Border Controls			Border controls and x-ineff.			Market segmentation			Trade *antimonde*			Full *antimonde*		
	1988	1991	1994	1988	1991	1994	1988	1991	1994	1988	1991	1994	1988	1991	1994
Marginal Costs	-0.15%	-0.18%	-0.17%	-0.15%	-0.18%	-0.18%	0.76%	0.52%	0.39%	0.76%	0.54%	0.41%	0.76%	0.54%	0.41%
Cost of Labour	-0.03%	-0.08%	-0.08%	-0.04%	-0.10%	-0.11%	-0.50%	-1.01%	-1.48%	-0.54%	-1.10%	-1.58%	-0.63%	-1.24%	-1.77%
Deflator of Absorption	-0.06%	-0.02%	-0.02%	-0.06%	-0.03%	-0.03%	1.97%	1.78%	1.60%	2.19%	2.09%	1.90%	2.17%	2.06%	1.87%
Price of Exports-RW	-0.18%	-0.25%	-0.24%	-0.18%	-0.25%	-0.25%	0.57%	0.12%	0.00%	0.57%	0.13%	0.00%	0.57%	0.12%	0.00%

Other Equipment

	Border Controls			Border controls and x-ineff.			Market segmentation			Trade *antimonde*			Full *antimonde*		
	1988	1991	1994	1988	1991	1994	1988	1991	1994	1988	1991	1994	1988	1991	1994
Marginal Costs	-0.16%	-0.19%	-0.19%	-0.16%	-0.20%	-0.20%	0.68%	0.46%	0.37%	0.67%	0.46%	0.36%	0.67%	0.45%	0.36%
Cost of Labour	-0.03%	-0.08%	-0.08%	-0.04%	-0.10%	-0.11%	-0.50%	-1.01%	-1.48%	-0.54%	-1.10%	-1.58%	-0.63%	-1.24%	-1.77%
Deflator of Absorption	-0.27%	-0.29%	-0.29%	-0.28%	-0.30%	-0.31%	1.56%	1.18%	1.01%	1.59%	1.26%	1.09%	1.57%	1.22%	1.04%
Price of Exports-RW	-0.16%	-0.20%	-0.20%	-0.16%	-0.20%	-0.20%	0.67%	0.44%	0.35%	0.66%	0.44%	0.35%	0.65%	0.44%	0.34%

Consumer goods

	Border Controls			Border controls and x-ineff.			Market segmentation			Trade *antimonde*			Full *antimonde*		
	1988	1991	1994	1988	1991	1994	1988	1991	1994	1988	1991	1994	1988	1991	1994
Marginal Costs	-0.21%	-0.25%	-0.25%	-0.21%	-0.25%	-0.25%	0.84%	0.63%	0.58%	0.80%	0.61%	0.56%	0.80%	0.61%	0.56%
Cost of Labour	-0.03%	-0.08%	-0.08%	-0.04%	-0.10%	-0.11%	-0.50%	-1.01%	-1.48%	-0.54%	-1.10%	-1.58%	-0.63%	-1.24%	-1.77%
Deflator of Absorption	-0.32%	-0.37%	-0.37%	-0.32%	-0.37%	-0.37%	1.38%	1.06%	0.96%	1.35%	1.05%	0.94%	1.33%	1.02%	0.91%
Price of Exports-RW	-0.21%	-0.25%	-0.25%	-0.21%	-0.25%	-0.25%	0.84%	0.63%	0.58%	0.80%	0.61%	0.56%	0.80%	0.61%	0.56%

Construction

	Border Controls			Border controls and x-ineff.			Market segmentation			Trade *antimonde*			Full *antimonde*		
	1988	1991	1994	1988	1991	1994	1988	1991	1994	1988	1991	1994	1988	1991	1994
Marginal Costs	-0.12%	-0.14%	-0.14%	-0.12%	-0.14%	-0.14%	0.47%	0.34%	0.32%	0.46%	0.34%	0.31%	0.45%	0.33%	0.31%
Cost of Labour	-0.03%	-0.08%	-0.08%	-0.04%	-0.10%	-0.11%	-0.50%	-1.01%	-1.48%	-0.54%	-1.10%	-1.58%	-0.63%	-1.24%	-1.77%
Deflator of Absorption	-0.12%	-0.14%	-0.14%	-0.12%	-0.14%	-0.14%	0.47%	0.34%	0.32%	0.46%	0.34%	0.31%	0.45%	0.33%	0.31%
Price of Exports-RW	-0.12%	-0.14%	-0.14%	-0.12%	-0.14%	-0.14%	0.47%	0.34%	0.32%	0.46%	0.34%	0.31%	0.45%	0.33%	0.31%

Telecommunications

	Border Controls			Border controls and x-ineff.			Market segmentation			Trade *antimonde*			Full *antimonde*		
	1988	1991	1994	1988	1991	1994	1988	1991	1994	1988	1991	1994	1988	1991	1994
Marginal Costs	-0.01%	-0.02%	-0.01%	-0.01%	-0.02%	-0.01%	-0.06%	-0.18%	-0.24%	-0.07%	-0.20%	-0.26%	-0.08%	-0.21%	-0.27%
Cost of Labour	-0.03%	-0.08%	-0.08%	-0.04%	-0.10%	-0.11%	-0.50%	-1.01%	-1.48%	-0.54%	-1.10%	-1.58%	-0.63%	-1.24%	-1.77%
Deflator of Absorption	-0.05%	-0.08%	-0.07%	-0.27%	-0.51%	-0.50%	0.10%	-0.03%	-0.09%	0.08%	-0.06%	-0.13%	-0.13%	-0.48%	-0.56%
Price of Exports-RW	-0.02%	-0.03%	-0.02%	-0.08%	-0.15%	-0.15%	-0.08%	-0.24%	-0.30%	-0.10%	-0.26%	-0.32%	-0.16%	-0.38%	-0.45%

Transports

	Border Controls			Border controls and x-ineff.			Market segmentation			Trade *antimonde*			Full *antimonde*		
	1988	1991	1994	1988	1991	1994	1988	1991	1994	1988	1991	1994	1988	1991	1994
Marginal Costs	-0.20%	-0.24%	-0.24%	-0.20%	-0.25%	-0.25%	0.54%	0.36%	0.30%	0.46%	0.28%	0.21%	0.43%	0.23%	0.15%
Cost of Labour	-0.03%	-0.08%	-0.08%	-0.04%	-0.10%	-0.11%	-0.50%	-1.01%	-1.48%	-0.54%	-1.10%	-1.58%	-0.63%	-1.24%	-1.77%
Deflator of Absorption	-0.21%	-0.26%	-0.26%	-0.21%	-0.26%	-0.27%	0.60%	0.40%	0.33%	0.53%	0.32%	0.25%	0.49%	0.27%	0.18%
Price of Exports-RW	-0.20%	-0.24%	-0.24%	-0.20%	-0.25%	-0.25%	0.54%	0.36%	0.30%	0.46%	0.28%	0.21%	0.43%	0.23%	0.15%

Banks

	Border Controls			Border controls and x-ineff.			Market segmentation			Trade *antimonde*			Full *antimonde*		
	1988	1991	1994	1988	1991	1994	1988	1991	1994	1988	1991	1994	1988	1991	1994
Marginal Costs	0.00%	-0.01%	-0.01%	0.00%	-0.01%	-0.02%	-0.10%	-0.18%	-0.20%	-0.11%	-0.20%	-0.22%	-0.12%	-0.21%	-0.25%
Cost of Labour	-0.03%	-0.08%	-0.08%	-0.04%	-0.10%	-0.11%	-0.50%	-1.01%	-1.48%	-0.54%	-1.10%	-1.58%	-0.63%	-1.24%	-1.77%
Deflator of Absorption	-0.03%	-0.05%	-0.05%	-0.09%	-0.17%	-0.17%	0.03%	-0.08%	-0.11%	0.01%	-0.11%	-0.14%	-0.05%	-0.23%	-0.28%
Price of Exports-RW	-0.01%	-0.02%	-0.02%	-0.02%	-0.05%	-0.05%	-0.15%	-0.26%	-0.29%	-0.16%	-0.28%	-0.31%	-0.19%	-0.32%	-0.36%

Services

	Border Controls			Border controls and x-ineff.			Market segmentation			Trade *antimonde*			Full *antimonde*		
	1988	1991	1994	1988	1991	1994	1988	1991	1994	1988	1991	1994	1988	1991	1994
Marginal Costs	-0.05%	-0.06%	-0.06%	-0.05%	-0.06%	-0.06%	0.22%	0.27%	0.41%	0.21%	0.28%	0.41%	0.19%	0.25%	0.38%
Cost of Labour	-0.03%	-0.08%	-0.08%	-0.04%	-0.10%	-0.11%	-0.50%	-1.01%	-1.48%	-0.54%	-1.10%	-1.58%	-0.63%	-1.24%	-1.77%
Deflator of Absorption	-0.06%	-0.08%	-0.08%	-0.06%	-0.07%	-0.08%	0.25%	0.29%	0.41%	0.24%	0.28%	0.41%	0.22%	0.26%	0.38%
Price of Exports-RW	-0.05%	-0.06%	-0.06%	-0.05%	-0.06%	-0.06%	0.22%	0.27%	0.41%	0.21%	0.28%	0.41%	0.19%	0.25%	0.38%

Non market

	Border Controls			Border controls and x-ineff.			Market segmentation			Trade *antimonde*			Full *antimonde*		
	1988	1991	1994	1988	1991	1994	1988	1991	1994	1988	1991	1994	1988	1991	1994
Marginal Costs	-0.08%	-0.13%	-0.13%	-0.09%	-0.14%	-0.15%	-0.07%	-0.49%	-0.84%	-0.11%	-0.55%	-0.91%	-0.14%	-0.60%	-0.98%
Cost of Labour	-0.03%	-0.08%	-0.08%	-0.04%	-0.10%	-0.11%	-0.50%	-1.01%	-1.48%	-0.54%	-1.10%	-1.58%	-0.63%	-1.24%	-1.77%
Deflator of Absorption	-0.08%	-0.13%	-0.13%	-0.09%	-0.14%	-0.15%	-0.07%	-0.49%	-0.84%	-0.11%	-0.55%	-0.91%	-0.14%	-0.60%	-0.98%
Price of Exports-RW	-0.08%	-0.13%	-0.13%	-0.09%	-0.14%	-0.15%	-0.07%	-0.49%	-0.84%	-0.11%	-0.55%	-0.91%	-0.14%	-0.60%	-0.98%

Table B9.1.

The full *antimonde* scenario: macroeconomic aggregates for the Netherlands

Macroeconomic Aggregates (vol.) (% change from *monde*)	Constraint Case			Flexible Case			Efficiency Case		
	1988	1991	1994	1988	1991	1994	1988	1991	1994
GDP fact. pr.	-1.08%	-1.26%	-1.66%	-0.69%	-1.21%	-1.54%	-0.71%	-1.31%	-1.72%
Priv. Consumption	-1.19%	-1.24%	-1.45%	-1.40%	-1.66%	-1.78%	-1.41%	-1.67%	-1.79%
Absorption	-1.32%	-1.41%	-1.69%	-1.88%	-2.50%	-2.71%	-1.89%	-2.51%	-2.73%
Total Investment	-5.20%	-5.38%	-6.11%	-4.29%	-4.49%	-4.64%	-4.29%	-4.49%	-4.64%
Total Exports to RW	-0.76%	-1.07%	-1.49%	1.45%	1.22%	1.01%	1.42%	1.12%	0.84%
Total Imports from RW	-1.96%	-2.12%	-2.37%	-3.28%	-3.20%	-2.93%	-3.24%	-3.03%	-2.63%
Total Intra-EU Trade	-1.38%	-1.41%	-1.64%	-0.59%	-2.60%	-2.82%	-0.61%	-2.65%	-2.92%
Employment (diff. from *monde*, 10³ persons)	-19	-21	-28	-33	-38	-44	-33	-38	-43
Disposable Income (deflated)	-1.24%	-1.29%	-1.51%	-1.46%	-1.72%	-1.84%	-1.46%	-1.73%	-1.86%

Macroeconomic Ratios (abs. diff. from *monde*)	Constraint Case			Flexible Case			Efficiency Case		
	1988	1991	1994	1988	1991	1994	1988	1991	1994
Current Account as % of GDP	0.00%	0.00%	0.00%	-0.69%	-0.54%	-0.54%	-0.68%	-0.52%	-0.50%
Public Deficit as % of GDP	-0.22%	-0.24%	-0.30%	-0.70%	-0.91%	-1.01%	-0.71%	-0.92%	-1.04%
Labour Productivity	-0.69%	-0.83%	-1.07%	0.00%	-0.41%	-0.63%	-0.03%	-0.53%	-0.83%
Investment/GDP	-0.86%	-0.87%	-0.94%	-1.79%	-1.78%	-1.77%	-1.79%	-1.75%	-1.73%
Priv.Cons./GDP	-0.06%	0.01%	0.13%	-0.42%	-0.27%	-0.14%	-0.41%	-0.21%	-0.04%

Deflators (% change from *monde*)	Constraint Case			Flexible Case			Efficiency Case		
	1988	1991	1994	1988	1991	1994	1988	1991	1994
Consumer Price Index	-0.21%	-0.08%	0.04%	1.22%	1.11%	0.99%	1.20%	1.03%	0.85%
Real Wage Rate	-1.18%	-1.38%	-1.84%	-1.06%	-1.57%	-1.96%	-1.08%	-1.66%	-2.12%
Marginal Costs	-0.47%	-0.31%	-0.15%	0.88%	0.81%	0.72%	0.86%	0.75%	0.62%
Producer Prices	-0.31%	-0.15%	0.01%	1.01%	0.99%	0.90%	1.00%	0.94%	0.81%
Average change in mark-ups (abs. diff.)	1.07%	1.14%	1.20%	1.09%	1.56%	1.63%	1.09%	1.56%	1.64%
Shadow Price of Capital	-1.11%	-0.74%	-0.24%	0.03%	0.19%	0.58%	0.01%	0.08%	0.39%
Terms-of-Trade RW	-1.01%	-0.85%	-0.70%	-4.81%	-4.07%	-3.38%	-4.73%	-3.74%	-2.80%

| Implicit change in real exchange rate | -0.84% | -0.62% | -0.43% | -4.34% | -3.46% | -2.62% | -4.24% | -3.07% | -1.93% |

| Trade Regime | Segmentation | | | Segmentation | | | Segmentation | | |

Table B9.2.
The full *antimonde* scenario: effects on IC sectors for the Netherlands

% change from *monde*

Metal Industries	Constraint Case			Flexible Case			Efficiency Case		
	1988	1991	1994	1988	1991	1994	1988	1991	1994
Production per firm	-19.57%	-19.63%	-19.78%	-15.25%	-22.63%	-22.80%	-15.27%	-22.68%	-22.87%
Real Marginal Costs	0.67%	0.80%	0.91%	-0.87%	0.54%	1.56%	-0.77%	0.95%	2.27%
Real Producer Prices	3.36%	3.49%	3.61%	0.82%	2.93%	3.96%	0.93%	3.34%	4.69%
Mark-ups domestic (abs. diff.)	9.38%	9.39%	9.41%	10.14%	12.20%	12.23%	10.14%	12.20%	12.24%
Fixed Costs per firm	0.71%	0.77%	0.77%	-1.71%	-0.85%	-0.33%	-1.64%	-0.59%	0.14%
Number of Firms	11.77%	11.73%	11.61%	13.33%	10.66%	10.05%	13.32%	10.58%	9.92%
Sigma of Love of Variety	0.00%	0.00%	0.00%	0.00%	0.00%	0.00%	0.00%	0.00%	0.00%

Chemical	Constraint Case			Flexible Case			Efficiency Case		
	1988	1991	1994	1988	1991	1994	1988	1991	1994
Production per firm	-7.74%	-7.84%	-8.03%	-8.79%	-13.96%	-14.12%	-8.80%	-14.00%	-14.20%
Real Marginal Costs	0.27%	0.41%	0.59%	-0.91%	0.47%	1.52%	-0.80%	0.88%	2.23%
Real Producer Prices	0.54%	0.68%	0.86%	-0.62%	0.92%	1.97%	-0.52%	1.32%	2.68%
Mark-ups domestic (abs. diff.)	0.83%	0.83%	0.84%	0.91%	1.28%	1.28%	0.91%	1.28%	1.29%
Fixed Costs per firm	0.24%	0.32%	0.37%	-1.71%	-0.90%	-0.34%	-1.65%	-0.64%	0.11%
Number of Firms	7.18%	7.10%	6.90%	9.16%	11.43%	11.26%	9.16%	11.49%	11.35%
Sigma of Love of Variety	0.00%	0.00%	0.00%	0.00%	0.00%	0.00%	0.00%	0.00%	0.00%

Other Intensive Industries	Constraint Case			Flexible Case			Efficiency Case		
	1988	1991	1994	1988	1991	1994	1988	1991	1994
Production per firm	-6.11%	-6.21%	-6.43%	-7.81%	-11.66%	-11.92%	-7.83%	-11.73%	-12.05%
Real Marginal Costs	-0.14%	0.00%	0.12%	-2.12%	-0.80%	0.29%	-2.01%	-0.36%	1.07%
Real Producer Prices	0.28%	0.43%	0.55%	-1.61%	-0.05%	1.05%	-1.50%	0.40%	1.84%
Mark-ups domestic (abs. diff.)	0.56%	0.56%	0.57%	0.70%	0.89%	0.90%	0.70%	0.89%	0.90%
Fixed Costs per firm	-0.14%	-0.07%	-0.09%	-3.04%	-2.32%	-1.74%	-2.97%	-2.02%	-1.21%
Number of Firms	6.37%	6.39%	6.25%	6.00%	9.61%	9.26%	6.00%	9.55%	9.15%
Sigma of Love of Variety	0.00%	0.00%	0.00%	0.00%	0.00%	0.00%	0.00%	0.00%	0.00%

Electrical goods	Constraint Case			Flexible Case			Efficiency Case		
	1988	1991	1994	1988	1991	1994	1988	1991	1994
Production per firm	-12.03%	-12.07%	-12.16%	-10.08%	-14.39%	-14.58%	-10.11%	-14.50%	-14.77%
Real Marginal Costs	-0.15%	-0.04%	0.00%	-2.12%	-0.88%	0.13%	-2.01%	-0.44%	0.89%
Real Producer Prices	1.01%	1.13%	1.16%	-1.25%	0.32%	1.35%	-1.14%	0.77%	2.13%
Mark-ups domestic (abs. diff.)	6.64%	6.65%	6.67%	6.61%	7.88%	7.89%	6.61%	7.88%	7.91%
Fixed Costs per firm	-0.18%	-0.13%	-0.20%	-3.12%	-2.47%	-1.94%	-3.05%	-2.18%	-1.44%
Number of Firms	8.21%	8.21%	8.12%	8.69%	8.51%	8.19%	8.66%	8.34%	7.90%
Sigma of Love of Variety	0.00%	0.00%	0.00%	0.00%	0.00%	0.00%	0.00%	0.00%	0.00%

Transport equipment	Constraint Case			Flexible Case			Efficiency Case		
	1988	1991	1994	1988	1991	1994	1988	1991	1994
Production per firm	-19.78%	-19.79%	-19.92%	-19.34%	-25.75%	-25.76%	-19.36%	-25.80%	-25.86%
Real Marginal Costs	0.70%	0.80%	0.85%	-1.22%	0.19%	1.16%	-1.11%	0.63%	1.92%
Real Producer Prices	2.64%	2.74%	2.80%	0.44%	2.36%	3.34%	0.55%	2.81%	4.12%
Mark-ups domestic (abs. diff.)	5.91%	6.02%	6.09%	6.27%	7.75%	7.76%	6.27%	7.76%	7.76%
Fixed Costs per firm	0.60%	0.66%	0.63%	-2.28%	-1.43%	-0.90%	-2.21%	-1.14%	-0.39%
Number of Firms	17.59%	17.13%	16.70%	18.08%	27.20%	27.26%	18.07%	27.17%	27.22%
Sigma of Love of Variety	0.00%	0.00%	0.00%	0.00%	0.00%	0.00%	0.00%	0.00%	0.00%

Other Equipment	Constraint Case			Flexible Case			Efficiency Case		
	1988	1991	1994	1988	1991	1994	1988	1991	1994
Production per firm	-15.53%	-15.59%	-15.70%	-15.03%	-20.59%	-20.73%	-15.05%	-20.65%	-20.84%
Real Marginal Costs	0.43%	0.54%	0.60%	-1.45%	-0.13%	0.86%	-1.35%	0.30%	1.61%
Real Producer Prices	1.41%	1.52%	1.59%	-0.67%	0.90%	1.89%	-0.57%	1.33%	2.65%
Mark-ups domestic (abs. diff.)	4.39%	4.39%	4.40%	5.11%	6.14%	6.15%	5.11%	6.14%	6.15%
Fixed Costs per firm	0.42%	0.46%	0.42%	-2.41%	-1.66%	-1.15%	-2.34%	-1.38%	-0.66%
Number of Firms	12.81%	12.74%	12.58%	9.62%	10.28%	10.09%	9.60%	10.21%	9.97%
Sigma of Love of Variety	0.00%	0.00%	0.00%	0.00%	0.00%	0.00%	0.00%	0.00%	0.00%

Telecommunications	Constraint Case			Flexible Case			Efficiency Case		
	1988	1991	1994	1988	1991	1994	1988	1991	1994
Production per firm	-2.81%	-2.06%	-2.29%	-3.78%	-6.53%	-6.89%	-3.79%	-6.61%	-7.02%
Real Marginal Costs	-0.61%	-0.86%	-0.65%	-3.30%	-1.98%	-0.69%	-3.18%	-1.50%	0.15%
Real Producer Prices	0.21%	0.16%	0.34%	-2.78%	-1.18%	0.11%	-2.66%	-0.70%	0.95%
Mark-ups domestic (abs. diff.)	0.90%	1.18%	1.13%	0.53%	0.32%	0.31%	0.53%	0.32%	0.30%
Fixed Costs per firm	0.00%	1.38%	1.22%	-5.84%	-6.64%	-6.14%	-5.77%	-6.34%	-5.61%
Number of Firms	2.90%	2.22%	2.34%	5.46%	11.41%	11.43%	5.46%	11.40%	11.41%
Sigma of Love of Variety	0.00%	0.00%	0.00%	0.00%	0.00%	0.00%	0.00%	0.00%	0.00%

Banks	Constraint Case			Flexible Case			Efficiency Case		
	1988	1991	1994	1988	1991	1994	1988	1991	1994
Production per firm	-0.73%	-0.21%	-0.40%	-1.63%	-2.87%	-3.28%	-1.65%	-2.94%	-3.39%
Real Marginal Costs	-0.65%	-0.81%	-0.57%	-3.31%	-1.98%	-0.68%	-3.19%	-1.51%	0.13%
Real Producer Prices	-0.47%	-0.58%	-0.38%	-3.22%	-1.88%	-0.57%	-3.10%	-1.41%	0.24%
Mark-ups domestic (abs. diff.)	0.14%	0.21%	0.18%	0.02%	-0.11%	-0.11%	0.02%	-0.11%	-0.11%
Fixed Costs per firm	-0.34%	0.30%	0.18%	-5.42%	-5.77%	-5.21%	-5.34%	-5.46%	-4.66%
Number of Firms	0.71%	0.44%	0.57%	1.65%	3.48%	3.44%	1.65%	3.47%	3.42%
Sigma of Love of Variety	0.00%	0.00%	0.00%	0.00%	0.00%	0.00%	0.00%	0.00%	0.00%

Table B9.3.
The full *antimonde* scenario: sectoral results for the Netherlands (volumes)

% change from *monde*

Agriculture	Constraint Case			Flexible Case			Efficiency Case		
	1988	1991	1994	1988	1991	1994	1988	1991	1994
Domestic Production - vol.	0.8%	0.5%	-0.3%	0.7%	0.9%	0.5%	0.7%	0.8%	0.3%
Imports - vol.	-2.0%	-2.0%	-1.9%	-3.3%	-2.9%	-2.4%	-3.2%	-2.6%	-2.0%
Exports - vol.	-1.7%	-2.3%	-3.2%	1.3%	1.1%	0.8%	1.3%	1.0%	0.6%
Absorption - vol.	0.6%	0.4%	0.1%	-0.7%	-1.3%	-1.5%	-0.7%	-1.3%	-1.5%
Investment - vol.	-0.6%	-0.8%	-2.6%	-3.8%	-3.8%	-4.0%	-3.9%	-3.8%	-4.0%
Labour Demand - vol.	1.0%	0.8%	0.2%	1.0%	1.3%	1.1%	1.0%	1.3%	1.1%
Private Consumption - vol.	-1.4%	-1.3%	-1.4%	-1.2%	-1.6%	-1.8%	-1.2%	-1.6%	-1.8%
Supply to domestic - vol.	2.4%	2.2%	1.5%	2.3%	3.0%	2.4%	2.2%	2.9%	2.2%
Intra-EU Trade - vol	0.0%	0.0%	0.0%	-1.0%	-2.7%	-2.9%	-1.0%	-2.7%	-3.0%

Energy	Constraint Case			Flexible Case			Efficiency Case		
	1988	1991	1994	1988	1991	1994	1988	1991	1994
Domestic Production - vol.	-0.8%	-1.3%	-2.0%	2.2%	2.0%	1.3%	2.2%	1.8%	1.1%
Imports - vol.	-1.1%	-1.2%	-1.4%	-1.2%	-1.1%	-1.0%	-1.1%	-1.1%	-0.9%
Exports - vol.	-1.4%	-2.0%	-2.9%	0.7%	0.5%	0.4%	0.7%	0.5%	0.3%
Absorption - vol.	-0.7%	-0.9%	-1.3%	0.6%	-0.1%	-0.5%	0.5%	-0.2%	-0.6%
Investment - vol.	-7.1%	-7.5%	-8.4%	-3.1%	-3.2%	-3.5%	-3.1%	-3.3%	-3.6%
Labour Demand - vol.	-0.7%	-1.1%	-1.7%	2.5%	2.3%	1.8%	2.5%	2.2%	1.6%
Private Consumption - vol.	-0.6%	-0.5%	-0.7%	-0.9%	-1.2%	-1.4%	-0.9%	-1.2%	-1.4%
Supply to domestic - vol.	-0.4%	-0.7%	-1.2%	1.6%	0.8%	0.3%	1.6%	0.7%	0.0%
Intra-EU Trade - vol	0.0%	0.0%	0.0%	1.3%	1.3%	0.9%	1.3%	1.2%	0.8%

Metal Industries	Constraint Case			Flexible Case			Efficiency Case		
	1988	1991	1994	1988	1991	1994	1988	1991	1994
Domestic Production - vol.	-10.1%	-10.2%	-10.5%	-4.0%	-14.4%	-15.0%	-4.0%	-14.5%	-15.2%
Imports - vol.	3.9%	3.8%	3.6%	-2.9%	-4.4%	-4.3%	-2.9%	-4.3%	-4.1%
Exports - vol.	-4.2%	-4.4%	-4.6%	1.4%	1.0%	0.8%	1.3%	0.9%	0.6%
Absorption - vol.	-4.0%	-4.0%	-4.3%	-3.4%	-7.9%	-8.4%	-3.4%	-8.0%	-8.4%
Investment - vol.	-14.4%	-14.5%	-15.2%	-5.9%	-10.6%	-10.9%	-5.9%	-10.7%	-11.0%
Labour Demand - vol.	-7.3%	-7.4%	-7.6%	-1.8%	-11.8%	-12.4%	-1.8%	-11.8%	-12.5%
Private Consumption - vol.	-0.7%	-0.7%	-0.7%	-0.5%	-0.9%	-0.9%	-0.5%	-0.8%	-0.9%
Supply to domestic - vol.	-22.5%	-22.6%	-22.9%	-12.4%	-23.7%	-24.7%	-12.5%	-23.9%	-24.9%
Intra-EU Trade - vol	0.0%	0.0%	0.0%	0.4%	-3.3%	-3.6%	0.4%	-3.4%	-3.7%

Chemical	Constraint Case			Flexible Case			Efficiency Case		
	1988	1991	1994	1988	1991	1994	1988	1991	1994
Domestic Production - vol.	-1.1%	-1.3%	-1.7%	-0.4%	-4.1%	-4.5%	-0.4%	-4.1%	-4.5%
Imports - vol.	-0.6%	-0.7%	-0.9%	-3.8%	-4.3%	-3.9%	-3.7%	-4.0%	-3.5%
Exports - vol.	-1.1%	-1.4%	-1.7%	1.4%	1.2%	1.0%	1.4%	1.1%	0.8%
Absorption - vol.	-0.7%	-0.9%	-1.1%	-0.7%	-3.2%	-3.4%	-0.7%	-3.1%	-3.4%
Investment - vol.	-5.9%	-6.0%	-6.9%	-4.2%	-5.9%	-6.1%	-4.2%	-5.9%	-6.0%
Labour Demand - vol.	-0.6%	-0.8%	-1.1%	0.2%	-3.2%	-3.5%	0.2%	-3.2%	-3.4%
Private Consumption - vol.	-1.3%	-1.2%	-1.3%	-0.9%	-1.3%	-1.5%	-0.9%	-1.3%	-1.5%
Supply to domestic - vol.	-0.9%	-1.1%	-1.5%	2.5%	4.5%	4.1%	2.5%	4.6%	4.2%
Intra-EU Trade - vol	0.0%	0.0%	0.0%	-1.0%	-4.8%	-5.0%	-1.0%	-4.8%	-5.0%

Other Intensive Industries	Constraint Case			Flexible Case			Efficiency Case		
	1988	1991	1994	1988	1991	1994	1988	1991	1994
Domestic Production - vol.	-0.1%	-0.2%	-0.6%	-2.3%	-3.2%	-3.8%	-2.3%	-3.3%	-4.0%
Imports - vol.	-4.8%	-4.9%	-5.0%	-5.3%	-4.7%	-4.2%	-5.2%	-4.4%	-3.7%
Exports - vol.	-1.4%	-1.7%	-2.0%	1.6%	1.4%	1.1%	1.6%	1.3%	1.0%
Absorption - vol.	-1.4%	-1.4%	-1.7%	-2.9%	-3.5%	-3.7%	-2.9%	-3.5%	-3.8%
Investment - vol.	-5.0%	-5.0%	-5.9%	-5.3%	-5.7%	-6.0%	-5.3%	-5.7%	-6.0%
Labour Demand - vol.	0.5%	0.4%	0.2%	-1.5%	-2.0%	-2.5%	-1.5%	-2.1%	-2.7%
Private Consumption - vol.	-0.9%	-0.9%	-1.1%	-1.4%	-1.3%	-1.3%	-1.4%	-1.3%	-1.3%
Supply to domestic - vol.	0.6%	0.6%	0.2%	-0.8%	1.3%	0.8%	-0.8%	1.2%	0.5%
Intra-EU Trade - vol	0.0%	0.0%	0.0%	-2.9%	-6.2%	-6.3%	-2.9%	-6.2%	-6.4%

Electrical goods	Constraint Case			Flexible Case			Efficiency Case		
	1988	1991	1994	1988	1991	1994	1988	1991	1994
Domestic Production - vol.	-4.8%	-4.8%	-5.0%	-2.3%	-7.1%	-7.6%	-2.3%	-7.4%	-8.0%
Imports - vol.	0.8%	0.7%	0.3%	-4.8%	-4.9%	-4.6%	-4.8%	-4.7%	-4.3%
Exports - vol.	-0.4%	-0.5%	-0.6%	2.1%	1.8%	1.5%	2.0%	1.7%	1.3%
Absorption - vol.	-3.7%	-3.7%	-4.1%	-4.9%	-6.3%	-6.4%	-4.9%	-6.3%	-6.5%
Investment - vol.	-7.2%	-7.2%	-8.3%	-5.3%	-7.5%	-7.8%	-5.3%	-7.6%	-7.9%
Labour Demand - vol.	-3.2%	-3.2%	-3.3%	-0.8%	-5.2%	-5.6%	-0.8%	-5.4%	-6.0%
Private Consumption - vol.	-2.1%	-1.4%	-2.1%	-4.6%	-3.1%	-2.6%	-4.6%	-3.1%	-2.6%
Supply to domestic - vol.	-17.8%	-17.7%	-18.1%	-12.5%	-19.7%	-20.3%	-12.6%	-20.0%	-20.9%
Intra-EU Trade - vol	0.0%	0.0%	0.0%	0.5%	-1.1%	-1.4%	0.5%	-1.3%	-1.6%

Transport equipment	Constraint Case			Flexible Case			Efficiency Case		
	1988	1991	1994	1988	1991	1994	1988	1991	1994
Domestic Production - vol.	-5.7%	-6.1%	-6.5%	-4.8%	-5.6%	-5.5%	-4.8%	-5.6%	-5.7%
Imports - vol.	0.9%	-0.2%	-1.3%	-6.0%	-5.0%	-4.6%	-5.9%	-4.8%	-4.2%
Exports - vol.	-2.3%	-2.4%	-2.6%	1.8%	1.7%	1.5%	1.8%	1.5%	1.2%
Absorption - vol.	-2.1%	-3.2%	-4.3%	-6.0%	-5.4%	-5.2%	-6.0%	-5.4%	-5.2%
Investment - vol.	-7.3%	-7.7%	-9.0%	-6.0%	-6.4%	-6.4%	-6.1%	-6.4%	-6.5%
Labour Demand - vol.	-3.2%	-3.6%	-4.0%	-2.3%	-2.5%	-2.4%	-2.4%	-2.5%	-2.5%
Private Consumption - vol.	4.4%	0.3%	-2.9%	-5.6%	-3.1%	-1.8%	-5.6%	-3.1%	-1.8%
Supply to domestic - vol.	-11.1%	-12.0%	-13.1%	-9.1%	-4.9%	-4.7%	-9.2%	-4.9%	-4.8%
Intra-EU Trade - vol	0.0%	0.0%	0.0%	-1.7%	-2.9%	-2.9%	-1.7%	-3.0%	-3.0%

Other Equipment	Constraint Case			Flexible Case			Efficiency Case		
	1988	1991	1994	1988	1991	1994	1988	1991	1994
Domestic Production - vol.	-4.7%	-4.8%	-5.1%	-6.9%	-12.4%	-12.7%	-6.9%	-12.6%	-12.9%
Imports - vol.	-1.6%	-1.7%	-2.3%	-4.7%	-5.1%	-4.9%	-4.7%	-4.9%	-4.6%
Exports - vol.	-2.3%	-2.4%	-2.6%	1.6%	1.3%	1.1%	1.5%	1.1%	0.8%
Absorption - vol.	-3.4%	-3.5%	-4.1%	-6.1%	-8.1%	-8.4%	-6.1%	-8.1%	-8.4%
Investment - vol.	-4.4%	-4.5%	-6.1%	-7.3%	-9.8%	-10.0%	-7.3%	-9.9%	-10.1%
Labour Demand - vol.	-3.2%	-3.3%	-3.4%	-5.4%	-10.7%	-10.9%	-5.4%	-10.8%	-11.1%
Private Consumption - vol.	-1.8%	-1.6%	-1.8%	-1.6%	-2.0%	-2.2%	-1.6%	-2.0%	-2.2%
Supply to domestic - vol.	-13.6%	-13.6%	-14.2%	-14.7%	-23.2%	-23.6%	-14.7%	-23.3%	-23.8%
Intra-EU Trade - vol	0.0%	0.0%	0.0%	-2.3%	-3.9%	-4.1%	-2.3%	-4.0%	-4.2%

Consumer goods	Constraint Case			Flexible Case			Efficiency Case		
	1988	1991	1994	1988	1991	1994	1988	1991	1994
Domestic Production - vol.	0.8%	0.6%	0.2%	-0.7%	-1.6%	-1.9%	-0.8%	-1.6%	-2.0%
Imports - vol.	-3.6%	-3.6%	-3.7%	-3.6%	-3.2%	-2.8%	-3.6%	-2.9%	-2.4%
Exports - vol.	-1.0%	-1.3%	-1.7%	1.9%	1.6%	1.3%	1.9%	1.4%	1.1%
Absorption - vol.	-1.1%	-1.1%	-1.3%	-1.5%	-1.9%	-2.1%	-1.5%	-1.9%	-2.1%
Investment - vol.	0.8%	0.6%	-1.1%	-4.5%	-4.9%	-5.1%	-4.5%	-4.9%	-5.1%
Labour Demand - vol.	1.2%	1.0%	0.7%	-0.2%	-0.9%	-1.1%	-0.2%	-0.9%	-1.1%
Private Consumption - vol.	-1.3%	-1.2%	-1.3%	-1.0%	-1.5%	-1.6%	-1.0%	-1.5%	-1.6%
Supply to domestic - vol.	5.8%	5.9%	5.5%	2.9%	7.5%	7.1%	2.9%	7.4%	7.0%
Intra-EU Trade - vol	0.0%	0.0%	0.0%	-1.3%	-3.3%	-3.5%	-1.3%	-3.4%	-3.6%

Construction	Constraint Case			Flexible Case			Efficiency Case		
	1988	1991	1994	1988	1991	1994	1988	1991	1994
Domestic Production - vol.	-4.1%	-4.2%	-4.7%	-6.6%	-6.5%	-6.8%	-6.6%	-6.5%	-6.7%
Imports - vol.	-	-	-	#VALUE!	#VALUE!	#VALUE!	#VALUE!	#VALUE!	#VALUE!
Exports - vol.	0.7%	0.6%	0.5%	0.5%	0.4%	0.3%	0.4%	0.3%	0.2%
Absorption - vol.	-4.2%	-4.3%	-4.8%	-6.7%	-6.6%	-6.9%	-6.7%	-6.6%	-6.9%
Investment - vol.	-6.8%	-7.0%	-8.3%	-7.4%	-7.4%	-7.6%	-7.4%	-7.4%	-7.5%
Labour Demand - vol.	-3.8%	-4.0%	-4.4%	-6.3%	-6.1%	-6.3%	-6.2%	-6.1%	-6.2%
Private Consumption - vol.	-1.4%	-1.3%	-1.4%	-0.9%	-1.4%	-1.7%	-0.9%	-1.5%	-1.7%
Supply to domestic - vol.	-4.1%	-4.2%	-4.7%	-6.6%	-6.5%	-6.8%	-6.6%	-6.5%	-6.7%
Intra-EU Trade - vol	0.0%	0.0%	0.0%	-3.0%	-3.1%	-3.2%	-3.0%	-3.1%	-3.2%

Telecommunications	Constraint Case			Flexible Case			Efficiency Case		
	1988	1991	1994	1988	1991	1994	1988	1991	1994
Domestic Production - vol.	0.0%	0.1%	0.0%	1.5%	4.1%	3.7%	1.5%	4.0%	3.6%
Imports - vol.	-6.0%	-6.3%	-6.1%	-5.6%	-5.5%	-5.1%	-5.6%	-5.3%	-4.8%
Exports - vol.	-3.3%	-3.0%	-3.3%	1.1%	1.1%	0.9%	1.1%	1.0%	0.8%
Absorption - vol.	-0.7%	-0.6%	-0.7%	-0.6%	-0.6%	-0.8%	-0.6%	-0.6%	-0.9%
Investment - vol.	-5.5%	-6.2%	-6.7%	-3.6%	-2.3%	-2.5%	-3.5%	-2.3%	-2.4%
Labour Demand - vol.	2.0%	2.5%	2.5%	2.3%	5.4%	5.2%	2.3%	5.4%	5.2%
Private Consumption - vol.	-1.8%	-1.7%	-1.8%	-1.2%	-1.8%	-2.1%	-1.2%	-1.8%	-2.1%
Supply to domestic - vol.	0.2%	0.3%	0.2%	2.2%	7.0%	6.7%	2.2%	7.0%	6.6%
Intra-EU Trade - vol	0.0%	0.0%	0.0%	-7.1%	-18.3%	-18.4%	-7.1%	-18.3%	-18.4%

Transports	Constraint Case			Flexible Case			Efficiency Case		
	1988	1991	1994	1988	1991	1994	1988	1991	1994
Domestic Production - vol.	0.1%	0.2%	0.2%	1.0%	1.2%	1.1%	1.0%	1.2%	1.0%
Imports - vol.	0.1%	0.2%	0.2%	0.5%	0.6%	0.5%	0.5%	0.6%	0.5%
Exports - vol.	1.0%	1.1%	1.2%	0.7%	0.6%	0.5%	0.7%	0.6%	0.5%
Absorption - vol.	-0.5%	-0.5%	-0.6%	-0.6%	-0.4%	-0.5%	-0.6%	-0.4%	-0.5%
Investment - vol.	-6.4%	-6.3%	-6.6%	-3.8%	-3.7%	-3.8%	-3.8%	-3.7%	-3.8%
Labour Demand - vol.	0.2%	0.3%	0.4%	1.2%	1.5%	1.4%	1.2%	1.5%	1.5%
Private Consumption - vol.	-1.6%	-1.5%	-1.5%	-1.1%	-1.6%	-1.9%	-1.1%	-1.7%	-1.9%
Supply to domestic - vol.	0.1%	0.2%	0.2%	1.0%	1.2%	1.1%	1.0%	1.2%	1.0%
Intra-EU Trade - vol	0.0%	0.0%	0.0%	2.1%	2.5%	2.3%	2.1%	2.4%	2.3%

Banks	Constraint Case			Flexible Case			Efficiency Case		
	1988	1991	1994	1988	1991	1994	1988	1991	1994
Domestic Production - vol.	0.0%	0.2%	0.2%	0.0%	0.5%	0.1%	0.0%	0.4%	-0.1%
Imports - vol.	-14.3%	-14.8%	-14.6%	-5.7%	-5.2%	-4.8%	-5.6%	-5.0%	-4.4%
Exports - vol.	-0.7%	0.1%	0.5%	1.1%	1.0%	0.8%	1.1%	0.9%	0.7%
Absorption - vol.	-0.5%	-0.3%	-0.3%	-0.4%	-0.2%	-0.6%	-0.4%	-0.2%	-0.7%
Investment - vol.	-4.3%	-4.7%	-5.2%	-4.2%	-3.9%	-4.1%	-4.2%	-3.9%	-4.1%
Labour Demand - vol.	0.8%	1.2%	1.2%	0.2%	0.8%	0.5%	0.2%	0.7%	0.5%
Private Consumption - vol.	-1.6%	-1.5%	-1.6%	-1.1%	-1.7%	-1.9%	-1.1%	-1.7%	-2.0%
Supply to domestic - vol.	0.0%	0.2%	0.2%	0.3%	1.5%	1.1%	0.3%	1.5%	1.0%
Intra-EU Trade - vol	0.0%	0.0%	0.0%	-4.5%	-11.6%	-11.8%	-4.5%	-11.6%	-11.9%

Services	Constraint Case			Flexible Case			Efficiency Case		
	1988	1991	1994	1988	1991	1994	1988	1991	1994
Domestic Production - vol.	-0.4%	-0.5%	-0.7%	-0.6%	-0.2%	-0.3%	-0.6%	-0.2%	-0.4%
Imports - vol.	-6.7%	-6.9%	-6.9%	-3.8%	-3.5%	-3.1%	-3.7%	-3.3%	-2.8%
Exports - vol.	2.3%	1.8%	1.6%	1.1%	0.9%	0.7%	1.1%	0.8%	0.6%
Absorption - vol.	-1.3%	-1.4%	-1.6%	-1.7%	-2.1%	-2.3%	-1.7%	-2.1%	-2.3%
Investment - vol.	-4.4%	-4.5%	-5.4%	-4.6%	-4.4%	-4.5%	-4.6%	-4.4%	-4.5%
Labour Demand - vol.	-0.2%	-0.3%	-0.3%	-0.4%	0.2%	0.2%	-0.4%	0.2%	0.2%
Private Consumption - vol.	-1.3%	-1.3%	-1.5%	-1.3%	-1.7%	-1.8%	-1.3%	-1.7%	-1.9%
Supply to domestic - vol.	-0.8%	-0.8%	-1.1%	-1.4%	-1.5%	-1.6%	-1.4%	-1.5%	-1.7%
Intra-EU Trade - vol	0.0%	0.0%	0.0%	0.9%	1.2%	1.1%	0.9%	1.2%	1.1%

Non market	Constraint Case			Flexible Case			Efficiency Case		
	1988	1991	1994	1988	1991	1994	1988	1991	1994
Domestic Production - vol.	-0.1%	-0.1%	-0.2%	-0.2%	-0.2%	-0.2%	-0.2%	-0.2%	-0.2%
Imports - vol.	-	-	-	#VALUE!	#VALUE!	#VALUE!	#VALUE!	#VALUE!	#VALUE!
Exports - vol.	1.5%	1.5%	1.5%	0.3%	0.2%	0.2%	0.3%	0.2%	0.2%
Absorption - vol.	-0.1%	-0.1%	-0.2%	-0.2%	-0.2%	-0.3%	-0.2%	-0.2%	-0.3%
Investment - vol.	-7.7%	-7.7%	-7.8%	-4.2%	-4.2%	-4.2%	-4.2%	-4.2%	-4.2%
Labour Demand - vol.	0.0%	0.0%	-0.1%	0.0%	0.0%	0.0%	0.0%	0.0%	0.1%
Private Consumption - vol.	-1.3%	-1.3%	-1.4%	-1.1%	-1.5%	-1.7%	-1.1%	-1.5%	-1.7%
Supply to domestic - vol.	-0.1%	-0.1%	-0.2%	-0.2%	-0.2%	-0.2%	-0.2%	-0.2%	-0.2%
Intra-EU Trade - vol	0.0%	0.0%	0.0%	0.4%	0.3%	0.3%	0.4%	0.3%	0.3%

Table B9.4.

The full *antimonde* scenario: sectoral results for the Netherlands (prices)

% change from *monde*

Agriculture	Constraint Case			Flexible Case			Efficiency Case		
	1988	1991	1994	1988	1991	1994	1988	1991	1994
Real Marginal Costs	-0.19%	0.04%	0.35%	1.38%	1.34%	1.36%	1.36%	1.27%	1.23%
Real Cost of Labour	-2.03%	-2.00%	-2.27%	-1.06%	-1.57%	-1.96%	-1.08%	-1.66%	-2.12%
Real Deflator of Absorption	0.23%	0.37%	0.55%	2.62%	2.44%	2.23%	2.58%	2.28%	1.96%
Real Price of Exports-RW	-0.19%	0.04%	0.35%	1.38%	1.34%	1.36%	1.36%	1.27%	1.23%

Energy	Constraint Case			Flexible Case			Efficiency Case		
	1988	1991	1994	1988	1991	1994	1988	1991	1994
Marginal Costs	-0.31%	-0.07%	0.26%	1.40%	1.33%	1.34%	1.37%	1.21%	1.14%
Cost of Labour	-2.03%	-2.00%	-2.27%	-1.06%	-1.57%	-1.96%	-1.08%	-1.66%	-2.12%
Deflator of Absorption	0.12%	0.25%	0.43%	2.70%	2.51%	2.30%	2.66%	2.33%	1.97%
Price of Exports-RW	-0.31%	-0.07%	0.26%	1.40%	1.33%	1.34%	1.37%	1.21%	1.14%

Metal Industries	Constraint Case			Flexible Case			Efficiency Case		
	1988	1991	1994	1988	1991	1994	1988	1991	1994
Marginal Costs	0.67%	0.80%	0.91%	2.41%	2.43%	2.22%	2.39%	2.35%	2.08%
Cost of Labour	-2.03%	-2.00%	-2.27%	-1.06%	-1.57%	-1.96%	-1.08%	-1.66%	-2.12%
Deflator of Absorption	3.11%	3.14%	3.18%	5.73%	6.17%	5.78%	5.69%	6.01%	5.49%
Price of Exports-RW	2.26%	2.39%	2.51%	1.41%	1.62%	1.45%	1.39%	1.55%	1.32%

Chemical	Constraint Case			Flexible Case			Efficiency Case		
	1988	1991	1994	1988	1991	1994	1988	1991	1994
Marginal Costs	0.27%	0.41%	0.59%	2.38%	2.36%	2.18%	2.36%	2.28%	2.04%
Cost of Labour	-2.03%	-2.00%	-2.27%	-1.06%	-1.57%	-1.96%	-1.08%	-1.66%	-2.12%
Deflator of Absorption	0.82%	0.88%	0.95%	3.70%	3.77%	3.46%	3.66%	3.63%	3.21%
Price of Exports-RW	0.40%	0.55%	0.73%	2.26%	2.20%	2.03%	2.24%	2.12%	1.89%

Other Intensive Industries	Constraint Case			Flexible Case			Efficiency Case		
	1988	1991	1994	1988	1991	1994	1988	1991	1994
Marginal Costs	-0.14%	0.00%	0.12%	1.16%	1.09%	0.95%	1.15%	1.05%	0.88%
Cost of Labour	-2.03%	-2.00%	-2.27%	-1.06%	-1.57%	-1.96%	-1.08%	-1.66%	-2.12%
Deflator of Absorption	0.66%	0.76%	0.84%	2.11%	2.13%	1.93%	2.09%	2.06%	1.80%
Price of Exports-RW	0.10%	0.25%	0.37%	1.05%	0.91%	0.78%	1.04%	0.87%	0.71%

Electrical goods	Constraint Case			Flexible Case			Efficiency Case		
	1988	1991	1994	1988	1991	1994	1988	1991	1994
Marginal Costs	-0.15%	-0.04%	0.00%	1.17%	1.01%	0.79%	1.15%	0.96%	0.70%
Cost of Labour	-2.03%	-2.00%	-2.27%	-1.06%	-1.57%	-1.96%	-1.08%	-1.66%	-2.12%
Deflator of Absorption	2.51%	2.53%	2.55%	4.57%	4.59%	4.15%	4.53%	4.42%	3.84%
Price of Exports-RW	0.85%	0.97%	1.01%	0.67%	0.51%	0.31%	0.66%	0.47%	0.24%

Transport equipment	Constraint Case			Flexible Case			Efficiency Case		
	1988	1991	1994	1988	1991	1994	1988	1991	1994
Marginal Costs	0.70%	0.80%	0.85%	2.06%	2.08%	1.82%	2.05%	2.03%	1.73%
Cost of Labour	-2.03%	-2.00%	-2.27%	-1.06%	-1.57%	-1.96%	-1.08%	-1.66%	-2.12%
Deflator of Absorption	3.21%	3.25%	3.28%	4.58%	5.32%	4.97%	4.56%	5.22%	4.80%
Price of Exports-RW	1.52%	1.64%	1.72%	1.18%	0.71%	0.44%	1.17%	0.66%	0.35%

Other Equipment	Constraint Case			Flexible Case			Efficiency Case		
	1988	1991	1994	1988	1991	1994	1988	1991	1994
Marginal Costs	0.43%	0.54%	0.60%	1.83%	1.76%	1.52%	1.82%	1.70%	1.42%
Cost of Labour	-2.03%	-2.00%	-2.27%	-1.06%	-1.57%	-1.96%	-1.08%	-1.66%	-2.12%
Deflator of Absorption	1.81%	1.82%	1.84%	3.69%	3.73%	3.33%	3.65%	3.58%	3.05%
Price of Exports-RW	1.06%	1.16%	1.23%	1.51%	1.40%	1.17%	1.49%	1.35%	1.07%

Consumer goods	Constraint Case			Flexible Case			Efficiency Case		
	1988	1991	1994	1988	1991	1994	1988	1991	1994
Marginal Costs	0.00%	0.15%	0.33%	1.77%	1.61%	1.45%	1.75%	1.54%	1.33%
Cost of Labour	-2.03%	-2.00%	-2.27%	-1.06%	-1.57%	-1.96%	-1.08%	-1.66%	-2.12%
Deflator of Absorption	0.93%	0.98%	1.03%	3.29%	3.10%	2.74%	3.25%	2.93%	2.45%
Price of Exports-RW	0.00%	0.15%	0.33%	1.77%	1.61%	1.45%	1.75%	1.54%	1.33%

Construction	Constraint Case			Flexible Case			Efficiency Case		
	1988	1991	1994	1988	1991	1994	1988	1991	1994
Marginal Costs	-0.33%	-0.20%	-0.12%	0.91%	0.75%	0.58%	0.90%	0.73%	0.53%
Cost of Labour	-2.03%	-2.00%	-2.27%	-1.06%	-1.57%	-1.96%	-1.08%	-1.66%	-2.12%
Deflator of Absorption	-0.33%	-0.20%	-0.12%	0.91%	0.75%	0.58%	0.90%	0.73%	0.53%
Price of Exports-RW	-0.33%	-0.20%	-0.12%	0.91%	0.75%	0.58%	0.90%	0.73%	0.53%

Telecommunications	Constraint Case			Flexible Case			Efficiency Case		
	1988	1991	1994	1988	1991	1994	1988	1991	1994
Marginal Costs	-0.61%	-0.86%	-0.65%	-0.01%	-0.09%	-0.03%	-0.01%	-0.10%	-0.04%
Cost of Labour	-2.03%	-2.00%	-2.27%	-1.06%	-1.57%	-1.96%	-1.08%	-1.66%	-2.12%
Deflator of Absorption	0.33%	0.30%	0.45%	0.97%	0.91%	0.91%	0.96%	0.87%	0.84%
Price of Exports-RW	2.79%	2.60%	2.80%	-0.48%	-1.09%	-1.03%	-0.49%	-1.10%	-1.06%

Transports	Constraint Case			Flexible Case			Efficiency Case		
	1988	1991	1994	1988	1991	1994	1988	1991	1994
Marginal Costs	-0.93%	-0.76%	-0.65%	0.33%	0.14%	0.03%	0.32%	0.08%	-0.06%
Cost of Labour	-2.03%	-2.00%	-2.27%	-1.06%	-1.57%	-1.96%	-1.08%	-1.66%	-2.12%
Deflator of Absorption	-0.93%	-0.76%	-0.64%	0.33%	0.14%	0.04%	0.32%	0.08%	-0.06%
Price of Exports-RW	-0.93%	-0.76%	-0.65%	0.33%	0.14%	0.03%	0.32%	0.08%	-0.06%

Banks	Constraint Case			Flexible Case			Efficiency Case		
	1988	1991	1994	1988	1991	1994	1988	1991	1994
Marginal Costs	-0.65%	-0.81%	-0.57%	-0.02%	-0.09%	-0.02%	-0.03%	-0.11%	-0.06%
Cost of Labour	-2.03%	-2.00%	-2.27%	-1.06%	-1.57%	-1.96%	-1.08%	-1.66%	-2.12%
Deflator of Absorption	-0.45%	-0.55%	-0.35%	0.07%	-0.09%	-0.02%	0.07%	-0.11%	-0.07%
Price of Exports-RW	0.74%	0.60%	0.83%	-0.09%	-0.23%	-0.16%	-0.09%	-0.25%	-0.20%

Services	Constraint Case			Flexible Case			Efficiency Case		
	1988	1991	1994	1988	1991	1994	1988	1991	1994
Marginal Costs	-0.98%	-0.78%	-0.61%	0.12%	-0.01%	-0.02%	0.11%	-0.05%	-0.09%
Cost of Labour	-2.03%	-2.00%	-2.27%	-1.06%	-1.57%	-1.96%	-1.08%	-1.66%	-2.12%
Deflator of Absorption	-0.83%	-0.64%	-0.48%	0.18%	0.07%	0.05%	0.17%	0.03%	-0.02%
Price of Exports-RW	-0.98%	-0.78%	-0.61%	0.12%	-0.01%	-0.02%	0.11%	-0.05%	-0.09%

Non market	Constraint Case			Flexible Case			Efficiency Case		
	1988	1991	1994	1988	1991	1994	1988	1991	1994
Marginal Costs	-1.23%	-1.15%	-1.24%	-0.11%	-0.44%	-0.70%	-0.12%	-0.47%	-0.75%
Cost of Labour	-2.03%	-2.00%	-2.27%	-1.06%	-1.57%	-1.96%	-1.08%	-1.66%	-2.12%
Deflator of Absorption	-1.23%	-1.15%	-1.24%	-0.11%	-0.44%	-0.70%	-0.12%	-0.47%	-0.75%
Price of Exports-RW	-1.23%	-1.15%	-1.24%	-0.11%	-0.44%	-0.70%	-0.12%	-0.47%	-0.75%

Table B9.5.
Decomposition of effects: macroeconomic aggregates for the Netherlands

Macroeconomic Aggregates (vol.) (% change from monde)	Border Controls 1988	Border Controls 1991	Border Controls 1994	Border controls and x-ineff. 1988	Border controls and x-ineff. 1991	Border controls and x-ineff. 1994	Market segmentation 1988	Market segmentation 1991	Market segmentation 1994	Trade antimonde 1988	Trade antimonde 1991	Trade antimonde 1994	Full antimonde 1988	Full antimonde 1991	Full antimonde 1994
GDP fact. pr.	-0.02%	-0.11%	-0.11%	-0.03%	-0.13%	-0.13%	-0.57%	-1.02%	-1.30%	-0.59%	-1.07%	-1.36%	-0.69%	-1.21%	-1.54%
Priv. Consumption	0.22%	0.15%	0.15%	0.22%	0.15%	0.15%	-1.46%	-1.63%	-1.74%	-1.38%	-1.62%	-1.73%	-1.40%	-1.66%	-1.78%
Absorption	-0.01%	-0.18%	-0.18%	-0.01%	-0.18%	-0.17%	-1.78%	-2.29%	-2.48%	-1.86%	-2.46%	-2.66%	-1.88%	-2.50%	-2.71%
Total Investment	0.03%	0.03%	0.03%	0.03%	0.03%	0.03%	-4.30%	-4.48%	-4.62%	-4.29%	-4.48%	-4.63%	-4.29%	-4.49%	-4.64%
Total Exports to RW	-0.52%	-0.56%	-0.57%	-0.52%	-0.57%	-0.58%	1.82%	1.62%	1.44%	1.50%	1.30%	1.12%	1.45%	1.22%	1.01%
Total Imports from RW	1.24%	1.26%	1.27%	1.25%	1.28%	1.30%	-4.62%	-4.68%	-4.48%	-3.41%	-3.40%	-3.19%	-3.28%	-3.20%	-2.93%
Total Intra-EU Trade	-0.73%	-1.90%	-1.90%	-0.74%	-1.92%	-1.92%	0.03%	-1.74%	-1.93%	-0.50%	-2.47%	-2.66%	-0.59%	-2.60%	-2.82%
Employment (diff. from monde, 10³ persons)	2	0	0	1	-1	-1	-33	-36	-42	-33	-37	-43	-33	-38	-44
Disposable Income (deflated)	0.23%	0.15%	0.15%	0.23%	0.15%	0.15%	-1.52%	-1.69%	-1.80%	-1.43%	-1.68%	-1.79%	-1.46%	-1.72%	-1.84%

Macroeconomic Ratios (abs. diff. from monde)	Border Controls 1988	Border Controls 1991	Border Controls 1994	Border controls and x-ineff. 1988	Border controls and x-ineff. 1991	Border controls and x-ineff. 1994	Market segmentation 1988	Market segmentation 1991	Market segmentation 1994	Trade antimonde 1988	Trade antimonde 1991	Trade antimonde 1994	Full antimonde 1988	Full antimonde 1991	Full antimonde 1994
Current Account as % of GDP	-0.09%	-0.03%	-0.03%	-0.09%	-0.03%	-0.02%	-0.70%	-0.62%	-0.63%	-0.72%	-0.59%	-0.59%	-0.69%	-0.54%	-0.54%
Public Deficit as % of GDP	0.13%	0.09%	0.09%	0.13%	0.08%	0.08%	-0.76%	-0.91%	-1.01%	-0.68%	-0.87%	-0.97%	-0.70%	-0.91%	-1.01%
Labour Productivity	-0.06%	-0.11%	-0.12%	-0.06%	-0.11%	-0.12%	0.10%	-0.27%	-0.44%	0.08%	-0.29%	-0.47%	0.00%	-0.41%	-0.63%
Investment/GDP	0.02%	0.04%	0.04%	0.02%	0.04%	0.04%	-1.82%	-1.81%	-1.82%	-1.81%	-1.80%	-1.81%	-1.79%	-1.78%	-1.77%
Priv.Cons./GDP	0.14%	0.15%	0.15%	0.15%	0.16%	0.16%	-0.52%	-0.36%	-0.26%	-0.46%	-0.32%	-0.22%	-0.42%	-0.27%	-0.14%

Deflators (% change from monde)	Border Controls 1988	Border Controls 1991	Border Controls 1994	Border controls and x-ineff. 1988	Border controls and x-ineff. 1991	Border controls and x-ineff. 1994	Market segmentation 1988	Market segmentation 1991	Market segmentation 1994	Trade antimonde 1988	Trade antimonde 1991	Trade antimonde 1994	Full antimonde 1988	Full antimonde 1991	Full antimonde 1994
Consumer Price Index	-0.32%	-0.30%	-0.30%	-0.33%	-0.32%	-0.32%	1.34%	1.20%	1.11%	1.26%	1.17%	1.08%	1.22%	1.11%	0.99%
Real Wage Rate	0.00%	-0.11%	-0.11%	-0.02%	-0.14%	-0.14%	-0.91%	-1.33%	-1.66%	-0.97%	-1.44%	-1.78%	-1.06%	-1.57%	-1.96%
Marginal Costs	-0.24%	-0.22%	-0.23%	-0.24%	-0.23%	-0.23%	0.96%	0.86%	0.79%	0.90%	0.84%	0.76%	0.88%	0.81%	0.72%
Producer Prices	-0.23%	-0.20%	-0.21%	-0.24%	-0.22%	-0.22%	1.10%	1.04%	0.97%	1.04%	1.04%	0.96%	1.01%	0.99%	0.90%
Real Shadow Price of Capital	-0.01%	0.01%	0.01%	0.01%	0.04%	0.03%	0.09%	0.27%	0.69%	0.10%	0.28%	0.71%	0.03%	0.19%	0.58%
Terms-of-Trade RW	2.06%	2.22%	2.24%	2.08%	2.26%	2.29%	-6.19%	-5.55%	-4.96%	-4.98%	-4.33%	-3.73%	-4.81%	-4.07%	-3.38%
Real Exchange Rate	4.21%	4.36%	4.38%	4.24%	4.40%	4.44%	-7.51%	-6.68%	-5.97%	-4.54%	-3.76%	-3.03%	-4.34%	-3.46%	-2.62%
Trade Regime	Integration			Integration			Segmentation			Segmentation			Segmentation		

Table B9.6.
Decomposition of effects: effects on IC sectors for the Netherlands

% change from *monde*

Metal Industries

	Border Controls			Border controls and x-ineff.			Market segmentation			Trade *antimonde*			Full *antimonde*		
	1988	1991	1994	1988	1991	1994	1988	1991	1994	1988	1991	1994	1988	1991	1994
Production per firm	-1.85%	-3.62%	-3.62%	-1.86%	-3.63%	-3.63%	-13.51%	-20.76%	-20.88%	-15.13%	-22.48%	-22.60%	-15.25%	-22.63%	-22.80%
Marginal Costs	3.73%	3.92%	3.94%	3.75%	3.96%	3.99%	-4.98%	-4.21%	-3.70%	-2.10%	-1.29%	-0.75%	-1.93%	-1.03%	-0.40%
Producer Prices	3.91%	4.24%	4.25%	3.93%	4.27%	4.30%	-3.54%	-2.14%	-1.61%	-0.42%	1.07%	1.63%	-0.23%	1.35%	2.00%
Mark-ups domestic (abs. diff.)	0.21%	0.43%	0.43%	0.21%	0.43%	0.43%	9.80%	11.79%	11.81%	10.11%	12.16%	12.18%	10.14%	12.20%	12.23%
Fixed Costs per firm	3.67%	3.86%	3.88%	3.69%	3.89%	3.91%	-4.70%	-3.97%	-3.53%	-1.84%	-1.05%	-0.59%	-1.71%	-0.85%	-0.33%
Number of Firms	-0.44%	-0.55%	-0.54%	-0.44%	-0.56%	-0.55%	14.50%	12.02%	11.45%	13.42%	10.78%	10.21%	13.33%	10.66%	10.05%
Sigma of Love of Variety	0.00%	0.00%	0.00%	0.00%	0.00%	0.00%	0.00%	0.00%	0.00%	0.00%	0.00%	0.00%	0.00%	0.00%	0.00%

Chemical

	Border Controls			Border controls and x-ineff.			Market segmentation			Trade *antimonde*			Full *antimonde*		
	1988	1991	1994	1988	1991	1994	1988	1991	1994	1988	1991	1994	1988	1991	1994
Production per firm	-1.16%	-2.58%	-2.58%	-1.16%	-2.60%	-2.60%	-8.12%	-13.06%	-13.19%	-8.70%	-13.85%	-13.97%	-8.79%	-13.96%	-14.12%
Marginal Costs	3.87%	4.11%	4.13%	3.89%	4.15%	4.18%	-5.14%	-4.45%	-3.89%	-2.14%	-1.37%	-0.79%	-1.96%	-1.10%	-0.44%
Producer Prices	3.90%	4.19%	4.20%	3.93%	4.22%	4.25%	-4.89%	-4.04%	-3.49%	-1.86%	-0.93%	-0.35%	-1.68%	-0.66%	0.01%
Mark-ups domestic (abs. diff.)	0.01%	0.09%	0.09%	0.01%	0.09%	0.09%	0.93%	1.27%	1.28%	0.91%	1.27%	1.28%	0.91%	1.28%	1.28%
Fixed Costs per firm	3.82%	4.07%	4.08%	3.84%	4.09%	4.12%	-4.85%	-4.20%	-3.73%	-1.85%	-1.11%	-0.62%	-1.71%	-0.90%	-0.34%
Number of Firms	0.82%	0.80%	0.80%	0.81%	0.77%	0.78%	8.86%	11.56%	11.43%	9.25%	11.58%	11.43%	9.16%	11.43%	11.26%
Sigma of Love of Variety	0.00%	0.00%	0.00%	0.00%	0.00%	0.00%	0.00%	0.00%	0.00%	0.00%	0.00%	0.00%	0.00%	0.00%	0.00%

Other Intensive Industries

	Border Controls			Border controls and x-ineff.			Market segmentation			Trade *antimonde*			Full *antimonde*		
	1988	1991	1994	1988	1991	1994	1988	1991	1994	1988	1991	1994	1988	1991	1994
Production per firm	-1.02%	-2.51%	-2.51%	-1.03%	-2.52%	-2.52%	-7.11%	-10.77%	-11.00%	-7.74%	-11.55%	-11.77%	-7.81%	-11.66%	-11.92%
Marginal Costs	3.98%	4.15%	4.17%	4.00%	4.19%	4.22%	-6.30%	-5.60%	-5.02%	-3.36%	-2.66%	-2.04%	-3.18%	-2.38%	-1.67%
Producer Prices	4.04%	4.30%	4.32%	4.06%	4.34%	4.37%	-5.86%	-4.94%	-4.34%	-2.86%	-1.91%	-1.29%	-2.67%	-1.63%	-0.91%
Mark-ups domestic (abs. diff.)	0.01%	0.04%	0.04%	0.01%	0.04%	0.04%	0.69%	0.87%	0.88%	0.70%	0.88%	0.89%	0.70%	0.89%	0.90%
Fixed Costs per firm	3.93%	4.10%	4.12%	3.95%	4.12%	4.15%	-6.11%	-5.47%	-4.99%	-3.18%	-2.53%	-2.02%	-3.04%	-2.32%	-1.74%
Number of Firms	0.58%	2.14%	2.13%	0.58%	2.15%	2.14%	6.14%	9.79%	9.45%	6.02%	9.64%	9.29%	6.00%	9.61%	9.26%
Sigma of Love of Variety	0.00%	0.00%	0.00%	0.00%	0.00%	0.00%	0.00%	0.00%	0.00%	0.00%	0.00%	0.00%	0.00%	0.00%	0.00%

Electrical goods

	Border Controls			Border controls and x-ineff.			Market segmentation			Trade *antimonde*			Full *antimonde*		
	1988	1991	1994	1988	1991	1994	1988	1991	1994	1988	1991	1994	1988	1991	1994
Production per firm	-1.37%	-2.75%	-2.75%	-1.37%	-2.76%	-2.77%	-9.02%	-13.06%	-13.21%	-9.98%	-14.24%	-14.37%	-10.08%	-14.39%	-14.58%
Marginal Costs	3.95%	4.10%	4.12%	3.97%	4.13%	4.16%	-6.28%	-5.64%	-5.13%	-3.35%	-2.72%	-2.19%	-3.18%	-2.45%	-1.83%
Producer Prices	4.06%	4.31%	4.33%	4.08%	4.34%	4.38%	-5.53%	-4.59%	-4.07%	-2.49%	-1.53%	-0.98%	-2.31%	-1.25%	-0.61%
Mark-ups domestic (abs. diff.)	0.16%	0.37%	0.36%	0.16%	0.37%	0.37%	6.50%	7.75%	7.76%	6.60%	7.86%	7.87%	6.61%	7.88%	7.89%
Fixed Costs per firm	3.92%	4.06%	4.08%	3.93%	4.08%	4.11%	-6.16%	-5.57%	-5.13%	-3.25%	-2.66%	-2.20%	-3.12%	-2.47%	-1.94%
Number of Firms	-0.16%	0.49%	0.50%	-0.16%	0.49%	0.49%	9.26%	9.18%	8.90%	8.78%	8.63%	8.35%	8.69%	8.51%	8.19%
Sigma of Love of Variety	0.00%	0.00%	0.00%	0.00%	0.00%	0.00%	0.00%	0.00%	0.00%	0.00%	0.00%	0.00%	0.00%	0.00%	0.00%

Transport equipment

	Border Controls			Border controls and x-ineff.			Market segmentation			Trade *antimonde*			Full *antimonde*		
	1988	1991	1994	1988	1991	1994	1988	1991	1994	1988	1991	1994	1988	1991	1994
Production per firm	-0.98%	-2.42%	-2.42%	-0.99%	-2.43%	-2.43%	-18.57%	-24.64%	-24.62%	-19.26%	-25.65%	-25.62%	-19.34%	-25.75%	-25.76%
Marginal Costs	3.91%	4.12%	4.14%	3.93%	4.15%	4.18%	-5.45%	-4.71%	-4.25%	-2.46%	-1.67%	-1.18%	-2.28%	-1.39%	-0.80%
Producer Prices	3.98%	4.28%	4.30%	4.00%	4.31%	4.35%	-3.92%	-2.73%	-2.26%	-0.82%	0.49%	0.98%	-0.62%	0.79%	1.38%
Mark-ups domestic (abs. diff.)	0.02%	0.16%	0.16%	0.02%	0.16%	0.16%	6.29%	7.76%	7.76%	6.27%	7.75%	7.75%	6.27%	7.75%	7.76%
Fixed Costs per firm	3.90%	4.10%	4.12%	3.91%	4.12%	4.15%	-5.40%	-4.68%	-4.24%	-2.42%	-1.64%	-1.18%	-2.28%	-1.43%	-0.90%
Number of Firms	1.06%	2.29%	2.30%	1.06%	2.31%	2.31%	17.94%	27.16%	27.21%	18.11%	27.25%	27.31%	18.08%	27.20%	27.26%
Sigma of Love of Variety	0.00%	0.00%	0.00%	0.00%	0.00%	0.00%	0.00%	0.00%	0.00%	0.00%	0.00%	0.00%	0.00%	0.00%	0.00%

Other Equipment

	Border Controls			Border controls and x-ineff.			Market segmentation			Trade *antimonde*			Full *antimonde*		
	1988	1991	1994	1988	1991	1994	1988	1991	1994	1988	1991	1994	1988	1991	1994
Production per firm	-1.37%	-2.69%	-2.69%	-1.38%	-2.70%	-2.70%	-13.64%	-18.84%	-18.93%	-14.93%	-20.45%	-20.54%	-15.03%	-20.59%	-20.73%
Marginal Costs	3.85%	4.05%	4.07%	3.87%	4.08%	4.12%	-5.61%	-4.95%	-4.46%	-2.69%	-1.97%	-1.47%	-2.51%	-1.70%	-1.10%
Producer Prices	3.92%	4.17%	4.18%	3.94%	4.20%	4.23%	-4.94%	-4.05%	-3.57%	-1.92%	-0.96%	-0.44%	-1.73%	-0.68%	-0.07%
Mark-ups domestic (abs. diff.)	0.06%	0.16%	0.16%	0.06%	0.16%	0.16%	5.02%	6.01%	6.02%	5.10%	6.13%	6.13%	5.11%	6.14%	6.15%
Fixed Costs per firm	3.81%	4.02%	4.03%	3.83%	4.03%	4.06%	-5.45%	-4.82%	-4.40%	-2.54%	-1.86%	-1.42%	-2.41%	-1.66%	-1.15%
Number of Firms	-0.22%	0.09%	0.09%	-0.22%	0.09%	0.09%	10.53%	11.53%	11.39%	9.69%	10.40%	10.24%	9.62%	10.28%	10.09%
Sigma of Love of Variety	0.00%	0.00%	0.00%	0.00%	0.00%	0.00%	0.00%	0.00%	0.00%	0.00%	0.00%	0.00%	0.00%	0.00%	0.00%

Telecommunications

	Border Controls			Border controls and x-ineff.			Market segmentation			Trade *antimonde*			Full *antimonde*		
	1988	1991	1994	1988	1991	1994	1988	1991	1994	1988	1991	1994	1988	1991	1994
Production per firm	0.07%	0.17%	0.16%	-0.51%	-1.11%	-1.13%	-3.27%	-5.49%	-5.82%	-3.19%	-5.41%	-5.75%	-3.78%	-6.53%	-6.89%
Marginal Costs	4.19%	4.33%	4.36%	4.21%	4.38%	4.43%	-7.50%	-6.75%	-5.98%	-4.55%	-3.86%	-3.05%	-4.35%	-3.55%	-2.65%
Producer Prices	4.15%	4.26%	4.29%	3.99%	3.96%	4.00%	-6.80%	-5.59%	-4.81%	-3.85%	-2.69%	-1.88%	-3.84%	-2.76%	-1.85%
Mark-ups domestic (abs. diff.)	-0.03%	-0.06%	-0.06%	-0.30%	-0.61%	-0.61%	0.84%	0.91%	0.89%	0.81%	0.88%	0.86%	0.53%	0.32%	0.31%
Fixed Costs per firm	4.10%	4.19%	4.21%	2.71%	1.41%	1.43%	-7.60%	-7.12%	-6.69%	-4.70%	-4.28%	-3.83%	-5.84%	-6.64%	-6.14%
Number of Firms	0.07%	0.25%	0.25%	0.75%	1.82%	1.82%	4.72%	9.93%	9.94%	4.79%	10.01%	10.01%	5.46%	11.41%	11.43%
Sigma of Love of Variety	0.00%	0.00%	0.00%	0.00%	0.00%	0.00%	0.00%	0.00%	0.00%	0.00%	0.00%	0.00%	0.00%	0.00%	0.00%

Banks

	Border Controls			Border controls and x-ineff.			Market segmentation			Trade *antimonde*			Full *antimonde*		
	1988	1991	1994	1988	1991	1994	1988	1991	1994	1988	1991	1994	1988	1991	1994
Production per firm	0.17%	0.38%	0.39%	-0.28%	-0.55%	-0.55%	-1.31%	-2.17%	-2.56%	-1.15%	-1.93%	-2.32%	-1.63%	-2.87%	-3.28%
Marginal Costs	4.18%	4.32%	4.33%	4.19%	4.34%	4.37%	-7.49%	-6.71%	-5.92%	-4.54%	-3.82%	-3.00%	-4.36%	-3.55%	-2.64%
Producer Prices	4.14%	4.23%	4.25%	4.07%	4.09%	4.12%	-7.30%	-6.42%	-5.61%	-4.38%	-3.57%	-2.73%	-4.28%	-3.46%	-2.53%
Mark-ups domestic (abs. diff.)	-0.04%	-0.08%	-0.08%	-0.15%	-0.29%	-0.29%	0.16%	0.14%	0.15%	0.13%	0.10%	0.10%	0.02%	-0.11%	-0.11%
Fixed Costs per firm	4.11%	4.20%	4.22%	3.15%	2.28%	2.31%	-7.58%	-7.03%	-6.55%	-4.67%	-4.20%	-3.70%	-5.42%	-5.77%	-5.21%
Number of Firms	0.16%	0.37%	0.37%	0.62%	1.34%	1.34%	1.07%	2.38%	2.35%	1.20%	2.56%	2.53%	1.65%	3.48%	3.44%
Sigma of Love of Variety	0.00%	0.00%	0.00%	0.00%	0.00%	0.00%	0.00%	0.00%	0.00%	0.00%	0.00%	0.00%	0.00%	0.00%	0.00%

Table B9.7.
Decomposition of effects: sectoral results for the Netherlands (volumes)

% change from *monde*

Agriculture

	Border Controls			Border controls and x-ineff.			Market segmentation			Trade *antimonde*			Full *antimonde*		
	1988	1991	1994	1988	1991	1994	1988	1991	1994	1988	1991	1994	1988	1991	1994
Domestic Production - vol.	-1.8%	-2.5%	-2.4%	-1.8%	-2.5%	-2.5%	2.5%	2.9%	2.5%	0.9%	1.0%	0.7%	0.7%	0.9%	0.5%
Imports - vol.	1.5%	1.3%	1.4%	1.5%	1.4%	1.4%	-4.7%	-4.3%	-3.9%	-3.4%	-3.1%	-2.7%	-3.3%	-2.9%	-2.4%
Exports - vol.	-0.7%	-0.7%	-0.7%	-0.7%	-0.8%	-0.8%	1.9%	1.6%	1.4%	1.4%	1.2%	0.9%	1.3%	1.1%	0.8%
Absorption - vol.	-0.6%	-1.3%	-1.2%	-0.6%	-1.3%	-1.3%	-0.2%	-0.6%	-0.8%	-0.7%	-1.2%	-1.5%	-0.7%	-1.3%	-1.5%
Investment - vol.	-0.9%	-1.3%	-1.3%	-0.9%	-1.3%	-1.3%	-3.0%	-2.9%	-3.0%	-3.8%	-3.8%	-3.9%	-3.8%	-3.8%	-4.0%
Labour Demand - vol.	-1.8%	-2.4%	-2.4%	-1.8%	-2.4%	-2.4%	2.6%	3.2%	3.0%	1.0%	1.4%	1.2%	1.0%	1.3%	1.1%
Private Consumption - vol.	0.2%	0.2%	0.2%	0.2%	0.2%	0.2%	-1.2%	-1.6%	-1.8%	-1.1%	-1.6%	-1.8%	-1.2%	-1.6%	-1.8%
Supply to domestic - vol.	-1.3%	-0.8%	-0.8%	-1.3%	-0.8%	-0.8%	3.6%	4.5%	4.0%	2.4%	3.2%	2.7%	2.3%	3.0%	2.4%
Intra-EU Trade - vol	-1.8%	-3.7%	-3.7%	-1.8%	-3.7%	-3.7%	0.6%	-0.7%	-1.0%	-1.0%	-2.6%	-2.8%	-1.0%	-2.7%	-2.9%

Energy

	Border Controls			Border controls and x-ineff.			Market segmentation			Trade *antimonde*			Full *antimonde*		
	1988	1991	1994	1988	1991	1994	1988	1991	1994	1988	1991	1994	1988	1991	1994
Domestic Production - vol.	-0.1%	0.0%	0.0%	-0.1%	-0.1%	-0.1%	2.3%	2.0%	1.4%	2.3%	2.1%	1.5%	2.2%	2.0%	1.3%
Imports - vol.	0.9%	1.0%	1.0%	0.9%	1.0%	1.0%	-1.8%	-1.8%	-1.7%	-1.2%	-1.2%	-1.1%	-1.2%	-1.1%	-1.0%
Exports - vol.	-0.3%	-0.4%	-0.4%	-0.3%	-0.4%	-0.4%	0.9%	0.8%	0.7%	0.7%	0.6%	0.5%	0.6%	0.5%	0.4%
Absorption - vol.	0.0%	-0.1%	-0.1%	0.0%	-0.1%	-0.1%	0.6%	0.0%	-0.4%	0.6%	0.0%	-0.4%	0.6%	-0.1%	-0.5%
Investment - vol.	-0.1%	0.0%	0.0%	-0.1%	0.0%	0.0%	-3.1%	-3.2%	-3.5%	-3.1%	-3.2%	-3.4%	-3.1%	-3.2%	-3.5%
Labour Demand - vol.	-0.1%	0.0%	0.0%	-0.1%	0.0%	0.0%	2.5%	2.2%	1.7%	2.5%	2.4%	1.8%	2.5%	2.3%	1.8%
Private Consumption - vol.	0.2%	0.1%	0.1%	0.2%	0.1%	0.1%	-0.9%	-1.3%	-1.4%	-0.9%	-1.2%	-1.4%	-0.9%	-1.2%	-1.4%
Supply to domestic - vol.	-0.3%	-0.4%	-0.4%	-0.3%	-0.5%	-0.5%	1.9%	1.1%	0.6%	1.7%	1.0%	0.4%	1.6%	0.8%	0.3%
Intra-EU Trade - vol	-0.2%	-0.1%	-0.1%	-0.2%	-0.1%	-0.1%	1.5%	1.4%	1.1%	1.4%	1.3%	1.0%	1.3%	1.3%	0.9%

Metal Industries

	Border Controls			Border controls and x-ineff.			Market segmentation			Trade *antimonde*			Full *antimonde*		
	1988	1991	1994	1988	1991	1994	1988	1991	1994	1988	1991	1994	1988	1991	1994
Domestic Production - vol.	-2.3%	-4.2%	-4.1%	-2.3%	-4.2%	-4.2%	-1.0%	-11.2%	-11.8%	-3.7%	-14.1%	-14.7%	-4.0%	-14.4%	-15.0%
Imports - vol.	0.9%	0.7%	0.7%	0.9%	0.7%	0.7%	-4.7%	-6.4%	-6.4%	-3.1%	-4.7%	-4.7%	-2.9%	-4.4%	-4.3%
Exports - vol.	-0.7%	-0.7%	-0.7%	-0.7%	-0.7%	-0.7%	1.9%	1.6%	1.4%	1.4%	1.1%	0.9%	1.4%	1.0%	0.8%
Absorption - vol.	-0.9%	-1.8%	-1.8%	-0.9%	-1.7%	-1.7%	-2.0%	-6.2%	-6.6%	-3.3%	-7.8%	-8.2%	-3.4%	-7.9%	-8.4%
Investment - vol.	-1.2%	-2.1%	-2.1%	-1.2%	-2.1%	-2.1%	-4.5%	-9.2%	-9.5%	-5.8%	-10.5%	-10.8%	-5.9%	-10.6%	-10.9%
Labour Demand - vol.	-2.1%	-3.8%	-3.8%	-2.1%	-3.8%	-3.8%	0.9%	-8.8%	-9.4%	-1.7%	-11.6%	-12.1%	-1.8%	-11.8%	-12.4%
Private Consumption - vol.	0.1%	0.1%	0.1%	0.1%	0.1%	0.1%	-0.6%	-0.8%	-0.8%	-0.5%	-0.8%	-0.8%	-0.5%	-0.8%	-0.9%
Supply to domestic - vol.	-0.7%	-0.3%	-0.3%	-0.7%	-0.3%	-0.3%	-10.7%	-21.9%	-22.8%	-12.3%	-23.5%	-24.4%	-12.4%	-23.7%	-24.7%
Intra-EU Trade - vol	-1.6%	-2.9%	-2.9%	-1.6%	-2.9%	-2.9%	2.7%	-0.9%	-1.1%	0.6%	-3.1%	-3.3%	0.4%	-3.3%	-3.6%

Chemical

	Border Controls			Border controls and x-ineff.			Market segmentation			Trade *antimonde*			Full *antimonde*		
	1988	1991	1994	1988	1991	1994	1988	1991	1994	1988	1991	1994	1988	1991	1994
Domestic Production - vol.	-0.3%	-1.8%	-1.8%	-0.4%	-1.8%	-1.8%	0.0%	-3.0%	-3.3%	-0.3%	-3.9%	-4.1%	-0.4%	-4.1%	-4.5%
Imports - vol.	0.9%	0.7%	0.7%	1.0%	0.7%	0.7%	-5.1%	-5.7%	-5.5%	-4.0%	-4.6%	-4.3%	-3.8%	-4.3%	-3.9%
Exports - vol.	-0.3%	-0.4%	-0.4%	-0.4%	-0.4%	-0.4%	1.6%	1.4%	1.3%	1.5%	1.3%	1.1%	1.4%	1.2%	1.0%
Absorption - vol.	-0.3%	-1.3%	-1.3%	-0.3%	-1.3%	-1.3%	-0.3%	-2.3%	-2.5%	-0.6%	-3.1%	-3.3%	-0.7%	-3.2%	-3.4%
Investment - vol.	-0.2%	-0.9%	-0.9%	-0.2%	-0.9%	-0.9%	-4.1%	-5.5%	-5.6%	-4.2%	-5.8%	-6.0%	-4.2%	-5.9%	-6.1%
Labour Demand - vol.	-0.3%	-1.7%	-1.7%	-0.3%	-1.8%	-1.7%	0.6%	-2.2%	-2.5%	0.3%	-3.1%	-3.3%	0.2%	-3.2%	-3.5%
Private Consumption - vol.	0.1%	0.1%	0.1%	0.1%	0.1%	0.1%	-0.9%	-1.3%	-1.5%	-0.8%	-1.3%	-1.5%	-0.9%	-1.3%	-1.5%
Supply to domestic - vol.	1.4%	3.1%	3.1%	1.3%	3.0%	3.0%	2.6%	5.1%	4.7%	2.7%	4.8%	4.4%	2.5%	4.5%	4.1%
Intra-EU Trade - vol	-0.9%	-2.7%	-2.7%	-0.9%	-2.7%	-2.7%	-0.3%	-3.7%	-3.8%	-0.9%	-4.6%	-4.8%	-1.0%	-4.8%	-5.0%

Other Intensive Industries

	Border Controls			Border controls and x-ineff.			Market segmentation			Trade *antimonde*			Full *antimonde*		
	1988	1991	1994	1988	1991	1994	1988	1991	1994	1988	1991	1994	1988	1991	1994
Domestic Production - vol.	-0.5%	-0.4%	-0.4%	-0.4%	-0.4%	-0.4%	-1.4%	-2.0%	-2.6%	-2.2%	-3.0%	-3.6%	-2.3%	-3.2%	-3.8%
Imports - vol.	1.9%	2.1%	2.1%	2.0%	2.2%	2.2%	-7.9%	-7.7%	-7.4%	-5.6%	-5.2%	-4.8%	-5.3%	-4.7%	-4.2%
Exports - vol.	-0.6%	-0.6%	-0.6%	-0.6%	-0.6%	-0.6%	2.0%	1.8%	1.6%	1.7%	1.5%	1.3%	1.6%	1.4%	1.1%
Absorption - vol.	-0.1%	-0.2%	-0.2%	-0.1%	-0.2%	-0.2%	-2.6%	-3.1%	-3.3%	-2.9%	-3.5%	-3.7%	-2.9%	-3.5%	-3.7%
Investment - vol.	-0.2%	-0.2%	-0.2%	-0.2%	-0.2%	-0.2%	-4.9%	-5.2%	-5.5%	-5.3%	-5.7%	-5.9%	-5.3%	-5.7%	-6.0%
Labour Demand - vol.	-0.4%	-0.2%	-0.3%	-0.4%	-0.2%	-0.2%	-0.7%	-1.0%	-1.3%	-1.4%	-1.9%	-2.4%	-1.5%	-2.0%	-2.5%
Private Consumption - vol.	0.2%	0.1%	0.1%	0.2%	0.1%	0.1%	-1.5%	-1.3%	-1.3%	-1.4%	-1.3%	-1.3%	-1.4%	-1.3%	-1.3%
Supply to domestic - vol.	0.7%	2.7%	2.7%	0.7%	2.7%	2.7%	-0.6%	1.6%	1.1%	-0.8%	1.4%	0.9%	-0.8%	1.3%	0.8%
Intra-EU Trade - vol	-1.6%	-3.6%	-3.6%	-1.6%	-3.6%	-3.6%	-1.6%	-4.7%	-4.8%	-2.8%	-6.0%	-6.2%	-2.9%	-6.2%	-6.3%

Electrical goods

	Border Controls			Border controls and x-ineff.			Market segmentation			Trade *antimonde*			Full *antimonde*		
	1988	1991	1994	1988	1991	1994	1988	1991	1994	1988	1991	1994	1988	1991	1994
Domestic Production - vol.	-1.5%	-2.3%	-2.3%	-1.5%	-2.3%	-2.3%	-0.6%	-5.1%	-5.5%	-2.1%	-6.8%	-7.2%	-2.3%	-7.1%	-7.6%
Imports - vol.	1.4%	1.4%	1.4%	1.4%	1.4%	1.4%	-6.7%	-6.9%	-6.8%	-5.0%	-5.2%	-5.0%	-4.8%	-4.9%	-4.6%
Exports - vol.	-0.6%	-0.7%	-0.7%	-0.7%	-0.7%	-0.7%	2.5%	2.3%	2.1%	2.1%	1.9%	1.7%	2.1%	1.8%	1.5%
Absorption - vol.	-0.2%	-0.6%	-0.6%	-0.2%	-0.6%	-0.6%	-4.4%	-5.6%	-5.7%	-4.8%	-6.2%	-6.3%	-4.9%	-6.3%	-6.4%
Investment - vol.	-0.7%	-1.1%	-1.1%	-0.7%	-1.1%	-1.1%	-4.5%	-6.6%	-6.8%	-5.2%	-7.4%	-7.6%	-5.3%	-7.5%	-7.8%
Labour Demand - vol.	-1.4%	-2.1%	-2.1%	-1.4%	-2.1%	-2.1%	0.8%	-3.4%	-3.7%	-0.6%	-5.0%	-5.4%	-0.8%	-5.2%	-5.6%
Private Consumption - vol.	0.8%	0.1%	0.2%	0.8%	0.1%	0.2%	-4.9%	-2.9%	-2.5%	-4.5%	-3.0%	-2.5%	-4.6%	-3.1%	-2.6%
Supply to domestic - vol.	0.3%	2.4%	2.4%	0.3%	2.4%	2.4%	-11.7%	-18.9%	-19.4%	-12.4%	-19.5%	-20.0%	-12.5%	-19.7%	-20.3%
Intra-EU Trade - vol	-1.7%	-3.1%	-3.1%	-1.7%	-3.1%	-3.1%	2.6%	1.4%	1.2%	0.7%	-0.9%	-1.0%	0.5%	-1.1%	-1.4%

Transport equipment

	Border Controls			Border controls and x-ineff.			Market segmentation			Trade *antimonde*			Full *antimonde*		
	1988	1991	1994	1988	1991	1994	1988	1991	1994	1988	1991	1994	1988	1991	1994
Domestic Production - vol.	0.1%	-0.2%	-0.2%	0.1%	-0.2%	-0.2%	-4.0%	-4.2%	-4.1%	-4.6%	-5.4%	-5.3%	-4.8%	-5.6%	-5.5%
Imports - vol.	1.8%	1.9%	2.0%	1.8%	2.0%	2.0%	-8.6%	-8.0%	-7.8%	-6.2%	-5.4%	-5.1%	-6.0%	-5.0%	-4.6%
Exports - vol.	-0.6%	-0.7%	-0.7%	-0.7%	-0.7%	-0.7%	2.3%	2.2%	2.0%	1.9%	1.8%	1.6%	1.8%	1.7%	1.5%
Absorption - vol.	0.5%	0.3%	0.3%	0.5%	0.3%	0.3%	-6.2%	-5.4%	-5.2%	-5.9%	-5.4%	-5.1%	-6.0%	-5.4%	-5.2%
Investment - vol.	0.0%	-0.1%	-0.1%	0.0%	-0.1%	-0.1%	-5.7%	-5.8%	-5.8%	-6.0%	-6.4%	-6.4%	-6.0%	-6.4%	-6.4%
Labour Demand - vol.	0.1%	0.0%	0.0%	0.1%	0.0%	0.0%	-1.6%	-1.3%	-1.2%	-2.3%	-2.4%	-2.3%	-2.3%	-2.5%	-2.4%
Private Consumption - vol.	0.7%	0.0%	0.1%	0.7%	0.0%	0.1%	-5.7%	-2.8%	-1.7%	-5.5%	-3.0%	-1.7%	-5.6%	-3.1%	-1.8%
Supply to domestic - vol.	2.7%	6.0%	6.0%	2.8%	6.0%	6.0%	-9.6%	-5.4%	-5.3%	-9.1%	-4.8%	-4.6%	-9.1%	-4.9%	-4.7%
Intra-EU Trade - vol	-0.7%	-1.7%	-1.7%	-0.7%	-1.7%	-1.7%	-0.8%	-1.7%	-1.7%	-1.6%	-2.8%	-2.8%	-1.7%	-2.9%	-2.9%

Other Equipment

	Border Controls			Border controls and x-ineff.			Market segmentation			Trade *antimonde*			Full *antimonde*		
	1988	1991	1994	1988	1991	1994	1988	1991	1994	1988	1991	1994	1988	1991	1994
Domestic Production - vol.	-1.6%	-2.6%	-2.6%	-1.6%	-2.6%	-2.6%	-4.5%	-9.5%	-9.7%	-6.7%	-12.2%	-12.4%	-6.9%	-12.4%	-12.7%
Imports - vol.	1.2%	1.2%	1.3%	1.2%	1.3%	1.3%	-6.8%	-7.4%	-7.3%	-4.9%	-5.3%	-5.3%	-4.7%	-5.1%	-4.9%
Exports - vol.	-0.8%	-0.9%	-0.9%	-0.8%	-0.9%	-0.9%	2.2%	2.0%	1.8%	1.6%	1.4%	1.2%	1.6%	1.3%	1.1%
Absorption - vol.	-0.5%	-1.0%	-0.9%	-0.5%	-0.9%	-0.9%	-5.3%	-7.0%	-7.3%	-6.1%	-8.0%	-8.3%	-6.1%	-8.1%	-8.4%
Investment - vol.	-0.8%	-1.3%	-1.3%	-0.8%	-1.3%	-1.3%	-6.2%	-8.5%	-8.7%	-7.2%	-9.8%	-9.9%	-7.3%	-9.8%	-10.0%
Labour Demand - vol.	-1.6%	-2.5%	-2.5%	-1.6%	-2.5%	-2.5%	-3.2%	-7.9%	-8.1%	-5.3%	-10.5%	-10.7%	-5.4%	-10.7%	-10.9%
Private Consumption - vol.	0.3%	0.2%	0.2%	0.3%	0.2%	0.2%	-1.7%	-2.0%	-2.1%	-1.6%	-1.9%	-2.1%	-1.6%	-2.0%	-2.2%
Supply to domestic - vol.	0.9%	4.0%	4.0%	0.9%	4.0%	4.0%	-13.7%	-22.1%	-22.4%	-14.6%	-23.1%	-23.4%	-14.7%	-23.2%	-23.6%
Intra-EU Trade - vol	-1.3%	-2.4%	-2.4%	-1.3%	-2.4%	-2.4%	-0.5%	-1.7%	-1.8%	-2.2%	-3.7%	-3.9%	-2.3%	-3.9%	-4.1%

Consumer goods

	Border Controls			Border controls and x-ineff.			Market segmentation			Trade *antimonde*			Full *antimonde*		
	1988	1991	1994	1988	1991	1994	1988	1991	1994	1988	1991	1994	1988	1991	1994
Domestic Production - vol.	-0.7%	-1.4%	-1.4%	-0.7%	-1.4%	-1.4%	-0.2%	-0.9%	-1.1%	-0.6%	-1.5%	-1.7%	-0.7%	-1.6%	-1.9%
Imports - vol.	1.4%	1.5%	1.6%	1.4%	1.6%	1.6%	-4.7%	-4.4%	-4.2%	-3.8%	-3.4%	-3.1%	-3.6%	-3.2%	-2.8%
Exports - vol.	-0.6%	-0.7%	-0.7%	-0.6%	-0.7%	-0.7%	2.3%	2.1%	1.8%	2.0%	1.7%	1.4%	1.9%	1.6%	1.3%
Absorption - vol.	-0.1%	-0.3%	-0.3%	-0.1%	-0.3%	-0.3%	-1.3%	-1.7%	-1.8%	-1.5%	-1.9%	-2.1%	-1.5%	-1.9%	-2.1%
Investment - vol.	-0.4%	-0.8%	-0.8%	-0.4%	-0.8%	-0.8%	-4.2%	-4.5%	-4.7%	-4.4%	-4.9%	-5.0%	-4.5%	-4.9%	-5.1%
Labour Demand - vol.	-0.8%	-1.5%	-1.4%	-0.8%	-1.5%	-1.5%	0.3%	-0.3%	-0.5%	-0.1%	-0.9%	-1.1%	-0.2%	-0.9%	-1.1%
Private Consumption - vol.	0.2%	0.2%	0.2%	0.2%	0.2%	0.2%	-1.1%	-1.5%	-1.6%	-1.0%	-1.4%	-1.6%	-1.0%	-1.5%	-1.6%
Supply to domestic - vol.	2.2%	7.3%	7.3%	2.2%	7.3%	7.3%	3.1%	7.7%	7.4%	3.0%	7.7%	7.4%	2.9%	7.5%	7.1%
Intra-EU Trade - vol	-1.4%	-3.3%	-3.3%	-1.4%	-3.3%	-3.3%	-0.7%	-2.5%	-2.7%	-1.3%	-3.3%	-3.4%	-1.3%	-3.3%	-3.5%

Construction

	Border Controls			Border controls and x-ineff.			Market segmentation			Trade *antimonde*			Full *antimonde*		
	1988	1991	1994	1988	1991	1994	1988	1991	1994	1988	1991	1994	1988	1991	1994
Domestic Production - vol.	0.2%	0.3%	0.3%	0.2%	0.3%	0.3%	-6.7%	-6.7%	-6.9%	-6.6%	-6.5%	-6.8%	-6.6%	-6.5%	-6.8%
Imports - vol.	#VALUE!	#VALUE!	#VALUE!	#VALUE!	#VALUE!	#VALUE!	0.7%	0.6%	0.6%	0.5%	0.4%	0.3%	0.5%	0.4%	0.3%
Exports - vol.	-0.3%	-0.3%	-0.3%	-0.3%	-0.3%	-0.3%	-6.8%	-6.8%	-7.1%	-6.7%	-6.7%	-6.9%	-6.7%	-6.6%	-6.9%
Absorption - vol.	0.2%	0.3%	0.3%	0.2%	0.3%	0.3%	-7.5%	-7.5%	-7.6%	-7.4%	-7.5%	-7.6%	-7.4%	-7.4%	-7.6%
Investment - vol.	0.1%	0.1%	0.1%	0.1%	0.1%	0.1%	-6.5%	-6.4%	-6.6%	-6.3%	-6.2%	-6.4%	-6.3%	-6.1%	-6.3%
Labour Demand - vol.	0.2%	0.3%	0.3%	0.2%	0.3%	0.3%	-1.0%	-1.4%	-1.7%	-0.9%	-1.4%	-1.6%	-0.9%	-1.4%	-1.7%
Private Consumption - vol.	0.2%	0.1%	0.1%	0.2%	0.1%	0.1%	-6.7%	-6.7%	-6.9%	-6.6%	-6.5%	-6.8%	-6.6%	-6.5%	-6.8%
Supply to domestic - vol.	0.2%	0.3%	0.3%	0.2%	0.3%	0.3%									
Intra-EU Trade - vol	0.6%	0.6%	0.6%	0.6%	0.6%	0.6%	-3.5%	-3.6%	-3.7%	-3.0%	-3.1%	-3.2%	-3.0%	-3.1%	-3.2%

Telecommunications

	Border Controls			Border controls and x-ineff.			Market segmentation			Trade *antimonde*			Full *antimonde*		
	1988	1991	1994	1988	1991	1994	1988	1991	1994	1988	1991	1994	1988	1991	1994
Domestic Production - vol.	0.1%	0.4%	0.4%	0.2%	0.7%	0.7%	1.3%	3.9%	3.5%	1.4%	4.1%	3.7%	1.5%	4.1%	3.7%
Imports - vol.	1.0%	1.1%	1.1%	0.9%	1.0%	1.0%	-6.3%	-6.1%	-5.8%	-5.7%	-5.6%	-5.3%	-5.6%	-5.5%	-5.1%
Exports - vol.	-0.2%	-0.3%	-0.3%	-0.2%	-0.2%	-0.2%	1.2%	1.2%	1.1%	1.2%	1.1%	1.0%	1.1%	1.1%	0.9%
Absorption - vol.	0.2%	0.3%	0.3%	0.3%	0.4%	0.4%	-0.8%	-0.8%	-1.0%	-0.6%	-0.7%	-0.9%	-0.6%	-0.6%	-0.8%
Investment - vol.	0.1%	0.3%	0.3%	0.2%	0.4%	0.4%	-3.7%	-2.5%	-2.7%	-3.6%	-2.4%	-2.6%	-3.6%	-2.3%	-2.5%
Labour Demand - vol.	0.1%	0.4%	0.4%	-0.3%	-0.3%	-0.3%	2.7%	6.3%	6.1%	2.8%	6.4%	6.2%	2.3%	5.4%	5.2%
Private Consumption - vol.	0.2%	0.2%	0.2%	0.2%	0.3%	0.2%	-1.3%	-1.9%	-2.1%	-1.3%	-1.9%	-2.1%	-1.2%	-1.8%	-2.1%
Supply to domestic - vol.	0.1%	0.3%	0.3%	0.2%	0.8%	0.8%	2.0%	6.8%	6.5%	2.1%	6.9%	6.6%	2.2%	7.0%	6.7%
Intra-EU Trade - vol	0.3%	0.1%	0.1%	0.0%	-1.0%	-1.0%	-7.1%	-18.2%	-18.3%	-7.0%	-18.1%	-18.2%	-7.1%	-18.3%	-18.4%

Transports

	Border Controls			Border controls and x-ineff.			Market segmentation			Trade *antimonde*			Full *antimonde*		
	1988	1991	1994	1988	1991	1994	1988	1991	1994	1988	1991	1994	1988	1991	1994
Domestic Production - vol.	1.3%	1.6%	1.6%	1.3%	1.6%	1.6%	-0.3%	-0.3%	-0.4%	1.0%	1.2%	1.1%	1.0%	1.2%	1.1%
Imports - vol.	0.6%	0.8%	0.8%	0.7%	0.8%	0.8%	-0.2%	-0.1%	-0.2%	0.5%	0.6%	0.5%	0.5%	0.6%	0.5%
Exports - vol.	-0.1%	-0.1%	-0.2%	-0.1%	-0.2%	-0.2%	0.7%	0.7%	0.6%	0.7%	0.6%	0.6%	0.7%	0.6%	0.5%
Absorption - vol.	0.5%	0.6%	0.6%	0.5%	0.6%	0.6%	-1.0%	-0.9%	-1.0%	-0.6%	-0.4%	-0.5%	-0.6%	-0.4%	-0.5%
Investment - vol.	0.6%	0.8%	0.8%	0.7%	0.8%	0.8%	-4.4%	-4.4%	-4.5%	-3.8%	-3.7%	-3.8%	-3.8%	-3.7%	-3.8%
Labour Demand - vol.	1.3%	1.6%	1.6%	1.3%	1.6%	1.6%	-0.2%	-0.1%	-0.2%	1.1%	1.4%	1.3%	1.2%	1.5%	1.4%
Private Consumption - vol.	0.2%	0.2%	0.2%	0.2%	0.2%	0.2%	-1.1%	-1.6%	-1.9%	-1.0%	-1.6%	-1.9%	-1.1%	-1.6%	-1.9%
Supply to domestic - vol.	1.3%	1.6%	1.6%	1.3%	1.6%	1.6%	-0.3%	-0.3%	-0.4%	1.0%	1.2%	1.1%	1.0%	1.2%	1.1%
Intra-EU Trade - vol	2.1%	2.6%	2.6%	2.1%	2.6%	2.6%	0.0%	0.0%	-0.1%	2.1%	2.5%	2.4%	2.1%	2.5%	2.3%

Banks

	Border Controls			Border controls and x-ineff.			Market segmentation			Trade *antimonde*			Full *antimonde*		
	1988	1991	1994	1988	1991	1994	1988	1991	1994	1988	1991	1994	1988	1991	1994
Domestic Production - vol.	0.3%	0.8%	0.8%	0.3%	0.8%	0.8%	-0.3%	0.2%	-0.3%	0.0%	0.6%	0.1%	0.0%	0.5%	0.1%
Imports - vol.	1.3%	1.5%	1.5%	1.2%	1.4%	1.4%	-6.8%	-6.4%	-6.1%	-5.9%	-5.5%	-5.2%	-5.7%	-5.2%	-4.8%
Exports - vol.	-0.2%	-0.3%	-0.3%	-0.2%	-0.2%	-0.3%	1.2%	1.1%	0.9%	1.1%	1.0%	0.9%	1.1%	1.0%	0.8%
Absorption - vol.	0.3%	0.5%	0.5%	0.3%	0.6%	0.5%	-0.5%	-0.4%	-0.8%	-0.3%	-0.1%	-0.5%	-0.4%	-0.2%	-0.6%
Investment - vol.	0.2%	0.4%	0.4%	0.2%	0.4%	0.4%	-4.3%	-4.1%	-4.3%	-4.2%	-3.9%	-4.1%	-4.2%	-3.9%	-4.1%
Labour Demand - vol.	0.3%	0.7%	0.7%	0.0%	0.1%	0.1%	0.2%	1.0%	0.7%	0.5%	1.4%	1.1%	0.2%	0.8%	0.5%
Private Consumption - vol.	0.2%	0.2%	0.2%	0.2%	0.2%	0.2%	-1.1%	-1.7%	-1.9%	-1.1%	-1.6%	-1.9%	-1.1%	-1.7%	-1.9%
Supply to domestic - vol.	0.2%	0.6%	0.6%	0.3%	0.7%	0.7%	0.1%	1.3%	0.9%	0.3%	1.6%	1.2%	0.3%	1.5%	1.1%
Intra-EU Trade - vol	0.7%	0.8%	0.9%	0.6%	0.3%	0.3%	-5.0%	-12.2%	-12.4%	-4.4%	-11.4%	-11.7%	-4.5%	-11.6%	-11.8%

Services

	Border Controls			Border controls and x-ineff.			Market segmentation			Trade *antimonde*			Full *antimonde*		
	1988	1991	1994	1988	1991	1994	1988	1991	1994	1988	1991	1994	1988	1991	1994
Domestic Production - vol.	0.4%	0.6%	0.6%	0.4%	0.6%	0.6%	-1.0%	-0.5%	-0.7%	-0.6%	-0.1%	-0.3%	-0.6%	-0.2%	-0.3%
Imports - vol.	1.9%	1.9%	1.9%	1.9%	2.0%	2.0%	-5.2%	-5.0%	-4.7%	-3.9%	-3.7%	-3.4%	-3.8%	-3.5%	-3.1%
Exports - vol.	-0.6%	-0.6%	-0.6%	-0.6%	-0.6%	-0.6%	1.5%	1.4%	1.2%	1.1%	1.0%	0.8%	1.1%	0.9%	0.7%
Absorption - vol.	0.1%	0.0%	0.0%	0.1%	0.0%	0.0%	-1.7%	-2.0%	-2.2%	-2.0%	-2.1%	-2.2%	-1.7%	-2.1%	-2.3%
Investment - vol.	0.2%	0.3%	0.3%	0.2%	0.3%	0.3%	-4.8%	-4.6%	-4.7%	-4.6%	-4.4%	-4.5%	-4.6%	-4.4%	-4.5%
Labour Demand - vol.	0.4%	0.6%	0.6%	0.5%	0.6%	0.6%	-0.8%	-0.3%	-0.3%	-0.4%	0.2%	0.1%	-0.4%	0.2%	0.2%
Private Consumption - vol.	0.2%	0.2%	0.1%	0.2%	0.2%	0.1%	-1.4%	-1.6%	-1.8%	-1.3%	-1.6%	-1.8%	-1.3%	-1.7%	-1.8%
Supply to domestic - vol.	0.0%	0.0%	0.0%	0.0%	0.0%	0.0%	-1.4%	-1.3%	-1.5%	-1.4%	-1.4%	-1.6%	-1.4%	-1.5%	-1.6%
Intra-EU Trade - vol	1.5%	2.0%	2.0%	1.5%	2.0%	2.0%	-0.4%	-0.4%	-0.5%	0.9%	1.2%	1.2%	0.9%	1.2%	1.1%

Non market

	Border Controls			Border controls and x-ineff.			Market segmentation			Trade *antimonde*			Full *antimonde*		
	1988	1991	1994	1988	1991	1994	1988	1991	1994	1988	1991	1994	1988	1991	1994
Domestic Production - vol.	#VALUE!	0.0%	0.0%	#VALUE!	0.0%	0.0%	-0.2%	-0.2%	-0.3%	-0.2%	-0.2%	-0.2%	-0.2%	-0.2%	-0.2%
Imports - vol.	-0.2%	-0.2%	#VALUE!	-0.2%	-0.2%	#VALUE!	0.4%	0.4%	0.3%	0.3%	0.3%	0.2%	#VALUE!	#VALUE!	#VALUE!
Exports - vol.	0.0%	0.0%	0.0%	0.0%	0.0%	0.0%	-0.2%	-0.2%	-0.3%	-0.2%	-0.1%	-0.2%	0.3%	0.2%	0.2%
Absorption - vol.	0.0%	0.0%	0.0%	0.0%	0.0%	0.0%	-0.2%	-0.2%	-0.3%	-0.2%	-0.2%	-0.2%	-0.2%	-0.2%	0.0%
Investment - vol.	0.0%	0.0%	0.0%	0.0%	0.0%	0.0%	-4.2%	-4.2%	-4.2%	-4.2%	-4.2%	-4.2%	-4.2%	-4.2%	-4.2%
Labour Demand - vol.	0.2%	0.1%	0.1%	0.2%	0.1%	0.1%	-0.1%	-0.1%	-0.1%	-0.1%	-0.1%	-0.1%	-0.1%	-0.1%	-0.1%
Private Consumption - vol.	0.0%	0.0%	0.0%	0.0%	0.0%	0.0%	-1.1%	-1.5%	-1.6%	-1.0%	-1.4%	-1.6%	-1.1%	-1.5%	-1.7%
Supply to domestic - vol.	0.0%	0.0%	0.0%	0.0%	0.0%	0.0%	-0.2%	-0.2%	-0.3%	-0.2%	-0.2%	-0.2%	-0.2%	-0.2%	-0.2%
Intra-EU Trade - vol	0.5%	0.5%	0.5%	0.5%	0.5%	0.5%	0.4%	0.3%	0.3%	0.4%	0.3%	0.3%	0.4%	0.3%	0.3%

Table B9.8.
Decomposition of effects: sectoral results for the Netherlands (prices)

% change from *monde*

Agriculture

	Border Controls			Border controls and x-ineff.			Market segmentation			Trade *antimonde*			Full *antimonde*		
	1988	1991	1994	1988	1991	1994	1988	1991	1994	1988	1991	1994	1988	1991	1994
Marginal Costs	-0.41%	-0.37%	-0.38%	-0.40%	-0.36%	-0.37%	1.53%	1.44%	1.47%	1.40%	1.37%	1.41%	1.38%	1.34%	1.36%
Cost of Labour	0.00%	-0.11%	-0.11%	-0.02%	-0.14%	-0.14%	-0.91%	-1.33%	-1.66%	-0.97%	-1.44%	-1.78%	-1.06%	-1.57%	-1.96%
Deflator of Absorption	-0.98%	-0.95%	-0.95%	-0.98%	-0.95%	-0.96%	3.09%	2.84%	2.69%	2.69%	2.54%	2.37%	2.62%	2.44%	2.23%
Price of Exports-RW	-0.41%	-0.37%	-0.38%	-0.40%	-0.36%	-0.37%	1.53%	1.44%	1.47%	1.40%	1.37%	1.41%	1.38%	1.34%	1.36%

Energy

	Border Controls			Border controls and x-ineff.			Market segmentation			Trade *antimonde*			Full *antimonde*		
	1988	1991	1994	1988	1991	1994	1988	1991	1994	1988	1991	1994	1988	1991	1994
Marginal Costs	-0.51%	-0.48%	-0.49%	-0.50%	-0.48%	-0.49%	1.67%	1.57%	1.62%	1.45%	1.41%	1.45%	1.40%	1.33%	1.34%
Cost of Labour	0.00%	-0.11%	-0.11%	-0.02%	-0.14%	-0.14%	-0.91%	-1.33%	-1.66%	-0.97%	-1.44%	-1.78%	-1.06%	-1.57%	-1.96%
Deflator of Absorption	-0.97%	-0.93%	-0.94%	-0.97%	-0.94%	-0.95%	3.22%	2.96%	2.82%	2.79%	2.64%	2.49%	2.70%	2.51%	2.30%
Price of Exports-RW	-0.51%	-0.48%	-0.49%	-0.50%	-0.48%	-0.49%	1.67%	1.57%	1.62%	1.45%	1.41%	1.45%	1.40%	1.33%	1.34%

Metal Industries

	Border Controls			Border controls and x-ineff.			Market segmentation			Trade *antimonde*			Full *antimonde*		
	1988	1991	1994	1988	1991	1994	1988	1991	1994	1988	1991	1994	1988	1991	1994
Marginal Costs	-0.48%	-0.44%	-0.44%	-0.48%	-0.45%	-0.45%	2.53%	2.46%	2.27%	2.43%	2.47%	2.27%	2.41%	2.43%	2.22%
Cost of Labour	0.00%	-0.11%	-0.11%	-0.02%	-0.14%	-0.14%	-0.91%	-1.33%	-1.66%	-0.97%	-1.44%	-1.78%	-1.06%	-1.57%	-1.96%
Deflator of Absorption	-0.83%	-0.69%	-0.70%	-0.84%	-0.71%	-0.72%	5.82%	6.06%	5.70%	5.78%	6.26%	5.90%	5.73%	6.17%	5.78%
Price of Exports-RW	-0.44%	-0.39%	-0.39%	-0.44%	-0.40%	-0.40%	1.49%	1.59%	1.44%	1.43%	1.65%	1.50%	1.41%	1.62%	1.45%

Chemical

	Border Controls			Border controls and x-ineff.			Market segmentation			Trade *antimonde*			Full *antimonde*		
	1988	1991	1994	1988	1991	1994	1988	1991	1994	1988	1991	1994	1988	1991	1994
Marginal Costs	-0.34%	-0.25%	-0.25%	-0.34%	-0.25%	-0.26%	2.37%	2.23%	2.08%	2.40%	2.39%	2.23%	2.38%	2.36%	2.18%
Cost of Labour	0.00%	-0.11%	-0.11%	-0.02%	-0.14%	-0.14%	-0.91%	-1.33%	-1.66%	-0.97%	-1.44%	-1.78%	-1.06%	-1.57%	-1.96%
Deflator of Absorption	-0.31%	-0.14%	-0.14%	-0.32%	-0.15%	-0.16%	3.53%	3.43%	3.16%	3.75%	3.86%	3.58%	3.70%	3.77%	3.46%
Price of Exports-RW	-0.36%	-0.26%	-0.27%	-0.36%	-0.27%	-0.27%	2.26%	2.08%	1.93%	2.28%	2.24%	2.08%	2.26%	2.20%	2.03%

Other Intensive Industries

	Border Controls			Border controls and x-ineff.			Market segmentation			Trade *antimonde*			Full *antimonde*		
	1988	1991	1994	1988	1991	1994	1988	1991	1994	1988	1991	1994	1988	1991	1994
Marginal Costs	-0.23%	-0.21%	-0.21%	-0.24%	-0.22%	-0.22%	1.21%	1.07%	0.95%	1.18%	1.11%	0.98%	1.16%	1.09%	0.95%
Cost of Labour	0.00%	-0.11%	-0.11%	-0.02%	-0.14%	-0.14%	-0.91%	-1.33%	-1.66%	-0.97%	-1.44%	-1.78%	-1.06%	-1.57%	-1.96%
Deflator of Absorption	-0.25%	-0.15%	-0.15%	-0.26%	-0.16%	-0.17%	2.08%	1.98%	1.80%	2.14%	2.17%	1.99%	2.11%	2.13%	1.93%
Price of Exports-RW	-0.24%	-0.26%	-0.26%	-0.25%	-0.26%	-0.27%	1.10%	0.90%	0.78%	1.07%	0.93%	0.81%	1.05%	0.91%	0.78%

Electrical goods

	Border Controls			Border controls and x-ineff.			Market segmentation			Trade antimonde			Full antimonde		
	1988	1991	1994	1988	1991	1994	1988	1991	1994	1988	1991	1994	1988	1991	1994
Marginal Costs	-0.26%	-0.26%	-0.26%	-0.27%	-0.27%	-0.27%	1.23%	1.04%	0.84%	1.19%	1.04%	0.84%	1.17%	1.01%	0.79%
Cost of Labour	0.00%	-0.11%	-0.11%	-0.02%	-0.14%	-0.14%	-0.91%	-1.33%	-1.66%	-0.97%	-1.44%	-1.78%	-1.06%	-1.57%	-1.96%
Deflator of Absorption	-0.71%	-0.61%	-0.61%	-0.72%	-0.63%	-0.64%	4.68%	4.56%	4.17%	4.65%	4.71%	4.32%	4.57%	4.59%	4.15%
Price of Exports-RW	-0.25%	-0.29%	-0.30%	-0.26%	-0.30%	-0.31%	0.72%	0.53%	0.34%	0.69%	0.54%	0.35%	0.67%	0.51%	0.31%

Transport equipment

	Border Controls			Border controls and x-ineff.			Market segmentation			Trade antimonde			Full antimonde		
	1988	1991	1994	1988	1991	1994	1988	1991	1994	1988	1991	1994	1988	1991	1994
Marginal Costs	-0.30%	-0.24%	-0.24%	-0.31%	-0.25%	-0.26%	2.06%	1.97%	1.72%	2.07%	2.09%	1.84%	2.06%	2.08%	1.82%
Cost of Labour	0.00%	-0.11%	-0.11%	-0.02%	-0.14%	-0.14%	-0.91%	-1.33%	-1.66%	-0.97%	-1.44%	-1.78%	-1.06%	-1.57%	-1.96%
Deflator of Absorption	-0.20%	0.00%	-0.01%	-0.21%	-0.02%	-0.02%	4.30%	4.76%	4.44%	4.61%	5.37%	5.04%	4.58%	5.32%	4.97%
Price of Exports-RW	-0.37%	-0.40%	-0.40%	-0.37%	-0.41%	-0.41%	1.21%	0.65%	0.39%	1.19%	0.73%	0.47%	1.18%	0.71%	0.44%

Other Equipment

	Border Controls			Border controls and x-ineff.			Market segmentation			Trade antimonde			Full antimonde		
	1988	1991	1994	1988	1991	1994	1988	1991	1994	1988	1991	1994	1988	1991	1994
Marginal Costs	-0.36%	-0.31%	-0.31%	-0.36%	-0.32%	-0.32%	1.90%	1.73%	1.51%	1.85%	1.79%	1.56%	1.83%	1.76%	1.52%
Cost of Labour	0.00%	-0.11%	-0.11%	-0.02%	-0.14%	-0.14%	-0.91%	-1.33%	-1.66%	-0.97%	-1.44%	-1.78%	-1.06%	-1.57%	-1.96%
Deflator of Absorption	-0.67%	-0.51%	-0.52%	-0.68%	-0.53%	-0.54%	3.83%	3.68%	3.32%	3.76%	3.84%	3.47%	3.69%	3.73%	3.33%
Price of Exports-RW	-0.35%	-0.31%	-0.31%	-0.36%	-0.32%	-0.33%	1.56%	1.35%	1.13%	1.52%	1.43%	1.20%	1.51%	1.40%	1.17%

Consumer goods

	Border Controls			Border controls and x-ineff.			Market segmentation			Trade antimonde			Full antimonde		
	1988	1991	1994	1988	1991	1994	1988	1991	1994	1988	1991	1994	1988	1991	1994
Marginal Costs	-0.56%	-0.53%	-0.53%	-0.56%	-0.53%	-0.54%	1.97%	1.75%	1.60%	1.78%	1.64%	1.49%	1.77%	1.61%	1.45%
Cost of Labour	0.00%	-0.11%	-0.11%	-0.02%	-0.14%	-0.14%	-0.91%	-1.33%	-1.66%	-0.97%	-1.44%	-1.78%	-1.06%	-1.57%	-1.96%
Deflator of Absorption	-0.73%	-0.63%	-0.63%	-0.74%	-0.64%	-0.65%	3.47%	3.15%	2.84%	3.35%	3.20%	2.88%	3.29%	3.10%	2.74%
Price of Exports-RW	-0.56%	-0.53%	-0.53%	-0.56%	-0.53%	-0.54%	1.97%	1.75%	1.60%	1.78%	1.64%	1.49%	1.77%	1.61%	1.45%

Construction

	Border Controls			Border controls and x-ineff.			Market segmentation			Trade antimonde			Full antimonde		
	1988	1991	1994	1988	1991	1994	1988	1991	1994	1988	1991	1994	1988	1991	1994
Marginal Costs	-0.22%	-0.21%	-0.21%	-0.22%	-0.22%	-0.22%	0.95%	0.75%	0.58%	0.91%	0.76%	0.59%	0.91%	0.75%	0.58%
Cost of Labour	0.00%	-0.11%	-0.11%	-0.02%	-0.14%	-0.14%	-0.91%	-1.33%	-1.66%	-0.97%	-1.44%	-1.78%	-1.06%	-1.57%	-1.96%
Deflator of Absorption	-0.22%	-0.21%	-0.21%	-0.22%	-0.22%	-0.22%	0.95%	0.75%	0.58%	0.91%	0.76%	0.59%	0.91%	0.75%	0.58%
Price of Exports-RW	-0.22%	-0.21%	-0.21%	-0.22%	-0.22%	-0.22%	0.95%	0.75%	0.58%	0.91%	0.76%	0.59%	0.91%	0.75%	0.58%

Telecommunications

	Border Controls			Border controls and x-ineff.			Market segmentation			Trade antimonde			Full antimonde		
	1988	1991	1994	1988	1991	1994	1988	1991	1994	1988	1991	1994	1988	1991	1994
Marginal Costs	-0.03%	-0.03%	-0.02%	-0.02%	-0.02%	-0.01%	0.01%	-0.07%	-0.01%	-0.01%	-0.10%	-0.03%	-0.01%	-0.09%	-0.03%
Cost of Labour	0.00%	-0.11%	-0.11%	-0.02%	-0.14%	-0.14%	-0.91%	-1.33%	-1.66%	-0.97%	-1.44%	-1.78%	-1.06%	-1.57%	-1.96%
Deflator of Absorption	-0.17%	-0.18%	-0.17%	-0.35%	-0.54%	-0.53%	1.21%	1.32%	1.33%	1.16%	1.28%	1.29%	0.97%	0.91%	0.91%
Price of Exports-RW	-0.03%	-0.06%	-0.04%	-0.10%	-0.21%	-0.20%	-0.39%	-0.92%	-0.87%	-0.43%	-0.98%	-0.92%	-0.48%	-1.09%	-1.03%

Transports

	Border Controls			Border controls and x-ineff.			Market segmentation			Trade antimonde			Full antimonde		
	1988	1991	1994	1988	1991	1994	1988	1991	1994	1988	1991	1994	1988	1991	1994
Marginal Costs	-0.23%	-0.25%	-0.25%	-0.23%	-0.26%	-0.26%	0.47%	0.28%	0.20%	0.36%	0.18%	0.10%	0.33%	0.14%	0.03%
Cost of Labour	0.00%	-0.11%	-0.11%	-0.02%	-0.14%	-0.14%	-0.91%	-1.33%	-1.66%	-0.97%	-1.44%	-1.78%	-1.06%	-1.57%	-1.96%
Deflator of Absorption	-0.23%	-0.25%	-0.25%	-0.23%	-0.26%	-0.26%	0.48%	0.28%	0.20%	0.37%	0.19%	0.10%	0.33%	0.14%	0.04%
Price of Exports-RW	-0.23%	-0.25%	-0.25%	-0.23%	-0.26%	-0.26%	0.47%	0.28%	0.20%	0.36%	0.18%	0.10%	0.33%	0.14%	0.03%

Banks

	Border Controls			Border controls and x-ineff.			Market segmentation			Trade antimonde			Full antimonde		
	1988	1991	1994	1988	1991	1994	1988	1991	1994	1988	1991	1994	1988	1991	1994
Marginal Costs	-0.03%	-0.04%	-0.05%	-0.04%	-0.06%	-0.07%	0.02%	-0.03%	0.05%	-0.01%	-0.06%	0.03%	-0.02%	-0.09%	-0.02%
Cost of Labour	0.00%	-0.11%	-0.11%	-0.02%	-0.14%	-0.14%	-0.91%	-1.33%	-1.66%	-0.97%	-1.44%	-1.78%	-1.06%	-1.57%	-1.96%
Deflator of Absorption	-0.08%	-0.12%	-0.13%	-0.19%	-0.33%	-0.34%	0.23%	0.18%	0.26%	0.18%	0.12%	0.20%	0.07%	-0.09%	-0.02%
Price of Exports-RW	-0.04%	-0.06%	-0.07%	-0.07%	-0.12%	-0.13%	-0.02%	-0.13%	-0.04%	-0.05%	-0.17%	-0.08%	-0.09%	-0.23%	-0.16%

Services

	Border Controls			Border controls and x-ineff.			Market segmentation			Trade antimonde			Full antimonde		
	1988	1991	1994	1988	1991	1994	1988	1991	1994	1988	1991	1994	1988	1991	1994
Marginal Costs	-0.10%	-0.12%	-0.12%	-0.10%	-0.12%	-0.12%	0.18%	0.05%	0.05%	0.14%	0.02%	0.02%	0.12%	-0.01%	-0.02%
Cost of Labour	0.00%	-0.11%	-0.11%	-0.02%	-0.14%	-0.14%	-0.91%	-1.33%	-1.66%	-0.97%	-1.44%	-1.78%	-1.06%	-1.57%	-1.96%
Deflator of Absorption	-0.15%	-0.16%	-0.16%	-0.15%	-0.16%	-0.16%	0.28%	0.16%	0.16%	0.20%	0.10%	0.10%	0.18%	0.07%	0.05%
Price of Exports-RW	-0.10%	-0.12%	-0.12%	-0.10%	-0.12%	-0.12%	0.18%	0.05%	0.05%	0.14%	0.02%	0.02%	0.12%	-0.01%	-0.02%

Non market

	Border Controls			Border controls and x-ineff.			Market segmentation			Trade antimonde			Full antimonde		
	1988	1991	1994	1988	1991	1994	1988	1991	1994	1988	1991	1994	1988	1991	1994
Marginal Costs	-0.11%	-0.17%	-0.16%	-0.12%	-0.18%	-0.18%	-0.03%	-0.33%	-0.57%	-0.08%	-0.39%	-0.64%	-0.11%	-0.44%	-0.70%
Cost of Labour	0.00%	-0.11%	-0.11%	-0.02%	-0.14%	-0.14%	-0.91%	-1.33%	-1.66%	-0.97%	-1.44%	-1.78%	-1.06%	-1.57%	-1.96%
Deflator of Absorption	-0.11%	-0.17%	-0.16%	-0.12%	-0.18%	-0.18%	-0.03%	-0.33%	-0.57%	-0.08%	-0.39%	-0.64%	-0.11%	-0.44%	-0.70%
Price of Exports-RW	-0.11%	-0.17%	-0.16%	-0.12%	-0.18%	-0.18%	-0.03%	-0.33%	-0.57%	-0.08%	-0.39%	-0.64%	-0.11%	-0.44%	-0.70%

Table B10.1.
The full *antimonde* scenario: macroeconomic aggregates for Portugal

Macroeconomic Aggregates (vol.) (% change from *monde*)	Constraint Case			Flexible Case			Efficiency Case		
	1988	1991	1994	1988	1991	1994	1988	1991	1994
GDP fact. pr.	-0.63%	-0.90%	-1.38%	-0.76%	-1.32%	-1.69%	-0.80%	-1.47%	-1.94%
Priv. Consumption	-0.97%	-0.90%	-1.13%	-1.34%	-1.59%	-1.80%	-1.35%	-1.64%	-1.90%
Absorption	-0.49%	-0.51%	-0.77%	-1.24%	-1.48%	-1.73%	-1.26%	-1.52%	-1.80%
Total Investment	-3.04%	-3.06%	-3.74%	-4.33%	-4.56%	-4.73%	-4.33%	-4.57%	-4.74%
Total Exports to RW	-0.18%	-1.36%	-2.22%	1.55%	1.23%	1.02%	1.52%	1.12%	0.83%
Total Imports from RW	-1.75%	-2.11%	-2.42%	-3.70%	-3.01%	-2.63%	-3.64%	-2.80%	-2.26%
Total Intra-EU Trade	-1.18%	-0.46%	-0.19%	-0.59%	-3.29%	-3.49%	-0.61%	-3.35%	-3.60%
Employment (diff. from *monde*, 10³ persons)	2	-1	-7	2	7	0	2	6	-1
Disposable Income (deflated)	-1.04%	-0.97%	-1.21%	-1.43%	-1.70%	-1.93%	-1.45%	-1.76%	-2.03%

Macroeconomic Ratios (abs. diff. from *monde*)	Constraint Case			Flexible Case			Efficiency Case		
	1988	1991	1994	1988	1991	1994	1988	1991	1994
Current Account as % of GDP	0.00%	0.00%	0.00%	-0.99%	-0.83%	-0.80%	-0.98%	-0.79%	-0.74%
Public Deficit as % of GDP	-0.03%	-0.04%	-0.08%	-0.39%	-0.52%	-0.58%	-0.39%	-0.54%	-0.61%
Labour Productivity	-0.68%	-0.88%	-1.19%	-0.81%	-1.50%	-1.69%	-0.84%	-1.62%	-1.91%
Investment/GDP	-0.60%	-0.54%	-0.60%	-2.13%	-2.12%	-2.12%	-2.12%	-2.08%	-2.06%
Priv.Cons./GDP	-0.24%	0.00%	0.18%	-0.41%	-0.19%	-0.08%	-0.39%	-0.13%	0.03%

Deflators (% change from *monde*)	Constraint Case			Flexible Case			Efficiency Case		
	1988	1991	1994	1988	1991	1994	1988	1991	1994
Consumer Price Index	-0.01%	0.50%	0.89%	0.89%	0.71%	0.67%	0.88%	0.65%	0.57%
Real Wage Rate	-0.59%	-0.88%	-1.47%	-0.69%	-1.06%	-1.55%	-0.73%	-1.22%	-1.82%
Marginal Costs	-0.56%	0.11%	0.61%	0.27%	0.18%	0.17%	0.26%	0.15%	0.12%
Producer Prices	-0.34%	0.33%	0.82%	0.41%	0.32%	0.31%	0.40%	0.28%	0.26%
Average change in mark-ups (abs. diff.)	1.49%	1.56%	1.59%	1.13%	1.14%	1.21%	1.13%	1.15%	1.22%
Shadow Price of Capital	-2.14%	-1.13%	-0.26%	-0.84%	-1.09%	-0.69%	-0.87%	-1.19%	-0.87%
Terms-of-Trade RW	-1.29%	-0.64%	-0.18%	-4.68%	-3.72%	-3.10%	-4.59%	-3.39%	-2.52%

Implicit change in real exchange rate	-0.58%	0.22%	0.76%	-3.27%	-2.15%	-1.47%	-3.18%	-1.78%	-0.82%

Trade Regime	*Segmentation*			*Segmentation*			*Segmentation*		

Table B10.2.
The full *antimonde* scenario: effects on IC sectors for Portugal

% change from *monde*

Metal Industries	Constraint Case			Flexible Case			Efficiency Case		
	1988	1991	1994	1988	1991	1994	1988	1991	1994
Production per firm	-18.54%	-18.80%	-19.17%	-15.78%	-20.85%	-20.97%	-15.79%	-20.90%	-21.06%
Real Marginal Costs	0.01%	0.64%	1.07%	-1.92%	-0.51%	0.63%	-1.80%	-0.02%	1.50%
Real Producer Prices	3.71%	4.42%	4.94%	0.92%	3.18%	4.35%	1.05%	3.69%	5.24%
Mark-ups domestic (abs. diff.)	6.75%	6.85%	6.98%	6.70%	8.28%	8.30%	6.70%	8.28%	8.30%
Fixed Costs per firm	0.20%	0.73%	1.01%	-2.41%	-1.37%	-0.83%	-2.34%	-1.08%	-0.32%
Number of Firms	13.97%	13.96%	13.59%	16.31%	20.70%	20.59%	16.31%	20.72%	20.64%
Sigma of Love of Variety	0.00%	0.00%	0.00%	0.00%	0.00%	0.00%	0.00%	0.00%	0.00%

Chemical	Constraint Case			Flexible Case			Efficiency Case		
	1988	1991	1994	1988	1991	1994	1988	1991	1994
Production per firm	-6.77%	-7.02%	-7.33%	-5.74%	-8.83%	-9.06%	-5.76%	-8.92%	-9.21%
Real Marginal Costs	-0.35%	0.29%	0.78%	-1.98%	-0.71%	0.46%	-1.86%	-0.22%	1.33%
Real Producer Prices	0.34%	1.00%	1.52%	-1.42%	0.15%	1.34%	-1.30%	0.65%	2.22%
Mark-ups domestic (abs. diff.)	0.85%	0.85%	0.87%	0.91%	1.13%	1.15%	0.91%	1.14%	1.16%
Fixed Costs per firm	-0.27%	0.27%	0.62%	-2.50%	-1.62%	-1.04%	-2.43%	-1.33%	-0.53%
Number of Firms	8.31%	8.27%	8.09%	11.19%	21.42%	21.13%	11.18%	21.31%	20.95%
Sigma of Love of Variety	0.00%	0.00%	0.00%	0.00%	0.00%	0.00%	0.00%	0.00%	0.00%

Other Intensive Industries	Constraint Case			Flexible Case			Efficiency Case		
	1988	1991	1994	1988	1991	1994	1988	1991	1994
Production per firm	-3.61%	-4.03%	-4.46%	-4.69%	-7.50%	-7.72%	-4.70%	-7.53%	-7.78%
Real Marginal Costs	-0.47%	0.22%	0.70%	-2.29%	-0.96%	0.22%	-2.17%	-0.47%	1.07%
Real Producer Prices	-0.18%	0.53%	1.03%	-1.95%	-0.42%	0.76%	-1.83%	0.07%	1.62%
Mark-ups domestic (abs. diff.)	0.25%	0.26%	0.28%	0.53%	0.66%	0.67%	0.53%	0.66%	0.67%
Fixed Costs per firm	-0.20%	0.35%	0.64%	-2.74%	-1.78%	-1.25%	-2.66%	-1.50%	-0.75%
Number of Firms	4.46%	4.35%	4.11%	2.56%	6.00%	5.89%	2.57%	6.05%	5.98%
Sigma of Love of Variety	0.00%	0.00%	0.00%	0.00%	0.00%	0.00%	0.00%	0.00%	0.00%

Electrical goods	Constraint Case			Flexible Case			Efficiency Case		
	1988	1991	1994	1988	1991	1994	1988	1991	1994
Production per firm	-18.12%	-18.54%	-19.08%	-15.87%	-22.30%	-22.55%	-15.89%	-22.37%	-22.67%
Real Marginal Costs	0.49%	1.08%	1.53%	-1.43%	0.10%	1.26%	-1.31%	0.60%	2.14%
Real Producer Prices	3.71%	4.41%	4.98%	0.76%	2.92%	4.13%	0.89%	3.44%	5.03%
Mark-ups domestic (abs. diff.)	7.89%	7.99%	8.33%	9.06%	11.15%	11.19%	9.06%	11.17%	11.22%
Fixed Costs per firm	0.73%	1.21%	1.51%	-1.86%	-0.69%	-0.12%	-1.79%	-0.39%	0.40%
Number of Firms	11.21%	11.53%	10.80%	4.73%	-5.13%	-5.67%	4.70%	-5.30%	-5.94%
Sigma of Love of Variety	0.00%	0.00%	0.00%	0.00%	0.00%	0.00%	0.00%	0.00%	0.00%

Transport equipment	Constraint Case			Flexible Case			Efficiency Case		
	1988	1991	1994	1988	1991	1994	1988	1991	1994
Production per firm	-21.89%	-22.24%	-22.75%	-19.32%	-22.58%	-22.64%	-19.34%	-22.62%	-22.72%
Real Marginal Costs	1.18%	1.80%	2.25%	-1.01%	0.57%	1.69%	-0.88%	1.08%	2.58%
Real Producer Prices	5.88%	6.67%	7.28%	2.48%	4.45%	5.59%	2.61%	4.97%	6.51%
Mark-ups domestic (abs. diff.)	13.26%	14.66%	15.75%	13.67%	15.58%	15.54%	13.68%	15.59%	15.56%
Fixed Costs per firm	1.29%	1.84%	2.18%	-1.56%	-0.35%	0.21%	-1.48%	-0.05%	0.73%
Number of Firms	17.70%	16.34%	14.62%	7.66%	-1.06%	-0.91%	7.64%	-1.12%	-0.98%
Sigma of Love of Variety	0.00%	0.00%	0.00%	0.00%	0.00%	0.00%	0.00%	0.00%	0.00%

Other Equipment	Constraint Case			Flexible Case			Efficiency Case		
	1988	1991	1994	1988	1991	1994	1988	1991	1994
Production per firm	-17.95%	-18.18%	-18.54%	-18.37%	-22.84%	-23.05%	-18.39%	-22.92%	-23.18%
Real Marginal Costs	-0.24%	0.42%	0.87%	-2.23%	-0.86%	0.29%	-2.10%	-0.35%	1.18%
Real Producer Prices	1.54%	2.24%	2.73%	-0.58%	1.16%	2.34%	-0.45%	1.68%	3.24%
Mark-ups domestic (abs. diff.)	3.08%	3.11%	3.17%	3.53%	4.27%	4.29%	3.53%	4.27%	4.29%
Fixed Costs per firm	-0.25%	0.34%	0.68%	-2.88%	-1.91%	-1.32%	-2.81%	-1.61%	-0.80%
Number of Firms	19.44%	19.32%	18.65%	14.24%	19.41%	18.93%	14.22%	19.32%	18.77%
Sigma of Love of Variety	0.00%	0.00%	0.00%	0.00%	0.00%	0.00%	0.00%	0.00%	0.00%

Telecommunications	Constraint Case			Flexible Case			Efficiency Case		
	1988	1991	1994	1988	1991	1994	1988	1991	1994
Production per firm	0.00%	0.77%	0.62%	-0.93%	-2.08%	-2.34%	-0.94%	-2.13%	-2.42%
Real Marginal Costs	-0.87%	-0.51%	-0.12%	-3.03%	-1.78%	-0.68%	-2.91%	-1.30%	0.16%
Real Producer Prices	-0.35%	0.33%	0.65%	-3.19%	-2.10%	-1.03%	-3.08%	-1.64%	-0.21%
Mark-ups domestic (abs. diff.)	0.74%	1.21%	1.10%	-0.32%	-0.77%	-0.80%	-0.33%	-0.79%	-0.83%
Fixed Costs per firm	0.70%	2.80%	2.84%	-5.11%	-5.80%	-5.53%	-5.05%	-5.58%	-5.13%
Number of Firms	-0.55%	-1.17%	-1.03%	1.02%	2.10%	2.16%	1.03%	2.13%	2.21%
Sigma of Love of Variety	0.00%	0.00%	0.00%	0.00%	0.00%	0.00%	0.00%	0.00%	0.00%

Banks	Constraint Case			Flexible Case			Efficiency Case		
	1988	1991	1994	1988	1991	1994	1988	1991	1994
Production per firm	-0.28%	0.46%	0.28%	-0.40%	-0.66%	-1.22%	-0.42%	-0.73%	-1.32%
Real Marginal Costs	-1.09%	-0.75%	0.04%	-3.24%	-1.97%	-0.52%	-3.11%	-1.46%	0.35%
Real Producer Prices	-0.87%	-0.51%	0.20%	-3.27%	-2.12%	-0.67%	-3.14%	-1.62%	0.19%
Mark-ups domestic (abs. diff.)	0.27%	0.28%	0.19%	-0.04%	-0.21%	-0.22%	-0.04%	-0.22%	-0.22%
Fixed Costs per firm	-0.10%	1.06%	1.24%	-4.48%	-4.50%	-4.10%	-4.41%	-4.24%	-3.65%
Number of Firms	-0.83%	-0.89%	-0.49%	0.60%	1.67%	1.68%	0.61%	1.69%	1.72%
Sigma of Love of Variety	0.00%	0.00%	0.00%	0.00%	0.00%	0.00%	0.00%	0.00%	0.00%

Table B10.3.
The full *antimonde* scenario: sectoral results for Portugal (volumes)

% change from *monde*

Agriculture	Constraint Case			Flexible Case			Efficiency Case		
	1988	1991	1994	1988	1991	1994	1988	1991	1994
Domestic Production - vol.	1.0%	0.8%	0.5%	3.1%	4.4%	3.8%	3.0%	4.2%	3.5%
Imports - vol.	-3.3%	-2.1%	-1.2%	-3.2%	-1.9%	-1.4%	-3.1%	-1.7%	-1.0%
Exports - vol.	1.1%	-0.5%	-1.8%	1.4%	1.2%	0.9%	1.4%	1.0%	0.7%
Absorption - vol.	0.0%	0.2%	0.2%	0.9%	1.9%	1.6%	0.9%	1.9%	1.5%
Investment - vol.	4.1%	4.0%	2.5%	-3.0%	-2.4%	-2.6%	-3.0%	-2.4%	-2.7%
Labour Demand - vol.	0.9%	0.8%	0.6%	3.1%	4.5%	4.1%	3.1%	4.4%	3.9%
Private Consumption - vol.	-2.6%	-1.7%	-1.2%	-0.7%	-1.3%	-1.7%	-0.7%	-1.3%	-1.7%
Supply to domestic - vol.	1.0%	0.9%	0.6%	3.1%	4.4%	3.8%	3.0%	4.2%	3.4%
Intra-EU Trade - vol	0.0%	0.0%	0.0%	-0.6%	-5.0%	-5.3%	-0.6%	-5.1%	-5.5%

Energy	Constraint Case			Flexible Case			Efficiency Case		
	1988	1991	1994	1988	1991	1994	1988	1991	1994
Domestic Production - vol.	0.2%	0.1%	-0.1%	1.2%	1.4%	1.1%	1.2%	1.3%	0.9%
Imports - vol.	-0.8%	-0.2%	0.1%	-1.4%	-1.0%	-0.9%	-1.4%	-0.9%	-0.7%
Exports - vol.	0.5%	-1.1%	-2.3%	0.7%	0.6%	0.4%	0.7%	0.5%	0.4%
Absorption - vol.	0.0%	0.1%	0.0%	0.4%	0.7%	0.3%	0.4%	0.6%	0.2%
Investment - vol.	-4.5%	-4.5%	-5.1%	-3.6%	-3.5%	-3.6%	-3.6%	-3.5%	-3.7%
Labour Demand - vol.	0.2%	0.2%	0.0%	1.3%	1.6%	1.3%	1.3%	1.5%	1.2%
Private Consumption - vol.	-1.4%	-0.5%	-0.1%	-0.7%	-1.3%	-1.6%	-0.7%	-1.3%	-1.7%
Supply to domestic - vol.	0.2%	0.2%	0.0%	1.0%	1.1%	0.8%	1.0%	1.0%	0.6%
Intra-EU Trade - vol	0.0%	0.0%	0.0%	1.4%	1.7%	1.6%	1.4%	1.6%	1.4%

Metal Industries	Constraint Case			Flexible Case			Efficiency Case		
	1988	1991	1994	1988	1991	1994	1988	1991	1994
Domestic Production - vol.	-7.2%	-7.5%	-8.2%	-2.0%	-4.5%	-4.7%	-2.1%	-4.5%	-4.8%
Imports - vol.	5.1%	4.4%	3.9%	-5.3%	-6.0%	-5.6%	-5.3%	-5.7%	-5.3%
Exports - vol.	-2.3%	-3.2%	-3.9%	1.6%	1.4%	1.2%	1.6%	1.3%	1.0%
Absorption - vol.	-2.0%	-2.3%	-2.9%	-4.1%	-7.1%	-7.3%	-4.1%	-7.1%	-7.4%
Investment - vol.	-9.6%	-9.8%	-11.0%	-5.1%	-6.2%	-6.3%	-5.1%	-6.2%	-6.3%
Labour Demand - vol.	-3.2%	-3.5%	-4.1%	1.3%	-0.2%	-0.4%	1.3%	-0.2%	-0.3%
Private Consumption - vol.	-1.3%	-0.9%	-0.7%	-0.4%	-0.6%	-0.8%	-0.4%	-0.7%	-0.9%
Supply to domestic - vol.	-9.1%	-9.2%	-10.0%	-5.3%	-7.2%	-7.5%	-5.3%	-7.2%	-7.5%
Intra-EU Trade - vol	0.0%	0.0%	0.0%	-0.4%	-2.4%	-2.5%	-0.4%	-2.4%	-2.5%

Chemical	Constraint Case			Flexible Case			Efficiency Case		
	1988	1991	1994	1988	1991	1994	1988	1991	1994
Domestic Production - vol.	1.0%	0.7%	0.2%	4.8%	10.7%	10.2%	4.8%	10.5%	9.8%
Imports - vol.	-2.6%	-2.3%	-2.0%	-3.8%	-2.5%	-2.2%	-3.7%	-2.3%	-1.8%
Exports - vol.	-0.4%	-1.4%	-2.3%	1.7%	1.5%	1.3%	1.7%	1.4%	1.1%
Absorption - vol.	0.0%	0.0%	-0.1%	1.0%	2.1%	1.8%	1.0%	2.1%	1.7%
Investment - vol.	-1.5%	-1.8%	-2.8%	-1.9%	0.8%	0.5%	-1.9%	0.7%	0.4%
Labour Demand - vol.	1.8%	1.5%	1.1%	5.6%	12.0%	11.5%	5.6%	11.8%	11.3%
Private Consumption - vol.	-3.0%	-2.0%	-1.4%	-0.7%	-1.4%	-1.8%	-0.7%	-1.4%	-1.9%
Supply to domestic - vol.	1.7%	1.6%	1.2%	5.4%	14.9%	14.3%	5.4%	14.7%	14.0%
Intra-EU Trade - vol	0.0%	0.0%	0.0%	-0.4%	-4.9%	-5.1%	-0.5%	-4.9%	-5.2%

Other Intensive Industries	Constraint Case			Flexible Case			Efficiency Case		
	1988	1991	1994	1988	1991	1994	1988	1991	1994
Domestic Production - vol.	0.7%	0.1%	-0.5%	-2.2%	-2.0%	-2.3%	-2.3%	-1.9%	-2.3%
Imports - vol.	-9.3%	-9.2%	-9.0%	-5.8%	-5.0%	-4.5%	-5.7%	-4.7%	-4.0%
Exports - vol.	-0.5%	-1.7%	-2.6%	1.5%	1.2%	1.0%	1.5%	1.1%	0.8%
Absorption - vol.	-1.0%	-1.1%	-1.4%	-3.4%	-3.8%	-4.0%	-3.4%	-3.8%	-4.0%
Investment - vol.	-1.8%	-2.2%	-3.5%	-5.3%	-5.1%	-5.3%	-5.3%	-5.1%	-5.2%
Labour Demand - vol.	1.0%	0.5%	0.0%	-1.8%	-1.2%	-1.4%	-1.7%	-1.1%	-1.3%
Private Consumption - vol.	0.0%	-0.1%	-0.7%	-1.6%	-1.5%	-1.5%	-1.6%	-1.6%	-1.6%
Supply to domestic - vol.	1.5%	1.4%	0.8%	-1.8%	1.1%	0.8%	-1.8%	1.2%	0.9%
Intra-EU Trade - vol	0.0%	0.0%	0.0%	-2.9%	-6.5%	-6.7%	-2.9%	-6.5%	-6.7%

Electrical goods	Constraint Case			Flexible Case			Efficiency Case		
	1988	1991	1994	1988	1991	1994	1988	1991	1994
Domestic Production - vol.	-8.9%	-9.1%	-10.3%	-11.9%	-26.3%	-26.9%	-11.9%	-26.5%	-27.3%
Imports - vol.	4.8%	4.5%	3.3%	-5.3%	-6.2%	-5.9%	-5.2%	-6.0%	-5.5%
Exports - vol.	-4.9%	-6.1%	-7.1%	1.6%	0.9%	0.7%	1.6%	0.8%	0.4%
Absorption - vol.	-2.5%	-2.1%	-3.4%	-6.9%	-11.8%	-11.9%	-6.9%	-11.9%	-12.1%
Investment - vol.	-7.2%	-7.4%	-9.5%	-9.5%	-16.1%	-16.4%	-9.5%	-16.1%	-16.5%
Labour Demand - vol.	-5.4%	-5.5%	-6.5%	-9.3%	-23.5%	-24.1%	-9.4%	-23.7%	-24.3%
Private Consumption - vol.	1.4%	3.7%	0.2%	-5.5%	-4.1%	-3.3%	-5.5%	-4.3%	-3.5%
Supply to domestic - vol.	-14.1%	-13.1%	-14.6%	-17.8%	-32.4%	-33.0%	-17.8%	-32.7%	-33.4%
Intra-EU Trade - vol	0.0%	0.0%	0.0%	-1.5%	-5.8%	-6.1%	-1.5%	-5.9%	-6.2%

Transport equipment	Constraint Case			Flexible Case			Efficiency Case		
	1988	1991	1994	1988	1991	1994	1988	1991	1994
Domestic Production - vol.	-8.1%	-9.5%	-11.5%	-13.1%	-23.4%	-23.3%	-13.2%	-23.5%	-23.5%
Imports - vol.	18.0%	12.4%	8.0%	-4.1%	-3.6%	-3.0%	-4.1%	-3.4%	-2.7%
Exports - vol.	-3.2%	-4.3%	-5.1%	1.6%	0.8%	0.6%	1.5%	0.7%	0.4%
Absorption - vol.	6.5%	2.3%	-1.7%	-5.5%	-6.5%	-6.1%	-5.5%	-6.5%	-6.1%
Investment - vol.	-5.9%	-7.4%	-10.3%	-9.9%	-14.6%	-14.6%	-9.9%	-14.6%	-14.6%
Labour Demand - vol.	-3.1%	-4.5%	-6.3%	-9.4%	-19.7%	-19.6%	-9.4%	-19.8%	-19.6%
Private Consumption - vol.	19.2%	10.4%	0.7%	-5.2%	-3.3%	-2.2%	-5.2%	-3.4%	-2.4%
Supply to domestic - vol.	-13.3%	-16.0%	-19.8%	-24.0%	-37.0%	-36.8%	-24.0%	-37.1%	-36.9%
Intra-EU Trade - vol	0.0%	0.0%	0.0%	2.0%	3.3%	3.3%	2.0%	3.2%	3.2%

Other Equipment	Constraint Case			Flexible Case			Efficiency Case		
	1988	1991	1994	1988	1991	1994	1988	1991	1994
Domestic Production - vol.	-2.0%	-2.4%	-3.3%	-6.7%	-7.9%	-8.5%	-6.8%	-8.0%	-8.8%
Imports - vol.	-1.9%	-1.9%	-2.6%	-6.2%	-6.1%	-5.9%	-6.1%	-5.9%	-5.6%
Exports - vol.	-0.8%	-1.7%	-2.4%	1.7%	1.4%	1.2%	1.7%	1.3%	1.0%
Absorption - vol.	-1.8%	-1.8%	-2.7%	-8.4%	-9.7%	-10.1%	-8.4%	-9.7%	-10.1%
Investment - vol.	3.5%	3.2%	0.8%	-7.3%	-7.8%	-8.1%	-7.3%	-7.8%	-8.2%
Labour Demand - vol.	0.0%	-0.3%	-1.1%	-4.8%	-5.5%	-6.0%	-4.8%	-5.6%	-6.1%
Private Consumption - vol.	-3.3%	-2.0%	-1.7%	-1.4%	-2.0%	-2.4%	-1.5%	-2.1%	-2.6%
Supply to domestic - vol.	-2.1%	-2.1%	-3.3%	-10.3%	-11.4%	-12.1%	-10.4%	-11.6%	-12.3%
Intra-EU Trade - vol	0.0%	0.0%	0.0%	-2.5%	-3.4%	-3.7%	-2.5%	-3.4%	-3.8%

Consumer goods	Constraint Case			Flexible Case			Efficiency Case		
	1988	1991	1994	1988	1991	1994	1988	1991	1994
Domestic Production - vol.	1.1%	0.9%	0.7%	1.9%	3.7%	3.4%	1.9%	3.6%	3.2%
Imports - vol.	-10.6%	-9.9%	-9.2%	-4.3%	-3.4%	-3.0%	-4.3%	-3.2%	-2.5%
Exports - vol.	0.7%	-0.6%	-1.6%	2.0%	1.7%	1.4%	2.0%	1.5%	1.1%
Absorption - vol.	-1.1%	-0.7%	-0.6%	-0.1%	0.0%	-0.3%	-0.1%	-0.1%	-0.4%
Investment - vol.	6.1%	6.0%	4.3%	-3.5%	-2.7%	-2.9%	-3.5%	-2.8%	-2.9%
Labour Demand - vol.	1.2%	1.0%	0.9%	2.1%	3.9%	3.8%	2.1%	3.9%	3.7%
Private Consumption - vol.	-2.5%	-1.7%	-1.2%	-0.7%	-1.2%	-1.6%	-0.7%	-1.2%	-1.6%
Supply to domestic - vol.	1.3%	1.6%	1.7%	1.6%	4.1%	3.8%	1.6%	4.0%	3.7%
Intra-EU Trade - vol	0.0%	0.0%	0.0%	-0.4%	-3.2%	-3.4%	-0.4%	-3.3%	-3.5%

Construction	Constraint Case			Flexible Case			Efficiency Case		
	1988	1991	1994	1988	1991	1994	1988	1991	1994
Domestic Production - vol.	-3.2%	-3.1%	-3.5%	-7.1%	-7.1%	-7.4%	-7.1%	-7.1%	-7.3%
Imports - vol.	-	-	-	#VALUE!	#VALUE!	#VALUE!	#VALUE!	#VALUE!	#VALUE!
Exports - vol.	-	-	-	#VALUE!	#VALUE!	#VALUE!	#VALUE!	#VALUE!	#VALUE!
Absorption - vol.	-3.2%	-3.1%	-3.5%	-7.1%	-7.1%	-7.4%	-7.1%	-7.1%	-7.3%
Investment - vol.	-2.1%	-2.1%	-3.5%	-7.5%	-7.5%	-7.7%	-7.5%	-7.5%	-7.7%
Labour Demand - vol.	-3.1%	-3.0%	-3.3%	-6.9%	-6.9%	-7.0%	-6.9%	-6.8%	-6.9%
Private Consumption - vol.	-3.1%	-2.1%	-1.5%	-0.7%	-1.4%	-1.9%	-0.7%	-1.5%	-2.0%
Supply to domestic - vol.	-3.2%	-3.1%	-3.5%	-7.1%	-7.1%	-7.4%	-7.1%	-7.1%	-7.3%
Intra-EU Trade - vol	0.0%	0.0%	0.0%	#DIV/0!	#DIV/0!	#DIV/0!	#DIV/0!	#DIV/0!	#DIV/0!

Telecommunications	Constraint Case			Flexible Case			Efficiency Case		
	1988	1991	1994	1988	1991	1994	1988	1991	1994
Domestic Production - vol.	-0.5%	-0.4%	-0.4%	0.1%	0.0%	-0.2%	0.1%	0.0%	-0.3%
Imports - vol.	-7.8%	-7.2%	-6.9%	-5.6%	-5.6%	-5.4%	-5.5%	-5.4%	-5.1%
Exports - vol.	-2.7%	-3.2%	-3.6%	1.0%	0.9%	0.8%	1.0%	0.8%	0.7%
Absorption - vol.	-0.6%	-0.5%	-0.5%	0.0%	-0.2%	-0.4%	-0.1%	-0.2%	-0.5%
Investment - vol.	-4.5%	-5.2%	-5.5%	-4.1%	-4.2%	-4.2%	-4.1%	-4.1%	-4.2%
Labour Demand - vol.	0.3%	1.0%	1.1%	-0.3%	-0.8%	-0.8%	-0.3%	-0.7%	-0.7%
Private Consumption - vol.	-2.7%	-2.0%	-1.6%	-0.8%	-1.3%	-1.7%	-0.8%	-1.3%	-1.8%
Supply to domestic - vol.	-0.5%	-0.4%	-0.4%	0.2%	0.5%	0.3%	0.2%	0.5%	0.3%
Intra-EU Trade - vol	0.0%	0.0%	0.0%	-6.6%	-17.9%	-18.1%	-6.6%	-17.9%	-18.1%

Transports	Constraint Case			Flexible Case			Efficiency Case		
	1988	1991	1994	1988	1991	1994	1988	1991	1994
Domestic Production - vol.	-0.6%	-0.4%	-0.3%	0.7%	0.5%	0.2%	0.7%	0.5%	0.2%
Imports - vol.	-0.6%	-0.4%	-0.3%	0.4%	0.2%	0.1%	0.4%	0.2%	0.1%
Exports - vol.	1.0%	0.6%	0.4%	0.6%	0.5%	0.4%	0.6%	0.5%	0.4%
Absorption - vol.	-1.4%	-1.0%	-0.7%	-0.2%	-0.6%	-0.9%	-0.2%	-0.6%	-0.9%
Investment - vol.	-5.3%	-5.1%	-5.5%	-3.8%	-4.0%	-4.1%	-3.8%	-4.0%	-4.1%
Labour Demand - vol.	-0.5%	-0.3%	-0.2%	0.8%	0.7%	0.5%	0.9%	0.7%	0.5%
Private Consumption - vol.	-3.5%	-2.4%	-1.7%	-0.8%	-1.5%	-2.0%	-0.8%	-1.6%	-2.1%
Supply to domestic - vol.	-0.6%	-0.4%	-0.3%	0.7%	0.5%	0.2%	0.7%	0.5%	0.2%
Intra-EU Trade - vol	0.0%	0.0%	0.0%	1.5%	1.7%	1.6%	1.5%	1.7%	1.5%

Banks	Constraint Case			Flexible Case			Efficiency Case		
	1988	1991	1994	1988	1991	1994	1988	1991	1994
Domestic Production - vol.	-1.1%	-0.4%	-0.2%	0.2%	1.0%	0.4%	0.2%	1.0%	0.4%
Imports - vol.	-20.0%	-20.1%	-19.3%	-5.7%	-4.9%	-4.5%	-5.7%	-4.7%	-4.1%
Exports - vol.	0.6%	0.4%	0.1%	1.0%	0.9%	0.7%	1.0%	0.8%	0.6%
Absorption - vol.	-1.3%	-0.6%	-0.4%	0.1%	0.6%	0.1%	0.1%	0.6%	0.0%
Investment - vol.	-3.2%	-3.1%	-3.4%	-4.1%	-3.7%	-3.9%	-4.1%	-3.7%	-3.9%
Labour Demand - vol.	-0.2%	0.5%	0.9%	-0.3%	-0.1%	-0.3%	-0.3%	-0.1%	-0.2%
Private Consumption - vol.	-3.7%	-2.5%	-1.8%	-0.9%	-1.7%	-2.3%	-0.9%	-1.8%	-2.4%
Supply to domestic - vol.	-1.1%	-0.5%	-0.2%	0.2%	1.1%	0.6%	0.2%	1.1%	0.5%
Intra-EU Trade - vol	0.0%	0.0%	0.0%	-5.5%	-14.8%	-14.9%	-5.6%	-14.8%	-14.9%

Services	Constraint Case			Flexible Case			Efficiency Case		
	1988	1991	1994	1988	1991	1994	1988	1991	1994
Domestic Production - vol.	0.3%	0.1%	-0.3%	-0.3%	-0.8%	-1.1%	-0.4%	-0.9%	-1.2%
Imports - vol.	-7.3%	-7.4%	-7.4%	-2.7%	-2.4%	-2.1%	-2.7%	-2.3%	-1.8%
Exports - vol.	4.1%	2.9%	2.3%	0.9%	0.7%	0.5%	0.9%	0.6%	0.4%
Absorption - vol.	0.1%	-0.1%	-0.5%	-0.4%	-0.9%	-1.2%	-0.4%	-1.0%	-1.3%
Investment - vol.	-0.5%	-0.7%	-1.9%	-4.4%	-4.6%	-4.7%	-4.4%	-4.6%	-4.8%
Labour Demand - vol.	0.2%	0.0%	-0.2%	-0.3%	-0.7%	-0.8%	-0.3%	-0.7%	-0.8%
Private Consumption - vol.	-0.3%	-0.7%	-1.3%	-1.7%	-1.9%	-2.1%	-1.7%	-2.0%	-2.2%
Supply to domestic - vol.	0.3%	0.1%	-0.3%	-0.4%	-0.8%	-1.1%	-0.4%	-0.9%	-1.2%
Intra-EU Trade - vol	0.0%	0.0%	0.0%	0.3%	-2.0%	-2.3%	0.3%	-2.1%	-2.5%

Non market	Constraint Case			Flexible Case			Efficiency Case		
	1988	1991	1994	1988	1991	1994	1988	1991	1994
Domestic Production - vol.	-0.1%	-0.1%	-0.1%	-0.1%	-0.1%	-0.1%	-0.1%	-0.1%	-0.1%
Imports - vol.	-	-	-	#VALUE!	#VALUE!	#VALUE!	#VALUE!	#VALUE!	#VALUE!
Exports - vol.	-	-	-	#VALUE!	#VALUE!	#VALUE!	#VALUE!	#VALUE!	#VALUE!
Absorption - vol.	-0.1%	-0.1%	-0.1%	-0.1%	-0.1%	-0.1%	-0.1%	-0.1%	-0.1%
Investment - vol.	-6.9%	-6.8%	-7.0%	-4.1%	-4.1%	-4.1%	-4.1%	-4.1%	-4.1%
Labour Demand - vol.	-0.1%	-0.1%	0.0%	0.0%	0.0%	0.1%	0.1%	0.1%	0.2%
Private Consumption - vol.	-2.0%	-1.6%	-1.4%	-1.1%	-1.5%	-1.9%	-1.1%	-1.6%	-2.0%
Supply to domestic - vol.	-0.1%	-0.1%	-0.1%	-0.1%	-0.1%	-0.1%	-0.1%	-0.1%	-0.1%
Intra-EU Trade - vol	0.0%	0.0%	0.0%	#DIV/0!	#DIV/0!	#DIV/0!	#DIV/0!	#DIV/0!	#DIV/0!

Table B10.4.
The full *antimonde* scenario: sectoral results for Portugal (prices)

% change from *monde*

Agriculture	Constraint Case			Flexible Case			Efficiency Case		
	1988	1991	1994	1988	1991	1994	1988	1991	1994
Real Marginal Costs	-0.90%	-0.11%	0.52%	0.00%	-0.22%	-0.09%	0.00%	-0.24%	-0.13%
Real Cost of Labour	-1.17%	-0.65%	-0.71%	-0.69%	-1.06%	-1.55%	-0.73%	-1.22%	-1.82%
Real Deflator of Absorption	-0.55%	0.07%	0.56%	0.96%	0.59%	0.55%	0.93%	0.50%	0.39%
Real Price of Exports-RW	-0.90%	-0.11%	0.52%	0.00%	-0.22%	-0.09%	0.00%	-0.24%	-0.13%

Energy	Constraint Case			Flexible Case			Efficiency Case		
	1988	1991	1994	1988	1991	1994	1988	1991	1994
Marginal Costs	-0.72%	0.01%	0.57%	0.19%	-0.09%	-0.08%	0.17%	-0.14%	-0.17%
Cost of Labour	-1.17%	-0.65%	-0.71%	-0.69%	-1.06%	-1.55%	-0.73%	-1.22%	-1.82%
Deflator of Absorption	-0.46%	0.12%	0.57%	0.87%	0.51%	0.43%	0.85%	0.41%	0.26%
Price of Exports-RW	-0.72%	0.01%	0.57%	0.19%	-0.09%	-0.08%	0.17%	-0.14%	-0.17%

Metal Industries	Constraint Case			Flexible Case			Efficiency Case		
	1988	1991	1994	1988	1991	1994	1988	1991	1994
Marginal Costs	0.01%	0.64%	1.07%	0.66%	0.58%	0.55%	0.65%	0.55%	0.50%
Cost of Labour	-1.17%	-0.65%	-0.71%	-0.69%	-1.06%	-1.55%	-0.73%	-1.22%	-1.82%
Deflator of Absorption	3.16%	3.48%	3.73%	3.46%	4.12%	4.11%	3.46%	4.09%	4.06%
Price of Exports-RW	1.54%	2.20%	2.66%	-0.44%	-0.83%	-0.85%	-0.45%	-0.86%	-0.92%

Chemical	Constraint Case			Flexible Case			Efficiency Case		
	1988	1991	1994	1988	1991	1994	1988	1991	1994
Marginal Costs	-0.35%	0.29%	0.78%	0.59%	0.38%	0.38%	0.58%	0.35%	0.33%
Cost of Labour	-1.17%	-0.65%	-0.71%	-0.69%	-1.06%	-1.55%	-0.73%	-1.22%	-1.82%
Deflator of Absorption	0.41%	0.80%	1.11%	1.71%	1.55%	1.49%	1.70%	1.48%	1.37%
Price of Exports-RW	0.32%	0.97%	1.47%	0.30%	-0.20%	-0.19%	0.29%	-0.22%	-0.24%

Other Intensive Industries	Constraint Case			Flexible Case			Efficiency Case		
	1988	1991	1994	1988	1991	1994	1988	1991	1994
Marginal Costs	-0.47%	0.22%	0.70%	0.29%	0.13%	0.14%	0.28%	0.10%	0.08%
Cost of Labour	-1.17%	-0.65%	-0.71%	-0.69%	-1.06%	-1.55%	-0.73%	-1.22%	-1.82%
Deflator of Absorption	0.05%	0.61%	1.01%	0.87%	0.82%	0.81%	0.86%	0.78%	0.73%
Price of Exports-RW	0.00%	0.69%	1.18%	0.24%	0.02%	0.03%	0.23%	-0.01%	-0.03%

Electrical goods	Constraint Case			Flexible Case			Efficiency Case		
	1988	1991	1994	1988	1991	1994	1988	1991	1994
Marginal Costs	0.49%	1.08%	1.53%	1.14%	1.18%	1.18%	1.14%	1.16%	1.15%
Cost of Labour	-1.17%	-0.65%	-0.71%	-0.69%	-1.06%	-1.55%	-0.73%	-1.22%	-1.82%
Deflator of Absorption	3.45%	3.65%	3.89%	4.07%	4.74%	4.62%	4.05%	4.66%	4.49%
Price of Exports-RW	2.27%	2.89%	3.41%	0.78%	1.58%	1.62%	0.78%	1.58%	1.61%

Transport equipment	Constraint Case			Flexible Case			Efficiency Case		
	1988	1991	1994	1988	1991	1994	1988	1991	1994
Marginal Costs	1.18%	1.80%	2.25%	1.57%	1.66%	1.61%	1.56%	1.64%	1.59%
Cost of Labour	-1.17%	-0.65%	-0.71%	-0.69%	-1.06%	-1.55%	-0.73%	-1.22%	-1.82%
Deflator of Absorption	5.11%	5.54%	5.91%	4.96%	5.68%	5.52%	4.95%	5.62%	5.42%
Price of Exports-RW	3.11%	3.94%	4.59%	0.83%	1.76%	1.70%	0.83%	1.75%	1.68%

Other Equipment	Constraint Case			Flexible Case			Efficiency Case		
	1988	1991	1994	1988	1991	1994	1988	1991	1994
Marginal Costs	-0.24%	0.42%	0.87%	0.35%	0.23%	0.21%	0.35%	0.21%	0.18%
Cost of Labour	-1.17%	-0.65%	-0.71%	-0.69%	-1.06%	-1.55%	-0.73%	-1.22%	-1.82%
Deflator of Absorption	1.58%	1.77%	1.92%	2.07%	2.07%	1.93%	2.05%	1.98%	1.79%
Price of Exports-RW	0.31%	0.98%	1.44%	-0.07%	-0.35%	-0.36%	-0.07%	-0.37%	-0.39%

Consumer goods	Constraint Case			Flexible Case			Efficiency Case		
	1988	1991	1994	1988	1991	1994	1988	1991	1994
Marginal Costs	-0.55%	0.13%	0.62%	0.36%	0.11%	0.09%	0.35%	0.09%	0.06%
Cost of Labour	-1.17%	-0.65%	-0.71%	-0.69%	-1.06%	-1.55%	-0.73%	-1.22%	-1.82%
Deflator of Absorption	-0.17%	0.38%	0.78%	0.77%	0.54%	0.49%	0.76%	0.49%	0.41%
Price of Exports-RW	-0.55%	0.13%	0.62%	0.36%	0.11%	0.09%	0.35%	0.09%	0.06%

Construction	Constraint Case			Flexible Case			Efficiency Case		
	1988	1991	1994	1988	1991	1994	1988	1991	1994
Marginal Costs	-0.19%	0.41%	0.78%	0.50%	0.39%	0.30%	0.49%	0.36%	0.25%
Cost of Labour	-1.17%	-0.65%	-0.71%	-0.69%	-1.06%	-1.55%	-0.73%	-1.22%	-1.82%
Deflator of Absorption	-0.19%	0.41%	0.78%	0.50%	0.39%	0.30%	0.49%	0.36%	0.25%
Price of Exports-RW	-0.19%	0.41%	0.78%	0.50%	0.39%	0.30%	0.49%	0.36%	0.25%

Telecommunications	Constraint Case			Flexible Case			Efficiency Case		
	1988	1991	1994	1988	1991	1994	1988	1991	1994
Marginal Costs	-0.87%	-0.51%	-0.12%	-0.45%	-0.70%	-0.76%	-0.46%	-0.74%	-0.83%
Cost of Labour	-1.17%	-0.65%	-0.71%	-0.69%	-1.06%	-1.55%	-0.73%	-1.22%	-1.82%
Deflator of Absorption	-0.35%	0.33%	0.64%	-0.60%	-1.12%	-1.20%	-0.61%	-1.17%	-1.30%
Price of Exports-RW	2.79%	3.24%	3.62%	-0.57%	-0.95%	-1.02%	-0.58%	-0.99%	-1.10%

Transports	Constraint Case			Flexible Case			Efficiency Case		
	1988	1991	1994	1988	1991	1994	1988	1991	1994
Marginal Costs	-0.46%	0.13%	0.38%	0.07%	-0.18%	-0.40%	0.06%	-0.24%	-0.50%
Cost of Labour	-1.17%	-0.65%	-0.71%	-0.69%	-1.06%	-1.55%	-0.73%	-1.22%	-1.82%
Deflator of Absorption	-0.11%	0.40%	0.63%	0.16%	-0.11%	-0.31%	0.14%	-0.17%	-0.42%
Price of Exports-RW	-0.46%	0.13%	0.38%	0.07%	-0.18%	-0.40%	0.06%	-0.24%	-0.50%

Banks	Constraint Case			Flexible Case			Efficiency Case		
	1988	1991	1994	1988	1991	1994	1988	1991	1994
Marginal Costs	-1.09%	-0.75%	0.04%	-0.66%	-0.88%	-0.60%	-0.67%	-0.90%	-0.65%
Cost of Labour	-1.17%	-0.65%	-0.71%	-0.69%	-1.06%	-1.55%	-0.73%	-1.22%	-1.82%
Deflator of Absorption	-0.83%	-0.48%	0.22%	-0.69%	-1.04%	-0.77%	-0.69%	-1.07%	-0.83%
Price of Exports-RW	0.18%	0.52%	1.31%	-0.69%	-0.95%	-0.67%	-0.69%	-0.97%	-0.72%

Services	Constraint Case			Flexible Case			Efficiency Case		
	1988	1991	1994	1988	1991	1994	1988	1991	1994
Marginal Costs	-0.95%	-0.17%	0.41%	-0.12%	-0.33%	-0.24%	-0.13%	-0.37%	-0.31%
Cost of Labour	-1.17%	-0.65%	-0.71%	-0.69%	-1.06%	-1.55%	-0.73%	-1.22%	-1.82%
Deflator of Absorption	-0.91%	-0.15%	0.42%	-0.12%	-0.33%	-0.24%	-0.13%	-0.37%	-0.31%
Price of Exports-RW	-0.95%	-0.17%	0.41%	-0.12%	-0.33%	-0.24%	-0.13%	-0.37%	-0.31%

Non market	Constraint Case			Flexible Case			Efficiency Case		
	1988	1991	1994	1988	1991	1994	1988	1991	1994
Marginal Costs	-0.75%	-0.20%	-0.09%	-0.18%	-0.46%	-0.78%	-0.20%	-0.52%	-0.90%
Cost of Labour	-1.17%	-0.65%	-0.71%	-0.69%	-1.06%	-1.55%	-0.73%	-1.22%	-1.82%
Deflator of Absorption	-0.75%	-0.20%	-0.09%	-0.18%	-0.46%	-0.78%	-0.20%	-0.52%	-0.90%
Price of Exports-RW	-0.75%	-0.20%	-0.09%	-0.18%	-0.46%	-0.78%	-0.20%	-0.52%	-0.90%

Table B10.5.
Decomposition of effects: macroeconomic aggregates for Portugal

Macroeconomic Aggregates (vol.) (% change from monde)	Border Controls			Border controls and x-ineff.			Market segmentation			Trade antimonde			Full antimonde		
	1988	1991	1994	1988	1991	1994	1988	1991	1994	1988	1991	1994	1988	1991	1994
GDP fact. pr.	-0.10%	-0.11%	-0.12%	-0.11%	-0.12%	-0.14%	-0.60%	-1.13%	-1.43%	-0.65%	-1.15%	-1.47%	-0.76%	-1.32%	-1.69%
Priv. Consumption	0.21%	0.26%	0.26%	0.21%	0.27%	0.26%	-1.41%	-1.67%	-1.85%	-1.28%	-1.51%	-1.69%	-1.34%	-1.59%	-1.80%
Absorption	0.10%	0.14%	0.14%	0.11%	0.16%	0.16%	-1.29%	-1.53%	-1.76%	-1.21%	-1.43%	-1.66%	-1.24%	-1.48%	-1.73%
Total Investment	0.06%	0.05%	0.05%	0.06%	0.05%	0.06%	-4.35%	-4.58%	-4.74%	-4.32%	-4.55%	-4.71%	-4.33%	-4.56%	-4.73%
Total Exports to RW	-0.60%	-0.69%	-0.70%	-0.61%	-0.70%	-0.71%	2.01%	1.77%	1.60%	1.61%	1.32%	1.14%	1.55%	1.23%	1.02%
Total Imports from RW	1.82%	2.11%	2.12%	1.84%	2.14%	2.16%	-5.48%	-5.12%	-4.84%	-3.86%	-3.27%	-2.96%	-3.70%	-3.01%	-2.63%
Total Intra-EU Trade	-0.55%	-1.83%	-1.84%	-0.55%	-1.84%	-1.85%	-0.32%	-2.98%	-3.13%	-0.50%	-3.16%	-3.32%	-0.59%	-3.29%	-3.49%
Employment (diff. from monde, 10³ persons)	-5	-5	-5	-6	-5	-5	6	11	4	2	8	2	2	7	0
Disposable Income (deflated)	0.22%	0.28%	0.27%	0.23%	0.29%	0.28%	-1.51%	-1.79%	-1.98%	-1.37%	-1.61%	-1.81%	-1.43%	-1.70%	-1.93%

Macroeconomic Ratios (abs. diff. from monde)	Border Controls			Border controls and x-ineff.			Market segmentation			Trade antimonde			Full antimonde		
	1988	1991	1994	1988	1991	1994	1988	1991	1994	1988	1991	1994	1988	1991	1994
Current Account as % of GDP	-0.12%	-0.16%	-0.16%	-0.12%	-0.16%	-0.15%	-0.92%	-0.75%	-0.75%	-1.02%	-0.88%	-0.87%	-0.99%	-0.83%	-0.80%
Public Deficit as % of GDP	0.12%	0.14%	0.14%	0.12%	0.14%	0.13%	-0.48%	-0.62%	-0.67%	-0.36%	-0.48%	-0.54%	-0.39%	-0.52%	-0.58%
Labour Productivity	0.04%	0.01%	0.00%	0.05%	0.02%	0.00%	-0.75%	-1.42%	-1.55%	-0.71%	-1.37%	-1.51%	-0.81%	-1.50%	-1.69%
Investment/GDP	0.06%	0.06%	0.06%	0.06%	0.06%	0.07%	-2.18%	-2.18%	-2.19%	-2.15%	-2.15%	-2.16%	-2.13%	-2.12%	-2.12%
Priv.Cons./GDP	0.22%	0.26%	0.26%	0.23%	0.27%	0.28%	-0.57%	-0.38%	-0.30%	-0.45%	-0.25%	-0.16%	-0.41%	-0.19%	-0.08%

Deflators (% change from monde)	Border Controls			Border controls and x-ineff.			Market segmentation			Trade antimonde			Full antimonde		
	1988	1991	1994	1988	1991	1994	1988	1991	1994	1988	1991	1994	1988	1991	1994
Consumer Price Index	-0.35%	-0.43%	-0.43%	-0.35%	-0.44%	-0.44%	1.07%	0.94%	0.91%	0.91%	0.75%	0.72%	0.89%	0.71%	0.67%
Real Wage Rate	-0.24%	-0.22%	-0.23%	-0.24%	-0.24%	-0.25%	-0.44%	-0.77%	-1.17%	-0.58%	-0.89%	-1.31%	-0.69%	-1.06%	-1.55%
Marginal Costs	-0.19%	-0.25%	-0.25%	-0.19%	-0.25%	-0.25%	0.37%	0.30%	0.31%	0.28%	0.20%	0.20%	0.27%	0.18%	0.17%
Producer Prices	-0.18%	-0.22%	-0.22%	-0.18%	-0.23%	-0.24%	0.51%	0.45%	0.45%	0.43%	0.35%	0.35%	0.41%	0.32%	0.31%
Real Shadow Price of Capital	0.22%	0.10%	0.09%	0.23%	0.12%	0.11%	-0.85%	-1.02%	-0.58%	-0.76%	-0.98%	-0.53%	-0.84%	-1.09%	-0.69%
Terms-of-Trade RW	2.26%	2.58%	2.60%	2.28%	2.61%	2.64%	-6.29%	-5.60%	-5.09%	-4.85%	-3.98%	-3.45%	-4.68%	-3.72%	-3.10%
Real Exchange Rate	4.35%	4.76%	4.78%	4.37%	4.79%	4.82%	-6.71%	-5.90%	-5.35%	-3.45%	-2.43%	-1.84%	-3.27%	-2.15%	-1.47%
Trade Regime	Integration			Integration			Segmentation			Segmentation			Segmentation		

Table B10.6.
Decomposition of effects: effects on IC sectors for Portugal

% change from *monde*

Metal Industries

	Border Controls			Border controls and x-ineff.			Market segmentation			Trade *antimonde*			Full *antimonde*		
	1988	1991	1994	1988	1991	1994	1988	1991	1994	1988	1991	1994	1988	1991	1994
Production per firm	-0.71%	-1.71%	-1.73%	-0.71%	-1.71%	-1.73%	-15.13%	-20.08%	-20.16%	-15.71%	-20.76%	-20.86%	-15.78%	-20.85%	-20.97%
Marginal Costs	4.18%	4.54%	4.56%	4.20%	4.57%	4.60%	-5.99%	-5.25%	-4.72%	-2.78%	-1.83%	-1.27%	-2.61%	-1.57%	-0.92%
Producer Prices	4.29%	4.79%	4.81%	4.30%	4.81%	4.85%	-3.37%	-1.85%	-1.30%	0.04%	1.84%	2.43%	0.23%	2.12%	2.81%
Mark-ups domestic (abs. diff.)	-0.02%	0.03%	0.03%	-0.03%	0.02%	0.03%	6.69%	8.27%	8.29%	6.70%	8.29%	8.30%	6.70%	8.28%	8.30%
Fixed Costs per firm	4.11%	4.47%	4.49%	4.12%	4.49%	4.52%	-5.73%	-4.97%	-4.52%	-2.55%	-1.58%	-1.10%	-2.41%	-1.37%	-0.83%
Number of Firms	0.60%	1.57%	1.54%	0.62%	1.62%	1.59%	16.33%	20.71%	20.61%	16.31%	20.68%	20.57%	16.31%	20.70%	20.59%
Sigma of Love of Variety	0.00%	0.00%	0.00%	0.00%	0.00%	0.00%	0.00%	0.00%	0.00%	0.00%	0.00%	0.00%	0.00%	0.00%	0.00%

Chemical

	Border Controls			Border controls and x-ineff.			Market segmentation			Trade *antimonde*			Full *antimonde*		
	1988	1991	1994	1988	1991	1994	1988	1991	1994	1988	1991	1994	1988	1991	1994
Production per firm	-0.04%	-0.63%	-0.63%	-0.04%	-0.63%	-0.64%	-5.92%	-9.09%	-9.27%	-5.66%	-8.71%	-8.90%	-5.74%	-8.83%	-9.06%
Marginal Costs	4.11%	4.43%	4.45%	4.13%	4.46%	4.50%	-6.01%	-5.39%	-4.83%	-2.85%	-2.04%	-1.45%	-2.68%	-1.77%	-1.09%
Producer Prices	4.10%	4.49%	4.50%	4.12%	4.52%	4.55%	-5.44%	-4.52%	-3.95%	-2.30%	-1.19%	-0.58%	-2.11%	-0.91%	-0.21%
Mark-ups domestic (abs. diff.)	-0.02%	-0.02%	-0.02%	-0.02%	-0.02%	-0.02%	0.93%	1.16%	1.18%	0.90%	1.13%	1.15%	0.91%	1.13%	1.15%
Fixed Costs per firm	4.02%	4.36%	4.37%	4.04%	4.38%	4.40%	-5.76%	-5.15%	-4.66%	-2.64%	-1.83%	-1.32%	-2.50%	-1.62%	-1.04%
Number of Firms	0.86%	2.53%	2.53%	0.87%	2.56%	2.55%	10.94%	21.13%	20.86%	11.23%	21.47%	21.20%	11.19%	21.42%	21.13%
Sigma of Love of Variety	0.00%	0.00%	0.00%	0.00%	0.00%	0.00%	0.00%	0.00%	0.00%	0.00%	0.00%	0.00%	0.00%	0.00%	0.00%

Other Intensive Industries

	Border Controls			Border controls and x-ineff.			Market segmentation			Trade *antimonde*			Full *antimonde*		
	1988	1991	1994	1988	1991	1994	1988	1991	1994	1988	1991	1994	1988	1991	1994
Production per firm	-0.54%	-1.70%	-1.70%	-0.54%	-1.70%	-1.71%	-4.37%	-7.10%	-7.30%	-4.64%	-7.44%	-7.65%	-4.69%	-7.50%	-7.72%
Marginal Costs	4.21%	4.55%	4.57%	4.23%	4.58%	4.62%	-6.35%	-5.68%	-5.11%	-3.15%	-2.27%	-1.68%	-2.98%	-2.02%	-1.33%
Producer Prices	4.24%	4.66%	4.68%	4.26%	4.70%	4.73%	-6.04%	-5.18%	-4.61%	-2.81%	-1.74%	-1.13%	-2.64%	-1.48%	-0.79%
Mark-ups domestic (abs. diff.)	-0.01%	0.01%	0.01%	-0.01%	0.01%	0.01%	0.54%	0.67%	0.68%	0.53%	0.67%	0.67%	0.53%	0.66%	0.67%
Fixed Costs per firm	4.10%	4.46%	4.48%	4.11%	4.47%	4.50%	-6.02%	-5.34%	-4.90%	-2.87%	-1.98%	-1.51%	-2.74%	-1.78%	-1.25%
Number of Firms	0.44%	1.03%	1.03%	0.45%	1.06%	1.05%	2.45%	5.90%	5.79%	2.55%	5.98%	5.86%	2.56%	6.00%	5.89%
Sigma of Love of Variety	0.00%	0.00%	0.00%	0.00%	0.00%	0.00%	0.00%	0.00%	0.00%	0.00%	0.00%	0.00%	0.00%	0.00%	0.00%

Electrical goods

	Border Controls			Border controls and x-ineff.			Market segmentation			Trade *antimonde*			Full *antimonde*		
	1988	1991	1994	1988	1991	1994	1988	1991	1994	1988	1991	1994	1988	1991	1994
Production per firm	-0.91%	-2.71%	-2.72%	-0.91%	-2.73%	-2.74%	-15.07%	-21.46%	-21.62%	-15.69%	-22.04%	-22.22%	-15.87%	-22.30%	-22.55%
Marginal Costs	4.16%	4.52%	4.54%	4.19%	4.55%	4.59%	-5.54%	-4.68%	-4.13%	-2.31%	-1.24%	-0.66%	-2.13%	-0.96%	-0.29%
Producer Prices	4.27%	4.80%	4.82%	4.29%	4.83%	4.87%	-3.53%	-2.08%	-1.51%	-0.14%	1.54%	2.15%	0.07%	1.86%	2.58%
Mark-ups domestic (abs. diff.)	-0.01%	0.18%	0.19%	-0.01%	0.18%	0.19%	9.03%	11.10%	11.11%	9.02%	11.10%	11.12%	9.06%	11.15%	11.19%
Fixed Costs per firm	4.09%	4.45%	4.47%	4.11%	4.47%	4.50%	-5.20%	-4.32%	-3.85%	-2.01%	-0.90%	-0.41%	-1.86%	-0.69%	-0.12%
Number of Firms	1.02%	1.53%	1.45%	1.03%	1.53%	1.44%	4.84%	-4.96%	-5.43%	4.84%	-5.00%	-5.49%	4.73%	-5.13%	-5.67%
Sigma of Love of Variety	0.00%	0.00%	0.00%	0.00%	0.00%	0.00%	0.00%	0.00%	0.00%	0.00%	0.00%	0.00%	0.00%	0.00%	0.00%

Transport equipment

	Border Controls			Border controls and x-ineff.			Market segmentation			Trade antimonde			Full antimonde		
	1988	1991	1994	1988	1991	1994	1988	1991	1994	1988	1991	1994	1988	1991	1994
Production per firm	-0.04%	-0.75%	-0.76%	-0.05%	-0.76%	-0.78%	-19.44%	-22.90%	-22.93%	-19.25%	-22.48%	-22.53%	-19.32%	-22.58%	-22.64%
Marginal Costs	4.15%	4.49%	4.51%	4.17%	4.52%	4.56%	-5.13%	-4.24%	-3.73%	-1.89%	-0.78%	-0.25%	-1.70%	-0.49%	0.14%
Producer Prices	4.15%	4.59%	4.61%	4.17%	4.62%	4.66%	-1.73%	-0.42%	0.10%	1.58%	3.08%	3.63%	1.79%	3.39%	4.04%
Mark-ups domestic (abs. diff.)	-0.05%	0.05%	0.06%	-0.05%	0.05%	0.06%	13.78%	15.69%	15.64%	13.65%	15.56%	15.52%	13.67%	15.58%	15.54%
Fixed Costs per firm	4.10%	4.45%	4.47%	4.12%	4.47%	4.50%	-4.92%	-4.01%	-3.56%	-1.70%	-0.57%	-0.09%	-1.56%	-0.35%	0.21%
Number of Firms	1.10%	2.27%	2.16%	1.11%	2.27%	2.16%	7.45%	-1.27%	-1.08%	7.71%	-1.01%	-0.85%	7.66%	-1.06%	-0.91%
Sigma of Love of Variety	0.00%	0.00%	0.00%	0.00%	0.00%	0.00%	0.00%	0.00%	0.00%	0.00%	0.00%	0.00%	0.00%	0.00%	0.00%

Other Equipment

	Border Controls			Border controls and x-ineff.			Market segmentation			Trade antimonde			Full antimonde		
	1988	1991	1994	1988	1991	1994	1988	1991	1994	1988	1991	1994	1988	1991	1994
Production per firm	-0.39%	-1.00%	-1.01%	-0.40%	-1.01%	-1.02%	-17.94%	-22.39%	-22.55%	-18.29%	-22.71%	-22.89%	-18.37%	-22.84%	-23.05%
Marginal Costs	4.21%	4.56%	4.58%	4.23%	4.60%	4.63%	-6.31%	-5.61%	-5.08%	-3.10%	-2.20%	-1.63%	-2.92%	-1.92%	-1.26%
Producer Prices	4.24%	4.64%	4.66%	4.26%	4.67%	4.70%	-4.76%	-3.71%	-3.15%	-1.46%	-0.19%	0.40%	-1.27%	0.10%	0.79%
Mark-ups domestic (abs. diff.)	0.01%	0.04%	0.04%	0.01%	0.04%	0.04%	3.52%	4.25%	4.27%	3.53%	4.27%	4.28%	3.53%	4.27%	4.29%
Fixed Costs per firm	4.17%	4.53%	4.55%	4.19%	4.56%	4.59%	-6.21%	-5.52%	-5.03%	-3.02%	-2.12%	-1.60%	-2.88%	-1.91%	-1.32%
Number of Firms	0.56%	2.08%	2.07%	0.56%	2.07%	2.06%	14.42%	19.63%	19.16%	14.27%	19.47%	19.00%	14.24%	19.41%	18.93%
Sigma of Love of Variety	0.00%	0.00%	0.00%	0.00%	0.00%	0.00%	0.00%	0.00%	0.00%	0.00%	0.00%	0.00%	0.00%	0.00%	0.00%

Telecommunications

	Border Controls			Border controls and x-ineff.			Market segmentation			Trade antimonde			Full antimonde		
	1988	1991	1994	1988	1991	1994	1988	1991	1994	1988	1991	1994	1988	1991	1994
Production per firm	0.01%	0.04%	0.03%	-0.58%	-1.18%	-1.18%	-0.32%	-0.86%	-1.10%	-0.30%	-0.85%	-1.09%	-0.93%	-2.08%	-2.34%
Marginal Costs	4.31%	4.68%	4.71%	4.33%	4.71%	4.75%	-7.09%	-6.50%	-5.99%	-3.87%	-3.08%	-2.54%	-3.72%	-2.84%	-2.22%
Producer Prices	4.24%	4.61%	4.64%	3.92%	3.97%	4.01%	-6.90%	-6.16%	-5.67%	-3.72%	-2.76%	-2.23%	-3.88%	-3.16%	-2.58%
Mark-ups domestic (abs. diff.)	-0.10%	-0.11%	-0.11%	-0.60%	-1.11%	-1.12%	0.25%	0.32%	0.30%	0.19%	0.25%	0.23%	-0.32%	-0.77%	-0.80%
Fixed Costs per firm	4.11%	4.51%	4.53%	2.50%	1.29%	1.31%	-6.83%	-6.29%	-6.07%	-3.70%	-2.94%	-2.69%	-5.11%	-5.80%	-5.53%
Number of Firms	0.13%	0.13%	0.13%	0.81%	1.53%	1.54%	0.25%	0.64%	0.69%	0.34%	0.73%	0.78%	1.02%	2.10%	2.16%
Sigma of Love of Variety	0.00%	0.00%	0.00%	0.00%	0.00%	0.00%	0.00%	0.00%	0.00%	0.00%	0.00%	0.00%	0.00%	0.00%	0.00%

Banks

	Border Controls			Border controls and x-ineff.			Market segmentation			Trade antimonde			Full antimonde		
	1988	1991	1994	1988	1991	1994	1988	1991	1994	1988	1991	1994	1988	1991	1994
Production per firm	-0.15%	-0.16%	-0.14%	-0.58%	-1.01%	-1.00%	0.14%	0.36%	-0.19%	0.08%	0.27%	-0.26%	-0.40%	-0.66%	-1.22%
Marginal Costs	4.52%	4.84%	4.85%	4.54%	4.89%	4.91%	-7.41%	-6.78%	-5.93%	-4.10%	-3.29%	-2.40%	-3.93%	-3.03%	-2.07%
Producer Prices	4.48%	4.81%	4.82%	4.42%	4.69%	4.71%	-7.34%	-6.76%	-5.92%	-4.05%	-3.28%	-2.40%	-3.96%	-3.18%	-2.22%
Mark-ups domestic (abs. diff.)	-0.04%	-0.03%	-0.03%	-0.14%	-0.23%	-0.24%	0.09%	0.01%	0.00%	0.06%	-0.01%	-0.02%	-0.04%	-0.21%	-0.22%
Fixed Costs per firm	4.15%	4.54%	4.55%	3.27%	2.75%	2.78%	-6.89%	-6.35%	-6.01%	-3.75%	-2.99%	-2.63%	-4.48%	-4.50%	-4.10%
Number of Firms	0.17%	0.09%	0.10%	0.59%	0.94%	0.95%	0.07%	0.76%	0.77%	0.19%	0.85%	0.86%	0.60%	1.67%	1.68%
Sigma of Love of Variety	0.00%	0.00%	0.00%	0.00%	0.00%	0.00%	0.00%	0.00%	0.00%	0.00%	0.00%	0.00%	0.00%	0.00%	0.00%

Table B10.7.
Decomposition of effects: sectoral results for Portugal (volumes)

% change from *monde*

Agriculture

	Border Controls			Border controls and x-ineff.			Market segmentation			Trade *antimonde*			Full *antimonde*		
	1988	1991	1994	1988	1991	1994	1988	1991	1994	1988	1991	1994	1988	1991	1994
Domestic Production - vol.	-1.0%	-1.0%	-1.0%	-1.0%	-1.0%	-1.0%	3.8%	5.3%	4.7%	3.2%	4.6%	4.1%	3.1%	4.4%	3.8%
Imports - vol.	2.3%	2.6%	2.6%	2.3%	2.6%	2.7%	-4.9%	-4.0%	-3.6%	-3.3%	-2.2%	-1.7%	-3.2%	-1.9%	-1.4%
Exports - vol.	-0.8%	-0.9%	-0.9%	-0.8%	-0.9%	-0.9%	2.1%	1.9%	1.7%	1.5%	1.2%	1.0%	1.4%	1.2%	0.9%
Absorption - vol.	0.1%	0.2%	0.2%	0.1%	0.2%	0.2%	0.8%	1.8%	1.5%	0.9%	2.0%	1.7%	0.9%	1.9%	1.6%
Investment - vol.	-0.5%	-0.5%	-0.4%	-0.5%	-0.5%	-0.4%	-2.7%	-2.0%	-2.3%	-2.9%	-2.3%	-2.5%	-3.0%	-2.4%	-2.6%
Labour Demand - vol.	-0.9%	-0.9%	-0.9%	-0.9%	-0.9%	-0.9%	3.8%	5.2%	4.9%	3.2%	4.6%	4.3%	3.1%	4.5%	4.1%
Private Consumption - vol.	0.2%	0.2%	0.3%	0.2%	0.2%	0.3%	-0.8%	-1.4%	-1.7%	-0.7%	-1.2%	-1.6%	-0.7%	-1.3%	-1.7%
Supply to domestic - vol.	-1.0%	-0.9%	-0.9%	-1.0%	-0.9%	-0.9%	3.8%	5.2%	4.7%	3.2%	4.6%	4.0%	3.1%	4.4%	3.8%
Intra-EU Trade - vol	-1.2%	-2.7%	-2.7%	-1.2%	-2.7%	-2.7%	0.7%	-3.6%	-3.9%	-0.5%	-4.9%	-5.1%	-0.6%	-5.0%	-5.3%

Energy

	Border Controls			Border controls and x-ineff.			Market segmentation			Trade *antimonde*			Full *antimonde*		
	1988	1991	1994	1988	1991	1994	1988	1991	1994	1988	1991	1994	1988	1991	1994
Domestic Production - vol.	-0.1%	-0.1%	-0.1%	-0.1%	0.0%	0.0%	1.4%	1.6%	1.3%	1.3%	1.6%	1.2%	1.2%	1.4%	1.1%
Imports - vol.	1.1%	1.3%	1.3%	1.1%	1.3%	1.3%	-2.2%	-1.9%	-1.8%	-1.5%	-1.0%	-0.9%	-1.4%	-1.0%	-0.9%
Exports - vol.	-0.4%	-0.4%	-0.4%	-0.4%	-0.4%	-0.4%	1.0%	0.9%	0.8%	0.7%	0.6%	0.5%	0.7%	0.6%	0.4%
Absorption - vol.	0.1%	0.2%	0.2%	0.1%	0.2%	0.2%	0.4%	0.6%	0.3%	0.5%	0.7%	0.5%	0.4%	0.7%	0.3%
Investment - vol.	-0.1%	0.0%	0.0%	-0.1%	0.0%	0.0%	-3.5%	-3.4%	-3.5%	-3.5%	-3.4%	-3.6%	-3.6%	-3.5%	-3.6%
Labour Demand - vol.	-0.1%	-0.1%	-0.1%	-0.1%	0.0%	0.0%	1.4%	1.7%	1.4%	1.4%	1.6%	1.4%	1.3%	1.6%	1.3%
Private Consumption - vol.	0.1%	0.2%	0.2%	0.1%	0.2%	0.2%	-0.8%	-1.3%	-1.7%	-0.7%	-1.2%	-1.5%	-0.7%	-1.3%	-1.6%
Supply to domestic - vol.	-0.2%	-0.1%	-0.1%	-0.2%	-0.1%	-0.1%	1.2%	1.3%	1.0%	1.1%	1.3%	0.9%	1.0%	1.1%	0.8%
Intra-EU Trade - vol	-0.2%	-0.1%	-0.1%	-0.2%	-0.1%	-0.1%	1.5%	1.9%	1.8%	1.5%	1.8%	1.7%	1.4%	1.7%	1.6%

Metal Industries

	Border Controls			Border controls and x-ineff.			Market segmentation			Trade *antimonde*			Full *antimonde*		
	1988	1991	1994	1988	1991	1994	1988	1991	1994	1988	1991	1994	1988	1991	1994
Domestic Production - vol.	-0.1%	-0.2%	-0.2%	-0.1%	-0.1%	-0.2%	-1.3%	-3.5%	-3.7%	-2.0%	-4.4%	-4.6%	-2.0%	-4.5%	-4.7%
Imports - vol.	2.1%	2.4%	2.4%	2.1%	2.4%	2.4%	-8.7%	-9.7%	-9.6%	-5.6%	-6.4%	-6.2%	-5.3%	-6.0%	-5.6%
Exports - vol.	-0.8%	-0.8%	-0.8%	-0.8%	-0.8%	-0.8%	2.2%	2.1%	1.9%	1.7%	1.5%	1.3%	1.6%	1.4%	1.2%
Absorption - vol.	0.2%	0.1%	0.1%	0.2%	0.2%	0.1%	-3.9%	-6.8%	-7.1%	-4.1%	-7.0%	-7.3%	-4.1%	-7.1%	-7.3%
Investment - vol.	0.0%	-0.1%	-0.1%	0.0%	-0.1%	-0.1%	-4.7%	-5.8%	-5.9%	-5.0%	-6.1%	-6.3%	-5.1%	-6.2%	-6.3%
Labour Demand - vol.	0.0%	0.1%	0.1%	0.1%	0.2%	0.1%	1.9%	0.5%	0.4%	1.3%	-0.2%	-0.4%	1.3%	-0.2%	-0.4%
Private Consumption - vol.	0.1%	0.1%	0.1%	0.1%	0.1%	0.1%	-0.4%	-0.7%	-0.9%	-0.3%	-0.6%	-0.8%	-0.4%	-0.6%	-0.8%
Supply to domestic - vol.	1.0%	2.2%	2.2%	1.0%	2.3%	2.2%	-5.3%	-7.2%	-7.5%	-5.2%	-7.2%	-7.5%	-5.3%	-7.2%	-7.5%
Intra-EU Trade - vol	-0.6%	-1.4%	-1.4%	-0.6%	-1.4%	-1.4%	0.3%	-1.6%	-1.7%	-0.3%	-2.3%	-2.4%	-0.4%	-2.4%	-2.5%

Chemical

	Border Controls			Border controls and x-ineff.			Market segmentation			Trade *antimonde*			Full *antimonde*		
	1988	1991	1994	1988	1991	1994	1988	1991	1994	1988	1991	1994	1988	1991	1994
Domestic Production - vol.	0.8%	1.9%	1.9%	0.8%	1.9%	1.9%	4.4%	10.1%	9.7%	4.9%	10.9%	10.4%	4.8%	10.7%	10.2%
Imports - vol.	1.3%	1.7%	1.8%	1.3%	1.8%	1.8%	-5.4%	-4.7%	-4.5%	-4.0%	-2.9%	-2.7%	-3.8%	-2.5%	-2.2%
Exports - vol.	-0.4%	-0.5%	-0.5%	-0.4%	-0.5%	-0.5%	2.0%	1.9%	1.7%	1.8%	1.6%	1.4%	1.7%	1.5%	1.3%
Absorption - vol.	0.2%	0.4%	0.4%	0.2%	0.4%	0.4%	1.0%	2.0%	1.7%	1.1%	2.2%	1.9%	1.0%	2.1%	1.8%
Investment - vol.	0.4%	0.9%	0.9%	0.4%	0.9%	0.9%	-2.1%	0.5%	0.3%	-1.9%	0.8%	0.6%	-1.9%	0.8%	0.5%
Labour Demand - vol.	0.8%	2.0%	2.0%	0.9%	2.0%	2.0%	5.1%	11.3%	10.9%	5.7%	12.1%	11.7%	5.6%	12.0%	11.5%
Private Consumption - vol.	0.1%	0.2%	0.2%	0.1%	0.2%	0.2%	-0.8%	-1.4%	-1.9%	-0.7%	-1.3%	-1.7%	-0.7%	-1.4%	-1.8%
Supply to domestic - vol.	0.9%	3.0%	3.0%	1.0%	3.1%	3.1%	5.2%	14.7%	14.2%	5.5%	15.1%	14.5%	5.4%	14.9%	14.3%
Intra-EU Trade - vol	-0.6%	-1.8%	-1.8%	-0.6%	-1.8%	-1.8%	-0.2%	-4.6%	-4.8%	-0.3%	-4.7%	-4.9%	-0.4%	-4.9%	-5.1%

Other Intensive Industries

	Border Controls			Border controls and x-ineff.			Market segmentation			Trade *antimonde*			Full *antimonde*		
	1988	1991	1994	1988	1991	1994	1988	1991	1994	1988	1991	1994	1988	1991	1994
Domestic Production - vol.	-0.1%	-0.7%	-0.7%	-0.1%	-0.7%	-0.7%	-2.0%	-1.6%	-1.9%	-2.2%	-1.9%	-2.2%	-2.2%	-2.0%	-2.3%
Imports - vol.	2.3%	2.6%	2.6%	2.3%	2.7%	2.7%	-8.9%	-8.6%	-8.3%	-6.1%	-5.5%	-5.1%	-5.8%	-5.0%	-4.5%
Exports - vol.	-0.7%	-0.7%	-0.8%	-0.7%	-0.8%	-0.8%	2.0%	1.8%	1.6%	1.6%	1.3%	1.1%	1.5%	1.2%	1.0%
Absorption - vol.	0.1%	0.0%	0.0%	0.1%	0.1%	0.1%	-3.4%	-3.8%	-4.0%	-3.4%	-3.8%	-4.0%	-3.4%	-3.8%	-4.0%
Investment - vol.	0.0%	-0.3%	-0.3%	0.0%	-0.3%	-0.3%	-5.2%	-5.0%	-5.2%	-5.3%	-5.1%	-5.3%	-5.3%	-5.1%	-5.3%
Labour Demand - vol.	0.0%	-0.5%	-0.5%	0.0%	-0.5%	-0.5%	-1.6%	-1.0%	-1.2%	-1.8%	-1.2%	-1.5%	-1.8%	-1.2%	-1.4%
Private Consumption - vol.	0.2%	0.2%	0.2%	0.2%	0.2%	0.2%	-1.6%	-1.6%	-1.5%	-1.5%	-1.4%	-1.4%	-1.6%	-1.5%	-1.5%
Supply to domestic - vol.	0.5%	1.3%	1.3%	0.5%	1.4%	1.4%	-1.9%	-1.6%	-1.5%	-1.8%	-1.4%	-1.4%	-1.8%	-1.5%	-1.5%
Intra-EU Trade - vol	-0.8%	-2.4%	-2.4%	-0.8%	-2.4%	-2.4%	-2.5%	-6.0%	-6.1%	-2.9%	-6.5%	-6.6%	-2.9%	-6.5%	-6.7%

Electrical goods

Electrical goods	Border Controls			Border controls and x-ineff.			Market segmentation			Trade antimonde			Full antimonde		
	1988	1991	1994	1988	1991	1994	1988	1991	1994	1988	1991	1994	1988	1991	1994
Domestic Production - vol.	0.1%	-1.2%	-1.3%	0.1%	-1.2%	-1.3%	-11.0%	-25.4%	-25.9%	-11.6%	-25.9%	-26.5%	-11.9%	-26.3%	-26.9%
Imports - vol.	2.0%	2.2%	2.2%	2.0%	2.2%	2.2%	-7.8%	-9.1%	-8.9%	-5.5%	-6.6%	-6.3%	-5.3%	-6.2%	-5.9%
Exports - vol.	-0.7%	-0.8%	-0.8%	-0.7%	-0.8%	-0.8%	2.2%	1.6%	1.3%	1.7%	1.0%	0.8%	1.6%	0.9%	0.7%
Absorption - vol.	0.4%	0.0%	-0.1%	0.4%	0.0%	-0.1%	-6.8%	-11.6%	-11.7%	-6.8%	-11.7%	-11.8%	-6.9%	-11.8%	-11.9%
Investment - vol.	0.1%	-0.6%	-0.6%	0.1%	-0.6%	-0.7%	-9.1%	-15.7%	-15.9%	-9.3%	-15.9%	-16.2%	-9.5%	-16.1%	-16.4%
Labour Demand - vol.	0.3%	-0.9%	-1.0%	0.3%	-0.9%	-1.0%	-8.6%	-22.8%	-23.2%	-9.1%	-23.3%	-23.7%	-9.3%	-23.5%	-24.1%
Private Consumption - vol.	0.8%	0.6%	0.4%	0.8%	0.6%	0.4%	-5.8%	-4.3%	-3.3%	-5.3%	-3.9%	-3.1%	-5.5%	-4.1%	-3.3%
Supply to domestic - vol.	1.2%	1.8%	1.7%	1.3%	1.8%	1.6%	-17.4%	-32.0%	-32.5%	-17.6%	-32.2%	-32.8%	-17.8%	-32.4%	-33.0%
Intra-EU Trade - vol	-0.7%	-1.7%	-1.7%	-0.7%	-1.7%	-1.8%	-0.5%	-4.8%	-4.9%	-1.3%	-5.5%	-5.7%	-1.5%	-5.8%	-6.1%

Transport equipment

Transport equipment	Border Controls			Border controls and x-ineff.			Market segmentation			Trade antimonde			Full antimonde		
	1988	1991	1994	1988	1991	1994	1988	1991	1994	1988	1991	1994	1988	1991	1994
Domestic Production - vol.	1.1%	1.5%	1.4%	1.1%	1.5%	1.4%	-13.4%	-23.9%	-23.8%	-13.0%	-23.3%	-23.2%	-13.1%	-23.4%	-23.3%
Imports - vol.	1.8%	2.0%	2.0%	1.8%	2.1%	2.0%	-6.7%	-6.7%	-6.3%	-4.3%	-3.9%	-3.5%	-4.1%	-3.6%	-3.0%
Exports - vol.	-0.7%	-0.8%	-0.8%	-0.7%	-0.8%	-0.8%	2.1%	1.5%	1.3%	1.6%	0.9%	0.7%	1.6%	0.8%	0.6%
Absorption - vol.	0.5%	0.6%	0.5%	0.6%	0.6%	0.5%	-5.7%	-6.7%	-6.3%	-5.4%	-6.4%	-6.0%	-5.5%	-6.5%	-6.1%
Investment - vol.	0.5%	0.7%	0.7%	0.5%	0.7%	0.7%	-10.1%	-14.8%	-14.8%	-9.9%	-14.6%	-14.5%	-9.9%	-14.6%	-14.6%
Labour Demand - vol.	1.1%	1.6%	1.5%	1.1%	1.6%	1.5%	-9.8%	-20.2%	-20.1%	-9.4%	-19.7%	-19.5%	-9.4%	-19.7%	-19.6%
Private Consumption - vol.	0.6%	0.4%	0.2%	0.6%	0.4%	0.2%	-5.3%	-3.4%	-2.2%	-5.0%	-3.2%	-2.1%	-5.2%	-3.3%	-2.2%
Supply to domestic - vol.	1.7%	3.2%	3.0%	1.7%	3.2%	3.0%	-24.2%	-37.2%	-36.9%	-23.9%	-36.9%	-36.6%	-24.0%	-37.0%	-36.8%
Intra-EU Trade - vol	-0.2%	-0.8%	-0.8%	-0.2%	-0.8%	-0.8%	2.4%	3.7%	3.8%	2.1%	3.4%	3.5%	2.0%	3.3%	3.3%

Other Equipment

Other Equipment	Border Controls			Border controls and x-ineff.			Market segmentation			Trade antimonde			Full antimonde		
	1988	1991	1994	1988	1991	1994	1988	1991	1994	1988	1991	1994	1988	1991	1994
Domestic Production - vol.	0.2%	1.1%	1.0%	0.2%	1.0%	1.0%	-6.1%	-7.2%	-7.7%	-6.6%	-7.7%	-8.2%	-6.7%	-7.9%	-8.5%
Imports - vol.	1.8%	2.0%	2.0%	1.8%	2.0%	2.0%	-8.9%	-9.2%	-9.2%	-6.4%	-6.4%	-6.3%	-6.2%	-6.1%	-5.9%
Exports - vol.	-0.9%	-1.0%	-1.0%	-0.9%	-1.0%	-1.0%	2.5%	2.3%	2.1%	1.8%	1.5%	1.3%	1.7%	1.4%	1.2%
Absorption - vol.	0.1%	-0.1%	-0.1%	0.1%	-0.1%	-0.1%	-8.4%	-9.7%	-10.1%	-8.4%	-9.7%	-10.0%	-8.4%	-9.7%	-10.1%
Investment - vol.	0.1%	0.6%	0.5%	0.1%	0.5%	0.5%	-7.0%	-7.5%	-7.8%	-7.2%	-7.7%	-8.0%	-7.3%	-7.8%	-8.1%
Labour Demand - vol.	0.2%	1.2%	1.1%	0.2%	1.1%	1.1%	-4.3%	-4.9%	-5.4%	-4.8%	-5.4%	-5.9%	-4.8%	-5.5%	-6.0%
Private Consumption - vol.	0.2%	0.3%	0.3%	0.2%	0.3%	0.3%	-1.5%	-2.1%	-2.5%	-1.4%	-1.9%	-2.3%	-1.4%	-2.0%	-2.4%
Supply to domestic - vol.	0.7%	2.8%	2.8%	0.7%	2.8%	2.8%	-10.1%	-11.1%	-11.7%	-10.3%	-11.3%	-11.9%	-10.3%	-11.4%	-12.1%
Intra-EU Trade - vol	-0.7%	-1.4%	-1.4%	-0.7%	-1.4%	-1.5%	-1.5%	-2.3%	-2.5%	-2.3%	-3.3%	-3.5%	-2.5%	-3.4%	-3.7%

Consumer goods

Consumer goods	Border Controls			Border controls and x-ineff.			Market segmentation			Trade antimonde			Full antimonde		
	1988	1991	1994	1988	1991	1994	1988	1991	1994	1988	1991	1994	1988	1991	1994
Domestic Production - vol.	-0.1%	0.0%	0.0%	-0.1%	0.0%	0.0%	1.9%	3.6%	3.4%	2.0%	3.8%	3.6%	1.9%	3.7%	3.4%
Imports - vol.	1.9%	2.3%	2.3%	1.9%	2.3%	2.4%	-5.8%	-5.3%	-4.9%	-4.5%	-3.7%	-3.3%	-4.3%	-3.4%	-3.0%
Exports - vol.	-0.8%	-0.9%	-0.9%	-0.8%	-0.9%	-0.9%	2.6%	2.4%	2.1%	2.1%	1.8%	1.5%	2.0%	1.7%	1.4%
Absorption - vol.	0.0%	0.1%	0.1%	0.1%	0.1%	0.1%	-0.1%	-0.1%	-0.4%	0.0%	0.0%	-0.2%	-0.1%	0.0%	-0.3%
Investment - vol.	-0.1%	-0.1%	0.0%	-0.1%	-0.1%	0.0%	-3.5%	-2.8%	-2.9%	-3.5%	-2.7%	-2.9%	-3.5%	-2.7%	-2.9%
Labour Demand - vol.	0.0%	0.0%	0.0%	0.0%	0.0%	0.0%	2.0%	3.7%	3.6%	2.2%	4.0%	3.8%	2.1%	3.9%	3.8%
Private Consumption - vol.	0.1%	0.2%	0.2%	0.1%	0.2%	0.2%	-0.7%	-1.3%	-1.6%	-0.6%	-1.1%	-1.5%	-0.7%	-1.2%	-1.6%
Supply to domestic - vol.	0.2%	1.1%	1.2%	0.2%	1.1%	1.2%	1.7%	4.2%	3.9%	1.7%	4.2%	4.0%	1.6%	4.1%	3.8%
Intra-EU Trade - vol	-0.7%	-2.6%	-2.6%	-0.7%	-2.6%	-2.6%	-0.5%	-3.4%	-3.6%	-0.3%	-3.1%	-3.3%	-0.4%	-3.2%	-3.4%

Construction

Construction	Border Controls			Border controls and x-ineff.			Market segmentation			Trade antimonde			Full antimonde		
	1988	1991	1994	1988	1991	1994	1988	1991	1994	1988	1991	1994	1988	1991	1994
Domestic Production - vol.	0.1%	0.1%	0.1%	0.1%	0.1%	0.1%	-7.1%	-7.1%	-7.4%	-7.1%	-7.1%	-7.3%	-7.1%	-7.1%	-7.4%
Imports - vol.	#VALUE!	#VALUE!	#VALUE!	#VALUE!	#VALUE!	#VALUE!	#VALUE!	#VALUE!	#VALUE!	#VALUE!	#VALUE!	#VALUE!	#VALUE!	#VALUE!	#VALUE!
Exports - vol.	#VALUE!	#VALUE!	#VALUE!	#VALUE!	#VALUE!	#VALUE!	#VALUE!	#VALUE!	#VALUE!	#VALUE!	#VALUE!	#VALUE!	#VALUE!	#VALUE!	#VALUE!
Absorption - vol.	0.1%	0.1%	0.1%	0.1%	0.1%	0.1%	-7.1%	-7.6%	-7.4%	-7.1%	-7.1%	-7.3%	-7.1%	-7.1%	-7.4%
Investment - vol.	0.1%	0.1%	0.1%	0.1%	0.1%	0.1%	-7.6%	-7.6%	-7.8%	-7.5%	-7.6%	-7.7%	-7.5%	-7.5%	-7.7%
Labour Demand - vol.	0.1%	0.1%	0.2%	0.1%	0.2%	0.2%	-7.1%	-7.0%	-7.2%	-7.0%	-6.9%	-7.1%	-6.9%	-6.9%	-7.0%
Private Consumption - vol.	0.1%	0.2%	0.2%	0.1%	0.2%	0.2%	-0.7%	-1.4%	-1.9%	-0.7%	-1.3%	-1.7%	-0.7%	-1.4%	-1.9%
Supply to domestic - vol.	0.1%	0.1%	0.2%	0.1%	0.2%	0.2%	-7.1%	-7.1%	-7.4%	-7.1%	-7.1%	-7.3%	-7.1%	-7.1%	-7.4%
Intra-EU Trade - vol	#DIV/0!	#DIV/0!	#DIV/0!	#DIV/0!	#DIV/0!	#DIV/0!	#DIV/0!	#DIV/0!	#DIV/0!	#DIV/0!	#DIV/0!	#DIV/0!	#DIV/0!	#DIV/0!	#DIV/0!

Telecommunications

	Border Controls			Border controls and x-ineff.			Market segmentation			Trade *antimonde*			Full *antimonde*		
	1988	1991	1994	1988	1991	1994	1988	1991	1994	1988	1991	1994	1988	1991	1994
Domestic Production - vol.	0.1%	0.2%	0.2%	0.2%	0.3%	0.3%	-0.1%	-0.2%	-0.4%	0.0%	-0.1%	-0.3%	0.1%	0.0%	-0.2%
Imports - vol.	1.1%	1.3%	1.3%	0.9%	1.0%	1.0%	-6.2%	-6.3%	-6.2%	-5.5%	-5.5%	-5.3%	-5.6%	-5.6%	-5.4%
Exports - vol.	-0.2%	-0.3%	-0.3%	-0.2%	-0.3%	-0.3%	1.1%	1.0%	0.9%	1.0%	0.9%	0.8%	1.0%	0.9%	0.8%
Absorption - vol.	0.2%	0.2%	0.2%	0.2%	0.4%	0.4%	-0.2%	-0.4%	-0.7%	-0.1%	-0.3%	-0.5%	0.0%	-0.2%	-0.4%
Investment - vol.	0.1%	0.1%	0.1%	0.1%	0.2%	0.2%	-4.2%	-4.3%	-4.4%	-4.2%	-4.3%	-4.4%	-4.1%	-4.2%	-4.2%
Labour Demand - vol.	0.2%	0.2%	0.2%	-0.4%	-0.9%	-0.9%	0.1%	0.2%	0.1%	0.2%	0.3%	0.2%	-0.3%	-0.8%	-0.8%
Private Consumption - vol.	0.1%	0.2%	0.2%	0.2%	0.4%	0.4%	-0.9%	-1.5%	-1.9%	-0.8%	-1.4%	-1.8%	-0.8%	-1.3%	-1.7%
Supply to domestic - vol.	0.1%	0.2%	0.2%	0.2%	0.4%	0.4%	0.1%	0.3%	0.1%	0.2%	0.4%	0.2%	0.2%	0.5%	0.3%
Intra-EU Trade - vol	0.4%	0.3%	0.3%	0.0%	-1.3%	-1.3%	-6.5%	-17.3%	-17.5%	-6.5%	-17.7%	-17.9%	-6.6%	-17.9%	-18.1%

Transports

	Border Controls			Border controls and x-ineff.			Market segmentation			Trade *antimonde*			Full *antimonde*		
	1988	1991	1994	1988	1991	1994	1988	1991	1994	1988	1991	1994	1988	1991	1994
Domestic Production - vol.	0.7%	0.9%	0.9%	0.7%	0.9%	0.9%	0.0%	-0.3%	-0.6%	0.7%	0.5%	0.3%	0.7%	0.5%	0.2%
Imports - vol.	0.4%	0.4%	0.4%	0.4%	0.5%	0.5%	0.0%	-0.2%	-0.3%	0.4%	0.3%	0.1%	0.4%	0.2%	0.1%
Exports - vol.	-0.1%	-0.2%	-0.2%	-0.1%	-0.2%	-0.2%	0.7%	0.6%	0.6%	0.6%	0.5%	0.5%	0.6%	0.5%	0.4%
Absorption - vol.	0.3%	0.4%	0.4%	0.3%	0.4%	0.5%	-0.4%	-0.9%	-1.2%	-0.2%	-0.6%	-0.9%	-0.2%	-0.6%	-0.9%
Investment - vol.	0.3%	0.4%	0.4%	0.4%	0.4%	0.5%	-4.2%	-4.4%	-4.5%	-3.9%	-4.0%	-4.1%	-3.8%	-4.0%	-4.1%
Labour Demand - vol.	0.7%	0.9%	0.9%	0.7%	0.9%	0.9%	0.1%	-0.3%	-0.5%	0.8%	0.6%	0.4%	0.8%	0.7%	0.5%
Private Consumption - vol.	0.2%	0.3%	0.3%	0.2%	0.3%	0.3%	-0.9%	-1.6%	-2.1%	-0.7%	-1.4%	-1.9%	-0.8%	-1.5%	-2.0%
Supply to domestic - vol.	0.7%	0.9%	0.9%	0.7%	0.9%	0.9%	0.0%	-0.3%	-0.6%	0.7%	0.5%	0.3%	0.7%	0.5%	0.2%
Intra-EU Trade - vol	1.5%	1.8%	1.8%	1.5%	1.8%	1.9%	0.0%	-0.1%	-0.2%	1.5%	1.7%	1.6%	1.5%	1.7%	1.6%

Banks

	Border Controls			Border controls and x-ineff.			Market segmentation			Trade *antimonde*			Full *antimonde*		
	1988	1991	1994	1988	1991	1994	1988	1991	1994	1988	1991	1994	1988	1991	1994
Domestic Production - vol.	0.0%	-0.1%	0.0%	0.0%	-0.1%	-0.1%	0.2%	1.1%	0.6%	0.3%	1.1%	0.6%	0.2%	1.0%	0.4%
Imports - vol.	1.4%	1.6%	1.7%	1.4%	1.5%	1.6%	-7.1%	-6.5%	-6.2%	-6.0%	-5.2%	-4.9%	-5.7%	-4.9%	-4.5%
Exports - vol.	-0.3%	-0.3%	-0.3%	-0.3%	-0.3%	-0.3%	1.2%	1.1%	0.9%	1.0%	0.9%	0.8%	1.0%	0.9%	0.7%
Absorption - vol.	0.0%	0.0%	0.0%	0.0%	0.0%	0.0%	0.1%	0.7%	0.2%	0.1%	0.7%	0.2%	0.1%	0.6%	0.1%
Investment - vol.	0.1%	0.0%	0.0%	0.1%	0.0%	0.0%	-4.1%	-3.7%	-4.0%	-4.1%	-3.7%	-3.9%	-4.1%	-3.7%	-3.9%
Labour Demand - vol.	0.2%	0.1%	0.1%	-0.4%	-1.0%	-1.0%	0.1%	0.9%	0.7%	0.2%	1.0%	0.8%	-0.3%	-0.1%	-0.3%
Private Consumption - vol.	0.2%	0.3%	0.3%	0.2%	0.3%	0.3%	-1.0%	-1.8%	-2.4%	-0.9%	-1.6%	-2.2%	-0.9%	-1.7%	-2.3%
Supply to domestic - vol.	0.0%	-0.1%	0.0%	0.0%	0.0%	0.0%	0.2%	1.2%	0.7%	0.3%	1.2%	0.7%	0.2%	1.1%	0.6%
Intra-EU Trade - vol	0.6%	1.0%	0.9%	0.4%	0.4%	0.3%	-5.5%	-14.3%	-14.4%	-5.5%	-14.7%	-14.8%	-5.5%	-14.8%	-14.9%

Services

	Border Controls			Border controls and x-ineff.			Market segmentation			Trade *antimonde*			Full *antimonde*		
	1988	1991	1994	1988	1991	1994	1988	1991	1994	1988	1991	1994	1988	1991	1994
Domestic Production - vol.	0.0%	0.1%	0.1%	0.0%	0.1%	0.1%	-0.3%	-0.8%	-1.0%	-0.3%	-0.7%	-1.0%	-0.3%	-0.8%	-1.1%
Imports - vol.	1.9%	2.2%	2.2%	2.0%	2.2%	2.2%	-4.4%	-4.2%	-4.0%	-2.8%	-2.6%	-2.3%	-2.7%	-2.4%	-2.1%
Exports - vol.	-0.6%	-0.7%	-0.7%	-0.6%	-0.7%	-0.7%	1.4%	1.3%	1.1%	0.9%	0.8%	0.6%	0.9%	0.7%	0.5%
Absorption - vol.	0.0%	0.1%	0.1%	0.0%	0.1%	0.1%	-0.3%	-0.9%	-1.2%	-0.3%	-0.9%	-1.2%	-0.4%	-0.9%	-1.2%
Investment - vol.	0.0%	0.0%	0.0%	0.0%	0.1%	0.1%	-4.4%	-4.6%	-4.8%	-4.4%	-4.6%	-4.7%	-4.4%	-4.6%	-4.7%
Labour Demand - vol.	0.1%	0.1%	0.1%	0.1%	0.2%	0.2%	-0.4%	-0.8%	-0.9%	-0.3%	-0.8%	-0.8%	-0.3%	-0.7%	-0.8%
Private Consumption - vol.	0.2%	0.3%	0.3%	0.2%	0.3%	0.3%	-1.8%	-2.0%	-2.1%	-1.6%	-1.8%	-2.0%	-1.7%	-1.9%	-2.1%
Supply to domestic - vol.	0.0%	0.0%	0.0%	0.0%	0.1%	0.1%	-0.3%	-0.8%	-1.0%	-0.3%	-0.8%	-1.0%	-0.4%	-0.8%	-1.1%
Intra-EU Trade - vol	1.4%	2.2%	2.2%	1.4%	2.2%	2.2%	-0.6%	-3.1%	-3.4%	0.4%	-2.0%	-2.3%	0.3%	-2.0%	-2.3%

Non market

	Border Controls			Border controls and x-ineff.			Market segmentation			Trade *antimonde*			Full *antimonde*		
	1988	1991	1994	1988	1991	1994	1988	1991	1994	1988	1991	1994	1988	1991	1994
Domestic Production - vol.	0.0%	0.0%	0.0%	#VALUE!	#VALUE!	#VALUE!	-0.1%	-0.1%	-0.1%	-0.1%	-0.1%	-0.1%	-0.1%	-0.1%	-0.1%
Imports - vol.	#VALUE!	#VALUE!	#VALUE!	#VALUE!	#VALUE!	#VALUE!	#VALUE!	#VALUE!	#VALUE!	#VALUE!	#VALUE!	#VALUE!	#VALUE!	#VALUE!	#VALUE!
Exports - vol.	#VALUE!	#VALUE!	#VALUE!	#VALUE!	#VALUE!	#VALUE!	#VALUE!	#VALUE!	#VALUE!	#VALUE!	#VALUE!	#VALUE!	#VALUE!	#VALUE!	#VALUE!
Absorption - vol.	0.0%	0.0%	0.0%	0.0%	0.0%	0.0%	-0.1%	-0.1%	-0.1%	-0.1%	-0.1%	-0.1%	-0.1%	-0.1%	-0.1%
Investment - vol.	0.0%	0.0%	0.0%	0.0%	0.0%	0.0%	-4.1%	-4.1%	-4.1%	-4.1%	-4.1%	-4.1%	-4.1%	-4.1%	-4.1%
Labour Demand - vol.	0.0%	0.0%	0.0%	0.1%	0.2%	0.2%	0.0%	0.0%	0.0%	0.0%	0.0%	0.0%	0.0%	0.0%	0.1%
Private Consumption - vol.	0.2%	0.2%	0.3%	0.2%	0.3%	0.3%	-1.1%	-1.6%	-1.9%	-1.0%	-1.5%	-1.8%	-1.1%	-1.5%	-1.9%
Supply to domestic - vol.	0.0%	0.0%	0.0%	0.0%	0.0%	0.0%	-0.1%	-0.1%	-0.1%	-0.1%	-0.1%	-0.1%	-0.1%	-0.1%	-0.1%
Intra-EU Trade - vol	#DIV/0!	#DIV/0!	#DIV/0!	#DIV/0!	#DIV/0!	#DIV/0!	#DIV/0!	#DIV/0!	#DIV/0!	#DIV/0!	#DIV/0!	#DIV/0!	#DIV/0!	#DIV/0!	#DIV/0!

Table B10.8.
Decomposition of effects: sectoral results for Portugal (prices)

% change from *monde*

Agriculture

	Border Controls			Border controls and x-ineff.			Market segmentation			Trade *antimonde*			Full *antimonde*		
	1988	1991	1994	1988	1991	1994	1988	1991	1994	1988	1991	1994	1988	1991	1994
Marginal Costs	-0.11%	-0.20%	-0.20%	-0.11%	-0.18%	-0.18%	0.07%	-0.12%	0.01%	0.01%	-0.21%	-0.09%	0.00%	-0.22%	-0.09%
Cost of Labour	-0.24%	-0.22%	-0.23%	-0.24%	-0.24%	-0.25%	-0.44%	-0.77%	-1.17%	-0.58%	-0.89%	-1.31%	-0.69%	-1.06%	-1.55%
Deflator of Absorption	-0.70%	-0.84%	-0.84%	-0.70%	-0.83%	-0.84%	1.38%	1.09%	1.09%	0.99%	0.64%	0.63%	0.96%	0.59%	0.55%
Price of Exports-RW	-0.11%	-0.20%	-0.20%	-0.11%	-0.18%	-0.18%	0.07%	-0.12%	0.01%	0.01%	-0.21%	-0.09%	0.00%	-0.22%	-0.09%

Energy

	Border Controls			Border controls and x-ineff.			Market segmentation			Trade *antimonde*			Full *antimonde*		
	1988	1991	1994	1988	1991	1994	1988	1991	1994	1988	1991	1994	1988	1991	1994
Marginal Costs	-0.30%	-0.39%	-0.40%	-0.30%	-0.38%	-0.39%	0.39%	0.16%	0.19%	0.21%	-0.06%	-0.04%	0.19%	-0.09%	-0.08%
Cost of Labour	-0.24%	-0.22%	-0.23%	-0.24%	-0.24%	-0.25%	-0.44%	-0.77%	-1.17%	-0.58%	-0.89%	-1.31%	-0.69%	-1.06%	-1.55%
Deflator of Absorption	-0.66%	-0.79%	-0.79%	-0.66%	-0.78%	-0.80%	1.31%	1.03%	0.98%	0.92%	0.58%	0.52%	0.87%	0.51%	0.43%
Price of Exports-RW	-0.30%	-0.39%	-0.40%	-0.30%	-0.38%	-0.39%	0.39%	0.16%	0.19%	0.21%	-0.06%	-0.04%	0.19%	-0.09%	-0.08%

Metal Industries

	Border Controls			Border controls and x-ineff.			Market segmentation			Trade *antimonde*			Full *antimonde*		
	1988	1991	1994	1988	1991	1994	1988	1991	1994	1988	1991	1994	1988	1991	1994
Marginal Costs	-0.17%	-0.22%	-0.22%	-0.17%	-0.22%	-0.22%	0.72%	0.65%	0.63%	0.67%	0.59%	0.57%	0.66%	0.58%	0.55%
Cost of Labour	-0.24%	-0.22%	-0.23%	-0.24%	-0.24%	-0.25%	-0.44%	-0.77%	-1.17%	-0.58%	-0.89%	-1.31%	-0.69%	-1.06%	-1.55%
Deflator of Absorption	-0.13%	-0.13%	-0.13%	-0.13%	-0.13%	-0.13%	3.30%	3.88%	3.88%	3.46%	4.12%	4.11%	3.46%	4.12%	4.11%
Price of Exports-RW	-0.22%	-0.36%	-0.35%	-0.22%	-0.36%	-0.36%	-0.34%	-0.71%	-0.72%	-0.43%	-0.81%	-0.83%	-0.44%	-0.83%	-0.85%

Chemical

	Border Controls			Border controls and x-ineff.			Market segmentation			Trade *antimonde*			Full *antimonde*		
	1988	1991	1994	1988	1991	1994	1988	1991	1994	1988	1991	1994	1988	1991	1994
Marginal Costs	-0.25%	-0.32%	-0.32%	-0.25%	-0.32%	-0.33%	0.70%	0.51%	0.52%	0.60%	0.39%	0.39%	0.59%	0.38%	0.38%
Cost of Labour	-0.24%	-0.22%	-0.23%	-0.24%	-0.24%	-0.25%	-0.44%	-0.77%	-1.17%	-0.58%	-0.89%	-1.31%	-0.69%	-1.06%	-1.55%
Deflator of Absorption	-0.30%	-0.37%	-0.37%	-0.30%	-0.37%	-0.38%	1.77%	1.64%	1.60%	1.74%	1.58%	1.53%	1.71%	1.55%	1.49%
Price of Exports-RW	-0.27%	-0.41%	-0.41%	-0.28%	-0.41%	-0.41%	0.42%	-0.03%	-0.02%	0.30%	-0.19%	-0.18%	0.30%	-0.20%	-0.19%

Other Intensive Industries

	Border Controls			Border controls and x-ineff.			Market segmentation			Trade *antimonde*			Full *antimonde*		
	1988	1991	1994	1988	1991	1994	1988	1991	1994	1988	1991	1994	1988	1991	1994
Marginal Costs	-0.15%	-0.20%	-0.21%	-0.15%	-0.20%	-0.21%	0.36%	0.22%	0.24%	0.30%	0.15%	0.17%	0.29%	0.13%	0.14%
Cost of Labour	-0.24%	-0.22%	-0.23%	-0.24%	-0.24%	-0.25%	-0.44%	-0.77%	-1.17%	-0.58%	-0.89%	-1.31%	-0.69%	-1.06%	-1.55%
Deflator of Absorption	-0.17%	-0.19%	-0.19%	-0.17%	-0.19%	-0.20%	0.92%	0.89%	0.89%	0.88%	0.84%	0.84%	0.87%	0.82%	0.81%
Price of Exports-RW	-0.16%	-0.22%	-0.23%	-0.16%	-0.22%	-0.23%	0.32%	0.12%	0.14%	0.25%	0.04%	0.06%	0.24%	0.02%	0.03%

Electrical goods

	Border Controls			Border controls and x-ineff.			Market segmentation			Trade antimonde			Full antimonde		
	1988	1991	1994	1988	1991	1994	1988	1991	1994	1988	1991	1994	1988	1991	1994
Marginal Costs	-0.19%	-0.24%	-0.24%	-0.19%	-0.24%	-0.24%	1.17%	1.22%	1.22%	1.14%	1.18%	1.18%	1.14%	1.18%	1.18%
Cost of Labour	-0.24%	-0.22%	-0.23%	-0.24%	-0.24%	-0.25%	-0.44%	-0.77%	-1.17%	-0.58%	-0.89%	-1.31%	-0.69%	-1.06%	-1.55%
Deflator of Absorption	-0.46%	-0.51%	-0.51%	-0.47%	-0.52%	-0.52%	4.13%	4.79%	4.69%	4.09%	4.77%	4.66%	4.07%	4.74%	4.62%
Price of Exports-RW	-0.27%	-0.36%	-0.35%	-0.27%	-0.35%	-0.35%	0.82%	1.59%	1.62%	0.77%	1.57%	1.60%	0.78%	1.58%	1.62%

Transport equipment

	Border Controls			Border controls and x-ineff.			Market segmentation			Trade antimonde			Full antimonde		
	1988	1991	1994	1988	1991	1994	1988	1991	1994	1988	1991	1994	1988	1991	1994
Marginal Costs	-0.21%	-0.27%	-0.27%	-0.21%	-0.26%	-0.26%	1.58%	1.66%	1.62%	1.56%	1.65%	1.59%	1.57%	1.66%	1.61%
Cost of Labour	-0.24%	-0.22%	-0.23%	-0.24%	-0.24%	-0.25%	-0.44%	-0.77%	-1.17%	-0.58%	-0.89%	-1.31%	-0.69%	-1.06%	-1.55%
Deflator of Absorption	-0.39%	-0.49%	-0.48%	-0.39%	-0.49%	-0.49%	4.93%	5.61%	5.46%	4.97%	5.69%	5.54%	4.96%	5.68%	5.52%
Price of Exports-RW	-0.33%	-0.49%	-0.48%	-0.33%	-0.49%	-0.48%	0.89%	1.78%	1.72%	0.82%	1.74%	1.68%	0.83%	1.76%	1.70%

Other Equipment

	Border Controls			Border controls and x-ineff.			Market segmentation			Trade antimonde			Full antimonde		
	1988	1991	1994	1988	1991	1994	1988	1991	1994	1988	1991	1994	1988	1991	1994
Marginal Costs	-0.14%	-0.19%	-0.19%	-0.14%	-0.19%	-0.19%	0.40%	0.29%	0.27%	0.35%	0.23%	0.21%	0.35%	0.23%	0.21%
Cost of Labour	-0.24%	-0.22%	-0.23%	-0.24%	-0.24%	-0.25%	-0.44%	-0.77%	-1.17%	-0.58%	-0.89%	-1.31%	-0.69%	-1.06%	-1.55%
Deflator of Absorption	-0.48%	-0.52%	-0.53%	-0.48%	-0.53%	-0.53%	2.26%	2.27%	2.16%	2.09%	2.11%	1.99%	2.07%	2.07%	1.93%
Price of Exports-RW	-0.16%	-0.27%	-0.27%	-0.16%	-0.27%	-0.27%	-0.01%	-0.28%	-0.28%	-0.07%	-0.35%	-0.36%	-0.07%	-0.35%	-0.36%

Consumer goods

	Border Controls			Border controls and x-ineff.			Market segmentation			Trade antimonde			Full antimonde		
	1988	1991	1994	1988	1991	1994	1988	1991	1994	1988	1991	1994	1988	1991	1994
Marginal Costs	-0.31%	-0.38%	-0.38%	-0.30%	-0.38%	-0.38%	0.52%	0.30%	0.29%	0.36%	0.11%	0.09%	0.36%	0.11%	0.09%
Cost of Labour	-0.24%	-0.22%	-0.23%	-0.24%	-0.24%	-0.25%	-0.44%	-0.77%	-1.17%	-0.58%	-0.89%	-1.31%	-0.69%	-1.06%	-1.55%
Deflator of Absorption	-0.39%	-0.46%	-0.46%	-0.39%	-0.46%	-0.46%	0.96%	0.77%	0.73%	0.78%	0.55%	0.51%	0.77%	0.54%	0.49%
Price of Exports-RW	-0.31%	-0.38%	-0.38%	-0.30%	-0.38%	-0.38%	0.52%	0.30%	0.29%	0.36%	0.11%	0.09%	0.36%	0.11%	0.09%

Construction

	Border Controls			Border controls and x-ineff.			Market segmentation			Trade antimonde			Full antimonde		
	1988	1991	1994	1988	1991	1994	1988	1991	1994	1988	1991	1994	1988	1991	1994
Marginal Costs	-0.17%	-0.20%	-0.21%	-0.17%	-0.20%	-0.20%	0.56%	0.46%	0.39%	0.50%	0.40%	0.32%	0.50%	0.39%	0.30%
Cost of Labour	-0.24%	-0.22%	-0.23%	-0.24%	-0.24%	-0.25%	-0.44%	-0.77%	-1.17%	-0.58%	-0.89%	-1.31%	-0.69%	-1.06%	-1.55%
Deflator of Absorption	-0.17%	-0.20%	-0.21%	-0.17%	-0.20%	-0.20%	0.56%	0.46%	0.39%	0.50%	0.40%	0.32%	0.50%	0.39%	0.30%
Price of Exports-RW	-0.17%	-0.20%	-0.21%	-0.17%	-0.20%	-0.20%	0.56%	0.46%	0.39%	0.50%	0.40%	0.32%	0.50%	0.39%	0.30%

Telecommunications

	Border Controls			Border controls and x-ineff.			Market segmentation			Trade *antimonde*			Full *antimonde*		
	1988	1991	1994	1988	1991	1994	1988	1991	1994	1988	1991	1994	1988	1991	1994
Marginal Costs	-0.04%	-0.08%	-0.07%	-0.04%	-0.07%	-0.07%	-0.38%	-0.60%	-0.64%	-0.42%	-0.66%	-0.70%	-0.45%	-0.70%	-0.76%
Cost of Labour	-0.24%	-0.22%	-0.23%	-0.24%	-0.24%	-0.25%	-0.44%	-0.77%	-1.17%	-0.58%	-0.89%	-1.31%	-0.69%	-1.06%	-1.55%
Deflator of Absorption	-0.13%	-0.17%	-0.17%	-0.47%	-0.86%	-0.86%	-0.16%	-0.32%	-0.37%	-0.25%	-0.42%	-0.48%	-0.60%	-1.12%	-1.20%
Price of Exports-RW	-0.06%	-0.09%	-0.09%	-0.15%	-0.27%	-0.27%	-0.41%	-0.68%	-0.72%	-0.46%	-0.74%	-0.79%	-0.57%	-0.95%	-1.02%

Transports

	Border Controls			Border controls and x-ineff.			Market segmentation			Trade *antimonde*			Full *antimonde*		
	1988	1991	1994	1988	1991	1994	1988	1991	1994	1988	1991	1994	1988	1991	1994
Marginal Costs	-0.28%	-0.32%	-0.32%	-0.28%	-0.33%	-0.34%	0.26%	0.04%	-0.15%	0.11%	-0.13%	-0.32%	0.07%	-0.18%	-0.40%
Cost of Labour	-0.24%	-0.22%	-0.23%	-0.24%	-0.24%	-0.25%	-0.44%	-0.77%	-1.17%	-0.58%	-0.89%	-1.31%	-0.69%	-1.06%	-1.55%
Deflator of Absorption	-0.34%	-0.40%	-0.41%	-0.35%	-0.42%	-0.42%	0.40%	0.20%	0.03%	0.19%	-0.05%	-0.23%	0.16%	-0.11%	-0.31%
Price of Exports-RW	-0.28%	-0.32%	-0.32%	-0.28%	-0.33%	-0.34%	0.26%	0.04%	-0.15%	0.11%	-0.13%	-0.32%	0.07%	-0.18%	-0.40%

Banks

	Border Controls			Border controls and x-ineff.			Market segmentation			Trade *antimonde*			Full *antimonde*		
	1988	1991	1994	1988	1991	1994	1988	1991	1994	1988	1991	1994	1988	1991	1994
Marginal Costs	0.16%	0.08%	0.07%	0.17%	0.10%	0.09%	-0.70%	-0.88%	-0.58%	-0.65%	-0.87%	-0.56%	-0.66%	-0.88%	-0.60%
Cost of Labour	-0.24%	-0.22%	-0.23%	-0.24%	-0.24%	-0.25%	-0.44%	-0.77%	-1.17%	-0.58%	-0.89%	-1.31%	-0.69%	-1.06%	-1.55%
Deflator of Absorption	0.12%	0.05%	0.03%	0.03%	-0.12%	-0.14%	-0.61%	-0.85%	-0.56%	-0.59%	-0.86%	-0.56%	-0.69%	-1.04%	-0.77%
Price of Exports-RW	0.16%	0.08%	0.06%	0.15%	0.06%	0.04%	-0.70%	-0.91%	-0.61%	-0.66%	-0.90%	-0.60%	-0.69%	-0.95%	-0.67%

Services

	Border Controls			Border controls and x-ineff.			Market segmentation			Trade *antimonde*			Full *antimonde*		
	1988	1991	1994	1988	1991	1994	1988	1991	1994	1988	1991	1994	1988	1991	1994
Marginal Costs	-0.07%	-0.15%	-0.15%	-0.07%	-0.14%	-0.15%	-0.05%	-0.23%	-0.13%	-0.09%	-0.30%	-0.20%	-0.12%	-0.33%	-0.24%
Cost of Labour	-0.24%	-0.22%	-0.23%	-0.24%	-0.24%	-0.25%	-0.44%	-0.77%	-1.17%	-0.58%	-0.89%	-1.31%	-0.69%	-1.06%	-1.55%
Deflator of Absorption	-0.09%	-0.17%	-0.17%	-0.09%	-0.16%	-0.16%	-0.03%	-0.21%	-0.11%	-0.09%	-0.29%	-0.19%	-0.12%	-0.33%	-0.24%
Price of Exports-RW	-0.07%	-0.15%	-0.15%	-0.07%	-0.14%	-0.15%	-0.05%	-0.23%	-0.13%	-0.09%	-0.30%	-0.20%	-0.12%	-0.33%	-0.24%

Non market

	Border Controls			Border controls and x-ineff.			Market segmentation			Trade *antimonde*			Full *antimonde*		
	1988	1991	1994	1988	1991	1994	1988	1991	1994	1988	1991	1994	1988	1991	1994
Marginal Costs	-0.24%	-0.25%	-0.25%	-0.25%	-0.26%	-0.27%	-0.01%	-0.27%	-0.56%	-0.14%	-0.39%	-0.69%	-0.18%	-0.46%	-0.78%
Cost of Labour	-0.24%	-0.22%	-0.23%	-0.24%	-0.24%	-0.25%	-0.44%	-0.77%	-1.17%	-0.58%	-0.89%	-1.31%	-0.69%	-1.06%	-1.55%
Deflator of Absorption	-0.24%	-0.25%	-0.25%	-0.25%	-0.26%	-0.27%	-0.01%	-0.27%	-0.56%	-0.14%	-0.39%	-0.69%	-0.18%	-0.46%	-0.78%
Price of Exports-RW	-0.24%	-0.25%	-0.25%	-0.25%	-0.26%	-0.27%	-0.01%	-0.27%	-0.56%	-0.14%	-0.39%	-0.69%	-0.18%	-0.46%	-0.78%

Table B11.1.
The full *antimonde* scenario: macroeconomic aggregates for Spain

Macroeconomic Aggregates (vol.) (% change from *monde*)	Constraint Case			Flexible Case			Efficiency Case		
	1988	1991	1994	1988	1991	1994	1988	1991	1994
GDP fact. pr.	-0.65%	-0.92%	-1.19%	-0.79%	-1.36%	-1.82%	-0.82%	-1.47%	-2.01%
Priv. Consumption	-0.60%	-0.64%	-0.84%	-1.32%	-1.57%	-1.90%	-1.33%	-1.61%	-1.96%
Absorption	-0.37%	-0.46%	-0.64%	-1.43%	-1.67%	-2.01%	-1.44%	-1.71%	-2.08%
Total Investment	-1.47%	-1.67%	-2.17%	-4.23%	-4.37%	-4.52%	-4.23%	-4.38%	-4.54%
Total Exports to RW	-1.28%	-2.64%	-2.93%	1.53%	1.13%	0.92%	1.50%	1.03%	0.74%
Total Imports from RW	-1.85%	-2.12%	-2.17%	-2.91%	-2.40%	-2.20%	-2.87%	-2.26%	-1.97%
Total Intra-EU Trade	-0.58%	0.00%	0.04%	-1.70%	-5.53%	-5.70%	-1.72%	-5.59%	-5.80%
Employment (diff. from *monde*, 10^3 persons)	-23	-28	-39	-30	-59	-82	-31	-60	-83
Disposable Income (deflated)	-0.61%	-0.66%	-0.87%	-1.35%	-1.61%	-1.94%	-1.36%	-1.65%	-2.01%

Macroeconomic Ratios (abs. diff. from *monde*)	Constraint Case			Flexible Case			Efficiency Case		
	1988	1991	1994	1988	1991	1994	1988	1991	1994
Current Account as % of GDP	0.00%	0.00%	0.00%	-0.99%	-0.98%	-0.92%	-0.98%	-0.95%	-0.87%
Public Deficit as % of GDP	0.09%	0.07%	0.03%	-0.17%	-0.23%	-0.35%	-0.17%	-0.24%	-0.38%
Labour Productivity	-0.45%	-0.67%	-0.85%	-0.52%	-0.83%	-1.09%	-0.54%	-0.94%	-1.27%
Investment/GDP	-0.17%	-0.15%	-0.20%	-1.70%	-1.64%	-1.61%	-1.69%	-1.62%	-1.57%
Priv.Cons./GDP	0.04%	0.20%	0.25%	-0.38%	-0.15%	-0.05%	-0.37%	-0.10%	0.04%

Deflators (% change from *monde*)	Constraint Case			Flexible Case			Efficiency Case		
	1988	1991	1994	1988	1991	1994	1988	1991	1994
Consumer Price Index	0.21%	0.92%	1.10%	0.77%	0.59%	0.57%	0.76%	0.54%	0.49%
Real Wage Rate	-0.78%	-1.06%	-1.40%	-1.01%	-1.71%	-2.29%	-1.03%	-1.81%	-2.48%
Marginal Costs	0.14%	0.91%	1.09%	0.54%	0.34%	0.29%	0.53%	0.31%	0.23%
Producer Prices	0.24%	1.03%	1.21%	0.63%	0.47%	0.42%	0.62%	0.44%	0.37%
Average change in mark-ups (abs. diff.)	0.67%	0.85%	0.88%	0.72%	1.14%	1.18%	0.73%	1.14%	1.19%
Shadow Price of Capital	-0.18%	0.60%	0.79%	0.13%	0.50%	0.92%	0.10%	0.40%	0.76%
Terms-of-Trade RW	-0.39%	0.34%	0.54%	-5.16%	-3.81%	-3.06%	-5.07%	-3.47%	-2.47%

	Constraint Case			Flexible Case			Efficiency Case		
Implicit change in real exchange rate	0.09%	0.98%	1.17%	-4.39%	-2.74%	-1.91%	-4.30%	-2.37%	-1.25%

Trade Regime	Segmentation	Segmentation	Segmentation

Table B11.2.
The full *antimonde* scenario: effects on IC sectors for Spain

% change from *monde*

Metal Industries	Constraint Case			Flexible Case			Efficiency Case		
	1988	1991	1994	1988	1991	1994	1988	1991	1994
Production per firm	-4.77%	-6.62%	-6.85%	-3.39%	-6.47%	-6.99%	-3.42%	-6.62%	-7.24%
Real Marginal Costs	0.95%	1.73%	1.99%	-1.62%	0.53%	1.89%	-1.51%	1.00%	2.72%
Real Producer Prices	1.81%	2.93%	3.22%	-1.02%	1.65%	3.09%	-0.90%	2.14%	3.96%
Mark-ups domestic (abs. diff.)	1.01%	1.22%	1.26%	1.04%	1.36%	1.47%	1.04%	1.39%	1.51%
Fixed Costs per firm	0.91%	1.59%	1.75%	-2.45%	-1.11%	-0.44%	-2.37%	-0.80%	0.12%
Number of Firms	4.64%	5.14%	4.98%	6.05%	8.55%	7.74%	6.02%	8.38%	7.45%
Sigma of Love of Variety	0.00%	0.00%	0.00%	0.00%	0.00%	0.00%	0.00%	0.00%	0.00%

Chemical	Constraint Case			Flexible Case			Efficiency Case		
	1988	1991	1994	1988	1991	1994	1988	1991	1994
Production per firm	-3.51%	-4.67%	-4.82%	-1.87%	-4.09%	-4.48%	-1.90%	-4.19%	-4.64%
Real Marginal Costs	0.24%	0.97%	1.17%	-2.47%	-0.38%	0.96%	-2.36%	0.07%	1.74%
Real Producer Prices	0.53%	1.35%	1.55%	-2.31%	-0.05%	1.30%	-2.20%	0.40%	2.09%
Mark-ups domestic (abs. diff.)	0.34%	0.38%	0.39%	0.26%	0.38%	0.41%	0.26%	0.39%	0.41%
Fixed Costs per firm	0.16%	0.76%	0.84%	-3.31%	-2.14%	-1.57%	-3.24%	-1.85%	-1.07%
Number of Firms	3.28%	3.92%	3.87%	6.41%	9.15%	8.67%	6.39%	9.06%	8.51%
Sigma of Love of Variety	0.00%	0.00%	0.00%	0.00%	0.00%	0.00%	0.00%	0.00%	0.00%

Other Intensive Industries	Constraint Case			Flexible Case			Efficiency Case		
	1988	1991	1994	1988	1991	1994	1988	1991	1994
Production per firm	-1.20%	-1.82%	-2.00%	-1.70%	-2.94%	-3.22%	-1.72%	-3.00%	-3.32%
Real Marginal Costs	0.25%	1.00%	1.16%	-2.69%	-0.60%	0.70%	-2.57%	-0.14%	1.51%
Real Producer Prices	0.30%	1.07%	1.24%	-2.61%	-0.48%	0.83%	-2.50%	-0.02%	1.63%
Mark-ups domestic (abs. diff.)	0.04%	0.04%	0.05%	0.09%	0.11%	0.12%	0.09%	0.11%	0.12%
Fixed Costs per firm	0.17%	0.82%	0.88%	-3.62%	-2.42%	-1.87%	-3.54%	-2.13%	-1.35%
Number of Firms	1.43%	1.63%	1.50%	0.42%	1.01%	0.81%	0.42%	1.00%	0.79%
Sigma of Love of Variety	0.00%	0.00%	0.00%	0.00%	0.00%	0.00%	0.00%	0.00%	0.00%

Electrical goods	Constraint Case			Flexible Case			Efficiency Case		
	1988	1991	1994	1988	1991	1994	1988	1991	1994
Production per firm	-2.64%	-4.07%	-4.44%	-3.88%	-6.24%	-6.63%	-3.91%	-6.35%	-6.81%
Real Marginal Costs	0.23%	0.97%	1.13%	-2.80%	-0.70%	0.59%	-2.68%	-0.24%	1.41%
Real Producer Prices	0.48%	1.36%	1.54%	-2.44%	-0.13%	1.19%	-2.32%	0.34%	2.01%
Mark-ups domestic (abs. diff.)	0.21%	0.28%	0.33%	0.51%	0.61%	0.63%	0.52%	0.62%	0.64%
Fixed Costs per firm	0.16%	0.81%	0.86%	-3.76%	-2.56%	-2.03%	-3.68%	-2.26%	-1.50%
Number of Firms	4.72%	5.13%	4.69%	3.80%	7.30%	6.81%	3.76%	7.16%	6.58%
Sigma of Love of Variety	0.00%	0.00%	0.00%	0.00%	0.00%	0.00%	0.00%	0.00%	0.00%

Transport equipment	Constraint Case			Flexible Case			Efficiency Case		
	1988	1991	1994	1988	1991	1994	1988	1991	1994
Production per firm	-5.83%	-9.19%	-9.56%	-6.51%	-10.27%	-10.39%	-6.54%	-10.36%	-10.56%
Real Marginal Costs	0.47%	1.19%	1.36%	-2.43%	-0.42%	0.79%	-2.31%	0.06%	1.63%
Real Producer Prices	1.02%	2.08%	2.27%	-1.86%	0.49%	1.71%	-1.74%	0.98%	2.56%
Mark-ups domestic (abs. diff.)	0.33%	0.43%	0.50%	1.00%	1.18%	1.19%	1.00%	1.18%	1.19%
Fixed Costs per firm	0.35%	0.99%	1.08%	-3.45%	-2.21%	-1.66%	-3.37%	-1.90%	-1.11%
Number of Firms	9.29%	10.52%	9.92%	6.43%	13.17%	13.03%	6.42%	13.10%	12.92%
Sigma of Love of Variety	0.00%	0.00%	0.00%	0.00%	0.00%	0.00%	0.00%	0.00%	0.00%

Other Equipment	Constraint Case			Flexible Case			Efficiency Case		
	1988	1991	1994	1988	1991	1994	1988	1991	1994
Production per firm	-9.53%	-12.30%	-12.51%	-10.01%	-13.94%	-14.32%	-10.04%	-14.03%	-14.48%
Real Marginal Costs	0.45%	1.16%	1.33%	-2.40%	-0.32%	0.99%	-2.29%	0.14%	1.80%
Real Producer Prices	0.90%	1.74%	1.93%	-1.95%	0.30%	1.62%	-1.84%	0.77%	2.44%
Mark-ups domestic (abs. diff.)	0.63%	0.71%	0.72%	0.78%	0.96%	0.98%	0.78%	0.97%	0.98%
Fixed Costs per firm	0.41%	0.99%	1.06%	-3.28%	-2.08%	-1.53%	-3.20%	-1.78%	-1.01%
Number of Firms	11.38%	13.94%	13.65%	9.71%	13.05%	12.30%	9.67%	12.91%	12.06%
Sigma of Love of Variety	0.00%	0.00%	0.00%	0.00%	0.00%	0.00%	0.00%	0.00%	0.00%

Telecommunications	Constraint Case			Flexible Case			Efficiency Case		
	1988	1991	1994	1988	1991	1994	1988	1991	1994
Production per firm	-0.57%	-0.39%	-0.56%	-1.65%	-4.26%	-4.71%	-1.66%	-4.32%	-4.82%
Real Marginal Costs	0.43%	1.52%	1.74%	-3.46%	-1.10%	0.40%	-3.34%	-0.62%	1.25%
Real Producer Prices	0.72%	2.04%	2.22%	-3.55%	-1.07%	0.41%	-3.43%	-0.60%	1.24%
Mark-ups domestic (abs. diff.)	0.21%	0.35%	0.31%	-0.24%	-0.59%	-0.63%	-0.24%	-0.60%	-0.66%
Fixed Costs per firm	1.06%	3.25%	3.17%	-6.42%	-6.83%	-6.49%	-6.35%	-6.56%	-6.01%
Number of Firms	-0.19%	-0.46%	-0.36%	0.93%	1.99%	2.09%	0.94%	2.02%	2.14%
Sigma of Love of Variety	0.00%	0.00%	0.00%	0.00%	0.00%	0.00%	0.00%	0.00%	0.00%

Banks	Constraint Case			Flexible Case			Efficiency Case		
	1988	1991	1994	1988	1991	1994	1988	1991	1994
Production per firm	-0.04%	0.14%	0.01%	-0.89%	-1.74%	-2.13%	-0.91%	-1.80%	-2.22%
Real Marginal Costs	0.18%	1.15%	1.29%	-3.54%	-1.27%	0.14%	-3.42%	-0.80%	0.96%
Real Producer Prices	0.23%	1.23%	1.36%	-3.59%	-1.39%	0.02%	-3.47%	-0.92%	0.84%
Mark-ups domestic (abs. diff.)	0.06%	0.07%	0.07%	-0.06%	-0.14%	-0.14%	-0.06%	-0.15%	-0.15%
Fixed Costs per firm	0.58%	1.91%	1.88%	-5.82%	-5.62%	-5.18%	-5.74%	-5.33%	-4.68%
Number of Firms	-0.18%	-0.29%	-0.26%	0.70%	1.44%	1.43%	0.70%	1.45%	1.44%
Sigma of Love of Variety	0.00%	0.00%	0.00%	0.00%	0.00%	0.00%	0.00%	0.00%	0.00%

Table B11.3.
The full *antimonde* scenario: sectoral results for Spain (volumes)

% change from *monde*

Agriculture	Constraint Case			Flexible Case			Efficiency Case		
	1988	1991	1994	1988	1991	1994	1988	1991	1994
Domestic Production - vol.	-0.4%	-0.5%	-0.6%	1.6%	0.3%	-0.2%	1.6%	0.2%	-0.4%
Imports - vol.	-1.9%	-0.7%	-0.4%	-4.3%	-3.2%	-2.7%	-4.2%	-3.0%	-2.2%
Exports - vol.	-2.5%	-4.2%	-4.7%	1.6%	1.1%	0.8%	1.6%	1.0%	0.6%
Absorption - vol.	-0.4%	-0.2%	-0.2%	0.3%	-0.3%	-0.7%	0.3%	-0.4%	-0.8%
Investment - vol.	5.8%	5.6%	4.8%	-3.6%	-4.2%	-4.4%	-3.6%	-4.2%	-4.5%
Labour Demand - vol.	-0.3%	-0.3%	-0.3%	1.9%	0.9%	0.6%	1.9%	0.8%	0.5%
Private Consumption - vol.	-1.2%	-0.8%	-0.8%	-0.9%	-1.3%	-1.6%	-0.9%	-1.3%	-1.7%
Supply to domestic - vol.	-0.2%	-0.1%	-0.2%	1.5%	0.6%	0.1%	1.5%	0.5%	-0.1%
Intra-EU Trade - vol	0.0%	0.0%	0.0%	0.2%	-3.5%	-3.7%	0.1%	-3.6%	-3.8%

Energy	Constraint Case			Flexible Case			Efficiency Case		
	1988	1991	1994	1988	1991	1994	1988	1991	1994
Domestic Production - vol.	-0.4%	-0.7%	-0.8%	1.0%	0.0%	-0.4%	0.9%	-0.1%	-0.5%
Imports - vol.	-0.3%	0.0%	0.0%	-1.2%	-1.1%	-1.1%	-1.1%	-1.0%	-1.0%
Exports - vol.	-2.0%	-3.0%	-3.3%	0.6%	0.4%	0.3%	0.6%	0.4%	0.3%
Absorption - vol.	-0.3%	-0.2%	-0.3%	-0.1%	-0.6%	-0.9%	-0.1%	-0.6%	-1.0%
Investment - vol.	-4.1%	-4.3%	-4.7%	-3.5%	-4.0%	-4.2%	-3.6%	-4.0%	-4.3%
Labour Demand - vol.	-0.3%	-0.6%	-0.7%	1.3%	0.4%	0.1%	1.3%	0.4%	0.0%
Private Consumption - vol.	-0.6%	0.0%	-0.1%	-1.2%	-1.6%	-1.9%	-1.2%	-1.6%	-1.9%
Supply to domestic - vol.	-0.2%	-0.4%	-0.5%	1.0%	0.2%	-0.3%	1.0%	0.1%	-0.5%
Intra-EU Trade - vol	0.0%	0.0%	0.0%	0.5%	-0.7%	-0.6%	0.5%	-0.7%	-0.6%

Metal Industries	Constraint Case			Flexible Case			Efficiency Case		
	1988	1991	1994	1988	1991	1994	1988	1991	1994
Domestic Production - vol.	-0.4%	-1.8%	-2.2%	2.5%	1.5%	0.2%	2.4%	1.2%	-0.3%
Imports - vol.	0.5%	0.9%	0.9%	-3.1%	-2.2%	-2.1%	-3.1%	-2.1%	-1.8%
Exports - vol.	-2.9%	-4.9%	-5.3%	1.4%	1.0%	0.7%	1.3%	0.8%	0.5%
Absorption - vol.	0.8%	-0.1%	-0.5%	0.9%	0.9%	0.0%	0.9%	0.7%	-0.2%
Investment - vol.	-1.3%	-2.8%	-3.5%	-2.9%	-3.3%	-3.9%	-2.9%	-3.5%	-4.1%
Labour Demand - vol.	0.7%	-0.4%	-0.7%	3.4%	3.1%	2.0%	3.3%	2.9%	1.6%
Private Consumption - vol.	#DIV/0!	#DIV/0!	#DIV/0!	#DIV/0!	#DIV/0!	#DIV/0!	#DIV/0!	#DIV/0!	#DIV/0!
Supply to domestic - vol.	0.8%	-0.5%	-0.9%	3.0%	4.7%	3.3%	2.9%	4.4%	2.8%
Intra-EU Trade - vol	0.0%	0.0%	0.0%	-1.5%	-6.2%	-6.4%	-1.5%	-6.3%	-6.5%

Chemical	Constraint Case			Flexible Case			Efficiency Case		
	1988	1991	1994	1988	1991	1994	1988	1991	1994
Domestic Production - vol.	-0.4%	-0.9%	-1.1%	4.4%	4.7%	3.8%	4.4%	4.5%	3.5%
Imports - vol.	-1.2%	-0.1%	0.0%	-4.3%	-3.5%	-3.2%	-4.3%	-3.3%	-2.8%
Exports - vol.	-1.0%	-2.2%	-2.4%	1.9%	1.5%	1.3%	1.9%	1.4%	1.1%
Absorption - vol.	-0.4%	-0.3%	-0.4%	0.5%	0.2%	-0.2%	0.5%	0.2%	-0.3%
Investment - vol.	-1.3%	-1.9%	-2.5%	-2.1%	-2.0%	-2.4%	-2.2%	-2.1%	-2.5%
Labour Demand - vol.	0.1%	-0.4%	-0.5%	4.8%	5.4%	4.7%	4.8%	5.3%	4.5%
Private Consumption - vol.	-1.5%	-0.9%	-0.9%	-1.0%	-1.5%	-1.9%	-1.0%	-1.6%	-2.0%
Supply to domestic - vol.	-0.1%	-0.5%	-0.7%	4.6%	6.5%	5.6%	4.6%	6.3%	5.3%
Intra-EU Trade - vol	0.0%	0.0%	0.0%	-1.5%	-6.4%	-6.6%	-1.6%	-6.5%	-6.7%

Other Intensive Industries	Constraint Case			Flexible Case			Efficiency Case		
	1988	1991	1994	1988	1991	1994	1988	1991	1994
Domestic Production - vol.	0.2%	-0.2%	-0.5%	-1.3%	-2.0%	-2.4%	-1.3%	-2.0%	-2.6%
Imports - vol.	-4.9%	-5.5%	-5.5%	-6.2%	-5.0%	-4.5%	-6.1%	-4.7%	-4.0%
Exports - vol.	-1.2%	-2.4%	-2.7%	1.7%	1.3%	1.1%	1.7%	1.2%	0.9%
Absorption - vol.	0.0%	-0.3%	-0.6%	-2.6%	-2.6%	-3.0%	-2.6%	-2.7%	-3.0%
Investment - vol.	-0.5%	-1.0%	-1.7%	-4.8%	-5.1%	-5.3%	-4.8%	-5.1%	-5.4%
Labour Demand - vol.	0.4%	0.0%	-0.3%	-1.0%	-1.5%	-1.9%	-1.0%	-1.5%	-1.9%
Private Consumption - vol.	0.4%	-0.2%	-0.6%	-1.4%	-1.2%	-1.3%	-1.4%	-1.2%	-1.4%
Supply to domestic - vol.	0.5%	0.2%	-0.1%	-1.4%	-1.0%	-1.5%	-1.5%	-1.1%	-1.6%
Intra-EU Trade - vol	0.0%	0.0%	0.0%	-3.4%	-7.6%	-7.8%	-3.4%	-7.7%	-7.8%

Electrical goods	Constraint Case			Flexible Case			Efficiency Case		
	1988	1991	1994	1988	1991	1994	1988	1991	1994
Domestic Production - vol.	1.9%	0.9%	0.0%	-0.2%	0.6%	-0.3%	-0.3%	0.4%	-0.7%
Imports - vol.	-4.5%	-6.9%	-7.4%	-6.6%	-5.4%	-5.1%	-6.6%	-5.2%	-4.6%
Exports - vol.	-1.9%	-3.7%	-4.0%	2.1%	1.6%	1.4%	2.1%	1.5%	1.1%
Absorption - vol.	0.9%	-0.4%	-1.2%	-4.4%	-3.9%	-4.2%	-4.4%	-4.0%	-4.3%
Investment - vol.	6.0%	4.7%	3.2%	-4.4%	-4.0%	-4.4%	-4.4%	-4.1%	-4.5%
Labour Demand - vol.	2.5%	1.6%	0.9%	0.6%	1.9%	1.2%	0.6%	1.7%	0.9%
Private Consumption - vol.	7.0%	1.9%	-1.0%	-5.3%	-2.7%	-2.8%	-5.3%	-2.8%	-2.9%
Supply to domestic - vol.	2.9%	2.1%	1.1%	-0.3%	2.6%	1.8%	-0.4%	2.4%	1.4%
Intra-EU Trade - vol	0.0%	0.0%	0.0%	-3.7%	-9.0%	-9.1%	-3.7%	-9.0%	-9.2%

Transport equipment	Constraint Case			Flexible Case			Efficiency Case		
	1988	1991	1994	1988	1991	1994	1988	1991	1994
Domestic Production - vol.	2.9%	0.4%	-0.6%	-0.5%	1.5%	1.3%	-0.5%	1.4%	1.0%
Imports - vol.	-4.2%	-11.3%	-12.2%	-6.3%	-5.2%	-4.9%	-6.2%	-5.0%	-4.5%
Exports - vol.	-2.9%	-5.1%	-5.5%	2.0%	1.6%	1.4%	2.0%	1.5%	1.1%
Absorption - vol.	4.3%	0.5%	-0.8%	-4.1%	-3.2%	-3.3%	-4.1%	-3.2%	-3.4%
Investment - vol.	7.3%	4.5%	2.9%	-4.2%	-3.3%	-3.5%	-4.3%	-3.4%	-3.6%
Labour Demand - vol.	3.8%	1.6%	0.7%	0.6%	3.2%	3.0%	0.6%	3.1%	2.9%
Private Consumption - vol.	18.6%	3.5%	-1.0%	-4.6%	-2.3%	-2.1%	-4.7%	-2.4%	-2.3%
Supply to domestic - vol.	7.0%	4.4%	3.0%	-0.4%	6.2%	5.9%	-0.4%	6.0%	5.7%
Intra-EU Trade - vol	0.0%	0.0%	0.0%	-3.1%	-7.5%	-7.6%	-3.1%	-7.5%	-7.6%

Other Equipment	Constraint Case			Flexible Case			Efficiency Case		
	1988	1991	1994	1988	1991	1994	1988	1991	1994
Domestic Production - vol.	0.8%	-0.1%	-0.6%	-1.3%	-2.7%	-3.8%	-1.3%	-2.9%	-4.2%
Imports - vol.	-0.5%	-0.7%	-1.1%	-4.6%	-4.1%	-3.9%	-4.5%	-3.9%	-3.6%
Exports - vol.	-1.9%	-3.2%	-3.5%	1.8%	1.3%	1.1%	1.8%	1.2%	0.8%
Absorption - vol.	1.1%	0.8%	0.3%	-4.3%	-4.8%	-5.3%	-4.3%	-4.8%	-5.4%
Investment - vol.	9.8%	8.6%	7.2%	-4.9%	-5.6%	-6.1%	-4.9%	-5.6%	-6.2%
Labour Demand - vol.	1.6%	0.9%	0.5%	-0.3%	-1.3%	-2.2%	-0.3%	-1.5%	-2.5%
Private Consumption - vol.	-0.9%	-0.8%	-1.2%	-1.9%	-2.1%	-2.5%	-1.9%	-2.1%	-2.6%
Supply to domestic - vol.	2.5%	2.0%	1.3%	-1.0%	0.0%	-1.1%	-1.0%	-0.2%	-1.6%
Intra-EU Trade - vol	0.0%	0.0%	0.0%	-2.5%	-4.9%	-5.2%	-2.5%	-5.0%	-5.3%

Consumer goods	Constraint Case			Flexible Case			Efficiency Case		
	1988	1991	1994	1988	1991	1994	1988	1991	1994
Domestic Production - vol.	-0.4%	-0.3%	-0.5%	0.7%	-0.1%	-0.6%	0.7%	-0.2%	-0.8%
Imports - vol.	-5.7%	-5.8%	-5.5%	-5.4%	-4.3%	-3.8%	-5.3%	-4.0%	-3.2%
Exports - vol.	-0.9%	-2.1%	-2.4%	2.4%	1.8%	1.4%	2.3%	1.6%	1.2%
Absorption - vol.	-0.8%	-0.5%	-0.6%	-0.7%	-1.1%	-1.4%	-0.7%	-1.1%	-1.4%
Investment - vol.	8.3%	8.2%	7.1%	-4.1%	-4.4%	-4.7%	-4.1%	-4.5%	-4.7%
Labour Demand - vol.	-0.3%	-0.1%	-0.2%	1.1%	0.4%	0.1%	1.0%	0.4%	0.1%
Private Consumption - vol.	-1.2%	-0.7%	-0.7%	-0.9%	-1.2%	-1.5%	-0.9%	-1.2%	-1.6%
Supply to domestic - vol.	-0.4%	-0.1%	-0.2%	0.3%	0.1%	-0.4%	0.3%	0.0%	-0.5%
Intra-EU Trade - vol	0.0%	0.0%	0.0%	-1.3%	-4.9%	-5.2%	-1.3%	-5.0%	-5.3%

Construction	Constraint Case			Flexible Case			Efficiency Case		
	1988	1991	1994	1988	1991	1994	1988	1991	1994
Domestic Production - vol.	-2.1%	-2.2%	-2.5%	-6.9%	-7.1%	-7.3%	-6.9%	-7.1%	-7.3%
Imports - vol.	-	-	-	#VALUE!	#VALUE!	#VALUE!	#VALUE!	#VALUE!	#VALUE!
Exports - vol.	-	-	-	#VALUE!	#VALUE!	#VALUE!	#VALUE!	#VALUE!	#VALUE!
Absorption - vol.	-2.1%	-2.2%	-2.5%	-6.9%	-7.1%	-7.3%	-6.9%	-7.1%	-7.3%
Investment - vol.	1.3%	1.1%	0.1%	-7.6%	-7.7%	-7.8%	-7.6%	-7.7%	-7.8%
Labour Demand - vol.	-2.0%	-2.0%	-2.3%	-6.7%	-6.7%	-6.8%	-6.7%	-6.7%	-6.7%
Private Consumption - vol.	-1.5%	-0.9%	-0.9%	-1.0%	-1.5%	-1.9%	-1.0%	-1.6%	-2.0%
Supply to domestic - vol.	-2.1%	-2.2%	-2.5%	-6.9%	-7.1%	-7.3%	-6.9%	-7.1%	-7.3%
Intra-EU Trade - vol	0.0%	0.0%	0.0%	#DIV/0!	#DIV/0!	#DIV/0!	#DIV/0!	#DIV/0!	#DIV/0!

Telecommunications	Constraint Case			Flexible Case			Efficiency Case		
	1988	1991	1994	1988	1991	1994	1988	1991	1994
Domestic Production - vol.	-0.8%	-0.9%	-0.9%	-0.7%	-2.4%	-2.7%	-0.7%	-2.4%	-2.8%
Imports - vol.	-3.4%	-3.0%	-2.9%	-5.4%	-4.9%	-4.5%	-5.3%	-4.7%	-4.2%
Exports - vol.	-3.0%	-5.8%	-6.0%	1.1%	0.8%	0.7%	1.1%	0.8%	0.6%
Absorption - vol.	-0.6%	-0.5%	-0.6%	-0.8%	-1.0%	-1.3%	-0.8%	-1.0%	-1.3%
Investment - vol.	-3.7%	-3.3%	-3.5%	-4.6%	-5.3%	-5.4%	-4.5%	-5.2%	-5.3%
Labour Demand - vol.	0.5%	1.2%	1.3%	-0.8%	-2.0%	-2.1%	-0.7%	-2.0%	-2.0%
Private Consumption - vol.	-1.7%	-1.2%	-1.2%	-1.0%	-1.5%	-1.9%	-1.0%	-1.5%	-2.0%
Supply to domestic - vol.	-0.6%	-0.5%	-0.5%	-0.5%	-0.5%	-0.8%	-0.5%	-0.5%	-0.9%
Intra-EU Trade - vol	0.0%	0.0%	0.0%	-4.1%	-15.3%	-15.5%	-4.2%	-15.3%	-15.6%

Transports	Constraint Case			Flexible Case			Efficiency Case		
	1988	1991	1994	1988	1991	1994	1988	1991	1994
Domestic Production - vol.	-0.6%	-0.5%	-0.6%	-0.3%	-0.6%	-0.9%	-0.3%	-0.6%	-1.0%
Imports - vol.	-0.6%	-0.5%	-0.6%	-0.2%	-0.3%	-0.5%	-0.2%	-0.3%	-0.5%
Exports - vol.	0.1%	-0.4%	-0.4%	0.6%	0.5%	0.4%	0.6%	0.5%	0.4%
Absorption - vol.	-0.8%	-0.6%	-0.7%	-1.0%	-1.4%	-1.7%	-1.0%	-1.4%	-1.8%
Investment - vol.	-4.3%	-4.3%	-4.5%	-4.3%	-4.4%	-4.6%	-4.3%	-4.4%	-4.6%
Labour Demand - vol.	-0.5%	-0.5%	-0.5%	-0.1%	-0.3%	-0.5%	-0.1%	-0.3%	-0.5%
Private Consumption - vol.	-1.8%	-1.1%	-1.1%	-1.4%	-1.9%	-2.3%	-1.4%	-1.9%	-2.4%
Supply to domestic - vol.	-0.6%	-0.5%	-0.6%	-0.3%	-0.6%	-0.9%	-0.3%	-0.6%	-1.0%
Intra-EU Trade - vol	0.0%	0.0%	0.0%	1.3%	1.5%	1.4%	1.3%	1.5%	1.3%

Banks	Constraint Case			Flexible Case			Efficiency Case		
	1988	1991	1994	1988	1991	1994	1988	1991	1994
Domestic Production - vol.	-0.2%	-0.1%	-0.2%	-0.2%	-0.3%	-0.7%	-0.2%	-0.4%	-0.8%
Imports - vol.	-9.9%	-12.3%	-12.2%	-6.2%	-5.3%	-4.9%	-6.1%	-5.0%	-4.5%
Exports - vol.	-0.9%	-2.0%	-1.7%	1.1%	0.8%	0.7%	1.1%	0.8%	0.6%
Absorption - vol.	-0.3%	-0.2%	-0.3%	-0.3%	-0.5%	-0.9%	-0.3%	-0.5%	-1.0%
Investment - vol.	-1.2%	-0.9%	-1.3%	-4.5%	-4.5%	-4.7%	-4.5%	-4.5%	-4.7%
Labour Demand - vol.	0.2%	0.6%	0.5%	-0.1%	-0.2%	-0.4%	-0.1%	-0.2%	-0.4%
Private Consumption - vol.	-1.8%	-1.1%	-1.1%	-1.3%	-1.9%	-2.3%	-1.3%	-1.9%	-2.4%
Supply to domestic - vol.	-0.2%	-0.1%	-0.2%	-0.2%	-0.3%	-0.7%	-0.2%	-0.3%	-0.8%
Intra-EU Trade - vol	0.0%	0.0%	0.0%	-4.0%	-10.6%	-10.8%	-4.0%	-10.6%	-10.8%

Services	Constraint Case			Flexible Case			Efficiency Case		
	1988	1991	1994	1988	1991	1994	1988	1991	1994
Domestic Production - vol.	-0.5%	-0.5%	-0.7%	-1.2%	-1.5%	-1.9%	-1.2%	-1.5%	-1.9%
Imports - vol.	-3.2%	-2.8%	-2.7%	-3.6%	-2.8%	-2.5%	-3.6%	-2.6%	-2.1%
Exports - vol.	3.3%	2.3%	2.1%	1.1%	0.7%	0.5%	1.0%	0.6%	0.4%
Absorption - vol.	-0.7%	-0.6%	-0.8%	-1.4%	-1.7%	-2.1%	-1.4%	-1.7%	-2.1%
Investment - vol.	0.7%	0.7%	0.0%	-4.7%	-4.9%	-5.0%	-4.7%	-4.9%	-5.0%
Labour Demand - vol.	-0.4%	-0.3%	-0.4%	-0.9%	-1.0%	-1.2%	-0.9%	-1.0%	-1.2%
Private Consumption - vol.	-0.9%	-0.8%	-0.9%	-1.3%	-1.7%	-2.0%	-1.3%	-1.7%	-2.1%
Supply to domestic - vol.	-0.6%	-0.6%	-0.7%	-1.4%	-1.7%	-2.1%	-1.4%	-1.7%	-2.1%
Intra-EU Trade - vol	0.0%	0.0%	0.0%	1.9%	2.8%	2.7%	1.9%	2.8%	2.7%

Non market	Constraint Case			Flexible Case			Efficiency Case		
	1988	1991	1994	1988	1991	1994	1988	1991	1994
Domestic Production - vol.	-0.1%	-0.1%	-0.1%	-0.1%	-0.1%	-0.1%	-0.1%	-0.1%	-0.1%
Imports - vol.	-	-	-	#VALUE!	#VALUE!	#VALUE!	#VALUE!	#VALUE!	#VALUE!
Exports - vol.	-	-	-	#VALUE!	#VALUE!	#VALUE!	#VALUE!	#VALUE!	#VALUE!
Absorption - vol.	-0.1%	-0.1%	-0.1%	-0.1%	-0.1%	-0.1%	-0.1%	-0.1%	-0.1%
Investment - vol.	-6.4%	-6.4%	-6.5%	-4.1%	-4.1%	-4.1%	-4.1%	-4.1%	-4.1%
Labour Demand - vol.	0.0%	0.0%	0.0%	0.1%	0.1%	0.1%	0.1%	0.1%	0.2%
Private Consumption - vol.	-1.2%	-0.8%	-0.9%	-1.1%	-1.5%	-1.8%	-1.1%	-1.5%	-1.9%
Supply to domestic - vol.	-0.1%	-0.1%	-0.1%	-0.1%	-0.1%	-0.1%	-0.1%	-0.1%	-0.1%
Intra-EU Trade - vol	0.0%	0.0%	0.0%	#DIV/0!	#DIV/0!	#DIV/0!	#DIV/0!	#DIV/0!	#DIV/0!

Table B11.4.
The full *antimonde* scenario: sectoral results for Spain (prices)

% change from *monde*

Agriculture	Constraint Case			Flexible Case			Efficiency Case		
	1988	1991	1994	1988	1991	1994	1988	1991	1994
Real Marginal Costs	0.18%	0.95%	1.17%	0.69%	0.57%	0.60%	0.68%	0.54%	0.55%
Real Cost of Labour	-0.70%	-0.08%	-0.23%	-1.01%	-1.71%	-2.29%	-1.03%	-1.81%	-2.48%
Real Deflator of Absorption	0.24%	0.92%	1.12%	1.19%	0.93%	0.88%	1.18%	0.87%	0.78%
Real Price of Exports-RW	0.18%	0.95%	1.17%	0.69%	0.57%	0.60%	0.68%	0.54%	0.55%

Energy	Constraint Case			Flexible Case			Efficiency Case		
	1988	1991	1994	1988	1991	1994	1988	1991	1994
Marginal Costs	0.31%	0.92%	1.12%	1.84%	1.32%	1.12%	1.81%	1.19%	0.88%
Cost of Labour	-0.70%	-0.08%	-0.23%	-1.01%	-1.71%	-2.29%	-1.03%	-1.81%	-2.48%
Deflator of Absorption	0.38%	0.77%	0.89%	3.16%	2.28%	1.88%	3.11%	2.07%	1.51%
Price of Exports-RW	0.31%	0.92%	1.12%	1.84%	1.32%	1.12%	1.81%	1.19%	0.88%

Metal Industries	Constraint Case			Flexible Case			Efficiency Case		
	1988	1991	1994	1988	1991	1994	1988	1991	1994
Marginal Costs	0.95%	1.73%	1.99%	1.76%	1.56%	1.51%	1.76%	1.55%	1.49%
Cost of Labour	-0.70%	-0.08%	-0.23%	-1.01%	-1.71%	-2.29%	-1.03%	-1.81%	-2.48%
Deflator of Absorption	1.57%	2.32%	2.56%	2.69%	2.55%	2.52%	2.69%	2.53%	2.48%
Price of Exports-RW	2.51%	4.83%	5.11%	1.44%	1.10%	1.09%	1.44%	1.10%	1.09%

Chemical	Constraint Case			Flexible Case			Efficiency Case		
	1988	1991	1994	1988	1991	1994	1988	1991	1994
Marginal Costs	0.24%	0.97%	1.17%	0.91%	0.66%	0.58%	0.90%	0.62%	0.52%
Cost of Labour	-0.70%	-0.08%	-0.23%	-1.01%	-1.71%	-2.29%	-1.03%	-1.81%	-2.48%
Deflator of Absorption	0.52%	1.06%	1.20%	2.19%	1.75%	1.56%	2.17%	1.66%	1.40%
Price of Exports-RW	0.79%	2.06%	2.25%	0.79%	0.48%	0.41%	0.78%	0.44%	0.35%

Other Intensive Industries	Constraint Case			Flexible Case			Efficiency Case		
	1988	1991	1994	1988	1991	1994	1988	1991	1994
Marginal Costs	0.25%	1.00%	1.16%	0.70%	0.44%	0.33%	0.69%	0.41%	0.28%
Cost of Labour	-0.70%	-0.08%	-0.23%	-1.01%	-1.71%	-2.29%	-1.03%	-1.81%	-2.48%
Deflator of Absorption	0.37%	1.04%	1.19%	1.09%	0.77%	0.63%	1.08%	0.73%	0.56%
Price of Exports-RW	0.44%	1.37%	1.54%	0.70%	0.43%	0.32%	0.69%	0.40%	0.27%

Electrical goods	Constraint Case			Flexible Case			Efficiency Case		
	1988	1991	1994	1988	1991	1994	1988	1991	1994
Marginal Costs	0.23%	0.97%	1.13%	0.59%	0.33%	0.22%	0.58%	0.31%	0.18%
Cost of Labour	-0.70%	-0.08%	-0.23%	-1.01%	-1.71%	-2.29%	-1.03%	-1.81%	-2.48%
Deflator of Absorption	0.70%	1.26%	1.39%	2.09%	1.60%	1.36%	2.07%	1.52%	1.21%
Price of Exports-RW	0.80%	2.16%	2.33%	0.51%	0.18%	0.07%	0.50%	0.16%	0.04%

Transport equipment	Constraint Case			Flexible Case			Efficiency Case		
	1988	1991	1994	1988	1991	1994	1988	1991	1994
Marginal Costs	0.47%	1.19%	1.36%	0.96%	0.62%	0.41%	0.96%	0.61%	0.40%
Cost of Labour	-0.70%	-0.08%	-0.23%	-1.01%	-1.71%	-2.29%	-1.03%	-1.81%	-2.48%
Deflator of Absorption	1.09%	1.68%	1.86%	2.24%	1.96%	1.71%	2.23%	1.93%	1.65%
Price of Exports-RW	1.18%	2.80%	2.99%	0.76%	0.21%	0.00%	0.76%	0.20%	-0.01%

Other Equipment	Constraint Case			Flexible Case			Efficiency Case		
	1988	1991	1994	1988	1991	1994	1988	1991	1994
Marginal Costs	0.45%	1.16%	1.33%	0.98%	0.72%	0.61%	0.98%	0.70%	0.57%
Cost of Labour	-0.70%	-0.08%	-0.23%	-1.01%	-1.71%	-2.29%	-1.03%	-1.81%	-2.48%
Deflator of Absorption	1.12%	1.46%	1.55%	2.66%	2.11%	1.81%	2.63%	2.00%	1.63%
Price of Exports-RW	0.74%	1.81%	1.99%	0.85%	0.54%	0.44%	0.85%	0.52%	0.40%

Consumer goods	Constraint Case			Flexible Case			Efficiency Case		
	1988	1991	1994	1988	1991	1994	1988	1991	1994
Marginal Costs	0.21%	0.97%	1.18%	0.69%	0.46%	0.41%	0.68%	0.45%	0.38%
Cost of Labour	-0.70%	-0.08%	-0.23%	-1.01%	-1.71%	-2.29%	-1.03%	-1.81%	-2.48%
Deflator of Absorption	0.29%	0.99%	1.18%	1.04%	0.73%	0.63%	1.03%	0.70%	0.57%
Price of Exports-RW	0.21%	0.97%	1.18%	0.69%	0.46%	0.41%	0.68%	0.45%	0.38%

Construction	Constraint Case			Flexible Case			Efficiency Case		
	1988	1991	1994	1988	1991	1994	1988	1991	1994
Marginal Costs	0.11%	0.87%	1.02%	0.40%	0.17%	0.07%	0.39%	0.14%	0.03%
Cost of Labour	-0.70%	-0.08%	-0.23%	-1.01%	-1.71%	-2.29%	-1.03%	-1.81%	-2.48%
Deflator of Absorption	0.11%	0.87%	1.02%	0.40%	0.17%	0.07%	0.39%	0.14%	0.03%
Price of Exports-RW	0.11%	0.87%	1.02%	0.40%	0.17%	0.07%	0.39%	0.14%	0.03%

Telecommunications	Constraint Case			Flexible Case			Efficiency Case		
	1988	1991	1994	1988	1991	1994	1988	1991	1994
Marginal Costs	0.43%	1.52%	1.74%	-0.08%	-0.07%	0.02%	-0.08%	-0.07%	0.02%
Cost of Labour	-0.70%	-0.08%	-0.23%	-1.01%	-1.71%	-2.29%	-1.03%	-1.81%	-2.48%
Deflator of Absorption	0.61%	1.79%	1.97%	-0.13%	-0.39%	-0.35%	-0.14%	-0.41%	-0.38%
Price of Exports-RW	3.73%	7.12%	7.34%	-0.16%	-0.24%	-0.16%	-0.16%	-0.25%	-0.17%

Transports	Constraint Case			Flexible Case			Efficiency Case		
	1988	1991	1994	1988	1991	1994	1988	1991	1994
Marginal Costs	0.09%	0.82%	0.98%	0.57%	0.31%	0.20%	0.56%	0.26%	0.12%
Cost of Labour	-0.70%	-0.08%	-0.23%	-1.01%	-1.71%	-2.29%	-1.03%	-1.81%	-2.48%
Deflator of Absorption	0.22%	0.90%	1.05%	0.73%	0.41%	0.29%	0.71%	0.36%	0.19%
Price of Exports-RW	0.09%	0.82%	0.98%	0.57%	0.31%	0.20%	0.56%	0.26%	0.12%

Banks	Constraint Case			Flexible Case			Efficiency Case		
	1988	1991	1994	1988	1991	1994	1988	1991	1994
Marginal Costs	0.18%	1.15%	1.29%	-0.15%	-0.24%	-0.24%	-0.15%	-0.25%	-0.27%
Cost of Labour	-0.70%	-0.08%	-0.23%	-1.01%	-1.71%	-2.29%	-1.03%	-1.81%	-2.48%
Deflator of Absorption	0.24%	1.23%	1.36%	-0.19%	-0.36%	-0.36%	-0.19%	-0.37%	-0.39%
Price of Exports-RW	1.03%	2.71%	2.84%	-0.17%	-0.28%	-0.28%	-0.17%	-0.29%	-0.31%

Services	Constraint Case			Flexible Case			Efficiency Case		
	1988	1991	1994	1988	1991	1994	1988	1991	1994
Marginal Costs	0.03%	0.84%	1.04%	0.24%	0.24%	0.35%	0.23%	0.22%	0.31%
Cost of Labour	-0.70%	-0.08%	-0.23%	-1.01%	-1.71%	-2.29%	-1.03%	-1.81%	-2.48%
Deflator of Absorption	0.05%	0.84%	1.04%	0.27%	0.26%	0.36%	0.26%	0.23%	0.31%
Price of Exports-RW	0.03%	0.84%	1.04%	0.24%	0.24%	0.35%	0.23%	0.22%	0.31%

Non market	Constraint Case			Flexible Case			Efficiency Case		
	1988	1991	1994	1988	1991	1994	1988	1991	1994
Marginal Costs	-0.32%	0.34%	0.33%	-0.31%	-0.81%	-1.19%	-0.32%	-0.85%	-1.26%
Cost of Labour	-0.70%	-0.08%	-0.23%	-1.01%	-1.71%	-2.29%	-1.03%	-1.81%	-2.48%
Deflator of Absorption	-0.32%	0.34%	0.33%	-0.31%	-0.81%	-1.19%	-0.32%	-0.85%	-1.26%
Price of Exports-RW	-0.32%	0.34%	0.33%	-0.31%	-0.81%	-1.19%	-0.32%	-0.85%	-1.26%

Table B11.5.
Decomposition of effects: macroeconomic aggregates for Spain

Macroeconomic Aggregates (vol.) (% change from monde)	Border Controls 1988	1991	1994	Border controls and x-ineff. 1988	1991	1994	Market segmentation 1988	1991	1994	Trade antimonde 1988	1991	1994	Full antimonde 1988	1991	1994
GDP fact. pr.	0.01%	-0.01%	-0.02%	0.00%	-0.03%	-0.03%	-0.70%	-1.21%	-1.63%	-0.69%	-1.22%	-1.64%	-0.79%	-1.36%	-1.82%
Priv. Consumption	0.23%	0.25%	0.25%	0.22%	0.24%	0.24%	-1.37%	-1.58%	-1.88%	-1.28%	-1.50%	-1.81%	-1.32%	-1.57%	-1.90%
Absorption	0.10%	0.11%	0.11%	0.10%	0.11%	0.11%	-1.42%	-1.62%	-1.93%	-1.40%	-1.62%	-1.93%	-1.43%	-1.67%	-2.01%
Total Investment	0.02%	0.03%	0.03%	0.02%	0.03%	0.03%	-4.23%	-4.36%	-4.51%	-4.23%	-4.36%	-4.51%	-4.23%	-4.37%	-4.52%
Total Exports to RW	-0.49%	-0.56%	-0.56%	-0.49%	-0.57%	-0.58%	1.85%	1.49%	1.30%	1.59%	1.22%	1.03%	1.53%	1.13%	0.92%
Total Imports from RW	1.07%	1.23%	1.24%	1.08%	1.25%	1.26%	-3.83%	-3.42%	-3.28%	-3.01%	-2.54%	-2.40%	-2.91%	-2.40%	-2.20%
Total Intra-EU Trade	-1.11%	-2.96%	-2.96%	-1.12%	-2.97%	-2.98%	-0.95%	-4.57%	-4.67%	-1.56%	-5.33%	-5.43%	-1.70%	-5.53%	-5.70%
Employment (diff. from monde, 10³ persons)	-2	-5	-5	-2	-7	-7	-28	-54	-77	-29	-56	-79	-30	-59	-82
Disposable Income (deflated)	0.23%	0.26%	0.26%	0.23%	0.25%	0.25%	-1.41%	-1.62%	-1.93%	-1.31%	-1.54%	-1.85%	-1.35%	-1.61%	-1.94%

Macroeconomic Ratios (abs. diff. from monde)	Border Controls 1988	1991	1994	Border controls and x-ineff. 1988	1991	1994	Market segmentation 1988	1991	1994	Trade antimonde 1988	1991	1994	Full antimonde 1988	1991	1994
Current Account as % of GDP	-0.11%	-0.12%	-0.12%	-0.11%	-0.12%	-0.12%	-0.93%	-0.93%	-0.88%	-1.01%	-1.01%	-0.96%	-0.99%	-0.98%	-0.92%
Public Deficit as % of GDP	0.16%	0.17%	0.17%	0.15%	0.16%	0.16%	-0.28%	-0.33%	-0.44%	-0.15%	-0.20%	-0.31%	-0.17%	-0.23%	-0.35%
Labour Productivity	0.02%	0.03%	0.03%	0.02%	0.03%	0.02%	-0.45%	-0.73%	-0.94%	-0.43%	-0.71%	-0.93%	-0.52%	-0.83%	-1.09%
Investment/GDP	0.01%	0.01%	0.01%	0.01%	0.02%	0.02%	-1.72%	-1.67%	-1.64%	-1.72%	-1.67%	-1.64%	-1.70%	-1.64%	-1.61%
Priv.Cons./GDP	0.16%	0.19%	0.19%	0.16%	0.19%	0.20%	-0.48%	-0.26%	-0.18%	-0.42%	-0.21%	-0.12%	-0.38%	-0.15%	-0.05%

Deflators (% change from monde)	Border Controls 1988	1991	1994	Border controls and x-ineff. 1988	1991	1994	Market segmentation 1988	1991	1994	Trade antimonde 1988	1991	1994	Full antimonde 1988	1991	1994
Consumer Price Index	-0.26%	-0.30%	-0.31%	-0.26%	-0.31%	-0.31%	0.87%	0.69%	0.69%	0.80%	0.63%	0.62%	0.77%	0.59%	0.57%
Real Wage Rate	0.02%	-0.02%	-0.02%	0.01%	-0.04%	-0.05%	-0.90%	-1.51%	-2.03%	-0.92%	-1.56%	-2.10%	-1.01%	-1.71%	-2.29%
Marginal Costs	-0.20%	-0.25%	-0.25%	-0.21%	-0.25%	-0.25%	0.62%	0.42%	0.38%	0.56%	0.36%	0.32%	0.54%	0.34%	0.29%
Producer Prices	-0.20%	-0.23%	-0.23%	-0.20%	-0.24%	-0.24%	0.71%	0.55%	0.52%	0.65%	0.50%	0.46%	0.63%	0.47%	0.42%
Real Shadow Price of Capital	-0.01%	-0.02%	-0.03%	-0.01%	-0.01%	-0.02%	0.19%	0.58%	1.03%	0.19%	0.59%	1.05%	0.13%	0.50%	0.92%
Terms-of-Trade RW	2.01%	2.29%	2.30%	2.03%	2.32%	2.35%	-6.43%	-5.19%	-4.56%	-5.36%	-4.10%	-3.45%	-5.16%	-3.81%	-3.06%

	Border Controls 1988	1991	1994	Border controls and x-ineff. 1988	1991	1994	Market segmentation 1988	1991	1994	Trade antimonde 1988	1991	1994	Full antimonde 1988	1991	1994
Real Exchange Rate	4.02%	4.36%	4.37%	4.04%	4.39%	4.43%	-7.35%	-5.83%	-5.14%	-4.61%	-3.06%	-2.34%	-4.39%	-2.74%	-1.91%
Trade Regime	Integration			Integration			Segmentation			Segmentation			Segmentation		

Table B11.6.
Decomposition of effects: effects on IC sectors for Spain

% change from *monde*

Metal Industries

	Border Controls			Border controls and x-ineff.			Market segmentation			Trade *antimonde*			Full *antimonde*		
	1988	1991	1994	1988	1991	1994	1988	1991	1994	1988	1991	1994	1988	1991	1994
Production per firm	-0.65%	-1.50%	-1.51%	-0.66%	-1.51%	-1.53%	-2.67%	-5.52%	-5.97%	-3.26%	-6.26%	-6.72%	-3.39%	-6.47%	-6.99%
Marginal Costs	3.67%	3.97%	3.98%	3.69%	4.01%	4.04%	-5.56%	-4.30%	-3.66%	-2.86%	-1.51%	-0.84%	-2.63%	-1.18%	-0.40%
Producer Prices	3.77%	4.22%	4.23%	3.80%	4.26%	4.29%	-5.09%	-3.37%	-2.67%	-2.27%	-0.42%	0.31%	-2.03%	-0.06%	0.80%
Mark-ups domestic (abs. diff.)	0.03%	0.06%	0.06%	0.03%	0.06%	0.06%	0.96%	1.26%	1.36%	1.02%	1.34%	1.44%	1.04%	1.36%	1.47%
Fixed Costs per firm	3.61%	3.91%	3.92%	3.63%	3.94%	3.96%	-5.34%	-4.17%	-3.61%	-2.64%	-1.39%	-0.80%	-2.45%	-1.11%	-0.44%
Number of Firms	0.28%	0.93%	0.90%	0.28%	0.92%	0.88%	6.32%	8.93%	8.15%	6.10%	8.64%	7.86%	6.05%	8.55%	7.74%
Sigma of Love of Variety	0.00%	0.00%	0.00%	0.00%	0.00%	0.00%	0.00%	0.00%	0.00%	0.00%	0.00%	0.00%	0.00%	0.00%	0.00%

Chemical

	Border Controls			Border controls and x-ineff.			Market segmentation			Trade *antimonde*			Full *antimonde*		
	1988	1991	1994	1988	1991	1994	1988	1991	1994	1988	1991	1994	1988	1991	1994
Production per firm	-0.28%	-0.82%	-0.82%	-0.29%	-0.83%	-0.84%	-1.84%	-4.03%	-4.37%	-1.78%	-3.96%	-4.30%	-1.87%	-4.09%	-4.48%
Marginal Costs	3.76%	4.04%	4.06%	3.78%	4.08%	4.10%	-6.36%	-5.09%	-4.47%	-3.68%	-2.38%	-1.72%	-3.48%	-2.08%	-1.33%
Producer Prices	3.77%	4.10%	4.12%	3.80%	4.14%	4.16%	-6.20%	-4.78%	-4.14%	-3.52%	-2.06%	-1.39%	-3.32%	-1.76%	-0.99%
Mark-ups domestic (abs. diff.)	0.00%	0.01%	0.01%	0.00%	0.01%	0.01%	0.27%	0.39%	0.41%	0.26%	0.38%	0.40%	0.26%	0.38%	0.41%
Fixed Costs per firm	3.67%	3.95%	3.96%	3.69%	3.97%	3.99%	-6.12%	-5.06%	-4.59%	-3.47%	-2.37%	-1.88%	-3.31%	-2.14%	-1.57%
Number of Firms	0.52%	1.51%	1.51%	0.51%	1.51%	1.51%	6.28%	9.02%	8.57%	6.46%	9.23%	8.77%	6.41%	9.15%	8.67%
Sigma of Love of Variety	0.00%	0.00%	0.00%	0.00%	0.00%	0.00%	0.00%	0.00%	0.00%	0.00%	0.00%	0.00%	0.00%	0.00%	0.00%

Other Intensive Industries

	Border Controls			Border controls and x-ineff.			Market segmentation			Trade *antimonde*			Full *antimonde*		
	1988	1991	1994	1988	1991	1994	1988	1991	1994	1988	1991	1994	1988	1991	1994
Production per firm	-0.29%	-0.73%	-0.74%	-0.29%	-0.74%	-0.75%	-1.48%	-2.63%	-2.88%	-1.64%	-2.84%	-3.09%	-1.70%	-2.94%	-3.22%
Marginal Costs	3.80%	4.10%	4.11%	3.82%	4.13%	4.16%	-6.59%	-5.34%	-4.75%	-3.90%	-2.61%	-1.99%	-3.70%	-2.31%	-1.59%
Producer Prices	3.81%	4.13%	4.14%	3.83%	4.16%	4.19%	-6.52%	-5.23%	-4.63%	-3.83%	-2.49%	-1.86%	-3.62%	-2.19%	-1.46%
Mark-ups domestic (abs. diff.)	0.00%	0.00%	0.00%	0.00%	0.00%	0.00%	0.09%	0.11%	0.11%	0.09%	0.11%	0.12%	0.09%	0.11%	0.12%
Fixed Costs per firm	3.74%	4.03%	4.04%	3.76%	4.05%	4.08%	-6.45%	-5.37%	-4.92%	-3.78%	-2.66%	-2.19%	-3.62%	-2.42%	-1.87%
Number of Firms	0.23%	0.58%	0.57%	0.24%	0.59%	0.58%	0.41%	1.02%	0.82%	0.43%	1.03%	0.83%	0.42%	1.01%	0.81%
Sigma of Love of Variety	0.00%	0.00%	0.00%	0.00%	0.00%	0.00%	0.00%	0.00%	0.00%	0.00%	0.00%	0.00%	0.00%	0.00%	0.00%

Electrical goods

	Border Controls			Border controls and x-ineff.			Market segmentation			Trade *antimonde*			Full *antimonde*		
	1988	1991	1994	1988	1991	1994	1988	1991	1994	1988	1991	1994	1988	1991	1994
Production per firm	-0.45%	-1.21%	-1.23%	-0.46%	-1.23%	-1.25%	-3.51%	-5.74%	-6.07%	-3.76%	-6.07%	-6.40%	-3.88%	-6.24%	-6.63%
Marginal Costs	3.86%	4.17%	4.18%	3.89%	4.20%	4.23%	-6.74%	-5.48%	-4.90%	-4.02%	-2.71%	-2.11%	-3.81%	-2.41%	-1.70%
Producer Prices	3.90%	4.28%	4.30%	3.93%	4.31%	4.35%	-6.42%	-4.98%	-4.38%	-3.66%	-2.16%	-1.53%	-3.45%	-1.84%	-1.11%
Mark-ups domestic (abs. diff.)	0.01%	0.02%	0.02%	0.01%	0.02%	0.02%	0.51%	0.59%	0.61%	0.51%	0.60%	0.62%	0.51%	0.61%	0.63%
Fixed Costs per firm	3.82%	4.12%	4.13%	3.84%	4.14%	4.16%	-6.64%	-5.56%	-5.13%	-3.92%	-2.80%	-2.35%	-3.76%	-2.56%	-2.03%
Number of Firms	0.37%	1.35%	1.31%	0.36%	1.34%	1.30%	3.92%	7.49%	7.03%	3.87%	7.40%	6.94%	3.80%	7.30%	6.81%
Sigma of Love of Variety	0.00%	0.00%	0.00%	0.00%	0.00%	0.00%	0.00%	0.00%	0.00%	0.00%	0.00%	0.00%	0.00%	0.00%	0.00%

Transport equipment

	Border Controls			Border controls and x-ineff.			Market segmentation			Trade antimonde			Full antimonde		
	1988	1991	1994	1988	1991	1994	1988	1991	1994	1988	1991	1994	1988	1991	1994
Production per firm	-0.46%	-1.72%	-1.73%	-0.47%	-1.73%	-1.74%	-6.28%	-9.90%	-9.98%	-6.39%	-10.10%	-10.17%	-6.51%	-10.27%	-10.39%
Marginal Costs	3.83%	4.14%	4.16%	3.85%	4.17%	4.20%	-6.40%	-5.24%	-4.76%	-3.66%	-2.45%	-1.93%	-3.44%	-2.12%	-1.50%
Producer Prices	3.87%	4.29%	4.30%	3.89%	4.32%	4.35%	-5.86%	-4.39%	-3.90%	-3.10%	-1.55%	-1.03%	-2.87%	-1.21%	-0.58%
Mark-ups domestic (abs. diff.)	-0.03%	0.01%	0.01%	-0.03%	0.01%	0.01%	1.02%	1.20%	1.21%	0.99%	1.18%	1.18%	1.00%	1.18%	1.19%
Fixed Costs per firm	3.81%	4.12%	4.14%	3.83%	4.14%	4.17%	-6.36%	-5.25%	-4.81%	-3.63%	-2.46%	-1.99%	-3.45%	-2.21%	-1.66%
Number of Firms	0.82%	1.83%	1.80%	0.82%	1.83%	1.81%	6.23%	12.98%	12.85%	6.47%	13.22%	13.08%	6.43%	13.17%	13.03%
Sigma of Love of Variety	0.00%	0.00%	0.00%	0.00%	0.00%	0.00%	0.00%	0.00%	0.00%	0.00%	0.00%	0.00%	0.00%	0.00%	0.00%

Other Equipment

	Border Controls			Border controls and x-ineff.			Market segmentation			Trade antimonde			Full antimonde		
	1988	1991	1994	1988	1991	1994	1988	1991	1994	1988	1991	1994	1988	1991	1994
Production per firm	-0.79%	-1.84%	-1.84%	-0.81%	-1.85%	-1.86%	-9.36%	-13.15%	-13.47%	-9.89%	-13.76%	-14.08%	-10.01%	-13.94%	-14.32%
Marginal Costs	3.80%	4.11%	4.12%	3.83%	4.14%	4.17%	-6.35%	-5.12%	-4.53%	-3.62%	-2.33%	-1.72%	-3.41%	-2.02%	-1.30%
Producer Prices	3.83%	4.18%	4.20%	3.86%	4.22%	4.25%	-5.94%	-4.55%	-3.95%	-3.18%	-1.72%	-1.09%	-2.96%	-1.40%	-0.67%
Mark-ups domestic (abs. diff.)	0.01%	0.03%	0.03%	0.01%	0.03%	0.03%	0.76%	0.95%	0.96%	0.77%	0.96%	0.97%	0.78%	0.96%	0.98%
Fixed Costs per firm	3.75%	4.04%	4.06%	3.76%	4.06%	4.09%	-6.16%	-5.10%	-4.65%	-3.44%	-2.32%	-1.85%	-3.28%	-2.08%	-1.53%
Number of Firms	0.54%	2.03%	2.03%	0.53%	2.02%	2.01%	10.03%	13.42%	12.72%	9.79%	13.17%	12.46%	9.71%	13.05%	12.30%
Sigma of Love of Variety	0.00%	0.00%	0.00%	0.00%	0.00%	0.00%	0.00%	0.00%	0.00%	0.00%	0.00%	0.00%	0.00%	0.00%	0.00%

Telecommunications

	Border Controls			Border controls and x-ineff.			Market segmentation			Trade antimonde			Full antimonde		
	1988	1991	1994	1988	1991	1994	1988	1991	1994	1988	1991	1994	1988	1991	1994
Production per firm	0.14%	0.17%	0.16%	-0.53%	-1.26%	-1.27%	-1.08%	-3.06%	-3.48%	-0.95%	-2.93%	-3.35%	-1.65%	-4.26%	-4.71%
Marginal Costs	4.03%	4.36%	4.40%	4.06%	4.40%	4.45%	-7.42%	-5.89%	-5.11%	-4.69%	-3.13%	-2.32%	-4.47%	-2.81%	-1.89%
Producer Prices	3.98%	4.30%	4.33%	3.79%	3.92%	3.96%	-7.27%	-5.41%	-4.65%	-4.57%	-2.68%	-1.88%	-4.56%	-2.78%	-1.88%
Mark-ups domestic (abs. diff.)	-0.05%	-0.06%	-0.07%	-0.36%	-0.69%	-0.69%	0.11%	0.08%	0.04%	0.08%	0.05%	0.01%	-0.24%	-0.59%	-0.63%
Fixed Costs per firm	3.96%	4.26%	4.28%	2.39%	1.10%	1.13%	-7.81%	-6.83%	-6.55%	-5.11%	-4.12%	-3.83%	-6.42%	-6.83%	-6.49%
Number of Firms	0.11%	0.14%	0.15%	0.80%	1.56%	1.57%	0.16%	0.50%	0.59%	0.22%	0.57%	0.66%	0.93%	1.99%	2.09%
Sigma of Love of Variety	0.00%	0.00%	0.00%	0.00%	0.00%	0.00%	0.00%	0.00%	0.00%	0.00%	0.00%	0.00%	0.00%	0.00%	0.00%

Banks

	Border Controls			Border controls and x-ineff.			Market segmentation			Trade antimonde			Full antimonde		
	1988	1991	1994	1988	1991	1994	1988	1991	1994	1988	1991	1994	1988	1991	1994
Production per firm	0.07%	0.10%	0.10%	-0.43%	-0.90%	-0.90%	-0.41%	-0.75%	-1.12%	-0.35%	-0.69%	-1.05%	-0.89%	-1.74%	-2.13%
Marginal Costs	4.01%	4.33%	4.34%	4.03%	4.36%	4.39%	-7.47%	-6.03%	-5.33%	-4.75%	-3.28%	-2.55%	-4.54%	-2.98%	-2.15%
Producer Prices	3.99%	4.31%	4.32%	3.96%	4.22%	4.24%	-7.46%	-6.02%	-5.32%	-4.74%	-3.28%	-2.55%	-4.60%	-3.10%	-2.27%
Mark-ups domestic (abs. diff.)	-0.01%	-0.02%	-0.02%	-0.08%	-0.16%	-0.16%	0.02%	0.00%	0.00%	0.01%	-0.01%	-0.01%	-0.06%	-0.14%	-0.14%
Fixed Costs per firm	3.97%	4.27%	4.28%	2.97%	2.24%	2.27%	-7.74%	-6.67%	-6.31%	-5.04%	-3.96%	-3.58%	-5.82%	-5.62%	-5.18%
Number of Firms	0.09%	0.14%	0.14%	0.58%	1.12%	1.12%	0.16%	0.40%	0.40%	0.22%	0.47%	0.46%	0.70%	1.44%	1.43%
Sigma of Love of Variety	0.00%	0.00%	0.00%	0.00%	0.00%	0.00%	0.00%	0.00%	0.00%	0.00%	0.00%	0.00%	0.00%	0.00%	0.00%

Table B11.7.
Decomposition of effects: sectoral results for Spain (volumes)

% change from *monde*

Agriculture

	Border Controls			Border controls and x-ineff.			Market segmentation			Trade *antimonde*			Full *antimonde*		
	1988	1991	1994	1988	1991	1994	1988	1991	1994	1988	1991	1994	1988	1991	1994
Domestic Production - vol.	-0.7%	-1.0%	-1.0%	-0.7%	-1.0%	-1.0%	2.1%	0.9%	0.4%	1.7%	0.5%	0.0%	1.6%	0.3%	-0.2%
Imports - vol.	2.1%	2.3%	2.3%	2.1%	2.3%	2.4%	-5.8%	-4.9%	-4.4%	-4.4%	-3.5%	-3.0%	-4.3%	-3.2%	-2.7%
Exports - vol.	-0.7%	-0.8%	-0.8%	-0.7%	-0.8%	-0.8%	2.1%	1.6%	1.4%	1.6%	1.2%	1.0%	1.6%	1.1%	0.8%
Absorption - vol.	-0.1%	-0.2%	-0.2%	-0.1%	-0.2%	-0.2%	0.4%	-0.2%	-0.5%	0.4%	-0.3%	-0.6%	0.3%	-0.3%	-0.7%
Investment - vol.	-0.3%	-0.5%	-0.5%	-0.3%	-0.5%	-0.5%	-3.4%	-3.9%	-4.1%	-3.6%	-4.1%	-4.3%	-3.6%	-4.2%	-4.4%
Labour Demand - vol.	-0.7%	-1.0%	-1.0%	-0.7%	-1.0%	-1.0%	2.3%	1.4%	1.1%	1.9%	0.9%	0.7%	1.9%	0.9%	0.6%
Private Consumption - vol.	0.2%	0.2%	0.2%	0.2%	0.2%	0.2%	-1.0%	-1.3%	-1.6%	-0.9%	-1.3%	-1.5%	-0.9%	-1.3%	-1.6%
Supply to domestic - vol.	-0.5%	-0.5%	-0.5%	-0.5%	-0.5%	-0.5%	1.8%	1.1%	0.5%	1.6%	0.8%	0.3%	1.5%	0.6%	0.1%
Intra-EU Trade - vol	-1.9%	-4.5%	-4.5%	-1.9%	-4.5%	-4.5%	1.7%	-1.6%	-1.7%	0.3%	-3.2%	-3.3%	0.2%	-3.5%	-3.7%

Energy

	Border Controls			Border controls and x-ineff.			Market segmentation			Trade *antimonde*			Full *antimonde*		
	1988	1991	1994	1988	1991	1994	1988	1991	1994	1988	1991	1994	1988	1991	1994
Domestic Production - vol.	-0.2%	-0.1%	-0.1%	-0.2%	-0.1%	-0.1%	1.1%	0.2%	-0.1%	1.0%	0.2%	-0.2%	1.0%	0.0%	-0.4%
Imports - vol.	0.6%	0.7%	0.7%	0.6%	0.7%	0.7%	-1.5%	-1.4%	-1.4%	-1.2%	-1.1%	-1.1%	-1.2%	-1.1%	-1.1%
Exports - vol.	-0.3%	-0.3%	-0.3%	-0.3%	-0.3%	-0.3%	0.8%	0.6%	0.5%	0.6%	0.5%	0.4%	0.6%	0.4%	0.3%
Absorption - vol.	0.1%	0.2%	0.2%	0.1%	0.2%	0.2%	-0.1%	-0.5%	-0.9%	0.0%	-0.5%	-0.8%	-0.1%	-0.6%	-0.9%
Investment - vol.	-0.2%	-0.1%	-0.1%	-0.2%	-0.1%	-0.1%	-3.4%	-3.9%	-4.1%	-3.5%	-4.0%	-4.2%	-3.5%	-4.0%	-4.2%
Labour Demand - vol.	-0.3%	-0.2%	-0.2%	-0.3%	-0.2%	-0.2%	1.4%	0.5%	0.3%	1.3%	0.5%	0.2%	1.3%	0.4%	0.1%
Private Consumption - vol.	0.3%	0.3%	0.3%	0.3%	0.3%	0.3%	-1.3%	-1.6%	-1.9%	-1.2%	-1.5%	-1.8%	-1.2%	-1.6%	-1.9%
Supply to domestic - vol.	-0.3%	-0.3%	-0.3%	-0.3%	-0.3%	-0.3%	1.3%	0.5%	0.1%	1.1%	0.3%	-0.1%	1.0%	0.2%	-0.3%
Intra-EU Trade - vol	0.0%	0.1%	0.1%	0.0%	0.2%	0.2%	0.5%	-0.7%	-0.6%	0.5%	-0.7%	-0.6%	0.5%	-0.7%	-0.6%

Metal Industries

	Border Controls			Border controls and x-ineff.			Market segmentation			Trade *antimonde*			Full *antimonde*		
	1988	1991	1994	1988	1991	1994	1988	1991	1994	1988	1991	1994	1988	1991	1994
Domestic Production - vol.	-0.4%	-0.6%	-0.6%	-0.4%	-0.6%	-0.7%	3.5%	2.9%	1.7%	2.6%	1.8%	0.6%	2.5%	1.5%	0.2%
Imports - vol.	1.5%	1.8%	1.8%	1.5%	1.8%	1.8%	-5.6%	-5.0%	-5.0%	-3.4%	-2.6%	-2.6%	-3.1%	-2.2%	-2.1%
Exports - vol.	-0.6%	-0.7%	-0.7%	-0.6%	-0.7%	-0.7%	1.9%	1.5%	1.3%	1.4%	1.1%	0.8%	1.4%	1.0%	0.7%
Absorption - vol.	-0.1%	-0.1%	-0.1%	-0.1%	-0.1%	-0.2%	1.5%	1.7%	0.9%	1.0%	1.1%	0.3%	0.9%	0.9%	0.0%
Investment - vol.	-0.2%	-0.3%	-0.3%	-0.2%	-0.3%	-0.3%	-2.5%	-2.7%	-3.3%	-2.8%	-3.2%	-3.8%	-2.9%	-3.3%	-3.9%
Labour Demand - vol.	-0.3%	-0.3%	-0.4%	-0.3%	-0.3%	-0.4%	4.2%	4.3%	3.2%	3.5%	3.3%	2.2%	3.4%	3.1%	2.0%
Private Consumption - vol.	#DIV/0!	#DIV/0!	#DIV/0!	#DIV/0!	#DIV/0!	#DIV/0!	#DIV/0!	#DIV/0!	#DIV/0!	#DIV/0!	#DIV/0!	#DIV/0!	#DIV/0!	#DIV/0!	#DIV/0!
Supply to domestic - vol.	0.3%	1.1%	1.0%	0.3%	1.1%	1.0%	3.5%	5.5%	4.1%	3.1%	4.9%	3.6%	3.0%	4.7%	3.3%
Intra-EU Trade - vol	-1.6%	-3.4%	-3.4%	-1.6%	-3.4%	-3.4%	0.1%	-4.3%	-4.4%	-1.4%	-6.0%	-6.0%	-1.5%	-6.2%	-6.4%

Chemical

	Border Controls			Border controls and x-ineff.			Market segmentation			Trade *antimonde*			Full *antimonde*		
	1988	1991	1994	1988	1991	1994	1988	1991	1994	1988	1991	1994	1988	1991	1994
Domestic Production - vol.	0.2%	0.7%	0.7%	0.2%	0.7%	0.7%	4.3%	4.6%	3.8%	4.6%	4.9%	4.1%	4.4%	4.7%	3.8%
Imports - vol.	0.9%	1.2%	1.2%	0.9%	1.2%	1.2%	-5.3%	-4.7%	-4.5%	-4.6%	-3.8%	-3.6%	-4.3%	-3.5%	-3.2%
Exports - vol.	-0.3%	-0.4%	-0.4%	-0.3%	-0.4%	-0.4%	2.0%	1.6%	1.4%	2.0%	1.6%	1.4%	1.9%	1.5%	1.3%
Absorption - vol.	0.0%	0.1%	0.1%	0.0%	0.1%	0.1%	0.5%	0.3%	-0.1%	0.5%	0.3%	-0.1%	0.5%	0.2%	-0.2%
Investment - vol.	0.1%	0.3%	0.3%	0.1%	0.3%	0.3%	-2.2%	-2.1%	-2.5%	-2.1%	-2.0%	-2.3%	-2.1%	-2.0%	-2.4%
Labour Demand - vol.	0.3%	0.8%	0.8%	0.3%	0.8%	0.8%	4.7%	5.3%	4.6%	4.9%	5.6%	4.9%	4.8%	5.4%	4.7%
Private Consumption - vol.	0.2%	0.2%	0.2%	0.2%	0.2%	0.2%	-1.1%	-1.5%	-1.9%	-1.0%	-1.5%	-1.8%	-1.0%	-1.5%	-1.9%
Supply to domestic - vol.	0.5%	1.7%	1.7%	0.5%	1.7%	1.7%	4.5%	6.5%	5.6%	4.7%	6.7%	5.8%	4.6%	6.5%	5.6%
Intra-EU Trade - vol	-1.6%	-3.7%	-3.7%	-1.6%	-3.7%	-3.7%	-0.7%	-5.4%	-5.4%	-1.4%	-6.2%	-6.3%	-1.5%	-6.4%	-6.6%

Other Intensive Industries

	Border Controls			Border controls and x-ineff.			Market segmentation			Trade *antimonde*			Full *antimonde*		
	1988	1991	1994	1988	1991	1994	1988	1991	1994	1988	1991	1994	1988	1991	1994
Domestic Production - vol.	-0.1%	-0.2%	-0.2%	-0.1%	-0.2%	-0.2%	-1.1%	-1.6%	-2.1%	-1.2%	-1.8%	-2.3%	-1.3%	-2.0%	-2.4%
Imports - vol.	1.9%	2.2%	2.2%	1.9%	2.2%	2.2%	-8.4%	-7.5%	-7.2%	-6.5%	-5.4%	-5.1%	-6.2%	-5.0%	-4.5%
Exports - vol.	-0.5%	-0.6%	-0.6%	-0.5%	-0.6%	-0.6%	2.1%	1.7%	1.5%	1.8%	1.4%	1.2%	1.7%	1.3%	1.1%
Absorption - vol.	0.1%	0.1%	0.1%	0.1%	0.1%	0.1%	-2.5%	-2.5%	-2.9%	-2.5%	-2.6%	-2.9%	-2.6%	-2.6%	-3.0%
Investment - vol.	0.0%	-0.1%	-0.1%	0.0%	-0.1%	-0.1%	-4.7%	-5.0%	-5.2%	-4.8%	-5.1%	-5.3%	-4.8%	-5.1%	-5.3%
Labour Demand - vol.	0.0%	-0.1%	-0.1%	0.0%	-0.1%	-0.1%	-0.9%	-1.3%	-1.6%	-1.0%	-1.5%	-1.8%	-1.0%	-1.5%	-1.9%
Private Consumption - vol.	0.2%	0.2%	0.2%	0.2%	0.2%	0.2%	-1.4%	-1.2%	-1.3%	-1.3%	-1.1%	-1.3%	-1.4%	-1.2%	-1.3%
Supply to domestic - vol.	0.3%	0.8%	0.8%	0.3%	0.8%	0.8%	-1.4%	-1.0%	-1.4%	-1.4%	-1.0%	-1.4%	-1.4%	-1.0%	-1.5%
Intra-EU Trade - vol	-1.8%	-4.4%	-4.4%	-1.8%	-4.4%	-4.4%	-2.2%	-6.1%	-6.2%	-3.3%	-7.5%	-7.6%	-3.4%	-7.6%	-7.8%

Aggregate results of the single market programme

Electrical goods

	Border Controls			Border controls and x-ineff.			Market segmentation			Trade *antimonde*			Full *antimonde*		
	1988	1991	1994	1988	1991	1994	1988	1991	1994	1988	1991	1994	1988	1991	1994
Domestic Production - vol.	-0.1%	0.1%	0.1%	-0.1%	0.1%	0.0%	0.3%	1.3%	0.5%	0.0%	0.9%	0.1%	-0.2%	0.6%	-0.3%
Imports - vol.	1.7%	1.9%	1.9%	1.7%	2.0%	2.0%	-8.3%	-7.3%	-7.1%	-6.8%	-5.8%	-5.5%	-6.6%	-5.4%	-5.1%
Exports - vol.	-0.6%	-0.7%	-0.7%	-0.6%	-0.7%	-0.7%	2.5%	2.1%	1.8%	2.2%	1.8%	1.5%	2.1%	1.6%	1.4%
Absorption - vol.	0.3%	0.2%	0.2%	0.3%	0.2%	0.2%	-4.4%	-3.7%	-4.0%	-4.4%	-3.8%	-4.1%	-4.4%	-3.9%	-4.2%
Investment - vol.	0.0%	0.1%	0.1%	0.0%	0.1%	0.0%	-4.2%	-3.7%	-4.1%	-4.3%	-3.9%	-4.3%	-4.4%	-4.0%	-4.4%
Labour Demand - vol.	-0.1%	0.2%	0.2%	-0.1%	0.2%	0.2%	1.0%	2.5%	1.8%	0.7%	2.1%	1.5%	0.6%	1.9%	1.2%
Private Consumption - vol.	1.0%	0.5%	0.3%	1.0%	0.5%	0.3%	-5.7%	-2.6%	-2.7%	-5.2%	-2.6%	-2.6%	-5.3%	-2.7%	-2.8%
Supply to domestic - vol.	0.4%	1.5%	1.4%	0.4%	1.5%	1.4%	-0.1%	3.0%	2.2%	-0.2%	2.9%	2.0%	-0.3%	2.6%	1.8%
Intra-EU Trade - vol	-1.9%	-4.2%	-4.2%	-1.9%	-4.2%	-4.3%	-1.9%	-7.0%	-7.0%	-3.5%	-8.7%	-8.8%	-3.7%	-9.0%	-9.1%

Transport equipment

	Border Controls			Border controls and x-ineff.			Market segmentation			Trade *antimonde*			Full *antimonde*		
	1988	1991	1994	1988	1991	1994	1988	1991	1994	1988	1991	1994	1988	1991	1994
Domestic Production - vol.	0.4%	0.1%	0.0%	0.3%	0.1%	0.0%	-0.4%	1.8%	1.6%	-0.3%	1.8%	1.6%	-0.5%	1.5%	1.3%
Imports - vol.	1.6%	1.8%	1.8%	1.6%	1.8%	1.8%	-8.5%	-7.7%	-7.6%	-6.5%	-5.6%	-5.4%	-6.3%	-5.2%	-4.9%
Exports - vol.	-0.6%	-0.7%	-0.7%	-0.6%	-0.7%	-0.7%	2.4%	2.1%	1.9%	2.1%	1.7%	1.5%	2.0%	1.6%	1.4%
Absorption - vol.	0.4%	0.3%	0.2%	0.4%	0.3%	0.2%	-4.2%	-3.2%	-3.4%	-4.1%	-3.1%	-3.3%	-4.1%	-3.2%	-3.3%
Investment - vol.	0.2%	0.0%	0.0%	0.2%	0.0%	0.0%	-4.2%	-3.3%	-3.4%	-4.2%	-3.3%	-3.4%	-4.2%	-3.3%	-3.5%
Labour Demand - vol.	0.4%	0.2%	0.2%	0.4%	0.2%	0.2%	0.6%	3.3%	3.2%	0.7%	3.3%	3.2%	0.6%	3.2%	3.0%
Private Consumption - vol.	0.8%	0.4%	0.2%	0.8%	0.3%	0.2%	-4.8%	-2.2%	-2.1%	-4.5%	-2.2%	-2.0%	-4.6%	-2.3%	-2.1%
Supply to domestic - vol.	1.2%	2.5%	2.4%	1.2%	2.5%	2.4%	-0.7%	5.9%	5.7%	-0.3%	6.3%	6.0%	-0.4%	6.2%	5.9%
Intra-EU Trade - vol	-1.0%	-2.6%	-2.6%	-1.0%	-2.6%	-2.6%	-2.5%	-6.7%	-6.7%	-2.9%	-7.3%	-7.3%	-3.1%	-7.5%	-7.6%

Other Equipment

	Border Controls			Border controls and x-ineff.			Market segmentation			Trade *antimonde*			Full *antimonde*		
	1988	1991	1994	1988	1991	1994	1988	1991	1994	1988	1991	1994	1988	1991	1994
Domestic Production - vol.	-0.3%	0.2%	0.1%	-0.3%	0.1%	0.1%	-0.3%	-1.5%	-2.5%	-1.1%	-2.4%	-3.4%	-1.3%	-2.7%	-3.8%
Imports - vol.	1.4%	1.7%	1.7%	1.4%	1.7%	1.7%	-6.7%	-6.4%	-6.4%	-4.8%	-4.3%	-4.3%	-4.6%	-4.1%	-3.9%
Exports - vol.	-0.8%	-0.9%	-0.9%	-0.8%	-0.9%	-0.9%	2.4%	1.9%	1.7%	1.9%	1.4%	1.2%	1.8%	1.3%	1.1%
Absorption - vol.	-0.1%	0.0%	-0.1%	-0.1%	0.0%	-0.1%	-4.1%	-4.4%	-4.9%	-4.3%	-4.7%	-5.2%	-4.3%	-4.8%	-5.3%
Investment - vol.	-0.1%	0.1%	0.1%	-0.1%	0.1%	0.1%	-4.4%	-5.0%	-5.5%	-4.8%	-5.4%	-5.9%	-4.9%	-5.6%	-6.1%
Labour Demand - vol.	-0.2%	0.2%	0.2%	-0.3%	0.2%	0.2%	0.7%	-0.2%	-1.0%	-0.1%	-1.1%	-1.9%	-0.3%	-1.3%	-2.2%
Private Consumption - vol.	0.3%	0.3%	0.3%	0.3%	0.3%	0.3%	-2.0%	-2.1%	-2.5%	-1.8%	-2.0%	-2.4%	-1.9%	-2.1%	-2.5%
Supply to domestic - vol.	0.7%	2.8%	2.8%	0.7%	2.8%	2.8%	-0.5%	0.5%	-0.6%	-0.8%	0.2%	-0.9%	-1.0%	0.0%	-1.1%
Intra-EU Trade - vol	-1.5%	-3.1%	-3.1%	-1.5%	-3.1%	-3.1%	-0.8%	-3.0%	-3.2%	-2.3%	-4.7%	-4.9%	-2.5%	-4.9%	-5.2%

Consumer goods

	Border Controls			Border controls and x-ineff.			Market segmentation			Trade *antimonde*			Full *antimonde*		
	1988	1991	1994	1988	1991	1994	1988	1991	1994	1988	1991	1994	1988	1991	1994
Domestic Production - vol.	-0.2%	-0.3%	-0.3%	-0.2%	-0.3%	-0.3%	0.9%	0.1%	-0.3%	0.8%	0.0%	-0.4%	0.7%	-0.1%	-0.6%
Imports - vol.	1.7%	2.0%	2.0%	1.7%	2.0%	2.0%	-6.5%	-5.5%	-5.1%	-5.6%	-4.6%	-4.2%	-5.4%	-4.3%	-3.8%
Exports - vol.	-0.7%	-0.8%	-0.8%	-0.7%	-0.8%	-0.8%	2.8%	2.2%	1.9%	2.5%	1.9%	1.6%	2.4%	1.8%	1.4%
Absorption - vol.	0.1%	0.1%	0.1%	0.1%	0.1%	0.1%	-0.7%	-1.0%	-1.3%	-0.7%	-1.0%	-1.3%	-0.7%	-1.1%	-1.4%
Investment - vol.	-0.1%	-0.2%	-0.2%	-0.1%	-0.2%	-0.2%	-4.0%	-4.3%	-4.6%	-4.0%	-4.4%	-4.6%	-4.1%	-4.4%	-4.7%
Labour Demand - vol.	-0.2%	-0.3%	-0.3%	-0.2%	-0.3%	-0.3%	1.2%	0.6%	0.3%	1.1%	0.5%	0.2%	1.1%	0.4%	0.1%
Private Consumption - vol.	0.1%	0.2%	0.2%	0.1%	0.2%	0.2%	-0.9%	-1.2%	-1.5%	-0.8%	-1.2%	-1.4%	-0.9%	-1.2%	-1.5%
Supply to domestic - vol.	0.1%	0.4%	0.4%	0.1%	0.4%	0.4%	0.4%	0.1%	-0.3%	0.4%	0.2%	-0.2%	0.3%	0.1%	-0.4%
Intra-EU Trade - vol	-2.0%	-4.9%	-4.9%	-2.0%	-4.9%	-4.9%	-0.5%	-3.9%	-4.1%	-1.1%	-4.7%	-4.9%	-1.3%	-4.9%	-5.2%

Construction

	Border Controls			Border controls and x-ineff.			Market segmentation			Trade *antimonde*			Full *antimonde*		
	1988	1991	1994	1988	1991	1994	1988	1991	1994	1988	1991	1994	1988	1991	1994
Domestic Production - vol.	0.1%	0.1%	0.1%	0.1%	0.1%	0.1%	-7.0%	-7.2%	-7.4%	-6.9%	-7.1%	-7.3%	-6.9%	-7.1%	-7.3%
Imports - vol.	#VALUE!	#VALUE!	#VALUE!	#VALUE!	#VALUE!	#VALUE!	#VALUE!	#VALUE!	#VALUE!	#VALUE!	#VALUE!	#VALUE!	#VALUE!	#VALUE!	#VALUE!
Exports - vol.	#VALUE!	#VALUE!	#VALUE!	#VALUE!	#VALUE!	#VALUE!	#VALUE!	#VALUE!	#VALUE!	#VALUE!	#VALUE!	#VALUE!	#VALUE!	#VALUE!	#VALUE!
Absorption - vol.	0.1%	0.1%	0.1%	0.1%	0.1%	0.1%	-7.0%	-7.2%	-7.4%	-6.9%	-7.1%	-7.3%	-6.9%	-7.1%	-7.3%
Investment - vol.	0.1%	0.1%	0.1%	0.1%	0.1%	0.1%	-7.6%	-7.8%	-7.9%	-7.6%	-7.7%	-7.9%	-7.6%	-7.7%	-7.8%
Labour Demand - vol.	0.1%	0.1%	0.1%	0.1%	0.1%	0.1%	-6.8%	-6.9%	-7.0%	-6.7%	-6.8%	-6.9%	-6.7%	-6.7%	-6.8%
Private Consumption - vol.	0.2%	0.2%	0.2%	0.2%	0.2%	0.2%	-1.1%	-1.5%	-1.9%	-1.0%	-1.5%	-1.8%	-1.0%	-1.5%	-1.9%
Supply to domestic - vol.	0.1%	0.1%	0.1%	0.1%	0.1%	0.1%	-7.0%	-7.2%	-7.4%	-6.9%	-7.1%	-7.3%	-6.9%	-7.1%	-7.3%
Intra-EU Trade - vol	#DIV/0!	#DIV/0!	#DIV/0!	#DIV/0!	#DIV/0!	#DIV/0!	#DIV/0!	#DIV/0!	#DIV/0!	#DIV/0!	#DIV/0!	#DIV/0!	#DIV/0!	#DIV/0!	#DIV/0!

Telecommunications

	Border Controls			Border controls and x-ineff.			Market segmentation			Trade antimonde			Full antimonde		
	1988	1991	1994	1988	1991	1994	1988	1991	1994	1988	1991	1994	1988	1991	1994
Domestic Production - vol.	0.2%	0.3%	0.3%	0.3%	0.3%	0.3%	-0.9%	-2.6%	-2.9%	-0.7%	-2.4%	-2.7%	-0.7%	-2.4%	-2.7%
Imports - vol.	0.9%	1.1%	1.2%	0.8%	0.9%	0.9%	-5.8%	-5.2%	-4.9%	-5.4%	-4.9%	-4.6%	-5.4%	-4.9%	-4.5%
Exports - vol.	-0.2%	-0.3%	-0.3%	-0.2%	-0.2%	-0.3%	1.2%	0.9%	0.8%	1.1%	0.9%	0.7%	1.1%	0.8%	0.7%
Absorption - vol.	0.2%	0.2%	0.2%	0.2%	0.3%	0.3%	-0.9%	-1.1%	-1.5%	-0.8%	-1.0%	-1.3%	-0.8%	-1.0%	-1.3%
Investment - vol.	0.2%	0.2%	0.2%	0.2%	0.2%	0.2%	-4.7%	-5.4%	-5.6%	-4.6%	-5.3%	-5.5%	-4.6%	-5.3%	-5.4%
Labour Demand - vol.	0.2%	0.2%	0.3%	-0.3%	-0.9%	-0.8%	-0.4%	-1.1%	-1.2%	-0.2%	-0.9%	-1.0%	-0.8%	-2.0%	-2.1%
Private Consumption - vol.	0.2%	0.2%	0.2%	0.2%	0.3%	0.3%	-1.1%	-1.6%	-2.0%	-1.0%	-1.5%	-1.9%	-1.0%	-1.5%	-1.9%
Supply to domestic - vol.	0.2%	0.2%	0.2%	0.2%	0.3%	0.4%	-0.6%	-0.7%	-1.0%	-0.5%	-0.5%	-0.9%	-0.5%	-0.5%	-0.8%
Intra-EU Trade - vol	1.0%	0.8%	0.8%	0.7%	-0.3%	-0.3%	-4.8%	-15.7%	-15.9%	-3.9%	-15.0%	-15.2%	-4.1%	-15.3%	-15.5%

Transports

	Border Controls			Border controls and x-ineff.			Market segmentation			Trade antimonde			Full antimonde		
	1988	1991	1994	1988	1991	1994	1988	1991	1994	1988	1991	1994	1988	1991	1994
Domestic Production - vol.	0.4%	0.4%	0.4%	0.4%	0.4%	0.4%	-0.6%	-0.9%	-1.2%	-0.3%	-0.5%	-0.9%	-0.3%	-0.6%	-0.9%
Imports - vol.	0.2%	0.2%	0.2%	0.2%	0.2%	0.2%	-0.3%	-0.5%	-0.6%	-0.1%	-0.3%	-0.4%	-0.2%	-0.3%	-0.5%
Exports - vol.	-0.1%	-0.1%	-0.1%	-0.1%	-0.1%	-0.1%	0.7%	0.6%	0.5%	0.7%	0.5%	0.5%	0.6%	0.5%	0.4%
Absorption - vol.	0.2%	0.2%	0.2%	0.2%	0.2%	0.2%	-1.1%	-1.4%	-1.7%	-1.0%	-1.3%	-1.7%	-1.0%	-1.4%	-1.7%
Investment - vol.	0.2%	0.2%	0.2%	0.2%	0.2%	0.2%	-4.4%	-4.6%	-4.7%	-4.3%	-4.4%	-4.6%	-4.3%	-4.4%	-4.6%
Labour Demand - vol.	0.3%	0.4%	0.4%	0.3%	0.4%	0.4%	-0.5%	-0.7%	-0.9%	-0.1%	-0.3%	-0.6%	-0.1%	-0.3%	-0.5%
Private Consumption - vol.	0.3%	0.3%	0.4%	0.3%	0.3%	0.4%	-1.5%	-2.0%	-2.3%	-1.3%	-1.8%	-2.2%	-1.4%	-1.9%	-2.3%
Supply to domestic - vol.	0.4%	0.4%	0.4%	0.4%	0.4%	0.4%	-0.6%	-0.9%	-1.2%	-0.3%	-0.5%	-0.9%	-0.3%	-0.6%	-0.9%
Intra-EU Trade - vol	1.4%	1.8%	1.8%	1.4%	1.8%	1.8%	-0.1%	-0.1%	-0.3%	1.3%	1.5%	1.4%	1.3%	1.5%	1.4%

Banks

	Border Controls			Border controls and x-ineff.			Market segmentation			Trade antimonde			Full antimonde		
	1988	1991	1994	1988	1991	1994	1988	1991	1994	1988	1991	1994	1988	1991	1994
Domestic Production - vol.	0.2%	0.2%	0.2%	0.1%	0.2%	0.2%	-0.2%	-0.4%	-0.7%	-0.1%	-0.2%	-0.6%	-0.2%	-0.3%	-0.7%
Imports - vol.	1.1%	1.4%	1.4%	1.1%	1.3%	1.3%	-7.1%	-6.3%	-6.1%	-6.4%	-5.6%	-5.3%	-6.2%	-5.3%	-4.9%
Exports - vol.	-0.2%	-0.3%	-0.3%	-0.2%	-0.3%	-0.3%	1.2%	0.9%	0.8%	1.1%	0.9%	0.8%	1.1%	0.8%	0.7%
Absorption - vol.	0.2%	0.2%	0.2%	0.1%	0.2%	0.2%	-0.3%	-0.5%	-0.9%	-0.3%	-0.4%	-0.8%	-0.3%	-0.5%	-0.9%
Investment - vol.	0.1%	0.2%	0.2%	0.1%	0.2%	0.2%	-4.5%	-4.6%	-4.8%	-4.5%	-4.5%	-4.7%	-4.5%	-4.5%	-4.7%
Labour Demand - vol.	0.2%	0.2%	0.2%	-0.1%	-0.2%	-0.2%	0.0%	0.0%	-0.1%	0.1%	0.2%	0.0%	-0.1%	-0.2%	-0.4%
Private Consumption - vol.	0.2%	0.3%	0.3%	0.2%	0.3%	0.3%	-1.4%	-1.9%	-2.3%	-1.3%	-1.8%	-2.2%	-1.3%	-1.9%	-2.3%
Supply to domestic - vol.	0.2%	0.2%	0.2%	0.1%	0.2%	0.2%	-0.2%	-0.3%	-0.7%	-0.2%	-0.2%	-0.6%	-0.2%	-0.3%	-0.7%
Intra-EU Trade - vol	0.7%	0.8%	0.8%	0.6%	0.3%	0.3%	-4.6%	-11.3%	-11.4%	-3.9%	-10.4%	-10.5%	-4.0%	-10.6%	-10.8%

Services

	Border Controls			Border controls and x-ineff.			Market segmentation			Trade antimonde			Full antimonde		
	1988	1991	1994	1988	1991	1994	1988	1991	1994	1988	1991	1994	1988	1991	1994
Domestic Production - vol.	0.3%	0.3%	0.3%	0.3%	0.3%	0.3%	-1.3%	-1.6%	-2.0%	-1.1%	-1.4%	-1.8%	-1.2%	-1.5%	-1.9%
Imports - vol.	1.8%	2.0%	2.0%	1.8%	2.0%	2.1%	-5.0%	-4.3%	-4.0%	-3.8%	-3.0%	-2.7%	-3.6%	-2.8%	-2.5%
Exports - vol.	-0.6%	-0.6%	-0.6%	-0.6%	-0.6%	-0.6%	1.5%	1.2%	1.0%	1.1%	0.8%	0.6%	1.1%	0.7%	0.5%
Absorption - vol.	0.2%	0.2%	0.2%	0.2%	0.2%	0.2%	-1.5%	-1.7%	-2.1%	-1.4%	-1.7%	-2.0%	-1.4%	-1.7%	-2.1%
Investment - vol.	0.1%	0.2%	0.2%	0.1%	0.2%	0.2%	-4.8%	-5.0%	-5.1%	-4.7%	-4.9%	-5.0%	-4.7%	-4.9%	-5.0%
Labour Demand - vol.	0.3%	0.4%	0.4%	0.3%	0.4%	0.4%	-1.1%	-1.3%	-1.4%	-0.9%	-1.0%	-1.2%	-0.9%	-1.0%	-1.2%
Private Consumption - vol.	0.2%	0.3%	0.3%	0.2%	0.2%	0.3%	-1.4%	-1.7%	-2.0%	-1.3%	-1.6%	-1.9%	-1.3%	-1.7%	-2.0%
Supply to domestic - vol.	0.2%	0.2%	0.2%	0.2%	0.2%	0.2%	-1.4%	-1.7%	-2.1%	-1.3%	-1.6%	-2.0%	-1.4%	-1.7%	-2.1%
Intra-EU Trade - vol	2.8%	3.8%	3.9%	2.8%	3.8%	3.9%	-0.8%	-0.6%	-0.7%	1.9%	2.8%	2.8%	1.9%	2.8%	2.7%

Non market

	Border Controls			Border controls and x-ineff.			Market segmentation			Trade antimonde			Full antimonde		
	1988	1991	1994	1988	1991	1994	1988	1991	1994	1988	1991	1994	1988	1991	1994
Domestic Production - vol.	0.0%	0.0%	0.0%	0.0%	0.0%	0.0%	-0.1%	-0.1%	-0.1%	-0.1%	-0.1%	-0.1%	-0.1%	-0.1%	-0.1%
Imports - vol.	#VALUE!	#VALUE!	#VALUE!	#VALUE!	#VALUE!	#VALUE!	#VALUE!	#VALUE!	#VALUE!	#VALUE!	#VALUE!	#VALUE!	#VALUE!	#VALUE!	#VALUE!
Exports - vol.	0.0%	0.0%	0.0%	0.0%	0.0%	0.0%	-0.1%	-0.1%	-0.1%	-0.1%	-0.1%	-0.1%	-0.1%	-0.1%	-0.1%
Absorption - vol.	0.0%	0.0%	0.0%	0.0%	0.0%	0.0%	-0.1%	-0.1%	-0.1%	-0.1%	-0.1%	-0.1%	-0.1%	-0.1%	-0.1%
Investment - vol.	0.0%	0.0%	0.0%	0.0%	0.0%	0.0%	-4.1%	-4.1%	-4.2%	-4.1%	-4.1%	-4.1%	-4.1%	-4.1%	-4.1%
Labour Demand - vol.	0.2%	0.2%	0.2%	0.2%	0.2%	0.2%	0.0%	0.0%	0.0%	0.0%	0.0%	0.0%	0.1%	0.1%	0.1%
Private Consumption - vol.	0.0%	0.2%	0.2%	0.0%	0.2%	0.2%	-1.1%	-1.5%	-1.8%	-1.1%	-1.4%	-1.8%	-1.1%	-1.5%	-1.8%
Supply to domestic - vol.	0.0%	0.0%	0.0%	0.0%	0.0%	0.0%	-0.1%	-0.1%	-0.1%	-0.1%	-0.1%	-0.1%	-0.1%	-0.1%	-0.1%
Intra-EU Trade - vol	#DIV/0!	#DIV/0!	#DIV/0!	#DIV/0!	#DIV/0!	#DIV/0!	#DIV/0!	#DIV/0!	#DIV/0!	#DIV/0!	#DIV/0!	#DIV/0!	#DIV/0!	#DIV/0!	#DIV/0!

Table B11.8.
Decomposition of effects: sectoral results for Spain (prices)

% change from *monde*

Agriculture

	Border Controls			Border controls and x-ineff.			Market segmentation			Trade *antimonde*			Full *antimonde*		
	1988	1991	1994	1988	1991	1994	1988	1991	1994	1988	1991	1994	1988	1991	1994
Marginal Costs	-0.23%	-0.28%	-0.28%	-0.23%	-0.27%	-0.27%	0.77%	0.64%	0.68%	0.70%	0.58%	0.62%	0.69%	0.57%	0.60%
Cost of Labour	0.02%	-0.02%	-0.02%	0.01%	-0.04%	-0.05%	-0.90%	-1.51%	-2.03%	-0.92%	-1.56%	-2.10%	-1.01%	-1.71%	-2.29%
Deflator of Absorption	-0.45%	-0.51%	-0.51%	-0.45%	-0.51%	-0.51%	1.38%	1.12%	1.09%	1.22%	0.97%	0.94%	1.19%	0.93%	0.88%
Price of Exports-RW	-0.23%	-0.28%	-0.28%	-0.23%	-0.27%	-0.27%	0.77%	0.64%	0.68%	0.70%	0.58%	0.62%	0.69%	0.57%	0.60%

Energy

	Border Controls			Border controls and x-ineff.			Market segmentation			Trade *antimonde*			Full *antimonde*		
	1988	1991	1994	1988	1991	1994	1988	1991	1994	1988	1991	1994	1988	1991	1994
Marginal Costs	-0.80%	-0.92%	-0.93%	-0.81%	-0.93%	-0.94%	2.29%	1.81%	1.66%	1.92%	1.44%	1.27%	1.84%	1.32%	1.12%
Cost of Labour	0.02%	-0.02%	-0.02%	0.01%	-0.04%	-0.05%	-0.90%	-1.51%	-2.03%	-0.92%	-1.56%	-2.10%	-1.01%	-1.71%	-2.29%
Deflator of Absorption	-1.35%	-1.53%	-1.54%	-1.36%	-1.55%	-1.57%	3.92%	3.10%	2.78%	3.29%	2.46%	2.13%	3.16%	2.28%	1.88%
Price of Exports-RW	-0.80%	-0.92%	-0.93%	-0.81%	-0.93%	-0.94%	2.29%	1.81%	1.66%	1.92%	1.44%	1.27%	1.84%	1.32%	1.12%

Metal Industries

	Border Controls			Border controls and x-ineff.			Market segmentation			Trade *antimonde*			Full *antimonde*		
	1988	1991	1994	1988	1991	1994	1988	1991	1994	1988	1991	1994	1988	1991	1994
Marginal Costs	-0.35%	-0.39%	-0.39%	-0.35%	-0.39%	-0.39%	1.78%	1.53%	1.48%	1.76%	1.55%	1.50%	1.76%	1.56%	1.51%
Cost of Labour	0.02%	-0.02%	-0.02%	0.01%	-0.04%	-0.05%	-0.90%	-1.51%	-2.03%	-0.92%	-1.56%	-2.10%	-1.01%	-1.71%	-2.29%
Deflator of Absorption	-0.37%	-0.38%	-0.38%	-0.37%	-0.38%	-0.38%	2.61%	2.37%	2.34%	2.69%	2.55%	2.51%	2.69%	2.55%	2.52%
Price of Exports-RW	-0.37%	-0.45%	-0.44%	-0.37%	-0.44%	-0.44%	1.46%	1.06%	1.05%	1.43%	1.09%	1.07%	1.44%	1.10%	1.09%

Chemical

	Border Controls			Border controls and x-ineff.			Market segmentation			Trade *antimonde*			Full *antimonde*		
	1988	1991	1994	1988	1991	1994	1988	1991	1994	1988	1991	1994	1988	1991	1994
Marginal Costs	-0.26%	-0.32%	-0.32%	-0.26%	-0.32%	-0.32%	0.99%	0.73%	0.67%	0.93%	0.68%	0.62%	0.91%	0.66%	0.58%
Cost of Labour	0.02%	-0.02%	-0.02%	0.01%	-0.04%	-0.05%	-0.90%	-1.51%	-2.03%	-0.92%	-1.56%	-2.10%	-1.01%	-1.71%	-2.29%
Deflator of Absorption	-0.33%	-0.40%	-0.41%	-0.34%	-0.41%	-0.42%	2.18%	1.71%	1.55%	2.24%	1.82%	1.65%	2.19%	1.75%	1.56%
Price of Exports-RW	-0.27%	-0.35%	-0.35%	-0.28%	-0.35%	-0.36%	0.87%	0.56%	0.51%	0.81%	0.50%	0.45%	0.79%	0.48%	0.41%

Other Intensive Industries

	Border Controls			Border controls and x-ineff.			Market segmentation			Trade *antimonde*			Full *antimonde*		
	1988	1991	1994	1988	1991	1994	1988	1991	1994	1988	1991	1994	1988	1991	1994
Marginal Costs	-0.22%	-0.26%	-0.26%	-0.22%	-0.26%	-0.26%	0.76%	0.49%	0.39%	0.71%	0.46%	0.35%	0.70%	0.44%	0.33%
Cost of Labour	0.02%	-0.02%	-0.02%	0.01%	-0.04%	-0.05%	-0.90%	-1.51%	-2.03%	-0.92%	-1.56%	-2.10%	-1.01%	-1.71%	-2.29%
Deflator of Absorption	-0.26%	-0.30%	-0.30%	-0.26%	-0.30%	-0.30%	1.14%	0.80%	0.68%	1.11%	0.80%	0.68%	1.09%	0.77%	0.63%
Price of Exports-RW	-0.22%	-0.27%	-0.27%	-0.22%	-0.27%	-0.27%	0.76%	0.48%	0.39%	0.71%	0.45%	0.35%	0.70%	0.43%	0.32%

Electrical goods

	Border Controls			Border controls and x-ineff.			Market segmentation			Trade antimonde			Full antimonde		
	1988	1991	1994	1988	1991	1994	1988	1991	1994	1988	1991	1994	1988	1991	1994
Marginal Costs	-0.15%	-0.19%	-0.19%	-0.16%	-0.19%	-0.19%	0.61%	0.34%	0.23%	0.60%	0.35%	0.24%	0.59%	0.33%	0.22%
Cost of Labour	0.02%	-0.02%	-0.02%	0.01%	-0.04%	-0.05%	-0.90%	-1.51%	-2.03%	-0.92%	-1.56%	-2.10%	-1.01%	-1.71%	-2.29%
Deflator of Absorption	-0.41%	-0.47%	-0.47%	-0.41%	-0.48%	-0.48%	2.14%	1.63%	1.42%	2.14%	1.66%	1.45%	2.09%	1.60%	1.36%
Price of Exports-RW	-0.16%	-0.22%	-0.22%	-0.16%	-0.22%	-0.22%	0.53%	0.19%	0.09%	0.52%	0.19%	0.09%	0.51%	0.18%	0.07%

Transport equipment

	Border Controls			Border controls and x-ineff.			Market segmentation			Trade antimonde			Full antimonde		
	1988	1991	1994	1988	1991	1994	1988	1991	1994	1988	1991	1994	1988	1991	1994
Marginal Costs	-0.19%	-0.22%	-0.22%	-0.19%	-0.22%	-0.22%	0.95%	0.58%	0.38%	0.96%	0.61%	0.41%	0.96%	0.62%	0.41%
Cost of Labour	0.02%	-0.02%	-0.02%	0.01%	-0.04%	-0.05%	-0.90%	-1.51%	-2.03%	-0.92%	-1.56%	-2.10%	-1.01%	-1.71%	-2.29%
Deflator of Absorption	-0.19%	-0.17%	-0.16%	-0.20%	-0.17%	-0.17%	2.13%	1.78%	1.54%	2.25%	1.98%	1.74%	2.24%	1.96%	1.71%
Price of Exports-RW	-0.22%	-0.29%	-0.28%	-0.22%	-0.29%	-0.29%	0.77%	0.19%	-0.01%	0.76%	0.20%	0.00%	0.76%	0.21%	0.00%

Other Equipment

	Border Controls			Border controls and x-ineff.			Market segmentation			Trade antimonde			Full antimonde		
	1988	1991	1994	1988	1991	1994	1988	1991	1994	1988	1991	1994	1988	1991	1994
Marginal Costs	-0.22%	-0.25%	-0.25%	-0.22%	-0.25%	-0.25%	1.00%	0.71%	0.61%	0.99%	0.73%	0.62%	0.98%	0.72%	0.61%
Cost of Labour	0.02%	-0.02%	-0.02%	0.01%	-0.04%	-0.05%	-0.90%	-1.51%	-2.03%	-0.92%	-1.56%	-2.10%	-1.01%	-1.71%	-2.29%
Deflator of Absorption	-0.52%	-0.56%	-0.57%	-0.53%	-0.57%	-0.58%	2.74%	2.12%	1.87%	2.72%	2.19%	1.93%	2.66%	2.11%	1.81%
Price of Exports-RW	-0.22%	-0.28%	-0.28%	-0.23%	-0.29%	-0.29%	0.87%	0.53%	0.44%	0.86%	0.55%	0.45%	0.85%	0.54%	0.44%

Consumer goods

	Border Controls			Border controls and x-ineff.			Market segmentation			Trade antimonde			Full antimonde		
	1988	1991	1994	1988	1991	1994	1988	1991	1994	1988	1991	1994	1988	1991	1994
Marginal Costs	-0.24%	-0.29%	-0.29%	-0.24%	-0.29%	-0.29%	0.76%	0.52%	0.47%	0.69%	0.46%	0.41%	0.69%	0.46%	0.41%
Cost of Labour	0.02%	-0.02%	-0.02%	0.01%	-0.04%	-0.05%	-0.90%	-1.51%	-2.03%	-0.92%	-1.56%	-2.10%	-1.01%	-1.71%	-2.29%
Deflator of Absorption	-0.31%	-0.36%	-0.36%	-0.31%	-0.36%	-0.36%	1.12%	0.80%	0.72%	1.05%	0.75%	0.66%	1.04%	0.73%	0.63%
Price of Exports-RW	-0.24%	-0.29%	-0.29%	-0.24%	-0.29%	-0.29%	0.76%	0.52%	0.47%	0.69%	0.46%	0.41%	0.69%	0.46%	0.41%

Construction

	Border Controls			Border controls and x-ineff.			Market segmentation			Trade antimonde			Full antimonde		
	1988	1991	1994	1988	1991	1994	1988	1991	1994	1988	1991	1994	1988	1991	1994
Marginal Costs	-0.15%	-0.18%	-0.18%	-0.15%	-0.19%	-0.19%	0.44%	0.21%	0.12%	0.41%	0.18%	0.09%	0.40%	0.17%	0.07%
Cost of Labour	0.02%	-0.02%	-0.02%	0.01%	-0.04%	-0.05%	-0.90%	-1.51%	-2.03%	-0.92%	-1.56%	-2.10%	-1.01%	-1.71%	-2.29%
Deflator of Absorption	-0.15%	-0.18%	-0.18%	-0.15%	-0.19%	-0.19%	0.44%	0.21%	0.12%	0.41%	0.18%	0.09%	0.40%	0.17%	0.07%
Price of Exports-RW	-0.15%	-0.18%	-0.18%	-0.15%	-0.19%	-0.19%	0.44%	0.21%	0.12%	0.41%	0.18%	0.09%	0.40%	0.17%	0.07%

Telecommunications

	Border Controls			Border controls and x-ineff.			Market segmentation			Trade antimonde			Full antimonde		
	1988	1991	1994	1988	1991	1994	1988	1991	1994	1988	1991	1994	1988	1991	1994
Marginal Costs	0.01%	0.01%	0.02%	0.01%	0.01%	0.02%	-0.07%	-0.06%	0.03%	-0.08%	-0.07%	0.02%	-0.08%	-0.07%	0.02%
Cost of Labour	0.02%	-0.02%	-0.02%	0.01%	-0.04%	-0.05%	-0.90%	-1.51%	-2.03%	-0.92%	-1.56%	-2.10%	-1.01%	-1.71%	-2.29%
Deflator of Absorption	-0.04%	-0.07%	-0.06%	-0.28%	-0.55%	-0.54%	0.12%	0.09%	0.15%	0.10%	0.06%	0.12%	-0.13%	-0.39%	-0.35%
Price of Exports-RW	0.00%	-0.01%	0.01%	-0.06%	-0.14%	-0.13%	-0.08%	-0.11%	-0.02%	-0.10%	-0.12%	-0.04%	-0.16%	-0.24%	-0.16%

Transports

	Border Controls			Border controls and x-ineff.			Market segmentation			Trade antimonde			Full antimonde		
	1988	1991	1994	1988	1991	1994	1988	1991	1994	1988	1991	1994	1988	1991	1994
Marginal Costs	-0.27%	-0.33%	-0.33%	-0.28%	-0.33%	-0.34%	0.72%	0.47%	0.39%	0.60%	0.35%	0.27%	0.57%	0.31%	0.20%
Cost of Labour	0.02%	-0.02%	-0.02%	0.01%	-0.04%	-0.05%	-0.90%	-1.51%	-2.03%	-0.92%	-1.56%	-2.10%	-1.01%	-1.71%	-2.29%
Deflator of Absorption	-0.30%	-0.36%	-0.36%	-0.30%	-0.37%	-0.37%	0.88%	0.58%	0.48%	0.76%	0.47%	0.37%	0.73%	0.41%	0.29%
Price of Exports-RW	-0.27%	-0.33%	-0.33%	-0.28%	-0.33%	-0.34%	0.72%	0.47%	0.39%	0.60%	0.35%	0.27%	0.57%	0.31%	0.20%

Banks

	Border Controls			Border controls and x-ineff.			Market segmentation			Trade antimonde			Full antimonde		
	1988	1991	1994	1988	1991	1994	1988	1991	1994	1988	1991	1994	1988	1991	1994
Marginal Costs	-0.01%	-0.03%	-0.03%	-0.01%	-0.03%	-0.04%	-0.13%	-0.20%	-0.19%	-0.14%	-0.22%	-0.21%	-0.15%	-0.24%	-0.24%
Cost of Labour	0.02%	-0.02%	-0.02%	0.01%	-0.04%	-0.05%	-0.90%	-1.51%	-2.03%	-0.92%	-1.56%	-2.10%	-1.01%	-1.71%	-2.29%
Deflator of Absorption	-0.02%	-0.05%	-0.05%	-0.10%	-0.19%	-0.20%	-0.10%	-0.19%	-0.17%	-0.12%	-0.21%	-0.20%	-0.19%	-0.36%	-0.36%
Price of Exports-RW	-0.01%	-0.03%	-0.04%	-0.03%	-0.07%	-0.07%	-0.13%	-0.21%	-0.20%	-0.14%	-0.23%	-0.22%	-0.17%	-0.28%	-0.28%

Services

	Border Controls			Border controls and x-ineff.			Market segmentation			Trade antimonde			Full antimonde		
	1988	1991	1994	1988	1991	1994	1988	1991	1994	1988	1991	1994	1988	1991	1994
Marginal Costs	-0.09%	-0.12%	-0.12%	-0.09%	-0.12%	-0.12%	0.28%	0.29%	0.40%	0.26%	0.26%	0.38%	0.24%	0.24%	0.35%
Cost of Labour	0.02%	-0.02%	-0.02%	0.01%	-0.04%	-0.05%	-0.90%	-1.51%	-2.03%	-0.92%	-1.56%	-2.10%	-1.01%	-1.71%	-2.29%
Deflator of Absorption	-0.11%	-0.14%	-0.15%	-0.11%	-0.14%	-0.14%	0.32%	0.31%	0.42%	0.29%	0.28%	0.39%	0.27%	0.26%	0.36%
Price of Exports-RW	-0.09%	-0.12%	-0.12%	-0.09%	-0.12%	-0.12%	0.28%	0.29%	0.40%	0.26%	0.26%	0.38%	0.24%	0.24%	0.35%

Non market

	Border Controls			Border controls and x-ineff.			Market segmentation			Trade antimonde			Full antimonde		
	1988	1991	1994	1988	1991	1994	1988	1991	1994	1988	1991	1994	1988	1991	1994
Marginal Costs	-0.07%	-0.11%	-0.11%	-0.07%	-0.12%	-0.12%	-0.25%	-0.72%	-1.06%	-0.28%	-0.76%	-1.12%	-0.31%	-0.81%	-1.19%
Cost of Labour	0.02%	-0.02%	-0.02%	0.01%	-0.04%	-0.05%	-0.90%	-1.51%	-2.03%	-0.92%	-1.56%	-2.10%	-1.01%	-1.71%	-2.29%
Deflator of Absorption	-0.07%	-0.11%	-0.11%	-0.07%	-0.12%	-0.12%	-0.25%	-0.72%	-1.06%	-0.28%	-0.76%	-1.12%	-0.31%	-0.81%	-1.19%
Price of Exports-RW	-0.07%	-0.11%	-0.11%	-0.07%	-0.12%	-0.12%	-0.25%	-0.72%	-1.06%	-0.28%	-0.76%	-1.12%	-0.31%	-0.81%	-1.19%

Table B12.1.

The full *antimonde* scenario: macroeconomic aggregates for the UK

Macroeconomic Aggregates (vol.) (% change from *monde*)	Constraint Case			Flexible Case			Efficiency Case		
	1988	1991	1994	1988	1991	1994	1988	1991	1994
GDP fact. pr.	-0.57%	-0.83%	-1.04%	-0.26%	-0.51%	-0.80%	-0.29%	-0.63%	-1.00%
Priv. Consumption	-0.59%	-0.68%	-0.86%	-1.09%	-1.13%	-1.29%	-1.09%	-1.16%	-1.36%
Absorption	-0.56%	-0.62%	-0.74%	-1.18%	-1.23%	-1.43%	-1.18%	-1.27%	-1.49%
Total Investment	-2.20%	-2.25%	-2.63%	-4.18%	-4.33%	-4.46%	-4.18%	-4.34%	-4.47%
Total Exports to RW	-1.18%	-1.97%	-2.18%	1.36%	1.09%	0.91%	1.34%	1.00%	0.75%
Total Imports from RW	-1.89%	-2.10%	-2.20%	-3.50%	-2.88%	-2.59%	-3.45%	-2.71%	-2.28%
Total Intra-EU Trade	-0.71%	-0.33%	-0.38%	-1.04%	-4.06%	-4.36%	-1.06%	-4.15%	-4.50%
Employment (diff. from *monde*, 10^3 persons)	0	-11	-26	-65	-81	-99	-65	-80	-97
Disposable Income (deflated)	-0.61%	-0.69%	-0.88%	-1.11%	-1.16%	-1.33%	-1.12%	-1.20%	-1.40%

Macroeconomic Ratios (abs. diff. from *monde*)	Constraint Case			Flexible Case			Efficiency Case		
	1988	1991	1994	1988	1991	1994	1988	1991	1994
Current Account as % of GDP	0.00%	0.00%	0.00%	-1.15%	-1.19%	-1.19%	-1.14%	-1.16%	-1.13%
Public Deficit as % of GDP	-0.04%	-0.05%	-0.07%	-0.26%	-0.28%	-0.36%	-0.27%	-0.31%	-0.39%
Labour Productivity	-0.57%	-0.78%	-0.94%	0.00%	-0.18%	-0.40%	-0.03%	-0.30%	-0.61%
Investment/GDP	-0.32%	-0.28%	-0.32%	-1.74%	-1.76%	-1.76%	-1.74%	-1.74%	-1.72%
Priv.Cons./GDP	-0.02%	0.09%	0.11%	-0.48%	-0.36%	-0.29%	-0.47%	-0.32%	-0.21%

Deflators (% change from *monde*)	Constraint Case			Flexible Case			Efficiency Case		
	1988	1991	1994	1988	1991	1994	1988	1991	1994
Consumer Price Index	0.59%	1.10%	1.18%	0.88%	0.72%	0.62%	0.87%	0.67%	0.53%
Real Wage Rate	-0.53%	-0.85%	-1.16%	-0.74%	-1.04%	-1.45%	-0.76%	-1.14%	-1.63%
Marginal Costs	0.47%	1.03%	1.13%	0.55%	0.44%	0.40%	0.54%	0.41%	0.35%
Producer Prices	0.59%	1.17%	1.27%	0.60%	0.52%	0.48%	0.59%	0.49%	0.42%
Average change in mark-ups (abs. diff.)	0.85%	0.99%	1.03%	0.39%	0.64%	0.67%	0.39%	0.64%	0.68%
Shadow Price of Capital	-0.22%	0.54%	0.81%	0.41%	0.78%	1.39%	0.39%	0.68%	1.22%
Terms-of-Trade RW	-0.24%	0.29%	0.39%	-4.96%	-4.00%	-3.32%	-4.88%	-3.67%	-2.74%

| Implicit change in real exchange rate | 0.38% | 1.04% | 1.13% | -3.93% | -2.80% | -2.03% | -3.84% | -2.44% | -1.39% |

Trade Regime	Segmentation			Segmentation			Segmentation		

Table B12.2.

The full *antimonde* scenario: effects on IC sectors for the UK

% change from *monde*

Metal Industries	Constraint Case			Flexible Case			Efficiency Case		
	1988	1991	1994	1988	1991	1994	1988	1991	1994
Production per firm	-5.38%	-7.11%	-7.26%	-4.29%	-7.34%	-7.64%	-4.31%	-7.42%	-7.78%
Real Marginal Costs	0.71%	1.23%	1.37%	1.96%	-0.64%	0.46%	-1.85%	-0.22%	1.21%
Real Producer Prices	1.01%	1.62%	1.76%	-1.73%	-0.26%	0.86%	-1.63%	0.17%	1.61%
Mark-ups domestic (abs. diff.)	0.41%	0.45%	0.46%	0.39%	0.54%	0.55%	0.39%	0.55%	0.56%
Fixed Costs per firm	0.68%	1.06%	1.08%	-2.61%	-1.72%	-1.17%	-2.55%	-1.45%	-0.70%
Number of Firms	5.30%	6.66%	6.59%	9.24%	15.61%	14.94%	9.22%	15.50%	14.75%
Sigma of Love of Variety	0.00%	0.00%	0.00%	0.00%	0.00%	0.00%	0.00%	0.00%	0.00%

Chemical	Constraint Case			Flexible Case			Efficiency Case		
	1988	1991	1994	1988	1991	1994	1988	1991	1994
Production per firm	-5.08%	-6.97%	-7.11%	-4.00%	-7.05%	-7.33%	-4.02%	-7.13%	-7.47%
Real Marginal Costs	0.64%	1.19%	1.35%	-2.04%	-0.71%	0.43%	-1.94%	-0.28%	1.19%
Real Producer Prices	0.80%	1.41%	1.57%	-1.92%	-0.49%	0.65%	-1.81%	-0.06%	1.41%
Mark-ups domestic (abs. diff.)	0.28%	0.31%	0.31%	0.24%	0.35%	0.36%	0.24%	0.36%	0.36%
Fixed Costs per firm	0.58%	1.00%	1.04%	-2.72%	-1.80%	-1.19%	-2.66%	-1.51%	-0.70%
Number of Firms	4.37%	5.70%	5.67%	8.37%	11.56%	11.10%	8.35%	11.46%	10.93%
Sigma of Love of Variety	0.00%	0.00%	0.00%	0.00%	0.00%	0.00%	0.00%	0.00%	0.00%

Other Intensive Industries	Constraint Case			Flexible Case			Efficiency Case		
	1988	1991	1994	1988	1991	1994	1988	1991	1994
Production per firm	-1.12%	-1.54%	-1.66%	-1.33%	-1.88%	-2.02%	-1.35%	-1.95%	-2.13%
Real Marginal Costs	0.56%	1.07%	1.13%	-2.61%	-1.33%	-0.29%	-2.50%	-0.88%	0.50%
Real Producer Prices	0.58%	1.10%	1.17%	-2.58%	-1.29%	-0.25%	-2.47%	-0.84%	0.54%
Mark-ups domestic (abs. diff.)	0.02%	0.03%	0.03%	0.03%	0.04%	0.04%	0.03%	0.04%	0.04%
Fixed Costs per firm	0.48%	0.89%	0.86%	-3.39%	-2.49%	-1.96%	-3.32%	-2.20%	-1.45%
Number of Firms	1.31%	1.50%	1.42%	1.31%	2.37%	2.26%	1.31%	2.34%	2.21%
Sigma of Love of Variety	0.00%	0.00%	0.00%	0.00%	0.00%	0.00%	0.00%	0.00%	0.00%

Electrical goods	Constraint Case			Flexible Case			Efficiency Case		
	1988	1991	1994	1988	1991	1994	1988	1991	1994
Production per firm	-3.20%	-4.43%	-4.59%	-3.73%	-6.16%	-6.32%	-3.75%	-6.24%	-6.47%
Real Marginal Costs	0.63%	1.10%	1.16%	-2.32%	-1.08%	-0.08%	-2.21%	-0.64%	0.68%
Real Producer Prices	0.78%	1.30%	1.36%	-2.16%	-0.81%	0.20%	-2.05%	-0.37%	0.96%
Mark-ups domestic (abs. diff.)	0.21%	0.24%	0.25%	0.26%	0.34%	0.35%	0.26%	0.34%	0.35%
Fixed Costs per firm	0.56%	0.93%	0.89%	-3.08%	-2.22%	-1.73%	-3.01%	-1.95%	-1.25%
Number of Firms	4.04%	4.99%	4.75%	5.00%	8.41%	8.21%	4.97%	8.30%	8.02%
Sigma of Love of Variety	0.00%	0.00%	0.00%	0.00%	0.00%	0.00%	0.00%	0.00%	0.00%

Transport equipment	Constraint Case			Flexible Case			Efficiency Case		
	1988	1991	1994	1988	1991	1994	1988	1991	1994
Production per firm	-7.36%	-9.37%	-9.54%	-7.92%	-10.95%	-11.04%	-7.95%	-11.04%	-11.19%
Real Marginal Costs	0.81%	1.26%	1.30%	-2.21%	-0.95%	-0.01%	-2.10%	-0.51%	0.77%
Real Producer Prices	1.21%	1.77%	1.82%	-1.80%	-0.38%	0.57%	-1.69%	0.07%	1.36%
Mark-ups domestic (abs. diff.)	0.68%	0.81%	0.83%	0.85%	1.08%	1.08%	0.85%	1.08%	1.08%
Fixed Costs per firm	0.68%	1.06%	1.03%	-3.00%	-2.08%	-1.58%	-2.93%	-1.80%	-1.09%
Number of Firms	10.18%	11.62%	11.28%	10.61%	20.07%	20.14%	10.60%	20.05%	20.11%
Sigma of Love of Variety	0.00%	0.00%	0.00%	0.00%	0.00%	0.00%	0.00%	0.00%	0.00%

Other Equipment	Constraint Case			Flexible Case			Efficiency Case		
	1988	1991	1994	1988	1991	1994	1988	1991	1994
Production per firm	-4.79%	-6.20%	-6.30%	-4.76%	-6.65%	-6.81%	-4.78%	-6.73%	-6.95%
Real Marginal Costs	0.62%	1.10%	1.15%	-2.44%	-1.18%	-0.18%	-2.33%	-0.74%	0.60%
Real Producer Prices	0.69%	1.19%	1.25%	-2.37%	-0.13%	-0.07%	-2.26%	-0.64%	0.70%
Mark-ups domestic (abs. diff.)	0.12%	0.13%	0.13%	0.14%	0.17%	0.17%	0.14%	0.17%	0.18%
Fixed Costs per firm	0.53%	0.91%	0.88%	-3.21%	-2.33%	-1.82%	-3.14%	-2.05%	-1.32%
Number of Firms	4.82%	6.09%	5.99%	4.55%	6.77%	6.52%	4.53%	6.67%	6.34%
Sigma of Love of Variety	0.00%	0.00%	0.00%	0.00%	0.00%	0.00%	0.00%	0.00%	0.00%

Telecommunications	Constraint Case			Flexible Case			Efficiency Case		
	1988	1991	1994	1988	1991	1994	1988	1991	1994
Production per firm	4.87%	5.00%	4.90%	-2.48%	-5.13%	-5.38%	-2.49%	-5.18%	-5.45%
Real Marginal Costs	0.60%	1.36%	1.48%	-3.06%	-1.63%	-0.40%	-2.94%	-1.17%	0.41%
Real Producer Prices	2.71%	3.66%	3.75%	-2.87%	-1.20%	0.02%	-2.76%	-0.75%	0.81%
Mark-ups domestic (abs. diff.)	2.53%	2.65%	2.61%	0.00%	-0.12%	-0.14%	-0.01%	-0.13%	-0.15%
Fixed Costs per firm	17.11%	19.12%	18.98%	-5.22%	-5.53%	-5.05%	-5.15%	-5.25%	-4.57%
Number of Firms	-5.90%	-6.01%	-5.90%	2.24%	3.97%	4.05%	2.24%	4.00%	4.10%
Sigma of Love of Variety	0.00%	0.00%	0.00%	0.00%	0.00%	0.00%	0.00%	0.00%	0.00%

Banks	Constraint Case			Flexible Case			Efficiency Case		
	1988	1991	1994	1988	1991	1994	1988	1991	1994
Production per firm	7.91%	7.78%	7.66%	-1.69%	-3.29%	-3.64%	-1.70%	-3.35%	-3.73%
Real Marginal Costs	0.64%	1.46%	1.61%	-2.93%	-1.43%	-0.12%	-2.81%	-0.97%	0.69%
Real Producer Prices	1.48%	2.32%	2.47%	-2.85%	-1.30%	0.02%	-2.74%	-0.84%	0.83%
Mark-ups domestic (abs. diff.)	0.94%	0.94%	0.93%	-0.02%	-0.04%	-0.05%	-0.02%	-0.04%	-0.05%
Fixed Costs per firm	19.40%	20.50%	20.41%	-4.45%	-4.12%	-3.57%	-4.38%	-3.82%	-3.05%
Number of Firms	-7.78%	-7.63%	-7.54%	1.38%	2.02%	2.03%	1.38%	2.02%	2.03%
Sigma of Love of Variety	0.00%	0.00%	0.00%	0.00%	0.00%	0.00%	0.00%	0.00%	0.00%

Table B12.3.
The full *antimonde* scenario: sectoral results for the UK (volumes)

% change from *monde*

Agriculture

	Constraint Case			Flexible Case			Efficiency Case		
	1988	1991	1994	1988	1991	1994	1988	1991	1994
Domestic Production - vol.	-0.5%	-0.7%	-0.8%	2.0%	0.2%	-0.1%	1.9%	0.0%	-0.5%
Imports - vol.	-1.1%	-0.3%	0.0%	-2.6%	-2.1%	-1.6%	-2.5%	-1.9%	-1.3%
Exports - vol.	-3.4%	-4.6%	-5.1%	1.3%	0.9%	0.7%	1.2%	0.8%	0.5%
Absorption - vol.	-0.4%	-0.1%	-0.1%	0.8%	0.0%	-0.1%	0.8%	-0.1%	-0.3%
Investment - vol.	2.8%	2.8%	2.1%	-3.3%	-4.1%	-4.3%	-3.3%	-4.2%	-4.4%
Labour Demand - vol.	-0.4%	-0.5%	-0.6%	2.4%	0.7%	0.5%	2.3%	0.5%	0.2%
Private Consumption - vol.	-1.4%	-0.9%	-0.8%	-0.8%	-1.0%	-1.2%	-0.8%	-1.0%	-1.2%
Supply to domestic - vol.	-0.2%	-0.2%	-0.3%	2.7%	1.4%	1.0%	2.7%	1.2%	0.5%
Intra-EU Trade - vol	0.0%	0.0%	0.0%	-0.8%	-2.9%	-3.0%	-0.8%	-3.0%	-3.2%

Energy

	Constraint Case			Flexible Case			Efficiency Case		
	1988	1991	1994	1988	1991	1994	1988	1991	1994
Domestic Production - vol.	-1.3%	-1.9%	-2.1%	1.6%	0.7%	0.0%	1.6%	0.5%	-0.3%
Imports - vol.	-0.7%	-0.4%	-0.3%	-1.2%	-1.0%	-0.9%	-1.2%	-1.0%	-0.8%
Exports - vol.	-3.0%	-4.3%	-4.9%	0.7%	0.5%	0.4%	0.7%	0.5%	0.3%
Absorption - vol.	-0.7%	-0.8%	-0.8%	0.7%	0.3%	-0.2%	0.6%	0.2%	-0.3%
Investment - vol.	-6.0%	-6.5%	-6.8%	-3.4%	-3.8%	-4.1%	-3.4%	-3.9%	-4.2%
Labour Demand - vol.	-1.3%	-1.8%	-2.0%	1.8%	1.0%	0.4%	1.8%	0.9%	0.2%
Private Consumption - vol.	-0.3%	0.2%	0.2%	-0.6%	-0.9%	-1.0%	-0.6%	-0.9%	-1.1%
Supply to domestic - vol.	-0.6%	-0.8%	-1.0%	1.3%	0.7%	0.2%	1.3%	0.6%	-0.1%
Intra-EU Trade - vol	0.0%	0.0%	0.0%	1.4%	0.3%	-0.4%	1.3%	0.1%	-0.7%

Metal Industries

	Constraint Case			Flexible Case			Efficiency Case		
	1988	1991	1994	1988	1991	1994	1988	1991	1994
Domestic Production - vol.	-0.4%	-0.9%	-1.1%	4.6%	7.1%	6.2%	4.5%	6.9%	5.8%
Imports - vol.	-0.6%	-0.7%	-0.8%	-2.2%	-1.1%	-1.0%	-2.2%	-1.0%	-0.7%
Exports - vol.	-1.8%	-2.6%	-2.8%	1.3%	1.0%	0.8%	1.3%	0.9%	0.6%
Absorption - vol.	0.2%	-0.1%	-0.2%	1.1%	2.4%	2.0%	1.1%	2.3%	1.9%
Investment - vol.	-3.1%	-3.6%	-4.0%	-2.1%	-0.9%	-1.3%	-2.1%	-1.0%	-1.4%
Labour Demand - vol.	0.0%	-0.4%	-0.6%	5.1%	7.9%	7.0%	5.0%	7.8%	6.8%
Private Consumption - vol.	-0.7%	-0.4%	-0.4%	-0.3%	-0.4%	-0.5%	-0.3%	-0.5%	-0.5%
Supply to domestic - vol.	0.8%	0.5%	0.3%	6.9%	15.0%	13.8%	6.9%	14.7%	13.3%
Intra-EU Trade - vol	0.0%	0.0%	0.0%	-1.3%	-6.5%	-6.7%	-1.3%	-6.5%	-6.8%

Chemical

	Constraint Case			Flexible Case			Efficiency Case		
	1988	1991	1994	1988	1991	1994	1988	1991	1994
Domestic Production - vol.	-0.9%	-1.7%	-1.8%	4.0%	3.7%	2.9%	4.0%	3.5%	2.6%
Imports - vol.	-0.4%	0.4%	0.5%	-3.4%	-2.8%	-2.5%	-3.4%	-2.6%	-2.1%
Exports - vol.	-1.2%	-2.0%	-2.3%	1.7%	1.4%	1.1%	1.7%	1.3%	1.0%
Absorption - vol.	-0.5%	-0.6%	-0.6%	1.2%	1.0%	0.7%	1.2%	0.9%	0.6%
Investment - vol.	-3.4%	-4.0%	-4.4%	-2.3%	-2.4%	-2.8%	-2.3%	-2.5%	-2.9%
Labour Demand - vol.	-0.7%	-1.3%	-1.5%	4.4%	4.2%	3.6%	4.4%	4.1%	3.4%
Private Consumption - vol.	-1.8%	-1.2%	-1.1%	-0.8%	-1.1%	-1.4%	-0.8%	-1.2%	-1.4%
Supply to domestic - vol.	-0.6%	-1.3%	-1.4%	5.7%	9.0%	8.2%	5.7%	8.8%	7.8%
Intra-EU Trade - vol	0.0%	0.0%	0.0%	-0.2%	-4.2%	-4.5%	-0.3%	-4.3%	-4.6%

Other Intensive Industries

	Constraint Case			Flexible Case			Efficiency Case		
	1988	1991	1994	1988	1991	1994	1988	1991	1994
Domestic Production - vol.	0.2%	-0.1%	-0.3%	0.0%	0.4%	0.2%	-0.1%	0.3%	0.0%
Imports - vol.	-2.9%	-3.0%	-3.1%	-5.4%	-4.5%	-4.0%	-5.4%	-4.2%	-3.5%
Exports - vol.	-1.3%	-2.0%	-2.1%	1.6%	1.3%	1.1%	1.6%	1.2%	0.9%
Absorption - vol.	-0.1%	-0.3%	-0.5%	-1.4%	-1.1%	-1.3%	-1.4%	-1.2%	-1.4%
Investment - vol.	-2.1%	-2.3%	-2.7%	-4.2%	-4.0%	-4.1%	-4.2%	-4.0%	-4.2%
Labour Demand - vol.	0.3%	0.1%	-0.1%	0.2%	0.7%	0.5%	0.2%	0.7%	0.5%
Private Consumption - vol.	1.5%	0.4%	-0.5%	-1.9%	-1.2%	-1.2%	-2.0%	-1.2%	-1.3%
Supply to domestic - vol.	0.4%	0.2%	0.0%	0.0%	1.1%	0.8%	0.0%	1.0%	0.7%
Intra-EU Trade - vol	0.0%	0.0%	0.0%	-2.8%	-6.4%	-6.6%	-2.8%	-6.5%	-6.6%

Electrical goods

	Constraint Case			Flexible Case			Efficiency Case		
	1988	1991	1994	1988	1991	1994	1988	1991	1994
Domestic Production - vol.	0.7%	0.3%	-0.1%	1.1%	1.7%	1.4%	1.0%	1.5%	1.0%
Imports - vol.	-2.5%	-3.5%	-4.0%	-5.1%	-4.1%	-3.8%	-5.0%	-3.9%	-3.5%
Exports - vol.	-1.1%	-1.8%	-1.9%	1.8%	1.5%	1.3%	1.8%	1.4%	1.1%
Absorption - vol.	0.0%	-0.5%	-1.1%	-2.8%	-2.1%	-2.2%	-2.8%	-2.1%	-2.3%
Investment - vol.	2.2%	1.8%	1.0%	-3.7%	-3.4%	-3.6%	-3.7%	-3.5%	-3.8%
Labour Demand - vol.	1.0%	0.8%	0.5%	1.7%	2.5%	2.3%	1.7%	2.4%	2.0%
Private Consumption - vol.	5.0%	2.2%	-0.6%	-4.6%	-2.2%	-2.1%	-4.6%	-2.3%	-2.2%
Supply to domestic - vol.	2.0%	1.9%	1.3%	1.9%	5.8%	5.3%	1.8%	5.6%	4.9%
Intra-EU Trade - vol	0.0%	0.0%	0.0%	-2.4%	-7.0%	-7.2%	-2.4%	-7.1%	-7.4%

Transport equipment

	Constraint Case			Flexible Case			Efficiency Case		
	1988	1991	1994	1988	1991	1994	1988	1991	1994
Domestic Production - vol.	2.1%	1.2%	0.7%	1.8%	6.9%	6.9%	1.8%	6.8%	6.7%
Imports - vol.	-1.3%	-3.8%	-4.6%	-5.5%	-4.6%	-4.3%	-5.4%	-4.4%	-4.0%
Exports - vol.	-0.6%	-1.3%	-1.3%	1.8%	1.5%	1.3%	1.8%	1.4%	1.1%
Absorption - vol.	1.7%	-0.1%	-0.9%	-3.6%	-2.7%	-2.8%	-3.6%	-2.8%	-2.8%
Investment - vol.	4.1%	3.2%	2.2%	-3.1%	-0.8%	-0.9%	-3.1%	-0.8%	-0.9%
Labour Demand - vol.	2.7%	1.9%	1.5%	2.8%	8.1%	8.1%	2.7%	8.1%	8.1%
Private Consumption - vol.	15.2%	4.4%	0.0%	-3.6%	-1.7%	-1.4%	-3.7%	-1.8%	-1.5%
Supply to domestic - vol.	4.3%	3.2%	2.4%	2.0%	12.0%	12.0%	1.9%	11.9%	11.9%
Intra-EU Trade - vol	0.0%	0.0%	0.0%	-3.5%	-8.3%	-8.4%	-3.5%	-8.3%	-8.5%

Other Equipment

	Constraint Case			Flexible Case			Efficiency Case		
	1988	1991	1994	1988	1991	1994	1988	1991	1994
Domestic Production - vol.	-0.2%	-0.5%	-0.7%	-0.4%	-0.3%	-0.7%	-0.5%	-0.5%	-1.1%
Imports - vol.	-2.1%	-2.3%	-2.5%	-4.4%	-3.9%	-3.7%	-4.4%	-3.7%	-3.4%
Exports - vol.	-1.2%	-1.8%	-1.9%	1.7%	1.3%	1.1%	1.7%	1.2%	0.9%
Absorption - vol.	-0.6%	-0.7%	-0.9%	-3.9%	-3.8%	-4.1%	-3.9%	-3.9%	-4.2%
Investment - vol.	5.4%	5.1%	4.3%	-4.4%	-4.4%	-4.7%	-4.5%	-4.5%	-4.8%
Labour Demand - vol.	0.0%	-0.2%	-0.3%	0.1%	0.3%	0.0%	0.0%	0.1%	-0.2%
Private Consumption - vol.	-0.8%	-0.8%	-1.2%	-1.9%	-1.6%	-1.8%	-1.9%	-1.7%	-1.9%
Supply to domestic - vol.	0.8%	0.8%	0.5%	-0.4%	2.3%	1.8%	-0.4%	2.1%	1.5%
Intra-EU Trade - vol	0.0%	0.0%	0.0%	-2.9%	-5.7%	-5.9%	-2.9%	-5.7%	-6.0%

Consumer goods

	Constraint Case			Flexible Case			Efficiency Case		
	1988	1991	1994	1988	1991	1994	1988	1991	1994
Domestic Production - vol.	-0.1%	0.0%	0.0%	1.3%	0.5%	0.3%	1.3%	0.4%	0.0%
Imports - vol.	-3.5%	-3.4%	-3.3%	-4.1%	-3.4%	-3.0%	-4.0%	-3.2%	-2.5%
Exports - vol.	-1.3%	-2.0%	-2.3%	2.0%	1.6%	1.3%	2.0%	1.5%	1.1%
Absorption - vol.	-0.9%	-0.6%	-0.6%	-0.6%	-0.8%	-1.0%	-0.6%	-0.9%	-1.1%
Investment - vol.	5.4%	5.6%	4.9%	-3.6%	-4.0%	-4.2%	-3.6%	-4.0%	-4.2%
Labour Demand - vol.	0.0%	0.2%	0.2%	1.7%	1.0%	0.9%	1.7%	0.9%	0.7%
Private Consumption - vol.	-1.4%	-0.9%	-0.8%	-0.7%	-1.0%	-1.1%	-0.7%	-1.0%	-1.2%
Supply to domestic - vol.	0.1%	0.5%	0.5%	1.3%	1.0%	0.8%	1.2%	0.8%	0.5%
Intra-EU Trade - vol	0.0%	0.0%	0.0%	-0.5%	-2.3%	-2.6%	-0.5%	-2.4%	-2.8%

Construction

	Constraint Case			Flexible Case			Efficiency Case		
	1988	1991	1994	1988	1991	1994	1988	1991	1994
Domestic Production - vol.	-2.0%	-2.0%	-2.3%	-6.8%	-7.1%	-7.3%	-6.8%	-7.1%	-7.3%
Imports - vol.	-	-	-	#VALUE!	#VALUE!	#VALUE!	#VALUE!	#VALUE!	#VALUE!
Exports - vol.	0.1%	-0.3%	-0.4%	0.5%	0.3%	0.3%	0.4%	0.3%	0.2%
Absorption - vol.	-2.0%	-2.0%	-2.3%	-6.9%	-7.1%	-7.3%	-6.8%	-7.1%	-7.3%
Investment - vol.	-1.2%	-1.0%	-1.7%	-7.6%	-7.7%	-7.8%	-7.6%	-7.7%	-7.8%
Labour Demand - vol.	-2.0%	-1.9%	-2.1%	-6.6%	-6.8%	-6.8%	-6.6%	-6.7%	-6.7%
Private Consumption - vol.	-1.7%	-1.1%	-1.1%	-0.7%	-1.0%	-1.3%	-0.7%	-1.1%	-1.3%
Supply to domestic - vol.	-2.0%	-2.0%	-2.3%	-6.8%	-7.1%	-7.3%	-6.8%	-7.1%	-7.3%
Intra-EU Trade - vol	0.0%	0.0%	0.0%	-3.0%	-3.1%	-3.2%	-3.0%	-3.1%	-3.2%

Telecommunications

	Constraint Case			Flexible Case			Efficiency Case		
	1988	1991	1994	1988	1991	1994	1988	1991	1994
Domestic Production - vol.	-1.3%	-1.3%	-1.3%	-0.3%	-1.4%	-1.5%	-0.3%	-1.4%	-1.6%
Imports - vol.	-2.2%	-2.2%	-2.1%	-5.3%	-5.1%	-4.8%	-5.3%	-4.9%	-4.5%
Exports - vol.	-3.7%	-5.6%	-5.7%	1.0%	0.8%	0.7%	1.0%	0.8%	0.6%
Absorption - vol.	-1.2%	-1.1%	-1.1%	-0.4%	-0.7%	-0.9%	-0.4%	-0.7%	-0.9%
Investment - vol.	-5.2%	-4.7%	-4.7%	-4.3%	-4.8%	-4.8%	-4.3%	-4.7%	-4.8%
Labour Demand - vol.	4.3%	4.9%	5.0%	0.0%	-0.8%	-0.9%	0.0%	-0.8%	-0.8%
Private Consumption - vol.	-2.2%	-1.8%	-1.7%	-0.9%	-1.2%	-1.4%	-0.9%	-1.2%	-1.5%
Supply to domestic - vol.	-1.2%	-1.0%	-1.0%	0.5%	1.3%	1.1%	0.5%	1.3%	1.1%
Intra-EU Trade - vol	0.0%	0.0%	0.0%	-7.6%	-18.6%	-18.7%	-7.7%	-18.7%	-18.8%

Transports

	Constraint Case			Flexible Case			Efficiency Case		
	1988	1991	1994	1988	1991	1994	1988	1991	1994
Domestic Production - vol.	-0.7%	-0.6%	-0.6%	0.2%	0.1%	-0.1%	0.2%	0.0%	-0.2%
Imports - vol.	-0.7%	-0.6%	-0.6%	0.1%	0.0%	-0.1%	0.1%	0.0%	-0.1%
Exports - vol.	0.0%	-0.2%	-0.1%	0.6%	0.5%	0.4%	0.6%	0.5%	0.4%
Absorption - vol.	-0.9%	-0.8%	-0.8%	-0.2%	-0.3%	-0.6%	-0.2%	-0.4%	-0.7%
Investment - vol.	-5.5%	-5.3%	-5.4%	-4.1%	-4.2%	-4.3%	-4.1%	-4.2%	-4.3%
Labour Demand - vol.	-0.7%	-0.6%	-0.5%	0.4%	0.3%	0.1%	0.4%	0.3%	0.2%
Private Consumption - vol.	-2.0%	-1.4%	-1.3%	-0.9%	-1.2%	-1.4%	-0.9%	-1.2%	-1.5%
Supply to domestic - vol.	-0.7%	-0.6%	-0.6%	0.2%	0.1%	-0.1%	0.2%	0.0%	-0.2%
Intra-EU Trade - vol	0.0%	0.0%	0.0%	0.4%	0.4%	0.3%	0.4%	0.4%	0.2%

Banks

	Constraint Case			Flexible Case			Efficiency Case		
	1988	1991	1994	1988	1991	1994	1988	1991	1994
Domestic Production - vol.	-0.5%	-0.4%	-0.5%	-0.3%	-1.3%	-1.7%	-0.3%	-1.4%	-1.8%
Imports - vol.	-6.9%	-8.7%	-8.6%	-5.8%	-5.2%	-4.7%	-5.7%	-5.0%	-4.3%
Exports - vol.	-1.0%	-1.5%	-1.3%	1.0%	0.8%	0.6%	0.9%	0.7%	0.5%
Absorption - vol.	-0.7%	-0.6%	-0.7%	-0.1%	-0.3%	-0.5%	-0.1%	-0.3%	-0.6%
Investment - vol.	-2.6%	-2.1%	-2.3%	-4.3%	-4.8%	-4.9%	-4.3%	-4.8%	-4.9%
Labour Demand - vol.	4.5%	4.8%	4.9%	-0.1%	-1.0%	-1.2%	-0.1%	-1.0%	-1.1%
Private Consumption - vol.	-2.0%	-1.3%	-1.2%	-0.9%	-1.2%	-1.5%	-0.9%	-1.3%	-1.6%
Supply to domestic - vol.	-0.5%	-0.4%	-0.4%	0.2%	0.2%	-0.1%	0.1%	0.1%	-0.2%
Intra-EU Trade - vol	0.0%	0.0%	0.0%	-5.3%	-12.6%	-12.8%	-5.3%	-12.6%	-12.9%

Services

	Constraint Case			Flexible Case			Efficiency Case		
	1988	1991	1994	1988	1991	1994	1988	1991	1994
Domestic Production - vol.	-0.3%	-0.5%	-0.6%	-0.7%	-0.9%	-1.0%	-0.7%	-0.9%	-1.1%
Imports - vol.	-2.1%	-1.5%	-1.6%	-3.2%	-2.6%	-2.2%	-3.1%	-2.4%	-1.9%
Exports - vol.	1.1%	0.5%	0.4%	1.0%	0.8%	0.6%	1.0%	0.7%	0.5%
Absorption - vol.	-0.6%	-0.6%	-0.8%	-1.0%	-1.1%	-1.3%	-1.0%	-1.1%	-1.3%
Investment - vol.	-0.9%	-1.0%	-1.5%	-4.5%	-4.6%	-4.7%	-4.5%	-4.6%	-4.7%
Labour Demand - vol.	-0.3%	-0.4%	-0.4%	-0.5%	-0.6%	-0.6%	-0.5%	-0.6%	-0.5%
Private Consumption - vol.	-0.7%	-0.8%	-1.0%	-1.1%	-1.2%	-1.3%	-1.1%	-1.2%	-1.4%
Supply to domestic - vol.	-0.5%	-0.6%	-0.7%	-1.1%	-1.3%	-1.5%	-1.1%	-1.4%	-1.5%
Intra-EU Trade - vol	0.0%	0.0%	0.0%	1.8%	2.9%	2.9%	1.8%	2.9%	2.8%

Non market

	Constraint Case			Flexible Case			Efficiency Case		
	1988	1991	1994	1988	1991	1994	1988	1991	1994
Domestic Production - vol.	-0.3%	-0.3%	-0.3%	-0.3%	-0.4%	-0.5%	-0.3%	-0.4%	-0.5%
Imports - vol.	-0.3%	-0.3%	-0.3%	-0.2%	-0.2%	-0.2%	-0.2%	-0.2%	-0.2%
Exports - vol.	0.2%	0.1%	0.1%	0.2%	0.2%	0.2%	0.2%	0.2%	0.1%
Absorption - vol.	-0.3%	-0.3%	-0.3%	-0.3%	-0.4%	-0.5%	-0.3%	-0.4%	-0.5%
Investment - vol.	-7.1%	-7.1%	-7.1%	-4.2%	-4.2%	-4.2%	-4.2%	-4.2%	-4.2%
Labour Demand - vol.	-0.3%	-0.2%	-0.2%	-0.2%	-0.2%	-0.2%	-0.2%	-0.2%	-0.1%
Private Consumption - vol.	-1.0%	-0.9%	-1.0%	-1.0%	-1.1%	-1.3%	-1.0%	-1.2%	-1.4%
Supply to domestic - vol.	-0.3%	-0.3%	-0.3%	-0.3%	-0.4%	-0.5%	-0.3%	-0.4%	-0.5%
Intra-EU Trade - vol	0.0%	0.0%	0.0%	0.1%	0.1%	0.1%	0.1%	0.1%	0.1%

Table B12.4.
The full *antimonde* scenario: sectoral results for the UK (prices)

% change from *monde*

Agriculture	Constraint Case			Flexible Case			Efficiency Case		
	1988	1991	1994	1988	1991	1994	1988	1991	1994
Real Marginal Costs	0.65%	1.23%	1.42%	1.24%	1.15%	1.16%	1.23%	1.12%	1.10%
Real Cost of Labour	-0.15%	0.19%	-0.03%	-0.74%	-1.04%	-1.45%	-0.76%	-1.14%	-1.63%
Real Deflator of Absorption	0.67%	1.08%	1.21%	2.24%	1.92%	1.75%	2.21%	1.81%	1.55%
Real Price of Exports-RW	0.65%	1.23%	1.42%	1.24%	1.15%	1.16%	1.23%	1.12%	1.10%

Energy	Constraint Case			Flexible Case			Efficiency Case		
	1988	1991	1994	1988	1991	1994	1988	1991	1994
Marginal Costs	0.43%	1.09%	1.34%	0.87%	0.90%	1.07%	0.86%	0.84%	0.97%
Cost of Labour	-0.15%	0.19%	-0.03%	-0.74%	-1.04%	-1.45%	-0.76%	-1.14%	-1.63%
Deflator of Absorption	0.45%	0.98%	1.17%	1.64%	1.47%	1.49%	1.61%	1.36%	1.29%
Price of Exports-RW	0.43%	1.09%	1.34%	0.87%	0.90%	1.07%	0.86%	0.84%	0.97%

Metal Industries	Constraint Case			Flexible Case			Efficiency Case		
	1988	1991	1994	1988	1991	1994	1988	1991	1994
Marginal Costs	0.71%	1.23%	1.37%	1.24%	1.12%	1.05%	1.23%	1.07%	0.97%
Cost of Labour	-0.15%	0.19%	-0.03%	-0.74%	-1.04%	-1.45%	-0.76%	-1.14%	-1.63%
Deflator of Absorption	1.02%	1.30%	1.38%	2.83%	2.54%	2.26%	2.80%	2.41%	2.02%
Price of Exports-RW	1.07%	1.94%	2.09%	1.11%	0.91%	0.85%	1.10%	0.86%	0.77%

Chemical	Constraint Case			Flexible Case			Efficiency Case		
	1988	1991	1994	1988	1991	1994	1988	1991	1994
Marginal Costs	0.64%	1.19%	1.35%	1.15%	1.05%	1.01%	1.14%	1.01%	0.95%
Cost of Labour	-0.15%	0.19%	-0.03%	-0.74%	-1.04%	-1.45%	-0.76%	-1.14%	-1.63%
Deflator of Absorption	0.79%	1.11%	1.21%	2.52%	2.33%	2.14%	2.49%	2.23%	1.96%
Price of Exports-RW	0.79%	1.56%	1.72%	1.08%	0.95%	0.91%	1.07%	0.91%	0.84%

Other Intensive Industries	Constraint Case			Flexible Case			Efficiency Case		
	1988	1991	1994	1988	1991	1994	1988	1991	1994
Marginal Costs	0.56%	1.07%	1.13%	0.58%	0.43%	0.30%	0.58%	0.41%	0.26%
Cost of Labour	-0.15%	0.19%	-0.03%	-0.74%	-1.04%	-1.45%	-0.76%	-1.14%	-1.63%
Deflator of Absorption	0.66%	1.09%	1.15%	1.07%	0.86%	0.68%	1.05%	0.81%	0.59%
Price of Exports-RW	0.61%	1.19%	1.26%	0.58%	0.43%	0.29%	0.57%	0.40%	0.25%

Electrical goods	Constraint Case			Flexible Case			Efficiency Case		
	1988	1991	1994	1988	1991	1994	1988	1991	1994
Marginal Costs	0.63%	1.10%	1.16%	0.88%	0.69%	0.51%	0.87%	0.65%	0.44%
Cost of Labour	-0.15%	0.19%	-0.03%	-0.74%	-1.04%	-1.45%	-0.76%	-1.14%	-1.63%
Deflator of Absorption	1.08%	1.35%	1.39%	2.52%	2.13%	1.79%	2.48%	2.00%	1.57%
Price of Exports-RW	0.74%	1.45%	1.51%	0.83%	0.61%	0.43%	0.82%	0.57%	0.37%

Transport equipment	Constraint Case			Flexible Case			Efficiency Case		
	1988	1991	1994	1988	1991	1994	1988	1991	1994
Marginal Costs	0.81%	1.26%	1.30%	0.98%	0.81%	0.58%	0.98%	0.78%	0.53%
Cost of Labour	-0.15%	0.19%	-0.03%	-0.74%	-1.04%	-1.45%	-0.76%	-1.14%	-1.63%
Deflator of Absorption	1.74%	2.04%	2.08%	2.62%	2.62%	2.32%	2.60%	2.54%	2.18%
Price of Exports-RW	1.21%	2.17%	2.22%	0.79%	0.44%	0.21%	0.79%	0.41%	0.16%

Other Equipment	Constraint Case			Flexible Case			Efficiency Case		
	1988	1991	1994	1988	1991	1994	1988	1991	1994
Marginal Costs	0.62%	1.10%	1.15%	0.76%	0.58%	0.41%	0.75%	0.55%	0.36%
Cost of Labour	-0.15%	0.19%	-0.03%	-0.74%	-1.04%	-1.45%	-0.76%	-1.14%	-1.63%
Deflator of Absorption	0.96%	1.21%	1.24%	2.19%	1.87%	1.55%	2.16%	1.75%	1.35%
Price of Exports-RW	0.69%	1.25%	1.31%	0.74%	0.56%	0.39%	0.74%	0.53%	0.34%

Consumer goods	Constraint Case			Flexible Case			Efficiency Case		
	1988	1991	1994	1988	1991	1994	1988	1991	1994
Marginal Costs	0.67%	1.18%	1.30%	1.05%	0.87%	0.73%	1.05%	0.84%	0.69%
Cost of Labour	-0.15%	0.19%	-0.03%	-0.74%	-1.04%	-1.45%	-0.76%	-1.14%	-1.63%
Deflator of Absorption	0.82%	1.18%	1.27%	1.92%	1.61%	1.38%	1.90%	1.53%	1.24%
Price of Exports-RW	0.67%	1.18%	1.30%	1.05%	0.87%	0.73%	1.05%	0.84%	0.69%

Construction	Constraint Case			Flexible Case			Efficiency Case		
	1988	1991	1994	1988	1991	1994	1988	1991	1994
Marginal Costs	0.49%	1.09%	1.22%	0.50%	0.44%	0.44%	0.50%	0.44%	0.42%
Cost of Labour	-0.15%	0.19%	-0.03%	-0.74%	-1.04%	-1.45%	-0.76%	-1.14%	-1.63%
Deflator of Absorption	0.49%	1.09%	1.22%	0.50%	0.44%	0.44%	0.50%	0.44%	0.42%
Price of Exports-RW	0.49%	1.09%	1.22%	0.50%	0.44%	0.44%	0.50%	0.44%	0.42%

Telecommunications	Constraint Case			Flexible Case			Efficiency Case		
	1988	1991	1994	1988	1991	1994	1988	1991	1994
Marginal Costs	0.60%	1.36%	1.48%	0.14%	0.13%	0.19%	0.14%	0.12%	0.16%
Cost of Labour	-0.15%	0.19%	-0.03%	-0.74%	-1.04%	-1.45%	-0.76%	-1.14%	-1.63%
Deflator of Absorption	2.59%	3.41%	3.49%	0.42%	0.32%	0.33%	0.42%	0.29%	0.28%
Price of Exports-RW	6.05%	8.70%	8.81%	-0.02%	-0.14%	-0.10%	-0.02%	-0.16%	-0.12%

Transports	Constraint Case			Flexible Case			Efficiency Case		
	1988	1991	1994	1988	1991	1994	1988	1991	1994
Marginal Costs	0.49%	1.01%	1.07%	0.36%	0.24%	0.15%	0.35%	0.21%	0.09%
Cost of Labour	-0.15%	0.19%	-0.03%	-0.74%	-1.04%	-1.45%	-0.76%	-1.14%	-1.63%
Deflator of Absorption	1.09%	1.44%	1.48%	0.64%	0.42%	0.31%	0.62%	0.37%	0.21%
Price of Exports-RW	0.49%	1.01%	1.07%	0.36%	0.24%	0.15%	0.35%	0.21%	0.09%

Banks	Constraint Case			Flexible Case			Efficiency Case		
	1988	1991	1994	1988	1991	1994	1988	1991	1994
Marginal Costs	0.64%	1.46%	1.61%	0.27%	0.33%	0.47%	0.27%	0.32%	0.45%
Cost of Labour	-0.15%	0.19%	-0.03%	-0.74%	-1.04%	-1.45%	-0.76%	-1.14%	-1.63%
Deflator of Absorption	1.59%	2.39%	2.53%	0.28%	0.31%	0.44%	0.28%	0.30%	0.41%
Price of Exports-RW	2.00%	3.35%	3.51%	0.24%	0.29%	0.43%	0.24%	0.28%	0.41%

Services	Constraint Case			Flexible Case			Efficiency Case		
	1988	1991	1994	1988	1991	1994	1988	1991	1994
Marginal Costs	0.34%	0.90%	0.97%	0.19%	0.12%	0.08%	0.19%	0.10%	0.04%
Cost of Labour	-0.15%	0.19%	-0.03%	-0.74%	-1.04%	-1.45%	-0.76%	-1.14%	-1.63%
Deflator of Absorption	0.37%	0.91%	0.97%	0.21%	0.13%	0.09%	0.20%	0.10%	0.04%
Price of Exports-RW	0.34%	0.90%	0.97%	0.19%	0.12%	0.08%	0.19%	0.10%	0.04%

Non market	Constraint Case			Flexible Case			Efficiency Case		
	1988	1991	1994	1988	1991	1994	1988	1991	1994
Marginal Costs	0.24%	0.75%	0.77%	0.14%	0.03%	-0.07%	0.13%	0.00%	-0.13%
Cost of Labour	-0.15%	0.19%	-0.03%	-0.74%	-1.04%	-1.45%	-0.76%	-1.14%	-1.63%
Deflator of Absorption	0.25%	0.75%	0.76%	0.18%	0.06%	-0.05%	0.17%	0.03%	-0.11%
Price of Exports-RW	0.24%	0.75%	0.77%	0.14%	0.03%	-0.07%	0.13%	0.00%	-0.13%

Table B12.5.
Decomposition of effects: macroeconomic aggregates for the UK

Macroeconomic Aggregates (vol.) (% change from *monde*)	Border Controls			Border controls and x-ineff.			Market segmentation			Trade *antimonde*			Full *antimonde*		
	1988	1991	1994	1988	1991	1994	1988	1991	1994	1988	1991	1994	1988	1991	1994
GDP fact. pr.	-0.06%	-0.08%	-0.09%	-0.07%	-0.09%	-0.10%	-0.11%	-0.29%	-0.54%	-0.17%	-0.37%	-0.62%	-0.26%	-0.51%	-0.80%
Priv. Consumption	0.19%	0.24%	0.23%	0.19%	0.23%	0.23%	-1.06%	-1.05%	-1.19%	-1.04%	-1.06%	-1.20%	-1.09%	-1.13%	-1.29%
Absorption	0.02%	0.04%	0.03%	0.02%	0.05%	0.05%	-1.10%	-1.12%	-1.29%	-1.15%	-1.19%	-1.37%	-1.18%	-1.23%	-1.43%
Total Investment	0.03%	0.03%	0.03%	0.04%	0.03%	0.03%	-4.19%	-4.34%	-4.46%	-4.18%	-4.33%	-4.45%	-4.18%	-4.33%	-4.46%
Total Exports to RW	-0.50%	-0.58%	-0.59%	-0.50%	-0.59%	-0.60%	1.69%	1.44%	1.29%	1.41%	1.17%	1.01%	1.36%	1.09%	0.91%
Total Imports from RW	1.22%	1.44%	1.45%	1.23%	1.46%	1.48%	-4.68%	-4.22%	-4.01%	-3.63%	-3.09%	-2.86%	-3.50%	-2.88%	-2.59%
Total Intra-EU Trade	-1.02%	-2.51%	-2.51%	-1.03%	-2.54%	-2.54%	-0.32%	-3.14%	-3.39%	-0.93%	-3.91%	-4.16%	-1.04%	-4.06%	-4.36%
Employment (diff. from *monde*, 10^3 persons)	11	18	18	10	17	17	-69	-86	-104	-64	-79	-97	-65	-81	-99
Disposable Income (deflated)	0.20%	0.24%	0.24%	0.20%	0.24%	0.24%	-1.09%	-1.07%	-1.22%	-1.07%	-1.09%	-1.24%	-1.11%	-1.16%	-1.33%

Macroeconomic Ratios (abs. diff. from *monde*)	Border Controls			Border controls and x-ineff.			Market segmentation			Trade *antimonde*			Full *antimonde*		
	1988	1991	1994	1988	1991	1994	1988	1991	1994	1988	1991	1994	1988	1991	1994
Current Account as % of GDP	-0.08%	-0.09%	-0.09%	-0.08%	-0.09%	-0.08%	-1.17%	-1.25%	-1.26%	-1.18%	-1.24%	-1.25%	-1.15%	-1.19%	-1.19%
Public Deficit as % of GDP	0.08%	0.09%	0.09%	0.07%	0.09%	0.09%	-0.27%	-0.27%	-0.33%	-0.24%	-0.25%	-0.31%	-0.26%	-0.28%	-0.36%
Labour Productivity	-0.11%	-0.15%	-0.16%	-0.11%	-0.16%	-0.17%	0.17%	0.05%	-0.12%	0.09%	-0.05%	-0.22%	0.00%	-0.18%	-0.40%
Investment/GDP	0.03%	0.03%	0.03%	0.03%	0.03%	0.04%	-1.78%	-1.81%	-1.81%	-1.76%	-1.79%	-1.79%	-1.74%	-1.76%	-1.76%
Priv.Cons./GDP	0.15%	0.18%	0.19%	0.15%	0.19%	0.19%	-0.56%	-0.44%	-0.38%	-0.51%	-0.40%	-0.34%	-0.48%	-0.36%	-0.29%

Deflators (% change from *monde*)	Border Controls			Border controls and x-ineff.			Market segmentation			Trade *antimonde*			Full *antimonde*		
	1988	1991	1994	1988	1991	1994	1988	1991	1994	1988	1991	1994	1988	1991	1994
Consumer Price Index	-0.27%	-0.32%	-0.32%	-0.27%	-0.33%	-0.33%	0.96%	0.79%	0.71%	0.91%	0.76%	0.68%	0.88%	0.72%	0.62%
Real Wage Rate	0.04%	0.08%	0.08%	0.03%	0.06%	0.06%	-0.60%	-0.85%	-1.19%	-0.64%	-0.90%	-1.26%	-0.74%	-1.04%	-1.45%
Marginal Costs	-0.17%	-0.21%	-0.21%	-0.17%	-0.21%	-0.21%	0.60%	0.48%	0.45%	0.56%	0.46%	0.42%	0.55%	0.44%	0.40%
Producer Prices	-0.17%	-0.20%	-0.20%	-0.17%	-0.21%	-0.21%	0.65%	0.57%	0.53%	0.61%	0.54%	0.51%	0.60%	0.52%	0.48%
Real Shadow Price of Capital	0.00%	-0.09%	-0.10%	0.02%	-0.05%	-0.07%	0.40%	0.78%	1.42%	0.47%	0.84%	1.50%	0.41%	0.78%	1.39%
Terms-of-Trade RW	1.96%	2.29%	2.31%	1.98%	2.32%	2.35%	-6.13%	-5.26%	-4.68%	-5.14%	-4.26%	-3.67%	-4.96%	-4.00%	-3.32%

	Border Controls			Border controls and x-ineff.			Market segmentation			Trade *antimonde*			Full *antimonde*		
	1988	1991	1994	1988	1991	1994	1988	1991	1994	1988	1991	1994	1988	1991	1994
Real Exchange Rate	4.05%	4.42%	4.45%	4.07%	4.45%	4.49%	-6.88%	-5.85%	-5.21%	-4.12%	-3.08%	-2.41%	-3.93%	-2.80%	-2.03%

Trade Regime	Integration	Integration	Segmentation	Segmentation	Segmentation

Table B12.6.
Decomposition of effects: effects on IC sectors for the UK

% change from *monde*

Metal Industries

	Border Controls			Border controls and x-ineff.			Market segmentation			Trade *antimonde*			Full *antimonde*		
	1988	1991	1994	1988	1991	1994	1988	1991	1994	1988	1991	1994	1988	1991	1994
Production per firm	-0.91%	-1.81%	-1.82%	-0.92%	-1.82%	-1.83%	-3.55%	-6.51%	-6.77%	-4.20%	-7.23%	-7.49%	-4.29%	-7.34%	-7.64%
Marginal Costs	3.66%	3.98%	4.00%	3.69%	4.01%	4.04%	-5.54%	-4.66%	-4.07%	-2.87%	-1.95%	-1.34%	-2.69%	-1.69%	-0.98%
Producer Prices	3.71%	4.07%	4.09%	3.73%	4.10%	4.13%	-5.35%	-4.32%	-3.73%	-2.65%	-1.57%	-0.95%	-2.47%	-1.30%	-0.59%
Mark-ups domestic (abs. diff.)	0.03%	0.06%	0.06%	0.03%	0.06%	0.06%	0.37%	0.51%	0.52%	0.39%	0.54%	0.55%	0.39%	0.54%	0.55%
Fixed Costs per firm	3.59%	3.91%	3.92%	3.61%	3.93%	3.95%	-5.38%	-4.59%	-4.13%	-2.75%	-1.92%	-1.44%	-2.61%	-1.72%	-1.17%
Number of Firms	-0.31%	0.16%	0.14%	-0.31%	0.17%	0.15%	9.91%	16.41%	15.77%	9.32%	15.72%	15.08%	9.24%	15.61%	14.94%
Sigma of Love of Variety	0.00%	0.00%	0.00%	0.00%	0.00%	0.00%	0.00%	0.00%	0.00%	0.00%	0.00%	0.00%	0.00%	0.00%	0.00%

Chemical

	Border Controls			Border controls and x-ineff.			Market segmentation			Trade *antimonde*			Full *antimonde*		
	1988	1991	1994	1988	1991	1994	1988	1991	1994	1988	1991	1994	1988	1991	1994
Production per firm	-0.65%	-1.70%	-1.71%	-0.66%	-1.71%	-1.72%	-3.77%	-6.71%	-6.95%	-3.92%	-6.93%	-7.18%	-4.00%	-7.05%	-7.33%
Marginal Costs	3.81%	4.13%	4.15%	3.83%	4.16%	4.19%	-5.72%	-4.83%	-4.21%	-2.96%	-2.02%	-1.38%	-2.78%	-1.75%	-1.02%
Producer Prices	3.83%	4.18%	4.20%	3.85%	4.22%	4.25%	-5.61%	-4.62%	-4.01%	-2.84%	-1.81%	-1.16%	-2.65%	-1.53%	-0.80%
Mark-ups domestic (abs. diff.)	0.01%	0.03%	0.03%	0.01%	0.03%	0.03%	0.25%	0.36%	0.36%	0.24%	0.35%	0.36%	0.24%	0.35%	0.36%
Fixed Costs per firm	3.77%	4.09%	4.11%	3.78%	4.11%	4.14%	-5.62%	-4.80%	-4.29%	-2.86%	-2.00%	-1.47%	-2.72%	-1.80%	-1.19%
Number of Firms	0.60%	1.30%	1.29%	0.60%	1.31%	1.30%	8.13%	11.37%	10.95%	8.44%	11.66%	11.22%	8.37%	11.56%	11.10%
Sigma of Love of Variety	0.00%	0.00%	0.00%	0.00%	0.00%	0.00%	0.00%	0.00%	0.00%	0.00%	0.00%	0.00%	0.00%	0.00%	0.00%

Other Intensive Industries

	Border Controls			Border controls and x-ineff.			Market segmentation			Trade *antimonde*			Full *antimonde*		
	1988	1991	1994	1988	1991	1994	1988	1991	1994	1988	1991	1994	1988	1991	1994
Production per firm	-0.20%	-0.42%	-0.43%	-0.20%	-0.43%	-0.43%	-1.17%	-1.68%	-1.80%	-1.28%	-1.81%	-1.93%	-1.33%	-1.88%	-2.02%
Marginal Costs	3.85%	4.20%	4.22%	3.87%	4.23%	4.26%	-6.25%	-5.38%	-4.87%	-3.53%	-2.64%	-2.10%	-3.35%	-2.37%	-1.73%
Producer Prices	3.86%	4.21%	4.23%	3.88%	4.23%	4.27%	-6.22%	-5.35%	-4.83%	-3.50%	-2.60%	-2.06%	-3.32%	-2.33%	-1.70%
Mark-ups domestic (abs. diff.)	0.00%	0.00%	0.00%	0.00%	0.00%	0.00%	0.03%	0.03%	0.04%	0.03%	0.04%	0.04%	0.03%	0.04%	0.04%
Fixed Costs per firm	3.83%	4.18%	4.20%	3.84%	4.19%	4.22%	-6.23%	-5.42%	-4.97%	-3.53%	-2.69%	-2.23%	-3.39%	-2.49%	-1.96%
Number of Firms	0.13%	0.48%	0.48%	0.15%	0.51%	0.50%	1.36%	2.42%	2.31%	1.32%	2.37%	2.27%	1.31%	2.37%	2.26%
Sigma of Love of Variety	0.00%	0.00%	0.00%	0.00%	0.00%	0.00%	0.00%	0.00%	0.00%	0.00%	0.00%	0.00%	0.00%	0.00%	0.00%

Electrical goods

	Border Controls			Border controls and x-ineff.			Market segmentation			Trade *antimonde*			Full *antimonde*		
	1988	1991	1994	1988	1991	1994	1988	1991	1994	1988	1991	1994	1988	1991	1994
Production per firm	-0.66%	-1.51%	-1.52%	-0.67%	-1.51%	-1.52%	-3.26%	-5.58%	-5.70%	-3.64%	-6.04%	-6.16%	-3.73%	-6.16%	-6.32%
Marginal Costs	3.79%	4.12%	4.15%	3.80%	4.15%	4.18%	-5.94%	-5.13%	-4.65%	-3.23%	-2.38%	-1.88%	-3.05%	-2.12%	-1.52%
Producer Prices	3.82%	4.19%	4.21%	3.83%	4.22%	4.25%	-5.80%	-4.89%	-4.41%	-3.07%	-2.11%	-1.61%	-2.89%	-1.85%	-1.25%
Mark-ups domestic (abs. diff.)	0.02%	0.04%	0.04%	0.02%	0.04%	0.04%	0.25%	0.33%	0.33%	0.25%	0.34%	0.34%	0.26%	0.34%	0.35%
Fixed Costs per firm	3.76%	4.10%	4.12%	3.77%	4.11%	4.14%	-5.90%	-5.14%	-4.73%	-3.20%	-2.41%	-1.99%	-3.08%	-2.22%	-1.73%
Number of Firms	0.08%	0.77%	0.75%	0.09%	0.80%	0.77%	5.34%	8.84%	8.67%	5.08%	8.52%	8.36%	5.00%	8.41%	8.21%
Sigma of Love of Variety	0.00%	0.00%	0.00%	0.00%	0.00%	0.00%	0.00%	0.00%	0.00%	0.00%	0.00%	0.00%	0.00%	0.00%	0.00%

Transport equipment

	Border Controls			Border controls and x-ineff.			Market segmentation			Trade *antimonde*			Full *antimonde*		
	1988	1991	1994	1988	1991	1994	1988	1991	1994	1988	1991	1994	1988	1991	1994
Production per firm	-0.47%	-1.14%	-1.15%	-0.47%	-1.14%	-1.15%	-7.70%	-10.69%	-10.75%	-7.85%	-10.86%	-10.92%	-7.92%	-10.95%	-11.04%
Marginal Costs	3.80%	4.16%	4.18%	3.82%	4.18%	4.22%	-5.86%	-5.05%	-4.62%	-3.13%	-2.26%	-1.82%	-2.95%	-1.99%	-1.45%
Producer Prices	3.83%	4.21%	4.24%	3.84%	4.24%	4.27%	-5.48%	-4.50%	-4.07%	-2.72%	-1.69%	-1.24%	-2.54%	-1.42%	-0.88%
Mark-ups domestic (abs. diff.)	0.01%	0.04%	0.04%	0.01%	0.04%	0.04%	0.85%	1.08%	1.08%	0.84%	1.07%	1.08%	0.85%	1.08%	1.08%
Fixed Costs per firm	3.80%	4.15%	4.17%	3.81%	4.17%	4.20%	-5.87%	-5.05%	-4.64%	-3.14%	-2.28%	-1.85%	-3.00%	-2.08%	-1.58%
Number of Firms	0.75%	2.05%	2.03%	0.76%	2.08%	2.06%	10.57%	20.00%	20.07%	10.64%	20.10%	20.18%	10.61%	20.07%	20.14%
Sigma of Love of Variety	0.00%	0.00%	0.00%	0.00%	0.00%	0.00%	0.00%	0.00%	0.00%	0.00%	0.00%	0.00%	0.00%	0.00%	0.00%

Other Equipment

	Border Controls			Border controls and x-ineff.			Market segmentation			Trade *antimonde*			Full *antimonde*		
	1988	1991	1994	1988	1991	1994	1988	1991	1994	1988	1991	1994	1988	1991	1994
Production per firm	-0.68%	-1.29%	-1.29%	-0.69%	-1.29%	-1.30%	-4.20%	-6.02%	-6.14%	-4.68%	-6.55%	-6.67%	-4.76%	-6.65%	-6.81%
Marginal Costs	3.80%	4.15%	4.17%	3.82%	4.17%	4.21%	-6.06%	-5.23%	-4.75%	-3.35%	-2.49%	-1.98%	-3.17%	-2.22%	-1.62%
Producer Prices	3.81%	4.17%	4.19%	3.83%	4.19%	4.23%	-6.00%	-5.14%	-4.66%	-3.28%	-2.39%	-1.88%	-3.10%	-2.12%	-1.52%
Mark-ups domestic (abs. diff.)	0.01%	0.01%	0.01%	0.01%	0.01%	0.01%	0.13%	0.17%	0.17%	0.14%	0.17%	0.17%	0.14%	0.17%	0.17%
Fixed Costs per firm	3.78%	4.13%	4.15%	3.79%	4.14%	4.17%	-6.04%	-5.25%	-4.83%	-3.34%	-2.53%	-2.08%	-3.21%	-2.33%	-1.82%
Number of Firms	-0.13%	0.27%	0.26%	-0.12%	0.30%	0.28%	5.04%	7.35%	7.13%	4.61%	6.86%	6.64%	4.55%	6.77%	6.52%
Sigma of Love of Variety	0.00%	0.00%	0.00%	0.00%	0.00%	0.00%	0.00%	0.00%	0.00%	0.00%	0.00%	0.00%	0.00%	0.00%	0.00%

Telecommunications

	Border Controls			Border controls and x-ineff.			Market segmentation			Trade *antimonde*			Full *antimonde*		
	1988	1991	1994	1988	1991	1994	1988	1991	1994	1988	1991	1994	1988	1991	1994
Production per firm	0.06%	0.07%	0.06%	-0.50%	-1.14%	-1.15%	-1.95%	-4.08%	-4.31%	-1.91%	-4.05%	-4.27%	-2.48%	-5.13%	-5.38%
Marginal Costs	4.02%	4.38%	4.41%	4.04%	4.41%	4.45%	-6.73%	-5.71%	-5.01%	-3.98%	-2.94%	-2.21%	-3.79%	-2.67%	-1.85%
Producer Prices	4.00%	4.37%	4.39%	3.89%	4.14%	4.18%	-6.41%	-5.02%	-4.33%	-3.65%	-2.25%	-1.53%	-3.60%	-2.24%	-1.43%
Mark-ups domestic (abs. diff.)	-0.02%	-0.01%	-0.02%	-0.19%	-0.37%	-0.37%	0.19%	0.26%	0.25%	0.18%	0.25%	0.23%	0.00%	-0.12%	-0.14%
Fixed Costs per firm	3.98%	4.35%	4.37%	2.70%	1.80%	1.82%	-6.88%	-6.06%	-5.66%	-4.16%	-3.34%	-2.91%	-5.22%	-5.53%	-5.05%
Number of Firms	0.06%	0.04%	0.04%	0.65%	1.27%	1.28%	1.59%	2.71%	2.79%	1.64%	2.76%	2.83%	2.24%	3.97%	4.05%
Sigma of Love of Variety	0.00%	0.00%	0.00%	0.00%	0.00%	0.00%	0.00%	0.00%	0.00%	0.00%	0.00%	0.00%	0.00%	0.00%	0.00%

Banks

	Border Controls			Border controls and x-ineff.			Market segmentation			Trade *antimonde*			Full *antimonde*		
	1988	1991	1994	1988	1991	1994	1988	1991	1994	1988	1991	1994	1988	1991	1994
Production per firm	0.03%	0.05%	0.05%	-0.29%	-0.63%	-0.63%	-1.36%	-2.65%	-2.99%	-1.34%	-2.63%	-2.96%	-1.69%	-3.29%	-3.64%
Marginal Costs	4.01%	4.35%	4.37%	4.03%	4.38%	4.41%	-6.62%	-5.54%	-4.75%	-3.85%	-2.76%	-1.94%	-3.66%	-2.48%	-1.56%
Producer Prices	4.00%	4.35%	4.36%	4.00%	4.33%	4.36%	-6.52%	-5.36%	-4.56%	-3.75%	-2.57%	-1.75%	-3.59%	-2.34%	-1.43%
Mark-ups domestic (abs. diff.)	0.00%	0.00%	0.00%	-0.04%	-0.07%	-0.07%	0.01%	0.02%	0.02%	0.01%	0.02%	0.01%	-0.02%	-0.04%	-0.05%
Fixed Costs per firm	3.95%	4.32%	4.34%	3.33%	3.06%	3.09%	-6.72%	-5.87%	-5.41%	-4.00%	-3.14%	-2.66%	-4.45%	-4.12%	-3.57%
Number of Firms	0.04%	0.02%	0.02%	0.36%	0.66%	0.66%	1.01%	1.33%	1.34%	1.07%	1.38%	1.40%	1.38%	2.02%	2.03%
Sigma of Love of Variety	0.00%	0.00%	0.00%	0.00%	0.00%	0.00%	0.00%	0.00%	0.00%	0.00%	0.00%	0.00%	0.00%	0.00%	0.00%

Table B12.7.
Decomposition of effects: sectoral results for the UK (volumes)

% change from *monde*

Agriculture

	Border Controls			Border controls and x-ineff.			Market segmentation			Trade *antimonde*			Full *antimonde*		
	1988	1991	1994	1988	1991	1994	1988	1991	1994	1988	1991	1994	1988	1991	1994
Domestic Production - vol.	-1.0%	-1.1%	-1.1%	-1.0%	-1.1%	-1.1%	2.9%	1.2%	1.0%	2.1%	0.4%	0.2%	2.0%	0.2%	-0.1%
Imports - vol.	1.7%	2.0%	2.1%	1.7%	2.1%	2.1%	-3.9%	-3.6%	-3.2%	-2.7%	-2.3%	-1.9%	-2.6%	-2.1%	-1.6%
Exports - vol.	-0.7%	-0.8%	-0.8%	-0.7%	-0.8%	-0.8%	1.8%	1.5%	1.2%	1.3%	1.0%	0.8%	1.3%	0.9%	0.7%
Absorption - vol.	-0.1%	0.1%	0.1%	-0.1%	0.1%	0.1%	1.0%	0.3%	0.1%	0.8%	0.1%	0.0%	0.8%	0.0%	-0.1%
Investment - vol.	-0.5%	-0.6%	-0.5%	-0.5%	-0.5%	-0.5%	-2.8%	-3.6%	-3.8%	-3.2%	-4.0%	-4.2%	-3.3%	-4.1%	-4.3%
Labour Demand - vol.	-1.1%	-1.1%	-1.1%	-1.1%	-1.1%	-1.1%	3.3%	1.6%	1.5%	2.5%	0.8%	0.7%	2.4%	0.7%	0.5%
Private Consumption - vol.	0.1%	0.2%	0.2%	0.1%	0.2%	0.2%	-0.8%	-1.0%	-1.1%	-0.7%	-1.0%	-1.1%	-0.8%	-1.0%	-1.2%
Supply to domestic - vol.	-0.9%	-0.4%	-0.4%	-0.9%	-0.4%	-0.4%	3.6%	2.4%	2.0%	2.9%	1.6%	1.3%	2.7%	1.4%	1.0%
Intra-EU Trade - vol	-1.9%	-4.2%	-4.2%	-1.9%	-4.1%	-4.1%	0.8%	-1.0%	-1.1%	-0.6%	-2.7%	-2.8%	-0.8%	-2.9%	-3.0%

Energy

	Border Controls			Border controls and x-ineff.			Market segmentation			Trade *antimonde*			Full *antimonde*		
	1988	1991	1994	1988	1991	1994	1988	1991	1994	1988	1991	1994	1988	1991	1994
Domestic Production - vol.	-0.6%	-1.1%	-1.1%	-0.6%	-1.1%	-1.1%	2.1%	1.4%	0.8%	1.7%	0.9%	0.2%	1.6%	0.7%	0.0%
Imports - vol.	0.8%	0.8%	0.8%	0.8%	0.8%	0.8%	-1.7%	-1.5%	-1.4%	-1.3%	-1.1%	-0.9%	-1.2%	-1.0%	-0.9%
Exports - vol.	-0.3%	-0.4%	-0.4%	-0.3%	-0.4%	-0.4%	0.9%	0.8%	0.6%	0.7%	0.5%	0.4%	0.7%	0.5%	0.4%
Absorption - vol.	-0.2%	-0.4%	-0.4%	-0.2%	-0.4%	-0.4%	0.8%	0.6%	0.2%	0.7%	0.4%	0.0%	0.7%	0.3%	-0.2%
Investment - vol.	-0.3%	-0.5%	-0.5%	-0.3%	-0.5%	-0.5%	-3.2%	-3.5%	-3.8%	-3.4%	-3.7%	-4.0%	-3.4%	-3.8%	-4.1%
Labour Demand - vol.	-0.6%	-1.1%	-1.1%	-0.6%	-1.1%	-1.1%	2.2%	1.6%	1.0%	1.9%	1.1%	0.5%	1.8%	1.0%	0.4%
Private Consumption - vol.	0.1%	0.2%	0.2%	0.1%	0.2%	0.2%	-0.6%	-0.8%	-1.0%	-0.6%	-0.8%	-1.0%	-0.6%	-0.9%	-1.0%
Supply to domestic - vol.	-0.5%	-0.7%	-0.7%	-0.5%	-0.7%	-0.7%	1.7%	1.2%	0.7%	1.4%	0.9%	0.4%	1.3%	0.7%	0.2%
Intra-EU Trade - vol	-0.6%	-1.2%	-1.2%	-0.6%	-1.2%	-1.2%	1.7%	1.0%	0.4%	1.5%	0.4%	-0.2%	1.4%	0.3%	-0.4%

Metal Industries

	Border Controls			Border controls and x-ineff.			Market segmentation			Trade *antimonde*			Full *antimonde*		
	1988	1991	1994	1988	1991	1994	1988	1991	1994	1988	1991	1994	1988	1991	1994
Domestic Production - vol.	-1.2%	-1.7%	-1.7%	-1.2%	-1.6%	-1.7%	6.0%	8.8%	7.9%	4.7%	7.4%	6.5%	4.6%	7.1%	6.2%
Imports - vol.	1.0%	1.2%	1.2%	1.0%	1.2%	1.2%	-3.7%	-2.8%	-2.7%	-2.4%	-1.3%	-1.3%	-2.2%	-1.1%	-1.0%
Exports - vol.	-0.6%	-0.7%	-0.7%	-0.6%	-0.7%	-0.7%	1.8%	1.5%	1.3%	1.4%	1.1%	0.9%	1.3%	1.0%	0.8%
Absorption - vol.	-0.4%	-0.4%	-0.5%	-0.4%	-0.4%	-0.4%	1.7%	3.1%	2.8%	1.2%	2.5%	2.1%	1.1%	2.4%	2.0%
Investment - vol.	-0.6%	-0.8%	-0.8%	-0.6%	-0.8%	-0.8%	-1.4%	-0.1%	-0.6%	-2.0%	-0.8%	-1.2%	-2.1%	-0.9%	-1.3%
Labour Demand - vol.	-1.2%	-1.6%	-1.6%	-1.2%	-1.6%	-1.6%	6.4%	9.5%	8.7%	5.2%	8.1%	7.2%	5.1%	7.9%	7.0%
Private Consumption - vol.	0.1%	0.1%	0.1%	0.1%	0.1%	0.1%	-0.3%	-0.4%	-0.5%	-0.3%	-0.4%	-0.5%	-0.3%	-0.4%	-0.5%
Supply to domestic - vol.	-0.5%	0.6%	0.5%	-0.5%	0.6%	0.5%	8.0%	16.2%	15.1%	7.1%	15.2%	14.1%	6.9%	15.0%	13.8%
Intra-EU Trade - vol	-1.8%	-3.5%	-3.6%	-1.8%	-3.5%	-3.6%	0.9%	-4.1%	-4.2%	-1.1%	-6.3%	-6.4%	-1.3%	-6.5%	-6.7%

Chemical

	Border Controls			Border controls and x-ineff.			Market segmentation			Trade *antimonde*			Full *antimonde*		
	1988	1991	1994	1988	1991	1994	1988	1991	1994	1988	1991	1994	1988	1991	1994
Domestic Production - vol.	-0.1%	-0.4%	-0.4%	-0.1%	-0.4%	-0.4%	4.1%	3.9%	3.2%	4.2%	3.9%	3.2%	4.0%	3.7%	2.9%
Imports - vol.	0.9%	1.2%	1.2%	0.9%	1.2%	1.2%	-4.6%	-4.3%	-4.0%	-3.6%	-3.1%	-2.9%	-3.4%	-2.8%	-2.5%
Exports - vol.	-0.3%	-0.4%	-0.4%	-0.3%	-0.4%	-0.4%	1.8%	1.5%	1.3%	1.7%	1.5%	1.3%	1.7%	1.4%	1.1%
Absorption - vol.	-0.1%	-0.1%	-0.1%	-0.1%	-0.1%	-0.1%	1.4%	1.2%	0.9%	1.3%	1.1%	0.8%	1.2%	1.0%	0.7%
Investment - vol.	0.0%	-0.2%	-0.2%	0.0%	-0.2%	-0.2%	-2.3%	-2.4%	-2.7%	-2.2%	-2.4%	-2.7%	-2.3%	-2.4%	-2.8%
Labour Demand - vol.	-0.1%	-0.4%	-0.4%	-0.1%	-0.4%	-0.4%	4.4%	4.4%	3.7%	4.5%	4.4%	3.8%	4.4%	4.2%	3.6%
Private Consumption - vol.	0.1%	0.2%	0.2%	0.1%	0.2%	0.2%	-0.8%	-1.0%	-1.2%	-0.7%	-1.1%	-1.3%	-0.8%	-1.1%	-1.4%
Supply to domestic - vol.	0.8%	2.3%	2.3%	0.8%	2.3%	2.3%	5.7%	8.9%	8.2%	5.9%	9.2%	8.4%	5.7%	9.0%	8.2%
Intra-EU Trade - vol	-1.3%	-3.3%	-3.3%	-1.3%	-3.3%	-3.3%	0.5%	-3.1%	-3.4%	-0.1%	-4.0%	-4.2%	-0.2%	-4.2%	-4.5%

Other Intensive Industries

	Border Controls			Border controls and x-ineff.			Market segmentation			Trade *antimonde*			Full *antimonde*		
	1988	1991	1994	1988	1991	1994	1988	1991	1994	1988	1991	1994	1988	1991	1994
Domestic Production - vol.	-0.1%	0.1%	0.0%	-0.1%	0.1%	0.1%	0.2%	0.7%	0.5%	0.0%	0.5%	0.3%	0.0%	0.4%	0.2%
Imports - vol.	1.8%	2.2%	2.2%	1.8%	2.2%	2.2%	-7.4%	-6.8%	-6.5%	-5.7%	-4.9%	-4.5%	-5.4%	-4.5%	-4.0%
Exports - vol.	-0.6%	-0.7%	-0.7%	-0.6%	-0.7%	-0.7%	2.0%	1.7%	1.5%	1.7%	1.4%	1.2%	1.6%	1.3%	1.1%
Absorption - vol.	0.0%	0.1%	0.1%	0.0%	0.1%	0.1%	-1.3%	-1.0%	-1.1%	-1.4%	-1.1%	-1.3%	-1.4%	-1.1%	-1.3%
Investment - vol.	0.0%	0.1%	0.1%	0.0%	0.1%	0.1%	-4.2%	-3.9%	-4.1%	-4.2%	-4.0%	-4.1%	-4.2%	-4.0%	-4.1%
Labour Demand - vol.	-0.1%	0.0%	0.0%	-0.1%	0.1%	0.1%	0.3%	0.9%	0.7%	0.2%	0.7%	0.5%	0.2%	0.7%	0.5%
Private Consumption - vol.	0.4%	0.3%	0.2%	0.4%	0.3%	0.2%	-1.9%	-1.1%	-1.1%	-1.9%	-1.1%	-1.1%	-1.9%	-1.2%	-1.2%
Supply to domestic - vol.	0.1%	0.6%	0.6%	0.1%	0.7%	0.6%	0.2%	1.2%	1.0%	0.1%	1.1%	0.9%	0.0%	1.1%	0.8%
Intra-EU Trade - vol	-1.8%	-4.1%	-4.1%	-1.8%	-4.1%	-4.1%	-1.4%	-4.8%	-4.9%	-2.7%	-6.3%	-6.4%	-2.8%	-6.4%	-6.6%

Electrical goods

	Border Controls			Border controls and x-ineff.			Market segmentation			Trade antimonde			Full antimonde		
	1988	1991	1994	1988	1991	1994	1988	1991	1994	1988	1991	1994	1988	1991	1994
Domestic Production - vol.	-0.6%	-0.7%	-0.8%	-0.6%	-0.7%	-0.8%	1.9%	2.8%	2.5%	1.3%	2.0%	1.7%	1.1%	1.7%	1.4%
Imports - vol.	1.4%	1.6%	1.6%	1.4%	1.6%	1.6%	-6.5%	-5.7%	-5.5%	-5.2%	-4.4%	-4.2%	-5.1%	-4.1%	-3.8%
Exports - vol.	-0.6%	-0.7%	-0.7%	-0.6%	-0.7%	-0.7%	2.2%	1.9%	1.7%	1.9%	1.6%	1.4%	1.8%	1.5%	1.3%
Absorption - vol.	0.0%	0.0%	-0.1%	0.0%	0.0%	-0.1%	-2.6%	-1.7%	-1.9%	-2.7%	-2.0%	-2.2%	-2.8%	-2.1%	-2.2%
Investment - vol.	-0.3%	-0.3%	-0.4%	-0.3%	-0.3%	-0.4%	-3.3%	-3.0%	-3.2%	-3.6%	-3.4%	-3.5%	-3.7%	-3.4%	-3.6%
Labour Demand - vol.	-0.6%	-0.8%	-0.8%	-0.6%	-0.7%	-0.8%	2.5%	3.5%	3.2%	1.8%	2.7%	2.5%	1.7%	2.5%	2.3%
Private Consumption - vol.	0.9%	0.6%	0.3%	0.9%	0.6%	0.3%	-4.6%	-1.9%	-1.9%	-4.5%	-2.0%	-1.9%	-4.6%	-2.2%	-2.1%
Supply to domestic - vol.	0.1%	1.3%	1.2%	0.1%	1.3%	1.3%	2.4%	6.5%	6.0%	2.1%	6.0%	5.6%	1.9%	5.8%	5.3%
Intra-EU Trade - vol	-1.9%	-4.1%	-4.2%	-1.9%	-4.1%	-4.2%	-0.5%	-4.8%	-5.0%	-2.2%	-6.8%	-6.9%	-2.4%	-7.0%	-7.2%

Transport equipment

	Border Controls			Border controls and x-ineff.			Market segmentation			Trade antimonde			Full antimonde		
	1988	1991	1994	1988	1991	1994	1988	1991	1994	1988	1991	1994	1988	1991	1994
Domestic Production - vol.	0.3%	0.9%	0.9%	0.3%	0.9%	0.9%	2.1%	7.2%	7.2%	1.9%	7.1%	7.1%	1.8%	6.9%	6.9%
Imports - vol.	1.4%	1.7%	1.7%	1.4%	1.7%	1.8%	-7.5%	-6.9%	-6.8%	-5.7%	-4.9%	-4.7%	-5.5%	-4.6%	-4.3%
Exports - vol.	-0.6%	-0.7%	-0.7%	-0.6%	-0.7%	-0.8%	2.2%	2.0%	1.8%	1.9%	1.6%	1.5%	1.8%	1.5%	1.3%
Absorption - vol.	0.2%	0.3%	0.2%	0.2%	0.3%	0.2%	-3.6%	-2.7%	-2.8%	-3.5%	-2.7%	-2.8%	-3.6%	-2.7%	-2.8%
Investment - vol.	0.1%	0.5%	0.5%	0.1%	0.5%	0.5%	-3.0%	-0.7%	-0.8%	-3.1%	-0.7%	-0.8%	-3.1%	-0.8%	-0.9%
Labour Demand - vol.	0.2%	0.9%	0.9%	0.2%	0.9%	0.9%	2.9%	8.3%	8.3%	2.8%	8.2%	8.2%	2.8%	8.1%	8.1%
Private Consumption - vol.	0.6%	0.4%	0.2%	0.6%	0.4%	0.3%	-3.5%	-1.5%	-1.2%	-3.5%	-1.6%	-1.3%	-3.6%	-1.7%	-1.4%
Supply to domestic - vol.	1.3%	3.3%	3.3%	1.3%	3.4%	3.3%	1.8%	11.8%	11.9%	2.0%	12.1%	12.2%	2.0%	12.0%	12.0%
Intra-EU Trade - vol	-1.4%	-2.7%	-2.7%	-1.4%	-2.7%	-2.7%	-2.4%	-7.0%	-7.1%	-3.4%	-8.1%	-8.2%	-3.5%	-8.3%	-8.4%

Other Equipment

	Border Controls			Border controls and x-ineff.			Market segmentation			Trade antimonde			Full antimonde		
	1988	1991	1994	1988	1991	1994	1988	1991	1994	1988	1991	1994	1988	1991	1994
Domestic Production - vol.	-0.8%	-1.0%	-1.0%	-0.8%	-1.0%	-1.0%	0.6%	0.9%	0.6%	-0.3%	-0.1%	-0.5%	-0.4%	-0.3%	-0.7%
Imports - vol.	1.3%	1.5%	1.5%	1.3%	1.5%	1.6%	-6.3%	-6.0%	-5.9%	-4.6%	-4.1%	-4.0%	-4.4%	-3.9%	-3.7%
Exports - vol.	-0.8%	-0.9%	-0.9%	-0.8%	-0.9%	-0.9%	2.2%	1.9%	1.7%	1.8%	1.4%	1.3%	1.7%	1.3%	1.1%
Absorption - vol.	-0.1%	-0.2%	-0.2%	-0.1%	-0.2%	-0.2%	-3.6%	-3.5%	-3.8%	-3.8%	-3.8%	-4.0%	-3.9%	-3.8%	-4.1%
Investment - vol.	-0.4%	-0.5%	-0.5%	-0.4%	-0.5%	-0.5%	-4.0%	-3.9%	-4.1%	-4.4%	-4.4%	-4.6%	-4.4%	-4.4%	-4.7%
Labour Demand - vol.	-0.9%	-1.1%	-1.1%	-0.8%	-1.0%	-1.1%	1.1%	1.4%	1.1%	0.2%	0.4%	0.1%	0.1%	0.3%	0.0%
Private Consumption - vol.	0.4%	0.3%	0.3%	0.3%	0.3%	0.3%	-1.8%	-1.5%	-1.7%	-1.8%	-1.5%	-1.7%	-1.9%	-1.6%	-1.8%
Supply to domestic - vol.	0.1%	1.4%	1.4%	0.1%	1.4%	1.4%	0.2%	2.8%	2.4%	-0.2%	2.4%	2.0%	-0.4%	2.3%	1.8%
Intra-EU Trade - vol	-1.5%	-3.2%	-3.2%	-1.5%	-3.2%	-3.2%	-1.2%	-3.7%	-3.8%	-2.8%	-5.5%	-5.6%	-2.9%	-5.7%	-5.9%

Consumer goods

	Border Controls			Border controls and x-ineff.			Market segmentation			Trade antimonde			Full antimonde		
	1988	1991	1994	1988	1991	1994	1988	1991	1994	1988	1991	1994	1988	1991	1994
Domestic Production - vol.	0.0%	0.3%	0.3%	0.0%	0.3%	0.3%	1.5%	0.8%	0.6%	1.4%	0.7%	0.5%	1.3%	0.5%	0.3%
Imports - vol.	1.5%	1.8%	1.9%	1.5%	1.9%	1.9%	-5.1%	-4.6%	-4.2%	-4.2%	-3.7%	-3.3%	-4.1%	-3.4%	-3.0%
Exports - vol.	-0.6%	-0.8%	-0.8%	-0.7%	-0.8%	-0.8%	2.4%	2.1%	1.8%	2.1%	1.7%	1.5%	2.0%	1.6%	1.3%
Absorption - vol.	0.0%	0.1%	0.2%	0.1%	0.2%	0.2%	-0.5%	-0.8%	-0.9%	-0.5%	-0.8%	-0.9%	-0.6%	-0.8%	-1.0%
Investment - vol.	0.0%	0.1%	0.1%	0.0%	0.1%	0.2%	-3.5%	-3.9%	-4.0%	-3.6%	-4.0%	-4.1%	-3.6%	-4.0%	-4.2%
Labour Demand - vol.	-0.1%	0.2%	0.2%	-0.1%	0.3%	0.3%	1.9%	1.1%	1.1%	1.7%	1.1%	1.0%	1.7%	1.0%	0.9%
Private Consumption - vol.	0.1%	0.2%	0.2%	0.1%	0.2%	0.2%	-0.7%	-0.9%	-1.0%	-0.7%	-0.9%	-1.1%	-0.7%	-1.0%	-1.1%
Supply to domestic - vol.	0.3%	1.2%	1.2%	0.3%	1.2%	1.2%	1.4%	1.2%	1.0%	1.4%	1.1%	1.0%	1.3%	1.0%	0.8%
Intra-EU Trade - vol	-2.0%	-4.4%	-4.4%	-2.0%	-4.4%	-4.4%	0.3%	-1.3%	-1.6%	-0.4%	-2.2%	-2.5%	-0.5%	-2.3%	-2.6%

Construction

	Border Controls			Border controls and x-ineff.			Market segmentation			Trade antimonde			Full antimonde		
	1988	1991	1994	1988	1991	1994	1988	1991	1994	1988	1991	1994	1988	1991	1994
Domestic Production - vol.	0.1%	0.1%	#VALUE!	0.1%	0.1%	#VALUE!	-6.9%	-7.2%	#VALUE!	-6.8%	-7.1%	#VALUE!	-6.8%	-7.1%	#VALUE!
Imports - vol.	-0.3%	-0.3%	-0.3%	-0.3%	-0.3%	-0.3%	0.7%	0.6%	0.5%	0.5%	0.4%	0.3%	0.5%	0.3%	0.3%
Exports - vol.	0.1%	0.1%	0.1%	0.1%	0.1%	0.1%	-6.9%	-7.2%	-7.4%	-6.9%	-7.1%	-7.3%	-6.9%	-7.1%	-7.3%
Absorption - vol.	0.1%	0.1%	0.1%	0.1%	0.1%	0.1%	-7.6%	-7.8%	-7.9%	-7.6%	-7.8%	-7.9%	-7.6%	-7.7%	-7.8%
Investment - vol.	0.1%	0.1%	0.1%	0.1%	0.1%	0.2%	-6.7%	-7.0%	-7.1%	-6.7%	-6.9%	-7.0%	-6.6%	-6.8%	-6.8%
Labour Demand - vol.	0.1%	0.2%	0.2%	0.1%	0.2%	0.2%	-0.7%	-0.9%	-1.2%	-0.7%	-0.9%	-1.2%	-0.7%	-1.0%	-1.3%
Private Consumption - vol.	0.1%	0.2%	0.1%	0.1%	0.2%	0.2%	-6.9%	-7.2%	-7.4%	-6.8%	-7.1%	-7.3%	-6.8%	-7.1%	-7.3%
Supply to domestic - vol.	0.1%	0.1%	0.1%	0.1%	0.1%	0.1%	-6.9%	-7.2%	-7.4%	-6.8%	-7.1%	-7.3%	-6.8%	-7.1%	-7.3%
Intra-EU Trade - vol	0.6%	0.6%	0.6%	0.6%	0.6%	0.6%	-3.5%	-3.6%	-3.7%	-3.0%	-3.1%	-3.2%	-3.0%	-3.1%	-3.2%

Telecommunications

	Border Controls			Border controls and x-ineff.			Market segmentation			Trade antimonde			Full antimonde		
	1988	1991	1994	1988	1991	1994	1988	1991	1994	1988	1991	1994	1988	1991	1994
Domestic Production - vol.	0.1%	0.1%	0.1%	0.1%	0.1%	0.1%	-0.4%	-1.5%	-1.6%	-0.3%	-1.4%	-1.6%	-0.3%	-1.4%	-1.5%
Imports - vol.	0.9%	1.1%	1.1%	0.8%	1.0%	1.0%	-5.8%	-5.6%	-5.3%	-5.4%	-5.2%	-4.9%	-5.3%	-5.1%	-4.8%
Exports - vol.	-0.2%	-0.3%	-0.3%	-0.2%	-0.3%	-0.3%	1.1%	0.9%	0.8%	1.0%	0.9%	0.8%	1.0%	0.8%	0.7%
Absorption - vol.	0.1%	0.1%	0.1%	0.1%	0.2%	0.2%	-0.5%	-0.8%	-0.9%	-0.4%	-0.7%	-0.9%	-0.4%	-0.7%	-0.9%
Investment - vol.	0.1%	0.1%	0.1%	0.1%	0.1%	0.1%	-4.4%	-4.9%	-5.0%	-4.4%	-4.9%	-4.9%	-4.3%	-4.8%	-4.8%
Labour Demand - vol.	0.1%	0.1%	0.1%	-0.2%	-0.6%	-0.6%	0.2%	-0.3%	-0.3%	0.3%	-0.2%	-0.2%	0.0%	-0.8%	-0.9%
Private Consumption - vol.	0.1%	0.2%	0.2%	0.2%	0.3%	0.3%	-0.9%	-1.1%	-1.4%	-0.8%	-1.1%	-1.4%	-0.9%	-1.2%	-1.4%
Supply to domestic - vol.	0.0%	0.0%	0.0%	0.1%	0.2%	0.2%	0.5%	1.2%	1.1%	0.5%	1.3%	1.1%	0.5%	1.3%	1.1%
Intra-EU Trade - vol	0.5%	0.4%	0.4%	0.2%	-0.6%	-0.6%	-7.8%	-18.7%	-18.8%	-7.5%	-18.5%	-18.6%	-7.6%	-18.6%	-18.7%

Transports

	Border Controls			Border controls and x-ineff.			Market segmentation			Trade antimonde			Full antimonde		
	1988	1991	1994	1988	1991	1994	1988	1991	1994	1988	1991	1994	1988	1991	1994
Domestic Production - vol.	0.1%	0.1%	0.1%	0.1%	0.1%	0.2%	0.1%	0.0%	-0.2%	0.2%	0.1%	-0.1%	0.2%	0.1%	-0.1%
Imports - vol.	0.0%	0.1%	0.1%	0.1%	0.1%	0.1%	0.1%	0.0%	-0.1%	0.1%	0.1%	0.0%	0.1%	0.0%	-0.1%
Exports - vol.	-0.1%	-0.2%	-0.2%	-0.1%	-0.2%	-0.2%	0.7%	0.6%	0.5%	0.6%	0.5%	0.5%	0.6%	0.5%	0.4%
Absorption - vol.	0.0%	0.0%	0.0%	0.0%	0.0%	0.0%	-0.1%	-0.2%	-0.5%	-0.2%	-0.3%	-0.5%	-0.2%	-0.3%	-0.6%
Investment - vol.	0.1%	0.1%	0.1%	0.1%	0.1%	0.1%	-4.2%	-4.2%	-4.3%	-4.1%	-4.2%	-4.3%	-4.1%	-4.2%	-4.3%
Labour Demand - vol.	0.1%	0.1%	0.1%	0.1%	0.1%	0.1%	0.2%	0.2%	0.0%	0.3%	0.3%	0.1%	0.4%	0.3%	0.1%
Private Consumption - vol.	0.2%	0.3%	0.3%	0.2%	0.3%	0.3%	-0.8%	-1.1%	-1.3%	-0.8%	-1.1%	-1.3%	-0.9%	-1.2%	-1.4%
Supply to domestic - vol.	0.1%	0.1%	0.1%	0.1%	0.1%	0.2%	0.1%	0.0%	-0.2%	0.2%	0.1%	-0.1%	0.2%	0.1%	-0.1%
Intra-EU Trade - vol	0.4%	0.4%	0.4%	0.4%	0.4%	0.4%	0.0%	0.0%	-0.1%	0.4%	0.4%	0.3%	0.4%	0.4%	0.3%

Banks

	Border Controls			Border controls and x-ineff.			Market segmentation			Trade antimonde			Full antimonde		
	1988	1991	1994	1988	1991	1994	1988	1991	1994	1988	1991	1994	1988	1991	1994
Domestic Production - vol.	0.1%	0.1%	0.1%	0.1%	0.0%	0.0%	-0.4%	-1.4%	-1.7%	-0.3%	-1.3%	-1.6%	-0.3%	-1.3%	-1.7%
Imports - vol.	1.0%	1.3%	1.3%	1.0%	1.3%	1.3%	-6.7%	-6.2%	-5.8%	-6.0%	-5.6%	-5.2%	-5.8%	-5.2%	-4.7%
Exports - vol.	-0.2%	-0.3%	-0.3%	-0.2%	-0.3%	-0.3%	1.0%	0.9%	0.7%	1.0%	0.8%	0.7%	1.0%	0.8%	0.6%
Absorption - vol.	0.0%	0.0%	0.0%	0.0%	0.0%	0.0%	0.0%	-0.2%	-0.4%	0.0%	-0.2%	-0.5%	-0.1%	-0.3%	-0.5%
Investment - vol.	0.1%	0.1%	0.1%	0.1%	0.1%	0.1%	-4.4%	-4.8%	-5.0%	-4.3%	-4.8%	-4.9%	-4.3%	-4.8%	-4.9%
Labour Demand - vol.	0.1%	0.1%	0.1%	-0.1%	-0.3%	-0.3%	0.0%	-0.8%	-1.0%	0.0%	-0.7%	-0.9%	-0.1%	-1.0%	-1.2%
Private Consumption - vol.	0.2%	0.2%	0.3%	0.2%	0.2%	0.3%	-0.9%	-1.2%	-1.4%	-0.8%	-1.2%	-1.4%	-0.9%	-1.2%	-1.5%
Supply to domestic - vol.	0.0%	0.0%	0.0%	0.0%	0.0%	0.0%	0.2%	0.3%	0.0%	0.2%	0.2%	-0.1%	0.2%	0.2%	-0.1%
Intra-EU Trade - vol	1.0%	0.9%	0.9%	0.8%	0.5%	0.5%	-6.1%	-13.4%	-13.6%	-5.2%	-12.5%	-12.7%	-5.3%	-12.6%	-12.8%

Services

	Border Controls			Border controls and x-ineff.			Market segmentation			Trade antimonde			Full antimonde		
	1988	1991	1994	1988	1991	1994	1988	1991	1994	1988	1991	1994	1988	1991	1994
Domestic Production - vol.	0.3%	0.3%	0.3%	0.3%	0.3%	0.3%	-0.9%	-1.1%	-1.2%	-0.6%	-0.8%	-1.0%	-0.7%	-0.9%	-1.0%
Imports - vol.	1.8%	2.0%	2.0%	1.8%	2.1%	2.1%	-4.6%	-4.0%	-3.7%	-3.3%	-2.7%	-2.5%	-3.2%	-2.6%	-2.2%
Exports - vol.	-0.6%	-0.6%	-0.6%	-0.6%	-0.6%	-0.7%	1.4%	1.2%	1.1%	1.0%	0.8%	0.7%	1.0%	0.8%	0.6%
Absorption - vol.	0.1%	0.1%	0.1%	0.1%	0.2%	0.1%	-1.0%	-1.0%	-1.2%	-1.0%	-1.0%	-1.2%	-1.0%	-1.1%	-1.3%
Investment - vol.	0.2%	0.2%	0.2%	0.2%	0.2%	0.2%	-4.6%	-4.7%	-4.8%	-4.5%	-4.6%	-4.7%	-4.5%	-4.6%	-4.7%
Labour Demand - vol.	0.3%	0.3%	0.3%	0.3%	0.3%	0.3%	-0.7%	-0.9%	-0.9%	-0.5%	-0.6%	-0.6%	-0.5%	-0.6%	-0.6%
Private Consumption - vol.	0.2%	0.2%	0.2%	0.2%	0.2%	0.2%	-1.1%	-1.1%	-1.2%	-1.0%	-1.1%	-1.2%	-1.1%	-1.2%	-1.3%
Supply to domestic - vol.	0.1%	0.1%	0.1%	0.1%	0.1%	0.1%	-1.1%	-1.2%	-1.4%	-1.1%	-1.3%	-1.4%	-1.1%	-1.3%	-1.5%
Intra-EU Trade - vol	2.1%	2.7%	2.7%	2.1%	2.7%	2.7%	-0.3%	0.4%	0.3%	1.8%	2.9%	2.9%	1.8%	2.9%	2.9%

Non market

	Border Controls			Border controls and x-ineff.			Market segmentation			Trade antimonde			Full antimonde		
	1988	1991	1994	1988	1991	1994	1988	1991	1994	1988	1991	1994	1988	1991	1994
Domestic Production - vol.	0.1%	0.1%	0.1%	0.1%	0.1%	0.1%	-0.3%	-0.4%	-0.4%	-0.3%	-0.4%	-0.4%	-0.3%	-0.4%	-0.5%
Imports - vol.	0.0%	0.0%	0.0%	0.0%	0.0%	0.0%	-0.2%	-0.2%	-0.2%	-0.2%	-0.2%	-0.2%	-0.2%	-0.2%	-0.2%
Exports - vol.	-0.1%	-0.2%	-0.2%	-0.1%	-0.2%	-0.2%	0.3%	0.3%	0.3%	0.3%	0.2%	0.2%	0.2%	0.2%	0.2%
Absorption - vol.	0.1%	0.1%	0.1%	0.1%	0.1%	0.1%	-0.3%	-0.4%	-0.4%	-0.3%	-0.4%	-0.4%	-0.3%	-0.4%	-0.5%
Investment - vol.	0.0%	0.0%	0.0%	0.0%	0.0%	0.0%	-4.2%	-4.3%	-4.3%	-4.2%	-4.2%	-4.3%	-4.2%	-4.2%	-4.2%
Labour Demand - vol.	0.0%	0.1%	0.1%	0.0%	0.0%	0.1%	-0.2%	-0.3%	-0.3%	-0.2%	-0.3%	-0.3%	-0.2%	-0.2%	-0.2%
Private Consumption - vol.	0.2%	0.2%	0.2%	0.1%	0.2%	0.2%	-1.0%	-1.1%	-1.2%	-1.0%	-1.1%	-1.2%	-1.0%	-1.1%	-1.3%
Supply to domestic - vol.	0.1%	0.1%	0.1%	0.1%	0.1%	0.1%	-0.3%	-0.4%	-0.4%	-0.3%	-0.4%	-0.4%	-0.3%	-0.4%	-0.5%
Intra-EU Trade - vol	0.2%	0.2%	0.2%	0.2%	0.2%	0.2%	-0.1%	-0.1%	-0.2%	0.1%	0.1%	0.1%	0.1%	0.1%	0.1%

Table B12.8.
Decomposition of effects: sectoral results for the UK (prices)

% change from *monde*

Agriculture

	Border Controls			Border controls and x-ineff.			Market segmentation			Trade *antimonde*			Full *antimonde*		
	1988	1991	1994	1988	1991	1994	1988	1991	1994	1988	1991	1994	1988	1991	1994
Marginal Costs	-0.34%	-0.42%	-0.42%	-0.34%	-0.41%	-0.41%	1.30%	1.18%	1.20%	1.24%	1.15%	1.16%	1.24%	1.15%	1.16%
Cost of Labour	0.04%	0.08%	0.08%	0.03%	0.06%	0.06%	-0.60%	-0.85%	-1.19%	-0.64%	-0.90%	-1.26%	-0.74%	-1.04%	-1.45%
Deflator of Absorption	-0.87%	-1.01%	-1.01%	-0.87%	-1.01%	-1.02%	2.59%	2.26%	2.12%	2.28%	1.99%	1.84%	2.24%	1.92%	1.75%
Price of Exports-RW	-0.34%	-0.42%	-0.42%	-0.34%	-0.41%	-0.41%	1.30%	1.18%	1.20%	1.24%	1.15%	1.16%	1.24%	1.15%	1.16%

Energy

	Border Controls			Border controls and x-ineff.			Market segmentation			Trade *antimonde*			Full *antimonde*		
	1988	1991	1994	1988	1991	1994	1988	1991	1994	1988	1991	1994	1988	1991	1994
Marginal Costs	-0.28%	-0.36%	-0.37%	-0.27%	-0.34%	-0.35%	0.97%	0.99%	1.18%	0.90%	0.93%	1.12%	0.87%	0.90%	1.07%
Cost of Labour	0.04%	0.08%	0.08%	0.03%	0.06%	0.06%	-0.60%	-0.85%	-1.19%	-0.64%	-0.90%	-1.26%	-0.74%	-1.04%	-1.45%
Deflator of Absorption	-0.65%	-0.77%	-0.78%	-0.65%	-0.77%	-0.78%	1.94%	1.78%	1.83%	1.69%	1.54%	1.59%	1.64%	1.47%	1.49%
Price of Exports-RW	-0.28%	-0.36%	-0.37%	-0.27%	-0.34%	-0.35%	0.97%	0.99%	1.18%	0.90%	0.93%	1.12%	0.87%	0.90%	1.07%

Metal Industries

	Border Controls			Border controls and x-ineff.			Market segmentation			Trade *antimonde*			Full *antimonde*		
	1988	1991	1994	1988	1991	1994	1988	1991	1994	1988	1991	1994	1988	1991	1994
Marginal Costs	-0.39%	-0.45%	-0.45%	-0.38%	-0.44%	-0.45%	1.34%	1.20%	1.14%	1.25%	1.13%	1.07%	1.24%	1.12%	1.05%
Cost of Labour	0.04%	0.08%	0.08%	0.03%	0.06%	0.06%	-0.60%	-0.85%	-1.19%	-0.64%	-0.90%	-1.26%	-0.74%	-1.04%	-1.45%
Deflator of Absorption	-0.89%	-0.99%	-0.99%	-0.89%	-0.99%	-1.01%	3.12%	2.79%	2.55%	2.88%	2.63%	2.37%	2.83%	2.54%	2.26%
Price of Exports-RW	-0.38%	-0.45%	-0.45%	-0.38%	-0.44%	-0.45%	1.22%	0.99%	0.93%	1.12%	0.92%	0.87%	1.11%	0.91%	0.85%

Chemical

	Border Controls			Border controls and x-ineff.			Market segmentation			Trade *antimonde*			Full *antimonde*		
	1988	1991	1994	1988	1991	1994	1988	1991	1994	1988	1991	1994	1988	1991	1994
Marginal Costs	-0.24%	-0.29%	-0.30%	-0.24%	-0.29%	-0.30%	1.16%	1.03%	1.00%	1.16%	1.06%	1.03%	1.15%	1.05%	1.01%
Cost of Labour	0.04%	0.08%	0.08%	0.03%	0.06%	0.06%	-0.60%	-0.85%	-1.19%	-0.64%	-0.90%	-1.26%	-0.74%	-1.04%	-1.45%
Deflator of Absorption	-0.29%	-0.35%	-0.35%	-0.29%	-0.35%	-0.36%	2.37%	2.12%	1.95%	2.56%	2.38%	2.22%	2.52%	2.33%	2.14%
Price of Exports-RW	-0.25%	-0.31%	-0.31%	-0.24%	-0.30%	-0.31%	1.08%	0.93%	0.90%	1.08%	0.96%	0.93%	1.08%	0.95%	0.91%

Other Intensive Industries

	Border Controls			Border controls and x-ineff.			Market segmentation			Trade *antimonde*			Full *antimonde*		
	1988	1991	1994	1988	1991	1994	1988	1991	1994	1988	1991	1994	1988	1991	1994
Marginal Costs	-0.20%	-0.22%	-0.23%	-0.20%	-0.23%	-0.23%	0.63%	0.47%	0.34%	0.59%	0.44%	0.31%	0.58%	0.43%	0.30%
Cost of Labour	0.04%	0.08%	0.08%	0.03%	0.06%	0.06%	-0.60%	-0.85%	-1.19%	-0.64%	-0.90%	-1.26%	-0.74%	-1.04%	-1.45%
Deflator of Absorption	-0.29%	-0.34%	-0.34%	-0.30%	-0.34%	-0.35%	1.11%	0.88%	0.72%	1.09%	0.89%	0.72%	1.07%	0.86%	0.68%
Price of Exports-RW	-0.20%	-0.23%	-0.23%	-0.20%	-0.23%	-0.23%	0.63%	0.46%	0.34%	0.59%	0.44%	0.31%	0.58%	0.43%	0.29%

Electrical goods

	Border Controls			Border controls and x-ineff.			Market segmentation			Trade *antimonde*			Full *antimonde*		
	1988	1991	1994	1988	1991	1994	1988	1991	1994	1988	1991	1994	1988	1991	1994
Marginal Costs	-0.26%	-0.30%	-0.30%	-0.27%	-0.30%	-0.31%	0.94%	0.73%	0.56%	0.89%	0.70%	0.53%	0.88%	0.69%	0.51%
Cost of Labour	0.04%	0.08%	0.08%	0.03%	0.06%	0.06%	-0.60%	-0.85%	-1.19%	-0.64%	-0.90%	-1.26%	-0.74%	-1.04%	-1.45%
Deflator of Absorption	-0.65%	-0.75%	-0.75%	-0.66%	-0.76%	-0.77%	2.65%	2.24%	1.95%	2.57%	2.22%	1.91%	2.52%	2.13%	1.79%
Price of Exports-RW	-0.26%	-0.31%	-0.31%	-0.27%	-0.31%	-0.31%	0.89%	0.65%	0.49%	0.84%	0.63%	0.46%	0.83%	0.61%	0.43%

Transport equipment

	Border Controls			Border controls and x-ineff.			Market segmentation			Trade *antimonde*			Full *antimonde*		
	1988	1991	1994	1988	1991	1994	1988	1991	1994	1988	1991	1994	1988	1991	1994
Marginal Costs	-0.25%	-0.27%	-0.27%	-0.25%	-0.27%	-0.27%	1.01%	0.81%	0.59%	0.99%	0.82%	0.59%	0.98%	0.81%	0.58%
Cost of Labour	0.04%	0.08%	0.08%	0.03%	0.06%	0.06%	-0.60%	-0.85%	-1.19%	-0.64%	-0.90%	-1.26%	-0.74%	-1.04%	-1.45%
Deflator of Absorption	-0.33%	-0.34%	-0.34%	-0.34%	-0.34%	-0.35%	2.52%	2.43%	2.16%	2.65%	2.67%	2.39%	2.62%	2.62%	2.32%
Price of Exports-RW	-0.26%	-0.31%	-0.31%	-0.27%	-0.32%	-0.32%	0.83%	0.45%	0.23%	0.80%	0.45%	0.22%	0.79%	0.44%	0.21%

Other Equipment

	Border Controls			Border controls and x-ineff.			Market segmentation			Trade *antimonde*			Full *antimonde*		
	1988	1991	1994	1988	1991	1994	1988	1991	1994	1988	1991	1994	1988	1991	1994
Marginal Costs	-0.25%	-0.28%	-0.28%	-0.25%	-0.28%	-0.28%	0.82%	0.62%	0.46%	0.77%	0.59%	0.43%	0.76%	0.58%	0.41%
Cost of Labour	0.04%	0.08%	0.08%	0.03%	0.06%	0.06%	-0.60%	-0.85%	-1.19%	-0.64%	-0.90%	-1.26%	-0.74%	-1.04%	-1.45%
Deflator of Absorption	-0.67%	-0.74%	-0.74%	-0.67%	-0.75%	-0.76%	2.38%	2.01%	1.73%	2.24%	1.94%	1.66%	2.19%	1.87%	1.55%
Price of Exports-RW	-0.25%	-0.28%	-0.28%	-0.25%	-0.28%	-0.28%	0.81%	0.60%	0.44%	0.75%	0.57%	0.41%	0.74%	0.56%	0.39%

Consumer goods

	Border Controls			Border controls and x-ineff.			Market segmentation			Trade *antimonde*			Full *antimonde*		
	1988	1991	1994	1988	1991	1994	1988	1991	1994	1988	1991	1994	1988	1991	1994
Marginal Costs	-0.33%	-0.38%	-0.38%	-0.33%	-0.38%	-0.39%	1.12%	0.91%	0.79%	1.05%	0.87%	0.74%	1.05%	0.87%	0.73%
Cost of Labour	0.04%	0.08%	0.08%	0.03%	0.06%	0.06%	-0.60%	-0.85%	-1.19%	-0.64%	-0.90%	-1.26%	-0.74%	-1.04%	-1.45%
Deflator of Absorption	-0.52%	-0.61%	-0.61%	-0.53%	-0.62%	-0.62%	2.02%	1.68%	1.47%	1.95%	1.65%	1.44%	1.92%	1.61%	1.38%
Price of Exports-RW	-0.33%	-0.38%	-0.38%	-0.33%	-0.38%	-0.39%	1.12%	0.91%	0.79%	1.05%	0.87%	0.74%	1.05%	0.87%	0.73%

Construction

	Border Controls			Border controls and x-ineff.			Market segmentation			Trade *antimonde*			Full *antimonde*		
	1988	1991	1994	1988	1991	1994	1988	1991	1994	1988	1991	1994	1988	1991	1994
Marginal Costs	-0.14%	-0.17%	-0.18%	-0.14%	-0.17%	-0.17%	0.51%	0.43%	0.42%	0.49%	0.43%	0.42%	0.50%	0.44%	0.44%
Cost of Labour	0.04%	0.08%	0.08%	0.03%	0.06%	0.06%	-0.60%	-0.85%	-1.19%	-0.64%	-0.90%	-1.26%	-0.74%	-1.04%	-1.45%
Deflator of Absorption	-0.14%	-0.17%	-0.18%	-0.14%	-0.17%	-0.17%	0.51%	0.43%	0.42%	0.49%	0.43%	0.42%	0.50%	0.44%	0.44%
Price of Exports-RW	-0.14%	-0.17%	-0.18%	-0.14%	-0.17%	-0.17%	0.51%	0.43%	0.42%	0.49%	0.43%	0.42%	0.50%	0.44%	0.44%

Telecommunications

	Border Controls			Border controls and x-ineff.			Market segmentation			Trade *antimonde*			Full *antimonde*		
	1988	1991	1994	1988	1991	1994	1988	1991	1994	1988	1991	1994	1988	1991	1994
Marginal Costs	-0.03%	-0.04%	-0.03%	-0.03%	-0.04%	-0.04%	0.15%	0.14%	0.20%	0.14%	0.14%	0.20%	0.14%	0.13%	0.19%
Cost of Labour	0.04%	0.08%	0.08%	0.03%	0.06%	0.06%	-0.60%	-0.85%	-1.19%	-0.64%	-0.90%	-1.26%	-0.74%	-1.04%	-1.45%
Deflator of Absorption	-0.10%	-0.13%	-0.13%	-0.24%	-0.41%	-0.41%	0.58%	0.62%	0.64%	0.57%	0.61%	0.63%	0.42%	0.32%	0.33%
Price of Exports-RW	-0.03%	-0.04%	-0.04%	-0.08%	-0.14%	-0.13%	0.04%	-0.04%	0.00%	0.03%	-0.05%	0.00%	-0.02%	-0.14%	-0.10%

Transports

	Border Controls			Border controls and x-ineff.			Market segmentation			Trade *antimonde*			Full *antimonde*		
	1988	1991	1994	1988	1991	1994	1988	1991	1994	1988	1991	1994	1988	1991	1994
Marginal Costs	-0.15%	-0.18%	-0.18%	-0.15%	-0.18%	-0.18%	0.42%	0.30%	0.22%	0.38%	0.26%	0.18%	0.36%	0.24%	0.15%
Cost of Labour	0.04%	0.08%	0.08%	0.03%	0.06%	0.06%	-0.60%	-0.85%	-1.19%	-0.64%	-0.90%	-1.26%	-0.74%	-1.04%	-1.45%
Deflator of Absorption	-0.24%	-0.33%	-0.34%	-0.24%	-0.33%	-0.34%	0.71%	0.51%	0.42%	0.67%	0.46%	0.36%	0.64%	0.42%	0.31%
Price of Exports-RW	-0.15%	-0.18%	-0.18%	-0.15%	-0.18%	-0.18%	0.42%	0.30%	0.22%	0.38%	0.26%	0.18%	0.36%	0.24%	0.15%

Banks

	Border Controls			Border controls and x-ineff.			Market segmentation			Trade *antimonde*			Full *antimonde*		
	1988	1991	1994	1988	1991	1994	1988	1991	1994	1988	1991	1994	1988	1991	1994
Marginal Costs	-0.04%	-0.07%	-0.08%	-0.04%	-0.07%	-0.08%	0.26%	0.31%	0.46%	0.27%	0.32%	0.47%	0.27%	0.33%	0.47%
Cost of Labour	0.04%	0.08%	0.08%	0.03%	0.06%	0.06%	-0.60%	-0.85%	-1.19%	-0.64%	-0.90%	-1.26%	-0.74%	-1.04%	-1.45%
Deflator of Absorption	-0.06%	-0.09%	-0.10%	-0.09%	-0.15%	-0.16%	0.31%	0.36%	0.50%	0.31%	0.37%	0.51%	0.28%	0.31%	0.44%
Price of Exports-RW	-0.04%	-0.07%	-0.08%	-0.05%	-0.08%	-0.09%	0.24%	0.29%	0.43%	0.25%	0.30%	0.44%	0.24%	0.29%	0.43%

Services

	Border Controls			Border controls and x-ineff.			Market segmentation			Trade *antimonde*			Full *antimonde*		
	1988	1991	1994	1988	1991	1994	1988	1991	1994	1988	1991	1994	1988	1991	1994
Marginal Costs	-0.08%	-0.10%	-0.11%	-0.08%	-0.10%	-0.11%	0.23%	0.16%	0.13%	0.21%	0.14%	0.12%	0.19%	0.12%	0.08%
Cost of Labour	0.04%	0.08%	0.08%	0.03%	0.06%	0.06%	-0.60%	-0.85%	-1.19%	-0.64%	-0.90%	-1.26%	-0.74%	-1.04%	-1.45%
Deflator of Absorption	-0.10%	-0.13%	-0.13%	-0.10%	-0.13%	-0.14%	0.25%	0.17%	0.15%	0.22%	0.15%	0.13%	0.21%	0.13%	0.09%
Price of Exports-RW	-0.08%	-0.10%	-0.11%	-0.08%	-0.10%	-0.11%	0.23%	0.16%	0.13%	0.21%	0.14%	0.12%	0.19%	0.12%	0.08%

Non market

	Border Controls			Border controls and x-ineff.			Market segmentation			Trade *antimonde*			Full *antimonde*		
	1988	1991	1994	1988	1991	1994	1988	1991	1994	1988	1991	1994	1988	1991	1994
Marginal Costs	-0.06%	-0.07%	-0.07%	-0.07%	-0.07%	-0.08%	0.17%	0.07%	-0.02%	0.16%	0.06%	-0.03%	0.14%	0.03%	-0.07%
Cost of Labour	0.04%	0.08%	0.08%	0.03%	0.06%	0.06%	-0.60%	-0.85%	-1.19%	-0.64%	-0.90%	-1.26%	-0.74%	-1.04%	-1.45%
Deflator of Absorption	-0.09%	-0.10%	-0.11%	-0.09%	-0.10%	-0.11%	0.23%	0.12%	0.02%	0.20%	0.10%	0.00%	0.18%	0.06%	-0.05%
Price of Exports-RW	-0.06%	-0.07%	-0.07%	-0.07%	-0.07%	-0.08%	0.17%	0.07%	-0.02%	0.16%	0.06%	-0.03%	0.14%	0.03%	-0.07%

Bibliography

Baldwin, R.E. (1992), 'Measurable Dynamic Gains from Trade', *Journal of Political Economy*, Vol. 100, No. 1, February.

Baldwin, R.E. and A.J. Venables (1995), *Methodologies for an Aggregate Ex Post Evaluation of the Completion of the Internal Market: Feasibility Study and Literature Survey*, Mimeo, European Commission, DG II, March.

Barro, R.J. and X. Sala-i-Martin (1995), *Economic Growth*, New York, McGraw-Hill.

Bourguignon, F., W.H. Branson and J. De Melo (1989), 'Macroeconomic Adjustment and Income Distribution: a Macro-Micro Simulation Model', Working Paper, World Bank, May.

Branson, W. and L.A. Winters (1990), 'Comments on "Assessing Trade and Welfare Effects of Trade Liberalization" by V. Norman', *European Economic Review*, Vol. 34, No. 4, June.

Burniaux, J.M. and J. Waelbroeck (1992), 'Preliminary Results of Two Experimental Models of General Equilibrium with Imperfect Competition', *Journal of Policy Modelling*, Vol. 14, pp. 65–92.

Capros, P., Karadeloglou P. and G. Mentzas (1989), 'Neo-Keynesian and Applied General Equilibrium Macroeconometric Models: New Developments for Greece', Paper presented at the IFAC Symposium on Modelling and Control of National Economies, 27–29 June, Edinburgh.

Capros, P., T. Georgakopoulos, D. van Regemorter, S. Proost, K. Conrad, T. Schmidt, Y. Smeers, N. Ladoux, M. Vielle and P. McGregor (1995), *GEM-E3: Computable General Equilibrium Model for Studying Economy-Energy-Environment Interactions*, European Commission, Luxembourg, Office for Official Publications of the EC.

Catinat, M. and A. Italianer (1988), 'Completing the Internal Market, Primary Economic Effects and their Implementation in Macroeconomic Models', Report prepared for the European Commission, DG II, 20 April.

Chamberlin, E.H. (1933), *The Theory of Monopolistic Competition: A Re-Orientation of the Theory of Value* (8th edn.), Cambridge, Mass., Harvard University Press, 1962.

Coe, D.T. and R. Moghadam (1993), 'Capital and trade as engines of growth in France', *IMF Staff Papers*, Vol. 40, No. 3, September.

Conrad K. and M. Schröder (1991), 'Demand for durable and nondurable goods, environmental policy and consumer welfare', *Journal of Applied Econometrics*, Vol. 6, pp. 271–286.

Deleau, M. and P. Malgrange (1981), 'Une maquette representative des modèles macroéconomiques', *Annales de l' INSEE*, Paris.

Dixit, A.K. and J.E. Stiglitz (1977), 'Monopolistic Competition and Optimum Product Diversity', *American Economic Review*, Vol. 67, pp. 297–308.

Emerson, M., M. Aujean, M. Catinat, P. Coybet and A. Jaquemin (1988), *The Economics of 1992*, Oxford, Oxford University Press.

European Commission (1985), *Completing the internal market*, COM(85) 310 final, Luxembourg, Office for Official Publications of the EC.

European Commission (1988), 'The Economics of 1992', *European Economy*, No. 35 (known as the Cecchini Report).

European Commission (1988), *Studies on the Economics of Integration: Research on the 'Cost of Non-Europe'*, Vol. 2, Luxembourg, Office for Official Publications of the EC, pp. 11–165.

European Commission (1994), 'The Community Internal Market – 1993 Report', COM(94) 55 final, Luxembourg, Office for Official Publications of the EC.

Gasiorek, M., A. Smith and A.J. Venables (1991), 'Completing the Internal Market in the EC: Factor Demand and Comparative Advantage', in L.A. Winters and A.J. Venables (eds.), *European Integration: Trade and Industry*, Cambridge, Cambridge University Press.

Gasiorek, M., A. Smith, and A.J. Venables (1992), '"1992": trade and welfare – a general equilibrium model' in L.A. Winters (ed.), *Trade Flows and Trade Policy after 1992*, Cambridge, Cambridge University Press.

Grossman, G.M. (1990), 'Book Review of Emerson *et al.*', in *Journal of International Economics*, Vol. 28, No. 3/4, May.

Haaland J. and I. Wooton (1991), 'Market integration, competition and welfare', CEPR discussion paper No. 574, London.

Haaland, J. and V.D. Norman (1992), 'Global production effects of European integration' in L.A. Winters (ed.), *Trade Flows and Trade Policy after 1992*, Cambridge, Cambridge University Press.

Harris, R. (1984), 'Applied general equilibrium analysis of small open economies with scale economies and imperfect competition', *American Economic Review*, Vol. 74, pp. 215–40.

Harrison G., Rutherford T. and D. Tarr (1994), 'Product standards, imperfect competition and completion of the market in the European Union', World Bank, International Economic Dept., policy research working paper 1293, April.

Helpman, E. and P.R. Krugman (1985), *Market Structure and Foreign Trade: Increasing Returns, Imperfect Competition and the International Economy*, Cambridge, Mass., MIT Press.

Hoeller, P., and M.-O. Louppe (1994), 'The EC's Internal Market: Implementation, Economic Consequences, Unfinished Business', OECD Economics Department, Working Paper No. 147, Paris.

Johansen, L. (1960), 'A Multi-Sectoral Study of Economic Growth', North-Holland, Amsterdam.

Markusen, J. and A. Venables (1988), 'Trade policy with increasing returns and imperfect competition', *Journal of International Economics*, Vol. 6, pp. 271–286.

Mercenier, J. (1994), 'Completing the European internal market: a general equilibrium evaluation under alternative market structure assumptions', in M. Dewatripont and V. Ginsburgh, (eds.), *European Economic Integration: a challenge in a changing world*, North-Holland, Amsterdam.

Norman, V.D. (1990), 'Assessing Trade and Welfare Effects of Trade Liberalization: A Comparison of Alternative Approaches to CGE Modelling With Imperfect Competition', *European Economic Review*, Vol. 34, No. 4, June.

Pelkmans, J., and L.A. Winters (1988), *The European Domestic Market*, Chatham House, London.

Pratten, C. (1988), 'A survey of the economies of scale' in *Studies on the economics of integration: Research on the 'costs of non-Europe'*, Vol. 2, European Commission, Luxembourg, Office for Official Publications of the EC.

Smith, A. and A.J. Venables (1988), 'Completing the internal market in the European Community: Some industry simulations', *European Economic Review*, Vol. 32, No. 7, September.

Willenbockel, D. (1994), *Applied General Equilibrium Modelling: Imperfect Competition and European Integration*, Chichester, John Wiley & Sons.

Winters, L.A. (ed.) (1992a), *Trade Flows and Trade Policy after 1992*, Cambridge, Cambridge University Press.

Winters, L.A. (1992b), 'The welfare and policy implications of the international trade consequences of "1992"', *American Economic Review* (Papers and Proceedings), Vol. 82, pp. 104–8.

Winters, L.A., and A.J. Venables (eds.) (1990), *European Integration: Trade and Industry*, Cambridge, Cambridge University Press.